Lecture Notes in Computer Science 4591

Commenced Publication in 1973
Founding and Former Series Editors:
Gerhard Goos, Juris Hartmanis, and Jan van Leeuwen

Jim Davies   Jeremy Gibbons (Eds.)

Integrated Formal Methods

6th International Conference, IFM 2007
Oxford, UK, July 2-5, 2007
Proceedings

 Springer

Volume Editors

Jim Davies
Oxford University Computing Laboratory
Wolfson Building
Oxford OX1 3QD, UK
E-mail: Jim.Davies@camlab.ox.ac.uk

Jeremy Gibbons
Oxford University Computing Laboratory
Wolfson Building
Oxford OX1 3QD, UK
E-mail: jeremy.gibbons@comlab.ox.ac.uk

Library of Congress Control Number: 2007928796

CR Subject Classification (1998): F.3, D.3, D.2, D.1

LNCS Sublibrary: SL 2 – Programming and Software Engineering

ISSN	0302-9743
ISBN-10	3-540-73209-8 Springer Berlin Heidelberg New York
ISBN-13	978-3-540-73209-9 Springer Berlin Heidelberg New York

Springer is a part of Springer Science+Business Media

springer.com

© Springer-Verlag Berlin Heidelberg 2007
Printed in Germany

Typesetting: Camera-ready by author, data conversion by Scientific Publishing Services, Chennai, India
Printed on acid-free paper   SPIN: 12080328   06/3180   5 4 3 2 1 0

Preface

The design and analysis of computing systems presents a significant challenge: systems need to be understood at many different levels of abstraction, and examined from many different perspectives. Formal methods—languages, tools, and techniques with a sound, mathematical basis—can be used to develop a thorough understanding and to support rigorous examination.

Further research into effective integration is required if these methods are to have a significant impact outside academia. The Integrated Formal Methods (IFM) series of conferences seeks to promote this research, to bring together the researchers carrying it out, and to disseminate the results of this research among the wider academic and industrial community.

Earlier meetings in the series were held at: York (1999); Dagstuhl (2000); Turku (2002); Kent (2004); Eindhoven (2005). IFM 2007 was the largest to date, with 32 technical papers (from 85 submissions), 3 invited talks, 3 workshops, and a tutorial. The success of the series reflects the enthusiasm and efforts of the IFM community, and the organizers would like to thank the speakers, the committee, and the reviewers for their contributions.

April 2007

Jim Davies
Jeremy Gibbons

Organization

Table of Contents

Verifying Temporal Properties of CommUnity Designs

Nazareno Aguirre[1], Germán Regis[1], and Tom Maibaum[2]

[1] Departamento de Computación, FCEFQyN, Universidad Nacional de Río Cuarto
and CONICET, Ruta 36 Km. 601, Río Cuarto (5800), Córdoba, Argentina
{naguirre,gregis}@dc.exa.unrc.edu.ar
[2] Department of Computing & Software, McMaster University,
1280 Main St. West, Hamilton, Ontario, Canada L8S 4K1
tom@maibaum.org

Abstract. We study the use of some verification techniques for reasoning about temporal properties of CommUnity designs. We concentrate on the verification of temporal properties in the context of branching-time temporal logic using the SMV tool.

We also discuss ways of modularising the temporal reasoning, by exploiting the various kinds of morphisms between designs available in CommUnity. Moreover, we combine SMV verification with some abstract interpretation mechanisms to overcome a limitation, with respect to the use of structure for simplification of verification, of CommUnity's refinement morphisms, the lack of support for data refinement.

1 Introduction

The constant increase in the complexity of software systems demands a continuous search for more and better modularisation mechanisms in software development processes, covering not only implementation, but also earlier stages, such as analysis and design. Indeed, many new modularisation mechanisms influence not only programming language constructs, but also their associated development methodologies. Modularisation mechanisms are also of a crucial importance for formal methods, and in particular for formal specification. Appropriate modularisation mechanisms allow us to *structure* our specifications, dividing the usually large specifications (due to the degree of detail that formal models demand) into manageable parts. Also, many modern software systems have an inherent structural nature, and for these, structured specifications are better suited. Finally, and more importantly for this paper, modularisation mechanisms allow us to apply some modularity principles to analyses of properties, taking advantage of the structure of the design itself, and making some automated and semi-automated verification techniques scale up and be applicable to larger systems specifications.

There exist many formal specification languages which put an emphasis on the way systems are built out of components (e.g., those reported in [15,6,20,14]), thus aiding the modularisation of specifications and designs. CommUnity is one of these languages; it is a formal program design language which puts special emphasis on ways of composing specifications of components to form specifications

J. Davies and J. Gibbons (Eds.): IFM 2007, LNCS 4591, pp. 1–20, 2007.

of systems [4]. CommUnity is based on Unity [1] and IP [5], and its foundations lie in the categorical approach to systems design [7]. Its mechanisms for composing specifications have a formal interpretation in terms of category theory constructs [4]. Moreover, CommUnity's composition mechanisms combine nicely with a sophisticated notion of refinement, which involves separate concepts of action blocking and action progress. CommUnity also has some tool support, the CommUnity Workbench [23]. The CommUnity Workbench supports the editing, compilation, colimit generation (as explained below, colimits represent the joint behaviour of interacting components in CommUnity) and execution of CommUnity programs. However, it currently does not support the verification of logical properties of designs. For this purpose, we propose the use of well known model checking tools, in order to verify *temporal* properties of designs. More precisely, and due to some particular characteristics of CommUnity, we propose the use of CTL based model checking to analyse temporal properties of CommUnity designs. We start by defining a translation from CommUnity designs into SMV specifications in a semantics preserving way; since our goal is to verify temporal properties of designs, we have to consider a semantics for CommUnity designs that is more restrictive than (but compatible with) the semantics of open CommUnity designs described in [12]. We then attempt to modularise the verification activities via the superposition and refinement morphisms available in CommUnity, as indicated in [13]. This is very important, since it allows us to exploit the structure of CommUnity designs for verification, a task that is crucial for the successful use of model checking and other automated analysis techniques. The idea is to check properties required of a component from the specification of that component, thus exponentially reducing the search space associated with these checks, as compared to the search space associated with the much larger specification of the system. Although not all properties are necessarily preserved by including a component in a system, by means of some structuring relationship, important categories of properties are. Thus economies of scale might be achieved by using this structuring information to structure verifications. We concentrate on the information supplied by superposition relationships, used in structuring designs, but also discuss refinements. Finally, we combine model checking with predicate abstraction [8] in order to overcome a limitation (with respect to the modularisation of verification) of CommUnity refinements, namely the lack of support for data refinement [13].

The paper proceeds as follows. In section 2 we describe CommUnity and the concepts of designs and programs, including the structuring principles used to build systems from components. We also summarise the transition systems semantics of designs. Then in section 3, we discuss the verification of CommUnity designs using SMV, how the required translation is defined, and how the verification can be modularised, in some cases, by using the structure defined by the superposition morphisms used in structuring the design. We also discuss the relationship between refinement morphisms and temporal properties, and describe how we complement the CTL model checking with predicate abstraction, which is necessary due to the fact that refinement morphisms do not allow for data refinement. We conclude with a discussion of results and future research. In order to illustrate the main ideas of the paper, we develop a case study based on a modular specification of a processor with a simple process scheduling mechanism.

2   CommUnity Designs

In this section, we introduce the reader to the CommUnity design language and its main features, by means of an example. The computational units of a system are specified in CommUnity through *designs*. Designs are abstract programs, in the sense that they describe a *class* of programs (more precisely, the class of all the programs one might obtain from the design by refinement), rather than a single program. In fact, when a design does not admit any further refinement, it is called a *program* [22].

Before describing in some detail the refinement and composition mechanisms of CommUnity, let us describe the main constituents of a CommUnity design. Assume that we have a fixed set $\mathcal{ADT}$ of datatypes, specified as usual via a first-order specification. A CommUnity design is composed of:

- A set V of *channels*, typed with sorts in $\mathcal{ADT}$. V is partitioned into three subsets V_{in}, V_{prv} and V_{out}, corresponding to input, private and output channels, respectively. Input channels are the ones controlled, from the point of view of the component, by the environment. Private and output channels are the local channels of the component. The difference between these is that output channels can be read by the environment, whereas private channels cannot.
- A first-order sentence $Init(V)$, describing the initial states of the design[1].
- A set Γ of actions, partitioned into private actions Γ_{prv} and public actions Γ_{pub}. Each action $g \in \Gamma$ is of the form:

$$g[D(g)] : L(g), U(g) \rightarrow R(g)$$

where $D(g) \subseteq V_{prv} \cup V_{out}$ is the (write) *frame* of g (the local channels that g modifies), $L(g)$ and $U(g)$ are two first-order sentences such that $U(g) \Rightarrow L(g)$, called the lower and upper bound guards, respectively, and $R(g)$ is a first-order sentence $\alpha(V \cup D(g)')$, indicating how the action g modifies the values of the variables in its frame ($D(g)$ is a set of channels and $D(g)'$ is the corresponding set of "primed" versions of the channels in $D(g)$, representing the new values of the channels after the execution of the action g.)

The two guards $L(g)$ and $U(g)$ associated with an action g are related to refinement, in the sense that the actual guard of an action g_r implementing the abstract action g, must lie between $L(g)$ and $U(g)$. As explained in [13], the negation of $L(g)$ establishes a blocking condition ($L(g)$ can be seen as a lower

---

[1] Some versions of CommUnity, such as the one presented in [13], do not include an initialisation constraint.

bound on the actual guard of an action implementing g), whereas $U(g)$ establishes a progress condition (i.e., an upper bound on the actual guard of an action implementing g).

Of course, $R(g)$ might not uniquely determine values for the variables $D(g)'$. As explained in [13], $R(g)$ is typically composed of a conjunction of implications *pre* $\Rightarrow$ *post*, where *pre* is a precondition and *post* defines a multiple assignment.

To clarify the definition of CommUnity designs, let us suppose that we would like to model a processor. We will abstract away from the actual code of the processes, and represent them simply by an ordered pair of non negative integers (denoted by **nat**), where the first integer represents a label for identifying the process and the second one the number of seconds of execution remaining. Then, a processor is a simple CommUnity design composed of:

- A local channel **curr_proc**:$\langle$**nat**, **nat**$\rangle$, representing the current process accessing the processor. We use a dummy value $(0,0)$ for indicating that the processor is idle.
- an input channel **in_proc**:$\langle$**nat**, **nat**$\rangle$, for obtaining a new process (from the environment, in an abstract sense) to be run by the processor.
- An action **load**, which loads a new process into the processor (reading the corresponding values from the input variable **in_proc**).
- An action **run**, that executes the current process for a second.
- An action **kill**, that removes the current process, replacing it by the dummy $(0,0)$.
- An action **switch**, which, if the current process is not the dummy $(0,0)$, replaces it by the incoming process **in_proc**.

The CommUnity design corresponding to this component is shown in Figure 1.

Design Processor
in
   in_proc: <nat, nat>
out
   curr_proc: <nat, nat>
init
   curr_proc $= (0,0)$
do
      load[curr_proc]: in_proc. snd $> 0 \land$ in_proc. fst $\neq 0 \land$ curr_proc$=(0,0)$
          $\longrightarrow$ curr_proc'$=$in_proc
[] *prv* run[curr_proc]: curr_proc. snd > 0, curr_proc. snd > 0
          $\longrightarrow$ curr_proc'$=$(curr_proc.fst , curr_proc. snd-1)
[]   kill [curr_proc]: curr_proc. fst $\neq 0$, false $\longrightarrow$ curr_proc'$=(0,0)$
[]   switch[curr_proc]: in_proc. snd $> 0 \land$ in_proc. fst $\neq 0 \land$
curr_proc. snd >0, false
        $\longrightarrow$ curr_proc'$=$in_proc

Fig. 1. An abstract CommUnity design for a simple processor

In Fig. 1, one can see the different kinds of guards that an action might have. For instance, action `kill` has safety and progress guards (`curr_proc.fst` $\neq 0$ and `false`, respectively). Since the progress guard for this action is `false`, the component is not obliged to execute the action when the environment requires it to do so.

Another important point to notice in the processor design is the apparent behaviour of action `switch`. After a switch, the previous value of `curr_proc` seems to be missing, since the component does not store it anywhere else, nor "sends" it to another component. It will become clearer later on that it will be the responsibility of other components in the architecture to "extract" the current process and store it when a switch takes place. This is basically due to the fact that communication between components is achieved by means of coordination, rather than by explicit invocation.

To complete the picture, let us introduce some further designs. One is a bounded queue of processes, with the traditional enqueue (`enq`) and dequeue (`deq`) operations, implemented over an array. The other is a process generator, a design that generates new processes to feed the system. These designs are shown in Figures 2 and 3, respectively.

Design Process_Queue
in
  in_proc: <nat, nat>
out
  out_proc: <nat, nat>
local
  queue: array(10,<nat, nat>)
  low, up, count: nat
init
  out_proc = (0,0) $\wedge$ $\forall$ x $\in$ [1..10] :
               queue[x] = (0,0) $\wedge$ low = 1 $\wedge$ up = 1 $\wedge$ count = 0
do
        enq[queue,out_proc,count,up]:   count<10 $\wedge$ in_proc.fst $\neq 0$
           $\longrightarrow$ queue'[up] = in_proc $\wedge$ up' = (up mod 10)+1 $\wedge$
             out_proc' = if(count=0,in_proc,queue[low]) $\wedge$ count'=count+1
[]   deq[queue,out_proc,count,low]: count>0 , count>5
           $\longrightarrow$ queue'[low] = (0,0) $\wedge$ low' = (low mod 10)+1 $\wedge$
             out_proc' = queue[(low mod 10)+1] $\wedge$count'=count$-$1

Fig. 2. An abstract CommUnity design for a process queue

---

the definition of action `enq` makes use of an if-then-else expression, in the syntax of the CommUnity Workbench. Notice that the progress guard for action `load` of the processor coincides with its blocking guard, which is too weak to guarantee a scheduling policy. Stronger progress guards for actions related to `load` will arise as a result of composing the processor with other components, to achieve

```
Design Process_Generator
out
  out_proc: <nat, nat>
local
  curr_id : nat
init
  curr_id  = 1 ∧ out_proc = (0,0)
do
  prv gen[ out_proc ]: out_proc.fst ≠ curr_id
        ⟶ out_proc'. fst  = curr_id ∧  out_proc'. snd > 0
[]    send[ out_proc, curr_id ]: out_proc.fst  = curr_id
        ⟶ out_proc'=(0,0) ∧  curr_id ' = curr_id+1
```

Fig. 3. An abstract CommUnity design for a process generator

a proper scheduling policy. In our case, for example, we require the dequeing of processes to be ready whenever the number of processes in the queue exceeds half the queue capacity (see the progress guard of action deq).

2.1   Component Composition

In order to build a system out of the above components, we need a mechanism for composition. The mechanism for composing designs in Community is based on action synchronisation and the "connection" of output channels to input channels (shared memory). Since our intention is to connect both the process generator and the processor to the queue (since processes to be enqueued might be generated by the generator, or come from a processor's currently executing process being "switched out"), and the queue has a single "incoming interface", we have a kind of *architectural mismatch*. In order to overcome it, we can use a duplexer, as specified in Figure 4. The duplexer enables us to design a system in which independent use of the operations of the queue can be made by components that are clients of the queue. Using this duplexer, we can form the architecture shown in Figure 5. In Fig. 5, the architecture is shown using the CommUnity Workbench graphical notation. In this notation, boxes represent designs, with its channels and actions, and lines represent the interactions ("cables" in the sense of [13]), indicating how input channels are connected to output channels, and which actions are synchronised.

2.2   Semantics of Architectures

CommUnity designs have a semantics based on (labelled) transition systems. Architectural configurations, of the kind shown in Fig. 5, also have a precise semantics; they are interpreted as categorical diagrams, representing the architecture [13]. The category has designs as objects and the morphisms are *superposition relationships*. A superposition morphism between two designs A and B

Design Duplexer
in
    in_1: <nat, nat>
    in_2: <nat, nat>
out
    out_proc: <nat, nat>
do
    read1[out_proc]: in_1 $\neq$ (0,0) $\wedge$ out_proc= (0,0) $\longrightarrow$ out_proc'=in_1
 [] read2[out_proc]: in_2 $\neq$ (0,0) $\wedge$ out_proc= (0,0) $\longrightarrow$ out_proc'=in_2
 [] send: out_proc $\neq$ (0,0) $\longrightarrow$ out_proc'=(0,0)

Fig. 4. An abstract CommUnity design for a simple duplexer

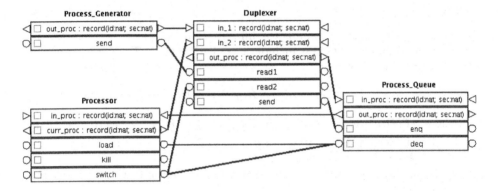

Fig. 5. A graphical view of the architecture of the system

indicates, in a formal way, that *B contains A*, and uses it while respecting the encapsulation of *A* (regulative superposition). The interesting fact is that the joint behaviour of the system can be obtained by taking the *colimit* of the categorical diagram corresponding to the architecture [4]. Therefore, one can obtain a single design (the colimit object), capturing the behaviour of the whole system.

2.3 Semantics for Abstract CommUnity Designs

In [13], the authors state that designs have an operational semantics when they are *closed* (i.e., they do not have input channels), the safety and progress guards for each action coincide, and the assignment for each action fully determines the value for each v', where v is in the frame of the action. For abstract CommUnity designs (i.e., not programs), it is not difficult to define a transition system semantics, by assuming that input channels can change arbitrarily and that, when no action occurs, the values of the local variables are preserved. This is exactly the idea followed in the definition of a denotational semantics for abstract CommUnity designs given in [12]. The semantics defined therein is, however, not

completely adequate for our purposes, since many labelled transition systems
might correspond to an open design. Since we want to verify temporal properties of designs, we are forced to interpret these, when they are opened, in a
particular way; we have been careful to do so in a way that is compatible with
the semantics of open CommUnity designs given in [12] (i.e., we interpret designs
as particular transition systems within the possible interpretations as described
in [12]). Moreover, when a design is a *program*, the interpretation coincides with
the operational semantics of these, as described in [13]. The semantics described
below, which is a specialisation of that defined in [12], will allow us to establish
a direct connection between arbitrary CommUnity designs (including programs)
and temporal logic, with the aim of verifying temporal properties of designs.

Let $\langle L_{\mathcal{ADT}}, \Phi \rangle$ be a first-order specification of datatypes, $\mathcal{U}_{\mathcal{ADT}}$ a model of
$\langle L_{\mathcal{ADT}}, \Phi \rangle$ and $P = \langle V_f, G \rangle$ a CommUnity design. Then, P defines a transition
system $T_P = \langle V_f, \theta, \mathcal{T} \rangle$ over $L_{\mathcal{ADT}}$ and $\mathcal{U}_{\mathcal{ADT}}$, where:

- the set of flexible variables is the set V_f of channels of P,
- the initialisation condition θ is the initialisation *Init* of P,
- for each action $g \in G$, we include a transition t_g in $\mathcal{T}$, whose transition
  relation is the following:

$$\rho_{t_g} : L(g) \wedge R(g) \wedge ST(\overline{D(g)})$$

  where $ST(\overline{D(g)})$ is the formula $\bigwedge_{v \in (Loc(V_f - D(g))}(v = v')$ (stuttering of the
  local variables not in the frame of g),
- $\mathcal{T}$ includes a stuttering transition t_I,
- $\mathcal{T}$ also includes a *local* stuttering transition *id*, whose transition relation is
  the following:

$$\rho_{id} : \bigwedge_{v \in Loc(V_f)} v = v'$$

The first two points in the above construction of the transition system T_P are
easy to understand. The third point indicates that the actions of P correspond to
transitions of T_P, as one might have expected. Notice that both the safety guard
and the precondition for an action g (the first captured by the conjunct $L(g)$
and the second is embedded in $R(g)$) are considered in the transition; moreover,
the corresponding assignment has to take place and the values of those local
variables not in the frame of g are required to be preserved. The fourth and
fifth points characterise the steps in which the design P is not actively involved
(computation steps of the environment); note that input channels are allowed to
change in a stuttering step of the design P.

The reader might notice that several constructs of CommUnity designs are
ignored in the above described construction of transition systems. The most notable case is that of progress guards. Progress guards are not taken into account
in the construction of transition systems for designs, because they represent
"readiness" constraints which are not part of the transition system definition,
but restrictions on the allowed models. For the particular models that we have
chosen as the interpretations for CommUnity designs, these trivially hold, as

long as the progress guards of actions are stronger than the corresponding safety ones. More precisely, when the progress guard $U(g)$ of an action g holds, g must be "available" to be executed (more formally, any state s in a computation of a design P in which $U(g)$ holds must have a t_g-successor state s'); since the enabling condition for actions, according to our interpretation, is the safety guard, whenever $L(g)$ is true the action is available, thus guaranteeing that $U(g)$ implies the availability of g. Clearly, the logical characterisation of progress constraints requires the use of path quantifiers. The reason for adopting a branching time temporal logic is to be able to express such constraints. These are useful, since the user might want to manually strengthen the enabling guards of actions, which is a sound activity (with respect to [12]) as long as they are not strengthened "beyond" the corresponding progress guards. Finally, according to [12], one must restrict runs of a transition system T_P for a design P to strongly fair runs with respect to private actions, taking as their enabling conditions their corresponding safety guards.

Notice also that the difference between private and shared actions does not have an impact in the construction of transition systems for designs. This is due to the fact that, as explained in [13], the difference between private and shared actions only has to do with the allowed forms of interaction between designs.

3   Verifying Temporal Properties of Designs

3.1   The SMV System

SMV (Symbolic Model Verifier) is one of the most widely used model checking tools. Originally developed at Carnegie Mellon [18], SMV was the first model checking tool that used a symbolic representation of transition systems based on binary decision diagrams, which allowed for the application of model checking techniques to larger finite state systems. SMV comprises a modular notation for describing transition systems, as well as a notation for describing properties of these, in the CTL temporal logic. We will not give a full description of SMV, but just a brief overview of the notation, so that the reader not familiar with it can straightforwardly follow our descriptions.

The SMV description of a system is organised in *modules*. Each module describes a portion of a finite state system, and its specification is given in terms of typed variables, initialisation constraints and a transition relation. More precisely, a module description starts with *declarations*, which are essentially given as a list of typed variables. These types for variables must be bounded. The variables in declarations can be accompanied by a declaration of new types or aliases of types, for variable typing. The state space associated with a module will then be given by all the combinations of values of the corresponding types for the declared variables. The *transition system* associated with the system corresponding to a module is defined in terms of:

 - a definition of the initial state, declared as initial values for each of the declared variables, and

– a definition of the transition relation, typically given as a "case" expression for the next value to be assumed for each of the declared variables.

Let us provide, as a simple example, the following module definition, which corresponds to a manual translation of the simplest CommUnity design of our example, the process generator: In our SMV models, `MAXINT` is a user provided

```
MODULE Process_Generator() {

  out_proc: array 0..1 of 0.. MAXINT;
  curr_id : array 0..1 of 0.. MAXINT;

  init(out_proc):= [0,0];
  init(curr_id ):= 1;

  next(curr_id):= case {
    out_proc[0]  = curr_id: curr_id +1;  -- action send
    out_proc[0] ~= curr_id: curr_id ;    -- action gen
  };

  next(out_proc):= case {
    out_proc[0]  = curr_id: [0,0];                  -- action send
    out_proc[0] ~= curr_id: [ curr_id ,1.. MAXINT]; -- action gen
  };
}
```

positive constant, representing the maximum positive integer we consider. Notice also that it is possible to represent nondeterministic assignment: in the above example, the second component of the `out_proc` variable is nondeterministically assigned a positive value, in the definition of its next value associated with action gen.

3.2   Translating CommUnity Designs into SMV

We now describe our general characterisation of CommUnity designs in the language of the SMV tool. We will illustrate the translation from CommUnity into SMV by means of a detailed example. It is worth mentioning that we have chosen Cadence SMV [19] because of its richer language, which allows us to describe transitions involving structured-typed variables, such as arrays, in a more concise way.

The translation we describe only involves designs and not architectural configurations. As explained before, any valid configuration is a representation of a single design (the colimit of the categorical diagram corresponding to the architecture), so we do not lose generality.

The simplest part is the characterisation of channels. These are simply translated as variables in SMV, and for obvious reasons we limit ourselves to the types supported by Cadence SMV. For our simple Processor design described before, the channels are represented as follows:

```
in_proc : array 0..1 of 0.. MAXINT; -- Input variable
curr_proc : array 0..1 of 0.. MAXINT;
```

The initialisation of channels is translated into "init" specifications for the corresponding variables in SMV, as one might expect:

```
-- Initialisation   of variables
init(in_proc) := [0.. MAXINT,0..MAXINT]; --Input variable
init(curr_proc):= [0,0];
```

The slightly more complicated part is the characterisation of actions. These need to be encoded into the "next" relationships for the variables. Since we need to simulate a scheduler for actions, which chooses nondeterministically one of the available actions, we introduce a "random variable". This variable randomly takes a numeric value corresponding to an action (including *skip*) to be executed in the next step as long as its safety guard is satisfied; if the safety guard of the chosen action is not true, then the action executed will be *skip*. For the Processor design, the scheduling of the actions is represented in the following way:

```
-- Definition of Scheduler
  -- Generation of random values used to schedule actions
init(rnd) := 0;
next(rnd) := 0..4;

init(curr_action ) := skip;
next(curr_action) := case{
  rnd = 0 : skip;
  rnd = 1 & (next(in_proc[1]) > 0 & next(in_proc[0]) ~= 0 &
                                      next(curr_proc) = [0,0] ) : load;
  rnd = 2 & (next(curr_proc[1]) > 0): run;
  rnd = 3 & true : kill ;
  rnd = 4 & (next(in_proc[1]) > 0 & next(in_proc[0]) ~= 0 &
                                      next(curr_proc[1]) > 0) : switch;
  1: skip;
};
```

A point worth noticing is that the execution of the system in the SMV representation of a design P starts with a *skip*. This simplifies the specification of the initialisation statement in the translation, since otherwise we would need to take into account the initialisation constraints in P for the scheduling of the first action to be executed. Our alternative does not restrict the executions of the system, which from the second instant onwards will evolve by randomly chosen (available) actions. Notice that safety guards are part of the scheduling. The assignments of the actions, on the other hand, appear on the "next" definitions for the channels, which are formed by a "case" expression which depends on the action executed:

```
-- Definition of next value of variables
next(in_proc) := [0.. MAXINT,0..MAXINT];  --Input variable

next(curr):= case{
  curr_action = skip : curr_proc;
  curr_action = load : in_proc;
  curr_action = run : [ curr_proc[0], curr_proc[1] - 1];
  curr_action = kill & curr_proc[0] = 0 : curr_proc;
  curr_action = kill & curr_proc[0] ~= 0 : [0,0];
  curr_action = switch : in_proc;
};
```

Notice that, since **in_proc** is an input variable, it can change arbitrarily in each step.

Finally, we need to represent the constraints corresponding to progress guards and strong fairness for private actions. These are easily characterised in CTL, using an ASSUME clause for progress guards constraints and a FAIRNESS clause for strong fairness on private actions:

```
-- Fairness for private actions
FAIRNESS
curr_action = {run};

-- Specification of progress guards as CTL formulae
ASSUME progress_switch;
 progress_switch : SPEC AG ((curr_proc[1] > 4 & in_proc ~= [0,0])
                                      → EX( curr_action = switch ));
```

Notice that progress guards are interpreted as (redundant) ASSUME clauses. If the user decides to strengthen some guards of actions in order to obtain more restrictive interpretations of a design, these must not go beyond the corresponding progress guards, in order not to make the SMV specification inconsistent.

Now we only need to provide the CTL formulae to be verified. For instance, we might want to check that if the id of the current process is 0 then it is the dummy process (i.e., the number of seconds remaining is also 0):

```
-- Properties to be verified
 NoInvalidProccess :SPEC AG (curr_proc[1] >0 →curr_proc[0]>0);
```

3.3   Modularising the Verification Through Morphisms

As put forward in [4] and later work, different notions of component relationships can be captured by morphisms, in the sense of category theory. We now exploit these morphisms in order to modularise the SMV-based verification, in the way indicated in [13].

Superposition Morphisms. We start by describing how superposition morphisms, which are used in the composition of CommUnity designs, are exploited. Let us first recall the formal notion of superposition morphism. A superposition morphism $\sigma : A \to B$ is a pair of mappings $\langle \sigma_{ch}, \sigma_{act} \rangle$ such that: *(i)* σ_{ch} is a total mapping from channels in A to channels in B, respecting the type and kind[2] of channels (except that input channels can be mapped to input or output channels), *(ii)* σ_{act} is a partial mapping from actions of B to actions of A, which preserves the kind (shared or private) of actions, does not reduce the write frame of actions of A, and the lower bound, upper bound and assignment for each action of A is strengthened in the corresponding actions of B; moreover, the encapsulation of A must be preserved, meaning that every action of B that modifies a channel v of $\text{ran}(\sigma_{ch})$ must "invoke" an action of A that includes $\sigma_{ch}^{-1}(v)$ in its write frame.

Basically, σ_{ch} indicates how the channels of A are embedded as channels of B. The mapping σ_{act}, on the other hand, indicates, for each action a of A, all the actions that use it in B (through $\sigma_{act}^{-1}(a)$).

The main result that enables us to modularise the verification via superposition morphisms is reported in [12]. Therein, the authors indicate that superposition morphisms preserve invariants, the effect of actions on channels and the restrictions to the occurrence of actions. More generally, we can affirm that superposition morphisms preserve safety properties, which is a direct consequence of the following theorem:

Theorem 1. *Let A and B be CommUnity designs, and $\langle \sigma_{ch}, \sigma_{act} \rangle : A \to B$ a superposition morphism. Let s be a computation of B, according to the above defined semantics of designs, and defined over an interpretation $\mathcal{U}$ for datatypes. The computation s^A, defined as the restriction of states in s to channels in $\sigma_{ch}(V_A)$, is a computation of A.*

Applied to our example, this means that we can reason locally about safety properties of the components of a system. We have some examples below in which we show the improvement that local verification of safety properties for our case study constitutes. Of course, as is well known, this does not hold for liveness properties, which are not necessarily preserved by superposition (it is well known that, when a component is put to interact with others, some of its liveness properties might be lost).

Notice also that, among all possible interpretations of an open CommUnity design, we choose the less restrictive one, i.e., that in which the actions are enabled under the weakest possible conditions. This has as a consequence that the safety properties of the design that are verified using our SMV translation are indeed properties of *all* the valid transition system interpretations (according to [12]) of the design.

---

[2] By the type of the channel we mean the sort with which it is associated; by the kind of a channel we mean its "input", "output" or "private" constraint.

Refinement Morphisms. An important relationship between designs is refinement. Refinement, besides relating abstract designs with more concrete "implementations", is also useful for characterising parametrisation and parameter instantiation. In [13], the authors present a characterisation of refinement in terms of category theory constructions. Essentially, they demonstrate that CommUnity designs and morphisms capturing the notion of refinement constitute a category. As defined in [13], a refinement σ between designs A and B is a pair of mappings $\langle \sigma_{ch}, \sigma_{act} \rangle$, such that *(i)* σ_{ch} is a total mapping from channels in A to channels in B, respecting the type and kind of channels, and injectively mapping different output and input channels of A to different output and input channels of B; *(ii)* σ_{act} is a partial mapping from actions of B to actions of A, which preserves the kind of actions, does not reduce the frame of actions of A, the lower bound and assignment for each action of A is strengthened in the corresponding actions of B; moreover, the upper bound of each action a of A must be weakened by the disjunction of the upper bounds of all actions in B refining a, meaning that every action of B that modifies a channel v of $\mathrm{ran}(\sigma_{ch})$ must "invoke" an action of A that includes $\sigma_{ch}^{-1}(v)$ in its frame. Also, shared actions of A must have at least one corresponding action in B, and all new actions of B do not modify the local channels of A.

Notice that, with respect to the assignment and lower bounds of actions, the refinement morphisms make them *stronger* when refining a design. Therefore, we again can affirm, as for superposition morphisms, that, if σ is a refinement morphism between designs A and B, then every execution trace of B, restricted to the channels originating in A, is an execution of A, and therefore safety properties are preserved along refinement morphisms. Moreover, as shown in [13], refinement morphisms also preserve properties expressing the readiness of actions (called *co-properties* in [13]). This does not mean, however, that refinement morphisms are theorem preserving morphisms, with respect to the logic CTL. Many liveness properties expressible in CTL, for example, are not necessarily preserved along refinement morphisms. Consider, as a trivial example, a design containing, among other things, a private action a:

```
Design P
...
out
    x : int
    ...
init
    x = 0 ∧ ...
do
    prv a[ x ]: true, false  ⟶ x'  = x + 1
    ...
```

where the variable x can only be modified by action a. Consider a refinement of this design, in which all actions and channels are maintained without modifications, except for a, which is refined as follows:

Design P'

...

out

   x : int

   ...

init

   x = 0 ∧ ...

do

     prv a[x]: false , false $\longrightarrow$ x' = x + 1

    ...

It is easy to see that, due to the strong fairness constraints imposed on private actions, the CTL liveness property $AF(x = 1)$ holds for the original design, but it does not hold for its described refinement.

One might be interested in exploiting refinement morphisms for simplifying the verification of properties of designs, since some safety and readiness properties might be easier to verify in more abstract designs, i.e., designs with fewer and simpler actions. However, the simplification one might obtain by moving from a design to more abstract (i.e., less refined) ones is limited, since refinement morphisms do not allow for data refinement (the types of channels must be preserved by refinement). This means, basically, that the state space of designs does not change through refinement morphisms. Thus, refinement morphisms are quite restricted for the simplification of verification, especially in the context of automated verification, where data abstraction is known to have a big impact on the verification times. For this reason, we complement below CommUnity's morphisms with abstraction mechanisms.

Abstraction. As we mentioned, abstraction is known to have a big impact in automated verification, especially for model checking [2]. Since refinement morphisms do not support data refinement, we considered the use of *predicate abstraction* [8], as a way of improving the SMV-based verification of CommUnity designs. Essentially, predicate abstraction consists of, given a (possibly infinite state) transition system, constructing an abstract version of it, whose abstract state space is determined by a number of predicates on the original state space. Basically, the state space of the abstract transition system is composed of equivalence classes of the original states, according to the provided (abstraction) predicates [8]. The more complex part is the construction of abstract transitions corresponding to the concrete ones, which requires checking to which of the equivalence class(es) the source and target states of each transition correspond. This can be computed automatically in many cases, and its complexity (not from a computational point of view) greatly depends on the provided predicates.

We used predicate abstraction in order to improve the verification for our example. For instance, we can concentrate on the processor design, and consider the following predicates to do the abstraction:

- the number of seconds remaining for curr_proc is 0,
- the process id for curr_proc is 0.

This leads us to the following four possibilities for `curr_proc`:

- *dummy*, if the number of seconds remaining is 0 and the process id is 0,
- *finished*, if the number of seconds remaining is 0 and the process id is not 0,
- *unfinished*, if the number of seconds remaining is not 0 and the process id is not 0,
- *invalid*, otherwise.

We can reproduce this abstraction for the `in_proc` variable, which leads us to a version of the SMV specification for the processor in which we do not distinguish the actual values of `curr_proc` and `in_proc`, but only whether their ids and remaining seconds are nil or not, which obviously makes the transition system for the design much smaller.

The corresponding abstract version of the SMV Processor module is the following:

```
typedef PROCCESS {dummy,finished,unfinished,invalid};
MODULE main (){
  rnd : 0..4;   -- used to schedule actions randomly
  curr_action : {skip, load, run, kill , switch1 };
-- Definition of the variables
    in_proc : PROCCESS;  --Input variable
    curr_proc : PROCCESS;
-- Definition of Scheduler
  init(rnd) := 0;
  next(rnd) := 0..4;
  init(curr_action ) := skip;
  next(curr_action) := case{
    rnd = 0 : skip;
    rnd = 1 & (next(in_proc) = unfinished & next(curr_proc) = dummy ) : load;
    rnd = 2 & (next(curr_proc) = unfinished) : run;
    rnd = 3 & true : kill ;
    rnd = 4 & (next(in_proc) = unfinished & next(curr_proc) = unfinished ) :
                                                      switch1;
    1: skip;  };
-- Initialisation   of variables
  init(in_proc) := { dummy,finished,unfinished,invalid};
  init(curr_proc):= dummy;
-- Definition of next value of variables
  next(in_proc) := { dummy,finished,unfinished,invalid};  --Input variable
  next(curr_proc):= case{
    curr_action = skip : curr_proc;
    curr_action = load : in_proc;
    curr_action = run : {unfinished , finished } ;
    curr_action = kill  & (curr_proc = dummy | curr_proc = invalid) : curr_proc;
    curr_action = kill  & (curr_proc = unfinished | curr_proc = finished ) : dummy;
    curr_action = switch1 : in_proc;  };
-- Fairness for private actions
  FAIRNESS curr_action = {run};
```

```
-- Specification of progress guards as CTL formulae
  ASSUME progress_switch1;
  progress_switch1 : SPEC AG ((curr_p = unfinished & in_p ~= dummy)
                                  → EX( curr_action = switch1 ));
}
```

We can verify the property that if the id of the current process is 0 then it is the dummy process, whose concrete and abstract versions are the following:

```
NoInvalidProccess :SPEC AG (curr_proc[1] >0 →curr_proc[0]>0);
```

```
NoInvalidProccess :SPEC AG (curr_proc ~= invalid);
```

The validity of the abstract version of this property implies the validity of its concrete version [2]. Since this is a safety property, it is guaranteed that it will also hold for the complete system (since superposition morphisms preserve safety properties).

A point regarding abstraction and readiness is worth noticing. As indicated in [2], all CTL formulae not involving existential path quantifiers are preserved through abstraction. Readiness assertions require existential path quantifiers to be expressed in CTL, and therefore these (expressing required non determinism of components) might not be preserved through abstractions.

3.4   Some Sample Properties

To end this section, we provide some sample properties we have been able to verify using our translation into SMV:

"Variables up and low are always valid positions of queue"

```
Bounds:SPEC AG(low_2 >= 1 & low_2 <= SIZE & up_2 >= 1 & up_2 <= SIZE);
```

"Variable count ranges from 0 (empty queue) to SIZE-1 (full queue)"

```
Count:SPEC AG(count_2 >= 0 & count_2 <= SIZE−1);
```

"Variable out_proc of the duplexer always holds a dummy process or a valid process (a positive process id and a positive number of seconds)"

```
NoInvalidDuplexerOut:SPEC AG(out_p_0 = [0,0] | (out_p_0[0] >0 & out_p_0[1] >0))
```

"All processes held in queue have a positive number of seconds remaining to be run" for (i =1;i<=SIZE;i=i+1){NoFinished[i]:**SPEC AG**(q_2[i][0] >0 →q_2[i][1]>0);}

"All live processes (in the processor) eventually finish"

for (i =1;i<=MAXINT;i=i+1){Proccessed[i]:
SPEC AG(curr_p_3[0]=i & curr_p_3[1] >0 →AF (curr_p_3[0]=i & curr_p_3[1]=0));}

Some of these properties can be verified locally within one component's design (for instance, the first two properties above are properties of the queue). This is so thanks to the fact that safety properties of designs are preserved through superposition morphisms. Other properties, such as the third one above, are *emergent properties*, in the sense of [3], i.e., they are properties of a design that emerge due to the interaction of it with other designs of the system.

4   Conclusions

We have presented a characterisation of CommUnity designs in SMV, defined with the aim of verifying temporal properties of these designs. We have experimented with the modularisation of the verification activities in SMV by exploiting Community's superposition morphisms, in the way indicated in [13]. We also observed that refinement morphisms, related to abstraction, are not powerful enough with respect to the improvement of automated verification, since they do not allow for data refinement. In order to overcome this limitation, we used an abstract interpretation mechanism known as predicate abstraction [8]. We also observed that, although predicate abstraction preserves a wide range of properties of designs, it does not necessarily preserve readiness properties of actions, related to the required non determinism of components. We developed a case study based on a modular specification of a processor with a simple process scheduling mechanism, and verified several temporal properties, including safety and liveness properties. Some of these were verified modularly, using abstraction and superposition morphisms.

We believe that CommUnity is an interesting language that deserves more attention. As we mentioned, it is a language that puts special emphasis on ways of composing specifications of components via their coordination, and clearly distinguishes action availability from action readiness. Moreover, there have been recently some extensions of it in order to capture complex notions such as mobility and dynamic reconfiguration. Of course, having appropriate tool support would improve the use of the language, and the work we report here is an initial attempt in this direction.

We are implementing a tool for verifying temporal properties of CommUnity designs. This tool is, at the moment, just a compiler that implements the translation of CommUnity designs into SMV. We are using the colimit generation procedure available in the CommUnity Workbench, and using a SAT solver to check the proof obligations associated to the construction of the abstract transition systems related to predicate abstraction. This is done manually, at the moment, but we plan to incorporate the generation and verification of these proof obligations to the tool. We also plan to exploit the hierarchical structure of SMV specifications in our translation (at the moment, our translations generate unstructured SMV specifications).

As work in progress, we are trying to characterise the abstraction associated with predicate abstraction in a categorical way (via an appropriate morphism capturing data refinement). We are also studying the verification of temporal properties of CommUnity's *dynamic software architectures* [22], i.e., architectural configuration that might change at run time (e.g., via the deletion or creation of components, and the deletion and creation of connectors between components). Reasoning about temporal properties of dynamic architectures is notably more complex, since it is necessary to characterise the architectural configuration of the system as part of the state of the system. We are also looking at how aspects, in the sense of [10], can be applied to CommUnity designs. Aspects, as already observed in [9] and later work, can be implemented via combinations of superimpositions. In [11], the authors show how several aspects can be successfully characterised and combined in an organised way in CommUnity, via the use of higher-order architectural connectors (aspect weaving would correspond to colimit construction). In fact, we believe that most aspects can be characterised as architectural transformation patterns, replacing some part of a system design, defined by a pattern of components and connectors, by another pattern of components and connectors. However, for this approach to be powerful enough, we believe it is necessary to use an additional kind of superposition, so called invasive superpositions, that can break encapsulation and weakens lower and upper guards, and generalise CommUnity's designs to allow the design of *hierarchical*, reconfigurable systems. Aspect "weaving" would still be realised by the colimit construction.

Acknowledgements

The first author was partially supported by the Argentinian Agency for Scientific and Technological Promotion (ANPCyT) and the Agencia Córdoba Ciencia, and his visits to McMaster University that contributed to this work were supported by McMaster University and the Canada Research Chair programme. The second author was partially supported by CONICET and the Agencia Córdoba Ciencia. The third author was partially supported by McMaster University, the Canada Research Chair programme, and the Natural Sciences and Engineering Council of Canada.

References

1. Chandy, K., Misra, J.: Parallel Program Design - A Foundation. Addison-Wesley, Reading (1988)
2. Clarke, E., Grumberg, O., Long, D.: Model Checking and Abstraction. In: ACM Trans. on Programming Languages and Systems, vol. 16(5), ACM Press, New York (1994)

3. Fiadeiro, J.: On the Emergence of Properties in Component-Based Systems. In: Nivat, M., Wirsing, M. (eds.) AMAST 1996. LNCS, vol. 1101, Springer, Heidelberg (1996)
4. Fiadeiro, J., Maibaum, T.: Categorical Semantics of Parallel Program Design. In: Science of Computer Programming, vol. 28(2-3), Elsevier, Amsterdam (1997)
5. Francez, N., Forman, I.: Interacting Processes. Addison-Wesley, Reading (1996)
6. Garlan, D., Monroe, R., Wile, D.: ACME: An Architecture Description Interchange Language. In: Proc. of CASCON'97, Toronto, Ontario (1997)
7. Goguen, J.: Categorical Foundations for General System Theory. In: Advances in Cybernetics anda Systems Research, Transcripta Books (1973)
8. Graf, S., Saidi, H.: Construction of abstract state graphs with PVS. In: Grumberg, O. (ed.) CAV 1997. LNCS, vol. 1254, Springer, Heidelberg (1997)
9. Katz, S., Gil, J.: Aspects and Superimpositions. In: Moreira, A.M.D., Demeyer, S. (eds.) Object-Oriented Technology. ECOOP'99 Workshop Reader. LNCS, vol. 1743, Springer, Heidelberg (1999)
10. Kiczales, G., Lamping, J., Mendhekar, A., Maeda, C., Lopes, C.V., Loingtier, J.-M., Irwin, J.: Aspect-Oriented Programming. In: Aksit, M., Matsuoka, S. (eds.) ECOOP 1997. LNCS, vol. 1241, Springer, Heidelberg (1997)
11. Lopes, A., Wermelinger, M., Fiadeiro, J.: Higher-Order Architectural Connectors. ACM Trans. on Software Engineering and Methodology, vol. 12(1). ACM Press, New York (2003)
12. Lopes, A., Fiadeiro, J.: Using Explicit State to Describe Architectures. In: Finance, J.-P. (ed.) ETAPS 1999 and FASE 1999. LNCS, vol. 1577, Springer, Heidelberg (1999)
13. Lopes, A., Fiadeiro, J.: Superposition: Composition vs. Refinement of Non-Deterministic, Action-Based Systems. In: Formal Aspects of Computing, vol. 16(1), Springer, Heidelberg (2004)
14. Luckham, D., Kenney, J., Augustin, L., Vera, J., Bryan, D., Mann, W.: Specification and Analysis of System Architecture Using Rapide. IEEE Trans. on Software Engineering. IEEE Press, New York (1995)
15. Magee, J., Dulay, N., Eisenbach, S., Kramer, J.: Specifying Distributed Software Architectures. In: Botella, P., Schäfer, W. (eds.) ESEC 1995. LNCS, vol. 989, Springer, Heidelberg (1995)
16. Manna, Z., Pnueli, A.: The Temporal Logic of Reactive and Concurrent Systems - Specification. Springer, Heidelberg (1991)
17. Manna, Z., Pnueli, A.: Temporal Verification of Reactive Systems - Safety. Springer, Heidelberg (1995)
18. McMillan, K.: Symbolic Model Checking - An Approach to the State Explosion Problem, PhD thesis, SCS, Carnegie Mellon University (1992)
19. McMillan, K.: The SMV Language, Cadence Berkeley Labs, Cadence Design Systems (1998)
20. Medvidovic, N., Oreizy, P., Robbins, J., Taylor, R.: Using Object-Oriented Typing to Support Architectural Design in the C2 Style. In: Proc. of ACM SIGSOFT '96, San Francisco, CA, ACM Press, New York (1996)
21. Wermelinger, M., Lopes, A., Fiadeiro, J.: Superposing Connectors. In: Proc. of the 10th International Workshop on Software Specification and Design, IEEE Press, Los Alamitos (2000)
22. Wermelinger, M., Lopes, A., Fiadeiro, J.: A Graph Based Architectural (Re)configuration Language. In: Proc. of ESEC/FSE'01, ACM Press, New York (2001)
23. Wermelinger, M., Oliveira, C.: The CommUnity Workbench. In: Proc. of ICSE 2002, Orlando (FL), USA, ACM Press, New York (2002)

Precise Scenarios – A Customer-Friendly Foundation for Formal Specifications

Oliver Au, Roger Stone, and John Cooke

Loughborough University, England
{o.t.s.au,r.g.stone,d.j.cooke}@lboro.ac.uk

Abstract. A formal specification, written in a mathematical notation, is beyond the comprehension of the average software customer. As a result, the customer cannot provide useful feedback regarding its correctness and completeness. To address this problem, we suggest the formalism expert to work with the customer to create precise scenarios. With only a few simple Z concepts, a precise scenario describes an operation by its effects on the system state. The customer would find a concrete precise scenario easier to understand than its corresponding abstract schema. The Z expert derives schemas based on the precise scenarios. Precise scenarios afford user involvement that improves the odds of a formal specification fully capturing the user requirements.

Keywords: precise scenario, formal method, requirements specification, use case, Z notation.

1 Introduction

The most important software project success factor is user involvement [1]. Specifications in mathematical notations are difficult for users to read and provide meaningful feedback [2]. Thus a formal specification may not truly reflect their requirements. This could explain the limited adoption of formal methods [3]. We hope to broaden the appeal of formal specification by integrating into it the intuitive scenarios. The result is increased user involvement in the application of formal methods.

Use cases and scenarios can involve customers in requirements elicitation. There should be a use case for each user task. A use case consists of several scenarios, one scenario for a situation. The most common way to describe the details of a scenario is by listing a sequence of steps. Each step names an actor and describes its action in a natural language. Due to the inherited ambiguity, the scenario descriptions are not a reliable basis for the formal specification.

We propose to describe a scenario by its precise effects on a state. A state is represented by its actual data expressed in a small subset of the specification language Z. For the layman, actual data are easier to understand than their abstract descriptions. A small number of Z symbols used in the precise scenarios make them easier to understand than the corresponding schemas. The customers can participate in the creation of the precise scenarios. But scenarios only partially

J. Davies and J. Gibbons (Eds.): IFM 2007, LNCS 4591, pp. 21–36, 2007.

describe the infinite behaviour of a software application. A Z expert will need to generalise the scenarios into schemas that form a complete Z specification. We could have demonstrated precise scenarios with another state-based specification language such as VDM-SL. However we find the *schema* operators in Z, for example, conjunction and disjunction, particular useful in the incremental development of a formal specification.

The idea of creating formal specifications from scenarios is not new. Amyot et al. express scenarios in Use Case Maps (UCM) and translate them into high-level LOTOS specifications [4]. Whittle and Schumann create statechart diagrams from UML sequence diagrams [5]. Uchitel et al. [6] and Damas et al. [7] use message sequence charts (MSC) to synthesize labeled transition system (LTS). System behaviour in the above research is limited to sequences of events. Being based on Z, precise scenarios can represent general computation beyond events.

In another strand of research, Grieskamp and Lepper combine use cases with Z [8]. Use cases relate operations of a Z specification in actual usage. Test dialogues, built with nondeterministic choice, repetition and interruption, are executed in ZETA [9]. In contrast to our research goal, their focus on black-box testing worsens the accessibility by software customers.

Structured-Object-based-Formal Language (SOFL) integrates structured methods, object-oriented methods and formal methods. Condition data flow diagrams are created with structured methods. Details are added with object-oriented methods. The formal part in VDM only provides partial constraints to the final specification [10, section 2]. Reviews, inspections and testing take the place of formal proofs. SOFL may be more appropriately considered a semi-formal methodology. SOFL overhauls the entire software development life cycle while precise scenarios only directly affect the specification activities.

Test First Design (TFD) or Test Driven Development (TDD) is a required practice of Extreme Progamming (XP) [11]. TDD is an iterative development approach with each iteration consists of five small steps: write a test, make it compile, run it to see that it fails, modify the code until the test succeeds, and refactor the code to remove any duplication introduced [12]. Tests, examples in disguise, are used to guide programming. We use precise scenarios to guide specification writing.

Framework for Integrated Tests (Fit) is a tool for enhancing collaboration among customers, programmers and testers [13]. Customers document sample computations in table form with HTML files. A row on a table, with specific input and output values, denotes an example. Programmers create classes called *fixture* to perform the necessary computing. The customer, programmer or tester can run the fixture against the table within the framework. It creates a similar table that highlights unexpected output values. New tests or examples can be easily added to the table for a rerun. A potential drawback in Fit is that only simple values are allowed in table cells. Though unnecessary for precise scenarios, we have presented them in this paper using table form. We allow a table cell to hold expressive data structures, for example, a set of relations.

We use a simple ordering problem to demonstrate our approach [14]. Section 2 describes the problem and a representation of the state space in Z. Each of sections 3 to 6 describes a user task, its precise scenarios and their use in the derivation of schemas. Section 7 discusses validation, underspecification, overspecification, nondeterminism, testing and tool support. Our conclusions are stated in section 8.

2   Ordering Problem and State Space

There are four user tasks in our ordering problem: create a new order, invoice an order, cancel an order and refill the stock. The following statement introduces basic types *OrderId* and *Product* for the identification of individual orders and products. Once defined, we can use them in the specification without worrying about their implementation.

[*OrderId, Product*]

When an order is newly created, it will be in the state *pending*. After the order has left the warehouse, its state changes to *invoiced*. These are the only two order states that concern us regarding the scenarios to be discussed. The following definition could be modified by adding the new state *paid* to deal with payment scenarios in an iterative development process which is beyond the scope of this paper.

OrderState ::= *pending* | *invoiced*

We declare the state space with schema *OrderSystem* which has four variables, and after a horizontal dividing line, two invariants.

$$
\begin{array}{l}
\underline{\quad OrderSystem \quad\quad\quad\quad\quad\quad\quad\quad\quad\quad\quad\quad\quad\quad\quad} \\
\quad stock : \text{bag } Product \\
\quad orders : OrderId \nrightarrow \text{bag } Product \\
\quad orderStatus : OrderId \nrightarrow OrderState \\
\quad freeIds : \mathbb{P}\, OrderId \\
\hline
\quad \text{dom } orders = \text{dom } orderStatus \\
\quad \text{dom } orders \cap freeIds = \varnothing \\
\end{array}
$$

A bag of *Product* is equivalent to a partial function from *Product* to the set of positive natural numbers $\mathbb{N}_1$. We use the function to keep track of a product's quantity in stock or in an order. The symbols $\nrightarrow$ and $\mathbb{P}$ represent partial function and power set respectively. The keyword dom stands for domain. The first invariant ensures that an order id in use must appear in both *orders* and *orderStatus* for an order cannot exist without its status. The second invariant prevents an order id from being used and at the same time available for new orders. Often, we don't know all the constraints until we have explored the scenarios. After an operation, we want to report whether it was successful.

$$Report ::= OK \mid no\_more\_ids \mid order\_not\_pending$$
$$\mid id\_not\_found \mid not\_enough\_stock$$

In an arbitrary state, we have 5 nuts and 6 bolts in stock. Order 1 was placed for 2 nuts and 2 bolts. Order 2 was placed for 3 bolts. Order 1 has been invoiced and order 2 is still pending. Ids 3 and 4 are free for future use. The state could be expressed with the following values in the variables of schema $OrderSystem$.

$$stock = \{nut \mapsto 5, bolt \mapsto 6\}$$
$$orders = \{1 \mapsto \{nut \mapsto 2, bolt \mapsto 2\}, 2 \mapsto \{bolt \mapsto 3\}\}$$
$$orderStatus = \{1 \mapsto invoiced, 2 \mapsto pending\}$$
$$freeIds = \{3, 4\}$$

3   New Order

The scenario $NewOrder$ documents a successful order creation using four Z concepts. They are input with the symbol ?, output with !, maplet with $\mapsto$, and set with { } and commas. The input parameter $order?$ places a new order for 4 $nuts$ and 4 $bolts$. Below the table headings are the pre-state followed by the post-state. In the post-state, the 3-dot symbol . . . is used to denote the unchanged function $stock$. Functions $orders$ and $orderStatus$ are extended by a map for $OrderId$ 3. The element 3 is removed from the set $freeIds$. The output parameters $id!$ and $report!$ return 3 and OK respectively.

scenario $NewOrder$
$order? = \{nut_a \mapsto 4_b, bolt_c \mapsto 4_d\}$

stock	orders	orderStatus	freeIds
$\{nut \mapsto 5,$ $bolt \mapsto 6\}$	$\{1 \mapsto \{nut \mapsto 2, bolt \mapsto 2\},$ $2 \mapsto \{bolt \mapsto 3\}\}$	$\{1 \mapsto invoiced,$ $2 \mapsto invoiced\}$	$\{3_e, 4\}$
. . .	$\{1 \mapsto \{nut \mapsto 2, bolt \mapsto 2\},$ $2 \mapsto \{bolt \mapsto 3\},$ $3_e \mapsto \{nut_a \mapsto 4_b, bolt_c \mapsto 4_d\}\}$	$\{1 \mapsto invoiced,$ $2 \mapsto invoiced,$ $3_e \mapsto pending\}$	$\{4\}$

$id! = 3_e, report! = OK$

Values referred in input/output parameters are subscripted allowing us to relate them to the state. When two pieces of data have the same subscript, for example, 3_e in the post-state of $orders$ and $orderStatus$, they must be identical. If two pieces of data have identical value but different subscripts, for example 4_b and 4_d, their equality is merely a coincidence. Value 4_d could have been 5_d throughout the scenario. The values allowed in a scenario are confined by earlier declarations in schema $OrderSystem$. For example, 4_b and 4_d must be taken from the set of positive natural numbers $\mathbb{N}_1$.

To generalise the above scenario to an operation schema, we need a type for the new order that maps $Product$ to a positive integer.

$$Order == \{order : \text{bag } Product \mid order \neq \varnothing\}$$

The scenario *NewOrder* can be converted to the equivalent Z schema below. The declaration part declares the variables, input/output parameters and their types. The symbol Δ alerts us that the state of *OrderSystem* is changed by this operation. The predicate part lists the constraints on the variables and parameters. The trailing symbol $'$ is used to denote a value after the operation.

NewOrderScenario

$\Delta\,OrderSystem$
$order? : Order$
$id! : OrderId$
$report! : Report$

$order? = \{nut_a \mapsto 4_b, bolt_c \mapsto 4_d\}$
$3_e \in freeIds$
$stock' = stock$
$orders' = orders \cup \{3_e \mapsto \{nut_a \mapsto 4_b, bolt_c \mapsto 4_d\}\}$
$orderStatus' = orderStatus \cup \{3_e \mapsto pending\}$
$freeIds' = freeIds \setminus \{3_e\}$
$id! = 3_e$
$report! = OK$

The first predicate specifies the value of the input parameter *order?*. The membership of 3_e in set *freeIds* gives rise to the second predicate. The third predicate states that *stock* is unchanged after the operation. The new maplets for 3_e, adding to *orders* and *orderStatus*, are captured in the fourth and fifth predicates. The removal of 3_e from the set *freeIds* is expressed next. The values for the output parameters are specified by the last two predicates.

Subscripted values, used to represent input/output parameters, are not fixed. For example, instead of picking 3_e in the pre-state, we could have picked 4_e. We may therefore replace the subscripted values with the input/output variables,

---
NewOrderGeneralised

$\Delta\,OrderSystem$
$order? : Order$
$id! : OrderId$
$report! : Report$

$order? = order?$
$id! \in freeIds$
$stock' = stock$
$orders' = orders \cup \{id! \mapsto order?\}$
$orderStatus' = orderStatus \cup \{id! \mapsto pending\}$
$freeIds' = freeIds \setminus \{id!\}$
$id! = id!$
$report! = OK$

---

for example, "3_e" with "$id!$" and "$\{nut_a \mapsto 4_b, bolt_c \mapsto 4_d\}$" with "$order?$", to have the generalised schema.

The generalised version of the Z schema can be simplified by removing the two identity predicates that always evaluate to *true*.

NewOrder
$\Delta\,OrderSystem$
$order? : Order$
$id! : OrderId$
$report! : Report$

$id! \in freeIds$
$stock' = stock$
$orders' = orders \cup \{id! \mapsto order?\}$
$orderStatus' = orderStatus \cup \{id! \mapsto pending\}$
$freeIds' = freeIds \setminus \{id!\}$
$report! = OK$

We now turn our attention to an unsuccessful attempt to create a new order. A separate post-state is not shown in the scenario because the state is unchanged. No subscripts are used because the input/output parameters do not relate to any data in the state. The precondition is an empty set *freeIds*.

scenario *NoMoreIdsError*
$order? = \{nut \mapsto 7\}$

stock	orders	orderStatus	freeIds
$\{nut \mapsto 5,$ $bolt \mapsto 6\}$	$\{1 \mapsto \{nut \mapsto 2, bolt \mapsto 2\},$ $2 \mapsto \{bolt \mapsto 3\},$ $3 \mapsto \{nut \mapsto 4, bolt \mapsto 4\},$ $4 \mapsto \{bolt \mapsto 8\}\}$	$\{1 \mapsto invoiced,$ $2 \mapsto invoiced,$ $3 \mapsto pending,$ $4 \mapsto pending\}$	$\{\ \}$

$report! = no\_more\_ids$

The symbol Ξ indicates that the state *OrderSystem* is unchanged by the schema.

NoMoreIdsError
$\Xi\,OrderSystem$
$order? : Order$
$report! : Report$

$freeIds = \varnothing$
$report! = no\_more\_ids$

The precondition of *NewOrder* is that there is some element in *freeIds*. Conversely, the precondition of *NoMoreIdsError* is that the set *freeIds* is empty. The disjunction of the two preconditions is *true*. Therefore operation *NewOrderOp* can handle all situations.

$$NewOrderOp == NewOrder \lor NoMoreIdsError$$

4 Invoice Order

The invoicing operation updates the order status from *pending* to *invoiced* and reduces the stock accordingly. The two preconditions, shown before the table, require the state to have sufficient stock to fill the order. The two postconditions, shown after the table, determine the updated stock quantities.

scenario *InvoiceOrder*

$id? = 2_a, 4_f \leq 5_c, 3_h \leq 9_e$

stock	orders	orderStatus	freeIds
$\{nut_b \mapsto 5_c,$ $bolt_d \mapsto 9_e\}$	$\{1 \mapsto \{nut \mapsto 2\},$ $2_a \mapsto \{nut_b \mapsto 4_f, bolt_d \mapsto 3_h\}\}$	$\{1 \mapsto invoiced,$ $2_a \mapsto pending\}$	$\{3, 4\}$
$\{nut_b \mapsto 1_i,$ $bolt_d \mapsto 6_j\}$	$\ldots$	$\{1 \mapsto invoiced,$ $2_a \mapsto invoiced\}$	$\ldots$

$report! = OK, 1_i = 5_c - 4_f, 6_j = 9_e - 3_h$

The Z mathematical toolkit provides the sub-bag symbol $\sqsubseteq$ that concisely expresses multiple $\leq$ relationships between corresponding quantities in two bags. Likewise, the bag difference symbol $\uplus$ expresses multiple pairwise subtractions. The updating of the order status to *invoiced* is expressed with the override symbol $\oplus$. Round brackets represent function application, for example, $orders(2_a)$ returns $\{nut_b \mapsto 4_f, bolt_d \mapsto 3_h\}$.

___ *InvoiceOrderScenario* _____

$\Delta OrderSystem$
$id? : OrderId$
$report! : Report$

$id? = 2_a$
$orders(2_a) \sqsubseteq stock$
$orderStatus(2_a) = pending$
$stock' = stock \uplus orders(2_a)$
$orders' = orders$
$orderStatus' = orderStatus \oplus \{2_a \mapsto invoiced\}$
$freeIds' = freeIds$
$report! = OK$

_____

After substitution and simplification, we have the following Z schema.

```
┌─ InvoiceOrder ──────────────────────────────────────────
│ Δ OrderSystem
│ id? : OrderId
│ report! : Report
├──────────────────────────────────────────────────────────
│ orders(id?) ⊑ stock
│ orderStatus(id?) = pending
│ stock' = stock ⊎ orders(id?)
│ orders' = orders
│ orderStatus' = orderStatus ⊕ {id? ↦ invoiced}
│ freeIds' = freeIds
│ report! = OK
└──────────────────────────────────────────────────────────
```

We have three unsuccessful scenarios for this operation. Explanations and intermediate steps are skimmed here due to their similarities to earlier scenarios.

scenario *IdNotFoundError*

$id? = 3_a, 3_a \neq 1_b, 3_a \neq 2_c$

stock	orders	orderStatus	freeIds
$\{nut \mapsto 5,$ $bolt \mapsto 9\}$	$\{1 \mapsto \{nut \mapsto 2, bolt \mapsto 2\},$ $2 \mapsto \{bolt \mapsto 3\}\}$	$\{1_b \mapsto invoiced,$ $2_c \mapsto pending\}$	$\{3, 4\}$

$report! = id\_not\_found$

```
┌─ IdNotFoundErrorScenario ───────────────────────────────
│ Ξ State
│ id? : OrderId
│ report! : Report
├──────────────────────────────────────────────────────────
│ id? = 3_a
│ 3_a ∉ {1_b, 2_c}
│ report! = id_not_found
└──────────────────────────────────────────────────────────
```

```
┌─ IdNotFoundError ───────────────────────────────────────
│ Ξ State
│ id? : OrderId
│ report! : Report
├──────────────────────────────────────────────────────────
│ id? ∉ dom orderStatus
│ report! = id_not_found
└──────────────────────────────────────────────────────────
```

scenario *OrderNotPendingError*

$id? = 1_a, invoiced_b \neq pending$

stock	orders	orderStatus	freeIds
$\{nut \mapsto 5,$ $bolt \mapsto 9\}$	$\{1 \mapsto \{nut \mapsto 2, bolt \mapsto 2\},$ $2 \mapsto \{bolt \mapsto 3\}\}$	$\{1_a \mapsto invoiced_b,$ $2 \mapsto pending\}$	$\{3, 4\}$

$report! = order\_not\_pending$

```
 ┌─ OrderNotPendingError ──────────────────────────────────
 │ Ξ State
 │ id? : OrderId
 │ report! : Report
 ├─────────────────────────────────────────────────────────
 │ orderStatus(id?) ≠ pending
 │ report! = order_not_pending
 └─────────────────────────────────────────────────────────
```

scenario *NotEnoughStockError*

$id? = 2_a, 77_c > 9_b$

stock	orders	orderStatus	freeIds
$\{nut \mapsto 5,$ $bolt_d \mapsto 9_b\}$	$\{1 \mapsto \{nut \mapsto 2, bolt \mapsto 2\},$ $2_a \mapsto \{bolt_d \mapsto 77_c\}\}$	$\{1 \mapsto invoiced,$ $2 \mapsto pending\}$	$\{3, 4\}$

$report! = not\_enough\_stock$

```
 ┌─ NotEnoughStockError ───────────────────────────────────
 │ Ξ State
 │ id? : OrderId
 │ report! : Report
 ├─────────────────────────────────────────────────────────
 │ ¬(orders(id?) ⊑ stock)
 │ report! = not_enough_stock
 └─────────────────────────────────────────────────────────
```

We define operation *InvoiceOrderOp* to deal with all situations. When multiple errors happen at the same time, the definition is unspecific about which error report to return. We will discuss nondeterminism in section 7.3.

$$InvoiceOrderOp == InvoiceOrder \lor IdNotFoundError \lor$$
$$OrderNotPendingError \lor NotEnoughStockError$$

5   Cancel Order

A *pending* order may be cancelled. Its order id is returned to the pool of free id's for future use.

scenario *CancelOrder*

$id? = 2_a$

stock	orders	orderStatus	freeIds
$\{nut \mapsto 5,$ $bolt \mapsto 6\}$	$\{1 \mapsto \{nut \mapsto 2, bolt \mapsto 2\},$ $2_a \mapsto \{bolt \mapsto 3\}\}$	$\{1 \mapsto invoiced,$ $2_a \mapsto pending_b\}$	$\{3, 4\}$
$\ldots$	$\{1 \mapsto \{nut \mapsto 2, bolt \mapsto 2\}\}$	$\{1 \mapsto invoiced\}$	$\{2_a, 3, 4\}$

$report! = OK$

The domain anti-restriction symbol $\lhd$ is used to remove maplets for order id 2_a from *orders* and *orderStatus*.

CancelOrderScenario _____

$\Delta OrderSystem$
$id? : OrderId$
$report! : Report$

$id? = 2_a$
$orderStatus(2_a) = pending$
$stock' = stock$
$orders' = \{2_a\} \lhd orders$
$orderStatus' = \{2_a\} \lhd orderStatus$
$freeIds' = \{2_a\} \cup freeIds$
$report! = OK$

We generalise the scenario schema by replacing 2_a with *id?*. After simplification, we have schema *CancelOrder*.

CancelOrder _____

$\Delta OrderSystem$
$id? : OrderId$
$report! : Report$

$orderStatus(id?) = pending$
$stock' = stock$
$orders' = \{id?\} \lhd orders$
$orderStatus' = \{id?\} \lhd orderStatus$
$freeIds' = \{id?\} \cup freeIds$
$report! = OK$

It is an error trying to cancel an order that does not exist or have already been *invoiced*. We can reuse error detecting schemas to handle all situations.

$$CancelOrderOp == CancelOrder \lor IdNotFoundError \lor$$
$$OrderNotPendingError$$

6   Enter Stock

Entering stock is the task of replenishing depleted stock. By assuming that there is always sufficient storage space, we don't worry about detecting an error for this task. The postconditions concerning the updated stock quantities are expressed with the bag addition symbol $\uplus$.

scenario *EnterStock*

$newStock? = \{nut_a \mapsto 80_b, bolt_c \mapsto 70_d\}$

stock	orders	orderStatus	freeIds
$\{nut_a \mapsto 5_e,$ $bolt_c \mapsto 9_f\}$	$\{1 \mapsto \{nut \mapsto 2, bolt \mapsto 2\},$ $2 \mapsto \{bolt \mapsto 3\}\}$	$\{1 \mapsto invoiced,$ $2 \mapsto pending\}$	$\{3, 4\}$
$\{nut_a \mapsto 85_g,$ $bolt_c \mapsto 79_h\}$	$\ldots$	$\ldots$	$\ldots$

$report! = OK, 85_g = 5_e + 80_b, 79_h = 9_f + 70_d$

$\_\_EnterStockScenario_____$
$\Delta OrderSystem$
$newStock? : Order$
$report! : Report$
$\rule{6cm}{0.4pt}$
$newStock? = \{nut_a \mapsto 80_b, bolt_c \mapsto 70_d\}$
$stock' = stock \uplus \{nut_a \mapsto 80_b, bolt_c \mapsto 70_d\}$
$orders' = orders$
$orderStatus' = orderStatus$
$freeIds' = freeIds$
$report! = OK$

$\_\_EnterStock_____$
$\Delta OrderSystem$
$newStock? : Order$
$report! : Report$
$\rule{6cm}{0.4pt}$
$stock' = stock \uplus newStock?$
$orders' = orders$
$orderStatus' = orderStatus$
$freeIds' = freeIds$
$report! = OK$

---

7 Validation

We can apply the values of input parameters and pre-states in a scenario to its operation schema. If the post-state and output parameters obtained are the same as in the original scenario, we know that the operation schema works correctly for the scenario.

Another type of validation we can perform is to apply new input parameters and pre-state values to an operation schema. This exercise in essence creates new scenarios. If the customer is satisfied with the newly created post-states and output parameters, we gain confidence that our Z schemas meet the user requirements. For instance, we can validate schema *InvoiceOrder* with the following input parameter and pre-state different from earlier scenarios.

$$id? = 3$$
$$stock = \{\ nut \mapsto 5, bolt \mapsto 9\}$$
$$orders = \{\ 1 \mapsto \{nut \mapsto 2\},$$
$$2 \mapsto \{nut \mapsto 4, bolt \mapsto 3\},$$
$$3 \mapsto \{nut \mapsto 5, bolt \mapsto 6\}\}$$
$$orderStatus = \{\ 1 \mapsto invoiced,\ 2 \mapsto invoiced,\ 3 \mapsto pending\}$$
$$freeIds = \{4\}$$

The first two predicates in schema *InvoiceOrder* specify its preconditions. They both evaluate to *true* with the above data. The next four predicates specify the resulting values of the four variables. The last predicate specifies the output parameter. To save space, we only show the evaluation of two predicates.

$$orders(id?) \sqsubseteq stock$$
$$orders(3) \sqsubseteq \{nut \mapsto 5, bolt \mapsto 9\}$$
$$\{nut \mapsto 5, bolt \mapsto 6\} \sqsubseteq \{nut \mapsto 5, bolt \mapsto 9\}$$
$$true$$

$$stock' = stock \uplus orders(id?)$$
$$stock' = \{nut \mapsto 5, bolt \mapsto 9\} \uplus \{nut \mapsto 5, bolt \mapsto 6\}$$
$$stock' = \{bolt \mapsto 3\}$$

After evaluating the schema predicates, we have a new scenario. Though without subscripts, preconditions and postconditions, there is enough information for the customer to decide if it matches his or her expectation.

scenario *InvoiceOrderNew*
$$id? = 3$$

stock	orders	orderStatus	ids
$\{nut \mapsto 5,$ $bolt \mapsto 9\}$	$\{1 \mapsto \{nut \mapsto 2\},$ $2 \mapsto \{nut \mapsto 4, bolt \mapsto 3\}$ $3 \mapsto \{bolt \mapsto 5, bolt \mapsto 6\}\}$	$\{1 \mapsto invoiced,$ $2 \mapsto invoiced,$ $3 \mapsto pending\}$	$\{4\}$
$\{bolt \mapsto 3\}$	...	$\{1 \mapsto invoiced,$ $2 \mapsto invoiced,$ $3 \mapsto invoiced\}$	...

$$report! = OK$$

7.1   Underspecification

Underspecification happens when a required condition is missing. Suppose we had omitted the following precondition of checking for sufficient stock in schema *InvoiceOrder*.

$$orders(id?) \sqsubseteq stock$$

When we validate the incorrect schema with an excessive ordered quantity, the operation may still succeed and yield a negative stock quantity which can easily be spotted by the customer as an error.

7.2 Overspecification

Overspecification happens when unnecessary conditions are included in a scenario. Recall scenario *NewOrder*. The quantities of the nuts and bolts in the input parameter were both 4 by coincidence. In our original scenario, they have different subscripts b and d to indicate that they need not be the same. Suppose we had made a mistake by using the same subscript b on both occurrences of 4. We would have a slightly different scenario.

scenario *OverSpecifiedNewOrder*

$order? = \{nut_a \mapsto 4_b, bolt_c \mapsto 4_b\}$

stock	orders		orderStatus	freeIds
$\{nut \mapsto 5,$ $bolt \mapsto 6\}$	$\{1 \mapsto \{nut \mapsto 2, bolt \mapsto 2\},$ $2 \mapsto \{bolt \mapsto 3\}\}$		$\{1 \mapsto invoiced,$ $2 \mapsto invoiced\}$	$\{3_e, 4\}$
...	$\{1 \mapsto \{nut \mapsto 2, bolt \mapsto 2\},$ $2 \mapsto \{bolt \mapsto 3\},$ $3_e \mapsto \{nut_a \mapsto 4_b, bolt_c \mapsto 4_b\}\}$		$\{1 \mapsto invoiced,$ $2 \mapsto invoiced,$ $3_e \mapsto pending\}$	$\{4\}$

$id! = 3_e, report! = OK$

The equality implied by the identical subscripts gives rise to the first predicate in the following schema. When we validate the schema with $order? = \{nut \mapsto 7, bolt \mapsto 9\}$, the new predicate would evaluate to *false*. Overspecification is caught when the operation fails on legitimate input and pre-state.

```
┌─ OverSpecifiedNewOrder ──────────────────────────────
│ ΔOrderSystem
│ order? : Order
│ id! : OrderId
│ report! : Report
├──────────────────────────────────────────────────────
│ ∀ p, q : Product | p ∈ dom order? ∧ q ∈ dom order? •
│                    order?(p) = order?(q)
│ id! ∈ freeIds
│ stock' = stock
│ orders' = orders ∪ {id! ↦ order?}
│ orderStatus' = orderStatus ∪ {id! ↦ pending}
│ freeIds' = freeIds \ {id!}
│ report! = OK
└──────────────────────────────────────────────────────
```

7.3 Nondeterminism

Recall that we have defined *InvoiceOrderOp* to catch errors.

$$InvoiceOrderOp == InvoiceOrder \lor IdNotFoundError \lor$$
$$OrderNotPendingError \lor NotEnoughStockError$$

If the preconditions of *OrderNotPendingError* and *NotEnoughStockError* are *true* at the same time, which error report are we going to get? In this nondeterministic definition of *InvoiceOrderOp*, we could get either one. If it is necessary to distinguish the two errors, we can eliminate nondeterminism by strengthening their preconditions so that their conjunction is *false*.

There are times that nondeterminism is a sign of error. In section 7.1, we discussed a situation where the checking for sufficient stock was omitted from schema *InvoiceOrder*. The omission causes nondeterminism between *InvoiceOrder* and *NotEnoughStockError*. Adding back the omitted predicate strengthens the preconditions of the incorrect version of schema *InvoiceOrder*. The conjunction of corrected *InvoiceOrder* and *NotEnoughStockError* is *false* and thus nondeterminism between them is removed. In general, we can detect nondeterminism by performing pairwise conjunction on the disjuncts used to define an operation. A non-*false* conjunction suggests nondeterminism.

7.4   Testing

The use of precise scenarios for the development and validation of schemas relates to a software testing technique called *equivalence partitioning* [15]. The technique ensures that a scenario is selected from every class of similar situations. For example, the operation *InvoiceOrder* can be partitioned into at least two classes of situations, one for ordered quantities being a sub-bag of stock quantities and one for otherwise. If necessary, we can divide them into more partitions. For example, we can add a class of situations where the ordered quantities equal to the stock quantities.

The research community has long held the attitude that formal methods reduce or eliminate the need for testing. But how do we know the formal specification is complete in the first place? Even for toy problems, it is hard to be certain that a formal specification is complete. Though the use of precise scenarios cannot guarantee completeness, the improved customer involvement will definitely help.

7.5   Tool Support Required

The success of a methodology relies heavily on the availability of good tools. There are many tools around, for example, CADiℤ [16], CZT (Community Z Tools) [17] and Z/EVES [18], useful for checking type consistency and proving theorems of a Z specification. In this paper, we have manually validated operation schemas against precise scenarios. Existing Z tools can improve the efficiency and reliability of the manual validation exercise by running an operation schema through test cases [18, section 3.2.5]. Specific input values are used to see if they can generate expected values in the state variables.

We need a tool to manage the operation schemas with their related scenarios. When a scenario is changed, we need to identify the affected operation schema to see if it still meets the new requirement described in the updated scenario. Conversely, when we decide to update an operation schema, we need to identify all the affected scenarios. If too many scenarios are affected, we may be better off creating a new operation schema than to update an existing one. A tool with such capabilities does not yet exist.

8   Conclusions

The Z specification we derived in this paper is almost identical to the one found in [14]. One notable difference is that our specification catches more errors. It is premature to conclude how the use of precise scenarios would shape a Z specification. However we do not seem to have lost any capability to create a generic Z specification.

Are precise scenarios more comprehensible than Z specifications by customers? Precise scenarios describe states with actual data; a few simple Z concepts are sufficient. On the other hand Z schemas describe operations with variables; additional Z concepts are needed. The example in this paper and our unpublished work on numerical computation, sorting and telephone system confirm that precise scenarios require fewer simpler concepts to describe than formal specifications. In addition, biologists and educationists suggest that understanding begins with concrete examples [19]. Every customer is unique. In the extreme case where the customer is a Z expert, he or she may actually prefer to reason directly in Z specification. But we think, as long as precise scenarios are not exceedingly lengthy, customers in general will have an easier time understanding them than formal specifications. As we continue to search for a better notation to write precise scenarios and gain experience in using it on real or toy problems, it will take some time before we learn the true value of precise scenarios in requirements elicitation.

In a real development project, there will be a great many precise scenarios because we need a few of them for each operation schema. However we should not be discouraged to use precise scenarios. With appropriate tool support, they are no harder to manage than test cases. In fact, the content that goes into a precise scenario is comparable to what goes into a test case. They differ in the time of creation and purpose. Precise scenarios are created earlier for requirements elicitation. They can be reused as test cases to reduce development costs.

Mistakes are not uncommon during the generalisation of precise scenarios to operation schemas. However underspecification and overspecification will be caught by appropriately written scenarios. The current paper shows only scenarios with pre- and post-states. Work in progress includes longer scenarios with intermediate states. We are also working on the use of precise scenarios with other languages. Eventually, we would like to field-test the approach with suitable tool support.

We propose to use precise scenarios as the foundation for formal specifications because they are simple enough for the customers to understand and yet precise enough for the validation of an implementation. While scenarios have been in use for long, the novelty of precise scenarios is precision without sacrificing simplicity and generality.

References

1. The Standish Group: The CHAOS Report, 5 (1994)
2. Zimmerman, M.K., Lundqvist, K., Leveson, N.: Investigating the Readability of State-Based Formal Requirements Specification Languages. ICSE'02: 24th International Conference on Software Engineering, May 2002, pp. 33–43 (2002)

3. Glass, R.L.: The Mystery of Formal Methods Disuse. Communications of the ACM 47(8), 15–17 (2004)
4. Amyot, D., Logrippo, L., Buhr, R.J.A., Gray, T.: Use Case Maps for the Capture and Validation of Distributed Systems Requirements. RE'99: 4th IEEE International Symposium on Requirements Engineering, June 1999, pp. 44–54 (1999)
5. Whittle, J., Schumann, J.: Generating Statechart Designs from Scenarios. ICSE'00: 22nd International Conference on Software Engineering, June 2000, pp. 314–323 (2000)
6. Uchitel, S., Kramer, J., Magee, J.: Synthesis of Behavioral Models from Scenarios. IEEE Transactions on Software Engineering 29(2), 99–115 (2003)
7. Damas, C., Lambeau, B., Dupont, P., van Lamsweerde, A.: Generating Annotated Behaviour Models from End-User Scenarios. IEEE Transactions on Software Engineering 31(12), 1056–1073 (2005)
8. Grieskamp, W., Lepper, M.: Using Use Cases. In: Executable, Z., Liu, S., McDermid, J.A., Hinchey, M.G. (eds.) ICFEM 2000: 3rd IEEE International Conference on Formal Engineering Methods, September 2000, pp. 111–119 (2000)
9. Büssow, R., Grieskamp, W.: A Modular Framework for the Integration of Heterogeneous Notations and Tools. In: Araki, K., Galloway, A., Taguchi, K. (eds.) IFM99: 1st International Conference on Integrated Formal Methods, June 1999, pp. 211–230 (1999)
10. Liu, S., Offutt, A.J., Ho-Stuart, C., Sun, Y., Ohba, M.: SOFL: A Formal Engineering Methodology for Industrial Applications. IEEE Transactions on Software Engineering 24(1), 24–45 (1998)
11. Beck, K.: Extreme Programming Explained: Embrace Change. Addison-Wesley, Reading (2000)
12. Beck, K.: Test-Driven Development: By Example, p. 24. Addison-Wesley, Reading (2003)
13. Mugridge, R., Cunningham, W.: Fit for Developing Software: Framework for Integrated Tests. Prentice-Hall, Englewood Cliffs (2005)
14. Bowen, J.P.: Chapter 1 - Z. In: Habrias, H., Frappier, M. (eds.) Software Specification Methods, ISTE, pp. 3–20 (2006)
15. Sommerville, I.: Software Engineering, 6th edn., pp. 444–447. Addison-Wesley, Reading (2001)
16. Toyn, I., McDermid, J.A.: CADiZ: An Architecture for Z Tools and its Implementation. Software – Practice and Experience 25(3), 305–330 (1995)
17. Malik, P., Utting, M.: CZT: A Framework for Z Tools. ZB2005: 4th International Conference of B and Z Users, April 2005, pp. 65–84 (2005)
18. Saaltink, M.: The Z/EVES 2.0 User's Guide, ORA Canada, pp. 31–32 (1999)
19. Zull, J.E.: The Art of Changing the Brain, pp. 102–103. Stylus Publishing (2002)

Automated Verification of Security Policies in Mobile Code*

Chiara Braghin[1], Natasha Sharygina[2,3], and Katerina Barone-Adesi[2]

[1] DTI, Università Statale di Milano, Crema, Italy
[2] Faculty of Informatics, Università della Svizzera Italiana, Lugano, Switzerland
[3] School of Computer Science, Carnegie Mellon University, Pittsburgh, USA

Abstract. This paper describes an approach for the automated verification of mobile programs. Mobile systems are characterized by the explicit notion of locations (e.g., sites where they run) and the ability to execute at different locations, yielding a number of security issues. We give formal semantics to mobile systems as Labeled Kripke Structures, which encapsulate the notion of the location net. The location net summarizes the hierarchical nesting of threads constituting a mobile program and enables specifying security policies. We formalize a language for specifying security policies and show how mobile programs can be exhaustively analyzed against any given security policy by using model checking techniques.

We developed and experimented with a prototype framework for analysis of mobile code, using the SATABS model checker. Our approach relies on SA-TABS's support for unbounded thread creation and enhances it with location net abstractions, which are essential for verifying large mobile programs. Our experimental results on various benchmarks are encouraging and demonstrate advantages of the model checking-based approach, which combines the validation of security properties with other checks, such as for buffer overflows.

1 Introduction

Despite the promising applications of mobile code technologies, such as web services and applet models for smart cards, they have not yet been widely deployed. A major problem is security: without appropriate security measures, a malicious applet could mount a variety of attacks against the local computer, such as destroying data (e.g., reformatting the disk), modifying sensitive data (e.g., registering a bank transfer via a home-banking software), divulging personal information over the network, or modifying other programs.

Moreover, programming over a wide area network such as the Internet introduces new issues to the field of multi-threaded programming and analysis. For example, during the execution of a mobile program, a given thread may stop executing at a site, and continue executing at another site. That is, threads may jump from site to site while retaining their conceptual identity. The following issues distinguish mobile systems from a more general case of multi-threaded programs:

---

* This work was done when the first author was staying at the Faculty of Informatics, Università della Svizzera Italiana, Lugano, Switzerland.

J. Davies and J. Gibbons (Eds.): IFM 2007, LNCS 4591, pp. 37–53, 2007.
© Springer-Verlag Berlin Heidelberg 2007

- threads may run in different locations (e.g., administrative domains, hosts, physical locations, etc.);
- communication among threads and threads migration take into account their geographical distribution (e.g., migration can only occur between directly linked net locations).

To protect mobile systems against security leaks, *security policies* are defined, i.e., rules or conditions that state which actions are permitted and which are prohibited in the system. The rules may concern access control or information flow, and are usually verified on the fly during the system execution. The dynamic approach has several drawbacks: it slows down the system execution, there is no formal proof that the dynamic checks are done properly, and the checks are not exhaustive.

This paper describes an approach for modeling and verifying mobile programs. We give formal semantics to mobile systems as Labeled Kripke Structures (LKSs), which encapsulate the notion of location and unbounded thread creation typical to mobile systems. We define the semantics of mobile programs where thread locations are hierarchically structured, where threads are always confined to locations and where threads may move within the Internet. The LKS notation allows modeling both data and communication structures of the multi-threaded systems. Consequently, it outperforms the traditional process algebra approach that captures only the communication behavior.

We formalize a language for specifying general-purpose and application-dependent security policies, and we show how mobile programs can be statically and exhaustively analyzed against those security policies by using model checking techniques. A policy configuration file, specifying what permissions (i.e., which types of system resource access) to deny, is given as an input to the model checker together with the program to be verified. To support features of mobile systems, the policy specification language defines rules for expressing and manipulating the code location.

We implemented a prototype framework for modeling and verifying mobile programs written in C. In our approach, a mobile program is annotated with information related to the security policy in such a way that if and when the security policy is violated, the model checker returns a counter-example that led to such an error. In such a way, we are able to discover both implementation and malicious errors. Our framework uses the SATABS model checker [1], which implements a SAT-based counterexample-guided abstraction refinement framework (CEGAR for short) for ANSI-C programs.

To cope with the computational complexity of verifying mobile programs, we define *projection* abstractions. Given a path of a multi-threaded program, one can construct projections by restricting the path to actions or states satisfying certain conditions. We exploit the explicit notion of locations and define location-based projections, which allow efficient verification of location-specific security policies.

In summary, our approach to modeling and verifying mobile programs has several advantageous features:

- it explicitly models thread location, location distribution and thread moving operations, which are essential elements of mobile programs;
- it preserves both data and communication structures of mobile systems;
- it defines a specification language for specifying security policies of mobile code;

- it integrates model checking technologies to support exhaustive analysis of security policies;
- it defines location-specific abstractions which enable the efficient verification of large mobile code applications.

We experimented with a number of mobile code benchmarks by verifying various security policies. The results of verifying security policies, dealing with both access permissions of system actions and tracing the location net with respect to permissible location configurations, were encouraging.

2 Related Work

The use of mobile systems raises a number of security issues, including access control (is the use of the resource permitted?), user authentication (to identify the valid users), data integrity (to ensure data is delivered intact), data confidentiality (to protect sensitive data), and auditing (to track uses of mobile resources). All but the first category are closely coupled with research in cryptography and are outside of the scope of this paper. Our techniques assume that the appropriate integrity checking and signature validation are completed before the security access policies are checked.

Trust management systems (TMS) [2] address the access control problem by requiring that security policies are defined explicitly in a specification language, and relying on an algorithm to determine when a specific request can be allowed. An extensive survey of trust management systems and various authorization problems can be found in [3,4,5]. The major difference from our work is that these techniques rely on encryption techniques or proof-carrying code certification. For example, in the SPKI/SDSI framework, all principals are represented by their public keys, and access control is established by checking the validity of the corresponding public keys. In contrast, our security analysis reduces access control problems to static reachability analysis.

Certified code [6] is a general mechanism for enforcing security properties. In this paradigm, untrusted mobile code carries annotations that allow a host to verify its trustworthiness. Before running the agent, the host checks the annotations and proves that they imply the host's security policy. Despite the flexibility of this scheme, so far, compilers that generate certified code have focused on simple type safety properties rather than more general security policies. The main difficulty is that automated theorem provers are not powerful enough to infer properties of arbitrary programs and constructing proofs by hand is prohibitively expensive. Unable to prove security properties statically, real-world security systems such as the Java Virtual Machine (JVM) have fallen back on run-time checking. Dynamic security checks are scattered throughout the Java libraries and are intended to ensure that applets do not access protected resources inappropriately. However, this situation is unsatisfying for a number of reasons: 1) dynamic checks are not exhaustive; 2) tests rely on the implementation of monitors which are error-prone; and 3) system execution is delayed during the execution of the monitor.

Modeling of Mobile Systems. The most common approach to modeling mobile programs is the process algebra-based approach. Various location-aware calculi, with an explicit notion of *location*, have arisen in the literature to directly model phenomena such as the distribution of processes within different localities, their migrations, or their failures [7,8,9,10].

The π calculus [11] is often referred to as *mobile* because it features the ability to dynamically create and exchange channel names. While it is a de facto standard for modeling concurrent systems, the mobility it supports encompasses only part of all the abstractions meaningful in a distributed system. In fact, it does not directly and explicitly model phenomena such as the distribution of processes within different localities, their migrations, or their failures. Moreover, mobility is not expressed in a sufficiently explicit manner since it basically allows processes only to change their interconnection structures, even if dynamically. Indeed, name mobility is often referred to as a model of labile processes or as link mobility, characterized by a dynamic interaction structure, and distinguished from calculi of mobile processes which exhibit explicit movement.

Seal [12] is one of the many variants spawned by π calculus. The principal ingredient added, the seal, is the generalization of the notions of agents and locations. Hierarchical locations are added to the syntax, and locations influence the possible interaction among processes. As in the π calculus, interaction takes place over named channels. Communication is constrained to take place inside a location, or to spread over two locations that are in a parent-child relationship. Locations are also the unit of movement, abstracting both the notions of site and agent: a location, together with its contents, can be sent over a channel, mimicking mobility of active computations.

Djoin [10] extends the π calculus with location, migration, remote communication and failure. The calculus allows one to express mobile agents roaming on the net, however, differently from the Mobile Ambient calculus, the details of message routing are hidden.

The most famous one is the Mobile Ambient calculus [13,7]: this specification language provides a very simple framework that encompasses mobile agents, the domains where agents interact and the mobility of the agents themselves. An ambient is a generalization of both agent and place notions. Like an agent, an ambient can move across places (also represented by ambients) where it can interact with other agents. Like a place, an ambient supports local undirected communication, and can receive messages (also represented by ambients) from other places [14]. The formal semantics we give to mobile systems draws many ideas from the ambient calculus.

The disadvantages of process algebra-based approaches, however, is that they model only limited details of the systems (they are restricted only to communication structures and do not preserve any information about data). This restricts the set of properties that can be analyzed to a set of control-specific properties. Additionally, process-algebraic techniques usually deal with coarse over approximations during the analysis of mobile systems. Over-approximations are useful to reduce the analysis complexity and guarantee that, if no errors are found in the abstract system, then no errors are present in the actual system. However, if errors are found, the verification techniques developed for process algebra fail to guarantee that they are real. In contrast to the process algebraic approach, our techniques not only model both data and communication structures but also (in the context of the abstraction-based model checking) simulate the errors on the actual system and, if the errors are found to be spurious, the approximated programs are refined. To the best of our knowledge, there are no abstraction-refinement techniques that would support the process algebraic analysis techniques.

3 Formal Semantics of Mobile Programs

3.1 Mobile Programs

This section gives the syntax of mobile programs using a C-like programming language (which we believe is one of the most popular general-purpose languages). We extend the standard definition of multi-threaded programs with an explicit notion of *location* and moving actions[1]. The syntax of a mobile program is defined using a finite set of *variables* (either local to a thread or shared among threads), a finite set of *constants*, and a finite set of *names*, representing constructs for thread synchronization, similar to the Java `wait` and `notify` constructs. It is specified by the following grammar:

$$
\begin{array}{lll}
LT ::= & & \text{location-aware threads} \\
\quad | & \ell[\,T\,] & \text{single thread} \\
\quad | & LT_1 \parallel LT_2 & \text{parallel composition} \\
T ::= & & \text{threads} \\
& T_1 \mid T_2 & \text{parallel comp.} \\
\quad | & Instr & \text{sequential exec.} \\
Instr ::= & & \text{instructions} \\
& Instr_1 \; ; \; Instr_2 & \text{sequential exec.} \\
\quad | & \texttt{x := e} & \text{assignment} \\
\quad | & \texttt{if}\,(Expr\,!=\,0)\,Instr & \text{condition} \\
\quad | & \texttt{while}\,(Expr\,!=\,0)\,Instr & \text{loop} \\
\quad | & \texttt{skip} & \text{skip} \\
\quad | & \texttt{m} & \text{sync. call} \\
\quad | & \texttt{fork} & \text{thread creation} \\
\quad | & M\_Instr & \text{moving action} \\
Expr ::= & & \text{expressions} \\
& \texttt{c} & \text{constant} \\
\quad | & Expr_1\,(\,+\mid-\mid\ast\mid/\,)\,Expr_2 & \text{arith. operation} \\
M\_Instr ::= & & \text{moving actions} \\
\quad | & \texttt{go\_in}\,(\ell)\mid\texttt{go\_out}\,(\ell) & \text{move in/out}
\end{array}
$$

In the grammar, x ranges over variables, c over constants, and m over the names of synchronization constructs. The meaning of the constructs for expressions and instructions is rather intuitive: an expression can be either a constant or an arithmetic operation (i.e., sum, difference, product and division). The instruction set mainly consists of the standard instructions for imperative languages: a sequential composition operator (;), the assignment instruction, the control flow instructions `if` and `while`, and the `skip` statement. The instructions specific to the threads package are the `fork` instruction, which spawns a new thread that is an exact copy of the thread executing the `fork` instruction, and the call to a synchronization method m.

We further assume a set of location names *Loc*, and we let $\ell, \ell_1, \ell_2, \ldots$ range over *Loc*. A thread is $\ell[\,T\,]$, with ℓ being the location name of thread T. More than one

---

[1] For detailed discussion on programming languages for mobile code and their syntax the reader can refer to [15].

thread may be identified by the same location, that is $\ell[T_1 \mid T_2]$ (examples will be shown later). A mobile program is defined by the parallel composition of multiple threads. A location can thus be seen as a bounded place, where mobile computation happens.

Conceptually, thread locations represent the geographical distribution of the Web. To capture this fact, we use a special structure, called a *location net*, which encapsulates the hierarchical nesting of the Web. We define the location net as a tree, whose nodes are labeled by unique location names, and the root is labeled by the special location name *env*, representing the external environment of the system under analysis. A tree t_ℓ is identified with the set of its paths.

Example 1. As a running example consider a *shopping agent* program, where several agents are sent out over the network to visit airline Web-sites to find the best airfare. Each agent is given various requirements, such as departure and destination time restrictions. After querying the airline database, it reports back the information to the user who made the request.

For simplicity, let's assume that the system is composed of threads $T_1...T_6$ which are distributed among various locations: $Loc = \{env, \ell_0, \ell_1, \ell_2, \ell_3, \ell_4\}$ and that a single thread is sent out. Here, ℓ_2, ℓ_3, ℓ_4 are the locations of various websites; ℓ_1 is the location of the agent, ℓ_0 is the program sending out the agent, and *env* the generalized environment location. Clearly, some of the locations are nested, and the location net corresponds to a tree, which can be defined by the set of its paths, i.e., $t_\ell = \{env.\ell_0.\ell_1, env.\ell_2, env.\ell_3, env.\ell_4\}$, or can be depicted as follows.

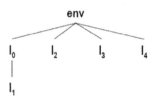

In the rest of the paper, when referring to nodes of the location net, we borrow standard vocabulary to define the relationship among tree nodes, such as father, child and sibling. For instance, in our example, ℓ_2 and ℓ_3 are siblings, whereas ℓ_0 is the father of ℓ_1 (and ℓ_1 is the child of ℓ_0).   ◇

The location net represents the topology of thread locations. In fact, it implicitly represents the distribution of threads. Location-aware threads can perform moving actions to change this distribution. These actions are the moving instructions, go_in and go_out. The explicit notion of location and the existence of moving actions affect the interaction among concurrent threads as follows (the formal definition will be given in Section 3.2):

- There are two types of composition: the parallel composition among threads identified by the same location (i.e., $\ell[T_1 \mid T_2]$), and the parallel composition among threads identified by different locations (i.e., $\ell_1[T_1] \parallel \ell_2[T_2]$) - see the example below.
- The execution of moving actions changes the location net, i.e., mobility can be described by updates of the location net.

- The execution of moving actions is constrained by the structure of the location net, i.e., moving actions can be performed only if the thread location and the target location has the father-child or siblings relationship.

Example 2. For example, if threads T_1 and T_2 represent a mail server and a browser running at site l_0 and threads $T_3...T_6$ are each running at sites $l_1...l_4$, then the shopping agent program of Example 1 can be formalized as follows:

$$\ell_0[T_1 \mid T_2] \quad \| \quad \ell_1[T_3] \quad \| \quad \ell_2[T_4] \quad \| \quad \ell_3[T_5] \quad \| \quad \ell_4[T_6]$$

In this program, threads T_1 and T_2 are running in parallel *locally* since $\ell_0[T_1 \mid T_2]$. On the contrary, T_3 and T_4 are running *remotely* since $\ell_1[T_3] \quad \| \quad \ell_2[T_4]$.   ◇

3.2   The Computational Model

In this section we formalize the semantics of mobile programs. We first define the semantics of a single thread, and then extend it to the case of a multi-threaded system. As done in the examples of the previous section, when discussing about multi-threaded systems consisting of n threads, we will use i, with $1 \le i \le n$, as a unique identifier of each thread T (i.e., we will write T_i).

Definition 1 (Location-aware Thread). *A thread is defined as a Labeled Kripke Structure $T = (S, Init, AP, \mathcal{L}, \Sigma, \mathcal{R})$ such that:*
- *S is a (possibly infinite) set of states;*
- *Init $\in S$ is the initial state;*
- *AP is the set of atomic propositions;*
- *$\mathcal{L} : S \rightarrow 2^{AP}$ is a state-labeling function;*
- *Σ is a finite set (alphabet) of actions;*
- *$\mathcal{R} \subseteq S \times \Sigma \times (S \cup \{ S \times S \})$ is a total labeled transition relation.*

A state $s \in S$ of a thread is defined as a tuple $(V_l, V_g, pc, \varphi, \eta)$, where V_l is the evaluation of the set of local variables, V_g is the evaluation of the set of global variables, pc is the program counter, $\varphi : Loc \hookrightarrow Loc$ is a partial function denoting the *location net* (where Loc is the set of location names as defined in Section 3.1), and $\eta : \mathbb{N} \hookrightarrow Loc$ is a partial function denoting the *thread location*. More specifically, φ describes the location net at a given state by recording the father-child relationship among all nodes of the net ($\bot$ in the case of env), whereas $\eta(i)$ returns the location name of T_i (i.e., the thread identified by i).

Example 3. Consider again the shopping agent program and its location net as defined in Example 2. In this case, the location net function is $\varphi(\ell_0) = env, \varphi(\ell_1) = \ell_0, \varphi(\ell_2) = env, \varphi(\ell_3) = env, \varphi(\ell_4) = env$. In addition, the thread location function for threads $T_1 \cdots T_6$ is defined as $\eta(1) = \ell_0, \eta(2) = \ell_0, \eta(3) = \ell_1, \eta(4) = \ell_2, \eta(5) = \ell_3, \eta(6) = \ell_4$.   ◇

The transition relation $\mathcal{R}$ is labeled by the *actions* of which there are four types: *moving*, *synchronization*, *thread creation*, and τ actions, which are contained in the mutually disjoint sets Σ^M, Σ^S, Σ^T, Σ^τ, respectively. We use Σ to identify the set of all actions. τ represents a generic action such as an assignment, a function call, etc. We write

$s \xrightarrow{a} s'$ to mean $(s, a, s') \in \mathcal{R}$, with $a \in \Sigma$. Moreover, we write $s \xrightarrow{a}_i s'$ to specify which thread performed the action. Note that, since we allow thread creation, if thread T_i performs a $\texttt{fork}$ action, s' can be defined as a pair of states s.t. $s \xrightarrow{\texttt{fork}}_i (s', \bar{s})$, where s' is the next state of s, and $\bar{s} = Init_i$ is an initial state of the newly created thread (which corresponds to the initial state of T_i).

Table 1 gives the inference rules for the labeled transition relation in the case of moving actions $(\texttt{go\_in}(\ell), \texttt{go\_out}(\ell))$, thread creation action, $\texttt{fork}$, and the synchronization action $\texttt{m}$. For the rules corresponding to the generic operations the reader is referred to [16]. The premises of the rules presented in Table 1 represent guarded conditions for the execution of the actions. All rules check the value of $Instr(s.pc)$, which determines the instruction to be executed by the running thread. Then, depending on the type of the action, they check further guarding conditions. In the consequences of the inference rules, we describe (within square brackets) the updates of the thread state caused by the execution of an action. We use the standard notation $\varphi \cup \{\ell_1 \mapsto \ell_2\}$ (with $\ell_1, \ell_2 \in Loc$) to indicate the update to function φ, i.e., the updates to the location net.

In the case of a "$\texttt{fork}$" action, thread T_i spawns a new thread that is an exact copy of itself. As a consequence, the program counter of T_i is updated, and a new thread is created with an initial state $\bar{s}$. The initial state is a copy of the initial state of T_i.

In the case of a "$\texttt{go\_in}(\ell)$" action, if ℓ is a sibling location to thread T_i location (i.e., $s.\varphi(s.\eta(i)) = s.\varphi(\ell)$), then the thread makes a transition and changes the state accordingly: the program counter pc is incremented, and the location net is updated (ℓ is now the father location of T_i location). If ℓ is not a sibling location, then the action is not performed because the guard does not hold.

In the case of a "$\texttt{go\_out}(\ell)$" action, if ℓ is the father location to thread T_i location (i.e., $s.\varphi(s.\eta(i)) = \ell$), then the thread makes a transition and changes the state accordingly: the program counter pc is incremented, and the location net is updated (ℓ is now a sibling location of T_i location). If ℓ is not the father location, then the action is not performed because the guard does not hold.

Note that the subtle features of mobile programs (namely, location, location net and unbounded thread creation) are modeled explicitly.

Let $T_1, \cdots, T_n$ be a set of threads initially present in the mobile program $\mathcal{P}$, then $\mathcal{P} = T_1 \parallel \cdots \parallel T_n$. The parallel composition operation is defined as follows.

Definition 2 (Mobile Program). *Let thread $T_1 = (S_1, Init_1, AP_1, \mathcal{L}_1, \Sigma_1, \mathcal{R}_1)$ and thread $T_2 = (S_2, Init_2, AP_2, \mathcal{L}_2, \Sigma_2, \mathcal{R}_2)$ be two Labeled Kripke structures. Then their composition is defined as follows: $T_1 \parallel T_2 = (S_1 \times S_2, Init_1 \times Init_2, AP, \mathcal{L}, \Sigma_1 \cup \Sigma_2, \mathcal{R})$ with the labeled transition relation defined in Table 2.*

In Table 2, a single state belonging to thread T_i is denoted by s^i, i.e., with i as superscript to indicate the thread number. When needed, we also use a subscript (and variable j) to indicate the position of an element in the path. For example, s^i_1 is the initial state of thread T_i. Given a state $s^i \in S_i$ of thread T_i, $s^i.V_l$, $s^i.V_g$, $s^i.pc$, $s^i.\varphi$ and $s^i.\eta$ are the values of local variables V_l, of global variables V_g, of program counter pc, of φ and of η, respectively. Moreover, $Instr(s^i.pc)$ denotes the instruction pointed by pc in thread T_i at state s^i. Note that $\forall i, j, i \neq j, \Sigma_i \cap \Sigma_j = \Sigma^S$, that is threads share only synchronization actions. In other words, threads proceed independently on local actions

Table 1. Inference rules for the labeled transition relation $\mathcal{R}$ for thread T_i

(FORK-ACTION)
$$Instr(s.pc) = \texttt{fork}$$
$$\frac{}{s \xrightarrow{\text{fork}}_i (s', \bar{s}) \;\; [s'.pc = s.pc + 1; \bar{s} = Init_i]}$$

(in-ACTION)
$$Instr(s.pc) = \texttt{go\_in}(\ell) \wedge (\exists \ell_1.\ell_1 := s.\eta(i) \wedge s.\varphi(\ell_1) = s.\varphi(\ell))$$
$$\frac{}{s \xrightarrow{\texttt{go\_in}(\ell)}_i s' \;\; [s'.pc = s.pc + 1; s'.\varphi = s.\varphi \cup \{\ell_1 \mapsto \ell\}]}$$

(out-ACTION)
$$Instr(s.pc) = \texttt{go\_out}(\ell) \wedge (\exists \ell_1.\ell_1 := s.\eta(i) \wedge s.\varphi(\ell_1) = \ell)$$
$$\frac{}{s \xrightarrow{\texttt{go\_out}(\ell)}_i s' \;\; [s'.pc = s.pc + 1; s'.\varphi = s.\varphi \cup \{\ell_1 \mapsto s.\varphi(\ell)\}]}$$

(SYNC-ACTION)
$$Instr(s.pc) = \texttt{m}$$
$$\frac{}{s \xrightarrow{\texttt{m}}_i s' \;\; [s'.pc = s.pc + 1]}$$

and synchronize on shared actions ($m \in \Sigma^S$), or on shared data (by definition of S_i, $S_1 \cap S_2 \neq \emptyset$). This notion of composition is derived from CSP [17].

The definition of a path of a mobile program reflects the possibility of unbounded thread creation during the execution of the `fork` instruction.

Definition 3 (Path). *A path* $\pi = \langle (s_1^1, s_1^2, \ldots, s_1^{n_1}), a_1, (s_2^1, s_2^2, \ldots, s_2^{n_2}), a_2, \ldots \rangle$ *of a mobile program is an alternating (possible infinite) sequence of tuples of states and events such that:*

(i) $n_j \in \mathbb{N}$ *and,* $\forall i, j \geq 1, s_1^i = Init_i, s_j^i \in S_i,$ *and* $a_j \in \cup_i \Sigma_i$;

(ii) *either* $s_j^i \xrightarrow{a_j} s_{j+1}^i$ *or* $s_j^i = s_{j+1}^i$ *for* $1 \leq i \leq n_{j+1}$;

(iii) *if* $a_j = \texttt{fork}$:

    – *then* $n_{j+1} = n_j + 1$ *and* $s_{j+1}^{n_{j+1}} = Init_k$ *with* $s_j^k \xrightarrow{a_j} s_{j+1}^k$

    – *else* $n_{j+1} = n_j$.

A path includes *tuples* of states, rather than a single state. The reason for that is that when a `fork` operation is executed, the state of the newly created thread must be recorded. Our notation indicates each state s_i^j by two indices, i and j, one to indicate the thread number, the other one to indicate the position in the path, respectively. The size of the tuple of states (i.e., the number of the currently existing threads) increases only if a `fork` is executed, otherwise it remains unchanged (case (iii)). In case of a `fork`, index k identifies the thread that performed the action. Thus, the state of the newly created thread is a copy of the initial state of thread T_k. Moreover, depending on the type of action (i.e., shared or local) one or more threads will change state, whereas the others do not change (case (ii)).

Table 2. The labeled transition relation for the parallel composition of two threads

---

(SYNC-ACTION)

$$\frac{a \in \Sigma_1^S \wedge s^1 \xrightarrow{a} {}_1 s'^1 \wedge a \in \Sigma_2^S \wedge s^2 \xrightarrow{a} {}_2 s'^2 \wedge s^1.\eta(1) = s^2.\eta(2)}{(s^1, s^2) \xrightarrow{a} (s'^1, s'^2)}$$

(L-PAR)

$$\frac{a \in \Sigma_1^M \wedge s \xrightarrow{a} {}_1 s'^1}{(s^1, s^2) \xrightarrow{a} {}_1 (s'^1, s^2)}$$

(R-PAR)

$$\frac{a \in \Sigma_2^M \wedge s^2 \xrightarrow{a} {}_2 s'^2}{(s^1, s^2) \xrightarrow{a} {}_2 (s^1, s'^2)}$$

---

4   Specifying Security Policies of Mobile Programs

In order to support features of mobile systems, we devised a policy specification language that defines rules for expressing also the code location. This security language primarily works at the level of method calls and variable accesses. Methods may be disallowed to an agent, either in general, or when invoked with specific arguments. (Global) variables may be marked as having a high security level, and they cannot be assigned to variables of a lower level; it is also possible to specify methods that may not be accessed within or passed to (no Read Up, no Write Down). In this way, it is possible to express both information flow and access control policies with the same language .

The BNF specification of the language follows, where terminals appear in Courier, non terminals are enclosed in angle brackets, optional items are enclosed in square brackets, items repeated one or more times are enclosed in curly brackets, and alternative choices in a production are separated by the | symbol. A policy might contain: (i) the definition of *security levels*; (ii) a list of *operation* definitions; and (iii) a list of *deny* statements, each one including one or more *permission* entries. In the definition of security levels, we enumerate the high level variables to specify a multi-level security policy. The definition of an *operation* collects together functions with the same meaning or side-effect (e.g., scanf and fread). A deny statement specifies which types of actions are not allowed to entities. By default, in the absence of deny statements, all actions are allowed to every possible user.

The *entities* to deny permissions to consist of processes (e.g., agents), identified by their current location. The keyword public means that the permission is denied to all entities. As we are dealing with mobile systems, an entity can also be identified by the host address (via codeBase), or by the location (via codeOrigin) it came from. The keyword remote identifies non-local locations.

A *permission* entry must begin with the keyword permission. It specifies *actions* to deny. An action can be a function (either user-defined or from the standard library), or an operation (a collection of functions). If it is a function, it is possible to also specify (i) formal parameters (variable names), (ii) actual parameters (the value of the arguments passed), (iii) an empty string, denying access to the function regardless of the arguments to it, or (iv) the keyword high (no high variables can be passed as arguments to this function). Notably, an actual parameter may be a location (a trailing $*$ prevents not only the location, but all sub-locations too).

$$\langle\text{policy}\rangle \longrightarrow \{\langle\text{sec\_levels}\rangle \mid \langle\text{operation\_def}\rangle \mid \langle\text{deny statement}\rangle\}$$

$$\langle\text{deny statement}\rangle \longrightarrow \texttt{deny\_to}\ \langle\text{deny\_target}\rangle\ [\langle\text{code base}\rangle]\ [\langle\text{code origin}\rangle]$$
$$\{\ \langle\text{permission entry}\rangle\ \{,\ \langle\text{permission entry}\rangle\}\ \}$$

$$\langle\text{deny\_target}\rangle \longrightarrow \texttt{public} \mid \langle\text{entity list}\rangle$$

$$\langle\text{entity list}\rangle \longrightarrow \langle\text{entity\_id}\rangle\ \{,\ \langle\text{entity\_id}\rangle\}$$

$$\langle\text{entity\_id}\rangle \longrightarrow \langle\text{location\_id}\rangle$$

$$\langle\text{location\_id}\rangle \longrightarrow \langle\text{identifier}\rangle$$

$$\langle\text{identifier}\rangle \longrightarrow (\langle\text{letter}\rangle \mid \langle\text{symbol}\rangle)\ \{\langle\text{letter}\rangle \mid \langle\text{digit}\rangle \mid \langle\text{symbol}\rangle\}$$

$$\langle\text{symbol}\rangle \longrightarrow \_ \mid \ .$$

$$\langle\text{code base}\rangle \longrightarrow \texttt{codeBase}\ \langle\text{IPv4 addr}\rangle$$

$$\langle\text{code origin}\rangle \longrightarrow \texttt{codeOrigin}\ (\langle\text{location}\rangle \mid \texttt{remote})$$

$$\langle\text{location}\rangle \longrightarrow \langle\text{location\_id}\rangle\ \{: \langle\text{location\_id}\rangle\}$$

$$\langle\text{permission entry}\rangle \longrightarrow \texttt{permission}\ \langle\text{action}\rangle$$

$$\langle\text{action}\rangle \longrightarrow \langle\text{function}\rangle \mid \langle\text{operation}\rangle$$

$$\langle\text{function}\rangle \longrightarrow \texttt{function}\ \langle\text{function\_id}\rangle\ \langle\text{parameters}\rangle$$

$$\langle\text{function\_id}\rangle \longrightarrow \langle\text{identifier}\rangle$$

$$\langle\text{parameters}\rangle \longrightarrow \langle\text{actual par}\rangle \mid \langle\text{formal par}\rangle \mid \texttt{high} \mid \varepsilon$$

$$\langle\text{actual par}\rangle \longrightarrow \texttt{"}\ \langle\text{string}\rangle\ \texttt{"}$$

$$\langle\text{formal par}\rangle \longrightarrow \texttt{args}\ \langle\text{vars}\rangle \mid \texttt{"}\ \langle\text{location\_id}\rangle\ \texttt{"}\ [*]$$

$$\langle\text{vars}\rangle \longrightarrow \langle\text{identifier}\rangle\ \{,\ \langle\text{identifier}\rangle\}$$

$$\langle\text{operation\_def}\rangle \longrightarrow \langle\text{operation}\rangle\ \{\ \langle\text{function\_id}\rangle\ \{,\ \langle\text{function\_id}\rangle\}\ \}$$

$$\langle\text{operation}\rangle \longrightarrow \texttt{operation}\ \langle\text{operation\_id}\rangle$$

$$\langle\text{operation\_id}\rangle \longrightarrow \langle\text{identifier}\rangle$$

$$\langle\text{receiver}\rangle \longrightarrow \langle\text{location\_id}\rangle$$

$$\langle\text{sec\_levels}\rangle \longrightarrow \texttt{High=\{}\ \langle\text{vars}\rangle\ \texttt{\}}$$

Consider the Java sandbox: it is responsible for protecting a number of resources by preventing applets from accessing the local hard disk and the network. In our language, a sketch of this security policy could be expressed as:

```
operation read_file_system { fread, read, scanf, gets}
deny to public codeOrigin remote
{ permission function connect_to_location,
  permission operation read_file_system }
```

A multi-level security policy could be expressed as:

```
High={confidential_var, x}
deny to public codeOrigin remote
{ permission function fopen high}
```

4.1 Security and Projection

To cope with the computational complexity of verifying mobile programs, we define *projection* abstractions. Given a path of a multi-threaded program $T_1 \parallel \cdots \parallel T_n$, one can construct projections by restricting the path to the actions in the alphabet of threads, or to states satisfying some conditions. We exploit the explicit notion of locations and define the location-based projections, which allow efficient verification of location-specific security policies (security policies in which `codeOrigin` or `codeBase` is present). With a location-specific policy, only processes which run on the indicated location need to be verified.

In the following, we assume only paths of finite length, as they are computed by the symbolic fix-point algorithm to handle verification of systems with an unbounded number of threads. In addition, we write $\langle\rangle$ for the empty path, and we use the dot notation to denote the concatenation of sequences. The concatenation of sequences will be used in the inductive definitions of projections to concatenate subsequences of paths. Notice that . is the concatenation operator for sequences of characters, thus it is not affected by the presence of mismatched parentheses.

Definition 4 (Location Projection, $\pi \downarrow \ell$). *Let $\mathcal{P}$ be $T_1 \parallel \cdots \parallel T_n$ and $\ell \in Loc$ be a location. The projection function $Proj_\ell : L(\mathcal{P})^* \to L(\mathcal{P})^*$ is defined inductively as follows (we write $\pi \downarrow \ell$ to mean $Proj_\ell(\pi)$):*

1. *$\langle\rangle \downarrow \ell = \langle\rangle$*
2. *If $s^i.\eta(i) = \ell$ then $(\langle s^i \rangle.\pi) \downarrow \ell = \langle s^i \rangle.(\pi \downarrow \ell)$*
3. *If $s^i.\eta(i) \neq \ell$ then $(\langle s^i \rangle.\pi) \downarrow \ell = \pi \downarrow \ell$*
4. *If $a \in \Sigma_i$, with i s.t. $s^i.\eta(i) = \ell$, then $(\langle a \rangle.\pi) \downarrow \ell = \langle a \rangle.(\pi \downarrow \ell)$*
5. *If $a \notin \Sigma_i$, with i s.t. $s^i.\eta(i) \neq \ell$, then $(\langle a, (s^1, s^2, \ldots, s^n) \rangle.\pi) \downarrow \ell = \pi \downarrow \ell$*

This projection traces the execution of threads for a particular location. The following information is collected: (i) states of threads whose location is ℓ (i.e., threads T_i such that $s^i.\eta(i) = \ell$), and (ii) actions that are performed by the threads whose location is ℓ (i.e., actions a such that $a \in \Sigma_i$, with $\ell[T_i]$). Here, the concatenation is done on each state element of the path, since each single state is examined to satisfy condition (i) (rules 2-3). On the contrary, once an action does not satisfy condition (ii), the next tuple is erased (rule 4).

With respect to what happens at a particular location during execution of a mobile program, there is no loss of precision in this projection-based abstraction. The projection removes only states and actions which are irrelevant to the particular location. Moreover, since security policies are defined in terms of a single location, this abstraction does not introduce spurious counterexamples during the verification of security policies using the `codeOrigin` entry.

5   A Model Checking Framework for Verification of Security Policies

A prototype framework for security analysis of mobile programs is shown in the picture below. A mobile program, P, and a security policy, S, are provided as an input to the model checking engine.

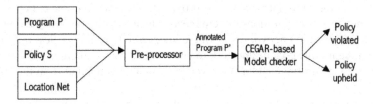

These inputs are processed, creating a new program, P', annotated with the security invariants. It has the following property: an assertion `assert(0)` (a security invariant) is not reachable in P' if and only if P enforces the security policy S. Thus, it is sufficient to give P' as an input to a model checker to statically determine whether or not an `assert(0)` is reachable in P.

The procedure for annotating the program with security invariants is a multi-step process. First, the intersection of methods in the security policy and methods used within the agent to verify is found. Then, a wrapper method is created for each of these methods. This wrapper contains an `assert(0)`, either unconditionally, or within a guard, based on the policy (this may check where the agent came from, and/or the arguments being passed to the method). The handling of high variable access is more complex (due to scoping and syntax), but analogous. This annotating procedure, as in SLIC [18], is the implementation of Schneider's security automata [19]. In fact, the annotated program P' consists of program P with inlined the reference monitor that enforces the security policy S.

Our framework uses a model checking toolset, SATABS [1]. Applying model checking to the analysis of mobile and multi-threaded systems is complicated by several factors, ranging from the perennial scalability problems to thread creation that is potentially unbounded and that thus leads to infinite state space. *Predicate abstraction* is one of the most popular and widely applied methods for systematic state-space reduction of programs. It abstracts data by only keeping track of certain predicates on the data. Each predicate is represented by a Boolean variable in the abstract program, while the original data variables are eliminated. The resulting Boolean program is an over-approximation of the original program. One starts with a coarse abstraction, and if it is found that an error-trace reported by the model checker is not realistic, the error trace is used to refine the abstract program, and the process proceeds until no spurious error traces can be found. The actual steps of the loop follow the *abstract-verify-refine* paradigm [20]. SATABS implements the abstraction refinement loop by computing and refining abstract programs. The procedure for the location-specific projections can be seen as the extension of SATABS's abstraction procedures. Among various techniques employed by SATABS, there is a model checker for Boolean programs (computed by the SATABS abstraction engine), BOPPO[16] that handles unbounded thread creation. The execution of a `fork` action corresponds to the migration of the code to the new sites and potentially leads to the creation of an unbounded number of new threads. SATABS implements a symbolic algorithm for over-approximating reachability in Boolean programs to support arbitrary thread creation which is guaranteed to terminate [21]. The devised algorithm is used as the underlying reachability engine in the CEGAR framework and is efficient. The SATABS ability to handle programs with arbitrary thread creation was the key reason for using it as a model checking engine of our security framework.

An initial configuration file can also be provided, to test whether the policy is upheld in specific network configurations (where the agent came from, both on the underlying network and the location network, and where it's currently running). Several functions exist within the mobile code framework to check these values; there is a dynamic version to be used at run-time, and a static version which is generated from the specified initial configuration. To check whether the policy holds under all possible conditions, it suffices to not provide these function definitions to SATABS, which then treats the results as non-deterministic; this can be accomplished by telling SATABS to use the run-time version of the definitions, not providing an initial configuration, or by not providing the generated location file as an input to SATABS.

SATABS supports C programs, thus our benchmarks have a C-base mobile language. Since serialization is not possible in C, we only allow code mobility (i.e., applet sending); running code cannot migrate. It is straightforward to extend our approach to benchmarks using other programming languages (e.g., Java, Telescript, etc.) by implementing a different front-end targeted to the language of choice.

5.1 Experimental Results

To validate the theoretical concepts presented in this paper, an experimental mobile code framework was developed, for which a number of examples of mobile code agents were generated. The mobile code agents were a shopping agent [22] and an updating agent [23].

The shopping example deals with a shopping query client, which sends several agents out to query simulated airline services in order to find available airfares. The agent is run on a simulated airline server, which is a distinct location on the location net from the original query client, and may be on a remote host. When the agent receives a reply, or fails to, it then tries to report back to the shopping query client.

The updating example specifies a central update server and several clients. The clients contact the server, and updates are sent, as an executable agent, whenever an update is available. This represents a way to keep the client software up to date, without forcing the client to poll the update server.

We verified a number of security policies ranging from file access control to policies that conditionally allowed the use of mobile code APIs based on the codeOrigin. The examples have been tested against different security policies, some general and some application dependent, as well as different initial location configurations. Both contain a "malicious" action (opening a connection to the location named "bad" and opening /etc/passwd, respectively), and one of the security policies for each checks this. The results of the experiments, with a location projection (where ℓ=the agent's location) on the whole system, are reported in Table 5.1.

The above policies are of a few forms, best shown by example. The updating agent opens /etc/passwd: Policy 2 (ua) disallows this action if and only if the agent came from a remote location, whereas every other argument to fopen is allowed.

```
deny to public codeOrigin remote
{ permission function fopen "/etc/passwd"}
```

Table 3. Agent benchmarks with deterministic configurations: pv = policy violated, ua = updating agent, sa = shopping agent

policy	time (s)	# iterations	# predicates	pv?	SATABS: pv?
none (ua)	0	1	0	no	no
1 (ua)	10.888	2	11	yes	yes
2 (ua)	34.812	14	18	yes	yes
3 (ua)	0.194	1	3	yes	yes
none (sa)	0.001	1	0	no	no
no_effect (sa)	0	1	0	no	no
1 (sa)	151.644	7	17	yes	yes
2 local (sa)	100.234	5	15	no	no
2 remote (sa)	524.866	12	36	yes	yes
3 codeBase (sa)	340.011	12	22	yes	yes
3 (sa)	108.564	6	16	yes	yes

Policy 3 codeBase in the shopping agent example is a variant on the policy above: it specifies codeBase (an IPv4 origin address) instead of codeOrigin, and is tailored to the "malicious action" found in the shopping agent.

```
deny to public codeBase 127.0.0.1
{ permission function connect_to_location bad}
```

Other policies are: "none" (verifying the agent without any security policy), the Java-like policy described in Section 4 (Policy 1 (ua)), and the security-level example policy also described in Section 4 (Policy 3 (ua)).

We were able to validate our technique on systems of different complexities, by changing the number of agents instantiated. Our tools correctly detected every security policy violation with no false positives. We observed that without performing projections the verification was problematic, whereas when using location projection the technique scaled gracefully and the complexity of the verification was highly reduced. Table 1 reports the total verification time (in sec) for the shopping agent and the updating examples; a number of predicates and a number of the CEGAR loop iterations indicate the complexity of the abstracted models.

6   Conclusion

In this paper, we introduced a framework for the modeling and verification of mobile programs. The system semantics were presented in terms of Labeled Kripke Structures, which encapsulated the essential features of mobile programs: namely, location and unbounded thread creation. The explicit modeling of these features enabled the specification of mobile systems security policies, which are otherwise difficult to define. The verification was based on model checking, exploiting abstraction-refinement techniques that not only allowed handling unbounded state space, but also deal effectively with large systems.

Acknowledgments. The authors thank Daniel Kroening for useful discussions and support during the implementation of the prototype framework for verifying security policies.

References

1. Clarke, E., Kroening, D., Sharygina, N., Yorav, K.: SATABS: SAT-based predicate abstraction for ANSI-C. In: Halbwachs, N., Zuck, L.D. (eds.) TACAS 2005. LNCS, vol. 3440, pp. 570–574. Springer, Heidelberg (2005)
2. Blaze, M., Feigenbaum, J., Ioannidis, J., Keromytis, A.D.: The role of trust management in distributed systems security, pp. 185–210 (1999)
3. Weeks, S.: Understanding trust management systems. In: IEEE Symposium on Security and Privacy, pp. 94–105 (2001)
4. Schwoon, S., Jha, S., Reps, T.W., Stubblebine, S.G.: On generalized authorization problems. In: CSFW, pp. 202–217 (2003)
5. Ganapathy, V., Jaeger, T., Jha, S.: Automatic placement of authorization hooks in the linux security modules framework. In: ACM Conf. on Comp.and Comm. Security., pp. 330–339 (2005)
6. Necula, G.C., Lee, P.: Research on proof-carrying code for untrusted-code security. In: IEEE Symposium on Security and Privacy, p. 204 (1997)
7. Cardelli, L., Gordon, A.D.: Mobile Ambients. In: Nivat, M. (ed.) ETAPS 1998 and FOSSACS 1998. LNCS, vol. 1378, pp. 140–155. Springer, Heidelberg (1998)
8. Hennessy, M., Riely, J.: Resource Access Control in Systems of Mobile Agents. In: HLCL '98. Journal of TCS, pp. 3–17. Elsevier, Amsterdam (1998)
9. De Nicola, R., Ferrari, G., Pugliese, R.: Klaim: a Kernel Language for Agents Interaction and Mobility. IEEE Transactions on Software Engineering 24(5), 315–330 (1998)
10. Fournet, C., Gonthier, G., Lévy, J.J., Maranget, L., Rémy, D.: A Calculus of Mobile Agents. In: Sassone, V., Montanari, U. (eds.) CONCUR 1996. LNCS, vol. 1119, pp. 406–421. Springer, Heidelberg (1996)
11. Milner, R., Parrow, J., Walker, D.: A Calculus of Mobile Processes, I and II. Information and Computation 100(1), 1–40, 41–77 (1992)
12. Vitek, J., Castagna, G.: Seal: A Framework for Secure Mobile Computations. In: Bal, H.E., Cardelli, L., Belkhouche, B. (eds.) Internet Programming Languages. LNCS, vol. 1686, pp. 47–77. Springer, Heidelberg (1999)
13. Cardelli, L.: Wide Area Computation. In: Wiedermann, J., van Emde Boas, P., Nielsen, M. (eds.) ICALP 1999. LNCS, vol. 1644, pp. 10–24. Springer, Heidelberg (1999) (Invited Paper)
14. Cardelli, L., Gordon, A.D.: Mobile Ambients. Theoretical Computer Science 240(1), 177–213 (2000)
15. Braghin, C., Sharygina, N.: Modeling and Verification of Mobile Systems. In: Proc. of TV 06 (2006)
16. Cook, B., Kroening, D., Sharygina, N.: Symbolic model checking for asynchronous boolean programs. In: Valmari, A. (ed.) Model Checking Software. LNCS, vol. 3925, pp. 75–90. Springer, Heidelberg (2006)
17. Roscoe, A.: The theory and practice of concurrency. Prentice-Hall, Englewood Cliffs (1997)
18. Ball, T., Rajamani, S.K.: SLIC: a Specification Language for Interface Checking (of C). Technical Report MSR-TR-2001-21, Microsoft Research (2002)
19. Schneider, F.B.: Enforceable security policies. ACM Transactions on Information and System Security, vol. 3(1) (2000)

20. Kurshan, R.: Computer-Aided Verification of Coordinating Processes. Princeton University Press, Princeton (1995)
21. Cook, B., Kroening, D., Sharygina, N.: Over-Approximating Boolean Programs with Unbounded Thread Creation. In: FMCAD 06: Formal Methods in System Design, Springer, Heidelberg (2006)
22. White, J.: Telescript technology: The foundation of the electronic marketplace. Technical report, General Magic Inc (1994)
23. Bettini, L., De Nicola, R., Loreti, M.: Software update via mobile agent based programming. In: SAC, pp. 32–36. ACM, New York (2002)

Slicing Concurrent Real-Time System Specifications for Verification*

Ingo Brückner

Universität Oldenburg, Department Informatik, 26111 Oldenburg, Germany
ingo.brueckner@informatik.uni-oldenburg.de

Abstract. The high-level specification language CSP-OZ-DC has been shown to be well-suited for modelling and analysing industrially relevant concurrent real-time systems. It allows us to model each of the most important functional aspects such as control flow, data, and real-time requirements in adequate notations, maintaining a common semantic foundation for subsequent verification. Slicing on the other hand has become an established technique to complement the fight against state space explosion during verification which inherently accompanies increasing system complexity. In this paper, we exploit the special structure of CSP-OZ-DC specifications by extending the dependence graph—which usually serves as a basis for slicing—with several new types of dependencies, including timing dependencies derived from the specification's DC part. Based on this we show how to compute a specification slice and prove correctness of our approach.

1 Introduction

When modelling and analysing complex systems, their various behavioural aspects need to be considered such as the admitted sequence of events taking place during operation, the associated modifications induced on the system state, or the real-time constraints that need to be imposed on the system's behaviour in order to achieve a functionally correct system model. In the area of safety-critical systems the application of formal methods with exactly defined semantics is advisable which are open to subsequent analysis and mathematical proof of certain desired properties. However, there is no single formalism which is equally well suited for each of the needed modelling tasks. Therefore, numerous combinations of different such modelling notations have been proposed in order to address each of the different system aspects with a dedicated technique [15,21,26,24].

The notation we consider in this paper is the high-level specification language CSP-OZ-DC [12], a formalism which has already been shown to be appropriate for modelling industrially relevant specifications such as parts of the European Train Control System (ETCS, [8]). CSP-OZ-DC combines three individually well-researched formalisms: *Communicating Sequential Processes* (CSP,

---

* This work was partly supported by the German Research Council (DFG) as part of the Transregional Collaborative Research Center "Automatic Verification and Analysis of Complex Systems" (SFB/TR 14 AVACS, www.avacs.org).

J. Davies and J. Gibbons (Eds.): IFM 2007, LNCS 4591, pp. 54–74, 2007.

[11]) to specify system behaviour in terms of ordering of events and communication between processes; *Object-Z* (OZ, [20]) to define a system's state space and modifications associated with the occurrence of events; *Duration Calculus* (DC, [9]) to define real-time properties over certain events or states. In CSP-OZ-DC, a common semantic basis is given to these three formalisms by extending the DC semantics such that it also covers the CSP and the OZ part. Furthermore, CSP-OZ-DC provides a compositional translation into phase event automata, a variant of timed automata which is appropriate for subsequent verification by model-checking [8,19,2].

One of the main obstacles for automated verification, however, is the problem of state space explosion, i.e., the exponential blow-up in the number of system states to be analysed. Many techniques have been proposed to tackle this problem and the frontier of systems being amenable to model checking has been pushed forward again and again throughout the last years by the—often complementary—application of various state reduction methods such as partial-order reduction [18] or predicate abstraction [6].

Aiming in the same direction is the method of *slicing*. It was originally introduced by Weiser [25] in the context of program analysis in order to determine those parts of a program which are relevant with respect to a specific debugging task. Having become an established method in the area of program analysis [23], slicing has found numerous further areas of application [28] in the past decades, among them the area of *software verification* where it has successfully been applied to various targets such as Java [10] and Promela [17]. As a syntax-based approach that operates at the source code level, slicing can exploit additional knowledge about the system structure. It has hence been shown to be effective in addition to complementary techniques working on the semantic level of the models generated from the source code [7].

Slicing in the context of verification is usually done in two steps. First, a *dependence graph* is constructed representing control and data dependencies present inside the source code. This first preparatory step is independent from the actual verification property and thus only needs to be performed once for a given verification target. Second, a backwards analysis is performed on the dependence graph with the verification property as *slicing criterion*, i.e., a starting point to identify elements that directly or indirectly affect the property to be verified. Computing the specification slice relevant to the verification property allows us to omit the irrelevant parts in the subsequent verification step such that the state space to be examined is already reduced before the verification actually starts. An important requirement in this context is the *correctness* of the slicing approach, i.e., the verification result must remain the same, regardless of whether verification is performed on the original target or on its slice.

In this paper we apply slicing to CSP-OZ-DC specifications as a preparatory step for subsequent verification with respect to *test formulas* [16], which form a subset of DC that is amenable to model-checking. The rich syntactical structure of CSP-OZ-DC specifications and their clear separation in different parts addressing different system aspects makes them an ideal target for the syntax-oriented technique of slicing. We exploit the special structure of CSP-OZ-DC specifications by introducing several new types of dependencies such as *predicate, synchronisation,* and *timing* dependencies into the dependence graph. In comparison to conventional dependence graphs these dependencies yield additional information about the specification allowing us to construct a more precise dependence graph and thus a more precise slicing outcome. Building upon previous work [4,3], we show correctness of our approach not only with respect to test formulas, but, more generally, with respect to any logic which is invariant under stuttering, i.e., which cannot distinguish between interpretations that are equivalent up to some stuttering steps (defined by sets of irrelevant variables and events obtained from slicing).

The paper is structured as follows. The next section introduces CSP-OZ-DC by giving a small example and roughly introducing the semantics of such specifications. In section 3 we present the dependence graph construction and the subsequent slicing algorithm, both illustrated by the running example. A sketch of the correctness proof of the slicing algorithm is given in section 4. The last section concludes and briefly discusses related work.

2   CSP-OZ-DC

For illustrating our approach we use a CSP-OZ-DC specification of an air conditioner system. It can operate in two modes, either heating or cooling. Initially the air conditioner is off. When it is switched on (*workswitch*), it starts to run. While running, the air conditioner either heats or cools its environment and simultaneously allows the user to switch the mode (*modeswitch*), refill fuel (*refill*) or switch it off again. Cooling or heating is modelled by a consumption of one unit of fuel (*consume*) and an emission of hot or cold air (*dtemp*). For the specification we first define the mode of operating (*TMode ::= heat | cool*).

The first part of the class defines its interface towards the environment by means of several communication channels (**chan**). The next part specifies its dynamic behaviour, i.e., the allowed ordering of method execution. It is defined via a set of CSP process equations, beginning with the initially active **main** process. The operators appearing here are prefixing →, sequential composition ⨟, interleaving ||| (parallel composition with no synchronisation) and external choice □. The third part of a CSP-OZ-DC class describes the attributes and methods of the class.

For every method we might have an **enable** schema fixing a guard for method execution (enabling schemas equivalent to *true* are left out) and an **effect** schema describing the effect of a method upon execution. For instance, the **enable** schema of method *consume* tells us that the air conditioner has to be on and a minimal amount of fuel is necessary for *consume* to take place. Upon execution one unit of fuel is consumed according to its **effect** schema. The method *level* on the other hand is always enabled, it just displays the current level of fuel.

The concluding *Duration Calculus* (DC) part of the class defines real-time properties of the system within a number of DC *counterexample formulas*, i.e., a subset of DC which is amenable for later verification. The only formula in the DC part of *AC* specifies that whenever the air conditioner is turned on for some time ($\lceil work = 1 \rceil$) and an event *workswitch* occurs, an event *off* must follow within at most one time unit (negatively defined by ... $\frown \boxminus off \wedge \ell > 1 \frown$ ... as part of the counterexample). The expression $\lceil work = 1 \rceil$ denotes a non-empty time interval throughout which predicate $work = 1$ holds. $\updownarrow$ *workswitch* refers to a point interval at which event *workswitch* occurs, while $\boxminus$ *off* refers to a non-empty time interval without any occurrence of event *off*. The chop operator $\frown$ connects all three intervals and surrounds them with initial and concluding **true** intervals of arbitrary length. These surrounding intervals enable the observation of the counterexample to happen at any point in time.

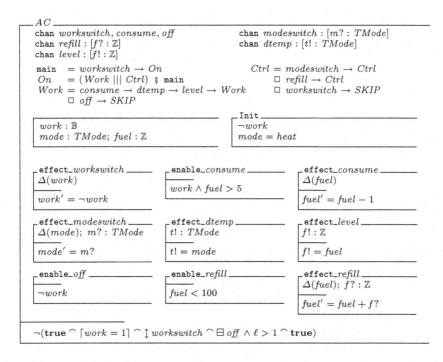

The air conditioner's environment is specified within a second class. Apart from modelling the temperature, this class also models the lighting situation (via type *LMode ::= brighten | darken*), possibly determined by some further components beyond the scope of our small example.

Intuitively, it is already quite obvious that in this specification the additional aspect of lighting is completely independent from the temperature. In section 3 we will see how to automatically obtain this observation as part of the slicing result.

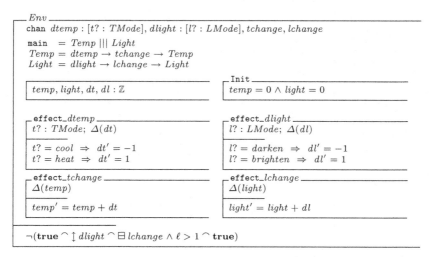

Finally, parallel composition of the air conditioner and the environment with synchronisation on the set of common events defines our complete example system:

$$System = AC \quad \| \quad Env$$
$$\{dtemp\}$$

The compositional semantics of such specifications [12] integrates the trace semantics for CSP [11], the history semantics for Object-Z [20], and the set of interpretations for Duration Calculus formulas [9].

Definition 1. *An* interpretation *is a function* $\mathcal{I}\colon Time \to Model$ *mapping the time domain* $Time == \mathbb{R}^+$ *to the set of Z models* $Model == NAME \nrightarrow \mathbb{W}$ *with* $NAME$ *being the set of all valid identifiers and* $\mathbb{W}$ *being the world, i.e., the set of all possible semantic values.*

An interpretation of a CSP-OZ-DC class defines a set of *observables*, i.e., time-dependent functions yielding valuations for

- all variables that are used in the CSP-OZ-DC class,
- boolean *channel variables* for all channels of the CSP-OZ-DC class changing its value at each point in time when the associated event occurs,
- *parameter variables* for all channels equipped with parameters containing the parameter values at the point in time when the associated event occurs.

The following definition yields an abstract view of interpretations where time is not taken into account.

Definition 2. *Let* $\mathcal{I}(t)$ *be an interpretation, changing its valuation at points in time* $0 = t_0 < t_1 < t_2 < \ldots$ *from* M_{i-1} *to* M_i *due to events* e_i *occurring at* t_i, $i \geq 1$. *Then* $\mathsf{Untime}(\mathcal{I}) = \langle M_0, e_1, M_1, e_2, M_2, \ldots \rangle$ *is the corresponding sequence of alternating states and events.*

An interpretation is fair *with respect to a set of events* $E' \subseteq Events$ *(or* E'-fair*) iff* $inf(\mathsf{Untime}(\mathcal{I})) \cap E' \neq \varnothing$ *where* $inf(\mathsf{Untime}(\mathcal{I})) = \{e \in Events \mid \exists$ *infinitely many* $i \in \mathbb{N}\colon e_i = e\}$.

The semantics of a CSP-OZ-DC class is provided by the set of interpretations that satisfy the given class, i.e., by interpretations $\mathcal{I}$ that satisfy all three parts comprising the class.

CSP part: $\mathcal{I} \models C_{CSP}$ iff Untime($\mathcal{I}$) corresponds to a run of the labelled transition system that is defined by the operational semantics of the CSP part [11].

Object-Z part: $\mathcal{I} \models C_{OZ}$ iff Untime($\mathcal{I}$) is in the history semantics of the Object-Z part [20], i.e., its first valuation satisfies the *Init* schema of the Object-Z part, all its valuations satisfy the *State* schema of the Object-Z part, and all its events together with their pre- and post-states satisfy the `enable` and `effect` schemas of the associated method.

DC part: $\mathcal{I} \models C_{DC}$ iff $\mathcal{I}$ satisfies each of the DC formulas according to the semantics of DC [9].

To argue about the events taking place at a given point in time, we use the following function.

Definition 3. *Let* $\mathcal{I}$: *Time* $\rightarrow$ *Model be an interpretation and* t *a point in time.* TakesPlace($\mathcal{I}, t$) *is the set of events that take place in* $\mathcal{I}$ *at time* t:

$$\text{TakesPlace}(\mathcal{I}, t) = \{e \in \text{Events} \mid \exists \varepsilon > 0:$$
$$\forall t_l \in [t - \varepsilon, t), t_r \in [t, t + \varepsilon]: \mathcal{I}(t_l)(e) \neq \mathcal{I}(t_r)(e)\}$$

The next definition allows us to refer to the CSP process term that remains in a given interpretation at a given point in time.

Definition 4. *Let* main *be the CSP part of a CSP-OZ-DC specification* C *and* $\mathcal{I}$ *an interpretation satisfying* C *with* $0 = t_0 < t_1 < t_2 < \dots$ *the points in time where* $\mathcal{I}$ *changes and* $e_i \in$ TakesPlace($\mathcal{I}, t_i$) *for* $i > 0$. *Then the residual CSP process term associated with a point in time, denoted by* $\text{CSP}_C(\mathcal{I}, t_i)$, *is defined as* $\text{CSP}_C(\mathcal{I}, t_i) = P_i$ *with* main $\equiv P_0 \xrightarrow{e_1} P_1 \xrightarrow{e_2} \dots \xrightarrow{e_i} P_i$ *being a valid transition according to the operational semantics of the CSP part of* C.

For describing properties of CSP-OZ-DC classes we can now use DC test formulas [16] which can be evaluated on the set of interpretations defined by the CSP-OZ-DC class. In this paper, we will not introduce this subset of DC, but instead only assume that our logic is invariant under projection, i.e., that it cannot distinguish interpretations where one is a projection of the other onto some set of observables. A precise definition of projection is given in section 4. One property of interest for our air conditioner specification could for instance be whether there are always at least 5 fuel units left when the air conditioner is on (which in fact is not true): $\varphi \equiv \neg\Diamond(\lceil work \wedge fuel < 5\rceil)$.

The main purpose of the technique proposed in this paper is to determine whether it is possible to check the property on a reduced specification C' such that the following holds[1]: $C \models \varphi$ iff $C' \models \varphi$.

As we will see it is possible to omit elements of the CSP part, the Object-Z part, and of the DC part of the example system for checking our property.

---

[1] $C \models \varphi$ stands for "the formula φ holds on all interpretations satisfying C".

3   Slicing

In general, the aim of program slicing is to determine those parts of a given program that are relevant with respect to a given slicing criterion such that only these relevant parts need to be considered when analysing the program with respect to the slicing criterion. This relevance analysis is usually based on the preceding construction of a program dependence graph (PDG) that comprises all dependence relations between elements of the program code. In preparation for the construction of the PDG for CSP-OZ-DC specifications we first construct the specification's control flow graph (CFG) which represents the execution order of the specification's schemas according to the CSP part.

3.1   Control Flow Graph

Starting with the $start.\texttt{main}$ node, representing the beginning of control flow according to the CSP $\texttt{main}$ process definition, its nodes ($n \in N_{CFG}$) and edges ($\longrightarrow_{CFG} \subseteq N_{CFG} \times N_{CFG}$) are derived from the syntactical elements of the specification's CSP part, based on an inductive definition for each CSP operator. Nodes either correspond

- to schemas of the Object-Z part (like $\texttt{enable\_}e$ and $\texttt{effect\_}e$),
- to operators in the CSP part (like nodes $interleave$ and $uninterleave$ for operator $|||$, nodes $extchoice$ and $unextchoice$ for operator $\square$, or nodes $pars_S$ and $unpars_S$ for operator $\|$), or
- to the structuring of the CSP process definitions (like $start.P$ and $term.P$ for entry and exit points of CSP process P, or $call.P$ and $ret.P$ for call and return points of references to process P).

For multiple occurrences of Object-Z methods inside the CSP process definitions unique CFG nodes are introduced, e.g. by a naming convention of the associated $\texttt{enable}$ and $\texttt{effect}$ nodes where the methods' names are extended by an ordinal referring to their syntactical occurrence inside the CSP process definitions.

Parallel Composition of Several Classes. When computing the PDG for the parallel composition of several classes, we start by constructing the CFG's for each individual class. These are then combined into one single global CFG for the entire parallel composition in the following steps:

1. The CFG nodes $start.\texttt{main}$ and $term.\texttt{main}$ of class C are renamed into $start.C$ and $term.C$ such that these nodes remain unique in the final CFG.
2. For each pair of classes (C_1, C_2) that should run in parallel composition, parallel synchronisation nodes $pars_S$ and $unpars_S$ are created and linked to the respective $start$ and $term$ nodes of each CFG. The synchronisation set S contains all events over which both classes need to synchronise.
3. Finally, new $start.\texttt{main}$ and $term.\texttt{main}$ nodes are created and connected to each of the newly created parallel synchronisation nodes.

Instead of constructing one PDG for each individual class as explained in the following section, the construction of the PDG for the parallel composition of all involved classes is then based on this previously constructed global CFG. Apart from this the construction for parallel composition of classes proceeds as usual.

3.2 Program Dependence Graph

The conventional program dependence graph (PDG) usually represents data and control dependencies that are present inside a program. In our case we derive several additional types of dependence from the rich syntactical structure of CSP-OZ-DC specifications, among them *predicate dependence* representing connections between schemas and associated predicates, *synchronisation dependence* representing mutual communication relations between processes, and *timing dependence* representing timing relations derived from DC formulas.

In addition to the nodes of the CFG, the PDG contains nodes for each predicate inside a specification schema: $N_{pred} = \{p_x \mid p \text{ predicate of schema node } x\}$. Again, predicate nodes are replicated for each occurrence of their associated event inside the CSP part, e.g., for each CFG schema node. Thus the set of nodes of the PDG is $N_{PDG} = N_{CFG} \cup N_{pred}$. Another important difference between both graphs is the set of edges they have. An edge connects two PDG nodes, if predicate, control, data or synchronisation dependencies exist between these nodes according to the definitions given below.

Before continuing with the construction of the PDG we first introduce some abbreviations. When reasoning about paths inside the CFG, we let $path_{CFG}(n, n')$ denote the set of sequences of CFG nodes that are visited when walking along CFG edges from node n to node n'. When we refer to schemas or predicates associated with a PDG node n, we let

- $out(n)$ denote all output variables (those decorated with a !),
- $in(n)$ denote all input variables (those decorated with a ?),
- $mod(n)$ denote $out(n)$ plus all variables being modified (those appearing in the Δ-list of the schema or in primed form in a predicate),
- $ref(n)$ denote $in(n)$ plus all referenced (unprimed) variables
- $vars(n) = mod(n) \cup ref(n)$ denote all variables.

Next, we proceed with definitions of the various kinds of dependence types that establish the program dependence graph for CSP-OZ-DC specifications. An example of each type of dependence can be found in the dependence graph of our example air conditioner system, depicted in figure 1.

Predicate Dependence. Each predicate that occurs in a CSP-OZ specification is located inside some schema. The idea of *predicate dependence* edges

$$\xrightarrow{pred} \subseteq (N_{CFG} \times N_{pred} \cup N_{pred} \times N_{CFG})$$

is to represent this relation between schemas and their associated predicates. An example can be seen in figure 1 between node $\boxed{\text{eff\_dtemp\_10}}$ and node $\boxed{\text{t?=cool => dt'=-1}}$.

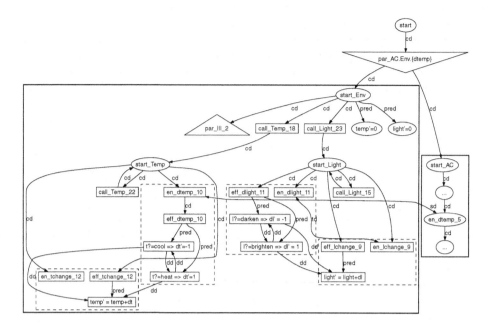

Fig. 1. Program dependence graph for the example system. Nodes inside bold bounding rectangles belong to the same class, nodes inside dashed bounding rectangles to the same event. Note, that most of the AC part is hidden, indicated by "..." nodes.

For predicates of **enable** schemas, these edges lead from the **enable** node to its predicates and vice versa, while for predicates of **effect** schemas there are only edges in the direction from the **effect** schema to its predicates. The different treatment of **enable** and **effect** schema predicates provides a way to represent the tighter connection between **enable** schemas and its predicates: **enable** predicates do not only depend on the event they are associated with but also serve as the event's guard, i.e., a mutual dependence exists, while this is not the case for events of an **effect** schema.

Predicate nodes belonging to the **Init** schema are attached to the associated *start*.main node in the way like predicate nodes belonging to an **effect** schema are attached to the associated **effect** node. This reflects the initial restriction of the state space according to the **Init** schema.

Finally, another type of predicate dependence exists for predicate nodes $n \equiv p_x$ implying modifications of variables mentioned in the DC part. Their so far unidirectional connection via the predicate dependence edge coming from their associated effect schema node $n' \equiv$ **effect_x** needs to be complemented by another predicate dependence edge in the opposite direction. This treats such predicate nodes in a similar way as predicate nodes of **enable** schemas, since they play—in conjunction with the DC formula—a similar role: They can be regarded as a guard for the associated event, since it can only take place if the predicate complies with the restrictions given in DC.

Control Dependence. The further construction of the PDG starts with the introduction of *control dependence* edges: $\xrightarrow{cd} \subseteq N_{CFG} \times N_{CFG}$

The idea behind these edges is to represent the fact that an edge's source node controls whether the target node will be executed. In particular, a node cannot be control dependent on itself. We distinguish the following types of control dependence edges:

- Control dependence due to *nontrivial precondition* exists between an `enable` node and its `effect` node iff the `enable` schema is non-empty (i.e., not equivalent to true).
- Control dependence due to *external (resp. internal) choice* or *parallel composition with synchronisation* exists between an *extch* (resp. *intch*) or *par$_S$* node and its immediate CFG successors.
- Control dependence due to *synchronisation* exists between an `enable` node and its associated `effect` node iff both nodes are located inside a branch attached to a parallel composition node and their associated event belongs to the synchronisation alphabet of this parallel composition node. Note, that even an event with an empty `enable` schema can be source of a control dependence edge, since synchronisation determines whether control flow continues.
- Control dependence due to *timing* exists between an `enable` node and its associated `effect` node iff there exists a DC formula that mentions the given event or variables that are modified by it. Again, even events with an empty `enable` schema can be source of a control dependence edge, since the DC part may restrict whether control flow continues.

An example of control dependence due to synchronisation can be seen in figure 1 between nodes en_dtemp_10 and eff_dtemp_10.

Additionally, some further control dependence edges are introduced in order to achieve a well-formed graph:

- *Call* edges exist between a *call* node and its associated *start* node.
- *Termination* edges exist between a *term* node and its associated *ret* node.
- *Start* edges exist between a *start* node and its immediate CFG successor.
- *Return* edges exist between a *ret* node and its immediate CFG successor.

Finally, all previously defined (direct) control dependence edges are extended to CFG successor nodes as long as they do not bypass existing control dependence edges. The idea of this definition is to integrate indirectly dependent nodes (that would otherwise be isolated) into the PDG.

- *Indirect control dependence* edges exist between two nodes n and n' iff

$$\exists \pi \in path_{CFG}(n, n'): \forall m, m' \in \text{ran}\,\pi : m \xrightarrow{cd} m' \Rightarrow m = n$$

An example of indirect control dependence can be seen in figure 1 between nodes start_Light and en_lchange_9.

Data Dependence. The idea of *data dependence* edges $\xrightarrow{dd} \subseteq N_{pred} \times N_{pred}$ is to represent the influence that one predicate might have on a different predicate by modifying some variable that the second predicate references. Therefore, the source node always represents a predicate located inside an `effect` schema, while the target node may also represent a predicate located inside an `enable` schema. We distinguish the following types of data dependence edges:

- *Direct data dependence* exists between two predicate nodes p_x and q_y (appearing in schemas x and y) iff there is a CFG path between both associated schema nodes without any further modification of the relevant variable, i.e., iff

$$\exists v \in (mod(p_x) \cap ref(q_y)), \exists \pi \in path_{CFG}(x,y):$$
$$\forall m \in \operatorname{ran} \pi: v \in mod(m) \Rightarrow (m = x \vee m = y)$$

- *Interference data dependence* exists between two nodes p_x and q_y iff the nodes of both associated schemas x and y are located in different CFG branches attached to the same interleaving or parallel composition operator, i.e., iff $mod(p_x) \cap ref(q_y) \neq \varnothing$ and $\exists m: (m \equiv interleave \vee m \equiv par_S)$ with

$$\exists \pi_x \in path_{CFG}(m,x) \wedge \exists \pi_y \in path_{CFG}(m,y): \operatorname{ran} \pi_x \cap \operatorname{ran} \pi_y = \{m\}$$

- *Symmetric data dependence* exists between two nodes p_x and q_y iff they are associated with the same schema and share modified variables, i.e., iff

$$mod(p_x) \cap mod(q_y) \neq \varnothing \wedge x = y$$

- *Synchronisation data dependence* exists between two predicate nodes p_x and q_y iff both are located inside `effect` schemas whose respective `enable` schemas are connected by a synchronisation dependence edge as defined below and one predicate has an output that the other predicate expects as input, i.e., iff $x = \texttt{effect\_}e \wedge y = \texttt{effect\_}e \wedge out(p_x) \cap in(q_y) \neq \varnothing$

An example of direct data dependence can be seen in figure 1 between nodes $\boxed{\texttt{t?=cool => dt'=1}}$ and $\boxed{\texttt{temp'=temp+dt}}$, where the modification of variable dt at the source node may directly reach the reference of this variable at the target node.

Synchronisation Dependence. The idea of *synchronisation dependence* edges $\xleftrightarrow{sd} \subseteq N_{CFG} \times N_{CFG}$ is to represent the influence that two `enable` schema nodes of the same event have on each other by being located inside two different branches of a parallel composition operator that has the schemas' associated event in its synchronisation alphabet. *Synchronisation dependence* exists between two nodes n and n' with $n \equiv n' \equiv \texttt{enable\_}e$ iff $\exists m \equiv par_S$ with $e \in S$:

$$\exists \pi \in path_{CFG}(m,n) \wedge \exists \pi' \in path_{CFG}(m,n'): \operatorname{ran} \pi \cap \operatorname{ran} \pi' = \{m\}$$

An example of synchronisation dependence can be seen in figure 1 between node $\boxed{\texttt{en\_dtemp\_5}}$ and node $\boxed{\texttt{en\_dtemp\_10}}$ which both belong to the synchronisation alphabet of AC and Env. If one of both events is relevant, this also applies to the other one, since both need to agree in order to occur.

Timing Dependence. The representation of dependencies arising from the DC part needs some additional preparation. The idea of *timing dependence* edges $\overset{td}{\longleftrightarrow} \subseteq N_{PDG} \times N_{PDG}$ is to represent the mutual influence between neighbouring elements of a DC counterexample formula.

According to [12], each formula DC occurring in the DC part of CSP-OZ-DC specifications can be represented as a sequence of *PhaseSpec* data structures:

$$DC \triangleq PhaseSpec_0^{DC}; \ PhaseSpec_1^{DC}; \ \ldots; \ PhaseSpec_n^{DC}$$

with $PhaseSpec_i^{DC}$ comprising all information specified in the associated phases of DC, i.e., invariants, time bounds, and forbidden or desired events. Dependencies are defined between nodes associated with the same or neighbouring *PhaseSpecs*. For each formula DC we then define a timing node sequence (TNS_{DC}) consisting of PDG nodes with relevance to the given formula, i.e.,

- predicate nodes implying modifications of variables mentioned in DC,
- **enable** nodes of events mentioned in DC, and
- the *start*.**main** node of the given class if the initial phase of DC has a time bound different from 0.

The nodes in each TNS_{DC} are ordered according to the syntactical occurrence of their associated specification elements inside DC with the exception of the *start*.**main** node. This node does never occur directly inside a DC formula but rather serves as a reference point for the length of the first phase which is the reason why this node—if present—will appear as the first element of the timing node sequence.

$$n \in \text{ran } TNS_{DC} \Leftrightarrow$$
$$n \equiv start.\textbf{main} \land timebound(PhaseSpec_0^{DC}) > 0$$
$$\lor \exists \, PhaseSpec_i^{DC} : mod(n) \cap vars(PhaseSpec_i^{DC}) \neq \varnothing$$
$$\lor \ n \equiv \textbf{enable\_}e \land e \in events(PhaseSpec_i^{DC})$$

Based on these timing node sequences, bidirectional *timing dependence* exists between two nodes n and n' iff there is a TNS_{DC} with two neighbouring timing nodes n and n'.

An example of timing dependence is the edge between nodes $\boxed{\text{en\_dlight\_11}}$ and $\boxed{\text{en\_lchange\_9}}$ in figure 1. This timing dependence is derived from the DC formula

$$DC \equiv \neg(\textbf{true} \frown \updownarrow dlight \frown \boxminus lchange \land \ell > 1 \frown \textbf{true})$$

which appears in the DC part of the environment specification and which relates both involved events *dlight* and *lchange*. This DC counterexample formula refers to initial and concluding intervals of arbitrary length (**true**), represented by $PhaseSpec_0^{DC}$ and $PhaseSpec_2^{DC}$. In between, it refers to a point interval ($\updownarrow dlight$) followed by a non-empty interval ($\boxminus lchange \land \ell > 1$) which are both represented by a single data structure, $PhaseSpec_1^{DC}$ with information about initial events (*dlight*), forbidden events (*lchange*), and interval length ($\ell > 1$).

3.3   Backward Slice

For our purpose, slicing is used to determine that part of the specification that is directly or indirectly relevant for the property φ to be verified and which therefore needs to remain in the specification. Computation of this slice starts from the set of events E_φ and the set of variables V_φ that appear directly in φ. Based on this *slicing criterion* (E_φ, V_φ) we determine the set of PDG nodes with direct influence on φ, i.e., the set of predicate nodes modifying variables from V_φ and the set of `enable` nodes belonging to events from E_φ:

$$N_\varphi = \{p_x \in N_{pred} \mid mod(p_x) \cap V_\varphi \neq \varnothing\} \cup \{\texttt{enable\_}e \in N_{CFG} \mid e \in E_\varphi\}$$

Starting from this initial set of nodes we compute the backward slice by a reachability analysis of the PDG. The resulting set of backwards reachable nodes contains all nodes that lead via an arbitrary number of predicate, control, data, synchronisation or timing dependence edges to one of the nodes that already are in N_φ. In addition to all nodes from N_φ, the backward slice contains therefore also all PDG nodes with indirect influence on the given property, i.e., it is the set of all relevant nodes for the specification slice:

$$N' = \{n' \in N_{PDG} \mid \exists n \in N_\varphi \colon n' \, (\xrightarrow{pred} \cup \xrightarrow{cd} \cup \xrightarrow{dd} \cup \xrightarrow{sd} \cup \xrightarrow{td})^* \, n\}$$

Thus relevant events are those associated with nodes from N' that represent `enable` or `effect` schemas

$$E' = \{e \mid \exists n \in N' \colon n \equiv \texttt{enable\_}e \vee n \equiv \texttt{effect\_}e\}$$

and relevant variables are those associated with nodes from N' that represent predicates:

$$V' = \bigcup_{p_x \in N'} vars(p_x).$$

3.4   Reduced Specification

Slicing concludes with the computation of the reduced specification, i.e., a version of the full specification without all details which are not relevant for the property that served as the slicing criterion. Verification with respect to this property can afterwards be performed on this reduced specification while the verification result will be the same.

To compute the CSP part of the reduced specification we need a notion of projection of CSP process definitions onto the set of relevant events:

Definition 5. *Let P be the right side of a process definition from the CSP part of a specification and E be the set of events that appear in the specification. The projection of P with respect to a set of events $E' \subseteq E$ is inductively defined:*

1. $SKIP|_{E'} := SKIP$ and $STOP|_{E'} := STOP$

2. $(e \rightarrow P)|_{E'} := \begin{cases} P|_{E'} & \text{if } e \notin E' \\ e \rightarrow P|_{E'} & \text{else} \end{cases}$

3. $(P \circ Q)|_{E'} := P|_{E'} \circ Q|_{E'}$ with $\circ \in \{; , \|\|, \sqcap, \square\}$

4. $(P \parallel_{S} Q)|_{E'} := P|_{E'} \parallel_{S \cap E'} Q|_{E'}$

The projection of the complete CSP part is defined by applying the above definition to the right side of each process definition.

Given the set N', V' and E' it is then straightforward to construct the reduced specification. For each class C its slice C' contains

- only channels from E'
- the projection of the original specification's CSP part onto E',
- a state schema with variables from V' only (same type as in C),
- schemas only for events in E' (plus *Init*),
- inside these schemas only predicates associated with nodes in N', and
- a DC part with only counterexample formulas that mention variables from V' and events from E'. (Note that due to the construction of timing dependence edges, for any given counterexample formula either all or none of its variables and events belong to the slice.)

When computing the slice of the complete system, i.e., the air conditioner specification in parallel composition with the environment with respect to the verification property $\varphi \equiv \Diamond(\lceil work \wedge fuel < 5 \rceil)$, we obtain the following results:

AC: Method *level* has been removed, which is sensible, since communicating the current amount of fuel (*level*) does not influence φ. Note that methods *modeswitch*, *dtemp* as well as variable *mode* have not been removed. The reason is that method *dtemp* belongs to the synchronisation alphabet, resulting in a control dependence edge due to synchronisation. However, when computing a slice of the air conditioner alone (without parallel composition with the environment), methods *dtemp* and *modeswitch* together with variable *mode* can be removed, since the amount of available fuel does not depend on the mode of operating.

Env: Methods *tchange*, *dlight* and *lchange* have been removed as well as variables *light*, *temp*, and *dl* and DC formula $\neg \Diamond(\updownarrow dlight \frown \boxminus lchange \wedge \ell > 1)$. This result is also sensible, since the actual effect imposed on the environment's temperature (*tchange* and *temp*) does not influence the verification property and the modelling of the environment's lighting behaviour (*dlight*, *lchange*, *light* and *dl*) is not related to the verification property at all.

To summarise, the specification's state space has not only been reduced with respect to its control flow space (events *level*, *tchange*, *dlight*, and *lchange*) but also with respect to its data state space (variables *light*, *temp*, and *dl*) and its timing requirements (the DC part of *Env*).

Note, that in both cases neither the original nor the sliced specification satisfy the given property, so the verification result will be negative in both cases. Nevertheless, this is exactly what we wanted to achieve: A specification slice must satisfy a slicing criterion if and only if the original specification does so.

4   Correctness

In this section we show correctness of the slicing algorithm, i.e., we show that the property (and slicing criterion) φ holds on the full specification if and only if it holds on the reduced specification. For proving this we will show that an interpretation of the reduced specification is a *projection* of an interpretation of the full specification onto some relevant subset of the variables and events, i.e., they only differ on variables and events that the formula does not mention.

Intuitively, when computing the projection of a given interpretation onto a set of relevant variables and a set of events, one divides the interpretation into blocks formed by time intervals beginning at one relevant event and ending at the next relevant event. The corresponding block in the projection refers to the same time interval, but does not contain any of the irrelevant events that may appear inside the block of the original interpretation. Furthermore, throughout both blocks the interpretation and its projection coincide in the valuation of all relevant variables.

Definition 6. *Let O' be a set of observables, $E' = O' \cap Events$ the set of events within O' and $\mathcal{I}, \mathcal{I}'$ be two E'-fair interpretations with $0 = t_0 < t_1 < t_2 < \ldots$ and $0 = t'_0 < t'_1 < t'_2 < \ldots$ the points in time where $\mathcal{I}$ and $\mathcal{I}'$ change, respectively. $\mathcal{I}'$ is in the* projection *of $\mathcal{I}$ with respect to O', denoted by* $\mathsf{Projection}_{O'}(\mathcal{I})$, *iff*

1. $\forall\, t \colon \mathcal{I}|_{O'}(t) = \mathcal{I}'|_{O'}(t)$
2. $\forall\, i \geq 0 \colon \exists j \colon (t_i = t'_j \wedge \mathsf{TakesPlace}(\mathcal{I}, t_i) = \mathsf{TakesPlace}(\mathcal{I}', t'_j))$
   $\qquad\qquad \vee\ (t'_j < t_i < t'_{j+1} \wedge \mathsf{TakesPlace}(\mathcal{I}, t_i) \cap E' = \varnothing)$

Given a logic which is invariant under projections, such a projection relationship between any two interpretations then guarantees that formulas which only mention observables from O' hold for either both or none of the interpretations. Note that projection is a particular form of stuttering.

Correctness proof. Now we start the actual correctness proof with several lemmas showing the relationships between CSP processes and events and variables which remain in the specification. Due to space restrictions we only present the main ideas of the proofs. The complete proofs can be found in [1].

Our first lemma states that the projection of each residual CSP process associated with a projection interval without relevant events as defined in definition 6 can mimic the behaviour of the residual CSP process associated with the last state of the projection block, i.e., the relevant event at the end of the block is enabled at any point inside the block when computing the CSP projection.

Lemma 1 (Transitions of CSP process projections). *Let $P_j, \ldots, P_{j+k+1}$ be CSP processes, E' a set of relevant events, $e_{j+1}, \ldots, e_{j+k-2}$ irrelevant events $(\notin E')$, and e_{j+k} a relevant event $(\in E')$, such that*

$$P_j \xrightarrow{e_{j+1}} P_{j+2} \xrightarrow{e_{j+3}} \ldots \xrightarrow{e_{j+k-2}} P_{j+k-1} \xrightarrow{e_{j+k}} P_{j+k+1}$$

is a valid transition sequence. Then the following holds[2]:

$$P \xrightarrow{e_{j+k}} P_{j+k+1}|_{E'} \text{ with } P \in \{P_j|_{E'}, \dots, P_{j+k-1}|_{E'}\}$$

Proof sketch: The proof builds up on another lemma considering the case of a single CSP transition: Either this transition is labelled with a relevant event $e \in E'$ or with an irrelevant event $e \notin E'$. In the former case it is easy to see that the associated projection also can perform this event e, while in the latter case some further considerations lead to the conclusion that the associated projection will finally perform the same relevant event as the original process. Both cases are shown by induction over the structure of the respective CSP processes. For the proof of the present lemma we then only need to combine both cases in an induction over the length of the projection block and come to the desired result.

Next, we bridge the gap between transition sequences that we can observe for CSP processes and paths that are present in the associated control flow graph.

Lemma 2 (CSP transition sequences and CFG paths). *Let C be a class specification, CFG its control flow graph, $\mathcal{I}$ an interpretation satisfying C with $0 = t_0 < t_1 < t_2 < \dots$ the points in time where $\mathcal{I}$ changes, t_i with $i > 0$ one of these points with $e \in \mathsf{TakesPlace}(\mathcal{I}, t_i)$ and $f \in \mathsf{TakesPlace}(\mathcal{I}, t_{i+1})$. Then the two corresponding nodes* enable_e *and* enable_f *of CFG are related in either one of the following ways:*

1. *There exists a path in CFG which leads from* enable_e *to* enable_f*:*

   $$path_{CFG}(\mathsf{enable\_}e, \mathsf{enable\_}f) \neq \varnothing$$

2. *There exists a CFG node* interleave[i] *or* par_S^i *with $S \cap \{e, f\} = \varnothing$ which has* enable_e *and* enable_f *as successors in different branches:*

   $$\exists n \in CFG: n \equiv interleave^i \vee (n \equiv par_S^i \wedge S \cap \{e, f\} = \varnothing):$$
   $$\exists \pi_e \in path_{CFG}(n, \mathsf{enable\_}e) \wedge \exists \pi_f \in path_{CFG}(n, \mathsf{enable\_}f):$$
   $$\pi_e \cap \pi_f = \{n\}$$

Proof sketch: The proof consists of two layers of induction over the structure of the residual CSP process terms $\mathsf{CSP}_C(\mathcal{I}, t_i)$ and $\mathsf{CSP}_C(\mathcal{I}, t_{i+1})$ such that each possible combination of CSP constructs is shown to be covered by one of the two cases mentioned in the lemma.

The following lemma states that the set of irrelevant events appearing inside a projection block does not have any influence on the relevant variables associated with the states inside the block.

Lemma 3 (No influence of irrelevant events on relevant variables). *Let C be a class specification, $\mathcal{I}$ an interpretation satisfying C with $0 = t_0 < t_1 < t_2 < \dots$ the points in time where $\mathcal{I}$ changes, associated with $e_i \in \mathsf{TakesPlace}(\mathcal{I}, t_i)$ for $i > 0$. Let furthermore E' be the set of relevant events computed by the slicing*

---

[2] Note, that $P_j|_{E'} = \dots = P_{j+k-1}|_{E'}$ does not necessarily hold.

algorithm with respect to some formula φ (with an associated set of variables V_φ), $e_{j+1}, \ldots, e_{j+k-1} \notin E'$, and $e_j, e_{j+k} \in E'$. Then the following holds:

$$\mathcal{I}(t_j)|_{\overline{V}} = \ldots = \mathcal{I}(t_{j+k-1})|_{\overline{V}} \quad \text{with } \overline{V} = V_\varphi \cup \bigcup_{e \in \{e_i \in E' | i \geq j\}} ref(e)$$

Proof sketch: We show this by contradiction: Supposed, the equality does not hold. This implies the existence of a data dependence between an event inside the block and the relevant event. In consequence, this leads to the event inside the block being a member of the set of relevant events.

Our last lemma states that DC formulas which the slicing algorithm identified to be irrelevant with respect to a property to be verified do not impose restrictions on any relevant event.

Lemma 4 (No influence of irrelevant DC formulas on relevant events).
Let C be a class specification, E' the set of relevant events obtained from slicing C with respect to some slicing criterion φ, and DC a counterexample formula from the DC part of C which is irrelevant with respect to φ. Let

$$E_{DC} = events(DC) \cup \{e \in Events \mid mod(e) \cap vars(DC) \neq \varnothing\}$$

be the set of events that DC refers to either directly or indirectly by referring to some variable that is modified by the respective event. Then the following holds:

1. *There exists no CFG path connecting events from E_{DC} with events from E'.*
2. *Timings of events from E_{DC} are not affected by timings of events from E'.*

Proof sketch: We show both claims by contradiction: Supposed, a path as in (1) exists, then this leads to the existence of a control dependence and thus to DC being relevant. Supposed, an irrelevant event as in (2) is forced to occur before a certain relevant event, then this leads to a connection between both nodes either via control flow edges, via a common DC formula, or via two DC formulas with a common reference point and thus in all cases to e and hence DC being relevant.

Now we come to our main theorem that states the existence of a projection relationship between any two interpretations associated with the original and to the sliced specification.

Theorem 1. *Let C be a class specification and C' the class obtained when slicing C with respect to a formula φ, associated with sets of events E_φ and variables V_φ. Let E' and V' be the set of events and variables, respectively, which the slicing algorithm delivers as those of interest (in particular $E_\varphi \subseteq E'$ and $V_\varphi \subseteq V'$). Then for any E'-fair interpretation $\mathcal{I}$ satisfying C there is a corresponding E'-fair interpretation $\mathcal{I}'$ satisfying C' such that*

$$\mathcal{I}' \in \mathsf{Projection}_{V' \cup E'}(\mathcal{I}).$$

Proof sketch: We need to consider two directions: (1) We have to show that for any interpretation of C we can construct a corresponding interpretation of C' and (2) vice versa. For both directions we define a set of variables $\overline{V}_i$ that contains all variables mentioned in the slicing criterion and for each $e_i \in$ TakesPlace$(\mathcal{I}, t_i) \cap E'$ all variables referenced by e_i or subsequent relevant events:

$$\overline{V}_i = V_\varphi \cup \bigcup_{e \in \{e_j \in E' | j \geq i\}} ref(e)$$

1. Let $\mathcal{I}$ be an interpretation satisfying C. We inductively construct an interpretation $\mathcal{I}'$ which coincides with $\mathcal{I}$ on relevant relevant events from E' and relevant variables from $\overline{V}_i$, i.e., intervals of $\mathcal{I}$ containing only irrelevant events correspond to intervals of $\mathcal{I}'$ containing no events but the same valuations of relevant variables.

   We have to show that $\mathcal{I}'$ satisfies C'. To this end we use induction over the length of $\mathcal{I}'$ where we apply lemma 3 and lemma 1 when showing that we can remove some intermediate sequences from the original interpretation such that all schemas, process definitions and timing constraints from the reduced specification are satisfied.

2. Let $\mathcal{I}'$ be an interpretation satisfying C' with $0 = t_0 < t_1 < t_2 < \ldots$ the points in time where $\mathcal{I}'$ changes and TakesPlace$(\mathcal{I}', t_i) \cap E' \neq \varnothing$.
   We inductively construct an interpretation $\mathcal{I}$ with

$$0 = t_0 < t_0^1 < t_0^2 < \ldots < t_0^{n_0} < t_1 < t_1^1 < t_1^2 < \ldots < t_1^{n_1} < t_2 < t_2^1 < \ldots$$

   the points in time where $\mathcal{I}$ changes, such that the same relevant events appear in $\mathcal{I}$ and $\mathcal{I}'$ at points in time t_i for $i > 0$, and additional (irrelevant) events appear in $\mathcal{I}$ at points in time $t_i^{j_i}$ for $i \geq 0$ and $1 \leq j_i \leq n_i$.

   In the induction we apply lemma 3 to show that we can safely insert the necessary additional steps in $\mathcal{I}$ such that the associated schemas of the full specification are satisfied. Furthermore, we apply lemma 2 to show that these additional steps are possible according to the process definitions from the full specification. Finally, we use lemma 4 to show that the additional DC formulas are satisfied by choosing appropriate points in time for the additional events in $\mathcal{I}$ such that $\mathcal{I}$ is indeed an interpretation of C.

5 Conclusion

We presented a slicing approach with the intention to use it as a preprocessing step in the verification of high-level specifications of concurrent real-time systems with respect to real-time properties. The overall aim of introducing slicing into the verification workflow is to complement other strategies to fight the problem of state space explosion. Our slicing algorithm is custom-tailored to the integrated specification language CSP-OZ-DC in order to exploit its particular features in the construction of an adequate dependence graph. Once this graph is constructed, it allows us to compute slices of the original specification with respect to a wide set of verification properties as we demonstrated for a small example specification. Subsequent verification runs can be performed on the slice instead of the full specification without changing the verification result.

Currently, we are integrating the proposed slicing technique as a plugin into the modelling environment Syspect [22] which was already used to automatically generate the dependence graph in figure 1. This tool gives (1) a precise CSP-OZ-DC semantics to a subset of UML notations such as state charts, class diagrams, and component diagrams, and (2) has a plugin-based connection to the verification tool chain for CSP-OZ-DC proposed in [13] and evaluated in [8], currently based on the abstraction-refinement model checker ARMC [19] and the deductive model checker SLAB [2].

Related Work. *Program slicing* as originally defined by Weiser in the field of program analysis and debugging [25] has been enhanced with respect to many different aspects, having found numerous additional fields of application at the same (for overview papers see [23,28]) and a similarly wide spectrum of targets, including Z-based specifications [5,27] as in our case.

Formal verification is an application area of slicing that has recently seen increasing interest, since slicing seems to be one technique that can help to tackle the problem of state space explosion during model checking. Empirical results [7] have shown that slicing can indeed effectively complement other strategies such as predicate abstraction [6] and partial order reduction [18] that are mostly applied on a different stage than slicing, namely either during or after model generation has already been performed. In contrast to that, slicing can be applied beforehand as a relatively cheap syntax-based method to reduce the input to model generation. Thus, the benefit of slicing can be seen in two directions: First, it enables an optimisation by accelerating the process of model generation, which is for larger systems already a substantial part of the complete verification process. Second, it yields smaller models to which subsequently the mentioned orthogonal strategies for state space reduction can still be applied.

Existing approaches to static slicing of formal specifications, however, do not consider verification, i.e., slicing is not carried out with respect to verification properties. Work on slicing used for reducing programs before verification has for instance been done for Java [7] and Promela [17]. Furthermore, we are not aware of any existing approaches that consider slicing of high-level specifications of *real-time* systems, while on the semantic level of timed automata slicing has been applied in [14].

References

1. Brückner, I.: Slicing CSP-OZ-DC Specifications for Verification. Technical report, Univ. Oldenburg (2007) http://csd.informatik.uni-oldenburg.de/~ingo/ifm07.pdf
2. Brückner, I., Dräger, K., Finkbeiner, B., Wehrheim, H.: Slicing Abstractions. In: FSEN'07. LNCS, Springer, Heidelberg (to appear, 2007)

3. Brückner, I., Wehrheim, H.: Slicing an Integrated Formal Method for Verification. In: Lau, K.-K., Banach, R. (eds.) ICFEM 2005. LNCS, vol. 3785, pp. 360–374. Springer, Heidelberg (2005)
4. Brückner, I., Wehrheim, H.: Slicing Object-Z Specifications for Verification. In: Treharne, H., King, S., Henson, M.C., Schneider, S. (eds.) ZB 2005. LNCS, vol. 3455, pp. 414–433. Springer, Heidelberg (2005)
5. Chang, D., Richardson, D.: Static and Dynamic Specification Slicing. In: SIGSOFT ISSTA, pp. 138–153. ACM Press, New York (1994)
6. Clarke, E.M., Grumberg, O., Jha, S., Lu, Y., Veith, H.: Counterexample-Guided Abstraction Refinement. In: CAV'00, pp. 154–169 (2000)
7. Dwyer, M.B., Hatcliff, J., Hoosier, M., Ranganath, V., Wallentine, R., Wallentine, T.: Evaluating the Effectiveness of Slicing for Model Reduction of Concurrent Object-Oriented Programs. In: Hermanns, H., Palsberg, J. (eds.) TACAS 2006 and ETAPS 2006. LNCS, vol. 3920, Springer, Heidelberg (2006)
8. Faber, J., Meyer, R.: Model Checking Data-Dependent Real-Time Properties of the European Train Control System. In: FMCAD'06, pp. 76–77. IEEE Computer Society Press, Los Alamitos (2006)
9. Hansen, M.R., Chaochen, Z.: Duration Calculus: Logical Foundations. Formal Aspects of Computing 9, 283–330 (1997)
10. Hatcliff, J., Dwyer, M., Zheng, H.: Slicing Software for Model Construction. Higher-order and Symbolic Computation 13(4), 315–353 (2000)
11. Hoare, C.A.R.: Communicating Sequential Processes. Prentice-Hall, Englewood Cliffs (1985)
12. Hoenicke, J.: Combination of Processes, Data, and Time. PhD thesis, Univ. of Oldenburg (2006)
13. Hoenicke, J., Maier, P.: Model-checking specifications integrating processes, data and time. In: Fitzgerald, J.A., Hayes, I.J., Tarlecki, A. (eds.) FM 2005. LNCS, vol. 3582, pp. 465–480. Springer, Heidelberg (2005)
14. Janowska, A., Janowski, P.: Slicing Timed Systems. Fundamenta Informaticae 60(1–4), 187–210 (2004)
15. Mahony, B., Dong, J.S.: Timed communicating Object-Z. IEEE Transactions on Software Engineering 26(2), 150–177 (2000)
16. Meyer, R., Faber, J., Rybalchenko, A.: Model Checking Duration Calculus: A Practical Approach. In: Barkaoui, K., Cavalcanti, A., Cerone, A. (eds.) ICTAC 2006. LNCS, vol. 4281, pp. 332–346. Springer, Heidelberg (2006)
17. Millett, L., Teitelbaum, T.: Issues in Slicing Promela and its Applications to Model Checking. STTT 2(4), 343–349 (2000)
18. Peled, D.A.: Ten years of partial order reduction. In: Vardi, M.Y. (ed.) CAV 1998. LNCS, vol. 1427, pp. 17–28. Springer, Heidelberg (1998)
19. Podelski, A., Rybalchenko, A.: ARMC: the logical choice for software model checking with abstraction refinement. In: Hanus, M. (ed.) PADL 2007. LNCS, vol. 4354, Springer, Heidelberg (2006)
20. Smith, G.: The Object-Z Specification Language. Kluwer Academic Publishers, Dordrecht (2000)
21. Smith, G., Hayes, I.J.: An introduction to Real-Time Object-Z. Formal Aspects of Computing 13(2), 128–141 (2002)
22. Syspect. Endbericht der Projektgruppe Syspect. Technical report, Univ. of Oldenburg (2006) http://syspect.informatik.uni-oldenburg.de/
23. Tip, F.: A Survey of Program Slicing Techniques. Journal of Programming Languages 3(3), 121–189 (1995)

24. Treharne, H., Schneider, S.A.: Communicating B Machines. In: Bert, D., Bowen, J.P., Henson, M.C., Robinson, K. (eds.) B 2002 and ZB 2002. LNCS, vol. 2272, pp. 416–435. Springer, Heidelberg (2002)
25. Weiser, M.: Programmers use slices when debugging. Communications of the ACM 25(7), 446–452 (1982)
26. Woodcock, J.C.P., Cavalcanti, A.L.C.: The Semantics of Circus. In: Bert, D., Bowen, J.P., Henson, M.C., Robinson, K. (eds.) B 2002 and ZB 2002. LNCS, vol. 2272, pp. 184–203. Springer, Heidelberg (2002)
27. Wu, F., Yi, T.: Slicing Z Specifications. SIGPLAN 39(8), 39–48 (2004)
28. Xu, B., Qian, J., Zhang, X., Wu, Z., Chen, L.: A brief survey of program slicing. SIGSOFT SEN 30(2), 1–36 (2005)

Slotted-Circus
A UTP-Family of Reactive Theories[*]

Andrew Butterfield[1], Adnan Sherif[2], and Jim Woodcock[3]

[1] Trinity College Dublin
Andrew.Butterfield@cs.tcd.ie
[2] Universidade Federal de Pernambuco
ams@cin.ufpe.br
[3] University of York
Jim.Woodcock@cs.york.ac.uk

Abstract. We present a generic framework of UTP theories for describing systems whose behaviour is characterised by regular time-slots, compatible with the general structure of the *Circus* language [WC01a]. This "slotted-*Circus*" framework is parameterised by the particular way in which event histories are observable within a time-slot, and specifies what laws a desired parameterisation must obey in order for a satisfactory theory to emerge.

Two key results of this work are: the need to be very careful in formulating the healthiness conditions, particularly **R2**; and the demonstration that synchronous theories like SCSP [Bar93] do not fit well with the way reactive systems are currently formulated in UTP and *Circus*.

1 Introduction

1.1 *Circus* and Slotted-*Circus*

The formal notation *Circus* [WC01a] is a unification of Z and CSP, and has been given a UTP semantics [WC02]. A *Circus* text describes behaviour as a collection of actions, which are a combination of processes with mutable state. However, apart from event sequencing, there is no notion of time in *Circus*.

A timed version of *Circus* (*Circus* Time Action or CTA) has been explored [SH02, She06] that introduces the notion of discrete time-slots in which sequences of events occur. In CTA, we have a two-level notion of history: the top-level views history as a sequence of time-slots; whilst the bottom-level records a history of events within a given slot. The key notion in this paper is that we can instantiate the bottom-level history in a variety of ways: as simple traces, or multisets of events, or as the more complex "micro-slot" structures used in the operational semantics of Handel-C [BW05].

This paper describes a generalisation of CTA called "slotted-*Circus*", which is a collection of theories parameterised by different ways to instantiate the

---

[*] Research reported in this paper was partially supported by QinetiQ.

J. Davies and J. Gibbons (Eds.): IFM 2007, LNCS 4591, pp. 75–97, 2007.

$$P; \ Q \ \widehat{=} \ \exists \, obs_0 \bullet P[obs_0/obs'] \wedge Q[obs_0/obs]$$
$$P \lhd c \rhd Q \ \widehat{=} \ c \wedge P \vee \neg \, c \wedge Q$$
$$P \sqcap Q \ \widehat{=} \ P \vee Q$$
$$\textstyle\bigsqcap_{i \in I} P_i \ \widehat{=} \ \exists \, i : I \bullet P_i$$
$$S \sqsubseteq P \ \widehat{=} \ [P \Rightarrow S]$$

Fig. 1. Basic UTP Operators

bottom-level event history within a time-slot. The motivation behind this work is the desire to re-cast existing semantics for Handel-C into the UTP framework so that *Circus* can be used as a specification language.

The Handel-C denotational [BW02] and operational semantics use this time-slot model, but with varying degrees of complexity in the slot structure, depending on which language constructs we wish to support. The slotted-*Circus* framework reported here is intended to be a foundation for formulating the common parts of these models, making it easier to explore the key differences.

1.2   UTP: General Principles

Theories in UTP are expressed as predicates over a pre-defined collection of free observation variables, referred to as the *alphabet* of the theory. The predicates are generally used to describe a relation between a before-state and an after-state, the latter typically characterised by dashed versions of the observation variables. A predicate whose free variables are all undashed is called a *(pre-)condition*. A given theory is characterised by its alphabet, and a series of *healthiness conditions* that constrain the valid assertions that predicates may make. In almost all cases there are some basic operators common to every theory (Figure 1). Sequential composition ($P; \ Q$) corresponds to relational composition, *i.e.*, the existence of an intermediate state (obs_0), such that P relates obs to obs_0, whilst Q relates obs_0 to obs'. The conditional $P \lhd c \rhd Q$ is generally used when c is a condition and asserts that P holds if c is true, otherwise it asserts Q. Nondeterminism between two predicates $P \sqcap Q$ is simply logical disjunction, which extends to an existential quantifier for a nondeterministic choice over an indexed set ($\bigsqcap_i P_i$). We capture the notion of refinement $\sqsubseteq$ as logical entailment between the implementation and specification predicates, quantified over all free variables.

We note that UTP follows the key principle that "programs are predicates" [Hoa85b], and so does not distinguish between the syntax of some language and its semantics as alphabetised predicates. In other words, we view the language constructs as being "syntactic sugar" for their predicate semantics, rather than defining some form of semantic function mapping some abstract syntax type to some domain capturing its meaning.

$$
\begin{aligned}
\text{Action} ::= \ & Skip \mid Stop \mid Chaos \\
\mid \ & \text{Name}^+ := \text{Expr}^+ \mid \text{Comm} \rightarrow \text{Action} \mid \text{Action} \ \square \ \text{Action} \\
\mid \ & \text{Action} \ [\![\, \text{VS} \mid \text{CS} \mid \text{VS}\,]\!] \ \text{Action} \mid \text{Action} \setminus \text{CS} \\
\mid \ & \mu\,\text{Name} \bullet F(\text{Name}) \mid Wait \ t \mid \ldots \\
\text{Comm} ::= \ & \text{Name.Expr} \mid \text{Name!Expr} \mid \text{Name?Name} \\
\text{Expr} ::= \ & \text{expression} \\
t ::= \ & \text{positive integer valued expression} \\
\text{Name} ::= \ & \text{channel or variable names} \\
\text{CS} ::= \ & \text{channel name sets} \\
\text{VS} ::= \ & \text{variable sets}
\end{aligned}
$$

Fig. 2. Slotted-*Circus* Syntax

1.3   Structure and Focus

The main technical emphasis of this paper is on the construction of the generic framework and the required healthiness conditions, with the semantics of the language constructs and a case study provided to give a feel for its utility. We first present the syntax §2, generic framework §3, healthiness conditions §4, and semantics §5. We then discuss instantiation §6 and describe a case-study §7, before mentioning related §8 and future §9 work, and concluding §10. Two appendices give supporting material.

2   Syntax

The syntax of Slotted-*Circus* is similar to that of *Circus*, and a subset is shown in Figure 2. The notation X^+ denotes a sequence of one of more X. We assume an appropriate syntax for describing expressions and their types, subject only to the proviso that booleans and non-negative integers are included.

The basic actions *Skip*, *Stop*, *Chaos* are similar to the corresponding CSP behaviours [Hoa85a, Sch00], respectively denoting actions that do nothing and terminate, do nothing and wait forever, or act unpredictably forever. We also introduce (multiple) assignment (:=) and event (communication) prefixes Comm → Action as basic actions. The communication prefixes range over communicating a value on a channel (Name.Expr), sending a value on a channel (Name!Expr), or receiving a value on a channel (Name?Name). The composite action operator $\square$ denotes external choice, whilst parallel composition of actions ($[\![\,\text{VS} \mid \text{CS} \mid \text{VS}\,]\!]$) is parameterised by three sets, the first and third denoting the variables the corresponding action may modify, while the middle one specifies the synchronisation channels. We require that parallel processes modify disjoint parts of the state. We also have hiding ($\setminus$ CS) and recursively defined actions (μ Name • F(Name)).

The key construct related to time-slots, and hence not part of *Circus*, is *Wait t* which denotes an action that simply waits for t time-slots to elapse, and then terminates.

3   Generic Slot-Theory

Both the semantics of Handel-C [BW05] and the timed extension to *Circus* called
"Circus Timed Actions (CTA)" [SH02, She06] have in common the fact that the
models involve a sequence of "slots" that capture the behaviour of the system
between successive clock ticks. These slots contain information about the events
that occurred during that time slot ("history") as well as the events being refused
at that point. A key feature of all these semantic models is that the progress
of events during a time-slot is observable, rather than just the overall outcome
for an entire slot. While the initial goal was to develop a synchronous variant
of *Circus*, it rapidly became clear that it was worth investing time in a generic
slot-based theory, which could then be specialised to cover synchronicity, CTA,
and the various slot-models that could be used to characterise Handel-C and
similar synchronous hardware languages at various levels of detail.

   We begin our description of the generic slotted theory by noting that it is
parametric in three inter-related aspects:

- A given set of events, E.
- A type constructor $\mathcal{H}$ that builds a slot's history-type from an event type.
- A collection of basic functions that work with $\mathcal{H}\ E$, which must satisfy
  certain laws.

Given $\mathcal{H}$, we then define the notion of a slot ($\mathcal{S}$) as being a pair: a history and
a set of events denoting a refusal:

$$\mathcal{S}\ E \mathrel{\hat{=}} (\mathcal{H}\ E) \times (\mathbb{P}\ E) \tag{1}$$

In a sense a slot is similar to the notion of a failure in CSP [Ros97], except that
it covers only the events within a single time-slot (*i.e.*, between two successive
clock ticks). Given a notion of time-slot, we then introduce the top-level notion
of event history as being a non-empty sequence of slots. The presence of clock-
ticks in the history is denoted by the adjacency of two slots, so a slot-sequence
of length $n + 1$ describes a situation in which the clock has ticked n times.

   We can now describe the observational variables of our generic UTP theory:

$ok : \mathbb{B}$ —True if the process is stable, *i.e.*, not diverging.
$wait : \mathbb{B}$ —True if the process is waiting, *i.e.*, not terminated.
$state : Var \nrightarrow Value$ —An environment giving the current values of slotted-*Circus*
   variables
$slots : (\mathcal{S}\ E)^+ :$ —A non-empty sequence of slots recording the behaviour of the
   system.

The variables ok, $wait$ play the same role as the in the reactive systems theory
in [HH98, Chp. 8], while $state$ follows the trend in [SH02] of grouping all the
program variables under one observational variable, to simplify the presentation
of the theory.

   In order to give the generic semantics of the language, we need to provide six
functions and two relations over $\mathcal{H}\ E$, listed in Figure 3. Function *Acc* returns the

$$Acc_{\mathcal{H}} : \mathcal{H} \, E \to \mathbb{P} \, E$$
$$EqvTrc_{\mathcal{H}} : E^* \leftrightarrow \mathcal{H} \, E$$
$$HNull_{\mathcal{H}} : \mathcal{H} \, E$$
$$\preceq_{\mathcal{H}} : \mathcal{H} \, E \leftrightarrow \mathcal{H} \, E$$
$$Hadd_{\mathcal{H}} : \mathcal{H} \, E \times \mathcal{H} \, E \to \mathcal{H} \, E$$
$$Hsub_{\mathcal{H}} : \mathcal{H} \, E \times \mathcal{H} \, E \twoheadrightarrow \mathcal{H} \, E$$
$$HHide_{\mathcal{H}} : \mathbb{P} \, E \to \mathcal{H} \, E \to \mathcal{H} \, E$$
$$HSync_{\mathcal{H}} : \mathbb{P} \, E \to \mathcal{H} \, E \times \mathcal{H} \, E \to \mathbb{P}(\mathcal{H} \, E)$$

Fig. 3. Generic Functions over $\mathcal{H} \, E$

set of events mentioned (*Accepted*) in its history argument. The relation *EqvTrc* relates a history to all event sequences (traces) compatible with it. *HNull* is a constant denoting an empty history. Infix symbol $\preceq$ captures the notion of one history being a prefix, of pre-history of another, and is required to be a pre-order. The functions *Hsub* and *Hadd* capture the notions of history subtraction and addition (extension). In particular we note that *Hsub* is partial and is only defined when the second argument is a pre-history of the first. Function *HHide* acts to remove a set of events from a history. Finally the *HSync* function generates all the possible histories that can result from the synchronisation of two histories over a given event set.

In order to produce a coherent theory, the functions have to obey a number of laws, listed in Appendix A. Most of the properties concerned capture reasonable behaviours that one would expect of histories, *e.g.*, that history addition is associative, or that the null history acts as a unit. Most of these laws where determined by the needs of the general theory, in particular the definitions and proofs needed to establish the required healthiness conditions.

As an example, a variation of the CTA theory of [She06] can be captured by defining an event history ($\mathcal{H}_{CTA} \, E$) to be a sequence of events, and instantiating most of the functions and relations as the corresponding ones for sequences.

$$\mathcal{H}_{CTA} \, E \cong E^* \tag{2}$$

3.1 Derived Types and Operators

Given the definition of $\mathcal{H}$, and the associated functions and relations, we need to use these to define the corresponding aspects for slots, and the slot-sequences that comprise our observational variables (see Figure 4). *EqvTrace*, defined in terms of *EqvTrc*, relates traces to slot-sequences with which they are compatible. The functions *Refs* and *EqvRef* extract refusals from slot-sequences, with the former returning a refusal-set list, whilst the latter singles out the last refusal set. A slot-sequence s is a slot-prefix of a slot-sequence t, written $s \preccurlyeq t$ if the front of s is a prefix of t and the history component of the last slot of s is a history-prefix of the corresponding component of the first slot of $t - s$. The

$$EqvTrace : E^* \leftrightarrow (S\ E)^*$$
$$Refs : (S\ E)^+ \rightarrow (\mathbb{P}\ E)^+$$
$$EqvRef : (S\ E)^+ \rightarrow \mathbb{P}\ E$$
$$\preccurlyeq\ :\ (S\ E)^+ \leftrightarrow (S\ E)^+$$
$$\approx\ :\ S\ E \leftrightarrow S\ E$$
$$\cong\ :\ (S\ E)^+ \leftrightarrow (S\ E)^+$$
$$Sadd_S : S\ E \times S\ E \rightarrow S\ E$$
$$Ssub_S : S\ E \times S\ E \nrightarrow S\ E$$
$$\sharp\ :\ ((S\ E)^+ \times (S\ E)^+) \rightarrow (S\ E)^+$$
$$\diagdown\ :\ ((S\ E)^+ \times (S\ E)^+) \nrightarrow (S\ E)^+$$

Fig. 4. Derived Functions and Relations

relation $\preccurlyeq$ is a pre-order. Slot equivalence $\approx$ and Slot-sequence equivalence ($\cong$) are the symmetric closure of $\preceq$ and $\preccurlyeq$ respectively, giving equivalence relations. An important point to note here is that if $s \cong t$, then s and t are identical, except for the refusal values in the last slot in each.

The notions of adding (extending) and subtracting histories are lifted to the slot level, but here an issue immediately arises as to how the refusal components are handled. If we consider history addition, then $Hadd(h_1, h_2)$ is intended to capture the history resulting from the events of history h_1, followed by those of h_2. We now note that in most CSP-like theories, a failure consisting of a trace/history of events (h) coupled with a refusal set (r), is to be interpreted as stating that the process under consideration is refusing the events in r, *after* having performed the events in h. Given this interpretation, we are then required to specify slot addition and subtraction as follows:

$$Sadd((h_1, \_), (h_2, r_2)) \widehat{=} (Hadd(h_1, h_2), r_2)$$
$$Ssub((h_1, r_1), (h_2, \_)) \widehat{=} (Hsub(h_1, h_2), r_1)$$

For history subtraction, the value $Hsub(h_1, h_2)$ is defined only if $h_2 \preceq h_1$, and denotes those events in h_1 that occurred after those in h_2. The significance of this interpretation is important, as will be made clear when we consider an attempt to model Synchronous CSP (SCSP) [Bar93] later in this paper. A consequence of this interpretation is that one of the healthiness conditions discussed in the next section (**R2**) becomes more complex.

Given slot addition and subtraction, these can then be lifted to act on slot-sequences, as $\sharp$ and $\diagdown$ respectively. The latter is only defined if its second argument is a $\preccurlyeq$-prefix of its first. Slot-sequence addition concatenates its two arguments, merging the last slot of the first with the first slot of the second:

$$slots_1 \sharp slots_2 \widehat{=} front(slots_1)^\frown \langle Sadd(last(slots_1), head(slots_2)) \rangle^\frown tail(slots_2) \quad (3)$$

Slot-sequence subtraction $s \setminus t$ is defined when $t \preccurlyeq s$, in which case both s and t can be written as

$$s = pfx \frown \langle slot_s \rangle \frown sfx$$
$$t = pfx \frown \langle slot_t \rangle$$

In this case, the subtraction becomes:

$$s \setminus t \mathrel{\hat{=}} \langle Ssub(slot_s, slot_t) \rangle \frown sfx \tag{4}$$

4   Healthiness Conditions

Given that we are defining semantics as predicates over before- and after- observations, we need to ensure that what we write is feasible, in that we do not describe behaviour that is computationally or physically infeasible (*e.g.*, undoing past events). In UTP, the approach to handling feasibility is to define a number of so-called healthiness conditions that characterise the sort of predicates which make sense in the intended interpretation of the theory.

While the notion of healthiness-conditions is well-understood in the UTP community, we are still going to take time for the presentation that follows, as we highlight a prevalent use of overloading that can have unexpected effects in inexperienced hands.

Given a healthiness condition called **H** we introduce two functions, **mkH** and **isH**. In order to denote a healthiness condition, we require that the former is an idempotent monotonic predicate transformer, w.rt. to the standard ordering used in UTP, namely that $S \sqsubseteq P$ iff $[P \Rightarrow S]$. The role of **mkH** is to convert an un-healthy predicate into a healthy one, in some fashion, but also to leave already healthy predicates unchanged (hence the need for idempotency, so that a healthy predicate is a fixed-point of **mkH**).

$$\mathbf{mkH} \; : \; Predicate \to Predicate$$
$$\mathbf{mkH} = \mathbf{mkH} \circ \mathbf{mkH}$$

Function **isH** asserts a healthiness condition, *i.e.*, is a higher order predicate that tests a given predicate to see if it is healthy:

$$\mathbf{isH} \; : \; Predicate \to \mathbb{B}$$
$$\mathbf{isH}(P) \mathrel{\hat{=}} P \equiv \mathbf{mkH}(P)$$

We can summarise by saying that a healthy predicate is a fixed-point of the corresponding healthiness predicate transformer. In most material on UTP, it is conventional to overload the notation **H** to refer to both **mkH** and **isH**, with the use usually being clear from context. In either case it is also conventional to refer in general to **H** as a healthiness condition, even in a context were it would actually be a predicate transformer. We shall adopt this convention in the sequel.

However a hazard can arise when alternative formulations of **H** are available; note that different functions may have the same set of fixed-points. We illustrate this later when discussing **R2**.

The healthiness conditions we introduce here for slotted-*Circus* parallel some of those in [HH98, Chp. 8] for general reactive systems, namely **R1**, **R2**, **R3** and **CSP1**.

4.1   Reactive Healthiness

We shall discuss **R1** and **R3** first, as these are fairly straightforward, while **R2** deserves some discussion, as its adaption for slotted-*Circus* was decidedly non-trivial.

R1 simply states that a slotted-*Circus* process cannot undo the past, or in other words, that the *slots'* observation must be an extension of *slots*, whilst **R3** deals with the situation when a process has not actually started to run, because a prior process has yet to terminate, characterised by $wait = \text{TRUE}$. In this case the action of a yet-to-be started process should simply be to do nothing, an action we call "reactive-skip" (II). Reactive skip has two behavioural modes: if started in an unstable state (i.e the prior computation is diverging), then all it guarantees is that the slots may get extended somehow; otherwise it stays stable, and leaves all other observations unchanged.

$$\textbf{R1}(P) \mathrel{\hat{=}} P \wedge slots \preccurlyeq slots'$$
$$\textbf{R3}(P) \mathrel{\hat{=}} \mathit{II} \vartriangleleft wait \vartriangleright P$$
$$\mathit{II} \mathrel{\hat{=}} \neg\, ok \wedge slots \preccurlyeq slots'$$
$$\vee$$
$$ok' \wedge wait' = wait \wedge state' = state \wedge slots' = slots$$

The purpose of the *slots* observation variable in slotted-*Circus*, and its trace analogue (tr) in UTP reactive-process theory, is to facilitate the definition of operators such as sequential composition. What is not permitted however, is for a process to be able to base its actions on the history of past events as recorded by this variable—any such "memory" of the past must be captured by the *state* observation. Healthiness condition **R2** is concerned with ensuring that a process can only specify how the history is extended, without reference to what has already happened. In [HH98, Chp. 8] this is captured by stating that P is **R2**-healthy if it is invariant under an arbitrary shift in the prehistory, or in other words, a non-deterministic choice over all possible values that tr might take:

$$\textbf{R2–UTP}(P) \mathrel{\hat{=}} \sqcap_s P[s, s \mathbin{\frown} (tr' - tr)/tr, tr']$$
$$\equiv \exists\, s \bullet P[s, s \mathbin{\frown} (tr' - tr)/tr, tr']$$

It would seem reasonable to expect the slotted-*Circus* version to simply replace tr by *slots* and use the slot-sequence analogues of sequence concatenation and subtraction. This would result in the following definition (here the **a** indicates "almost"):

$$\textbf{R2a}(P) \mathrel{\hat{=}} \exists\, ss \bullet P[ss, ss \mathbin{\sharp} (slots' \smallsetminus slots)/slots, slots'] \tag{5}$$

Whilst this looks plausible, there is in fact a problem with it, which only becomes apparent when we attempt to apply the definition later on in the semantics and then prove certain key desirable properties. Consider the predicate $slots' = slots$ which asserts that no events occur. This predicate should be **R2**-healthy, as it describes a process that chooses to do nothing, regardless of the value of $slots$. However calculation shows that

$$\mathbf{R2a}(slots' = slots) \equiv slots' \cong slots\,.$$

The equality gets weakened to the slot-sequence equivalence introduced earlier. An immediate consequence of this is that $\mathbb{I}$ is not healthy by this definition, as calculation shows that the slot-equality is weakened to slot-equivalence (underlined below).

$$\mathbf{R2a}(\mathbb{I}) \equiv \neg\, ok \wedge slots \preccurlyeq slots' \vee ok' \wedge wait' = wait \wedge state' = state \wedge \underline{slots' \cong slots}$$

Original work explored keeping **R2a** as is, and redefining $\mathbb{I}$ to be that version shown above. However this then weakened a number of key properties of $\mathbb{I}$, most notably to do with its role as an identity for sequential composition under appropriate circumstances.

The underlying problem with **R2a** has to do with the fact that in slotted-*Circus*, unlike UTP, we have refusals interleaved with events in *slots*, and slot-sequence operators that treat refusals, particularly the last, in a non-uniform way. The problem is that **R2a** weakens the predicate a little too much, so we need to find a way to strengthen its result appropriately. The appropriate way to handle this issue has turned out to be to modify the definition of **R2** to require that we only quantify over ss values that happen to agree with $slots$ on the very last refusal. This has no impact on predicates like $\preccurlyeq$ and $\cong$ which are not concerned with the last refusals, but provides just enough extra information to allow slot-sequence equality be considered as **R2**-healthy. The slightly strengthened version now reads:

$$\mathbf{R2}(P) \,\hat{=}\, \exists\, ss \bullet P[ss, ss \,\sharp\, (slots' \smallsetminus slots)/slots, slots'] \wedge Ref(last(slots)) = Ref(last(ss))$$

The proof that **R2** is idempotent is somewhat more involved than those for **R1** and **R3**. Calculations show that predicates $slots \preccurlyeq slots'$, $slots' \cong slots$, $slots' = slots$ (se Appendix B) and $\mathbb{I}$, are all **R2**-healthy. It also distributes through disjunction, which is very important.

It is worth pointing out that two versions of **R2** are presented in [HH98]. The second, which we shall call **R2'** is shown in an appendix:

$$\mathbf{R2'}(P) \,\hat{=}\, P[\langle\rangle, tr' - tr/tr, tr']$$

Both **R2** and **R2'** have the same set of fixed points, so can be used interchangeably as a test for healthiness. However, if used to make a predicate healthy, then **R2** is more forgiving than **R2'**:

$$\mathbf{R2}(tr = \langle a\rangle \wedge tr' = \langle a, b\rangle) \equiv (tr' - tr) = \langle b\rangle$$
$$\mathbf{R2'}(tr = \langle a\rangle \wedge tr' = \langle a, b\rangle) \equiv \mathbf{false}$$

This is an example of where overloading the notation **H** to stand for both **mkH** and **isH** can be misleading. We note that the version of **R2** used in [She06] is the CTA equivalent of **R2'**.

Reactive Healthiness. A reactive slotted-*Circus* process is one that satisfies all three of the above healthiness conditions, so we define an overall condition **R** as their composition:

$$\mathbf{R} \mathrel{\widehat{=}} \mathbf{R3} \circ \mathbf{R2} \circ \mathbf{R1} \tag{6}$$

In fact all three conditions commute with each other, so we re-order the above composition to suit.

4.2 CSP Healthiness

In addition to the reactive-healthiness just introduced, shared by a range of concurrent theories including ACP and CSP, there are a number of aspects of healthiness specific to CSP-like theories. In [HH98, Chp. 8] there are five of these presented, but for our purposes it suffices to consider only the first one.

A process is **CSP1** healthy if *all* it asserts, when started in an unstable state (due to some serious earlier failure), is that the event history may be extended:

$$\mathbf{CSP1}(P) \mathrel{\widehat{=}} P \vee \neg\, ok \wedge slots \preccurlyeq slots' \tag{7}$$

5 Slotted Semantics

We are now in a position to give the semantics of the slotted-Circus language which is presented for completeness in Figures 5 & 6.

We shall not give a detailed commentary to all the definitions shown but instead will focus on some key points.

The *STOP* action refuses all events, but does allow the clock to keep ticking. Assignment and channel-communication take less than a clock-cycle, so we can sequence arbitrarily many in a time-slot. This does raise the possibility of Zeno processes (infinite events within a time-slot), so some care will be required here (disallowing infinite histories). This is more power than that required for synchronous hardware, where we expect these actions to synchronise with the clock, but we can model that by postfixing a *Wait* 1 statement, as used in the case study shown later. An important point to note is the definition of channel input ($c?x \to P$), not only involves an event $c.e$ for some e, but also updates the state. This is exploited later to allow shared variables.

The definition of external choice is quite complex —see [She06, p69] for a discussion.

We define slotted-parallel in a direct fashion, similar to that used for *Circus*, avoiding the complexities of the UTP/CTA approaches, and also handling error cases in passing. An error occurs in $P \,[\![\, s_A \mid C \mid s_B \,]\!]\, Q$ if P (Q) modifies any variable in s_B (s_A).

5.1 Laws

The language constructs displayed here obey a wide range of laws, many of which have been described elsewhere [HH98, WC01b, SH02, She06] for those constructs

$$Chaos \mathrel{\widehat{=}} \mathbf{R}(\mathbf{true})$$

$$Stop \mathrel{\widehat{=}} \mathbf{CSP1}(\mathbf{R3}(ok' \wedge wait' \wedge EqvTrace(\langle\rangle, slots' \setminus\!\!\setminus slots)))$$

$$b\&A \mathrel{\widehat{=}} A \mathbin{\lhd} b \mathbin{\rhd} Stop$$

$$Skip \mathrel{\widehat{=}} \mathbf{R}(\exists\, ref \bullet ref = EqvRef(slots) \wedge Skip)$$

$$Wait\ t \mathrel{\widehat{=}} \mathbf{CSP1}(\mathbf{R}(ok' \wedge delay(t) \wedge EqvTrace(\langle\rangle, slots' \setminus\!\!\setminus slots)))$$

$$delay(t) = (\#slots' - \#slots < t) \mathbin{\lhd} wait' \mathbin{\rhd} (\#slots' - \#slots = t \wedge state' = state)$$

$$x := e \mathrel{\widehat{=}} \mathbf{CSP1}\left(\mathbf{R}\left(\begin{array}{c} ok = ok' \wedge wait = wait' \wedge slots = slots' \\ \wedge\, state' = state \oplus \{x \mapsto val(e, state)\} \end{array}\right)\right)$$

$$val : \mathsf{Expr} \times (\mathsf{Name} \to Value) \nrightarrow Value$$

$$c.e \to Skip \mathrel{\widehat{=}} \mathbf{CSP1}\left(ok' \wedge \mathbf{R}\left(wait\_com(c) \vee complete\_com(c.e)\right)\right)$$

$$wait\_com(c) = wait' \wedge possible(c)(slots, slots') \wedge EqvTrace(\langle\rangle, slots' \setminus\!\!\setminus slots)$$

$$possible(c)(slots, slots') = c \notin \bigcup Refs(slots' - front(slots))$$

$$term\_com(c.e) = \neg\, wait' \wedge \#slots = \#slots' \wedge EqvTrace(\langle c\rangle, slots' \setminus\!\!\setminus slots)$$

$$complete\_com(c.e) = term\_com(c.e) \vee wait\_com(c);\ term\_com(c.e)$$

$$c!e \to Skip \mathrel{\widehat{=}} c.e \to Skip$$

$$c?x \to Skip \mathrel{\widehat{=}} \exists\, e \bullet \left(c.e \to Skip[state_0/state] \wedge state' = state_0 \oplus \{x \mapsto e\}\right)$$

$$comm \to A \mathrel{\widehat{=}} (comm \to Skip);\ A$$

$$A \mathbin{\square} B \mathrel{\widehat{=}} \mathbf{CSP2}(ExtChoice1(A, B) \vee ExtChoice2(A, B))$$

$$ExtChoice1(A, B) \mathrel{\widehat{=}} A \wedge B \wedge Stop$$

$$ExtChoice2(A, B) \mathrel{\widehat{=}} (A \vee B) \wedge DifDetected(A, B)$$

$$DifDetected(A, B) \mathrel{\widehat{=}} \neg\, ok' \vee \left(\begin{array}{c} \left(\begin{array}{c} (ok \wedge \neg\, wait) \wedge \\ \left(\left(\begin{array}{c} A \wedge B \wedge ok' \wedge \\ wait' \wedge slots = slots' \end{array}\right) \vee \right) \\ Skip \end{array}\right);\ \\ \left(\begin{array}{c} (ok' \wedge \neg\, wait' \wedge slots' = slots) \vee \\ (ok' \wedge ImmEvts(slots, slots')) \end{array}\right) \end{array}\right)$$

$$ImmEvts(slots, slots') \mathrel{\widehat{=}} \neg\, EqvTrc(\langle\rangle, head(slots' \setminus\!\!\setminus slots))$$

Fig. 5. Slotted-*Circus* Semantics (part I)

that slotted-*Circus* shares with other languages (e.g. non-deterministic choice, sequential composition, conditional, guards, *STOP*, *SKIP*). Here we simply indicate some of the laws regarding *Wait* that peculiar to slotted-*Circus* (Figure 7).

5.2   Links

In [HH98, §1.6,pp40–1], a general Galois connection between an abstract theory with observational variable a and a concrete theory over observation c is:

$$[(\exists\, c \bullet D(c) \wedge \ell(c, a)) \Rightarrow S(a)]\ \textbf{iff}\ [D(c) \Rightarrow (\forall\, a \bullet \ell(c, a) \Rightarrow S(a))]$$

Here D and S are corresponding design (concrete) and specification (abstract) predicates respectively, while $\ell(c, a)$ is the linking predicate connecting observations at the two worlds. Of interest to us in the main are links between *Circus*

$$A \, [\![\, s_A \mid \{\!| \, cs \, |\!\} \mid s_B \,]\!] \, B$$

$$\widehat{=} \; \exists \, obs_A, obs_B \; \bullet$$

$$A[obs_A/obs'] \wedge B[obs_B/obs'] \wedge$$

$$\left(\begin{array}{l} \mathbf{if} \; \left(\begin{array}{l} s_A \lhd state_A \neq s_A \lhd state \; \vee \\ s_B \lhd state_B \neq s_B \lhd state \; \vee \\ s_A \cap s_B \neq \emptyset \end{array} \right) \\ \mathbf{then} \; \neg \, ok' \wedge slots \preccurlyeq slots' \\ \mathbf{else} \; \left(\begin{array}{l} ok' = ok_A \wedge ok_B \wedge \\ wait' = (wait_A \vee 1.wait_B) \wedge \\ state' = (s_B \lhd state_A) \oplus (s_A \lhd state_B) \wedge \\ ValidMerge(cs)(slots, slots', slots_A, slots_B) \end{array} \right) \end{array} \right)$$

$$ValidMerge : \mathbb{P}\,E \rightarrow ((\mathcal{S}\,E)^+)^4 \rightarrow \mathbb{B}$$

$$ValidMerge(cs)(, s, s', s0, s_1) = dif(s', s) \in TSync(cs)(dif(s0, s), dif(s_1, s))$$

$$TSync : \mathbb{P}\,E \rightarrow (\mathcal{S}\,E)^* \times (\mathcal{S}\,E)^* \rightarrow \mathbb{P}((\mathcal{S}\,E)^+)$$

$$TSync(cs)(s_1, s_2) = TSync(cs)(s_2, s_1)$$

$$TSync(cs)(\langle\rangle, \langle\rangle) = \{\}$$

$$TSync(cs)(\langle s \rangle, \langle\rangle) = \{ \, \langle s' \rangle \mid s' \in SSync(cs)(s, SNull(Ref(s))) \, \}$$

$$TSync(cs) \left(\begin{array}{l} s_1 \, \fatsemi \, S_1, \\ s_2 \, \fatsemi \, S_2 \end{array} \right) = \left\{ \begin{array}{l} s' \, \fatsemi \, S' \\ \mid s' \in SSync(cs)(s_1, s_2) \wedge \\ \quad S' \in TSync(cs)(S_1, S_2) \end{array} \right\}$$

$$A \setminus hidn \; \widehat{=} \; \mathbf{R} \left(\begin{array}{l} \exists \, s \bullet A[s/slots'] \wedge \\ slots' \diagdown slots = map(SHide(hidn))(dif(s, slot)) \end{array} \right) ; \; Skip$$

$$\mu\, X \bullet F(X) \, \widehat{=} \, \sqcap \{ X \mid F(X) \sqsubseteq X \}$$

Fig. 6. Slotted-*Circus* Semantics (II)

$$Wait \; n; \; Wait \; m = Wait \; (m + n)$$

$$Wait \; n \; \Box \; Wait \; n + m = Wait \; n$$

$$(Wait \; n; \; P) \; \Box \; (Wait \; n; \; Q) = Wait \; n; \; (P \; \Box \; Q)$$

$$(Skip \; \Box \; (Wait \; n; \; P)) = Skip, \quad n > 0$$

$$(a \rightarrow P) \; \Box \; (Wait \; n; \; (a \rightarrow P)) = (a \rightarrow P)$$

Fig. 7. Laws of slotted-*Circus Wait*

(playing the role of the abstract theory with observations a) and various instantiations of slotted-*Circus* (concrete, with obsevations c). The difference between *Circus* and slotted-*Circus* is that the former has observations tr and ref, whilst the latter subsumes both into *slots*. However we can immediately exploit the method just presented by using the following relationship to define ℓ, which here relates the *Circus* observational variables to those of slotted-*Circus*:

$$EqvTrace(tr, slots) \wedge ref = EqvRef(slots) \tag{8}$$

So we get a Galois-link between *Circus* and any instantiation of slotted-*Circus* for free. Similarly, a given relationship between different $\mathcal{H}$ types allows us to generate Galois-links between different slotted-*Circus* instantiations.

6   Instantiating Slotted-*Circus*

We now look at the issue of giving one or more concrete instantiations to the slotted-*Circus* framework just described. Originally, this work was aimed at producing a synchronous version of *Circus*, in which all events in a time-slot were to be considered as simultaneous. One motivation for this was to support the Handel-C language, which maps programs to synchronous hardware in which all variable updates are synchronised with a global clock edge marking the end of a computation cycle [Cel02]. However, there were two main difficulties with this approach.

The first was that the formal semantics developed for Handel-C outside of the UTP framework [BW02, BW05] actually modelled activity within a time-slot as a series of decision-making events spread out in time, all culminating in a set of simultaneous variable updates at the end of the slot. This approach, adopted in both the operational and denotational semantics, gives a very natural and intuitive description of what is taking place during Handel-C execution.

The second difficulty is more fundamental in nature, and exposed a key assumption underlying the UTP reactive theories, and those for CSP in general. Early work looked at the Ph.D thesis of Janet Barnes [Bar93] which introduced a synchronous version of CSP (SCSP). The key observation was a sequence of slots, each comprising two event sets, one denoting the events occurring in that slot (Acceptances) and the other describing the events refused (Refusals). A healthiness condition required that the acceptances and refusals in any slot be disjoint. However, implicit in this disjointedness condition is the notion that both the acceptances and refusals are truly simultaneous. However, in the failures of CSP, and the corresponding *tr* and *ref* observations of UTP, the key interpretation involved is that the refusals describe what is being refused given that the event history has just taken place. As a specific example, consider the process $a \rightarrow b \rightarrow P$. A possible (failure) observation of this process is $(\langle a \rangle, \{a\})$, *i.e.*, we have observed the occurrence of the a event and the fact that the process is now refusing to perform an a.

Consider trying to instantiate a slot where the history is simply an event-set, as per SCSP:

$$A \in \mathcal{SCSP}\ E \;\widehat{=}\; \mathbb{P}\,E$$
$$HNull_{\mathcal{SCSP}} \;\widehat{=}\; \emptyset$$
$$Hadd_{\mathcal{SCSP}}(A_1, A_2) \;\widehat{=}\; A_1 \cup A_2$$
$$Hsub_{\mathcal{SCSP}}(A_1, A_2) \;\widehat{=}\; A_1 \setminus A_2$$

$$\cdots$$

We find that we cannot guarantee law [Sadd:unit] (Appendix A), even if the SCSP invariant is not required. This property is required to demonstrate that

$slots \cong slots'$ is **R2**-healthy. The underlying problem is that the definition of **R2** relies on being able to deduce that $slots$ is empty if subtracting $slots$ from $slots'$ leaves $slots'$ unchanged. However at the history-as-set level, we cannot deduce $H = \emptyset$, given that $H' \setminus H = H'$.

6.1 Multiset History Instantiation

We can define an instantiation where the event history is a multiset or bag of events ($\mathcal{H}_{\mathcal{MSA}}$), so event ordering is unimportant, but multiple event occurrences in a slot do matter (Figure 8). The bag notation used here is that of Z [Spi87]. The events accepted are simply the bag domain. A trace corresponds to a bag if it contains the same number of events as that bag. A null history is simply an empty bag. A bag is a prefix if smaller than another bag. History addition and subtract are the bag equivalents. History synchronisation merges the parts of the two bags disjoint from the synchronisation set, with the intersection of all three. Hiding is modelled by bag restriction.

The proofs that the above instantiation satisfy the properties in Appendix A are all straightforward. The proof of law [ET:pfx] for $\mathcal{MSA}$ is shown in Appendix B.

$$\mathcal{H}_{\mathcal{MSA}} \, E \,\hat{=}\, E \twoheadrightarrow \mathbb{N}_1$$
$$Acc(bag) \,\hat{=}\, dom(bag)$$
$$EqvTrc(tr, bag) \,\hat{=}\, items(tr) = bag$$
$$HNull \,\hat{=}\, [\![\,]\!]$$
$$bag_1 \preceq bag_2 \,\hat{=}\, bag_1 \sqsubseteq bag_2$$
$$Hadd(bag_1, bag_2) \,\hat{=}\, bag_1 \oplus bag_2$$
$$Hsub(bag_1, bag_2) \,\hat{=}\, bag_1 \ominus bag_2$$
$$HSync(cs)(bag_1, bag_2) \,\hat{=}\, \{(cs \ntriangleleft (bag_1 \oplus bag_2)) \oplus (cs \triangleleft (bag_1 \cap bag_2))\}$$
$$\textbf{where} \quad \cap \text{ is bag interesection}$$
$$HHide(hdn)\,bag \,\hat{=}\, hdn \ntriangleleft bag$$

Fig. 8. Multiset Action Instantiation ($\mathcal{MSA}$)

7 Example *Circus* Process

We illustrate slotted *Circus* using an example originally due to Hoare [Hoa85a]. The problem is to compute the weighted sums of consecutive pairs of inputs. Suppose that the input stream contains the following values: $x_0, x_1, x_2, x_3, x_4, \ldots$; then the output stream will be

$$(a * x_0 + b * x_1), (a * x_1 + b * x_2), (a * x_2 + b * x_3), (a * x_3 + b * x_4), \cdots$$

for weights a and b. We specify this problem with a synchronous process with two channels: *left*, used for input, and *right* used for output. Since each output requires two consecutive values from the input stream, the first output cannot occur before the third clock cycle.

clock	0	1	2	3	4	5	
left	x_0	x_1	x_2	x_3	x_4	x_5	$\cdots$
right			$a * x_0 + b * x_1$	$a * x_1 + b * x_2$	$a * x_2 + b * x_3$	$a * x_3 + b * x_4$	$\cdots$

Hoare's solution performs the two multiplications in parallel and then adds the results. Suppose the implementation technology is a single field-programmable gate array; the circuitry for the computation of the output would then be inherently parallel anyway. Let's assume instead that we want to implement the two multiplications on separate FPGAs. It's clear that the a-product is always ready one clock cycle before we need to perform the addition. Let's keep this intermediate result in the variable m: First however, note we are going to tar-

clock	0	1	2	3	4	5	
left	x_0	x_1	x_2	x_3	x_4	x_5	$\cdots$
m		$a * x_0$	$a * x_1$	$a * x_2$	$a * x_3$	$a * x_4$	$\cdots$
right			$m + b * x_1$	$m + b * x_2$	$m + b * x_3$	$m + b * x_4$	$\cdots$

get a Handel-C-like scenario where channel communication and assignment take one-clock cycle, and we have shared variables. We need to reason about interleavings of assignments, but rather than re-work the whole theory to have state-sequences, we simply convert assignments into channel communications. So for the following case study, we have the following shorthands:

shorthand	expansion
$c?_1 x$	$c?x \rightarrow Wait\,1.$
$c!_1 x$	$c!x \rightarrow Wait\,1.$
$x :=_1 e$	$(a!_1 e \,[\![\, \emptyset \mid a \mid x \,]\!]\, a?_1 x)$ where a is fresh.
δP	variables modified by P i.e used in $x := \ldots$ or $c?x$
$P \,[\![\!] \, Q$	$P \,[\![\, \delta P \mid \emptyset \mid \delta Q \,]\!] \, Q$

In effect the clock-cycle wait is built into the communication and assignment notations, effectively avoid any Zeno hazards. Now we're ready to specify the problem as a slotted *Circus* process. The process *WS* is clearly deadlock and

$$WS \;\widehat{=}\; \textsf{var}\; x, m : \mathbb{N} \bullet (\, \textit{left}?_1 x \;;\; (\, \textit{left}?_1 x \,[\![\!]\, m :=_1 a * x \,);$$
$$(\, \mu X \bullet (\, \textit{left}?_1 x \,[\![\!]\, m :=_1 a * x \,[\![\!]\, \textit{right}!_1 (m + b * x)\,)\;;\; X\,))$$

livelock free: it is a non-stopping process with no internal synchronisations; and it is hiding and chaos-free, with guarded recursion. Now we need to decompose *WS* into two parallel processes with encapsulated state. We can replace the use of m by a channel communication that passes the intermediate value. One process (*WSL*) will receive the input stream and compute the a-product; the other (*WSR*) will compute the b-product and the sum, and generate the output stream. But now we see a problem with WS. The value x_1 is received by WSL in the first clock cycle, and so it can be communicated to WSR in the second cycle. So it can't be used by WSR until the third clock cycle. So we need to delay the output on the *right* by another clock cycle. Our timing diagram shows this more clearly.

clock	0	1	2	3	4	5	
left	x_0	x_1	x_2	x_3	x_4	x_5	$\cdots$
w		x_0	x_1	x_2	x_3	x_4	$\cdots$
m			$a * x_0$	$a * x_1$	$a * x_2$	$a * x_3$	$\cdots$
right				$m + b * x_1$	$m + b * x_2$	$m + b * x_3$	$\cdots$

Here's another version of WS that does this.

$WS' \ \hat{=} \ $ **var** $w, x, m : \mathbb{N} \bullet$
$\qquad left?_1 x \ ; \ (\ left?_1 x \parallel\!\parallel w :=_1 x\ );$
$\qquad (\ left?_1 x \parallel\!\parallel w :=_1 x \parallel\!\parallel m :=_1 a * w\ );$
$\qquad (\mu X \bullet (\ left?_1 x \parallel\!\parallel w :=_1 x \parallel\!\parallel m :=_1 a * x \parallel\!\parallel right!_1 (m + b * w))\ ) \ ; \ X\ )$

Our refinement strategy is to split into two processes. The variable x belongs in WSL, since it is used to store the current input. The variable m can be placed in WSR, since it is used directly in producing outputs, but its value must be computed in WSL, and so the value will have to be communicated from left to right. The variable w records the previous input, and this is used in both left and right processes; so we duplicate its value using a ghost variable v. The ghost variable can then be used in the right-hand process in the calculation of the output on the right. Our refinement starts with organising the variables. (To reduce clutter, we abbreviate $left?_1 x$ by $?_1 x$ and $right!_1 e$ by $!_1 e$. We also separate the beginning and end of variable scopes.)

$\qquad$ **var** w, x, m ;
$\qquad\qquad ?_1 x \ ; \ (?_1 x \parallel\!\parallel w :=_1 x) \ ; \ (?_1 x \parallel\!\parallel w, m :=_1 x, a * w) \ ;$
$\qquad\qquad (\mu X \bullet (?_1 x \parallel\!\parallel w, m :=_1 x, a * w \parallel\!\parallel !_1 (m + b * w)) \ ; \ X) \ ;$
$\qquad$ **end** w, x, m

$= \{\, v \ ghosts \ w \,\}$

$\qquad$ **var** w, x, m ;
$\qquad\qquad ?_1 x \ ; \ (?_1 x \parallel\!\parallel w :=_1 x) \ ;$
$\qquad\qquad$ **var** v ;
$\qquad\qquad\qquad (?_1 x \parallel\!\parallel v, w, m :=_1 x, x, a * w) \ ;$
$\qquad\qquad\qquad (\mu X \bullet (?_1 x \parallel\!\parallel v, w, m :=_1 x, x, a * w \parallel\!\parallel !_1 (m + b * v)) \ ; \ X) \ ;$
$\qquad\qquad$ **end** v ;
$\qquad$ **end** w, x, m

$= \{\, widen \ scope \,\}$

$\qquad$ **var** v, w, x, m ;
$\qquad\qquad ?_1 x \ ; \ (?_1 x \parallel\!\parallel w :=_1 x) \ ; \ (?_1 x \parallel\!\parallel v, w, m :=_1 x, x, a * w) \ ;$
$\qquad\qquad (\mu X \bullet (?_1 x \parallel\!\parallel v, w, m :=_1 x, x, a * w \parallel\!\parallel !_1 (m + b * v)) \ ; \ X) \ ;$
$\qquad$ **end** v, w, x, m

Our next step is to insert some hidden events to prepare for the communication of values between the two processes. We add two hidden channels: c communicates x's value; and mid communicates m's value. These events are not needed in the first two steps.

$= \{ \, hiding \, \}$

$(\, var \; v, w, x, m \; ;$
$\qquad ?_1 x \; ; (?_1 x \; ||| \; w :=_1 x) \; ; (?_1 x \; ||| \; c.x \; ||| \; mid.a * w \; ||| \; v, w, m :=_1 x, x, a * w) \; ;$
$\qquad (\mu X \bullet$
$\qquad\qquad (?_1 x \; ||| \; c.x \; ||| \; mid.a * w \; ||| \; v, w, m :=_1 x, x, a * w \; ||| \; !_1(m + b * v)) \; ; X) \; ;$
$\quad end \; v, w, x, m \,) \setminus \{\!| c, mid |\!\}$

Now we can prepare for the parallel split by organising each step into parallel parts, examining each atomic action and assigning it to the left or right component. The right-hand process doesn't need to do anything during the first two steps, so we make it wait. In the third step, the the input belongs on the left. The pair of actions $(c.x \; ||| \; v :=_1 x)$ can be replaced by a communication: the left performs the output $c!_1 x$ and the right performs the input $c?_1 v$. Similarly, $(mid.a * w \; ||| \; m :=_1 a * w)$ can be replaced by $mid!_1 a * w$ and $mid?_1 m$.

Finally, the assignment to w belongs on the left. The body of the recursion is split in exactly the same way, with the addition of the output being assigned to the right-hand process.

$= \{ \, parallel \, \}$

$(\, var \; v, w, x, m \; ;$
$\qquad (?_1 x \; || \; Wait \, 1) \; ;$
$\qquad ((?_1 x \; ||| \; w :=_1 x) \; || \; Wait \, 1) \; ;$
$\qquad ((?_1 x \; ||| \; c!_1 x \; ||| \; mid!_1 a * w \; ||| \; w :=_1 x) \; || \; (c?_1 v \; ||| \; mid?_1 m)) \; ;$
$\qquad (\mu X \bullet ((?_1 x \; ||| \; c!_1 x \; ||| \; mid!_1 a * w \; ||| \; w :=_1 x)$
$\qquad\qquad || \; (c?_1 v \; ||| \; mid?_1 m \; ||| \; !_1(m + b * v)) \; ; X)) \; ;$
$\quad end \; v, w, x, m \,) \setminus \{\!| c, mid |\!\}$

We also need to split the recursion into two parallel parts. Since the body comprises two atomic steps in parallel, the fixed-point operator distributes cleanly through the parallel operator.

$= \{ \, parallel \, \}$

$(\, var \; v, w, x, m \; ;$
$\qquad (?_1 x \; || \; Wait \, 1) \; ;$
$\qquad ((?_1 x \; ||| \; w :=_1 x) \; || \; Wait \, 1) \; ;$
$\qquad ((?_1 x \; ||| \; c!_1 x \; ||| \; mid!_1 a * w \; ||| \; w :=_1 x) \; || \; (c?_1 v \; ||| \; mid?_1 m)) \; ;$
$\qquad ((\mu X \bullet (?_1 x \; ||| \; c!_1 x \; ||| \; mid!_1 a * w \; ||| \; w :=_1 x) \; ; X)$
$\qquad || \; (\mu X \bullet (c?_1 v \; ||| \; mid?_1 m \; ||| \; !_1(m + b * v)) \; ; X)) \; ;$
$\quad end \; v, w, x, m \,) \setminus \{\!| c, mid |\!\}$

Now we can perform the parallel split, using an interchange law for sequence and parallel that is similar to the spreadsheet rules in UTP. We create the left-hand process by encapsulating w and x, retaining the left-hand parts, and discarding the right-hand parts. We create the right-hand process similarly.

$$= \{ \textit{parallel split} \}$$
$$((\textit{var } w, x ;$$
$$?_1 x ;$$
$$(?_1 x \;|||\; w :=_1 x) ;$$
$$(?_1 x \;|||\; c!_1 x \;|||\; mid!_1 a * w \;|||\; w :=_1 x) ;$$
$$(\mu X \bullet (?_1 x \;|||\; c!_1 x \;|||\; mid!_1 a * w \;|||\; w :=_1 x) ; X) ;$$
$$\textit{end } w, x)$$
$$||$$
$$(\textit{var } v, m ;$$
$$Wait\, 1 ; Wait\, 1 ;$$
$$(c?_1 v \;|||\; mid?_1 m) ;$$
$$(\mu X \bullet (c?_1 v \;|||\; mid?_1 m \;|||\; !_1(m + b * v)) ; X) ;$$
$$\textit{end } v, m)$$
$$) \setminus \{| c, mid |\}$$

Now we can tidy up the processes for our final result.

$$(\textit{var } w, x : \mathbb{N} \bullet$$
$$left?_1 x ; (left?_1 x \;|||\; w :=_1 x) ; (left?_1 x \;|||\; c!_1 x \;|||\; mid!_1 a * w \;|||\; w :=_1 x) ;$$
$$(\mu X \bullet (left?_1 x \;|||\; c!_1 x \;|||\; mid!_1 a * w \;|||\; w :=_1 x) ; X) ;$$
$$||$$
$$\textit{var } v, m : \mathbb{N} \bullet (Wait\, 2 ; (c?_1 v \;|||\; mid?_1 m) ;$$
$$(\mu X \bullet (c?_1 v \;|||\; mid?_1 m \;|||\; right!_1(m + b * v)) ; X) ;)$$
$$) \setminus \{| c, mid |\}$$

Of course, since this is equal to WS, it is deadlock and livelock-free and computes the right results.

A key point of the above case-study is that it works in any of the instantiations mentioned so far for slotted-$\mathcal{C}irc us$, namely $\mathcal{CTA}$ or $\mathcal{MSA}$.

8 Related Work

During the development of Handel-C at Oxford, a lot of the principles and theory was developed and published [PL91, HIJ93]. Here the emphasis was very much on the verified compilation into hardware of an occam-like language. However with the commercialisation of this as the language Handel-C the formal aspects and hardware compilation parted company, and the Handel-C language acquired new constructs like "prialt" that were not treated in the literature.

Modern Handel-C [Cel02] also has the idea of connecting hardware with different clocks together using tightly controlled asynchronous interfaces. Modelling this kind of behaviour requires a theory that mixes time and asynchronicity, such as timed-CSP [Sch00].

There has been work done on hardware semantics, ranging from the "reFLect" language used by Intel for hardware verification [GJ06], to the language Esterel used mainly for the development of flight avionics [BG92]. The Intel approach is a suite of hardware description languages, model-checkers and theorem provers all written and/or integrated together using the reFLect language, aimed mainly at the verification of computer datapath hardware. The Esterel language is a hardware description language with a formal semantics, and so is quite low-level in character, and so in the context of this research could be considered a potential replacement of Handel-C as an implementation technology. However, it is unclear how well it would link to the kind of specification and refinement style of work that we are proposing to support.

9 Future Work

We have described a generic framework for instantiating a wide range of slotted-theories, capturing their common features. An important aspect that has yet to be covered is what distinguishes the the various instantiations from one another, i.e. how do the laws of $\mathcal{CTA}$ differ from those of $\mathcal{MSA}$, for instance. We know for example that the following is a law of $\mathcal{MSA}$, but not of $\mathcal{CTA}$, or slotted-$Circus$ in general:

$$a \rightarrow b \rightarrow P = b \rightarrow a \rightarrow P$$

Also worthy of exploration are the details of the behaviour of the Galois links inbetween different instances of slotted-$Circus$, and between those and standard $Circus$. These details will provide a framework for a comprehensive refinement calculus linking all these reactive theories together.

In order to deal with the asynchronously interfaced multiple-clock hardware now supported by Handel-C we will need to exploit the link from the slotted theories to the generally asynchronous $Circus$ theory itself.

Also of interest will be to consider to what extent the work on "generic composition" [Che02, Che06] can contribute to a clear and or tractable presentation of this theory.

10 Conclusions

A framework for giving UTP semantics to a class of reactive systems whose execution is demarcated by regular clock ticks has been presented. The general nature of the observational variables and the key operations on same have been discussed, showing how they are used build to both the healthiness conditions and the language semantics. A key result of this work has been the care needed to get a satisfactory definition of **R2**, and exposing the fact that certain synchronous theories like SCSP do not fit this particular UTP pattern for describing reactive systems.

Acknowledgement

We would like to thank the Dean of Research at TCD and QinetiQ for their support of this work, and the comments of the anonymous reviewers, which helped improve key material in this paper.

References

[Bar93] Barnes, J.E.: A Mathematical Theory of Synchronous Communication. Technical Monograph PRG-112, Oxford University Computing Laboratory Programming Research Group, Hilary Term (1993)

[BG92]   Berry, G., Gonthier, G.: The ESTEREL synchronous programming language: design, semantics, implementation. Science of Computer Programming 19, 87–152 (1992)

[BW02]   Butterfield, A., Woodcock, J.: Semantic domains for handel-C. Electr. Notes Theor. Comput. Sci, vol. 74 (2002)

[BW05]   Butterfield, A., Woodcock, J.: prialt in Handel-C: an operational semantics. International Journal on Software Tools for Technology Transfer (STTT) 7(3), 248–267 (2005)

[Cel02] Celoxica Ltd. Handel-C Language Reference Manual, v3.0, (2002) URL: www.celoxica.com

[Che02] Chen, Y.: Generic composition. Formal Asp. Comput 14(2), 108–122 (2002)

[Che06] Chen, Y.: Hierarchical organisation of predicate-semantic models. In: Dunne, S., Stoddart, B. (eds.) UTP 2006. LNCS, vol. 4010, pp. 155–172. Springer, Heidelberg (2006)

[GJ06]   Melham, T., Grundy, J., O'Leary, J.: A reflective functional language for hardware design and theorem proving. Journal of Functional Programming 16(2), 157–196 (2006)

[HH98]   Hoare, C.A.R., He, J.: Unifying Theories of Programming. Series in Computer Science. Prentice-Hall, Englewood Cliffs (1998)

[HIJ93] Jifeng, H., Page, I., Bowen, J.: Towards a provably correct hardware implementation of Occam. In: Milne, G.J., Pierre, L. (eds.) CHARME 1993. LNCS, vol. 683, pp. 214–225. Springer, Heidelberg (1993) IFIP WG10.2

[Hoa85a] Hoare, C.A.R.: Communicating Sequential Processes. Intl. Series in Computer Science. Prentice-Hall, Englewood Cliffs (1985)

[Hoa85b] Hoare, C.A.R.: Programs are predicates. In: Proc. of a discussion meeting of the Royal Society of London on Mathematical logic and programming languages, Upper Saddle River, NJ, USA, pp. 141–155. Prentice-Hall, Inc, Englewood Cliffs (1985)

[PL91]   Page, I., Luk, W.: Compiling Occam into field-programmable gate arrays. In: Moore, W., Luk, W. (eds.) FPGAs, Oxford Workshop on Field Programmable Logic and Applications, 15 Harcourt Way, Abingdon OX14 1NV, UK, pp. 271–283 Abingdon EE&CS Books (1991)

[Ros97] Roscoe, A.W.: The Theory and Practice of Concurrency. international series in computer science. Prentice-Hall, Englewood Cliffs (1997)

[Sch00] Schneider, S.: Concurrent and Real-time Systems — The CSP Approach. Wiley, Chichester (2000)

[SH02]   Sherif, A., He, J.: Towards a time model for circus. In: George, C.W., Miao, H. (eds.) ICFEM 2002. LNCS, vol. 2495, pp. 613–624. Springer, Heidelberg (2002)

[She06]   Sherif, A.: A Framework for Specification and Validation of Real Time Systems using Circus Action. Ph.d. thesis, Universidade Federale de Pernambuco, Recife, Brazil (2006)

[Spi87]   Spivey,: The Z Notation: A Reference Manual. Prentice Hall, Englewood Cliffs (1987)

[WC01a]   Woodcock, J.C.P., Cavalcanti, A.L.C.: A Concurrent Language for Refinement. In: Butterfield, A., Pahl, C. (eds.) IWFM'01: 5th Irish Workshop in Formal Methods, Dublin, Ireland, July 2001. BCS Electronic Workshops in Computing (2001)

[WC01b]   Woodcock, J., Cavalcanti, A.: Circus: a concurrent refinement language. Technical report, University of Kent at Canterbury (October 2001)

[WC02]   Woodcock, J., Cavalcanti, A.: The semantics of circus. In: ZB, pp. 184–203 (2002)

A   Generic Laws

The functions and relations over $\mathcal{H}\,E$ required to define a slotted-*Circus* theory, need to satisfy the following laws:

[ET:elems] $EqvTrc(tr, hist) \Rightarrow elems(tr) = Acc(hist)$

[HIST:eq] $(h_1 = h_2) \equiv \forall\, tr \bullet EqvTrc(tr, h_1) \equiv EqvTrc(tr, h_2)$

[HN:null] $Acc(HNull) = \{\}$

[pfx:refl] $hist \preceq hist = \mathrm{TRUE}$

[pfx:trans] $hist_1 \preceq hist_2 \wedge hist_2 \preceq hist_3 \Rightarrow hist_1 \preceq hist_3$

[pfx:anti-sym] $hist_1 \preceq hist_2 \wedge hist_2 \preceq hist_1 \Rightarrow hist_1 = hist_2$

[SN:pfx] $HNull \preceq hist$

[ET:pfx] $hist_1 \preceq hist_2 \Rightarrow \exists\, tr_1, tr_2 \bullet EqvTrc(tr_1, hist_1) \wedge EqvTrc(tr_2, hist_2) \wedge tr_1 \leq t$

[Sadd:events] $Acc(Sadd(h_1, h_2)) = Acc(h_1) \cup Acc(h_2)$

[Sadd:unit] $Sadd(h_1, h_2) = h_1 \equiv h_2 = HNull$

[Sadd:assoc] $Sadd(h_1, Sadd(h_2, h_3)) = Sadd(Sadd(h_1, h_2), h_3)$

[Sadd:prefix] $h \preceq Sadd(h, h')$

[Ssub:pre] $\mathrm{pre}\ Ssub(h_1, h_2) = h_2 \preceq h_1$

[Ssub:events] $h_2 \preceq h_1 \wedge h' = Ssub(h_1, h_2) \Rightarrow$
$$Acc(h_1) \setminus Acc(h_2) \subseteq Acc(h') \subseteq Acc(h_1)$$

[SSub:self] $Ssub(h, h) = HNull$

[SSub:nil] $Ssub(h, HNull) = h$

[SSub:same] $hist \preceq hist'_a \wedge hist \preceq hist'_b \Rightarrow$
$$Ssub(hist'_a, hist) = Ssub(hist'_b, hist) \equiv hist'_a = hist'_b$$

[SSub:subsub] $hist_c \preceq hist_a \wedge hist_c \preceq hist_b \wedge hist_b \preceq hist_a$
$$\Rightarrow Ssub(Ssub(hist_a, hist_c), Ssub(hist_b, hist_c)) = Ssub(hist_a, hist_b)$$

[Sadd:Ssub] $hist \preceq hist' \Rightarrow Sadd(hist, Ssub(hist', hist)) = hist'$

[Ssub:Sadd] $Ssub(Sadd(h_1, h_2), h_1) = h_2$

[SHid:evts] $Acc(SHide(hid)(h)) = Acc(h) \setminus hid$

[SNC:sym] $SSync(cs)(h_1, h_2) = SSync(cs)(h_2, h_1)$

[SNC:one] $\forall h' \in SSync(cs)(h_1, HNull) \bullet Acc(h') \subseteq Acc(h_1) \setminus cs$

[SNC:only] $h' \in Acc(SSync(cs)(h_1, h_2)) \Rightarrow Acc(h') \subseteq Acc(h_1) \cup Acc(h_2)$

[SNC:sync] $h' \in Acc(SSync(cs)(h_1, h_2)) \Rightarrow cs \cap Acc(h') \subseteq cs \cap (Acc(h_1) \cap Acc(h_2))$

[SNC:assoc] $SyncSet(cs)(h_1)(SSync(cs)(h_2, h_3)) = SyncSet(cs)(h_3)(SSync(cs)(h_1, h_2))$

B   Proofs for R2-ness of = and $\mathcal{MSA}$ Prefix

$\qquad \mathbf{R2}(slots' = slots)$

$\equiv$ " defn. $\mathbf{R2}$, apply substitution, shorthand $RL(s) = Ref(last(s))$ "

$\qquad \exists ss \bullet ss \sharp (slots' \diagdown slots) = ss \wedge RL(slots) = RL(ss)$

$\equiv$ " Property 1 (below) "

$\qquad \exists ss \bullet slots' \diagdown slots = \langle SNull(RL(ss)) \rangle \wedge RL(slots) = RL(ss)$

$\equiv$ " Property 2 (below) "

$\qquad \exists ss \bullet front(slots') = front(slots) \wedge tail(slots').1 = tail(slots).1$
$\qquad\qquad \wedge RL(slots') = RL(ss) \wedge RL(slots) = RL(ss)$

$\equiv$ " Liebniz, restrict quantification scope "

$\qquad front(slots') = front(slots) \wedge tail(slots').1 = tail(slots).1$
$\qquad \wedge RL(slots') = RL(slots) \wedge \exists ss \bullet RL(slots) = RL(ss)$

$\equiv$ " defn. of equality, witness $ss = slots$ "

$\qquad slots = slots'$

Property 1: $(ss \sharp tt = ss) \equiv tt = \langle SNull(RL(ss)) \rangle$

Property 2: $(tt' \diagdown tt) = \langle SNull(r) \rangle \equiv front(tt) = front(tt') \wedge last(tt).1 = last(tt').1 \wedge RL(t$

$\quad bag_1 \preceq bag_2$

$\equiv$ " defn. of prefix "

$\quad bag_1 \sqsubseteq bag_2$

$\equiv$ " bag property "

$\quad \exists bag_\Delta \bullet bag_2 = bag_1 \oplus bag_\Delta$

$\equiv$ " bag property: $\forall bag \bullet \exists tr \bullet items(tr) = bag$ "

$\quad \exists bag_\Delta, tr_\Delta, tr_1, \bullet bag_2 = bag_1 \oplus bag_\Delta \wedge items(tr_\Delta) = bag_\Delta \wedge items(tr_1) = bag_1$

$\equiv$ " One-point rule backwards $tr_2 = tr_1 \frown tr_\Delta$ "

$\quad \exists bag_\Delta, tr_\Delta, tr_1, tr_2 \bullet bag_2 = bag_1 \oplus bag_\Delta \wedge items(tr_\Delta) = bag_\Delta \wedge items(tr_1) = bag_1 \wedge tr_2 = tr$

$\equiv$ " One-point rule bag_Δ, Liebniz bag_1 "

$\exists\, tr_\Delta, tr_1, tr_2 \bullet bag_2 = items(tr_1) \oplus items(tr_\Delta) \wedge items(tr_1) = bag_1 \wedge tr_2 = tr_1 \frown tr_\Delta$

$\equiv$ " $items$ is a sequence homomorphism "

$\exists\, tr_\Delta, tr_1, tr_2 \bullet bag_2 = items(tr_2) \wedge bag_1 = items(tr_1) \wedge tr_2 = tr_1 \frown tr_\Delta$

$\equiv$ " sequence property "

$\exists\, tr_\Delta, tr_1, tr_2 \bullet bag_2 = items(tr_2) \wedge bag_1 = items(tr_1) \wedge tr_\Delta = tr_2 - tr_1$

$\equiv$ " One point rule: tr_Δ, requires definedness of $tr_2 - tr_1$ "

$\exists\, tr_1, tr_2 \bullet bag_2 = items(tr_2) \wedge bag_1 = items(tr_1) \wedge tr_1 \leq tr_2$

$\equiv$ " def. of $EqvTrc$, backwards "

$\exists\, tr_1, tr_2 \bullet EqvTrc(tr_2, bag_2) \wedge EqvTrc(tr_1, bag_1) \wedge tr_1 \leq tr_2$

Bug Hunting with False Negatives[*]

Jens Calamé[1], Natalia Ioustinova[1], Jaco van de Pol[1,2], and Natalia Sidorova[2]

[1] Centrum voor Wiskunde en Informatica,
P.O.Box 94079, 1090 GB Amsterdam, The Netherlands
[2] Eindhoven University of Technology,
P.O.Box 513, 5600 MB Eindhoven, The Netherlands
jens.calame@cwi.nl, ustin@cwi.nl,
jaco.van.de.pol@cwi.nl, n.sidorova@tue.nl

Abstract. Safe data abstractions are widely used for verification purposes. Positive verification results can be transferred from the abstract to the concrete system. When a property is violated in the abstract system, one still has to check whether a concrete violation scenario exists. However, even when the violation scenario is not reproducible in the concrete system (a false negative), it may still contain information on possible sources of bugs.

Here, we propose a bug hunting framework based on abstract violation scenarios. We first extract a violation pattern from one abstract violation scenario. The violation pattern represents multiple abstract violation scenarios, increasing the chance that a corresponding concrete violation exists. Then, we look for a concrete violation that corresponds to the violation pattern by using constraint solving techniques. Finally, we define the class of counterexamples that we can handle and argue correctness of the proposed framework.

Our method combines two formal techniques, model checking and constraint solving. Through an analysis of contracting and precise abstractions, we are able to integrate overapproximation by abstraction with concrete counterexample generation.

1 Introduction

Abstractions [5,6,7,9,13,18] are widely used to reduce the state space of complex, distributed, data-oriented and thus large systems for verification purposes. We focus on abstractions that are used to check satisfaction rather than the violation of properties. These abstractions are constructed in such a way that we can transfer positive verification results from the abstract to the concrete model, but not the negative ones. Counterexamples found on the abstract system may have no counterpart in the concrete system. We further refer to this kind of counterexamples as *false negatives*. False negatives are usually used to refine the abstraction and iteratively call the model checking algorithm on the refined abstraction [4,10,17].

---

[*] Part of this research has been funded by the Dutch BSIK/BRICKS project.

J. Davies and J. Gibbons (Eds.): IFM 2007, LNCS 4591, pp. 98–117, 2007.

Fig. 1. Abstracted timer

In this paper, we consider false negatives in the context of *data abstractions*, i.e. abstractions that substitute actual data values by abstract ones and operations on concrete data by operations on abstract data, depending on the property being verified. We use the timer abstraction from [8] as an illustrating example in this paper. This abstraction leaves all values of a discrete timer below k unchanged and maps all higher values to the abstract value k^+. Note that the deterministic time progress operation *tick* (decreasing the values of active timers by one), becomes non-deterministic in the abstract model (see Fig. 1). But this abstraction allows us to only regard the k smallest values and the constant k^+ in order to prove that a property holds for any value n.

Consider a system, where every timer setting $set(n)$ is followed by n *tick* steps before the timer is set again, for some constant value n. Being set to a value n above k, the abstract timer can do an arbitrary number of *tick* steps, before it reaches value $k - 1$. From there, it decreases until it expires at 0.

We now use this k^+ timer abstraction to verify an action-based *LTL* property $\Box(a \rightarrow \Diamond b)$ and obtain the following trace as a counterexample for the abstract system: $a.set(k^+).tick^3.b.(a.set(k^+).tick^2.d)^\star$. Note that the timer abstraction affected the parameter of the *set* action, so that the number of *tick* steps following $set(k^+)$ is not fixed anymore. This trace obviously is a *false negative* since it does not reflect any possible trace of the original system (remember the constant n).

Assuming that the trace $a.set(n).tick^n.b.(a.set(n).tick^n.d)^\star$ exists in the original system, the false negative still contains a clue for finding this concrete counterexample. We can relax the found abstract counterexample by using the information that the operations on timers are influenced by the timer abstraction and check whether the concrete system contains a trace matching the pattern $a.any^\star.b.(a.any^\star.d)^\star$ where *any* represents any action on timers. We call such a pattern a *violation pattern*. Note that any trace matching the violation pattern violates our property of interest. The pattern contains a cyclic part, and it is more restrictive than the negation of the property. Therefore, when enumerative model checking is concerned, it is easier to find a trace of the concrete system satisfying the pattern than one that violates the property.

In this paper, we propose a framework that supports the bug hunting process described in the above example. In this framework, we apply a combination of abstraction, refinement and constraint solving techniques to process algebraic specifications. The framework is illustrated in Fig. 2 where $\mathcal{M}$ denotes the concrete system, $\mathcal{M}^\alpha$ stands for an abstraction of $\mathcal{M}$, ϕ is the property in question and ϕ^α is its abstraction. When checking whether the abstract system satisfies the abstract property, we may obtain a counterexample having no counterpart in the concrete system (the set $(\mathcal{M}^\alpha \backslash \mathcal{M}) \cap \neg\phi$). Given the counterexample, we relax actions influenced by the data abstraction and construct a violation pattern that represents

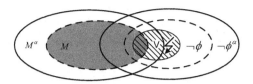

Fig. 2. Violation pattern approach

a set of traces violating the property and resembling the counterexample. For this to work, we need an accurate analysis of contracting and precise abstractions [16]. In short, contracting abstractions abstract a system property in a way, that less traces fulfill this property, while precise abstractions do not affect fulfilling traces.

To check whether there is a concrete trace matching the violation pattern, we transform the violation pattern and the specification of the concrete system into a constraint logic program. Subsequently, a constraint solver is used to find a concrete trace matching the violation pattern, if such a trace exists.

The rest of the paper is organized as follows: In the remainder of this section, we compare our work with related work. In Section 2, we define the class of systems we are working with. Furthermore, we define a next-free action-based *LTL (ALTL)* and extend it by data (*eALTL*). In Section 3, we work out abstractions of labeled transition systems and of *eALTL* properties. In Section 4, we present a taxonomy of counterexamples, of which we select the false negatives to build up a bug hunting framework and discuss its correctness in Section 5. In Section 6, we give an example for the implementation of this framework. Finally, we conclude with Section 7.

Related Work

First, we compare our method with the more traditional CEGAR approach (Counter-Example-Guided Abstraction Refinement) [4,17], which has recently been extended to state- and event-based software by the ComFoRT framework [3]. In both methods, abstractions preserve properties in one direction only: if the abstract system satisfies the property, so does the concrete system; a counterexample may however be a real one or a false negative. In the CEGAR method, the abstraction is refined based on abstract counterexamples, and model checking is iteratively applied to the refined abstractions of the system. Our method is to generalize false negatives and then to find violations in the concrete specification, which are similar to the original false negative. Note that in principle both methods can be combined: given a false negative, one could search for a concrete violation using our method. If it is found, the CEGAR loop can be terminated early. If still no concrete counterexample is found, one can proceed by refining the abstraction as in the CEGAR approach and iterate verification.

For counterexamples that have been produced when model checking the abstract model, it has to be determined whether they represent real system defects. In [21], the problem of automating this analysis has been addressed. For this purpose, the authors propose two techniques: model checking on choice-free paths and abstract counterexample guided concrete simulation. In [20], an approach based on test generation is proposed for searching for concrete instances of abstract counterexamples. Only counterexamples for safety properties are addressed by those approaches, i.e. it works only for finite counterexamples, while we deal with infinite traces. Unlike these approaches, we look for a concrete trace that does not match a counterexample itself, but a violation pattern that has been generated from it.

Finally, [15] and [22] are orthogonal to ours, because there model checking methods are proposed that rely on a refinement of an *underapproximation* of the system behavior. These methods aim at the falsification of a desired property and apply a refinement when no counterexample is found. In contrast, we try to prove the property and, if we do not succeed, try to find a concrete counterexample.

2   The Specification Framework

We did our research in the setting of the process-algebraic language μCRL [14]. As graphical notation, we will use symbolic transition systems (STSs, cf. [24]). A specification S over an alphabet of actions Act (defined below), is given as the parallel composition $\Pi_{i=1}^{n} P_i$ of a finite number of processes. A process definition P is given by a four-tuple ($Var, Loc, Edg, (\ell_{\text{init}}, \eta_{\text{init}})$), where Var denotes a finite set of variables, and Loc denotes a finite set of *locations* ℓ, or control states. A mapping of variables to values is called a valuation; we denote the set of valuations by $Val = \{\eta \mid \eta \colon Var \to \mathbb{D}\}$. We assume standard data domains such as $\mathbb{N}$ or $\mathbb{B}$. The set $Expr$ denotes the set of *expressions*, built from variables and function symbols in the usual way. An expression can be evaluated to a value, given a valuation for the variables. We write $\mathbb{D}$ when leaving the data-domain unspecified and silently assume all expressions to be well-typed. The initial location and valuation are given by ($\ell_{\text{init}}, \eta_{\text{init}}$). The set $Edg \subseteq Loc \times Act \times Loc$ denotes the set of edges. An *edge* describes changes of configurations specified by an *action* from Act.

Let $Event$ be a set of system events (cf. channel names, action names). As actions, we distinguish (1) the *input* of an event s together with a local variable to which the received value can be assigned, (2) the *output* of an event s together with a value described by an expression, and (3) *internal actions*, like assignments. Every action is *guarded* by a boolean expression g. This guard decides, whether the action may be executed (when the guard evaluates to true) or not. So we define the set Act to consist of: $g \triangleright ?s(x)$, $g \triangleright !s(e)$, or $g \triangleright \tau, x := e$, resp., and we use $\iota, \iota' \ldots$ when leaving the action unspecified. For an edge $(\ell, \iota, \hat{\ell}) \in Edg$, we write more suggestively $\ell \to_\iota \hat{\ell}$.

Examples of specifications can be found in Fig. 6 later in this paper. There, the system on the left-hand side awaits an input $in(x)$, with a variable x that will be instantiated at runtime. Depending on the value of x, the system will then output the event out with either the value of x or 0.

Before we define the semantics of our specifications, we introduce the notion of labeled transition systems and traces.

Definition 1 (Total *LTS*). *A labeled transition system* (*LTS*) *is a quadruple* $\mathcal{M} = (\Sigma, Lab, \Delta, \sigma_{\text{init}})$ *where* Σ *is a set of* states, *Lab is a set of* action labels, $\Delta \subseteq \Sigma \times Lab \times \Sigma$ *is a labeled* transition relation *and* $\sigma_{\text{init}} \in \Sigma$ *is the* initial state. *A total LTS does not contain any deadlocks.*

Further we write $\sigma \rightarrow_{\lambda} \sigma'$ for a triple $(\sigma, \lambda, \sigma') \in \Delta$ and refer to it as a λ-*step of* $\mathcal{M}$. For the rest of the paper, we assume *LTS*s to be *total*.

Definition 2 (Traces). *Let* $\mathcal{M} = (\Sigma, Lab, \Delta, \sigma_{\text{init}})$ *be an LTS. A trace* β *of* $\mathcal{M}$ *is a mapping* $\beta \colon \mathbb{N} \setminus \{0\} \rightarrow Lab$, *such that there is a mapping* $\beta' \colon \mathbb{N} \rightarrow \Sigma$ *and for any* $i, (i+1) \in \mathbb{N} \colon \beta'[i] \rightarrow_{\beta[i+1]} \beta'[i+1] \in \Delta$ *with* $\beta'[0] = \sigma_{\text{init}}$. *We further refer to the suffix of* β *starting at* $\beta[i]$ *as* β^i. *By* $[\![\mathcal{M}]\!]_{\text{trace}}$, *we denote the set of all traces in* $\mathcal{M}$.

The step semantics of $\mathcal{S}$ is given by an *LTS* $\mathcal{M} = (\Sigma, Lab, \Delta, \sigma_{\text{init}})$. Here, the set of states is $\Sigma := Loc \times Val$ with the initial state $\sigma_{\text{init}} := (\ell_{\text{init}}, \eta_{\text{init}}) \in \Sigma$. The (possibly infinite) set of labels is $Lab := \{s(d) \mid s \in Event, d \in \mathbb{D}\}$. Finally, the transitions $\Delta \subseteq \Sigma \times Lab \times \Sigma$ are given as a labeled transition relation between states. The labels differentiate internal actions and communication steps, either input or output, which are labeled by an event and a value being transmitted, i.e. τ, $?s(v)$ or $!s(v)$, respectively.

Receiving an event s with a communication parameter x, $\ell \rightarrow_{g \rhd ?s(x)} \hat{\ell} \in Edg$, results in updating the valuation $\eta_{[x \mapsto v]}$ according to the parameter of the event and changing current location to $\hat{\ell}$. The possible input values are limited by the guard. Output, $\ell \rightarrow_{g \rhd !s(e)} \hat{\ell} \in Edg$, is guarded, so sending a message involves evaluating the guard and the expression according to the current valuation. It leads to the change of the location of the process from ℓ to $\hat{\ell}$. Assignments, $\ell \rightarrow_{g \rhd \tau, x := e} \hat{\ell} \in Edg$, result in the change of a location and the update of the valuation $\eta_{[x \mapsto v]}$, where $[\![e]\!]_{\eta} = v$. Assignment transitions are labeled by the corresponding action label τ. Firing such a transition also involves evaluating the guard and the expression according to the current valuation.

2.1 *ALTL* with Data (*eALTL*)

To specify properties of a system, we propose a data extension for action-based Linear Temporal Logic (*ALTL* [12]). This logic specifies system properties in terms of events parameterized with data. Here, we first define *action formulae*, their satisfaction and then define *extended ALTL, eALTL*.

Definition 3 (Action Formulae). *Let* x *be a variable from Var, expr be a boolean expression from Expr, a be an event from Event, then the syntax of an action formula* ζ *is defined as follows:*

$$\zeta ::= \top \mid \{a(x) \mid expr(x)\} \mid \neg \zeta \mid \zeta \wedge \zeta$$

We will use $a(x)$ as an abbreviation for $\{a(x) \mid \mathsf{true}\}$ and $a(d)$ as an abbreviation for $\{a(x) \mid x = d\}$. We do not impose any limitations on the set of boolean expressions.

Definition 4 (Interpretation of an action formula). *Let $act \in Lab$ and ζ be an action formula, then the satisfaction of ζ on act is defined as follows:*

$$
\begin{aligned}
act &\models \top & &\textit{always (\textnormal{true})} \\
act &\models \{a(x) \mid expr(x)\} & &\textit{if there exists some } d \in \mathbb{D} \textit{ s.t.} \\
& & &act = a(d) \textit{ and } [\![expr]\!]_{[x \mapsto d]} = \textnormal{true} \\
act &\models \zeta_1 \wedge \zeta_2 & &\textit{if } act \models \zeta_1 \textit{ and } act \models \zeta_2 \\
act &\models \neg\zeta & &\textit{if not } act \models \zeta
\end{aligned}
$$

Definition 5 (*eALTL* Formulae). *Let ζ be an action formula. The syntax of eALTL formulae is defined by the following grammar:*

$$
\phi ::= \zeta \mid \neg\phi \mid \phi \wedge \phi \mid \phi \mathbf{U} \phi
$$

Definition 6 (Semantics of *eALTL*). *Let β be a (infinite) trace, ϕ, ϕ_1, ϕ_2 be eALTL formulae, ζ be an action formula then*

$$
\begin{aligned}
\beta &\models \zeta & &\textit{if } \beta[1] \models \zeta \\
\beta &\models \neg\phi & &\textit{if not } \beta \models \phi \\
\beta &\models \phi_1 \wedge \phi_2 & &\textit{if } \beta \models \phi_1 \textit{ and } \beta \models \phi_2 \\
\beta &\models \phi_1 \mathbf{U} \phi_2 & &\textit{if there exists } k \in \mathbb{N} \textit{ such that} \\
& & &\textit{for all } 0 \leq i < k : \beta^i \models \phi_1 \textit{ and } \beta^k \models \phi_2
\end{aligned}
$$

Let $\mathcal{M} = (\Sigma, Lab, \Delta, \sigma_{\text{init}})$ be an *LTS*. We say that $\mathcal{M} \models \phi$ iff $\beta \models \phi$ for all traces β of $\mathcal{M}$ starting at σ_{init}. We introduce the following shorthand notations: $\bot$ for $\neg\top$; $\Diamond\phi$ for $\top\mathbf{U}\phi$; $\Box\phi$ for $\neg\Diamond\neg\phi$; $\phi_1 \vee \phi_2$ for $\neg(\neg\phi_1 \wedge \neg\phi_2)$; $\phi_1 \Rightarrow \phi_2$ for $\neg\phi_1 \vee \phi_2$; $\phi_1 \mathbf{R} \phi_2$ for $\neg(\neg\phi_1 \mathbf{U} \neg\phi_2)$. *eALTL* is suitable to express a broad range of property patterns like occurrence, bounded response or absence [11]. For our further work on abstracting properties of systems, we will require that property formulae are in positive normal form, i.e. all negations are pushed inside, right before action formulae.

3   Abstraction of Systems and Properties

In this section, we present an abstraction mechanism based on homomorphisms as in [5,16], and adapted to an action-based setting. Abstracting a system leads to a smaller state space which can thus be examined easier. However, model checking an abstracted system also requires the abstraction of the properties that have to be checked. We will first present the abstraction of systems and then the abstraction of *eALTL* properties.

3.1   Abstraction of a System

The basis for the abstraction is a homomorphism $\alpha = \langle h_s, h_a \rangle$ defining two abstraction functions which regard states and actions of an *LTS* [5,23]. The function $h_s : \Sigma \to \Sigma^\alpha$ maps the states of a concrete system $\mathcal{M}$ to abstract states. The function $h_a : Lab \to Lab^\alpha$ does the same with action labels of $\mathcal{M}$.

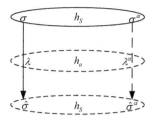

Fig. 3. Abstraction requirement for *LTS*s

Definition 7. *Let abstraction* $\alpha = \langle h_s, h_a \rangle$ *for automaton* $\mathcal{M} = (\Sigma, Lab, \Delta, \sigma_{\text{init}})$ *be given. We define* $\alpha(\mathcal{M})$ *to be* $(\Sigma^\alpha, Lab^\alpha, \Delta^\alpha, h_s(\sigma_{\text{init}}))$, *where* $\sigma^\alpha \rightarrow_{\lambda^\alpha} \hat{\sigma}^\alpha \in \Delta^\alpha$ *if and only if* $\sigma \rightarrow_\lambda \hat{\sigma} \in \Delta$, *for some* σ, $\hat{\sigma}$ *and* λ *such that* $h_s(\sigma) = \sigma^\alpha$, $h_s(\hat{\sigma}) = \hat{\sigma}^\alpha$, *and* $h_a(\lambda) = \lambda^\alpha$.

Now, we define a *homomorphic relation on traces*, $\equiv_\alpha \subseteq Lab^\star \times Lab^{\alpha\star}$, which relates concrete traces from $Lab^\star$ to their abstract counterparts in $Lab^{\alpha\star}$.

Definition 8 (Trace Inclusion w.r.t. α). *Let* $\alpha = \langle h_s, h_a \rangle$ *be a homomorphism. For a trace* β *of* $Lab^\star$ *and trace* β^α *of* $Lab^{\alpha\star}$, *we say* $\beta \equiv_\alpha \beta^\alpha$ *iff for all* $i \in \mathbb{N}$: $\beta^\alpha[i] = h_a(\beta[i])$.

We say that $\mathcal{M} \sqsubseteq_\alpha \mathcal{M}^\alpha$ *iff for every trace* β *of* $\mathcal{M}$ *there exists a trace* β^α *of* $\mathcal{M}^\alpha$ *such that* $\beta \equiv_\alpha \beta^\alpha$.

It is well known that homomorphic abstractions lead to overapproximations. Notably, the abstract system covers at least the traces of the concrete system:

Lemma 9. *Let* $\mathcal{M}$ *be an* LTS *with homomorphism* α. *Then* $\mathcal{M} \sqsubseteq_\alpha \alpha(\mathcal{M})$.

It is often more convenient to apply abstractions directly on a system specification $\mathcal{S}$ than on its transition system $\mathcal{M}$. Such an abstraction on the level of $\mathcal{S}$ is well-developed within the *Abstract Interpretation* framework [6,7,9]. Abstract Interpretation imposes a requirement on the relation between the concrete specification $\mathcal{S}$ and its abstract interpretation $\mathcal{S}^\alpha$. This takes the form of a safety requirement on the relation between data and operations of the concrete system and their abstract counterparts (we skip the details). Each value of the concrete domain $\mathbb{D}$ is related by a data abstraction function h_d to a value from the abstract domain $\mathbb{D}^\alpha$. For every operation (function) f on the concrete data domain, an abstract function f^α is defined, which overapproximates f. For reasons of simplicity, we assume f to be a unary operation. Furthermore, we apply only data abstraction. This means that the names of actions in a system are not affected by the abstraction, i.e. $h_a(a(d)) = a(h_d(d))$ such that two actions $a(x)$ and $b(y)$ cannot be mapped to the same abstract action.

However, applying abstractions directly on a system's specification $\mathcal{S}$ rather than on its *LTS* leads to a loss of precision. Let $\mathcal{S}^\alpha$ be the abstract interpretation of $\mathcal{S}$, and let $\mathcal{M}^\alpha$ and $\mathcal{M}$ be their underlying *LTS*s. It is well known that $\mathcal{M}^\alpha$ is only an overapproximation of $\alpha(\mathcal{M})$ (cf. [5]). In particular, we will still have trace inclusion up to α: $\mathcal{M} \sqsubseteq_\alpha \alpha(\mathcal{M}) \sqsubseteq_\alpha \mathcal{M}^\alpha$.

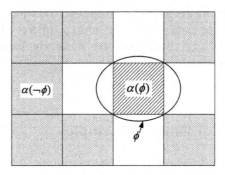

Fig. 4. Contracting Abstraction

3.2   Abstraction of *eALTL* Formulae

The abstraction of *eALTL* formulae is based on the notions of *contracting and precise abstractions* as it has been introduced in [16]. In a contracting abstraction, a property ϕ^α holds for a trace β^α iff the property ϕ holds for *all* concrete traces β with $\beta^\alpha = \alpha(\beta)$. Note that for soundness of abstract model checking, we need contracting abstractions. This does, however, not imply that all properties that hold for the original system, *must* also hold in the abstract system (see Fig. 4, ellipse vs. hatched square). In *precise* abstractions, this cannot happen.

Definition 10 (Contracting and Precise Abstraction). *Let ϕ be a property over an action alphabet λ. Its abstraction ϕ^α is*

- contracting *iff:* $\forall \beta \in Lab^\star : \alpha(\beta) \models \phi^\alpha \Rightarrow \beta \models \phi$.
- precise *iff:* $\forall \beta \in Lab^\star : \alpha(\beta) \models \phi^\alpha \Leftrightarrow \beta \models \phi$.

In the following, we define an abstraction of *eALTL* formulae that is guaranteed to be contracting. We assume all formulae to be in positive normal form.

Definition 11 (Abstraction of Action Formulae). *Action formulae as defined in Def. 3 are abstracted as follows:*

$$\alpha(\top) := \top$$
$$\alpha(\{a(x) \mid expr(x)\}) := \{a(x^\alpha) \mid \forall x : h_d(x) = x^\alpha \rightarrow expr(x))\}$$
$$\alpha(\neg\{a(x) \mid expr(x)\}) := \bigvee_{b \neq a} \{b(x^\alpha)\} \vee \{a(x^\alpha) \mid \forall x : h_d(x) = x^\alpha \rightarrow \neg expr(x)\}$$
$$\alpha(\zeta_1 \wedge \zeta_2) := \alpha(\zeta_1) \wedge \alpha(\zeta_2)$$

The abstraction of *eALTL* formulae is more straightforward, since we do not have to regard negations on this level.

Definition 12 (Abstraction of *eALTL* Formulae). eALTL *formulae as defined in Def. 5 are abstracted as follows:*

$$\alpha(\phi_1 \wedge \phi_2) := \alpha(\phi_1) \wedge \alpha(\phi_2)$$
$$\alpha(\phi_1 \mathbf{U} \phi_2) := \alpha(\phi_1)\mathbf{U}\alpha(\phi_2)$$

In order to have precise abstractions, we need a restriction on the homomorphism α. We define that α is *consistent* with ϕ, iff for all action formulae ζ occuring in ϕ, $\{h_a(act)|act \models \zeta\} \cap [\![\neg\alpha(\zeta)]\!] = \emptyset$, i.e. the hatched square and the ellipse in Figure 4 coincide.

Lemma 13. *If α is consistent with ϕ, then $\alpha(\phi)$ is precise.*

4 Classification of Counterexamples

We can now explain model checking by abstraction for *eALTL* formulae. Let a specification $\mathcal{S}$ (with underlying *LTS* $\mathcal{M}$) and an *eALTL* property ϕ be given. Let us investigate whether a contracting abstraction α suffices for our needs. We compute $\alpha(\phi)$ and $\mathcal{S}^\alpha$, generate its underlying *LTS* $\mathcal{M}^\alpha$ and use a model checking algorithm to check $\mathcal{M}^\alpha \models \phi^\alpha$. If this holds, we can derive by our previous results, that also $\mathcal{M} \models \phi$, without ever generating $\mathcal{M}$. If it does not hold, we obtain a counterexample. Here we provide a classification of abstract counterexamples and demonstrate their relationship with contracting and precise abstractions of *eALTL* formulae.

Given a concrete system $\mathcal{M}$, its abstraction $\mathcal{M}^\alpha$, a property ϕ and its abstraction ϕ^α, we differentiate between three classes of abstract counterexamples (see Fig. 5). Given a counterexample χ^α, we refer to a concrete trace $\chi \in [\![\mathcal{M}]\!]_{\text{trace}}$ such that $\chi \equiv_\alpha \chi^\alpha$ as a *concrete counterpart* of χ^α. The first class (see counterexample 1 in Fig. 5) consists of the counterexamples having *no* concrete counterparts in the concrete system. These counterexamples are referred to as *false negatives*.

The second class (see counterexample 2 in Fig. 5) consists of counterexamples having (at least one) concrete counterpart *satisfying* the original property. We further refer to this class as *spurious counterexamples*.

The third class (see counterexample 3 in Fig. 5) consists of the counterexamples having at least one counterpart in the concrete system; moreover all concrete counterparts violate the concrete property. Counterexamples from this class are referred to as *ideal counterexamples*.

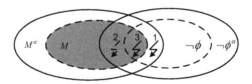

Fig. 5. Classification of counterexamples

Definition 14. *Let χ^α be a counterexample obtained by verifying an abstraction ϕ^α of a property ϕ on the abstraction $\mathcal{M}^\alpha$ of a system $\mathcal{M}$ w.r.t. the homomorphism h. We distinguish the following three cases:*

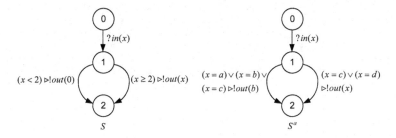

Fig. 6. Concrete and Abstracted Specifications from Example 15

1. We call χ^α a false negative, if there is no $\chi \in [\![\mathcal{M}]\!]_{\text{trace}}$ such that $\chi \equiv_\alpha \chi^\alpha$.
2. We call χ^α a spurious counterexample if there exists $\chi \in [\![\mathcal{M}]\!]_{\text{trace}}$ such that $\chi \equiv_\alpha \chi^\alpha$ and $\chi \models \phi$.
3. Otherwise, we call χ^α an ideal counterexample.

Contracting abstractions may lead to spurious counterexamples. The following example illustrates this case.

Example 15. Let S in Fig. 6 be the specification of a concrete system. We abstract $\mathbb{Z}$ into $\mathbb{Z}^\alpha = \{a, b, c, d\}$ where a stands for the numbers from $(-\infty, -3)$; b stands for the numbers from $[-3, 0]$; c stands for the numbers from $(0, 3]$; and d stands for the numbers from $(3, +\infty)$. By applying this abstraction to S we obtain S^α (see Fig. 6).

Consider the property $\phi = \Diamond(\{out(x) \mid (x \geq 2)\})$. We compute the contracting abstraction of ϕ as follows:

$$\phi = \Diamond(\{out(x) \mid (x \geq 2)\})$$
$$\phi^\alpha = \Diamond(\{out(x^\alpha) \mid \forall x : h_d(x) = x^\alpha \rightarrow (x \geq 2)\})$$
$$= \Diamond(out(d))$$

Verifying ϕ^α on S^α we may obtain the trace $in(c).out(c)$ as a counterexample, because it is a trace in S^α, but does not satisfy ϕ. However, the concrete trace $in(2).out(2)$ corresponding to the abstract counterexample satisfies $\Diamond(out(x) \wedge (x \geq 2))$. Hence, $\neg\phi^\alpha$ is not precise enough.

Such spurious counterexamples are problematic for tracking real bugs. Therefore, we will use *precise* abstractions, in order to avoid spurious counterexamples. A contracting abstraction can be made precise, by fitting the abstraction to the predicates in the specification and the formula:

Example 16. Let S in Fig. 7 be the specification of a concrete system. We abstract $\mathbb{Z}$ into $\mathbb{Z}^\alpha = \{a, b, c, d\}$ where the interpretation of a and b remains the same as in Example 15 while c represents the numbers from the interval $(0, 2)$ and d represents those from $[2, +\infty)$. By applying this abstraction to S we obtain S^α (see Fig. 7).

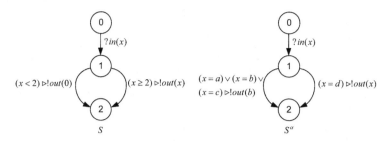

Fig. 7. Concrete and Abstracted Specifications from Example 16

Consider again the property $\phi = \Diamond(\{out(x) \mid (x \geq 2)\})$ and its abstraction $\phi^\alpha = \Diamond(out(d))$. Verifying ϕ^α on $\mathcal{S}^\alpha$ we may obtain the following counterexamples: $in(a).out(b)$, $in(b).out(b)$, and $in(c).out(b)$. In this example it is straightforward to see that any concretization of these traces is a counterexample for ϕ. So in this case, the abstraction is precise.

5   Bug Hunting with False Negatives

Counterexamples that are false negatives still have a value for detecting bugs in specifications. By relaxing them, i.e. making them even more abstract, false negatives cover a larger part of the system, which can contain bugs. In this manner, they can serve as a starting point for bug hunting.

In this section, we provide an overview of our framework for bug hunting with false negatives. This process comprises the following steps:

1. Specify a requirement as a formula ϕ of *eALTL*.
2. Choose and apply a data abstraction, which is consistent with ϕ, to the specification of the concrete system and to the concrete property.
3. Abstract counterexamples for the property are (automatically) determined using model checking.
4. Generalize the false negative further by *relaxing* actions, which are not directly relevant for our search. This results in a violation pattern. The relaxing process itself is automatic, only the counterexample and the set of directly relevant actions have to be given as input to the algorithm (see Alg. 1).
5. The concrete counterexamples are automatically computed by finding the intersection of the original system and the violation pattern.

Since the first three steps of the framework can be handled by existing data abstraction and model checking techniques, our contribution concerns the steps 4 and 5 of the framework.

5.1   Constructing a Violation Pattern

A counterexample that we obtain in case the property is violated on our abstract model is an infinite trace of the form $\beta_p \beta_s^\omega$ where β_p is a finite prefix and β_s^ω is a cyclic suffix with a finite *cycle base* β_s.

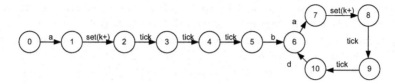

Fig. 8. A concrete counterexample

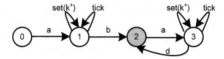

Fig. 9. The violation pattern for the counterexample

Although the counterexample χ^α may have no counterpart in the concrete system, it can contain a clue about a counterexample present in the concrete system. Therefore we transform a counterexample χ^α into a *violation pattern* $\mathcal{V}$, considering only *infinite* counterexamples.

A violation pattern is an *LTS* that accepts all traces hitting a distinguished *cyclic* state infinitely often. The violation pattern accepts only traces which are *similar* to the counterexample and *violate* the abstract property. The actions mentioned in the property are essential for the property violation. Therefore we keep this information in the violation pattern. For actions influenced by the abstraction, the order and the number of actions in a similar trace may differ from those of the counterexample. We will now first illustrate the idea of similarity on a simple example and then generalize it.

Example 17. Let us come back to the example from the introduction. Assume that we model-check the property $\square(a \to \Diamond b)$ and obtain the abstract counterexample $a.set(k^+).tick^3.b.(a.set(k^+).tick^2.d)^\omega$ (see Fig. 8). The k^+ is in this case an abstraction of a timer: The original value of the timer is preserved up to k; any value above k is abstracted to the constant value k^+. To guarantee that the property is violated by any trace accepted by the pattern, we keep *at least* the actions a and b, because they are mentioned in the property (see Fig. 9). Since we are searching for similar traces with an infinite *cyclic* suffix β_s, we may also decide to keep information about some actions of this cycle. Here we also provide the action step d in the cycle (see Fig. 9). The actions *tick* and $set(k^+)$ are not mentioned in the property and are definitely influenced by the timer abstraction. Therefore, we *relax* these actions, meaning, we allow these actions to occur an arbitrary number of times in an arbitrary order (see states 1 and 3 of the violation pattern in Fig. 9).

We refer to the set of action labels that we do not want to relax by Lab_{keep}. This set includes *at least* all the labels mentioned in the abstract (and also the concrete) property. In the violation pattern, we distinguish a *cyclic* state which corresponds to the first state in the cyclic suffix. The last action in the cycle base of an infinite counterexample leads to this cyclic state.

Ideally, we would like to relax more actions influenced by data abstraction. These actions can be found by applying static analysis techniques. The more actions we keep, the more concrete the counterexample is and the faster we can check whether there is a concrete trace matching the pattern. By keeping too many actions, however, we might end up with a violation pattern that specifies traces having no counterparts in the concrete system.

Definition 18 (Non-relaxed Actions). *Given a set Act^{ϕ^α} of actions appearing in a property ϕ^α, we define that some set Lab_{keep} of non-relaxed actions in a violation pattern is* consistent *if and only if $Lab_{\text{keep}} \supseteq Act^{\phi^\alpha}$.*

Lab_{keep} can optionally contain additional actions, like the last action of a cyclic suffix, or actions not influenced by the data abstraction, to make the violation pattern more specific.

Definition 19 (Violation Pattern). *Given an abstract counterexample $\chi^\alpha = \beta_p \beta_s^\omega$ and a set Lab_{keep} of non-relaxed actions, a* violation pattern *is an extended LTS $\mathcal{V} = (\Sigma, Lab, \Delta, \sigma_{\text{init}}, \sigma_{\text{cyclic}})$ constructed by Algorithm 1, where σ_{cyclic} is the cyclic state.*

The set of traces visiting the cyclic state infinitely often, is further referred to as the set $[\![\mathcal{V}]\!]_{\text{trace}}$ of accepted traces.

Given a counterexample $\chi^\alpha = \beta_p \beta_s^\omega$ and a set Lab_{keep} of actions to keep, Algorithm 1 constructs the violation pattern $\mathcal{V}$. The algorithm starts with creating the initial state $\sigma_{\text{init}} := 0$ of $\mathcal{V}$ and goes through $\beta_p \beta_s$. When the algorithm encounters an action to relax, it adds a self-loop transition labeled with this action to the current state of $\mathcal{V}$. When it encounters an action to keep, it adds a transition from the current state to the (new) next state labeled by this action or, if the algorithm has reached the end of the cycle base, back to the cyclic state. The first state of β_s is assigned to σ_{cyclic}.

Lemma 20. *Let Lab_{keep} be consistent with ϕ^α, let χ^α be a counterexample for ϕ^α, and $\mathcal{V}$ be a violation pattern generated from χ^α and Lab_{keep}. Every trace $\beta^\alpha \in [\![\mathcal{V}]\!]_{\text{trace}}$ satisfies: $\beta^\alpha \not\models \phi^\alpha$.*

Proof Sketch. *If a counterexample χ^α is relaxed, at least all actions from the property's alphabet are in Lab_{keep} (see Def. 18), i.e. they are not relaxed. This means, that if a trace β^α is in $[\![\mathcal{V}]\!]_{\text{trace}}$, it contains all actions from ϕ^α in the same order as they appear in the counterexample χ^α.*

Since we are considering next-free properties, the absolute position of the actions in question in the particular trace is not required, to keep violating the property ϕ^α. Preserving the cyclic state σ_{cyclic} for an infinite counterexample also allows us to preserve the cyclicity of the infinite suffix of such a counterexample.

Algorithm 1. Build Violation Pattern

Require: $\chi^\alpha = \beta_p \beta_s^\omega, Lab_{keep}$	// trace, actions to keep
Ensure: $\mathcal{V} = (\Sigma, Lab, \Delta, \sigma_{init}, \sigma_{cyclic})$	// violation pattern
1: $\sigma_{init} := 0;\ \Sigma := \{\sigma_{init}\};$	// initialization
2: $st := 0;$	// current state st of $\mathcal{V}$
3: **for all** $i = 1..|\beta_p \beta_s|$ **do**	// for all steps of $\beta_p \beta_s$
4: **if** $\chi^\alpha[i] \notin Lab_{keep}$ **then**	
5: $\Delta := \Delta \cup \{(st, \chi^\alpha[i], st)\};$	// add a relaxed step
6: **fi**	
7: **if** $i = |\beta_p| + 1$ **then**	
8: $\sigma_{cyclic} := \{st\};$	// indicate the first state of the cycle
9: **fi**	
10: **if** $\chi^\alpha[i] \in Lab_{keep} \vee i = |\beta_p \beta_s|$ **then**	// if step to be kept or last one
11: **if** $i = |\beta_p \beta_s|$ **then**	// if last state in cycle base
12: $st' := \sigma_{cyclic};$	// next state is the cyclic one
13: **else**	
14: $st' := st + 1;$	// next state is arbitrary
15: **fi**	
16: $\Sigma := \Sigma \cup \{st'\};$	// add a new state,
17: $\Delta := \Delta \cup \{(st, \chi^\alpha[i], st')\};$	// add the step to the new state
18: $st := st';$	// proceed with the next state of $\mathcal{V}$
19: **fi**	
20: **od**	

5.2 Looking for a Concrete Counterexample

After we have constructed the violation pattern $\mathcal{V}$, we check whether there is a concrete counterexample $\chi = \chi_p \chi_s^\omega$, such that the corresponding abstract counterexample $\chi^\alpha \in [\![\mathcal{V}]\!]_{trace}$.

For infinite counterexamples we need to check that some state of χ_s corresponds to σ_{cyclic}. We employ constraint solving [19] to find a concrete counterexample, which allows us to check this condition for infinite (but cyclic) traces, and also for certain infinite and parameterized systems.

To find a concrete trace matching the violation pattern $\mathcal{V}$, we transform the specification of the concrete system and the violation pattern into a *constraint program* and formulate a *query* to find such a trace. This transformation is similar to the one described in [2]. Note that for a concrete system with an infinite state space, it is possible that the constraint solver will not terminate. Moreover, it is possible that the only traces that match the violation pattern are spiral traces, not cyclic ones (i.e. we do have a loop with respect to control locations, but some variable is infinitely growing) and we will not be able to find them.

The transformation of the specification of the concrete system into a rule system $\mathcal{R}_\mathcal{S}$ is defined in Table 1. Each edge of the specification $\mathcal{S}$ is mapped into a rule $\varrho \leftarrow g$. In the rule, g is a guard and ϱ is a user-defined constraint of the form $s(state(\ell, \overline{Var}), state(\hat{\ell}, \overline{Var}'), param(Y))$. The first parameter *state* of the user-defined constraint describes the source states corresponding to the edge in terms of control locations of a process and valuations of process variables. The second

Table 1. From specification $\mathcal{S}$ to rule system $\mathcal{R}_\mathcal{S}$

$$\text{ROUTPUT} \frac{\ell \rightarrow_{g\triangleright!s(e)} \hat{\ell} \in Edg}{s(state(\ell, \overline{Var}), state(\hat{\ell}, \overline{Var}), param(e)) \leftarrow g}$$

$$\text{RINPUT} \frac{\ell \rightarrow_{g\triangleright?s(x)} \hat{\ell} \in Edg}{s(state(\ell, \overline{Var}), state(\hat{\ell}, \overline{Var}_{[x \mapsto Y]}), param(Y)) \leftarrow g}$$

$$\text{RASSIGN} \frac{\ell \rightarrow_{g\triangleright\tau, x:=e} \hat{\ell} \in Edg}{\tau(state(\ell, \overline{Var}), state(\hat{\ell}, \overline{Var}_{[x \mapsto e]}), param) \leftarrow g}$$

Table 2. From violation pattern $\mathcal{V}$ to rule system $\mathcal{R}_\mathcal{V}$

$$(1) \frac{\sigma \rightarrow_{!s(v)} \hat{\sigma} \vee \sigma \rightarrow_{?s(v)} \hat{\sigma} \vee \sigma \rightarrow_\tau \hat{\sigma} \quad \sigma \neq \sigma_{\text{cyclic}}}{\sigma(state(\vec{X}), \bar{C}, \bar{\beta}) \leftarrow s(state(\vec{X}), state(\vec{X}'), param(Y)) \wedge \\ v = \alpha(Y) \wedge \hat{\sigma}(state(\vec{X}'), \bar{C}, [\bar{\beta}, s(Y)])}$$

$$(2) \frac{\sigma \rightarrow_{!s(v)} \hat{\sigma} \vee \sigma \rightarrow_{?s(v)} \hat{\sigma} \vee \sigma \rightarrow_\tau \hat{\sigma} \quad \sigma = \sigma_{\text{cyclic}}}{\sigma(state(\vec{X}), \bar{C}, \bar{\beta}) \leftarrow s(state(\vec{X}), state(\vec{X}'), param(Y)) \wedge \\ v = \alpha(Y) \wedge (\vec{X} \in \bar{C} \vee \hat{\sigma}(state(\vec{X}'), [\vec{X} \mid \bar{C}], [\bar{\beta}, s(Y)]))}$$

parameter *state* describes the destination states in terms of control locations of a process and valuations of process variables. The third parameter *param* contains parameters representing input and output values. The constraint is satisfied iff the guard g is satisfied. This means, that there is a transition $(\ell, \eta) \rightarrow_{g\triangleright s(d)} (\hat{\ell}, \hat{\eta})$, if and if only the rule $s(state(\ell, \overline{Var}), state(\hat{\ell}, \overline{Var}'), param(Y)) \leftarrow g$ holds, for some substitution $\overline{Var} = \eta$, $\overline{Var}' = \hat{\eta}$, $Y = d$ that makes guard g become true.

In ROUTPUT, the name of the constraint coincides with the event s. Note that the values of the process variables $\overline{Var}$ remain unmodified and the output value is represented by the parameter Y whose value is given by the expression e. In RINPUT, the input leads to the substitution of the value of process variable x by the value of the input parameter Y. In RASSIGN, an assignment is represented by substituting the value of the process variable x by the valuation of expression e. These rules have no local parameters, so the parameter structure is empty.

Transformation of the edges of $\mathcal{V} = (\Sigma, Lab, \Delta, \sigma_{\text{init}}, \sigma_{\text{cyclic}})$ into the rules of the rule system $\mathcal{R}_\mathcal{V}$ is defined in Table 2. Here, we abbreviate $(\ell, \overline{Var})$ by $\vec{X}$ and $(\hat{\ell}, \overline{Var}')$ by $\vec{X}'$. Intuitively, given a step of $\mathcal{V}$, a rule of $\mathcal{R}_\mathcal{V}$ checks whether the concrete system may make this step. The rules also take into account the information about the cyclic state and the data abstraction.

The rules in Table 2 transform the steps of a violation pattern into rules of the form: $\varrho \leftarrow \xi \wedge g_\alpha \wedge v$. ϱ is a user-defined constraint of the form $\sigma(state(\vec{X}), \bar{C}, \bar{\beta})$ specifying the source state $state(\vec{X})$ of the concrete system, the set of states, which are *possibly* on a cycle, in the set $\bar{C}$. This set is accumulatively constructed, and it contains concrete candidate cyclic states that match with σ_{cyclic} in the violation pattern. The third parameter, $\bar{\beta}$, contains the trace that has already been visited while examining $\mathcal{V}$ and will contain the end result.

ξ is a user-defined constraint of the form $s(state(\vec{X}), state(\vec{X'}), param(Y))$ as defined above. It represents a step on which the concrete system and the violation pattern can potentially synchronize.

The guard g_α checks whether the data parameters of the concrete action are a concretization of the data parameters of the abstract action.

Finally, ν determines whether and how the violation pattern has to be examined further. We will explain this in more detail shortly. Simplified, ν stops the further examination of $\mathcal{V}$, if we have reached the cyclic state of $\mathcal{V}$. Otherwise, it decides that the next step in $\mathcal{V}$ will be taken and sets the parameters accordingly.

We will now describe the rules in more detail. Rule 1 of Table 2 transforms steps of the violation pattern whose actual state σ is not the beginning of the cycle base. The step specified by the constraint $s(state(\vec{X}), state(\vec{X'}), param(Y))$ changes the state to $\hat{\sigma}$ in the violation pattern and to $state(\vec{X'})$ in the concrete system. That is captured by the constraint $\hat{\sigma}(state(\vec{X'}), \bar{C}, [\bar{\beta}, s(Y)])$ in ϱ. The constraint is satisfied only if both the violation pattern and the concrete system can make the specified step and the action labeling the step of the concrete system satisfies the constraint $v = \alpha(Y)$. When doing the next examination step, $\bar{C}$ is left unchanged, while the actual event s together with a concretization Y of its parameter v, is added to the examination trace $\bar{\beta}$.

Rule 2 transforms those steps of the violation pattern, which start from a state corresponding to the beginning of the cycle. If the actual corresponding state in the system is found in $\bar{C}$, the state is cyclic and has already earlier been visited during the examination. In this case, examination ends successfully. If the state is not yet in $\bar{C}$, it is *potentially cyclic*. In this case, the step is treated like in Rule 1, just that the actual state of the system is added to $\bar{C}$. Logging potentially cyclic states and examining the violation pattern further allows us to not only detect obvious cycles, i.e. cycles in the system which are also immediately visible in the violation pattern. We can also detect those cycles, where the system spirals before entering a real cycle. In this case, the system first runs through a cycle with respect to the location, but differing in the data part of the system state, before finally returning to a previously visited state. In such a case, the cyclic state of the violation pattern is visited more than once.

The rule system $\mathcal{R}_\mathcal{V}$, together with the rule system $\mathcal{R}_\mathcal{S}$, forms the constraint program. In order to check whether we can find a concrete counterexample matching the violation pattern, we transform the pair of the initial state of the violation pattern and the initial state of the concrete system into the query $q_{init} := \sigma_{init}(state(\vec{X}_{init}), [], [])$ (initial state without any potentially cyclic states and without action steps yet in the counterexample trace) and ask a constraint solver, whether it finds a solution in the constraint program formed by $\mathcal{R}_\mathcal{S}$ and $\mathcal{R}_\mathcal{V}$. If yes, it provides us a counterexample as a list of actions and violation pattern states, which has been collected over the examination of $\mathcal{V}$. If constraint solving does not find a solution, we cannot give a conclusive answer and have to use e.g. abstraction refinement techniques to find out, whether the property holds on the concrete system or not.

Lemma 21. *If the query q_{init} to the rule system $\mathcal{R}_{\mathcal{V}}$ holds for some trace β, then $\beta \in \llbracket \mathcal{M} \rrbracket_{\mathrm{trace}}$, and $\alpha(\beta) \in \mathcal{V}$.*

Proof Sketch. *Assume, that q_{init} holds in rule system $\mathcal{R}_{\mathcal{V}}$ for a trace β. Then, this trace is in $\llbracket \mathcal{M} \rrbracket_{\mathrm{trace}}$, since the conditions for the execution of particular actions in $\mathcal{R}_{\mathcal{V}}$ are based on $\mathcal{R}_{\mathcal{S}}$, an exact specification of the operational semantics of the specification language as defined in Section 2.*

The abstraction of the trace β, $\alpha(\beta)$, however, is in the violation pattern $\mathcal{V}$. The reason therefore is, that the rule system $\mathcal{R}_{\mathcal{V}}$ is generated from this violation pattern and thus only reflects steps (and inductively: traces), which appear in $\mathcal{V}$. Thus, the rule system only holds for those traces β, where $\alpha(\beta) \in \mathcal{V}$.

5.3   Correctness of the Framework

In this section, we argue the correctness of the framework, which has been worked out in the previous two subsections on the derivation of a violation pattern and the search for further counterexamples using constraint solving.

Theorem 22. *Let $\alpha = \langle h_s, h_a \rangle$ be an abstraction consistent with eALTL-property ϕ. Let LTSs $\mathcal{M}$ and $\mathcal{M}^{\alpha}$ be given, such that $\mathcal{M} \subseteq_{\alpha} \mathcal{M}^{\alpha}$. Furthermore, assume that the counterexample $\chi^{\alpha} \in \llbracket \mathcal{M}^{\alpha} \rrbracket_{\mathrm{trace}}$ and $\chi^{\alpha} \not\models \phi^{\alpha}$. Let $\mathcal{V}$ be a violation pattern built from χ^{α} and a consistent Lab_{keep} by the algorithm in Fig. 1. Let β be a trace for which q_{init} holds, according to the constraint solving procedure defined in Subsection 5.2. Then β is a counterexample: $\beta \in \llbracket \mathcal{M} \rrbracket_{\mathrm{trace}}$ and $\beta \not\models \phi$.*

Proof Sketch. *By Lemma 21, $\beta \in \llbracket \mathcal{M} \rrbracket_{\mathrm{trace}}$ and $\alpha(\beta) \in \llbracket \mathcal{V} \rrbracket_{\mathrm{trace}}$. By Lemma 20, $\alpha(\beta) \not\models \phi^{\alpha}$. By Lemma 13, as α is a precise abstraction, we have $\beta \not\models \phi$.*

6   Implementation

To check the applicability of our framework we performed a number of verification experiments with μCRL specifications [14]. For constraint solving, we used Eclipse Prolog [1].

We took a mutant of the *Positive Acknowledgment Retransmission Protocol* (*PAR*) [25] as our case study. The usual scenario for *PAR* includes a sender, a receiver, a message channel and an acknowledgment channel. The sender receives a frame from the upper layer, i.e. from its environment, sends it to the receiver via the message channel, the receiver delivers the frame to the upper layer and sends a positive acknowledgment via the acknowledgment channel to the sender. *PAR* depends on timers, which we have chosen too low for our experiments.

We tried to verify that for any setting of the sender timer exceeding some value k, all messages sent by the upper layer to the sender are eventually received by the upper layer from the receiver. To prove that the property holds for any setting of the sender timer exceeding k, we applied the timer abstraction described in Section 1 to the sender timer. The property was not satisfied on the abstract system (since the k we took was less than the sum of the channel delays) and we obtained a counterexample.

The abstract counterexample was not reproducible on the concrete system, since the number of *tick* steps from a setting of the sender timer till its expiration varied along the trace due to the use of the abstraction. We transformed the counterexample into a violation pattern by relaxing the actions on the sender timer as influenced by the abstraction. The specification of the system was transformed from μCRL into a set of Prolog constraint rules, while the violation pattern was immediately formulated as a set of Prolog rules according to our theory (Def. 18, 19 and Fig. 9). The constraint solver was then able to find a concrete counterexample for our property.

7 Conclusion

We proposed a novel framework for interpreting negative verification results obtained with the help of data abstractions. Existing approaches to handling abstract counterexamples try to find an exact counterpart of the counterexample (e.g. [21]). When no concrete counterpart can be found, data abstraction is considered to be not fine enough and abstraction refinement is applied (e.g. [4]).

In our framework we look for useful information in false negatives, combining the two formal methods model checking and constraint solving. Given a specification of a system and a property (formulated as an $eALTL$ formula), we first choose and apply data abstraction to both of them and then verify the abstract property on the abstract system. If the verification results in a violation of the abstract property and the obtained counterexample has no counterpart in the concrete system, we transform the counterexample into a violation pattern, which is further used to guide the search for concrete counterexamples.

The framework allows to handle counterexamples obtained when verifying safety properties, but also counterexamples for liveness properties. Moreover, the framework can be applied for searching concrete counterexamples in parameterized and infinite state systems. Success is not always guaranteed – the violation pattern can be too strict, concrete counterexamples can have a spiral form (i.e. a loop in the specification, that does not lead back to a state fully identical to its starting state), or there could be no counterexample at all since the property just holds on the concrete system. Still, our approach can help in finding counterexamples in those cases when a data abstraction influences the order and the number of some actions, e.g. as timer and counter abstractions do. Even though, we defined the framework for homomorphistic abstractions in this paper, it seems to be possible to generalize abstraction and refinement on the basis of Galois-connections and so define a framework for bughunting with false negatives based on abstract interpretation.

The approach to the generation of a violation pattern leaves a certain freedom in the sense that the set of actions to relax can be more/less restrictive. Tuning the violation pattern or using the expertise of system developers to pick an appropriate set of actions to relax can be potentially less costly than repeating the abstraction/refinement cycle immediately. More case studies comparing both approaches and trying their combinations are still needed.

References

1. Brisset, P., et al.: ECLIPSe Constraint Library Manual, version 5.9 edn. (May 2006) http://eclipse.crosscoreop.com/eclipse/doc/libman.pdf
2. Calamé, J.R., Ioustinova, N., v.d. Pol, J.C.: Towards Automatic Generation of Parameterized Test Cases from Abstractions. Technical Report SEN-E0602, Centrum voor Wiskunde en Informatica (March 2006) (To appear in ENTCS)
3. Chaki, S., Clarke, E., Grumberg, O., Ouaknine, J., Sharygina, N., Touili, T., Veith, H.: State/Event Software Verification for Branching-Time Specifications. In: Romijn, J.M.T., Smith, G.P., van de Pol, J. (eds.) IFM 2005. LNCS, vol. 3771, pp. 53–69. Springer, Heidelberg (2005)
4. Clarke, E.M., Grumberg, O., Jha, S., Lu, Y., Veith, H.: Counterexample-guided Abstraction Refinement for Symbolic Model Checking. Journ. of the ACM 50(5), 752–794 (2003)
5. Clarke, E.M., Grumberg, O., Long, D.E.: Model Checking and Abstraction. ACM Transactions on Programming Languages and Systems 16(5), 1512–1542 (1994) A preliminary version appeared in the Proc. of the POPL'92
6. Cousot, P., Cousot, R.: Abstract Interpretation: A Unified Lattice Model for Static Analysis of Programs by Construction or Approximation of Fixpoints. In: Proc. of the 4th ACM SIGACT-SIGPLAN Symp. on Principles of programming languages (POPL'77), pp. 238–252. ACM Press, New York (1977)
7. Dams, D.: Abstract Interpretation and Partition Refinement for Model Checking. PhD dissertation, Eindhoven University of Technology (July 1996)
8. Dams, D., Gerth, R.: The Bounded Retransmission Protocol Revisited. Electronic Notes in Theoretical Computer Science 9, 26 (1999)
9. Dams, D., Gerth, R., Grumberg, O.: Abstract Interpretation of Reactive Systems. ACM Transactions on Programming Languages and Systems (TOPLAS) 19(2), 253–291 (1997)
10. Das, S., Dill, D.L.: Counter-Example Based Predicate Discovery in Predicate Abstraction. In: FMCAD, pp. 19–32 (2002)
11. Dwyer, M.B., Avrunin, G.S., Corbett, J.C.: Patterns in Property Specifications for Finite-state Verification. In: Proc. of the 21st Intl. Conf. on Software Engineering, pp. 411–420. IEEE Computer Society Press, Los Alamitos (1999)
12. Giannakopoulou, D.: Model Checking for Concurrent Software Architectures. PhD thesis, Imperial College of Science Techn. and Med., Univ. of London (March 1999)
13. Graf, S., Saïdi, H.: Construction of Abstract State Graphs with PVS. In: Proc. of the 9th Intl. Conf. on Computer-Aided Verification, pp. 72–83 (1997)
14. Groote, J.F., Ponse, A.: The Syntax and Semantics of μCRL. In: Ponse, A., Verhoef, C., van Vlijmen, S. (eds.) Algebra of Communicating Processes. Workshops in Computing, pp. 26–62. Springer, Heidelberg (1994)
15. Grumberg, O., Lerda, F., Strichman, O., Theobald, M.: Proof-guided Underapproximation-Widening for Multi-Process Systems. In: Proc. of the Ann. Symp. on Principles of Programming Languages, pp. 122–131 (2005)

16. Kesten, Y., Pnueli, A.: Control and Data Abstraction: The Cornerstones of Practical Formal Verification. Intl. Journ. on Software Tools for Technology Transfer 2(4), 328–342 (2000)
17. Lakhnech, Y., Bensalem, S., Berezin, S., Owre, S.: Incremental Verification by Abstraction. In: Proc. of the Intl. Conf. on Tools and Algorithms for the Construction and Analysis of Systems, pp. 98–112 (2001)
18. Loiseaux, C., Graf, S., Sifakis, J., Bouajjani, A., Bensalem, S.: Property Preserving Abstractions for the Verification of Concurrent Systems. Formal Methods in System Design 6(1), 11–44 (1995)
19. Marriott, K., Stuckey, P.J.: Programming with Constraints – An Introduction. MIT Press, Cambridge (1998)
20. Pace, G., Halbwachs, N., Raymond, P.: Counter-example Generation in Symbolic Abstract Model-Checking. Intl. Journ. on Software Tools for Technology Transfer 5(2), 158–164 (2004)
21. Pasareanu, C.S., Dwyer, M.B., Visser, W.: Finding Feasible Counter-examples when Model Checking Abstracted Java Programs. In: Proc. of the Intl. Conf. on Tools and Algorithms for the Construction and Analysis of Systems, pp. 284–298 (2001)
22. Pasareanu, C.S., Pelánek, R., Visser, W.: Concrete Model Checking with Abstract Matching and Refinement. In: Proc. of the Intl. Conf. on Computer-Aided Verification, pp. 52–66 (2005)
23. v.d. Pol, J.C., Espada, M.A.V.: Modal Abstractions in μCRL. In: Rattray, C., Maharaj, S., Shankland, C. (eds.) AMAST 2004. LNCS, vol. 3116, Springer, Heidelberg (2004)
24. Rusu, V., du Bousquet, L., Jéron, T.: An Approach to Symbolic Test Generation. In: Grieskamp, W., Santen, T., Stoddart, B. (eds.) IFM 2000. LNCS, vol. 1945, pp. 338–357. Springer, Heidelberg (2000)
25. Tanenbaum, A.S.: Computer Networks. Prentice Hall International, Englewood Cliffs (1981)

Behavioural Specifications from Class Models

Alessandra Cavarra and James Welch

Oxford University Computing Laboratory
Wolfson Building, Parks Road, Oxford OX1 3QD UK

Abstract. This paper illustrates a technique to automatically derive intra-object behaviours (in the form of state diagrams) from an object model. We demonstrate how we may take specifications, written in a restricted language of pre- and postconditions, and generate protocols of usage that represent possible behaviours of the generated program. We discuss how to use these state diagrams to analyse the specification for errors, and how to produce correct abstractions to show a particular class of properties of a system. This approach proves successful and scalable for specific domains of application such as database systems and e-commerce websites.

1   Introduction

Techniques for automatically generating programmes from their specifications has been a goal of research in software engineering for many years. Techniques such as automatic programming [12,15,16] met with limited success, but the growth of model-driven development has led to a renewed effort, most notably in the form of Model Driven Architecture (MDA)[11].

Much of this work has been on the *static* properties of programs—in the conversion of the structure of the specification into an equivalent structure in the program code. In particular, the class diagrams of the Unified Modeling Language (UML)[14] are commonly translated into Java class 'stubs', where default create, read, update and destroy methods can be created, but further functionality is typically required to be added manually by the programmer.

In general, dynamic properties of the system are much harder than static properties to translate into code, not least because algorithmic code is often difficult to express using specification languages such as UML, since a suitable abstraction is harder to find. The wide variety of ways in which dynamic properties may be expressed (states, events, interactions, use cases, etc.) is also a hindrance—the interaction between types of specification is not clearly defined and detailed specifications prove hard to consistently refine.

A typical specification or requirements document is expressed in many ways— for example domain artifacts in a class diagram, business rules in terms of invariants, pre- and postconditions, and protocols in terms of state and sequence diagrams. Whilst each individual part of the specification may be validated independently, the interaction between parts of the specification is less easily understood and harder to reason about. This also leads to the problem of requirements traceability.

J. Davies and J. Gibbons (Eds.): IFM 2007, LNCS 4591, pp. 118–137, 2007.

When generating systems in such a manner, we must test their functionality by testing the resulting application, validating the functionality of the system with respect to the intended functionality. However, exhaustive testing is infeasible, and so a more logical solution is to validate the correctness of the specification, on the assumption that the system functionality is correctly refined from the specification.

For some predicate P or sequence of transitions S, we may like to ask the following questions of our specification:

- Is it possible that a state satisfying P might occur during the operation of the system?
- Is it possible that S may be performed?
- Is it S the only sequence of transactions that may occur?

Moreover, we may wish to enforce these conditions: P must never hold of any state of the system; S must be an allowed sequence; S must never be allowed to happen; S must be the only sequence of transactions that may occur. In many cases, as discussed in [4], such properties may not be expressed explicitly in terms of invariants, since to do so would make the specification too restrictive for use in real-life.

In previous works [2,5,4] we have introduced *Booster*, a domain-specific language for specifying information-driven systems. The language is an integrated formal specification language, based upon object-oriented constructs, and defines functionality in a declarative style—in terms of pre- and post-conditions. Whilst the correctness of each method individually may be determined, it is harder to prove that a system comprising of these methods is correct.

In this paper, we provide a solution to this problem in a domain-specific setting, by automatically generating protocols for usage. These allow us to "step through" the proposed system, checking for allowable states, and validating sequences of transactions.

Whilst the ideas presented here are specific to the *Booster* language, they may be usefully adapted for a more generic class of specification, although automation may not always be possible. In particular, these ideas can be applied to systems specified using UML class diagrams annotated with constraints written in a restricted version of the Object Constraint Language. However, as described in [4], the Object Constraint Language is in some ways less expressive *Booster* as it lacks the ability to compose method specifications.

We start this paper by introducing the Unified Modeling Language—in particular the notions of Class and State Diagrams. Next we give an overview of the key features of the *Booster* language, and compare it with the UML. In section 4 we discuss the process of automatically generating workflows from *Booster* specifications; in section 5 we illustrate this theory with an example, showing how the technique can be useful. The paper concludes with a brief discussion of the validity of this work and how the process may be applied with more general specifications, an orientation of this work amongst recent related work, and a discussion of future research goals in this area.

2 UML

The Unified Modeling Language [14] has gained popularity in the last decade and is now widely used in industry, despite a number of continuing challenges (most notably the lack of a universally-accepted precise semantics). UML contains a vast set of notations to describe the structure and the dynamics of a software system. The language is composed of two different categories of diagrams representing the two views of a system: the static view, modeling information that does not evolve with time, and the dynamic view, where the evolution of the components of the system is shown.

However, most of the notation provided by UML is actually seldom adopted in practice, while the parts that are mainly used are those that were already well established before the advent of UML: class, state, and sequence diagrams. For the purpose of this work we concentrate on class and state diagrams.

2.1 Class Diagrams and OCL

Class diagrams provide a static structural view of the system; they depict the classes of the system, their inter-relationships, and the operations and attributes of the classes.

The application concepts are modelled in UML as classes, each of which describes a set of objects that hold information and communicate to implement a behaviour. The information they hold is modelled as attributes; the behaviour they perform is modelled as operations. Structural relationships between objects of different classes are represented by associations. The definition of associations may be enhanced by a name, role names and cardinality (multiplicity).

Class diagrams can be annotated with constraints written using the Object Constraint Language [17]. OCL is a declarative language for describing rules that apply to UML models; it allows the definition of invariants on classes and sets of associated classes, and pre- and postconditions on classes' operations. In previous work [4] we have discussed the differences between the UML and *Booster*, and described how techniques in *Booster* may be usefully applied to models in the UML and OCL.

2.2 State Diagrams

UML state diagrams are a variation of Harel's statecharts [8]. They focus on the event-ordered behaviour of an object. A state diagram shows the event triggered flow of control due to transitions which lead from state to state, i.e. it describes the possible sequences of states and actions through which a model element can go during its lifetime as a result of reacting to discrete events.

In UML 2.0 in addition to expressing the behaviour of a part of the system, state diagrams can also be used to express the usage protocol of part of a system. These kinds of state diagrams are referred to as *behavioural state diagrams* and *protocol state diagrams* (PSD - introduced in UML 2.0) respectively. A PSD specifies which operations of the class can be called in which state and under which condition, thus specifying the allowed call sequences on the operations of the class. A protocol state machine presents the possible and permitted transitions on the instances of a class, together with the operations that carry the transitions. A protocol transition specifies a legal transition for an operation. Transitions of protocol state machines have the following information: a precondition, a trigger, and a postcondition. The protocol transition specifies that the associated operation can be called for an instance in the origin state under the initial condition, and that at the end of the transition, the destination state will be reached under the final condition (post).

3 The *Booster* Language

The *Booster* notation, first described in [2], combines key features of three earlier formal methods—the Z notation, the B method, and the Refinement Calculus—with the aim of automatically generating software components whose design is:

- *transformational*—the intended effect of an operation can be described in terms of values of inputs, outputs, and attributes immediately before, and immediately after, the operation has been performed.
- *sequential*—at most one operation may be acting upon the data within the component at any one time; the current operation must finish reading or updating the data before the next can begin.

In particular, this encompasses components based upon an object database, accessed through transactions and queries.

Specifications are structured in an object-based style—using classes, associations and inheritance. On each class attributes may be defined, which may be of primitive type or may define end-points for associations. Invariants may be defined in the scope of a class, but their effect may extend to associated classes.

Methods are defined on each class to update the attributes of the current class and also any associated classes. Such methods are defined *declaratively* in terms of pre- and postconditions. Preconditions may be any arbitrary predicate defined in terms of the state of input values and attribute values before the execution of the method.

Postconditions are more restricted however, and are limited to the syntax provided in Fig. 1.

A postcondition is a series of conjuncts, separated by the symbol '&'. A conjunct may be an implication, a universal quantification, or a primitive postcondition. The antecedent of an implication is an arbitrary predicate, interpreted as a constraint upon the values of attributes before the operation is performed. The consequent of an implication is a conjunction of primitives. The range of a universal quantification is a collection of objects of the same class, constrained by the antecedent of an implication. A primitive postcondition is an assertion of equality between a variable and an expression, of set membership, or of its negation.

⟨postcondition⟩ ::=
     ⟨conjunct⟩ | ⟨conjunct⟩ "&" ⟨postcondition⟩

⟨conjunct⟩ ::=
     ⟨implication⟩ | ⟨forall⟩ | ⟨primitive⟩

⟨implication⟩ ::=
     ⟨antecedent⟩ "=>" ⟨consequent⟩

⟨forall⟩ ::=
     "forall(" ⟨class⟩ ")." ⟨implication⟩

⟨consequent⟩ ::=
     ⟨primitive⟩ | ⟨primitive⟩ "&" ⟨consequent⟩

⟨primitive⟩ ::=
     ⟨variable⟩ "=" ⟨expression⟩ |
     ⟨expression⟩ ":" ⟨variable⟩ |
     ⟨expression⟩ "/:" ⟨variable⟩

Fig. 1. Syntax of postconditions in *Booster*

We may also create new methods from existing specifications. For example, given methods M1 and M2 we may create a new method M1 AND M2 which has the effect of schema conjunction from Z—the new method has the effect of calling both M1 and M2 at the same time. Similarly we may use OR for schema disjunction, THEN for sequential composition, and ALL which has the effect of an iterated conjunction. Compound methods may be expanded to form primitive methods; for example M1 AND M2 has a precondition that is the conjunction of the individual preconditions, postconditions are similarly conjoined. There are restrictions upon the use of AND to ensure preconditions are not automatically *false*; this is explained in [5].

The restriction imposed upon postconditions is powerful in that we may reason about methods without having to concern ourselves with non-determinism and algorithmic detail. We may automatically generate applications from specifications written in the *Booster* language; this is a two phase process. The first stage is that of expansion, where a specification is automatically transformed into an equivalent specification, also written in the *Booster* language. This expansion includes:

- Providing specifications for "default methods" such as *Create* and *Destroy*;
- Inheritance hierarchies are flattened[3];
- Compound methods are reduced to primitive methods[5]
- Adding scoping information for attributes;
- Inferring types and adding preconditions to ensure the type-correctness of all reference and input values;
- Automatically maintaining association invariants[18];
- Automatically guarding against breaking other invariants[4]

This expansion allows the programmer to specify only the intended effect of a method. Any consequences implied by the rest of the model will be automatically included, and if the intention of the method is impossible in the context of the model a false precondition will always be generated.

The second phase takes the expanded specification and produces imperative code—this stage has been explained in [5] and [3]. Method specifications are compiled into sequential transactions; two methods cannot update the same piece of data at the same time. These transactions are "atomic" - they are assumed to occur instantaneously and model states during execution are not of interest. Preconditions are translated into guards for the transaction; a transaction cannot be called if its guard evaluates to *false*. Postconditions are translated into independent substitutions upon attribute values; the execution of all substitutions is guaranteed to terminate in a state satisfying the postcondition, changing only the values mentioned in the postcondition.

An extract from an example *Booster* specification is shown in Fig. 2. This describes a class of Reader objects—people who are registered on a system for registering library borrowing. A Reader object has values for his name (of type String), and for his age (a natural number). The next attribute denotes an association between the classes `Reader` and `Library`—a Reader may belong to a number of libraries. The association is bi-directional—there is an attribute `Readers` in the class `Library`—whenever `Reader.Libraries` is updated then `Library.Readers` must be too, and vice-versa. Similarly, the final attribute denotes an association between `Reader` and `Book`. The definition of these other classes will be given later in the paper.

```
CLASS Reader
 ATTRIBUTES
  Name : STRING
  Age  : NAT
  Libraries : SET(Library.Readers)
  Books : SET(Book.Reader)
 METHODS
  Create,
  Destroy,
  Borrow( Book_in.Library : Libraries
        | Book_in : Books)
```

Fig. 2. An example of a class in *Booster*

There are three methods defined on the `Reader` class: `Create` and `Destroy`, which are both to be given default implementations, and `Borrow`, which associates a new `Book` with this reader. The precondition ensures that the reader is a member of the same library as the book (an input-value); the postcondition states that the new book is a member of the set of books that this reader has borrowed.

This information could have been presented in the UML, although, as explained in [4], the *Booster* language is more appropriate for our purposes. The language is more restricted, less verbose, and allows us to form new methods by combining existing specifications, something currently not possible in the OCL. However the work presented in this paper could equally be done using a subset of the UML and OCL, with the same refinement semantics that is provided in *Booster*.

4   The Generation of State Diagrams

Given a specification in *Booster*, consisting of classes, attributes and methods with pre- and postconditions, we would like to be able to explore the dynamic properties inherent in the model. In particular this paper addresses those of state and usage protocols—we generate a UML protocol state diagram—and from this we can validate some dynamic properties of our models. From the state machine we can find out whether a particular state is allowed by our system, and which sequence of transactions will achieve that state. We can decide whether a sequence of transactions is allowed by our intended system, or whether some sequence of transactions is the *only* allowed interaction. Moreover, just viewing a state machine for a system can give us a better idea of its functionality and we may gain insight into how the system may be used. In this section, we describe how this can be achieved and in Section 5 we illustrate the application of this technique.

4.1   Abstraction

When generating a state machine we must first consider which parts of the system we are interested in. Generating the entire state machine for a system of classes will be computationally expensive, in that there may be many states and transitions to consider. Additionally, such a state machine would be difficult to view or to manually reason about.

Instead, we must generate a sub-graph of the entire state machine—an abstraction that represents particular properties—and we begin this process by choosing a particular subset of state that we are interested in. We must choose a particular subset of attributes that are relevant to the dynamic properties that we wish to validate—the smallest such subset will create the smallest possible state chart.

Additionally, where attributes may take on a large number of values (e.g. attributes of natural number type, or set-valued attributes), we must restrict the states of these attributes to a smaller number that represents values that we are interested in. For example, we may restrict our interest in a particular attribute, that is of type natural number, to the values $\{0, 1, 2, > 2\}$. Here we consider states in which the attribute takes the values 0, 1, 2 or any natural number greater than 2. The abstraction must not restrict the values of the attribute, but provide a state for every possible value. Such restrictions are usually intuitive from the validation we are interested in; as with all automatic processes it is easy to adjust the restrictions and re-generate the state machine if the restrictions are too weak or too strong.

This abstraction process may be automated by considering the semantics of the property we are interested in, however in general further abstraction is necessary since some system state, initial conditions and input variable may need choosing according to an envisaged scenario.

Having reduced the number of states that we are interested in, it is now possible to automatically reduce the number of transitions that are relevant. *Booster* has a notion of a *change list*, similar to the frame in the refinement calculus—denoting a set of attributes which are subject to change in the course of a method. This change list may be specified explicitly by the modeller as syntactic sugar, but is usually deduced from the postcondition. A postcondition in *Booster* is refined into a combination of substitutions on attribute values, each of which may be guarded. Each substitution is a simple deduction from the postcondition, and the attribute on the left-hand-side of the substitution is part of the change-list. For example, the postcondition:

```
value_in : this.att
```

gives rise to the substitution:

$$this.att := this.att \cup value\_in$$

and we deduce that `this.att` is part of the change-list. From this analysis we can calculate the change-list of every method, and restrict our transitions to those corresponding to methods whose change-list includes part of the state that we are interested in.

Additionally, we may wish to include those methods whose precondition includes a restriction upon any part of our chosen state, and any others which may be of interest. We could alternatively choose to ignore certain methods which lead to sub-sections of the state machine that are uninteresting—for example the creation of extra objects—that may increase the size of the state machine without adding to our understanding of the system.

Typically the state machine we are interested in will be based upon the life-cycle of an object—from its creation to its destruction. We may wish to further restrict our interest to a particular circumstance though, and choose initial values for the system. For example, we may wish to only consider the system after a particular event has occurred, or after a particular state has been reached. This additional restriction can form part of the validation, or may assist in viewing particular behaviours of the system—especially when the generated state machine is still large.

Other initial values are necessary for providing the state machine an environment. We might need to assume existence of other objects in the system so that interactions may take place—we may need to make assumptions on the attributes and associations of these objects too. For example, if we are looking at the lifecycle of an object, and a transition causes it to be linked with another object, we might prefer to assume that it already exists, rather than cluttering our state machine with the creation and lifecycle of that object too.

Our example in section 5 illustrates these restriction and initialisation choices, explains why they are important and discusses how optimal choices can be made.

4.2 Transitions

Having made assumptions about the environment for our state machine, and made restrictions on the states and the transitions, we can now show how to build a state machine. Initially we shall consider a particular state and explain how transitions may be created from methods to leave this state. In the next subsection we discuss how new states may be created so that an entire graph may be constructed.

We analyse the precondition in the context of the current subset of state—this state includes the attributes we have singled out as in our scope of interest, the values assigned to any input values this method may require, and the state of any objects that we have made assumptions about previously. We may attempt to evaluate a precondition in this state and we get three possibilities:

– the precondition is a restriction upon the part of the state we know nothing about;
– the precondition is partly a restriction upon the state we do know about, but based upon a part of the state that is outside our scope of interest;
– or that the precondition may be entirely evaluated (to either *true* or *false*) based upon the current subset of state.

In the first situation, we have a method which is only applicable in conditions which are outside our scope of interest. However, its effect may be within our scope of interest so it still must be considered. There is a transition corresponding to this state but it is annotated with a precondition—this precondition corresponds to the entire precondition of the method. Our experience shows that this kind of transition is rare—generally a precondition for a method provides conditions to ensure that the effect is achievable and so some parts of the precondition can be evaluated, as in the next case.

In the second case, we have a method whose precondition may be partially evaluated in the current subset of state. By lazy evaluation we can determine whether such a precondition is guaranteed to be true, false, or still indeterminable. If the precondition is still indeterminable, we create a transition between this state and the next, and add a precondition to the transition, asserting that the parts of the precondition that cannot be evaluated hold true. If the precondition is evaluable, and is either true or false, then we may proceed as for the next case.

In the final case, we have a method whose precondition either evaluates to *true* or *false*. With the latter, this method is never applicable in the current state and so no transition corresponds to it from this state. In the former, we create a transition from this state to the next, which corresponds to this method. There may be a precondition on this transition though, which corresponds with restrictions to input variables, assumptions about objects in our environment, and parts of the state which fall outside our area of scope.

We choose to ignore those methods that only manipulate the state of other objects in the system—those that are in our environment. This is because we only care about the other objects when they become part of the current scope—before this time their interactions and updates are uninteresting.

4.3   States

When we create a state machine we expect the modeller to provide some initial conditions—in particular the initial state from which we begin generation. Alternatively, when considering the life-cycle of an object, we may wish to start in an initial pseudo-state such as those defined in the UML, where the first transition is always the `Create` method.

From the first state we find all the transitions that are possible, as described above. These may have preconditions attached to them, that restrict their operation in certain states outside our scope of interest. Each transition corresponds to a method in the system, and it is from the method that we construct the next state. Since every postcondition in *Booster* can be translated into a collection of substitutions, we can evaluate each in the context of the current state, any inputs, our assumed environment, and the fact that the precondition is true.

Such substitutions may either alter the value of an attribute we are interested in, or it may leave it unchanged. Since new values may be entirely determined, we can calculate the new state of the system. This may be a new state, unseen by us in the course of this generation, or it may be a state we have already seen—perhaps even the current state—in which case the transition takes us back to that state.

In some cases the new value in the substitution may be indeterminable, because the expression uses attributes outside the scope of interest. In this case we have three options available to us:

- add transitions leading to every feasible state in the diagram—states in which the other attributes correspond to the correct substitution—adding the precondition that the expression evaluates to the value determined by the new state;
- the modeller must make an assumption about the value of the new expression, and this must be factored in elsewhere in the state diagram as well;
- or the modeller must choose to increase the number of attributes in the scope of interest, to allow the expression to be evaluated—in this case the generation of the state-diagram must restart.

Generation of a state machine can be performed in a breadth-first or depth-first manner, depending on the type of validation required.

4.4   Validation and Verification

The purpose of creating a state machine may vary—typically it will be to verify some dynamic property of the specified system, although they may also be helpful for customers to look at, or for the modeller to get a better idea of the system they are building. In the first instance the verification can be performed automatically; the type of verification required can be split into two distinct cases.

In the first case, the question asked is of the form: "What sequence of events leads to the system state satisfying a particular predicate?". This is a reachability problem –we are looking for one or more states that satisfy a particular condition and we can evaluate each state as we generate it. We can present each sequence that starts in an initial state and ends in a state satisfying the condition.

In the second case, we answer questions of the form: "Is this particular sequence of transactions S allowed to occur in the generated system?". S may also include splitting and joining, and so may be a state diagram itself. Therefore the problem may be solved by deciding whether S is a sub-graph of the generated state machine G. The states of S must be a subset of the states of G, and for any transition between states s_1 and s_2 there must be the equivalent transition in G. Any preconditions on the generated transitions must be examined by the modeller—to decide whether the abstraction is appropriate.

For a particular sequence of transactions, or protocol of usage S we can ensure:

- that S is available during the operation of the system;
- that S is the only sequence of states available;
- or that S is never allowed to happen during the operation of the system.

We can achieve these in obvious ways—by changing the preconditions or postconditions of already defined methods such that extra conditions are enforced, and adding extra attributes to represent the state of the system. In such modifications however, we may only strengthen preconditions and postconditions, never weakening constraints that have already been specified by the modeller. Of course, such guarantees are only applicable in the context of the abstraction, and it is up to the modeller to decide whether the abstraction is sufficient.

5   A Worked Example

We now present an example to show the validity of our work. In this example we will start with an initial system, and show how we may generate a state machine from it to verify a particular property. We show an extract from the generated state machine that is sufficient to show the property does not hold, and discuss how we might change the model accordingly.

5.1   An Example Specification

The initial system is that of a library system, first introduced in [18]. Whilst just a simple problem, it is hopefully complex enough to examine issues that apply to the kind of systems in the application domain of *Booster*. The specification is presented in Fig. 3.

In the library system there are objects representing libraries, readers and books. A reader may be a member of any number of libraries, and as a member of a library is entitled to borrow books from that library. A book belongs to one library, and may be in the possession of at most one reader at any one time.

We describe this system using three classes: Library, Reader and Book. A Book object has many attributes, representing such details as the title, the author's name, the publisher, the ISBN number, however these are not of interest in this example. We consider only the attributes Library and Borrower here. The attribute Library denotes a mandatory end to an association with the class Library—the other end of the association is the reference attribute Books in the class Library. The attribute Borrower is an optional (denoted by square brackets []) end of an association with the class Reader and the attribute Books—this is an optional-to-many association.

The system also defines a many-to-many association between the classes Library and Reader. These associations define the only attributes that we are interested in for the purposes of this example. Similarly, we just present a certain number of methods that are interesting for the purpose of this example—those that manipulate these particular associations. This is a part of the abstraction process—focusing on particular attributes for the properties we are interested in.

In Fig. 3 we present the *expanded* version of all methods, and for reasons of space and clarity we've omitted parts of the precondition that are irrelevant for this presentation (such as those pertaining to type checking of references or setting of other attributes).

The first method defined on the Library class is one that adds a reader to its membership (note that every person in this system is represented by a Reader object). The precondition for this method is that there are still some readers in the system that are not already members of this current library, and that the input variable, Member_in is not already a member of the library. The postcondition states that Member_in has this library in its set of libraries, and that this current library has Member_in in the set of members.

As an aside, this method in *Booster* could have been specified simply by specifying the intention: Member_in : Members and the expansion process would have produced the additional pre- and postconditions, and provided scoping as explained in section 3. The next method on the class Library, RemoveMember is similarly defined—the method is unavailable if the input is not a current member of the library, the effect is that both ends of the association are updated.

Class Reader has three methods that are relevant to this example. The first, Create, is always available and simply creates a new object. The set Reader is the extension of the class Reader, that is the set of all objects of that class. Since the attributes Books and Libraries are not mentioned in the postcondition, they take on default values, namely the empty set. The Destroy method is always available, and removes every link it has with other objects and removes itself from the extension.

Finally the class Book has two methods of interest. The first, Transfer, moves a book from one library to another. The precondition is that there is at least one more library in the system where it can be transferred, and that the input Library_in is not the current location of the book. The postcondition is made

```
CLASS Library
 ATTRIBUTES
  ...
  Books      : SET ( Book . Library )
  Members    : SET ( Reader . Libraries )
 METHODS
  AddMember( 0 < (Reader.card - Library_this.Members.card) &
             Member_in /: Library_this.Members
           | Library_this : Member_in.Libraries &
             Member_in   : Library_this.Members )
  RemoveMember( Member_in : Library_this.Members
              | Library_this /: Member_in.Libraries &
                Member_in /: Library_this.Members )

CLASS Reader
 ATTRIBUTES
  ...
  Books     : SET ( Book . Borrower )
  Libraries : SET ( Library . Members )
 METHODS
  Create( true | Reader_new : Reader)
  Destroy( true
         | forall (Book_each).(Book_each : Reader_this.Books
                          => Reader_this /: Book_each.Borrower) &
           forall (Library_each).(Library_each : Reader_this.Libraries
                          => Reader_this /: Library_each.Members) &
           Reader_this /: Reader )
  Borrow( 0 < (Book.card - Reader_this.Books.card) &
          Book_in.Borrower = {} &
          Book_in.Library : Reader_this.Libraries
        | Book_in.Borrower = Reader_this &
          Book_in : Reader_this.Books )

CLASS Book
 ATTRIBUTES
  ...
  Borrower  : [ Reader . Books ]
  Library   : Library . Books
 METHODS
  Transfer( 2 > Library.card &
            Library_in /= Book_this.Library
          | Book_this /: Book_this.Library_0.Books &
            Book_this : Library_in.Books &
            Book_this.Library = Library_in )
  Return( Book_this.Borrower /= {}
        | Book_this.Borrower = {} &
          Book_this /: Book_this.Borrower_0.Books)
```

Fig. 3. An extract from the Library System Specification in *Booster*

up of three parts: that the book is removed from the **Books** attribute of the old library (variables in the pre-state are denoted with _0). Secondly, the method **Return** is only available when the book is loaned to a reader; its effect is to remove the link between the current book and the reader it was loaned to.

The specification as it stands is enough to generate a system, and dynamic properties of the generated system are inherent in the pre- and postconditions. However to decide whether the specification is correct with respect to the dynamic properties, we must make these properties more explicit. For this example, we are interested in the question: "Can a reader have a book on loan that does not belong to a library he is a member of?". This is a typical question that might be asked of such a system. We may have decided to disallow such a scenario by creating an invariant in the class **Book**:

```
Book_this.Borrower /= {}
        => Book_this.Borrower : Book_this.Library.Readers
```

However, as we described in [4], such an invariant may be too strong—for example a reader may be banned from a library before he has returned all his books. For the purposes of this example, we will find all the scenarios where such a situation may occur, so we can strengthen our specification accordingly.

5.2   Generation

We begin by choosing an abstraction that is relevant to our particular problem. In presenting this example we have already partly achieved this: we have only presented the attributes and methods that we might be interested in.

For this example we are going to produce the state machine of the object life-cycle for the class **Reader**. The property we are interested in can be expressed using the attributes **Reader.Books** and **Reader.Libraries**, and the *derived* value **Reader.Books.Library** which contains the set of all libraries that own the books that the current reader has on loan. This uses the attribute **Book.Library**, which gives three system attributes that we are interested in. We can therefore restrict our analysis to just the methods that modify these attributes. This is exactly the set of methods presented in Fig. 3. We assume the lack of **Create** and **Destroy** methods for libraries and books for clarity and simplicity, however in the full generation we would expect them to appear.

We must also make some initial assumptions about the environment in which this **Reader** object is to live. We assume that there is one **Book** object, B_1, and two **Library** objects in scope, L_1 and L_2, and these are the only other objects in the system. This will largely decrease the state space, but hopefully not so much that no useful information can be obtained from the state machine. We will assume that B_1 belongs to L_1. These assumptions can be modified if the generated state machine does not show us enough information; however the authors' experience is that a small environment such as this is generally suitable. When generating the state machine, we do not consider updates to these objects unless they directly update our three attributes—these objects only become of interest when they are accessible through association.

We can now choose an abstraction for the state, so that the generated state machine will be small enough to view. For the attribute `Reader.Libraries` we choose the set of states $\{\{\}, \{L_1\}, \{L_2\}, \{...\}\}$ where $\{...\}$ is any other state. We choose the same abstraction for `Reader.Books.Library` and $\{\{\}, \{B_1\}, \{...\}\}$ for the attribute `Reader.Books`.

Our final configuration is that of the initial state. Since we are interested in the object-lifecycle, we begin in the initial pseudo-state and the first transition will always be the `Create` method.

An extract from the generated state machine is shown in Fig. 4. The entire state-machine is just over twice the size of this, and can be easily viewed on a screen, but is not suitable for presentation in this format. Properties are typically verified automatically, so there is often no need to present the state machine in its entirety. However the modeller can gain a better understanding of his model by viewing the whole thing.

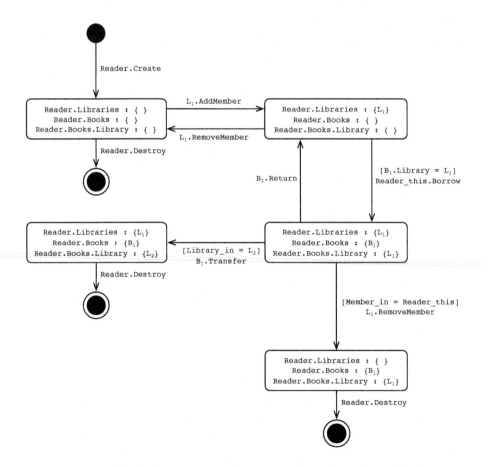

Fig. 4. An extract of the generated state machine

Observe that the generated state machine is actually a protocol state machine where states are labeled by the postcondition of their incoming transitions rather than by abstract names.

The original question, "Can a reader have a book on loan that does not belong to a library he is a member of?", can be solved by searching for a state in which the derived set `Reader.Books.Library` is not a subset of `Reader.Libraries`.

Automatic analysis of the generated state diagram can show that there are two ways of reaching the specific state. The two usage protocols are:

$$Reader.Create \rightarrow L_1.AddMember \rightarrow Reader\_this.Borrow \rightarrow B_1.Transfer$$

and

$$Reader.Create \rightarrow L_1.AddMember \rightarrow Reader\_this.Borrow \rightarrow L_1.RemoveMember$$

Either a book may be transferred to a different library while a reader is borrowing it (and the reader is not a member of the new library), or a library may remove a reader before he has returned his books from that library. The modeller may now add preconditions to the methods if they wish to prevent such scenarios from happening.

The modeller may also look at the state machine for themselves and notice other dynamic properties that they weren't expecting—for example that a reader can be removed from the system (using `Destroy`), whilst still holding books. This may not have been their intention and so they can add preconditions appropriately. It is the authors' experience that this process can be helpful before generating a system so that modelling errors can be eliminated.

The process as it stands relies a lot upon the intuition of the modeller to provide a useful abstraction upon the attributes and their states. However, as an automatic process, a new state machine can easily be generated if the current one does not provide the intended answers. The examination of preconditions on the transitions is also important—to help decide whether the state machine is an accurate representation of what may happen in the system.

6   Discussion

In this section we discuss the implications of this work in relation to the *Booster* language, Model-Driven Development, and Model-Driven Architecture. We give an overview of related work, and discuss why our methods are novel. Finally we provide details of our future research plans regarding *Booster* and software modelling.

The practice of model-driven development is becoming increasingly popular. A strong design and build process centered on refinement and verification can increase the quality of software applications. Techniques for automatic refinement are slowly being developed. Such tools increase the speed of development as well as reducing the scope for manually-introduced errors.

In *Booster*, the refinement process is entirely automated—this is possible by restricting the specification language and the application domain. This restriction is not overly inhibiting though, as the application domain covers a broad range of information systems, including database systems and e-commerce websites.

This level of automation makes the *Booster* language essentially a higher-level programming language, and this becomes the artifact which is used for correctness proofs. Such proofs ensure that the model is consistent with the requirements of the system, as opposed to traditional proof techniques which ensure consistency between specification and program code.

Whilst the static structure of the specification is relatively easy to verify, dynamic properties may be expressed in a wider variety of forms and so are much harder to verify. In *Booster*, dynamic properties are expressed in terms of pre- and postconditions. Such constraints imply restrictions on usage scenarios, but these restrictions must be made explicit in order for them to be validated against a specification. In this paper we have shown how we may automatically translate pre- and postconditions in *Booster* into state machines that more explicitly depict workflows and object-life cycles.

This is possible through the restricted nature of the *Booster* specification language—that we may automatically derive state substitutions from postconditions. Such substitutions allow us to determine exactly when a method is applicable, and what the resultant state will be. The technique is not possible where postconditions are unrestricted constraints, where the method that satisfies them may be non-deterministic or algorithmic in nature. *Booster* also ensures that methods are refined into sequential atomic transactions, where a single piece of data cannot be updated by two methods at the same time. In such a way the state machines generated are dependent on the actions of one user at a time, keeping the machines simple.

This technique proves to be scalable: the state machine generation is not affected by the number of classes in the model, but depends only on the chosen abstraction. The abstraction techniques used here are not new—indeed they are commonly used in model-checking to reduce the state space[1], and have also been used in a similar context by Gupta[7].

The result of this work is that the activity of software development can be raised to a higher level–testing can be performed at the level of specification rather than code. The code from which the application is built is brought closer to the abstractions of customer requirements, and so may be more easily understood by non-experts. Indeed, the generation of state machines and the presentation of specifications in a variety of graphic forms is a useful tool in narrowing the gap between customers and system developers, as well as aiding the documentation process.

6.1 Related Work

The work most closely related to ours is that of Gupta[7]. In this work the author also takes specifications written in the form of class diagrams and pre- and postconditions. In this respect our work is very similar; however there are important differences between our work and his.

Firstly our pre- and postconditions define the complete constraints upon an object, not just a partial restriction. Using the *Booster* expander, we can ensure that all constraints take account of the whole model and do not just specify the intended effect of the model. In this respect we do not treat classes independently, but analyse all methods of associated classes that may change the attributes of the current class. Such a distinction is important, since invariants generally affect more attributes than just those of the current class—in particular association invariants[18].

Most importantly, the restricted nature of *Booster* postconditions means that instead of considering the constraints upon the after-state of a method, we can consider the actions of the methods themselves by calculating the substitutions that satisfy the constraints. In Gupta's work, restrictions are necessary on the types of predicate—they need to be in Disjunctive Normal Form—and he makes no mention of non-determinism or partiality.

We perform a similar abstraction step to that in Gupta's work, in order to reduce the number of states and transitions that we need consider. However, in our work we can make additional reductions to the number of transitions because we know which substitutions are to take place—we can calculate exactly which variables are to change and consider just the methods which change attributes that we are interested in. In the more general setting, methods have no notion of a change list and so every method must be considered at every step.

This abstraction technique is also subject to considerable research—in particular that of *slicing* state machines[13,20,9], and model-checking[1]. Whilst our approach is to produce the abstraction as it is generated, an alternative method would be to generate the whole state machine and then use the techniques in these papers to perform the abstraction. However this would be computationally expensive, since the number of states and transitions in the complete state machine would normally be too great to analyse automatically.

Other research has explored the relationship between object-state and dynamic behaviour, notably that of Holt et al[10] and Graham[6]. However, this work has been focussed on testing implementations, and has been manually implemented in a wider application domain.

Other related work includes [19] where state charts are generated from sequence diagrams. These links between types of specification diagrams are useful in allowing the modeller and customer to explore a system before it is built. Other types of dynamic modelling with *Booster* is the subject of further research, as explained below.

6.2   Further Work

Further work is centered around the ongoing research into the *Booster* language and toolset—the main focus of which is the integration with the UML. We are currently in the process of developing a UML profile—restricting the syntax of the OCL and providing a semantics similar to that of *Booster*, and extending the OCL to allow method composition. This integration will allow us to exploit interesting existing work on UML, in particular tools, IDEs, and to appeal to practitioners who are more familiar with the graphical notation.

In relation to the work presented here, we wish to be able to factorise the generated state machines, by using sequential composite states. This would decrease the size of the generated diagrams and make them easier to read by the specifier or a customer.

Another interesting area of exploration is that of validation and correction of class models or *Booster* specifications against state machines. We want to allow the users to be able to modify the generated state machines, for example by adding preconditions or extra transitions, and see these changes automatically reflected in the *Booster* model.

Such further research will increase the applicability of the work presented here, and increase our knowledge of the relationship between static and dynamic properties of system specifications.

References

1. Clarke, E.M., Grumberg, O., Long, D.E.: Model checking and abstraction. ACM Trans. Program. Lang. Syst. 16(5), 1512–1542 (1994)
2. Davies, J., Crichton, C., Crichton, E., Neilson, D., Sørensen, I.H.: Formality, evolution, and model-driven software engineering. In: Mota, A., Moura, A. (eds.) Proceedings of SBMF 2004. ENTCS (2005)
3. Davies, J., Faitelson, D., Welch, J.: Domain-specific Semantics and Data Refinement of Object Models. In: Moreira, A.M., Ribeiro, L. (eds.) SBMF 2006: Brazilian Symposium on Formal Methods, pp. 185–200 (2006)
4. Davies, J., Welch, J., Cavarra, A., Crichton, E.: On the generation of object databases using booster. In: ICECCS '06: Proceedings of the 11th IEEE International Conference on Engineering of Complex Computer Systems, Washington, DC, USA, pp. 249–258. IEEE Computer Society, Los Alamitos (2006)
5. Faitelson, D., Welch, J., Davies, J.: From predicates to programs: the semantics of a method language. Electronic Notes in Theoretical Computer Science (to appear 2006)
6. Graham, I.: Graham/SOMA (Semantic Object Modeling Approach) method, pp. 73–83. Wiley-QED Publishing, Somerset, NJ (1994)
7. Gupta, A.: Automated Object's Statechart Generation from Class Method Contract. In: Proceedings of the 3rd Workshop on Model design and Validation (MoDeV2a'06): Perspectives on Integrating MDA and V&V, Genoa, Italy, October 2006, ACM/IEEE, New York (2006)
8. Harel, D.: Statecharts: A visual formalism for complex systems. Science of Computer Programming 8(3), 231–274 (1987)
9. Heimdahl, M.P.E., Whalen, M.W.: Reduction and slicing of hierarchical state machines. In: Jazayeri, M., Schauer, H. (eds.) FSE 1997. LNCS, vol. 1267, pp. 450–467. Springer, Heidelberg (1997)
10. Holt, N.E., Anda, B.C.D., Asskildt, K., Briand, L.C.L., Endresen, J., FrØystein, S.: Experiences with precise state modeling in an industrial safety critical system. In: Houmb, S.H., Georg, G., France, R., Petriu, D.C., Jürjens, J. (eds.) Critical Systems Development Using Modeling Lanuguages, CSDUML'06, pp. 68–77. Springer, Heidelberg (2006)

11. Kleppe, A., Warmer, J., Bast, W.: MDA Explained. The Model Driven Architecture: Practice and Promise. Addison-Wesley, Reading, MA (2003)
12. Manna, Z., Waldinger, R.J.: Toward automatic program synthesis. Commun. ACM, vol. 14(3) (1971)
13. Nowack, A.: Slicing abstract state machines. In: Zimmermann, W., Thalheim, B. (eds.) ASM 2004. LNCS, vol. 3052, pp. 186–201. Springer, Heidelberg (2004)
14. Object Management Group. UML 2.0 superstructure specification (2005) http://www.omg.org/cgi-bin/doc?ptc/05-07-04
15. Prywes, N., Amir, S., Shastry, S.: Use of a nonprocedural specification language and associated program generator in software development. ACM Trans. Program. Lang. Syst., vol. 1(2) (1979)
16. Ruth, G.R.: Automatic programming: Automating the software system development process. In: ACM '77: Proceedings of the 1977 annual conference, ACM Press, New York (1977)
17. Warmer, J., Kleppe, A.: The Object Constraint Language: Getting Your Models Ready for MDA, 2nd edn. Addison Wesley, Reading, MA (2003)
18. Welch, J., Faitelson, D., Davies, J.: Automatic maintenance of association invariants. In: SEFM '05: Proceedings of the Third IEEE International Conference on Software Engineering and Formal Methods, Washington, DC, pp. 282–292. IEEE Computer Society, Los Alamitos (2005)
19. Whittle, J., Schumann, J.: Generating statechart designs from scenarios. In: ICSE '00: Proceedings of the 22nd international conference on Software engineering, New York, pp. 314–323. ACM Press, New York (2000)
20. Xie, T., Notkin, D.: Automatic extraction of sliced object state machines for component interfaces. In: Proceedings of the 3rd Workshop on Specification and Verification of Component-Based Systems at ACM SIGSOFT 2004/FSE-12 (SAVCBS 2004), October 2004, pp. 39–46 (2004)

Inheriting Laws for Processes with States

Yifeng Chen

Department of Computer Science,
University of Durham, Durham DH1 3LE, UK
Yifeng.Chen@dur.ac.uk

Abstract. This paper studies the laws of communicating sequential processes (CSP) with Z-like initial and final states. Instead of defining a large semantics including all observable aspects, we incrementally develop the model in three stages: partially correct relational model, then totally correct sequential model and finally the reactive-process model with states. The properties of each model are captured as algebraic laws. A law in one model may or may not be true in its submodels. We apply a technique based on healthiness conditions to identify the conditions for law inheritance. Such abstract conditions themselves can be captured as pattern laws of commutativity. The model uses a new approach to define parallel compositions using just the primitive commands, nondeterministic choice, conjunction and some unary (hiding) operators.

1 Introduction

This paper studies the laws of communicating sequential processes with Z-like initial and final states. Instead of defining a large semantics including all observable aspects, we incrementally develop the model in three stages: partially correct relational model, then totally correct sequential model and finally the reactive-process model with states. The intended model then becomes a submodel with more healthiness conditions. In particular, we aim at reusing the laws of predicate calculus and sequential models. Many laws of sequential languages also hold in CSP, but there are exceptions. For example, SKIP is the unit of sequential composition: $(\text{SKIP} \, \mathbin{;} A) = A = (A \, \mathbin{;} \text{SKIP})$ in both sequential and parallel models. On the other hand, we have $(A \, \mathbin{;} \text{CHAOS}) = \text{CHAOS}$ in sequential models but not in CSP. For a counterexample, we have $(a \rightarrow \text{SKIP}) \, \mathbin{;} \text{CHAOS} = (a \rightarrow \text{CHAOS})$ in which the following divergences cannot undo the action that is already performed.

How do we know which laws are inheritable and which are not? In previous approaches and also Unifying Theories of Programming [12], this is done by checking and re-proving laws individually. For example, a conditional test can be moved ahead of a proceeding assignment statement if the condition is substituted for the assignment:

$$(s := e \, \mathbin{;} \text{if } b \text{ then } A \text{ else } B) \;=\; \text{if } b[e/s] \text{ then } (s := e \, \mathbin{;} A) \text{ else } (s := e \, \mathbin{;} B). \quad (1)$$

J. Davies and J. Gibbons (Eds.): IFM 2007, LNCS 4591, pp. 138–155, 2007.

This law holds in both the partially correct relational model and the totally correct sequential model. However, because an assignment statement is denoted as different predicates in the two models, the law had to be re-proved in UTP ([12] Section 3.1). Such re-proof not only leads to tedious proof obligations but also raises question over the benefit of theory linking.

We will use a new technique first outlined in [6] and later further developed in [7]. The technique is based on a meta-theory about healthiness conditions. We are able to identify some abstract conditions on the structures of laws. Such conditions are captured in the form of *pattern laws* for semantic embedding's commutativity with respect to program operators. For example, we will show that if in a law of sequential programs, the first argument of every sequential composition terminates successfully, and its second argument does not deadlock or diverge, then the law also holds in CSP with states.

The contribution of this paper is to apply the techniques to integrate event-based parallel specifications and state-based sequential specifications. Some results of [7] are repeated here for coherent presentation.

Integrating event-based and state-based specifications has long been of intense research interests due to its importance in applications as well as its technical challenges. States are originally abstracted from process calculi because shared variables cause interference between processes, and such concurrent specifications (e.g. in action systems) are not compositional at observational level. On the other hand, pure process calculi are found too restrictive for various applications. A typical area is verification of security protocols. Most security protocols do depend on states. The problem is a matter of tradeoff between compositionality and flexibility.

Morgan [13] first studied failures-divergences modelling of action systems. The linking theory was further developed in [3] and applied to the combination of CSP and B-Method [15]. Another line of research integrates CSP with Z-style specifications [12,4]. A CSP process is extended with an initial state for the start of the process and a final state for its end. Unlike action systems, intermediate states are not represented. This formalism is more abstract. Parallelism is compositional and entirely handled by CSP. This paper follows the second approach and studies laws and law inheritance in such a model. We will show that although the formalism does not model action systems directly, action systems become special specifications, as states can be used to determine the actions performed by a process.

CSP, as a language, has too many different binary operators. There has been effort in unifying different kinds of parallelism. The most basic form of parallelism is conjunction (e.g. [8]). Conjunction is useful in specification, but realistic parallel compositions are not as simple. UTP uses a technique called *parallel-by-merge*. The idea is to define parallel compositions as a parallel-by-merge composition with a certain parameter M. The parameter is a three-way relation that connects to the non-conjunctive observables of the composition, hides them and generates the observable for the composition. A slightly more general notation called parallel-via-medium was introduced in [5]. The notation is general and powerful but unfortunately difficult to manipulate. Hoare [11] recently expresses the view that it is desirable to unify various parallel compositions using conjunction. In this paper, by temporarily dropping some healthiness conditions of CSP (C1-C7 Chapter 7 of [10]), we are able to define all the CSP parallel compositions using just the primitive commands, disjunction (nondeterministic choice), conjunction and a number of unary hiding operators. The dropped healthiness conditions can be restored at the end without affecting any established laws. For each model, we will study its healthiness conditions, the corresponding semantic construction and an algebraic normal form.

Section 2 reviews Unifying Theories of Programming. Section 3 defines healthiness conditions, commands, laws and fixpoints. Section 4 introduces the models of partially correct relational model and the totally correct sequential model. Section 5.2 studies the CSP model with states.

2   Unifying Theories of Programming

This section is prepared for those readers who are unfamiliar with the notations of this style of algebraic semantics. UTP, the latest development in relational semantics, is aimed at linking different computational models with predicates and functions on predicates. Each program or specification is represented as a predicate, or simply a set of value assignments over some free logical variables. For example, a predicate $x' = x + 1$ denotes a sequential program $x := x + 1$ that increases x by 1. Two predicates are considered the same if they describe the same relation. Both universal disjunction (set union) and conjunction (set intersection) are allowed. Thus the underlying logic is infinitary.

A healthiness condition classifies predicates into the groups of healthy and unhealthy ones. A general programming theory can be specialised by adding new healthiness conditions. It has been shown that if the additional healthiness condition of a submodel is *well-formed* as the fixpoint equation $A = h(A)$ of a monotonic and idempotent predicate function h, then the inter-model mapping between the original model and the submodel is entirely characterised by the predicate function h. Any predicate A is transformed by h into a healthy predicate $h(A)$.

Healthiness condition is a complementary technique to the more traditional semantic construction in denotational semantics and abstract interpretation. For example, a binary relation $r \subseteq \mathbb{N} \times \mathbb{N}$ has a *downwards closed* range iff it satisfies a healthiness condition $r = (r \,\dot{,}\, s)$ where $s \,\hat{=}\, \{(n, m) \mid n \geqslant m\}$. Alternatively, given arbitrary $S \subseteq \mathbb{N}$ and $k \in \mathbb{N}$, we can *construct* such a relation as $S \times \{n \mid n \leqslant k\}$ in correspondence. Sometimes the two approaches are used in a combination.

In UTP's sequential models, a binary relation is a predicate on undashed and dashed variables in pairs. For example, $(x' := x + 1 \land y' = y)$ represents an assignment $x := x + 1$ with program variables x and y. The *sequential composition* $(A \,\dot{,}\, B)$ is defined as $(\exists v_0 \cdot A[v_0/v'] \land B[v_0/v])$ where $v = x, y$. *Nondeterministic choice* $A \sqcap B \,\hat{=}\, A \lor B$ is disjunction. The constant predicates $\bot \,\hat{=}\, \mathtt{tt}$ and $\top \,\hat{=}\, \mathtt{ff}$ represent chaos and magic, respectively. The refinement order $A \sqsubseteq B$ corresponds to reduction of nondeterminism and set containment. The semantics of a recursion $A = f(A)$ is defined as Tarski's weakest fixpoint $\mu f \; \widehat{=} \; \bigsqcap \{A \mid A \sqsupseteq f(A)\}$ where f is a monotonic predicate function closed in the complete lattice of healthy predicates.

The above simple model is not totally correct for sequential computation, as it does not distinguish termination and nontermination. UTP introduces another model with two special logical variables ok and ok' where ok, not appearing in any program, records the observation that the program has been started, and ok' records that the program has terminated. The assignment $x := x + 1$ is now represented as $ok \Rightarrow (x' = x + 1 \land y' = y \land ok')$. To achieve an appropriate set of laws, undesirable predicates must be excluded from the semantic space. Four healthiness conditions have been introduced incrementally: H1 $A = (ok \Rightarrow A)$ (denoted as h_{ok} in this paper), H2 $A = (A \lor \exists ok' \cdot (A \land \neg ok'))$, H3 $A = (A \; \s%; \; (ok \Rightarrow ((x', y', ok') = (x, y, ok))))$ and H4 $(A \; \s%; \; \mathtt{tt}) = \mathtt{tt}$. H1 states that if a computation has not started, it behaves chaotically. H2 describes the downward closure of ok'. A model satisfying H1 and H2 can be extended into a reactive parallel model incorporating intermediate states between the initial state and the final state [12]. H3 states that if a computation may not terminate from some initial state, then in the final state, x', y' and ok' are chaotic. H4 excludes infeasible specification and guarantees some final state from every initial state. The last one is not in the regular form $A = h(A)$ and yields a CPO [1] instead of a complete lattice. We leave such a healthiness condition to be included at last. As long as it yields a property-preserving sub-language, all results from the complete-lattice model of specifications can be inherited.

We accept two classes of logical variables: non-overlined variables such as $u, v, u', v', \cdots$ and overlined ones such as $\overline{u}, \overline{v}, \overline{u'}, \overline{v'}, \cdots$. Healthiness conditions are best defined with generic compositions. A generic composition [5] is a relational composition with a designated interface of non-overlined variables.

Definition 1. $A :_v C \; \widehat{=} \; \exists v_0 \cdot A[v_0/v] \land C[v_0/\overline{v}]$

A *fresh* variable list v_0 is used to connect the list v of A and the list $\overline{v}$ of C with the interface v_0 hidden by the existential quantifier. For example, the following composition relates two predicates on only x (and $\overline{x}$ for the second predicate): $(x = 10 \land y = 20) :_x (\overline{x} \leqslant x \land z = 30) = (10 \leqslant x \land y = 20 \land z = 30)$. Generic composition and its inverse form a Galois connection and satisfy the algebraic laws of strictness, distributivity and associativity. The notation is especially useful when the interfaces of the operators in a predicate are not identical. For example, the interface can be expanded with new logical variables: $A :_v C = A :_{v,u} (C \land \overline{u} = u)$ where $\{v\} \cap \{u\} = \emptyset$. Many healthiness conditions can now be simplified using the notation.

3   A Meta-theory of Predicative Modelling

3.1   Set-Theoretic Predicate Calculus

Let ν denote the set of all logical variables and $\mathbb{C}$ be a set of all constants. When a variable list is expected, we assume the variables in ν to be ordered alphabetically. For example $(\nu = \nu')$ describes pairwise equality. A *value assignment* a is a total function $a \in (\nu \to \mathbb{C})$. A predicate is a set of assignments. Let PRED $\hat{=} \wp(\nu \to \mathbb{C})$ denote the complete lattice of all predicates whose (refinement) order is $\supseteq$ (also written as $\sqsubseteq$), lub is $\cap$, glb is $\cup$, top is the empty set $\emptyset$ and bottom is $(\nu \to \mathbb{C})$. Here we are following the convention of UTP in which the complete lattice is "upside-down". Let $s, t, u, \cdots$ denote (finite and order-sensitive) lists of variables and let $\{s\}$ denote the set of variables from the list. Let $A, B, C, \cdots$ denote predicates in PRED. The following table lists the predicate commands including functional equality, substitution, existential quantification, universal disjunction and negation:

Command	Set-theoretic definition
$s = e(t)$	$\hat{=} \{a \mid a(s) = e \circ a(t)\}$
$A[e(t)/s]$	$\hat{=} \{a' \mid a \in A,\ a' = a \dagger \{s \mapsto e \circ a'(t)\}\}$
$\exists s \cdot A$	$\hat{=} \{a' \mid a \in A,\ a(u) = a'(u)\}$
$\bigvee \mathrm{S}$	$\hat{=} \bigcup \mathrm{S}$
$\neg A$	$\hat{=} (\nu \to \mathbb{C}) \setminus A$

where e is a list of (total) expressions, s, t, u are variable lists, and $\mathrm{S} \subseteq \wp(\nu \to \mathbb{C})$ is a set of predicates. We use $a(s)$ to denote the tuple of constants from the assignment a on the list s of variables. Other predicate commands can be derived: universal conjunction $\bigwedge \mathrm{S} \hat{=} \neg \bigvee \{\neg A \mid A \in \mathrm{S}\}$, binary disjunction $A \vee B \hat{=} \bigvee \{A, B\}$, implication $A \Rightarrow B \hat{=} \neg A \vee B$, true $\mathtt{tt} \hat{=} (s = s)$, false $\mathtt{ff} \hat{=} \neg \mathtt{tt}$ and universal quantifier $\forall x \cdot A \hat{=} \neg \exists x \cdot \neg A$. We assume that $\mathtt{ff} = \bigvee \emptyset$.

We prefer program notations in semantic models: the bottom $\bot \hat{=} \mathtt{tt}$ (or abort and chaos), the top $\top \hat{=} \mathtt{ff}$ (or magic), the glb (or universal nondeterministic choice) $\bigsqcap \mathrm{S} \hat{=} \bigvee \mathrm{S}$, the lub $\bigsqcup \mathrm{S} \hat{=} \bigwedge \mathrm{S}$, the binary nondeterministic choice $A \sqcap B \hat{=} A \vee B$, conjunctive parallel composition $A \sqcup B \hat{=} A \wedge B$ and the binary conditional (or if b then A else B) $A \lhd b \rhd B \hat{=} (b \wedge A) \vee (\neg b \wedge B)$ where the boolean expression $b = b(t)$ is a parameter. The basic laws of glb, lub and conditional are listed as follows. All distributivities also hold for universal glb and lub.

Law 1 (PRED...)   (1) $\bot \sqcap A = \bot$ (2) $\top \sqcap A = A$
                        (3) $\bot \sqcup A = A$ (4) $\top \sqcup A = \top$

Law 2 (PRED...) *The operators $\sqcap$ and $\sqcup$ are idempotent, commutative and associative and distribute each other.*

Law 3 (PRED...) (1) $A \lhd b \rhd A = A$ (2) $A \lhd \mathtt{tt} \rhd B = A$
                    (3) $A \lhd b \rhd B = B \lhd \neg b \rhd A$
                    (4) $A \lhd c \rhd (B \lhd b \rhd C) = (A \lhd c \rhd B) \lhd b \rhd (A \lhd c \rhd C)$
                    (5) $A \lhd c \rhd (B \lhd b \rhd C) = (A \lhd c \rhd B) \lhd c \vee b \rhd C$
                    (6) $(A \sqcap B) \lhd b \rhd C = (A \lhd b \rhd C) \sqcap (B \lhd b \rhd C)$
                    (7) $(A \lhd b \rhd \top) \sqcap (A \lhd c \rhd \top) = A \lhd b \vee c \rhd \top$
                    (8) $(A \lhd b \rhd B) \sqcup C = (A \sqcup C) \lhd b \rhd (B \sqcup C)$

3.2   Predicate Functions

Let $f, g, h, \cdots$ denote (total) *predicate functions*. We use $f(\text{PRED})$ to denote the range of a unary predicate function f. Let $f \circ g(A) \mathrel{\hat{=}} f(g(A))$.

Definition 2. *A function f* commutes *with another function g for a predicate A, if we have $f \circ g(A) = g \circ f(A)$. They commute in a semantic space $h(\text{PRED})$ if we have $f \circ g \circ h = g \circ f \circ h$. They are simply called commutative if they commute in* PRED*. A unary function f commutes with an n-arg function g for the arguments $A_1, A_2, \cdots, A_n$, if we have: $f(g(A_1, A_2, \cdots, A_n)) = g(f(A_1), f(A_2), \cdots, f(A_n))$. A unary function f is* idempotent*, if we have $f \circ f = f$. A unary function is called a* healthiness *function if it is monotonic and idempotent. A unary function f is called* linear*, if it distributes universal disjunction $f(\bigvee M) = \bigvee \{f(A) \mid A \in M\}$ for any $M \subseteq$ PRED. A function f* absorbs *another function g, if we have $f \circ g = f$. A function f is* closed *with respect to a unary function g, if we have $f \circ g = g \circ f \circ g$.*

Linearity implies monotonicity. The range of a linear function is always a complete lattice whose glb and lub are disjuction and conjunction, respectively. Absorption characterises the link between the healthiness conditions of a model and its submodels. Closure is a necessary property relating program operators and healthiness conditions. A command is called a *primitive*, if it is a healthy predicate in the semantic space. Assignment statements are primitives. A *program operator* is an n-ary *monotonic* predicate function closed in the semantic space. A program operator is closed in a semantic space $h(\text{PRED})$ iff it is closed with respect to the healthiness function h.

3.3   Semantic Inheritance

The healthiness function h_2 of a submodel must absorb that h_1 of the original abstract model to render an embedding, i.e. $h_2 \circ h_1 = h_2$. If h_2 is also closed with respect to h_1 (i.e. $h_1 \circ h_2 = h_2$), then the submodel becomes a sublattice. Such sublattice extension is assumed in the original meta-theory of UTP ([12] Section 4.1), although some semantic extensions are not sublattices. For example, the extension from the sequential model to reactive processes (such as CSP) is a Galois embedding satisfying an additional healthiness condition $A = (A \wedge tr \leqslant tr')$ (i.e. R1 of UTP). It prevents any computation (even chaos) from unwinding the actions already performed. The healthiness function h_{tr} transforms the primitive $\perp = \mathbf{tt}$ into $tr \leqslant tr'$. Related laws and fixpoints can be affected by such transformation.

A primitive C in the original model satisfying $C = h_1(C)$ is inherited by the submodel as $h_2(C)$. That means, in general, an inherited primitive is not the original predicate! For example, assignment statement $x := x + 1$ is denoted by a predicate $x' = x + 1$ in the partially correct relational model with the only program variable x. The healthiness function h_{ok} transforms the predicate to a different one $ok \Rightarrow (x' = x + 1)$. On the other hand, we follow a principle of UTP and assume that an operator is always inherited exactly as its original definition. Violating this requirement may lead to unnecessary complexity in future studies.

The law $A \sqcap B = B \sqcap A$ holds in every model with a linear healthiness function. Another law $(\bot \,\mathring{,}\, \top) = \top$ holds in the partially correct relational model but not in the totally correct sequential model where $(\bot \,\mathring{,}\, \top) = \bot$. The law (1) provides another example. We now address this important issue and consider the simplest case first.

Theorem 1 (Simple inheritance of laws). *Let h_1 and h_2 be the healthiness functions of a model and its submodel, respectively. If $h_2 \circ h_1 = h_2 = h_1 \circ h_2$, and every primitive in a law of the original model is also healthy in the submodel, then the law also holds in the submodel.*

For example, if disjunction is closed in a model, then the law $A \sqcap B = B \sqcap A$ of PRED must hold, as every semantic space is a sublattice of PRED. The following theorem handles the general case when a submodel may not be a sublattice, or the primitives in the law are not healthy in the submodel.

Theorem 2 (Inheritance of laws). *Let h_1 and h_2 be the healthiness functions of a model and its submodel, respectively. If we have $h_2 \circ h_1 = h_2$, and h_2 commutes with every operator for its arguments in a law, then that law also holds in the submodel.*

Note that the healthiness function h_2 only needs to commute with the operators *for their arguments* in the law. The program letters, as arguments, are already h_1-healthy.

4   Basic Models

4.1   Partially Correct Relational Model

Model $\text{REL}(v)$ is a property-preserving sub-language of PRED. The undashed variables v and the dashed variables v' record the observation about the start and the end of a computation, respectively. $\text{REL}(v)$ inherits the commands $\bot$, $\top$, $\sqcap$, $\sqcup$, and $\triangleleft b(t, s') \triangleright$ where s and t are variable lists such that no single variable appears twice in each list and $\{s, t\} \subseteq \{v\}$. Note that the binary conditional $\triangleleft b(t, s') \triangleright$ may test the variables s' about the final state. This flexibility is convenient for future extension to reactiveness. We introduce two new commands:

$$
\begin{array}{lll}
s := e(t) & \widehat{=} \;\; (s' = e(t) \wedge v_1 = v_1') & \text{assignment} \\
A \,\mathring{,}\, B & \widehat{=} \;\; \exists v_0 \cdot (A[v_0/v'] \wedge B[v_0/v]) & \text{sequential composition}
\end{array}
$$

where $v_1 \widehat{=} v \setminus \{s\}$, and v_0 is a fresh list of variables. An assignment statement keeps variables not in s unchanged. We use a convention $\text{I\!I}_s \widehat{=} \bigsqcap_e s := e$ to denote the terminating program that assign arbitrary values to s and makes it chaotic, and SKIP to denote $\text{I\!I}_s$ with the empty list s. The sequential composition is standard relational composition. Predicates in this model only depend on the variables v, v'. The following healthiness condition is a mathematical representation of this frame restriction:

HC 1 (h_v) $A = \exists \xi \xi' \cdot A$ $(\xi \mathrel{\widehat{=}} \nu \setminus \{v, v'\})$.

As a convention, we write $A = A(v, v')$ to denote such a healthy predicate. Note that the condition is semantical not syntactical: a predicate $(v' = v \land y = y)$ is healthy even if $y \notin \{v, v'\}$. The corresponding healthiness function $h_v(A) \mathrel{\widehat{=}} \exists \xi \xi' \cdot A$ forces any variable not in $\{v, v'\}$ to be chaotic (and hence unobservable). All related laws of PRED are inherited.

The basic laws concerning assignments and sequential composition are listed as follows. Some laws are shared by submodels, while others may be more specific to this model.

Law 4 (REL,SEQ,CSPZ)

(1) $s := e = s, t := e, t$ (2) $s, t := e, f = t, s := f, e$
(3) $u, s, t := e, f, g = s, t, u := f, g, e$
(4) $(s := e \,\mathbin{\raise.15ex\hbox{$\scriptstyle\circ$}}\hskip-.3em\raise-.6ex\hbox{$\scriptstyle\circ$}\; s := f(u)) = s := f(u[e/s])$
(5) $(s := e \,\mathbin{\raise.15ex\hbox{$\scriptstyle\circ$}}\hskip-.3em\raise-.6ex\hbox{$\scriptstyle\circ$}\; t := f(u)) = s, t := e, f(u[e/s])$
(6) $(s := e \sqcup s := f) = (s := e) \mathbin{\lhd} e = f \mathbin{\rhd} \top$
(7) $s := e(t) \mathbin{\lhd} b \mathbin{\rhd} \top = s := e(t) \mathbin{\lhd} b[e(t)/s'] \mathbin{\rhd} \top$

Law 5 (REL,SEQ,CSPZ)

(1) $\bot \,\mathbin{\raise.15ex\hbox{$\scriptstyle\circ$}}\hskip-.3em\raise-.6ex\hbox{$\scriptstyle\circ$}\; \bot = \bot$ (2) $(\top \,\mathbin{\raise.15ex\hbox{$\scriptstyle\circ$}}\hskip-.3em\raise-.6ex\hbox{$\scriptstyle\circ$}\; A) = \top$
(3) $(\,\mathbin{\raise.15ex\hbox{$\scriptstyle\circ$}}\hskip-.3em\raise-.6ex\hbox{$\scriptstyle\circ$}\,)$ is associative, distributes $\sqcap$ and has left unit SKIP.
(4) $u := e \,\mathbin{\raise.15ex\hbox{$\scriptstyle\circ$}}\hskip-.3em\raise-.6ex\hbox{$\scriptstyle\circ$}\; (A \mathbin{\lhd} b \mathbin{\rhd} B) = (u := e \,\mathbin{\raise.15ex\hbox{$\scriptstyle\circ$}}\hskip-.3em\raise-.6ex\hbox{$\scriptstyle\circ$}\; A) \mathbin{\lhd} b[e/u] \mathbin{\rhd} (u := e \,\mathbin{\raise.15ex\hbox{$\scriptstyle\circ$}}\hskip-.3em\raise-.6ex\hbox{$\scriptstyle\circ$}\; B)$
(5) $(A \mathbin{\lhd} b(v) \mathbin{\rhd} B) \,\mathbin{\raise.15ex\hbox{$\scriptstyle\circ$}}\hskip-.3em\raise-.6ex\hbox{$\scriptstyle\circ$}\; C = (A \,\mathbin{\raise.15ex\hbox{$\scriptstyle\circ$}}\hskip-.3em\raise-.6ex\hbox{$\scriptstyle\circ$}\; C) \mathbin{\lhd} b(v) \mathbin{\rhd} (B \,\mathbin{\raise.15ex\hbox{$\scriptstyle\circ$}}\hskip-.3em\raise-.6ex\hbox{$\scriptstyle\circ$}\; C)$

Law 6 (REL,SEQ)   (1) $(v := e \,\mathbin{\raise.15ex\hbox{$\scriptstyle\circ$}}\hskip-.3em\raise-.6ex\hbox{$\scriptstyle\circ$}\; \bot) = \bot$
                       (2) $(v := f \,\mathbin{\raise.15ex\hbox{$\scriptstyle\circ$}}\hskip-.3em\raise-.6ex\hbox{$\scriptstyle\circ$}\; \top) = \top$

Law 7 (REL,CSPZ) $(A \,\mathbin{\raise.15ex\hbox{$\scriptstyle\circ$}}\hskip-.3em\raise-.6ex\hbox{$\scriptstyle\circ$}\; \text{SKIP}) = A$

Law 8 (REL) $(A \,\mathbin{\raise.15ex\hbox{$\scriptstyle\circ$}}\hskip-.3em\raise-.6ex\hbox{$\scriptstyle\circ$}\; \top) = \top$

4.2 Sequential Specifications

The model $\text{SEQ}(w)$ is a submodel of $\text{REL}(w, ok)$ and inherits all commands with the only restriction that the special variable ok does not appear in any program, i.e. $\{s, t\} \subseteq \{w\}$. Here the original variable list v has split into the special variable ok and a smaller variable list w. The syntactical restriction immediately leads to a new healthiness condition:

HC 2 $(h_{ok_=})$ $A = A :_{ok, ok'} (\overline{ok = ok'} \Rightarrow ok = ok')$

This condition states that the logical variables ok and ok' are either equal, representing a terminating computation, or chaotic, representing nontermination. A predicate A satisfies $A = h_{ok} \circ h_{ok_=}(A)$, iff there exist $B = B(w, w')$ and $C = C(w, w')$ such that $B \land C = \mathbf{ff}$, $A = \Phi(B, C)$ $\Phi(B, C) \mathrel{\widehat{=}} (B \lor (C \land ok = ok'))$. The closure of operators can be shown using this constructive form.

Adding the healthiness condition alone will not change the laws, because all primitives (i.e. chaos, magic and syntax-restricted assignments) remain unchanged, and the space is a sublattice, according to Theorem 1. That means although the additional healthiness condition has already distinguished termination and nontermination, it does not generate the desirable set of laws. For example, we would still have $(\bot \,\ {}_{9}\, x := 1) = (x := 1)$, which violates the intuition that no computation after nontermination is observable. To make sure $(\bot \,\ {}_{9}\, A) = A$, we need to weaken every healthy predicate so that when a computation does not start, it behaves chaotically. This leads us to H1 of UTP:

HC 3 (h_{ok}) $A = (ok \Rightarrow A)$.

Let $h_{seq} \,\widehat{=}\, h_{ok} \circ h_{ok_=}$. A sequential specification is a predicate A that satisfies $h_{seq}(A) = A$. A predicate A satisfies $A = h_{seq}(A)$, iff there exist $B = B(w, w')$ and $C = C(w, w')$ such that $B \wedge C = \mathbf{ff}$, $A = \neg ok \vee \Phi(B, C)$.

In fact, the healthiness condition h_{seq} is exactly the same as the composition of H1 and H2 in UTP. The condition H2 $A = h_{ok'}(A) \,\widehat{=}\, A :_{ok'} (\overline{ok'} \Rightarrow ok')$ states that if a computation may not terminate (i.e. $\neg ok'$) then ok' must be entirely chaotic, and we have $h_{ok'} \circ h_{ok} = h_{ok} \circ h_{ok'} = h_{ok} \circ h_{ok_=}$! Why do we prefer $h_{ok} \circ h_{ok_=}$ to H1 and H2? That is because this way of introducing healthiness functions highlights the healthiness condition that preserves laws and the condition that alters them. As we have explained, $h_{ok_=}$ reflects a syntactical restriction over the language and preserves all laws, while h_{ok} alters them. Firstly, it changes magic from $\mathbf{ff}$ into $\neg ok$; secondly, the new space is no longer a sublattice as $\neg ok$ is not $h_{ok_=}$-healthy; finally, h_{ok} does sometimes but not always commute with sequential composition. For example, we have a counterexample:

$$h_{ok}(\bot \,\ {}_{9}\, x := 1) = \neg ok \vee (x' := 1 \wedge v_0' = v_0) \neq \mathbf{tt} = h_{ok}(\bot) \,\ {}_{9}\, h_{ok}(x := 1)$$

where $v_0 \,\widehat{=}\, v \setminus \{x\}$. This is exactly the reason why, by adding h_{ok}, we deny some laws from $\mathrm{REL}(v)$ and at the same time render some new laws!

An interesting question is: how do we know which laws will be inherited and which will be denied? The method used in UTP is to re-prove the laws individually. For example the law (1) is re-proved. A more general solution is to use Theorem 2. In fact if the first argument of a sequential composition always terminates from any initial state, the function h_{ok} does distribute sequential composition. In the relational model $\mathrm{SEQ}(w)$, a predicate that always terminates satisfies the healthiness condition $A = (A \wedge ok = ok')$. Remember that $\mathbb{II}_w = (ok = ok')$. Thus we essentially need to show the following equality

$$h_{seq}((A \wedge \mathbb{II}_w) \,\ {}_{9}\, B) = h_{seq}((A \wedge \mathbb{II}_w) \,\ {}_{9}\, h_{seq}(B)$$

for any h_{seq}-healthy predicates A and B. We use a convention $[A] \,\widehat{=}\, h_{seq}(A)$. Then such commutativity corresponds to a pattern law that links semantic denotations in both models.

Law 9 ($\mathrm{REL} \rightarrow \mathrm{SEQ}$) (1) $[(A \sqcup \mathbb{II}_w) \,\ {}_{9}\, B] = [A \sqcup \mathbb{II}_w] \,\ {}_{9}\, [B]$
(2) $[\cdot]$ *commutes with* $\sqcap, \sqcup,$ *and* $\lhd b \rhd$.

Other commutativities of Law 9(2) are readily provable. We can directly apply these pattern laws of inheritance on the law (1):

$$[s := e] \; \mathbin{\mathring{,}} [A] \lhd b \rhd [B]$$
$$= [s := e \mathbin{\mathring{,}} A \lhd b \rhd B]$$
$$= [(s := e \mathbin{\mathring{,}} A) \lhd b[e/s] \rhd (s := e \mathbin{\mathring{,}} B)]$$
$$= ([s := e] \mathbin{\mathring{,}} [A]) \lhd b[e/s] \rhd ([s := e] \mathbin{\mathring{,}} [B])$$

Similarly, Law 1-6 are inherited. When the first argument does not always terminate, we need a new law to make the law set complete:

Law 10 (SEQ,CSPZ) $(\bot \lhd b \rhd \top) \mathbin{\mathring{,}} A = (\bot \lhd \exists w' \cdot b \rhd \top)$.

Evidently $(\bot \mathbin{\mathring{,}} A) = \bot$ becomes a special case. For completeness, Law 1-7 and 10 are complete for transformation of any SEQ program to a normal form:

$$\bot \lhd B \rhd \bigsqcap\nolimits_{e : C(w, e(w))} (w := e(w) \lhd \exists w' \cdot C \rhd \top)$$

where $B = B(w, w')$ and $C = C(w, w')$ are two predicates. The healthiness condition $h_{seqok}(A)$ is also *complete* and cannot be stronger, as every healthy predicate is the semantics of some program.

If we impose an additional restriction that the condition $b = b(t)$ in binary conditionals $(A \lhd b(t) \rhd B)$ does not contain dashed variables. This syntactical restriction leads to a further healthiness condition $A = (A \mathbin{\mathring{,}} (ok \Rightarrow v = v'))$ (H3 of UTP). This condition states that if a computation does not terminate, then both ok' and the final state w' become chaotic. The seuqential model with this healthiness condition is totally correct and satisfies the law $A = (A \mathbin{\mathring{,}} \text{SKIP})$. The semantic construction is still $\neg ok \vee \Phi(B, C)$ although $B = B(w)$ no longer depends on dashed variables, reflecting the syntactical restriction. As $h_{w'}$ commutes with h_{seq}, adding this healthiness condition renders a sublattice. All primitives are unchanged. According to Theorem 1, all laws of SEQ(w, ok) are inherited. We can further impose the feasibility condition H4 (leaving out $\top$ and $\sqcup$, see Section 2) and Dijkstra's finitary condition [9,5]. These conditions are of higher order and form a CPO instead of a complete lattice. Nevertheless, they will not deny any existing laws as long as such healthiness conditions are added after the regular healthiness conditions.

5   CSP-Z Specifications

5.1   The Model

CSPZ(u) is a submodel of SEQ$(tr, wait, ref, u)$ in which the original variable list w splits up into three special variables and a smaller list u of state variables. The variable tr represents the (finite) trace record of actions and $tr, tr' \in \mathcal{A}^*$ where the alphabet $\mathcal{A}$ is a non-empty finite set of actions. The variable $wait$ was first introduced by Hoare and He [12] to replace the tick action $\checkmark$ in the original CSP model. If a process does not diverge i.e. ok' is true, then $wait'$

denotes deadlock, and $\neg wait'$ denotes a successful termination. The variable ref represents the refusal set of actions ($ref, ref' \subseteq \mathcal{A}$). The refusals help distinguish external choice and nondeterministic choice. The variable list u contains all variables of state-based sequential computation.

As a sub-language, $\text{CSP}Z(u)$ only inherits the primitives chaos $\bot$, magic $\top$, state-variable assignment $s := e(t)$ where $\{s, t\} \subseteq \{u\}$, stop $(ref, wait := \mathcal{B}, \neg wait)$ and action $(tr := tr \,^\frown \langle a \rangle)$, and the operators $\sqcap$, $\sqcup$, $(\,\fatsemi\,)$, and $\triangleleft b \triangleright$ where $\mathcal{B} \subseteq \mathcal{A}$ and the conditionals only depend on the values of state variables at the start: $b = b(u)$. We will use these restricted commands to define CSP processes.

Further healthiness conditions are needed. The healthiness condition $h_{w'}$ states that if a computation diverges, then all of $wait', ref', u'$ become chaotic while tr' is arbitrarily extending tr. Evidently, $h_{w'}$ is similar but different from H3 of UTP, as the following skipping command maintains the monotonicity of tr, tr' even if the previous computation does not terminate. This healthiness condition denies Law 6, as no following computation can unwind the actions already performed. The condition h_{tr} ensures the monotonicity of trace extension. Note that chaos is now strengthened from $\mathtt{tt}$ to $tr \leqslant tr'$. The condition $h_{\Delta tr}$ (i.e. R2 of UTP) requires a process to depend only on the trace record during the lifespan. The healthiness condition h_{ref} requires a computation not to depend on ref (CSP3 of UTP), rendering the law $A = (\mathtt{SKIP} \,\fatsemi\, A)$. The condition $h_{wait'}$ states that, after succussful termination, a process always refuses all actions, rendering the law $A = (A \,\fatsemi\, \mathtt{SKIP})$, and after deadlock, the state variables are chaotic. This corresponds to the CSP property that if a process ends with the action $\checkmark$, then it can refuse all actions in the end. This condition (CSP4 of UTP [12]) was neglected in earlier models [10,14]. The condition h_{wait} requires every healthy predicate to skip and preserve the refusals if the previous process stops in waiting, rendering the law $(\mathtt{STOP} \,\fatsemi\, A) = \mathtt{STOP}$.

HC 4 $(h_{w'})$ $\quad A \;=\; A \,\fatsemi\, (v' = v \triangleleft ok \triangleright tr \leqslant tr')$

HC 5 (h_{tr}) $\quad A \;=\; (A \wedge tr \leqslant tr')$.

HC 6 $(h_{\Delta tr})$ $\quad A \;=\; A :_{tr, tr'} (\overline{tr' - tr} \;=\; tr' - tr)$

HC 7 (h_{ref}) $\quad A \;=\; \exists ref \cdot A$

HC 8 $(h_{wait'})$ $\quad A \;=\; A :_{ref', u'} (\overline{ref'} = ref' \triangleleft wait' \triangleright \overline{u}' = u')$

HC 9 (h_{wait}) $\quad A \;=\; h_{w'}(v' = v) \triangleleft wait \triangleright A$

Let $h_{cspz} \;\widehat{=}\; h_{wait} \circ h_{wait'} \circ h_{ref} \circ h_{\Delta tr} \circ h_{w'} \circ h_{seq}$ be the healthiness function of $\text{CSP}Z(u)$. A predicate A satisfies $A = h_{cspz}(A)$, iff there exist predicates of divergences $D = D(dtr, u)$, failures $F = F(dtr, ref', u)$ and terminating behaviours $T = T(dtr, u, u')$ such that $D = \exists s \cdot (D[s/dtr] \wedge s \leqslant dtr)$, $F \sqcup T \sqsubseteq D$, and

$$A \;=\; h_{wait} \circ h_{tr} \circ h_{ok} \big(\varPhi(D, F \triangleleft wait' \triangleright T)[tr' - tr/dtr] \big).$$

Note that the refinement of such specifications corresponds to refinement for every of D, F and T for uniqueness of the representation. The closure of operators can be shown using this constructive form. Most primitives have different semantic denotations now. For example, skip is changed from $(ok \Rightarrow v' = v)$ into $(v' = v \lhd wait \rhd \exists ref \cdot v' = v) \lhd ok \rhd tr \leqslant tr'$.

5.2   CSP Commands and Action System

The following table lists a few inherited primitives as CSP-style convention commands:

CHAOS	$\widehat{=}$	$\perp$	divergences
VOID	$\widehat{=}$	$\top$	magic
$STOP_{\mathcal{B}}$	$\widehat{=}$	$ref, wait := \mathcal{B}, \neg wait$	immediate waiting
DOa	$\widehat{=}$	$tr := tr ^\frown \langle a \rangle$	doing action a

where $\mathcal{B} \subseteq \mathcal{A}$ and $a \in \mathcal{A}$. CHAOS is the weakest process that can do everything, although it must extend traces. Note that CHAOS is already transformed by h_{cspz}. VOID is the strongest specification and will erase all previous successfully terminating behaviours. $STOP_{\mathcal{B}}$ deadlocks and refuses to engage in any action from $\mathcal{B}$ (without downward closure). SKIP immediately terminates successfully and refuses all actions after termination. DOa performs an action a and terminates successfully (without any waiting before the action).

Let the convention $DO_{\langle\rangle} \widehat{=}$ SKIP and $DO_{s ^\frown t} \widehat{=} DO_s \,\mathbf{;}\, DO_t$ denote the processes terminating after a sequence of actions, $DO_p \widehat{=} \bigsqcap_{s \in p} DO_s$ be a process that nondeterministically chooses an action sequence to perform, $DO^* \widehat{=} DO_{\mathcal{A}^*}$ be the process with chaotic action sequences, $STOP_{\subseteq \mathcal{B}} \widehat{=} \bigsqcap_{\mathcal{C} \subseteq \mathcal{B}} STOP_{\mathcal{C}}$ be the waiting process with downwards-closed refusals, STOP $\widehat{=} STOP_{\subseteq \mathcal{A}}$ be deadlock, and MOVE $\widehat{=} (\mathbb{II}_u \,\mathbf{;}\, DO^* \,\mathbf{;}\, (\text{SKIP} \sqcap \text{STOP}))$ be the weakest convergent process with chaotic states. We need other useful commands in specifications:

$a \to A$	$\widehat{=}$	$(DOa \sqcap STOP_{\subseteq \mathcal{A} \backslash \{a\}}) \,\mathbf{;}\, A$	action followed by a process
ACT_ℓ	$\widehat{=}$	$\bigsqcap_a DOa \lhd \ell(u) = a \rhd$ VOID	state-controlled action
$b \overset{\ell}{\rightsquigarrow} A$	$\widehat{=}$	$(A \,\mathbf{;}\, ACT_\ell) \lhd b \rhd$ VOID	guarded process

where $\ell : \mathbb{C}^{|u|} \to \mathcal{A}$ is a mapping from states to actions. The process $a \to A$ behaves like A after performing as action a. ACT_ℓ performs an action, which is controlled by the initial state and the state-event mapping ℓ. A guarded process $b \overset{\ell}{\rightsquigarrow} A$ first checks the guard condition on the initial state. If the guard is true, then it behaves like A and then performs an action according to the final state of A. Normally A in a guarded process is a state-variable assignment. Such a guarded process is called a guarded assignment, which can be used to link events and states.

An action system [2], in state-based parallelism, can be represented as a loop of guarded commands after some initialisation:

$$B_0 \; ; \; \text{do} \; b_1 \, B_1 [] \cdots [] b_n \, B_n \; \text{od}$$

where each B_i is an assignment, and each b_j is a guard on the state. Semantically, intermediate states are observable and interleaved. Action systems are not representable in sequential model $\text{SEQ}(w)$, which does not represent the intermediate states. Such an action system is now represented using guarded assignments in $\text{CSPZ}(u)$ as follows:

$$B_0 \; ; \; \mu X \cdot ((b_1 \overset{\ell}{\rightsquigarrow} B_1) \sqcap \cdots \sqcap (b_n \overset{\ell}{\rightsquigarrow} B_n) \sqcap (\neg b_1 \wedge \cdots \wedge \neg b_n) \overset{\ell}{\rightsquigarrow} \text{SKIP})) \; ; \; X$$

where ℓ extracts some information about the intermediate states. If the alphabet can be infinite and contain all possible states, then we can use an identity function $\ell(u) = u$ to represent the action system faithfully. In most systems, the set of observable actions depend on states but the intermediate states of local variables are not directly observable. The mapping ℓ can be used to determine the state influence on observable intermediate actions. Communication and concurrency are still model-checkable if the alphabet is finite, and then the above definition becomes attractive. Such systems can be composed in parallel using CSP operators. Note that $\text{CSPZ}(u)$ is essentially an integration of CSP and Z rather than that of CSP and action system. The modelling of alphabetical hiding is a technical complication in CSP-style action system. But it is not a problem here, as we do not need to merge adjacent intermediate states after hiding the actions between them, because such intermediate states do not exist.

Action systems is essentially variable-sharing parallelism. Parallel action systems may interfere with each other's state. Our approach is essentially to restrict variable-sharing within individual processes and use CSP parallel compositions to compose them and make use of the normal-form technique in verification and refinement calculus.

5.3   Law Inheritance

The simple inheritance Theorem 1 is no longer applicable. The more general Theorem 2 works when h_{cspz} commutes with the operators. The following laws identify the patterns for such commutativity where $[A] \; \widehat{=} \; h_{cspz}(A)$:

Law 11 (SEQ→CSPZ)   (1) $[A \sqcup \text{DO}^* \; ; \; B \sqcup \text{MOVE}] = [A \sqcup \text{DO}^*] \; ; \; [B \sqcup \text{MOVE}]$
(2) $[\text{CHAOS} \; ; \; B] = [\text{CHAOS}] \; ; \; [B]$
(3) $[s := e \; ; \; B] = [s := e] \; ; \; [B]$
(4) $[\cdot]$ *commutes with* $\sqcap$, $\sqcup$ *and* $\triangleleft b(u) \triangleright$.

According these patterns, some laws are directly inheritable. For example, we still have the algebraic-unit law $[\text{SKIP} \; ; \; [A] = [\text{SKIP} \; ; \; A] = [A]$, and $[\text{DO}_s] \; ;$ $[\text{DO}_t] = [\text{DO}_s \; ; \; \text{DO}_t] = [\text{DO}_{s \frown t}]$. On the other hand, the model $\text{SEQ}(w)$'s laws $(\text{STOP}_\mathcal{B} \; ; \; \text{CHAOS}) = \text{CHAOS}$ and $(\text{DO}a \; ; \; \text{CHAOS}) = \text{CHAOS}$ no longer hold in the new model. Instead, we have $[\text{STOP}_\mathcal{B}] \; ; \; [\text{CHAOS}] = [\text{STOP}_\mathcal{B}]$ and $[\text{DO}a] \; ; \; [\text{CHAOS}] \neq$ $[\text{CHAOS}]$ due to the new property-altering healthiness functions. Law 1, 2, 4, 5 and 10 are inherited. New laws will be introduced in the next subsection.

5.4   Parallelism as Conjunction

We have temporarily neglected several healthiness conditions of CSP, including some closure and feasibility requirements. The reason is that we intend to define all CSP binary compositions using just disjunction, conjunction and some unary operators:

$\delta(A)$	$\widehat{=}$ $h_{cspz}(A \wedge \neg ok')$	extracting divergences
$\tau(A)$	$\widehat{=}$ $h_{cspz}(\exists tr' \cdot A)$	hiding traces
$\omega(A)$	$\widehat{=}$ $h_{cspz}(\exists wait' \cdot A)$	hiding wait
$\rho(A)$	$\widehat{=}$ $h_{cspz}(\exists ref' \cdot A)$	hiding refusals

where the function h_{cspz} is employed to force semantic healthiness. The idea is perhaps best explained in an analogy to predicate calculus in which we usually define a binary operator with just disjunction, conjunction and existential hiding:

$$A \oplus B \; \widehat{=} \; \exists ab \cdot (A[a/x] \wedge B[b/x] \wedge x = a \oplus b)$$

where $\oplus$ is some merging operator. We may re-write this as follows:

$$A \oplus B \; = \; \bigsqcap\nolimits_{a,b} (x = a \oplus b \sqcup \exists x \cdot (A \sqcup x = a) \sqcup \exists x \cdot (B \sqcup x = b)). \qquad (2)$$

The three unary operators are just like the existential quantifier and can help hide the observation on traces, waiting and refusals, respectively. The three operators can be merged into one, although it is more flexible to have them separately. We temporarily drop the downward-closure healthiness conditions (C2 and C3 of CSP). Thus $\text{STOP}_{\mathcal{B}}$ with a fixed (i.e. not downwards-closed) refusal is a valid command. Such a specification can be used to extract the refusal of a computation by conjunction, playing a similar role as $x = a$ and $x = b$ in (2). We have a new Law 12 for deadlock-led sequential compositions, and other laws for operator elimination into the normal form. Distributivities also hold for universal glb and lub.

Law 12 (CSPZ)   (1) $(\text{STOP}_{\mathcal{B}} \;\raise0.5ex\hbox{$\scriptscriptstyle\circ$}\kern-0.3em\raise-0.5ex\hbox{$\scriptscriptstyle\circ$}\; A) \; = \; \text{STOP}_{\mathcal{B}}$
                     (2) $(A \;\raise0.5ex\hbox{$\scriptscriptstyle\circ$}\kern-0.3em\raise-0.5ex\hbox{$\scriptscriptstyle\circ$}\; \text{SKIP}) \; = \; A$
                     (3) $(s := e \;\raise0.5ex\hbox{$\scriptscriptstyle\circ$}\kern-0.3em\raise-0.5ex\hbox{$\scriptscriptstyle\circ$}\; \text{DO}_a) \; = \; (\text{DO}_a \;\raise0.5ex\hbox{$\scriptscriptstyle\circ$}\kern-0.3em\raise-0.5ex\hbox{$\scriptscriptstyle\circ$}\; s := e)$

Law 13 (CSPZ)   (1) $(\text{DO}_a \;\raise0.5ex\hbox{$\scriptscriptstyle\circ$}\kern-0.3em\raise-0.5ex\hbox{$\scriptscriptstyle\circ$}\; A) \sqcup \text{STOP}_{\mathcal{B}} \; = \; (\text{DO}_a \;\raise0.5ex\hbox{$\scriptscriptstyle\circ$}\kern-0.3em\raise-0.5ex\hbox{$\scriptscriptstyle\circ$}\; A) \sqcup \text{SKIP} \; = \; \text{VOID}$
                     (2) $(\text{DO}_a \;\raise0.5ex\hbox{$\scriptscriptstyle\circ$}\kern-0.3em\raise-0.5ex\hbox{$\scriptscriptstyle\circ$}\; A) \sqcup (\text{DO}_a \;\raise0.5ex\hbox{$\scriptscriptstyle\circ$}\kern-0.3em\raise-0.5ex\hbox{$\scriptscriptstyle\circ$}\; B) \; = \; \text{DO}_a \;\raise0.5ex\hbox{$\scriptscriptstyle\circ$}\kern-0.3em\raise-0.5ex\hbox{$\scriptscriptstyle\circ$}\; (A \sqcup B)$
                     (3) $(\text{DO}_a \;\raise0.5ex\hbox{$\scriptscriptstyle\circ$}\kern-0.3em\raise-0.5ex\hbox{$\scriptscriptstyle\circ$}\; A) \sqcup (\text{DO}_b \;\raise0.5ex\hbox{$\scriptscriptstyle\circ$}\kern-0.3em\raise-0.5ex\hbox{$\scriptscriptstyle\circ$}\; B) \; = \; \text{VOID} \qquad (a \neq b)$

Law 14 (CSPZ)   (1) $\delta(\text{CHAOS}) = \text{CHAOS}$
                     (2) $\delta(\text{VOID}) = \delta(\text{STOP}_{\mathcal{B}}) = \delta(\text{SKIP}) = \delta(s := e) = \text{VOID}$
                     (3) $\delta(\text{DO}_a \;\raise0.5ex\hbox{$\scriptscriptstyle\circ$}\kern-0.3em\raise-0.5ex\hbox{$\scriptscriptstyle\circ$}\; A) = \text{DO}_a \;\raise0.5ex\hbox{$\scriptscriptstyle\circ$}\kern-0.3em\raise-0.5ex\hbox{$\scriptscriptstyle\circ$}\; \delta(A)$
                     (4) δ *distributes* $\sqcap$ *and* $\triangleleft b \triangleright$.

Law 15 (CSPZ) (1) $\sigma(\text{CHAOS}) = \text{CHAOS}$ (2) $\sigma(\text{VOID}) = \text{VOID}$
(3) $\sigma(\text{STOP}_\mathcal{B}) = (\text{DO}^* \mathbin{\mathring{,}} \text{STOP}_\mathcal{B})$ (4) $\sigma(\text{SKIP}) = \text{DO}^*$
(5) $\sigma(s := e) = (\text{DO}^* \mathbin{\mathring{,}} s := e)$ (6) $\sigma(\text{DO}_a \mathbin{\mathring{,}} A) = \sigma(A)$
(7) σ *distributes* $\sqcap$ *and* $\vartriangleleft b \vartriangleright$.

Law 16 (CSPZ) (1) $\rho(\text{CHAOS}) = \text{CHAOS}$ (2) $\rho(\text{VOID}) = \text{VOID}$
(3) $\rho(\text{STOP}_\mathcal{B}) = \text{STOP}$ (4) $\rho(\text{SKIP}) = \text{SKIP}$
(5) $\rho(s := e) = s := e$ (6) $\rho(\text{DO}_a \mathbin{\mathring{,}} A) = \text{DO}_a \mathbin{\mathring{,}} \rho(A)$
(7) ρ *distributes* $\sqcap$ *and* $\vartriangleleft b \vartriangleright$.

Law 17 (CSPZ)
(1) $\omega(\text{CHAOS}) = \text{CHAOS}$ (2) $\omega(\text{STOP}_\mathcal{B}) = (\text{STOP}_\mathcal{B} \sqcap \text{SKIP})$
(3) $\omega(\text{VOID}) = \text{VOID}$ (4) $\omega(\text{SKIP}) = (\text{STOP} \sqcap \text{SKIP})$
(5) $\omega(s := e) = (\text{STOP} \sqcap s := e)$ (6) $\omega(\text{DO}_a \mathbin{\mathring{,}} A) = \text{DO}_a \mathbin{\mathring{,}} \omega(A)$
(7) ω *distributes* $\sqcap$ *and* $\vartriangleleft b \vartriangleright$.

CSP-Z specifications have a normal form:

$$\bigsqcap\nolimits_{s,a:D(s,a)} (\text{DO}_s \mathbin{\mathring{,}} \text{CHAOS}) \vartriangleleft u = a \vartriangleright \text{VOID}$$
$$\sqcap \quad \bigsqcap\nolimits_{s,\mathcal{B},a:F(s,\mathcal{B},a)} (\text{DO}_s \mathbin{\mathring{,}} \text{STOP}_\mathcal{B}) \vartriangleleft u = a \vartriangleright \text{VOID}$$
$$\sqcap \quad \bigsqcap\nolimits_{s,a,b:T(s,a,b)} (\text{DO}_s \mathbin{\mathring{,}} u := b) \vartriangleleft u = a \vartriangleright \text{VOID}.$$

where $D = D(dtr, u)$, $F = F(dtr, ref', u)$ and $T = T(dtr, u, u')$. Every specification is transformable to this normal form. Proof is standard application of the laws by induction on the structure of an arbitrary specification.

5.5 Binary Compositions

We now define external choice $\square$ that diverges if either argument diverges, conjoins (i.e. intersects, for downwards-closed processes) the refusals during actionless waiting, or otherwise behaves nondeterministically, a convention of constant choice A^b between A and SKIP according to the constant boolean b, fixed-alphabet parallel composition $\parallel$ that conjoins traces, disjoins the waiting status and takes union of refusals when being convergent, and the interleaving composition $\interleave$ that interleaves traces, disjoins waiting status and conjoins (i.e. intersects, for downwards-closed processes) refusals:

$A \square B \;\widehat{=}\; \delta(A \sqcap B) \sqcap ((A \sqcap B) \sqcup \text{MOVE}) \sqcap (A \sqcup B)$
$A^b \quad \widehat{=}\; \bigsqcap(\{A \mid b\} \cup \{\text{SKIP} \mid \neg b\})$
$A \parallel B \;\widehat{=}\; \delta(A \sqcap B) \sqcap \bigsqcap\nolimits_{b,c,\mathcal{B},\mathcal{C}} (\omega \circ \rho(A \sqcup \text{DO}^* \mathbin{\mathring{,}} \text{STOP}_\mathcal{B}^b) \sqcup$
$\omega \circ \rho(B \sqcup \text{DO}^* \mathbin{\mathring{,}} \text{STOP}_\mathcal{C}^c) \sqcup (\text{DO}^* \mathbin{\mathring{,}} \text{STOP}_{\mathcal{B}\cup\mathcal{C}}^{b\vee c}))$
$A \interleave B \;\widehat{=}\; \delta(A \sqcap B) \sqcap \bigsqcap\nolimits_{s,t,b,c} (\omega \circ \tau(A \sqcup \text{DO}_s \mathbin{\mathring{,}} \text{STOP}^b) \sqcup$
$\omega \circ \tau(B \sqcup \text{DO}_t \mathbin{\mathring{,}} \text{STOP}^c) \sqcup (\text{DO}_{s \interleave t} \mathbin{\mathring{,}} \text{STOP}^{b\vee c}))$

---

where $s \interleave t$ is the set of all interleavings of two traces s and t.

The following table lists some algebraic properties of various compositions:

	$\sqcap$	$\sqcup$	$\,\fatsemi\,$	$\square$	$\|$	$\|\|\|$
zero	CHAOS	VOID	VOID, STOP$_\mathcal{B}$, CHAOS	CHAOS	CHAOS	CHAOS
unit	VOID	CHAOS	SKIP	STOP		SKIP

where we note that VOID, STOP$_\mathcal{B}$, CHAOS are only the left zeros of sequential composition, which has no right zero.

Although all laws about these compositions are derivable from the laws of the hiding operators, we still list some interesting ones, as they can be useful in reasoning.

Law 18 (CSPZ)

(1) $(A \fatsemi \text{CHAOS}) \square (B \fatsemi \text{CHAOS}) = (A \fatsemi \text{CHAOS}) \sqcap (B \fatsemi \text{CHAOS})$
(2) $(A \sqcup \text{STOP}) \square (B \sqcup \text{STOP}) = (A \sqcup B \sqcup \text{STOP})$
(3) $(A \sqcup \text{STOP}) \square (B \sqcup \text{MOVE}) = (B \sqcup \text{MOVE})$
(4) $(A \sqcup \text{MOVE}) \square (B \sqcup \text{MOVE}) = (A \sqcap B) \sqcup \text{MOVE}$
(5) $\square$ *is idempotent, commutative and associative, and distributes* $\sqcap$ *and* $\lhd b \rhd$.

Law 19 (CSPZ)

(1) $(A \fatsemi \text{CHAOS}) \| (B \fatsemi \text{CHAOS}) = (A \fatsemi \text{CHAOS}) \sqcap (B \fatsemi \text{CHAOS})$
(2) $(\text{DO}_a \fatsemi A) \| (\text{DO}_a \fatsemi B) = (\text{DO}_a \fatsemi A \| B)$
(3) $(\text{DO}_a \fatsemi A) \| (\text{DO}_b \fatsemi B) = \text{VOID} \quad (a \neq b)$
(4) $(\text{STOP}_\mathcal{B} \| \text{STOP}_\mathcal{C}) = \text{STOP}_{\mathcal{B} \cup \mathcal{C}}$
(5) $(\text{STOP}_\mathcal{B} \| s := e) = (\text{STOP}_\mathcal{B} \| \text{SKIP}) = \text{STOP}_{\mathcal{B} \subseteq}$
(6) $(s := e \| t := f) = (s := e \sqcup t := f)$
(7) $\|$ *is idempotent, commutative and associative, and distributes* $\sqcap$ *and* $\lhd b \rhd$.

Law 20 (CSPZ)

(1) $(A \fatsemi \text{CHAOS}) \|\|\| (B \fatsemi \text{CHAOS}) = (A \fatsemi \text{CHAOS}) \sqcap (B \fatsemi \text{CHAOS})$
(3) $(\text{DO}_a \fatsemi A) \|\|\| (\text{DO}_b \fatsemi B) = (\text{DO}_a \fatsemi A \|\|\| (\text{DO}_b \fatsemi B)) \sqcap (\text{DO}_b \fatsemi (\text{DO}_a \fatsemi A) \|\|\| B)$
(4) $(\text{STOP}_\mathcal{B} \|\|\| \text{STOP}_\mathcal{C}) = \text{STOP}_\mathcal{B} \lhd \mathcal{B} = \mathcal{C} \rhd \text{VOID}$
(5) $(\text{STOP}_\mathcal{B} \|\|\| s := e) = (\text{STOP}_\mathcal{B} \|\|\| \text{SKIP}) = \text{STOP}_\mathcal{B}$
(6) $(s := e \|\|\| t := f) = (s := e \sqcup t := f)$
(7) $\|\|\|$ *is commutative and associative, and distributes* $\sqcap$ *and* $\lhd b \rhd$.

5.6 CSP

CSP is a submodel of CSPZ(u) where the state-variable list u is empty. Only standard CSP commands are inherited: CHAOS, SKIP, STOP, $a \to A$, $A \square B$, $A \| B$ and $A \|\|\| B$. Because of the syntatical restriction, CSP satisfies more healthiness conditions. The condition $h_\emptyset$ (C1 of CSP) states that a process at least can deadlock immediately without refusing any action. The condition $h_{ref'}$ (C3 of CSP) requires subset closure for ref' so that intersection of refusals corresponds to simple predicative conjunction. The condition $h_{\Delta tr\downarrow}$ (C2 of CSP) describes the prefix closure of traces with the empty refusal. The healthiness condition $h_{ref \bullet tr}$ (i.e. C4 of CSP) states that if a process cannot refuse an action, it must be able to perform it. This condition is of higher order [5] and renders a CPO instead of a complete lattice – just like the feasibility healthiness condition of sequential programming. Because a $h_{ref \bullet tr}$-healthy predicate in $\text{CSPZ}(u)$ is still h_{cspz}-healthy, no difficulty is caused if we always impose it at last, and the semantic extension is still property-preserving. All $\text{CSPZ}(u)$ laws (for the sublanguage) are inherited. Details are abbreviated, as our focus is on property-altering extensions.

HC 10 $(h_\emptyset)$ $A \ = \ A \vee (\neg wait \wedge wait' \wedge tr = tr' \wedge ref' = \emptyset)$

HC 11 $(h_{ref'})$ $A \ = \ A :_{ref'} (\overline{ref'} \supseteq ref')$

HC 12 $(h_{\Delta tr \downarrow})$
$A \ = \ A \vee A :_{wait',ref',tr'} (\overline{tr'} - tr > tr' - tr \wedge \neg wait \wedge wait' \wedge ref' = \emptyset)$

HC 13 $(h_{ref \bullet tr})$
$A[tr_0, ref_0 / tr', ref'] \Rightarrow \forall a \in \mathcal{A} \cdot (A[ref_0 \cup \{a\} / ref'] \vee A[tr_0 ^\frown \langle a \rangle, \emptyset / tr', ref'])$

6   Conclusions and Future Work

The handling of fixed points is a challenging issue, which has been addressed in [7] by two major theorems. Note that the fixed-point theory of UTP no longer works for our model development, because sequential model is not a sublattice of the relational model, neither is it the case for the process-state model to the sequential model. More preconditions are needed to link fixed points in a model and those in its submodels. Many results and theorems can be found in [7].

The discussions of this paper remain at the theoretical level. More case studies need to be carried out. If all state-event mappings in a `CspZ` specification have finite ranges, then it becomes model-checkable. Tools like FDR can be applied without modification. Another possible way of application is to use the algebraic laws in verifying static analysers. A static analyser can be defined in abstract interpretation as a partial semantic function. We can apply the function on the normal form to illustrate its effect on any arbitrary process. Similar application has been successfully achieved for Bulk-Synchronous Parallel programming [16].

References

1. Abramsky, S., Jung, A.: Domain theory. In: Abramsky, S., Gabbay, D., Maibaum, T.S.E. (eds.) Handbook of Logic in Computer Science, pp. 1–168. Oxford University Press, New York (1994)
2. Back, R.J., von Wright, J.: Trace refinement of action systems. In: International Conference on Concurrency Theory, pp. 367–384 (1994)
3. Butler, M.: A CSP Approach To Action Systems. PhD thesis, OUCL, University of Oxford, Oxford (1992)

4. Cavalcanti, A., Woodcock, J.: Predicate transformers in the semantics of Circus. IEE Proceedings - Software 150(2), 85–94 (2003)
5. Chen, Y.: Generic composition. Formal Aspects of Computing 14(2), 108–122 (2002)
6. Chen, Y.: Hierarchical organisation of predicate-semantic models. In: Dunne, S., Stoddart, B. (eds.) UTP 2006. LNCS, vol. 4010, pp. 155–172. Springer, Heidelberg (2006)
7. Chen, Y.: Sharing properties between programming models. Technical report, Department of Computer Science, Durham University (2007)
8. Chen, Y., Sanders, J.W.: Logic of global synchrony. ACM Transactions on Programming Languages and Systems 26(2), 221–262 (2004)
9. Dijkstra, E.W.: Guarded commands, nondeterminacy and the formal derivation of programs. Communications of the ACM 18(8), 453–457 (1975)
10. Hoare, C.A.R.: Communicating Sequential Processes. Prentice-Hall, Englewood Cliffs (1985)
11. Hoare, C.A.R.: Dicussions about parallel composition as conjunction. Private communication (2006)
12. Hoare, C.A.R., He, J.: Unifying Theories of Programming. Prentice-Hall, Englewood Cliffs (1998)
13. Morgan, C.C.: Beauty is our business: a birthday salute to Edsger W. Dijkstra. chapter Of wp and CSP, pp. 319–326. Springer, Heidelberg (1990)
14. Roscoe, A.W.: The Theory and Practice of Concurrency. Prentice-Hall, Englewood Cliffs (1998)
15. Schneider, S., Treharne, H.: Verifying controlled components. In: Boiten, E.A., Derrick, J., Smith, G.P. (eds.) IFM 2004. LNCS, vol. 2999, pp. 87–107. Springer, Heidelberg (2004)
16. Zhou, J., Chen, Y.: Generating C code from LOGS specifications. In: Liu, Z., Araki, K. (eds.) ICTAC 2004. LNCS, vol. 3407, pp. 195–210. Springer, Heidelberg (2005)

Probabilistic Timed Behavior Trees

Robert Colvin, Lars Grunske, and Kirsten Winter

ARC Centre for Complex Systems,
School of Information Technology and Electrical Engineering
University of Queensland, Australia

Abstract. The *Behavior Tree* notation has been developed as a method
for systematically and traceably capturing user requirements. In this paper we extend the notation with *probabilistic* behaviour, so that reliability, performance, and other dependability properties can be expressed.
The semantics of probabilistic timed Behavior Trees is given by mapping
them to probabilistic timed automata. We gain advantages for requirements capture using Behavior Trees by incorporating into the notation an
existing elegant specification formalism (probabilistic timed automata)
which has tool support for formal analysis of probabilistic user requirements.

Keywords: Behavior Trees, probabilities, timed automata, model
checking.

1 Introduction

Representing the user requirements of a large and complex system in a manner that is readable by the client and preserves their vocabulary and intention
(validatable), while also having a formal underpinning (verifiable), is an important task for systems engineering. The *Behavior Tree* (BT) notation [Dro03]
is a graphical language that supports a behaviour-oriented design method for
handling real-world systems [WD04]. The notation facilitates systematic and
traceable translation of natural language requirements which structures the compositional and behavioural information. The notation includes a core subset
which has a formal basis [Win04] and can be model checked [GLWY05].

Currently the Behavior Tree notation does not have a syntax for expressing probabilistic behaviour. Such behaviour is important in system specification
as many systems specify, for instance, hardware dependability requirements or
probabilistic measures on performance. In this paper, we extend the Behavior
Tree (BT) notation to include probabilistic choice, thereby increasing the expressiveness of the language and also allowing stochastic properties to be model
checked. The new notation, which we call *probabilistic timed Behavior Trees*
(ptBTs), is an extension of *timed Behavior Trees* (tBTs), which are introduced
in [GWC07]. It allows the user to model timed as well as probabilistic behaviour.

The contributions of the paper are: 1) an operational semantics for timed
Behavior Trees in terms of timed transition systems, based on their mapping

J. Davies and J. Gibbons (Eds.): IFM 2007, LNCS 4591, pp. 156–175, 2007.

to *timed automata* [BW04] given in [GWC07]; and 2) the syntax and semantics of probabilistic timed Behavior Trees, which extend those for timed Behavior Trees, and are based on *probabilistic timed automata* [Bea03] and probabilistic timed transition systems. We use two examples to demonstrate the extension, and describe how probabilistic timed Behavior Trees can be model checked.

The paper is structured as follows. Section 2 introduces Behavior Trees and their timed extension, and in Section 3 their semantics is given in terms of timed automata. In Section 4 probabilities are introduced to the timed BT notation and a semantics is given in terms of probabilistic timed automata. Section 5 gives two examples of probabilistic timed Behavior Trees and explains how they were model checked using PRISM [HKNP06].

2   Preliminaries on Behavior Trees

As preliminaries we introduce the Behavior Tree notation and their extension to timed Behavior Trees.

2.1   Behavior Trees

The *Behavior Tree* (BT) notation [Dro03] is a graphical notation to capture the functional requirements of a system provided in natural language. The strength of the BT notation is two-fold: Firstly, the graphical nature of the notation provides the user with an intuitive understanding of a BT model - an important factor especially for use in industry. Secondly, the process of capturing requirements is performed in a stepwise fashion. That is, single requirements are modelled as single BTs, called *individual requirements trees*. In a second step these individual requirement trees are composed into one BT, called the *integrated requirements tree*. Composition of requirements trees is done on the graphical level: an individual requirements tree is merged with a second tree (which can be another individual requirements tree or an already integrated tree) if its root node matches one of the nodes of the second tree. Intuitively, this merging step is based on the matching node providing the point at which the preconditions of the merged individual requirement tree are satisfied. This structured process provides a successful solution for handling very large requirements specifications [Dro03,WD04].

The syntax of the BT notation comprises nodes and arrows. The notation contains a rich variety of node types for expressing behaviour; in this paper we

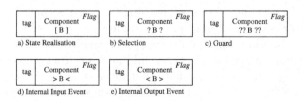

Fig. 1. BT node types

focus on a core subset of the language which models state tests and updates and event initiation and response. Each BT node type in Figure 1 refers to a particular *component*, C, and a *behaviour*, B, and is optionally marked by one or more *flags*. Nodes also contain a *tag*, which is used for traceability; since the tags have no effect on the semantics, we will ignore them for the purposes of this paper. The nodes types in Figure 1 are described below.

(a) A *state realisation*, where B is either a simple state name or an expression. A state realisation node models that C realises (enters) state B. For example, the root node of Figure 2 models that initially the *Power* component is in state *on*.

(b) A *selection*, where B is a condition on C's state; the control flow terminates if the condition evaluates to false.

(c) A *guard*, where B is a condition on C's state, as with (b); however, the control flow can only pass the guard when the condition holds, otherwise it is blocked and waits until the condition becomes true.

(d-e) An event modelling communication and data flow between components within the system, where B specifies an event; the control flow can pass the internal event node when the event occurs (the message is sent), otherwise it is blocked and waits; the communication is synchronous.

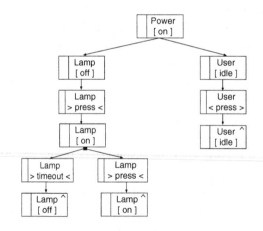

Fig. 2. Example: A simple lamp and its user

The control flow of the system is specified by either a single arrow leaving a node, for *sequential* flow, or multiple arrows leaving a node, for *concurrent* or *alternative* flow. In addition, *atomic* flow is specified by line with no arrowhead; this indicates that the behaviour of the child node occurs immediately after the behaviour of the parent node. We note that more than one input/output event is not allowed within an atomic block of nodes, since this could induce deadlock (for a more detailed discussion see [GWC07]).

The example in Figure 2 shows three types of edges: after the initialisation the control flow branches into two concurrent threads, the left modelling the behaviour of the lamp, and the right modelling an abstract user. The lamp thread contains alternative flow, when either a timeout event happens which causes the lamp to switch off, or another press signal is send by the user. The lamp waits for either of these events to occur. The first one to happen determines the flow of control. This alternative flow is marked by the black box on the branching edges.

A flag in BT node can specify: (a) a *reversion* node, marked by ' ^', if the node is a leaf node, indicating that the control flow loops back to the closest matching ancestor node (a matching node is a node with the same component name, type and behaviour) and all behaviour begun at that node initially is terminated; (b) a *referring* node, marked by '~', indicating that the flow continues from the matching node; (c) a *thread kill* node, marked by '−−', which kills the thread that starts with the matching node, or (d) a *synchronisation* node, marked by '=', where the control flow waits until all other threads with a matching synchronisation node have reached the synchronisation point. Every leaf node in Figure 2 is marked as a reversion node; we do not utilise the other flags in the examples in this paper.

2.2   Timed Behavior Trees

Timed Behavior Trees (tBTs), originally introduced in [GWC07], extend BTs with the notion of real-valued clocks for expressing timing behaviour. The timing information expressed by timed automata [BW04] was adopted. All clocks are initialised to zero and progress simultaneously with the same rate. Clocks can be reset at any time, and they can constrain the behaviour in terms of guards and invariants: a guard over a clock restricts the time when a step can be taken, and an invariant restricts the time a component can remain in a state without changing to the next state. The tBT notation therefore extends a BT node by three slots: a *guard* **G** over clock values, a *reset* **R** of clocks, and an *invariant* **I** over clocks. (If not relevant to a particular node, the slots may be omitted.) As with timed automata, we restrict clock invariants to be expressions of the form $x \oplus t$, where x is a clock, t evaluates to an integer value, and $\oplus$ is one of $<, \leq, =, \geq, >$.

As an example, in Figure 3 we augment the lamp Behavior Tree of Figure 2 with explicit timing constraints. The thread on the left hand side introduces the clock variable x, which is reset as soon as the event *press* is received. When the lamp realises the state *on* it must satisfy the invariant $x \leq 5$, modelling that the lamp can remain in state *on* for at most 5 time units before switching off (after exactly 5 time units) or the user presses the button. If the user presses the button while the lamp is on, the lamp may stay on for an additional 5 time units, as indicated by the reset of clock x. In the right-hand thread, a second clock y enforces a more specific timed behaviour in that the user cannot press the button twice within 1 time unit.

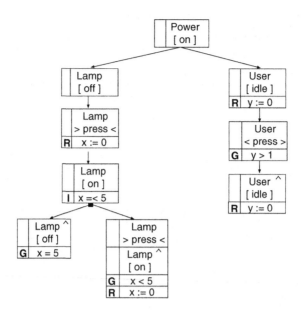

Fig. 3. Timed system of a lamp and its user in tBT

3   Semantics of Timed Behavior Trees

A timed Behavior Tree (tBT) can be defined as a finite automaton, which contains state variables and clock variables, a finite set of *locations*, and a finite set of labelled *edges*. Locations model the states of the system, abstracting from the evaluation of state and clock variables. Edges symbolise the transitions between the locations. A transition from one location to the next can be guarded and it can perform one or more actions as well as a number of clock resets. Each edge also has an optional synchronisation event.

Components in a tBT are treated as state variables in a timed automaton, while events are treated as timed automaton synchronisations. A Behavior Tree node represents an *edge* in a timed automaton, as nodes embody state changes and events. Each arrow in a BT (except for atomic flow) corresponds to a *location* in a timed automaton. The guards and updates (including resets) of clock and state variables, and synchronisation events, are therefore added to the edges, though clock invariants are pushed to the location following the edge. The general mapping for a node is given in Figure 4.

Nodes. More concretely, the nodes in Figure 1 may be represented as follows (altering the *component_behaviour* section in Figure 4). State realisations are mapped to an update of the relevant component, while a guard node is mapped to a guard on the component. Both input and output events are mapped to synchronisations of the same name, with input events decorated with '?' and output events with '!'. The transfer of data through events may be modelled

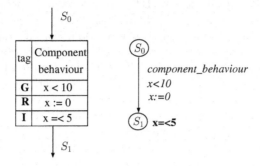

Fig. 4. tBT node (left) and corresponding timed automaton (right)

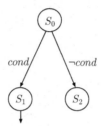

Fig. 5. Behaviour for selections

using state variables. A selection node requires the addition of an extra edge and terminal state (S_2) for the case where the condition is not satisfied; this is shown in Figure 5.

Control flow. Sequential flow, as mentioned above, maps to a location, while alternative flow maps straightforwardly to nondeterministic choice. Nodes joined by atomic flow are joined together so that their updates and guards are combined into one transition. Because we restrict atomic flow in tBTs to contain only one synchronisation, this representation is straightforward.

Concurrency. We will call tBTs without concurrent flow of control *sequential tBTs.* A sequential tBT maps to a single timed automaton as described above. Timed BTs with concurrent branching, called *concurrent tBTs*, map to a network of automata, acting concurrently and synchronising on events. Each thread maps to a single automaton, which has to be invoked at a particular point in the control flow, namely the branching point that starts the thread. Therefore, each single automata has an initial location which models the thread being disabled. The location *disabled* can be exited only via an edge that is labelled with the special synchronisation event *invoke?*. The process that starts the thread sends the matching synchronisation event *invoke!* and terminates, i.e., goes itself to the location *disabled.*

Flags. We may now specify how a tBT node's flags are represented. Firstly we note that both reversion nodes and thread kill nodes terminate the behaviour of processes at an arbitrary point in their execution. For each automaton p that may be killed by process q, we introduce a synchronisation event $kill\_q?$, and augment p with edges labelled with $kill\_q?$ leading from each location in p to the disabled location (this approach introduces less overhead than if we were to take the approach of associating *kill?* events with the process being killed). This way, an automaton's behaviour is terminated whenever the corresponding $kill\_q!$ event is received. In Figure 6 we depict the user thread from Figure 3 as a timed automaton in a network system, assuming that it may be killed by process q at any time.

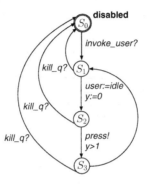

Fig. 6. Timed automaton simulating the user thread within the lamp system

A node with a reversion flag is typically modelled as a transition from the current location to the location immediately after the edge representing the target node. In general we choose the after-location rather than the before-location to allow for resetting of local clocks (see [GWC07] for why reversions may have different clock resets to their matching node). However, when there are no resets in the reversion node, or if the resets are identical, we can more simply represent reversions as an edge to the before-location. For the examples in this paper, we adopt this more straightforward approach. The reversion transition is labelled with $kill\_q!$, which terminates the behaviour of all automata, if any, that are invoked after the matching node (in Figure 6 there are none). A node with a referring flag is modelled simply as a transition from the current location to the location preceding the target node. A node with a kill flag generates a *kill!* event, and a node with a synchronisation flag is modelled directly as a synchronisation transition in a timed automaton.

3.1 Operational Semantics

The semantics of a sequential tBT is given as as a timed automaton. To a large extent our definitions follow the definitions of the operational semantics of timed automata in [BW04]. We divert from these, however, where it is suitable for modelling Behavior Trees, e.g., we separate actions (state updates) from synchronisations, and explicitly define state variables to represent components, which can be of any type, whereas in [BW04] state variables are treated as a special kind of clock variable.

Let $\mathcal{V}$ be a finite set of state variables, and $\mathcal{C}$ be a finite set of clocks. Let $\Sigma(\mathcal{V})$ denote the set of actions (representing state updates), and let $\mathcal{G}(\mathcal{V})$ denote the set of conditions over state variables (representing guards and selections). Let $\mathcal{G}(\mathcal{C})$ be a set of guards over clocks, $\mathcal{R}(\mathcal{C})$ a set of clock resets, and $\mathcal{I}(\mathcal{C})$ a set of clock invariants. We write *skip* to represent an action or clock reset which does has no effect, and *true* for variable and clock guards which are always satisfied. Let Θ be the synchronisation events, with $\varepsilon \in \Theta$ a distinguished element which represents an internal step, i.e., no synchronisation.

Definition 1. *A sequential tBT is a tuple* $\langle L, l_0, E, I \rangle$ *where*

  - *L is a finite set of locations*
  - $l_0 \in L$ *is the initial location*
  - $E \subseteq L \times \Theta \times \mathcal{G}(\mathcal{C}) \times \mathcal{G}(\mathcal{V}) \times \mathcal{R}(\mathcal{C}) \times \Sigma(\mathcal{V}) \times L$ *is the set of edges*
  - $I : L \to \mathcal{I}(\mathcal{C})$ *is the mapping that assigns clock invariants to locations.*

We use the notation $l \xrightarrow{s,g,c,r,a} l'$ *if* $(l, s, g, c, r, a, l') \in E$.

As an example, consider the sequential tBT representing the user in Figure 6. There are four locations, with the initial location S_0. The invocation edge is the tuple $(S_0, invoke\_user?, true, true, skip, skip, S_0)$. The $User[idle]$ edge is the tuple $(S_1, \varepsilon, true, true, (y := 0), (User := idle), S_2)$, while the $User\langle press \rangle$ edge is the tuple $(S_2, press!, (y > 1), true, skip, skip, S_3)$. The reversion is represented as an edge back to the location S_1, i.e., $(S_3, \varepsilon, true, true, skip, skip, S_1)$. The edge corresponding to a $kill\_q$ event occurring while the lamp process is in location S_3 is $(S_3, kill\_q?, true, true, skip, skip, S_0)$.

Before giving the operational semantics we introduce some notation. We use *clock assignments* to denote the progress of time and with it changing clock values, and *variable assignments* to monitor the evaluation of the state variables. A clock assignment is a mapping from clocks $\mathcal{C}$ to non-negative real numbers $\mathbb{R}_+$. If u is a clock assignment, then $u + d$ denotes the clock assignment that maps all $c \in \mathcal{C}$ to $u(c) + d$. Resetting clocks is denoted as $[\overline{r} \mapsto 0]u$ which maps all clocks in $\overline{r} \subseteq \mathcal{C}$ to 0 and leaves all other clocks in $\mathcal{C} \setminus \overline{r}$ unchanged. Let v be a variable assignment mapping all variables in $\mathcal{V}$ to a value in their domain. Updating state variables is denoted as $[\overline{x} \mapsto \overline{e}]v$ which changes the variable assignment to map variables $\overline{x} \subseteq \mathcal{V}$ to corresponding values in $\overline{e}$ and leaves all other variables unchanged.

The semantics of a sequential tBT can be given as a timed transition system, in which a state of a sequential tBT can be given as a tuple consisting of a location, a variable assignment, and a clock assignment, i.e., $\langle l, v, u \rangle$.

There are two types of transitions possible: the system either delays for some time (*delay step*) or takes one of the enabled transitions (*action step*).

Definition 2. *The semantics of a sequential tBT is a timed transition system with states $\langle l, v, u \rangle$ and transitions as follows.*

- $\langle l, v, u \rangle \xrightarrow{d} \langle l, v, u + d \rangle$ *(delay step)*
     if u and $u + d$ satisfy $I(l)$ for a $d \in \mathbb{R}_+$
- $\langle l, v, u \rangle \xrightarrow{\alpha} \langle l', v', u' \rangle$ *(action step)*
     if $l \xrightarrow{s,g,c,r,a} l'$, u satisfies g, v satisfies c,
     $v' = [\overline{x} \mapsto \overline{e}]v$ *if* $a = (\overline{x} \mapsto \overline{e})$,
     $u' = [\overline{r} \mapsto 0]u$, *and* u' *satisfies* $I(l')$.

According to this definition, if a process is in a location from where no action step is enabled by the time the clock evaluation violates the location invariant, no further step is possible (the delay step is also disabled) and the process halts. Furthermore, this definition allows for indefinitely many delay steps if the automaton is in a state for which no location invariant is specified (i.e., any u and $u + d$ will satisfy *true*).

3.2 Concurrent Timed Behavior Trees

The semantics of a concurrent tBT can now be given as a *network* of timed automata, i.e., parallel automata that operate in an interleaving fashion using a handshake synchronisation mechanism. A state of a network with n concurrent processes is formalised as a tuple $\langle ls, v, u \rangle$ with ls being a vector of length n of the current locations in each process, v the variable assignment[1] and u the clock assignment. Let l_i denote the i-th element of location vector ls and $ls[l'_i/l_i]$ denote the vector ls with the element l_i being substituted by l'_i. With $I(ls)$ we denote the conjunction of invariants on all locations, i.e., $I(ls) = \bigwedge_i I(l_i)$.

Let $s?, s! \in \Theta$ symbolise reading and sending of a synchronisation event, respectively, also recalling $\varepsilon \in \Theta$ denotes an internal action of the system.

A network can perform three types of steps: a delay step and an action step, both similar to the steps in a single automaton, and also a synchronisation step.

Definition 3. *The semantics of a concurrent tBT is a network of timed transition systems with states $\langle ls, v, u \rangle$ and transitions as follows.*

- $\langle ls, v, u \rangle \xrightarrow{d} \langle ls, v, u + d \rangle$ *(delay step)*
     if u and $u + d$ satisfy $I(ls)$ for a $d \in \mathbb{R}_+$
- $\langle ls, v, u \rangle \xrightarrow{\varepsilon} \langle ls[l'_i/l_i], v', u' \rangle$ *(action step)*
     if $l_i \xrightarrow{\varepsilon,g,c,r,a} l'_i$,
     u satisfies g, v satisfies c,
     $v' = [\overline{x} \mapsto \overline{e}]v$ *if* $a = (\overline{x} \mapsto \overline{e})$,
     $u' = [\overline{r} \mapsto 0]u$, *and* u' *satisfies* $I(ls[l'_i/l_i])$.

---

[1] State variables are not related to a particular process but treated as global and are therefore accessible by any process.

- $\langle ls, v, u \rangle \xrightarrow{\varepsilon} \langle ls[l'_i/l_i][l'_j/l_j], v', u' \rangle$ *(synchronisation step)*
    if there exists $i \neq j$ such that

    1. $l_i \xrightarrow{s?, g_i, c_i, r_i, a_i} l'_i, \quad l_j \xrightarrow{s!, g_j, c_j, r_j, a_j} l'_j$
       and u satisfies $g_i \wedge g_j$ and v satisfies $c_i \wedge c_j$
       and
    2. $v' = [\overline{x_i}/\overline{e_i}]([\overline{x_j}/\overline{e_j}]v)$
       if $a_i = (\overline{x_i} \mapsto \overline{e_i})$ and $a_j = (\overline{x_j} \mapsto \overline{e_j})$ and
    3. $u' = [\overline{r_i} \cup \overline{r_j} \mapsto 0]u$ and u' satisfies
       $I(ls[l'_i/l_i][l'_j/l_u])$.

Note that in a synchronisation step the sending process updates the state variables (if its action a contains updates) before the receiving process, facilitating synchronous message passing.

4   Probabilistic Timed Behavior Trees

In this section we extend timed Behavior Trees to *probabilistic timed Behavior Trees* (ptBTs). We follow the well-established and expressive approach of annotating transitions with a *probability* that the transition will take place. In the Behavior Tree notation, this means we associate with each node an optional probability slot which contains a number from 0 to 1, i.e., in the range $[0, 1]$. As an example, in which probabilistic choice is used to model component failures, consider the ptBT in Figure 7 which extends the lamp example with a 1% chance that the lamp will fail (e.g., blow a fuse) whenever it is switched from off to on.

For clarity, and without loss of generality, we impose a well-formedness condition on ptBTs that either every *child* node of a node has an associated probability, or none do (a child node is a direct descendant). We have therefore introduced *probabilistic branching* in addition to alternative and concurrent branching. The probabilities in the child nodes must sum to less than or equal to 1. If the probabilities sum to P, and P is less than one, it is understood that with probability $1 - P$ no transition is taken.[2] In the lamp example, the probabilities of the child nodes of the *Lamp⟨press⟩* node sum to 1, indicating that one of the actions must be taken. In the user thread, however, the probability of the user pressing the button is 0.3. Thus it is implicit there is a 70% chance that the user will not press the button as time passes.

The mapping of ptBTs to probabilistic timed automata follows that of tBTs for the non-probabilistic constructs in the language, with the addition that probabilities are added to the corresponding edges in the automaton, if the sum of the probabilities is 1. If the probabilities of all the edges leaving a location sum to P for $P < 1$, in general an additional edge looping back to itself with probability

---

[2] This models an exponentially distributed delay before the next action is taken. In continuous timed systems, such behaviour can also be represented using real-valued *rates*, giving the expected incidence of events per time unit. For simplicity we define ptBTs to contain probabilities only (values in the range $[0,1]$), but in Section 5 we describe how rates may be introduced for model checking.

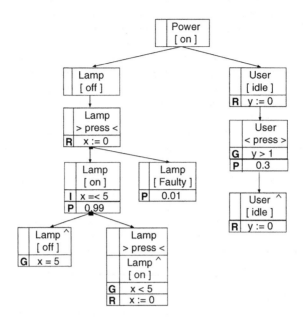

Fig. 7. Probabilistic timed system of a lamp and its user

$1 - P$ is added, which includes any clock guards – see Figure 8 for an example. An exception to this is if the node is an output event. Because it is not possible to label only one edge in a probabilistic choice in a timed automaton with a synchronisation, an intermediate location is added between the probabilistic choice and the synchronisation – an example is given later in Figure 9.

To specify probabilistic properties we may choose from several different specification languages: continuous stochastic logic (CSL) [ASSB96], if the model is deterministic and uses continuous time; probabilistic computation tree logic (PCTL) [HJ94], if the model uses discrete time; or PCTL's extension to probabilistic timed computation tree logic (PTCTL) [KNSS02], if the model is nondeterministic and uses continuous time. As an example, if the global time is recorded in clock G, the dependability property "with what probability will the Lamp enter the faulty state before X time units" can be formally stated in PCTL as

$$\mathcal{P}_{=?}(true \; \mathcal{U} \; (lamp = faulty \land G \le X))$$

where $\mathcal{U}$ is the temporal *until* operator, and a property *true* $\mathcal{U} \; \phi$ models *eventually* ϕ.

4.1   Semantics of Probabilistic Timed Behavior Trees

We give the meaning of ptBTs as probabilistic timed automata. There are several ways in which probabilities may be added to the timed automaton model, e.g., by associating them with edges [KNPS06] or with locations [KNSS00]. We follow

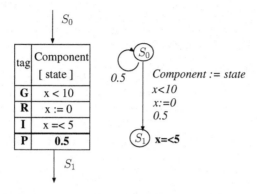

Fig. 8. ptBT node (left) and corresponding probabilistic timed automaton (right)

the former approach, and replace the target locations in edges with a *probability mapping* on clock resets, variable updates, and target locations. A probability mapping on type T is a partial function from elements of T to values in the range $[0, 1]$, which sum to 1, i.e.,

$$\mathsf{Dist}(T) \triangleq \{p : T \nrightarrow [0, 1] \mid \sum_{t:\, \mathrm{dom}\, p} p(t) = 1\}$$

Definition 4. *A sequential probabilistic tBT is a tuple $\langle L, l_0, E, I \rangle$ where*

- *L is a finite set of locations*
- *$l_0 \in L$ is the initial location*
- *$E \subseteq L \times \Theta \times \mathcal{G}(\mathcal{C}) \times \mathcal{G}(\mathcal{V}) \times \mathsf{Dist}(\mathcal{R}(\mathcal{C}) \times \Sigma(\mathcal{V}) \times L)$ is the set of edges*
- *$I : L \to \mathcal{I}(\mathcal{C})$ is the mapping that assigns clock invariants to locations.*

In Figure 9 we give the graphical representation of the sequential probabilistic timed automaton for the user process in the lamp example, alongside its representation as a tuple. By including resets and updates with the target locations in the distribution we may enforce differing resets and updates depending on how the probabilistic choice is resolved.

The semantics of a probabilistic timed automaton is updated so that an *action step* from location l_1 to l_2 may be taken only if the associated probability is greater than 0. This is given by the second line in the action step constraint below, which is otherwise identical to Definition 2.

Definition 5. *The semantics of a sequential ptBT is a probabilistic timed transition system with states $\langle l, v, u \rangle$ and transitions as follows.*

- $\langle l, v, u \rangle \xrightarrow{d} \langle l, v, u + d \rangle$ *(delay step)*
     if u and $u + d$ satisfy $I(l)$ for a $d \in \mathbb{R}_+$

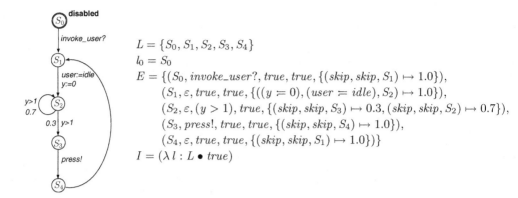

$$L = \{S_0, S_1, S_2, S_3, S_4\}$$
$$l_0 = S_0$$
$$E = \{(S_0, invoke\_user?, true, true, \{(skip, skip, S_1) \mapsto 1.0\}),$$
$$(S_1, \varepsilon, true, true, \{((y := 0), (user := idle), S_2) \mapsto 1.0\}),$$
$$(S_2, \varepsilon, (y > 1), true, \{(skip, skip, S_3) \mapsto 0.3, (skip, skip, S_2) \mapsto 0.7\}),$$
$$(S_3, press!, true, true, \{(skip, skip, S_4) \mapsto 1.0\}),$$
$$(S_4, \varepsilon, true, true, \{(skip, skip, S_1) \mapsto 1.0\})\}$$
$$I = (\lambda\, l : L \bullet true)$$

Fig. 9. Sequential ptBT of the user process as a probabilistic timed automaton, with its representation as a tuple

- $\langle l, v, u \rangle \xrightarrow{a} \langle l', v', u' \rangle$ *(action step)*
  if $(l, s, g, c, D) \in E$,
  $(r, a, l') \in dom\ D$ and $D(r, a, l') > 0$, and
  u satisfies g, v satisfies c,
  $v' = [\overline{x} \mapsto \overline{e}]v$ if $a = (\overline{x} \mapsto \overline{e})$,
  $u' = [\overline{r} \mapsto 0]u$, and u' satisfies $I(l')$

By augmenting edges with distributions, which therefore represent a set of "probable" edges, rather than assigning a *single* probability for that edge, we are able to more succinctly capture the "sum to one" property, and express nondeterministic behaviour. A non-probabilistic timed automaton can be mapped to a probabilistic timed automaton by replacing each edge (l, s, g, c, r, a, l') with the edge (l, s, g, c, D), where the distribution D maps (r, a, l') to 1.0. Such distributions are called *point distributions*. When a nondeterministic choice is made between two locations, this is represented by two edges, each of which has a point distribution on the target edge.

4.2   Semantics of Concurrent Probabilistic Timed Behavior Trees

The semantics of concurrent ptBTs must also be extended in a similar way to Definition 3, so that both probabilities in a synchronisation step are greater than 0. The definition below differs from Definition 3 in that probabilities are checked to be non-zero in action and synchronisation steps.

Definition 6. *The semantics of a concurrent ptBT is a network of probabilistic timed transition systems with states $\langle ls, v, u \rangle$ and transitions as follows.*

- $\langle ls, v, u \rangle \xrightarrow{d} \langle ls, v, u + d \rangle$ *(delay step)*
  if u and $u + d$ satisfy $I(ls)$ for a $d \in \mathbb{R}_+$

- $\langle ls, v, u \rangle \xrightarrow{\varepsilon} \langle ls[l_i'/l_i], v', u' \rangle$ *(action step)*
  if $(l_i, \varepsilon, g, c, D) \in E_i$,
  $(r, a, l_i') \in dom\ D$ and $D(r, a, l_i') > 0$,
  u satisfies g, v satisfies c,
  $v' = [\overline{x} \mapsto \overline{e}]v$ if $a = (\overline{x} \mapsto \overline{e})$,
  $u' = [\overline{r} \mapsto 0]u$, and u' satisfies $I(ls[l_i'/l_i])$.

- $\langle ls, v, u \rangle \xrightarrow{\varepsilon} \langle ls[l_i'/l_i][l_j'/l_j], v', u' \rangle$ *(synchronisation step)*
  if there exists $i \neq j$ such that

  1. $(l_i, s?, g_i, c_i, D_i) \in E_i$ and
     $(l_j, s!, g_j, c_j, D_j) \in E_j$ and
     $(r_i, a_i, l_i') \in dom\ D_i \wedge (r_j, a_j, l_j') \in dom\ D_j$ and
     $D_i(r_i, a_i, l_i') \cdot D_j(r_j, a_j, l_j') > 0$ and
     u satisfies $g_i \wedge g_j$ and v satisfies $c_i \wedge c_j$ and
  2. $v' = [\overline{x_i}/\overline{e_i}]([\overline{x_j}/\overline{e_j}]v)$
     if $a_i = (\overline{x_i} \mapsto \overline{e_i})$ and $a_j = (\overline{x_j} \mapsto \overline{e_j})$ and
  3. $u' = [\overline{r_i} \cup \overline{r_j} \mapsto 0]u$ and u' satisfies
     $I(ls[l_i'/l_i][l_j'/l_u])$.

The addition of probabilities does not greatly affect the semantics, however it has important implications for model checking. In an execution of the probabilistic Lamp system in Figure 7, the probability of each transition is recorded, and hence it is possible, in exhaustive analysis, to determine the probabilities of each execution. We explore this in more detail in the next section.

5   Model Checking Probabilistic Timed Behavior Trees

In this section we describe how probabilistic timed Behavior Trees may be model checked using the model checker PRISM [HKNP06], and provide two examples. PRISM (Probabilistic Symbolic Model Checker) provides model checking facilities for three types of probabilistic models: deterministic time Markov chains (DTMCs), continuous time Markov chains (CTMCs), and Markov decision processes (MDPs) (for an overview of the three models and how they may be model checked, see [Kwi03]). To utilise PRISM, we must therefore translate ptBTs into one of the three model types. DTMCs and CTMCs are deterministic, and hence are suitable for deterministic ptBTs. MDPs, which are generalisations of DTMCs, contain nondeterministic choice, though, like DTMCs, are limited to discrete time. Because ptBTs contain nondeterministic choice, we will typically translate a ptBT model into a PRISM MDP for model checking, following guidelines given in [KNPS06]; in Section 5.1 we give an example of this using the Lamp ptBT. In Section 5.2 we give a deterministic ptBT, which we model check as a PRISM CTMC.

5.1   Case Study 1 - Lamp Example

Consider the user probabilistic timed automaton given in Figure 9. Its translation into a PRISM MDP is given below.

```
module user
  L: [0..4] init 0;
  user: [0..1] init 0;
  y: [0..MAX_Y] init 0;

  [invoke_user] L=0            -> (L'=1);
  []            L=1            -> (L'=2) & (y'=0) & (user' = 1);
  [time]        L=2 & y>1  -> 0.3: (L'=3) & INC(y)  +
                              0.7: (L'=2) & INC(y);
  [press]       L=3            -> (L'=4);
  []            L=4            -> (L'=1);
  [time]        !(L=2 & y> 1) and !(L=3)
                              -> INC(y);
endmodule
```

The variable L represents the locations, and *user* the user component (0 representing the user's initial state, and 1 representing the *idle* state). We also declare local clock y, which for efficiency reasons is at most MAX_Y. (Within the code, the abbreviation $INC(Y)$ increments y up to the maximum MAX_Y.) Each action line corresponds to an element of E, and is of the form

[sync] *guard* -> *action*

for non-probabilistic behaviour, or

[sync] *guard* -> *prob1* : *action1* + *prob2* : *action2* + ...

for probabilistic behaviour. The start of a line gives the synchronisation event enclosed in square brackets (which are empty for internal actions), and the guards combine the conditions on clocks and state variables (there is no distinction in PRISM). The action part updates variables and clocks. The translation is straightforward, except that we must explicitly model the advancement of time, as observed in local clock y. Any action which results in the passing of time is synchronised with the global clock (see below) on the event *time*, and any local clocks are incremented (since this is a discrete time model). In addition, the last action line allows time to advance with no action being taken (the guard is used to prevent doubling up of time increments, and to ensure no time passes between the probabilistic choice and the *press* event occurring).

Global time is maintained via the *time* module. After invocation, the *time* module increments the global clock synchronously with all modules which maintain their own local clocks.

```
module time
    time_L : [0..1] init 0;
    global_clock: [0..MAX_GLOBAL_CLOCK] init 0;

    [invoke_clock]  time_L=0 -> (time_state'=1);
    [time]          time_L=1 -> (time_state'=1) & INC(global_clock);
endmodule
```

The full PRISM model also contains a process representing the lamp, and a process which initiates the lamp, timer, and user processes. Having translated the model into an MDP, we may check whether it satisfies reliability requirements written in probabilistic computation tree logic (PCTL) [HJ94]. For example, "The probability that the lamp fails within 100 time units should be less than 10 percent" is given as

```
Pmin<0.1 [ true U (lamp_state = faulty & global_clock <= 100) ]
```

where *faulty* is an abbreviation for the corresponding integer-valued lamp state.

Given a failure probability of 0.01 for the lamp, and that the user presses the button with a probability of 0.3, the model checking showed the model fulfils this requirement.

5.2   Case Study 2 - Viking Example

In this section we give a model with no nondeterminism or local clocks, which can be model checked as a PRISM CTMC. The example involves a group of four Vikings attempting to cross a bridge, from the "unsafe" side to the "safe" side, though the bridge may hold only one at a time – see Figure 10. An individual Viking can step on to the bridge, and then cross to the safe side. However if more than one steps on to the bridge at the same time, they begin arguing, which may result in one or more of the Vikings backing down and returning to the unsafe side of the bridge. (The behaviour of the system can be likened to processes competing for access to a critical section.) For reasons of space we show the thread for only one Viking – the other three are similar.

The Viking BT is specified as follows: initially each Viking is unsafe, and with a *rate* (described below) given by **enter_rt** they enter the bridge. Note that the

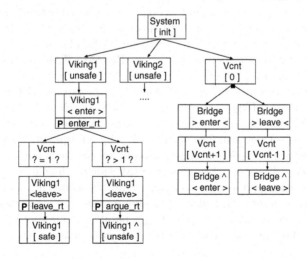

Fig. 10. Viking Behavior Tree

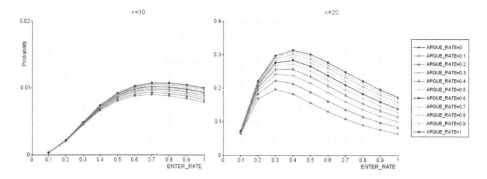

Fig. 11. Result of PRISM model checking for the Viking example with a parameter sweep over the enter and arguing probabilities

passage of time is implicit in this model, and that as time passes it becomes more and more likely that an individual Viking will enter the bridge. Entering a bridge is modelled by a synchronisation with the bridge process, which is described below. After entering the bridge, the Viking may leave if he is the only occupant, and does so at the rate given by `leave_rt`. If there is more than one Viking on the bridge, he begins "arguing" with the other Vikings, and may back down and leave the bridge, returning to the unsafe side, at a rate given by `argue_rt`. The bridge process simply maintains a count of the number of Vikings on the bridge by synchronising on leave and enter events from each Viking.

This model may be translated into a CTMC, because it is deterministic and does not contain local clocks. However, CTMCs operate on *rates*, rather than probabilities, and thus the value in the probability slot must be interpreted as a rate. This is straightforward, unless the rate of an event occurring is more than once per time unit (since this would require a value greater than one, i.e., could not be interpreted as a probability). In this example we set our rates to be less than once per second, and leave the extension of ptBTs to use rates as future work. The translation of the Viking ptBT to a PRISM CTMC is straightforward, since time does not need to be explicitly modelled.

We may check various properties of the Viking model, as with the lamp. Because the model is a CTMC, we use continuous stochastic logic (CSL) [ASSB96] instead of PCTL. In this case, we may determine which combination of probabilities gives the best performance, as measured by how quickly all Vikings make it to the safe side of the bridge. As an example, we fix the leaving probability at 1.0, i.e., Vikings will exit the bridge to the safe side at the earliest opportunity, and observe the change in probability that results from varying the probabilities of entering and arguing (also called a parameter sweep). This is checked against the following property, which queries the probability of all four Vikings becoming safe within G time units (*all_safe* is an abbreviation for each Viking being in the safe state).

```
P=? [true U<G all_safe]
```

The results of the analysis in PRISM are presented in Figure 11. The graphs show the probabilities that all Vikings are safe for varying values of the argue and enter rates with the leave rate set at 1. The graph on the left gives the probabilities for the case where $G = 10$, i.e., all Vikings are safe within 10 time units, while the graph on the right is for the case where $G = 20$. In both cases a higher argue rate gives better performance, but over a longer time span a less aggressive enter strategy gives better performance (optimal enter rate for $G = 10$ is approximately 0.8, while for $G = 20$ it is approximately 0.4).

6   Related Work

Various notations have been extended to enable modelling of probabilistic behaviour, e.g., stochastic Petri Nets [MBC+95], probabilistic timed CSP [Low95], stochastic π calculus [Pri95], probabilistic action systems [Tro99], and probabilistic statecharts [JHK02].

From the perspective of probabilistic requirements capture, the closest work to our own is that of Jansen et al. [JHK02], who extend UML statecharts with probabilities. Statecharts, like Behavior Trees, is a graphical notation to support modelling of system requirements. Similarly to our work, the semantics of probabilistic statecharts, which is given in terms of Markov Decision Processes (MDP), provides an interface to the model checker PRISM. In contrast to probabilistic timed BTs, however, probabilistic statecharts do not allow modelling timed behaviour since a notion of clocks is not included. Furthermore, the Behavior Tree approach allows individual requirements to be successively integated by grafting them onto the growing design tree as branches, as outlined in Section 2. Because Behavior Trees have been specifically designed for this purpose, they provide a simpler and more straightforward mechanism for building the system model from its individual requirements than is possible using other notations.

7   Conclusion and Future Work

In this paper we have given a probabilistic extension to the timed Behavior Tree notation and a semantics in terms of probabilistic timed automata (see, e.g., [Bea03]), as well as given a more rigorously defined semantics of timed Behavior Trees [GWC07]. The extension was demonstrated with two examples, which were also model checked in PRISM [HKNP06]. The notation extension was designed to be straightforward for system modellers to incorporate when capturing probabilistic requirements, as well as allow the probabilistic behaviour of faulty components to be specified. Probabilistic system properties may then be formally verified after translation to probabilistic timed automata.

The addition of probabilistic choice to Behavior Trees was particularly motivated by the need for modelling faulty behaviour of safety-critical embedded systems. Consequently, in future work, we will enhance the automatic Failure Mode and Effect Analysis (FMEA) for Behavior Trees [GLWY05]. The procedure currently uses fault injection experiments and model checking of the resulting Behavior Tree to determine whether the injected failure leads to a hazard condition, which is specified as a normal temporal logical formula. However, a limitation of this procedure is that the model checker will generate counter examples that are relatively improbable. With the results presented in this paper, we propose to assign to each of these injected faults an occurrence rate, and perform an analysis of the resulting behaviour with probabilistic model checking. We will then be able to analyse hazard conditions together with their tolerable hazard probabilities.

As it stands, current probabilistic model checking approaches work with exponential distributions only, but in practice, many faults are distributed differently; in particular, many faults are Weibull distributed [Bir99], and follow the common "bathtub" curve which models a burn-in and wear-out phase. Consequently, we will investigate how to include arbitrary distributions in the probabilistic timed BT notation, and in what way these distributions can be supported by model checking tools.

Acknowledgements. This work was produced with the assistance of funding from the Australian Research Council (ARC) under the ARC Centres of Excellence program within the ARC Centre for Complex Systems (ACCS). The authors wish to thank their colleagues in the Dependable Complex Computer-based Systems project and the anonymous reviewers for their constructive suggestions.

References

ASSB96.   Aziz, A., Sanwal, K., Singhal, V., Brayton, R.K.: Verifying continuous time markov chains. In: Alur, R., Henzinger, T.A. (eds.) CAV 1996. LNCS, vol. 1102, pp. 269–276. Springer, Heidelberg (1996)

Bea03.   Beauquier, D.: On probabilistic timed automata. Theoretical Computer Science 292(1), 65–84 (2003)

Bir99.   Birolini, A.: Reliability Engineering: Theory and Practice, 3rd edn. Springer, Heidelberg (1999)

BW04.   Bengtsson, J., Wang, Y.: Timed automata: Semantics, algorithms and tools. In: Desel, J., Reisig, W., Rozenberg, G. (eds.) Lectures on Concurrency and Petri Nets. LNCS, vol. 3098, Springer, Heidelberg (2004)

Dro03.   Dromey, R.G.: From requirements to design: Formalizing the key steps. In: Int. Conference on Software Engineering and Formal Methods (SEFM 2003), pp. 2–13. IEEE Computer Society Press, Los Alamitos (2003)

GLWY05.   Grunske, L., Lindsay, P., Winter, K., Yatapanage, N.: An automated failure mode and effect analysis based on high-level design specification with Behavior Trees. In: Romijn, J.M.T., Smith, G.P., van de Pol, J. (eds.) IFM 2005. LNCS, vol. 3771, pp. 129–149. Springer, Heidelberg (2005)

GWC07.   Grunske, L., Winter, K., Colvin, R.: Timed Behavior Trees and their Application to Verifying Real-time Systems. In: Proc. of 18th Australian Conference on Software Engineering (ASWEC 2007), April 2007, accepted for publication (2007)

HJ94.   Hansson, H., Jonsson, B.: A logic for reasoning about time and reliability. Formal Aspects of Computing 6(5), 512–535 (1994)

HKNP06.   Hinton, A., Kwiatkowska, M., Norman, G., Parker, D.: PRISM: A tool for
          automatic verification of probabilistic systems. In: Hermanns, H., Palsberg,
          J. (eds.) TACAS 2006 and ETAPS 2006. LNCS, vol. 3920, pp. 441–444.
          Springer, Heidelberg (2006)
JHK02.   Jansen, D.N., Hermanns, H., Katoen, J.-P.: A probabilistic extension of
          UML Statecharts. In: Damm, W., Olderog, E.-R. (eds.) FTRTFT 2002.
          LNCS, vol. 2469, pp. 355–374. Springer, Heidelberg (2002)
KNPS06.   Kwiatkowska, M., Norman, G., Parker, D., Sproston, J.: Performance anal-
          ysis of probabilistic timed automata using digital clocks. Formal Methods
          in System Design 29, 33–78 (2006)
KNSS00.   Kwiatkowska, M., Norman, G., Segala, R., Sproston, J.: Verifying quantita-
          tive properties of continuous probabilistic timed automata. In: Palamidessi,
          C. (ed.) CONCUR 2000. LNCS, vol. 1877, pp. 123–137. Springer, Heidelberg
          (2000)
KNSS02.   Kwiatkowska, M., Norman, G., Segala, R., Sproston, J.: Automatic verifica-
          tion of real-time systems with discrete probability distributions. Theoretical
          Computer Science 282(1), 101–150 (2002)
Kwi03.   Kwiatkowska, M.: Model checking for probability and time: From theory to
          practice. In: Proc. 18th Annual IEEE Symposium on Logic in Computer
          Science (LICS'03), Invited Paper, pp. 351–360. IEEE Computer Society
          Press, Los Alamitos (2003)
Low95.   Lowe, G.: Probabilistic and prioritized models of timed CSP. Theoretical
          Computer Science 138(2), 315–352 (1995)
MBC$^+$95. Marsan, M.A., Balbo, G., Conte, G., Donatelli, S., Franceschinis, G.: Mod-
          elling with Generalized Stochastic Petri Nets. Wiley Series in Parallel Com-
          puting. Wiley, Chichester (1995)
Pri95.   Priami, C.: Stochastic π calculus. The. Computer Journal 38(6), 578–589
          (1995)
Tro99.   Troubitsyna, E.: Reliability assessment through probabilistic refinement.
          Nordic Journal of Computing 6(3), 320–342 (1999)
WD04.   Wen, L., Dromey, R.G.: From requirements change to design change: A for-
          mal path. In: Int. Conference on Software Engineering and Formal Methods
          (SEFM 2004), pp. 104–113. IEEE Computer Society Press, Los Alamitos
          (2004)
Win04.   Winter, K.: Formalising Behaviour Trees with CSP. In: Boiten, E.A., Der-
          rick, J., Smith, G.P. (eds.) IFM 2004. LNCS, vol. 2999, pp. 148–167.
          Springer, Heidelberg (2004)

Guiding the Correction of Parameterized Specifications

Jean-François Couchot[1,2] and Frédéric Dadeau[3]

[1] INRIA Futurs, ProVal, Parc Orsay Université, F-91893
[2] LRI, Univ Paris-Sud, CNRS, Orsay F-91405

[3] Lab. d'Informatique de Grenoble, BP. 72, Saint-Martin d'Hères F-38402

Abstract. Finding inductive invariants is a key issue in many domains such as program verification, model based testing, etc. However, few approaches help the designer in the task of writing a correct and meaningful model, where correction is used for consistency of the formal specification w.r.t. its inner invariant properties. Meaningfulness is obtained by providing many explicit views of the model, like animation, counter-example extraction, and so on. We propose to ease the task of writing a correct and meaningful formal specification by combining a panel of provers, a set-theoretical constraint solver and some model-checkers.

1 Introduction

When designing safe softwares, writing formal specifications is a hard but valuable task, since consistency between the program and its inner properties can be translated into Proof Obligations (POs) that can then be discharged into some more or less automated prover.

The B method [1] ranges in this scope, by providing a formal development framework. It starts from often parameterized abstract specifications, called abstract machines, that are later refined until a parameter-free implementation is obtained. Intuitively, an abstract machine is composed of state variables, an initialisation operation, some operations that modify the values of state variables and an invariant that represents properties that must hold for each state of the execution.

Invariant verification techniques can be divided into two main categories: model-checking (Spin [28], SMV [35]), which exhaustively explores the states of the execution graph, and deductive approaches, based on automatic provers (Simplify [21], Yices [23], haRVey [20]) or interactive ones (COQ [34], PVS [37], HOL [27]). Intuitively, model-checking aims at checking whether all reachable states satisfy a given property, which is then called an invariant. On the other hand, deductive approaches try to show that a property is inductive, i.e., established by initialisation and preserved through each operation. The B method is conceived as a deductive approach, in which the generated POs

J. Davies and J. Gibbons (Eds.): IFM 2007, LNCS 4591, pp. 176–194, 2007.
© Springer-Verlag Berlin Heidelberg 2007

are discharged into a set-theoretical prover [16,2]. Some model-checkers for B machines have been developed, such as ProB [31] or the BZ-Testing-Tools [3] animator, but all of them require finite and enumerated data structures to work.

Each inductive property is obviously an invariant, whereas an invariant is, seldom if ever, inductive. If the invariant is not inductive, invariance proofs fail. In an interactive mode, the modeler is asked to manually end the proof, which might be useless since the errors are located in the specification. In an automatic mode, the proof may end. When it does, it generally answers "not valid", sometimes while extracting the subformula that originates this answer. This allows the engineer to modify either the invariant, or the code of the operation, or both. When the proof does not terminate, the validity of the considered formula is unknown. Thus, the engineer is left with unknown results concerning the inductivity of the invariants he wrote.

This paper presents an original framework relying on the efficient combination of deductive and model-checking approaches, in order to be able to help the engineer in the process of designing, automatically checking the correctness and (eventually) correcting a formal specification.

This framework is depicted in Fig. 1. We first consider the translation of the formal specification into the Why language. Why [24] is a verification tool that is dedicated to build POs for a variety of provers, and runs them to perform the verification. In case of failure of all the provers, our approach aims at providing a concrete counter-examples for the induction property. This task starts with an instantiation of the parameters, by using recent results in proof techniques applied on software verification [26]. It makes it possible to use CLPS [3], a set-theoretical constraint solver, to solve the instantiated constraint, which results in a counter-example if the formula is invalid. In addition, B animators [31,11] are employed to automatically produce an execution trace leading to this counter-example when it exists. The modeler obtains, for free, some guidance information that helps her/him to modify the incriminated part of her/his formal specification. Furthermore, in order to be able to give a feedback on the PO validity, when the proof does not terminate, or when the prover is unable to decide the theory involved within the formula, we also propose to instantiate the formula before checking its consistency with CLPS.

This paper is organized as follows. Section 2 presents the consistency checking of B machines, that makes it possible to establish their correction, and presents the running example that will illustrate our approach throughout the following sections. We give in Sect. 3 the translation of B machines into the Why language. Then, we present in Sect. 4 the instantiation techniques that are sufficient to compute a counter-example. In Sect. 5, we show how to help the designer in the task of correcting her/his specification by computing an execution trace that leads to the counter-example. Finally, we draw a comparison with some related works in Sect. 6, before we conclude and present future works in Sect. 7.

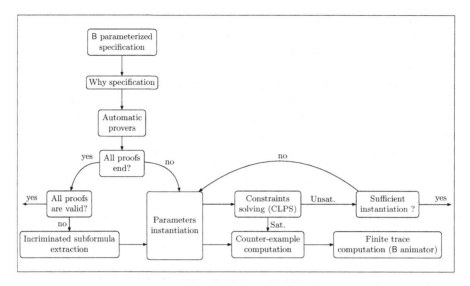

Fig. 1. Combining deductive and constraint-satisfaction approaches

2   Correction of a B Machine

The B formal method [1] was developed by J.-R. Abrial. It scopes the whole software development process, from the abstract specification to the automatic code generation into a classical programming language, such as C or Ada, by using successive refinement steps. The first step details the software as a *machine*, called abstract machine. It may contain abstract data, such as abstract sets or parameters, which makes its behaviors undeterministic. These parameters have to be precised in subsequent refinement steps.

Fig. 2 gives an example of an abstract parameterized machine in the scope of this study.

Semantically, the abstract machine of Fig. 2 simulates the global behavior of a set of processors running in parallel the distributed MESI [38] cache coherence protocol. In this protocol, each processor manages its own cache that can be in one of the following control states M, E, S and I. The global machine state is then defined by the sets m, e, s and i that precise which cache among those of c are respectively in the M, E, S and I control states.

Syntactically, such a B machine is composed of the following clauses:

- the MACHINE clause specifies the machine name and its parameters, that may be finite sets. In the example, the machine is parameterized by c which is the finite set of processors that follow the transition system detailed by the machine.
- The VARIABLES clause contains all the machine state variables, that may be modified by the operations.

```
MACHINE                                    ANY  p WHERE p ∈ c ∧  p ∈ s THEN
   mesiSet(c)                                   m, e, s, i :=
VARIABLES                                       ∅, {p}, ∅, i ∪ m  e ∪ (s \ {p})
   m, e, s, i                              END;
INVARIANT                                  sendRead =
   m, e, s, i ∈ ℙ(c) ∧                        ANY  p WHERE p ∈ c ∧  p ∈ i THEN
   m ∪ e ∪ s ∪ i = c ∧                           m, e, s, i :=
   ⋀ⱼ≠ᵏⱼ,ₖ∈{m,e,s,i} j ∩ k = ∅ ∧                 ∅, ∅, m ∪ e ∪ s ∪ {p}, i \ {p}
   ((∃ p₁ . p₁ ∈ c ∧ p₁ ∈ s) ⇒              END;
      ¬(∃ p₂ . p₂ ∈ c ∧ p₂ ∈ m))          write =
INITIALISATION                                ANY  p WHERE p ∈ c ∧ p ∈ e THEN
   m, e, s, i := ∅, ∅, ∅, c                      e, m := e \ {p}, m ∪ {p}
OPERATIONS                                    END
   sendWriteInvalidate =                  END
```

$$m, e, s, i \in \mathbb{P}(c) \wedge$$
$$m \cup e \cup s \cup i = c \wedge$$
$$\bigwedge_{j,k \in \{m,e,s,i\}}^{j \neq k} j \cap k = \emptyset \wedge$$

Fig. 2. Set-Theoretical B Specification of the MESI Protocol

- The INVARIANT clause contains the I predicate that defines the properties on the state variables that must be initially established and preserved by each operation.

  The first three lines of the INVARIANT specify that set variables m, e, s and i describe a partition of set c, which means that each processor is only in one control state at any time. These lines will be referred as $Inv\_type(m, e, s, i, c)$ in the remainder of the paper. The last two lines of the INVARIANT express a cache coherence property: when a processor is reading, (i.e., in the S control state), no other processor can modify its cache (i.e., is in M). This property will be referred as $Inv\_read(m, e, s, i, c)$ in the following sections. Of course, Inv is the conjunction of Inv_type and Inv_read.

- The INITIALISATION and OPERATIONS clauses contain respectively a (generalized) substitution U assigning an initial value to each state variable and a collection $SUBSTS$ of generalized substitutions that modify their values.

  Any processor can read in its own cache, except if it is in the *Invalidate* state (I), which means that its content is not consistent with central memory. In the *Shared* state (S), the cache content is a copy of central memory. Before it is modified, a cache in state S asks others to be invalidated, by invoking operation sendWriteInvalidate, and switches to *Exclusive* (E state). This control state means that it owns the exclusiveness of writing into the central memory and into the cache. This writing step is represented by the write operation, that moves each cache into the *Modified* state (M). The sendRead operation expresses that a processor with an invalidated cache (i.e. in I state) that requires to read in central memory moves all the *Modified* and *Exclusive* processors to the *Shared* state. Initially, all the processors are *Invalidated*.

Notice that this example illustrates that sets are convenient structures to express local transitions (by adding and removing a singleton), rendez-vous transitions (by adding and removing two singletons), and broadcast transitions (by building the union of sets), commonly used in distributed cache-coherence algorithms.

The POs of a B abstract machine ensure its consistency with respect to the invariant. They are syntactically based on a weakest precondition calculus (syntactically written [ ]) that transforms a predicate according to a generalized substitution. Intuitively, $[S]\,I$ represents the set of states where all successors by S verify I.

POs can be separated into two classes. First, the PO $[U]\,I$ that is valid if and only if the invariant is established by the initialisation. Next, for each substitution $S \in SUBSTS$, the PO $I \Rightarrow [S]\,I$ ensures that the operation defined by S preserves the invariant.

The next section presents how we translate the B machines for the PO generator.

3   Translation into Why Language

In a previous work [19], we have shown how the POs expressing the consistency of a B machine can be discharged into the haRVey prover. Even if this technique is scalable, it is constrained to the evolution of this prover. Instead of developing as many PO generators as there exists provers, we translate the B machine into a Hoare-Floyd style program annotated with assertions corresponding to the invariant and we let a generic tool producing the POs and sending them to several provers.

The Why [24] tool presents this combination of features, allowing to discharge the generated POs into a variety of provers such as Simplify, Zenon [22], CVC-lite [8], Ergo [18], or SMT provers (Yices [23], mathsat [12], rv-sat [25]). Furthermore, it makes it possible to declare logical models as sets of types, functions, predicates and axioms declarations. The axiomatized symbols can be used in both programs and annotations.

Intuitively, the translation of a B machine into the Why language consists, in a first step, in axiomatizing the symbols and, in a second step, in translating the general substitution language into an annotated language. We present hereafter the intuitions of these two steps.

First of all, the theories that are commonly used in B are axiomatized in Why syntax. For instance, here is how we define set theory with a set of axioms, called $SSET$ in [19]

$$\forall\, e\,.\,(e \notin \emptyset), \tag{1}$$

$$\forall\, e\,.\,(e \in \{e\}), \tag{2}$$

$$\forall\, e, f\,.\,(e \neq f \Rightarrow \neg e \in \{f\}), \tag{3}$$

$$\forall\, e, s_1, s_2\,.\,(e \in s_1 \cup s_2 \Leftrightarrow (e \in s_1 \vee e \in s_2)), \tag{4}$$

$$\forall\, e, s_1, s_2\,.\,(e \in s_1 \cap s_2 \Leftrightarrow (e \in s_1 \wedge e \in s_2)), \tag{5}$$

$$\forall\, e, s_1, s_2 \,.\, (e \in s_1 \setminus s_2 \Leftrightarrow (e \in s_1 \wedge \neg e \in s_2)), \tag{6}$$

$$\forall\, s_1, s_2 \,.\, (s_1 \subseteq s_2 \Leftrightarrow \forall\, e.(e \in s_1 \Rightarrow e \in s_2)), \tag{7}$$

$$\forall\, s_1, s_2 \,.\, (s_1 = s_2 \Leftrightarrow \forall\, e.(e \in s_1 \Leftrightarrow e \in s_2)). \tag{8}$$

Such axioms are polymorphic in the sense that they are defined for any element e, f of sort α and any set s_1, s_2 is of sort $\alpha\,\mathrm{SET}$. The typing variable α is instantiated according to the formula it is applied to.

Each symbol of this theory gives rise to two symbols in Why, one for the expression part and one for the predicative part.

For instance, union_ : $\alpha\,\mathrm{SET} \times \alpha\,\mathrm{SET} \rightarrow \alpha\,\mathrm{SET}$, which expresses the union function, is given by

```
parameter union_ : s1: 'a set → s2: 'a set →
  { } 'a set { set_equal(result,union(s1,s2)) }
```

which signifies that, given two sets of α elements, s1 and s2, the result of (union_ s1 s2) is a set of α elements that is equal to the union which is axiomatized with

```
axiom union_def :
  forall s1: 'a set . forall s2: 'a set . forall el : 'a.
    member(union(s1,s2),el) ↔ member(s1,el) or member(s2,el),
```

where member is also axiomatized, according to axioms (1), (2) and (3).

Total function theory is axiomatized by the theory of arrays [6], given by

$$\forall\, a, i, e \,.\, \mathrm{rd}(\mathrm{wr}(a, i, e), i) = e \tag{9}$$

$$\forall\, a, i, j, e \,.\, i \neq j \Rightarrow \mathrm{rd}(\mathrm{wr}(a, i, e), j) = \mathrm{rd}(a, j) \tag{10}$$

$$\forall\, a, b \,.\, (\forall\, i \,.\, \mathrm{rd}(a, i) = \mathrm{rd}(b, i)) \Leftrightarrow a = b \tag{11}$$

where a, b are arrays of sort $(\alpha, \beta)\,\mathrm{ARRAY}$, i, j are indexes of sort α, which allows arrays to be indexed with any sorts, and e is a value of sort β. Other relations (e.g. partial functions) are rewritten into sets of pairs, using symbols defined in *SSET* and the theory of pairs [39],

$$\forall\, i, j \,.\, \pi_1(\langle i, j \rangle) = i$$

$$\forall\, i, j \,.\, \pi_2(\langle i, j \rangle) = j$$

$$\forall\, p \,.\, \langle \pi_1(p), \pi_2(p) \rangle = p$$

where i is of sort α, j is of sort β, p is of sort $(\alpha, \beta)\,\mathrm{PAIR}$ and $\langle\rangle$ has the following signature $\langle\rangle : \alpha \times \beta \rightarrow (\alpha, \beta)\,\mathrm{PAIR}$.

We sketch here the translation of B operations into functions. First of all, the predicate describing the INVARIANT clause is duplicated both in the precondition and in the postcondition of each function encoding an operation. The parameters of the function are those of the operation, plus the local variables in the scope of an ANY operator. The generalized substitutions are directly translated into their counterpart in the Why programming language with assertions.

For instance, the precondition is moved in the precondition part of the function, the if ... then ... else ... structure is translated into its equivalent in Why. The any... where... then ... choice becomes an if ... then ... in Why as follows: the declared variable is introduced as a parameter of the function and the condition of the any is duplicated as in the if condition.

$$S \parallel (S' \parallel S'') = (S \parallel S') \parallel S''$$
$$S \parallel S' = S' \parallel S$$
$$\text{skip} \parallel S = S$$
$$(P \Longrightarrow S) \parallel S' = P \Longrightarrow (S \parallel S')$$
$$(S \, [] \, S') \parallel S'' = (S \parallel S'') \, [] \, (S' \parallel S'')$$
$$(\text{if } P \text{ then } S \text{ else } S') \parallel S'' = \text{if } P \text{ then } (S \parallel S'') \text{ else } (S' \parallel S'')$$
$$(@x \, . \, S) \parallel S' = (@x \, . \, (S \parallel S')) \text{ if } x \text{ is not free in } S'$$

where S, S', S'' are generalized substitutions, P is a predicate, x is a variable.

Fig. 3. Reduction of the $\parallel$ operator

We now focus on the parallel substitution ($\parallel$), classically present in abstract machines. Since this feature is not taken into account by the Why language, we reduce this substitution following a method that is twofold. First, the parallel substitution is reduced until it only concerns assignments, following the rules [9] given in Fig. 3. Next, multiple assignments are classically rewritten into sequential ones by introducing temporary variables storing the expression on the right part of the assignment. Such local variables declarations are encoded with a let... in ... structure in Why.

Back to MESI. The following code is the `write` function translated from the `write` operation where the function parameter p results from the any translation and the local variable t originates from $\parallel$.

```
let write (p : elem) =
{ Inv(m,e,s,i,c) }
if ((member_ !c p) && (member_ !e p) then
 begin
  let t = (minus_ !e  (singleton_ p)) in
  m := (union_ !m  (singleton_ p));
  e := t
 end
{ Inv(m,e,s,i,c) }
```

The results of our experiments on discharging proof with provers that can be plugged into Why are given in Fig. 4 with a timeout (TO) set to 10s for an Intel Pentium 4, 1.7GHz with 756Mb of memory. They reveal how hard it is

Proof Obligations	Simplify	Ergo	Yices	Zenon	haRVey-sat	haRVey-fol	CVC-lite
sendWriteInvalidate	yes	yes	yes	TO	no	unknown	unknown
sendRead	yes	yes	yes	TO	no	unknown	unknown
write	unknown	no	unknown	TO	no	unknown	unknown

Fig. 4. Results of discharging POs

to write a correct specification for first order provers that are not complete but hopefully correct. They show that the `write` function does not seem to respect the invariant: no prover succeeds in establishing the validity of the corresponding proof obligation. In other words, the unsatisfiability of its negation, i.e.

$$Inv(m, e, s, i, c) \land$$
$$\big(\exists\, p\,.\, (p \in c \land p \in e \land \neg Inv(m, e, s, i, c))\big)\big[m \leftarrow m \cup \{p\}, e \leftarrow e \setminus \{p\}\big], \qquad (12)$$

can not be established by any prover.

The designer is then invited to correct the `write` operation or to strengthen the invariant. If she/he guesses that the invariant is not inductive and uses an automated method to strengthen it according to the `write` operation, she/he obtains the following assertion

$$Inv(me, e, s, i, c) \land (\forall\, p\,.\, (p \in c \land p \in e) \Rightarrow Inv(m \cup \{p\}, e \setminus \{p\}, s, i, c))\,. $$
$$(13)$$

Although this approach is correct, it usually leads to invariance formulae that do not make sense and, thus, produces what we absolutely want to avoid, namely meaningless specifications.

The next section shows how to exhibit a counter-example, as a starting point for debugging a specification.

4   Parameter Instantiation

This section suggests two methods for providing a counter-example from a (satisfiable) formula. The first method combines a result in model theory with a constraint solving procedure. The second one, coarser, follows the intuition by applying incremental approach.

4.1   Sort-Based Instantiation

Intuitively, the sets used in a specification often originate from a partitioning of a more general set, and hence, are generally pairwise disjoint. Such sets can be seen as sorts and we are left to check the satisfiability of a formula in a multi-sorted logic. For this formula, the Herbrand satisfiability method takes the sorts into account and produces a finite model when it exists. Such model can be seen as an instantiation of the initial set-theoretical formula. We now detail this approach, composed of five steps.

The first step consists in syntactically extracting the sorts of the formula. Sets declared as machine parameters are considered as primary sorts in a first phase. Then, all abstract sets that are defined as subsets of a primary sort are checked to be pairwise disjoint, and are considered as sorts in a second phase. Predicates that define the sorts are then removed from the invariant formula and in the inherited proof obligations.

The second step is a reduction of set-theoretical symbols: in the remaining formula, all the uninterpreted symbols from the set-theory, except membership (e.g. inclusion, union) are translated into formulas where the sole predicates are equality between two elements of sort α and membership (by applying axioms from (5) to (8) in the left to the right direction of implication). Similarly, equality of arrays is reduced to equality between values by applying axiom (11).

The third step consists in assigning one sort to each variable. The two non obvious cases are when a variable should have two sorts, which results from the union of two sets, and when the variable belongs to a singleton. The former case gives rise to splitting by introducing a fresh variable and duplicating the corresponding subformula. The latter is interpreted by the fact that the variable has the same sort as the element in the singleton. In what follows, $p : \tau$ denotes that p is of sort τ.

Back to MESI. The PO corresponding to (12) in which sets are translated into sorts is

$$((\exists\, p_1 : s) \Rightarrow \neg(\exists\, p_2 : m)) \wedge$$
$$(\exists\, p : e) \wedge (\exists\, p_3 : s) \wedge$$
$$(\exists\, p_{4_a} : m) \vee (\exists\, p_{4_b} : e)$$

where the last line is the result of the interpretation of $(\exists\, p_4 \in m \cup \{p\})$.

The fourth step exploits the multi-sorted Herbrand satisfiability method: we classically start by considering a Skolem form of the formula and use the following quantifier elimination result.

Theorem 1. ([26, Cor. 1]) *Let τ be a sort such that there is no function symbol f of signature $\tau_1 \times \cdots \times \tau_n \rightarrow \tau$, $n \geqslant 1$, and let x be a variable of sort τ. Suppose that $\forall\, x\,.\,\Phi(x)$ is a closed formula in Skolem form, then $\forall\, x\,.\,\Phi(x)$ is satisfiable if and only if the finite conjunction $\bigwedge_{c \in H_\tau} \Phi(c)$ is satisfiable, where H_τ is the set of all well-sorted terms of sort τ.*

Notice that this method might not be complete since all variables do not necessarily occur in the formula. In that case, the remaining set variables are supposed to be the empty set.

Furthermore, in addition to giving a counter-example when validity is not automatically proved, this instantiation technique provides an enumerated specification as general as the parameterized one, since it yields an over approximation of the specification parameters. For the details of the method, see [26]. Such specification is called a *general bounded specification* in the following.

Back to MESI. The multi-sorted Herbrand universe calculus gives the following instantiation

$$m \subseteq \{p_{4_a}\} \wedge e \subseteq \{p_{4_b}, p\} \wedge s \subseteq \{p_3\} \wedge i = \emptyset \wedge c \subseteq \{p, p_3, p_{4_a}, p_{4_b}\} \qquad (14)$$

for PO (12). When applied on other proof obligations, this calculus shows that a set c of cardinality less or equal to 8 is sufficient to make the MESI be a general bounded specification.

The fifth and last step uses the set-theoretical CLPS constraint solver [11] in order to return a counter-example as explicit as possible. CLPS is natively able to manage set-theoretical and relational structures based on the notion of pairs. Thus, it manages relations and all kinds of functions. The native CLPS operators are given in Fig. 5. All other operators from the B notation are rewritten in order to match the solver syntax. For example, let X and Y two relations and consider the B left overriding function $X \lhd\!\!\!\!- Y$ which defines the union between Y and all the pairs $(x, y) \in X$ such that x does not belong to the domain of X. Such expression is substituted with the fresh variable Z, which is constraint by the following set of literals:

$$\{D2 = dom(Y), D1 = dom(X), D3 = D1{-}D2, D4 = D3 \lhd X, Z = D4 \cup Y\}$$

In this formula, dom and $\lhd$ are native CLPS operators.

This solver uses an AC-3 arc consistency algorithm, meaning that the consistency of a constraint system can only be ensured by checking that a solution to the constraint system described by this formula exists. Its strongest requirement is the finiteness of the data domains, which is ensured by previous step.

Solver Primitive	Usual definition	Mathematical notation
A eq B	Equality	$A = B$
A neq B	Disequality	$A \neq B$
A ins S	Membership	$A \in S$
A nin S	Non Membership	$A \notin S$
S sub T	Inclusion	$S \subseteq T$
S # N	Cardinality	$N = card(S)$
rdom(Q,S,R)	Domain Restriction	$Q = S \lhd R$
dom(S,R)	Domain	$S = dom(R)$
ran(S,R)	Range	$S = ran(R)$
inv(Q,R)	Inverse relation	$Q = R^{-1}$
power(T,S)	Powerset	$T = \mathbb{P}(S)$
pcart(S,T,U)	Cartesian product	$S = T \times U$
couple(X,Y)	Couple	$X \mapsto Y$
S union T	Union	$S \cup T$
S inter T	Intersection	$S \cap T$
S setminus T	Set difference	$S \setminus T$

Fig. 5. Operators of the CLPS set solver

Back to MESI. The ground formula (14) $\wedge$ (12) is given to CLPS which concludes that it is satisfiable for $m = \emptyset$, $e = \{p\}$, $s = \{p_3\}$ and $i = \emptyset$.

4.2   Incremental Instantiation

The instantiation technique presented in Sect. 4.1 is obtained by applying the theorem given in [26]. This theorem requires several conditions to be applied. When it is not applicable, our proposal is to automatically perform an incremental instantiation of the abstract sets.

The idea is to consider arbitrarily finite sets for each abstract set. These sets must be finite and contain a large number of constants. For instance, one can start from a partial Herbrand instantiation if this one is infinite. Thus, the data domains are finite. The conjunction of the formula with this instantiation constraint is then given to CLPS, as previously, to check its satisfiability.

Back to MESI. Suppose that the prover was unable to conclude on the example, an instantiation of $c = \{\widetilde{q}_1, \widetilde{q}_2, \widetilde{q}_3, \ldots, \widetilde{q}_N\}$ is computed by iterating over the values of N. The instantiated formula is then given to CLPS which checks its satisfiability.

Figure 6 shows the results of this experiment on PO formula (12), for which we iterated over the size of c from 1 to 4. In this figure, each $\widetilde{q}_i$, $1 \leqslant i \leqslant 4$, is a fresh constant. The minimal counter-example is obtained for a set c containing two elements, as in Sect. 4.1.

Value of c	Satisfiability of (12)	Example
$\{\widetilde{q}_1\}$	no	none
$\{\widetilde{q}_1, \widetilde{q}_2\}$	yes	$s = \{\widetilde{q}_1\}, e = \{\widetilde{q}_2\}$
$\{\widetilde{q}_1, \widetilde{q}_2, \widetilde{q}_3\}$	yes	$s = \{\widetilde{q}_1, \widetilde{q}_2\}, e = \{\widetilde{q}_3\}$
$\{\widetilde{q}_1, \widetilde{q}_2, \widetilde{q}_3, \widetilde{q}_4\}$	yes	$s = \{\widetilde{q}_1, \widetilde{q}_2, \widetilde{q}_3\}, e = \{\widetilde{q}_4\}$

Fig. 6. Results using an iterative instantiation on the example

The designer is left with the choice of strengthening the invariant or modifying the operations. The next section shows how we can guide her/him in this choice.

5   Reaching the Counter-Example

The previous section ends with an instantiation of the state variables that makes the invariant not inductive. Thus, all data in the B specification are finite and different techniques, such as model-checking may be applied. We propose to first integrate ProB [31] to find a counter-example. If the system is too complex for the model-checking to be applied, we propose to use symbolic animation to reach a counter-example. In this latter case, we use the symbolic animation engine of the BZ-Testing-Tools [3,11] framework, in order to compute an execution trace that leads to the violation of the invariant. This engine has already been put into practice in the framework of automated generation of boundary test cases from set-theoretical B models [4,5].

The two animators impose a strong requirement that the model must be finite. Such a requirement is compliant with our method, as presented in the previous section which may produce a general bounded specification When the method cannot be applied, an incremental instantiation of the parameters is repeatly applied to check the reachability of the counter-example.

In this section, we first introduce ProB and we present its application on the MESI example (Sect. 5.1). Then, in order to demonstrate the scalability of our approach, we formalize the notion of symbolic animation (Sect. 5.2), we give some efficiency keynotes on the BZ-Testing-Tools animator (Sect. 5.3) and we show how to interpret the animation results, by pointing out of which part of the specification should be modified (Sect. 5.4).

5.1   Using the ProB Model-Checker

ProB [31] is a model checker that relies on constraint solving technologies to compute the transitions between states. From a given state, ProB compute all the successors and checks whether the invariant is true or false within these states. If the invariant is checked as false, it returns an execution path that provides a counter-example. ProB offers heuristics to detect permutations in states and is optimized to handle relatively large states spaces [32,33].

Back to MESI. We instantiate the MESI machine, setting the parameter c to 8 elements. ProB computes in 10 seconds the 270 states of the system execution, and does not find a violation of the invariant. Thus, we conclude that the invariant is not inductive, but still, it is an invariant, which can not be violated during the possible executions of the system.

Since ProB enumerates the complete reachability graph of the B specification execution, it may face the problem of combinatorial explosion, when applied to large systems. Therefore, we propose to use symbolic animation in order to handle large state spaces.

5.2   Symbolic Animation

Symbolic animation consists in using an underlying constraint solver for representing symbolic states, each of which gather a possibly large number of concrete states. Thus, it avoids the exhaustive enumeration of possible states, as done in ProB [31], by providing an optimization that increases the scalability of the approach.

A *symbolic state* is a constraints system over the state variables, that represents a set of concrete states, whose state variable values are the solutions of this constraint system. Thus, a symbolic state is seen as a set of constraints over the state variables. The consistency of these constraints guarantees that the symbolic state represents at least one concrete state; there are as many concrete state as solutions to the constraint system.

5.3 Efficiency Keynotes on the BZ-Testing-Tools Animator

This section presents the keynotes on the BZ-Testing-Tools animator. To show how convenient the animator is for the task of checking the reachability of a counter-example, we focus on its relevant features: behavior extraction and behavior animation heuristic.

First of all, the possible transitions are extracted from the B operations, as a path through the control-flow graph of the considered operation. Intuitively, an if ... then ... else ... structure is split into two subparts, the first one representing the if ... then part, the second one representing the else part.

Each B operation is then decomposed into *behaviors*, which represent a path in the control-flow graph of the operation. A behavior $b(P, X, X')$ is expressed as a predicate over P, X and X' which respectively stand for the operation parameters, the current values of state variables and their next values. Consider for instance the B operation in Fig. 7, where x is a state variable of type BOOL. It is composed of the two behaviors $(p \in 0..1000 \land p \leq 500 \land x' = TRUE)$ and $(p \in 0..1000 \land p > 500 \land x' = FALSE)$. Notice that on the MESI example, given in Fig. 2, each operation has only one behavior.

Activating a behavior of an operation from a functional model is seen as solving a constraint satisfaction problem between the state before the operation and the constraints given by the transition of the operation. More formally, let $\rho_1(X)$ be a symbolic state and let $b(P, X, X')$ be a behavior extracted from an operation, symbolic state $\rho_2(X')$ resulting from the activation of b in ρ_1 is defined by

$$\rho_2(X') = \rho_1(X) \land \exists P . b(P, X, X').$$

The behavior b is said to be activable in ρ_1 if and only if the resulting constraint system is satisfiable.

Back to MESI. Consider the MESI example, with a finite set c arbitrarily instantiated to $c = \{\tilde{q}_1, \tilde{q}_2, \tilde{q}_3, \tilde{q}_4\}$. Let $\rho_1(m_0, e_0, s_0, i_0)$ be

$$m_0 = \emptyset \land e_0 = \emptyset \land s_0 = \emptyset \land i_0 = \{\tilde{q}_1, \tilde{q}_2, \tilde{q}_3, \tilde{q}_4\}$$

```
op1(p)  ≙
    PRE
            p  ∈    0..1000
    THEN
            IF  p  ≤    500  THEN
                    x  :=  TRUE
            ELSE
                    x  :=  FALSE
            END
    END
```

Fig. 7. A simple B operation with two behaviors

i.e. the symbolic state representing the initial state. The set of symbolic states resulting from the activation of the sendRead operation is defined by

$$\rho_2(m_1, e_1, s_1, i_1) \equiv \rho_1(m_0, e_0, s_0, i_0) \wedge \exists\, p_0 \cdot p_0 \in i_0 \wedge$$
$$m_1 = m_0 \wedge e_1 = e_0 \wedge s_1 = s_0 \cup \{p_0\} \wedge i_1 = i_0 \backslash \{p_0\}$$

which is satisfiable, if and only if

$$\rho_2(m_1, e_1, s_1, i_1) \equiv \rho_1(m_0, e_0, s_0, i_0) \wedge \widetilde{p}_0 \in \{\widetilde{q}_1, \widetilde{q}_2, \widetilde{q}_3, \widetilde{q}_4\} \wedge$$
$$m_1 = \emptyset \wedge e_1 = \emptyset \wedge s_1 = \{\widetilde{p}_0\} \wedge i_1 = \{\widetilde{q}_1, \widetilde{q}_2, \widetilde{q}_3, \widetilde{q}_4\} \backslash \{\widetilde{p}_0\}$$

is, where $\widetilde{p}_0$ is the Skolem constant of p_0. Such a predicate implicitly represents 4 concrete states, according to the value of $\widetilde{p}_0$ in $\{\widetilde{q}_1, \widetilde{q}_2, \widetilde{q}_3, \widetilde{q}_4\}$.

Symbolic animation consists in repeating this process at will, for each operation, until a pertinent state is reached. Notice that symbolic states are never enumerated. This technique reduces the reachability graph size and delays combinatorial explosion. The BZ-Testing-Tools animator implements these principles. It is provided with a Graphical User Interface, that makes it possible to validate a B model. Nevertheless, it is also possible to use the API of the animator to automatically animate a B model. In this case, the animation can be randomized, or guided by a target, reached by using heuristics as it is now described. The heuristic aims at guiding the choice of behaviors –and, as the consequence, of operations– to activate in order to reach the counter-example.

The counter-example trace computation uses the symbolic animation guided by a "best-first" algorithm and a customized heuristic function. This algorithm aims at defining whether a symbolic state is pertinent w.r.t. the given target or not. The trace computation aims at reaching a state that satisfies the constraints given by the predicate describing the counter-example. The parameters of the activated operation are left unspecified until the search ends with a counter-example that instantiates them. The heuristic we use consists in computing the distance from the current symbolic state to the target to reach, also considered as a symbolic state. The *distance between two symbolic states* is evaluated as sum of the distances between the symbolic values of all variables in these states.

A symbolic variable is defined by a domain and associated constraints depending on other variables. The *distance between two symbolic variables* (represented by Diff in the Fig. 8) is evaluated to 0 if and only if the domains of the two variables intersect. Otherwise, the distance depends on the type of the data, and the proximity of the two domains.

Figure 8 illustrates the concept of distance between two domains. In this figure, "VarDom" represents the variable domain, "CurrVarDom" is the domain of the current state variable, "TargetVarDom" is the domain of the variable in the targeted state, and "UnifiedDom" is the unification of the two variables, i.e., the intersection of the latter two domains. Such heuristic has been shown to beat other approaches in symbolic animation [17].

Back to MESI. Running the counter-example search algorithm does not detect any counter-example for a depth of 6, in 17 seconds.

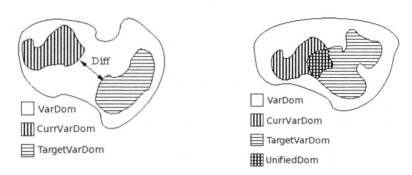

Fig. 8. Distance between two variables

Compared to ProB, this algorithm does not produce a better result on a small example. Moreover, the result of the algorithm is partial (since it is bounded), whereas in ProB it is absolute. Indeed, the computational complexity of the algorithm is $\mathcal{O}(n^d)$ where n is the number of behaviors extracted from the B machine operations, and d is the search depth. Nevertheless, this heuristic is useful. First, it makes it possible to handle large systems, and thus, it is possible to provide a result even when ProB fails. In addition, it is important to notice that this algorithm only aims at quickly and efficiently finding a trace, when it exists. If the trace does not exist, as in the MESI example, the computation of all symbolic paths of a given depth has to be performed before concluding, matching the worst case computational complexity.

5.4   Interpreting the Reachability Result

Basically, there are three possible issues for the animation. The first case is when the animator ends after having reached the counter-example. In this case, the formula claimed to be an invariant is not one, let-alone an inductive invariant. The spurious operations may be corrected by strengthening their guards.

The second case is when the analysis ends on the general bounded specification with an unreachable counter-example, when the graph is small enough to be completely explored. In this case, the method has computed the strongest invariant, which is indeed inductive but may be meaningless for the specifier (in the running example, it contains 270 states!). We propose that the specifier strenghten the invariant by removing the states corresponding to the counter-example.

The third case is when the bounded animator gives an unreachability answer for an arbitrarily instantiated specification: since reachability is undecidable, the search depth is bounded, and so, it is possible that no counter-example trace will be found. What does it mean if the invariant has not been checked as inductive? The states that cause the invariant to be violated can simply be unreachable, and the B specification is still correct.

The answer depends on the goal of the specification. If the specification aims at establishing B refinement properties, it is mandatory that the invariant is strengthened to be inductive. If the specification aims at verifying safety properties or generating test cases, the guarantee that the invariant cannot be violated for a given execution depth k may be sufficient. Even in a test generation process, it is still possible to run the generated tests (whose size is greater than k) on the specification, and to check that no test provokes a violation of the invariant.

Back to MESI. We give to the animator the general bounded specification MESI, such that c has cardinality less than or equal to 8. It concludes that the counter-example cannot be reached. The designer is then invited to strenghten the invariant by removing states where s and e are simultaneously non empty, which is given by the new invariant

$$Inv\_type(m, e, s, i, c) \wedge ((\exists\, p_1 . p_1 \in c \wedge p_1 \in s) \Rightarrow$$
$$(\neg(\exists\, p_2 . p_2 \in c \wedge p_2 \in m) \wedge \neg(\exists\, p_3 . p_3 \in c \wedge p_3 \in e))).$$

This invariant is both meaningful and inductive.

6   Related Work

To the best of our knowledge, the approach we present here is original and has never been introduced previously.

Several works [7,13,26] have shown cases where all subtleties of a parameterized system are already present in some instantiated version of it. As done in this paper, these work strongly rely on the fact that the correctness of a small instantiated system implies the correctness of the parameterized one. Unfortunately, such methods build a consistency proof by providing strengthened invariants which may be to involved for the designer to understand (it is even referred as *invisible invariants* in [7] since they may not be seen). In this work, less ambitious but more pragmatic, the model instantiation is computed thanks to sorts. By translating sets into sorts, we follow the idea previously developed in [10].

Similar work exists on combining test generation and proof. In [30], the authors describe a process that aims at increasing the confidence in a Java program that has not been proved correct w.r.t. its JML specification. Indeed, when the prover fails to establish the correctness of a piece of code, a large suite of tests cases is produced. The process is different from our approach, since we systematically compute a reachable counter-example. Moreover, we only focus on the specification itself, without having to take a particular implementation into account.

The work we present in this paper is also related to bounded model-checking (BMC) [14], in which a model execution is computed until a given depth to check whether different properties are satisfied. In practice, BMC has been applied to the verification of safety properties [40]. Our work differs from the other animation/model-checking approaches, such as [15,36,31,35], in the sense that, for us, the animation is only employed to find a counter-example. Indeed, most of the other approaches consider animation itself as the answer to the verification problem. For us, animation is complementary to proof techniques. Moreover, our proposal makes it possible to deal with a parameterized models, that cannot be treated by classical animators without being first instantiated. From that point of view, the trinity Proof-Instantiation-Animation proposed here is clearly original.

7   Conclusion and Future Work

This paper has presenteed strategies of collaboration between provers and symbolic animators using constraint solving, in order to help the specifier dealing with the answers given by these tools. The relevance of this help is illustrated in the context of the correction of parameterized B machines.

First, the provers have to be automated, in order to avoid the hazard of having to manually deal with some subtle proof obligations, that dismiss the modeller from her/his initial specification work. Second, the goal of checking parameterized systems makes it mandatory to resort to theorem proving techniques. Third, parameter-related data are a burden for all theorem provers. Even when the termination of the computation is experimentally observed, it cannot in general be theoretically determined. Thus, it is sometimes necessary to stop the execution of the prover if it seems to diverge. Fourth, the unavoidable instantiation of parameters makes it possible to compute a counter-example, and an associated execution trace, using advanced constraint solving techniques.

Among the tools we have considered, the Why tool is especially interesting, since it addresses a large variety of provers, working on different theories. This increases the chances for a proof obligation not checked by one of the provers to be checked by another one.

For the future, we are curently implementing a complete tool chain that aims at automatically checking the correctness of B invariants by combining proof and constraint solving, as described in Fig. 1. This will make it possible for us to validate our approach on realistic and industrial case studies. Separated experiments with Why tool [29] and BZ-Testing-Tools [3] that target the verification or validation of large-scale systems are very promising.

References

1. Abrial, J.-R.: The B Book - Assigning Programs to Meanings, August 1996. Cambridge University Press, Cambridge (1996)
2. Abrial, J.-R., Cansell, D.: Click'n'prove: Interactive proofs within set theory. In: Basin, D., Wolff, B. (eds.) TPHOLs 2003. LNCS, vol. 2758, pp. 1–24. Springer, Heidelberg (2003)
3. Ambert, F., Bouquet, F., Chemin, S., Guenaud, S., Legeard, B., Peureux, F., Vacelet, N., Utting, M.: BZ-TT: A tool-set for test generation from Z and B using constraint logic programming. In: Proc. of Formal Approaches to Testing of Software FATES 2002, co-located with CONCUR '02, pp. 105–120, INRIA Technical Report (August 2002)

4. Ambert, F., Bouquet, F., Legeard, B., Peureux, F.: Automated boundary-value test generation from specifications - method and tools. In: 4th Int. Conf. on Software Testing, ICSTEST 2003, pp. 52–68 (2003)
5. Ambert, F., Bouquet, F., Legeard, B., Peureux, F., Py, L., Torrebore, E.: Automated Test Case and Test Driver Generation for Embedded Software. In: ICSSEA - Int. Conf. on Software, System Engineering and Applications, December 2004, pp. 34–49 (2004)
6. Armando, A., Ranise, S., Rusinowitch, M.: A rewriting approach to satisfiability procedures. Journal of Information and computation 183, 140–164 (2003) Special Issue on the 12th International Conference on Rewriting Techniques and Applications (RTA'01) (2003)
7. Arons, T., Pnueli, A., Ruah, S., Xu, J., Zuck, L.D.: Parameterized verification with automatically computed inductive assertions. In: Berry, G., Comon, H., Finkel, A. (eds.) CAV 2001. LNCS, vol. 2102, pp. 221–234. Springer, Heidelberg (2001)
8. Barrett, C., Berezin, S.: CVC Lite: A new implementation of the cooperating validity checker. In: Alur, R., Peled, D.A. (eds.) CAV 2004. LNCS, vol. 3114, Springer, Heidelberg (2004)
9. Bert, D., Potet, M.-L.: La méthode B. École Jeunes chercheurs en programmation (May 2003)
10. Bodeveix, J.-P., Filali, M., Munoz, C.: A Formalization of the B method in Coq Available at http://www.csl.sri.com/papers/pbs2/
11. Bouquet, F., Legeard, B., Peureux, F.: A constraint solver to animate a B specification. International Journal on Software Tools for Technology Transfer 6(2), 143–157 (2004)
12. Bozzano, M., Bruttomesso, R., Cimatti, A., Junttila, T., van Rossum, P., Schulz, S., Sebastiani, S.: MathSAT: Tight integration of SAT and decision procedures. Journal of Automated Reasoning 35, 265–293 (2005)
13. Chou, C.-T., Mannava, P.K., Park, S.: A simple method for parameterized verification of cache coherence protocols. In: Hu, A.J., Martin, A.K. (eds.) FMCAD 2004. LNCS, vol. 3312, pp. 382–398. Springer, Heidelberg (2004)
14. Clarke, E., Biere, A., Raimi, R., Zhu, Y.: Bounded model checking using satisfiability solving. Formal Methods in System Design 19(1), 7–34 (2001)
15. Clarke, E.M., Grumberg, O., Peled, A.: Model Checking (CLA e 99:1 1.Ex). MIT Press, Cambridge (1999)
16. ClearSy. Manuel de référence du langage B v.1.8.5. (2004) Available at http://www.atelierb.societe.com/ressources/manrefb.185.fr.pdf
17. Colin, S.: Procédures de recherche en génération de tests à partir de modéles de spécifications. PhD thesis, LIFC - University of Franche-Comté (2005)
18. Conchon, S., Contejean, E.: The Ergo automatic theorem prover (2006) Available at http://ergo.lri.fr/
19. Couchot, J.-F., Déharbe, D., Giorgetti, A., Ranise, S.: Scalable automated proving and debugging of set-based specifications. Journal of the Brazilian Computer Society 9(2), 17–36 (2003) ISSN 0104-6500
20. Déharbe, D., Ranise, S.: Light-weight theorem proving for debugging and verifying units of code. In: 1st International Conference on Software Engineering and Formal Methods (SEFM'03), pp. 220–228 (2003)
21. Detlefs, D., Nelson, G., Saxe, J.B.: Simplify: a theorem prover for program checking. J. ACM 52(3), 365–473 (2005)
22. Doligez, D.: The zenon prover. Distributed with the Focal Project, at http://focal.inria.fr/

23. Dutertre, B., de Moura, L.M.: A Fast Linear-Arithmetic Solver for DPLL(T). In: Ball, T., Jones, R.B. (eds.) CAV 2006. LNCS, vol. 4144, pp. 81–94. Springer, Heidelberg (2006)
24. Filliâtre, J.-C.: Why: a multi-language multi-prover verification tool. Research Report 1366, LRI, Université Paris Sud (March 2003)
25. Fontaine, P.: haRVey-sat (2006) Available at http://harvey.loria.fr/haRVey.html
26. Fontaine, P., Gribomont, E.P.: Decidability of invariant validation for parameterized systems. In: Garavel, H., Hatcliff, J. (eds.) ETAPS 2003 and TACAS 2003. LNCS, vol. 2619, pp. 97–112. Springer, Heidelberg (2003)
27. Gordon, M.J.C., Melham, T.F. (eds.): Introduction to HOL (A theorem-proving environment for higher order logic). Cambridge University Press, Cambridge (1993)
28. Holzmann, G.: The model checker SPIN. Software Engineering 23(5), 279–295 (1997)
29. Hubert, T., Marché, C.: A case study of C source code verification: the Schorr-Waite algorithm. In: 3rd IEEE International Conference on Software Engineering and Formal Methods (SEFM'05), pp. 190–199. IEEE Computer Society Press, Los Alamitos (2005)
30. Ledru, Y., du Bousquet, L., Dadeau, F., Allouti, F.: A case study in matching test and proof coverage. In: Proceedings of the Third International Workshop on Model-Based Testing (MBT'07), co-located with ETAPS'07, to be pubilshed in ENTCS (2007)
31. Leuschel, M., Butler, M.: Pro B: A model checker for B. In: Araki, K., Gnesi, S., Mandrioli, D. (eds.) FME 2003. LNCS, vol. 2805, pp. 855–874. Springer, Heidelberg (2003)
32. Leuschel, M., Butler, M., Spermann, C., Turner, E.: Symmetry reduction for B by permutation flooding. In: Julliand, J., Kouchnarenko, O. (eds.) B 2007. LNCS, vol. 4355, pp. 79–93. Springer, Heidelberg (2006)
33. Leuschel, M., Turner, E.: Visualising Larger State Spaces in ProB. In: Treharne, H., King, S., Henson, M.C., Schneider, S. (eds.) ZB 2005. LNCS, vol. 3455, pp. 6–23. Springer, Heidelberg (2005)
34. The Coq development team. The Coq proof assistant reference manual. LogiCal Project, Version 8.0 (2004)
35. McMillan, K.L.: The SMV system. Carnegie-Mellon University (1992)
36. Miller, T., Strooper, P.: Animation can show only the presence of errors, never their absence. In: ASWEC '01: Proceedings of the 13th Australian Conference on Software Engineering, p. 76. IEEE Computer Society Press, Los Alamitos (2001)
37. Owre, S., Rushby, J.M., Shankar, N.: PVS: a prototype verification system. In: Kapur, D. (ed.) Automated Deduction - CADE-11. LNCS, vol. 607, pp. 748–752. Springer, Heidelberg (1992)
38. Papamarcos, M.S., Patel, J.H.: A low-overhead coherence solution for multiprocessors with private cache memories. In: ISCA '84: Proceedings of the 11th annual international symposium on Computer architecture, pp. 348–354. ACM Press, New York (1984)
39. Ranise, S.: Satisfiability solving for program verification: towards the efficient combination of Automated Theorem Provers and Satisfiability Modulo Theory Tools. In: Ahrendt, W., Baumgartner, P., de Nivelle, H. (eds.) Proc. of the DISPROVING: Non-Validity, Non-Provability, co-located with IJCAR 2006, pp. 49–58 (2006)
40. Sheeran, M., Singh, S., Stålmarck, G.: Checking safety properties using induction and a sat-solver. In: Johnson, S.D., Hunt Jr., W.A. (eds.) FMCAD 2000. LNCS, vol. 1954, pp. 108–125. Springer, Heidelberg (2000)

Proving Linearizability Via Non-atomic Refinement

John Derrick[1], Gerhard Schellhorn[2], and Heike Wehrheim[3]

[1]Department of Computing, University of Sheffield, Sheffield, UK
J.Derrick@dcs.shef.ac.uk
[2]Universität Augsburg, Institut für Informatik, 86135 Augsburg, Germany
schellhorn@informatik.uni-augsburg.de
[3]Universität Paderborn, Institut für Informatik, 33098 Paderborn, Germany
wehrheim@uni-paderborn.de

Abstract. Linearizability is a correctness criterion for concurrent objects. In this paper, we prove linearizability of a concurrent lock-free stack implementation by showing the implementation to be a *non-atomic refinement* of an abstract stack. To this end, we develop a generalisation of non-atomic refinement allowing one to refine a single (Z) operation into a CSP process. Besides this extension, the definition furthermore embodies a termination condition which permits one to prove *starvation freedom* for the concurrent processes.

Keywords: Object-Z, CSP, refinement, concurrent access, linearizability.

1 Introduction

Linearizability was defined by Herlihy and Wing [14] as a correctness criterion for objects shared by concurrent processes. Like serialisability for database transactions, it permits one to view concurrent operations on objects as though they occur in some sequential order. As Herlihy and Wing put it,

> Linearizability provides the illusion that each operation applied by concurrent processes takes effect instantaneously at some point between its invocation and its response.

Recently, Groves et al. [9,4] started work on verifying correctness (and more specifically linearizability) of concurrent data structures using forward and backward simulations between I/O-automata. Concurrent data structures allow concurrent access by several processes, the only atomic operations being the reading of variables and an atomic *compare-and-swap* (atomically comparing the values of two variables plus setting a variable). In general concurrent access increases the level of parallelism in the use of the data structure but potentially introduces flaws due to individual atomic operations being applied out of order (with respect to what was required by the design). Linearizability is a correctness condition that is used to check whether such flaws have been introduced, it is, however, not

J. Davies and J. Gibbons (Eds.): IFM 2007, LNCS 4591, pp. 195–214, 2007.

trivial to demonstrate that linearizability holds. The approach taken by Groves et al. uses I/O-automata to model the concurrent implementation as well as an abstract data structure in which operations are taken to be atomic. Correctness of the implementation is shown via forward and backward simulations between these automata (with proofs conducted in PVS), that is, the simulations guarantee linearizability, and the allowable orderings of concrete operations is described via program counters.

In this paper, we investigate the use of (Object-)Z refinement [7,20] as a means for showing the correctness, and in particular linearizability, of concurrent implementations of abstract data structures. However, in moving between an abstract data structure and its concurrent implementation the granularity of operations completely change, we therefore have to employ *non-atomic refinement* as the correctness criteria. Non-atomic refinement as defined in [5,6] allows an abstract operation to be implemented by a *sequence* of concrete operations. We generalise this here since our objective is to encode the orderings of concrete operations not via program counters or sequences but more naturally by *process* descriptions, and we use CSP [15] to model this. The description of the concurrent implementation is thus given in a combination of CSP and Object-Z (in CSP-OZ [11]). As a consequence, the existing definition of non-atomic refinement (only allowing for fixed sequences of concrete operations) is generalised to include operation decompositions given as CSP processes. We prove that this definition of non-atomic refinement guarantees linearizability.

In addition to linearizability, we study *progress* properties for concurrent data structures. As the concurrent implementations need to guarantee interference-freedom for concurrent accesses, operations which have already been partly carried out might need to be reset or retried. This potentially introduces starvation of processes. While Groves et al. are concerned with proving safety properties, i.e. linearizability, we, in addition, show that a particular form of starvation freedom to be also guaranteed by definition of non-atomic refinement that we use. To do this, we introduce a condition on a *variant* in our simulation rules, similar to variants employed in Event_B [2]. The whole approach is exemplified by the example of a concurrent stack implementation from [4].

The paper is structured as follows. The next section introduces our running example of a concurrent stack modelled in a combination of Object-Z and CSP. Section 3 sets the ground for our investigations, giving amongst others the existing definition of non-atomic refinement in Z, more specifically the forward simulation rules. This definition is then generalised in Section 4 to allow refinements of a single operation into a whole CSP process. In Section 5 we show that this generalised definition of non-atomic refinement guarantees linearizability. The last section concludes and discusses related work.

2 An Abstract and a Concrete Stack

As an example of a data structure and its concurrent implementation we take the lock-free implementation of a stack as treated in [4]. Abstractly, the stack is a sequence of elements of some given type T (containing some dedicated element *empty*) together with two operations *push* and *pop*. Here, we will use plain Object-Z [10,19] to describe the abstract stack and a combination of Object-Z and CSP (CSP-OZ [11]) for the implementation.

In Object-Z, a class specification consists of a state schema defining the variables of the class, an initialisation schema giving constraints for initial states and a number of operation schemas. An operation schema defines the variables to be changed by the operation (in a Δ-list), declares inputs and outputs (with ? and !, respectively) and gives constraints on the allowed changes. Primed variables in these predicates refer to after states. For instance, operation *pop* below is allowed to change *stack*, has an output variable $v!$ and defines the output to be *empty* when the stack is empty, and to be the head of the stack otherwise. In the former case the stack remains unchanged, in the latter the top element is removed.

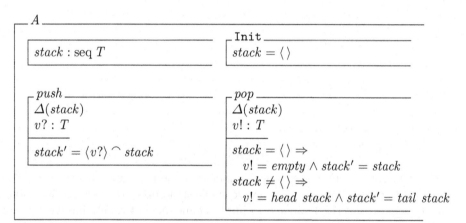

Next, the stack is implemented by a linked list of nodes. A node consists of a value *val* : T and a pointer *next* to the next node in the list. The pointer may also be empty (value *null*). A variable *head* is used to keep track of the current head of the list. Operations *push* and *pop* are split into several smaller operations, making new nodes, swapping pointers etc.. There is one operation atomically carrying out a comparison of values and an assignment: $CAS(mem, exp, new)$ (Compare-and-swap) compares *mem* to *exp*; if this succeeds *mem* is set to *new* and CAS returns *true*, otherwise the CAS fails, leaves *mem* unchanged and returns *false*. Below the implementations of *pop* and *push* are first given in pseudo-code. (Note, that *pop* continues on the next page.)

```
push(v : T):              pop(): T:
1   n:= new(Node);        1   repeat
2   n.val := n;           2       ss:= Head;
3   repeat                3       if ss = null then
4       ss:= Head;        4           return empty;
5       n.next := ss;     5       ssn := ss.next;
```

```
6  until CAS(Head,ss,n)              6       lv := ss.val
                                     7       until CAS(Head,ss,ssn);
                                     8       return lv
```

The *push* operation first creates a new node with the value to be pushed onto the stack. It then repeatedly sets a local variable *ss* to *head* and the pointer of the new node to *ss*. This ends once the final *CAS* detects that *head* (still) equals *ss* upon which *head* is set to the new node *n*. Note that the *CAS* in *push* does not necessarily succeed: in case of a concurrent pop, *head* might have been changed in between. The *pop* is similar: it memorizes the head it started with in *ss*, then determines the remaining list and the output value. If *head* is still equal to *ss* in the end, the pop takes effect and the output value is returned.

For an Object-Z description of this, we first have to define an appropriate free type for the linked list and operations for extracting values from nodes in the list.

$$Node ::= node\langle\!\langle T \times Node \rangle\!\rangle \mid null$$

$$
\begin{array}{l}
\mline first : Node \nrightarrow T \\
\hline
\forall t : T, n : Node \bullet \\
\quad first\ node(t, n) = t
\end{array}
\qquad
\begin{array}{l}
second : Node \nrightarrow T \\
\hline
\forall t : T, n : Node \bullet \\
\quad second\ node(t, n) = n
\end{array}
$$

$$
\begin{array}{l}
collect : Node \nrightarrow seq\,T \\
\hline
collect = \lambda N.\ \textbf{if}\ N = null\ \textbf{then}\ \langle\rangle\ \textbf{else}\ \langle first(N)\rangle \frown collect(second(N))
\end{array}
$$

$collect(N)$ constructs the sequence of nodes reachable from N. It is undefined for cyclic structures. Since in our example cyclic structures are not used, we assume all equations $collect(N) = stack$ to imply definedness of $collect$ implicitly.

The class specifying the implementation of the stack contains an Object-Z part describing all the operations of the above given pseudo-code. The numbering is according to line numbers in the pseudo-code, but where we have sometimes merged two operations into one (e.g., *psh2* incorporates lines 1 and 2).

In addition to the Object-Z, we have a number of CSP process equations describing the possible orderings of these operations. We use a small fragment of CSP, specifically, $\rightarrow$ stands for the prefix operator of CSP (sequencing) and $\Box$ is the external choice. The main process, $\texttt{main} = U \;|||\; O$, specifies that the push and pop operations are to be executed concurrently, since processes O and U specify that every stack object should continously allow *pop*'s and *push*'s. Finally, the CSP processes *PUSH* and *POP* model one execution of the above pseudo-code programs, respectively.

$$
\begin{array}{l}
\underline{C}\rule{8cm}{0.4pt} \\
\texttt{main} = U \;|||\; O \qquad U = PUSH;\ U \qquad O = POP;\ O \\
PUSH = psh2 \rightarrow Rep \\
Rep = psh4 \rightarrow psh5 \rightarrow (CAS_t psh \rightarrow Skip \\
\qquad\qquad\qquad\qquad\quad \Box\ CAS_f psh \rightarrow Rep)
\end{array}
$$

$POP = pop2 \rightarrow (pop3t \rightarrow Skip$
$\qquad\qquad \Box\; pop3f \rightarrow pop5 \rightarrow pop6 \rightarrow (CAS_t pop \rightarrow Skip$
$\qquad\qquad\qquad\qquad\qquad\qquad\qquad\qquad \Box\; CAS_f pop \rightarrow POP))$

$head, sso, ssu, ssn, n : Node$
$lv : T$

__Init_____
$head = null$

__psh2_____
$\Delta(n)$
$v? : T$

$n' = node(v?, null)$

__psh4_____
$\Delta(ssu)$

$ssu' = head$

__psh5_____
$\Delta(n)$

$n' = node(first\; n, ssu)$

__$CAS_t psh$_____
$\Delta(head)$

$head = ssu$
$head' = n$

__$CAS_f psh$_____

$head \neq ssu$

__pop2_____
$\Delta(sso)$

$sso' = head$

__pop3t_____
$v! : T$

$sso = null \wedge v! = empty$

__pop3f_____

$sso \neq null$

__pop5_____
$\Delta(ssn)$

$ssn' = second\; sso$

__pop6_____
$\Delta(lv)$

$lv' = first\; sso$

__$CAS_t pop$_____
$\Delta(head)$
$v! : T$

$head = sso \wedge head' = ssn$
$v! = lv$

__$CAS_f pop$_____

$head \neq sso$

The semantics of this combination of CSP and Object-Z can best be understood as a parallel composition of the CSP and the Object-Z semantics: at any point in time there are certain operations which the CSP process currently allows and others which the Object-Z part allows; if an operation is allowed by both the object can execute it and thereby progresses to a new Object-Z state and a new (the remaining) CSP process. Note that the CSP process is making no restrictions on the values of inputs and outputs, these solely depend on the Object-Z part. For a formal definition of the semantics see [11].

The objective in this paper is to show that the data structure C is linearizable with respect to A. Linearizability requires that each operation appears to occur atomically at some point between its invocation and its response. For this, we first have to fix a *linearization point* for every operation, saying which operation in the implementation is the one where the effect "seemingly instantaneous" takes place. For both *push* and *pop* these are the CAS_t operations, and for *pop* it is, in addition, *pop3t*. Once the linearization operation has been executed the effect has taken place. For the proof of linearizability we proceed in two steps: we first show that C is a non-atomic refinement of A (in a sense yet to be defined) and then in general prove that non-atomic refinements imply linearizability.

3   Background

The general idea of the correctness proof is to show linearizability via a refinement proof. A prominent property of the stack example is the fact that a single abstract operation is split into several concrete operations. There are currently two notions of refinement for Z (or Object-Z) which can cope with this issue: *weak refinement* [8,7] and *non-atomic refinement* [5,6]. The former assumes that all but one of these operations abstractly correspond to a *skip*, that is, has no effect. The latter, however, allows one to really split an abstract operation, here into a sequence of two concrete operations. This latter definition is thus our starting point, however, one which we will later generalise to allow a concrete decomposition where several concrete operations are ordered according to a CSP process. We thus start by explaining the current version of non-atomic refinement as given in [5,6].

The following definition applies to pure Object-Z specifications C and A, where we (as usual) use a blocking interpretation of preconditions. It assumes that every abstract operation AOp is split into exactly two operations $COp_1 \, \S \, COp_2$. It extends the standard conditions of forward simulation with additional conditions dealing with the new states where the sequence $COp_1 \, \S \, COp_2$ has been started but not yet terminated, where we record this information in a sequence S. For example, S might be $\langle COp_1 \rangle$ denoting the fact that $COp_1 \, \S \, COp_2$ has begun but not yet terminated. Furthermore, at the concrete level, these decompositions might well be interleaved. Thus, DOp_1, say, occurs after COp_1 but before COp_2, S would then be $\langle COp_1, DOp_1 \rangle$. For every such sequence we use a specific retrieve relation R^S, which records the partial effects which might already have been achieved in the concrete specification.

Definition 1
A specification C is a non-atomic forward simulation of the specification A if there is a retrieve relation R such that every abstract operation AOp is recast into a sequence of concrete operations $COp_1 \,\sempty\, COp_2$, and there is a family of retrieve relations R^S such that the following hold.

I $CState \bullet CInit \Rightarrow (\exists\, AState \bullet AInit \bullet R)$
C $R^{\langle\rangle} = R$
S1. $\forall\, AState, CState, CState' \bullet R^S \wedge COp_1 \Rightarrow \exists\, AState' \bullet \Xi AState \wedge (R^{S^\frown \langle COp_1\rangle})'$
S2 Start.
  $\forall\, AState;\ CState \bullet R \Rightarrow (pre\, AOp \iff pre\, COp_1)$
S2 Continue.
  $\forall\, AState, CState \bullet R^S \wedge COp_1 \in S \Rightarrow pre\, COp_2$
S3. $\forall\, AState, CState, CState' \bullet R^S \wedge COp_2 \Rightarrow$
  $COp_1 \in S \wedge \exists\, AState' \bullet AOp \wedge (R^{S\setminus\langle COp_1\rangle})'$ □

We briefly explain every condition. Condition **I** is the usual initialisation and condition **C** describes a *coupling* between the retrieve relations: when the sequence S is empty, R^S coincides with the usual retrieve relation. Condition **S1** is used to record the started but not yet finished refinements in R^S: once a COp_1 has been executed we are in an intermediate state which is related to the same abstract state as before, however, under a retrieve relation R^S with COp_1 attached to the end of the sequence. The conditions **S2** are applicability conditions: the **start** condition guarantees that COp_1 can be executed whenever the corresponding abstract operation is enabled, and the **continue** condition guarantees that started refinement may always be completed. Condition **S3** (correctness condition) rules out that refinements can be started "in the middle", i.e., that a COp_2 occurs with no previous (uncompleted) COp_1, and in addition does the matching with the abstract operation. It furthermore (upon completion of the sequence) removes the first operation from R^S. These conditions are schematically represented in Figure 1.

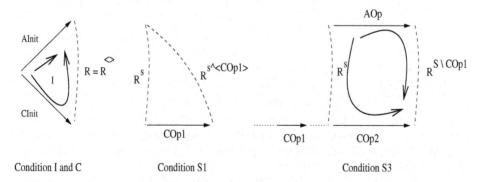

Fig. 1. Conditions required for non-atomic refinement

Examples of the definition of non-atomic refinement are given in [6], which also shows that it is sound with respect to an action refinement definition of CSP failures refinement.

Our aim is to derive a definition of non-atomic refinement that is (i) applicable to examples such as the stack, and (ii) guarantees linearizability. For Definition 1, linearizability is already guaranteed: if a concrete specification has executions where operations interfere in an undesired way, it is not possible to match the concrete operations with the abstract specification and the conditions for this non-atomic refinement are not satisfied. However, this notion of non-atomic refinement isn't applicable to our example as it stands: we need to split abstract operations into CSP processes, not just sequences of two operations.

In the next section, we generalise Definition 1 to derive a definition of non-atomic forward simulation that ensures linearizability. Before doing so we first have to define some notations about CSP processes that we need later in the paper.

Notation and Conventions. We assume that the abstract operation to be split will always be named AOp, its CSP process is AOP. The operations in AOP are usually $COp_1, \ldots, COp_n$. In our example, AOp might be *push* and the CSP process $PUSH$ would then be AOP. In the CSP process describing the refinement of an abstract operation we only use the CSP fragment consisting of $\rightarrow$, ; (sequencing), $\square$ (external choice) and process calls to occur. Hence we essentially allow regular expressions here. These CSP processes are then combined using interleaving ($\|\|\|$, parallel composition with no synchronisation). In the CSP terms we will only have operation *names*, never values of inputs and outputs. We assume the main process of our specification to be defined as $\mathtt{main} = Q_1 \| \ldots \| Q_n$, where every Q_k is $Q_k = AOP_k; Q_k$. Thus all implementations of abstract operations are running in parallel, AOP_k describes one execution of the abstract operation's implementation.

Definition 2

The traces (viz: executions) of CSP processes are defined via its operational semantics (see e.g., [18]). The set of terminating traces of a CSP process P is $Term(P) = \{tr \mid tr \frown \langle\sqrt{}\rangle \in traces(P)\}$. An operation op itself is terminal if it is last in a terminal trace: $op = last(tr)$ for some $tr \in Term(P)$, otherwise it is non-terminal.

The initial operations of some CSP process P are denoted by $init(P) = \{Op \mid P \xrightarrow{Op}\}$, and the CSP processes after executing a trace tr are P after $tr = \{P' \mid P \xrightarrow{tr} P'\}$. We let init be defined on sets of processes as well. □

For example, terminated traces of $PUSH$ include $\langle psh2, psh4, psh5, CAS_t psh \rangle$ as well as $\langle psh2, psh4, psh5, CAS_f psh, psh4, psh5, CAS_t psh \rangle$, and $CAS_t psh$ is the only terminal operation of $PUSH$.

For POP we have, e.g., $init(POP) = \{pop2\}$, and POP after $\langle pop2, pop3f, pop5 \rangle$ is $pop6 \rightarrow (CAS_t pop \rightarrow skip \square CAS_f pop \rightarrow POP)$.

4   Generalised Non-atomic Refinement

There are several aspects we need to take into account when we generalise non-atomic refinement from a decomposition of two operations in sequence to arbitrary CSP processes. The most important point is that when an arbitrary CSP process is used, it may restrict the allowed order of operations (over and above a fixed sequential decomposition). Hence for the applicability and correctness conditions we have to look at both the current Z state and the current CSP process.

Definition 3 below is based on the same ideas as the previous definition of non-atomic refinement: we have a family of relations R^S, $R^{\langle\rangle}$ representing the usual abstraction relation and for a nonempty S, R^S are retrieve relations for the intermediate states in the concrete implementation.

The sequence S represents initial parts of the CSP processes, where operations coming from different abstract operations can be mixed (depending on the order in which they have taken place). For instance, a possible sequence S for our stack example could be $\langle psh2, psh4, pop2, psh5 \rangle$ (i.e., the parts of $PUSH$ and POP that have already been executed). When projecting such a sequence onto the alphabet of a particular CSP process (i.e., $S \upharpoonright \alpha(AOP)$), we see the projection to the operations belonging to one abstract operation.

In deriving the correct forward simulation conditions there are different situations which have to be covered:

S2 Start. $S \upharpoonright \alpha(AOP)$ might be empty for some AOP, that is, there is currently no refinement started for AOP. In this situation we have to guarantee that the process AOP can start if and only if the abstract operation is enabled.

S2 Continuation. $S \upharpoonright \alpha(AOP)$ might not be empty but also is not a terminated trace, and here we need to ensure continuation.

S1 and S3. Some started but not yet terminated trace in a refinement is continued with a concrete operation (note that this requires the operation to be enabled in the current state as well as allowed next in the CSP process). If this continuation does not lead to termination, this is abstractly matched by an empty step, however, we record the effect of the operation in R^S.

If this continuation leads to termination, the correct match with a corresponding abstract operation has to take place and the whole completed trace is removed from S (condition S3).

We are led to the following definition, where conditions **C** and **I** are the coupling of abstraction relations and the initialisation condition, respectively. Condition **S4** is discussed below.

Definition 3. *A specification C is a generalised non-atomic forward simulation of the specification A if there is a retrieve relation R such that every abstract operation AOp is recast into a CSP process AOP, and there is a family of simulation relations R^S and an ordering relation $<_{WF}$ such that the following hold.*

C $R^{\langle\rangle} = R$

I $\forall\, CState \bullet CInit \Rightarrow (\exists\, AState \bullet AInit \wedge R^{\langle\rangle})$

S1 $\forall\ non\text{-}terminal\ COp_i \bullet \forall\, AState;\ CState;\ CState' \bullet$
$\quad R^S \wedge COp_i \wedge (S \,^\frown \langle COp_i\rangle) \upharpoonright \alpha(AOP) \in traces(AOP)$

$\qquad \Rightarrow \exists\, AState' \bullet \varXi AState \wedge (R^{S^\frown\langle COp_i\rangle})'$

S2 Start
$\quad \forall\, AState;\ CState \bullet$
$\quad R^S \wedge (S \upharpoonright \alpha(AOP) = \langle\rangle) \Rightarrow (preAOp \Leftrightarrow \exists\, COp_i \in init(AOP) \bullet preCOp_i)$

S2 Continuation
$\quad \forall\, AState;\ CState \bullet R^S \wedge S \upharpoonright \alpha(AOP) \notin Term(AOP) \wedge (S \upharpoonright \alpha(AOP) \neq \langle\rangle)$
$\qquad \Rightarrow \exists\, COp_i \in init(AOP\ after\ (S \upharpoonright \alpha(AOP))) \bullet pre\ COp_i$

S3 $\forall\ terminal\ COp_t \bullet \forall\, AState;\ CState;\ CState' \bullet$
$\quad R^S \wedge COp_t \wedge (S \,^\frown \langle COp_t\rangle \upharpoonright \alpha(AOP) \in Term(AOP)$

$\qquad \Rightarrow \exists\, AState' \bullet AOp \wedge (R^{S\backslash(S^\frown\langle COp_t\rangle \upharpoonright\alpha(AOP))})'$

S4 $\forall\, AState;\ CState;\ CState' \bullet$
$\quad R^S \wedge COp_i \wedge S \upharpoonright \alpha(AOP) \neq \langle\rangle \wedge (S \,^\frown \langle COp_i\rangle) \upharpoonright \alpha(AOP) \in traces(AOP)$
$\qquad \Rightarrow (S \,^\frown \langle COp_i\rangle, CState') <_{WF} (S, CState)$ $\qquad\qquad\qquad \square$

Condition S4 is a completely new condition ensuring progress in a refinement. To understand the need for a progress condition, consider the following 'decomposition' of a single abstract operation AOp, given here as a CSP process:

$$P = Invoke \rightarrow (COp_1 \rightarrow P$$
$$\square$$
$$COp_2 \rightarrow skip)$$

It is easy to define $R = R^{\langle\rangle}$ and a family of simulations $R^{\langle Invoke\rangle}$ $= R^{\langle Invoke, COp_1\rangle} = R^{\langle Invoke, COp_1, COp_1\rangle} = \ldots$ pictured as in Figure 2. Without condition S4 this example satisfies the requirements of a generalised forward simulation, and thus would be seen as an acceptable implementation of AOp, even though we have introduced non-termination - potentially $Invoke$ and COp_1 can be applied indefinitely.

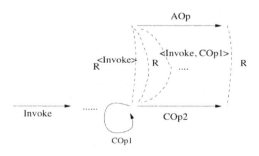

Fig. 2. Potential non-termination in a non-atomic refinement

Condition S4 ensures that this type of non-progression cannot be introduced, not even when several operations are in progress. It requires the existence of a well-founded ordering over $S \times CState$ (that is, the existence of a well-founded set $(WF, <_{WF})$) such that every 'progression' lowers its value, and S4 expresses this requirement. The precondition $S \upharpoonright \alpha(AOP) \neq \langle\rangle$ excludes invoking operations that start a new process from this condition.

Taken together, the roles of the individual conditions can be expressed as in Figure 3.

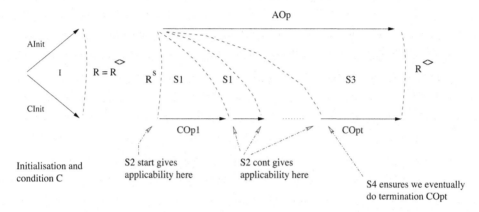

Fig. 3. The roles of the conditions in a generalised forward simulation

We now show how the definition can be applied to our running example of a concurrent implementation of a stack.

4.1   Example

The definition of generalised non-atomic forward simulation requires, in addition to the standard retrieve relation between abstract and concrete states, the existence of a number of simulation relations for each abstract operation being decomposed. To derive these, one needs to understand how the concurrent implementation evolves as it performs its individual steps.

Consider first *push*. This first performs the updates as pictured in Figure 4.

Initially, and after every completed *push* and *pop*, *head* in C should point to the same list as *stack*, we thus have:

$$
\begin{array}{|l}
\hline
\underline{\;R\;} \\
\quad AState \\
\quad CState \\
\hline
\quad collect(head) = stack \\
\hline
\end{array}
$$

The effect of any of the concrete components *psh2*, *psh4* and *psh5* is to update the concrete state, but still preserving the invariant $collect(head) = stack$. The

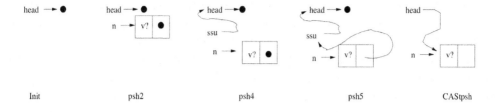

Fig. 4. The concrete *push* operation

latter can only change after a 'visible' concrete effect, that is, a linearisation point. We thus have the following.

```
┌─ R⟨psh2⟩ ──────────────────────
│ AState
│ CState
│ v? : T
├─────────────────────────────────
│ collect(head) = stack
│ n = node(v?, null)
└─────────────────────────────────
```

```
┌─ R⟨psh2,psh4⟩ ─────────────────
│ AState
│ CState
│ v? : T
├─────────────────────────────────
│ collect(head) = stack
│ n = node(v?, null)
└─────────────────────────────────
```

```
┌─ R⟨psh2,psh4,psh5⟩ ────────────────────────────────────────────
│ AState
│ CState
│ v? : T
├──────────────────────────────────────────────────────────────
│ collect(head) = stack
│ ssu = head
│ n = node(first v?, ssu)
└──────────────────────────────────────────────────────────────
```

$$R^{\langle psh2,psh4,psh5,CAS_f psh\rangle} = R^{\langle psh2\rangle}$$
$$R^{\langle psh2,psh4,psh5,CAS_t psh\rangle} = R$$

Note that $head = ssu$ is established by $psh4$ but not recorded in $R^{\langle psh2,psh4\rangle}$, since executing $CAS_t pop$ will destroy this property. We do not need this property since $CAS_t psh$ checks if the $head$ is still ssu. Note also that we record and preserve the input value $v?$ received in $psh2$ in the simulation relations. Thereby we are able to move it forwards through the triangular diagrams set up by condition **S1** until we are able to check equality with the abstract input in condition **S3**.

The relations for *push* are conjunctively combined with simulations for *pop*. These latter ones can be derived in a similar fashion where $R = R^{\langle pop2\rangle}$, and others such as

$R^{\langle pop2,pop3f \rangle}$ _____

| $AState$ |
$CState$
$collect(head) = stack$
$sso \neq null$

$R^{\langle pop2,pop3f,pop5 \rangle}$ _____

| $AState$ |
$CState$
$collect(head) = stack$
$sso \neq null$
$ssn = second\ sso$

$R^{\langle pop2,pop3f,pop5,pop6 \rangle}$ _____

| $AState$ |
$CState$
$collect(head) = stack$
$sso \neq null$
$ssn = second\ sso$
$lv = first\ sso$

$R^{\langle pop2,pop3f,pop5,pop6,CAS_f pop \rangle}$ ___

| $AState$ |
$CState$
$collect(head) = stack$
$sso \neq head$

Note that at the end of the loop, when $CAS_f pop$ has just been executed, we need the information that the test has been negative[1]. Again:

$$R^{\langle pop2,pop3f,pop5,pop6,CAS_f pop,pop2 \rangle} = R^{\langle pop2 \rangle}$$
$$R^{\langle pop2,pop3f,pop5,pop6,CAS_t pop \rangle} = R = R^{\langle pop2,pop3t \rangle}$$

The superscripts of the simulations intuitively correspond to values of the program counter of the pseudo-code for *push* and *pop* given in Section 2. Given any $S \in init(PUSH \ ||| \ POP)$ the necessary superscript S_1 for the push operation is the longest postfix of $S \upharpoonright \alpha(PUSH)$ that is a prefix of $\langle psh2, psh4, psh5, CAS_t push \rangle$ or $\langle psh2, psh4, psh5, CAS_f psh \rangle$. Similarly S_2 is defined as the longest postfix of $S \upharpoonright \alpha(POP)$ that is a prefix of one of $\langle pop2, pop3t \rangle$, $\langle pop2, pop3f, pop5, pop6, CAS_f pop \rangle$ or $\langle pop2, pop3f, pop5, pop6, CAS_t pop \rangle$. The family R^S of relations needed for the proof obligations is defined as

$$R^S := R^{S_1} \wedge R^{S_2}$$

It is easy, but tedious, to verify conditions **C, I, S1, S2 start, S2 continuation** and **S3**.

The basic idea to establish termination via condition **S4** is that starting the push loop will establish $head = ssu$ in $psh4$. The equation will subsequently be invalidated only when the pop process executes $CAS_t pop$. But then the POP process has terminated, and the next iteration of the push loop will terminate too, since an intervening $CAS_t pop$ is no longer possible.

This fact can be exploited to define an order that decreases in every step as follows:

– first, the number of instructions left that the push/pop process must execute to reach the end of the push/pop loop is relevant, since it decreases during

_____

[1] This is required for the lifeness proof only. For safety $R^{\langle\rangle}$ would be sufficient.

execution of every instruction within the loop. This distance to the end of the loop can be defined as

$$pushdist(S) := 4 - length(S_1),$$
$$popdist(S) = 5 - length(S_2)$$

- second, the pop loop (5 instructions) will be executed once more, when the push program is in its "critical section" after ssu has been set to be $head$ in $psh4$, but when $head = ssu$ is false again. Therefore we define a predicate $critpush(S)$ which is true, if $last(S_1)$ is one of $psh4$ or $psh5$. Dually, predicate $critpop(S)$ is true iff $last(S_2) \in \{pop3f, pop5, pop6, CAS_f pop\}$.
- Finally, if none of the two processes has finished, then as argued above, one of them can modify $head$, so that the other must go once more through the loop (4 or 5 instructions). That the push processes has finished is characterised by $last(S_1) = CAS_t psh$ and similarly for the pop process as $last(S_2) \in \{pop3t, CAS_t pop\}$.

Altogether we can define an upper bound on the maximal number of instruction needed to finish both loops (identifying boolean values true and false with 1 and 0)

$$\#(S, CState) := \quad pushdist(S) + popdist(S)$$
$$+ \, 4 * (head \neq ssu \land critpush(S))$$
$$+ \, 5 * (head \neq sso \land critpop(S))$$
$$+ \, 5 * (last(S_1) \neq CAS_t psh \land last(S_2) \notin \{pop3t, CAS_t pop\})$$

and use this number to define

$$(S', CState') <_{WF} (S, CState) \text{ iff } \#(S', CState') < \#(S, CState)$$

The order decreases for every step executed by the pop process.

- For $CAS_t pop$ and $pop3t$ $popdist(S)$ decreases and $head \neq ssu$ may become true. This may add 4 when $critpush(S)$ holds, but then $last(S_1) \neq CAS_t psh$, so the last summand no longer adds 5, since $last(S_2)$ enters $\{pop3t, CAS_t pop\}$.
- When $pop3f, pop5$ or $pop6$ are executed, $popdist(S)$ decreases and everything else remains constant.
- Executing $pop2$ has only to be considered when the loop is repeated, i.e. when $S_2 = \langle pop2, pop3f, pop5, pop6, CAS_f pop \rangle$. In this case R^{S_2} implies $head \neq sso$ ($CAS_f pop$ has just been executed) and $popdist(S)$ increases from 0 to 4. The critical section of pop is entered, and $pop2$ sets $sso = head$. Therefore the fourth summand no longer adds 5 and $\#(S, CState)$ decreases in this case too.

For $push$ operations the argument is as follows:

- For $CAS_t psh$ $pushdist(S)$ decreases and $head \neq sso$ may become true. This may add 5 when $critpop(S)$ holds, but then $last(S_2) \notin \{pop3t, CAS_t pop\}$. Since $last(S_1)$ enters $CAS_t psh$, the last summand no longer adds 5.

- When $psh4$ or $psh5$ are executed $pushdist(S)$ decreases. All other summands remain unchanged: for $psh4$ $citpush(S)$ becomes true, but since $head = ssu$ after the operation, the third summand remains unchanged.
- Executing CAS_fpsh restarts the loop of the push program, and increases $pushdist(S)$ from 1 to 3. Since $head \neq ssu$ remains true and $critpush(S)$ becomes false, the third summand no longer adds 4.
- Executing $psh2$ does not need not to be considered, since it is only executed to start a push (when $S \restriction \alpha(PUSH) = \langle \rangle$).

Summarising this proves condition **S4**: every step that does not start a new *push* or *pop* process leads to a smaller pair $(S, CState)$. With no new processes started the running ones will terminate after a finite number of steps, livelock is absent.

5 Linearizability

Finally, we come to linearizability. Rather than attempt an additional proof, we show linearizability by proving that generalised non-atomic refinement implies it. The results of the previous section are then enough to show all we set out to do.

For the rest of this section we assume that $A = (AState, AInit, (AOp_j)_{j \in J})$ is the Z component of the abstract specification. A is implemented by a specification C which includes a CSP component. Then, for every abstract operation AOp_j we have some CSP process AOP which consists of a number of concrete operations from $\alpha(AOP)$ implementing it. The set of operations $(COp_i)_{i \in I}$ is thus partitioned into a disjoint set of operations, one for each abstract operation.

To prove that refinement implies linearizability, we need to formalize the latter, which we do by realising that it is a correctness criterion which requires a comparison of histories or runs of specifications. Thus we need to give an operational semantics defining the *runs* of our classes, and we do this now.

Definition 4. *Let C be a a combined CSP and Object-Z specification with some dedicated main process* main *and some Object-Z part $(CState, CInit, (COp_i)_{i \in I})$. A* run *of C is a transition sequence*

$$(cs_0, P_0) \xrightarrow{COp_{i_0}.in_0.out_0} (cs_1, P_1) \xrightarrow{COp_{i_1}.in_1.out_1} \dots$$

such that

- *initialisation: $cs_0 \in CInit$ and $P_0 = $* main*, and*
- *succession: $(cs_j, in_j, out_j, cs_{j+1}) \in COp_{i_j}$ and $P_j \xrightarrow{COp_{i_j}} P_{j+1}$.*

From a run $(cs_0, P_0) \xrightarrow{COp_{i_0}.in_0.out_0} (cs_1, P_1) \xrightarrow{COp_{i_1}.in_1.out_1} \dots$ we can derive its history $H = COp_{i_0}.in_0.out_0 \; COp_{i_1}.in_1.out_1 \dots$. $\square$

Note that the in's and out's can also be empty. The difference between the histories and traces of a CSP process is that the former include input and output values.

We write $traces(H)$ to denote the sequence of operation names, without any input and output values. We assume that there are no τ-transitions generated from the CSP part, that is, the Object-Z and CSP components progress jointly, which can be guaranteed if we exclude internal choice from the CSP fragment used, and use a specific semantics for process identifiers. For specifications without a CSP process, *runs* are defined similarly, simply leaving out the CSP component.

For linearizability we have to fix when an operation starts and when it ends. Thus we assume that we have fixed operations standing for the *invocation* and the *return* of an abstract operation. For instance, $pop2$ is the invocation of an abstract Pop and $pop3t$ and $CAS_t pop$ are possible returns. Inputs are passed upon invocation and outputs upon return. Particular instantiations of operations with inputs or outputs give us *events*: for example, $pop2.5$ and $pop3t.empty$ are possible events. The set of all invocation events is Inv, those specific to some operation AOp are $Inv(AOp)$, i.e., $Inv = \bigcup_{j \in J} Inv(AOp_j)$. Similarly, Ret is the set of all return events and $Ret(AOp)$ those of some operation AOp.

Definition 5. *A history is* sequential *if it can be divided into subsequences belonging to one abstract operation AOp, such that they start with an invocation from $Inv(AOp)$, end with a return from $Ret(AOp)$ and, in between, have only operations of $\alpha(AOP)$ (this is the* completed *part). The last such subsequence can possibly end without being completed (a* pending *operation). The history is* complete *if every invocation operation is eventually followed by a corresponding return.* □

For example, $H = \langle psh2.2, psh4, pop2, psh5, CAS_t psh, pop3f, psh2.8 \rangle$ is not sequential since in the initial subsequence $\langle psh2.2, psh4 \rangle$, although $psh2.2 \in Inv(Push)$, $psh4$ is not a return of $Push$.

In general, histories need not be sequential but might contain arbitrary interleavings of implementations of (abstract) operations (as far as the specification allows). A history H is thus an interleaving of some sequential histories, each describing the invocations of one operation which currently have taken place. Some invocations can be completed (viz. followed by a return), but others cannot. We let $rem(H)$ denote those subsequences of H containing only the non-completed parts. For instance, for $H = \langle psh2.2, psh4, pop2, psh5, CAS_t psh, pop3f, psh2.8 \rangle$ the remaining non-completed part is $rem(H) = \langle pop2, pop3f, psh2.8 \rangle$. This is almost those part of the current run that we keep in the sequence S of our relations R^S. Almost, but not quite, since we do not have values of inputs and outputs in S. We let $rem'(H)$ be the sequence without input and output values.

For linearizability, we are interested in the global order of abstract operation execution, and this will be determined by the order of their linearization points, which - in our case - are the terminal operations. This gives rise to the following notion of equivalence on histories.

Definition 6. *Two histories H_1 and H_2 are equivalent iff the following hold:*

1. *$H_1 \upharpoonright Ret = H_2 \upharpoonright Ret$ and*
2. *$\forall AOp \bullet H_1 \upharpoonright Inv(AOp) = H_2 \upharpoonright Inv(AOp)$.* □

Requirement (2) states that the individual operations are invoked with the same inputs. Requirement (1) states a similar property for returns and outputs (thus the same inputs lead to the same outputs), and, in addition, requires that the overall ordering of returns is the same in H_1 and H_2. Strictly speaking, this is a little stronger than is required by linearizability (which only requires that the partial orders defined by returns and invocations are consistent), but it is guaranteed by non-atomic refinement and easier to state.

Definition 7. *A history H is linearizable if it can be extended by zero or more events to give a history H' such that*

1. *H' is complete, and*
2. *H' is equivalent to some complete sequential history G.*

A specification is linearizable *if all its histories are.*   □

This allows us to finally state the result.

Theorem 1. *Let A, C be Object-Z specifications, C with and A without a CSP component. If C is a generalised non-atomic refinement of A, then C is linearizable.*

Proof
We show that

1. every history H of C can be completed to some history H',
2. for H' there is some corresponding history H_A of A,
3. from H_A we can easily construct a sequential history G of C which is equivalent to H'.

Proof of 2):
Let H be a complete history and R^S the family of retrieve relations proving C to be a generalised non-atomic refinement of A. For the history H there is an associated run

$$(cs_0, P_0) \xrightarrow{COp_0.in_0, out_0} (cs_1, P_1) \ldots$$

We inductively show that we can construct a corresponding run of A.

Base case. Using condition **I** we can find a state as_0 such that $as_0 \in AInit$ and $(as_0, cs_0) \in R^{\langle\rangle}$.

Induction step. For our induction step we assume the following hypothesis (which is also fulfilled by the base case). The current CSP process is always of the form $P_k = P_{k,1}; \; Q_1 \; || \; \ldots \; || \; P_{k,n}; \; Q_n$. If we have constructed the abstract run $as_0 \xrightarrow{COp_0.in_0, out_0} as_1 \ldots as_k$ and have a history H_k so far, then we have for $S = rem'(H_k)$ that $(as_k, cs_k) \in R^S$, $\mathtt{main} \xrightarrow{trace(H_k)} P_k$ and for all j, $1 \le j \le n$, $AOP_j \xrightarrow{trace(H_k) \restriction \alpha(AOP_j)} P_{k,j}$.

By definition of the semantics we know that $P_k \xrightarrow{COp_k} P_{k+1}$ and $(cs_k, in_k, out_k, cs_{k+1}) \in COp_k$. Assume $COp_k \in \alpha(AOp_j)$. Since $AOP_j \xrightarrow{S \restriction \alpha(AOP_j)} P_{k,j}$ we get $(S \frown \langle COp_k \rangle) \restriction \alpha(AOP_j) \in traces(AOP_j)$. Now we have to consider two cases:

– COp_k is non-terminal:

Then by condition **S1** of the refinement $(as_k, cs_{k+1}) \in R^{S^\frown COp_k}$ and the abstract run is not extended further.

– COp_k is terminal:
We know $P_k \xrightarrow{COp_k} P_{k+1}$ and hence (definition of terminal) $P_{k,j} \xrightarrow{COp_k} skip$ and $(S^\frown \langle COp_k \rangle) \upharpoonright \alpha(AOP_j) \in Term(AOP_j)$. By condition **S3** of the refinement we thus find as_{k+1} such that for in_k being the input value of the last invocation stored in R^S and out_k being the output value in $COp_k.out_k$ we have $(as_k, in_k, out_k, as_{k+1}) \in AOP_j$ and $(as_{k+1}, cs_{k+1}) \in R^{S \backslash ((S^\frown \langle COp_k \rangle) \upharpoonright \alpha(AOP_j))}$.

Proof of 1):
Let H be a non-completed history of C. Consider its run, ending in state cs_k. With the same argument as above we can construct a corresponding abstract run of A, i.e., we have a state as_k and a relation R^S such that $(as_k, cs_k) \in R^S$ and S has all the properties we assumed in the induction above. Let AOp_j be an operation whose implementation is not completed. Then $S \upharpoonright \alpha(AOP_j) \notin Term(AOP_j)$ nor is $S \upharpoonright \alpha(AOP_j) = \langle \rangle$. Hence by condition **S2 Continuation** there is a $COp_i \in \alpha(AOP_j)$ which is enabled and the run can be continued with this operation. By condition **S4** this continuation of one abstract operation eventually ends; then we continue with the next pending operation.
Proof of 3):
Straightforward: the abstract sequence constructed in 2) has an ordering consistent with the returns and has the same inputs and outputs. Thus we just construct the corresponding sequential run out of it; its history will be equivalent to the one we started with.   □

This completes the proof that generalized non-atomic refinement implies linearizability, and that, for example, our concrete implementation of the stack possesses this property.

6   Conclusion

There are a number of (related) approaches to showing that concurrent implementations are correct. To some extent these depend on the mechanisms used in the algorithms, for example whether locks are used to provide critical sections.

Our starting point is the recent work of Groves and Colvin who have been considering verification of concurrent implementations which use 'compare and swap' instructions to avoid the potential bottlenecks of lock-based algorithms.

Specifically, we have taken the core of the algorithm in [4] and reformulated it using an integration of Object-Z and CSP. In [4] specifications are based on two IO-automata. One roughly corresponds to our concrete model with interleaved runs, while the other corresponds to runs with sequential histories G that we construct in the linearization proof of Section 5. Linearization is shown using refinement of IO Automata using forwards and backwards simulation and was mechanized in PVS. The basic proof principle common to our and their approach is induction over the length of histories.

However, our approach differs from theirs, in that we start with an abstract level containing atomic stack operations. We also have embedded sufficient conditions into our generalised forward simulation so that it alone guarantees both refinement as well as linearizability.

Further work by Groves and Colvin includes [12], where they verify an improved version of an algorithm of Hendler et al [13] (which in turn extends the algorithm of [4]) using a new approach based on action systems. This approach, like ours starts with an abstract level of atomic push and pop operations.

The approach uses a different proof technique than our and their earlier work. Specifically, it works by induction over the number of completed abstract runs (traces in $Term(POP)$ or $Term(PUSH)$) contained in a history, and it is based on the approaches of Lipton [17] and Lamport and Schneider [16].

Both [4] and [12] consider safety only, while we also consider absence of livelock. For action systems, the extension of the framework of [16] to considering termination described in [3] should be analogous to our consideration of livelock.

Additional relevant work in state-based formalisms includes [1], where the correctness of a concurrent queue algorithm using Event_B is shown. There, instead of verifying a given implementation, correctness is achieved by construction involving only correct refinement steps.

Acknowledgements

We would like to thank Simon Bäumler for discussions on ideas in this paper. John Derrick was supported by the Leverhulme Trust via a Research Fellowship for this work.

References

1. Abrial, J.-R., Cansell, D.: Formal Construction of a Non-blocking Concurrent Queue Algorithm (a Case Study in Atomicity). Journal of Universal Computer Science 11(5), 744–770 (2005)
2. Abrial, J.-R., Cansell, D., Mery, D.: Refinement and Reachability in Event_B. In: Treharne, H., King, S., Henson, M.C., Schneider, S. (eds.) ZB 2005. LNCS, vol. 3455, pp. 222–241. Springer, Heidelberg (2005)
3. Back, R.-J.: Atomicity refinement in a refinement calculus framework. Reports on Computer Science and Mathematics 141, Abo Akademi (1993)
4. Colvin, R., Doherty, S., Groves, L.: Verifying concurrent data structures by simulation. ENTCS 137, 93–110 (2005)
5. Derrick, J., Wehrheim, H.: Using coupled simulations in non-atomic refinement. In: Bert, D., Bowen, J.P., King, S. (eds.) ZB 2003. LNCS, vol. 2651, pp. 127–147. Springer, Heidelberg (2003)
6. Derrick, J., Wehrheim, H.: Non-atomic refinement in Z and CSP. In: Treharne, H., King, S., Henson, M.C., Schneider, S. (eds.) ZB 2005. LNCS, vol. 3455, Springer, Heidelberg (2005)

7. Derrick, J., Boiten, E. (eds.): Refinement in Z and Object-Z: Foundations and Advanced Applications, May 2001. Formal Approaches to Computing and Information Technology. Springer, Berlin Heidelberg (2001)
8. Derrick, J., Boiten, E., Bowman, H., Steen, M.: Specifying and Refining Internal Operations in Z. Formal Aspects of Computing 10, 125–159 (1998)
9. Doherty, S., Groves, L., Luchangco, V., Moir, M.: Formal verification of a practical lock-free queue algorithm. In: de Frutos-Escrig, D., Núñez, M. (eds.) FORTE 2004. LNCS, vol. 3235, pp. 97–114. Springer, Heidelberg (2004)
10. Duke, R., Rose, G., Smith, G.: Object-Z: A specification language advocated for the description of standards. Computer Standards and Interfaces 17, 511–533 (1995)
11. Fischer, C.: CSP-OZ - a combination of CSP and Object-Z. In: Bowman, H., Derrick, J. (eds.) Second IFIP International conference on Formal Methods for Open Object-based Distributed Systems, July 1997, pp. 423–438. Chapman & Hall, Sydney (1997)
12. Groves, L., Colvin, R.: Derivation of a scalable lock-free stack algorithm. ENTCS (To appear, 2007)
13. Hendler, D., Shavit, N., Yerushalmi, L.: A scalable lock-free stack algorithm. In: SPAA '04: Proceedings of the sixteenth annual ACM symposium on Parallelism in algorithms and architectures, pp. 206–215. ACM Press, New York (2004)
14. Herlihy, M., Wing, J.M.: Linearizability: A correctness condition for concurrent objects. ACM Transactions on Programming Languages and Systems 12(3), 463–492 (1990)
15. Hoare, C.A.R.: Communicating Sequential Processes. Prentice-Hall, Englewood Cliffs (1985)
16. Lamport, L., Schneider, F.B.: Pretending atomicity. Technical Report TR89-1005, SRC Digital (1989)
17. Lipton, R.J.: Reduction: a method of proving properties of parallel programs. Commun. ACM 18(12), 717–721 (1975)
18. Roscoe, A.W.: The Theory and Practice of Concurrency. International Series in Computer Science. Prentice-Hall, Englewood Cliffs (1998)
19. Smith, G.: The Object-Z Specification Language. Kluwer Academic Publishers, Dordrecht (2000)
20. Woodcock, J.C.P., Davies, J.: Using Z: Specification, Refinement, and Proof. Prentice-Hall, Englewood Cliffs (1996)

Lifting General Correctness into Partial Correctness is *ok*

Steve Dunne and Andy Galloway

School of Computing, University of Teesside
Middlesbrough, TS1 3BA, UK
`s.e.dunne@tees.ac.uk`
High Integrity Systems Engineering, Department of Computer Science,
University of York, UK
`andyg@cs.york.ac.uk`

Abstract. Commands interpreted in general correctness are usually characterised by their wp and wlp predicate transformer effects. We describe a way to ascribe to such commands a *single* predicate transformer semantics which embodies both their wp and wlp characteristics. The new single predicate transformer describes an everywhere-terminating "lifted" computation in an *ok*-enriched variable space, where *ok* is inspired by Hoare and He's UTP but has the novelty here that it enjoys the same status as the other state variables, so that it can be manipulated directly in the lifted computation itself.

The relational model of this lifted computation is not, however, simply the canonical UTP relation of the original underlying computation, since this turns out to yield too cumbersome a lifted computation to permit reasoning about efficiently with the mechanised tools available. Instead we adopt a slightly less constrained model, which we are able to show is nevertheless still effective for our purpose, and yet admits a much more efficient form of mechanised reasoning with the tools available.

1   Introduction

We adopt a general-correctness[1] [21] perspective on computations and reconcile the UTP-style relational characterisation of computations in this perspective as described in [11] with their more familiar Dijkstra-style predicate-transformer characterisation. This general-correctness perspective allows us to describe accurately the behaviour of what we might call *contingently-terminating* computations, which are guaranteed to terminate with specified results from some starting states, permitted but not guaranteed to terminate with specified results from certain other states, and guaranteed not to terminate from yet other starting states.

To provide a concrete syntax in which to describe these computations we will employ the Abstract Command Language [12,10]. We will describe a way to ascribe

---

[1] Chen [4] calls it *factual correctness*, while Hesselink [19] and Nelson [26] both use a similar semantics in their analyses of programs without explicitly naming it.

J. Davies and J. Gibbons (Eds.): IFM 2007, LNCS 4591, pp. 215–232, 2007.

to such commands a *single* predicate-transformer semantics which embodies both their wp and wlp characteristics. The new single predicate transformer describes an everywhere-terminating "lifted" computation in an *ok*-enriched variable space, where *ok* is inspired by Hoare and He's Unifying Theories of Programming (UTP) [20] but with the novelty that it enjoys the same status as the other state variables, so that it can be manipulated directly by the lifted computation itself.

The relational model of this lifted computation is not, however, simply the canonical UTP relation of the original underlying computation, since this turns out to yield too cumbersome a lifted computation to permit reasoning about efficiently with the mechanised tools available. Instead we adopt a slightly less constrained model, which we will prove is nevertheless still effective for our purpose, yet admits a much more efficient form of mechanised reasoning with the tools available. We seek to model our contingently-terminating computations in this way so that to reason about them we can thereby make direct use of existing support tools such as the BToolkit [2], AtelierB [5] or ProB [22] without any modification, even though they were all designed to support only total-correctness reasoning. We do this by using such tools to reason about the corresponding lifted computations rather than directly about the underlying computations themselves.

In Section 2 we set out some necessary terminology, definitions and notation that we employ in the rest of the paper. In Section 3 we review the notion of general correctness and introduce abstract commands as a formal language for writing contingently-terminating programs, together with some elements of the theory which underpins them. In Section 4 we summarise the alternative UTP-inspired representation of contingently-terminating computations originally given in [11], and show how to reconcile this with the wp-wlp predicate-transformer representation. We also extend the class of relations called prescriptions identified in [11] by introducing the new notion of pseudo-prescription, and show that this extended class is closed under disjunction and relational composition as well as retaining a vital property we call compositionality. In Section 5 we reach the heart of the matter where we explore what we actually require of any lifting scheme. Finally, we propose our particular lifting scheme, showing that this does indeed fulfil our requirements, and illustrate its application by means of a small example.

2   Preliminaries

Following established UTP practice we deal extensively in this paper with alphabetised relations, *i.e.* relations expressed as predicates over an explicitly given or understood alphabet of variables. Often this alphabet includes Boolean-valued variables ok and ok', and then for conciseness we frequently take the liberty of treating these variables themselves as predicates, for example writing just $\neg\ ok'$ instead of $ok' = \text{FALSE}$. We refer interchangeably to a relation and its predicate providing its alphabet is understood. We define the following partial order on relations A and B sharing the same alphabet α:

Definition 1. (Implication Ordering on Predicates)

$$A \leq B \quad =_{df} \quad \forall \alpha.\ B \Rightarrow A$$

The constant predicates true and false are respectively the bottom and top of this lattice. For any predicate A we therefore have $\text{true} \leq A \leq \text{false}$. We deem relations A and B to be equal if their predicates are true of precisely the same bindings of the variables of their common alphabet:

Definition 2. (Equality for predicates)

$$A \ = \ B \quad =_{df} \quad (A \leq B) \ \wedge \ (B \leq A)$$

Binary Relations and Conditions. A homogeneous binary relation is one whose alphabet is of the form (v, v') where v is a list of undashed variables and v' is a corresponding list of dashed versions of these. The undashed variables v represent the relation's input states while the dashed variables v' represent its output states. A *condition* is a relation whose predicate constrains only undashed variables.

Syntactic Substitution. If A is a predicate expression over an alphabet which includes a list of variables u, and E is list of appropriately typed expressions corresponding to u, we write $A[E/u]$ to denote the predicate derived from A by replacing each free occurrence of each of the variables of u with the corresponding expression from E. Note that syntactic substitution distributes through the basic logical connectives such as conjunction and disjunction, so that for example

$$(A \vee B)[E/u] \quad = \quad A[E/u] \vee B[E/u]$$

Some Convenient Relational Abbreviations. If A is a predicate expression over alphabet (w, ok, w', ok') we will write A_{tt}, A_{tf}, A_{ft} and A_{ff} as abbreviations for $A[\text{true}, \text{true}/ok, ok']$, $A[\text{true}, \text{false}/ok, ok']$, $A[\text{false}, \text{true}/ok, ok']$ and $A[\text{false}, \text{false}/ok, ok']$ respectively.

Composition of Relations. Let A and B be homogeneous binary relations with a common alphabet (v, v'). Then we have

Definition 3. (Relational Composition)

$$A\,;\,B \quad =_{df} \quad \exists v''.\ A[v''/v'] \wedge B[v''/v]$$

where v'' is a fresh list of variables corresponding with those of v. In particular, relational composition gives us a convenient way of formally expressing that a relation A is a condition, namely that $A\,;\,\text{true} = A$. Among the important algebraic properties of relational composition are that it is associative and left- and right-distributes through disjunction, so that, for example, for homogeneous binary relations A, B and C on a common alphabet we have

$$\begin{aligned}
(A\,;\,B)\,;\,C &= A\,;\,(B\,;\,C) \\
(A \vee B)\,;\,C &= (A\,;\,C) \vee (B\,;\,C) \\
A\,;\,(B \vee C) &= (A\,;\,B) \vee (A\,;\,C)
\end{aligned}$$

Relational Algebra. We will make use of the identities expressed by the following proposition

Proposition 2.1. (Some useful relational identities)

$$
\begin{array}{llll}
(1) & (A\,;B)_{tt} & = & (A_{tt}\,;B_{tt}) \vee (A_{tf}\,;B_{ft}) \\
(2) & (A\,;B)_{tf} & = & (A_{tf}\,;B_{ff}) \vee (A_{tt}\,;B_{tf}) \\
(3) & (A\,;B)_{ft} & = & (A_{ft}\,;B_{tt}) \vee (A_{ff}\,;B_{ft}) \\
(4) & (A\,;B)_{ff} & = & (A_{ff}\,;B_{ff}) \vee (A_{ft}\,;B_{tf})
\end{array}
$$

Proof: By defn of "$;$" and appropriate true and false case splits for ok and ok'.

□

3   General Correctness and Abstract Commands

General correctness separates for a computation the respective issues of (a) its reliable termination and (b) the correctness of its result should it (whether reliably or even fortuitously) terminate, treating these two concerns quite orthogonally. As such it discriminates between computations more finely than *total correctness*, which simply superimposes (a) on (b), thereby equating all behaviour other than reliably terminating as indistinguishably pathological. Thus general correctness not only allows the specifier to express the conditions required for guaranteed termination of a computation and constrain its result in those circumstances, it also allows him to constrain its result in cases where termination is not guaranteed, even to the point of sometimes forbidding fortuitous termination altogether, thereby demanding actual non-termination.

3.1   The Interactive Era

One of the reviewers of the draft version of this paper was sceptical of the value of considering general correctness at all, describing it as "a mere *cul-de-sac* in the history of computing". While it is certainly true that total correctness has predominated almost absolutely until recently in all the prominent refinement and program-correctness theories such as [24,1,3,20], we believe this reflects a historical pre-occupation with pure sequential computation, which has in fact been largely superseded by the current focus on interactive computing. Even in 1998 Milner [23] was already pointing out that computing *is* interaction. This has important implications for software developers. No longer are we always necessarily exclusively concerned with the result of executing our sequential programs through to successful termination. Such programs now often provide the individual interacting threads of today's complex distributed processing systems, and thus we may require them to behave reliably even in situations where termination is not even in prospect. A channel-listener, for example, must idle until it detects an incoming message, then deal effectively with such a message if and when it arrives. But since there is never a guarantee that such a message will ever arrive, our channel-listener must be capable in principle of idling indefinitely. There are circumstances, therefore, where non-termination *is* precisely what we demand. As formal software specifiers and designers we must have a specification language in which we can formally articulate such a requirement, and a design calculus with which we can prove that a given program meets such a specification. To quote from [18]:

> With the addition of communication, non-terminating executions can perform useful computation, so a semantics that does not insist on termination is useful.

We might go further and say we need a semantics in which we can insist on non-termination in certain conditions. In short, we must learn to work in the context of general correctness. In this regard it is also salient to point to work undertaken by various authors in the field of timed refinement, for example [14,15], and [16,17]. Such work invariably exhibits the quintessential general-correctness characteristic that actual non-termination is precisely characterisable. Total correctness, on the other hand, can only subsume non-termination into the completely unpredictable behaviour known as divergence or chaos.

3.2   Abstract Commands

We first introduced abstract commands [12], as an adaptation of Abrial's generalised substitutions [1], to express computations in general correctness, and subsequently further developed them by introducing the notion of frames [10]. Dawson [6] later formalised our resulting theory of abstract commands in Isabelle/HOL to confirm its soundness. In this paper, however, we confine ourselves to commands sharing a common frame w of all state variables in the context of discourse. Each such command S is fully characterised by its termination predicate $\mathrm{trm}(S)$, which defines from which starting states it can be relied on to terminate, and its weakest liberal precondition $\mathrm{wlp}(S, Q)$ which defines from which starting states it must if it does terminate establish any particular postcondition Q. The trm-wlp semantics of each of our basic abstract commands is given in Table 1. The weakest-precondition (wp) and weakest-liberal-precondition (wlp) predicate transformers were of course invented by Dijkstra [8,9] who linked them by the healthiness rule

$$\mathrm{wp}(S, Q) \quad = \quad \mathrm{wp}(S, \mathrm{true}) \wedge \mathrm{wlp}(S, Q)$$

In our approach, however, we choose to treat $\mathrm{wp}(S, \mathrm{true})$ as primitive and denote it by $\mathrm{trm}(S)$, so that $\mathrm{wp}(S, Q)$ can then be obtained using Dijkstra's rule as

$$\mathrm{wp}(S, Q) \quad =_{df} \quad \mathrm{trm}(S) \wedge \mathrm{wlp}(S, Q)$$

3.3   Normal Form of an Abstract Command

The *before-after* predicate $\mathrm{prd}(S)$ of an abstract command S operating in a state space characterised by state variable(s) w is defined as

$$\mathrm{prd}(S) \quad =_{df} \quad \neg \, \mathrm{wlp}(S, w' \neq w)$$

Table 1. Basic abstract commands

name of C	syntax	trm(C)	wlp(C, Q)
skip	skip	true	Q
assignment	$u := E$	true	$Q[E/u]$
termination precondition	$P \mid S$	$P \wedge \text{trm}(S)$	wlp(S, Q)
guard	$P \longrightarrow S$	$P \Rightarrow \text{trm}(S)$	$P \Rightarrow \text{wlp}(S, Q)$
bounded choice	$S \sqcap T$	trm$(S) \wedge \text{trm}(T)$	wlp$(S, Q) \wedge \text{wlp}(T, Q)$
unbounded choice	$@z.\ S$	$\forall z.\ \text{trm}(S)$	$\forall z.\ \text{wlp}(S, Q)$
sequential composition	$S\ ;\ T$	trm$(S)\ \wedge$ wlp$(S, \text{trm}(T))$	wlp$(S, \text{wlp}(T, Q))$

It relates each initial state w to the possible final states w' which of S might yield. Indeed S can be expressed in normal form as

$$S\ =\ \text{trm}(S) \mid @\, w'.\ \text{prd}(S) \longrightarrow w := w'$$

This normal form embodies the following identities which follow from our definitions of prd(S) and wp(S, Q):

$$\text{wlp}(S, Q)\ =\ \forall w'.\ \text{prd}(S) \Rightarrow Q[w'/w]$$
$$\text{wp}(S, Q)\ =\ \text{trm}(S) \wedge \forall w'.\ \text{prd}(S) \Rightarrow Q[w'/w]$$

3.4   Indeterminate Assignment

Given a relation R on (w, w') we also define the following useful derived command we call an *indeterminate assignment*:

$$w : R\quad =_{df}\quad @\, w'.\ R \longrightarrow w := w'$$

Our operational intuition of $w : R$ is that from each starting state it assigns to w a nondeterministically-chosen final state from among those related by R to that starting state. Where the starting state in question has no related final states the assignment is miraculous (*i.e.* unenabled). We note that trm$(w : R) = \text{true}$ and prd$(w : R) = R$. Our indeterminate assignment $w : R$ corresponds with what Back and von Wright [3], working in total correctness, call the *demonic relational update* on R and denote by $[R]$.

Using indeterminate assignment we can express the normal form of an abstract command S more succinctly as

$$S\ =\ \text{trm}(S) \mid w : \text{prd}(S)$$

4   General Correctness and UTP

In [11] we introduced the notion of a *prescription* as the general-correctness counterpart of Hoare and He's total-correctness notion of a design [20], and developed a corresponding theory for these. They have subsequently attracted the interest of other authors [13,7] who have incorporated them into their own investigations.

Let w be the state variable(s) of our state space and ok be an auxiliary Boolean variable which when initially true signifies the computation has started and when finally true signifies it has terminated. We recall from [11] that a prescription is an alphabetised relation over (w, ok, w', ok') whose predicate can be expressed in the form

$$(ok \wedge P \ \Rightarrow \ ok') \ \wedge \ (ok' \ \Rightarrow \ R \wedge ok)$$

where P and R are subsidiary predicates not containing ok or ok'. We abbreviate it as $P \Vdash R$. Conversely, for any prescription A over (w, ok, w', ok') we have that

$$A \ = \ \neg A_{tf} \Vdash A_{tt}$$

If P is simply a *condition* – *i.e.* it constrains only the undashed state variables w– then we call $P \Vdash R$ a *normal* prescription, and interpret it operationally as *If the program starts in a state satisfying P it must eventually terminate; moreover, if it terminates R will be satisfied, and it must have started, though not necessarily from a state satisfying P.* In this case we call P the termination condition of $P \Vdash R$. In the rest of this paper all the prescriptions we encounter will be normal ones in this sense.

4.1   Prescriptions *versus* Predicate Transformers

We can reconcile the predicate-transformer (abstract command) and relational (prescription) representations of a computation in general correctness by noting that the computation represented imperatively by any abstract command S is represented relationally by the normal prescription $\mathrm{trm}(S) \Vdash \mathrm{prd}(S)$.

Conversely, we know that any normal prescription A represents a computation in general correctness, and that this is also characterised by its pair of predicate transformers wp and wlp, which can be derived from A by

$$\mathrm{wp}(A, Q) \quad =_{df} \quad \neg\, (A \,;\, \neg\, (ok \wedge Q))[\mathrm{true}/ok]$$
$$\mathrm{wlp}(A, Q) \quad =_{df} \quad \neg\, (A \,;\, \neg\, (ok \Rightarrow Q))[\mathrm{true}/ok]$$

Equivalently, we could instead first introduce the notion of a *rich condition* as a predicate over (w, ok) and then define a *weakest-rich-precondition* (**wrp**) predicate transformer for A, such that for any rich postcondition R

$$\mathbf{wrp}(A, R) \quad =_{df} \quad \neg\, (A \,;\, \neg\, R)$$

A's wp and wlp can then be derived from its wrp as

$$\text{wp}(A, Q) \quad = \quad \mathbf{wrp}(A, (ok \wedge Q))[\text{true}/ok]$$
$$\text{wlp}(A, Q) \quad = \quad \mathbf{wrp}(A, (ok \Rightarrow Q))[\text{true}/ok]$$

thus achieving a unification of wp and wlp arguably more transparent than that offered in [25]. And indeed since $(ok \Rightarrow Q) \leq Q \leq (ok \wedge Q)$ in the lattice of rich conditions we might even be tempted to define an intermediate predicate transformer "whp", as it were "halfway" between wp and wlp, by

$$\text{whp}(A, Q) \quad =_{df} \quad \mathbf{wrp}(A, Q)[\text{true}/ok]$$

Curiously, it turns out this is indistinguishable from wp, save that unlike wp it has the property that $\text{whp}(A, \text{true}) = \text{true}$ for every A.

4.2   Pseudo-prescriptions

Prescriptions are canonical relational representations of computations in general correctness, in the sense that any two distinct normal prescriptions will represent distinct computations. There are several equivalent convenient healthiness tests to determine whether a relation over (w, ok, w', ok') is actually a prescription. For example, a relation A over (w, ok, w', ok') is a prescription if and only if $A[\text{false}/ok'] = \neg\, ok'$ [11, Thm 1]. Equivalently, A is a prescription if and only if $A_{ft} = \text{false}$ and $A_{ff} = \text{true}$.

We note that *any* relation A over (w, ok, w', ok') in a sense "encodes" the normal prescription $\neg\, (A_{tf}\, ;\, \text{true}) \Vdash A_{tt}$. We call the latter A's *intrinsic* prescription and denote it more compactly by $P(A)$. Indeed, echoing established UTP practice in [20] we can regard our $P(\,)$ as an idempotent "healthifying" function on relations whose fixed points are precisely the normal prescriptions over (w, ok, w', ok').

Unfortunately arbitrary relations suffer the shortcoming that their intrinsic prescriptions are not in general compositional with respect to relational composition. That is to say, for arbitrary relations A and B over (w, ok, w', ok') it is not always the case that $P(A\, ;\, B) = P(A)\, ;\, P(B)$. We can, however, define a class of relations called *pseudo-prescriptions* somewhat larger than that of prescriptions, which *are* compositional with respect to their intrinsic prescriptions. We say that a relation A over (w, ok, w', ok') is a pseudo-prescription if and only if $A_{ft} = \text{false}$ and $A_{ff}\, ;\, \text{true} = \text{true}$. Our pseudo-prescriptions enjoy some important properties as expressed in the following two propositions:

Proposition 4.2.1 (Closure of pseudo-prescriptions)
Pseudo-prescriptions are closed under disjunction and relational composition.

Proof: The closure of pseudo-prescriptions under disjunction follows trivially from the distributivity of syntactic substitution through disjunction, giving that $(A \vee B)_{ft} = A_{ft} \vee B_{ft}$, and $(A \vee B)_{ff} = A_{ff} \vee B_{ff}$, and then the left-distributivity of ";" through disjunction, giving that

$$(A \vee B)_{ff}\, ;\, \text{true} = (A_{ff} \vee B_{ff})\, ;\, \text{true} = (A_{ff}\, ;\, \text{true}) \vee (B_{ff}\, ;\, \text{true})$$

Their closure under relational composition is shown by

$(A \,;\, B)_{ft}$

$= \{$ Prop 2.1.(3) $\}$

$(A_{ft} \,;\, B_{tt}) \lor (A_{ff} \,;\, B_{ft})$

$= \{$ A and B are pseudo-prescriptions so $A_{ft} = B_{ft} =$ false $\}$

$(\text{false} \,;\, B_{tt}) \lor (A_{ff} \,;\, \text{false})$

$= \{$ relational algebra and logic $\}$

false

and then

$(A \,;\, B)_{ff} \,;\, \text{true}$

$= \{$ Prop 2.1.(4) $\}$

$((A_{ff} \,;\, B_{ff}) \lor (A_{ft} \,;\, B_{tf})) \,;\, \text{true}$

$= \{$ A is pseudo-prescription so $A_{ft} =$ false $\}$

$((A_{ff} \,;\, B_{ff}) \lor (\text{false} \,;\, B_{tf})) \,;\, \text{true}$

$= \{$ relational algebra and logic $\}$

$(A_{ff} \,;\, B_{ff}) \,;\, \text{true}$

$= \{$ ";" is associative $\}$

$A_{ff} \,;\, B_{ff} \,;\, \text{true}$

$= \{$ B is pseudo-prescription so $B_{ff} \,;\, \text{true} = \text{true}$ $\}$

$A_{ff} \,;\, \text{true}$

$= \{$ A is pseudo-prescription so $A_{ff} \,;\, \text{true} = \text{true}$ $\}$

true   □

The next proposition establishes that, at least when applied to pseudo-prescriptions, our intrinsic-prescription extractor function P( ) is compositional with respect to ";". The significance of this is that we can safely use pseudo-prescriptions as surrogates for the computations embodied in their intrinsic prescriptions, since when we compose them we know the result will accurately encode the actual compositions of the original underlying computations.

Proposition 4.2.2 (Compositionality of pseudo-prescriptions)
Let A and B be relations over (w, ok, w', ok') such that $A_{ft} = B_{ft} =$ false and $A_{ff} \,;\, \text{true} = B_{ff} \,;\, \text{true} = \text{true}$. Then $P(A \,;\, B) = P(A) \,;\, P(B)$.

Proof:

$P(A \,;\, B)$

$= \{$ defn of intrinsic prescription $\}$

$\neg ((A \,;\, B)_{tf} \,;\, \text{true}) \Vdash (A \,;\, B)_{tt}$

$= \{$ Props. 2.1.(1), 2.1.(2) $\}$

$\neg (((A_{tf} \,;\, B_{ff}) \lor (A_{tt} \,;\, B_{tf})) \,;\, \text{true}) \Vdash (A_{tt} \,;\, B_{tt}) \lor (A_{tf} \,;\, B_{ft})$

$= \{$ composition distributes through $\lor$ $\}$

$\neg ((A_{tf} \,;\, B_{ff} \,;\, \text{true}) \lor (A_{tt} \,;\, B_{tf} \,;\, \text{true})) \Vdash (A_{tt} \,;\, B_{tt}) \lor (A_{tf} \,;\, B_{ft})$

$= \{\, B_{\!f\!f} \,;\, \text{true} = \text{true and } B_{\!f\!t} = \text{false} \,\}$

$\qquad \neg\,((A_{t\!f}\,;\,\text{true}) \vee (A_{tt}\,;\,B_{t\!f}\,;\,\text{true})) \ \Vdash\ (A_{tt}\,;\,B_{tt}) \vee (A_{t\!f}\,;\,\text{false})$

$= \{\, \text{relational algebra and logic} \,\}$

$\qquad \neg\,(A_{t\!f}\,;\,\text{true}) \wedge \neg\,(A_{tt}\,;\,B_{t\!f}\,;\,\text{true}) \ \Vdash\ A_{tt}\,;\,B_{tt}$

$= \{\, \text{composition of normal prescriptions [11, Cor. 6.1]} \,\}$

$\qquad (\neg\,(A_{t\!f}\,;\,\text{true}) \Vdash A_{tt})\ ;\ (\neg\,(B_{t\!f}\,;\,\text{true}) \Vdash B_{tt})$

$= \{\, \text{defn of intrinsic prescription} \,\}$

$\qquad \mathrm{P}(A)\,;\,\mathrm{P}(B)$ $\qquad\qquad\qquad\qquad\qquad\qquad\qquad\qquad\quad\square$

Pseudo-prescriptions certainly still represent computations in general correctness, though those representations are clearly no longer canonical since distinct pseudo-prescriptions can share the same intrinsic prescription and therefore represent the same computation. In the next section we will see how pseudo-prescriptions play a fundamental role in validating that our lifting of abstract commands into partial-correctness computations is sound.

5   Lifting a Computation

The notion of *lifting* a computation is motivated by the crucial insight that a computation on an underlying space w with a contingent termination behaviour can be modelled by an always-terminating one on the enriched state (w, ok). Providing our lifting scheme is sound, then by reasoning about its lifted counterpart we can thereby indirectly arrive at valid conclusions about the underlying computation itself.

Because the lifted computation is acting on the enriched state it can manipulate ok as an ordinary program variable. An always-terminating computation is of course completely described by its partial-correctness semantics, and is therefore fully characterised in predicate-transformer terms by its wlp, and in relational terms by its before-after state relation.

Since we now have two state spaces so to speak in play at the same time, namely an underlying state space characterised by w alone and an enriched one characterised by (w, ok). we must be careful to keep track over which of these our various predicate transformers are ranging. To help us do this we adopt the convention that the bold-font version **wlp** of our weakest-liberal-precondition predicate transformer ranges over the enriched state (w, ok), thereby characterising computations on this enriched state, whereas the ordinary-font wp and wlp predicate transformers range over the underlying state w and so characterise ordinary computations on that underlying state.

Note that if C is an abstract command over enriched state (w, ok), then

$$
\begin{aligned}
\mathrm{prd}(C) \ &=\ \neg\,\mathbf{wlp}(C,\,(w, ok) \neq (w', ok'))\\
&=\ \neg\,\mathbf{wlp}(C,\,w \neq w' \vee ok \neq ok')
\end{aligned}
$$

Table 2 lists the explicitly derived prds of some typical commands over the enriched state (w, ok).

Table 2. Derived prds of commands over enriched state (w, ok)

name	syntax	prd
skip	skip	$w' = w \wedge ok' = ok$
assignment	$u := E$ where $u \subseteq w$	$u' = E \wedge y' = y \wedge ok' = ok$ where y is $w \backslash u$
assignment	$ok :=$ false	$w' = w \wedge \neg\, ok'$
termination precondition	$P \mid C$	$\mathrm{prd}(C)$
guard	$G \longrightarrow C$	$G \wedge \mathrm{prd}(C)$
bounded choice	$C \sqcap D$	$\mathrm{prd}(C) \vee \mathrm{prd}(D)$
unbounded choice	$@z.\ C$	$\exists\, z, z'.\ \mathrm{prd}(C)$
sequential composition	$C\,;D$	$\mathrm{prd}(C)\,;\mathrm{prd}(D)$

5.1 Lifting Abstract Commands

We seek to associate with each abstract command S acting on a state w an always-terminating one C acting on an enriched state (w, ok), in such a way that S's wp and wlp effects can be recovered from C by

$$
\begin{aligned}
\mathrm{wp}(S, Q) &= \textbf{wlp}(C, ok \wedge Q)[\mathrm{true}/ok] \\
\mathrm{wlp}(S, Q) &= \textbf{wlp}(C, ok \Rightarrow Q)[\mathrm{true}/ok]
\end{aligned}
$$

In relational terms this is equivalent to requiring that

$$
\mathrm{trm}(S) \Vdash \mathrm{prd}(S) \quad = \quad \mathrm{P}(\mathrm{prd}(C))
$$

We will call a lifting scheme with this property *effective*. A canonical way to derive such an C would be to define it as an indeterminate assignment based on the characteristic prescription of S, as in

$$
C \quad =_{df} \quad w, ok : (\mathrm{trm}(S) \Vdash \mathrm{prd}(S))
$$

since then $\mathrm{prd}(C)$ would be $\mathrm{trm}(S) \Vdash \mathrm{prd}(S)$ which as a normal prescription is a fixed point of $\mathrm{P}()$. Such a lifting scheme, though, is impractical since it yields cumbersome lifted computations which cannot be reasoned about efficiently with the available mechanised support tools.

Instead we propose the lifting scheme L detailed in Table 3. The merit of this scheme is that it is very easy to mechanise, and yields lifted commands hardly any

Table 3. Lifting Scheme L for Abstract Commands

name of C	syntax	L(C)
skip	skip	skip
assignment	$u := E$	$u := E$
termination precondition	$P \mid S$	$(\neg P \longrightarrow ok := \text{false}) \sqcap L(S)$
guard	$G \longrightarrow S$	$(ok \Rightarrow G) \longrightarrow L(S)$
bounded choice	$S \sqcap T$	$L(S) \sqcap L(T)$
unbounded choice	$@z . S$	$@z . L(S)$
sequential composition	$S ; T$	$L(S) ; L(T)$

more complex in form than the underlying commands concerned, which are thus very amenable to efficient mechanised reasoning via the tools available. Clearly, though, our lifting scheme L is not canonical since it lifts some semantically-equivalent commands to distinct lifted commands. For example, it is easy to show that skip and $w : w' = w$ are semantically equivalent, yet L(skip) is skip while L($w : w' = w$) turns out to be

$$(\neg ok \longrightarrow @w' . w := w') \sqcap \text{skip}$$

which is clearly not the same as skip. Nevertheless, our lifting scheme does have the vital property expressed by the following proposition:

Proposition 5.1.1   (Compositionality of lifting scheme L)

For any abstract command expression S the lifting scheme L in Table 3 ensures that $\text{prd}(L(S))$ is a pseudo-prescription.

Proof: By structural induction over the syntax of abstract commands. For example, in the case of $P \mid S$ we have

$\text{prd}(L(P \mid S))$
$= \{ \text{Table 3} \}$
   $\text{prd}((\neg P \longrightarrow ok := \text{false}) \sqcap L(S))$
$= \{ \text{Table 2} \}$
   $\text{prd}(\neg P \longrightarrow ok := \text{false}) \lor \text{prd}(L(S))$
$= \{ \text{Table 2} \}$
   $(\neg P \land \text{prd}(ok := \text{false})) \lor \text{prd}(L(S))$

$= \{$ Table 2 $\}$

$\qquad (\neg P \wedge w' = w \wedge \neg ok') \ \vee \ \mathrm{prd}(\mathrm{L}(S))$ (1)

and now substituting $[\mathrm{false}, \mathrm{true}/ok, ok']$ in (1) yields

$\qquad (\neg P \wedge w' = w \wedge \neg \, \mathrm{true}) \ \vee \ \mathrm{prd}(\mathrm{L}(S))_{ft}$

$= \{$ logic $\}$

$\qquad \mathrm{false} \ \vee \ \mathrm{prd}(\mathrm{L}(S))_{ft}$

$= \{$ logic $\}$

$\qquad \mathrm{prd}(\mathrm{L}(S))_{ft}$

$= \{$ by inductive assumption $\mathrm{prd}(\mathrm{L}(S))$ is a pseudo-prescription $\}$

$\qquad \mathrm{false} \quad \{$ thus establishing that $\mathrm{prd}(\mathrm{L}(P \mid S))_{ft} \ = \ \mathrm{false} \}$

On the other hand, substituting $[\mathrm{false}, \mathrm{false}/ok, ok']$ in (1) yields

$\qquad (\neg P \wedge w' = w \wedge \neg \, \mathrm{false}) \ \vee \ \mathrm{prd}(\mathrm{L}(S))_{f\!f}$

$= \{$ logic $\}$

$\qquad (\neg P \wedge w' = w) \ \vee \ \mathrm{prd}(\mathrm{L}(S))_{f\!f}$ (2)

and then composing (2) with true yields

$\qquad ((\neg P \wedge w' = w) \ \vee \ \mathrm{prd}(\mathrm{L}(S))_{f\!f}) \, ; \mathrm{true}$

$= \{$ ";" left-distributes through $\vee$ $\}$

$\qquad ((\neg P \wedge w' = w) \, ; \mathrm{true}) \ \vee \ (\mathrm{prd}(\mathrm{L}(S))_{f\!f} \, ; \mathrm{true})$

$= \{$ by inductive assumption $\mathrm{prd}(\mathrm{L}(S))$ is a pseudo-prescription $\}$

$\qquad ((\neg P \wedge w' = w) \, ; \mathrm{true}) \ \vee \ \mathrm{true}$

$= \{$ logic $\}$

$\qquad \mathrm{true} \quad \{$ thus also establishing that $\mathrm{prd}(\mathrm{L}(P \mid S))_{f\!f} \, ; \mathrm{true} \ = \ \mathrm{true} \}$

We conclude that $\mathrm{prd}(\mathrm{L}(P \mid S))$ is indeed a pseudo-prescription if $\mathrm{L}(S)$ is.   □

This in turn leads to our main result:

Proposition 5.1.2 (Effectiveness of lifting scheme L)

For any abstract command expression S the lifting scheme L in Table 3 ensures that

$$
\begin{aligned}
\mathrm{wp}(S, Q) &= \mathbf{wlp}(\mathrm{L}(S), ok \wedge Q)[\mathrm{true}/ok] \\
\mathrm{wlp}(S, Q) &= \mathbf{wlp}(\mathrm{L}(S), ok \Rightarrow Q)[\mathrm{true}/ok]
\end{aligned}
$$

Proof: Again, by structural induction over the syntax of abstract commands. In particular, the demonstration for sequential composition follows from the compositionality of pseudo-prescriptions *via* Props 4.2.1, 4.2.2 and 5.1.1.   □

5.2 An Example

The archetypal extreme contingently-terminating computation is perhaps the infinite loop known variously as loop [26], never [11] or abort[2] [9,25]. which is

---

[2] Not to be confused with its total-correctness namesake which may or may not terminate.

in fact nowhere allowed to terminate. It is expressed in UTP relational terms by the prescription false ⊢ false, or equivalently in abstract-command terms as false | false ⟶ skip. It is never actually obliged to terminate (termination condition false), and in fact to do so it would have to achieve the impossible (postcondition false), so we can conclude it never does so. Reasoning formally directly in the abstract-command semantics of Table 1 we have

$$\text{trm(never)}$$
= { defn of never as an abstract command }
$$\text{trm(false | false} \longrightarrow \text{skip)}$$
= { defn of termination precondition in Table 1 }
$$\text{false} \wedge \text{trm(false} \longrightarrow \text{skip)}$$
= { logic }
$$\text{false}$$

meaning it is never guaranteed to terminate, while

$$\text{wlp(never, false)}$$
= { defn of never as an abstract command }
$$\text{wlp(false | false} \longrightarrow \text{skip, false)}$$
= { defn of termination precondition in Table 1 }
$$\text{wlp(false} \longrightarrow \text{skip, false)}$$
= { defn of guard in Table 1 }
$$\text{false} \Rightarrow \text{wlp(skip, false)}$$
= { logic }
$$\text{true}$$

meaning if it did so it would always establish the impossible (postcondition false), from which we can conclude it can never do so.

Now we repeat our reasoning, but this time we proceed indirectly. First we lift never using Table 3 and then we extract trm(never) and wlp(never, false) from its lifted counterpart using Prop. 5.1.2:

$$\text{L(never)}$$
= { defn of never }
$$\text{L(false | false} \longrightarrow \text{skip)}$$
= { Table 3 lifting a termination precondition }
$$(\neg \text{ false} \longrightarrow ok := \text{false}) \sqcap \text{L(false} \longrightarrow \text{skip)}$$
= { logic }
$$(\text{true} \longrightarrow ok := \text{false}) \sqcap \text{L(false} \longrightarrow \text{skip)}$$
= { discard trivial guard }
$$ok := \text{false} \sqcap \text{L(false} \longrightarrow \text{skip)}$$
= { Table 3 lifting a guard }
$$ok := \text{false} \sqcap (ok \Rightarrow \text{false}) \longrightarrow \text{L(skip)}$$

= { logic }

    $ok :=$ false $\sqcap \neg ok \longrightarrow$ L(skip)

= { Table 3 lifting skip }

    $ok :=$ false $\sqcap \neg ok \longrightarrow$ skip

And now having obtained L(never) we proceed to derive trm(never) and wlp(never, false):

    trm(never)

= { for any command S trm(S) = wp$(S,$ true$)$ }

    wp(never, true)

= { Prop. 5.1.2 }

    $\mathbf{wlp}$(L(never), $ok \wedge$ true)[true/ok]

= { logic }

    $\mathbf{wlp}$(L(never), ok)[true/ok]

= { derivation of L(never) above }

    $\mathbf{wlp}(ok :=$ false $\sqcap \neg ok \longrightarrow$ skip, ok)[true/ok]

= { defn of $\sqcap$ in Table 1 }

    $(\mathbf{wlp}(ok :=$ false, $ok) \wedge \mathbf{wlp}(\neg ok \longrightarrow$ skip, $ok))$[true/ok]

= { defn of := in Table 1 }

    (false $\wedge \mathbf{wlp}(\neg ok \longrightarrow$ skip, $ok))$[true/ok]

= { logic }

    false

as we would expect. And then we have

    wlp(never, false)

= { Prop. 5.1.2 }

    $\mathbf{wlp}$(L(never), $ok \Rightarrow$ false)[true/ok]

= { logic }

    $\mathbf{wlp}$(L(never), $\neg ok$)[true/ok]

= { derivation of L(never) above }

    $\mathbf{wlp}(ok :=$ false $\sqcap \neg ok \longrightarrow$ skip, $\neg ok$)[true/ok]

= { defn of $\sqcap$ in Table 1 }

    $(\mathbf{wlp}(ok :=$ false, $\neg ok) \wedge \mathbf{wlp}(\neg ok \longrightarrow$ skip, $\neg ok))$[true/ok]

= { defn of := in Table 1 }

    $(\neg$ false $\wedge \mathbf{wlp}(\neg ok \longrightarrow$ skip, $\neg ok))$[true/ok]

= { logic }

    $\mathbf{wlp}(\neg ok \longrightarrow$ skip, $\neg ok$)[true/ok]

= { defn of guard in Table 1 }

    $(\neg ok \Rightarrow \mathbf{wlp}($skip, $\neg ok))$[true/ok]

= { defn of skip in Table 1 }

$$(\neg\ ok \Rightarrow \neg\ ok)[\text{true}/ok]$$
$$= \{\ \text{logic}\ \}$$
    true

again as we would expect. This illustrates how reasoning about our infinite loop never, as it were vicariously, through its lifted always-terminating counterpart $ok := \text{false}\ \sqcap\ \neg\ ok \longrightarrow \text{skip}$ is both effective and sound.

6 Conclusion

We have shown how a contingently-terminating computation expressed by an abstract command can be equivalently expressed as a prescription. Conversely, we have shown how a prescription can be interpreted as an abstract command by extracting its wp and wlp predicate-transformer effects. We also showed how each of these can be regarded as particular cases of a higher-level predicate transformer **wrp** also extractible from the prescription, which works on "rich conditions" rather than ordinary conditions, thus achieving a interesting unification of wp and wlp.

We defined the new notion of the intrinsic prescription encoded within an arbitrary relation over (w, ok, w', ok') and used this to define our idempotent "healthifying" function P( ) applying to all such relations and yielding normal prescriptions. We identified a class of relations over (w, ok, w', ok') called pseudo-prescriptions subsuming prescriptions and showed that not only are these closed under disjunction and relational composition, but that they also have the important property of compositionality with respect to their intrinsic prescriptions. We defined an efficient easily-mechanisable lifting scheme for abstract commands whose lifted counterparts correspond to pseudo-prescriptions whose compositionality guarantees the effectiveness of the scheme. The importance of such a scheme is that it gives us the means to reason in general correctness about our abstract-command programs with existing support tools only designed to reason in total or partial correctness, without needing to modify these at all.

From a theoretical point of view it is interesting to note that we know our pseudo-prescriptions are not the least-constrained effective encodings of our contingently-terminating computations. It remains to characterise these least-constrained such encodings, and investigate whether they might offer any advantages over pseudo-prescriptions.

References

1. Abrial, J.-R.: The B-Book: Assigning Programs to Meanings. Cambridge University Press, Cambridge (1996)
2. B-Core. The B-Toolkit. http://www.b-core.com
3. Back, R.-J., von Wright, J.: Refinement Calculus: A Systematic Introduction. Springer, Berlin Heidelberg (1998)
4. Chen, Y.: A fixpoint theory for non-monotonic parallelism. Theoretical Computer Science 308, 367–392 (2003)

5. ClearSy. Atelierb. `http://www.atelierb.societe.com`
6. Dawson, J.E.: Formalising general correctness. In: Computing: The Australasian Theory Symposium 2004. Electronic Notes in Theoretical Computer Science, vol. 91, pp. 46–65. Elsevier, Amsterdam (2004)
7. Deutsch, M., Henson, M.C.: A relational investigation of UTP designs and per-scriptions. In: Dunne, S.E., Stoddart, W.J. (eds.) UTP 2006. LNCS, vol. 4010, pp. 101–122. Springer, Heidelberg (2006)
8. Dijkstra, E.W.: A Discipline of Programming. Prentice-Hall, Englewood Cliffs (1976)
9. Dijkstra, E.W., Scholten, C.S.: Predicate Calculus and Program Semantics. Springer, Berlin Heidelberg (1990)
10. Dunne, S.E.: Abstract commands: a uniform notation for specifications and implementations. In: Fidge, C.J. (ed.) Computing: The Australasian Theory Symposium 2001. Electronic Notes in Theoretical Computer Science, vol. 42, Elsevier, Amsterdam (2001) `http://www.elsevier.nl/locate/entcs`
11. Dunne, S.E.: Recasting Hoare and He's unifying theory of programs in the context of general correctness. In: Butterfield, A., Strong, G., Pahl, C. (eds.) Proceedings of the 5th Irish Workshop in Formal Methods, IWFM 2001, Workshops in Computing, British Computer Society, Vancouver (2001), `http://ewic.bcs.org/conferences/2001/5thformal/papers`
12. Dunne, S.E., Stoddart, W.J., Galloway, A.J.: Specification and refinement in general correctness. In: Evans, A., Duke, D., Clark, A. (eds.) Proceedings of the 3rd Northern Formal Methods Workshop. BCS Electronic Workshops in Computing (1998) `http://www.ewic.org.uk/ewic/workshop/view.cfm/NFM-98`
13. Guttmann, W., Möller, B.: Modal design algebra. In: Dunne, S.E., Stoddart, W.J. (eds.) UTP 2006. LNCS, vol. 4010, pp. 236–256. Springer, Heidelberg (2006)
14. Hayes, I.J.: Separating timing and calculation in real-time refinement. In: Grundy, J., Schwenke, M., Vickers, T. (eds.) International Refinement Workshop and Formal Methods Pacific 1998, pp. 1–16. Springer, Heidelberg (1998)
15. Hayes, I.J.: Reasoning about non-terminating loops using deadline commands. In: Backhouse, R., Oliveira, J. (eds) Mathematics of Program Construction (MPC2000), (2000) Also available as Technical Report UQ-SVRC-00-02, `http://svrc.it.uq.edu.au`
16. Hehner, E.C.R.: Termination is timing. In: van de Snepscheut, J.L.A. (ed.) Mathematics of Program Construction. LNCS, vol. 375, pp. 36–47. Springer, Heidelberg (1989)
17. Hehner, E.C.R.: A Practical Theory of Programming. Springer, Heidelberg (1993)
18. Hehner, E.C.R., Gravell, A.M.: Refinement semantics and loop rules. In: Woodcock, J.C.P., Davies, J., Wing, J.M. (eds.) FM 1999. LNCS, vol. 1709, pp. 1497–1510. Springer, Heidelberg (1999)
19. Hesselink, W.H.: Programs, Recursion and Unbounded Choice. Cambridge Tracts in Theoretical Computer Science, vol. 27. Cambridge University Press, Cambridge (1992)
20. Hoare, C.A.R., Jifeng, H.: Unifying Theories of Programming. Prentice Hall, Englewood Cliffs (1998)
21. Jacobs, D., Gries, D.: General correctness: a unification of partial and total correctness. Acta. Informatica 22, 67–83 (1985)
22. Leuschel, M., Butler, M.: ProB: a model checker for B. In: Araki, K., Gnesi, S., Mandrioli, D. (eds.) FME 2003. LNCS, vol. 2805, pp. 855–874. Springer, Heidelberg (2003)

23. Milner, A.J.R.G.: Computing is interaction. Invited address FACS 21st Anniversary Symposium, December 2, 1998. The Royal Society, London (1998)
24. Morgan, C.C.: Programming from Specifications, 2nd edn. Prentice Hall International, Englewood Cliffs (1994)
25. Morgan, C.C., McIver, A.: Unifying wp and wlp. Information Processing Letters 59, 159–163 (1996)
26. Nelson, G.: A generalisation of Dijkstra's calculus. ACM Transactions on Programmg Languages and Systems, vol. 11(4) (1989)

Verifying CSP-OZ-DC Specifications with Complex Data Types and Timing Parameters*

Johannes Faber[1], Swen Jacobs[2], and Viorica Sofronie-Stokkermans[2]

[1] Department of Computing Science, University of Oldenburg, Germany
j.faber@uni-oldenburg.de
[2] Max-Planck-Institut Informatik, Saarbrücken, Germany
{sjacobs,sofronie}@mpi-sb.mpg.de

Abstract. We extend existing verification methods for CSP-OZ-DC to reason about real-time systems with complex data types and timing parameters. We show that important properties of systems can be encoded in well-behaved logical theories in which hierarchic reasoning is possible. Thus, testing invariants and bounded model checking can be reduced to checking satisfiability of ground formulae over a simple base theory. We illustrate the ideas by means of a simplified version of a case study from the European Train Control System standard.

1 Introduction

Complex real-time systems, consisting of several components that interact, arise in a natural way in a wide range of applications. In order to verify these systems, one needs, on the one hand, to find a suitable specification language, and on the other hand, to develop efficient techniques for their verification.

In the *specification of complex systems*, one needs to take several aspects into account: control flow, data changes, and timing aspects. Motivated by this necessity, in [HO02, Hoe06] a specification language CSP-OZ-DC (COD) is defined, which combines Communicating Sequential Processes (CSP), Object-Z (OZ) and the Duration Calculus (DC). *Verification tasks* (e.g., invariant checking or bounded model checking) can usually be reduced to proof tasks in theories associated to the COD specification. These theories can be combinations of concrete theories (e.g., integer, rational or real numbers) and abstract theories (e.g., theories of functions or of data structures). Existing verification techniques for COD [HM05, MFR06] do not incorporate efficient reasoning in complex theories, which is essential to perform such verification tasks efficiently.

In this paper, we analyse both aspects mentioned above. We use COD specifications of systems, with complex data types and timing parameters, and analyse possibilities for efficient invariant checking and bounded model checking in these systems. The main contributions of the paper can be described as follows.

---

* This work was partly supported by the German Research Council (DFG) under grant SFB/TR 14 AVACS. See http://www.avacs.org for more information.

J. Davies and J. Gibbons (Eds.): IFM 2007, LNCS 4591, pp. 233–252, 2007.

Specification: We extend existing work in which COD specifications were used [HO02, Hoe06, MFR06] in two ways:

(i) We use abstract data structures for representing and storing information about an unspecified *parametric* number of components of the systems. This allows us to pass in an elegant way from verification of several finite instances of a verification problem (for 2, 3, 4, ... components) to general verification results, in which the number of components is a parameter.

(ii) In order to refer to time constants also within the specification's data (OZ) part, we introduce timing parameters. This allows for more flexible specifications of timing constraints.

Verification: We show that, in this context, invariant checking or bounded model checking can be reduced to proving in complex theories. We analyse the theories that occur in relationship with a given COD specification, and present a sound and efficient method for hierarchic reasoning in such theories. We identify situations where the method is sound and complete (i.e., where the specific properties of systems define chains of local theory extensions).

Applications: Our running example is an extension of a case study that we considered in [JSS07] (in which we first applied hierarchic reasoning in the verification of train control systems). Here, we additionally encompass efficient handling of emergency messages and illustrate the full procedure – starting from a COD description of the case study to the verification.

Structure of the paper. We illustrate the idea of our approach by means of a case study, which will be our running example (Sect. 1.1). Section 2 introduces the specification language COD and discusses an extension with timing parameters. Section 3 presents an operational semantics of COD specifications, in terms of Phase Event Automata (PEA), and discusses some simplifications for PEA. Section 4 presents a verification method for COD specifications: the associated PEA are translated into transition constraint systems; verification is reduced to satisfiability checking in combinations of theories. We identify some theories, in which hierarchic reasoning is possible, occurring frequently in applications.

1.1   Illustration

We here give a general description of a case study inspired by the specification of the European Train Control System (ETCS) standard [ERT02]. We explain the tools we used for modelling the example and give the idea of the method for checking safety. This will be used as a running example throughout the paper. Related ETCS scenarios have been studied in [HJU05, FM06, MFR06, TZ06].

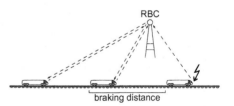

Fig. 1. Emergencies in the ETCS

The example we consider has a less complicated control structure than those in [FM06, MFR06]. Instead, it considers an arbitrary number of trains, and hence, needs to use more realistic and sophisticated data types.

The RBC Case Study. We consider a radio block centre (RBC), which communicates with all trains on a given track segment. The situation is sketched in Fig. 1. Every train reports its position to the RBC in given time intervals and the RBC communicates to every train how far it can safely move, based on the position of the preceding train; the trains adjust their speed between given minimum and maximum speeds. If a train has to stop suddenly, it sends an emergency message. The RBC handles the message sent by a train (which we refer to as emergency train) by instructing each train behind the emergency train on the track to stop too.

Idea. In this case study, the following aspects need to be considered:

(1) The scenario describes processes running in parallel.
(2) We need to specify the state space and the pre- and postconditions of actions.
(3) There are timing constraints on the duration of system states.

For encompassing all these aspects, we use the specification language COD, that allows to express the control flow of the systems (expressed in CSP), data structures used for modelling state and state change (OZ) and time constraints (DC). We pass from specification to verification as follows:

- We associate so-called *Phase Event Automata* A_{CSP}, A_{OZ}, A_{DC} with the CSP, OZ and DC part, respectively. Their parallel composition A represents the semantics of the COD specification.
- From A we derive a family of transition constraints that describe the properties of the transitions in the system.
- We use this set of transition constraints for checking given safety properties.

This last verification step is highly non-trivial. Transition constraints may combine constraints over various theories. In our case, we need to reason in a combination of a theory of integers (indices of trains), reals (for modelling speeds or distances), arrays (in which the current speed and reported positions of the trains are stored), and functions (e.g., associating with each speed an upper bound for the optimal braking distance at that speed). Many of these data structures have additional properties, which need to be specified as axioms in first-order logic with quantifiers. We show that properties of systems can be encoded in well-behaved logical theories in which efficient reasoning is possible.

2   CSP-OZ-DC: A High-Level Specification Language

In order to capture the control flow, data changes, and timing aspects of the systems we want to verify, we use the high-level specification language CSP-OZ-DC (COD) [HM05, Hoe06], which integrates three well-investigated formalisms: *Communicating Sequential Processes* [Hoa85], *Object-Z* [Smi00], and *Duration Calculus* [ZH04], allowing the compositional and declarative specification of each aspect by means of the best-suited formalism. In particular, data and data changes are specified in a constraint-based representation (using OZ). In this paper, we use this advantage of the COD representation and extend the known verification procedures for COD [HM05, MFR06] to combination of theories.

We give an intuition of the formalism and its advantages using our case study: We model a *radio block centre* (RBC) that controls the railway traffic on a single (to simplify matters infinite) track segment. This RBC controls n consecutive trains, represented by their position and speed values. The full COD specification is given in Fig. 2, that we explain in the remainder of this section.

The specification begins with the declaration of a timing parameter T_PR (cf. Sect. 2.1), followed by the *interface part*, in which methods are declared. These methods are used in all parts (CSP, OZ, DC) of the COD specification, and provide the functionality of the COD class.

Interface: ————————————————————————————
method *positionReport*
method *detectEmergency* : $[trainNumber : \mathbb{N}]$

CSP. We use CSP [Hoa85] to specify the control flow of a system using processes over events. The interface part declares all possible events.

CSP: ————————————————————————————
$$\mathtt{main} \stackrel{c}{=} Driveability \parallel\parallel\parallel Detection$$
$$Driveability \stackrel{c}{=} positionReport \rightarrow Driveability$$
$$Detection \stackrel{c}{=} detectEmergency \rightarrow Detection$$

The **main** process of our specification comprises an interleaving of two subprocesses, *Driveability* and *Detection*, for controlling the trains and incoming emergency messages synchronously. The *Detection* process detects emergencies using *detectEmergency* events, while the *Driveability* process regularly updates the train positions using *positionReport* events.

OZ. The data space and its changes are specified with OZ schemata [Smi00]. The OZ part of the running example begins with the state schema defining the state space of the RBC. Positions and speed values of the trains are given by sequences $train : \text{seq}\, Position$ and $speed : \text{seq}\, Speed$, where the types are given by reals: $Position == \mathbb{R}$, $Speed == \mathbb{R}^+$. Sequences, in the sense of OZ, are partial functions $train : \mathbb{N} \rightarrow Position$, that are defined for all $i \leq n$. A third data type is *Acceleration*, which is also real-valued: $Acceleration == \mathbb{R}^+$.

State space: ————————————————————————————
$train : \text{seq}\, Position$	$emergencyTrain : \mathbb{N}$
$speed : \text{seq}\, Speed$	$maxDec : Acceleration$
$maxSpeed, minSpeed : Speed$	$d : Position$
$brakingDist : Speed \rightarrow Position$	$n : \mathbb{N}$

The variable *emergencyTrain* is a pointer to the first train on the track that reported an emergency. We also define some important constants, for the maximal speed, for the minimal speed (without emergencies), the number of trains n, and the safety margin between trains d. Next follow axioms for the data structures defined in the state schema.

Axioms: ——

$0 < minSpeed < maxSpeed$
$n = \#train = \#speed$
$0 < d = brakingDist(maxSpeed)$
$\forall s : Speed \bullet brakingDist(s) \geq \frac{s^2}{2*maxDec}$
$\forall s_1, s_2 : Speed \mid s_1 < s_2 \bullet brakingDist(s_1) < brakingDist(s_2)$
$brakingDist(0) = 0$

——

The latter three axioms ensure a safety distance between the trains. The function *brakingDist* yields for a given speed value the distance needed by a train in order to stop if the emergency brakes are applied. For the constant maximal deceleration *maxDec*, the minimal braking distance for a speed value *spd* is $\frac{spd^2}{2*maxDec}$. Since the trains can not always reach their maximal deceleration, we define this term as a lower bound for our braking function. We require monotonicity of *brakingDist* and specify its value for a speed value of 0.

Every COD class has an `Init` schema (cf. Fig. 2) that constrains initial values of state variables, and communication schemata which define state changes. Every communication schema (prefix `com`) belongs to a CSP event as given by the interface of a class. Every time a CSP event occurs the state space is changed according to the constraints of the appropriate communication schema.

———— `com`_*detectEmergency* ————————————————————————————
$\Delta(speed, emergencyTrain)$
$newEmergencyTrain? : \mathbb{N}$
——
$newEmergencyTrain? \leq n$
$emergencyTrain' = min\{newEmergencyTrain?, emergencyTrain\}$
$speed'(emergencyTrain') = 0$
$\forall i \in \mathbb{N} \mid i \neq emergencyTrain' \bullet speed'(i) = speed(i)$
——

Consider for instance the schema for *detectEmergency*. The first line identifies state variables that are changed by this schema, the remaining variables implicitly stay unchanged. The expression *newEmergencyTrain?* (second line) represents an input variable. The following lines constrain state changes (primed variables denote the post-state while unprimed variables refer to the pre-state). For example $emergencyTrain' = min\{newEmergencyTrain?, emergencyTrain\}$ sets the new value for *emergencyTrain*. (The train with the lowest number is the first on the track. So, *emergencyTrain* always points to the first train on the track that reported an emergency.) The schema `com`_*positionReport* (Fig. 2) sets the speed values for all trains and calculates their new positions: without an emergency train in front, the speed can be arbitrary between *minSpeed* and *maxSpeed*, unless the distance to the previous train is too small ($< d$); in this case the speed is set to *minSpeed*. In case of an emergency, the trains behind the emergency train brake with maximal deceleration.

DC. The duration calculus (DC) is an interval-based dense real-time logic [ZH04]. Important operators of the DC are the *chop* operator $\frown$ that splits an interval into subintervals, the operator ℓ yielding the length of an interval, and the *every-where* operator $\lceil p \rceil$ specifying that a predicate p holds everywhere on an interval. An explicit time constant $t \in \mathbb{Q}^+$ or a symbolic constant T are used to define interval lengths. Since DC is undecidable we use a decidable sub-class (counter-example formulae). We apply the algorithm of [Hoe06] to generate automata from DC specifications of this subclass.

$DC:$ ───

$\neg(true \frown \updownarrow positionReport \frown (\ell < T\_PR) \frown \updownarrow positionReport \frown true)$
$\neg(true \frown \boxminus positionReport \wedge (\ell > T\_PR) \frown true)$

───

In the DC specification above, the first formula specifies that it will never be the case ($\neg$) that two *positionReport* events ($\updownarrow$) are separated ($\frown$) by an interval with a length (ℓ) smaller than T_PR. (So there will be at least T_PR time units between two position reports.) In the second formula, $\boxminus$ describes an interval in which no position report event is detected. The formula states that there is no interval of a length greater than T_PR without a *positionReport* event. Together the formulae define the exact periodicity of *positionReport*.

2.1   Timing Parameters in COD

The original definition of COD in [Hoe06] only allows for using rational numbers to define interval lengths. This restriction results in a loss of generality: a developer always has to define exact values for every interval, even if the specification does not depend on an exact length. In our example, one has to replace the T_PR constant in the DC formulae with a fixed rational to get a valid COD specification. To overcome this problem, we introduce *timing parameters* as an extension for COD. That is, we allow the usage of symbolic constants for the interval definitions in the DC part, like T_PR in our example. These symbolic constants are declared as generic constants (parameters of the class) and also are accessible in the OZ part. For instance, we use T_PR in the schema of *positionReport*. That allows us to use the same (undetermined) interval length in the OZ and in the DC part.

3   Operational Semantics of COD Specifications

In this section, we present a translation from COD specifications to PEA. We extend existing translations from COD to PEA to also deal with timing parameters and study possibilities of simplifying the PEA obtained this way.

3.1   Translation of COD Specifications into PEA

Phase Event Automata (PEA) are timed automata [AD94] involving both data and timing aspects. Our definition of PEA is based on [Hoe06], but differs in that we also allow symbolic constants to occur in clock invariants $\mathcal{L}^c(C)$. In what follows, let $\mathcal{L}(V)$ be a subset of the language of OZ predicates.[1] For a

───────────────────────────

[1] Ideally, $\mathcal{L}(V)$ should be expressive enough so that specifications with complex data types can be translated, but should permit automatic verification.

```
┌─ RBC[T_PR : ℚ⁺] ──────────────────────────────────────────────────┐
│  method positionReport                                             │
│  method detectEmergency : [trainNumber : ℕ]                        │
│         main ≙ Driveability ||| Detection                          │
│  Driveability ≙ positionReport → Driveability                      │
│    Detection ≙ detectEmergency → Detection                         │
```

$$train : \text{seq } Position \qquad\qquad emergencyTrain : \mathbb{N}$$
$$speed : \text{seq } Speed \qquad\qquad maxDec : Acceleration$$
$$maxSpeed, minSpeed : Speed \qquad d : Position$$
$$brakingDist : Speed \to Position \qquad n : \mathbb{N}$$

$$0 < minSpeed < maxSpeed$$
$$n = \#train = \#speed$$
$$0 < d = brakingDist(maxSpeed) \qquad\qquad (1)$$
$$\forall s : Speed \bullet brakingDist(s) \geq \frac{s^2}{2*maxDec}$$
$$\forall s_1, s_2 : Speed \mid s_1 < s_2 \bullet brakingDist(s_1) < brakingDist(s_2)$$
$$brakingDist(0) = 0$$

Init
$$emergencyTrain > n$$
$$\forall i : \text{dom } speed \bullet minSpeed \leq speed(i) \leq maxSpeed$$
$$\forall i : \text{dom } train \mid i \neq 1$$
$$\bullet train(i) < train(i-1) - brakingDist(speed(i))$$

com_positionReport
$$\Delta(train, speed)$$

$$\forall i : \text{dom } train \mid i = 1 \wedge i < emergencyTrain$$
$$\bullet minSpeed \leq speed'(i) \leq maxSpeed$$
$$\forall i : \text{dom } train \mid 1 < i < emergencyTrain \wedge train(i-1) - train(i) \geq d$$
$$\bullet minSpeed \leq speed'(i) \leq maxSpeed$$
$$\forall i : \text{dom } train \mid 1 < i < emergencyTrain \wedge train(i-1) - train(i) < d$$
$$\bullet minSpeed = speed'(i)$$
$$\forall i : \text{dom } train \mid i \geq emergencyTrain$$
$$\bullet speed'(i) = max\{speed(i) - maxDec * T\_PR, 0\}$$
$$\forall i : \text{dom } train \bullet train'(i) = train(i) + speed'(i) * T\_PR$$

com_detectEmergency
$$\Delta(speed, emergencyTrain)$$
$$newEmergencyTrain? : \mathbb{N}$$

$$newEmergencyTrain? \leq n$$
$$emergencyTrain' = min\{newEmergencyTrain?, emergencyTrain\}$$
$$speed'(emergencyTrain') = 0$$
$$\forall i \in \mathbb{N} \mid i \neq emergencyTrain' \bullet speed'(i) = speed(i)$$

$$\neg(true ^\frown \text{\textcommabelow{}} positionReport ^\frown (\ell < T\_PR) ^\frown \text{\textcommabelow{}} positionReport ^\frown true)$$
$$\neg(true ^\frown \boxminus positionReport \wedge (\ell > T\_PR) ^\frown true)$$

CSP Inter-part face

OZ part

DC part

Fig. 2. The COD specification for the emergency case study

set C of clock variables and timing parameters T, the set $\mathcal{L}^c(C, T)$ of (convex) *clock constraints* with constants is defined by the following BNF grammar:

$$\delta ::= c < t \mid c \leq t \mid c < z \mid c \leq z \mid \delta \wedge \delta,$$

where $c \in C$ is a clock, $t \in \mathbb{Q}^+$ is a rational constant, and $z \in T$ is a timing parameter. The semantics is given by clock valuations $\gamma : C \to \mathbb{R}^+$ assigning non-negative reals to clocks. The semantics of a timing parameter z is an interpretation $\mathcal{I} : T \to \mathbb{Q}^+$. We write $\gamma, \mathcal{I} \models \delta$ iff δ holds for γ and $\mathcal{I}$. For a set of clocks X, we denote by $(\gamma + t)$ the increasing of clocks, i.e., $(\gamma + t)(c) := \gamma(c) + t$, and by $\gamma[X := 0]$ the valuation, where each clock in X is set to zero and the values of the remaining clocks are given by γ.

Definition 1 (Phase Event Automaton). *A phase event automaton (PEA) is a tuple* $(P, V, A, C, E, s, I, P^0)$*, where* P *is a finite set of locations (phases) with initial locations* $P^0 \subseteq P$*;* V, A, C *are finite sets of real-valued variables, events, and real-valued clocks, respectively;* $s : P \to \mathcal{L}(V)$*,* $I : P \to \mathcal{L}^c(C, T)$ *assign state invariants resp. clock invariants to phases. The set of edges is* $E \subseteq P \times \mathcal{L}(V \cup V' \cup A \cup C) \times \mathbb{P}(C) \times P$*. We assume that a* stuttering edge $(p, \bigwedge_{e \in A} \neg e \wedge \bigwedge_{v \in V} v' = v, \varnothing, p)$ *(empty transition) exists for every phase* p*.*

   The operational semantics of PEA is defined by infinite runs of configurations $\langle (p_0, \beta_0, \gamma_0, t_0, Y_0), (p_1, \beta_1, \gamma_1, t_1, Y_1), \cdots \rangle$*, where initially* $p_0 \in P^0$ *and* $\gamma_0(c) = 0$ *for* $c \in C$*. For* $i \in \mathbb{N}$ *and variable valuations* β_i *(with* $\beta_i(v) = \beta'_i(v')$*) we demand* $\beta(i) \models s(p_i)$ *and* $\gamma_i + t_i, \mathcal{I} \models I(p_i)$ *and* $t_i > 0$*. For transitions* $(p_i, g, X, p_{i+1}) \in E$ *we further require* $\beta_i, \beta'_{i+1}, \gamma_i + t_i, Y_i \models g$ *and* $\gamma_{i+1} = (\gamma_i + t_i)[X := 0]$*.*

Thus, a PEA is an automaton enriched by constraints to define data changes and clocks to measure time (similar to a timed automaton). An edge (p_1, g, X, p_2) represents a transition from p_1 to p_2 with a guard g over (possibly primed) variables, clocks, and events, and a set X of clocks that are to be reset. Primed variables v' denote the post-state of v whereas the unprimed v always refers to the pre-state. In the parallel composition of PEA, we consider conjunctions of guards of transitions and invariants of locations.

Definition 2 (Parallel Composition). *The parallel composition of two PEA* $\mathcal{A}_1$ *and* $\mathcal{A}_2$*, where* $\mathcal{A}_i = (P_i, V_i, A_i, C_i, E_i, s_i, I_i, P_i^0)$*, is defined by*

$$\mathcal{A}_1 \parallel \mathcal{A}_2 := (P_1 \times P_2, V_1 \cup V_2, A_1 \cup A_2, C_1 \cup C_2, E, s_1 \wedge s_2, I_1 \wedge I_2, P_1^0 \times P_2^0),$$

where $((p_1, p_2), g_1 \wedge g_2, X_1 \cup X_2, (p'_1, p'_2)) \in E$ *iff* $(p_i, g_i, X_i, p'_i) \in E_i$ *with* $i = 1, 2$*.*

The translation of COD specifications into PEA is compositional: every part of the specification is translated separately into PEA; the semantics for the entire specification is the parallel composition of the automata for every part: $\mathcal{A}(COD) = \mathcal{A}(CSP) \parallel \mathcal{A}(OZ) \parallel \mathcal{A}(DC)$.

Translation of the CSP part. The translation of the CSP part into PEA is based on the structured operational semantics of CSP [Ros98]. If this semantics of the CSP part is given as a labelled transition system $(Q, A, q_0, \longrightarrow)$ with locations Q and events A from the COD specification, its PEA is $\mathcal{A}(CSP) = (Q, \varnothing, A, \varnothing, E, s, I, \{q_0\})$, where $s(q) = true$, $I(q) = true$ for all $q \in Q$ and

$$E = \{(p, only(e), \varnothing, p') \mid p \xrightarrow{e} p'\} \cup \{(p, only(\tau), \varnothing, p) \mid p \in Q\}.$$

The predicate $only(e)$ demands that only the event e is communicated whereas $only(\tau)$ demands that no event is communicated. That is, E consists of transitions for every transition in the original transition system and of stuttering edges for every location. The PEA of our example's CSP part is pictured in Fig. 3.

Translation of the OZ part. The OZ part of a COD specification is translated into a PEA with two locations: one for setting the initial values of state variables and one for the running system, with a transition for each state changing event. The variables of the PEA are the variables $Var(State)$ declared in the state schema. The set A of events of the PEA consists of all COD events for which a communication schema $\mathtt{com\_c}$ exists. For each such event the automaton has a transition executing the state change as defined in the associated communication schema. The resulting PEA is $\mathcal{A}(OZ) = (\{p_0, p_1\}, Var(State), A, \varnothing, E, s, I, \{q_0\})$, where $s(p_0) = \mathtt{Init}$ (invariant from the initial schema), $s(p_1) = State$ (invariant from the state schema), $I(p_i) = true$ for i $= 1,2$, and

$$E = \{(p_1, only(c) \wedge \mathtt{com\_c}, \varnothing, p_1) \mid c \in A\} \cup$$
$$\{(p_i, only(\tau) \wedge \varXi State, \varnothing, p_i) \mid i = 1, 2\} \cup \{(p_0, only(\tau) \wedge \varXi State, \varnothing, p_1)\}.$$

The OZ predicate $\varXi State$ demands that the state space is not changed: $\varXi State :\Leftrightarrow \bigwedge_{v \in Var(State)} v' = v$. The formula $\mathtt{com\_c}$ only changes the state of the variables occurring in the $\varDelta$ list of the corresponding operation schema; the remaining variables remain implicitly unchanged. The OZ part PEA of the RBC is illustrated in Fig. 3. Formula (1) refers to the state schema from Fig. 2. The operation schemata, e.g., $\mathtt{com\_}positionReport$ refer to the constraints of the specification.

Translation of the DC part. Each formula of the DC part is translated into an individual PEA. The translation of counter-example formulae (cf. Sect. 2), e.g., $\neg(phase_0 \frown event_1 \frown phase_1 \frown \cdots \frown phase_n)$, into PEA is similar to the translation of a non-deterministic finite automaton into a deterministic one: every location of the resulting automaton represents a subset of DC phases. Every run of the automaton leading to a location labelled with $phase_i$ accepts the prefix of the DC counter-example up to $phase_i$. In addition, $phase_i$ may have an upper or lower time bound. In this case, the automaton includes a clock c_i measuring the duration of the phase. Event expressions $event_i$ separating two DC phases constitute the guards that restrict transitions from $phase_{i-1}$ to $phase_i$. Technical details of the construction can be found in [Hoe06]. The automata for the DC part of the RBC specification are displayed in Fig. 3(c). For instance, the upper automaton enforces the behaviour defined by the second DC formulae of our example (Fig. 2). It consists of one location with a clock invariant, i.e, the automaton stays in this location for at most T_PR time units – the only way to reset the clock $c1$ is the transition that synchronises on $positionReport$. By this, every $positionReport$ event has to occur in time.

3.2   PEA with Timing Parameters

As we allow timing parameters to occur in the DC part and in convex clock expressions, we need to adapt the translation of the DC part into PEA given in [Hoe06]: since the original translation does not depend on concrete values of rational constants, we can treat timing parameters exactly like rational constants. The clock constraints generated by the translation are then convex as before.

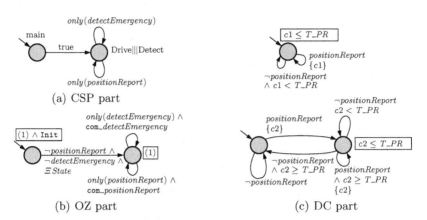

Fig. 3. PEA for the RBC case study. Boxes around formulae indicate state invariants; braces ($\{c1\}$,$\{c2\}$) indicate clock resets.; Ξ is defined on page 241.

Important properties of PEA, e.g., the translation into TCS (cf. Sect. 4), only depend on the convexity of clock constraints. We thus obtain:

Theorem 1. *The translation from COD with complex data types and timing parameters to PEA described here is sound (i.e., the PEA runs are exactly the system runs admitted by the CSP, OZ, and DC part) and compositional.*

3.3   Simplifications of PEA

As mentioned in Section 3.1, the operational semantics of the whole COD specification is given by the parallel product of the individual PEA. This product can grow very large: theoretically, its size is the product of the size of all individual automata, both in terms of locations and in terms of transitions. We propose the following simplifications for the product PEA:

- Transitions whose combined guards evaluate to `false` can be removed, as can be locations that are not connected to an initial state. We can also remove all events from the PEA, as these are only used for synchronising the individual automata [Hoe06].
- Consider the case that we have several clocks in the product automaton. All clocks run at the same speed and can be reset to 0 by transitions. If we have two (or more) clocks for which the set of transitions that resets them is the same, we can identify them, i.e., remove one clock and replace it by the other in all guards. This not only gives us a system with one variable less, but may also remove additional transitions by making their guards `false`.

Theorem 2. *Let $\mathcal{A} = (P, V, A, C, E, s, I, P^0)$ be a PEA, $c_1, c_2 \in C$. If $\{(p_1, g, X, p_2) \in E \mid c_1 \in X\} = \{(p_1, g, X, p_2) \in E \mid c_2 \in X\}$, then $\mathcal{A}$ is equivalent to $\mathcal{A}' = (P, V, A, C \setminus \{c_2\}, E', s', I', P^0)$, where E', s' and I' result from E, s and I by replacing all occurrences of c_2 by c_1.*

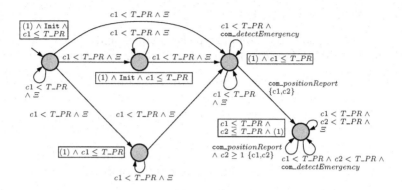

Fig. 4. Simplified product PEA

Applied to the running example, the first simplification reduces the product automaton from 8 locations and 90 transitions (without stuttering edges) to 5 locations and 10 transitions. With the second one, we remove one clock variable and one additional transition from the product automaton. The entire product automaton with simplifications is pictured in Fig. 4. It basically comprises four locations representing slightly different possibilities to initialise the system and one dead end location in the lower right corner. The latter is eventually entered and can be interpreted as the main state of the system. Here the trains periodically report their positions to the RBC and emergencies may be detected.

4   Verification of COD Specifications

In this section, we elaborate on verifying safety properties of systems with complex data types specified in COD, based on their translation to PEA. We define transition constraint systems (TCS) and show how to extract a TCS from a PEA. We introduce the verification tasks that we consider. After an intuitive presentation of our idea for efficient verification, we formally analyse situations where verification problems can be reduced to checking satisfiability of ground formulae over a simple theory. The method is illustrated on the running example.

Language and theory associated with a COD specification. Let S be a COD specification. The *signature of S*, Σ_S consists of all sorts, functions and predicates declared in the OZ specification either implicitly (by mentioning standard theories) or explicitly. The theory of S, $\mathcal{T}_S$ is constructed by extending the (many-sorted) combination $\mathcal{T}_0$ of all standard theories used in the OZ and DC specification with the functions declared in the OZ part and the axioms for the data structures specified at the beginning of the OZ part (which we will denote by Ax). In what follows, the theory $\mathcal{T}_S$ will be considered to be a background theory: even if we do not refer to it explicitly, it is always taken into account.

4.1   Translation of PEA to TCS

Let Σ be a signature, $\mathcal{V}$ a set of (typed) variables, and $\mathcal{V}'$ a copy of corresponding primed variables. Let $\mathcal{F}(X)$ be the family of all Σ-formulae in the variables X.

Definition 3 (Transition Constraint Systems). *A transition constraint system T is a tuple $(\mathcal{V}, \Theta, \Phi)$ with $\Theta \in \mathcal{F}(\mathcal{V})$ and $\Phi \in \mathcal{F}(\mathcal{V} \cup \mathcal{V}')$. The formula Θ characterises the* initial states *of T, Φ the* transition constraints *of T (i.e., the relationships between the variables $\mathcal{V}$ and $\mathcal{V}'$ – before and after transitions).*

A translation from PEA to TCS has been developed by Hoenicke and Maier [HM05, Hoe06]. We use the simplified translation from [Hoe06].

Let S be a COD specification and $\mathcal{A}_S = (P, V, A, C, E, s, I, P_0)$ the PEA associated with S. We associate with $\mathcal{A}_S$ the TCS $T(\mathcal{A}_S) = (\mathcal{V}, \Theta, \Phi)$, where:

- $\mathcal{V} = V \cup A \cup C \cup \{\mathsf{len}, \mathsf{pc}\}$, where len is a real-valued variable representing the time spent in the current state, and pc is the *program counter* that is interpreted over P and represents the current location (phase) of the system.
- $\Theta = \bigvee_{p \in P_0} \mathsf{pc}{=}p \wedge \mathsf{len}{>}0 \wedge \bigwedge_{c \in C} c{=}\mathsf{len} \wedge s(p) \wedge I(p)$. Θ requires that there exists an initial location p in which a positive time len is spent, all clocks are set to len and both the state and the clock invariant of the location p hold.
- $\Phi = \bigvee_{(p_1, g, X, p_2) \in E} \mathsf{pc}{=}p_1 \wedge \mathsf{pc}'{=}p_2 \wedge g \wedge s'(p_2) \wedge I'(p_2) \wedge \mathsf{len}'{>}0 \wedge \bigwedge_{c \in X} c'{=}\mathsf{len}' \wedge \bigwedge_{c \in C \setminus X} c'{=}c + \mathsf{len}'$, where s' and I' represent s and I with unprimed variables replaced by primed ones. The formula Φ states that there exists a transition (p_1, g, X, p_2) such that the program counter is p_1 before and p_2 after the transition, the guard g of the transition as well as the state and clock invariant of location p_2 are satisfied, the system will remain in p_2 for some positive time, and clocks are incremented by len' if they are not reset by the transition (otherwise they are set to len').

We thus obtain a representation of the original COD specification S in terms of first-order formulae over the signature Σ_S and theory $\mathcal{T}_S$ of S. We encode states of the system by formulae over $\mathcal{V}$. If σ, σ' are states (encoded as formulae over $\mathcal{V}$, and $\mathcal{V}'$ respectively), we say that σ is reachable in one step from σ in $T_S = (\mathcal{V}, \Theta, \Phi)$ w.r.t. $\mathcal{T}_S$ if $\mathcal{T}_S, \sigma, \sigma' \models \Phi$. A run of T_S is a sequence of states $\langle \sigma_1, \dots \sigma_m \rangle$ such that $\mathcal{T}_S, \sigma_1 \models \Theta$ and σ_{i+1} is reachable in one step from σ_i.

As a consequence of the results in [Hoe06] we obtain:

Corollary 1. *The translation from PEA to TCS preserves the semantics: every run in the TCS can be mapped to a run of the PEA; the mapping is surjective.*

Example 1. Consider the RBC example discussed in Sect. 1.1. We use the simplified PEA $\mathcal{A} = (P, V, A, C, E, s, I, P_0)$ developed in Sect. 3.3, where $A = \varnothing$ and $C = \{x_1\}$. The TCS $T(\mathcal{A}) = (\mathcal{V}, \Theta, \Phi)$ associated with $\mathcal{A}$ is defined as follows[2]:

(1) $\mathcal{V} = V \cup A \cup C \cup \{\mathsf{len}, \mathsf{pc}\}$. For technical reasons we model the variables of type sequence (e.g. $\mathsf{train}, \mathsf{speed}$) as functions of sort $\mathsf{i} \to \mathsf{num}$.

---

[2] We will use a sans serif font for all symbols in the signature of the TCS $T(\mathcal{A})$.

The following formulae (extracted from the OZ specification) help define $T(\mathcal{A})$:

$\phi_{\text{input}} = \text{newEmergencyTrain}' > 0,$

$\phi_{\text{clock}} = x_1 < 1 \wedge \text{len}' > 0 \wedge x_1' = x_1 + \text{len}' \wedge x_1' \leq 1,$

$\phi_{\text{init}} = (\forall\, i : 1 < i \leq n \rightarrow \text{train}(i) < \text{train}(i-1) - \text{brakingDist}(\text{speed}(i))) \wedge$
$\qquad (\forall\, i : 1 \leq i \leq n \rightarrow \text{minSpeed} \leq \text{speed}(i) \leq \text{maxSpeed}) \wedge (\text{emergencyTrain} > n),$

$\phi_{\text{emerg}} = \text{newEmergencyTrain} \leq n \wedge$
$\qquad \text{emergencyTrain}' = \min\{\text{newEmergencyTrain}, \text{emergencyTrain}\} \wedge$
$\qquad \text{speed}'(\text{emergencyTrain}') = 0 \wedge$
$\qquad \forall\, i : i \neq \text{emergencyTrain}' \rightarrow \text{speed}'(i) = \text{speed}(i),$

$\phi_{\text{posRep}} = \forall\, i : i=1 \wedge \text{emergencyTrain} > i \rightarrow \text{minSpeed} \leq \text{speed}'(i) \leq \text{maxSpeed} \wedge$
$\qquad \forall\, i : 1 < i < \text{emergencyTrain} \wedge \text{train}(i-1) - \text{train}(i) \geq d$
$\qquad\qquad \rightarrow \text{minSpeed} \leq \text{speed}'(i) \leq \text{maxSpeed} \wedge$
$\qquad \forall\, i : 1 < i < \text{emergencyTrain} \wedge \text{train}(i-1) - \text{train}(i) < d$
$\qquad\qquad \rightarrow \text{speed}'(i) = \text{minSpeed} \wedge$
$\qquad \forall\, i : i \geq \text{emergencyTrain} \rightarrow \text{speed}'(i) = \max\{\text{speed}(i) - \text{maxDec} * T\_PR, 0\} \wedge$
$\qquad \forall\, i : 1 \leq i \leq n \rightarrow \text{train}'(i) = \text{train}(i) + \text{speed}'(i) * T\_PR,$

$\phi_{\text{const}} = \bigwedge_{c \in \text{const}} c' = c,$ where $\text{const} = \{\text{maxDec}, \text{maxSpeed}, \text{minSpeed}, n, d, T\_PR\}$
is the set of all variables in $\mathcal{V}$ that do not change during execution.

(2) The initial predicate is $\Theta = \text{pc} = 1 \wedge \text{len} > 0 \wedge x_1 = \text{len} \wedge \phi_{\text{init}}$.

(3) We describe the transition relation Φ in terms of the individual transitions. Several transitions change only the clock, but no state variables. Let $S_1 = \{(1,1), (1,3), (3,3)\}$, $S_2 = \{(1,2), (1,4), (2,2), (2,4), (4,4)\} \subset P \times P$, and

$$\phi_{(i,j)} = \begin{cases} (\text{pc}=i \wedge \text{pc}'=j \wedge \phi_{\text{clock}} \wedge \phi_{\text{init}} \wedge \phi_{\text{const}} \wedge \phi_{\text{input}}) & \text{if } (i,j) \in S_1 \\ (\text{pc}=i \wedge \text{pc}'=j \wedge \phi_{\text{clock}} \wedge \phi_{\text{const}} \wedge \phi_{\text{input}}) & \text{if } (i,j) \in S_2 \end{cases}.$$

Finally, we have the following transitions that change the state variables:

$\phi_1 = (\text{pc}=4 \wedge \text{pc}'=4 \wedge \phi_{\text{emerg}} \wedge \phi_{\text{clock}} \wedge \phi_{\text{const}} \wedge \phi_{\text{input}}),$

$\phi_2 = (\text{pc}=4 \wedge \text{pc}'=5 \wedge \phi_{\text{posRep}} \wedge \text{len}' > 0 \wedge x_1'=0 \wedge x_1' \leq 1 \wedge \phi_{\text{const}} \wedge \phi_{\text{input}}),$

$\phi_3 = (\text{pc}=5 \wedge \text{pc}'=5 \wedge \phi_{\text{emerg}} \wedge \phi_{\text{clock}} \wedge \phi_{\text{const}} \wedge \phi_{\text{input}}),$

$\phi_4 = (\text{pc}=5 \wedge \text{pc}'=5 \wedge \phi_{\text{posRep}} \wedge \text{len}' > 0 \wedge x_1'=0 \wedge x_1' \leq 1 \wedge \phi_{\text{const}} \wedge \phi_{\text{input}}).$

Altogether, $\Phi = \bigvee_{(i,j) \in S_1 \cup S_2} \phi_{(i,j)} \vee \bigvee_{i=1}^{4} \phi_i$.

4.2   Verification of TCS

The verification problems we consider are invariant checking and bounded model checking. We explain the problems which occur in this context, and present an idea that allows to solve these problems in certain situations. We illustrate the problems as well as the verification methods on our case study.

Invariant checking. We can check whether a formula Ψ is an inductive invariant of a TCS $T=(\mathcal{V}, \Theta, \Phi)$ in two steps: (1) prove that $\mathcal{T}_S, \Theta \models \Psi$; (2) prove that $\mathcal{T}_S, \Psi, \Phi \models \Psi'$, where Ψ' results from Ψ by replacing every $x \in \mathcal{V}$ by x'. Failure to prove (2) means that Ψ is not an invariant, or Ψ is not inductive w.r.t. T.[3]

---

[3] Proving that a Ψ is an invariant of the system in general requires to find a stronger formula Γ (i.e., $\mathcal{T}_0 \models \Gamma \rightarrow \Psi$) and prove that Γ is an inductive invariant.

Example 2. For the system described in Sect. 1.1, let Ψ be the formula that states that the distance between two trains must always be greater than the sum of the braking distances of the trains in between (Ψ is a safety condition):

$$\Psi = \forall\, i : 1 < i \leq \mathsf{n} \to \mathsf{train}(i) < \mathsf{train}(i - 1) - \mathsf{brakingDist}(\mathsf{speed}(i)).$$

To check that Ψ is an inductive invariant, we need to check that:

(1) The initial states of the system, given by Θ, satisfy the safety property Ψ.
(2) Assuming that a given state σ satisfies Ψ, any state σ' reachable from σ using the transition predicate Φ satisfies Ψ'.

Checking (1) is not a problem. For (2) we need to show $\mathcal{T}_S \models \Psi \wedge \Phi \to \Psi'$, where $\mathcal{T}_S$ is the theory associated with the COD specification, an extension of $\mathcal{T}_0$ (many-sorted combination of real arithmetic (sort num) with an index theory describing precedence of trains (sort i)), with the set of definitions $\mathsf{Def} \subseteq \mathsf{Ax}$ for global constants of the system (Ax are the axioms in the OZ specification) and with function symbols $\mathsf{brakingDist}, \mathsf{train}, \mathsf{train}', \mathsf{speed}, \mathsf{speed}'$ fulfilling the axioms specified in $\mathsf{Ax}, \Psi,$ and Φ. We need to show that $\mathcal{T}_0 \wedge \mathsf{Ax} \wedge \Psi \wedge \Phi \wedge \neg\Psi' \models \perp$.

Bounded model checking. We check whether, for a fixed k, unsafe states are reachable by runs of $T = (\mathcal{V}, \Theta, \Phi)$ of length at most k. Formally, we check whether:

$$\mathcal{T}_S \wedge \Theta_0 \wedge \bigwedge_{i=1}^{j} \Phi_i \wedge \neg\Psi_j \models \perp \quad \text{ for all } 0 \leq j \leq k,$$

where Φ_i is obtained from Φ by replacing all variables $x \in \mathcal{V}$ by x_i, and all variables $x' \in \mathcal{V}'$ by x_{i+1}; Θ_0 is Θ with x_0 replacing $x \in \mathcal{V}$; and Ψ_i is Ψ with x_i replacing $x \in \mathcal{V}$.

Problem. Standard combination methods [NO79, Ghi04] allow for testing satisfiability in certain combinations of theories, but only for ground formulae. Our problem contains several non-ground formulae: the global axioms Ax, the invariant Ψ and the transition relation Φ. Only $\neg\Psi'$ corresponds to a ground set of clauses. Thus, standard methods are not directly applicable. We want to reduce the problem above to a ground satisfiability problem over decidable theories. To this end, we may replace quantified formulae by a number of ground instances, giving a decidable ground satisfiability problem over the base theory $\mathcal{T}_0$ (plus free function symbols). This approach is sound, but in general not complete. In what follows, we identify situations when this method is complete.

Our idea. In order to overcome the problem mentioned above we proceed as follows. We start from a base theory $\mathcal{T}_0$ associated with the COD specification S (usually a many-sorted combination of standard theories, e.g., integers or reals). For the case of invariant checking we consider the following successive extensions of $\mathcal{T}_0$ and study possibilities of efficient reasoning in these extensions:

– the extension $\mathcal{T}_1$ of $\mathcal{T}_0$ with the definitions and axioms in the OZ part of the COD specification for variables which do not occur in Φ (i.e., do not change);

- the extension $\mathcal{T}_2$ of $\mathcal{T}_1$ with the remaining variables in a set $\mathcal{V}$ (including those of sort sequence, modelled by functions) which occur in Φ and satisfy Ψ (together with the corresponding definitions and axioms);
- the extension $\mathcal{T}_3$ of $\mathcal{T}_2$ with primed variables $\mathcal{V}'$ (including primed versions of functions for the variables of sort sequence) satisfying Φ.

Example 3. Again consider the running example. We consider successive extensions of $\mathcal{T}_0$, a many-sorted combination of real arithmetic (for reasoning about time, positions and speed, sort num) with an index theory (for describing precedence between trains, sort i). For the case of invariant checking, we have:

- the extension $\mathcal{T}_1$ of $\mathcal{T}_0$ with a monotone and bounded function brakingDist as well as global constants, defined by Def $\subseteq$ Ax,
- the extension $\mathcal{T}_4$ of $\mathcal{T}_1$ with $\mathcal{V}$-variables from Φ, satisfying Ψ, defined by:
  - Let $\mathcal{T}_2$ be the extension of $\mathcal{T}_1$ with the (free) function speed.
  - Let $\mathcal{T}_3$ be the extension of $\mathcal{T}_2$ with the binary function secure defined for every $0 < i < j < n$ by $\mathsf{secure}(i,j) = \sum_{k=i+1}^{j} \mathsf{brakingDist}(\mathsf{speed}(k))$.
  - $\mathcal{T}_4$ is the extension of $\mathcal{T}_3$ with function train satisfying $\overline{\Psi}$ (equivalent to Ψ):

$$\overline{\Psi} = \forall\, i,j\,(0 < i < j \leq \mathsf{n} \to \mathsf{train}(j) < \mathsf{train}(i) - \mathsf{secure}(i,j)),$$

- the extension $\mathcal{T}_5$ of $\mathcal{T}_4$ with functions train$'$ and speed$'$ satisfying Φ.

We show that for all of these extensions hierarchic reasoning is possible (cf. Sect. 4.3).[4] This allows us to reduce problem (2) to testing satisfiability of ground clauses in $\mathcal{T}_0$, for which standard methods for reasoning in combinations of theories can be applied. A similar method can be used for bounded model checking.

4.3 Efficient Reasoning in Complex Theories: Locality

In the following, we identify situations in which we can give sound, complete and efficient methods for reasoning in theory extensions.

Local theory extensions. Let $\mathcal{T}_0$ be a theory with signature $\Pi_0 = (S_0, \Sigma_0, \mathsf{Pred})$. We consider extensions with new sorts S_1 and new function symbols Σ_1 constrained by a set $\mathcal{K}$ of (universally quantified) clauses in signature $\Pi = (S, \Sigma, \mathsf{Pred})$, where $S = S_0 \cup S_1$ and $\Sigma = \Sigma_0 \cup \Sigma_1$. We are interested in checking satisfiability of sets of ground clauses G with respect to such theory extensions.

When referring to sets G of ground clauses we assume they are in the signature $\Pi^c = (S, \Sigma \cup \Sigma_c, \mathsf{Pred})$ where Σ_c is a set of new constants. An extension $\mathcal{T}_0 \subseteq \mathcal{T}_0 \cup \mathcal{K}$ is *local* if satisfiability of a set G of clauses w.r.t. $\mathcal{T}_0 \cup \mathcal{K}$ only depends on $\mathcal{T}_0$ and those instances $\mathcal{K}[G]$ of $\mathcal{K}$ in which the terms starting with extension functions are in the set $\mathsf{st}(\mathcal{K}, G)$ of ground terms which already occur in G or $\mathcal{K}$. Formally, the extension $\mathcal{T}_0 \subseteq \mathcal{T}_0 \cup \mathcal{K}$ is local if condition (Loc) holds:

---

[4] We consider extensions with axiom $\overline{\Psi}$ instead of Ψ since $\overline{\Psi}$ defines a local theory extension, and hence it allows for hierarchic reasoning (cf. Sect. 4.3), whereas Ψ does not have this property. We are currently studying possibilities of automatically recognising local theory extensions, and of automatically generating (equivalent) sets of axioms defining local extensions from given sets of axioms.

(Loc)   For every set G of ground clauses, $\mathcal{T}_0 \wedge \mathcal{K} \wedge G$ is unsatisfiable iff $\mathcal{T}_0 \wedge$
$\mathcal{K}[G] \wedge G$ has no partial model where all terms in $\mathsf{st}(\mathcal{K}, G)$ are defined

A partial model of $\mathcal{T}_0 \wedge \mathcal{K}[G] \wedge G$ is a partial Π^c-structure P s.t. $P_{|\Pi_0}$ is a total
model of $\mathcal{T}_0$ and P satisfies all clauses in $\mathcal{K}[G] \wedge G$ where all terms are defined.
    We give examples of local theory extensions relevant for the verification tasks
we consider. Some appear in [GSSW06, SS05, SS06], some are new.

Theorem 3. *The extension of any theory with* free function symbols *is local.*
In addition, assume the base theory has a reflexive partial ordering $\leq$. Then:

(1) Extensions of $\mathcal{T}_0$ with axioms of the following type are also local:

(GBound$_f^t$) $\forall x_1, \ldots, x_n (\phi(x_1, \ldots, x_n) \to f(x_1, \ldots, x_n) \leq t(x_1, \ldots, x_n))$

where $t(x_1, \ldots, x_n)$ is a term, $\phi(x_1, \ldots, x_n)$ a conjunction of literals, both in the base signature Π_0 and with variables among $x_1, \ldots, x_n$.

(2) For $i \in \{1, \ldots, m\}$, let $t_i(x_1, \ldots, x_n)$ and $s_i(x_1, \ldots, x_n)$ be terms and let $\phi_i(x_1, \ldots, x_n)$ be conjunctions of literals, all of them in the base signature Π_0, with variables among $x_1, \ldots, x_n$, such that for every $i \neq j$, $\phi_i \wedge \phi_j \models_{\mathcal{T}_0} \bot$. Any "piecewise-bounded" extension $\mathcal{T}_0 \wedge (\mathsf{GBound}_f)$, where f is an extension symbol, is local. Here $(\mathsf{GBound}_f) = \bigwedge_{i=1}^m (\mathsf{GBound}_f^{[s_i, t_i], \phi_i})$;

(GBound$_f^{[s_i, t_i], \phi_i}$) $\forall \overline{x}(\phi_i(\overline{x}) \to s_i(\overline{x}) \leq f(\overline{x}) \leq t_i(\overline{x}))$.

(3) For many ordered theories including the reals (for a complete list see [SS05, SS06, JSS07]), extensions with (possibly strictly) monotone functions are local. Combinations with boundedness axioms (GBound$_f^t$), where t has the same monotonicity as f, do not destroy locality.

Hierarchic reasoning in local theory extensions. Let $\mathcal{T}_0 \subseteq \mathcal{T}_1 = \mathcal{T}_0 \cup \mathcal{K}$ be
a local theory extension. To check the satisfiability of a set G of ground clauses
w.r.t. $\mathcal{T}_1$ we can proceed as follows (for details cf. [SS05]):

Step 1: Use locality. By the locality condition, G is unsatisfiable w.r.t. $\mathcal{T}_1$ iff
$\mathcal{K}[G] \wedge G$ has no partial model in which all the subterms of $\mathcal{K}[G] \wedge G$ are defined,
and whose restriction to Π_0 is a total model of $\mathcal{T}_0$.

Step 2: Flattening and purification. We purify and flatten $\mathcal{K}[G] \wedge G$ by introducing new constants for the arguments of the extension functions as well as for the (sub)terms $t = f(g_1, \ldots, g_n)$ starting with extension functions $f \in \Sigma_1$, together with corresponding new definitions $c_t \approx t$. The set of clauses thus obtained has the form $\mathcal{K}_0 \wedge G_0 \wedge D$, where D is a set of ground unit clauses of the form $f(c_1, \ldots, c_n) \approx c$, where $f \in \Sigma_1$ and $c_1, \ldots, c_n, c$ are constants, and $\mathcal{K}_0, G_0$ are clause sets without function symbols in Σ_1.

Step 3: Reduction to testing satisfiability in $\mathcal{T}_0$. We reduce the problem to testing
satisfiability in $\mathcal{T}_0$ by replacing D with the following set of clauses:

$$N_0 = \bigwedge \{ \bigwedge_{i=1}^n c_i = d_i \to c = d \mid f(c_1, \ldots, c_n) = c, f(d_1, \ldots, d_n) = d \in D \}.$$

Theorem 4 ([SS05]). *Assume that $\mathcal{T}_0 \cup \mathcal{K}$ is a local extension of $\mathcal{T}_0$. With the notations above, G is satisfiable in $\mathcal{T}_0 \cup \mathcal{K}$ iff $\mathcal{K}_0 \wedge G_0 \wedge N_0$ is satisfiable in $\mathcal{T}_0$.*

The method above is easy to implement and efficient. If all the variables in $\mathcal{K}$ are guarded by extension functions then the size of $\mathcal{K}_0 \wedge G_0 \wedge N_0$ is polynomial in the size of G. Thus, the complexity of checking the satisfiability of G w.r.t. $\mathcal{T}_0 \wedge \mathcal{K}$ is $g(n^k)$ (where k depends on $\mathcal{K}$ cf. e.g. [SS05]) where $g(n)$ is the complexity of checking the satisfiability of a set of ground clauses of size n in $\mathcal{T}_0$.

Application to parametric verification of COD specifications. A sound but potentially incomplete method for checking whether $\mathcal{T}_0 \wedge \mathsf{Ax} \wedge \Psi \wedge \Phi \wedge \neg \Psi' \models \bot$, which can always be used, is to take into account only certain ground instances of the universally quantified formulae in $\mathsf{Ax} \wedge \Psi \wedge \Phi$, related to the ground formula $G = \neg \Psi'$. However *complete* approaches can often be obtained, because many axioms used in verification problems define chains of local extensions of $\mathcal{T}_0$:

- definitions for constants can be expressed by axioms of the type GBound_f^t;
- often, transition relations which reflect updates of variables or of a sequence f according to mutually exclusive "modes of operation" are axiomatised by axioms of the form (GBound_f) as defined in Theorem 3(2) and 3(3).

If a complete approach can be given, the method for hierarchic reasoning described above can be used in two ways. If the constraints on the parameters of the systems are completely specified in the COD specification, then it allows us to reduce the problem of checking whether a system property Ψ is an inductive invariant to the problem of deciding satisfiability of a set of constraints in $\mathcal{T}_0$. Alternatively, we may choose not to specify all constraints on the parameters. As a side effect, after the reduction of the problem to a satisfiability problem in the base theory, one can automatically determine constraints on the parameters (in the running example these are, e.g., $T\_PR, \mathsf{minSpeed}, \mathsf{maxSpeed}, ...$), which guarantee that the property is an inductive invariant and are sufficient for this. (This can be achieved for instance using quantifier elimination.)

4.4   Example: The RBC Case Study

We show how the verification method based on hierarchic reasoning can be applied to our case study. The following is a consequence of Theorem 3.

Theorem 5. *Let $\mathcal{T}_0$ be the (many-sorted) combination of real arithmetic (for reasoning about time, positions and speed, sort* num*) with an index theory (for describing precedence between trains, sort* i*).*

(1) The extension $\mathcal{T}_1$ of $\mathcal{T}_0$ with a monotone and bounded function brakingDist *as well as global constants, with definitions* Def $\subseteq$ Ax*, is local.*
(2) The extension $\mathcal{T}_2$ of $\mathcal{T}_1$ with the (free) function speed *is local.*
(3) The extension $\mathcal{T}_3$ of $\mathcal{T}_2$ with the function secure *(cf. Example 3) is local.*
(4) The extension $\mathcal{T}_4$ of $\mathcal{T}_3$ with functions train *satisfying $\overline{\Psi}$ (Example 3) is local.*
(5) The extension $\mathcal{T}_5$ of $\mathcal{T}_4$ with functions train′ *and* speed′ *satisfying Φ is local.*

We follow the steps in the method for hierarchic reasoning in Sect. 4.3 and reduce the verification task to a satisfiability problem in the base theory $\mathcal{T}_0$. To make our task slightly simpler, we split the transition relation and look at every ϕ_i separately. Those ϕ_i that do not change the state variables train and speed are sure to preserve the invariant. Furthermore, the program counters do not interfere with the invariant. As a result, we have two interesting cases:

$$\Phi_1 = \phi_{\text{emerg}} \wedge \phi_{\text{clock}} \wedge \phi_{\text{const}} \wedge \phi_{\text{input}},$$
$$\Phi_2 = \phi_{\text{posRep}} \wedge \text{len}' > 0 \wedge x_1' = 0 \wedge x_1' \leq 1 \wedge \phi_{\text{const}} \wedge \phi_{\text{input}}.$$

We start with the first transition. We have to prove $\mathcal{T}_0 \wedge \text{Def} \wedge \text{Def}_{\text{secure}} \wedge \overline{\Psi} \wedge \Phi_1 \wedge \neg\Psi' \models \bot$. This is a satisfiability problem over $\mathcal{T}_4 \wedge \Phi_1$. In a first reduction, this problem is reduced to a problem over $\mathcal{T}_4 = \mathcal{T}_0 \wedge \text{Def} \wedge \text{Def}_{\text{secure}} \wedge \overline{\Psi}$:

Step 1: Use locality. For this step, the set of ground clauses we consider is $G = \neg\Psi' = \{1 < k_1, k_1 \leq \text{n}, k_2 = k_1 + 1, s = \text{speed}'(k_1), \text{train}'(k_1) \geq \text{train}'(k_2) - \text{brakingDist}(s)\}$. Of the extension symbols train' and speed', only speed' occurs in Φ_1. Ground terms with speed' are speed'(k_1) in G and speed'(emergencyTrain') in Φ_1. Thus, $\Phi_1[G]$ consists of two instances of Φ_1: one with i instantiated to k_1, the other with i instantiated to emergencyTrain' (we remove clauses that are generated in both instantiations such that they only appear once):

$$\begin{aligned}
\Phi_1[G] = \ &\phi_{\text{clock}} \wedge \phi_{\text{input}} \wedge \phi_{\text{const}} \wedge \text{newEmergencyTrain} \leq \text{n} \wedge \\
&\text{emergencyTrain}' = \min\{\text{newEmergencyTrain}, \text{emergencyTrain}\} \wedge \\
&\text{speed}'(\text{emergencyTrain}') = 0 \wedge \\
&k_1 \neq \text{emergencyTrain}' \rightarrow \text{speed}'(k_1) = \text{speed}(k_1) \wedge \\
&\text{emergencyTrain}' \neq \text{emergencyTrain}' \\
&\rightarrow \text{speed}'(\text{emergencyTrain}') = \text{speed}(\text{emergencyTrain}').
\end{aligned}$$

Step 2: Flattening and purification. $\Phi_1[G] \wedge G$ is already flat with respect to speed' and train'. We purify the set of clauses by replacing every ground term with speed' or train' at the root with new constants $c_1, \ldots, c_4$ and obtain a set of definitions $D = \{\text{speed}'(\text{emergencyTrain}') = c_1, \text{speed}'(k_1) = c_2, \text{train}'(k_1) = c_3, \text{train}'(k_2) = c_4\}$, together with the purified sets of clauses

$$G_0 = \{1 < k_1, k_1 \leq \text{n}, k_2 = k_1 + 1, s = c_2, c_3 \geq c_4 - \text{brakingDist}(s)\}$$

$$\begin{aligned}
\Phi_1[G]_0 = \ &\phi_{\text{clock}} \wedge \phi_{\text{input}} \wedge \phi_{\text{const}} \wedge \text{newEmergencyTrain} \leq \text{n} \wedge \\
&\text{emergencyTrain}' = \min\{\text{newEmergencyTrain}, \text{emergencyTrain}\} \wedge \\
&c_1 = 0 \wedge k_1 \neq \text{emergencyTrain}' \rightarrow c_2 = \text{speed}(k_1) \wedge \\
&\text{emergencyTrain}' \neq \text{emergencyTrain}' \rightarrow c_1 = \text{speed}(\text{emergencyTrain}').
\end{aligned}$$

Step 3: Reduction to satisfiability in $\mathcal{T}_4$. We add the set of clauses $N_0 = \{\text{emergencyTrain}' = k_1 \rightarrow c_1 = c_2, k_1 = k_2 \rightarrow c_3 = c_4\}$. This allows us to remove D and obtain a ground satisfiability problem in $\mathcal{T}_4$: $\Phi_1[G]_0 \wedge G_0 \wedge N_0$. In four further reduction steps, we reduce this problem (using a similar procedure) to a ground satisfiability problems over $\mathcal{T}_0$. This set of clauses can now directly be handed to a decision procedure for the combination of the theories of reals and indices. In the same way, the transition Φ_2 can be handled.

5   Conclusions

In this paper, we presented a method for invariant checking and bounded model checking for complex specifications of systems containing information about processes, data, and time. In order to represent these specifications in full generality, we used the specification language CSP-OZ-DC (COD) [HO02, Hoe06]. Similar combined specification formalisms are, e.g., [MD99, Smi02, Süh02] but we prefer COD due to its strict separation of control, data, and time, and to its compositionality (cf. Sect. 3), that is essential for automatic verification.

One of our goals was to model complex systems with a parametric number of components. For this, it was essential to use complex data structures (e.g., arrays, functions). Therefore, in this paper we needed to extend existing verification techniques for COD [HM05, MFR06] to situations when abstract data structures appear. Also, in order to achieve a tighter binding of the OZ to the DC part, we introduced timing parameters, allowing for more flexible specifications.

We showed that, in this context, invariant checking or bounded model checking can be reduced to proving in complex theories. This was done using translations from COD to PEA (and then to simplified PEA) and from PEA to TCS (these translations can be fully automated – we already have tool support for them). We then analysed the type of theories that occur in relationship with a given COD specification, and presented a sound method for efficient reasoning in these theories. At the same time, we identified situations when the method is sound and complete (i.e., when the specific properties of "position updates" can be expressed by using chains of local theory extensions). All these ideas were illustrated by means of a running example complementing scenarios studied in [FM06, MFR06] (as now we consider an arbitrary number of trains) and in [JSS07] (as now we also encompass efficient handling of emergency messages). We kept the running example relatively easy in order to ensure clarity of presentation. More complicated scenarios can be handled similarly (we also considered, e.g., situations in which time passes between position and speed updates).

In ongoing work, we investigate possibilities to use methods for abstraction-based model checking and invariant generation for this type of models.

References

[AD94]   Alur, R., Dill, D.L.: A theory of timed automata. Theoretical Computer Science 126(2), 183–235 (1994)

[ERT02]   ERTMS User Group, UNISIG. ERTMS/ETCS System requirements specification. Version 2.2.2 (2002) http://www.aeif.org/ccm/default.asp

[FM06]   Faber, J., Meyer, R.: Model checking data-dependent real-time properties of the European Train Control System. In: FMCAD, pp. 76–77. IEEE Computer Society Press, Los Alamitos (2006)

[Ghi04]   Ghilardi, S.: Model theoretic methods in combined constraint satisfiability. Journal of Automated Reasoning 33(3–4), 221–249 (2004)

[GSSW06]   Ganzinger, H., Sofronie-Stokkermans, V., Waldmann, U.: Modular proof systems for partial functions with Evans equality. Information and Computation 204(10), 1453–1492 (2006)

[HJU05]   Hermanns, H., Jansen, D.N., Usenko, Y.S.: From StoCharts to MoDeST: a comparative reliability analysis of train radio communications. In: Workshop on Software and Performance, pp. 13–23. ACM Press, New York (2005)

[HM05]   Hoenicke, J., Maier, P.: Model-checking of specifications integrating processes, data and time. In: Fitzgerald, J.A., Hayes, I.J., Tarlecki, A. (eds.) FM 2005. LNCS, vol. 3582, Springer, Heidelberg (2005)

[HO02]   Hoenicke, J., Olderog, E.-R.: CSP-OZ-DC: A combination of specification techniques for processes, data and time. Nordic Journal of Computing 9(4), 301–334 (March 2003)

[Hoa85]   Hoare, C.A.R.: Communicating Sequential Processes. Prentice-Hall, Englewood Cliffs (1985)

[Hoe06]   Hoenicke, J.: Combination of Processes, Data, and Time. PhD thesis, University of Oldenburg, Germany (2006)

[JSS07]   Jacobs, S., Sofronie-Stokkermans, V.: Applications of hierarchic reasoning in the verification of complex systems. ENTCS (special issue dedicated to PDPAR 2006), 15 pages (To appear, 2007)

[MD99]   Mahony, B.P., Dong, J.S.: Overview of the semantics of TCOZ. In: IFM, pp. 66–85. Springer, Heidelberg (1999)

[MFR06]   Meyer, R., Faber, J., Rybalchenko, A.: Model checking duration calculus: A practical approach. In: Barkaoui, K., Cavalcanti, A., Cerone, A. (eds.) ICTAC 2006. LNCS, vol. 4281, pp. 332–346. Springer, Heidelberg (2006)

[NO79]   Nelson, G., Oppen, D.C.: Simplification by cooperating decision procedures. ACM TOPLAS 1(2), 245–257 (1979)

[Ros98]   Roscoe, A.W.: Theory and Practice of Concurrency. Prentice-Hall, Englewood Cliffs (1998)

[Smi00]   Smith, G.: The Object Z Specification Language. Kluwer Academic Publishers, Dordrecht (2000)

[Smi02]   Smith, G.: An integration of real-time Object-Z and CSP for specifying concurrent real-time systems. In: Butler, M., Petre, L., Sere, K. (eds.) IFM 2002. LNCS, vol. 2335, pp. 267–285. Springer, Heidelberg (2002)

[SS05]   Sofronie-Stokkermans, V.: Hierarchic reasoning in local theory extensions. In: Nieuwenhuis, R. (ed.) Automated Deduction – CADE-20. LNCS (LNAI), vol. 3632, pp. 219–234. Springer, Heidelberg (2005)

[SS06]   Sofronie-Stokkermans, V.: Interpolation in local theory extensions. In: Furbach, U., Shankar, N. (eds.) IJCAR 2006. LNCS (LNAI), vol. 4130, pp. 235–250. Springer, Heidelberg (2006)

[Süh02]   Sühl, C.: An overview of the integrated formalism RT-Z. Formal Asp. Comput 13(2), 94–110 (2002)

[TZ06]   Trowitzsch, J., Zimmermann, A.: Using UML state machines and petri nets for the quantitative investigation of ETCS. In: VALUETOOLS, pp. 1–34. ACM Press, New York (2006)

[ZH04]   Zhou, C., Hansen, M.R.: Duration Calculus. Springer, Heidelberg (2004)

Modelling and Verification of the LMAC Protocol for Wireless Sensor Networks

Ansgar Fehnker[1,*], Lodewijk van Hoesel[2], and Angelika Mader[2,**]

[1] National ICT Australia and University of New South Wales, Australia
ansgar.fehnker@nicta.com.au
[2] Department of Computer Science, University of Twente, The Netherlands
l.f.w.vanhoesel@utwente.nl, mader@ewi.utwente.nl

Abstract. In this paper we report on modelling and verification of a medium access control protocol for wireless sensor networks, the LMAC protocol. Our approach is to systematically investigate all possible connected topologies consisting of four and of five nodes. The analysis is performed by timed automaton model checking using Uppaal. The property of main interest is detecting and resolving collision. Evaluation of this property for all connected topologies requires more than 8000 model checking runs. Increasing the number of nodes would not only lead increase the state space, but to a greater extent cause an instance explosion problem. Despite the small number of nodes this approach gave valuable insight in the protocol and the scenarios that lead to collisions not detected by the protocol, and it increased the confidence in the adequacy of the protocol.

1 Introduction

In this paper we report about modelling and verification of a medium access control protocol for wireless sensor networks, the LMAC protocol [10]. The LMAC protocol is designed to function in a multi-hop, energy-constrained wireless sensor network. It targets especially energy-efficiency, self-configuration and distributed operation. In order to avoid energy-wasting effects, like idle listening, hidden terminal problem or collision of packets, the communication is scheduled. Each node gets periodically a time interval (slot) in which it is allowed to control the wireless medium according its own requirements and needs. Here, we concentrate on the part of the protocol that is responsible for the distributed and localised strategy of choosing a time slot for nodes.

Although, the basic idea of the protocol is quite simple, the possible behaviours get quickly too complex to be overseen by pure insight. Therefore, we chose a model checking technique for the formal analysis of the protocol. We apply model checking in an experimental approach [4,6]: formal analysis can only increase the *confidence* in the correctness of an implementation, but not

---

* National ICT Australia is funded through the Australian Government's *Backing Australia's Ability* initiative, in part through the Australian Research Council.
** supported by NWO project 632.001.202, Methods for modelling embedded systems.

J. Davies and J. Gibbons (Eds.): IFM 2007, LNCS 4591, pp. 253–272, 2007.

guarantee it. This has two reasons: first, a formal correctness proof is only about a model, and not about the implementation. Second, we will (and can) not prove correctness for the general case, but only for instances of topologies.

Model checking as a way to increase the confidence comes also into play, as we do not aim to prove that the protocol is correct for all considered topologies. This is in contrast to related work on verification of communication protocols, such as [1]. It is known beforehand that there exist problematic topologies for which the LMAC protocol cannot satisfy all relevant properties. The aim is to iteratively improve the model, and to reduce the number of topologies for which the protocol may fail. This is an important quantitative aspect of the model checking experiments presented in this paper.

In order to get meaningful results from model checking we follow two lines:

Model checking experiments: We systematically investigate all possible connected topologies of 4 and 5 nodes, which are in total 11, and 61 respectively. For 12 different models and 6 properties we performed about 8000 model checking runs using the model checker Uppaal [2,3]. There are the following reasons for the choice of the model checking approach considering all topologies:

(1) Relevant faults appear already in networks with a small number of nodes. Of course, possible faults that involve more nodes are not detected here.

(2) It is not enough to investigate only representative topologies, because it is difficult to decide what "representative" is. It turned out that topologies that look very "similar" behave differently, in the sense that in one collision can occur, which does not in the other. This suggests that the systematic way to investigate all topologies gives more reliable results. This forms a contrast to similar approaches such as [8] which considers only representative topologies, and the work in [5], which considers only very regular topologies.

(3) By model checking all possible scenarios are traversed exhaustively. It turned out that scenarios leading to collisions are complex, and are unlikely to be found by a simulator. On the other hand, simulations can deal with much higher numbers of nodes. We believe that both, verification and simulation, can increase the confidence in a protocol, but in complementary ways.

Systematic model construction: The quality of results gained from model checking cannot be higher than the quality of models that is used. We constructed the models systematically, which is presented in sufficient detail. We regard it as relevant that the decisions that went into the model construction are explicit, such that they can be questioned and discussed. It also makes it easier to interpret the result of the model checking experiments, i.e. to identify what was proven, and what not. The reader who is not interested in the details of the model should skip therefore Section 4.

The goal of the protocol is to find a mapping of time slots to nodes that prevents collisions. To this end it is necessary that not only direct neighbours have different slots, but also that all neighbours of a node have pairwise different slots. Neighbours of neighbours will be called *second-order* neighbours. The problem is at least NP-hard [7,9]: each solution to the slot-mapping problem is also a solution to the graph colouring problem, but not vice versa.

When starting the protocol analysis using Uppaal, the protocol had been developed [10], implemented and analysed by simulation. The specification consisted of the publication mentioned, and personal explanations. Our analysis here restricts to the fragment of the protocol concerned with the slot distribution mechanism trying to avoid collision. Other aspects, as time synchronisation or sleeping modes of nodes, are covered by the protocol, but are not addressed in the analysis here. During our modelling and verification efforts we found that the implementation covered more aspects than the specification did. The main results of our analysis were an improvement of the protocol, such that less collisions remain undetected, and an analysis of possible undetected collisions showing that undetected collisions do not prevent connection to the gateway.

The paper is structured as follows. In Section 2 we give a short description of the LMAC protocol, and in Section 3 a brief introduction to timed automata. The models and properties are described in detail in Section 4. The model checking results are discussed in Section 5. We conclude with discussions in Section 6.

2   The LMAC Protocol

In schedule-based MAC protocols, time is organised in *time slots*, which are grouped into *frames*. Each frame has a fixed length of a (integer) number of time slots. The number of time slots in a frame should be adapted to the expected network node density or system requirements.

The scheduling principle in the LMAC protocol [10] is very simple: every node gets to control one time slot in every frame to carry out its transmission. When a node has some data to transmit, it waits until its time slot comes up, and transmits the packet without causing collision or interference with other transmissions. In the LMAC protocols, nodes always transmit a short control message in their time slot, which is used to maintain synchronisation.

The control message of the LMAC protocol plays an important role in obtaining a local view of the network within a two-hop distance. With each transmission a node broadcasts a bit vector of slots occupied by its (first-order) neighbours . When a node receives a message from a neighbour, it marks the respective time slots as occupied. To maintain synchronisation other nodes always listen at the beginning of time slots to the control messages of other nodes.

In the remainder we will briefly describe the part of LMAC concerned with the choice of a time slot. We define four operational phases (Fig. 1):

Initialisation phase (I) — The node samples the wireless medium to detect other nodes. When a neighbouring node is detected, the node synchronizes (i.e. the node knows the current slot number), and proceeds to the wait phase W, or directly to the discover phase D.

Wait phase (W) — We observed that ,especially at network setup, many nodes receive an impulse to synchronize at the same time. The protocol introduces randomness in reaction time between synchronising with the network and

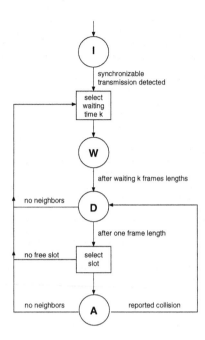

Fig. 1. Control flow diagram of the protocol

actually choosing a free time slot, to reduce the likelihood that nodes select slots at the same time. This is achieved by inserting a random wait time after the initialisation phase I and before the discover phase D.

Discover phase (D) — The node collects first-order neighbourhood information during one entire frame and records the occupied time slots. If all information is collected, the node chooses a time slot and advances to the active phase A.

By performing an 'OR'-operation between all received bit vectors, a node in the discover phase D can determine which time slots in its second-order neighbourhood are unoccupied and can be freely used. At this moment the node can choose *any* time slot that it marked as unoccupied. To reduce the probability of collisions, the protocol is to randomly choose one of the available slots.

Active phase (A) — The node transmits a message in its own time slot. It listens in all other time slots and accepts data from neighbouring nodes. The node also keeps its view on the network up-to-date. When a neighbouring node informs that there was a collision in the time slot of the node, it will return to the wait phase W. Collisions can occur when two or more nodes choose the same time slot for transmission simultaneously. This can happen with small probability at network setup or when network topology changes due to mobility of nodes.

The nodes that cause a collision cannot detect the collision by themselves; they need to be informed by their neighbouring nodes. These neighbouring nodes use their own time slot to inform the network that they detected a collision. When a node is informed that it is in a collision it will give up its time slot and return to the discover phase D.

3   Timed Automata

Systems are modelled in Uppaal as a parallel composition of timed automata [3]. Time is modelled using real-valued clocks and time only progresses in the locations of the automata: transitions are instantaneous. The guards on transitions between locations in the automata and the invariants in the various locations may contain both integer-valued variables and real-valued clocks. Clocks can be reset to zero on transitions. Several automata can synchronize on transitions using handshake and broadcast synchronisation. Shared variables can be used to model data transfer between automata. Locations can be declared urgent, which means time is not allowed to progress, or committed, which means time is not allowed to progress and interleaving is restricted. If only one automaton is in a committed location at any one time, its transitions are guaranteed to be atomic.

Properties of systems are checked by the Uppaal model checker, which performs an exhaustive search through the state space of the system for the validity of these properties. It can check for invariant, reachability, and liveness properties of the system, specified in a fragment of TCTL.

4   Models and Properties

4.1   Model Decomposition

Uppaal models are, as mentioned in the previous section, parallel compositions of timed automata, and allow for compositional modeling of complex systems. The LMAC protocol is naturally distributed over the different nodes. The Uppaal model reflects this by including exactly one timed automaton model for each node. Each of these timed automata models is then organised along the lines of the flow chart in Section 2.

The Uppaal model of the LMAC protocol will be used to analyse the behaviour, correctness and performance of the protocol. Since the LMAC protocol builds on an assumed time synchronisation, the Uppaal model will also assume an existing synchronisation on time. Although it would be interesting to analyse the timing model in detail, it falls outside of the scope of the protocol and this investigation.

The LMAC protocols divides time into frames, which are subdivided into slots. Within a slot, each node communicates with its neighbours and updates its local state accordingly. We model each slot to take two time units. Each node has a local clock. Nodes communicate when their local clock equals 1, and update information when their clocks equals 2. At this time the clock will be reset to zero.

Based on this timing model, the protocol running on one node is modelled as a single timed automaton. The complete model contains one of these automata for each node in the network. The timed automata distinguish between 4 phases, as shown in the control flow graph in Figure 1. The first phase is the initialisation phase, the second the optional wait phase. The next part models the discover phase which gathers neighbourhood information. At the end of the discover phase a node chooses a slot, and proceeds to the fourth and last phase, the active phase. Figure 2 to 6 depict the models for each phase. Details of the different parts will be discussed later in this section. Note, that the model presented here serves as a baseline for an iterative improvement of model and protocol.

Channels and Variables

Global channels and variables. The wireless medium and the topology of the network are modelled by a broadcast channel sendWM, and a connectivity matrix can_hear. A sending node i synchronises on transitions labeled sendWM!. The receiving nodes j then synchronizes on label sendWM? if can_hear[j][i] is true. This model of *sending* is used in the active phase (Fig. 6), and the model of *receiving* during initialisation (Fig. 2), discover (Fig. 4) and active phase (Fig. 6).

The model uses three global arrays to maintain a list of slot numbers and neighbourhood information for each node. Array slot_no records for each node the current slot number. Array first and second record for each node information on the first and second-order neighbours, respectively. Note, that the entries of these arrays are bit vectors, and will be manipulated using bit-wise operations. All nodes have read access to each of the elements in the arrays, but only write access to its own. The arrays are declared globally to ease read access.

The model uses two additional global variables aux_id and aux_col. These are one place buffers, used during communication to exchange information on IDs and collisions.

Local variables. Each node has five local variables. Variable rec_vec is a local copy of received neighbourhood information, counter counts the number of slots a node has been waiting, and current the current slot number, with respect to the beginning to the frame. Variable col records the reported collisions, while detected is used to record detected collisions. Finally, each node has a local clock t.

The node model. The remainder of this section will discuss each part of the node model in detail.

Initialisation phase. The model for the initialisation phase is depicted in Figure 2. As long a node does not receive any message it remains in the initial node. If a node receives a message, i.e. if it can hear (can_hear[id][aux_id]==1) and synchronise with the sender (sendWM?), it sets its current slot number to the slot number of the sender (current=slot_no[aux_id]), and resets its local clock (t=0). The slot number of the sender is part of the message that is send. From this time on the receiver will update the current slot number at the same rate as the sender. They are equal whenever either of them sends. This synchronisation is the subject of one of the properties that will be verified later.

If the receiver receives a second packet before the end of the slot a collision has occurred. The node will discard the received information and return to the initial

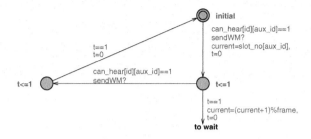

Fig. 2. Model of the initialisation phase

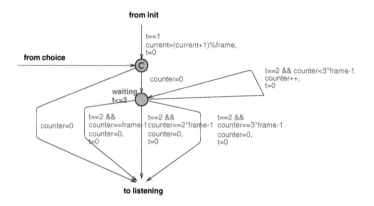

Fig. 3. Model of the wait phase

location. If no collision occurs, the node will proceed to the next slot, increment the current slot counter modulo the length of the frame (**current=current+1% frame**), and proceed to the wait phase (Figure 3).

Wait Phase. When a node enters the wait phase, it may decide (non-deterministically) to skip this phase. A node waits for at most 3 frames in this location **waiting**. Waiting is implemented as a self loop, which is guarded by **counter<3*frame-1**. The loop increments the counter at the end of a slot (**t==2**). A node can proceed to the discover phase when it waited for exactly one, two or three frames.

Discover Phase. The model for the discover phase consists of four locations (Figure 4). The entry location **listening0** models when a node is sensing the medium. Location **rec_one0** models that a node continues sensing after reception of a first message. Location **done0** is reached when a node detected a collision. Finally, the model contains a committed location, in which the node checks if it listened to the medium for a full frame. If it did, it proceeds to choose a free slot, otherwise it continues listening.

Clocks and variables will be updated as follows. When a node enters location **listening0**, the local clock will be zero. It will wait in this location for at

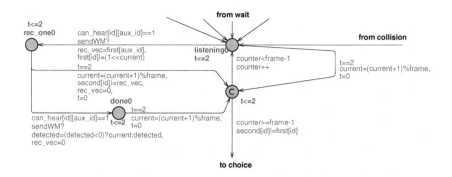

Fig. 4. Model of the discover phase

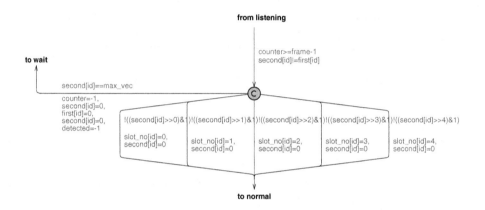

Fig. 5. Model of the choice

most 2 time units, enforced by invariant `t<=2`. If it receives a message from a neighbouring node, it will record the neighbour information of that neighbour (`rec_vec=first[aux_id]`). The node sets the bit for the current slot in its own neighbourhood vector to true (`first[id]|=1<<current`). If the node does not receive any message by the end of the slot (`t==2`), it will increment the current slot number, and move to a committed location.

When the node received one message, it waits in location `rec_one0` either until it receives a second message (collision), or until the end of the slot (`t==2`). The node uses the received neighbourhood information only in the latter case to update the information on slots occupied by the second-order neighbours (`second[id]|=rec_vec`). In the first case the node records if a collision occurred if it was the first collision since the beginning of the discover phase (`detected=(detected<0)?current:detected`). Note, that `detected` has value −1 if no collision has been detected yet. At the end of a slot(`t==2`) the node enters the committed location. If it listened for less than a frame length, it will return to `listening0`, otherwise it will choose a slot.

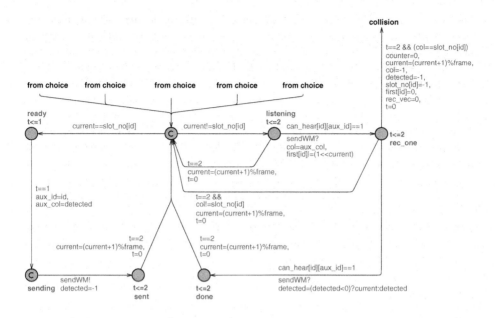

Fig. 6. Model of the active phase

Choosing. Choosing is not a actual phase, but an important intermediate state. Choosing a slot is modelled by a single committed location (Figure 5). Before entering this location the node computes the slots that are neither occupied by the (first-order) neighbours, nor by the second-order neighbours (second[id] |= first[id]). If all slots are reported occupied, the node returns to the wait phase (second[id]==max_vec)[1]. If there are available slots, i.e the corresponding bits in the bit-vector second[id] are equal to zero, the node will select non-deterministically one of these slots.

Active Phase. The main phase of a node is the active phase. The model for this phase is depicted in Figure 6. Locations ready, sending, and sent deal with the transmission of a message, locations listening, rec_one, and done deal with receiving messages.

From the central committed location, which is entered at the beginning of a slot, the node proceeds to send, if the chosen slot number is equal to current slot number (current==slot_no[id]), and proceeds to the discover phase otherwise (current!=slot_no[id]).

If a node wants to send it waits for one time unit in location ready. After one time unit, the node first copies its ID and collision information into global buffers aux_id, aux_col, and then triggers all nodes in it neighbourhood to update their local information through broadcast channel sendWM!. The node then stays in location sent until the end of the slot.

---

[1] Constant max_vec is a bit-vector where all elements are set to true.

If a node is ready to receive a message it waits in location `listening`. It remains in that location either until the end of the slot, or until it receives a message. In the former case it increments the slot number at the end of the slot, and proceed with the next slot. In the latter case, if it receives a message, it updates its local information and enter location `rec_one`. If a second message arrives while in `rec_one`, it discards the received information, records the collision (`detected=(detected<0)?current:detected`), and waits for the remaining time of the slot in `done`. If no collision occurred while in `rec_one`, the node proceeds at the end of the slot (`t==2`) depending on the received collision information `col`. If a collision has been reported and it is equal to its slot number (`col==slot_no[id]`), the node returns to the discover phase, and resets all local information. Otherwise, it updates its neighbourhood information, and proceeds with the next slot.

The next section briefly discusses some properties of the timed automaton model of the LMAC protocol, in particular a property that ensures that after a collision nodes involved will choose a new slot.

4.2 Properties

The timed automata model of the LMAC protocol should guarantee basic safety properties. The most basic property is freedom from deadlocks, which can be checked in Uppaal by verifying the following:

$$AG\neg deadlock \tag{1}$$

In addition, we require that the model successfully implements synchronisation of nodes. First, nodes should be synchronised halfway the duration of a slot, since at this time they will send and receive information. We prove for each pair (i,j) of first-order neighbours

$$AG(node_i.t == 1 \Rightarrow node_j.t == 1) \tag{2}$$

In addition neighbours should agree on the current slot number, to ensure that received information is interpreted correctly.

$$AG(node_i.t == 1 \Rightarrow node_i.current == node_j.current) \tag{3}$$

Since we only consider completely connected networks, pairwise synchronisation implies synchronisation of the entire network. The nodes do not to be synchronised when $node_i.t \neq 1$. This can happen when one node increments its current slot number before the other.

In addition to these safety properties the protocol should satisfy a very basic reachability property: There should exist a path to a state, such that all nodes are active, and such that they have a chosen a slot number that is distinct from their first and second-order neighbour's slot. Let $\mathcal{N}$ be the set of all pairs of first and second-order neighbours. We then verify

$$EF \bigwedge_{(i,j)\in\mathcal{N}} (slot\_no(i) \neq slot\_no(j) \wedge active(i) \wedge active(j)) \tag{4}$$

where $active(i)$ is true if a node is its active phase. If the model cannot satisfy this property, it is not even possible to reach a configuration without collision, i.e the related colouring problem has no solution.

The previous property guarantees that there exists a solution, but it does not guarantee that the protocol find this solution. The LMAC protocol chooses slots randomly from the available slots. This is implemented in the timed automaton model as a non-deterministic choice. It is therefore possible that two nodes will repeatedly choose the same slot. For a probabilistic model we could try to prove that with probability one distinct slots will eventually be chosen. Unfortunately, we cannot use the timed automaton model to prove this directly.

Alternatively, we verify two liveness properties to show that the protocol will eventually resolve all conflicts, if satisfied. The first is to show that whenever two first or second-order neighbours choose the same slot number, they will eventually choose a new slot number. We show for each pair (i,j) in $\mathcal{N}$

$$AG \ (slot\_no(i) == slot\_no(j) \wedge sending(i) \wedge sending(j)) \qquad (5)$$
$$\Rightarrow AF(\neg active(i) \vee \neg active(j))$$

A node may leave the active phase eventually due to a third node reporting the collision or a triggered timeout.

The second liveness property is, that if a node is about to choose a slot, and if it can only choose from one available slot, its neighbours who are in the discover phase are not forced to the make the same choice. The neighbour should eventually be able to choose a different slot. The latter requirement can be dropped, if the neighbour that was forced to a choice, left the active phase and either waits or discovers. For all pairs (i,j) in $\mathcal{N}$ we show

$$AG \ (choosing(i) \wedge available\_slot(i) == 1 \wedge discover(j)) \Rightarrow \qquad (6)$$
$$AF(choosing(j) \wedge (slot\_no(i) \neq slot\_no(j) \vee wait(i) \vee discover(i)))$$

This means that, even if a node is forced to a certain choice ($choosing(i) \wedge available\_slot(i) == 1$), neighbours can eventually choose a different slot.

4.3   Simplification

The model described in Section 4.1 was close to the informal description of the protocol as presented in Section 2. As such each node was equipped with its own clock, and its internal actions completely independent from other nodes.

Checking the reachability probability property (4) was easy, and checking the safety properties (1) to (3) was possible, although demanding in terms of memory and time constraints, while proving the liveness properties (5) and (6) turned out to exceed the memory and time constraints for most topologies. To be able to verify the protocol for all topologies with up to 5 nodes for all properties, we had to simplify the model. The simplification reduced the number of clocks and non-essential interleaving, while keeping the essential behavior.

The simplification builds on two observations. Firstly, that all clocks are synchronised, and secondly that all updates are local. We introduce a scheduler, with its own clock, that synchronizes the internal update of the nodes at the end of a slot. Without loss of subsequent behavior this scheduler realises a local partial order reduction.

Given that the local clocks of the nodes are only reset during the update of a node, and given that we can safely synchronize all updates, as mentioned before, we find that all clocks are now perfectly synchronised. This means that for clocks t_1 and t_2 holds the invariant $t_1 == t_2$. We can therefore safely replace the local clocks of the nodes by the single clock of the scheduler.

The simplification reduced number of clocks and manually introduced a partial order reduction on internal transitions. It should be noted that the scheduler added to the model to achieve this reduction has no equivalent in the actual LMAC protocol. It was purely introduced to reduce the complexity of the model checking problem. If anything it reflects that the LMAC protocol builds on an existing time synchronisation.

5   Results

This section reports on the model checking results for the properties defined in Section 4.2.

While the safety and reachability properties should be satisfied by all models, it is known beforehand that the LMAC protocol is not able to resolve all collisions. This is the subject of the first liveness property (5). Two neighbouring nodes will remain in a collision perpetually, if no third node is able to report this collision, either because there is no third node, or because the third node is unable to send a message without collision. This is a fundamental shortcoming of collision detection algorithms. The aim of the model checking experiments is to iteratively improve the model, and thus the protocol, to reduce the number of topologies that suffer from this problem. This means to reduce the number of topologies and pairs of neighbours that do not satisfy property (5). The improvements deal with modelling bugs, clarification of an ambiguous informal protocol description, to improvements of the protocol.

The model checking experiments have been performed on a Mac Pro with 2 x 3 GHz Dual-Core processor, and a 4 GB 667 MHz memory. We used Uppaal version 4.0. Checking property (5) for a five-node model, i.e. ca. 500 runs of the model checker, took about an hour. This machine outperformed different other PCs, the weakest ones taking a week for the same set of verifications without solving them all, or the better ones, doing the job in a few hours, but still failing due to memory limitations for some experiments, which had to be killed when using too much memory.

5.1   Safety and Reachability Properties

For basic model we assume a network of 4 nodes, and a frame length of 5 slots. For this basic model there are 11 topologies, with 64 pairs of first and second-order neighbours. The experiments show that the basic model (and all models

model 1, topology 4, pair (0,2)

node	0	1	2	3	4	5	6	7	8	9	10	11	12	13	14	15	16	17	18	19	20	21	22	23	24	25	26	27	28	29	30	31	32	33	34
0	0	0	0	0	0	*0*	0	0	0	0	0	0	0	0	0	0	0	*0*	0	0	0	0	d	d	d	d	d	d	**3**	3	3	3	3	**3**	3
1	i	d	d	d	d	d	**d**	1	1	1	**1**	d	d	d	d	d	**d**	2	2	2	2	**2**	2	2	2	2	2	2	**2**	2	2	2	2	**2**	2
2	i	d	d	d	d	d	**d**	1	1	1	**1**	d	d	d	d	d	**d**	2	2	2	2	**2**	d	d	d	d	d	d	3	3	**3**	3	3	3	3	**3**	3
3	i	i	i	i	i	i	i	**i**	w	w	w	w	w	d	d	d	d	d	**0**	0	0	0	0	**0**	d	d	d	d	d	**d**	4	4	4	4	4

Fig. 7. Scenario of an unresolved collision between node 0 and 2. The y-axis shows the different nodes, the x-axis the time. Each slot contains whether the node is in the initialisation (i), waiting (w), discover (d), or active phase. In the latter case the current slot number is shown. White bold face indicates that the node is sending, black bold face that a node is receiving. Bold italics on a dark (red) background indicate collisions.

that will be derived in the process) satisfy the safety and reachability properties (1) to (4). This means that the models are deadlock free, that the nodes are synchronised, and that for each topology there exist a path that assigns the slots without collision, i.e. that there exists a solution of the related graph colouring problem.

5.2   Liveness Properties

The main liveness property (5) deals with unresolved collisions. In the basic model unresolved collisions may occur for in 3 topologies, for a total of 6 pairs of neighbours. From this basic model for 4 nodes we arrive in 12 iterations at a model that satisfactory resolves collisions for topologies with 5 nodes.

Model 1. This is the basic model for 4 nodes, and a frame length of 5 slots. Among the collisions that are not resolved are collisions that separate a node from the other nodes. An example scenario of such behavior is depicted in Figure 7. It belongs to topology 4, depicted in Figure 8.

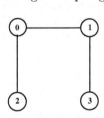

Fig. 8. Topology 4

At time 0 the gateway, node 0, sends a first message. This message is received by node 1 and 2 and they start listening to the medium. One frame later node 1 and 2 both select slot 1, and send at time 6. This leads to a collision at node 0. Node 0 reports the collision at time 10, and node 1 and 2 return to the discover phase. At the end of the scenario node 0 and node 2 collide, perpetually, since there is no neighbour to witness the collision. Node 2 does not receive any message from then on, since it cannot listen while sending. Node 2 entered this collision, because it chose a slot, while it had insufficient information. Node 2 listened from time 21 to time 26, but received not a single message. It had no information about its neighbours, when it made its choice, and any choice had the potential to lead to a collision.

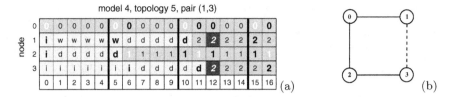

Fig. 9. (a) Scenario of an unresolved collision between node 1 and 3 in topology 5. (b) Topology 5. Node 1 and 3 may fail to resolve a collision.

Model 2. The second model improves on the first model, by introducing the rule that a node may not choose if it received no information in the discover phase. This additional rule successfully deals with the collision depicted in Figure 7.

This model run into problems because it does not reset its first-order neighbour information. After a few repeated choices some node assume that all slots are occupied. They cannot enter the active phase, and consequently cannot report collisions between other nodes. This bug was in the model because of an incomplete informal specification.

Model 3. Model 3 improves on model 2, in that it resets all neighbourhood information after it sends a message. It propagates in the active phase only information collected during the last frame length of slots.

The additional rules in Model 2 and 3 do not eliminate the possibility that a nodes may become disconnected from the network. It may still happen if a node only receives messages while it sends, and no third node witnesses or reports the collision.

Model 4. The fourth model improves on the third model in that a node chooses anew if it does not receive any message in a frame length. This last additional rule resolves all remaining collisions for topologies with 4 nodes which are not ring topology bugs. There is one ring topology, and only two pairs of nodes in it are affected. A scenario leading to this bug is depicted in Figure 9. This kind of collision is however not problematic, since all nodes are able to communicate with the gateway.

Model 5. The fifth model is identical to Model 4, except that it is instantiated for topologies with 5 nodes. There are 61 different topologies, with 571 pairs of neighbours. Although Model 4 was able to resolve all collisions except for the ring topology bug, applied to topologies of 5 nodes many other unresolved collisions suddenly occur. Model checking revealed 56 unresolved collisions, affecting 18 topologies. Also, the model checker was not able to complete for 26 topologies due to memory and time constraints. Once the computer starts swapping memory, progress typically stalls.

Model 6. The sixth model improves on the fifth model by an additional rule. If a node has chosen a slot, and it is active, but has not sent its first message yet,

model 10, topology 31, pair (2,4)

node	20	21	22	23	24	25	26	27	28	29	30	31	32	33	34	35	36	37	38	39	40	41	42	43	44	45	46	47	48	49	50	51	52	53	54	55	56	57	58	59
0	0	0	0	0		0	0	d	d	d	d	d	d	0	0		0	0	0	0		0	0	0	0		0	0	0	0		0	0	0	0		0	0	0	0
1	3	d	d	d	d	d	2	2	2	2	2	2	2	2	2	2	w	w	w	w	w	w	w	w	w	w	w	w	w	w	w	d	d	d	d	d	w	w	w
2	3	d	d	d	d	d	d	1	1	1	1	1	1	d	d	d	d	d	d	4	4	4	4	4	4	4	4	4	4	4	4	4	4	4	4	4	4	4
3	d	d	d	d	d	d	0	0	d	d	d	d	d	d	0	0	0	0	0	0	0	0	0	0	0	0	0	0	0	0	0	0	0	0	0	0	0	0	0
4	1		1	1	1	1	1	1	1	1	1	1	d	d	d	d	d	d	4	4	4	4	4	4	4	4	4	4	4	4	4	4	4	4	4	4	4	4	4

Fig. 10. Scenario of an unresolved collision between node 0 and 3

and if it then receives from a neighbour information that it slot is occupied by a second-order neighbour, then the node proceeds to choose a new slot.

Model 7. The seventh model modifies a rule introduced in Model 2. If it receives in the listing phase only collisions, it does not have sufficient information about its second-order neighbours to make a choice that avoids collisions. The new rule states that a node will not choose if it did not receive a single message, except for collisions.

In the seventh model the following could occur. First, a node reported a collision to all neighbours. Next, these neighbours proceeded to the discover phase. As a consequence, the node which reported the collision would receive no message for a frame length of slots, and incorrectly conclude that it is was disconnected from the network.

Model 8. Model 8 modifies a rule, which was introduced earlier, to avoid the scenario described for model 7. A node concludes that it is alone if it does not hear a neighbour in **two** frame lengths. This prevents a node that reported a collision to conclude that it is disconnected, just because its neighbours went to the discover phase for one frame length.

Model 9. Model 9 further refines the rule about when nodes conclude that they are alone and disconnected. If a node is active, but has not sent yet, it concludes that it disconnected if it has received no message in the frame length of slots right before its first transmission.

Model 10. Model 10 fixes a problem that occurs right after choosing a slot. Model 3 introduced that neighbour information is reset once in a frame length of slots during the active phase. When a mode transitions from the discover phase to the active phase it does not reset the neighbourhood information. As a consequence it may reflect the state of up to two frames length in the past by the time a node is sending. Model 10 fixes this by resetting all information, even if collected during the discover phase, after one frame length. In addition a node concludes that is alone if it hears nothing but collisions for two frame lengths.

Model 11. The eleventh model also refines the rules about when a node has to conclude that it is in a collision. It tackles the problem depicted in Figure 10. Nodes 0 and 3 enter a perpetual collision, since node 1 wrongly concluded at time

model 11, topology 41, pair (1,4)

node	0	1	2	3	4	5	6	7	8	9	10	11	12	13	14	15	16	17	18	19	20	21	22	23	24	25	26	27	28	29	30	31	32	33	34	35	36	37	38	39
0	0	0	0	0		0	0	0	0		0	0	0	0		0	0	0	0		0	0	0	0		0	0	0	0		0	0	0	0		0	0	0	0	
1	i	w	w	w	w	w	d	d	d	d	d	2	2	2	2	d	d	d	d	d	3	3	3	3	3	d	d	d	d	d	2	2	2	2	2	d	d	d	d	d
2	i	w	w	w	w	w	d	d	d	d	d	4	4	4	4	4	4	4	4	4	4	4	4	4	4	4	4	4	4	4	4	4	4	4	4	4	4	4	4	4
3	i	d	d	d	d	d	d	1	1	1	1	1	1	1	1	1	1	1	1	1	1	1	1	1	1	1	1	1	1	1	1	1	1	1	1	1	1	1	1	1
4	i	i	i	i	i	i	i	d	d	d	d	d	2	2	2	2	d	d	d	d	d	3	3	3	3	3	d	d	d	d	d	2	2	2	2	2	d	d	d	d

Fig. 11. Node 1 and 4 are perpetually forced to make the same choice

36 that it was disconnected. Node 1 assumed to be alone, since it only heard collisions for two frame lengths. However, the collisions in the frame running from time 27 to 31 differ from the collisions between 33 and 36. Node 1 is not disconnected, and it actually successfully reported a collision at time 32.

Model 11 introduces a new rule about when to conclude that it is in a collision. A node chooses anew if it either receives nothing for two frames or if it witnesses the same collision for the second time. The rational for the latter case is, that if a node observes a collision for the second time, it apparently unsuccessfully reported the collision, likely because it is in a collision itself.

Model 11 resolves all remaining perpetual collisions that happen not in ring topology. The remaining perpetual collisions happen in the ring of 5 nodes, or topologies that contain a ring of 4 nodes. Overall, this are 35 pairs of nodes in 13 topologies that potentially end up in an perpetual collision. These are depicted in Figure 12.

As it comes to the second liveness property – that if a node is forced to choose a slot, all nodes in the discover phase will eventually be able to choose a different slot – it turns out that Model 11 fails for 42 pairs in 14 topologies. Figure 11 depicts an example scenario. First node 1 and 4 both choose the slot 2. This collision is reported at time 14 by node 2. At time 15 node 0 sends its neighbourhood information to node 1. Based on information collected in the frame from time 10 to 14, it reports that all slots but slot 3 are occupied. Node 1 hence has to choose slot 3 at time 19. Node 4 receives in its discover phase messages in slot 1 and 4. In slot 1, it also learns from node 3 that slots 2 and 0 are occupied. Hence, node 4 has to choose node 3 as well, leading to a collision at time 23. This collision gets reported at time 24.

During the next discover phase, both, node 1 and 4 learn that all but slot 2 are occupied. Node 1 and 4 have therefore to choose slot 2 at the end of their discover phase. They end up in a collision again, which gets reported, and at the end of the next discover phase they both have to choose slot 3 again. Etcetera.

Model 12. Model 12 is identical to model 11 except that it assumes a frame length of 6 slots. Increasing the frame size does not influence the number of potential collisions in ring topologies. However, since it increases the number of available slots, all pairs in all topologies now satisfy the second liveness property. If one node is forced to choose a certain slot, the second can eventually choose a slot that differs from the first nodes slot.

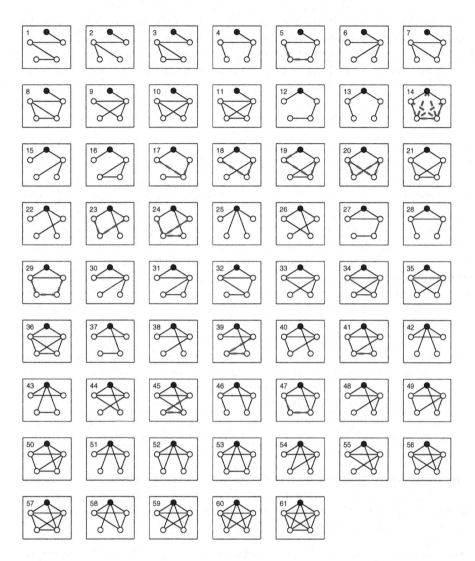

Fig. 12. Final results for all 61 topologies with 5 nodes. The gateway is the solid node. Dashed lines depict pairs of neighbours that **may** end up in an perpetual collision. Only in the ring topology 14 this may happen also between second-order neighbours.

6   Conclusion

In this paper we reported about the analysis of a medium access protocol for wireless networks, the LMAC protocol. The analysis technique we applied was model checking, using the timed automaton model checker Uppaal [3]. Our approach was a systematic analysis of all possible connected network topologies with 4 and with 5 nodes. The most relevant property we investigated was, whether collisions are detected and a new choice of slots is initiated afterwards. We checked 12 different models, four for all topologies of four nodes, eight for all topologies consisting of five nodes. The sequence of models reflects the increments in insight in the protocol, and in the improvements of the protocol. Figure 12 shows the results for the last of the models.

Checking the models against a number of properties summed up to more than 8000 model checking runs in total. For example, in each of the eight five node models there are 571 pairs of nodes. For each pair it needs to be investigate whether a possible collision is detected by the protocol or not. This results in 4568 instances of property 5 alone that need to be model checked.

Extending the systematic analysis to 6 node topologies would not only increase the model checking time for each instance, but also the number of instances to investigate. With 6 nodes we would have 486 different topologies and 6273 pairs of nodes to analyse. This would lead not only to a state space explosion problem within one model, but to a much higher extent to a instance explosion problem. For the state space explosion fully symbolic model checking techniques could be helpful, but not for the instance explosion problem. Furthermore, it seems to be difficult to parameterise topologies, having parametric model checking techniques in mind. An alternative approach for showing correctness for a class of topologies, using a combination of model-checking and abstract interpretation, was presented in [1]. Here however, we face the additional problem that essential properties are not valid for a number of instances. Therefore, we argue that with straightforward model checking techniques, not much more can be done. A possible extension could be stochastic analysis with a probabilistic model checker, which will be discussed below.

There are three main results: (1) the description of the protocol is improved, (2) the protocol itself is improved, and (3), problematic topologies with possible scenarios of unresolved collision have been identified.

Improvement of the protocol description. We had a quite usual experience here: several "bugs" found in first rounds of analysis turned out to be present in the documentation of the protocol, but not in the implementation. The respective "patches" were added to the documentation.

Protocol improvements. Some scenarios leading to unresolved collisions helped to improve the protocol, and were absent in the later protocol versions:

- There is an additional trigger for the choice of a new slot: if a node hears nothing, it concludes that it is isolated or participating itself in an collision, and starts a new choice.
- If a node hears the same collision twice, it concludes that its collision report has not been heard. The only reason for this is that this node itself is in a collision. Therefore it starts a new choice in this situation.
- Some situations of collision detected could be solved by a change in parameters in the protocol, e.g., the time that a node listens before it chooses a new slot, was extended from one frame to two frames.

– The frequency of information update was increased, e.g. slots where collisions were heard are only stored for one frame. Timely resets seem to be crucial for the protocol.

Protocol faults. It is the case that collisions are not detected if there is not a third node which can observe the collision. This situation occurs in all topologies containing a square. Fortunately, even when there is a collision, all nodes are still connected to the gateway, which makes these collisions less dramatic. The only exception to this pattern is the ring-topology of five nodes, where also unresolved collision can occur.

As mentioned, the colouring problem that the LMACprotocol tries to solve is NP-hard. It cannot be expected that a light-weight, distributed algorithm finds a solution in all cases.

Further results are:

Justification of the verification approach. The real faults found in the protocol were detected in non-trivial scenarios, generated by Uppaal-counterexamples and, for readability, transformed to a graphic by a Matlab procedure. Figure 10 contains an example of such a scenario. It is obvious that these scenarios, due to complexity, are unlikely to be found during a simulation run.

Justification of the analysis of *all* possible topologies. We found that small changes in the topology can lead to different results. Intuitively, one would expect that "similar" topologies give similar results. Unfortunately, any intuition of this kind was proved wrong. Also another intuition, that most collisions occur when the connectivity is higher turned out to be wrong. It turns out the collisions get resolved when the connectivity is high. This justifies our approach of systematically investigating all topologies. Selecting "representative" topologies is misleading, because there are no criteria for what "representative" could be.

Quantification of the success rate. For the 61 topologies we investigated 571 pairs of nodes for collision detection. 35 pairs of these showed a possible unresolved collision. There are two aspects of probability present: first, for a fixed topology we could determine the probability of an undetected collision. This exceeds the possibilities of Uppaal, and would require a probabilistic model checker (what we have not done). The second aspect is the probability of a certain topology. This cannot be answered in general, because it depends on the application domain, and the level of mobility in the network investigated.

Future work. We have not considered the probabilistic aspects of the protocol. There are two sources of probabilities in the protocol: the choice of a new slot out of all free slots, and the waiting time before choosing a new slot. We see two different approaches to treat these aspects: one is by simple meta-argumentation, based on combinatorics and elementary stochastics (e.g., "What is the probability that two nodes keep choosing the same waiting times?"). The other possibility is by using a probabilistic model checker, like PRISM. However, probabilistic models are typically even more complex than the ones we considered, which decreases the limit of what can be analysed. In this case a number of effective abstraction steps have to be applied to the model, to decrease its complexity.

We have not yet considered aspects of energy efficiency in the choice of new slots. One source of energy consumption is the number of iterations are necessary, to choose a slot without creating a collision. To answer this question probabilistic analysis is necessary. Another source of energy consumption is in the number of hops that a packet needs to reach the gateway. The choice of a slot can influence latency. Here, it seems that the "more deterministic" choice for a latency-minimizing slot increases the chance for collision during the slot selection phase. In contrary, when we apply a uniformly distributed choice of slots during the selection phase, the latency will not be optimal. What the right balance is between these parameters is subject to further analysis.

References

1. Bauer, J., Schaefer, I., Toben, T., Westphal, B.: Specification and verification of dynamic communication systems. In: Application of Concurrency to System Design (ACSD'06), pp. 189–200. IEEE Computer Society, Los Alamitos (2006)
2. Behrmann, G., David, A., Larsen, K.G.: A tutorial on uppaal. In: Bernardo, M., Corradini, F. (eds.) Formal Methods for the Design of Real-Time Systems: SFM-RT 2004. LNCS, vol. 3185, Springer, Heidelberg (2004)
3. Behrmann, G., David, A., Larsen, K.G., Hakansson, J., Petterson, P., Yi, W., Hendriks, M.: Uppaal 4.0. In: Quantitative Evaluation of Systems - (QEST'06), pp. 125–126. IEEE Computer Society Press, Los Alamitos (2006)
4. Brinksma, E.: Verification is experimentation! Int. J. on Software Tools for Technology Transfer 3(2), 107–111 (2001)
5. Cardell-Oliver, R.: Why Flooding is Unreliable (Extended Version). Technical Report UWA-CSSE-04-001, CSSE, University of Western Australia (2004)
6. Mader, A., Wupper, H., Boon, M.: The construction of verification models for embedded systems. Technical report TR-CTIT-07-02, Centre for Telematics and Information Technology, Univ. of Twente, The Netherlands (January 2007)
7. Moscibroda, T., Wattenhofer, R.: Coloring unstructured radio networks. In: Proc. of 17th Symposium on Parallelism in Algorithms and Architectures (2005)
8. Olveczky, P., Thorvaldsen, S.: Formal modeling and analysis of wireless sensor network algorithms in real-time maude. In: Proceedings of the 14th International Workshop on Parallel and Distributed Real-Time Systems (WPDRTS 2006), IEEE Computer Society Press, Los Alamitos (2006)
9. Sridharan, A., Krishnamachari, B.: Max-min fair collision-free scheduling for wireless sensor networks. In: Workshop on multi-hop wireless networks (2004)
10. van Hoesel, L.F.W., Havinga, P.J.M.: A lightweight medium access protocol (lmac) for wireless sensor networks: Reducing preamble transmissions and transceiver state switches. In: In 1st International Workshop on Networked Sensing Systems (INSS 2004), pp. 205–208 (June 2004)

Finding State Solutions to Temporal Logic Queries

Mihaela Gheorghiu, Arie Gurfinkel, and Marsha Chechik

Department of Computer Science, University of Toronto,
Toronto, ON M5S 3G4, Canada
{mg,arie,chechik}@cs.toronto.edu

Abstract. Different analysis problems for state-transition models can be uniformly treated as instances of temporal logic query-checking, where solutions to the queries are restricted to states. In this paper, we propose a symbolic query-checking algorithm that finds exactly the state solutions to a query. We argue that our approach generalizes previous specialized techniques, and this generality allows us to find new and interesting applications, such as finding stable states. Our algorithm is linear in the size of the state space and in the cost of model checking, and has been implemented on top of the model checker NuSMV, using the latter as a black box. We show the effectiveness of our approach by comparing it, on a gene network example, to the naive algorithm in which all possible state solutions are checked separately.

1 Introduction

In the analysis of state-transition models, many problems reduce to questions of the type: "What are all the states that satisfy a property φ?". Symbolic model checking can answer some of these questions, provided that the property φ can be formulated in an appropriate temporal logic. For example, suppose the erroneous states of a program are characterized by the program counter (pc) being at a line labeled ERROR. Then the states that may lead to error can be discovered by model checking the property EF (pc = ERROR), formalized in the branching temporal logic CTL [10].

There are many interesting questions which are not readily expressed in temporal logic and require specialized algorithms. One example is finding the reachable states, which is often needed in a pre-analysis step to restrict further analysis only to those states. These states are typically found by computing a forward transitive closure of the transition relation [8]. Another example is the computation of "procedure summaries". A *procedure summary* is a relation between states, representing the input/output behavior of a procedure. The summary answers the question of which inputs lead to which outputs as a result of executing the procedure. They are computed in the form of "summary edges" in the control-flow graphs of programs [21,2]. Yet another example is the algorithm for finding *dominators/postdominators* in program analysis, proposed in [1]. A state t is a postdominator of a state s if all paths from s eventually reach t, and t is a dominator of s if all paths to s pass through t.

Although these problems are similar, their solutions are quite different. Unifying them into a common framework allows reuse of specific techniques proposed for each problem, and opens a way for creating efficient implementations to other problems of

J. Davies and J. Gibbons (Eds.): IFM 2007, LNCS 4591, pp. 273–292, 2007.

a similar kind. We see all these problems as instances of *model exploration*, where properties of a model are *discovered*, rather than checked. A common framework for model exploration has been proposed under the name of *query checking* [5].

Query checking finds *which* formulas hold in a model. For instance, a query EF ? is intended to find all propositional formulas that hold in the reachable states. In general, a CTL query is a CTL formula with a missing propositional subformula, designated by a placeholder ("?"). A *solution* to the query is any propositional formula that, when substituted for the placeholder, makes a CTL formula that holds in the model. The general query checking problem is: given a CTL query on a model, find all of its propositional solutions. For example, consider the model in Figure 1(a), where each state is labeled by the atomic propositions that hold in it. Here, some solutions to EF ? are $(p \wedge \neg q \wedge r)$, representing the reachable state s_0, and $(q \wedge r)$, representing the set of states $\{s_1, s_2\}$. On the other hand, $\neg r$ is not a solution: $EF \ \neg r$ does not hold, since no states where r is false are reachable. Query checking can be solved by repeatedly substituting each possible propositional formula for the placeholder, and returning those for which the resulting CTL formula holds. In the worst case, this approach is exponential in the size of the state space and linear in the cost of CTL model checking.

Each of the analysis questions described above can be formulated as a query. Reachable states are solutions to EF ?. Procedure summaries can be obtained by solving $EF ((\text{pc} = \text{PROC\_END}) \wedge \text{?})$, where $\text{pc} = \text{PROC\_END}$ holds in the return statement of the procedure. Dominators/postdominators are solutions to the query AF ? (*i.e.*, what propositional formulas eventually hold on all paths). This insight gives us a uniform formulation of these problems and allows for easy creation of solutions to other, similar, problems. For example, a problem reported in genetics research [4,12] called for finding *stable states* of a model, that are those states which, once reached, are never left by the system. This is easily formulated as $EFAG$?, meaning "what are the reachable states in which the system will remain forever?".

These analysis problems further require that solutions to their queries be states of the model. For example, a query AF ? on the model in Figure 1(a) has solutions $(p \wedge \neg q \wedge r)$ and $(q \wedge r)$. The first corresponds to the state s_0 and is a state solution. The second corresponds to a set of states $\{s_1, s_2\}$ but neither s_1 nor s_2 is a solution by itself. When only state solutions are needed, we can formulate a restricted *state query-checking* problem by constraining the solutions to be single states, rather than arbitrary propositional formulas (that represent *sets* of states). A naive state query checking algorithm is to repeatedly substitute each state of the model for the placeholder, and return those for which the resulting CTL formula holds. This approach is linear in the size of the state space and in the cost of CTL model checking. While significantly more efficient than general query checking, this approach is not "fully" symbolic, since it requires many runs of a model-checker.

While several approaches have been proposed to solve general query checking, none are effective for solving the state query-checking problem. The original algorithm of Chan [5] was very efficient (same cost as CTL model checking), but was restricted to *valid* queries, *i.e.*, queries whose solutions can be characterized by a single propositional formula. This is too restrictive for our purposes. For example, neither of the queries EF ?, AF ?, nor the stable states query EF AG ? are valid. Bruns and Godefroid [3] generalized query checking to all CTL queries by proposing an automata-based CTL model checking algorithm over a lattice of sets of all possible solutions. This algorithm is exponential in the size of the state space. Gurfinkel and Chechik [15] have also provided a symbolic algorithm for general query checking. The algorithm is based on reducing query checking to multi-valued model checking and is implemented in a tool TLQSolver [7]. While empirically faster than the corresponding naive approach of substituting every propositional formula for the placeholder, this algorithm still has the same worst-case complexity as that in [3], and remains applicable only to modest-sized query-checking problems. An algorithm proposed by Hornus and Schnoebelen [17] finds solutions to any query, one by one, with increasing complexity: a first solution is found in time linear in the size of the state space, a second, in quadratic time, and so on. However, since the search for solutions is not controlled by their shape, finding all state solutions can still take exponential time. Other query-checking work is not directly applicable to our state query-checking problem, as it is exclusively concerned either with syntactic characterizations of queries[23], or with extensions, rather than restrictions, of query checking [24,26].

In this paper, we provide a symbolic algorithm for solving the state query-checking problem, and describe an implementation using the model-checker NuSMV [8]. The algorithm is formulated as model checking over a lattice of sets of states, but its implementation is done by modifying only the interface of NuSMV. Manipulation of the lattice sets is done directly by NuSMV. While the running time of this approach is the same as in the corresponding naive approach, we show empirical evidence that our implementation can perform better than the naive, using a case study from genetics [12].

The algorithms proposed for the program analysis problems described above are special cases of ours, that solve only EF ? and AF ? queries, whereas our algorithm solves any CTL query. We prove our algorithm correct by showing that it *approximates* general query checking, in the sense that it computes exactly those solutions, among all given by general query checking, that are states. We also generalize our results to an approximation framework that can potentially apply to other extensions of model checking, *e.g.*, vacuity detection, and point to further applications of our technique, *e.g.*, to querying XML documents.

There is a also a very close connection between query-checking and sanity checks such as vacuity and coverage [19]. All these problems require checking several "mutants" of the property or of the model to obtain the final solution. The algorithm for solving state queries presented in this paper bears many similarities to the algorithms described in [19]. Since query-checking is more general, we believe it can provide a uniform framework for studying all these problems.

The rest of the paper is organized as follows. Section 2 provides the model checking background. Section 3 describes the general query-checking algorithm. We formally define the state query-checking problem and describe our implementation in Section 4. Section 5 presents the general approximation technique for model checking over lattices of sets. We present our case study in Section 6, and conclude in Section 7.

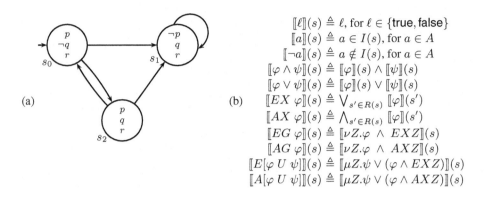

(a)

(b)

$$[\![\ell]\!](s) \triangleq \ell, \text{ for } \ell \in \{\text{true}, \text{false}\}$$
$$[\![a]\!](s) \triangleq a \in I(s), \text{ for } a \in A$$
$$[\![\neg a]\!](s) \triangleq a \notin I(s), \text{ for } a \in A$$
$$[\![\varphi \wedge \psi]\!](s) \triangleq [\![\varphi]\!](s) \wedge [\![\psi]\!](s)$$
$$[\![\varphi \vee \psi]\!](s) \triangleq [\![\varphi]\!](s) \vee [\![\psi]\!](s)$$
$$[\![EX \; \varphi]\!](s) \triangleq \bigvee_{s' \in R(s)} [\![\varphi]\!](s')$$
$$[\![AX \; \varphi]\!](s) \triangleq \bigwedge_{s' \in R(s)} [\![\varphi]\!](s')$$
$$[\![EG \; \varphi]\!](s) \triangleq [\![\nu Z.\varphi \; \wedge \; EXZ]\!](s)$$
$$[\![AG \; \varphi]\!](s) \triangleq [\![\nu Z.\varphi \; \wedge \; AXZ]\!](s)$$
$$[\![E[\varphi \; U \; \psi]]\!](s) \triangleq [\![\mu Z.\psi \vee (\varphi \wedge EXZ)]\!](s)$$
$$[\![A[\varphi \; U \; \psi]]\!](s) \triangleq [\![\mu Z.\psi \vee (\varphi \wedge AXZ)]\!](s)$$

Fig. 1. (a) A simple Kripke structure; (b) CTL semantics

2   Background

In this section, we review some notions of lattice theory, minterms, CTL model checking, and multi-valued model checking.

Lattice theory. A *finite lattice* is a pair $(\mathcal{L}, \sqsubseteq)$, where $\mathcal{L}$ is a finite set and $\sqsubseteq$ is a partial order on $\mathcal{L}$, such that every finite subset $B \subseteq \mathcal{L}$ has a least upper bound (called *join* and written $\sqcup B$) and a greatest lower bound (called *meet* and written $\sqcap B$). Since the lattice is finite, there exist $\top = \sqcup \mathcal{L}$ and $\bot = \sqcap \mathcal{L}$, that are the maximum and respectively minimum elements in the lattice. When the ordering $\sqsubseteq$ is clear from the context, we simply refer to the lattice as $\mathcal{L}$. A lattice if *distributive* if meet and join distribute over each other. In this paper, we work with lattices of propositional formulas. For a set of atomic propositions P, let $\mathcal{F}(P)$ be the set of propositional formulas over P. For example, $\mathcal{F}(\{p\}) = \{\text{true}, \text{false}, p, \neg p\}$. This set forms a finite lattice ordered by implication (see Figure 2(a)). Since $p \Rightarrow \text{true}$, p is under true in this lattice. Meet and join in this lattice correspond to logical operators $\wedge$ and $\vee$, respectively.

A subset $B \subseteq \mathcal{L}$ is called *upward closed* or an *upset*, if for any $a, b \in \mathcal{L}$, if $b \in B$ and $b \sqsubseteq a$, then $a \in B$. In that case, B can be identified by the set M of its minimal elements ($b \in B$ is minimal if for all $a \in B$ if $a \sqsubseteq b$, then $a = b$), and we write $B = \uparrow M$. For example, for the lattice $(\mathcal{F}(\{p\}), \Rightarrow)$ shown in Figure 2(a), $\uparrow\{p, \neg p\} = \{p, \neg p, \text{true}\}$. The set $\{p, \neg p\}$ is not an upset, whereas $\{p, \neg p, \text{true}\}$ is. For singletons, we write $\uparrow a$ for $\uparrow\{a\}$. We extend the $\uparrow$ notation to any set $A \subseteq \mathcal{L}$ by $\uparrow A = \uparrow M$, where M is the set of minimal elements in A. We write $\mathcal{U}(\mathcal{L})$ for the set of all upsets of $\mathcal{L}$, *i.e.*, $A \subseteq \mathcal{L}$ iff $\uparrow A \in \mathcal{U}(\mathcal{L})$. $\mathcal{U}(\mathcal{L})$ is closed under union and intersection, and therefore forms a lattice ordered by set inclusion. We call $(\mathcal{U}(\mathcal{L}), \subseteq)$ the *upset lattice* of $\mathcal{L}$. The upset lattice of $\mathcal{F}(\{p\})$ is shown in Figure 2(b).

An element j in a lattice $\mathcal{L}$ is *join-irreducible* if $j \neq \bot$ and j cannot be decomposed as the join of other lattice elements, *i.e.*, for any x and y in $\mathcal{L}$, $j = x \sqcup y$ implies $j = x$ or $j = y$ [11]. For example, the join-irreducible elements of the lattice in Figure 2(a) are p and $\neg p$, and of the one in Figure 2(b) — $\uparrow\text{true}$, $\uparrow p$, $\uparrow\neg p$, and $\uparrow\text{false}$.

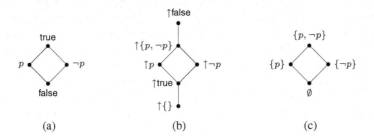

Fig. 2. Lattices for $P = \{p\}$: (a) $(\mathcal{F}(P), \Rightarrow)$; (b) $(\mathcal{U}(\mathcal{F}(P)), \subseteq)$; (c) $(2^{\mathcal{M}(P)}, \subseteq)$

Minterms. In the lattice of propositional formulas $\mathcal{F}(P)$, a join-irreducible element is a conjunction in which every atomic proposition of P appears, positive or negated. Such conjunctions are called *minterms* and we denote their set by $\mathcal{M}(P)$. For example,

$$\mathcal{M}(\{p, q\}) = \{p \wedge q, p \wedge \neg q, \neg p \wedge q, \neg p \wedge \neg q\}.$$

CTL model checking. CTL model checking is an automatic technique for verifying temporal properties of systems expressed in a propositional branching-time temporal logic called *Computation Tree Logic* (CTL) [9]. A system model is a *Kripke structure* $\mathcal{K} = (S, R, s_0, A, I)$, where S is a set of states, $R \subseteq S \times S$ is a (left-total) transition relation, $s_0 \in S$ is the initial state, A is a set of atomic propositions, and $I : S \rightarrow 2^A$ is a labeling function, providing the set of atomic propositions that are true in each state. CTL formulas are evaluated in the states of $\mathcal{K}$. Their semantics can be described in terms of infinite execution paths of the model. For instance, a formula $AG\ \varphi$ holds in a state s if φ holds in every state, on every infinite execution path $s, s_1, s_2, \ldots$ starting at s; $AF\ \varphi$ $(EF\ \varphi)$ holds in s if φ holds in some state, on every (some) infinite execution path $s, s_1, s_2, \ldots$. The formal semantics of CTL is given in Figure 1(b). Without loss of generality we consider only CTL formulas in *negation normal form*, where negation is applied only to atomic propositions [9]. In Figure 1(b), the function $[\![\varphi]\!] : S \rightarrow \{\text{true}, \text{false}\}$ indicates the result of checking a formula φ in state s; the set of successors for a state s is $R(s) \triangleq \{s' | (s, s') \in R\}$; $\mu Z.f(Z)$ and $\nu Z.f(Z)$ are least and greatest fixpoints of f, respectively, where $\mu Z.f(Z) = \bigvee_{i>0} f^i(\text{false})$ and $\nu Z.f(Z) = \bigwedge_{i>0} f^i(\text{true})$. Other temporal operators are derived from the given ones, for example: $EF\ \varphi = E[\text{true}\ U\ \varphi]$, $AF\ \varphi = A[\text{true}\ U\ \varphi]$. The operators in pairs $(AX, EX), (AG, EF), (AF, EG), \ldots$ are duals of each other.

A formula φ holds in a Kripke structure $\mathcal{K}$, written $\mathcal{K} \models \varphi$, if it holds in the initial state, *i.e.*, $[\![\varphi]\!](s_0) = \text{true}$. For example, on the model in Figure 1(a), where $A = \{p, q, r\}$, properties $AG\ (p \vee q)$ and $AF\ q$ are true, whereas $AX\ p$ is not. The complexity of model-checking a CTL formula φ on a Kripke structure $\mathcal{K}$ is $O(|\mathcal{K}| \times |\varphi|)$, where $|\mathcal{K}| = |S| + |R|$.

Multi-valued model checking. *Multi-valued* CTL model checking [6] is a generalization of model checking from a classical logic to an arbitrary *De Morgan* algebra $(\mathcal{L}, \sqsubseteq, \neg)$, where $(\mathcal{L}, \sqsubseteq)$ is a finite distributive lattice and $\neg$ is any operation that is an involution ($\neg\neg\ell = \ell$) and satisfies De Morgan laws. Conjunction and disjunction are the meet and join operations of $(\mathcal{L}, \sqsubseteq)$, respectively. When the ordering and the negation operation of an algebra $(\mathcal{L}, \sqsubseteq, \neg)$ are clear from the context, we refer to it as $\mathcal{L}$. In this paper, we only use a version of multi-valued model checking where the model remains classical, *i.e.*, both the transition relation and the atomic propositions are two-valued, but properties are specified in a multi-valued extension of CTL over a given De Morgan algebra $\mathcal{L}$, called $\mathcal{X}\text{CTL}(\mathcal{L})$. The logic $\mathcal{X}\text{CTL}(\mathcal{L})$ has the same syntax as CTL, except that the allowed constants are all $\ell \in \mathcal{L}$. Boolean values true and false are replaced by the $\top$ and $\bot$ of $\mathcal{L}$, respectively. The semantics of $\mathcal{X}\text{CTL}(\mathcal{L})$ is the same as of CTL, except $[\![\varphi]\!]$ is extended to $[\![\varphi]\!] : S \to \mathcal{L}$ and the interpretation of constants is: for all $\ell \in \mathcal{L}$, $[\![\ell]\!](s) \triangleq \ell$. The other operations are defined as their CTL counterparts (see Figure 1(b)), where $\vee$ and $\wedge$ are interpreted as lattice operators $\sqcup$ and $\sqcap$, respectively. The complexity of model checking a $\mathcal{X}\text{CTL}(\mathcal{L})$ formula φ on a Kripke structure $\mathcal{K}$ is still $O(|\mathcal{K}| \times |\varphi|)$, *provided that* meet, join, and quantification can be computed in constant time [6], which depends on the lattice.

3   Query Checking

In this section, we review the query-checking problem and a symbolic method for solving it.

Background. Let $\mathcal{K}$ be a Kripke structure with a set A of atomic propositions. A CTL query, denoted by $\varphi[?]$, is a CTL formula containing a *placeholder* "?" for a propositional subformula (over the atomic propositions in A). The CTL formula obtained by substituting the placeholder in $\varphi[?]$ by a formula $\alpha \in \mathcal{F}(A)$ is denoted by $\varphi[\alpha]$. A formula α is a *solution* to a query if its substitution into the query results in a CTL formula that holds on $\mathcal{K}$, *i.e.*, if $\mathcal{K} \models \varphi[\alpha]$. For example, $(p \wedge \neg q \wedge r)$ and $(q \wedge r)$ are among the solutions to the query $AF\ ?$ on the model of Figure 1(a), whereas $\neg r$ is not.

In this paper, we consider queries in *negation normal form* where negation is applied only to the atomic propositions, or to the placeholder. We further restrict our attention to queries with a single placeholder, although perhaps with multiple occurrences. For a query $\varphi[?]$, a substitution $\varphi[\alpha]$ means that all occurrences of the placeholder are replaced by α. For example, if $\varphi[?] = EF\ (? \wedge AX\ ?)$, then $\varphi[p \vee q] = EF\ ((p \vee q) \wedge AX\ (p \vee q))$. We assume that occurrences of the placeholder are either non-negated everywhere, or negated everywhere, *i.e.*, the query is either *positive* or *negative*, respectively. Here, we limit our presentation to positive queries; see Section 5 for the treatment of negative queries.

The general CTL query-checking problem is: given a CTL query on a model, find all its propositional solutions. For instance, the answer to the query $AF\ ?$ on the model in Figure 1(a) is the set consisting of $(p \wedge \neg q \wedge r), (q \wedge r)$ and every other formula implied by these, including $p, (q \vee r)$, and true. If α is a solution to a query, then any β such that $\alpha \Rightarrow \beta$ (*i.e.*, any weaker β) is also a solution, due to the monotonicity of positive queries [5]. Thus, the set of all possible solutions is an upset; it is sufficient for the query-checker to output the strongest solutions, since the rest can be inferred from them.

One can restrict a query to a subset $P \subseteq A$ [3]. We then denote the query by $\varphi[?P]$, and its solutions become formulas in $\mathcal{F}(P)$. For instance, checking $AF\ ?\{p, q\}$ on the model of Figure 1(a) should result in $(p \wedge \neg q)$ and q as the strongest solutions, together with all those implied by them. We write $\varphi[?]$ for $\varphi[?A]$.

If P consists of n atomic propositions, there are 2^{2^n} possible distinct solutions to $\varphi[?P]$. A "naive" method for finding all solutions would model check $\varphi[\alpha]$ for every possible propositional formula α over P, and collect all those α's for which $\varphi[\alpha]$ holds in the model. The complexity of this naive approach is 2^{2^n} times that of usual model-checking.

Symbolic algorithm. A symbolic algorithm for solving the general query-checking problem was described in [15] and has been implemented in the TLQSolver tool [7]. We review this approach below.

Since an answer to $\varphi[?P]$ is an upset, the upset lattice $\mathcal{U}(\mathcal{F}(P))$ is the space of all possible answers [3]. For instance, the lattice for $AF\ ?\{p\}$ is shown in Figure 2(b). In the model in Figure 1(a), the answer to this query is $\{p, \mathsf{true}\}$, encoded as $\uparrow\{p\}$, since p is the strongest solution.

Symbolic query checking is implemented by model checking over the upset lattice. The algorithm is based on a state semantics of the placeholder. Suppose query $?\{p\}$ is evaluated in a state s. Either p holds in s, in which case the answer to the query should be $\uparrow p$, or $\neg p$ holds in s, in which case the answer is $\uparrow\neg p$. Thus we have:

$$[\![?\{p\}]\!](s) = \begin{cases} \uparrow p & \text{if } p \in I(s), \\ \uparrow\neg p & \text{if } p \notin I(s). \end{cases}$$

This case analysis can be logically encoded by the formula $(p \wedge \uparrow p) \vee (\neg p \wedge \uparrow\neg p)$.

Let us now consider a general query $?P$ in a state s (where $?$ ranges over a set of atomic propositions P). We note that the case analysis corresponding to the one above can be given in terms of minterms. Minterms are the strongest formulas that may hold in a state; they also are mutually exclusive and complete — exactly one minterm j holds in any state s, and then $\uparrow j$ is the answer to $?P$ at s. This semantics is encoded in the following translation of the placeholder:

$$\mathcal{T}(?P) = \bigvee_{j \in \mathcal{M}(P)} (j \wedge \uparrow j).$$

The symbolic algorithm is defined as follows: given a query $\varphi[?P]$, first obtain $\varphi[\mathcal{T}(?P)]$, which is a $\mathcal{X}$CTL formula (over the lattice $\mathcal{U}(\mathcal{F}(P))$), and then model check this formula. The semantics of the formula is given by a function from S to $\mathcal{U}(\mathcal{F}(P))$, as described in Section 2. Thus model checking this formula results in a value from $\mathcal{U}(\mathcal{F}(P))$. That value was shown in [15] to represent all propositional solutions to $\varphi[?P]$. For example, the query $AF\ ?$ on the model of Figure 1(a) becomes

$$\begin{aligned}
AF\ ((p \wedge q \wedge r \wedge \uparrow(p \wedge q \wedge r)) \vee \\
(p \wedge q \wedge \neg r \wedge \uparrow(p \wedge q \wedge \neg r)) \vee \\
(p \wedge \neg q \wedge r \wedge \uparrow(p \wedge \neg q \wedge r)) \vee \\
(p \wedge \neg q \wedge \neg r \wedge \uparrow(p \wedge \neg q \wedge \neg r)) \vee \\
\ldots).
\end{aligned}$$

The result of model-checking this formula is $\uparrow\{p \wedge \neg q \wedge r, q \wedge r\}$.

The complexity of this algorithm is the same as in the naive approach. In practice, however, TLQSolver was shown to perform better than the naive algorithm [15,7].

4   State Solutions to Queries

Let $\mathcal{K}$ be a Kripke structure with a set A of atomic propositions. In general query checking, solutions to queries are arbitrary propositional formulas. On the other hand, in *state query checking*, solutions are restricted to be single states. To represent a single state, a propositional formula needs to be a minterm over A. In *symbolic* model checking, any state s of $\mathcal{K}$ is uniquely represented by the minterm that holds in s. For example, in the model of Figure 1(a), state s_0 is represented by $(p \wedge \neg q \wedge r)$, state s_2 by $(p \wedge q \wedge r)$, etc. Thus, for state query checking, an answer to a query is a set of minterms, rather than an upset of propositional formulas. For instance, for the query AF ?, on the model of Figure 1(a), the state query-checking answer is $\{p \wedge \neg q \wedge r\}$, whereas the general query-checking one is $\uparrow\{r \wedge q, p \wedge \neg q \wedge r\}$. While it is still true that if j is a solution, everything in $\uparrow j$ is also a solution, we no longer view answers as upsets, since we are interested only in minterms, and j is the only minterm in the set $\uparrow j$ (minterms are incomparable by implication). We can thus formulate state query checking as *minterm query checking*: given a CTL query on a model, find all its minterm solutions. We show how to solve this for any query $\varphi[?P]$, and any subset $P \subseteq A$. When $P = A$, the minterms obtained are the state solutions.

Given a query $\varphi[?P]$, a naive algorithm would model check $\varphi[\alpha]$ for every minterm α. If n is the number of atomic propositions in P, there are 2^n possible minterms, and this algorithm has complexity 2^n times that of model-checking. Minterm query checking is thus much easier to solve than general query checking.

Of course, any algorithm solving general query checking, such as the symbolic approach described in Section 3, solves minterm query checking as well: from all solutions, we can extract only those which are minterms. This approach, however, is much more expensive than needed. Below, we propose a method that is tailored to solve just minterm query checking, while remaining symbolic.

4.1   Solving Minterm Query Checking

Since an answer to minterm query checking is a set of minterms, the space of all answers is the powerset $2^{\mathcal{M}(P)}$ that forms a lattice ordered by set inclusion. For example, the lattice $2^{\mathcal{M}(\{p\})}$ is shown in Figure 2(c). Our symbolic algorithm evaluates queries over this lattice. We first adjust the semantics of the placeholder to minterms. Suppose we evaluate $?\{p\}$ in a state s. Either p holds in s, and then the answer should be $\{p\}$, or $\neg p$ holds, and then the answer is $\{\neg p\}$. Thus, we have

$$[\![?\{p\}]\!](s) = \begin{cases} \{p\} & \text{if } p \in I(s), \\ \{\neg p\} & \text{if } p \notin I(s). \end{cases}$$

This is encoded by the formula $(p \land \{p\}) \lor (\neg p \land \{\neg p\})$. In general, for a query $?P$, exactly one minterm j holds in s, and in that case $\{j\}$ is the answer to the query. This gives the following translation of placeholder:

$$\mathcal{A}_m(?P) \triangleq \bigvee_{j \in \mathcal{M}(P)} (j \land \{j\}).$$

Our minterm query-checking algorithm is now defined as follows: given a query $\varphi[?P]$ on a model $\mathcal{K}$, compute $\varphi[\mathcal{A}_m(?P)]$, and then model check this over $2^{\mathcal{M}(P)}$.

For example, for AF ?, on the model of Figure 1(a), we model check

$$
\begin{aligned}
AF\ (&(p \land q \land r \land \{p \land q \land r\}) \lor \\
&(p \land q \land \neg r \land \{p \land q \land \neg r\}) \lor \\
&(p \land \neg q \land r \land \{p \land \neg q \land r\}) \lor \\
&(p \land \neg q \land \neg r \land \{p \land \neg q \land \neg r\}) \lor \\
&\cdots),
\end{aligned}
$$

and obtain the answer $\{p \land \neg q \land r\}$, that is indeed the only minterm solution for this model.

To prove our algorithm correct, we need to show that its answer is the set of all minterm solutions. We prove this claim by relating our algorithm to the general algorithm in Section 3. We show that, while the general algorithm computes the set $B \in \mathcal{U}(\mathcal{F}(P))$ of all solutions, ours results in the subset $M \subseteq B$ that consists of only the minterms from B. We first establish an "approximation" mapping from $\mathcal{U}(\mathcal{F}(P))$ to $2^{\mathcal{M}(P)}$ that, for any upset $B \in \mathcal{U}(\mathcal{F}(P))$, returns the subset $M \subseteq B$ of minterms.

Definition 1 (Minterm approximation). *Let P be a set of atomic propositions. Minterm approximation $f_m : \mathcal{U}(\mathcal{F}(P)) \to 2^{\mathcal{M}(P)}$ is $f_m(B) \triangleq B \cap \mathcal{M}(P)$, for any $B \in \mathcal{U}(\mathcal{F}(P))$.*

With this definition, $\mathcal{A}_m(?P)$ is obtained from $\mathcal{T}(?P)$ by replacing $\uparrow j$ with $f_m(\uparrow j) = \{j\}$. The minterm approximation preserves set operations; this can be proven using the fact that any set of propositional formulas can be partitioned into minterms and non-minterms.

Proposition 1. *The minterm approximation $f_m : \mathcal{U}(\mathcal{F}(P)) \to 2^{\mathcal{M}(P)}$ is a lattice homomorphism, i.e., it preserves the set operations: for any $B, B' \in \mathcal{U}(\mathcal{F}(P))$, $f_m(B) \cup f_m(B') = f_m(B \cup B')$ and $f_m(B) \cap f_m(B') = f_m(B \cap B')$.*

By Proposition 1, and since model checking is performed using only set operations, we can show that the approximation preserves model-checking results. Model checking $\varphi[\mathcal{A}_m(?P)]$ is the minterm approximation of checking $\varphi[\mathcal{T}(?P)]$. In other words, our algorithm results in set of all minterm solutions, which concludes the correctness argument.

Theorem 1 (Correctness of minterm approximation). *For any state s of $\mathcal{K}$,*

$$f_m(\llbracket \varphi[\mathcal{T}(?P)] \rrbracket(s)) = \llbracket \varphi[\mathcal{A}_m(?P)] \rrbracket(s).$$

In summary, for $P = A$, we have the following correct symbolic state query-checking algorithm : given a query $\varphi[?]$ on a model $\mathcal{K}$, translate it to $\varphi[\mathcal{A}_m(?A)]$, and then model check this over $2^{\mathcal{M}(A)}$.

The worst-case complexity of our algorithm is the same as that of the naive approach. With an efficient encoding of the approximate lattice, however, our approach can outperform the naive one in practice, as we show in Section 6.

4.2 Implementation

Although our minterm query-checking algorithm is defined as model checking over a lattice, we can implement it using a classical symbolic model checker. This is done by encoding the lattice elements in $2^{\mathcal{M}(P)}$ such that lattice operations are already implemented by a symbolic model checker. The key observation is that the lattice $(2^{\mathcal{M}(P)}, \subseteq)$ is isomorphic to the lattice of propositional formulas $(\mathcal{F}(P), \Rightarrow)$. This can be seen, for instance, by comparing the lattices in Figures 2(a) and 2(c). Thus, the elements of $2^{\mathcal{M}(P)}$ can be encoded as propositional formulas, and the operations become propositional disjunction and conjunction. A symbolic model checker, such as NuSMV [8], which we used in our implementation, already has data structures for representing propositional formulas and algorithms to compute their disjunction and conjunction — BDDs [25]. The only modifications we made to NuSMV were parsing the input and reporting the result.

While parsing the queries, we implemented the translation $\mathcal{A}_m$ defined in Section 4.1. In this translation, for every minterm j, we give a propositional encoding to $\{j\}$. We cannot simply use j to encode $\{j\}$. The lattice elements need to be *constants* with respect to the model, and j is not a constant — it is a propositional formula that contains model variables. We can, however, obtain an encoding for $\{j\}$, by renaming j to a similar propositional formula over fresh variables. For instance, we encode $\{p \wedge \neg q \wedge r\}$ as $x \wedge \neg y \wedge z$. Thus, our query translation results in a CTL formula with double the number of propositional variables compared to the model. For example, the translation of $AF\ ?\{p, q\}$ is

$$AF\ ((p \wedge q \wedge x \wedge y)\vee$$
$$(p \wedge \neg q \wedge x \wedge \neg y)\vee$$
$$(\neg p \wedge q \wedge \neg x \wedge y)\vee$$
$$(\neg p \wedge \neg q \wedge \neg x \wedge \neg y)).$$

We input this formula into NuSMV, and obtain the set of minterm solutions as a propositional formula over the encoding variables $x, y, \ldots$. For $AF\ ?\{p, q\}$, on the model in Figure 1(a), we obtain the result $x \wedge \neg y$, corresponding to the only minterm solution $p \wedge \neg q$.

4.3 Exactness of Minterm Approximation

In this section, we address the applicability of minterm query checking to general query checking. When the minterm solutions are the strongest solutions to a query, minterm query checking solves the general query-checking problem as well, as all solutions to that query can be inferred from the minterms. In that case, we say that the minterm approximation is *exact*. We would like to identify those CTL queries that admit exact minterm approximations, independently of the model. The following can be proven using the fact that any propositional formula is a disjunction of minterms.

Proposition 2. *A positive query $\varphi[?P]$ has an exact minterm approximation in any model iff $\varphi[?P]$ is distributive over disjunction, i.e., $\varphi[\alpha \vee \beta] = \varphi[\alpha] \vee \varphi[\beta]$.*

An example of a query that admits an exact approximation is EF ?; its strongest solutions are always minterms, representing the reachable states. In [5], Chan showed that deciding whether a query is distributive over *conjunction* is EXPTIME-complete. We obtain a similar result by duality.

Theorem 2. *Deciding whether a CTL query is distributive over disjunction is EXPTIME-complete.*

Since the decision problem is hard, it would be useful to have a grammar that is guaranteed to generate queries which distribute over disjunction. Chan defined a grammar for queries distributive over conjunction, that was later corrected by Samer and Veith [22]. We can obtain a grammar for queries distributive over disjunction, from the grammar in [22], by duality.

5 Approximations

The efficiency of model checking over a lattice is determined by the size of the lattice. In the case of query checking, by restricting the problem and approximating answers, we have obtained a more manageable lattice. In this section, we show that our minterm approximation is an instance of a more general approximation framework for reasoning over any lattice of sets. Having a more general framework makes it easier to accommodate other approximations that may be needed in query checking. For example, we use it to derive an approximation to *negative* queries. This framework may also apply to other analysis problems that involve model checking over lattices of sets, such as vacuity detection [14].

We first define general approximations that map larger lattices into smaller ones. Let U be any finite set. Its powerset lattice is $(2^U, \subseteq)$. Let $(\mathcal{L}, \subseteq)$ be any sublattice of the powerset lattice, *i.e.*, $\mathcal{L} \subseteq 2^U$.

Definition 2 (Approximation). *A function $f : \mathcal{L} \rightarrow 2^U$ is an* approximation *if:*

1. *it satisfies $f(B) \subseteq B$ for any $B \in \mathcal{L}$ (i.e., $f(B)$ is an under-approximation of B), and*
2. *it is a lattice homomorphism, i.e., it respects the lattice operations: $f(B \cap C) = f(B) \cap f(C)$, and $f(B \cup C) = f(B) \cup f(C)$.*

From the definition of f, the image $f(\mathcal{L})$ of $\mathcal{L}$ through f is a sublattice of 2^U, having $f(\top)$ and $f(\bot)$ as its maximum and minimum elements, respectively.

We consider an approximation to be correct if it is preserved by model checking: reasoning over the smaller lattice is the approximation of reasoning over the larger one. Let φ be a $\mathcal{X}CTL(\mathcal{L})$ formula. We define its translation $\mathcal{A}(\varphi)$ into $f(\mathcal{L})$ to be the $\mathcal{X}CTL(f(\mathcal{L}))$ formula obtained from φ by replacing any constant $B \in \mathcal{L}$ occurring in φ by $f(B)$. The following theorem simply states that the result of model checking $\mathcal{A}(\varphi)$ is the approximation of the result of model checking φ. Its proof follows by structural induction from the semantics of $\mathcal{X}CTL$, and uses the fact that approximations are homomorphisms. [18] proves a similar result, albeit in a somewhat different context.

Theorem 3 (Correctness of approximations). *Let $\mathcal{K}$ be a classical Kripke structure, $\mathcal{L}$ be a De Morgan algebra of sets, f be an approximation function on $\mathcal{L}$, and φ be a $\mathcal{X}CTL(\mathcal{L})$ formula. Let $\mathcal{A}(\varphi)$ be the translation of φ into $f(\mathcal{L})$. Then for any state s of $\mathcal{K}$,*

$$f([\![\varphi]\!](s)) = [\![\mathcal{A}(\varphi)]\!](s).$$

Theorem 1 is a corollary to Theorem 3. Our minterm approximation satisfies condition (1) of Definition 2, since $f_m(B) = B \cap \mathcal{M}(P) \subseteq B$, and it also satisfies condition (2) by Proposition 1. Thus, f_m is an approximation to which Theorem 3 applies, yielding Theorem 1.

The minterm approximation defined in Section 4.1 was restricted to positive queries. The general approximation framework defined above makes it easy to derive a minterm approximation for negative queries. We denote a negative query by $\varphi[\neg?P]$. To obtain the minterm solutions to $\varphi[\neg?P]$, we can check $\varphi[?P]$, that is, ignore the negation and treat the query as positive. For example, to check the negative query $AF \neg?\{p, q\}$, we check $AF \ ?\{p, q\}$ instead. The minterm solutions to the original negative query are the duals of the *maxterm* solutions to $\varphi[?P]$. A maxterm is a *disjunction* where all the atomic propositions are, positive or negated. We denote by $\mathcal{X}(P)$ the set of maxterms over a set P of atomic propositions. For example, $\mathcal{X}(\{p, q\}) = \{p \vee q, p \vee \neg q, \neg p \vee q, \neg p \vee \neg q\}$. A minterm j is a solution to $\varphi[\neg?P]$ iff its negation $\neg j$ is a maxterm solution to $\varphi[?P]$. We thus need to define a *maxterm approximation* $f_x : \mathcal{U}(\mathcal{F}(P)) \rightarrow 2^{\mathcal{X}(P)}$ for positive queries. We define f_x such that, for any upset B, it returns the subset of maxterms in that set, *i.e.*, $f_x(B) = B \cap \mathcal{X}(P)$. According to Definition 2, f_x is an approximation: (1) holds by f_x's definition, and (2) follows from the fact that any set of propositional formulas can be partitioned into maxterms and non-maxterms. We define the translation:

$$\mathcal{A}_x(?P) \triangleq \bigvee_{j \in \mathcal{M}(P)} (j \wedge f_x(\uparrow j)).$$

Then, by Theorem 3, model-checking $\varphi[\mathcal{A}_x(?P)]$ results in all the maxterm solutions to $\varphi[?P]$. By negating every resulting maxterm, we obtain all minterm solutions to $\varphi[\neg?P]$. For example, maxterm solutions to $AF \ ?\{p, q\}$ for the model of Figure 1(a) is the set $\mathcal{X}(\{p, q\})$; thus, the minterm solutions to $AF \ \neg?\{p, q\}$ are the entire set $\mathcal{M}(\{p, q\})$.

In summary, we have shown that minterm approximations can be generalized to an approximation framework over any lattices of sets, which is applicable, for instance, to finding minterm solutions to negative queries.

6   Case Study

In this section, we study the problem of finding stable states of a model, and evaluate the performance of our implementation by comparing it to the naive approach to state query checking.

In a study published in plant research, a model of gene interaction has been proposed to compute the "stable states" of a system of genes [12]. This work defined stable states as reachable gene configurations that no longer change, and used discrete dynamical systems to find such states. A different publication, [4], advocated the use of Kripke structures as appropriate models of biological systems, where model checking can answer some of the relevant questions about their behaviour. [4] also noted that query-checking might be useful as well, but did not report any applications of this technique. Motivated by [4], we repeated the study of [12] using our state query-checking approach.

The model of [12] consists of 15 genes, each with a "level of expression" that is either boolean (0 or 1), or ternary (0,1, or 2). The laws of interaction among genes have been established experimentally and are presented as logical tables. The model was translated into a NuSMV model with 15 variables, one per gene, of which 8 are boolean and the rest are ternary, turning the laws into NuSMV next-state relations. The model has 559,872 states and is in the Appendix.

The problem of finding all stable states of the model and the initial states leading to them is formulated as the minterm query checking of $EFAG?$, where ? ranges over all variables. Performance of our symbolic algorithm (Section 4) and the naive state query-checking algorithm for this query is summarized in the top row of the table in Figure 3(a), where the times are reported in minutes. Our algorithm was implemented using NuSMV as described in Section 4.2. The naive algorithm was also implemented using NuSMV by generating all possible minterms over the model variables, replacing each for the placeholder in $EFAG?$ and calling NuSMV to check the resulting formulas. Both algorithms were run on a Pentium 4 processor with 2.8GHz and 1 GB of RAM. Our algorithm gave an answer in under two hours, being about 20% faster than the naive.

To have a larger basis of comparison between the two algorithms, we varied the model (see rows 2-4), and the checked queries (see rows 5-7). Each "mutant" was obtained by permanently switching a different gene off (see Appendix), as indicated in [12]. The performance gain of our algorithm is robust to these changes.

Discussion. Performance improvements observed in our case study may not be attainable for every model. If the model is sufficiently small, our algorithm is likely to be faster. As models grow, however, the naive algorithm, which uses fewer BDD variables, will be more scalable. For more challenging models, a combination of the two approaches may yield the best results.

Another alternative is an iterative approach. Suppose we are interested in checking a query AF ? with two propositions, a and b. We first check AF ?$\{a\}$ and AF ?$\{b\}$. If no value is found for a proposition, then the query has no minterm solutions. Otherwise, the results correspond to the values each proposition has in all minterm solutions. For example, suppose we obtain $a = $ false, whereas b can be either true or false. We proceed

	Model	Query	Algorithms	
			Ours	Naive
1	original	$EF\ AG\ ?$	117	145
2	mutant 1	$EF\ AG\ ?$	116	144
3	mutant 2	$EF\ AG\ ?$	117	145
4	mutant 3	$EF\ AG\ ?$	117	146
5	original	$AG\ ?$	116	145
6	original	$EF\ ?$	118	146
7	original	$AF\ ?$	117	145

(a)

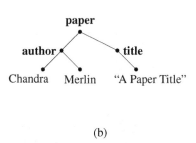

(b)

Fig. 3. (a) Experimental results; (b) An XML example (adapted from [13])

by checking a query for each pair of propositions, using for the placeholder replacement only those values found in the previous step. For example, we check $AF?\{a, b\}$, replacing ? by $(\neg a \wedge b \wedge \{\neg a \wedge b\}) \vee (\neg a \wedge \neg b \wedge \{\neg a \wedge \neg b\})$. We continue with checking triples of propositions using the valued obtained for pairs, and so on, until the query is checked on all atomic propositions, or it has been established that no answer exists. In this iterative process, there is place for heuristics that would switch between checking queries by our algorithm or the naive one, based on the resources available (time vs. memory). We will address such improvements in future optimizations of our implementation.

7   Conclusions

We have identified and formalized the state query-checking problem, which is of practical interest and can be solved more efficiently than general query checking. We have presented a symbolic algorithm that solves this problem, described a simple implementation using the NuSMV model checker, and showed its effectiveness on a realistic case study. We proved our algorithm correct by introducing the notion of approximation, which we have extended to reasoning over any lattice of sets. Our state query-checking algorithm generalizes techniques previously proposed for computing procedure summaries [2] and postdominators [1]. In essence, we generalized these algorithms, specialized for EF ? and AF ? queries, respectively, to arbitrary CTL queries. Our algorithm solves general state-based queries by computing fixpoints over *pre*-image computations, *i.e.*, iterating over EX and AX. While some of these queries can be solved by fixpoints over *post*-image computations, such as the query EF ? for discovering the reachable states, not every state-based CTL query can be solved that way, and this impossibility result follows from the work in [16].

We have also presented the application of state query checking to finding stable states in gene networks. In the rest of this section we present another application, that we are currently investigating.

State query checking can be applied to querying XML documents, which are modelled as trees. A simple example, of a fragment from a document containing information about research papers and adapted from [13], is shown in Figure 3(b). An example query is "what are the titles of all papers authored by Chandra?". Viewing tree nodes as states and edges as transitions yields a state-transition model, on which CTL properties can be evaluated [20]. Unfortunately, our example, like many other XML queries, needs to refer to both past and future, and is expressed as a CTL+Past formula as follows [13]:

$$EX^{\text{past}} \ (\text{title} \wedge EX^{\text{past}} \ (\text{paper} \wedge EX \ (\text{author} \wedge EX \ \text{Chandra}))).$$

Such formulas cannot be evaluated without modifying the internals of standard model-checkers. Formulating this question as a query yields

$$\text{paper} \wedge EX \ (\text{title} \wedge EX \ ?) \wedge EX \ (\text{author} \wedge EX \ \text{Chandra}),$$

whose desired solutions are states (here, the node labeled "A Paper Title"), and which avoids the use of the past, and can be solved by our approach, without modifying existing model checkers.

Acknowledgements. We are grateful to Miguel Carrillo Barajas of the Universidad Nacional Autónoma de México (UNAM), for providing us with the gene model, relevant references, and helpful clarifications. We thank Jocelyn Simmonds for helping us with implementation, and Shiva Nejati for comments on this paper. This research was supported in part by NSERC.

References

1. Aminof, B., Ball, T., Kupferman, O.: Reasoning About Systems with Transition Fairness. In: Baader, F., Voronkov, A. (eds.) LPAR 2004. LNCS (LNAI), vol. 3452, pp. 194–208. Springer, Heidelberg (2005)
2. Ball, T., Rajamani, S.: Bebop: A Symbolic Model Checker for Boolean Programs. In: Havelund, K., Penix, J., Visser, W. (eds.) SPIN Model Checking and Software Verification. LNCS, vol. 1885, pp. 113–130. Springer, Heidelberg (2000)
3. Bruns, G., Godefroid, P.: Temporal Logic Query-Checking. In: Proc. of LICS'01, pp. 409–417 (2001)
4. Chabrier-Rivier, N., Chiaverini, M., Danos, V., Fages, F., Schachter, V.: Modeling and Querying Biomolecular Interaction Networks. Theor. Comp. Sci. 325(1), 25–44 (2004)
5. Chan, W.: Temporal-Logic Queries. In: Emerson, E.A., Sistla, A.P. (eds.) CAV 2000. LNCS, vol. 1855, pp. 450–463. Springer, Heidelberg (2000)
6. Chechik, M., Devereux, B., Easterbrook, S., Gurfinkel, A.: Multi-Valued Symbolic Model-Checking. ACM Trans. on Soft. Eng. and Meth. 12(4), 1–38 (2003)
7. Chechik, M., Gurfinkel, A.: TLQSolver: A Temporal Logic Query Checker. In: Hunt Jr., W.A., Somenzi, F. (eds.) CAV 2003. LNCS, vol. 2725, pp. 210–214. Springer, Heidelberg (2003)
8. Cimatti, A., Clarke, E.M., Giunchilia, E., Giunchiglia, F., Pistore, M., Roveri, M., Sebastiani, R., Tacchella, A.: NuSMV Version 2: An Open Source Tool for Symbolic Model Checking. In: Brinksma, E., Larsen, K.G. (eds.) CAV 2002. LNCS, vol. 2404, pp. 359–364. Springer, Heidelberg (2002)
9. Clarke, E., Grumberg, O., Peled, D.: Model Checking (1999)

10. Clarke, E.M., Emerson, E.A., Sistla, A.P.: Automatic Verification of Finite-State Concurrent Systems Using Temporal Logic Specifications. ACM Trans. on Prog. Lang. and Sys. 8(2), 244–263 (1986)

11. Davey, B.A., Priestley, H.A.: Introduction to Lattices and Order (1990)

12. Espinosa-Soto, C., Padilla-Longoria, P., Alvarez-Buylla, E.R.: A Gene Regulatory Network Model for Cell-Fate Determination during Arabidopsis thaliana Flower Development That Is Robust and Recovers Experimental Gene Expression Profiles. The. Plant Cell. 16, 2923–2939 (2004)

13. Gottlob, G., Koch, C.: Monadic Queries over Tree-Structures Data. In: Proc. of LICS'02, pp. 189–202 (2002)

14. Gurfinkel, A., Chechik, M.: How Vacuous Is Vacuous? In: Jensen, K., Podelski, A. (eds.) TACAS 2004. LNCS, vol. 2988, pp. 451–466. Springer, Heidelberg (2004)

15. Gurfinkel, A., Chechik, M., Devereux, B.: Temporal Logic Query Checking: A Tool for Model Exploration. IEEE Trans. on Soft. Eng. 29(10), 898–914 (2003)

16. Henzinger, T.A., Kupferman, O., Qadeer, S.: From Pre-Historic to Post-Modern Symbolic Model Checking. Form. Meth. in Syst. Des. 23(3), 303–327 (2003)

17. Hornus, S., Schnoebelen, P.: On Solving Temporal Logic Queries. In: Kirchner, H., Ringeissen, C. (eds.) AMAST 2002. LNCS, vol. 2422, pp. 163–177. Springer, Heidelberg (2002)

18. Konikowska, B., Penczek, W.: Reducing Model Checking from Multi-Valued CTL* to CTL*. In: Brim, L., Jančar, P., Křetínský, M., Kucera, A. (eds.) CONCUR 2002. LNCS, vol. 2421, Springer, Heidelberg (2002)

19. Kupferman, O.: Sanity Checks in Formal Verification. In: Baier, C., Hermanns, H. (eds.) CONCUR 2006. LNCS, vol. 4137, Springer, Heidelberg (2006)

20. Miklau, G., Suciu, D.: Containment and Equivalence for an XPath fragment. In: Proc. of PODS'02, pp. 65–76 (2002)

21. Reps, T.W., Horwitz, S., Sagiv, M.: Precise Interprocedural Dataflow Analysis via Graph Reachability. In: Proc. of POPL'95, pp. 49–61 (1995)

22. Samer, M., Veith, H.: Validity of CTL Queries Revisited. In: Baaz, M., Makowsky, J.A. (eds.) CSL 2003. LNCS, vol. 2803, pp. 470–483. Springer, Heidelberg (2003)

23. Samer, M., Veith, H.: A Syntactic Characterization of Distributive LTL Queries. In: Díaz, J., Karhumäki, J., Lepistö, A., Sannella, D. (eds.) ICALP 2004. LNCS, vol. 3142, pp. 1099–1110. Springer, Heidelberg (2004)

24. Samer, M., Veith, H.: Parameterized Vacuity. In: Hu, A.J., Martin, A.K. (eds.) FMCAD 2004. LNCS, vol. 3312, pp. 322–336. Springer, Heidelberg (2004)

25. Somenzi, F.: Binary Decision Diagrams. In: Somenzi, F. (ed.) Calculational System Design. NATO Science Series F: Computer and Systems Sciences, vol. 173, pp. 303–366. Sciences, Sciences (1999)

26. Zhang, D., Cleaveland, R.: Efficient Temporal-Logic Query Checking for Presburger Systems. In: Proc. of ASE'05, pp. 24–33 (2005)

Appendix

```
-- flower gene network model
-- created by Miguel Carrillo Barajas of UNAM
   (miguel_carrillob@yahoo.com)
-- according to the paper [12]
```

```
MODULE main
VAR
ft   : {0,1};
emf1: {0,1};
tfl1: {0,1,2};
lfy : {0,1,2};
ful : {0,1,2};
ap1 : {0,1,2};
ap3 : {0,1,2};
pi  : {0,1,2};
ag  : {0,1,2};
ufo : {0,1}; --No change
wus : {0,1};
ap2 : {0,1};
sep : {0,1};
lug : {0,1}; --No change
clf : {0,1}; --No change
ASSIGN
-- FUL
next(ful):= case
tfl1=1 | tfl1=2           : 0;
ap1=0 & tfl1=0           : 2;
ap1=1 & tfl1=0           : 1;
ap1=2 & tfl1=0           : 0;
                       1 : ful;

esac;
--FT
next(ft):= case
emf1=0   : 1;
emf1=1   : 0;
       1 : ft;
esac;
--AP1
next(ap1):= case
ag=2                                      : 0;
ag=0                         & ft=1       : 2;
ag=1                         & ft=1       : 1;
ag=0            & lfy>=tfl1 & ft=0        : 2;
ag=1            & lfy>=tfl1 & ft=0        : 1;
(ag=0 | ag=1) & lfy<tfl1   & ft=0         : 0;
                                    1 : ap1;

esac;
--EMF1
next(emf1):=case
lfy=0                : 1;
```

```
(lfy=1 | lfy=2) : 0;
                1 : emf1;
esac;
--LFY
next(lfy):=case
                  tfl1=0                    & emf1=0 : 2;
ap1=0 & ful=0 & tfl1=0                      & emf1=1 : 1;
ap1=0 & ful=0 & (tfl1=1 | tfl1=2) & emf1=0 : 1;
ap1=0 & ful=0 & (tfl1=1 | tfl1=2) & emf1=1 : 0;
ap1=0 & ful=1 & (tfl1=1 | tfl1=2) & emf1=0 : 1;
ap1=0 & ful=1 & tfl1=0                      & emf1=1 : 1;
ap1=0 & ful=2 & (tfl1=0 | tfl1=1) & emf1=0 : 2;
ap1=0 & ful=2 & tfl1=0                      & emf1=1 : 1;
ap1=0 & ful=2 & tfl1=2                      & emf1=0 : 1;
ap1=0 & ful=2 & (tfl1=1 | tfl1=2) & emf1=1 : 1;
ap1=0 & ful=1 & (tfl1=1 | tfl1=2) & emf1=1 : 0;
ap1=1          & (tfl1=0 | tfl1=1) & emf1=0 : 2;
ap1=1          & tfl1=2                      & emf1=1 : 0;
ap1=1          & (tfl1=0 | tfl1=1) & emf1=1 : 1;
ap1=1          & tfl1=2                      & emf1=0 : 1;
ap1=2          & tfl1=2                      & emf1=1 : 1;
ap1=2          & (tfl1=0 | tfl1=1)              : 2;
ap1=2                                & emf1=0 : 2;
                                          1 : lfy;
esac;
--AP2; in mutant1 this is fixed to 0
next(ap2):=case
tfl1=0            : 1;
tfl1=1 | tfl1=2  : 0;
            1 : ap2;
esac;
--WUS
next(wus):=case
wus=0                            : 0;
wus=1 & ag=2          & sep=1    : 0;
wus=1 & ag=2          & sep=0    : 1;
wus=1 & (ag=0 | ag=1)           : 1;
                        1 : wus;
esac;
--AG
next(ag):=case
(lfy >= tfl1)                        & ap2=0 : 2;
(lfy < tfl1)                                 : 0;
(lfy > tfl1)                  & wus=1 & ap2=1 : 2;
lfy=2      & tfl1=2           & wus=1 & ap2=1 : 2;
```

```
(lfy = tfl1)   & (tfl1 <2)                            & ap2=1              : 0;
(lfy> tfl1)          & (ag=0 | ag=1) & wus=0 & ap2=1 & clf=0   : 1;
(lfy> tfl1)          & ag=2  & wus=0 & ap2=1 & sep=0 & clf=0   : 1;
(lfy> tfl1)          & (ag=0 | ag=1) & wus=0 & ap2=1 & lug=0   : 1;
(lfy> tfl1)          & ag=2 & wus=0 & ap2=1 & sep=0 & lug=0    : 1;
(lfy> tfl1) & ap1=0  & (ag=0 | ag=1) & wus=0 & ap2=1           : 1;
(lfy> tfl1) & ap1=0  & ag=2          & wus=0 & ap2=1 & sep=0   : 1;
lfy=2 & tfl1=2      & (ag=0 | ag=1) & wus=0 & ap2=1 & clf=0    : 1;
lfy=2 & tfl1=2      & ag=2 & wus=0 & ap2=1 & sep=0  & clf=0    : 1;
lfy=2 & tfl1=2      & (ag=0 | ag=1) & wus=0 & ap2=1 & lug=0    : 1;
lfy=2 & tfl1=2      & ag=2 & wus=0 & ap2=1 & sep=0 & lug=0     : 1;
lfy=2 & tfl1=2 & ap1=0 & (ag=0 | ag=1) & wus=0 & ap2=1         : 1;
lfy=2 & tfl1=2 & ap1=0 & ag=2 & wus=0 & ap2=1 & sep=0          : 1;
lfy> tfl1 & (ap1=1 | ap1=2) & (ag=0 | ag=1) &
                          wus=0 & ap2=1 & lug=1 & clf=1 : 0
lfy> tfl1 & (ap1=1 | ap1=2) & ag=2 &
                       wus=0 & ap2=1 & sep=0 & lug=1 & clf=1 : 0
lfy=2 & tfl1=2 & (ap1=1 | ap1=2) &
               (ag=0 | ag=1) & wus=0 & ap2=1 & lug=1 & clf=1 : 0
lfy=2 & tfl1=2 & (ap1=1 | ap1=2) &
                   ag=2 & wus=0 & ap2=1 & sep=0 & lug=1 & clf=1 : 0
lfy > tfl1 & ag=2       & wus=0 & ap2=1 & sep=1               : 2
lfy=2 & tfl1=2 & ag=2   & wus=0 & ap2=1 & sep=1               : 2
                                               1 : a
esac;
--TFL1
next(tfl1):=case
                                          emf1=0 : 0;
ap1=2                                     & emf1=1 : 0;
(ap1=0 | ap1=1) & lfy=2                   & emf1=1 : 0;
ap1=1           & (lfy=0 | lfy=1) & ap2=1 & emf1=1 : 0;
ap1=1           & (lfy=0 | lfy=1) & ap2=0 & emf1=1 : 1;
ap1=0           & (lfy=0 | lfy=1)         & emf1=1 : 2;
                                               1 : tfl1;
esac;
--PI
next(pi):=case
lfy=0 & ap3=0                                                 : 0
lfy=0 & (ap3=1 | ap3=2) & pi=0                                : 0
lfy=0 & ap1=0 & (ap3=1 | ap3=2) & (pi=1 | pi=2) & ag=0        : 0
lfy=0 & ap1=0 & (ap3=1 | ap3=2) &
                    (pi=1 | pi=2) & (ag=1 | ag=2) & sep=0 : 0
lfy=0 & (ap1=1 | ap1=2) & (ap3=1 | ap3=2) &
                              (pi=1 | pi=2) & sep=0 : 0
(lfy=1 | lfy=2)  & ap3=0                  & ag=0              : 0
```

```
(lfy=1 | lfy=2)  & ap3=0              & (ag=1 | ag=2)            : 1
(lfy=1 | lfy=2)  & (ap3=1 | ap3=2) & pi=0                       : 1
(lfy=1 | lfy=2)  & ap1=0 & (ap3=1 | ap3=2) &
                                     (pi=1 | pi=2) & ag=0: 1
(lfy=1 | lfy=2)  & ap1=0 & (ap3=1 | ap3=2) &
                        (pi=1 | pi=2) & (ag=1 | ag=2) & sep=0 : 1
(lfy=1 | lfy=2)  & (ap1=1 | ap1=2) & (ap3=1 | ap3=2) &
                                     (pi=1 | pi=2)& sep=0 : 1
 ap1=0           & (ap3=1 | ap3=2) &
                        (pi=1 | pi=2) & (ag=1 | ag=2) & sep=1 : 2
 (ap1=1 | ap1=2) & (ap3=1 | ap3=2) & (pi=1 | pi=2)   & sep=1 : 2
                                                           1 : p
esac;
--SEP
next(sep):=case
tfl1=0                      : 1;
(tfl1=1 | tfl1=2)    : 0;
                       1 : sep;
esac;
--AP3; in mutant3 this is fixed at 0
next(ap3):=case
ag in {1,2} & pi in {1,2} & sep= 1  & ap3 in {1,2} : 2;
ap1 in {1,2} & pi in {1,2} & sep= 1 & ap3 in {1,2} : 2;
lfy in {1,2}                & sep= 0       & ufo= 1 : 1;
lfy in {1,2}                        & ap3= 0 & ufo= 1 : 1;
lfy in {1,2} & pi= 0                       & ufo= 1 : 1;
ap1= 0 & lfy in {1,2} & ag= 0              & ufo= 1 : 1;
                            sep= 0       & ufo= 0 : 0;
                                ap3= 0   & ufo= 0 : 0;
            pi= 0                         & ufo= 0 : 0;
ap1= 0 & ag= 0                           & ufo= 0 : 0;
lfy= 0                      & sep= 0               : 0;
lfy= 0                            & ap3= 0         : 0;
lfy= 0 & pi= 0                                     : 0;
ap1= 0 & lfy= & ag= 0                              : 0;
                                           1 : ap3;
esac;
--UFO no change
next(ufo):=ufo;
--LUG no change; in mutant2 this is fixed at 0
next(lug):=lug;
--CLF no change
next(clf):=clf;
----------------------------------------------------
```

Qualitative Probabilistic Modelling in Event-B*

Stefan Hallerstede and Thai Son Hoang

ETH Zurich
Switzerland
{halstefa,htson}@inf.ethz.ch

Abstract. Event-B is a notation and method for discrete systems modelling by refinement. We introduce a small but very useful construction: qualitative probabilistic choice. It extends the expressiveness of Event-B allowing us to prove properties of systems that could not be formalised in Event-B before. We demonstrate this by means of a small example, part of a larger Event-B development that could not be fully proved before. An important feature of the introduced construction is that it does not complicate the existing Event-B notation or method, and can be explained without referring to the underlying more complicated probabilistic theory. The necessary theory [18] itself is briefly outlined in this article to justify the soundness of the proof obligations given. We also give a short account of alternative constructions that we explored, and rejected.

1   Introduction

We consider modelling of software systems and more generally of complex systems to be an important development phase. We also believe that more complex models can only be written when the method of stepwise refinement [9] is used. Formal notation is indispensable in such a modelling activity. It provides the foundation on which building models can be carried out. Simply writing a formal text is insufficient, though, to achieve a model of high quality. The only serious way to analyse a model is to reason about it, proving in a mathematically rigorous way that all required properties are satisfied.

Event-B [7] is a formalism and method for discrete systems modelling. It has been developed from the B-Method [1] using many ideas of Action Systems [8]. The semantics of an Event-B model is characterised by *proof obligations*. In fact, proof obligations have a two-fold purpose. On the one hand, they show that a model is sound with respect to some behavioural semantics. On the other hand, they serve to verify properties of the model. This goes so far that we only focus on the proof obligations and do not present a behavioural semantics at all. This approach permits us to use the same proof obligations for very

---

* This research was carried out as part of the EU research project IST 511599 RODIN (Rigorous Open Development Environment for Complex Systems) http://rodin.cs.ncl.ac.uk.

J. Davies and J. Gibbons (Eds.): IFM 2007, LNCS 4591, pp. 293–312, 2007.

different modelling domains, e.g., reactive, distributed and concurrent systems [5], sequential programs [3], electronic circuits [11], or mixed designs [2], not being constrained to semantics tailored to a particular domain. Event-B is a calculus for modelling that is independent of the various models of computation.

The standard reasoning in Event-B is based on (demonic) nondeterminism which is usually sufficient for systems modelling. However, some system behaviours are more appropriately modelled probabilistically. Event-B is extensible, that is, it can be extended when more expressiveness is needed. In this article, we focus on extending Event-B with means for qualitative modelling of probability. This extension grew out of the need for "almost-certain termination" properties used in some communication protocols, e.g. [5]. We use it to demonstrate how Event-B can be extended and discuss what problems we encountered. The extension has been made so that the impact on the notation is minimal, and the resulting proof obligations are as simple as possible. We also discuss some alternatives that may appear attractive to achieve convenient notation: they would lead, however, to more complicated proof obligations. We consider this a serious drawback because we think reasoning is the main purpose of modelling.

Some probabilistic models can only be expressed in terms of numerical measures, e.g., certain reliability problems [21, Chapter 4.4], or performance problems [13]. Yet, there is also a large class of problems where the exact numerical measures are not of importance, e.g., when modelling communication protocols [16], or human behaviour [2]. When modelling these, stating exact probabilities would be over-specific: all we need is a termination property making use of a strong local fairness property associated with probabilistic choice [14]. In this article we restrict our attention to this qualitative aspect of probability.

In Event-B, simplicity and efficiency are favoured over completeness and generality [7]. Generality comes at the price of intricate reasoning and, in particular, much reduced possibilities for automated tool support [4]. The available theory [21] for probabilistic reasoning about models is very rich but associated with intricate reasoning. So, a probabilistic Event-B will have to use a simplified theory. Our requirements on probabilistic Event-B are threefold:

  (i) it should be *simple*, i.e., easy to understand;
 (ii) it should be *useful*, i.e., solve a commonly encountered class of problems;
(iii) and it should permit *efficient tool support*.

Simplicity of the notation is very important because an Event-B model is understood as a means of reasoning and communication: we must not have doubts about the meaning of a model. We also require that we have good reason for the extension: if we would not know of any problem that we could solve –only or better– by means of the extended method, there would be little point in extending Event-B.

Overview. The paper is structured as follows. In Section 2, we give an overview of the Event-B modelling notation, along with the proof obligations that give meanings to Event-B constructs. In Section 3, we consider a probabilistic extension of Event-B for *almost-certain convergence*. In particular, Section 3.1 discusses the necessary additions to the notation and the proof obligations in order to accommodate the extension, and in Section 3.2, we consider the rejected alternatives. An example of a communication protocol is given in Section 4 to illustrate our approach. In Section 5, we give justifications of our proof obligations. Finally, a summary and some conclusions are presented in Section 6.

2   The Event-B Modelling Notation

Event-B [7], unlike classical B [1], does not have a concrete syntax [12]. Still, we present the basic notation for Event-B using some syntax. We proceed like this to improve legibility and help the reader remember the different constructs of Event-B. The syntax should be understood as a convention for presenting Event-B models in textual form rather than defining a language.

Event-B models are described in terms of the two basic constructs: *contexts* and *machines*. Contexts contain the static part of a model whereas machines contain the dynamic part. Contexts may contain *carrier sets, constants, axioms,* where carrier sets are similar to types [7]. In this article, we simply assume that there is some context and do not mention it explicitly. Machines are presented in Section 2.1, and machine refinement in Section 2.2.

2.1   Machines

Machines provide behavioural properties of Event-B models. Machines may contain *variables, invariants, theorems, events,* and *variants.* Variables v define the state of a machine. They are constrained by invariants $I(v)$. Possible state changes are described by means of events. Each event is composed of a *guard* $G(t, v)$ and an *action* $S(t, v)$, where t are *local variables* the event may contain. The guard states the necessary condition under which an event may occur, and the action describes how the state variables evolve when the event occurs. An event can be represented by the term

$$\text{any } t \text{ where } G(t, v) \text{ then } S(t, v) \text{ end}. \tag{1}$$

The short form

$$\text{when } G(v) \text{ then } S(v) \text{ end} \tag{2}$$

is used if event e does not have local variables, and the form

$$\text{begin } S(v) \text{ end} \tag{3}$$

if in addition the guard equals *true*. A dedicated event of the form (3) is used for *initialisation*. The action of an event is composed of several *assignments* of the form

$$x := E(t, v) \tag{4}$$

$$x :\in E(t, v) \tag{5}$$

$$x :| Q(t, v, x') \quad , \tag{6}$$

where x are some variables, $E(t, v)$ expressions, and $Q(t, v, x')$ a predicate. Assignment form (4) is *deterministic*, the other two forms are *nondeterministic*. Form (4) assigns x to an element of a set, and form (5) assigns to x a value satisfying a predicate. The effect of each assignment can also be described by a before-after predicate:

$$BA\big(x := E(t, v)\big) \quad \widehat{=} \quad x' = E(t, v) \tag{7}$$

$$BA\big(x :\in E(t, v)\big) \quad \widehat{=} \quad x' \in E(t, v) \tag{8}$$

$$BA\big(x :\mid Q(t, v, x')\big) \quad \widehat{=} \quad Q(t, v, x') \quad . \tag{9}$$

A before-after predicate describes the relationship between the state just before an assignment has occurred (represented by unprimed variable names x) and the state just after the assignment has occurred (represented by primed variable names x'). All assignments of an action $S(t, v)$ occur simultaneously which is expressed by conjoining their before-after predicates, yielding a predicate $A(t, v, x')$. Variables y that do not appear on the left-hand side of an assignment of an action are not changed by the action. Formally, this is achieved by conjoining $A(t, v, x')$ with $y' = y$, yielding the before-after predicate of the action:

$$BA\big(S(t, v)\big) \quad \widehat{=} \quad A(t, v, x') \wedge y' = y \quad . \tag{10}$$

In proof obligations we represent the before-after predicate $BA\big(S(t, v)\big)$ of an action $S(t, v)$ directly by the predicate

$$\boldsymbol{S}(t, v, v') \quad .$$

Proof obligations serve to verify certain properties of a machine. All proof obligations in this article are presented in the form of sequents: "antecedent" $\vdash$ "succedent".

For each event of a machine, *feasibility* must be proved:

$$\vdash \begin{array}{l} I(v) \\ G(t, v) \\ (\exists v' \cdot \boldsymbol{S}(t, v, v')) \end{array} \quad . \tag{11}$$

By proving feasibility, we achieve that $\boldsymbol{S}(t, v, v')$ provides an after state whenever $G(t, v)$ holds. This means that the guard indeed represents the enabling condition of the event.

Invariants are supposed to hold whenever variable values change. Obviously, this does not hold a priori for any combination of events and invariants and, thus, needs to be proved. The corresponding proof obligation is called *invariant preservation*:

$$\vdash \begin{array}{l} I(v) \\ G(t, v) \\ \boldsymbol{S}(t, v, v') \\ I(v') \end{array} \quad . \tag{12}$$

Similar proof obligations are associated with the initialisation event of a machine. The only difference is that the invariant does not appear in the antecedent of the proof obligations (11) and (12). For brevity, we do not treat initialisation differently from ordinary events of a machine. The required modifications of the concerned proof obligations are obvious.

2.2   Machine Refinement

Machine refinement provides a means to introduce more details about the dynamic properties of a model [7]. For more on the well-known theory of refinement, we refer to the Action System formalism that has inspired the development of Event-B [8]. We present some important proof obligations for machine refinement. As mentioned before, the user of Event-B is not presented with a behavioural model but only with proof obligations. The proof obligations describe the semantics of Event-B models.

A machine CM can refine at most one other machine AM. We call AM the *abstract* machine and CM a *concrete* machine. The state of the abstract machine is related to the state of the concrete machine by a *glueing invariant* $J(v, w)$, where v are the variables of the abstract machine and w the variables of the concrete machine.

Each event ea of the abstract machine is *refined* by one or more concrete events ec. Let abstract event ea and concrete event ec be:

$$ea \quad \widehat{=} \quad \text{any } t \text{ where } G(t, v) \text{ then } S(t, v) \text{ end} \tag{13}$$

$$ec \quad \widehat{=} \quad \text{any } u \text{ where } H(u, w) \text{ then } T(u, w) \text{ end} \quad . \tag{14}$$

Somewhat simplified, we can say that ec refines ea if the guard of ec is stronger than the guard of ea, and the glueing invariant $J(v, w)$ establishes a simulation of ec by ea:

$$
\begin{array}{l}
I(v) \\
J(v, w) \\
H(u, w) \\
\boldsymbol{T}(u, w, w') \\
\vdash \\
\quad (\exists t, v' \cdot G(t, v) \;\wedge\; \boldsymbol{S}(t, v, v') \;\wedge\; J(v', w'))
\end{array}
\quad . \tag{15}
$$

In the course of refinement, often *new events* ec are introduced into a model. New events must be proved to refine the implicit abstract event *skip* that does nothing. Moreover, it may be proved that new events do not collectively diverge by proving that a *variant* $V(w)$ is bounded below:

$$
\begin{array}{l}
I(v) \\
J(v, w) \\
H(u, w) \\
\vdash \\
\quad V(w) \in \mathbb{N} \quad ,
\end{array}
\tag{16}
$$

and is decreased by each new event. We refer to the corresponding proof obligation as *progress*:

$$
\begin{array}{l}
I(v) \\
J(v,w) \\
H(u,w) \\
\boldsymbol{T}(u,w,w') \\
\vdash \quad V(w') < V(w) \quad,
\end{array}
\tag{17}
$$

where we assume that the variant is an integer expression. It can be more elaborate [7] but this is not relevant here. We call events that satisfy (16) and (17) *convergent*.

3   Qualitative Probabilistic Event-B

The purpose of qualitative probabilistic reasoning is to provide the concept of *almost-certain convergence* [14,18][1]. Similarly to [14,18] qualitative probabilistic reasoning is introduced into Event-B by means of the *qualitative probabilistic choice*[2]:

$$
S \oplus T \quad,
$$

where S or T are chosen with some positive probability (see Section 5). The probabilistic extension should not depart from the existing structure of Event-B machines. Hence, we only consider introducing probabilistic choice in places where we already have nondeterministic choice. In Event-B nondeterministic choice appears in three places:

(i)   choice among different events,
(ii)   choice of local variables of events,
(iii)   nondeterministic assignments.

In each of these, we could also use probabilistic choice. We present our favoured solution based on (iii) in Section 3.1, and discuss the alternatives based on (i) and (ii) in Section 3.2.

3.1   Almost Certain Convergence in Event-B

In this section, we introduce step by step the proof obligations for almost-certain convergence in Event-B. Although we treat probability on the level of assignments, we actually do not mix probabilistic assignments and nondeterministic assignments in the same event. This saves us from having to define the meaning of their simultaneous joint effect. Hence, we say the *action* of an event is either

---

[1] The authors of [14,18] use the term "almost-certain termination".
[2] We do not use the term "abstract probabilistic choice" to avoid clashes with other refinement terminology, e.g., "concrete abstract probabilistic choice".

probabilistic or *nondeterministic*. Still, for better readability, we introduce some notation for qualitative probabilistic assignments corresponding to (5):

$$x \ \oplus|\ Q(t,v,x') \ \ .\tag{18}$$

With respect to invariant preservation a probabilistic action behaves identically to a nondeterministic action, i.e., demonically (see Section 5). However, it behaves angelically with respect to progress. We can rephrase the progress proof obligation (17) as follows:

$$\vdash \begin{array}{l} I(v) \\ J(v,w) \\ H(u,w) \\ (\forall w' \cdot \boldsymbol{T}(u,w,w') \ \Rightarrow\ V(w') < V(w)) \end{array} \ ,$$

i.e. the action *must* decrease the variant $V(w)$. The corresponding proof obligation for a new event with a probabilistic action follows from the angelic interpretation of the action. This means it *may* decrease the variant $V(w)$:

$$\vdash \begin{array}{l} I(v) \\ J(v,w) \\ H(u,w) \\ (\exists w' \cdot \boldsymbol{T}(u,w,w') \ \wedge\ V(w') < V(w)) \end{array} \ .\tag{19}$$

Note, that proof obligation (19) subsumes feasibility (11).

For convergence of an event, (16) and (17) are sufficient. For almost-certain convergence of an event, on the other hand, the corresponding proof obligations (16) and (19) are not sufficient. An upper bound $U(w)$ is required that dominates the variant $V(w)$:

$$\vdash \begin{array}{l} I(v) \\ J(v,w) \\ H(u,w) \\ V(w) \le U(w) \end{array} \ ,\tag{20}$$

for all new events.

Figure 1 shows the evolution of the variant $V(w)$ and the upper bound $U(w)$ in a concrete machine for a new nondeterministic event *nd* and a new probabilistic event *pr*: event *nd* *must* decrease the variant $V(w)$ whereas *pr* *may* decrease it. However, the possible variation of $V(w)$ by event *pr* is limited below by the constant 0 –proved by means of (16)– and above by $U(w)$. The upper bound $U(w)$ itself is bound below by 0 as a consequence of (16) and (20). Given that $U(w)$ is constant or, at least, not increasing, this is sufficient for almost-certain convergence of *nd* and *pr*. For all new events of the concrete machine we have to prove:

$$\vdash \begin{array}{l} I(v) \\ J(v,w) \\ H(u,w) \\ \boldsymbol{T}(u,w,w') \\ U(w') \le U(w) \end{array} \ ,\tag{21}$$

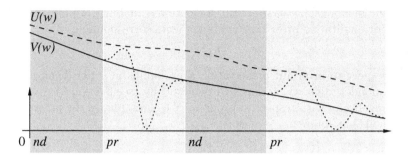

Fig. 1. Almost-certain convergence

Note, that proof obligation (21) is based on the demonic interpretation of the actions of all new events, i.e. all new events *must* not increase the upper bound. Hence, the following fact makes the difference to "certain" convergence: new events with probabilistic actions *may* decrease the variant but *must* not increase the upper bound.

The infimum probability associated with the probabilistic action $\boldsymbol{T}(u, w, w')$ must be greater than zero [18]. Using qualitative probabilistic assignment (18), we can only achieve this by requiring finiteness of the possible choices for w' of the probabilistic action $\boldsymbol{T}(u, w, w')$:

$$\vdash \begin{array}{l} I(v) \\ J(v, w) \\ H(u, w) \\ \text{finite}(\{w' \mid \boldsymbol{T}(u, w, w')\}) \end{array} \quad . \tag{22}$$

Events with probabilistic actions that satisfy (19) to (22) are called *almost-certainly convergent*. Note, that almost-certain convergence also imposes proof obligations (20) and (21) on new nondeterministic events, and that if we have new events with nondeterministic actions and new events with probabilistic actions, we prove their joint almost-certain convergence.

3.2   The Rejected Alternatives

In order to see the advantages of the approach to almost-certain convergence presented in the Section 3.1, we discuss the two alternatives: probabilistic choice among different events or probabilistic choice of local variables of events. We begin with the discussion with the latter.

It seems natural to introduce probabilistic choice at the level of local variables, say:

$$ec \quad \widehat{=} \quad \text{prob any } u \text{ where } H(u, w) \text{ then } T(u, w) \text{ end}$$

However, treating probabilistic choice on this level would lead to unnecessarily complicated proof obligations while our aim is to keep them simple. In particular, probabilistic progress proof obligations would be difficult compared to (19):

$$\begin{array}{l} I(v) \\ J(v,w) \\ \vdash \quad (\exists u \cdot H(u,w) \, \land \, (\forall w' \cdot \boldsymbol{T}(u,w,w') \, \Rightarrow \, V(w') < V(w))) \end{array} \qquad (23)$$

We would have to think about two quantifiers, whereas in (19) only one existential quantification needs to be discarded.

Probabilistic choice among different events has been discussed in [20]. This approach does only require little modification to the Event-B notation. It requires the introduction of additional variables to group probabilistic choices, say:

$$\begin{array}{ll} ec_1 & \widehat{=} \quad \textsf{prob } a \textsf{ any } u_1 \textsf{ where } H_1(u_1,w) \textsf{ then } T_1(u_1,w) \textsf{ end} \\ ec_2 & \widehat{=} \quad \textsf{prob } a \textsf{ any } u_2 \textsf{ where } H_2(u_2,w) \textsf{ then } T_2(u_2,w) \textsf{ end} \quad , \end{array}$$

denoting the abstract probabilistic choice $ec_1 \oplus ec_2$. For probabilistic progress we would obtain a proof obligation with two disjuncts ($i = 1, 2$):

$$(\exists u_i \cdot H_i(u_i,w) \, \land \, (\forall w' \cdot \boldsymbol{T}_i(u_i,w,w') \, \Rightarrow \, V(w') < V(w)))$$

in its succedent.

More problems may appear when trying to specify more general probabilistic choices, say, between n components where n is a positive number, e.g., in the dining philosophers [21, Chapter 3]. We also need to determine the order in which probabilistic choices and nondeterministic choices are resolved: there are still nondeterministic choices among events and of local variables. Given the intricate relationship of probabilistic and nondeterministic choice this could potentially lead to models very difficult to comprehend. Then perhaps, the best would be to restrict the body of the event to being entirely deterministic. It appears that we would have to make decisions that may seem arbitrary or introduce restrictions that make the notation more complex.

3.3 Preliminary Study of Refinement

As mentioned in the introduction, we consider refinement to be crucial in the development of complex systems. A theory of probabilistic refinement is available [21], but it is intricate too. Hence, to use it with Event-B, we need to simplify it first. We do not want to complicate the reasoning associated with Event-B refinement.

In qualitative probabilistic Event-B we have to address refinement of events with non-deterministic actions and events with probabilistic actions. As usual, it should be possible to refine a nondeterministic action by a probabilistic action [19]. Concerning refinement of events with probabilistic actions, we have two major possibilities: either we permit probabilistic choice to be refined or we do not permit it.

The second alternative appears attractive because we could reason about probabilistic models with minimal extra effort. We would have to learn less proof obligations, and we could use standard Event-B refinement. We could ignore probability most of the time, avoiding data-refinement of probabilistic actions, for instance. Probabilistic proofs would only occur where they are necessary, not complicating entire developments. To achieve this, some techniques presented in [6] could be used to delay probabilistic proofs. Only at a very late stage probabilistic concerns would enter the scene, at a stage where refinement of probabilistic actions would no longer be necessary.

By contrast, if we need to refine probabilistic actions, we have to take into account the angelic interpretation for probabilistic progress (19). We are uncertain whether refinement of probabilistic actions is needed in practice, or whether the techniques discussed in the preceding paragraph would suffice. This remains to be investigated. Which techniques are more appropriate only (more) experience will show.

4   Example: Contention Resolution in the Firewire Protocol

The Contention problem in the Firewire tree identify protocol [16,17] is one example of a use of probability to break symmetry. The example has been treated in classical B [14,18]. In this section, we will look at how we can achieve a similar result in Event-B.

We use the contention problem in the Firewire protocol to demonstrate the usefulness of qualitative probabilistic modelling in a practical problem [5]. In our presentation, we do not deal with the full model but focus on almost-certain convergence which allows us to prove a probabilistic termination property of the Firewire protocol left open in [5].

In this section, we first give an overview of the Firewire protocol. Then we give the specification of the contention problem in Event-B. We show the failure of an attempt to use nondeterministic resolution and how to solve the problem by the approach proposed in Section 3.1.

4.1   Overview of the Firewire Protocol

Purpose. A set of devices is linked by a network of bidirectional connections. The network is an acyclic graph with devices as nodes (Figure 2a). The protocol provides a symmetric and distributed solution for finding a node that will be the leader of the network in a *finite* amount of time. All devices run the same algorithm to find the leader of the network. Figure 2b shows a possible state of the network of Figure 2a after a leader has been elected. The Firewire tree identify protocol for achieving this is described below.

Protocol. Any node with only one connection can send the message "**req**" via that connection requesting the neighbouring node to be leader. Also, any node that has already received the message "**req**" via all its connections except one, can send the message "**req**" via that last remaining connection. Message sending

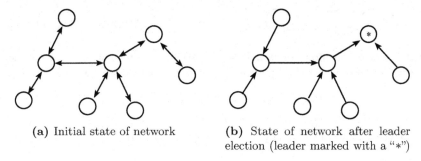

(a) Initial state of network

(b) State of network after leader election (leader marked with a "*")

Fig. 2. Abstraction of leader election protocol

happens distributed and nondeterministically, i.e., there is no supervisory coordination. Eventually, there will be one node that received the message "**req**" via all its connections: that node will become the leader of the network. An example of the initial state and possible final state is shown in Figure 2.

Contention. At the final stage of the protocol, there are two nodes left that are linked to each other and have not yet sent the message "**req**". If both nodes try to send the message "**req**" via that (bidirectional) connection, a livelock occurs where it cannot be decided which node should become the leader. Each node

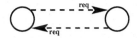

Fig. 3. Contention

detects the problem by receiving the message "**req**" from the node to which it has just sent the same message. We identify this as the *contention problem* illustrated in Figure 3.

Fortunately, there exists a probabilistic protocol to resolve the contention within finite time; this is proved in Event-B by means of almost-certain convergence in Section 4.4 below. Before it is proved, we present the protocol and show that (demonic) nondeterminism is unsuitable to model the probabilistic behaviour. The protocol works as follows:

Each node independently chooses with the same non-zero probability, either to send the message after a **short** delay or after a **long** delay (the assumption for the **long** delay being that it is long enough for the message to be transferred from one node to another). Eventually, it is "almost certain" that one of them will choose to send the message after a **short** delay, while the other node will choose to send the message after a **long** delay. The message that was sent after a **short** delay will then be received before the other is sent (according to the assumption). An example for solving contention can be seen in Figure 4, where one process has chosen to send a message after a **short** delay and the other after a **long** delay.

(a) Message sent after **short** wait is received, the other message not sent

(b) State after contention resolution (leader marked with a "∗")

Fig. 4. Probabilistic contention resolution

4.2 Event-B Model of the Contention Problem

An Event-B model of the Firewire tree identify protocol has already been developed in [5]. We do not repeat the model but focus only on the contention problem that is only partially modelled in [5] leaving the termination property of the protocol unproved. In this sense, we complete the model within the Event-B framework. We take the abstract view of the contention problem only presenting what is essential. We define a carrier set $WAIT$ containing the two constants: *short* and *long*.

$$\textbf{sets:} \quad WAIT = \{short, long\}$$

Two variables x and y represent the state of the two nodes in contention: either sending the message after a *short* or *long* delay.

$$\textbf{variables:} \quad x, y$$

$$\textbf{invariants:} \\ x \in WAIT \\ y \in WAIT$$

There is only one event which resolves the contention (in one shot) by assigning different values to x and y. This only specifies that the problem is to be resolved but not how.

```
(abstract_)resolve
    when
        x = y
    then
        x, y    :|   x' ≠ y'
    end
```

4.3 Attempting Nondeterministic Contention Resolution

We attempt to achieve contention resolution by nondeterminism. We will see why it fails and see better what is gained by probabilistic reasoning. We refine the abstract model, introducing two new variables, namely u and v, in the refinement. They represent the intermediate states of the two nodes during contention resolution.

variables: x, y, u, v

invariants:
$$u \in WAIT$$
$$v \in WAIT$$

A new event draw models (nondeterministically) the effect of randomly choosing for both of the two nodes either sending messages after a *long* or a *short* delay. The new event is enabled while the values of u and v are the same. It draws new values until they are different.

Event resolve has an additional guard $u \neq v$ (compared to the initial model of Section 4.2) indicating that two *different* delay times u and v have been successfully drawn. In this case, x and y will be assigned to u and v, respectively, and the contention is resolved.

draw
  when
    $u = v$
  then
    $u :\in WAIT$
    $v :\in WAIT$
  end

(concrete_)resolve
  when
    $u \neq v$
    $x = y$
  then
    $x, y := u, v$
  end

The concrete event resolve refines the abstract event resolve because the concrete event contains the guard $u \neq v$. We obtain the following proof obligation, see (15), that is trivially discharged:

$$\vdash \frac{\begin{array}{c} x' = u \\ y' = v \\ u \neq v \end{array}}{x' \neq y'} \ .$$

Failure of Demonic Nondeterminism. We are left to prove that the new event draw does not take control of the system forever. However, we cannot state a variant that would satisfy proof obligation (17). The problem is that the new event draw may behave like *skip*, doing nothing: the new event draw can be always enabled: the nondeterministic choice in event draw can always set u and v to their old values leaving draw always enabled. Using nondeterminism, we stuck and the termination property of the protocol cannot be proved.

4.4   Probabilistic Contention Resolution

Probabilistic choice (18) is appropriate to model contention resolution and prove (almost-certain) termination of the protocol, thus, fully solving the problem of contention. Using probabilistic choice, we can model the event draw as follows:

$$
\begin{array}{l}
\textsf{draw} \\
\quad \textsf{when} \\
\qquad u = v \\
\quad \textsf{then} \\
\qquad u \ \oplus\!| \ u' \in WAIT \\
\qquad v \ \oplus\!| \ v' \in WAIT \\
\quad \textsf{end}
\end{array}
$$

The meaning of the new event draw is that u and v are chosen from the set $WAIT$ probabilistically. The choices must be proper (see [18]), in other words, the probability should not be 0 or 1.

Based on the probabilistic draw, we can prove that the event draw converges almost-certainly. According to Section 3.1, we have to show (19), (20), and (21). We take as variant the *embedded predicate* $\langle u = v \rangle$, where $\langle P \rangle$ is defined to have value 1 if P holds and 0 if P does not hold. A suitable upper bound is the constant 1.

$$
\begin{array}{ll}
\textbf{variant:} & \langle u = v \rangle \\
\textbf{bound:} & 1
\end{array}
$$

For (21) there is nothing to prove. The proof that the variant is dominated by the bound (20) follows from the definition of the embedded predicate above:

$$
\vdash \frac{\cdots}{\langle u = v \rangle \leq 1} \quad .
$$

Finally, one has to prove (probabilistic) progress (19). This is where nondeterminism failed: we were not able to prove progress by means of (17). We have to prove that event draw may decrease the variant $\langle u = v \rangle$:

$$
\vdash \frac{\begin{array}{l} u \in WAIT \\ v \in WAIT \\ u = v \end{array}}{\exists u', v' \ \cdot \ u' \in WAIT \ \wedge \ v' \in WAIT \ \wedge \ \langle u' = v' \rangle < \langle u = v \rangle} \quad .
$$

This is easy: we instantiate u' to *short* and v' to *long*, yielding for the left hand side of the inequation

$$
\langle u' = v' \rangle \ = \ \langle long = short \rangle \ = \ 0
$$

by definition of the embedded predicate. Also, from $u = v$, we infer for the right hand side

$$\langle u = v \rangle \;=\; 1 \;.$$

Hence, the claim follows from $0 < 1$. Note, that the possible instantiations for u' and v' just correspond to the solutions of the contention resolution.

5 Soundness

In this section, we give justifications for the proof obligations of Section 3.1. We sketch the derivation of the proof obligations from the underlying theory. The theory is based on predicate and expectation transformers [21]. The gap left to the relational model used can be bridged by the well-known relationship between predicate transformers and before-after predicates, see e.g. [1].

The probabilistic reasoning presented in this article is based on qualitative probabilistic choice $\oplus$ (see [14, Chapter 3.2]). It is characterised by the following demonic and angelic distribution laws:

$$\lfloor S \oplus T \rfloor P \quad \widehat{=} \quad [S]P \wedge [T]P \tag{24}$$

$$\lceil S \oplus T \rceil P \quad \widehat{=} \quad [S]P \vee [T]P \;. \tag{25}$$

The first law, called *demonic distribution*, is used when proving invariant preservation and the second, called *angelic distribution*, is used when proving almost-certain termination. The above can be easily extended to qualitative probabilistic choice with multiple branches

$$S_1 \oplus \ldots \oplus S_n \;.$$

It is interpreted similarly to qualitative probabilistic choice: it is a probabilistic choice between substitutions $S_1, \ldots, S_n$ where the probability of each branch is "proper". The definition of "proper" can be found in [14, Chapter 3.2]. Note, that it is essential that the choice is between a finite number of branches. The reason for this is to get "definite" probabilistic predicate transformers (see [18, Definition 3]).

In Section 3.1, we introduce the notion of probabilistic choice $x \oplus| P(x, x')$, which is interpreted similarly to the qualitative multiple probabilistic choice. However, we use the choice between all possible values x' satisfying $P(x, x')$. To achieve definiteness, we require $finite(\{x' \mid P(x, x')\})$. The corresponding demonic and angelic distribution laws are:

$$\lfloor x \oplus| \; P(x, x') \rfloor Q(x) \quad \widehat{=} \quad (\forall x' \cdot P(x, x') \Rightarrow Q(x')) \tag{26}$$

$$\lceil x \oplus| \; P(x, x') \rceil Q(x) \quad \widehat{=} \quad (\exists x' \cdot P(x, x') \wedge Q(x')) \tag{27}$$

Almost-certain convergence. We derive almost certain convergence for
Event-B using the standard model of a generalised loop [10,21] as a basis. For
ease of presentation we consider a simple Event-B machine with two new events
of the form

$$\text{when } G(v) \text{ then } S(v) \text{ end}$$

$$\text{when } H(v) \text{ then } T(v) \text{ end} \quad ,$$

where $S(v)$ is probabilistic and $T(v)$ is nondeterministic (and non-probabilistic).
The loop consisting of the new events is defined by:

$$
\begin{array}{ll}
loop \quad \widehat{=} \quad \text{do} & \\
& G(v) \Longrightarrow S(v) \\
& \| \\
& H(v) \Longrightarrow T(v) \\
\text{end} &
\end{array}
$$

We state without proof the zero-one law for probabilistic loops (Lemma 2 in
[14]) adapted to our needs:

Lemma 1. *Let $I(v)$ be the invariant of the construct. Let δ be a number strictly
greater than zero. If we have that*

$$I(v) \quad \Rightarrow \quad \lfloor G(v) \Longrightarrow S(v) \ \| \ H(v) \Longrightarrow T(v) \rfloor I \quad , \qquad (28)$$

and

$$\delta \times \langle I \rangle \quad \Rightarrow \quad [loop]\langle true \rangle \qquad (29)$$

both hold, then in fact $\langle I \rangle \Rightarrow [loop]\langle I \rangle$.

Since $\lfloor \cdot \rfloor$ distributes through $\|$, the first condition (28) can be decomposed as
follows:

$$I(v) \quad \Rightarrow \quad \lfloor G(v) \Longrightarrow S(v) \ \| \ H(v) \Longrightarrow T(v) \rfloor I(v)$$

$\Leftrightarrow$ \hfill Distribution of $\lfloor \cdot \rfloor$ through $\|$

$$I(v) \quad \Rightarrow \quad (\lfloor G(v) \Longrightarrow S(v) \rfloor I(v) \ \wedge \ \lfloor H(v) \Longrightarrow T(v) \rfloor I(v))$$

$\Leftrightarrow$ \hfill Distribution of $\lfloor \cdot \rfloor$ through $\Longrightarrow$

$$I(v) \quad \Rightarrow \quad (G(v) \Rightarrow \lfloor S(v) \rfloor I(v) \ \wedge \ H(v) \Rightarrow \lfloor T(v) \rfloor I(v))$$

$\Leftrightarrow$ \hfill Logic

$$(I(v) \wedge G(v) \Rightarrow \lfloor S(v) \rfloor I(v)) \ \wedge \ (I(v) \wedge H(v) \Rightarrow \lfloor T(v) \rfloor I(v))$$

$\Leftrightarrow$ \hfill $T(v)$ is standard

$$(I(v) \wedge G(v) \Rightarrow \lfloor S(v) \rfloor I(v)) \ \wedge \ (I(v) \wedge H(v) \Rightarrow [T(v)]I(v))$$

From this calculation, we can see that the standard simulation proof obligation (15) applies to events with nondeterministic and probabilistic actions. Probabilistic actions are interpreted demonically using (26). The need for definiteness stems from condition (29). With the precautions we have taken, the whole construct *loop* is definite.

Probabilistic Progress. For the second condition (29) in Lemma 1, we introduce the notion of variant. Let $V(v)$ and $U(v)$ be two natural number expressions over the state v. It can be proved that, as a consequence of Lemma 5 in [14], condition (29) is equivalent to the following conditions (30) to (32):

$$I(v) \;\wedge\; (G(v) \vee H(v))$$
$$\Rightarrow \tag{30}$$
$$V(v) \leq U(v) \quad,$$

$$I(v) \;\wedge\; V(v) = N$$
$$\Rightarrow \tag{31}$$
$$\lceil G(v) \implies S(v) \;\|\; H(v) \implies T(v) \rceil\, (V(v) < N) \quad,$$

$$I(v) \;\wedge\; U(v) = N$$
$$\Rightarrow \tag{32}$$
$$\lceil G(v) \implies S(v) \;\|\; H(v) \implies T(v) \rceil\, (U(v) \leq N) \quad,$$

where N is a logical constant.

The condition (30) can be decomposed as follows:

$$I(v) \;\wedge\; (G(v) \vee H(v)) \Rightarrow V(v) \leq U(v)$$
$$\Leftrightarrow \qquad\qquad\qquad\qquad\qquad\qquad\qquad\qquad\qquad\qquad \text{Logic}$$
$$(I(v) \wedge G(v) \;\Rightarrow\; V(v) \leq U(v)) \;\wedge\; (I(v) \wedge H(v) \;\Rightarrow\; V(v) \leq U(v))$$

The two conjuncts in the last line correspond to proof obligation (20). It must be proved that whenever a new event, nondeterministic or probabilistic, is enabled, the variant $V(v)$ must be dominated by the upper bound $U(v)$.

Furthermore, using that $\lceil \cdot \rceil$ distributes through $\|$, condition (31) can be decomposed as follows:

$$I(v) \;\wedge\; V(v) = N$$
$$\Rightarrow$$
$$\lceil G(v) \implies S(v) \;\|\; H(v) \implies T(v) \rceil\, (V(v) < N)$$

$$\Leftrightarrow \qquad\qquad\qquad\qquad\qquad\qquad \text{Distribution of } \lceil \cdot \rceil \text{ through } \|$$

$$I(v) \;\wedge\; V(v) = N$$
$$\Rightarrow$$
$$(\lceil G(v) \implies S(v) \rceil\, (V(v) < N) \;\wedge\; \lceil H(v) \implies T(v) \rceil\, (V(v) < N))$$

$$\Leftrightarrow \qquad\qquad\qquad\qquad\qquad\qquad \text{Distribution of } \lceil \cdot \rceil \text{ through } \implies$$

$$I(v) \;\wedge\; V(v) = N$$

$$\Rightarrow$$

$$\quad (G(v) \;\Rightarrow\; \lceil S(v) \rceil\, (V(v) < N) \quad\wedge\quad H(v) \;\Rightarrow\; \lceil T(v) \rceil\, (V(v) < N))$$

$$\Leftrightarrow \qquad\qquad\qquad\qquad\qquad\qquad\qquad\qquad\qquad\qquad\qquad\qquad\text{Logic}$$

$$\quad (I(v) \;\wedge\; V(v) = N \;\wedge\; G(v) \;\Rightarrow\; \lceil S(v) \rceil\, (V(v) < N))$$

$$\wedge$$

$$\quad (I(v) \;\wedge\; V(v) = N \;\wedge\; H(v) \;\Rightarrow\; \lceil T(v) \rceil\, (V(v) < N))$$

$$\Leftrightarrow \qquad\qquad\qquad\qquad\qquad\qquad\qquad\qquad\qquad\qquad\qquad T(v) \text{ is standard}$$

$$\quad (I(v) \;\wedge\; V(v) = N \;\wedge\; G(v) \;\Rightarrow\; \lceil S(v) \rceil\, (V(v) < N))$$

$$\wedge$$

$$\quad (I(v) \;\wedge\; V(v) = N \;\wedge\; H(v) \;\Rightarrow\; [T(v)](V(v) < N))$$

The above reasoning yields for the event with nondeterministic action the progress proof obligation (17). For the event with probabilistic action, the action $S(v)$ is interpreted angelically, yielding the probabilistic progress proof obligation (19). The derivation of proof obligation (21) from condition (32) proceeds similarly.

6   Conclusion

The method of qualitative probabilistic reasoning in Event-B that we propose comes at very little cost of extra proof effort. The introduced concept of almost-certain convergence is easy to explain, and useful for common termination proofs based on probabilistic system behaviour. The method preserves the simplicity of Event-B proof obligations only requiring a modest extension to existing proof obligations. Furthermore, it is not necessary to make some sort of syntactic extension. We believe that this is an important advantage. Almost-certain convergence is reduced to a problem of proof. The modelling style of Event-B is not touched. We plan to implement the extension in the RODIN platform for Event-B [4].

We have not introduced concrete probabilities, see e.g. [21]. We believe that the qualitative approach already brings many benefits without the extra complication of numerical probabilistic reasoning. In most cases where only convergence is needed, specifying probabilities could be regarded as over-specification (at the cost of much more difficult proofs). Having said this, we do not dispute the usefulness of numerical probabilistic derivations. Note, that in that context the method we have presented in this article still applies – but some additional proof obligations would be needed [15]. We intend to work on such extensions to Event-B when we have more experience with the associated modelling in Event-B.

Note, that the formalisation of qualitative probabilistic choice we have chosen reflects closely the structure of Markov decision processes [23]. Hence, it should be possible to use some body of theory from this area with only little adaptation.

In particular, our approach should be open to use techniques of performance analysis used with Markov decision processes [13].

We have briefly discussed refinement in the context of qualitative probabilistic choice. It is not clear yet whether Event-B refinement should be extended or whether the present theory is sufficient. Future extensions concerning refinement of qualitative probabilistic choice should be defined to offer an alternative to existing techniques but not replace them. We think the Event-B technique of using anticipated events is very attractive because it allows us reason in a standard (non-probabilistic) way as much as possible.

Acknowledgement

We want to thank Jean-Raymond Abrial and Carroll Morgan for the discussions about this article, and suggestions for some improvements.

References

1. Abrial, J.-R. (ed.): The B-Book: Assigning Programs to Meanings. Cambridge University Press, Cambridge (1996)
2. Abrial, J.-R.: Event driven system construction (1999)
3. Abrial, J.-R.: Event based sequential program development: Application to constructing a pointer program. In: Araki, K., Gnesi, S., Mandrioli, D. (eds.) FME 2003. LNCS, vol. 2805, pp. 51–74. Springer, Heidelberg (2003)
4. Abrial, J.-R., Butler, M., Hallerstede, S., Voisin, L.: An open extensible tool environment for Event-B. In: Liu, Z., He, J. (eds.) ICFEM 2006. LNCS, vol. 4260, pp. 588–605. Springer, Heidelberg (2006)
5. Abrial, J.-R., Cansell, D., Méry, D.: A mechanically proved and incremental development of IEEE 1394 tree identify protocol. Formal Aspects of Computing 14(3), 215–227 (2003)
6. Abrial, J.-R., Cansell, D., Méry, D.: Refinement and Reachability in Event B. In: Treharne, H., King, S., Henson, M.C., Schneider, S. (eds.) ZB 2005. LNCS, vol. 3455, pp. 222–241. Springer, Heidelberg (2005)
7. Abrial, J.-R., Hallerstede, S.: Refinement, Decomposition and Instantiation of Discrete Models: Application to Event-B. Fundamentae Informatica, vol. 77(1-2) (2007)
8. Back, R.-J.: Refinement Calculus II: Parallel and Reactive Programs. In: de Bakker, J.W., de Roever, W.-P., Rozenberg, G. (eds.) Stepwise Refinement of Distributed Systems. LNCS, vol. 430, pp. 67–93. Springer, Heidelberg (1990)
9. Back, R.-J., von Wright, J.: Refinement Calculus: A Systematic Introduction. Graduate Texts in Computer Science. Springer, Heidelberg (1998)
10. Dijkstra, E.W.: A Discipline of Programming. Prentice-Hall, Englewood Cliffs, NJ (1976)
11. Hallerstede, S.: Parallel hardware design in B. In: Bert, D., Bowen, J.P., King, S., Waldén, M.A. (eds.) ZB 2003. LNCS, vol. 2651, pp. 101–102. Springer, Heidelberg (2003)
12. Hallerstede, S.: Justifications for the Event-B Modelling Notation. In: Julliand, J., Kouchnarenko, O. (eds.) B 2007. LNCS, vol. 4355, pp. 49–63. Springer, Heidelberg (2006)

13. Hallerstede, S., Butler, M.J.: Performance analysis of probabilistic action systems. Formal Aspects of Computing 16(4), 313–331 (2004)
14. Hoang, T.S.: The Development of a Probabilistic B-Method and a Supporting Toolkit. PhD thesis, School of Computer Science and Engineering — The University of New South Wales (July 2005)
15. Hoang, T.S., Jin, Z., Robinson, K., McIver, A., Morgan, C.: Probabilistic Invariants for Probabilistic Machines. In: Bert, D., Bowen, J.P., King, S., Waldén, M. (eds.) ZB 2003. LNCS, vol. 2651, pp. 240–259. Springer, Heidelberg (2003)
16. IEEE. IEEE Standard for a High Performance Serial Bus. Std 1394-1995 (1995)
17. IEEE. IEEE Standard for a High Performance Serial Bus (supplement). Std 1394a-2000 (2000)
18. McIver, A., Morgan, C., Hoang, T.S.: Probabilistic termination in B. In: Bert, D., Bowen, J.P., King, S., Waldén, M. (eds.) ZB 2003. LNCS, vol. 2651, pp. 216–239. Springer, Heidelberg (2003)
19. Morgan, C.: The Generalised Substitution Language Extended to Probabilistic Programs. In: Bert, D. (ed.) B 1998. LNCS, vol. 1393, Springer, Heidelberg (1998) Also available at [22, B98]
20. Morgan, C., Hoang, T.S., Abrial, J.-R.: The challenge of probabilistic event B - extended abstract. In: Treharne, H., King, S., Henson, M.C., Schneider, S.A. (eds.) ZB 2005. LNCS, vol. 3455, pp. 162–171. Springer, Heidelberg (2005)
21. Morgan, C., McIver, A.: Abstraction, Refinement and Proof for Probabilistic Systems. Monographs in Computer Science. Springer, Heidelberg (2005)
22. PSG. Probabilistic Systems Group: Collected Reports. At, http://web.comlab.ox.ac.uk/oucl/research/areas/probs/bibliography.html
23. Puterman, M.L.: Markov Decision Processes: Discrete Stochastic Dynamic Programming. Wiley-Interscience, New York (1994)

Verifying Smart Card Applications: An ASM Approach[*]

Dominik Haneberg, Holger Grandy, Wolfgang Reif, and Gerhard Schellhorn

Lehrstuhl für Softwaretechnik und Programmiersprachen
Institut für Informatik, Universität Augsburg
86135 Augsburg Germany
{haneberg,grandy,reif,schellhorn}@informatik.uni-augsburg.de

Abstract. We present PROSECCO[1], a formal model for security protocols of smart card applications, based on Abstract State Machines (ASM)
[BS03],[Gur95], and a suitable method for verifying security properties
of such protocols. The main part of this article describes the structure
of the protocol ASM and all its relevant parts. Our modeling technique
enables an attacker model exactly tailored to the application, instead of
only an attacker similar to the Dolev-Yao model. We also introduce a
proof technique for security properties of the protocols. Properties are
proved in the KIV system using symbolic execution and invariants. Furthermore we describe a graphical notation based on UML diagrams that
allows to specify the important parts of the application in a simple way.

Our formal approach is exemplified with a small e-commerce application. We use an electronic wallet to demonstrate the ASM-based protocol
model and we also show what the proof obligations of some of the security
properties look like.

1 Introduction

Smart cards are computers fitting in a wallet. They store information and independently execute specific programs. Their most exceptional characteristic is
the fact that they are tamper-proof. This predestines them for storage of security critical information. They are used for digital signatures, access control,
electronic wallets, e-ticketing and so on. Communication is an integral part of
such applications, the transmitted data contains such crucial data as customer
data or electronic business goods. Such data must be protected while in transfer. This is generally done using security protocols. Unfortunately an application
can have very specific security demands that are not fulfilled by standard protocols. The security properties guaranteed by standard protocols are often just
building blocks for the real security properties of the application, so the need for
application specific security protocols arises.

Unfortunately designing cryptographic protocols is very error-prone, i.e., it is
very hard to design them correctly [AN95]. This article presents PROSECCO[1], an

---

[*] This work is sponsored by the Deutsche Forschungsgemeinschaft.

[1] **Pro**tocols for **Se**cure **Co**mmunication.

J. Davies and J. Gibbons (Eds.): IFM 2007, LNCS 4591, pp. 313–332, 2007.
© Springer-Verlag Berlin Heidelberg 2007

approach for security protocol verification that uses an Abstract State Machine (ASM) as application model [Han06]. The ASM comprises the static aspects of the application, like the internal state of the different types of agents and the abilities of the attacker, a malicious participant, as well as the dynamic aspects, i.e., the different protocol steps that the agents can perform. Our approach offers a flexible attacker model in order to tailor the attacker to the investigated application. Proofs of security properties are generally invariant or inductive proofs and performed with the KIV system [BRS+00], our interactive theorem prover. Verification is simplified through the use of Dynamic Logic (DL) [HKT00] invariants.

PROSECCO is a generic approach which can be used to verify smart card applications and other e- and m-commerce applications, like electronic ticketing [GHRS06], as well as normal cryptographic protocols. Furthermore, it is not limited to standard properties like secrecy. A graphical notation to model the scenario and the protocols [HRS02] simplifies the construction of the formal model. PROSECCO's attacker model is generic and can be tailored to the application, so we are not limited to the Dolev-Yao attacker [DY81].

PROSECCO is part of a larger project, which has the overall goal of a seamless verification of security protocols, beginning with an abstract protocol model and ending with verified program code. Implementation correctness is verified using a refinement of the abstract protocols to Java code and a calculus for proving properties of Java Card programs [Ste04]. The verification of a Java implementation of the application complements PROSECCO because it establishes a connection between the abstract description of cryptographic protocols and their actual implementations. Therefore it is possible to verify the correspondence between the code deployed on the real smart cards and the abstract model of the security protocols. Java Card as the target platform for the smart card applications was chosen because the Java Card framework is an interesting and forward-looking platform for the development of smart card applications: it allows the programming of smart cards in a high-level object-oriented language, it supports multi-applicative smart cards as wells as field-loadable code, i.e., adding new applications to already deployed smart cards. In order to correspond to Java, the PROSECCO model contains agent states explicitly.

The paper is organized as follows: Section 2 presents the important concepts of the application model, Section 3 describes how the agents are modeled. Section 4 introduces the attacker and Section 5 describes the structure of the protocol ASM. The graphical notation of PROSECCO is described in Section 6. In Section 7 the technique is exemplified with a small example. Section 8 discusses related work and Section 9 concludes.

2   Concepts of the Application Model

The abstract model of the smart card applications combines algebraic specifications to describe the static aspects of the application with an Abstract State

Machine (ASM) which describes the dynamic ones. The algebraic specification contains fundamental definitions, like data types and the attacker's abilities. We use a detailed model of the communication between the agents in order to be able to specify different attacker types. Within this article we use the term agent to denote a participant (system or person) of the application under investigation. Each agent has one or more communication ports. Ports can be linked by channels and the agents communicate by sending messages (described by a freely generated data type *document* similar to msg used in [Pau98]) over these channels.

The specification framework is generic in the sense that the abilities of the attacker and the possible communication between the agents are defined application specific and therefore they are not fixed, like in other approaches for cryptographic protocol verification. This is important for the smart card scenarios because, depending on the attacker model chosen for the application, the attacker may eavesdrop into some communication links, e.g., over the Internet, but he cannot eavesdrop into the communication between smart card and card reader.

Built on top of the algebraic specification is an ASM describing the protocols. Every function of a smart card application is realized by a specific communication protocol (e.g., transfering money between wallets). Each protocol consists of different steps. All such protocol steps, that may be performed by one type of agent, are combined into an ASM rule that specifies this agent type's behavior. The ASM rules for the different agent types are integrated into the protocol ASM which selects nondeterministically the next active agent and then performs one protocol step for the selected agent. Through this nondeterministic selection all possible traces of the application are represented by this ASM.

More details on the algebraic specification can be found in a Technical Report [HGRS06] as well as in the Web presentation of the case study. The Web presentation of the specifications, theorems, and proofs can be found as project E-WALLET in [KIV].

3   Modeling the Agents

Distinct from most other approaches to security protocol verification (for example [Pau98]) which model the state of an agent implicitly by the history of the steps it has performed, we explicitly model the internal state of the agents. Each agent has its own state described by the fields in which it stores values, e.g., its private key. Modeling the state of the agents increases the complexity of the model but is necessary for the future refinement of the abstract protocol specifications to real code [GHRS06],[GSR06]. An implementation of course has a notion of program state and, in order to express a refinement relation, a corresponding notion of state, like the balance of an electronic purse, seems natural for the abstract model too. Each agent has a set of fields to store the application data, e.g., a cryptographic key. Each field contains data of an algebraically specified data type. As usual in ASM the state of the agents is stored in dynamic functions. This means that for an agent type with fields $f_1, \ldots, f_m$ of sorts $s_1, \ldots, s_m$ the ASM uses dynamic functions f_1: $agent \rightarrow s_1$, ..., f_m: $agent \rightarrow s_m$ to store the values of the fields of the agents of this type and the state of a given agent, $agent$, of this type is defined by $f_1(agent), \ldots, f_m(agent)$.[2]

An agent has a unique type. Each agent (including the attacker) is of one of the agent types $at \in agent\text{-}types$. For example in a smart card based electronic wallet, there are the smart card itself and different terminals, e.g., a point-of-sale terminal for paying and a terminal for loading additional money on the card, as well as the attacker and the owners of the smart cards. For this example we have $agent\text{-}types = \{$attacker, user, terminal, card$\}$.

4 The Attacker

The attacker model describes the assumed threat in the application scenario. Usually cryptographic protocols are analyzed with a powerful attacker in mind, which is similar to the Dolev-Yao attacker [DY81]. Nevertheless in certain applications the Dolev-Yao attacker is not adequate. Sometimes a reduced attacker model is more realistic. For example, certain high security smart card terminals are protected against intrusion and prevent the attacker from eavesdropping into the communication between terminal and smart card. Also sending MMS[3] over the GSM network can be considered secure, because the GSM communication is encrypted. An attacker cannot learn the contents of the sent MMS by eavesdropping. If an application has such specific properties and its security relies on them, a Dolev-Yao attacker cannot be used for verification (cf., e.g., the Cindy electronic ticketing application in [GHRS06]). Such an attacker with reduced abilities can be realized easily in our model, because our model determines individually for every communication channel how the attacker can manipulate it. The reason why one wants to rely on the properties of the used communication technique is that securing communication against a more powerful attacker usually leads to more complex protocols with more cryptography used. In the case of smart card applications this may enforce the usage of more expensive smart cards. Realistic assumptions about the attacker can crucially influence whether the application is economically feasible.

The description of the attacker in our ASM model consists of two parts. One part is an ASM rule describing the possible steps of the attacker (eavesdropping and sending messages). The second part is contained in the underlying algebraic specification, which contains formalizations of the attacker's treatment of messages (analysis and generation) and an exact determination which operations the attacker can perform on which communication links.

---

[2] Variables of basic data types are typeset in *italic*, whereas variables of functional types are typeset in a sans serif font. Typewriter is used for information given in a diagram of the graphical notation (cf. Section 6).

[3] Multimedia Messaging Service.

5   The ASM

This section describes the dynamic aspects of the model, i.e ., how the steps of the different agent types are described as ASM rules and how the protocol ASM is built out of these protocol steps.

The protocol ASM describes all steps that may be performed by the agents. Therefore the repeated execution of this rule, starting in a well-formed initial state, represents all traces of the application. Because in a given state more than one agent might be able to perform a step and the rule of the protocol ASM must guarantee that all these steps could be performed, the ASM nondeterministically chooses one of the agents which can perform a step and executes the step for the selected agent:

APPLICATION = **choose** *agent* **with** ready(*agent*) **in** STEP

where STEP is the ASM rule that describes the actions of the agents.

After choosing the agent for the next step, the ASM branches into the code describing the possible actions of the selected agent. Given that R_i is the rule for agents of type at_i $(i = 1, \ldots, n)$ this is done by a **case**-statement[4]:

STEP =
    case agent-type(*agent*) **of**
    at_1: R_1
    $\ldots$
    at_n: R_n

5.1   The Attacker

The main actions of the attacker are eavesdropping and sending messages. First we present the ASM rule that describes how the attacker sends messages to other agents. The attacker sending documents is captured by this ASM rule:

ATTACKER-SEND =
    choose *docs* **with** $\forall$ *doc* $\in$ *docs. attacker-known* $\rightsquigarrow$ *doc* **in**
        choose *agent, port* **with**
            ($\exists$ (*agent, port, remote-agent, remote-port*) $\in$ *connections.*
                can-write(*agent, port, remote-agent, remote-port*))
        in inputs(*agent, port*) := *docs*

The infix predicate $\cdot \rightsquigarrow \cdot$: *set(document)* $\times$ *document* determines if a certain document can be produced using a given attacker's knowledge[5]. The ASM-rule chooses a list of documents (*docs*) that can be produced by the attacker and then chooses an existing agent and a port of this agent which can be modified by the attacker and replaces the list of messages on this port with *docs*. Ports

---

[4] **case**-statements are not part of traditional ASM syntax but can easily be defined as an abbreviation for a sequence of **if**-statements.

[5] *docset* $\rightsquigarrow$ *doc* is equivalent to *doc* $\in$ synth(*docset*) in [Pau98].

represent the communication interfaces of the agents. To enable communication between two agents, a connection must be established between two ports. Each connection allows bidirectional communication between two agents. Whether the attacker can modify messages sent over a connection or not is determined by the predicate can-write($agent_1$, $port_1$, $agent_2$, $port_2$). This predicate is true iff communication using a connection between port $port_1$ of $agent_1$ and port $port_2$ of $agent_2$ can be manipulated by the attacker.

Eavesdropping is done by the rule ATTACKER-ADD:

ATTACKER-ADD =
   if   agent-type(*remote-agent*) = attacker
     ∨ can-read(*agent, outport, remote-agent, remote-port*)
   then *attacker-known* := *attacker-known* ∫+ *outdoc*

ATTACKER-ADD adds a document to the attacker's knowledge if the attacker has access to the used communication link and decomposes all documents in the attacker's knowledge as far as possible. The modification of the attacker's knowledge is expressed by the function ∫+ : *set(document)* × *document* → *set(document)*. *docset* ∫+ *doc* is the set of documents that results from adding *doc* to *docset* and applying the decomposition rules for documents until a fixpoint is reached. *docset* ∫+ *doc* is analz(*docset* ∪ {*doc*}) in [Pau98]. ATTACKER-ADD is used in rule SEND (cf. Section 5.2), which the other agents use to send documents.

5.2   Regular Agents

This section describes how the ASM rules for the normal agents (e.g., the smart card programs) are built. Every agent has a set of possible protocol steps he may perform. Each such step is characterized by a pair, consisting of a condition C and a rule R. The condition C describes under which conditions it is possible to execute the step, e.g., the received document contains a certain information. In well-formed protocols the conditions of the different protocol steps of an agent exclude each other. The rule R consists of a set of assignments, that modify the state functions for the agent and produce a response. All the protocol steps of an agent type are put together into an **if**-statement. Assume the agent of type at has m possible steps $R_1, \ldots, R_m$ with corresponding conditions $C_1, \ldots, C_m$, then the rule for this agent type has the following structure:

R_{at} =
  if $C_1(agent)$ **then** R_1
  . . .
  else if $C_m(agent)$ **then** R_m
  SEND

The R_i describe the modifications to the internal state of the agent. This is done by a sequence of assignments to the state functions. If an agent has fields $f_1, \ldots, f_n$ the rules R_i have the following form:

$R_i =$
$\quad$ $f_1(agent) := \ldots$
$\quad$ $\ldots$
$\quad$ $f_n(agent) := \ldots$
$\quad$ $outdoc := \ldots$
$\quad$ $outport := \ldots$

It is not necessary that all fields of an agent are modified in a step, instead it is also possible that just a subset of all fields of the agent is changed. The variable *outport* stores the port that should be used to send the response, *outdoc* stores the response document.

At the end of the ASM rule of the regular agents, the rule SEND is used to transfer the response to its destined receiver. The rule SEND is the following:

SEND =
$\quad$ **if** $(agent,\ outport,\ \cdot,\ \cdot) \in connections$ **then**
$\quad\quad$ **choose** $(agent,\ outport,\ remote\text{-}agent,\ remote\text{-}port) \in connections$ **in**
$\quad\quad\quad$ inputs($remote\text{-}agent,\ remote\text{-}port$) :=
$\quad\quad\quad\quad$ inputs($remote\text{-}agent,\ remote\text{-}port$) + $outdoc$
$\quad\quad$ ATTACKER-ADD

SEND selects an active connection, that belongs to *outport* and puts the generated document at the end of the list of unprocessed documents of the receiver's (*remote-agent*) input port (*remote-port*) belonging to the selected connection. If no appropriate connection exists, the message is lost. SEND is completed by using ATTACKER-ADD to ensure that the attacker receives the document, if the attacker can eavesdrop on the connection.

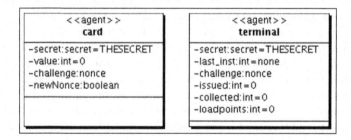

Fig. 1. Class diagram describing the agents of an electronic wallet application

6   Graphical Notation

The full formal model of an application in PROSECCO consists of fixed parts, like the axioms for cryptographic operations and application specific parts, like the protocols and the attacker's abilities. The fixed parts are taken from a reusable library and therefore do not require specification effort, when modeling a new

320   D. Haneberg et al.

application but the application specific parts do. The application specific part
consists of a couple of axioms, describing the communication infrastructure,
i.e., possible communication channels and how the attacker can influence them,
the composition if the agents' states, and of course a description of the actual
protocols, given as an ASM (cf. Section 5).

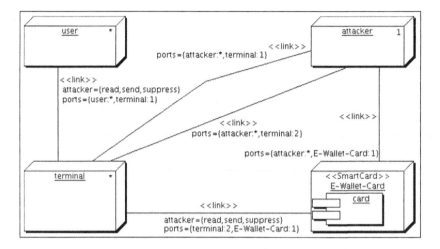

Fig. 2. Deployment diagram of the e-wallet application

The modeler should focus on the relevant parts of the application, especially
the protocols. To spare him the necessity to write all axioms by hand and to
develop the ASM from scratch PROSECCO offers a graphical notation. The graphical model uses 3 types of UML diagrams [RJB98],[OMG03] to describe the application. The formal model is generated via transformation from the diagrams.

A class diagram is used to describe the composition of the internal state of the
different agent types and how the state of an agent is initialized. Figure 1 shows
the class diagram for the electronic wallet case study described in Section 7.
The diagram describes two application specific agent types (indicated by the
stereotype «agent»), card and terminal. The diagram also states that initially
the value of the field value of a card is 0. Generated from the class diagram we
get the dynamic functions to store the agents' states and an axiom describing
admissible initial states.

The structure of the communication network used by the application is described by a deployment diagram. The deployment diagram contains the agents
of the application (including the users and the attackers). Smart card programs
are represented by components contained in a node representing their smart card
(stereotype «SmartCard»). Figure 2 shows the deployment diagram for the electronic wallet. Communication associations with stereotype «link» describe the
possible communication channels. The deployment diagram in Figure 2 defines 5
channels. The user interface of the terminals is represented by a link between the

user node and the terminal node. The link between the terminal node and the smart card node represents the card reader of the terminal. The links between the attacker node and the smart card and the terminal nodes represent a part of the application specific attacker model. The link between the attacker node and the smart card node states that the attacker can send data to a card, e.g., using a PC with card reader. The channel between the attacker and port 1 of the terminal states that the attacker can use the terminal like a normal customer. Finally the link between the attacker and port 2 of the terminal states that the attacker can send data to the card reader of the terminal, e.g., using a smart card with a malicious smart card program.

Tagged values associated with a link specify which ports of which agent types can be connected by the communication channel (tag **ports**) and what the attacker can do with this channel (tag **attacker**). The deployment diagram furthermore specifies if there may be multiple instances of an agent type or just a single one (e.g., the ticket issuing server in an electronic ticketing application). The transformation extracts the relevant information from the deployment diagram and generates axioms for various predicates describing the communication network, e.g., for the predicate can-read. In the deployment diagram a channel into which the attacker can eavesdrop is annotated with 'read' as element of the value of the tag **attacker**. In Figure 2 there are 2 such annotations: for the channels between users and terminals and for the channels between terminals and smart cards. The generated axiom describing which channels the attacker can eavesdrop into is therefore:

can-read:

$$\text{can-read}(\text{mk-connection}(agent \odot port, agent_1 \odot port_1))$$
$$\leftrightarrow \quad \text{user?}(agent) \land \text{terminal?}(agent_1) \land port_1 = 1$$
$$\lor \text{terminal?}(agent) \land port = 2 \land \text{card?}(agent_1) \land port_1 = 1$$

The axiom states that the attacker can eavesdrop into a given connection, mk-connection($agent \odot port, agent_1 \odot port_1$), between port $port$ of agent $agent$ and port $port_1$ of agent $agent_1$ if it is either a connection between a user and the user interface of the terminal (port 1 of a terminal) or a connection between the card reader of a terminal (port 2 of a terminal) and the interface of a smart card (port 1 of a card). There is no reason for the attacker to eavesdrop into the other 3 types of channels, for he is an endpoint of those channels and therefore has access to them without eavesdropping.

The protocols used in the application are described with activity diagrams. Each agent participating in a protocol is modeled by its own swimlane. The execution of a protocol run starts at the initial state and follows the control flow of the activity diagram until the protocol completes successfully or an error is noticed. The swimlanes can contain branch nodes, representing case distinctions in the protocol (e.g., signature is good respectively bogus), activity nodes, describing changes to the internal state of an agent (as sequences of assignments), and signal sending nodes, which represent the sending of a message to another

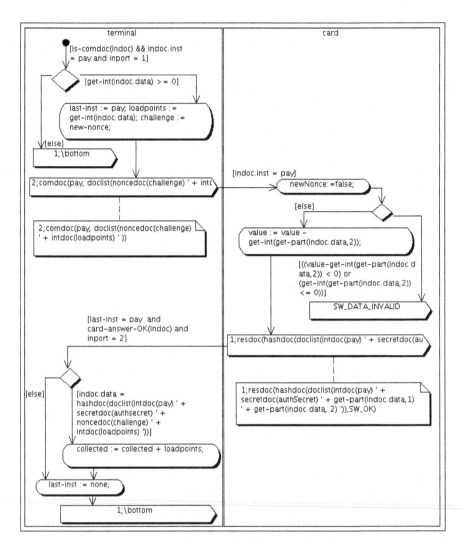

Fig. 3. Activity diagram of the payment protocol

agent. Figure 3 shows the activity diagram specifying the protocol to load additional money on a smart card of the e-wallet application described in Section 7.

For example the protocol step beginning at the topmost branch node in the terminal swimlane of Figure 3 leads to the following ASM code, which represents the branch as an **if**-statement, the contents of the activity node as a sequence of assignments, and the signal sending node as fixing of the output (*outdoc*) and the port used to send the message (*outport*):

if get-int(*indoc*.data) ≥ 0 **then**
   last-inst(*agent*) := pay;
   loadpoints(*agent*) := get-int(*indoc*.data);
   let *nonce* = [?] **in**
      NEW-NONCE (all-nonces; *next-nonce, nonce*);
      challenge(*agent*) := *nonce*
   outdoc := commanddoc(pay, challenge(*agent*) + loadpoints(*agent*))
   outport := 2
else
   outdoc := ⊥
   outport := 1

NEW-NONCE is a macro which returns a previously unused random number in the variable *nonce*. In the positive case of the **if**-statement the output is a commanddoc[6], otherwise it is an empty document ⊥. The instruction associated with the command is 'pay' and the data part of the command contains the newly generated nonce (challenge(*agent*)) and the number of points (loadpoints(*agent*)).

7   An Electronic Wallet

In this section we illustrate our modeling technique using a small smart card application. The application is an electronic wallet similar to the Mondex system, i.e., a smart card that can store money and be used for payment, for example in a university cafeteria or at copying machines. The smart card program (cardlet for short) stores the money as so-called *value points*. The application scenario was already described in [HRS02] but the protocols considered here are different, since they are designed to be secure against a more powerful attacker. The example is not very complicated and only serves as illustration of the kind of applications we are interested in, what our formal model looks like, what type of security properties we want to verify, and what proof technique is used. Larger applications we verified are the Mondex case study [SGHR06],[SGH+07],[SGH+06],[HSGR06] and Cindy [GHRS06], an electronic ticketing application.

As agents in this application we have the smart cards with the e-wallet application, card terminals (used for loading money on the cards and for payment), the owners of the cards, and the attacker. For reasons of simplicity we combined the functions of the load and the point-of-sale terminals into one agent type.

As described in Section 5 the main ASM rule of the application chooses an agent and then the ASM rule for this agent is used to perform a protocol step. The ASM rule for the electronic wallet example is as follows:

E-WALLET =
   choose *agent* ∈ {attacker, user, term, card} **with** ready(*agent*) **in**
      case agent-type(*agent*) **of**

---

[6] commanddocs represent the so-called Command-APDUs which are used to send commands to smart cards.

attacker : ATTACKER
user : USER
term : TERMINAL
card : CARDLET

ATTACKER, USER, TERMINAL, and CARDLET are the ASM rules for the four agent types. USER just sends commands to start protocol runs to the terminal, ATTACKER uses ATTACKER-SEND (cf. Section 5.1) to send messages, TERMINAL is the ASM rule for agents of type terminal, and CARDLET is the rule for the e-wallet cards.

7.1   Internal State of the Agents

The state of an agent comprises of the data needed by the agent to perform the functions of the application. For example, in our electronic wallet the smart card application must store its current amount of value points and both, the terminals and the cards must know a common secret used for message authentication. In KIV the dynamic functions storing the state of the ASM are represented as higher-order variables, e.g., the field secret which stores the common authentication secret is represented by the dynamic function secret with type $agent \rightarrow secret$. The other fields of the agents are represented by similar functions.

7.2   The Terminal

In this section we show a part of the ASM rule TERMINAL. We focus on the protocol step that generates the document to load additional points on the smart card. First the terminal selects an input to process and then performs the step consistent with the input and its internal state. The conditions for the different protocol steps should be mutually exclusive, so there is always exactly one step possible for a given input.

TERMINAL =
  if newConnection
  then ...
  else choose *port* with inputs $\neq$ [] in
        let *indoc* = head(inputs) in
          /* block */
          inputs := tail(inputs)
          if response-OK(*indoc*) $\land$ *port* = 2 $\land$ last-inst = auth then
            /* block */
            last-inst := load
            issued := issued + loadpoints
            outdoc := commanddoc(load, loadpoints +
                        hashdoc(secret + *indoc*.doc + loadpoints))
            outport := 2
            /* block end */
          else ...
          /* block end */

In this ASM rule the state functions are used as abbreviations, e.g., issued stands for issued(*agent*) where *agent* denotes the currently active agent, i.e., in this case a terminal. As mentioned above, this part of the ASM rule for the terminal is responsible for the last step of the protocol for loading points. In the condition it is tested among other things, that the last document presumably received from the smart card reported a successful completion of the last protocol step of the card (response-OK(*indoc*)) and that the terminal is currently running the load protocol (last-inst = auth). The state of the terminal is modified by incrementing the number of issued points and by storing the instruction that will be sent to the card. The document that will be sent to the smart card is a commanddoc with instruction 'load' and a data part that contains the number of points to load and the hash value of a list of documents, containing a nonce to prevent replays, a common secret for authentication, and the number of points to load. The nonce to prevent replays is *indoc*.doc, a part of the document currently processed by the terminal.

A similar ASM rule exists for the cardlets. It is omitted due to space restrictions but can be found in the Technical Report [HGRS06].

7.3   Proving Properties

Given our formal model of the application one can start to prove the desired security properties of the application. These can be typical properties of cryptographic protocols, such as secrecy or authenticity, but primarily we are interested in the more important application specific demands. In the described electronic wallet, the application specific security goal is that the users cannot defraud. In order to prove this, one needs to know that the shared secret (denoted THESECRET) is never disclosed to the attacker, so one auxiliary property needed for the proof of the main security property is:

secret-unknown:
$$(\quad \neg \text{ THESECRET} \in \textit{attacker-known}$$
$$\wedge \ \forall \ \textit{agent}, \textit{port}. \ (\neg \text{ THESECRET} \in \text{inputs}(\textit{agent}, \textit{port})))$$
$$\rightarrow \langle\!| \text{E-WALLET} |\!\rangle$$
$$(\quad \neg \text{ THESECRET} \in \textit{attacker-known}$$
$$\wedge \ \forall \ \textit{agent}, \textit{port}. \ (\neg \text{ THESECRET} \in \text{inputs}(\textit{agent}, \textit{port})))$$

E-WALLET was defined at the beginning of Section 7 and is the ASM rule of the application. $\langle\!|\cdot|\!\rangle$ is the strong diamond operator of DL. The meaning of a formula $\langle\!|\alpha|\!\rangle \ \varphi$ is that all runs of the program α terminate and the condition φ holds afterwards.[7] Therefore, the theorem **secret-unknown** states that if initially the secret is not in the knowledge of the attacker and not contained in the unprocessed messages of any agent, then this will still be the case after execution of E-WALLET. This means that the secrecy is invariant with respect to all possible steps of the application. With some simplifier rules this property can be proved automatically by the KIV system using symbolic execution. The

---

[7] $\langle\!|\alpha|\!\rangle \ \varphi$ corresponds to wp(α, φ) in Dijkstra's wp-calculus.

symbolic execution heuristic of the KIV system automatically executes all case-splits resulting from the nondeterminism of the ASM and step-by-step removes the ASM program from the proof goals until the resulting proof goals are plain higher-order formulas.

7.4   Main Security Property

A noteworthy aspect of our approach is that our main interest are not low level security properties like confidentiality (as, e.g., in Section 7.3). Instead we focus on application dependent properties like the exclusion of fraud, although of course the low level properties are often necessary preconditions for the interesting properties. In our electronic wallet example the informal security property of the application provider is: 'It is impossible that more money is spent with the cards than previously was loaded onto the cards'. This property rules out fraud because it guarantees that only value points which were correctly loaded onto the smart cards (in exchange for real money) can be spent, i.e., 'the users cannot get more than they have paid for'[8].

To easily express this property, we added two fields (`collected` and `issued`) to the state of the terminals which accumulate the sum of the points loaded onto the cards and the points spent with the cards. For the proof it is useful to consider the points currently on the cards as well. The points on the cards are stored in the field `value` of the cards. With these three fields the security property can be expressed as $\sum_{t \in Terminals}\mathsf{collected}(t) + \sum_{c \in Cards}\mathsf{value}(c) \leq \sum_{t \in Terminals}\mathsf{issued}(t)$. What we must prove actually is that this inequality holds after all possible finite sequences of steps of the application. This can be expressed in a DL formula that states that this property will not be violated in any state reachable after a finite number of steps of the ASM.

7.5   Verification Technique

This property is proven basically by showing that the inequality is invariant relative to a step of the application. As the invariant necessary to establish the property is quite complicated for a direct proof attempt, we used a different approach with an invariant that itself contains a program. We use a basic strategy of Dynamic Logic not possible, e.g., in Hoare-calculus: A program formula is used as an invariant. This formula says informally that 'for every well-formed state even after the worst possible attack the desired property holds'. The advantage of such an invariant is that the main property must not be established for all intermediate states, instead we can focus on such states (called *states of interest* in [Bör03],[Sch05]) in which certain operations are completed. Using such invariants with ASM rule applications spares us the effort of dealing with the complex interdependencies between the states of the agents in intermediate

---

[8] Note that 'the users get exactly as much as they have paid for' is not provable. The attacker can always intercept the transfer of points and delete them. The Mondex case study [SCW00] improves the situation by keeping track of lost money using exception logs.

states, i.e., in states in which unfinished runs of the load or the pay protocol exist. The state invariant is clearly simplified by not having to express which of the unfinished protocol runs are allowed to reach a successful end and why. Interestingly establishing this invariant after an attacker step is trivial, because the invariant especially says that attacker steps do no harm. A related idea is used in [Sch01] to express that two states are related through a coupling invariant if two finite sequences of state transitions starting in those states lead to two similar successor states. A dual idea used in [DW03],[Sch05] is to use predecessor states.

INV-definition:
INV $\leftrightarrow$ ⟨|begin
ATTACK-CARDS; CARD-STEPS;
ATTACK-TERMINALS; TERMINAL-STEPS;
end|⟩ ($\sum_{t \in Terminals}$ collected(t) + $\sum_{c \in Cards}$ value(c) $\leq$ $\sum_{t \in Terminals}$ issued(t))

The invariant, given by theorem **INV-definition**, is proved by symbolic execution of E-WALLET in the DL-calculus of KIV. The symbolic execution results in some open goals, one for each step of E-WALLET. These goals are then closed by showing that INV still holds.

The program part of the invariant consists of four parts: ATTACK-CARDS and ATTACK-TERMINALS are programs in which the attacker performs an attack on each smart card respectively terminal he can attack, i.e., when the attacker can create a document that causes a cardlet to load additional points respectively a terminal to accept a payment, this document is sent to the cardlet respectively the terminal. CARD-STEPS and TERMINAL-STEPS are loops which iterate over all cards respectively terminals and force these agents to process the documents that attacker has created for them.

Given a well-formed initial state of the ASM, the invariance of INV guarantees that in any state, reachable by a finite sequence of steps, even if the attacker does the worst he can, the security property holds, i.e., in any reachable state after some additional steps, the security property holds. But the initial proof obligation was that the inequality holds in every reachable state. So finally we have to prove that the inequality propagates backwards over the program part of the invariant, i.e., if the inequality holds after a run of the program, it also holds in the state in which the program started. But this is simple, because an attack could modify the agents' states only in such a way that the security property gets violated but not in a way that undoes a violation of the property.

We have proven the security property with KIV, which offers good proof support through mature heuristics for DL and a powerful simplifier which can handle thousands of rewrite rules. The overall degree of automation was approximately 85 %. The high degree of nondeterminism of the protocol model led to a considerable number of goals in the proof but most of them were quite similar and could be closed with a few appropriate lemmas. The few remaining difficult goals required a more detailed analysis and some complex lemmas.

7.6   Protocols and Their Expected Functionalities

Besides the security property we also proved that the protocols for the different functions serve their purpose, e.g., it is possible to increment the points stored on a card using the load protocol. Showing that a protocol has successful runs is important, since a protocol that does nothing would trivially satisfy the security invariant. For example the functioning of the load protocol can be expressed by theorem **load-works**. $\langle \alpha \rangle \; \psi$ means there exists a terminating run of α such that ψ holds afterwards.

load-works:

$\qquad \mathsf{value}(\mathrm{CARD}) = i_0 \wedge \mathsf{issued}(\mathrm{TERM}) = j_0 \wedge \varphi$
$\rightarrow \forall \, i. \quad i > 0 \wedge \mathsf{value}(\mathrm{CARD}) + i \; \leq \; 32767$
$\qquad \rightarrow \exists \, n. \langle \mathrm{E\text{-}WALLET}^n \rangle \; (\mathsf{value}(\mathrm{CARD}) = i_0 + i \wedge \mathsf{issued}(\mathrm{TERM}) = j_0 + i)$

Assuming a well-formed initial state described by φ in which the card CARD currently contains i_0 value points and the terminal TERM currently has issued j_0 points, this theorem states that for each value i, which is positive and that would not cause an overflow when added to the value points on the card, there exists a finite sequence of steps of the application E-WALLET that loads i points on the card, i.e., that leads to a state in which the number of points stored on the card is incremented by i and the terminal has issued i additional value points.

8   Related Work

Formal methods that analyze security protocols on an abstract level are used for quite some time. A lot of different approaches have been proposed.

Rather different from PROSECCO is the usage of specialized logics, such as the BAN logic of belief [BAN89]. In [ABV01] Accorsi, Basin and Viganò describe an approach that combines security logics with inductive methods.

Many approaches to the verification of protocols are model-checking based. In [Low96] an analysis of the Needham-Schroeder Public-Key protocol is described. The protocol is described in CSP and the Failure Divergences Refinement Checker (FDR) is used to check the protocol description. An enhancement to the usage of general-purpose model-checkers is the usage of model-checkers specifically designed for reasoning about security protocols, e.g., OFMC, developed by Basin et al. [BMV03]. The model checking based approaches usually focus on standard properties like secrecy or authenticity while our interactive approach can deal with arbitrary properties.

The CSP approach is not limited to model-checking anymore. [RSG+01] describes, among other things, an embedding of the CSP trace semantics in PVS. It also describes *rank functions* as a mean to simplify reasoning about the availability of certain messages. Such a technique could be combined with our model of the possible runs of the application, but so far reasoning based on [Pau98] was sufficient. We just formulate theorems stating the unavailability of a certain message or the conditions under which the message is available to the attacker.

Strand spaces [FHG99] are also an approach to abstract specification of cryptographic protocols. The model is quite elegant and easy to understand. The attacker model corresponds to a Dolev-Yao attacker and does not use a detailed model of different communication channels as we do. The method also focuses on standard goals for cryptographic protocols and therefore the main concepts of the model are production and consumption of messages. Application specific goals, like the one described in this paper, and therefore the treatment of application specific data are not modeled.

Paulson uses Isabelle to verify security protocols [Pau98]. This approach is quite successful and can cope with large protocols such as SET [Pau01]. Our representation of documents and the attacker's knowledge is inspired by this approach: we use documents and functions very similar to analz and synth in [Pau98]. Our approach differs in how system runs are described. First, [Pau98] describes protocol runs declaratively using an inductive definition of the set of possible traces while our approach describes runs using iterative application of (operationally specified) ASM rules. There is a close connection, since iterative rule application can be defined using inductive relations (for while loops and recursion this has, e.g., been done in [Nip02]). We prefer an operational definition using ASM rules where the inductive nature is encoded in the semantics, since it offers the full possibilities of structured programs which can be exploited for proof automation using symbolic execution [RSSB98]. A second difference is that we use an explicit representation of the agents' states, while [Pau98] instead defines an explicit system trace consisting of all messages that have been sent. The difference is that of state based vs. event based representation: recovering the current points loaded onto a card could be done in [Pau98] by accumulating the points of all successful load and pay messages and adding/subtracting them.

A middle ground between [Pau98] and our approach is also possible as the case study [BR98] on the Needham-Schroeder protocol shows: there an ASM is used to formalize runs, but a global execution trace is used instead of agent states. [BR97] analyzes the Kerberos protocol using distributed ASMs with an agent state similar to ours. Proofs have been done manually though in both cases. Also between our and Paulson's inductive approach is [Bel01]. Bella extends the inductive approach to deal with smart card applications. He allows inputs to and outputs from smart cards which the attacker cannot observe. This reflects that the Dolev-Yao model is inappropriate in some cases. What remains of Paulson's original approach is that the state of the agents is derived from the trace.

Concerning the graphical modeling of security critical applications and especially security protocols, UMLsec [Jür02],[Jür05] is most similar to PROSECCO. UMLsec is a UML profile which extends several UML diagrams with security relevant annotations. UMLsec allows the investigation of various security properties, not just security of cryptographic protocols. To specify cryptographic protocols, UMLsec uses sequence diagrams to describe the messages of the protocol and class diagrams to describe the state of the agents and add annotations marking security relevant information. UMLsec focuses on modeling, proof support for the verification of properties of cryptographic protocols is offered by exporting parts of the model into inputs for a model-checker. The verification also focuses on some standard properties of security protocols (e.g., secrecy). In PROSECCO the formal model is completely embedded in the KIV system. The PROSECCO approach also does not suffer from the limitations of model-checkers (finite state space) and is not limited to standard properties. [Jür05] reports on the verification of CEPS, a proposal for a smart card-based electronic payment system. The proof of the security property for the payment system as presented in [Jür05] is done by hand, i.e., without tool-support.

9   Conclusion

We presented an approach to specify security protocols in smart card applications, to allow their formal analysis, and an example illustrating our approach.

Summarizing, our approach offers a detailed model of the communication to support an application specific attacker which is important for smart card applications. The verification framework is generic and can be used for different applications. Our proof strategy, proving state invariants by symbolic execution is supported by the KIV system with a high degree of automation. Using DL programs in the invariants simplifies them by focusing on the interesting states.

The approach itself is suitable for the verification of security properties of different kinds of communication protocols. Our approach can be used to model various protocol scenarios, such as smart card applications as well as distributed systems, communicating over the Internet or over other insecure networks like WLAN or GSM, as well as common cryptographic protocols. Besides the protocols of the presented e-wallet application we already formalized other cryptographic protocols, e.g., the Needham-Schroeder Public-Key protocol and other m-commerce applications [GHRS06]. Furthermore PROSECCO offers a graphical notation for the description of the application, that simplifies the modeling.

Our goal is to have a verification approach that starts with proofs of security properties in an abstract specification and continues all the way down to the verification of correctness of an implementation of the agents in real Java code. Besides using PROSECCO in more case studies in the future, we will continue the development of the concept for the refinement to Java [GSR06].

References

[ABV01]   Accorsi, R., Basin, D., Viganò, L.: Towards an awareness-based semantics for security protocol analysis. In: Goubault-Larrecq, J. (ed.) Workshop on Logical Aspects of Cryptographic Protocol Verification, Elsevier, Amsterdam (2001)

[AN95]   Anderson, R.J., Needham, R.M.: Programming Satan's Computer. In: van Leeuwen, J. (ed.) Computer Science Today. LNCS, vol. 1000, Springer, Heidelberg (1995)

[BAN89]   Burrows, M., Abadi, M., Needham, R.M.: A Logic of Authentication. Technical report, SRC Research Report 39 (1989)

[Bel01]   Bella, G.: Mechanising a Protocol for Smart Cards. In: Attali, S., Jensen, T. (eds.) E-smart 2001. LNCS, vol. 2140, Springer, Heidelberg (2001)

[BMV03]   Basin, D., Mödersheim, S., Viganò, L.: An On-The-Fly Model-Checker for Security Protocol Analysis. In: Snekkenes, E., Gollmann, D. (eds.) ES-ORICS 2003. LNCS, vol. 2808, pp. 253–270. Springer, Heidelberg (2003)

[Bör03]   Börger, E.: The ASM Refinement Method. Formal Aspects of Computing, vol. 15(1–2) (2003)

[BR97]   Bella, G., Riccobene, E.: Formal Analysis of the Kerberos Authentication System. Journal of Universal Computer Science 3(12), 1337–1381 (1997)

[BR98]   Bella, G., Riccobene, E.: A Realistic Environment for Crypto-Protocol Aalyses by ASMs. In: Glässer, U., Schmitt, P. (eds.) Proc. 5th Int. Workshop on Abstract State Machines, Magdeburg University (1998)

[BRS+00]   Balser, M., Reif, W., Schellhorn, G., Stenzel, K., Thums, A.: Formal system development with KIV. In: Maibaum, T.S.E. (ed.) ETAPS 2000 and FASE 2000. LNCS, vol. 1783, Springer, Heidelberg (2000)

[BS03]   Börger, E., Stärk, R.F.: Abstract State Machines—A Method for High-Level System Design and Analysis. Springer, Heidelberg (2003)

[DW03]   Derrick, J., Wehrheim, H.: Using Coupled Simulations in Non-atomic Refinement. In: Bert, D., Bowen, J.P., King, S., Walden, M. (eds.) ZB 2003. LNCS, vol. 2651, Springer, Heidelberg (2003)

[DY81]   Dolev, D., Yao, A.C.: On the security of public key protocols. In: Proc. 22th IEEE Symposium on Foundations of Computer Science, IEEE, Los Alamitos (1981)

[FHG99]   Fábrega, F.J.T., Herzog, J.C., Guttman, J.D.: Strand Spaces: Proving Security Protocols Correct. Journal of Computer Security 7, 191–230 (1999)

[GHRS06]   Grandy, H., Haneberg, D., Reif, W., Stenzel, K.: Developing Provably Secure M-Commerce Applications. In: Müller, G. (ed.) ETRICS 2006. LNCS, vol. 3995, Springer, Heidelberg (2006)

[GSR06]   Grandy, H., Stenzel, K., Reif, W.: A Refinement Method for Java Programs. Technical Report 2006-29, University of Augsburg (December 2006)

[Gur95]   Gurevich, Y.: Evolving algebras 1993: Lipari guide. In: Börger, E. (ed.) Specification and Validation Methods, Oxford Univ. Press, New York (1995)

[Han06]   Haneberg, D.: Sicherheit von Smart Card – Anwendungen. PhD thesis, University of Augsburg, Augsburg, Germany (in German) (2006)

[HGRS06]   Haneberg, D., Grandy, H., Reif, W., Schellhorn, G.: Verifying Smart Card Applications: An ASM Approach. Technical Report 2006-08, Universität Augsburg (2006)

[HKT00]   Harel, D., Kozen, D., Tiuryn, J.: Dynamic Logic. MIT Press, Cambridge (2000)

[HRS02]   Haneberg, D., Reif, W., Stenzel, K.: A Method for Secure Smartcard Applications. In: Kirchner, H., Ringeissen, C. (eds.) AMAST 2002. LNCS, vol. 2422, Springer, Heidelberg (2002)

[HSGR06]   Haneberg, D., Schellhorn, G., Grandy, H., Reif, W.: Verification of Mondex Electronic Purses with KIV: From Transactions to a Security Protocol. Technical Report 2006-32, University of Augsburg (December 2006)

[Jür02]   Jürjens, J.: UMLsec: Extending UML for Secure Systems Development. In: Jézéquel, J.-M., Hussmann, H., Cook, S. (eds.) UML 2002 - The Unified Modeling Language 5th International Conference. LNCS, vol. 2460, Springer, Heidelberg (2002)

[Jür05]   Jürjens, J.: Secure Systems Development with UML. Springer, Heidelberg (2005)

[KIV]   Web presentation of KIV projects. URL: http://www.informatik.uniaugsburg.de/swt/projects/

[Low96]   Lowe, G.: Breaking and fixing the Needham-Schroeder public-key protocol using FDR. In: Margaria, T., Steffen, B. (eds.) TACAS 1996. LNCS, vol. 1055, pp. 147–166. Springer, Heidelberg (1996)

[Nip02]   Nipkow, T.: Hoare logics for recursive procedures and unbounded nondeterminism. In: Bradfield, J.C. (ed.) CSL 2002 and EACSL 2002. LNCS, vol. 2471, Springer, Heidelberg (2002)

[OMG03]   The Object Management Group (OMG). OMG Unified Modeling Language Specification Version 1.5 (2003)

[Pau98]   Paulson, L.C.: The inductive approach to verifying cryptographic protocols. Journal of Computer Security 6, 85–128 (1998)

[Pau01]   Paulson, L.C.: Verifying the SET Protocol. In: Goré, R.P., Leitsch, A., Nipkow, T. (eds.) IJCAR 2001. LNCS (LNAI), vol. 2083, Springer, Heidelberg (2001)

[RJB98]   Rumbaugh, J., Jacobson, I., Booch, G.: The Unified Modeling Language Reference Manual. Addison-Wesley, Reading (1998)

[RSG+01]   Ryan, P.Y.A., Schneider, S.A., Goldsmith, M.H., Lowe, G., Roscoe, B.: The Modelling and Analysis of Security Protocols: the CSP Approach. Addison-Wesley, Reading (2001)

[RSSB98]   Reif, W., Schellhorn, G., Stenzel, K., Balser, M.: Structured specifications and interactive proofs with KIV. In: Bibel, W., Schmitt, P. (eds.) Automated Deduction—A Basis for Applications, Kluwer, Dordrecht (1998)

[Sch01]   Schellhorn, G.: Verification of ASM Refinements Using Generalized Forward Simulation. Journal of Universal Computer Science (J.UCS) 7(11), 952–979 (2001) URL: http://www.jucs.org

[Sch05]   Schellhorn, G.: ASM Refinement and Generalizations of Forward Simulation in Data Refinement: A Comparison. Journal of Theoretical Computer Science 336(2-3), 403–435 (2005)

[SCW00]   Stepney, S., Cooper, D., Woodcock, J.: AN ELECTRONIC PURSE Specification, Refinement, and Proof. In: Technical monograph PRG-126, July 2000, Oxford University Computing Laboratory, Oxford (2000)

[SGH+06]   Schellhorn, G., Grandy, H., Haneberg, D., Möbius, N., Reif, W.: A systematic verification Approach for Mondex Electronic Purses using ASMs. Technical Report 2006-27, Universität Augsburg, Augsburg (2006)

[SGH+07]   Schellhorn, G., Grandy, H., Haneberg, D., Möbius, N., Reif, W.: A Systematic Verification Approach for Mondex Electronic Purses using ASMs. In: Abrial, J.-R., Glässer, U. (eds.) Proceedings of the Dagstuhl Seminar on Rigorous Methods for Software Construction and Analysis. LNCS, Springer, Heidelberg (submitted, 2007)

[SGHR06]   Schellhorn, G., Grandy, H., Haneberg, D., Reif, W.: The Mondex Challenge: Machine Checked Proofs for an Electronic Purse. In: Misra, J., Nipkow, T., Sekerinski, E. (eds.) FM 2006. LNCS, vol. 4085, Springer, Heidelberg (2006)

[Ste04]   Stenzel, K.: A formally verified calculus for full Java Card. In: Rattray, C., Maharaj, S., Shankland, C. (eds.) AMAST 2004. LNCS, vol. 3116, Springer, Heidelberg (2004)

Verification of Probabilistic Properties in HOL Using the Cumulative Distribution Function

Osman Hasan and Sofiène Tahar

Dept. of Electrical & Computer Engineering, Concordat University
1455 de Maisonette W., Montreal, Quebec, H3G 1M8, Canada
{o_hasan,tahar}@ece.concordia.ca

Abstract. Traditionally, computer simulation techniques are used to perform probabilistic analysis. However, they provide inaccurate results and cannot handle large-scale problems due to their enormous CPU time requirements. To overcome these limitations, we propose to complement simulation based tools with higher-order-logic theorem proving so that an integrated approach can provide exact results for the critical sections of the analysis in the most efficient manner. In this paper, we illustrate the practical effectiveness of our idea by verifying numerous probabilistic properties associated with random variables in the HOL theorem prover. Our verification approach revolves around the fact that any probabilistic property associated with a random variable can be verified using the classical *Cumulative Distribution Function* (CDF) properties, if the CDF relation of that random variable is known. For illustration purposes, we also present the verification of a couple of probabilistic properties, which cannot be evaluated precisely by the existing simulation techniques, associated with the Continuous Uniform random variable in HOL.

Keywords: Interactive Theorem Proving, Higher-Order-Logic, Probabilistic Systems, Cumulative Distribution Function, HOL.

1 Introduction

Probabilistic analysis has become a tool of fundamental importance to virtually all engineers and scientists as they often have to deal with systems that exhibit significant random or unpredictable elements. The main idea behind probabilistic analysis is to model these uncertainties by random variables and then judge the performance and reliability issues based on the corresponding probabilistic properties.

Random variables are basically functions that map random events to numbers. Every random variable gives rise to a probability distribution, which contains most of the important information about this random variable. The probability distribution of a random variable can be uniquely described by its *Cumulative Distribution Function* (CDF), which is sometimes also referred to as the probability distribution function. The CDF of a random variable R, $F_R(x)$, represents

J. Davies and J. Gibbons (Eds.): IFM 2007, LNCS 4591, pp. 333–352, 2007.

the probability that the random variable R takes on a value that is less than or equal to a real number x

$$F_R(x) = Pr(R \leq x) \tag{1}$$

where Pr denotes the probability. The CDF of a random variable contains complete information about the probability model of the random variable and one of its major significance is that it can be used to characterize both discrete and continuous random variables. A distribution is called discrete if its CDF consists of a sequence of finite or countably infinite jumps, which means that it belongs to a random variable that can only attain values from a certain finite or countably infinite set. Discrete random variables can also be characterized by their *probability mass function* (PMF), which represents the probability that the given random variable R is exactly equal to some value x, i.e., $Pr(R = x)$. A distribution is called continuous if its CDF is continuous, which means that it belongs to a random variable that ranges over a continuous set of numbers that contains all real numbers between two limits. A Continuous random variable can also be characterized by its *probability density function* (PDF), which represents the slope of its CDF, i.e., $\frac{dF_R(x)}{dx}$. Besides characterizing both discrete and continuous random variables, the CDF also allows us to determine the probability that a random variable falls in any arbitrary interval of the real line. Because of these reasons, the CDF is regarded as one of the most useful characteristic of random variables in the field of probabilistic analysis where the main goal is to determine the probabilities for various events.

Today, simulation is the most commonly used computer based probabilistic analysis technique. Most simulation softwares provide a programming environment for defining functions that approximate random variables for probability distributions. The random elements in a given system are modeled by these functions and the system is analyzed using computer simulation techniques, such as the Monte Carlo Method [17], where the main idea is to approximately answer a query on a probability distribution by analyzing a large number of samples. The inaccuracy of the probabilistic analysis results offered by simulation based techniques poses a serious problem in highly sensitive and safety critical applications, such as space travel, medicine and military, where a mismatch between the predicted and the actual system performance may result in either inefficient usage of the available resources or paying higher costs to meet some performance or reliability criteria unnecessarily. Besides the inaccuracy of the results, another major limitation of simulation based probabilistic analysis is the enormous amount of CPU time requirement for attaining meaningful estimates. This approach generally requires hundreds of thousands of simulations to calculate the probabilistic quantities and becomes impractical when each simulation step involves extensive computations.

In order to overcome the limitations of the simulation based approaches, we propose to use higher-order logic interactive theorem proving [9] for probabilistic analysis. Higher-order logic is a system of deduction with a precise semantics and can be used for the development of almost all classical mathematics theories. Interactive theorem proving is the field of computer science and mathematical logic concerned with computer based formal proof tools that require some sort of human assistance. We believe that probabilistic analysis can be performed by specifying the behavior of systems which exhibit randomness in higher-order logic and formally proving the intended probabilistic properties within the environment of an interactive theorem prover. Due to the inherent soundness of this approach, the probabilistic analysis carried out in this way will be capable of providing exact answers. It is important to note here that higher-order-logic theorem proving cannot be regarded as the golden solution in performing probabilistic analysis because of its own limitations. Even though theorem provers have been successfully used for a variety of tasks, including some that have eluded human mathematicians for a long time, but these successes are sporadic, and work on hard problems usually requires a proficient user and a lot of formalization. On the other hand, simulation based techniques are at least capable of offering approximate solutions to these problems. Therefore, we consider simulation and higher-order-logic theorem proving as complementary techniques, i.e., the methods have to play together for a successful probabilistic analysis framework. For example, the proposed theorem proving based approach can be used for the safety critical parts of the design which can be expressed in closed mathematical forms and simulation based approaches can handle the rest.

The foremost conditions for conducting probabilistic analysis within the environment of a higher-order-logic theorem prover are (1) the higher-order-logic formalization of random variables; and (2) to be able to formally verify the probabilistic properties of these random variables within the theorem prover. This paper is mainly targeted towards the second condition above, though the formalization of random variables is also discussed briefly. Our approach for the verification of probabilistic properties, illustrated in Figure 1, is primarily based on the fact that if a random variable is formally specified and its CDF relation is formally verified in a higher-order-logic theorem prover then the classical CDF properties [16] can be used to prove any of its probabilistic properties. The paper presents the verification of these classical CDF properties and the formal proofs for the facts that any probabilistic property for a given random variable, including the PMF and the PDF, can be expressed in terms of its CDF.

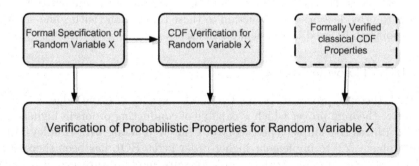

Fig. 1. Framework for Verifying Probabilistic Properties

We have selected the HOL theorem prover [10] for the current formalization mainly in order to build upon the existing mathematical theories of *Measure* and *Probability*. Hurd [14] developed these theories and also presented a framework for the formalization of probabilistic algorithms in his PhD thesis. Random variables are basically probabilistic algorithms and Hurd's thesis also contains the formalization of some discrete random variable which are verified by proving their corresponding PMF relations in the HOL theorem prover.

The rest of the paper is organized as follows. In Section 2, we present a brief introduction to the HOL theorem prover and an overview of Hurd's methodology for the formalization of probabilistic algorithms in HOL . Then in Section 3, we show how Hurd's formalization framework can be extended to formalize continuous random variables as well by defining the Standard Uniform random variable and proving its CDF relation in the HOL theorem prover. The benefit of the formal definition of the Standard Uniform random variable is that it can be used along with nonuniform random number generation techniques [7] to formalize other continuous random variables in HOL. In Section 4, we formally specify the CDF by a real valued higher-order-logic function and provide the formal verification of its classical properties within the HOL theorem prover. Section 5 illustrates the usefulness of the formally verified CDF properties in constructing a higher-order-logic theorem prover based probabilistic analysis framework. In this section, we have included the HOL proofs for the facts that the CDF relation of a random variable can be used along with the formally verified CDF properties to determine any of its associated probabilistic quantities. Then in Section 6, we outline the process of verifying a couple of probabilistic properties associated with the Continuous Uniform random variable within the HOL theorem prover to illustrate the practical effectiveness of the proposed approach. A review of the related work in the literature is given in Section 7 and we finally conclude the paper in Section 8.

2   Preliminaries

In this section, we provide an overview of the HOL theorem prover and Hurd's methodology [14] for the formalization of probabilistic algorithms in HOL. The intent is to provide a brief introduction to these topics along with some notation that is going to be used in the next sections.

2.1   HOL Theorem Prover

The HOL theorem prover, developed at the University of Cambridge, UK, is an interactive theorem prover which is capable of conducting proofs in higher-order logic. It utilizes the simple type theory of Church [5] along with Hindley-Milner polymorphism [22] to implement higher-order logic. HOL has been successfully used as a verification framework for both software and hardware as well as a platform for the formalization of pure mathematics. It supports the formalization of various mathematical theories including sets, natural numbers, real numbers, measure and probability. The HOL theorem prover includes many proof assistants and automatic proof procedures. The user interacts with a proof editor and provides it with the necessary tactics to prove goals while some of the proof steps are solved automatically by the automatic proof procedures.

In order to ensure secure theorem proving, the logic in the HOL system is represented in the strongly-typed functional programming language ML [24]. The ML abstract data types are then used to represent higher-order-logic theorems and the only way to interact with the theorem prover is by executing ML procedures that operate on values of these data types. Users can prove theorems using a natural deduction style by applying inference rules to axioms or previously generated theorems. The HOL core consists of only basic 5 axioms and 8 primitive inference rules, which are implemented as ML functions. Soundness is assured as every new theorem must be created from these basic axioms and primitive inference rules or any other pre-existing theorems/inference rules.

We selected the HOL theorem prover for the proposed formalization mainly because of its inherent soundness and ability to handle higher-order logic and in order to benefit from the built-in mathematical theories for measure and probability.

2.2   Verifying Probabilistic Algorithms in HOL

Hurd [14] proposed to formalize the probabilistic algorithms in higher-order logic by thinking of them as deterministic functions with access to an infinite Boolean sequence $\mathbb{B}^\infty$; a source of infinite random bits. These deterministic functions make random choices based on the result of popping the top most bit in the infinite Boolean sequence and may pop as many random bits as they need for their computation. When the algorithms terminate, they return the result along with the remaining portion of the infinite Boolean sequence to be used by other programs. Thus, a probabilistic algorithm which takes a parameter of type α and ranges over values of type β can be represented in HOL by the function

$$\mathcal{F} : \alpha \to B^\infty \to \beta \times B^\infty$$

For example, a $Bernoulli(\frac{1}{2})$ random variable that returns 1 or 0 with equal probability $\frac{1}{2}$ can be modeled as follows

$\vdash$ bit = λs. (if shd s then 1 else 0, stl s)

where s is the infinite Boolean sequence and shd and stl are the sequence equivalents of the list operation 'head' and 'tail'. The function bit accepts the infinite Boolean sequence and returns a random number, which is either 0 or 1 together with a sequence of unused Boolean sequence, which in this case is the tail of the sequence. The above methodology can be used to model most probabilistic algorithms. All probabilistic algorithms that compute a finite number of values equal to 2^n, each having a probability of the form $\frac{m}{2^n}$: where m represents the HOL data type nat and is always less than 2^n, can be modeled, using Hurd's framework, by well-founded recursive functions. The probabilistic algorithms that do not satisfy the above conditions but are sure to terminate can be modeled by the *probabilistic while loop* proposed in [14].

The probabilistic programs can also be expressed in the more general state-transforming monad where the states are the infinite Boolean sequences.

```
⊢ ∀ a,s. unit a s = (a,s)
⊢ ∀ f,g,s. bind f g s = let (x,s')← f(s) in g x s'
```

The unit operator is used to lift values to the monad, and the bind is the monadic analogue of function application. All the monad laws hold for this definition, and the notation allows us to write functions without explicitly mentioning the sequence that is passed around, e.g., function *bit* can be defined as

```
⊢ bit_monad = bind sdest (λb. if b then unit 1 else unit 0)
```

where sdest gives the head and tail of a sequence as a pair (*shd* s,*stl* s).

Hurd [14] also formalized some mathematical measure theory in HOL in order to define a probability function $\mathbb{P}$ from sets of infinite Boolean sequences to real numbers between 0 and 1. The domain of $\mathbb{P}$ is the set $\mathcal{E}$ of events of the probability. Both $\mathbb{P}$ and $\mathcal{E}$ are defined using the Carathéodory's Extension theorem, which ensures that $\mathcal{E}$ is a σ-algebra: closed under complements and countable unions. The formalized $\mathbb{P}$ and $\mathcal{E}$ can be used to derive the basic laws of probability in the HOL prover, e,g., the additive law, which represents the probability of two disjoint events as the sum of their probabilities:

$$⊢ ∀ A B. A \in \mathcal{E} \wedge B \in \mathcal{E} \wedge A \cap B = \emptyset \Rightarrow$$
$$\mathbb{P}(A \cup B) = \mathbb{P}(A) + \mathbb{P}(B)$$

The formalized $\mathbb{P}$ and $\mathcal{E}$ can also be used to prove probabilistic properties for probabilistic programs such as

$$⊢ \mathbb{P} \{s \mid fst (bit s) = 1\} = \tfrac{1}{2}$$

where the function fst selects the first component of a pair and $\{x|C(x)\}$ represents a set of all x that satisfy the condition C in HOL.

The measurability of a function is an important concept in probability theory and also a useful practical tool for proving that sets are measurable [3]. In Hurd's formalization of probability theory, a set of infinite Boolean sequences, S, is said to be measurable if and only if it is in $\mathcal{E}$, i.e., $S \in \mathcal{E}$. Since the probability measure $\mathbb{P}$ is only defined on sets in $\mathcal{E}$, it is very important to prove that sets that arise in verification are measurable. Hurd [14] showed that a function is guaranteed to be measurable if it accesses the infinite boolean sequence using only the unit, bind and sdest primitives and thus leads to only measurable sets.

Hurd formalized four discrete random variables and proved their correctness by proving the corresponding PMF relations [14]. Because of their discrete nature, all these random variables either compute a finite number of values or are sure to terminate. Thus, they can be expressed using Hurd's methodology by either well formed recursive functions or the probabilistic while loop [14]. On the other hand, continuous random variables always compute an infinite number of values and therefore would require all the random bits in the infinite Boolean sequence if they are to be represented using Hurd's methodology. The corresponding deterministic functions cannot be expressed by either recursive functions or the probabilistic while loop and it is mainly for this reason that the specification of continuous random variables needs to be handled differently than their discrete counterparts.

3   Formalization of the Standard Uniform Distribution

In this section, we present the formalization of the Standard Uniform distribution in the HOL theorem prover. The Standard Uniform random variable is a continuous random variable and can be characterized by the CDF as follows:

$$Pr(X \leq x) = \begin{cases} 0 \text{ if } x < 0; \\ x \text{ if } 0 \leq x < 1; \\ 1 \text{ if } 1 \leq x. \end{cases} \tag{2}$$

One of the significant aspects of formalizing the Standard Uniform random variable is that it can be utilized along with the nonuniform random number generation techniques [7] to model other continuous random variables in the HOL theorem prover as well. Therefore, it opens the doors of formally verifying the probabilistic properties of systems that exhibit randomness of continuous nature.

3.1   Formal Specification of Standard Uniform Random Variable

The Standard Uniform random variable can be formally expressed in terms of an infinite sequence of random bits as follows [13]

$$\lim_{n \to \infty} (\lambda n. \sum_{k=0}^{n-1} (\frac{1}{2})^{k+1} X_k) \tag{3}$$

where, X_k denotes the outcome of the kth random bit; *true* or *false* represented as 1 or 0 respectively. The mathematical relation of Equation (3) can be formalized in the HOL theorem prover in two steps. The first step is to define a discrete Standard Uniform random variable that produces any one of the equally spaced 2^n dyadic rationals in the interval $[0, 1 - (\frac{1}{2})^n]$ with the same probability $(\frac{1}{2})^n$ using Hurd's methodology

```
Definition 3.1:
⊢ (std_unif_disc 0 = unit 0) ∧
     ∀ n. (std_unif_disc (n+1) =
         bind (std_unif_disc n) (λm. bind sdest
    (λb. unit (if b then ((½)ⁿ⁺¹ + m) else m)))))
```

The function *std_unif_disc* allows us to formalize the real sequence of Equation (3) in the HOL theorem prover. Now, the formalization of the mathematical concept of limit of a real sequence in HOL [12] can be used to formally specify the Standard Uniform random variable of Equation (3) as follows

Definition 3.2:
⊢ ∀ s. std_unif_cont s = lim (λn. fst(std_unif_disc n s))

where, *lim M* represents the HOL formalization of the limit of a real sequence [12], such that *lim M* is the limit value of the real sequence M (i.e., $\lim_{n \to \infty} M(n) = lim\ M$).

3.2   Formal Verification of Standard Uniform Random Variable

The formalized Standard Uniform random variable, *std_unif_cont*, can be verified to be correct by proving its CDF to be equal to the theoretical value given in Equation (2). The first step in this verification is to prove the measurability of the set under consideration, i.e., to prove that the set $\{s \mid std\_unif\_cont\ s \leq x\}$ is in $\mathcal{E}$. Since, the function *std_unif_disc* accesses the infinite boolean sequence using only the **unit**, **bind** and **sdest** primitives, Hurd's formalization framework can be used to prove

Lemma 3.1:
⊢ ∀ x,n. {s | FST (std_unif_disc n s) ≤ x} ∈ $\mathcal{E}$

On the other hand, the definition of the function *std_unif_cont* involves the *lim* function and thus the corresponding sets cannot be proved to be measurable in a very straightforward manner. Therefore, in order to prove this, we leveraged the fact that each set in the sequence of sets $(\lambda n.\{s \mid FST(std\_unif\_disc\ n\ s) \leq x\})$ is a subset of the set before it, in other words, this sequence of sets is a monotonically decreasing sequence. Thus, the countable intersection of all sets in this sequence can be proved to be equal to the set $\{s \mid std\_unif\_cont\ s \leq x\}$

Lemma 3.2:
⊢ ∀ x. {s | std_unif_cont s ≤ x} =
     ∩ₙ (λ n. {s | FST (std_unif_disc n s) ≤ x})

Now the set $\{s \mid std\_unif\_cont\ s \leq x\}$ can be proved to be measurable since $\mathcal{E}$ is closed under countable intersections [14] and all the sets in the sequence $(\lambda n.\{s \mid FST(std\_unif\_disc\ n\ s) \leq x\})$ are measurable according to Lemma 3.1.

Theorem 3.1:
⊢ ∀ x. {s | std_unif_cont s ≤ x} ∈ $\mathcal{E}$

Theorem 3.1 can now be used along with the real number theories [12] to verify the CDF of the probabilistic function *std_unif_cont* in the HOL theorem prover and the verification details can be found in [13].

Theorem 3.2:
⊢ ∀ x. ℙ{s | std_unif_cont s ≤ x} =
     if (x < 0) then 0 else (if (x < 1) then x else 1)

4   Formalization of the Cumulative Distribution Function

In this section, we present the formal specification of the CDF and the verification of CDF properties in the HOL theorem prover. The CDF and its properties have been an integral part of the classical probability theory since its early development in the 1930s. The properties are mentioned in most of the probability theory texts, e.g, [16] and have been used successfully in performing analytical analysis of random systems using paper-pencil proofs. Our main contribution is the formalization of these properties in a mechanical theorem prover. The proof process was long and tedious requiring a deep understanding and proficiency in both the mathematical backgrounds (Boolean Algebra, Set Theory, Real Theory, Measure Theory and Probability Theory) as well as the HOL theorem prover. The motivation, on the other hand, is that these formalized properties can now be utilized to obtain a complete, rigorous and communicable description of random components in a system. Also, the formalization allows us to perform machinized proofs regarding probabilistic properties within the framework of a sound theorem-prover environment.

4.1   Formal Specification of CDF

It follows from Equation (1) that the CDF can be formally specified in HOL by a higher-order-logic function that accepts a random variable and a real argument and returns the probability of the event when the given random variable is less than or equal to the value of the given real number. Hurd's formalization of the probability function $\mathbb{P}$, which maps sets of infinite Boolean sequences to real numbers between 0 and 1, can be used to formally specify the CDF as follows:

> Definition 4.1:
> $\vdash \forall$ R x. cdf R x = $\mathbb{P}$ {s | R s $\leq$ x}

where, R represents the random variable that accepts an infinite Boolean sequence and returns a real number and the set $\{s \mid R\ s \leq x\}$ is the set of all infinite Boolean sequences, s, that satisfy the condition $(R\ s \leq x)$.

4.2   Formal Verification of CDF Properties

Using the formal specification of the CDF, we are able to verify the classical CDF properties [16] within the HOL theorem prover. The formal proofs for these properties not only ensure the correctness of our CDF specification but also play a vital role in proving various probabilistic properties associated with random variables as shown in Figure 1. All properties in the following sections are verified under the assumption that the set $\{s \mid R\ s \leq x\}$, where R represents the random variable under consideration, is measurable for all values of x.

CDF Bounds. *For any real number x,*

$$0 \leq F_R(x) \leq 1 \tag{4}$$

This property states that if we plot the CDF against its real argument x, then the graph of the CDF, F_R, is between the two horizontal lines $y = 0$ and $y = 1$. In other words, the lines $y = 0$ and $y = 1$ are the bounds for the CDF F_R.

The above characteristic can be verified in HOL using the fact that the CDF is basically a probabilistic quantity along with the basic probability law, verified in [14], that states that the probability of an event is always less than 1 and greater than 0 ($\forall S.\ S \in \mathcal{E} \Rightarrow 0 \leq \mathbb{P}(S) \leq 1$).

```
Theorem 4.1:
⊢ ∀ R x. (0 ≤ CDF R x) ∧ (CDF R x ≤ 1)
```

CDF is Monotonically Increasing. *For any two real numbers a and b,*

$$if\ a < b,\ then\ F_R(a) \leq F_R(b) \tag{5}$$

In mathematics, functions between ordered sets are monotonic if they preserve the given order. Monotonicity is an inherent characteristic of CDFs and the CDF value for a real argument a can never exceed the CDF value of a real argument b if a is less than b.

Using the set theory in HOL, it can be proved that for any two real numbers a and b, if $a < b$ then the set of infinite Boolean sequences $\{s \mid R\ s \leq a\}$ is a subset of the set $\{s \mid R\ s \leq b\}$. Then, using the monotone law of the probability function ($\forall S\ T.\ S \in \mathcal{E} \land T \in \mathcal{E} \land S \subseteq T \Rightarrow (\mathbb{P}(S) \leq \mathbb{P}(T))$), verified in [14], we proved the monotonically increasing property of the CDF in HOL.

```
Theorem 4.2:
⊢ ∀ R a b. a < b ⇒ (CDF R a ≤ CDF R b)
```

Interval Probability. *For any two real numbers a and b,*

$$if\ a < b,\ then\ Pr(a < R \leq b) = F_R(b) - F_R(a) \tag{6}$$

This property is very useful for evaluating the probability of a random variable, R, lying in any given interval (a,b] in terms of its CDF.

Using the set theory in HOL, it can be proved that for any two real numbers a and b, if $a < b$ then the set of infinite Boolean sequences $\{s \mid R\ s \leq b\}$ is equal to the union of the sets $\{s \mid R\ s \leq a\}$ and $\{s \mid (a < R\ s) \land (R\ s \leq b)\}$. Now, the above CDF property can be proved in HOL using the additive law of the probability function ($\forall S\ T.\ S \in \mathcal{E} \land T \in \mathcal{E} \land S \cap T = \emptyset \Rightarrow (\mathbb{P}(S \cup T) = \mathbb{P}(S) + \mathbb{P}(T))$), verified in [14], along with the closed under complements and countable unions property of $\mathcal{E}$.

```
Theorem 4.3:
⊢ ∀ R a b. a < b ⇒
    (ℙ {s | (a < R s) ∧ (R s ≤ b) } = CDF R b - CDF R a)
```

CDF at Negative Infinity

$$\lim_{x \to -\infty} F_R(x) = 0; \ that \ is, \ F_R(-\infty) = 0 \qquad (7)$$

This property states that the value of the CDF tends to 0 as its real argument approaches negative infinity or in other words the graph of CDF must eventually approach the line $y = 0$ at the left end of the real axis.

We used the formalization of limit of a real sequence [12] along with the formalization of the mathematical measure theory [14] in HOL to prove this property. The first step is to prove a relationship between the limit value of the probability of a monotonically decreasing sequence of events A_n (i.e, $A_{n+1} \subseteq A_n$ for every n) and the probability of the countable intersection of all events that can be represented as A_n.

$$\forall A_n. \lim_{n \to \infty} Pr(A_n) = Pr(\bigcap_n A_n) \qquad (8)$$

This relationship, sometimes called the *Continuity Property of Probabilities*, can be used to prove the above CDF property by instantiating it with a decreasing sequence of events represented in Lambda calculus as $(\lambda n.\{s \mid R \ s \leq -(\&n)\})$; where n has the HOL data type nat: $\{0, 1, 2, \ldots\}$ and "$\&$" converts it to its corresponding real number. The left hand side of Equation 8, with this sequence, represents the CDF for the random variable R when its real argument approaches negative infinity and thus is equal to the left hand side of our proof goal in Equation 7. Using the monotonically decreasing nature of the events in the sequence $(\lambda n.\{s \mid R \ s \leq -(\&n)\})$, the right hand side of Equation 8, with this sequence, can be proved to be equal to the probability of an empty set. The CDF at negative infinity property can now be proved using the basic probability law $(\mathbb{P}(\{\}) = 0)$, verified in [14], which states that the probability of an empty set is 0.

> **Theorem 4.4:**
> $\vdash \forall$ R. lim (λ n. CDF R (-&n)) = 0

where, *lim* is the HOL function for the limit of a real sequence [12].

CDF at Positive Infinity

$$\lim_{x \to \infty} F_R(x) = 1; \ that \ is, \ F_R(\infty) = 1 \qquad (9)$$

This property, quite similar to the last one, states that the value of the CDF tends to 1 as real argument approaches positive infinity or in other words the graph of CDF must eventually approach the line $y = 1$ at the right end of the real axis.

The HOL proof steps for this property are also quite similar to the last one and this time we use the Continuity Property of Probabilities which specifies the relationship between the limit value of the probability of a monotonically increasing sequence of events A_n (i.e, $A_n \subseteq A_{n+1}$ for every n) and the probability of the countable union of all events that can be represented as A_n.

$$\forall A_n. \lim_{n \to \infty} Pr(A_n) = Pr(\bigcup_n A_n) \tag{10}$$

In this case, we instantiate Equation 10 with an increasing sequence of events represented in Lambda calculus as $(\lambda n.\{s \mid R \ s \leq (\&n)\})$. The countable union of all events in this sequence is the universal set. The CDF at positive infinity property can now be proved in the HOL theorem prover using the basic probability law ($\mathbb{P}(\text{UNIV}) = 1$), verified in [14], which states that the probability of the universal set is 1.

Theorem 4.5:
⊢ ∀ R. lim (λ n. CDF R (&n)) = 1

CDF is Continuous from the Right. *For every real number a,*

$$\lim_{x \to a^+} F_R(x) = F_R(a) \tag{11}$$

where $\lim_{x \to a^+} F_R(x)$ is defined as the limit of $F_R(x)$ as x tends to a through values greater than a. Since F_R is monotone and bounded, this limit always exists.

In order to prove this property in HOL, we used a decreasing sequence of events represented in Lambda calculus as $(\lambda n.\{s \mid R \ s \leq a + \frac{1}{\&(n+1)}\})$. This sequence of events has been selected in such a way that if the Continuity Property of Probabilities, given in Equation 8, is instantiated with this sequence then its left hand side represents the CDF for a random variable, R, when its real argument approaches a through values greater than a. Therefore, with this sequence, the left hand side of the Continuity Property of Probabilities is equal to the left hand side of our proof goal in Equation 11. Using the monotonically decreasing nature of the events in the sequence $(\lambda n.\{s \mid R \ s \leq a + \frac{1}{\&(n+1)}\})$, it can also be proved that the countable intersection of all events in this sequence is the set $\{s \mid R \ s \leq a\}$. The CDF can now be proved to be continuous from the right as the right hand side of the Continuity Property given in Equation 8, with the sequence $(\lambda n.\{s \mid R \ s \leq a + \frac{1}{\&(n+1)}\})$, represents the CDF of random variable at real argument a.

Theorem 4.6:
⊢ ∀ R a. lim (λ n. CDF R (a + $\frac{1}{\&(n+1)}$)) = CDF R a

CDF Limit from the Left. *For every real number a,*

$$\lim_{x \to a^-} F_R(x) = Pr(R < a) \tag{12}$$

where $\lim_{x \to a^-} F_R(x)$ is defined as the limit of $F_R(x)$ as x tends to a through values less than a.

This property is quite similar to the previous one and can be proved by instantiating the Continuity Property of Probabilities, given in Equation 10, with an increasing sequence of events represented in Lambda calculus as $(\lambda n.\{s \mid R\ s \leq a - \frac{1}{\&(n+1)}\})$. The left hand side of Equation 10, with this sequence, represents the CDF for the random variable R when its real argument approaches a through values less than a and is thus equal to the left hand side of our proof goal in Equation 12. Using the monotonically increasing nature of the events in the sequence $(\lambda n.\{s \mid R\ s \leq a - \frac{1}{\&(n+1)}\})$, it can be proved that the countable union of all the events in this sequence is the set $\{s \mid R\ s < a\}$ which led us to prove the theorem stating the CDF limit from the left.

Theorem 4.7:
$\vdash \forall R\ a.\ \lim\ (\lambda\ n.\ \text{CDF R (a - } \frac{1}{\&(n+1)})) = \mathbb{P}\ \{s \mid (R\ s < a\})$

5 CDF Properties and Probabilistic Analysis

As mentioned in Section 1, probabilistic analysis is basically the process of evaluating performance and/or reliability of a given system by representing its uncertain elements in terms of random variables and characterizing the results in terms of the corresponding probabilistic quantities. We have already seen in Sections 2 and 3 of this paper that both discrete and continuous random variables can be formalized in the HOL theorem prover. In this section, we illustrate the usefulness of the formally verified CDF properties in relevance to evaluating probabilistic quantities while performing probabilistic analysis within the HOL theorem prover.

5.1 Determining Interval Probabilities

The CDF of a random variable, R, along with the CDF properties verified in Section 4 can be used to determine the probability that R will lie in any specified interval of the real line. In this section, we verify this statement in the HOL theorem prover by dividing the real line in three disjoint intervals; $(-\infty, a]$, $(a, b]$ and (b, ∞), and determining the probabilities that a random variable lies in these intervals in terms of its CDF.

Determining the probability for the first interval is quite straightforward since the CDF for a random variable, R, with a real argument, a, can be used directly to find the probability that a random variable, R, will lie in the interval $(-\infty, a]$. Whereas, the probability that a random variable, R, will lie in the interval $(a, b]$ can be determined by its CDF values for the real arguments a and b as has been proved in Theorem 4.3. For the third interval, we first use the set theory in HOL to prove that for any real value b, the set of infinite Boolean sequences $\{s \mid b < R\ s\}$ is the complement of the set $\{s \mid R\ s \leq b\}$. The probability that a random variable, R, lies in the interval (b, ∞) can now be represented in terms of its CDF by using the complement law of the probability function $(\forall S.\ S \in \mathcal{E} \Rightarrow \mathbb{P}(S) = 1 - \mathbb{P}(\bar{S}))$, verified in [14], under the assumption that the set $\{s \mid Rs \leq a\}$ is measurable.

Theorem 5.1:
⊢ ∀ R b. ℙ {s | b < R s} = 1 - (CDF R b)

5.2   Representing PMF in Terms of the CDF

The PMF can be expressed in terms of the CDF of the corresponding random variable by using the fact that for any real value a the set of infinite Boolean sequences {s | R s ≤ a} is equal to the union of the sets {s | R s < a} and {s | R s = a}. Now, using Theorems 4.6 and 4.7, the additive law of the probability function ℙ and the closed under complements and countable unions property of $\mathcal{E}$, the desired relationship can be proved under the assumption that the sets {s|Rs = a} and {s|Rs ≤ a} are measurable.

Theorem 5.2:
⊢ ∀ R a. ℙ {s | R s = a} = lim (λ n. CDF R (a + $\frac{1}{\&(n+1)}$)) -
lim (λ n. CDF R (a - $\frac{1}{\&(n+1)}$))

A unique characteristic for all continuous random variables is that their PMF is equal to 0. Theorem 5.2 along with the formalization of continuous functions allowed us prove this property in the HOL theorem prover.

Theorem 5.3:
⊢ ∀ R a. (∀x. (λx. CDF R x) contl x) ⇒ ℙ {s | R s = a} = 0)

where, $(\forall x.f \; contl \; x)$ represents the HOL function definition for a continuous function [12] such that the function f is continuous for all x.

5.3   Representing PDF in Terms of the CDF

The PDF, which is the slope of the CDF, represents the probability distribution of a continuous random variable in terms of integrals. It can be expressed in the HOL theorem prover by using the formal definition of the CDF and the formalization of the mathematical concept of a derivative [12].

Definition 5.1:
⊢ ∀ R x. pdf R x = @l. ((λx. CDF R x) diffl l) x

where $(f \; diffl \; l) \; x$ represents the HOL formalization of the derivative [12], such that l is the derivative of the function f with respect to the variable x, and @x.t represents the Hilbert choice operator in HOL ($\varepsilon x.t$ term), that represents the value of x such that t is true.

Using the above definition of the PDF, we were able to prove the following classical properties of the PDF [16] in the HOL theorem prover under the assumption that the set {s | R s ≤ x}, where R represents the random variable under consideration, is measurable for all values of x.

PDF Lower Bound. *For any real number x,*

$$0 \leq f_R(x) \tag{13}$$

This property states that if we plot the PDF against its real argument x, then the graph of the PDF, f_R, will never go below the horizontal line $y = 0$. In other words, the line $y = 0$ is the lower bound for the PDF f_R.

We utilized the monotonically increasing property of the CDF proved in Theorem 4.2 along with the nonnegative characteristic of the derivative of nondecreasing functions to prove this property in the HOL theorem prover.

> Theorem 5.4:
> ⊢ ∀ R x. (∀x.(λx. CDF R x) differentiable x) ⇒ (0 ≤ pdf R x)

where, the condition (*f differentiable x*) ensures in HOL that a derivative exists for the function f for the variable x.

Interval Probability in Terms of PDF. *For any two real numbers a and b,*

$$if \ a < b, \ then \ Pr(a < R \leq b) = \int_a^b f_R(x)dx \tag{14}$$

We used the HOL formalization of the gauge integral [21], which has all the attractive convergence properties of the Lesbesgue integral, along with the interval property of the CDF, verified in Theorem 4.3, to prove the above property in the HOL theorem prover.

> Theorem 5.5:
> ⊢ ∀ R x.(∀x. (λx. CDF R x) differentiable x) ⇒
>   (Dint (a,b) (λx. pdf R x)
>   (ℙ {s | (a ≤ R s) ∧ (R s ≤ b)}))

where *Dint(a,b) f k* represents the HOL formalization of the gauge integral [12] such that the definite integral of the function f over the interval [a,b] is k.

6   Illustrative Example

In this section, we illustrate the practical effectiveness of our approach by presenting a simplified probabilistic analysis example of roundoff error in a digital processor within the HOL theorem prover.

Assume that the roundoff error for a particular digital processor is uniformly distributed over the interval $[-5\text{x}10^{-12}, 5\text{x}10^{-12}]$. An engineering team is interested in verifying that the probability of the event when the roundoff error in this digital processor is greater than $2\text{x}10^{-12}$ is less than 0.33 and the probability that the final result fluctuates by $\pm 1\text{x}10^{-12}$ with respect to the actual value is precisely equal to 0.2. We now verify these properties in HOL by following the steps mentioned in Figure 1.

6.1   Formal Specification of the Continuous Uniform Distribution

The first step, in the higher-order-logic theorem proving based formal verification of probabilistic properties, is the formalization of the random variable that is required in the probabilistic analysis under consideration. The example under consideration calls for the Continuous Uniform random variable, which can be characterized by the CDF as follows

$$\mathbb{P}(X \leq x) = \begin{cases} 0 & \text{if } x \leq a; \\ \frac{x-a}{b-a} & \text{if } a < x \leq b; \\ 1 & \text{if } b < x. \end{cases} \tag{15}$$

The Continuous Uniform random variable can be formally expressed in terms of the formalized Standard Uniform random variable of Section 3 using the Inverse Transform Method (ITM) [7]. The ITM is a commonly used nonuniform random number generation technique for generating continuous random variants for probability distributions for which the inverse of the CDF can be expressed in a closed mathematical form.

```
Definition 6.1:
⊢ ∀ a b s. uniform_cont a b s = (b - a) * std_unif_cont s) + a
```

The function $uniform\_cont$, which formally represents the Continuous Uniform random variable, accepts two real valued parameters a, and b and the infinite Boolean sequence s and returns a real number in the interval [a,b].

6.2   CDF Verification of the Continuous Uniform Random Variable

The second step in our approach for the verification of probabilistic properties associated with a random variable is the verification of its CDF relationship, as shown in Figure 1. This can be done by proving the CDF of the function $uniform\_cont$ to be equal to the theoretical value of the CDF of the Continuous Uniform random variable given in Equation 15.

The definition of the function $uniform\_cont$ and elementary real arithmetic operations may be used to transform the set $\{s|uniform\_cont\ a\ b\ s\ \leq\ x\}$ in such a way that $(std\_unif\_cont\ s)$ is the only term that remains on the left hand side of the inequality, i.e., $(\mathbb{P}\{s|std\_unif\_cont\ s \leq \frac{x-a}{b-a}\})$. Now, the CDF property for the function std_unif_cont, proved in Theorem 3.2, along with some simple arithmetic reasoning can be used to prove the desired CDF relationship.

```
Theorem 6.1:
⊢ ∀ a b x. (a < b) ⇒ ℙ{s | uniform_cont a b s ≤ x} =
        if (x ≤ a) then 0 else (if (x ≤ b) then x−a/b−a else 1)
```

Similarly, the measurability property proved in Theorem 3.1 can be used to prove the measurability property for the set that corresponds to the CDF of the probabilistic function $uniform\_cont$ in the HOL theorem prover.

```
Theorem 6.2:
⊢ ∀ a b x. (a < b) ⇒ measurable {s | uniform_cont a b s ≤ x}
```

6.3   Verification of Probabilistic Properties

After the completion of the above steps, we are now in the position of formally verifying the given probabilistic properties by modeling the roundoff error as a Continuous Uniform random variable in the interval $[-5\text{x}10^{-12}, 5\text{x}10^{-12}]$.

We proceed to verify the first probabilistic property, which checks if the probability of the event when the roundoff error in this digital processor is greater than $2\text{x}10^{-12}$ is less than 0.33, by instantiating Theorem 5.1 with the random variable ($\lambda s.\ uniform\_cont\ -5x10^{-12}\ 5x10^{-12}\ s$) and the real value $2\text{x}10^{-12}$. Now the property can be verified by simplifying the result using the formal definition of the CDF, given in Definition 4.1, Theorems 6.1 and 6.2 and the real number theories in HOL [12].

> **Theorem 6.3:**
> $\vdash \mathbb{P}$ {s | $2\text{x}10^{-12}$ < uniform_cont $-5\text{x}10^{-12}$ $5\text{x}10^{-12}$ s } < 0.33

Similarly the second property, which checks if the probability of the final result fluctuating by $\pm 1\text{x}10^{-12}$ with respect to the actual value is precisely equal to 0.2, can be verified by checking if the probability of the Continuous Uniform random variable, defined in the interval $[-5\text{x}10^{-12}, 5\text{x}10^{-12}]$, falling in the interval $[-1\text{x}10^{-12}, 1\text{x}10^{-12}]$ is equal to 0.2. This can be done by using the definition of CDF, Theorems 6.1 and 6.2 and instantiating the CDF property verified in Theorem 4.3 by the real values $-1\text{x}10^{-12}$, $1\text{x}10^{-12}$ for variables a, b and the random variable ($\lambda s.\ uniform\_cont\ -5x10^{-12}\ 5x10^{-12}\ s$) for variable R.

> **Theorem 6.4:**
> $\vdash \mathbb{P}$ {s | (-1x10^{-12} < uniform_cont $-5\text{x}10^{-12}$ $5\text{x}10^{-12}$ s) $\wedge$
> (uniform_cont $-5\text{x}10^{-12}$ $5\text{x}10^{-12}$ s $\leq$ 1x10^{-12})} = 0.2

The above example illustrates the fact that the interactive theorem proving based approach is capable to verify probabilistic quantities, which can be expressed in a closed mathematical form, with 100% precision; a novelty which is not available in the simulation based techniques. Thus, by integrating the higher-order-logic theorem proving capability to the simulation based tools, the level of the overall accuracy of the results can be raised. This added benefit comes at the cost of a significant amount of time and effort spent, while formalizing the system behavior, by the user.

7   Related Work

Due to the vast application domain of probability, many researchers around the world are trying to improve the quality of computer based probabilistic analysis. The ultimate goal is to come up with tools that are capable of providing accurate analysis, can handle large-scale problems and are easy to use. In this section, we provide a brief account of the state-of-the-art and discuss some related work in the field of probabilistic analysis.

Modern probability and statistics is supported by computers to perform some of the very large and complex calculations using simulation techniques. All commonly used commercial probabilistic and statistical software packages available these days, e.g., SAS [27], SPSS [28], Microsoft's Excel [8], etc. contain a large collection of discrete and absolutely continuous univariate and multivariate distributions which in turn can be used to form complicated random models. The models can then be analyzed using simulation techniques. These packages are capable of automatically evaluating probabilistic quantities but the results are less accurate. McCullough [18] proposed a collection of intermediate-level tests for assessing the numerical reliability of a statistical package and uncovered flaws in most of the mainframe statistical packages [19] and [20]. Our proposed approach, on the other hand, is capable of determining precise probabilistic quantities at the cost of significant user interaction.

A number of *probabilistic languages*, e.g., Probabilistic cc [11], λ_o [23] and IBAL [25], have been proposed that are capable of modeling random variables. Probabilistic languages treat probability distributions as primitive data types and abstract from their representation schemes. Therefore, they allow programmers to perform probabilistic computations at the level of probability distributions rather than representation schemes. These probabilistic languages are quite expressive and can be used to perform probabilistic analysis based on the distribution properties of random variables but they have their own limitations. For example, either they require a special treatment such as the lazy list evaluation strategy in IBAL and the limiting process in Probabilistic cc or they do not support precise reasoning as in the case of λ_o. The theorem proving based approach proposed in this paper, on the other hand, is capable of modeling most probability distributions due to the high expressive of the higher-order-logic and also provides precise reasoning based on its inherent soundness.

Another alternative for the formal verification of probabilistic properties is to use probabilistic model checking techniques, e.g., [2], [26]. Like the traditional model checking, it involves the construction of a precise mathematical model of the probabilistic system which is then subjected to exhaustive analysis to verify if it satisfies a set of formal probabilistic properties. This approach is capable of providing precise solutions in an automated way; however it is limited for systems that can only be expressed as a probabilistic finite state machine and is incapable of handling large systems due to the state space explosion [6] problem. Our proposed theorem proving based approach, in contrast, is capable of handling all kinds of probabilistic systems because of the high expressiveness of the higher-order-logic and the verification of probabilistic properties is independent of the size of the model since state space explosion is not an issue.

Hurd's PhD thesis [14] can be regarded as one of the pioneering works in regards to formalizing probabilistic systems in higher-order-logic. The thesis also presents the tools, based on the mathematical probability theory, for reasoning about the correctness of probabilistic systems and this is the area that we extended to verify interval properties of probabilistic systems in HOL. Hurd *et. al* [15] also formalized the *probabilistic guarded-command language (pGCL)* in HOL. The *pGCL* contains both demonic and probabilistic nondeterminism and thus makes it suitable for reasoning about distributed random algorithms. Celiku [4] built upon the formalization of the *pGCL* to mechanize the quantitative

Temporal Logic (*qtl*) and demonstrated the ability to verify temporal properties of probabilistic systems in HOL.

8 Conclusions

In this paper, we propose to use higher-order-logic theorem proving as a complement to state-of-the-art simulation based approaches for a more reliable and efficient probabilistic analysis framework. The inherent soundness of the theorem-proving based analysis allows us to acquire exact answers to probabilistic properties, which can be expressed in a closed mathematical form, in an interactive manner and is thus quite useful for the analysis of safety critical and highly sensitive sections of the system under test. Simulation techniques, on the other hand, are capable of handling analytically complex sections in an automated way but provide approximate answers and thus can be used to efficiently handle the less critical sections of the system.

We presented a formal definition of the *Cumulative Distribution Function* of random variables along with the verification of its properties in the HOL theorem prover. This is a very significant step towards verification of probabilistic properties in a formalized probabilistic analysis framework, as has been shown in Section 5 of this paper. We also briefly described the formalization of the Standard Uniform random variable in the HOL theorem prover and illustrated with an example that it can be used to formalize other continuous random variables as well.

To the best of our knowledge, the paper presents the first attempt to formally verify the CDF properties in a higher-order-logic theorem prover. For this verification, we utilized the HOL theories of *Sets, Boolean Algebra, Natural Numbers, Real Analysis, Measure* and *Probability*. Our results can therefore be used as an evidence for the usefulness of theorem provers in proving pure mathematics and the soundness of the existing HOL libraries. Besides being the first step towards a formalized probabilistic analysis framework, the presented formalization is also a significant step towards an attempt to reconstruct mathematical knowledge in a computer-oriented environment and therefore is also a contribution to the QED project, which calls for a computer system that effectively represents all important mathematical knowledge and techniques [1].

References

1. The QED Manifesto. In: CADE-12: Proceedings of the 12th International Conference on Automated Deduction, pp. 238–251. Springer, Heidelberg (1994)
2. Baier, C., Haverkort, B., Hermanns, H., Katoen, J.P.: Model Checking Algorithms for Continuous time Markov Chains. IEEE Transactions on Software Engineering 29(4), 524–541 (2003)
3. Billingsley, P.: Probability and Measure. John Wiley, Chichester (1995)
4. Celiku, O.: Quantitative Temporal Logic Mechanized in HOL. In: International Colloquium Theoretical Aspects of Computing, pp. 439–453 (2005)
5. Church, A.: A Formulation of the Simple Theory of Types. Journal of Symbolic Logic 5, 56–68 (1940)

6. Clarke, E.M., Grumberg, O., Peled, D.A.: Model Checking. The MIT Press, Cambridge (2000)
7. Devroye, L.: Non-Uniform Random Variate Generation. Springer, Heidelberg (1986)
8. Microsoft Excel (2007) http://office.microsoft.com
9. Gordon, M.J. C.: Mechanizing Programming Logics in Higher-Order Logic. In: Current Trends in Hardware Verification and Automated Theorem Proving, pp. 387–439. Springer, Heidelberg (1989)
10. Gordon, M.J.C., Melham, T.F.: Introduction to HOL: A Theorem Proving Environment for Higher-Order Logic. Cambridge University Press, Cambridge (1993)
11. Gupta, V.T., Jagadeesan, R., Panangaden, P.: Stochastic Processes as Concurrent Constraint Programs. In: Principles of Programming Languages, pp. 189–202. ACM Press, New York (1999)
12. Harrison, J.: Theorem Proving with the Real Numbers. Springer, Heidelberg (1998)
13. Hasan, O., Tahar, S.: Formalization of Standard Uniform Random Variable. Technical Report, Concordia University, Montreal, Canada (December 2006) http://hvg.ece.concordia.ca/Publications/TECH_REP/SURV_TR06
14. Hurd, J.: Formal Verification of Probabilistic Algorithms. PhD Thesis, University of Cambridge, Cambridge, UK (2002)
15. Hurd, J., McIver, A., Morgan, C.: Probabilistic Guarded Commands Mechanized in HOL. Theoretical Computer Science 346, 96–112 (2005)
16. Khazanie, R.: Basic Probability Theory and Applications. Goodyear (1976)
17. MacKay, D.J.C.: Introduction to Monte Carlo methods. In: Learning in Graphical Models. NATO Science Series, pp. 175–204. Kluwer Academic Publishers, Dordrecht (1998)
18. McCullough, B.D.: Assessing the Reliability of Statistical Software: Part I. The. American Statistician 52(4), 358–366 (1998)
19. McCullough, B.D.: Assessing the Reliability of Statistical Software: Part II. The. American Statistician 53(2), 149–159 (1999)
20. McCullough, B.D., Wilson, B.: On the Accuracy of Statistical Procedures in Microsoft Excel 2003. Computational Statistics and Data. Analysis 49, 1244–1252 (2005)
21. McShane, E.J.: A Unified Theory of Integration. The. American Mathematical Monthly 80, 349–357 (1973)
22. Milner, R.: A Theory of Type Polymorphism in Programming. Journal of Computer and System Sciences 17, 348–375 (1978)
23. Park, S., Pfenning, F., Thrun, S.: A Probabilistic Language based upon Sampling Functions. In: Principles of Programming Languages, pp. 171–182. ACM Press, New York (2005)
24. Paulson, L.C.: ML for the Working Programmer. Cambridge University Press, Cambridge (1996)
25. Pfeffer, A.: IBAL: A Probabilistic Rational Programming Language. In: International Joint Conferences on Artificial Intelligence, pp. 733–740. Morgan Kaufmann Publishers, San Francisco (2001)
26. Rutten, J., Kwaiatkowska, M., Normal, G., Parker, D.: Mathematical Techniques for Analyzing Concurrent and Probabilisitc Systems. CRM Monograph, 23, (2004)
27. SAS. (2007) http://sas.com/technologies/analytics/statistics/stat/index.html
28. SPSS (2007) http://www.spss.com/

UTP Semantics for Web Services

He Jifeng*

Software Engineering Institute
East China Normal University, Shanghai

Abstract. Web services are increasingly being applied in solving many universal interoperability problems. Business Process Execution Language (BPEL) is a de facto standard for specifying the behaviour of business process. It contains several interesting features, including scope-based compensation, fault handling and shared label synchronisation. This paper presents a design-based formalism for specifying the behaviour of Web services, and provides new healthiness conditions to capture these new programming features. The new models for handling fault and compensation are built as conservative extension of the standard relational model in the sense that the algebraic laws presented in [14] remain valid. The paper also discusses the links between the new model with the design model, and shows that programs can be transformed to the normal forms within the algebraic framework.

1 Introduction

With the development of the Internet Technology, Web services and Web-based applications increasingly play an important role in information systems. The aim of Web services is to achieve universal interoperability between different WEb-based applications. In recent years, various business modelling languages have been in troduced. such as XLANG [24], WSFL [15] and BPEL [9] and StAC [7]. BPEL is to be a standard for describing the behaviour of a business process based on interactions between the process and its partner [9]. It contains several interesting features, including compensation and fault handling, which can be used to deal with business transactions. To ensure the correct development of service-based systems, the precise understanding of the language features is apparently important.

Compensation is one of typical features for long-running transactions. Butler introduced Compensating CSP to describe this feature and also provided a trace semantics [6,7,8] In [4,5], Bruni discussed the StAC [6] programs, and invented a process calculi in the form of Java API, namely Java Transactional Web Services. Qiu investigated the fault behaviour of the BPEL-like processes [22]. In [21], Pu formalised an operational semantics for BPEL, where the bisimulation technique was adopted to relate programs with their specifications.

---

* This work was supported by the National Basic Research Program of China (Grant No. 2005CB321904).

J. Davies and J. Gibbons (Eds.): IFM 2007, LNCS 4591, pp. 353–372, 2007.
© Springer-Verlag Berlin Heidelberg 2007

The π-calculus has been applied in describing various Web service models. Lucchi and Mazzara formalised the semantics of BPEL within the framework of the π-calculus [18]. Laneve and Zavattaro explored the application of the π-calculus in the formalisation of the transactional constructs of BPEL and the standard pattern of Web service compisition [16]. Gordon and Pucella validated a Web service security abstraction using the spi calculus [1,11].

This paper is an attempt at taking a step forward to gain some perspectives on service-oriented languages within the design calculus [14] as well as to identify the links among various models for the following language features

- Fault handling
- Compensation mechanism
- Transaction

Our contributions include

- providing a conservative extension of the standard relational model to deal with fault handling and compensation, which can be characterised by additional halthiness conditions.
- expanding the algebraic system for the Guarded Command Language [10] by adding new left zero laws to support the normal form reduction.
- constructing a Galois connection (retract) to link the new model with the design model.

The paper is organised as follows: Section 2 introduces a new healthiness condition into the design calculs to deal with fault handling. Section 3 provides an observation-oriented semantics for a simple imperative language with fault handling mechanism. Section 4 explores the Galois link between this model with the design model. We examine a language with the compensation mechanism. in Section 5. Section 6 is devoted to a transaction-based language. The paper concludes with a short discussion on the linking theories.

In the rest of this section we introduce some notations which will be used in the later discussion.

Definition 1.1 (Merge)

Let P and Q be designs. The notation $P \oplus Q$ denotes the program which merges the outcomes of P and Q.

$$P \oplus Q \ =_{df} \ \mathbf{if}(\mathbf{pre}.P \to P, \ \mathbf{pre}.Q \to Q)\mathbf{fi}$$

where $\mathbf{pre}.P \ =_{df} \ \neg P[true, \ false/ok, \ ok']$.

Theorem 1.1

$$(b \vdash S) \oplus (c \vdash T) \ =_{df} \ (b \vee c) \vdash (b \wedge S \vee c \wedge T)$$

$\oplus$ is idempotent, symmetric and associative. It distributes over both nondeterministic choice and conditional.

Theorem 1.2

(1) $P \sqcap (Q \oplus R) = (P \sqcap Q) \oplus (P \sqcap R)$

(2) $(P \lhd e \rhd Q) \oplus R = (P \oplus R) \lhd e \rhd (Q \oplus R)$

(3) $(P \oplus Q) \lhd b \rhd R = (P \lhd b \rhd R) \oplus (Q \lhd b \rhd R)$

Proof. Let $P =_{df} (b \vdash S)$ and $Q =_{df} (c \vdash T)$ and $R =_{df} (d \vdash U)$.

$$
\begin{array}{lll}
(1) \quad LHS & & \{\text{Def of } \oplus\} \\
\quad = P \sqcap (c \lor d) \vdash (c \land T \lor d \land U) & & \{\text{def of } \sqcap\} \\
\quad = (b \land (c \lor d)) \vdash (b \land S) \lor (c \land T) \lor (d \land U) & & \{\text{Ordering of designs}\} \\
\quad = b \land (c \lor d) \vdash & & \\
\qquad (b \land (c \lor d) \land S \lor (b \land c) \land T \lor b \land d \land U) & & \{\text{Def of } \oplus\} \\
\quad = (b \land c) \vdash (S \lor T) \oplus (b \land d) \vdash (S \lor U) & & \{\text{def of } \sqcap\} \\
\quad = RHS & &
\end{array}
$$

Definition 1.2

Designs $b \vdash S$ and $c \vdash T$ are domain-disjoint if $b \land c = false$.

Theorem 1.3

If P and Q are domain-disjoint, then

(1) $P \oplus Q = P \sqcup Q$

(2) $(P \oplus Q); R = (P; R) \oplus (Q; R)$

Proof

$$
\begin{array}{lll}
(1) \, RHS & & \{\text{Refinement calculus}\} \\
= (b \lor c) \vdash ((b \Rightarrow S) \land (c \Rightarrow T)) & & \{\text{ordering of designs}\} \\
= b \lor c \vdash (b \lor c) \land (\neg c \land S \lor \neg b \land T) & & \{b \land c = false\} \\
= LHS & &
\end{array}
$$

$$
\begin{array}{lll}
(2) \, LHS & & \{\text{def of } \oplus\} \\
= (b \lor c) \vdash (b \land S \lor c \land T); R & & \{\text{refinement calculus}\} \\
= (b \lor c) \land \neg((b \land S \lor c \land T); \neg d) \vdash (b \land S \lor c \land T); U & & \{b \land c = false\} \\
= b \land (\neg(b \land S); \neg d) \lor c \land \neg((c \land T); \neg d) \vdash & & \\
\quad (b \land S \lor c \land T); U & & \{\text{def of } \oplus\} \\
= b \land \neg((b \land S); \neg d) \vdash (b \land S); U \oplus & & \\
\quad c \land \neg(c \land T); \neg d)) \vdash (c \land T); U & & \{\text{refinement calculus}\} \\
= RHS & &
\end{array}
$$

Theorem 1.4

If $R = true \vdash U$, then $(P \oplus Q); R = (P; R) \oplus (Q; R)$

2 A Model for Fault Handling

In this section we work towards a precise characterisation of the class of *designs* [14] that are most useful in fault handling. As usual, we follow the standard practice of mathematics, which is to classify the basic concepts by their most important properties. The classification of the basic concepts of a design is essential to our goal of unifying theories of programming.

A subclass of designs may be defined in a variety of ways. Sometimes it is done by a syntactic property. Sometimes the definition requires satisfaction of a particular collection of algebraic laws. In general, the most useful definitions are these that are given in many different forms, together with a proof that all of them are equivalent.

To handling fault cases requires a more explicit analysis of the phenomena of program execution. We therefore introduce into the alphabet of our designs a pair of Boolean variables to denote the relevant observations.

Definition 2.1 ($eflag$ and $eflag'$)

$eflag$ records the observation that the program is asked to start when the execution of its predcessor halts due to an occurrence of error.
$eflag'$ records the observation that an error occurs during the execution of the program.

The variables $eflag$ and $eflag'$ are not global variables held in the store of any program, and it is assumed that they will never be mentioned in any expression or assignment of the program text.

The introduction of error states has implication for sequential composition: all the exception cases of program P are of course also the exception cases of $P; Q$. Control can pass P to Q only when P terminates successfully. Rather than change the definition of sequential composition given in [14], we enforce these rules by means a healthiness condition. If the program Q is asked to start in an exception case of its predecessor, it leaves the state unchanged

$(\mathbf{Req_1})\ Q\ =\ II \lhd eflag \rhd Q$

when the design II adopts the following definition

$$II =_{df}\ true \vdash ((v' = v) \land (eflag' = eflag))$$

A design is $\mathbf{Req_1}$-healthy if it satisfies the healthiness condition $\mathbf{Req_1}$.

Theorem 2.1

$\mathbf{Req_1}$-healthy designs form a complete lattice.

Proof. Clearly the mapping $\mathcal{H}_1 =_{df} \lambda Q \bullet (II \lhd eflag \rhd Q)$ is monotonic. The conclusion follows from Tarski's Fixed Point Theorem [23].

The following theorem indicates $\mathbf{Req_1}$-healthy designs are closed under conventional programming combinators.

Theorem 2.2

(1) $\mathcal{H}_1(P \sqcap Q)\ =\ \mathcal{H}_1(P) \sqcap \mathcal{H}_1(Q)$

(2) $\mathcal{H}_1(P \triangleleft b \triangleright Q) = \mathcal{H}_1(P) \triangleleft b \triangleright \mathcal{H}_1(Q)$

(3) $\mathcal{H}_1(P; \mathcal{H}_1(Q)) = \mathcal{H}_1(P); \mathcal{H}_1(Q)$

Proof of (3) RHS {; distributes over cond}

$\qquad = \mathcal{H}_1(Q) \triangleleft eflag \triangleright (P; \mathcal{H}_1(Q))$ {Cond is associative}

$\qquad = II \triangleleft eflag \triangleright (P; \mathcal{H}_1(Q))$ {Def of $\mathcal{H}_1$}

$\qquad = LHS$

The basic concept of a **Req$_1$**-healthy design deserves a notation of its own.

Definition 2.2

Let b_1 and b_2 be Boolean expressions of program variables, and R_1 and R_2 predicates not containing $eflag$ or $eflag'$. Define

$$\begin{pmatrix} b_1 \\ b_2 \end{pmatrix} \Vdash \begin{pmatrix} R_1 \\ R_2 \end{pmatrix} =_{df} \mathcal{H}_1 \begin{pmatrix} (b_1 \vdash R_1); \mathbf{succ}_1 \oplus \\ (b_2 \vdash R_2); \mathbf{fail}_1 \end{pmatrix}$$

where

$$\mathbf{succ}_1 =_{df} true \vdash (v' = v \wedge \neg eflag')$$

$$\mathbf{fail}_1 =_{df} true \vdash (v' = v \wedge eflag')$$

This predicate states that

- if the program starts in a state satisfying b_1, it will terminate successfully, and on termination R_1 will hold.
- if it is activated in a state satisfying b_2, an error may occur during its execution and R_2 will be true when the program terminates.

Theorem 2.3

$$\begin{pmatrix} b_1 \\ b_2 \end{pmatrix} \Vdash \begin{pmatrix} R_1 \\ R_2 \end{pmatrix} = \mathcal{H}_1 \left((b_1 \vee b_2) \vdash \begin{pmatrix} (b_1 \wedge R_1) \\ \triangleleft \neg eflag' \triangleright \\ (b_2 \wedge R_2) \end{pmatrix} \right)$$

In the interpretation of programs and specifications as single predicates, correctness is identified with implication. In the refinement calculus, the corresponding ordering is known as refinement. The following theorem shows that the two ordering are the same. The notation $P[e, f/x, y]$ denotes the result of simultaneously substituting e for x and f for y in P.

Theorem 2.4 (Ordering)

Let $P = \begin{pmatrix} b_1 \\ b_2 \end{pmatrix} \Vdash \begin{pmatrix} R_1 \\ R_2 \end{pmatrix}$ and $Q = \begin{pmatrix} c_1 \\ c_2 \end{pmatrix} \Vdash \begin{pmatrix} S_1 \\ S_2 \end{pmatrix}$.

$P \sqsupseteq Q$ iff

$[c \Rightarrow b]$ **and** $[(c \wedge b_1 \wedge R_1) \Rightarrow (c_1 \wedge S_1)]$ **and** $[(c \wedge b_2 \wedge R_2) \Rightarrow (c_2 \wedge S_2)]$

where $b =_{df} b_1 \vee b_2$ and $c =_{df} c_1 \vee c_2$.

3 Programming Language

Definition 3.1 (Chaos)

The chaotic program $\perp$ is defined as usual

$$\mathbf{beh}_1(\perp) \ =_{df} \ \mathcal{H}_1(true)$$

Theorem 3.1 (Left zero)

If Q is a $\mathbf{Req}_1$-healthy design, then $\perp; Q \ = \ \perp$

Proof. From Theorem 2.2(3).

There is a class of programs which never end the execution with a meaningful outcome. The assignment $x := 1/0$ belongs to this category.

Definition 3.2 (halt)

We use the notation halt to denote the program which always throws an error case, and leaves all variables unchanged.

$$\mathbf{beh}_1(\mathtt{halt}) \ =_{df} \ \begin{pmatrix} false \\ true \end{pmatrix} \Vdash \begin{pmatrix} x' = x \wedge y' = y \wedge .. \wedge z' = z \\ x' = x \wedge y' = y \wedge ... \wedge z' = z \end{pmatrix}$$

Theorem 3.2 (Algebraic characterisation of $\mathbf{Req}_1$-healthy)

A design P is $\mathbf{Req}_1$-healthy iff it satisfies the left zero law

$$\mathtt{halt}; P \ = \ \mathtt{halt}$$

Proof. Assume that P is a $\mathbf{Req}_1$-healthy design:

$\mathtt{halt}; P$	{Def of halt}
$= \mathtt{halt}; (eflag)_\perp; P$	{; distributes over cond}
$= \mathtt{halt}; (P \lhd eflag \rhd \perp)$	{assumption}
$= \mathtt{halt}; ((II \lhd eflag \rhd P) \lhd eflag \rhd \mathtt{chaos})$	{cond is assoc}
$= \mathtt{halt}; (eflag)_\perp$	{Def of halt}
$= \mathtt{halt}$	

Suppose that P is a design satisfying the left zero law

P	{the left unit law}
$= \mathtt{skip}; P$	{Def of skip}
$= (\mathtt{halt} \lhd eflag \rhd \mathtt{skip}); P$	{; distributes over cond}
$= (\mathtt{halt}; P) \lhd eflag \rhd (\mathtt{skip}; P)$	{assumption}
$= \mathtt{halt} \lhd eflag \rhd P$	{Def of halt}
$= \mathtt{skip} \lhd eflag \rhd P$	

The nonderterminic choice and sequential composition have exactly the same meaning as operators on the single predicates defined in [14].

Theorem 3.3

Let $b = b_1 \vee b_2$ and $c = c_1 \vee c_2$. Then

(1) $\begin{pmatrix} b_1 \\ b_2 \end{pmatrix} \Vdash \begin{pmatrix} S_1 \\ S_2 \end{pmatrix} \sqcap \begin{pmatrix} c_1 \\ c_2 \end{pmatrix} \Vdash \begin{pmatrix} T_1 \\ T_2 \end{pmatrix} =$

$\begin{pmatrix} b_1 \wedge c \vee c_1 \wedge b \\ b_2 \wedge c \vee c_2 \wedge b \end{pmatrix} \Vdash \begin{pmatrix} b_1 \wedge S_1 \vee c_1 \wedge T_1 \\ b_2 \wedge S_2 \vee c_1 \wedge T_2 \end{pmatrix}$

(2) $\begin{pmatrix} b_1 \\ b_2 \end{pmatrix} \Vdash \begin{pmatrix} S_1 \\ S_2 \end{pmatrix} ; \begin{pmatrix} c_1 \\ c_2 \end{pmatrix} \Vdash \begin{pmatrix} T_1 \\ T_2 \end{pmatrix} =$

$\begin{pmatrix} b_1 \wedge \neg(R_1; \neg c) \\ b_1 \wedge \neg(R_1; \neg c) \vee b_2 \end{pmatrix} \Vdash \begin{pmatrix} S_1; (c_1 \wedge T_1) \\ b_1 \wedge \neg(S_1; \neg c) \wedge (R_1; (c_2 \wedge T_2)) \vee b_2 \wedge S_2 \end{pmatrix}$

(3) $\begin{pmatrix} b_1 \\ b_2 \end{pmatrix} \Vdash \begin{pmatrix} S_1 \\ S_2 \end{pmatrix} \lhd d \rhd \begin{pmatrix} c_1 \\ c_2 \end{pmatrix} \Vdash \begin{pmatrix} T_1 \\ T_2 \end{pmatrix} =$

$\begin{pmatrix} b_1 \lhd d \rhd c_1 \\ b_2 \lhd d \rhd c_2 \end{pmatrix} \Vdash \begin{pmatrix} S_1 \lhd d \rhd T_1 \\ S_2 \lhd d \rhd T_2 \end{pmatrix}$

The definition of the assignment needs to take into account the possibility that evalation of the expression is undefined..

Definition 3.3 (Assignment)

For each expression e of a reasonable programming language, it is possible to calculate a condition $\mathcal{D}(e)$, which is true in just those circumstances in which e can be successfully evaluated [20]. For example

$$\begin{aligned}
\mathcal{D}(17) &= true \\
\mathcal{D}(true) &= \mathcal{D}(false) = true \\
\mathcal{D}(b \vee c) &= \mathcal{D}(b) \wedge \mathcal{D}(c) \\
\mathcal{D}(x) &= true \\
\mathcal{D}(e + f) &= \mathcal{D}(e) \wedge \mathcal{D}(f) \\
\mathcal{D}(e/f) &= \mathcal{D}(e) \wedge \mathcal{D}(f) \wedge f \neq 0 \\
\mathcal{D}(e \lhd b \rhd f) &= (b \Rightarrow \mathcal{D}(e)) \wedge (\neg b \Rightarrow \mathcal{D}(f)) \quad \text{if } b \text{ is well-defined}
\end{aligned}$$

For any expression e, $\mathcal{D}(e)$ is a well-defined Boolean expressuion.

Successful execution of an assignment relies on the assumption that the expression will be successfully evaluated. So we formulate our definition of assignment

$$\mathbf{beh}_1(x := e) =_{df} \begin{pmatrix} \mathcal{D}(e) \\ \neg \mathcal{D}(e) \end{pmatrix} \Vdash \begin{pmatrix} x' = e \wedge y' = y \wedge .. \wedge z' = z \\ x' = x \wedge y' = y \wedge ... \wedge z' = z \end{pmatrix}$$

Expressed in words, this definition states that

- Either the initial values of the variables are such that evaluation of e fails ($\neg\mathcal{D}(e)$), and the execution halts with all variables unchanged.
- or the program terminates successfully, and the value of x' is e, and the final values of all the other variables are the same as their initial values.

The following laws express the basic properties of assignment: that variables not mentioned on the left of := remain unchanged, that the order of the listing is immaterial.

Theorem 3.4 (Algebraic laws for assignment)

(1) $(x := e) = (x, y := e, y)$

(2) $(x, y, z := e, f, g) = (y, x, z, := f, e, g)$

Guarded choice is defined as usual, and will be shown as the finite normal form in the later discussion.

Definition 3.4 (Guarded choice)

Let $\{b_i \mid 1 \le i \le n\}$ be a set of boolean expressions, and $\{P_i \mid 1 \le i \le n\}$ a set of programs.

$$\mathbf{beh}_1(\mathbf{if}\, b_1 \to P_1, .., b_n \to P_n\, \mathbf{fi}) =_{df} \begin{pmatrix} \bigvee_i (b_i \wedge \mathcal{D}(b) \wedge P_i) \,\vee \\ (\bigwedge_i \neg b_i) \wedge \mathcal{D}(b) \wedge \bot \,\vee \\ \neg\mathcal{D}(b) \wedge \mathtt{halt} \end{pmatrix}$$

The following theorem enables us to focus on the guarded choices with well-defined boolean guards in the rest of this section.

Theorem 3.5

$\mathbf{if}(b_1 \to P_1, ..., b_n \to P_n)\mathbf{fi} =$

$\mathbf{if}((b_1 \lhd \mathcal{D}(b) \rhd false) \to P_1, .., (b_n \lhd \mathcal{D}(b) \rhd false) \to P_n, \neg\mathcal{D}(b) \to \mathtt{halt})\mathbf{fi}$

The next theorem collects a set of well-known algebraic laws for guarded choice, which will be used in the normal form reduction later.

Theorem 3.6

(1) $\mathbf{if}(b_1 \to P_1, .., b_n \to P_n)\mathbf{fi} = \mathbf{fi}(b_{\pi(1)} \to P_{\pi(1)}, .. b_{\pi(n)} \to P_{\pi(n)})\mathbf{fi}$

where π is any permutation of the list $\{1, 2, .., n\}$.

(2) $\mathbf{if}(b \to P, b \to Q, \underline{G})\mathbf{fi} = \mathbf{if}(b \to (P \sqcap Q), \underline{G})\mathbf{fi} =$
$\quad \mathbf{if}(b \to P, \underline{G})\mathbf{fi} \sqcap \mathbf{if}(b \to Q, \underline{G})\mathbf{fi}$

(3) $\mathbf{if}(b_1 \to P_1, .., b_n \to P_n)\mathbf{fi}; Q = \mathbf{if}(b_1 \to (P_1; Q), .., b_n \to (P_n; Q))\mathbf{fi}$

(4) $\mathbf{if}(b \to \mathbf{if}(c_1 \to Q_1, .., c_n \to Q_n)\mathbf{fi}, \underline{G})\mathbf{fi} =$
$\quad \mathbf{if}(b \wedge c_1 \to Q_1, ..., b \wedge c_n \to Q_n, \underline{G})\mathbf{fi}$ provided that $\bigvee_i c_i = true$

(5) $\mathbf{if}(b \to P, c \to P, \underline{G})\mathbf{fi} = \mathbf{if}((b \vee c) \to P, \underline{G})\mathbf{fi}$

(6) $\mathbf{if}(false \to P, \underline{G})\mathbf{fi} = \mathbf{if}(\underline{G})\mathbf{fi}$

(7) $\mathbf{if}()\mathbf{fi} = \bot$

(8) $\mathbf{if}(b_1 \rightarrow P_1, .., b_n \rightarrow P_n)\mathbf{fi}$ $=$ $\mathbf{if}(b_1 \rightarrow P_1, .., b_n \rightarrow P_n, \bigwedge_i \neg b_i \rightarrow \bot))\mathbf{fi}$

(9) P $=$ $\mathbf{if}(true \rightarrow P)\mathbf{fi}$

Conditional choice is a special kind of guarded choice.

$$P \lhd b \rhd Q =_{df} \mathbf{if}(b \rightarrow P, \neg b \rightarrow Q)\mathbf{fi}$$

Definition 3.5 (Total assignment)

An assignment is a total one if all the variables of the program appear on the left hand side in some standard order

$$x, y, .., z := e, f, .., g$$

and all the expressions on the right hand side are well-defined.

Total assignments satisfy the algebraic laws given in [14], for example

Theorem 3.7 (Algebraic laws for total assignment)

(1) $\mathtt{skip} = (v := v)$

(2) $(v := e\,;\, v := f) = (v := f(e))$

$$\text{(3)}\; v := e;\, \mathbf{if} \begin{pmatrix} b_1(v) \rightarrow P_1, \\ .., \\ b_n(v) \rightarrow P_n \end{pmatrix} \mathbf{fi} = \mathbf{if} \begin{pmatrix} b_1(e) \rightarrow (v := e; P_1), \\ ..., \\ b_n(e) \rightarrow (v := e; P_n) \end{pmatrix} \mathbf{fi}$$

We can transform an assignment into a total one by using guarded choice.

Theorem 3.8

$$x := e = \mathbf{if} \begin{pmatrix} \mathcal{D}(e) \rightarrow x := (e \lhd \mathcal{D}(e) \rhd x), \\ \neg \mathcal{D}(e) \rightarrow \mathtt{halt} \end{pmatrix} \mathbf{fi}$$

In the following we will use $v := e$ to denote a total assignment. The following laws enable us to merge alternatives of a guarded choice.

Theorem 3.9

(1) $\mathbf{if}(b \rightarrow v := e,\, c \rightarrow v := f,\, \underline{G})\mathbf{fi} =$

$\mathbf{if}(b \vee c \rightarrow (v := (e \lhd b \rhd (f \lhd c \rhd v)) \sqcap v := (f \lhd c \rhd (e \lhd b \rhd v))),\, \underline{G})\mathbf{fi}$

(2) $\mathbf{if}(b \rightarrow v := e; \mathtt{halt},\, c \rightarrow v := f; \mathtt{halt},\, \underline{G})\mathbf{fi} =$

$\mathbf{if}(b \vee c \rightarrow (v := (e \lhd b \rhd (f \lhd c \rhd v)) \sqcap v := (f \lhd c \rhd (e \lhd b \rhd v))); \mathtt{halt},\, \underline{G})\mathbf{fi}$

Definition 3.6 (Finite normal form)

A finite normal form has the following structure

$$\mathbf{if}\, (b \rightarrow \sqcap_i(v := e_i),\, c \rightarrow \sqcap_j(v := f_j); \mathtt{halt})\, \mathbf{fi}$$

where
- b and c are well-defined.
- all assignments are total assignment.

Theorem 3.10 (Normal form reduction)

Any finite program can be transformed into a normal form using the laws given previously.

Proof. First we show how to convert primitive commands into normal form.

(1) Chaos:

$$\bot \qquad\qquad\qquad\qquad \{\text{Theorem 3.6(7)}\}$$

$$= \mathbf{if}()\mathbf{fi} \qquad\qquad\qquad\qquad \{\text{Theorem 3.6(6)}\}$$

$$= \mathbf{if}(false \to v := v,\ false \to v := v; \mathtt{halt})\mathbf{fi}$$

(2) Halt:

$$\mathtt{halt} \qquad\qquad\qquad\qquad \{\text{Theorem 3.6(9)}\}$$

$$= \mathbf{if}(true \to \mathtt{halt})\mathbf{fi} \qquad\qquad\qquad\qquad \{\text{Theorem 3.6(6)}\}$$

$$= \mathbf{if}(false \to v := v,\ true \to \mathtt{halt})\mathbf{fi} \qquad\qquad\qquad\qquad \{\text{left unit}\}$$

$$= \mathbf{if}(false \to v := v,\ true \to (v := v; \mathtt{halt}))\mathbf{fi}$$

(3) Assignment:

$$x := e \qquad\qquad\qquad\qquad \{\text{Theorem 3.8}\}$$

$$= \mathbf{if}(\mathcal{D}(e) \to x := e \lhd \mathcal{D}(e) \rhd x,\ \neg\mathcal{D}(e) \to \mathtt{halt})\mathbf{fi} \qquad\qquad\qquad\qquad \{\text{Theorem 3.4}\}$$

$$= \mathbf{if}(\mathcal{D}(e) \to x, y, .., z := e \lhd \mathcal{D}(e) \rhd x, y, ..., z,$$

$$\neg\mathcal{D}(e) \to \mathtt{halt})\mathbf{fi}$$

In the following we show how to eliminate programming combinators betwen normal forms.

(4) Nondeterministic choice.

$$\mathbf{if}\begin{pmatrix} b_1 \to \sqcap_i(v := e_i), \\ b_2 \to \sqcap_j(v := f_j); \mathtt{halt} \end{pmatrix}\mathbf{fi} \sqcap$$

$$\mathbf{if}\begin{pmatrix} c_1 \to \sqcap_l(v := g_l), \\ c_2 \to \sqcap_m(v := h_m); \mathtt{halt} \end{pmatrix}\mathbf{fi} \qquad\qquad \{\text{Theorem 3.6(2), (9)}\}$$

$$= \mathbf{if}\begin{pmatrix} true \to \mathbf{if}\begin{pmatrix} b_1 \to \sqcap_i(v := e_i), \\ b_2 \to \sqcap_j(v := f_j); \mathtt{halt} \end{pmatrix}\mathbf{fi}, \\ true \to \mathbf{if}\begin{pmatrix} c_1 \to \sqcap_l(v := g_l), \\ c_2 \to \sqcap_m(v := g_m); \mathtt{halt} \end{pmatrix}\mathbf{fi} \end{pmatrix}\mathbf{fi} \qquad \{\text{Theorem 3.6(4), (8)}\}$$

$$= \mathbf{if}\begin{pmatrix} b_1 \to \sqcap_i(v := e_i),\ c_1 \to \sqcap_l(v := g_l), \\ b_2 \to \sqcap_j(v := f_j); \mathtt{halt},\ c_2 \to \sqcap_m(v := g_m); \mathtt{halt}, \\ \neg c \to \bot,\ \neg b \to \bot \end{pmatrix}\mathbf{fi} \quad \{\text{Theorem 3.6(1), (2)}\}$$

$$= \sqcap_{i,\,j,\,l,\,m}\mathbf{if}\begin{pmatrix} b_1 \to (v := e_i),\ c_1 \to (v := g_l), \\ b_2 \to (v := f_j); \mathtt{halt},\ c_2 \to (v := g_m); \mathtt{halt}, \\ \neg c \to \bot,\ \neg b \to \bot \end{pmatrix}\mathbf{fi} \qquad \{\text{Theorem 3.9}\}$$

$$= \sqcap_{i,j,l,m}\mathbf{if}((b_1 \vee c_1) \to \begin{pmatrix} (v := (e_i \lhd b_1 \rhd (g_l \lhd c_1 \rhd v))) \sqcap \\ v := (g_l \lhd c_1 \rhd (e_i \lhd b_1 \rhd v))) \end{pmatrix},$$

$$(b_2 \vee c_2) \to \begin{pmatrix} ((v := f_j \lhd b_2 \rhd (h_m \lhd c_2 \rhd v))) \sqcap \\ ((v := h_m \lhd c_2 \rhd (f_j \lhd b_2 \rhd v))) \end{pmatrix}; \mathbf{halt})\mathbf{fi} \quad \{\text{Theorem 3.6(2), (8)}\}$$

$$= \mathbf{if}((b_1 \wedge c \vee c_1 \wedge b) \to$$

$$\sqcap_{i,j} \begin{pmatrix} (v := (e_i \lhd b_1 \rhd (g_l \lhd c_1 \rhd v))) \sqcap \\ (v := (g_l \lhd c_1 \rhd (e_i \lhd b_1 \rhd v))) \end{pmatrix},$$

$$(b_2 \wedge c \vee c_2 \wedge b) \to$$

$$\sqcap_{j,m} \begin{pmatrix} (v := f_j \lhd b_2 \rhd (h_m \lhd c_2 \rhd v)) \sqcap \\ (v := h_m \lhd c_2 \rhd (f_j \lhd b_2 \rhd v)) \end{pmatrix}; \mathbf{halt})\mathbf{fi}$$

(5) Composition: From (4) we are only required to consider the case $P; Q$ where

$$P = \mathbf{if}(b_1 \to v := e, \, b_2 \to v := f; \mathbf{halt})\mathbf{fi}$$

$$Q = \mathbf{if}(c_1(v) \to v := g(v), \, c_2(v) \to v := h(v); \mathbf{halt})\mathbf{fi}$$

$P; Q$ {Theorem 3.1 and 3.6(3)}

$$= \mathbf{if} \begin{pmatrix} b_1 \to (v := e); Q, \\ b_2 \to (v := f); \mathbf{halt} \end{pmatrix} \mathbf{fi} \quad\quad\quad \{\text{Theorem 3.7(2), (3)}\}$$

$$= \mathbf{if} \begin{pmatrix} b_1 \to \mathbf{if} \begin{pmatrix} c_1(e) \to (v := g(e)) \\ c_2(e) \to (v := h(e); \mathbf{halt}) \end{pmatrix} \mathbf{fi} \\ b_2 \to (v := f); \mathbf{halt} \end{pmatrix} \quad \{\text{Theorem 3.6(4), (8)}\}$$

$$= \mathbf{if} \begin{pmatrix} b_1 \wedge c_1(e) \to (v := g(e)) \\ b_1 \wedge c_2(e) \to (v := h(e); \mathbf{halt}) \\ b_1 \to \neg c(e) \to \bot \\ b_2 \to (v := f); \mathbf{halt} \end{pmatrix}$$

from which and Theorem 3.9 follows the conclusion.

(6) Guarded choice: From (4) and Theorem 3.6(2) we will only examine the case $\mathbf{if}(c_1 \to P_1, .., c_n \to P_n)\mathbf{fi}$ where

$$P_i = \mathbf{if}(b_1^i \to (v := e_i), \, b_2^i \to (v := f_i; \mathbf{halt}))\mathbf{fi}$$

Let $b^i = (b_1^i \vee b_2^i$.

$\mathbf{if}(c_1 \to P_1, .., c_n \to P_n)\mathbf{fi}$ {Theorem 3.6(4), (8)}

$$= \mathbf{if} \begin{pmatrix} c_1 \wedge b_1^1 \to (v := e_1), \\ c_1 \wedge b_2^1 \to (v := f_1; \mathbf{halt}), \\ c_1 \wedge \neg b^1 \to \bot, \\ ... \\ c_n \wedge b_1^n \to (v := e_n), \\ c_n \wedge b_2^n \to (v := f_n; \mathbf{halt}), \\ c_n \wedge \neg b^n \to \bot, \end{pmatrix} \mathbf{fi}$$

from which and Theorem 3.9 follows the conclusion.

4   Link with the Design Calculus

This section discusses the relationship between the design calculus in [14] with
the refinement calculs for fault handling. We will show there exists a retract to
link these two calculi.

First we define a mapping $\mathcal{G}_1$ from design to $\mathbf{Req}_1$-healthy designs:

$$\mathcal{G}_1(D) \ =_{df} \ \mathcal{H}_1(D \parallel (true \vdash (eflag' = eflag)))$$

where $\parallel$ stands for disjoint parallel combinator [14]:

$$(b \vdash R)\parallel(c \vdash S) \ =_{df} \ (b \wedge c) \vdash (R \wedge S)$$

Theorem 4.1

$$\mathcal{G}_1(b \vdash R) \ = \ \begin{pmatrix} b \\ false \end{pmatrix} \models \begin{pmatrix} R \\ false \end{pmatrix}$$

$\quad LHS$ $\hfill$ {Def of disjoint parallel}

$= \mathcal{H}_1(b \vdash (R \wedge eflag' = eflag))$ $\hfill$ {Def of $\mathcal{H}_1$}

$= \mathcal{H}_1(b \vdash R \wedge \neg eflag')$ $\hfill$ {ordering of design calculus}

$= \mathcal{H}_1(b \vdash (b \wedge R \wedge eflag'))$ $\hfill$ {Def 2.2}

$= RHS$

$\mathcal{G}_1$ distributes over the standard programming combinators.

Theorem 4.2 (Homomorphism)

(1) $\mathcal{G}_1(D_1; D_2) \ = \ \mathcal{G}_1(D_1); \mathcal{G}_1(D_2)$

(2) $\mathcal{G}_1(D_1 \sqcap D_2) \ = \ \mathcal{G}_1(D_1) \sqcap \mathcal{G}_1(D_2)$

(3) $\mathcal{G}_1(D_1 \lhd b \rhd D_2) \ = \ \mathcal{G}_1(D_1) \lhd b \rhd \mathcal{G}_1(D_2)$ provided that b is well-defined.

Now we define a function $\mathcal{F}_1$ which maps a $\mathbf{Req}_1$-healthy design to a design

$$\mathcal{F}_1(P) \ =_{df} \ P[false/eflag]; (\neg eflag \vdash v' = v)$$

Theorem 4.3

$$\mathcal{F}_1\left(\begin{pmatrix} b_1 \\ b_2 \end{pmatrix} \models \begin{pmatrix} R_1 \\ R_2 \end{pmatrix} \right) \ = \ ((b_1 \vee b_2) \wedge \neg(b_2 \wedge R_2; true)) \vdash (b_1 \wedge R_1)$$

Proof. LHS $\hfill$ {Def of $\mathcal{F}_1$}

$\quad = (b_1 \vee b_2) \vdash (b_1 \wedge R_1) \lhd \neg eflag' \rhd (b_2 \wedge R_2) ;$

$\qquad (\neg eflag \vdash (v' = v))$ $\hfill$ {Refinement calculus}

$\quad = RHS$

Corollary. If $[b_2 \Rightarrow \exists v' R_2]$, then

$$\mathcal{F}_1\left(\begin{pmatrix} b_1 \\ b_2 \end{pmatrix} \models \begin{pmatrix} R_1 \\ R_2 \end{pmatrix} \right) \ = \ (b_1 \wedge \neg b_2) \vdash R_1$$

Theorem 4.4

Let $P =_{df} \begin{pmatrix} b_1 \\ b_2 \end{pmatrix} \Vvdash \begin{pmatrix} R_1 \\ R_2 \end{pmatrix}$ and $Q =_{df} \begin{pmatrix} c_1 \\ c_2 \end{pmatrix} \Vvdash \begin{pmatrix} S_1 \\ S_2 \end{pmatrix}$

If $[b_2 \Rightarrow \exists v' \bullet R_2]$ and $[c_2 \Rightarrow \exists v' \bullet S_2]$, then

(1) $\mathcal{F}_1(P \sqcap Q) = \mathcal{F}_1(P) \sqcap \mathcal{F}_1(Q)$

(2) $\mathcal{F}_1(P; Q) = \mathcal{F}_1(P); \mathcal{F}_1(Q)$

(3) $\mathcal{F}_1(P \lhd d \rhd Q) = \mathcal{F}_1(P) \lhd d \rhd \mathcal{F}_1(Q)$ provided that d is well-defined.

Finally we show that the pair $(\mathcal{F}_1, \mathcal{G}_1)$ is a *retract*.

Theorem 4.5 (Retract)

$(\mathcal{F}_1, \mathcal{G}_1)$ is a Galois connection satisfying

(1) $\mathcal{F}_1(\mathcal{G}_1(D)) = D$

(2) $\mathcal{G}_1(\mathcal{F}_1(P)) \sqsubseteq P$

Proof

(1) $\mathcal{F}_1(\mathcal{G}_1(b \vdash R))$ {Theorem 4.1}

$= \mathcal{F}_1\left(\begin{pmatrix} b \\ false \end{pmatrix} \Vvdash \begin{pmatrix} R \\ false \end{pmatrix} \right)$ {Corollary}

$= b \vdash R$

(2) $\mathcal{G}_1(\mathcal{F}_1(P))$ {Theorem 4.3}

$= \mathcal{G}_1((b_1 \vee b_2) \wedge \neg(b_2 \wedge R_2; true) \vdash (b_1 \wedge R_1))$ {Theorem 4.1}

$= \begin{pmatrix} (b_1 \vee b_2) \wedge \neg(b_2 \wedge R_2; true) \\ false \end{pmatrix} \Vvdash \begin{pmatrix} b_1 \wedge R_1 \\ false \end{pmatrix}$ {Theorem 2.3}

$\sqsubseteq P$

5   Rollback

To equip a program with compensation mechanism, it is necessary to characterise the cases when the control has to be passed to the compensation components. Following the line adopted by the fault handling model, we introduce a new logical variable *forward* to describe the status of control flow of the execution of a program:

- *forward'* = *true* indicates successful termination of the execution of the program. In this case, its successor will carry on with the initial state set up by the program.
- *forward'* = *false* indicates the program has to roll back its execution to the original state. In this case, its corresponding compensation module will be invoked.

As a result, when a program Q is asked to start in a state where $forward = false$, it has to remain silent, i.e., Q is required to meet the following healthiness condition:

(Req_2) $Q = II \lhd \neg forward \rhd Q$

This condition can be captured by the following mapping

$$\mathcal{H}_2(Q) =_{df} II \lhd \neg forward \rhd Q$$

in the sense that a program satisfies Req_2 iff it is a fixed point of $\mathcal{H}_2$

Theorem 5.1

$\mathcal{H}_2 \circ \mathcal{H}_1 = \mathcal{H}_1 \circ \mathcal{H}_2$ where $\circ$ denotes functional composition.

Proof. From the fact that

$$\mathcal{H}_1(\mathcal{H}_2(Q)) = II \lhd eflag \vee \neg foward \rhd Q = \mathcal{H}_2(\mathcal{H}_1(Q))$$

Let et $\mathcal{H} =_{df} \mathcal{H}_1 \circ \mathcal{H}_2$.

Theorem 5.2

A design satisfies both Req_1 and Req_2 iff it is a fixed point of $\mathcal{H}$.

Like the mapping $\mathcal{H}_1$, $\mathcal{H}$ is also a homomorphism.

Theorem 5.3

(1) $\mathcal{H}(P \sqcap Q) = \mathcal{H}(P) \sqcap \mathcal{H}(Q)$

(2) $\mathcal{H}(P \lhd b \rhd Q) = \mathcal{H}(P) \lhd b \rhd \mathcal{H}(Q)$

(3) $\mathcal{H}(P; \mathcal{H}(Q)) = \mathcal{H}(P); \mathcal{H}(Q)$

Similar to the Req_1-healthy designs in Section 2, we introduce the following notation to specify both error handling and rollback mechanism. Define

$$\begin{pmatrix} b_1 \\ b_2 \\ b_3 \end{pmatrix} \Vdash \begin{pmatrix} R_1 \\ R_2 \\ R_3 \end{pmatrix} =_{df} \mathcal{H} \begin{pmatrix} (b_1 \vdash R_1); \mathbf{succ} \oplus \\ (b_2 \vdash R_2); \mathbf{fail} \oplus \\ (b_3 \vdash R_3); \mathbf{rollback} \end{pmatrix}$$

where

$$\mathbf{succ} =_{df} (\mathbf{succ}_1 \parallel (true \vdash forward'))$$

$$\mathbf{fail} =_{df} (\mathbf{fail}_1 \parallel (true \vdash forward'))$$

$$\mathbf{rollback} =_{df} true \vdash ((v' = v) \wedge \neg forward')$$

We add a primitive command undo into our language, whose execution gives rise to the change of control flow

$$\mathbf{beh}(\text{undo}) =_{df} \begin{pmatrix} false \\ false \\ true \end{pmatrix} \Vdash \begin{pmatrix} false \\ false \\ v' = v \end{pmatrix}$$

Theorem 5.4

A program Q is a fixed point of $\mathcal{H}$ iff it satisfies the left zero laws

$$\text{undo}; Q = \text{undo} \quad \text{and} \quad \text{halt}; Q = \text{halt}$$

The definitions of the programming language of Section 3 remain the same except that we have to take $\mathbf{Req_2}$ into account:

$$\mathbf{beh}(Q) =_{df} \mathcal{H}_2(\mathbf{beh_1}(Q)) \parallel (true \vdash (forward' = forward))$$

The new model preserves all the algebraic laws given in Section 3. Our extended language has a new normal form

Definition 5.1 (Finite normal form)

A finite normal form has the following structure

$$\textbf{if } (b \to \sqcap_i(v := e_i), \; c \to \sqcap_j(v := f_j); \textbf{halt}, \; d \to \sqcap_k(v := g_k); \textbf{undo}) \textbf{ fi}$$

Theorem 5.5 (Normal form reduction)

Any finite program can be transformed into a normal form using the laws given previously.

Proof. Similar to Theorem 3.10.

We define the following mappings to link the new model with the model of Section 2

$$\mathcal{G}_2(P) =_{df} \mathcal{H}_2(P \parallel (true \vdash forward'))$$

$$\mathcal{F}_2(Q) =_{df} Q[true/forward]; (forward \vdash ((v' = v) \wedge (eflag' = eflag)))$$

Theorem 5.6

$$(1) \; \mathcal{F}_2\left(\begin{pmatrix} b_1 \\ b_2 \\ b_3 \end{pmatrix} \Vdash \begin{pmatrix} R_1 \\ R_2 \\ R_3 \end{pmatrix}\right) = \left(\begin{pmatrix} b_1 \wedge \neg b_3 \\ b_2 \wedge \neg b_3 \end{pmatrix} \vdash \begin{pmatrix} R_1 \\ R_2 \end{pmatrix}\right)$$

$$(2) \; \mathcal{G}_2\left(\begin{pmatrix} b_1 \\ b_2 \end{pmatrix} \vdash \begin{pmatrix} R_1 \\ R_2 \end{pmatrix}\right) = \left(\begin{pmatrix} b_1 \\ b_2 \\ false \end{pmatrix} \vdash \begin{pmatrix} R_1 \\ R_2 \\ false \end{pmatrix}\right)$$

Theorem 5.7

$(\mathcal{F}_2, \mathcal{G}_2)$ is a retract, i.e. it is a Galois connection satisfying

(1) $\mathcal{F}_2(\mathcal{G}_2(P)) = P$

(2) $\mathcal{G}_2(\mathcal{F}_2(Q)) \sqsubseteq Q$

6   Compensation

The ability to declare compensation logic alongside forware-working logic is the underpinning of the application-controlled error-handling framework of

WS-BPEL. This section will provide a design-based model for transation which consists of forware activity (for application task) and backward activity (for compensation).

Definition 6.1 (Forward and Backward Activities)

Let P be a design with $forward, forward' \in \alpha(P)$. Its forward activity $\overrightarrow{P}$ and backward activity $\overleftarrow{P}$ are defined by

$$\overrightarrow{P} =_{df} P \lhd forward \rhd II$$

$$\overleftarrow{P} =_{df} II \lhd forward \rhd (P; (\neg forward)_{\perp})$$

The definition states that

1. P exhibits its forward-working behaviour when it is activated with $forward = true$.
2. P performs compensation when $forward$ is false initially. However, this compensation-logic is irreversible.

Theorem 6.1

(1) $\overrightarrow{\overrightarrow{P}} = \overrightarrow{P}$

(2) $\overleftarrow{\overleftarrow{P}} = \overleftarrow{P}$

(3) $\overleftarrow{\overrightarrow{P}} = II = \overrightarrow{\overleftarrow{P}}$

$\rightarrow$ and $\leftarrow$ distribute over the standard programming combinators.

Theorem 6.2

(1) $\overrightarrow{P \sqcap Q} = \overrightarrow{P} \sqcap \overrightarrow{Q}$

(2) $\overrightarrow{P \lhd b \rhd Q} = \overrightarrow{P} \lhd b \rhd \overrightarrow{Q}$

(3) $\overrightarrow{P; Q} = \overrightarrow{P}; \overrightarrow{Q}$

(4) $\overrightarrow{\overrightarrow{P}; Q} = \overrightarrow{P; Q}$

Theorem 6.3

(1) $\overleftarrow{P \sqcap Q} = \overleftarrow{P} \sqcap \overleftarrow{Q}$

(2) $\overleftarrow{P \lhd b \rhd Q} = \overleftarrow{P} \lhd b \rhd \overleftarrow{Q}$

(3) $\overleftarrow{P; Q} = \overleftarrow{P}; \overleftarrow{Q} = \overleftarrow{\overleftarrow{P}; Q}$

The following laws enable us to eliminate the nested $\leftarrow$ and $\rightarrow$

Theorem 6.4

(1) $\overrightarrow{\overleftarrow{P}; Q} \;=\; \overrightarrow{Q}$

(2) $\overleftarrow{\overrightarrow{P}; Q} \;=\; \overleftarrow{Q}$

(3) $\overrightarrow{P}; \overleftarrow{Q} \;=\; \overleftarrow{Q}; \overrightarrow{\overleftarrow{P}; Q}$

Definition 6.2 (Transaction)

T is a transaction if it satisfies

$$T \;=\; \overrightarrow{T} \vartriangleleft forward \vartriangleright \overleftarrow{T}$$

Clearly transactions form a complete lattice.

Theorem 6.5

The set of transactions is closed under conditional and nondeterministic choices.

Definition 6.3 (Chain)

Let P and Q be transactions. Their chain $P \gg Q$ is defined by

$$P \gg Q \;=_{df}\; (\overrightarrow{P}; \overrightarrow{(Q; \overleftarrow{P})}) \vartriangleleft forward \vartriangleright (\overleftarrow{Q}; \overleftarrow{P})$$

Theorem 6.6 (Associativity)

$(P \gg Q) \gg R \;=\; P \gg (Q \gg R)$

Proof. $\overrightarrow{LHS}$ {Def 6.3}

$= \overrightarrow{P \gg Q}\,;\, R; \overleftarrow{P \gg Q}$ {Def 6.3}

$= \overrightarrow{P; Q; \overleftarrow{P}}; R; \overleftarrow{Q}; \overleftarrow{P}$ {Theorem 6.2(4)}

$= \overrightarrow{P; \overrightarrow{Q; \overleftarrow{P}}}; R; \overleftarrow{Q}; \overleftarrow{P}$ {Theorem 6.2(3)}

$= \overrightarrow{P}; (\overrightarrow{Q}; \overleftarrow{P}; \overrightarrow{(R; \overleftarrow{Q}; \overleftarrow{P})})$ {Theorem 6.4(3)}

$= \overrightarrow{P}; (\overrightarrow{Q}; \overrightarrow{(R; \overleftarrow{Q})}; \overleftarrow{P})$ {Theorem 6.2(4)}

$= \overrightarrow{RHS}$

Definition 6.4 (Forward transaction)

T is a forward transaction if its forward-working thread never rolls back its execution:

$$\overrightarrow{T} = \overrightarrow{T}; (forward)_{\perp}$$

Forward transactions form a complete lattice, and are are closed under $\sqcap$, $\triangleleft b \triangleright$ and $>>$.

Theorem 6.7

If P and Q are forward transactions, then

$$P >> Q \; = \; (\overrightarrow{P}; \overrightarrow{Q}) \; \triangleleft forward \triangleright \; (\overleftarrow{Q}; \overleftarrow{P})$$

Theorem 6.8

Let P, Q and R be forward transactions. If $\overleftarrow{P} = \overleftarrow{Q}$, then

(1) $(P \triangleleft b \triangleright Q) >> R \; = \; (P >> R) \triangleleft b \triangleright (Q >> R)$

(2) $(P \sqcap Q) >> R \; = \; (P >> R) \sqcap (Q >> R)$

Definition 6.5 (Parallel)

Let P and Q be transactions with disjoint alphabets. The notation $P \times Q$ denotes the program which runs P and Q in parallel, and rolls back its forware-working activities when either P or Q does so.

$$P \times Q \; =_{df} \; \left(\begin{array}{l} \left(\begin{array}{l} P[ok_1', foward_1', eflag_1'/ok', forward', eflag'] \wedge \\ Q[ok_2', foward_2', eflag_2'/ok', forward', eflag'] \end{array} \right) ; \\ ok_1 \wedge ok_2 \Rightarrow \left(\begin{array}{l} ok' \wedge (v' = v) \\ forward' = forward_1 \wedge forward_2 \\ eflag' = eflag_1 \vee eflag_2 \end{array} \right) \end{array} \right)$$

Theorem 6.9 (Properties)

(1) $P \times Q \; = \; Q \times P$

(2) $P \times (Q \times R) \; = \; (P \times Q) \times R$

(3) $(P \sqcap Q) \times R \; = \; (P \times R) \sqcap (Q \times R)$

(4) $(P \triangleleft b \triangleright Q) \times R \; = \; (P \times R) \triangleleft b \triangleright (Q \times R)$

7   Conclusion

A theory of programming is intended to support the practice of programming by relating each program to the specification of what it is intended to achieve. An unifying theory is one that is applicable to a general paradigm of computing, supporting the classification of many programming languages as correct instances ofthe paradigm. This paper indicates that the UTP approach is effective in the following aspects

- a new model can be built by adding healthiness conditions:

  1. the model of designs is characterised by the left zero law $\bot; P = \bot$ and the unit laws $\mathtt{skip}; P = P = P; \mathtt{skip}$

2. the model of $\mathbf{Req}_1$-healthy designs is captured as a subset of designs that meet the new left zero law $\mathtt{halt}; P = \mathtt{halt}$

3. the model in dealing with compensation is seen as a submodel of the $\mathbf{Req}_1$-healthy designs which satisfies the left zero law $\mathtt{undo}; P = P$.

– we can explore the links among the models by providing the Galois retracts.

– the model extension is ecnomical since the original algebraic laws remain valid.

References

1. Abadi, M., Gordon, A.D.: A calculus for cryptographic protocols: The spi calculus. Information and Computation 148(1), 1–70 (1999)

2. Alonso, G., Kuno, H., Casati, F., et al.: Web Services: Concepts, Architectures and Applications. Springer, Heidelberg (2003)

3. Bhargavan, K., et al.: A Semantics for Web Service Authentication. Theoretical Computer Science 340(1), 102–153 (2005)

4. Bruni, R., Montanari, H.C., Montannari, U.: Theoretical foundation for compensation in flow composition languages. In: Proc. POPL 2005, 32nd ACM SIGPLAN-SIGACT symposium onprinciple of programming languages, pp. 209–220. ACM Press, New York (2004)

5. Bruni, R., et al.: From Theory to Practice in Transactional Composition of Web Services. In: Bravetti, M., Kloul, L., Zavattaro, G. (eds.) Formal Techniques for Computer Systems and Business Processes. LNCS, vol. 3670, pp. 272–286. Springer, Heidelberg (2005)

6. Bulter, M.J., Ferreria, C.: A process compensation language. In: Grieskamp, W., Santen, T., Stoddart, B. (eds.) IFM 2000. LNCS, vol. 1945, pp. 61–76. Springer, Heidelberg (2000)

7. Bulter, M.J., Ferreria, C.: An Operational Semantics for StAC: a Lanuage for Modelling Long-Running Business Transactions. In: De Nicola, R., Ferrari, G.L., Meredith, G. (eds.) COORDINATION 2004. LNCS, vol. 2949, pp. 87–104. Springer, Heidelberg (2004)

8. Butler, M.J., Hoare, C.A.R., Ferreria, C.: A Trace Semantics for Long-Running Transactions. In: Abdallah, A.E., Jones, C.B., Sanders, J.W. (eds.) Communicating Sequential Processes. LNCS, vol. 3525, pp. 133–150. Springer, Heidelberg (2005)

9. Curbera, F., Goland, Y., Klein, J. et al.: Business Process Execution Language for Web Service (2003) http://www.siebei.com/bpel

10. Dijkstra, E.W.: A Discipline of Programming. Prentice-Hall, Englewood Cliffs (1976)

11. Gordon, A.D., et al.: Validating a Web Service Security Abstraction by Typing. Formal Aspect of Computing 17(3), 277–318 (2005)

12. Jifeng, H., Huibiao, Z., Geguang, P. (eds.): A model for BPEL-like languages. Frontiers of Computer Science in China, vol. 1(1), pp. 9–20. Higher Education Press (2007)

13. Hoare, C.A.R.: Communicating Sequential Language. Prentice-Hall, Englewood Cliffs (1985)

14. Hoare, C.A.R., Jifeng, H.: Unifying theories of programming. Prentice-Hall, Englewood Cliffs (1998)

15. Leymann, F.: Web Service Flow Language (WSFL1.0). IBM (2001)

16. Laneve, C., et al.: Web-pi at work. In: De Nicola, R., Sangiorgi, D. (eds.) TGC 2005. LNCS, vol. 3705, pp. 182–194. Springer, Heidelberg (2005)
17. Jing, L., Jifeng, H., Geguang, P.: Towards the Semantics for Web Services Choreography Description Language. In: Liu, Z., He, J. (eds.) ICFEM 2006. LNCS, vol. 4260, pp. 246–263. Springer, Heidelberg (2006)
18. Lucchi, R., Mazzara, M.: A Pi-calculus based semantics for WS-BPEL. Journal of Logic and Algebraic Programming (in press)
19. Milner, R.: Communication and Mobile System: the π-calculus. Cambridge University Press, Cambridge (1999)
20. Morris, J.M.: Non-deterministic expressions and predicate transformers. Information Processing Letters 61, 241–246 (1997)
21. Geguang, P., et al.: Theoretical Foundation of Scope-based Compensation Flow Language for Web Service. In: Ning, P., Qing, S., Li, N. (eds.) ICICS 2006. LNCS, vol. 4307, pp. 251–266. Springer, Heidelberg (2006)
22. Qiu, Z.Y., et al.: Semantics of BPEL4WS-Like Fault and Compensation Handling. In: Fitzgerald, J.A., Hayes, I.J., Tarlecki, A. (eds.) FM 2005. LNCS, vol. 3582, pp. 350–365. Springer, Heidelberg (2005)
23. Tarski, A.: A lattice-theoretical fixpoint theorem and its applications. Pacific Journal of Mathematics 5, 285–309 (1955)
24. Thatte, S.: XLANG: Web Service for Business Process Design. Microsoft (2001)

Combining Mobility with State

Damien Karkinsky, Steve Schneider, and Helen Treharne

Department of Computing, University of Surrey

Abstract. Our work is motivated by practice in Peer-to-Peer networks and Object-Oriented systems where instantiation and dynamically reconfigurable interconnection are essential paradigms. For example, in a Peer-to-Peer network nodes can exchange data to complete tasks. Nodes can leave or join the network at any time. In Object-Oriented systems, an object can be uniquely identified and will communicate with other objects. In this paper we outline a formal framework which supports this kind of interaction so that the integrity of each active object or node is preserved, and so that we can reason about the overall behaviour of the system. The formal framework is based on a combination of the π-calculus and the B-Method.

1 Introduction

Implementations of distributed systems involve setting up a network or networks, managing the communication that occur between the nodes in a network and transferring data between nodes. Networks can be static and comprise a fixed number of nodes or they can be more dynamic in which the number of nodes in a network may vary over time. Peer-to-Peer (P2P) networks are typically large-scale with potentially millions of nodes which join and leave a network regularly; the nodes are autonomous but co-operate to share and retrieve resources. Much of the research conducted in the area of P2P networks has focused on describing possible network architectures [4] and also on simulations to reason about the performance of networks [10]. Orthogonally, the formal methods community has also contributed to reasoning about dynamic distributed systems which can evolve in their architecture but has focused on proving the correctness of their communication protocols. For example, the π-calculus [9] has been used to prove properties of communication protocols and P2P algorithms [2,3]. The research emphasis to date is based on a high level of abstraction of the data being transferred across systems. We are interested in exploring how to specify systems which are dynamic in nature and to ensure the integrity of the data being transferred between nodes. The inherent difficulty with this is that when data is transferred between nodes the receiving node has no control over the data, but may need to make some assumptions about it before it can be used reliably. It is clear that there are two aspects to such a specification: the patterns of behaviour and state information.

The Formal Methods Group at the University of Surrey has been working on developing techniques for specifying and verifying distributed systems so that

J. Davies and J. Gibbons (Eds.): IFM 2007, LNCS 4591, pp. 373–392, 2007.

the patterns of behaviour are made explicit and captured separately from the specification of the data in the system. The approach is referred to as CSP‖B. CSP [6] is a process algebra that is concerned with the evolution of systems as they execute sequences of events. The B Method [1] focuses on defining how the data within a system can be managed through operations.

Early research detailing the CSP‖B approach [15] focused on the sequential aspects of CSP and was concerned with identifying how sequences of events could control the way the data were being updated. Both B and CSP were chosen because they were individually mature notations with strong tool support. The goal in their integration was to preserve the original semantics of both languages whilst building a framework for defining and reasoning about a combined system. The overhead of keeping both descriptions separate is the additional proof obligations that need to be proved for each particular system in order to show that the combined views are consistent. Consistency in the CSP ‖ B approach means demonstrating divergence freedom and deadlock freedom of the process/machines pairs [16,11]. Inappropriate behaviour (such as calling operations outside their preconditions) is modelled as divergence, so divergence freedom is at the core of the approach and this must be established before considering any other safety and liveness properties of interest. The CSP ‖ B approach adopts a particular style of specification constraining the architecture of a system to be static. The data held within B machines are tightly coupled with their corresponding CSP processes, and this relationship is fixed from the outset. Therefore, the approach does not support dynamic reconfiguration.

Our research aim is to model P2P architectures using the π-calculus and B but we begin by developing techniques to support a model of a simplified server-node network. In this paper we explore the use of the π-calculus to describe the dynamic patterns of behaviour of a system and model the data within a system separately using the B method. We use a behavioural type-system with variant types, introduced in [8] and in Section 2, to maintain server/client style interaction between instances of machines and π processes. The interactions enable π processes to call operations of instances of B machines. We provide a proof obligation framework to show that none of these operation calls violate the operations' preconditions. The proof obligation framework is formally underpinned by the π-calculus semantic framework. In order to achieve this formal justification we provided a π operational semantics for B machines in [7], which is informally discussed in this paper. The novelty in the work is that we can verify that the state within a system will always be dynamically transferred in a way which ensures that the operations which manage the state can be called safely.

The paper is organised as follows: Section 2 provides some background notation on B and the π-calculus, Section 3 discusses how to construct combined specifications using B and the π-calculus, Section 4 illustrates the concepts of constructing and verifying a combined specification using a running example, Section 5 defines how to ensure that B machines and π processes are combined in a consistent way, i.e. divergence free, and Section 6 provides a summary, a discussion of related work and future plans.

2   Notation

B specifications are structured into units called *machines*. Each machine contains some *state* describing the data of interest, and *operations* to manipulate the state. A B machine also contains an *invariant* that declares properties of the state variables, and specifies what must be preserved by the execution of operations. The B Toolkit automatically generates *proof obligations* that must be discharged in order to verify that the invariant is preserved.

An operation takes the form **PRE** R **THEN** S **END** where R is a predicate and S represents the statements that update the variables. In CSP ‖ B we use classical B which supports operations with preconditions. In this paper we focus on operations without input and outputs for simplicity, as an initial step towards developing a general framework for combining π with B. We discuss the future incorporation of input/output in operations in Section 6.2.

Following [8], we use variant type extensions to the π-calculus [9]. The π-calculus classifies channels and values as being drawn from a set of names $\mathcal{N}$. A process can be defined in terms of channels and values as follows:

Definition 1

$$P :: = 0 \mid a(w).P \mid \overline{a}\langle w \rangle.P \mid \tau.P \mid$$
$$P_1 + P_2 \mid (P_1 \mid P_2) \mid (\nu\, v)(P) \mid !P$$

The process 0 cannot perform any action. For a channel a, the process $a(w).P$ initially performs an input action where w is bound to the value input along a, and the process $\overline{a}\langle w \rangle.P$ initially performs an output action where the name w is sent along a. The process $\tau.P$ initially performs an internal action. Different processes can be executed using choice and they can execute in parallel. $(\nu\, v)(P)$ creates a new name v with scope P. The replication process $(!P)$ is an unbounded number of Ps running concurrently. We will use free and bound names, and α-renaming in the usual way. In the syntax, the binding constructs are the ν operator and input prefix $a(w)$.

The behavioural type system in [8] separates channel communications into capabilities for inputting and outputting. This will enable us to specify how the environment may use a channel it has received. The benefit of using the variant type extensions from our point of view will be to prevent π processes from making calls to non-existent B-operations.

A process term without free names (*closed*) can be typed by assigning types to every channel bound by the ν operator. Such processes can be type checked using inference style rules. For example, in the process $(\nu v)(P)$, we can express the requirement that v is of type T with the term $(\nu v : T)(P)$. The most basic type for T is $\sharp unit$. A channel of type iV represents the requirement that it can be used only to input a value of type V. Similarly, oV permits the use of the channel only to output a value of type V. The type $\sharp V$ permits both input and output.

The construct $[l_1\_Y_1, \ldots, l_n\_Y_n]$ in π represents a variant type, and can be thought of as a set of label/value pairs. In our case the labels will correspond to B

operation names, and there will be no values (since there are no inputs/outputs). Thus, we define a simplified variant type associated with a machine M:
$V_M = [l_1, \ldots, l_n]$ where l_1 to l_n are the operations of machine M.

3 Combining B Machines and π Processes

In this section we consider how to structure the communication between a B machine and a π process. We can think of a machine as a node servicing requests to execute its operations. The operations (services) are offered via a single channel drawn from a special set of channels, $\mathcal{MR}$, that are used to communicate with B machines. A particular channel is referred to as a *machine reference* to an instance of a machine M. We allow multiple instances of M and they each have a unique machine reference and their own local copy of the state.

A machine reference is given a particular type, $\sharp V_M$, and when a machine reference z is used to make an operation call, that call is considered to be a variant label of V_M. In order to execute an operation a π process selects an operation and sends it along the appropriate machine reference channel. For example $\bar{z}\,GetBusy$ represents a machine reference z and a call to the operation *GetBusy*.

From the point of view of a B machine the type of a machine reference is iV_M because it is only permitted to service incoming requests whereas a π process considers a machine reference to be of type oV_M because it is only permitted to issue operation calls (i.e. output on the machine reference channel).

In our specifications we want the flexibility of being able to dynamically create instances of B machines. In order to achieve this we define a process which can be interpreted as having the capability of infinitely supplying machine instances and we refer to this process as *MGEN*, defined below. The process is replicated infinitely and each replication can engage in an interaction on the *create* channel and then engage in initialising a new instance of a machine M.

In order to allow B machines to be considered in parallel with π processes they are given a π-wrapper, i.e. a machine is packaged up so that it can synchronise on special channels *createM* and *initM* so that it can be created with a unique machine reference, and initialised and after that it can receive operation calls via a unique machine reference.

The π-wrapped machine M, ready to be created, is denoted by $[\![BEGIN]\!]_M(z)$ within the process *MGEN* and we will elaborate on its definition in Section 5.1. Note that the type of *initM* is $\sharp unit$, and the π-wrapped machine, $[\![BEGIN]\!]_M(z)$, can only receive requests to create a machine instance.

Definition 2

$$MGEN =\,!(\nu\ z : \sharp V_M,\ initM : \sharp unit)$$
$$(\overline{createM}\langle z\rangle.\overline{initM}.0\ \mid\ [\![BEGIN]\!]_M(z))$$

We can extend the *MGEN* process to enable a supply of different B machines, $M_1 \ldots M_n$, which we may want to use in our combined specifications. This is expressed as follows:

Definition 3

$$MGEN \; =!(\nu \; z : \sharp V_{M_1}, \; initM_1 : \sharp unit)$$
$$(\overline{createM_1}\langle z\rangle.\overline{initM_1}.0 \; | \; [\![BEGIN]\!]_{M_1}(z))$$
$$| \; \ldots$$
$$|!(\nu \; z : \sharp V_{M_n}, \; initM_n : \sharp unit)$$
$$(\overline{createM_n}\langle z\rangle.\overline{initM_n}.0 \; | \; [\![BEGIN]\!]_{M_n}(z))$$

Furthermore, in practice we may use a global $MGEN$ process across the system, or we may use several local copies, as illustrated in Figure 5 within Section 4.

3.1 Mediators

Now we consider how to define the π processes which communicate with the B machines. We refer to these processes as *mediators* since they control the operation calls made to machines instances. Mediators can engage in three kinds of events: they can synchronise internally or with other mediators, they can issue operation calls, and they can take control or relinquish control of machines instances. We identify specific channels, referred to as *control points*, in order to identify the latter two kinds of communication. Control points are formally defined as follows:

Definition 4. *A channel is a* control point *if and only if*

1. *it is used to transmit machine references only,*
2. *it is a monadic channel,*
3. *it always transmits the same kind of machine.*

Control points, machine references, and other synchronisations are all modelled as names within the π-calculus. However, the need to distinguish between them necessitates the identification of various disjoint subsets of the set of π names:

- $\mathcal{SN}$ is the set of *standard names*,
- $\mathcal{CP}$ is the set of *control points*,
- $\mathcal{MR}$ is the set of *machine references*.

In a particular specification, elements of these sets are given types as follows: machine references are channels which carry a type $\sharp V_M$, as stated earlier; control points are channels which carry the output capability of machine references and are of type $\sharp o V_M$; and channels from $\mathcal{SN}$ are not concerned with the B machine framework and thus carry names from $\mathcal{SN}$.

Controllers for machines are constructed in a particular way, in order to ensure that a machine reference is held by no more than one execution thread at a time. This enables us to manage the operation calls to machines through the design of the controllers, to ensure that state updates to machines occur only in a structured way by tracking the locus of control over the machine. As we will illustrate, this makes it possible to verify the combined system with respect to correctness of operation calls.

Controllers which are of the right form are termed *mediators*. Mediators are constructed from *sequential finite controllers* (SFCs), which are processes constructed from the sequential parts of the language (prefix and choice) with conditions on the handling of machine references. Informally, the conditions amount to the following:

1. an SFC should not contain any free machine references. This means that any machine reference occurring in the SFC must be bound by a control point input.
2. whenever an SFC outputs a machine reference z (i.e. on a control point) then the subsequent process description should not contain any free occurrences of z.

Definition 5 (Sequential finite controller (SFC)). *We define SFC terms using the following clauses.*

1. *0 is an SFC term;*
2. *If P is an SFC term then*
    (a) *if $a \in \mathcal{SN}$ or $a \in \mathcal{CP}$ then $a(w).P$ is an SFC term,*
    (b) *if $a \in \mathcal{SN}$ then $\overline{a}\langle w \rangle.P$ is an SFC term,*
    (c) *if $cp \in \mathcal{CP}$ and z is not free in P then $\overline{cp}\langle z \rangle.P$ is an SFC term,*
    (d) *if $z \in \mathcal{MR}$ and l is a label for z then $\overline{z\,l}.P$ is an SFC term,*
    (e) *$\tau.P$ is an SFC term,*
    (f) *if $x \in \mathcal{SN}$ then $(\nu x)(P)$ is an SFC term*
3. *if P_1 and P_2 are SFC terms then $(P_1 + P_2)$ is an SFC term.*

Then a sequential finite controller *(SFC) is an SFC term with no free occurrences of any machine references.*

Example 1. To illustrate the definition we give some examples of what is permitted and what is not permitted:

– $cp_1(z).\overline{z\,l}.\overline{cp_2}\langle z \rangle.0$ is an SFC.
– $cp_1(z).\overline{z\,l}.\overline{cp_2}\langle z \rangle.\overline{z\,l}.0$ is not an SFC: there should not be any occurrence of $\overline{z\,l}$ following the output of z on cp_2. For the same reason, it is not an SFC term.
– $\overline{z\,l}.\overline{cp_2}\langle z \rangle.0$ is not an SFC, since the machine reference z is free. However, it is an SFC term.
– $cp_1(z).cp_1(w).\overline{z\,l}.\overline{cp_2}\langle z \rangle.\overline{w\,m}.\overline{cp_2}\langle w \rangle.0$ is an SFC.
– $(\nu z)(\overline{z\,l}.\overline{cp_2}\langle z \rangle.0)$ is not an SFC or an SFC term: ν bindings of machine references are not permitted.

Types have been omitted for simplicity in this example, and in Example 2 below.

Mediators are then constructed by composing sequential finite controllers by means of parallel composition, replication, and restriction.

Definition 6 (Mediator). *We define mediators using the following clauses.*

1. *If P is an SFC then P is a mediator.*
2. *If D_1 and D_2 are mediators, then $D_1 \mid D_2$ is a mediator.*
3. *If P is an SFC then $!P$ is a mediator.*
4. *If D is a mediator then $(\nu w)(D)$ is a mediator.*

Example 2. To illustrate the definition we give some examples of mediators:

- $cp_1(z).\overline{z}\ \overline{l.\overline{cp_1}}\langle z \rangle.0$ is a mediator, since it is an SFC.
- $!(cp_1(z).\overline{z}\ \overline{l.\overline{cp_1}}\langle z \rangle.0)$ is a mediator.
- $(cp_0(z).cp_1\langle z \rangle.0) \mid !(cp_1(z).\overline{z}\ \overline{l.\overline{cp_1}}\langle z \rangle.0)$ is a mediator.
- $(\nu cp_1)((cp_0(z).\overline{cp_1}\langle z \rangle.0) \mid !(cp_1(z).\overline{z}\ \overline{l.\overline{z}\ \overline{m}.\overline{cp_1}}\langle z \rangle.a(w).0))$ is a mediator.

The last mediator on the list has one free control point, cp_0, and then one internal control point cp_1. A machine reference z can be accepted on cp_0, and then passed along cp_1 to the replicated component. Observe that only one thread in the replicated component can be in possession of z at any point.

We are now in a position to define control systems for generating and controlling mobile B machine instances. These are made up of two parts: mediators, which are responsible for managing machine references and passing them around; and machine generators, which are responsible for creating new machine references and introducing them into the system.

Given a mediator D, the associated control system $CSYSTEM_D$ therefore consists of the mediator composed with an $MGEN$ with matching vector $\widetilde{createM}$ and corresponding vector of types $\sharp o \widetilde{V_M}$ as follows:

$$CSYSTEM_D = (\nu\ \widetilde{createM} : \sharp o \widetilde{V_M})(D \mid MGEN)$$

4   Example

To illustrate the treatment of mobile B processes presented in this paper, we consider an example of allocating resources within a network. Resources are passed around a network, to service areas of high demand. Servers in the network autonomously decide how best to respond to a request for further resources, either by creating a fresh resource, by allocating one from a local pool of free resources, or by passing a request to another server. The description presented below abstracts away the decision making process of the servers, and focuses purely on the range of possibilities open to them.

The system is called the Resource Allocation Service (RAS). It offers clients the opportunity to request increases and decreases in the quantity of resource currently allocated. The interface between an individual client and the RAS consists of two channels, *inc* and *dec*, which are used to request an increase of a resource, and a decrease of a resource, respectively. We will model resources as B 'Node' machines which can be allocated to particular tasks. Figure 1 gives the description of the Node machine. The machine has three possible states, and operations for switching between them. It is initially in state *Fresh*, and once it is activated it alternates between *Busy* and *Free*, by means of the operations *GetBusy* and *GetFree*. The preconditions of these operations introduce the requirement that an operation should only be called from the appropriate state, and it will be important to ensure that the RAS does not violate this requirement when activating Node machines. A particular Node machine with machine reference z will have its operations called through occurrences of z *GetBusy* and z *GetFree*.

```
MACHINE          Node
SETS             STATUS = {Fresh, Busy, Free}
VARIABLES        status
INVARIANT        status : STATUS
INITIALISATION   status := Fresh
OPERATIONS
  GetBusy = PRE (status = Free) or (status = Fresh)
            THEN status := Busy
            END;
  GetFree = PRE status = Busy
            THEN status := Free
            END
END
```

Fig. 1. The B description of a Node

The *SERVER* Mediators

The system will be controlled by a collection of *SERVER* mediators. These mediators will provide the external interface (*inc* and *dec*) with the clients, and they will activate and manage resources. They will also transfer resources in order to meet areas of high demand.

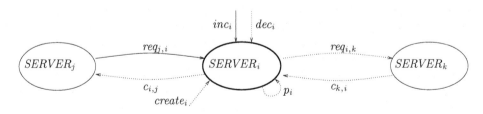

Fig. 2. $SERVER_i$ in its start state

The architecture of a *SERVER* mediator is given in Figure 2, and the description in the π-calculus is given in Figure 3. The mediator $SERVER_i$ is able to handle requests for a resource from an external client, through the particular channel inc_i. Requests can also arrive along req channels from other servers; the

$$SERVER_i = (\nu p_i : \sharp o V_{Node})$$

$$(\,!\,(inc_i\;.\;(\,create_i(z)\;.\;WORK_i(z)$$
$$+\;p_i(z)\;.\;WORK_i(z)$$
$$+\;\Sigma_{k \in S_i}\overline{req_{i,k}}\;.\;c_{k,i}(z)\;.\;WORK_i(z))$$
$$+\;\Sigma_{j \in C_i}(req_{j,i}\;.\;(\,create_i(z)\;.\;SEND_i(j,z)$$
$$+\;p_i(z)\;.\;SEND_i(j,z)$$
$$+\;\Sigma_{k \in S_i}\overline{req_{i,k}}\;.\;c_{k,i}(z)\;.\;SEND_i(j,z)))))$$

$$WORK_i(z) = \bar{z}\;GetBusy\;.\;dec_i\;.\;\bar{z}\;GetFree\;.\;\overline{p_i}\langle z \rangle\;.\;0$$
$$SEND_i(j,z) = \overline{c_{i,j}}\langle z \rangle\;.\;0$$

Fig. 3. Description of a server controller

channel $req_{j,i}$ is used to pass a request from $SERVER_j$ to $SERVER_i$. When a request has been received (from either of these sources), there are three ways of obtaining the resource required. The first is through the creation of a new resource, provided by a machine generator on channel $create_i$ (we use $create_i$ rather than $createNode$ for readability within the example); the second is by identifying a free resource currently in the local pool of available resources, and this is done through the server's internal channel p_i; and the third is by passing the request to another server k, along channel $req_{i,k}$, and then receiving the response along channel $c_{k,i}$. These three possible reactions to inc_i (and also to $req_{j,i}$) are illustrated in Figure 4.

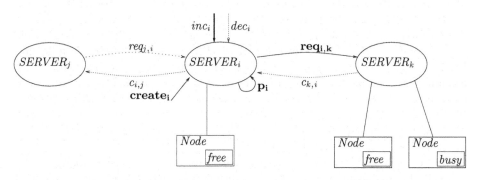

Fig. 4. Possible responses to inc_i (and also to $req_{j,i}$) from $SERVER_i$

Each of the channels $create_i$, p_i, and $c_{k,i}$ are used to communicate a machine channel z, and so they are all *control points* of the mediators. Observe that the description of $SERVER_i$ is consistent with the requirement on a mediator: that when a machine reference is output on a control point then the subsequent description should not contain any free occurrence of the machine reference. In the case of $SERVER_i$ we see that when machine reference z is output along control point p_i or $c_{i,j}$, then the subsequent description on that thread of control is in fact 0, which indeed does not contain z.

When $SERVER_i$ has control of a Node through a link z, it is able to activate it and shut it down by use of z *GetBusy* and z *GetFree*. Requests to reduce resource usage along the dec_i channel result in the closing down of node activity, and the release of the node into the local pool of available resources along the channel p_i.

The use of replication in the server description indicates that any number of inc_i or $req_{j,i}$ requests can be handled. However, observe that dec_i is possible only when there are active nodes, and it will be blocked otherwise.

The set C_i denotes the other servers which can make a resource request of $SERVER_i$: it is those j's for which a $req_{j,i}$ will be allowed. Conversely, the set S_i denotes the servers from which $SERVER_i$ can request a resource, and for consistency we require that $j \in C_i \Leftrightarrow i \in S_j$ for any i and j. If the set S_i is empty then it will not be possible for $SERVER_i$ to pass the request on, and it will have to be serviced either by recycling a resource, or by creating a new one. Conversely, if C_i is empty then $SERVER_i$ will not receive requests from any other servers.

The sets C_i or S_i will correspond to a network structure or hierarchy of resource allocators, which will vary according to the considerations of the RAS design. For example, it may be a requirement that there should be no cycles in the graph of request links.

Servers and Nodes

The $SERVER_i$ mediators are combined with a mechanism for generating Node machines, which may be thought of as a Node factory. The process $MGEN_i$ is used to generate and initialise Node machines, raising a fresh machine reference z for that node, and passing that machine reference to $SERVER_i$ along their joint channel $create_i$. The description of $MGEN_i$ is given in Figure 5, following Definition 2. The process $[\![BEGIN]\!]_{Node}(z)$ is the Node machine inside a π-calculus wrapper, with machine reference z, awaiting initialisation through the channel $initNode$. The reference z is passed along $create_i$ (to $SERVER_i$), and the Node machine is initialised. The encapsulation ensures that z is fresh and so is known only within $MGEN_i$. The combination of $SERVER_i$ and a newly generated Node is illustrated in Figure 6.

We consider a $RESOURCER_i$ to consist (initially) of a $SERVER_i$ and the associated machine generator $MGEN_i$. Observe that $RESOURCER_i$ is a control system for $SERVER_i$, $CSYSTEM_{SERVER_i}$. The Resource Allocation System will then consist of the parallel composition of all the nodes, as shown in Figure 5.

Figure 7 illustrates a scenario of a Node instance being passed from one server to another. The first event in this scenario is a request inc_i for another resource at $SERVER_i$. In this case the request results in a request to a neighbouring server $SERVER_k$ along $req_{i,k}$. That server picks up a machine reference z from the pool of local free machines, and then passes z along channel $c_{k,i}$ in response to $SERVER_i$'s request $req_{i,k}$. Once this last communication has occurred,

$$MGEN_i = !(\nu z_i : \natural V_{Node}, \; initNode : \natural unit)$$

$$(\overline{create_i}\langle z_i \rangle.\overline{initNode}.0 \mid [\![BEGIN]\!]_{Node}(z_i))$$

$$RESOURCER_i = (\nu create_i : \natural o V_{Node})(SERVER_i \mid MGEN_i)$$

$$RAS = (\nu C : \natural o V_{Node}, R : \natural unit)(RESOURCER_1 \mid \ldots \mid RESOURCER_n)$$

where

$$C = \bigcup_{i \in I}\{c_{i,j} \mid j \in C_i\}$$

$$R = \bigcup_{i \in I}\{req_{i,j} \mid j \in S_i\}$$

Fig. 5. The architecture of RAS

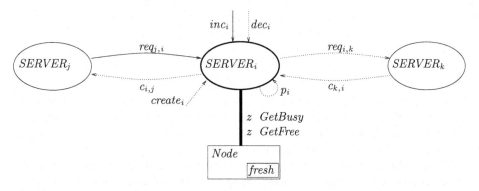

Fig. 6. $SERVER_i$ following creation of a node

$SERVER_k$ no longer has access to z. Thus the node becomes wholly under the control of $SERVER_i$, which is now able to issue the instruction z $GetBusy$ and make use of this resource.

Assertions

Now we consider the behaviour of RAS, and introduce the notion of *assertions* on control points. Section 5 will provide the formal approach, but we motivate it informally here.

It is necessary to ensure that z $GetBusy$ is invoked only when the Node instance referenced by z is not already busy, since this requirement is encapsulated by the precondition of the operation. In order to guarantee this, we identify assertions on the states of the machine instances whose references are passed across control points. We can see that any machine reference passed along $create_i$ must have $status = Fresh$ for the associated machine instance, since such an instance will still be in its initial state. Further, any machine whose unique reference z is

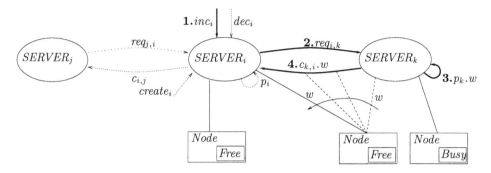

Fig. 7. Requesting and passing a node from $SERVER_k$ to $SERVER_i$

Control Point	Assertion
$create_i$	$status = Fresh$
p_i	$status = Free$
$c_{i,j}$	$status \neq Busy$

Fig. 8. Assertions associated with the control points within RAS

passed on p_i must have $status = Free$, since it can only appear on p_i following $z\ GetFree$. Finally, we can associate the assertion $status \neq Busy$ with machine references passed along the $c_{i,j}$ control points. The collection of assertions on the control points is given in Figure 8.

We are then able to use rely/guarantee style reasoning to ensure the control point assertions are respected, and that operations are never called out of their preconditions. Whenever a machine reference is input at a control point we may assume that the machine instance satisfies the corresponding assertion. This is then enough to ensure (1) that the mediator receiving the machine reference calls operations appropriately; and (2) that it can guarantee the assertion is true at any control point where it outputs the machine reference. The nature of mediators ensures that a machine reference is always located at no more than one mediator, ensuring that state updates are strictly controlled, and are the responsibility of a single mediator from the point the machine reference is received on the control point. Hence there can be no interference on the updates of the machine's state.

In $SERVER_i$, the event inc_i is followed by the input of a machine reference z on one of three control points. If it is on $create_i$, then the assertion for $create_i$ states that $status = Fresh$ for the machine instance when z is input. This is ensured by the initialisation clause of the Node machine. It is then enough to guarantee that $z\ GetBusy$ is called within its precondition, and subsequently that $z\ GetFree$ is called within its own precondition, and finally that the state of the machine instance is $status = Free$ at the point z is output on p_i, ensuring the assertion associated with p_i. If the input of z is on p_i then the corresponding assertion tells us that the associated machine instance is in state $status = Free$, and this is sufficient to provide the same guarantees as in the previous case. Finally, if the input of z is on $c_{k,i}$ for some k (in response to a request $req_{i,k}$) then the assertion tells us that the corresponding machine instance has $status \neq Busy$, which is again sufficient to provide the necessary guarantees.

The other behaviour possible for $SERVER_i$ is in response to a $req_{j,i}$ event. This is again followed by the input of a machine reference z on one of the three control points. If z is input on $create_i$, then the corresponding assertion $status = Fresh$ on the machine instance is sufficient to ensure that $status \neq Busy$ when z is immediately passed as output on $c_{i,j}$. Similarly, if z is received on p_i, then the assertion $status = Free$ again is sufficient to ensure that $status \neq Busy$. Finally, if z is received on $c_{k,i}$ then the machine instance has $status \neq Busy$, which remains true when z is output on $c_{i,j}$.

Hence in $SERVER_i$, if machine references are consistent with assertions on inputs, then operations will only ever be called within their preconditions, and machine references are consistent with assertions on outputs.

5   Identifying and Discharging Assertions

In the above example we identified assertions on the states of machine instances at control points within the mediators, i.e. when the instances were created, when they were passed from one mediator to another, and during internal communication. When a mediator receives a reference to a newly created machine instance then we can assume that the instance is in its initial state. When a machine instance is received by a mediator we may assume the instance will be a particular state. It is the responsibility of the mediator relinquishing control of the instance to guarantee that this assumption is met.

We use tags to associate control points with their corresponding assertions.

Definition 7 (Tags). *A tag t is a mapping from control points to predicates on the states of machine instances. The notation t_{cp_z} denotes the assertion associated with control point cp, on the specific machine instance referenced by z.*

Definition 8 (Tagged SFC). *For a given tag t and SFC P, P_t is a tagged SFC if t has a predicate for each of the control points in P.*

A similar definition is given for mediators:

Definition 9 (Tagged Mediator). *A mediator M is a tagged mediator M_t if each (bound or free) control point within its definition is tagged with t.*

The purpose of introducing tags is to give a definition of consistency between mediators and machine instances. The key idea is that we extract a sequence of B operations and assertions from each SFC P_t within a tagged mediator. The tagged SFC P_t will be consistent with the assertions on its control points and the sequence of its B operations, if the sequence of operations assumes the assertions for any input control points, and then ensures the assertions on any output control points. Input assertions are translated to *rely* assertions, which can be assumed. Within B this is modelled as a blocking (SELECT) assertion. Output assertions are translated to *guarantee* assertions, which will need to be established. Within B this is modelled as a diverging (PRE) assumption.

We extract the relevant sequence of B operations from a P_t by examining the structure of the syntax of P_t as follows:

Definition 10. *Given a tagged sequential finite controller, P_t, its corresponding sequence of operations and assertions, $bseq(P_t)$ is defined recursively below. Assume $bseq(P_{1t})$, $bseq(P_{2t})$ are defined, where P_1 and P_2 are SFCs tagged with t.*

$$bseq(0) = skip$$
$$bseq(cp(b).P_{1t}) = SELECT\ t_{cp_b}\ THEN\ skip\ END;\ bseq(P_{1t})$$
$$bseq(\overline{z}\ l.P_{1t}) = l_z\ ;\ bseq(P_{1t})$$
$$bseq(\overline{cp}\langle z \rangle.P_{1t}) = PRE\ t_{cp_z}\ THEN\ skip\ END;\ bseq(P_{1t})$$
$$bseq(\pi.P_{1t}) = bseq(P_{1t})\ for\ any\ prefix\ \pi\ not\ covered\ by\ above\ cases$$
$$bseq((\nu\ v : S)(P_{1t})) = bseq(P_{1t})\ where\ v \in \mathcal{SN}$$
$$bseq(P_{1t} + P_{2t}) = CHOICE\ bseq(P_{1t})OR\ bseq(P_{2t})END$$

The process 0 is converted to *skip* as it does not perform any actions. At an input control point we identify the appropriate assertion, and introduce a corresponding guard. An operation call $\overline{z}\ l$ is converted to the AMN l_z, which means the operation l for the particular machine reference z. Tracking the machine reference z is necessary because an SFC P_t may perform sequences of operations from different instances and we need to be able to distinguish between those instances. At an output control point we embed the assertion as a precondition predicate. A correctness proof will require this assertion to be established.

All other syntactic constructs are ignored by *bseq* since they are not concerned with the execution of operations, they are related to communication between mediators.

Example 3. Consider the control point *cp* which handles machine references which refer to instances of the Node machine. A tag t associates *cp* with the assertion *status = Fresh*. The tagged SFC given by

$$(cp(z)\ .\ cp(w)\ .\ z\ GetBusy\ .\ w\ GetBusy\ .\ 0)_t$$

translates as follows:

$$bseq((cp(z).cp(w).z\ GetBusy.w\ GetBusy.0)_t)$$
$$= SELECT\ t_{cp_z}\ THEN\ skip\ END\ ;\ SELECT\ t_{cp_w}\ THEN\ skip\ END\ ;$$
$$GetBusy_z\ ;\ GetBusy_w\ ;\ skip$$

$= SELECT\ status_z = Fresh\ THEN\ skip\ END$;

$SELECT\ status_w = Fresh\ THEN\ skip\ END$;

$PRE\ (status_z = Free)\ or\ (status_z = Fresh)\ THEN\ status_z := Busy\ END$;

$PRE\ (status_w = Free)\ or\ (status_w = Fresh)\ THEN\ status_w := Busy\ END$;

$skip$

Observe the two machine references received along cp are handled separately so that the two calls of $GetBusy$ are to two different instances of the $Node$ machine, and in both cases the precondition is true.

We now define consistency of a tagged SFC as follows:

Definition 11 (Tagged SFC Consistency). *A tagged sequential finite controller P_t is sfc-consistent if $wp(bseq(P_t), true)$ holds.*

By discharging the weakest precondition proof obligation we can conclude that P_t is divergence-free and hence that it guarantees all the output assertions and valid operation calls.

Mediator consistency is then defined as follows:

Definition 12 (Tagged Mediator Consistency). *A tagged mediator D_t is m-consistent if each tagged SFC P_t in D_t is sfc-consistent. Consistency of a tagged mediator can be defined inductively through the four mediator clauses:*

- P_t is m-consistent if P_t is SFC consistent
- $(!P)_t$ is m-consistent if P_t is SFC consistent
- $(D_1 \mid D_2)_t$ is m-consistent if $(D_1)_t$ and $(D_2)_t$ are m-consistent
- $(\nu cp)(D)_t$ is m-consistent if D_t is m-consistent

Once we have shown *mediator consistency* then we have ensured that all the operation calls within the mediator D will be within their precondition. The other requirement for consistency of a control system is that the generated machines should initially meet the assertions on their associated *create* channels. Thus, we introduce the additional requirements that each initialisation clause T_{M_i} of any generated M_i should establish the assertion on the $createM_i$ channel. This is captured in Definition 13.

Definition 13 (Tagged $CSYSTEM_D$ consistency). *A $CSYSTEM_{Dt}$ is consistent if D_t is m-consistent and $wp(T_{M_i}, t_{createM_i})$ holds for each M_i which MGEN can generate.*

Then a $CSYSTEM_D$ is consistent if we can find a tag t for which $CSYSTEM_{Dt}$ is consistent. An important result from [7] is the following theorem:

Theorem 1. *If $CSYSTEM_D$ is consistent then $CSYSTEM_D$ is divergence-free.*

5.1 Underlying Semantics

This proof obligation framework above is underpinned by the π-calculus semantic framework, and a π semantics for B machines is provided to support reasoning about π mediators and B machines within a single semantic framework. In [7] we defined an approach which enables the interpretation of a B machine as a π-calculus labelled transition system.

Initially, we consider a B machine M to be uninitialised and $[\![BEGIN]\!]_M(z)$ represents an uninitialised machine which will be able to receive operations calls along z. The only transition possible in this state is the initialisation transition. This will be executed in parallel with $\overline{initM}$ when machines are created in $MGEN$.

Once a machine is initialised, we consider the execution of an operation (without inputs and outputs) in two stages. First, the precondition of the operation is checked and this is represented by a transition labelled by $z\ l$. Second, if the precondition holds then the state is updated with respect to the operation's definition otherwise the operation has diverged and the state of the B machine is mapped to $\bot$ since no further guarantees can be made about the state. This second stage is associated with two different transitions: an internal transition which can be performed when the precondition holds and a div transition otherwise.

When the π wrapped B machine instance is placed in parallel with a π process all communications between them become internal transitions apart from the div transition, and this is significant when proving Theorem 1 above. The key feature of its proof is the argument that no execution of the mediators in D leads to an operation from any of its instances being called outside its precondition. This is established by examining the possible transitions of a $CSYSTEM_D$ and showing that at each step no divergence has occurred. We can achieve this by appealing to the fact that we have already demonstrated $CSYSTEM_D$ consistency and therefore the div transition will never be a possible transition for the B machines in $CSYSTEM_D$.

The benefit of this theorem is that, in practice, we can focus on examining the individual sequential finite controllers and their corresponding machine instances but that these individual results can be composed together to ensure divergence freedom of the whole system.

6   Discussion

In this paper we have shown that state and the operations which update and query the state can be described in conjunction with a mobile paradigm. We have extended the notion of B machines with unique references so that they can be instantiated at run-time by a π process. We defined a syntactic framework for π processes in order to control the execution of B operations. We used a behavioural type system within the π-calculus to provide guarantees on the way machine instances and processes should interact. We converted the signature of a machine instance into a variant type which specifies the operations a π process can execute. Without such a type system it would be difficult to specify the interface of a machine instance and ensure that π processes do not call operations which are not in that interface. The typing system provides the guarantee that any operation call will always be serviced appropriately by a machine instance and not by another π processes (pretending to be a machine).

We have established that the behavioural requirements on π processes together with discharging the weakest-precondition proof obligations ensure that B machine instances do not diverge when controlled by π processes. We outlined that this rely-guarantee style of reasoning is formally justified using the operational semantics.

6.1   Related Work

In our CSP ∥ B [15] approach we also introduced wp proof obligations to show that CSP controllers were consistent with B machines. We considered each controller as a collection of sequential CSP processes. These sequential processes are similar to the sequential finite controllers presented in this paper but they do not have control points and there is no notion of being able to create instances of machines. In order to demonstrate consistency we examined each sequential CSP process separately, extracted the B operations from each process and this was done in a similar way to how *bseq* is used. In CSP ∥ B we had to introduce the notion of a control loop invariant so that we could make assumptions about the state at the beginning and end of each recursive call. In the approach presented in this paper we do not have a global notion of an invariant that we are trying to preserve after a sequence of operations calls. However, the assertions on the control points play a similar role. We can simply check that a sequence terminates and this check incorporates verifying any rely/guarantee assertions to deal with dynamic behaviour. We have added another wp obligation, which is not needed in CSP ∥ B, to deal with ensuring that machines are created in an appropriate state.

Taguchi *et al.* [13] have integrated Object-Z and the π-calculus into a single formal framework (PiOZ). In their framework they have extended the π-calculus syntax to allow operations to be called explicitly within π processes and to include guards which can refer to the Object-Z state. Their syntax is limited and does not include the $(\nu\ v)$ operator and !, and therefore the framework relies on channel generation from the Object-Z semantics. This is visible in their π descriptions because a π channel is semantically identified as an Object-Z state variable. In essence it resonates with our work but we believe that they are not making the best use of the dynamic features of the π-calculus.

Smith [12] also used Object-Z to model mobile systems. A Node class in [12] is similar to a $SERVER_i$ process together with a Node machine in our example. The Object-Z framework allows the network architecture to be explicitly defined. In our example, the topology of the servers is governed by the way the request and control point channels are defined. It would be interesting to investigate how we could also make this more explicit in our models.

The notion of mobility is also introduced in [14] so that the Circus [18] framework can be extended to deal with dynamic behaviour. In [14] processes are assigned to variables and these variables can be passed around using mobile output channels. We can compare a mobile output channel to a control point output in our framework. The authors in [14] also note that if a process outputs a process variable then any subsequent reference to it may provide unpredictable behaviour. In our framework we disallow any further interaction after a machine reference has been output from a process because we cannot provide any guarantees about the state of the instance following the output of the reference (unless, of course, control is returned).

The mobile channels introduced by Welch and Barnes in Occam-π [17] are more flexible than our control points. In Occam-π communication via channels also has a notion of an originator and recipient but they allow their channels to change ownership during run-time, which we have currently disallowed in order to enable our rely/guarantee proofs. The motivation for Occam-π originally came from CSP. However, CSP does not explicitly define which process has the responsibility for its channel ends. Therefore, Welch proposed that mobile channels be modelled as CSP processes, and each process is produced on demand. Each of these processes has an unique identifier number and the mobility in a formal model comes from communicating the index. The formal model presented in [17] is very low level and reflects how it has been implemented successfully in Occam-π .

6.2   Future Work

We illustrated our ideas by using a running example which highlighted dynamic instantiation and control passing communication. We could extend the notion of dynamic instantiation so that the servers, as well as workers, could also be generated dynamically, possibly by some kind of server controller, and they could even dynamically change the network by adding new links allowing them to pass requests for resource to new servers. Furthermore, we could consider descriptions of a P2P network overlay, as in [2], where the complex topology of the servers was stored in the B and this information passed to the π processes.

One of the principal motivations for this work was to draw out the complex issues related to dynamic interactions so that it could inform potential extensions to CSP $\parallel$ B . We now also feel that the work is interesting in its own right and there are many extensions to be explored and open issues to be addressed.

Firstly, we need to consider how the weakest-precondition proof obligations, identified in Definitions 11 and 13, would be generated in practice and how they would be proved using tool support. We would also need to determine whether there could be problems in general with circularity.

Secondly, we could extend the framework to allow control points to be passed along channels. In our RAS specification, the control points between servers are static. For example, currently a B machine reference can be passed from oneserver to another one via an intermediate server but the receiving server must have included an explicit control point in its description to enable references of that kind to be passed to it from the intermediate server. We would want to consider allowing servers to receive machine instances via control points which had been set up dynamically. In the example, this would mean that instance would then not be required to be passed via an intermediate server; instead a control point could be set up dynamically between the two servers who could then send and receive a machine reference between each other, eliminating the need to go via the intermediate server. The introduction of mobile control points would impact on the definitions of the weakest-precondition proof obligations and this would need to be investigated.

Thirdly, we need to allow the framework to support operations which have input and output parameters. This could be achieved by extending the type system to include linearly receptive types [9]. Operations in a B machine can receive input, update state, and provide output simultaneously. The π calculus would not support this using one action in a process and therefore we would need to split an operation call into a sequence of actions. By using linearly receptive types we can ensure that if an operation has an output then it will be received by a mediator. We anticipate the need to define private channels $((\nu q)(\overline{z}\ op\_\langle x, q \rangle \mid q(y).P))$ to gather the output from an operation. Without such strict typing the mediator would not be under any obligation to pick up the output of an operation.

Fourthly, we may want to weaken the behavioural requirement of only allowing one π process to interact with a machine instance at any one time. We could allow other processes to execute query operations on the machine instance while one process retained overall control of the instance. We could support the definition of a control point that outputs a machine reference so that the process receiving the reference has the ability to call a reduced set of operations from that machine instance's interface. The type system, with variant sub-typing, would be integral to facilitate this extension. The challenge with this extension will be how to maintain the guarantees that can be made about the state of a machine instance. Such an extension would mean that each B machine instance could be viewed more autonomously in order to make the approach more compatible with a component-oriented view of a system.

Finally, by incorporating session types [5] into the type system we can add further constraints on how operations of a machine instance should be called when a mediator passes control of instances from itself to another mediator. For example, given $D_1 = \overline{cp}.0$ and $D_2 = cp(z).\overline{z}\ inc.\overline{z}\ inc.0$ and the session type of the control point cp permitting only the sequence of inc followed by dec operation calls, then $D_1 \mid D_2$ is not typeable. This could be useful in specifying access control properties on B machine instances.

Acknowledgments. The authors are grateful to AWE for funding a research studentship in order to conduct this work. Thanks also to the anonymous referees for their detailed comments.

References

1. Abrial, J-R.: The B Book: Assigning Programs to Meaning, CUP (1996)
2. Bakhshi, R., Gurov, D.: Verification of Peer-to-Peer Algorithms: a Case Study. In: Proceedings of 2nd International Workshop on Methods and Tools for Coordinating Concurrent, Distributed and Mobile Systems (MTCoord'06). ENTCS (2006)

3. Berger, M., Honda, K.: The Two-Phase Commitment Protocol in an Extended pi-Calculus. In: Proceedings of EXPRESS'00. ENTCS, vol. 39(1) (2003)
4. Eng, K.L., Crowcroft, J., Pias, M., Sharma, R., Lim, S.: A Survey and Comparison of Peer-to-Peer Overlay Network Schemes. IEEE Communications Surveys and Tutorials 7(2), 72–93 (2005)
5. Gay, S.J., Hole, M.J.: Types and Subtypes for Client-Server Interactions. In: Swierstra, S.D. (ed.) ESOP 1999 and ETAPS 1999. LNCS, vol. 1576, pp. 74–90. Springer, Heidelberg (1999)
6. Hoare, C.A.R.: Communicating Sequential Processes. Prentice-Hall, Englewood Cliffs (1985)
7. Karkinsky, D.: Mobile B machines. PhD thesis, University of Surrey (2007)
8. Pierce, B.C., Sangiorgi, D.: Typing and Subtyping for Mobile Processes. Mathematical Structures in Computer Science 6(5), 409–454 (1996)
9. Sangiorgi, D., Walker, D.: The π-calculus: a Theory of Mobile Processes. CUP (2001)
10. Saroiu, S., Gummadi, P.K., Gribble, S.D.: A Measurement Study of Peer-to-Peer File Sharing Systems. In: Kienzle, M.G., Shenoy, P.J. (eds.) Proceedings of Multimedia Computing and Networking 2002. SPIE, vol. 4673, pp. 156–170 (2002)
11. Schneider, S., Treharne, H.: CSP Theorems for Communicating B machines. Formal Aspects of Computing 17(4), 390–422 (2005)
12. Smith, G.: A Framework for Modelling and Analysing Mobile Systems. In: Australasian Computer Science Conference (ACSC), pp. 193–202 (2004)
13. Taguchi, K., Dong, J.S., Ciobanu, G.: Relating π-calculus to Object-Z. In: Bellini, P., Bohner, S., Steffen, B. (eds.) Proceedings of IEEE International Conference on Engineering Complex Computer Systems (ICECCS'04), pp. 97–106. IEEE Press, New York (2004)
14. Tang, X., Woodcock, J.: Towards Mobile Processes in Unifying Theories. SEFM 2004, pp. 44–55. IEEE Computer Society Press, Los Alamitos (2004)
15. Treharne, H., Schneider, S.: Using a Process Algebra to Control B OPERATIONS. IFM, pp. 437–456. Springer, Heidelberg (1999)
16. Treharne, H., Schneider, S., Bramble, M.: Composing Specifications using Communication. In: Bert, D., Bowen, J.P., King, S. (eds.) ZB 2003. LNCS, vol. 2651, pp. 58–78. Springer, Heidelberg (2003)
17. Welch, P., Barnes, F.: Communicating mobile processes: introducing occam-pi. In: Abdallah, A.E., Jones, C.B., Sanders, J.W. (eds.) Communicating Sequential Processes. LNCS, vol. 3525, pp. 175–210. Springer, Heidelberg (2005)
18. Woodcock, J.C.P., Cavalcanti, A.L.C.: A Concurrent Language for Refinement. In: 5th Irish Workshop on Formal Methods (2001)

Algebraic Approaches to Formal Analysis of the Mondex Electronic Purse System

Weiqiang Kong, Kazuhiro Ogata, and Kokichi Futatsugi

Graduate School of Information Science
Japan Advanced Institute of Science and Technology (JAIST)
{weiqiang,ogata,kokichi}@jaist.ac.jp

Abstract. Mondex is a payment system that utilizes smart cards as electronic purses for financial transactions. This paper first reports on how the Mondex system can be modeled, specified and interactively verified using an equation-based method – the OTS/CafeOBJ method. Afterwards, the paper reports on, as a complementarity, a way of automatically falsifying the OTS/CafeOBJ specification of the Mondex system, and how the falsification can be used to facilitate the verification. Differently from related work, our work provides alternative ways of (1) modeling the Mondex system using an OTS (Observational Transition System), a kind of transition system, and (2) expressing and verifying (and falsifying) the desired security properties of the Mondex system directly in terms of invariants of the OTS.

1   Introduction

Mondex [1] is a payment system that utilizes smart cards as electronic purses for financial transactions. The system has recently been chosen as a challenge for formal methods [2,4], after it was originally specified and manually proved for correctness (of refinement) using the Z notation described in [9]. The purpose of setting up this challenge is to see what the current state-of-the-art is in mechanizing the specification, refinement, and proof, and ultimately to contribute to the Grand Challenge – Dependable Software Evolution [2,3,4]. As a response, different formal methods have been applied to tackle this same problem, including, for example, KIV [5,6], RAISE [7], Alloy [8] etc.

In this paper, we report on how this problem can be tackled by using an equation-based method – the OTS/CafeOBJ method [10]. Specifically, we describe how the Mondex system is modeled as an OTS (Observational Transition System), a kind of transition system that can be straightforwardly written in terms of equations; and how to specify the OTS in CafeOBJ [11,12], an algebraic specification language; and finally how to express the desired security properties of the Mondex system as invariants of the OTS, and to verify the invariants by writing and executing proof scores using CafeOBJ system.

As a complement to the interactive verification of the OTS/CafeOBJ method, we also report on a way of automatically falsifying (finding counterexamples) the OTS/CafeOBJ specification of the Mondex system by using Maude `search` command [13]. The basis of this way of falsification is an automatic translation

J. Davies and J. Gibbons (Eds.): IFM 2007, LNCS 4591, pp. 393–412, 2007.

from the OTS/CafeOBJ specification into the corresponding Maude specification [14,15]. The falsification has been shown, from our experience, to be useful for facilitating the OTS/CafeOBJ method in its different verification stages.

Differently from related work, our work provides an alternative way of modeling the Mondex system in an operational style (in terms of transition system), which is inspired by [5,6], rather than in a relational style as used in [7,8,9]; and our work also provides an alternative way of expressing and verifying (and falsifying) desired properties of the Mondex system directly in terms of invariants, rather than using the refinement construction and proof that were originally used in the Z method [9] and then also used in [5,6,7,8]. This work therefore provides a different way of viewing the Mondex analysis problem, and can be used to compare different modeling and proof strategies.

The rest of the paper is organized as follows: Section 2 outlines the main parts of the Mondex electronic purse system. Section 3 introduces the OTS/CafeOBJ method. Sections 4 and 5 describe how to model and specify the Mondex system, and how to express the desired security properties of the Mondex system as invariants and their corresponding verification method. Section 6 discusses the motivation of falsifying the OTS/CafeOBJ specification of the Mondex system, and our proposed method for doing so. Section 7 discusses related work. And finally Section 8 concludes the paper and mentions future work.

2   Overview of the Mondex Electronic Purse System

In the Mondex system, cards, which are used as electronic purses, store monetary value as electronic information, and exchange value with each other through a communication device without using a central controller (such as a remote database). The communication protocol, which is used for transferring electronic values between two cards, say FromPurse (the paying purse) and ToPurse (the receiving purse), is as follows:

1. The communication device ascertains a transaction by collecting cards' information and sending two messages *startFrom* and *startTo*.
2. FromPurse receives the *startFrom* message that contains information of the ToPurse, and the amount of value to be transferred.
3. ToPurse receives the *startTo* message that contains information of the FromPurse, and the amount to be transferred. As a result, ToPurse sends a *Req* message to FromPurse requesting that amount.
4. FromPurse receives the *Req* message and decreases its balance, and then sends a message *Val* to ToPurse for transferring value.
5. ToPurse receives the *Val* message and increases its balance, and then sends a message *Ack* to FromPurse acknowledging the transaction.

Although the communication protocol seems to be simple, it is complicated by several facts as pointed out in [8,9]: (1) the protocol can be stopped at any time, either due to internal reasons of cards, or due to card-holders intentionally doing so; (2) a message can be lost and replayed in the communication channel, and (3) a message can be read by any card. Note, however, that it is assumed that the *Req*, *Val* and *Ack* messages cannot be forged, which is guaranteed by some (unclear) means of cryptographic system [9].

Two key security properties demanded by the Mondex system are ([9]):

1. No value may be created in the system,
2. All value is accounted for in the system (no value is lost).

Note that in this paper, we omit another protocol of the Mondex system that deals with uploading exception logs[1] onto a central archive, since it is not directly related to the above properties.

3   The OTS/CafeOBJ Method

3.1   CafeOBJ: Algebraic Specification Language

Abstract machines as well as abstract data types can be specified in CafeOBJ [11,12] mainly based on hidden and initial algebras. CafeOBJ has two kinds of sorts: visible and hidden sorts that denote abstract data types and the state spaces of abstract machines, respectively. There are two kinds of operators for hidden sorts: action and observation operators. Action operators denote state transitions of abstract machines, and observation operators let us know the situation where abstract machines are located. Both an action operator and an observation operator take a state of an abstract machine and zero or more data, and return the successor state of the state and a value that characterizes the situation where the abstract machine is located.

Declarations of action and observation operators start with bop, and those of other operators with op. Declarations of equations start with eq, and those of conditional ones with ceq. The CafeOBJ system rewrites a given term by regarding equations as left-to-right rewrite rules.

Basic units of CafeOBJ specifications are modules. The CafeOBJ built-in module BOOL that specifies proposition logic is automatically imported by almost every module unless otherwise stated. In the module BOOL, visible sort Bool denoting truth values, and the constants true and false, and some logical operators such as not_ (negation), _and_ (conjunction), and _implies_ (implication) are declared. The operator if_then_else_fi is also available.

3.2   Observational Transition Systems (OTSs)

We assume that there exists a universal state space called Υ, and also that data types used, including the equivalence relation (denoted by $=$) for each data type, have been defined in advance. An OTS $\mathcal{S}$ [10] consists of $\langle \mathcal{O}, \mathcal{I}, \mathcal{T} \rangle$, where:

- $\mathcal{O}$: A finite set of observers. Each $o \in \mathcal{O}$ is a function $o : \Upsilon \to D$, where D is a data type and may differ from observer to observer. Given an OTS $\mathcal{S}$ and two states $\upsilon_1, \upsilon_2 \in \Upsilon$, the equivalence (denoted by $\upsilon_1 =_{\mathcal{S}} \upsilon_2$) between them wrt $\mathcal{S}$ is defined as $\forall o \in \mathcal{O}, o(\upsilon_1) = o(\upsilon_2)$.

---

[1] Exception logs are used to record information of those failed transactions in which value may be lost (detailed in Section 4).

- $\mathcal{I}$: The set of initial states such that $\mathcal{I} \subseteq \Upsilon$.
- $\mathcal{T}$: A finite set of conditional transitions. Each $\tau \in \mathcal{T}$ is a function $\tau : \Upsilon \to \Upsilon$, provided that $\tau(v_1) =_{\mathcal{S}} \tau(v_2)$ for each $[v] \in \Upsilon/ =_{\mathcal{S}}$ and each $v_1, v_2 \in [v]$. $\tau(v)$ is called the successor state of $v \in \Upsilon$ wrt τ. The condition c_τ of τ is called the effective condition. For each $v \in \Upsilon$ such that $\neg c_\tau(v)$, $v =_{\mathcal{S}} \tau(v)$.

Reachable states wrt $\mathcal{S}$ are inductively defined: (1) each $v_0 \in \mathcal{I}$ is reachable, and (2) for each $\tau \in \mathcal{T}$, $\tau(v)$ is reachable if $v \in \Upsilon$ is reachable. An invariant wrt $\mathcal{S}$ is a state predicate $p : \Upsilon \to Bool$, which holds in all reachable states wrt $\mathcal{S}$.

Observers and transitions may be parameterized. Generally, observers and transitions are denoted by $o_{i_1,\ldots,i_m}$ and $\tau_{j_1,\ldots,j_n}$, provided that $m, n \geq 0$ and there exists a data type D_k such that $k \in D_k$ $(k = i_1, \ldots, i_m, j_1, \ldots, j_n)$.

3.3   Specification of OTSs in CafeOBJ

The universal state space Υ is denoted by a hidden sort, say H. An observer $o_{i_1,\ldots,i_m} \in \mathcal{O}$ is denoted by a CafeOBJ observation operator and declared as bop $o : H\ V_{i_1} \ldots V_{i_m} \text{-> } V$., where $V_{i_1}, \ldots, V_{i_m}$ and V are visible sorts.

Any initial state in $\mathcal{I}$ is denoted by a constant, say $init$, which is declared as op $init : \text{-> } H$. The equation expressing the initial value of $o_{i_1,\ldots,i_m}$ is as follows:

eq $o(init, X_{i_1}, \ldots, X_{i_m}) = f(X_{i_1}, \ldots, X_{i_m})$.

X_k is a CafeOBJ variable of V_k, where $k = i_1, \ldots, i_m$, and $f(X_{i_1}, \ldots, X_{i_m})$ is a CafeOBJ term denoting the initial value of $o_{i_1,\ldots,i_m}$.

A transition $\tau_{j_1,\ldots,j_n} \in \mathcal{T}$ is denoted by a CafeOBJ action operator and declared as bop $a : H\ V_{j_1} \ldots V_{j_n} \text{-> } H$., where $V_{j_1}, \ldots, V_{j_n}$ are visible sorts. $\tau_{j_1,\ldots,j_n}$ may change the value returned by $o_{i_1,\ldots,i_m}$ if it is applied in a state v such that $c_{\tau_{j_1,\ldots,j_n}}(v)$, which can be written generally as follows:

ceq $o(a(S, X_{j_1}, \ldots, X_{j_n}), X_{i_1}, \ldots, X_{i_m})$
$= $ e-a$(S, X_{j_1}, \ldots, X_{j_n}, X_{i_1}, \ldots, X_{i_m})$ if c-a$(S, X_{j_1}, \ldots, X_{j_n})$.

S is a CafeOBJ variable for H and X_k is a CafeOBJ variable of V_k, where $k = i_1, \ldots, i_m, j_1, \ldots, j_n$. a$(S, X_{j_1}, \ldots, X_{j_n})$ denotes the successor state of S wrt $\tau_{j_1,\ldots,j_n}$. e-a$(S, X_{j_1}, \ldots, X_{j_n}, X_{i_1}, \ldots, X_{i_m})$ denotes the value returned by $o_{i_1,\ldots,i_m}$ in the successor state. c-a$(S, X_{j_1}, \ldots, X_{j_n})$ denotes the effective condition $c_{\tau_{j_1,\ldots,j_n}}$.

$\tau_{j_1,\ldots,j_n}$ changes nothing if it is applied in a state v such that $\neg c_{\tau_{j_1,\ldots,j_n}}(v)$, which can be written generally as follows:

ceq a$(S, X_{j_1}, \ldots, X_{j_n}) = S$ if not c-a$(S, X_{j_1}, \ldots, X_{j_n})$.

3.4   Verification of Invariants of OTSs

Some invariants may be proved by case analysis only. But we often need to do induction on the reachable state space of an OTS $\mathcal{S}$ (the number of transitions applied). We describe how to prove a predicate p_1 is invariant to $\mathcal{S}$ using induction by writing proof scores in CafeOBJ. The proof that p_1 is invariant to $\mathcal{S}$

often needs other predicates. We suppose that $p_2, \ldots, p_n$ are such predicates. We then prove $p_1 \wedge \ldots \wedge p_n$ invariant to $\mathcal{S}$. Let $x_{i_1}, \ldots, x_{i_{m_i}}$ of types $D_{i_1}, \ldots, D_{i_{m_i}}$ be all free variables in p_i ($i = 1, \ldots, n$) except for v whose type is Υ.

We first declare the operators denoting $p_1, \ldots, p_n$. Their defining equations in a module INV (which imports the module where $\mathcal{S}$) are written as follows:

```
op invᵢ  :  H Vᵢ₁ ... Vᵢₘᵢ  -> Bool
eq  invᵢ(S, Xᵢ₁, ..., Xᵢₘᵢ)  =  pᵢ(S, Xᵢ₁, ..., Xᵢₘᵢ) .
```

where $i = 1, \ldots, n$. V_k ($k = i_1, \ldots, i_{m_i}$) is a visible sort denoting D_k, and X_k is a CafeOBJ variable whose sort is V_k. $p_i(S, X_{i_1}, \ldots, X_{i_{m_i}})$ is a CafeOBJ term denoting p_i. In INV, we also declare a constant x_k denoting an arbitrary value of V_k ($k = 1, \ldots, n$). We then declare the operators denoting basic formulas to show in the inductive cases and their defining equations in a module ISTEP (which imports INV) as follows:

```
op istepᵢ  :  Vᵢ₁ ... Vᵢₘᵢ  -> Bool
eq  istepᵢ(Xᵢ₁, ..., Xᵢₘᵢ)  =  invᵢ(s, Xᵢ₁, ..., Xᵢₘᵢ) implies invᵢ(s', Xᵢ₁, ..., Xᵢₘᵢ) .
```

where $i = 1, \ldots, n$. s and s' are constants of H, denoting an arbitrary state and a successor state of s.

The proof of each inductive case often requires case analysis. Let us consider the inductive case where it is shown that $\tau_{j_1, \ldots, j_n}$ preserves p_i. Suppose that the state space is split into l sub-spaces for the proof of the inductive case, and that each sub-space is characterized by a predicate $case_k$ ($k = 1, \ldots, l$) such that $(case_1 \vee \ldots \vee case_l) \Leftrightarrow$ true. Also suppose that $\tau_{j_1, \ldots, j_n}$ is denoted by an action operator a, and visible sorts $V_{j_1}, \ldots, V_{j_n}$ correspond to data types $D_{j_1}, \ldots, D_{j_n}$ of the parameters of $\tau_{j_1, \ldots, j_n}$. The proof for case $case_k$ is shown here:

```
open ISTEP
   -- arbitrary objects
   op yⱼ₁ :-> Vⱼ₁ .      ...      op yⱼₙ :-> Vⱼₙ .
   -- assumptions
   Declarations of equations denoting caseₖ.
   -- successor state
   eq s' = a(s, yⱼ₁, ..., yⱼₙ) .
   -- check if the predicate is true
   red SIHᵢ implies istepᵢ(xᵢ₁, ..., xᵢₘᵢ) .
close
```

where $i = 1, \ldots, n$. A comment starts with -- and terminates at the end of the line. SIH_i is a CafeOBJ term denoting what strengthens the inductive hypothesis $inv_i(s, X_{i_1}, \ldots, X_{i_{m_i}})$ and can be the (and) concatenation of different predicates ranging from $inv_1(\ldots)$ to $inv_n(\ldots)$. The CafeOBJ command red is used to reduce a term denoting a proposition to its truth value. open creates a temporary module that imports a module given as an argument, and close destroys the temporary module. Parts enclosed with open and close are basic units of proof scores, which are called proof passages.

4   Formalization of the Mondex System

4.1   Basic Data Types

Key data types used in the OTS model of the Mondex system include: `Purse`,
`Message` and `Ether`. Each `Purse` of the Mondex system is constructed using the
CafeOBJ operator `mk-purse` that takes the following arguments:

(1) `Name`: the name of the purse, which is used as identifier of the purse.
(2) Previous `Balance`: the balance before a coming transaction. Note that this
    component is introduced and used by us only with the purpose to express and
    verify the desired properties directly as invariants, while this component is
    not used in the Z method and its follow-up work. The value of this component
    is set (updated) to the current balance when a transaction is going to happen.
(3) Current `Balance`: the current balance of the purse.
(4) `Seqnum`: the sequence number, which is globally unique and is to be used in
    the next transaction. This number is increased during any transaction, and
    thus it is necessary in avoiding replay attacks.
(5) `Status`: the status of the purse. Possible status of a purse includes: `idle`,
    `epr`, `epv`, and `epa`. `idle` denotes that a purse is in a status either before
    or after a transaction. The other three status labels denote that a purse is
    expecting a value-request message, expecting a value-transfer message, and
    expecting an acknowledgement message, respectively.
(6) `Paydetail`: the payment detail of a transaction that the purse is currently in-
    volved in or just finished. A payment detail is constructed using the CafeOBJ
    operator `mk-pay` that takes five arguments: the name of the `FromPurse`
    and its sequence number, the name of the `ToPurse` and its sequence num-
    ber, and the amount of value (also of sort `Bal` for simplicity) to be trans-
    ferred. Given a payment detail `mk-pay(FN:Name, FS:Seqnum, TN:Name,`
    `TS:Seqnum, V:Bal)`, projection operators `from`, `fromno`, `to`, `tono`, and
    `value` are defined to obtain each of its components.
(7) `Exlog`: the exception log, which is a list of payment details of failed trans-
    actions. A transaction can fail since a message may be lost, and cards may
    abort a transaction, etc. If there are possibilities that money may be lost
    during a failed transaction, the current payment detail will be recorded into
    the exception log. A predicate `_/inexlog_` is defined to check whether a
    payment detail is in the exception log or not.

Given a purse `mk-purse(N:Name, PB:Bal, CB:Bal, SE:Seqnum, ST:Status,`
`P:Paydetail, E:Exlog)`, projection operators `name`, `pbal`, `bal`, `seq`, `sta`, `pay`,
and `exlog` are defined to obtain each of its components.

According to the communication protocol, there are five kinds of `Message`s:
`startfrom(N:Name, V:Bal, S:Seqnum)`, `startto(N:Name, V:Bal, S:Seqnum)`,
`req(P:Paydetail)`, `val(P:Paydetail)`, and `ack(P:Paydetail)`. For each kind
of message, there exists a predicate to check the attribution of the message, such
as `isstartfrom` and `isreq` etc. For the first two messages, projection operators
`nameofm`, `valueofm` and `seqofm` are defined, and for the remaining three messages,
projection operators `pdofm` are defined.

The Ether is considered as a bag (multi-set) of messages, which is used to formalize the communication channel. All messages sent are put into the ether and a purse receives a message by selecting one from the ether. In this way, we model that a message can be read by any purse. The constructors of Ether are CafeOBJ operators nil and _,_ (of Ethers, where Message is declared as a sub-sort of Ether). And there are two predicates_/in_ and empty? checking whether a message is in ether or whether the ether is empty. Another two operators, get and top, are defined to remove the first element and obtain the first element of ether, respectively.

4.2   OTS Model and Its CafeOBJ Specification

Two observers denoted by CafeOBJ observation operators purse and ether are declared as follows:

```
bop purse : Sys Name -> Purse.          bop ether : Sys -> Ether.
```

where sort Sys is a hidden sort denoting the universal state space Υ of the OTS model of the Mondex system. Given a state and a purse name, observer purse returns the content (components) of the purse in this state, and given a state, observer ether returns the content (messages) of the ether in this state.

Given a constant init:Sys denoting any initial state of the Mondex system, the initial state is characterized by the following equations:

```
eq purse(init,P)
  = mk-purse(P,ib(P,seedv),ib(P,seedv),is(P,seedn),idle,none,emptyexlog).
eq ether(init) = nil.
```

In the first equation, variable P:Name denotes an arbitrary purse; ib(P,seedv) is a term denoting the previous balance of P, which is equal to its current balance in initial state; is(P,seedn) is a term denoting the initial sequence number of P; and any purse denoted by P is initially in the status idle, and there are no payment details or exception logs for P (denoted by none and emptylog, respectively). The second equation says that initially the ether is empty (denoted by nil), namely that no message exists in the ether.

Nine transitions, which characterize sending and receiving messages, and also the security features of the Mondex system, are declared as follows:

```
bop startpay      : Sys Name Name Bal -> Sys
bop recstartfrom : Sys Name Message   -> Sys
bop recstartto    : Sys Name Message   -> Sys
bop recreq        : Sys Name Message   -> Sys
bop recval        : Sys Name Message   -> Sys
bop recack        : Sys Name Message   -> Sys
bop drop          : Sys -> Sys
bop duplicate     : Sys -> Sys
bop abort         : Sys Name -> Sys
```

(1) Transition denoted by the CafeOBJ action operator startpay characterizes that the communication device ascertains a transaction and sends the startfrom and startto messages.

```
op c-startpay : Sys Name Name Bal -> Bool
eq c-startpay(S,P1,P2,V)
  = sta(purse(S,P1)) = idle and sta(purse(S,P2)) = idle and not(P1 = P2).
ceq purse(startpay(S,P1,P2,V),Q) = purse(S,Q)      if c-startpay(S,P1,P2,V).
ceq ether(startpay(S,P1,P2,V))
  = startfrom(P2,V,seq(purse(S,P2))),
    startto(P1,V,seq(purse(S,P1))),ether(S)     if c-startpay(S,P1,P2,V).
ceq startpay(S,P1,P2,V) = S                     if not c-startpay(S,P1,P2,V).
```

The effective condition denoted by `c-startpay` demands that (the first equation): the two purses denoted by `P1` and `P2` be in the `idle` status, namely that they are currently not involved in any other transactions; and that they be different purses. If `startpay` is applied when the condition holds: the components of any purse denoted by `Q` are not changed (the second conditional equation); and two messages `startfrom` and `startto` are put into the ether (the third conditional equation). The last conditional equation says that even if `startpay` is applied when the condition does not hold, nothing changes.

(2) Transition denoted by the CafeOBJ action operator `recstartfrom` characterizes that a purse receives the message `startfrom`.

```
op c-recstartfrom : Sys Name Message -> Bool
eq c-recstartfrom(S,P,M)
  = M /in ether(S) and isstartfrom(M) and sta(purse(S,P)) = idle and
    not(P = nameofm(M)) and valueofm(M) <= bal(purse(S,P)) .
ceq purse(recstartfrom(S,P,M),Q)
  = mk-purse(Q,(if (P=Q) then bal(purse(S,Q)) else pbal(purse(S,Q))fi),
              bal(purse(S,Q)),(if (P=Q) then nextseqnum(seq(purse(S,Q)))
                                         else seq(purse(S,Q)) fi),
          (if (P = Q) then epr else sta(purse(S,Q)) fi),
          (if (P = Q) then mk-pay(Q,seq(purse(S,Q)),
                              nameofm(M),seqofm(M),valueofm(M))
                       else pay(purse(S,Q)) fi),
          exlog(purse(S,Q)))              if c-recstartfrom(S,P,M).
ceq ether(recstartfrom(S,P,M)) = ether(S)      if c-recstartfrom(S,P,M).
ceq recstartfrom(S,P,M) = S                    if not c-recstartfrom(S,P,M).
```

The effective condition denoted by `c-recstartfrom` demands that: there exist a `startfrom` message in the ether; the purse P that is going to receive the message be in the status `idle`; the name argument of the `startfrom` message be other than P (namely that P is not going to do a transaction with itself); and last P have enough value for this request.

If `recstartfrom` is applied when the condition holds: the previous balance of P is updated to its current balance, namely to record the current balance before a coming transaction as the previous balance; increase the sequence number; change the status of P to `epr`; and generate a payment detail. Note that two variables P and Q both denote purses. However, P denotes the purse receiving the message `startfrom` (executing the transition `recstartfrom`), and Q denotes the purse that the observer `purse` are "observing" on. After applying `recstartfrom`, P becomes the `FromPurse` of a transaction denoted by its payment detail.

(3) Transition denoted by the CafeOBJ action operator `recstartto` character-izes that a purse receives the message `startto`.

```
op c-recstartto : Sys Name Message -> Bool
eq c-recstartto(S,P,M)
   = M /in ether(S) and isstartto(M) and sta(purse(S,P)) = idle and
     not(P = nameofm(M)) .
ceq purse(recstartto(S,P,M),Q)
   = mk-purse(Q,(if (P=Q) then bal(purse(S,Q)) else pbal(purse(S,Q))fi),
                 bal(purse(S,Q)),(if (P=Q) then nextseqnum(seq(purse(S,Q)))
                                           else seq(purse(S,Q)) fi),
              (if (P = Q) then epv else sta(purse(S,Q)) fi),
              (if (P = Q) then mk-pay(nameofm(M),seqofm(M),
                                      Q,seq(purse(S,Q)),valueofm(M))
                          else pay(purse(S,Q)) fi),
              log(purse(S,Q)))                    if c-recstartto(S,P,M).
ceq ether(recstartto(S,P,M))
   = req(pd(nameofm(M),seqofm(M),P,seq(purse(S,P))),valueofm(M))),
       ether(S)                                   if c-recstartto(S,P,M).
ceq recstartto(S,P,M) = S                     if not c-recstartto(S,P,M).
```

Equations defining effective condition and application of transition `recstartto` are similar to those of transition `recstartfrom`, except that: the condition de-mands a `startto` message in the ether; the status of the purse is changed to `epv`; and a `req` message is put into the ether. After applying `recstartto`, P becomes the `ToPurse` of the transaction denoted by its payment detail.

(4) Transition denoted by the CafeOBJ action operator `recreq` characterizes that a purse receives the message `req`.

```
op c-recreq : Sys Name Message -> Bool
eq c-recreq(S,P,M)
   = M /in ether(S) and isreq(M) and sta(purse(S,P)) = epr and
     pay(purse(S,P)) = pdofm(M) .
ceq purse(recreq(S,P,M),Q)
   = mk-purse(Q,pbal(purse(S,Q)),
              (if (P = Q) then (bal(purse(S,Q)) - value(pdofm(M)))
                          else bal(purse(S,Q)) fi),
              seq(purse(S,Q)),
              (if (P = Q) then epa else sta(purse(S,Q)) fi),
              pay(purse(S,Q)),log(purse(S,Q)))      if c-recreq(S,P,M).
ceq ether(recreq(S,P,M)) = val(pdofm(M)),ether(S)   if c-recreq(S,P,M).
ceq recreq(S,P,M) = S                           if not c-recreq(S,P,M).
```

The effective condition denoted by `c-recreq` demands that: there exist a `req` message in the ether; the purse P that is going to receive the `req` message be in the status `epr`; and the payment detail of the `req` message be equal to the payment detail of P. If `recreq` is applied when the condition holds, the current balance of P is deceased with the requested amount of value; the status of P is changed to `epa`; and a `val` message is put into the ether.

(5) Transition denoted by the CafeOBJ action operator `recval` characterizes that a purse receives the message `val`.

```
op c-recval : Sys Name Message -> Bool
eq c-recval(S,P,M)
   = M /in ether(S) and isval(M) and sta(purse(S,P)) = epv and
     pay(purse(S,P)) = pdofm(M) .
ceq purse(recval(S,P,M),Q)
   = mk-purse(Q,pbal(purse(S,Q)),
                (if (P = Q) then (bal(purse(S,Q)) + value(pdofm(M)))
                            else bal(purse(S,Q)) fi),
              seq(purse(S,Q)),
              (if (P = Q) then idle else sta(purse(S,Q)) fi),
              pay(purse(S,Q)),log(purse(S,Q)))       if c-recval(S,P,M).
ceq ether(recval(S,P,M)) = ack(pdofm(M)),ether(S)    if c-recval(S,P,M).
ceq recval(S,P,M) = S                             if not c-recval(S,P,M).
```

The effective condition denoted by `c-recval` demands that: there exist a `val` message in the ether; the purse P that is going to receive the message be in the status `epv`; and the payment detail of the `val` message be equal to the payment detail of the purse P. If `recval` is applied when the condition holds: the current balance of P is increased with the transferred amount of value; the status of P is changed to `idle`, which means that the transaction is completed at the ToPurse's side; and an `ack` message is put into the ether.

(6) Transition denoted by the CafeOBJ action operator `recack` characterizes that a purse receives the message `ack`.

```
op c-recack : Sys Purse Message -> Bool
eq c-recack(S,P,M)
   = M /in ether(S) and isack(M) and sta(purse(S,P)) = epa and
     pay(purse(S,P)) = pdofm(M) .
ceq purse(recack(S,P,M),Q)
   = mk-purse(Q,pbal(purse(S,Q)),bal(purse(S,Q)),seq(purse(S,Q)),
                (if (P = Q) then idle else sta(purse(S,Q)) fi),
                pay(purse(S,Q)),log(purse(S,Q))) if c-recack(S,P,M).
ceq ether(recack(S,P,M)) = ether(S)             if c-recack(S,P,M).
ceq recack(S,P,M) = S                        if not c-recack(S,P,M).
```

The effective condition denoted by `c-recack` demands that: there exist an `ack` message in the ether; the purse P that is going to receive the `ack` message be in the status `epa`; and the payment detail of the `ack` message be equal to the payment detail of P. If `recack` is applied when the condition holds: the status of P is changed to `idle`, which denotes that a transaction is successfully completed.

Besides the above described transitions that correspond to sending and receiving messages of the communication protocol of the Mondex system, there are three more transitions to characterize security features of the Mondex system, which include: the ether is unreliable, and a transaction can be stopped at any time.

(7) To characterize that the messages in the ether may be lost and replayed, we define two more transitions: drop and duplicate. As long as the ether is not empty, transition drop can remove a message from the ether, and transition duplicate can duplicate a message in the ether. Equations defining these two transitions are as follows:

```
op c-drop : Sys -> Bool
eq c-drop(S) = not empty?(ether(S)) .
ceq purse(drop(S),Q) = purse(S,Q)                      if c-drop(S).
ceq ether(drop(S)) = get(ether(S))                     if c-drop(S).
ceq drop(S) = S                                    if not c-drop(S).

op c-duplicate : Sys -> Bool
eq c-duplicate(S) = not empty?(ether(S)) .
ceq purse(duplicate(S),Q) = purse(S,Q)            if c-duplicate(S).
ceq ether(duplicate(S)) = top(ether(S)),ether(S) if c-duplicate(S).
ceq duplicate(S) = S                          if not c-duplicate(S).
```

(8) To characterize that a transaction can be stopped at any time, namely that a purse can abort a transaction at any time the card-holder wishes, we define the transition abort as follows:

```
eq purse(abort(S,P),Q)
   = mk-purse(Q,pbal(purse(S,Q)),bal(purse(S,Q)),
             (if (P = Q) then nextseqnum(seq(purse(S,Q)))
                         else seq(purse(S,Q)) fi),
             (if (P = Q) then idle else sta(purse(S,Q)) fi),
             pay(purse(S,Q)),
             (if (P = Q) then
                 (if (sta(purse(S,Q)) = epa or sta(purse(S,Q)) = epv)
                             then pay(purse(S,Q)) @ log(purse(S,Q))
                             else log(purse(S,Q)) fi)
                         else log(purse(S,Q)) fi)).
eq ether(abort(S,P)) = ether(S) .
```

Note that no effective condition is defined for transition abort, which means that the transition abort can be executed at any time. When a purse aborts a transaction, the status of the purse is changed to idle, and its sequence number is increased. In addition, if a purse aborts a transaction in status epa or epv, the payment detail of this transaction must be recorded to the exception log of the aborting purse (through concatenation operator @). This is because that there exist possibilities that value may be lost when a FromPurse has transferred value (in epa) or a ToPurse is waiting for value being transferred (in epv, namely that it has not received the value). Note that a same payment detail may be logged in both FromPurse and ToPurse, although a value is only lost once. The purpose of this is to analyze the exception logs in the future by comparing the two logs and refund value if value did be lost.

5   Verification of the Mondex System

5.1   Formal Definitions of the Properties

Through making use of the introduced component "previous balance", we are able to define the two desired security properties of the Mondex system as invariants. Formal definitions of the properties are below.

1. For any reachable state s, any two purses denoted by p_1 and p_2:

$(\mathtt{sta}(\mathtt{purse}(s,p_1))) = \mathtt{idle}$ and $\mathtt{sta}(\mathtt{purse}(s,p_2)) = \mathtt{idle}$ and
$\mathtt{pay}(\mathtt{purse}(s,p_1)) = \mathtt{pay}(\mathtt{purse}(s,p_2))$ and $\mathtt{not}(p_1 = p_2))$
implies
$(\mathtt{bal}(\mathtt{purse}(s,p_1)) + \mathtt{bal}(\mathtt{purse}(s,p_2))$ <= $\mathtt{pbal}(\mathtt{purse}(s,p_1)) + \mathtt{pbal}(\mathtt{purse}(s,p_2)))$.

In the premise of Property 1, two arbitrary different purses denoted by p_1 and p_2 are both in the status $\mathtt{idle}$, which means that p_1 and p_2 are currently not involved in any transactions; additionally, the equality of their payment details expresses that either they are never involved in any transactions (thus the payment details are both $\mathtt{none}$), or a transaction between them has just finished (finished normally or abnormally by aborting the transaction does not matter). Therefore, Property 1 can be stated as: for two arbitrary different purses, (1) if no transaction ever happens for each of the two purses, or (2) after any one transaction between them, the sum of their current balances will not be increased (less than or equal to the sum of their balances before the transaction). This implies the informal description of Property 1 that covers all possible purses for any number of transactions.

2. For any reachable state s, any two purses denoted by p_1 and p_2:

$(\mathtt{sta}(\mathtt{purse}(s,p_1))) = \mathtt{idle}$ and $\mathtt{sta}(\mathtt{purse}(s,p_2)) = \mathtt{idle}$ and
$\mathtt{pay}(\mathtt{purse}(s,p_1)) = \mathtt{pay}(\mathtt{purse}(s,p_2))$ and $\mathtt{not}(p_1 = p_2))$
implies
$(\mathtt{if}\ \mathtt{pay}(\mathtt{purse}(s,p_1))\ \mathtt{/inexlog}\ \mathtt{log}(\mathtt{purse}(s,p_1))$ and
$\quad \mathtt{pay}(\mathtt{purse}(s,p_2))\ \mathtt{/inexlog}\ \mathtt{log}(\mathtt{purse}(s,p_2))$
$\ \mathtt{then}\ \mathtt{bal}(\mathtt{purse}(s,p_1)) + \mathtt{bal}(\mathtt{purse}(s,p_2)) + \mathtt{lost}(\mathtt{pay}(\mathtt{purse}(s,p_1)))$
$\qquad = \mathtt{pbal}(\mathtt{purse}(s,p_1)) + \mathtt{pbal}(\mathtt{purse}(s,p_2))$
$\ \mathtt{else}\ \mathtt{bal}(\mathtt{purse}(s,p_1)) + \mathtt{bal}(\mathtt{purse}(s,p_2))$
$\qquad = \mathtt{pbal}(\mathtt{purse}(s,p_1)) + \mathtt{pbal}(\mathtt{purse}(s,p_2))\ \mathtt{fi})$.

The premise of Property 2 is exactly same as Property 1. To understand the conclusion of Property 2, let us see the following table, which analyzes, under the property's premise, whether value is lost or not during a transaction.[2]

A $\mathtt{FromPurse}$ can be in the status $\mathtt{idle}$, $\mathtt{epr}$ or $\mathtt{epa}$, and a $\mathtt{ToPurse}$ can be in the status $\mathtt{idle}$ or $\mathtt{epv}$. Since aborting transaction by either the $\mathtt{FromPurse}$ or the $\mathtt{ToPurse}$ in status $\mathtt{idle}$ only increases its sequence number, and the current and previous balances remain unchanged, we only analyze the situations that

---

[2] As to the situation where two purses are never involved in any transactions, it is trivial that no value is lost. So this situation is omitted in the following discussion.

from \ to		abort	non-abort
abort	log	*lost* (a)	not lost (b)
	non-log	not lost (c)	*impossible* (d)
non-abort		*impossible* (e)	not lost (f)

a purse aborts in the status epr, epa (for FromPurse) and epv (for ToPurse). non-abort in the table denotes that a purse successfully finished the transaction on its side, and abort denotes that a purse finished the transaction (on its side) by aborting it. log and non-log are used to distinguish that FromPurse aborts the transaction on status epa or epr (only aborting in epa will be logged). The ToPurse will always log the transaction when aborting the transaction (in epv). The items of the table (labeled (a) – (f)) are explained as follows:

(a) The FromPurse aborts the transaction after it decreases its current balance and sends the val message (in epa), and the ToPurse aborts the transaction before it receives the val message (in epv). Therefore value is lost.

(b) The FromPurse aborts the transaction after it decreases its current balance and sends the val message, and the ToPurse does not abort the transaction. Since the ToPurse is in status idle (as the premise says), it has successfully received the val message and therefore no value is lost.

(c) The FromPurse aborts the transaction before it decreases its current balance (in epr), and the ToPurse aborts while waiting for the val message (in epv). Therefore no value is lost.

(d) The FromPurse aborts the transaction before it decreases its current balance, and the ToPurse finishes the transaction successfully. This situation is impossible since no val message was sent.

(e) The FromPurse successfully finished the transaction, and the ToPurse aborts the transaction while waiting for the val message. This situation is impossible since no ack message was sent.

(f) Both the FromPurse and ToPurse finish the transaction successfully. Therefore no value is lost.

The above analyzed situations from (a) – (f) are reflected in the formula for Property 2, in which lost is a function that counts the lost value of a transaction (denoted by the payment detail). Therefore, for any one transaction between two arbitrary different purses, if value is lost, the value is logged in the exception logs of both the FromPurse and ToPurse, and the sum of their current balances plus the lost value is equal to the sum of their previous balances before this transaction; otherwise, value is not lost, and the sum of their current balances is equal to the sum of their previous balances before this transaction.

5.2 Verification of the Properties

We describe partly an inductive case of the proof of Property 2, which shows that transition abort preserves the property. Among those invariants that are used as lemmas to strengthen the inductive hypothesis of Property 2, we introduce two of them (which are called Properties 3 and 4), and a proof passage that uses these two lemmas. Formal definition of Properties 3 and 4 are as follows:

3. For any reachable state s and any purse denoted by p :

    `sta(purse(`s`,`p`)) = epv implies bal(purse(`s`,`p`)) = pbal(purse(`s`,`p`)).`

4. For any reachable state s and any purse denoted by p :

    `pay(purse(`s`,`p`)) /inexlog log(purse(`s`,`p`)) and from(pay(purse(`s`,`p`))) =` p
    `implies`
    `bal(purse(`s`,`p`)) = pbal(purse(`s`,`p`)) - value(pay(purse(`s`,`p`))).`

As introduced in Section 2, we declare the operators denoting Properties 2, 3 and 4 in a module `INV` as follows:

```
op inv2 : Sys Name Name -> Bool
op inv3 : Sys Name -> Bool                    op inv4 : Sys Name -> Bool
```

The operators are defined with equations to denote the properties. We also declare the operator denoting the basic formula to prove in each inductive case of the proof of Property 2 and its defining equation in a module `ISTEP` as follows:

```
op istep2 : Name Name -> Bool
eq istep2(P1,P2) = inv2(s,P1,P2) implies inv2(s',P1,P2) .
```

where `s` and `s'` are constants of sort `Sys`. `s` denotes an arbitrary state and `s'` denotes a successor state of `s`.

The proof passage for proving the inductive case **abort** of Property 2, which uses Properties 3 and 4 to strengthen the inductive hypothesis, is as follows:

```
open ISTEP
  -- arbitrary objects
  op q : -> Name.
  -- assumption
  eq (p1 = q) = false.              eq p2 = q.
  eq sta(purse(s,q)) = epv.
  eq (pay(purse(s,p1)) /inexlog log(purse(s,p1))) = true.
  eq sta(purse(s,p1)) = idle .      eq pay(purse(s,q)) = pay(purse(s,p1)).
  eq (bal(purse(s,q)) = pbal(purse(s,q))) = false.
  -- successor state
  eq s' = abort(s,q).
  -- check if the predicate is true.
  red inv3(s,q) and inv4(s,p1) implies istep2(p1,p2).
close
```

The equations in the "assumption" part characterize the case being analyzed. In this proof passage, `inv3(s,q)` and `inv4(s,p1)` are used to strengthen the inductive hypothesis denoted by `inv2(p1,p2)`. Proof passages for the other cases of the inductive case **abort** are written similarly, and some other properties are used as lemmas to prove this inductive case.

Here is a brief summarization of the OTS/CafeOBJ specification and verification of the Mondex system. The CafeOBJ specification of the OTS model of the Mondex system is approximately 1100 lines. And 53 other invariant properties are proved and used as lemmas to prove the two desired properties of the Mondex system. The proof scores are approximately 47000 lines. Although the proof scores seem to be long, most of the work is "copy-and-paste" work, and the difficult task in verification is to come up with some of those 53 lemmas. It took about 5 minutes to have the CafeOBJ system load the CafeOBJ specification and execute all the proof scores on a computer with 3.2GHz processor and 2GB memory. It took a couple of weeks to complete the case study.

6   Falsification of the Mondex System

As a complement to the interactive verification of the OTS/CafeOBJ method, we report on a way of automatically falsifying the Mondex system by employing Maude model checking facilities (in particular the Maude `search` command [13]) to take advantage of (1) the fully automatic verification/falsification procedure, and (2) informative counterexamples.

An implemented prototype translator [15] that translates the OTS/CafeOBJ specifications into corresponding Maude specifications is used as the basis for this falsification. As a sibling language of CafeOBJ, Maude is a specification and programming language based on rewrite logic, which is equipped with model checking facilities. The primary reason for choosing Maude is that it supports model checking on abstract data types, including inductively defined data types, and does not require the state space of a system to be finite, although the reachable state space of the system should be finite. This finiteness restriction can be abandoned when using Maude `search` command to explicitly explore a finite reachable state space of a system for counterexamples (namely falsification).

One may wonder why we need falsification of the Mondex system, since we have already verified it using the OTS/CafeOBJ method. The reasons are that falsification can be used to facilitate, in different stages, the interactive verification of the two security properties:

1. Before carrying out the interactive verification, falsifying the two properties can help obtain a certain degree of confidence of the correctness (within a finite reachable state space) of the system and property specifications.
2. While conducting the interactive verification, generating good and correct lemmas is not a simple task. Falsification can help, in this stage, to filter out those lemmas generated which are essentially wrong.

6.1   Maude Specification of the Mondex System

We show directly the translated Maude specification for transition `recack` as a demonstration example. More technical details (translation rules and soundness proof wrt counterexamples [3]) can be found in [14,15].

---

[3] i.e. for any counterexample reported by Maude for the translated specification, there exists a corresponding counterexample in the original OTS/CafeOBJ specification.

Consider two different purses denoted by Maude constants `p1` and `p2` of sort `Name`, the Maude specification of the OTS/CafeOBJ transition `recack` is:

```
crl[recack_p1]:
  (purse[p1] : PS1) (purse[p2] : PS2) (ether : (M,EH)) (steps : C)
  =>
  (purse[p1] :
  mk-purse(p1,pbal(PS1),bal(PS1),seq(PS1),idle,pay(PS1),log(PS1)))
  (purse[p2] :
  mk-purse(p2,pbal(PS2),bal(PS2),seq(PS2),sta(PS2),pay(PS2),log(PS2)))
  (ether : (M,EH)) (steps : (C + 1))
if (isack(M) and sta(PS1) = epa and pay(PS1) = pdofm(M) and C < bound).
```

The set of equations of the OTS/CafeOBJ specification that characterizes the transition `recack` is translated into Maude conditional rewrite rules. `crl` is the keyword to declare a conditional rewrite rule, and `recack_p1` in the bracket is the label of this rule, which denotes that `p1` receives the message `ack`.

The left-hand side of the rule (before `=>`) denotes the current state of the OTS, which consists of four terms of observations. Maude variables `PS1` and `PS2` of sort `Purse` denote the return values of observer `purse` on purses `p1` and `p2`, respectively. The term `(M,EH)` of sort `Ether` denotes that current ether consists of a message `M` and the remaining part `EH` of the ether. The right-hand side of the rule (after `=>`) denotes the successor state of the OTS wrt the execution of the rule. The component `status` of purse `p1` is changed to `idle`, and other components remain unchanged. The return value of observer `purse` on purse `p2`, and the return value of observer `ether` remain unchanged.

Note that an additional observer `steps` is introduced in the rule. The return value of `steps` is increased by 1 after the execution of the rule. Through defining a predicate `C < bound` in the condition of the rule, we can restrict execution of the OTS within finite steps (less than `bound`, a natural number determined by human verifiers), which is inspired by Bounded Model Checking.

Predicates in the condition of the rule check that: there exists an `ack` message in the ether; the purse `p1` that is going to receive the message is in the status `epa`; and the payment detail of the `ack` message is equal to the payment detail of `p1`. Note that another similar Maude rewrite rule is also generated to characterize the situation in which purse `p2` receives the `ack` message.

6.2   Falsification of the Mondex System

We show the translated Maude specification of Property 1 of the Mondex system as follows, and Property 2 is translated similarly:

```
search [1] in MONDEX :
init =>* (purse[P1] : PS1) (purse[P2] : PS2) S
      such that not((sta(PS1) = idle and sta(PS2) = idle and
                     pay(PS1) = pay(PS2) and not(P1 = P2))
                     implies
                     (bal(PS1) + bal(PS2) <= pbal(PS1) + pbal(PS2))).
```

Maude `search` command explores the tree of possible rewrites starting at an initial state `init` to a final state that matches pattern `(purse[P1] : PS1)` (purse[P2] : PS2) S and satisfies the condition denoted by the term after such that. In the above command, MONDEX is a Maude module that describes the OTS of the Mondex system (in which the equation defining init and those rewrite rules are defined). P1 and P2 are variables of sort Name denoting two arbitrary purses. S is a variable of sort Sys denoting an arbitrary state of the OTS. Note that in the condition part, we use the negation operator not in front of the term denoting Property 1, since we aim at falsification of the property.

Setting bound to 9, and considering two purses p1 and p2 in the initial state init, we feed the above search command into Maude system, and No Solution is returned, which denotes that no counterexample is found.

We now give a simple example showing that the falsification can help filter out a lemma generated during interactive verification of the OTS/CafeOBJ method. The lemma, named here as Property 5, is as follows:

5. For any reachable state s, any two purses denoted by p_1 and p_2:

pay(purse(s,p_1)) = none and from(pay(purse(s,p_2))) = p_1 and not($p_1 = p_2$)
implies
fromno(pay(purse(s,p_2))) = seq(purse(s,p_1)).

Intuitively Property 5 says that: if a purse p1's payment detail is none, and the from component of the payment detail of another purse p2 is equal to p1, then the fromno component of the payment detail of p2 is equal to p1's current sequence number. This seems to be reasonable since, when p1's payment detail is none, this means that p1 has never been involved in any transactions. And thus p1's sequence number has never increased. The property describes the situation when two purses p1 and p2 are going to have a transaction, and p2 has received the startto message, but p1 has not yet received the startfrom message.

However, Property 5 is actually incorrect, because even if p1's payment detail is none, it could execute the abort transition freely before it receives the startfrom message, since no condition is defined for abort. Therefore, p1's sequence number may increase. A correct conclusion of Property 5 should be fromno(pay(purse(s,p_2))) <= seq(purse(s,p_1)).

To realize this incorrectness of Property 5 by using the interactive verification of the OTS/CafeOBJ method, a certain amount of proof effort is needed, however, the incorrectness can be immediately reported by Maude system as a counterexample as follows:

```
state 0: ...
        ===[ crl ... [label startpay_p1_p2_con] ]===>
state 1: ...
        ===[ crl ... [label recstartto_p2] ]===>
state 8: ...
        ===[ crl ... [label abort_p1] ]===>
state 51: ...
```

where state 0 denotes the initial state and state 51 denotes the state where a counterexample is found. The omitted parts after each numbered state are terms denoting corresponding states, and the omitted parts after crl are terms denoting the rewrite rules with corresponding labels. In state 51, the fromno component of p2 is is(p1,seedn), but the sequence number of p1 is nextseqnum (is(p1, seedn)), which is contrary to Property 5.

7   Related Work

The Mondex system was originally specified and manually proved for correctness using the Z method [9]. In [9], two models of the Mondex system were developed, where the first is an abstract model that models value exchanges between purses as atomic transaction, and the second is a concrete model that models value exchanges between purses following the communication protocol. It is then proved that the two security properties hold for the abstract model, and the concrete model is a refinement of the abstract one.

Following the original Z work, a number of other formal methods, such as KIV [5,6], RAISE [7] and Alloy [8] etc, have been employed for the Mondex problem. We discuss these related work regarding the aspects of modeling, refinement proof (or verification) and falsification, respectively.

The RAISE and Alloy work seem to intentionally follow closely the modeling methods of the original Z work, while keeping their own features. The KIV work provides an alternative operational style formalization of the Mondex system using (two) abstract state machines, and makes several simplifications and modifications, which include, for example: removed of the global input while obtaining the input from the ether; removed of the ignore operation that does nothing (which is needed by the refinement theory used in Z work); and merging the purses' two idling status, eaFrom and eaTo, into one idle status, etc.

Our work of modeling the Mondex system as an OTS in an operational style is inspired by the KIV work, which from our point of view is simpler than the Z modeling method (a similar statement is made in the KIV work). In addition, we made several further modifications to the KIV modeling as follows:

1. Since messages existing in ether can be lost, we abandoned the assumption made in KIV modeling that startfrom and startto messages are always available in ether. In our model, no message exists in the initial ether.
2. To reflect that a purse can abort a transaction at any time, as the cardholder wishes, we did not define any effective condition for the transition abort, while a condition was defined for abort in KIV modeling.
3. We explicitly defined two transitions, duplicate and drop, to characterize that messages in the ether can be replayed or lost. The KIV modeling used ether' ⊆ ether to characterize that messages can be lost, but did not explicitly show that messages can be replayed.

To show the correctness of the properties to the Mondex system, refinement proofs are developed in Z, KIV, RAISE and Alloy work in different forms and with different features. Although the refinement construction and proof strategies are suitable for the Mondex problem, we employ an alternative way of expressing and verifying the security properties of the Mondex system directly as invariants, through using an introduced component "previous balance" into purses. Note, however, that even if different proof strategies are used, we share some similar or exactly same proof obligations. First, for the property of payment details that `from` and `to` components should be different (Section. 4.3.2 of [9]), and for the properties P-2 to P-4 for purses (Section. 4.6 of [9]), which are used in the refinement proofs of the Z and KIV work, we have proved and used as lemmas exactly the same properties in our verification; and second, for some of the properties B-2 to B-12 expressing constraints on ether (Section 5.3 of [9]), we have proved and used as lemmas very similar properties in our work.

In the RAISE and Alloy work, two different ways of falsification of the Mondex system are described, by means of translating the RSL (RAISE Specification Language) specification of the Mondex system into SAL, and appealing the Alloy analyzer (model-finding technique), respectively. In our work, Maude `search` command is used for conducting falsification through a translation into Maude specification of the Mondex system. Our work is similar to the above two work in the sense that we all consider a finite reachable state space (called finite scope in Alloy terminology), such as finite number of purses. However, our work is different from the RAISE work in the sense that we do not need to make those changes of the Mondex system as RAISE work did: (1) the possible loss of messages was not modeled in RAISE work to reduce possible changes to the ether, and (2) ranges of money and sequence numbers were restricted to 0..3, etc. Possible reason for these may be that we are able to do falsification on inductively defined data types. For example, `Ether` is defined using constructors `nil` and `_,_`. This point is also a possible difference between our work and Alloy work.

8   Conclusion

We have described two algebraic approaches to both verification and falsification of the Mondex system, and how the latter can be used to facilitate the former. We have employed alternative ways of (1) modeling the Mondex system in an operational style, rather than in a relational style, and (2) expressing and verifying (and falsifying) security properties of the Mondex system directly in terms of invariants. This work therefore provides a different way of viewing the Mondex analysis problem, and can be used to compare different modeling and proof strategies. In addition, our model of the Mondex system makes several simplifications to the original Z model (as inspired by the KIV model), and several further modifications to the KIV model to keep closer to the real problem. For more information about our work on Mondex, please visit URL: http://www.ldl.jaist.ac.jp/mondex/.

Future Work. In our modeling and verification of the Mondex system, we did not consider intruder purses that may send fake messages based on possibly gleaned information. This is because it is assumed that the *Req*, *Val* and *Ack* messages cannot be forged, which is guaranteed by some (unclear) means of cryptographic system. In the KIV work, a possible communication protocol using cryptographic algorithm was developed. Our first future work is to extend our verification by considering possible intruder purses. Our second future work relates to falsification. We are going to investigate the technical issue of how many entities (such as purses) are enough to uncover possible counterexamples when the number of entities has to be made finite for falsification.

Acknowledgements

This research is conducted as a program for the "21st Century COE Program" in Special Coordination Funds for promoting Science and Technology by Ministry of Education, Culture, Sports, Science and Technology. We would like to thank Chris George and Anne E. Haxthausen for kindly sharing their RSL specification of Mondex with us, and Mary Ann Mooradian for proof-reading the paper.

References

1. MasterCard International Inc. Mondex. URL: http://www.mondex.com/.
2. Mondex Case Study. URL: http://qpq.csl.sri.com/vsr/private/repository/Mondex-CaseStudy
3. UK Computing Research Committee, Grand Challenges in Computer Research. URL: http://www.ukcrc.org.uk/grand_challenges/index.cfm
4. Woodcock, J.: Grand Challenges 6: Dependable Systems Evolution. URL: http://www.fmnet.info/gc6/
5. Schellhorn, G., Grandy, H., Haneberg, D., Reif, W.: The Mondex challenge: machine checked proofs for an electronic purse. Technical Report, University of Augsburg (2006)
6. Schellhorn, G., Grandy, H., Haneberg, D., Reif, W.: The Mondex challenge: machine checked proofs for an electronic purse. In: Misra, J., Nipkow, T., Sekerinski, E. (eds.) FM 2006. LNCS, vol. 4085, pp. 16–31. Springer, Heidelberg (2006)
7. Haxthausen, A., George, C., Schütz, M.: Specification and proof of the Mondex electronic purse. In: AWCVS'06, UNU-IIST Report No. 347, pp. 209–224 (2006)
8. Ramananandro, T.: Mondex, An Electronic Purse: Specification and refinement checks with the Alloy model-finding method. Internship Report (2006) http://www.eleves.ens.fr/home/ramanana/work/mondex/
9. Stepney, S., Cooper, D., Woodcock, J.: An electronic purse specification, refinement, and proof. Technical monograph PRG-126, Oxford University Computing Laboratory (July 2000)
10. Ogata, K., Futatsugi, K.: Proof scores in the OTS/CafeOBJ method. In: Najm, E., Nestmann, U., Stevens, P. (eds.) FMOODS 2003. LNCS, vol. 2884, pp. 170–184. Springer, Heidelberg (2003)
11. CafeOBJ Web Site (2007) URL: http://www.ldl.jaist.ac.jp/cafeobj/
12. Diaconescu, R., Futatsugi, R.K.: CafeOBJ report. AMAST Series in Computing, vol. 6. World Scientific, Singapore (1998)
13. Clavel, M., Durán, F., Eker, S., Lincoln, P., Martí-Oliet, N., Meseguer, J., Talcott, C.: Maude manual (Version 2.2) (2007) URL: http://maude.cs.uiuc.edu/maude2-manual/
14. Nakamura, M., Kong, W., Ogata, K., Futatsugi, K.: A complete specification translation from OTS/CafeOBJ into OTS/Maude. IEICE TR, SS2006 13, 1–6 (2006)
15. Kong, W., Ogata, K., Futatsugi, K.: A lightweight integration of theorem proving and model checking for system verification. In: APSEC'05, pp. 59–66. IEEE CS, Washington, DC (2005)

Capturing Conflict and Confusion in CSP

Christie Marr (née Bolton)

SALTIRE
University of St Andrews
Fife KY16 9AJ
`christie.marr@st-andrews.ac.uk`

Abstract. Traditionally, developers of concurrent systems have adopted two distinct approaches: those with *truly concurrent* semantics and those with *interleaving* semantics. In the coarser interleaving interpretation parallelism can be captured in terms of non-determinism whereas in the finer, truly concurrent interpretation it cannot. Thus processes $a \parallel b$ and $a.b + b.a$ are identified within the interleaving approach but distinguished within the truly concurrent approach.

In [5] we explored the truly concurrent notions of *conflict*, whereby transitions can occur individually but not together from a given state, and *confusion*, whereby the conflict set of a given transition is altered by the occurrence of another transition with which it does not interfere. We presented a translation from the truly concurrent formalism of Petri nets to the interleaving process algebra CSP and demonstrated how the CSP model-checker FDR can be used to detect the presence of both conflict and confusion in Petri nets. This work is of interest firstly because, to the author's knowledge, no existing tool for Petri nets can perform these checks, and secondly (and perhaps more significantly) because we bridged the gap between truly concurrent and interleaving formalisms, demonstrating that true concurrency can be captured in what is typically considered to be an interleaving language.

In this paper we build on the work presented in [5] further embedding the truly concurrent notions of conflict and confusion in the interleaving formalism CSP by extending the domain of our translation from the simplistic subset of *safe* Petri nets, in which each place can hold at most one token, to standard Petri nets, in which the number of tokens in each place is unbounded.

Keywords: True Concurrency, Interleaving Concurrency, Petri Nets, CSP, Conflict, Confusion, Automatic Verification.

1 Introduction

Software is increasingly used in critical systems (financially critical, environmentally critical, or safety critical) where correctness is paramount. For such systems it is desirable, indeed it is often a legal requirement, to formally design, specify and analyse models of the system. Testing alone is insufficient as it simply enables us to detect the presence of errors not prove their absence. Rather, we

J. Davies and J. Gibbons (Eds.): IFM 2007, LNCS 4591, pp. 413–438, 2007.

must formally, and preferably automatically, prove that the system meets its requirements. This is especially important for concurrent systems since their high levels of complexity make them particularly vulnerable to errors.

Within concurrency theory two distinct approaches have arisen: those with *truly concurrent* semantics and those with *interleaving* semantics. Examples of the former include trace theory [13], Petri net theory [17], prime event structures [25], pomsets [18], and others (cf. e.g., [16,3]). Examples of the latter include CSP [10], CCS [14,15] and ACP [2]. Advocates of the true concurrency argue that their approach is a more accurate model of "reality" whilst advocates of the interleaving approach argue that their model is an adequate abstraction. A more in depth comparison of the merits of these approaches is given in e.g. [18].

The main difference between true concurrency and the coarser interleaving approach is that in truly concurrent formalisms we can distinguish between the concurrent execution of actions and the non-deterministic choice between the possible orders of their executions, whereas within the interleaving approach we cannot. Thus processes $a \parallel b$ and $a.b + b.a$ are identified within the interleaving approach but distinguished within the truly concurrent approach.

Three notions central to true concurrency are *causal dependency*, *conflict* and *confusion*. Causal dependence is when one action is enabled only when another has occurred. Conflict is when two or more actions are enabled but if one occurs the others cannot, that is the actions can occur individually but not together. Confusion can arise when there is a mixture of conflict and concurrency.

In [5] we presented a translation from safe nets, a simple interpretation of the truly concurrent formalism of Petri Nets [17] in which places can hold at most one token, to the interleaving semantics of CSP [10,21]. Through this translation we explored the relationship between true concurrency and the interleaving approach. We demonstrated how this simple class of nets could be captured as CSP processes and, more specifically, went on to show how the truly concurrent concepts of conflict and confusion could be detected in safe nets using FDR [8], the model-checker for CSP. The contribution of [5] was two-fold. Firstly, and from a practical perspective, we demonstrated how conflict and confusion, ideas central to true concurrency, can be automatically detected in Petri nets: to the author's knowledge, no existing tool for modelling Petri nets can perform these checks [24,1]. Secondly, and perhaps more significantly, from a theoretical perspective, we demonstrated how the gap between truly concurrent and interleaving formalisms can be bridged and in particular how true concurrency can be captured, and truly concurrent properties reasoned about, in what is traditionally considered to be an interleaving language.

In this paper, we build on the work presented in [5], revising, developing and extending definitions for safe nets to cope with the less simplistic generalised (unsafe) nets [17,20] thereby strengthening the links between these formalisms, further cementing the truly concurrent notions of conflict and confusion into the toolbox of users of CSP. Where appropriate, and to facilitate understanding, we present corresponding definitions for safe and unsafe nets side-by-side and discuss how the structures of our model for the latter mirror those for the former.[1]

The paper begins with an introduction to Petri net theory, identifying in particular the differences between safe and unsafe nets. This is followed by a discussion of the concepts of concurrency, causal dependency, conflict and confusion. After an introduction to the subset of the language of CSP that is needed for the rest of the paper we present our translations from safe and unsafe Petri nets to CSP. We then develop tests for using the CSP model-checker to automatically detect conflict and both conflict-increasing and conflict-decreasing confusion in unsafe Petri nets, building on techniques presented in [5]. We conclude with a discussion of this and related work.

2   Petri Nets

Petri net theory was first proposed by Carl Petri in the early 1960s [17]. His intention was to develop a technique for modelling distributed systems and in particular notions of concurrency and non-determinism, that was at the same time both graphical and intuitive, and formal and mathematical.

As discussed in e.g. [19] there are a number of different categories of Petri net. Here we restrict ourselves to safe Petri nets in which each place contains at most one token and standard (unsafe) nets in which places can contain more than one token.

2.1   Graphical Representation

In their graphical representation, Petri's nets are built using collections of three types of object: circles or *places* denoting local state; boxes or *transitions* denoting actions; and directed arcs, or arrows, from places to transitions and transitions to places denoting flow. Thus a net is an ordered bipartite directed graph. Places may or may not be named within the graphical representation of a Petri net. In a *marked graph*, places within the graph may contain *tokens* (filled circles), indicating which transitions are enabled.

Safe Nets. In *safe* nets, places can contain at most one token and a transition is enabled precisely when all the places that directly precede the transition contain a token, and none of the places that the transition directly precedes contain tokens: that is, all of its preconditions and none of its postconditions are satisfied. By way of an example, Figures 1 (a) and (c) illustrate the safe nets corresponding to $a \parallel b$, the parallel composition of a and b, and $a.b + b.a$, the non-deterministic choice between their possible orderings. Note that this is the simplest example of two processes that are distinguished in true concurrency but not in the interleaving approach.

---

[1] Although the definitions and discussion regarding safe nets have already been published in [5] they are included here as they illuminate the more complex definitions regarding unsafe nets.

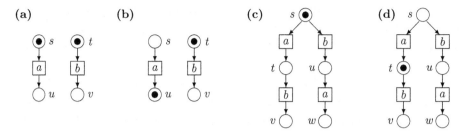

Fig. 1. Safe Petri nets modelling $a \parallel b$ and $a.b + b.a$ before and after transition a

When a transition fires in a safe net, tokens are removed from all places directly preceding the transition, and tokens are placed in all (empty) places that the transition precedes. Thus, if transition a fires then the nets illustrated in Figures 1 (a) and (c) will be transformed to the nets illustrated in Figures 1 (b) and (d).

Unsafe Nets. In standard (*unsafe*) nets, places may contain multiple tokens. Transitions may require multiple tokens in a single place in order to be enabled and, upon firing, may provide multiple transitions to a single place. These multiplicities may be indicated either by labelling the arcs with the appropriate multiplicity or by allowing multiple arcs between pairs of places and transitions. We adopt the latter approach here. By way of an example, consider Figure 2.

Fig. 2. A unsafe net before and after the firing of transition q

When transition b fires, two tokens are removed from place s, one is added to place u, and two are added to place v.

Provided they do not interfere (that is they share no common preconditions and, in the case of safe nets, share no common postconditions) a set of transitions, all of which are enabled, may fire together in a single atomic step. Tokens are removed from all places in the disjoint union of their presets and put in all places in their postsets.

2.2   Formal Representation

As we have already observed, Petri nets not only have an intuitive, graphical representation, as described above. They also have a fully formal mathematical representation which we will discuss in this section.

Safe Petri Nets. As discussed in [19], there are a variety of formal representations of Petri Nets. In this paper a safe Petri Net $\mathcal{N}_S$ is represented by the quintuple $(P_{\mathcal{N}_S}, T_{\mathcal{N}_S}, Pre_{\mathcal{N}_S}, Post_{\mathcal{N}_S}, L_{\mathcal{N}_S})$ where $P_{\mathcal{N}_S}$ is the set of places and $T_{\mathcal{N}_S}$ is the set of transitions. Partial functions $Pre_{\mathcal{N}_S} : T_{\mathcal{N}_S} \nrightarrow P_{\mathcal{N}_S}$ and $Post_{\mathcal{N}_S} : T_{\mathcal{N}_S} \nrightarrow P_{\mathcal{N}_S}$ respectively link transitions with their presets (or preconditions) and postsets (or postconditions), whilst total function $L_{\mathcal{N}_S} : T_{\mathcal{N}_S} \rightarrow Action$ links transitions and actions thereby facilitating one set of behaviours to be enabled by the occurrence of an action in one context and another set of behaviours to be enabled by the occurrence of the same action in a different context. Where the labelling function $L_{\mathcal{N}_S}$ is injective it can either be represented as the identity function or can be elided. This definition is the same as that presented in [5] with the exception that the flow relation $F_{\mathcal{N}_S} \subseteq (P_{\mathcal{N}_S} \times T_{\mathcal{N}_S}) \cup (T_{\mathcal{N}_S} \times P_{\mathcal{N}_S})$ linking places and transitions has been split into $Pre_{\mathcal{N}_S}$ and $Post_{\mathcal{N}_S}$.

The healthiness conditions for safe Petri Nets are as follows.

- $P_{\mathcal{N}_S} \cap T_{\mathcal{N}_S} = \emptyset$ (S-H1)
- $\operatorname{dom} Pre_{\mathcal{N}_S} = \operatorname{dom} Post_{\mathcal{N}_S} = T_{\mathcal{N}_S}$ (S-H2)
- $\operatorname{ran} Pre_{\mathcal{N}_S} \cup \operatorname{ran} Post_{\mathcal{N}_S} = P_{\mathcal{N}_S}$ (S-H3)
- $\operatorname{dom} L_{\mathcal{N}_S} = T_{\mathcal{N}_S}$ (S-H4)

Condition S-H1 states that no place is also a transition. Condition S-H2 states that every transition has a before state and an after state whilst condition S-H3 states that every place is attached to at least one transition. Finally, condition S-H4 states that every transition has an associated action.

Marked Safe Nets. A marked net records not only the structural relationship between places and transitions but also the positions of the tokens. Thus a marked safe net, where each place can hold at most one token, can be represented by the a pair $(\mathcal{N}_S, M_{\mathcal{N}_S})$ where $\mathcal{N}_S$ is as defined above and $M_{\mathcal{N}_S} \subseteq P_{\mathcal{N}}$ is the set of all initially marked places.

Unsafe Nets. The difference between safe and standard (unsafe) nets is that places can contain more than one token in an unsafe net. Rather than simply identifying those places that contain tokens we must record the number of tokens in each place. Moreover, more than one token may be required by or produced in a single place by a single transition. Thus unsafe net $\mathcal{N}_U$ is represented by $(P_{\mathcal{N}_U}, T_{\mathcal{N}_U}, Pre_{\mathcal{N}_U}, Post_{\mathcal{N}_U}, L_{\mathcal{N}_U})$ where total functions $Pre_{\mathcal{N}_U} : (T_{\mathcal{N}_U} \times P_{\mathcal{N}_U}) \rightarrow \mathbb{N}$ and $Post_{\mathcal{N}_U} : (T_{\mathcal{N}_U} \times P_{\mathcal{N}_U}) \rightarrow \mathbb{N}$ record the number of tokens in each place in the preset and postset of each transition. As with safe nets, $P_{\mathcal{N}_U}$, $T_{\mathcal{N}_U}$, and $L_{\mathcal{N}_U} : T_{\mathcal{N}_U} \rightarrow Action$ respectively describe the set of places, the set of transitions, and the labeling function relating transitions and actions. The associated healthiness conditions mirror those of safe nets.[2]

---

[2] Throughout this paper we use $(\forall x : X \bullet bool)$ to denote that Boolean *bool* holds for all x in X. Further we use $(\exists x : X \bullet bool)$ to state that there exists an element x in set X such that Boolean *bool* holds.

- $P_{\mathcal{N}_U} \cap T_{\mathcal{N}_U} = \emptyset$ (U-H1)
- $\forall t : T_{\mathcal{N}_U} \bullet (\exists p_i : P_{\mathcal{N}_U} \bullet Pre_{\mathcal{N}_U}(t, p_i) \geq 1) \wedge$ (U-H2)
  $(\exists p_o : P_{\mathcal{N}_U} \bullet Post_{\mathcal{N}_U}(t, p_o) \geq 1)$
- $\forall p : P_{\mathcal{N}_U} \bullet \exists t : T_{\mathcal{N}_U} \bullet (Pre_{\mathcal{N}_U}(t, p) \geq 1 \vee Post_{\mathcal{N}_U}(t, p) \geq 1)$ (U-H3)
- $\operatorname{dom} L_{\mathcal{N}_S} = T_{\mathcal{N}_S}$ (U-H4)

Once more the second and third conditions respectively state that every transition has a before state and an after state and that every place is attached to at least one transition.

Marked Unsafe Nets. We introduce a marking function, a total function from places to integers identifying each place with the number of tokens in that place. Hence a marked, unsafe net is captured by the pair $(\mathcal{N}_U, M_{\mathcal{N}_U})$ where $\mathcal{N}_U$ is as defined above and where total function $M_{\mathcal{N}_U} : P_{\mathcal{N}_U} \to \mathbb{N}$ records the number of tokens initially in each place.

Examples. The marked safe nets modelling $a \parallel b$ and $a.b + b.a$, as illustrated in Figures 1 (a) and (c) can respectively be captured as $(\mathcal{N}, \{s, t\})$ and $(\mathcal{N}', \{s\})$ as follows.

$$\mathcal{N} = (\{s, t, u, v\}, \{a, b\}, \{(a, s), (b, t)\}, \{(a, u), (b, v)\})$$
$$\mathcal{N}' = (\{s, t, u, v, w\}, \{a_1, a_2, b_1, b_2\},$$
$$\{(a_1, s), (b_1, t), (b_2, s), (a_2, u), \}, \{(a_1, t), (b_1, v), (b_2, u), (a_2, w)\},$$
$$\{(a_1, a), (a_2, a), (b_1, b), (b_2, b)\}).$$

Note that the definition of $\mathcal{N}'$ illustrates how the labelling function is used to capture varying behaviour after different occurrences of the same transition. In particular, although transitions a_1 and a_2 both correspond to action a, transition b_1, corresponding to action b, can occur after transition a_1 but not after a_2.

Setting all preconditions and postconditions to 0 and then, where necessary, over-riding using the operator $\oplus$, the marked unsafe net depicted in Figure 2 can be captured as the pair $(\mathcal{N}'', \{(s, 3), (t, 0), (u, 1), (v, 0)\})$ where $\mathcal{N}''$ is defined as follows.

$$\mathcal{N}'' = (\{s, t, u, v\}, \{a, b\},$$
$$((\{a, b\} \times \{s, t, u, v\}) \times \{0\}) \oplus \{((a, s), 1), ((b, s), 2)\},$$
$$((\{a, b\} \times \{s, t, u, v\}) \times \{0\}) \oplus \{((a, t), 3), ((b, u), 1), ((b, v), 2)\})$$

3 Concurrency, Conflict and Confusion

In this section we introduce and formally define the concurrent notions of conflict and confusion in the context of both safe and unsafe nets.

3.1 Purity

In this paper we consider only *pure* nets, that is nets in which no place lies in the preset and the postset of the same transition. In particular, safe and unsafe nets $\mathcal{N}_S$ and $\mathcal{N}_U$ must respectively satisfy the following conditions.

$$\forall\, t : T_{\mathcal{N}_S} \bullet Pre_{\mathcal{N}_S}(t) \cap Post_{\mathcal{N}_S}(t) = \emptyset$$
$$\forall\, t : T_{\mathcal{N}_U} \bullet \forall\, p : P_{\mathcal{N}_U} \bullet (\, Pre_{\mathcal{N}_U}(t, u) > 0 \Rightarrow Post_{\mathcal{N}_U}(t, u) = 0\,)$$

3.2   Enabled Transitions and Pre- and Post-Conditions

A transition is enabled in a safe net precisely when all of its preset and none of its postset is marked. Conversely, in an unsafe net in which places can contain more than one token, a transition is enabled simply when its preset contains sufficient tokens. More formally, given pure net $\mathcal{N}$, transition $t \in T_{\mathcal{N}}$, and marking C (that is $C_S : \mathbb{P}\, P_{\mathcal{N}_S}$ and $C_U : P_{\mathcal{N}_U} \to \mathbb{N}$), we write $C[t\rangle_{\mathcal{N}}$ to indicate that t is enabled from state C in $\mathcal{N}$. Thus

$$C[t\rangle_{\mathcal{N}_S} \equiv Pre_{\mathcal{N}_S}(t) \subseteq C \wedge Post_{\mathcal{N}_S} \cap C = \emptyset$$
$$C[t\rangle_{\mathcal{N}_U} \equiv \forall\, p : P_{\mathcal{N}_U} \bullet Pre_{\mathcal{N}_U}(t, p) \le C(p).$$

Further, we write $C[t\rangle_{\mathcal{N}} C'$ to indicate not only that t is enabled from state C in $\mathcal{N}$ but also that should t occur, then $\mathcal{N}$ is transformed state C to state C'. Thus

$$C[t\rangle_{\mathcal{N}_S} C' \equiv C[t\rangle_{\mathcal{N}_S} \wedge C' = (C \setminus Pre_{\mathcal{N}_S}(t)) \cup Post_{\mathcal{N}_S}(t)$$
$$C[t\rangle_{\mathcal{N}_U} C' \equiv C[t\rangle_{\mathcal{N}_U} \wedge$$
$$\forall\, p : P_{\mathcal{N}_U} \bullet C'(p) = C(p) - Pre_{\mathcal{N}_U}(t, p) + Post_{\mathcal{N}_U}(t, p).$$

Note that the above notation can be used in Boolean expressions. Hence expression $\neg\, C[t\rangle_{\mathcal{N}}$ states that transition t is not enabled from marking C.

3.3   Interference

Two transitions interfere with one another in a safe net $\mathcal{N}_S$ when there is overlap between the preset and postset of one and the preset and postset of the other. This condition may be relaxed for unsafe nets as a transition is not prevented from occurring by the presence of a token in its postset.

More formally, given pure net $\mathcal{N}$, transitions $t, t' : T_{\mathcal{N}}$ interfere precisely when the function *Interfere* holds, where *Interfere* is defined as follows for safe and unsafe nets $\mathcal{N}_S$ and $\mathcal{N}_U$.

$$Interfere(safe, \mathcal{N}_S, t, t') \equiv$$
$$t \ne t' \wedge (Pre_{\mathcal{N}_S}(t) \cup Post_{\mathcal{N}_S}(t)) \cap (Pre_{\mathcal{N}_S}(t') \cup Post_{\mathcal{N}_S}(t')) \ne \emptyset$$
$$Interfere(unsafe, \mathcal{N}_U, t, t') \equiv$$
$$t \ne t' \wedge \exists\, p : P_{\mathcal{N}_U} \bullet (\, Pre_{\mathcal{N}_U}(t, p) > 0 \wedge Pre_{\mathcal{N}_U}(t', p) > 0\,) \vee$$
$$(\, Pre_{\mathcal{N}_U}(t, p) > 0 \wedge Post_{\mathcal{N}_U}(t', p) > 0\,) \vee$$
$$(\, Post_{\mathcal{N}_U}(t, p) > 0 \wedge Pre_{\mathcal{N}_U}(t', p) > 0\,)$$

Having considered pairwise interference, we next introduce the function *IntFree* for safe and unsafe nets that returns true precisely when there is no interference between transitions in a given set. More formally, given sets of transitions $A_S : T_{\mathcal{N}_S}$ and $A_U : T_{\mathcal{N}_U}$,

$$IntFree(safe, \mathcal{N}_S, A_S) \equiv \forall\, t, t' : A_S \bullet t \neq t' \Rightarrow \neg\ Interfere(safe, \mathcal{N}_S, t, t')$$
$$IntFree(unsafe, \mathcal{N}_U, A_U) \equiv \forall\, t, t' : A_U \bullet t \neq t' \Rightarrow \neg\ Interfere(unsafe, \mathcal{N}_U, t, t').$$

Note that for later convenience we choose to parametrise functions *Interfere* and *IntFree* with values *safe* and *unsafe*.

3.4   Concurrency

In Section 3.2 we introduced the notation $C[t\rangle_{\mathcal{N}}$ to denote that transition t is enabled in net $\mathcal{N}$ given marking C. To facilitate concurrency, we extend this to sets of enabled transitions, insisting only that they do not interfere. Hence, $C[A\rangle_{\mathcal{N}}$ indicates that the set of transitions $A \subset T_{\mathcal{N}}$ can occur individually and without interference, and hence *concurrently* in $\mathcal{N}$ given marking C. More formally, given sets of transitions $A_S : T_{\mathcal{N}_S}$ and $A_U : T_{\mathcal{N}_U}$,

$$C[A_S\rangle_{\mathcal{N}_S} \equiv IntFree(safe, \mathcal{N}_S, A_S) \wedge \forall\, t : A_S \bullet C[t\rangle_{\mathcal{N}_S}$$
$$C[A_U\rangle_{\mathcal{N}_U} \equiv IntFree(unsafe, \mathcal{N}_U, A_U) \wedge \forall\, t : A_U \bullet C[t\rangle_{\mathcal{N}_U}.$$

For later use we introduce the functions Req_U and $Yield_U$ for unsafe nets. Given interference-free set of transitions $A_U : T_{\mathcal{N}_U}$ and place $p : P_{\mathcal{N}_U}$, they respectively return the number of tokens required in the given place for the whole set of transitions to be enabled, and the number of tokens yielded in the given place should the whole set of transitions fire. More formally,

$$IntFree(unsafe, \mathcal{N}_U, A_U) \;\Rightarrow\; (\,Req_U(\mathcal{N}_U, A_U, p) \equiv \Sigma_{t \in A_U}\, Pre_{\mathcal{N}_U}(t, p)$$
$$\wedge$$
$$Yield_U(\mathcal{N}_U, A_U, p) \equiv \Sigma_{t \in A_U}\, Post_{\mathcal{N}_U}(t, p)\,).$$

We use these functions in the definition of $C[A_U\rangle_{\mathcal{N}_U} C'$, the concurrent extensions of $C[t\rangle_{\mathcal{N}_U} C'$. Hence,

$$IntFree(safe, \mathcal{N}_S, A_S) \Rightarrow$$
$$C[A_S\rangle_{\mathcal{N}_S} C' \equiv C[A_S\rangle_{\mathcal{N}_S} \wedge\ C' = (C \setminus (\bigcup_{t \in T_{\mathcal{N}_S}} Pre_{\mathcal{N}_S}(t))) \cup (\bigcup_{t \in T_{\mathcal{N}_S}} Post_{\mathcal{N}_S}(t))$$

$$IntFree(unsafe, \mathcal{N}_U, A_U) \Rightarrow$$
$$C[A_U\rangle_{\mathcal{N}_U} C' \equiv C[A_U\rangle_{\mathcal{N}_U} \wedge$$
$$\forall\, p : P_{\mathcal{N}_U} \bullet C'(p) = C(p) - Req_U(\mathcal{N}_U, A_U, p) + Yield_U(\mathcal{N}_U, A_U, p)$$

3.5   Conflict

Two transitions t and t' are in *conflict* in net $\mathcal{N}$ at a given marking C if they can occur individually but not together at C. In particular predicates $C[t\rangle_{\mathcal{N}}$ and $C[t'\rangle_{\mathcal{N}}$ both hold but $\neg\ C[\{t, t'\}\rangle_{\mathcal{N}}$. Consider Figure 3 below in which we explore the different conditions for conflict in safe and unsafe nets. We see that

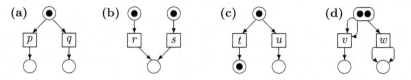

Fig. 3. Examples of conflict in safe nets ((a) and (b)) and unsafe nets ((c) and (d))

transitions p and q are in conflict in the safe net in Figure 3a since if one fires then the preconditions of the other are no longer satisfied. Similarly, transitions r and s are in conflict in the safe net in Figure 3b since if one fires then the postset of the other will already contain a token. Transitions t and u are in conflict in the unsafe net in Figure 3c since if one fires then the preconditions of the other are no longer satisfied.[3] Finally, we observe that transitions v and w are in conflict in the unsafe net in Figure 3d since if either fires then there will be insufficient tokens in the preset to enable the other.

For both safe and unsafe nets, we define *Conflicts* to be the set of all transitions that are in conflict with a given enabled transition from a given marking. More formally, given nets $\mathcal{N}_S$ and $\mathcal{N}_U$, markings $C_S : \mathbb{P} \, P_{\mathcal{N}_S}$ and $C_U : (T_{\mathcal{N}_U} \times P_{\mathcal{N}_U}) \to \mathbb{N}$, and transitions $t_S : T_{\mathcal{N}_S}$ and $t_U : T_{\mathcal{N}_U}$, such that $C_S[t_S\rangle_{\mathcal{N}_S}$ and $C_U[t_U\rangle_{\mathcal{N}_U}$,

$$Conflicts_S(\mathcal{N}_S, C_S, t_S) \equiv \{t'_S : T_{\mathcal{N}_S} \mid C_S[t'_S\rangle_{\mathcal{N}_S} \wedge \neg \, C_S[\{t_S, t'_S\}\rangle_{\mathcal{N}_S}\}$$

$$Conflicts_U(\mathcal{N}_U, C_U, t_U) \equiv \{t'_U : T_{\mathcal{N}_U} \mid C_U[t'_U\rangle_{\mathcal{N}_U} \wedge \neg \, C_U[\{t_U, t'_U\}\rangle_{\mathcal{N}_U}\}$$

Note that whilst these definitions are syntactically identical they are semantically different: the differences are simply embedded within the definitions of $C_S[t'_S\rangle_{\mathcal{N}_S}$, $C_S[\{t_S, t'_S\}\rangle_{\mathcal{N}_S}$, $C_U[t'_U\rangle_{\mathcal{N}_U}$, and $C_U[\{t_U, t'_U\}\rangle_{\mathcal{N}_U}$.

3.6   Confusion

A mixture of concurrency and conflict may result in a system reaching a *confused* state whereby the conflict set of one transition is altered by the occurrence of another apparently unrelated transition. In particular, transition t is confused at state C from which it is enabled in net $\mathcal{N}$ if there is another transition t' also enabled at C and with which it does not interfere such that the conflict set of t before the occurence of t' is not equal to the conflict set of t after the occurence of t'. More formally, given nets $\mathcal{N}_S$ and $\mathcal{N}_U$, markings $C_S : \mathbb{P} \, P_{\mathcal{N}_S}$ and $C_U : (T_{\mathcal{N}_U} \times P_{\mathcal{N}_U}) \to \mathbb{N}$, and transitions $t_S : T_{\mathcal{N}_S}$ and $t_U : T_{\mathcal{N}_U}$, such that $C_S[t_S\rangle_{\mathcal{N}_S}$ and $C_U[t_U\rangle_{\mathcal{N}_U}$,

$$Confused_S(\mathcal{N}_S, t_S, C_S) \equiv$$
$$\exists \, t'_S : T_{\mathcal{N}_S}; \; C'_S : \mathbb{P} \, P_{\mathcal{N}_S} \mid C_S[t_S\rangle_{\mathcal{N}_S} C'_S \bullet$$
$$C_S[\{t_S, t'_S\}\rangle_{\mathcal{N}_S} \wedge Conflicts_S(\mathcal{N}_S, C_S, t_S) \neq Conflicts_S(\mathcal{N}_S, C_S, t'_S)$$

---

[3] Note that were the net in Figure 3c a safe net, transitions t and u would not be in conflict since t would not be enabled since its postset already contains a token.

422   C. Marr

$Confused_U(\mathcal{N}_U, t_U, C_U) \equiv$
$\exists\, t'_U : T_{\mathcal{N}_U}; \ C'_U : \mathbb{P}\,P_{\mathcal{N}_U} \mid C_U[t_U\rangle_{\mathcal{N}_U} C'_U \bullet$
$\quad C_U[\{t_U, t'_U\}\rangle_{\mathcal{N}_U} \wedge Conflicts_U(\mathcal{N}_U, C_U, t_U) \neq Conflicts_U(\mathcal{N}_U, C_U, t'_U).$

Once again the differences between the functions are embedded within their subfunctions.

There are two types of confusion: conflict-increasing (asymmetric) confusion and conflict-decreasing (symmetric) confusion, although a single net can contain instances or combinations of both.

Conflict-Increasing Confusion. Conflict-increasing confusion occurs when conflict is introduced into the system: that is

$$Conflicts(\mathcal{N}, C, t) \subset Conflicts(\mathcal{N}, C, t').$$

Examples of conflict-increasing confusion in *safe* nets are illustrated in Figures 4 (a) and (b). The confusion in Figure 4 (a) arises from the *preconditions* of q not being satisfied initially whilst the confusion in Figure 4 (b) arises from the *postconditions* of q not being satisfied initially.[4] An example of conflict-increasing

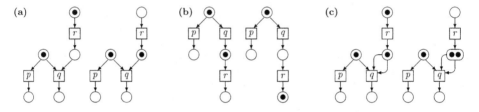

Fig. 4. (a) and (b) illustrate conflict-increasing confusion in safe nets: in both cases, transitions p and q are not initially in conflict, although after the occurrence of r, transition q becomes enabled and conflict is introduced. (c) illustrates conflict-increasing confusion in an unsafe net: initially transitions p and q are not in conflict, however after the occurrence of r, transition q becomes enabled and conflict is introduced.

confusion in an *unsafe* net is illustrated in Figure 4 (c). Observe that since there are no contraints on the postconditions in unsafe nets, confusion cannot arise from postconditions not being satisfied initially.

Conflict-Decreasing Confusing. Conflict-decreasing confusion occurs when conflict is eliminated from the system: that is

$$Conflicts(\mathcal{N}, C, t) \supset Conflicts(\mathcal{N}, C, t').$$

Examples of conflict-decreasing confusion in *safe* nets are illustrated Figure 5. The confusion in Figure 5a arises from the *preconditions* of q not being satisfied

---
[4] Note that were the net in Figure 4 (b) an *unsafe* net, there would be no confusion since transitions p and q would not initially be in conflict.

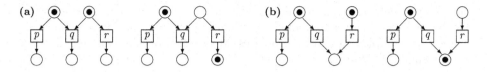

Fig. 5. Examples of conflict-decreasing confusion in safe nets. Transitions p and q are initially in conflict. After the occurrence of r they are no longer in conflict since q is no longer enabled.

after the occurence of r whilst the confusion in Figure 5b arises from the *post-conditions* of q not being satisfied after the occurence of r.[5]

An example of conflict-decreasing confusion in an *unsafe* net is illustrated in Figure 6. Observe once again that since there are no contraints on the post-conditions in unsafe nets, confusion cannot arise from postconditions not being satisfied after the occurence of another transition.

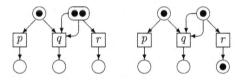

Fig. 6. An example of conflict-decreasing confusion in an unsafe net. Transitions p and q are initially in conflict. After the occurrence of r they are no longer in conflict since q is no longer enabled.

4   CSP

The process algebra Communicating Sequential Processes (CSP) [10,21] is a mathematical language for capturing the behaviour of systems by recording the occurrence of events. Analysis of the system can then be performed by using the model-checker FDR to *compare* a formal specification *SPEC*, a simple process capturing specific desired properties of the system, with the process describing the model itself.

4.1   Syntax

In this section we give a brief introduction to the subset of the CSP syntax that we will be using throughout the rest of the paper, as well as the traces semantic model for the language [21].

A *process*, as defined in [10], is a pattern of communication that describes the behaviour of a system. Behaviour is described in terms of *events* or *synchronous* atomic communications, marking points in the evolution of the system. Compound events can be constructed using '.' the dot operator, and a family of

---

[5] Note, once again, that were the net in Figure 5b an *unsafe* net, there would be no confusion since p and q would still be in conflict after the occurence of r.

compound events is called a *channel*. Channels can be used to represent the passing of values between components. Simple processes may be combined to create more complex composite processes. Moreover processes can be defined in terms of mutually-recursive equations.

The simplest process is *Stop*, the process that denotes deadlock. No events can be performed and this process marks the end of a pattern of communication. For any event a and process P, the process $a \rightarrow P$ is willing to communicate event a and, if that event occurs, will subsequently behave as P.

The *choice operator*[6] comes in two forms: the binary operator, and the choice over an indexed set of processes. Given processes P and Q, a set of processes $R(i)$ indexed over some set I, and a predicate $p(i)$ for $i \in I$, the following processes are as described:

$P \square Q$ a choice between P and Q;

$\square\, i : I \mid p(i) \bullet R(i)$ a choice over the set of processes $R(i)$ such that $p(i)$.

There are various representations of the parallel operator in CSP. Throughout the paper we will use the following: given processes P and Q and set of events X, the process $P \parallel_X Q$ denotes the *parallel* combination of P and Q synchronised on set X. Events in the alphabet of P but not in X can be performed without the cooperation of Q and similarly events in the alphabet of Q but not in X can be performed without the cooperation of P. No event in X can occur without the cooperation of both P and Q. We write $\parallel i : I \bullet [A(i)]\, P(i)$ to denote an *indexed parallel* combination of processes in which each process $P(i)$ can evolve independently but must synchronise upon every event from the set $A(i)$. In an *interleaving* parallel combination no synchronisation is required; therefore in the combination $P \parallel\!\parallel Q$, processes P and Q evolve independently.

Renaming is a useful technique. The process $P[[a'/a]]$ behaves exactly as process P except that every occurrence of the event a is replaced by the event a'. Multiple renamings are performed in the natural way.

4.2   Semantics

There are various ways of describing the behaviour of CSP processes: we may give them an *algebraic semantics* defined by a set of algebraic laws; we may give them an *operational semantics* describing programs using transition diagrams; or we may give them a *denotational semantics* mapping the language into an abstract model based on sets of behaviours.

---

[6] There are in fact two choice operators in CSP: one denoting internal choice and the other denoting external choice. An *internal choice* is resolved between the processes involved without reference to the environment, whereas an *external choice* may be influenced by the environment and is resolved by the first event to occur. These operators are indistinguishable within the traces semantic model with which we are concerned here and which we will formally introduce in Section 4.2. Hence we consider only external choice throughout this paper.

Various denotational semantic models have been proposed for CSP. Three established models are the *traces* model, the *stable failures* model and the *failures-divergences* model as defined by Roscoe [21]. In addition the *singleton failures* model was introduced in [4] and a further family of failures-based models was discussed in [6]. In this paper we are concerned only with the traces model, $\mathcal{T}$.

The Traces Model. A *trace* records a history of behaviour. It is expressed as a sequence of events in which the process has engaged with the head of the sequence being the first event that was communicated. Given a process P, the set $\mathcal{T}[\![P]\!]$ is the set of all possible finite traces of P. Thus the semantic domain of the traces model is the set $\mathbb{P}(\Sigma^*)$ where Σ is the set of all events.

Healthiness Conditions. The healthiness conditions of $\mathcal{T}$ are given below:

- $\langle\rangle \in \mathcal{T}[\![P]\!]$, $\qquad\qquad\qquad\qquad\qquad\qquad\qquad\qquad\qquad$ (T1)
- $tr \frown tr' \in \mathcal{T}[\![P]\!] \Rightarrow tr \in \mathcal{T}[\![P]\!]$. $\qquad\qquad\qquad\qquad\qquad$ (T2)

Condition (T1) states that the empty trace is a possible trace of every process and condition (T2) states that the set of traces of any process is prefix-closed.

Semantic Laws.
The semantic laws for the traces model are then as follows:

$$\mathcal{T}[\![Stop]\!] = \{\langle\rangle\}$$
$$\mathcal{T}[\![a \rightarrow P]\!] = \{tr : \mathcal{T}[\![P]\!] \bullet \langle a\rangle \frown tr\} \cup \{\langle\rangle\}$$
$$\mathcal{T}[\![P \,\square\, Q]\!] = \mathcal{T}[\![P]\!] \cup \mathcal{T}[\![Q]\!]$$
$$\mathcal{T}[\![P \parallel_X Q]\!] = \{tr : \Sigma^* \mid \operatorname{ran} tr \subseteq \alpha(P) \cup \alpha(Q) \;\wedge$$
$$tr \restriction (\alpha(P) \cup X) \in \mathcal{T}[\![P]\!] \;\wedge$$
$$tr \restriction (\alpha(Q) \cup X) \in \mathcal{T}[\![Q]\!]\}$$

where $\alpha(P)$ is the alphabet of process P and where sequence $tr \restriction X$ is the longest subsequence of tr containing only elements from the set X.

4.3   Refinement

The refinement ordering induced by the traces model is based upon reverse containment. One process is traces-refined by another if every trace of the second is also a trace of the first. Given processes P and Q we write

$$P \sqsubseteq_\mathcal{T} Q \Leftrightarrow \mathcal{T}[\![Q]\!] \subseteq \mathcal{T}[\![P]\!].$$

The model-checker FDR [8] is used for automatically analysing large or complex systems in CSP. Typically a process *IMPL* modelling the system in question is compared with a more abstract model *SPEC*: thus $SPEC \sqsubseteq_\mathcal{T} IMPL$. Model-checker FDR will perform an exhaustive breadth-first search identifying any trace of *IMPL* that is not also a trace of *SPEC*.

5   Capturing Marked Petri Nets as CSP Processes

Used in the conventional manner, the process algebra CSP which adopts an interleaving approach to concurrency cannot model truly concurrent systems. However, in this section we demonstrate that this restriction, the inability to distinguish between the concurrent execution of actions and the non-deterministic choice between the possible orders of their executions, can be overcome if presets and postsets are taken into consideration.

5.1   Capturing Places

A net can be captured as the parallel combination of a collection of simple processes, one for each place. In the case of safe nets, each such process records the presence or absence of a token. It permits the execution of an event corresponding to a transition it lies in the preset of only if that transition is currently enabled, or equivalently if the place contains a token. Moreover, it permits the execution of an event corresponding to a transition it lies in the postset of only if that transition is currently enabled, or equivalently if the place contains no token. To accomodate the truly concurrent behaviour of Petri nets, we permit the atomic execution of *sets* of transitions provided there is no interference. Hence, the process corresponding to place $p_S \in P_{\mathcal{N}_S}$ in a *safe* net can be captured by the following pair of mutually recursive processes.

$$FullPlace_S(\mathcal{N}_S, p_S) =$$
$$\square\, A_S : \mathbb{P}\, T_{\mathcal{N}_S} \mid p_S \in (\bigcup_{t_S \in A_S} Pre_{\mathcal{N}_S}(t_S)) \bullet trans.A_S \rightarrow EmptyPlace_S(\mathcal{N}_S, p_S)$$
$$EmptyPlace_S(\mathcal{N}_S, p_S) =$$
$$\square\, A_S : \mathbb{P}\, T_{\mathcal{N}_S} \mid p_S \in (\bigcup_{t_S \in A_S} Post_{\mathcal{N}_S}(t_S)) \bullet trans.A_S \rightarrow FullPlace_S(\mathcal{N}_S, p_S)$$

Unsafe nets can also be captured as the parallel combination of a collection of simple processes, one for each place. In the case of unsafe nets, it is insufficient to record simply the presence or absence of a token: we must record the number of tokens. The process corresponding to a given place then permits the execution of an event corresponding to a transition it lies in the preset of only if it contains sufficient tokens. As with safe nets, to accomodate the concurrent behaviour of Petri nets, we permit the atomic execution of sets of transitions provided there is no interference. It therefore follows that the process corresponding to place $p_U \in P_{\mathcal{N}_U}$ in *unsafe* net $\mathcal{N}_U$ is modelled as follows:

$$Place_U(\mathcal{N}_U, p_U, tokens) =$$
$$\square\, A_U : \mathbb{P}\, T_{\mathcal{N}_U} \mid Req_U(net_U, A_U, p_U) \leq tokens \bullet$$
$$trans.A \rightarrow Place_U(\mathcal{N}_U, p_U, tokens - Req_U(net_U, A_U, p_U) + Yield_U(net_U, A_U, p_U))$$

where parameter *tokens* indicates the number of tokens in the place and where functions *Req* and *Yield* are as defined in Section 3.4.

We observe that the alphabet, or set of events with which the processes corresponding to given place is concerned, contains all events *trans.ts* such that the set $ts : \mathbb{P}\, T_\mathcal{N}$ contains a transition that the given place lies in the preset or (in the case of safe nets) in the postset of. More formally,[7] we define

$$\alpha_S(\mathcal{N}_S, p_S) = \{A_S : \mathbb{P}\, T_{\mathcal{N}_S};\ t_S : T_{\mathcal{N}_S}\ |$$
$$p \in (Pre_{\mathcal{N}_S}(t_S) \cup Post_{\mathcal{N}_S}(t_S)) \bullet trans.(\{t_S\} \cup A_S)\}.$$

$$\alpha_U(\mathcal{N}_U, p_U) = \{A_U : \mathbb{P}\, T_{\mathcal{N}_U};\ t_U : T_{\mathcal{N}_U}\ |$$
$$(Pre_{\mathcal{N}_U}(t_U, p_U) \geq 1 \bullet trans.(\{t_U\} \cup A_U)\}.$$

We initialise the above processes corresponding to places $p_S : P_{\mathcal{N}_S}$ and $p_U : P_{\mathcal{N}_U}$ according to initial markings. Thus

$$StartingPlace_S(\mathcal{N}_S, M_{\mathcal{N}_S}, p_S) =$$
$$\text{if } p_S \in M_{\mathcal{N}_S} \text{ then } FullPlaces(\mathcal{N}_S, p_S) \text{ else } EmptyPlaces(\mathcal{N}_S, p_S)$$
$$StartingPlace_U(\mathcal{N}_U, M_{\mathcal{N}_U}, p_U) = Place_U(\mathcal{N}_U, p_U, M_{\mathcal{N}_U}(p_U)).$$

5.2   Eliminating Interference

The processes corresponding to individual places ensure that the event corresponding to a given transition can fire only if that transition is enabled. However, since we permit *sets* of transitions to occur provided they do not interfere, thereby mirroring the concurrency afforded by Petri nets, we need a further process that restricts this behaviour to intereference-free sets.

$$NoInterference_S(\mathcal{N}_S) =$$
$$\square\, A_S : \mathbb{P}\, T_{\mathcal{N}_S}\ |\ IntFree(safe, \mathcal{N}_S, A_S) \bullet trans.A_S \rightarrow NoInterference(\mathcal{N}_S)$$
$$NoInterference_U(\mathcal{N}_U) =$$
$$\square\, A_U : \mathbb{P}\, T_{\mathcal{N}_U}\ |\ IntFree(unsafe, \mathcal{N}_U, A_U) \bullet trans.A_U \rightarrow NoInterference_U(\mathcal{N}_U)$$

where *IntFree* is defined in Section 3.3.

5.3   Capturing Nets

The process corresponding to a given marked net $(\mathcal{N}, M_\mathcal{N})$ is therefore the parallel combination of the correctly initialised processes corresponding to each of its places ($StartingPlace(\mathcal{N}, M_\mathcal{N}, p)$ for each $p : P_\mathcal{N}$), each synchronising on the set of events with which it is concerned ($\alpha(net, p)$), and further constrained by the process $NoInterference(\mathcal{N})$ to ensure that only interference-free sets of transitions may occur concurrently. Thus,

$$N_{(\mathcal{N}_S, M_{\mathcal{N}_S})} = (\ \|_{p_S \in P_{\mathcal{N}_S}}\ [\alpha(\mathcal{N}_S, p_S)]\, StartingPlace(\mathcal{N}_S, M_{\mathcal{N}_S}, p_S)\ )$$
$$\|_{\Sigma_{\mathcal{N}_S}}$$
$$NoInterference_S(\mathcal{N}_S)$$

---

[7] We use the notation $\{a_1 : A_1;\ \ldots a_n : A_n\ |\ p(a_1, \ldots, a_n) \bullet t(a_1, \ldots, a_n)\}$ to denote the set of terms $t(a_1, \ldots, a_n)$ where tuple $(a_1, \ldots a_n)$ is an element from the set $A_1 \times \ldots \times A_n$ subject to constraining predicate $p(a_1, \ldots a_n)$.

$$N_{(\mathcal{N}_U, M_{\mathcal{N}_U})} = (\|_{p_U \in P_{\mathcal{N}_U}} [\alpha(\mathcal{N}_U, p_U)] \, StartingPlace(\mathcal{N}_U, M_{\mathcal{N}_U}, p_U))$$
$$\|_{\Sigma_{\mathcal{N}_U}}$$
$$NoInterference_U(\mathcal{N}_U)$$

where $\Sigma_{\mathcal{N}_S} = \{trans.A_S \mid A_S \in \mathbb{P} \, T_{\mathcal{N}_S}\}$ and $\Sigma_{\mathcal{N}_U} = \{trans.A_U \mid A_U \in \mathbb{P} \, T_{\mathcal{N}_U}\}$.

6 Testing for Conflict

We observed in Section 3.5 that conflict occurs when a pair of transitions that are both enabled from a reachable state interfere: thus we have conflict in marked net $(\mathcal{N}, M_{\mathcal{N}})$ modelled by process $N_{(\mathcal{N}, M_{\mathcal{N}})}$ if we can find a sequence of transition events, $tr \in \Sigma_{\mathcal{N}}^*$ and a pair of distinct transitions $t, t' \in T_{\mathcal{N}}$ that interfere such that $tr \frown \langle trans.\{t\}\rangle \in \mathcal{T} [\![\, N_{(\mathcal{N}, M_{\mathcal{N}})} \,]\!]$ and $tr \frown \langle trans.\{t'\}\rangle \in \mathcal{T} [\![\, N_{(\mathcal{N}, M_{\mathcal{N}})} \,]\!]$.

Recalling that given command $LHS \sqsubseteq_{\mathcal{T}} RHS$ the model-checker FDR [8] performs a breadth-first search to check for the existence of a trace of process RHS that is not also a trace of process LHS.[8] Our goal is therefore to construct processes LHS and RHS, both functions of the process corresponding to our given net, that differ precisely when conflict is present.

Since FDR cannot perform backtracking we interleave two copies of the process corresponding to the given net, one primed and one unprimed, and, for both LHS and RHS, keep them in step through parallel combination with a control process.

6.1 The *Control* Processes

In [5], whilst testing for conflict, conflict-decreasing and conflict-increasing confusion in safe nets, we defined six distinct *Control* processes—a pair (one for LHS and one for RHS) for detecting conflict, a pair for detecting conflict-decreasing confusion, and a pair for detecting conflict-increasing confusion—all of which had very similar behaviour. In each case the control process kept two or three copies of the process corresponding to the given net (in the case of detecting conflict, two copies, one primed and one unprimed, and in the case of detecting confusion, three copies, one unprimed, one primed and one double primed) in step until the occurrence of a *check* event.

Here we are concerned not only with the six *Control* processes mentioned above but also with their six counterparts for unsafe nets. Because of the similarities between each of these processes and to facilitate understanding we choose in this paper to define a single parametrised *Control* process encompassing all twelve. The parameters of *Control* are as follows: the first parameter, LR, takes values *left* or *right* to indicate whether it is a control process for LHS or RHS; the second parameter, SU, takes values *safe* or *unsafe* to indicate whether it is a safe or unsafe net; the

---

[8] Note that processes LHS and RHS are typically referred to as $SPEC$ and $IMPL$, denoting the specification and implementation: FDR searches for any behaviour in the implementation that is not permitted by the specification. However, since in this paper we are comparing two functions of the process corresponding to a given net, these names are unhelpful.

third parameter, *test*, takes values *conflict*, *dec* or *inc* to indicate whether we are testing for conflict, conflict-decreasing confusion, or conflict-increasing confusion; finally the fourth parameter is the net under consideration.

Regardless of whether it is controlling the left-hand side or the right-hand side or whether it is concerned with a safe or an unsafe net, when testing for conflict the control process keeps the primed and unprimed copies of the process corresponding to the given net in step until the occurrence of the *check* event. After the check event, the *Control* process behaves as its associated *AfterCheck* process since all parameters are preserved. Hence:

$$Control(LR, SU, test, \mathcal{N}) =$$
$$\text{if } (test == conflict) \text{ then}$$
$$\square \, ts : \mathbb{P} \, T_{\mathcal{N}} \bullet trans.ts \rightarrow trans'.ts \rightarrow Control(LR, SU, test, \mathcal{N})$$
$$\square$$
$$check \rightarrow AfterCheck(LR, SU, test, \mathcal{N})$$
$$\text{else} \ldots$$

Obviously, since we are concerned only with detecting *conflict* in this section, we define only the parts of the *Control* processes concerned with this particular test. We will complete the definition of *Control* in Sections 7 and 8 when we consider conflict-decreasing and conflict-increasing confusion.

6.2   The *AfterCheck* Processes

The purpose of the *Control* process before the *check* event was to ensure that all copies of the process corresponding to the given net reached the same state, that is they had all performed the same transition events. The purpose of the *AfterCheck* process is then to check subsequent availability of transition events. In particular, when testing for conflict, we need to show that two *interfering* transitions can occur from the current state, one to be performed by the unprimed copy of the process corresponding to the net and the other to be performed by the primed copy. This is the case for both safe and unsafe nets, although the specific conditions for interference, as defined in Section 3.3, are different.

The *AfterCheck* processes for both *LHS* and *RHS* permit one *trans* event, $trans.\{t_1\}$ for some $t_1 \in T_{\mathcal{N}}$. The left-hand side then deadlocks whilst the right-hand side allows a further event $trans'.\{t_2\}$ if there exists an available transition $t_2 \in T_{\mathcal{N}}$ that interferes with t_1: thus the right-hand side can extend its trace where the left-hand side cannot precisely when there is conflict. Hence we define the process *AfterCheck* as follows:

$$AfterCheck(LR, SU, test, \mathcal{N}) =$$
$$\text{if } (test == conflict) \text{ then } (\square \, t_1 : T_{\mathcal{N}} \bullet trans.\{t_1\} \rightarrow$$
$$(\text{if } (LR == left) \text{ then } Stop$$
$$\text{else } (\square \, t_2 : T_{\mathcal{N}} \mid Interfere(SU, \mathcal{N}, t_1, t_2) \bullet trans'.\{t_2\} \rightarrow Stop)))$$
$$\text{else} \ldots$$

Once again we will complete this definition in subsequent sections when we consider conflict-decreasing and conflict-increasing confusion.

6.3 Processes *LHS* and *RHS*

We have already observed that we need a second, primed copy of the process corresponding to the given net to overcome the fact that FDR cannot perform backtracking. For both safe and unsafe nets we define the primed variants of processes $N_{(\mathcal{N}, M_{\mathcal{N}})}$ as follows:

$$N'_{(\mathcal{N}, M_{\mathcal{N}})} = N_{(\mathcal{N}, M_{\mathcal{N}})}\left[\left[trans'.ts / trans.ts \mid ts \in \mathbb{P}\, T_{\mathcal{N}}\right]\right]$$

The alphabet of the primed process is defined in the natural way. Thus $\Sigma'_{\mathcal{N}} = \{trans'.ts \mid ts \in \mathbb{P}\, T_{\mathcal{N}}\}$.

For both safe and unsafe nets, processes *LHS* and *RHS* comprise the parallel combination of the relevant control process with an interleaving of the primed and unprimed copies of the process corresponding to the given net. As above we parametrise our processes: the first parameter, SU, takes values *safe* or *unsafe* to indicate whether the net is safe or unsafe; the second, *test*, takes values *conflict*, *dec* or *inc* to indicate whether we are testing for conflict, conflict-decreasing confusion, or conflict-increasing confusion; the third is the net under consideration; and the fourth is the initial marking of that net.

$LHS(SU, test, \mathcal{N}, M_{\mathcal{N}}) =$
  if $(test == conflict)$ then
    $\left(\left(N_{(\mathcal{N}, M_{\mathcal{N}})} \;||| \; N'_{(\mathcal{N}, M_{\mathcal{N}})}\right) \;||_{\Sigma_{\mathcal{N}_S} \cup \Sigma'_{\mathcal{N}_S}} \; Control(left, SU, conflict, \mathcal{N})\right)$

  else ...

$RHS(SU, test, \mathcal{N}, M_{\mathcal{N}}) =$
  if $(test == conflict)$ then
    $\left(\left(N_{(\mathcal{N}, M_{\mathcal{N}})} \;||| \; N'_{(\mathcal{N}, M_{\mathcal{N}})}\right) \;||_{\Sigma_{\mathcal{N}_S} \cup \Sigma'_{\mathcal{N}_S}} \; Control(right, SU, conflict, \mathcal{N})\right)$

  else ...

Once again we will complete these definitions in subsequent sections when we consider conflict-decreasing and conflict-increasing confusion.

6.4 The Test

We have constructed our processes so that the right-hand side will be able to execute a trace that the left-hand side cannot precisely when conflict is present. Model-checker FDR will detect this discrepancy and the appropriate refinement check, that corresponding to either safe or unsafe nets, will fail.

$$LHS(safe, conflict, \mathcal{N}_S, M_{\mathcal{N}_S}) \sqsubseteq_T RHS(safe, conflict, \mathcal{N}_S, M_{\mathcal{N}_S})$$
$$LHS(unsafe, conflict, \mathcal{N}_U, M_{\mathcal{N}_U}) \sqsubseteq_T RHS(unsafe, conflict, \mathcal{N}_U, M_{\mathcal{N}_U})$$

7 Testing for Conflict-Decreasing Confusion

As observed in Section 3.5, conflict-decreasing confusion can arise when there is a mixture of concurrency and conflict. We need to demonstrate that the conflict set of a given transition is *reduced* by the occurrence of another transition with which it does not interfere. More specifically, we have conflict-decreasing confusion in net $\mathcal{N}$ modelled by process $N_{(\mathcal{N},M_{\mathcal{N}})}$ after sequence of transitions $tr \in \mathcal{T}[\![\, N_{(\mathcal{N},M_{\mathcal{N}})} \,]\!]$ if we can find transitions $t_1, t_2, t_3 \in T_{\mathcal{N}}$ where t_1 and t_3 do not interfere such that t_1, t_2 and t_3 are all enabled after tr and such that t_1 and t_2 conflict after trace tr but not after trace $tr ^\frown \langle trans.\{t_3\}\rangle$.

7.1 Processes LHS and RHS

Recall that in Section 6 when testing for conflict we needed to check the availability of *two* transition events after the same trace and hence required *two* copies, one primed and one unprimed, of the process corresponding to the given net. Here we need to check the availability of *three* events and hence need a *third*, double primed copy of the process corresponding to the given net. For both safe and unsafe nets we define the double primed variant and its associated alphabet in the natural way.

$$N''_{(\mathcal{N},M_{\mathcal{N}})} \;=\; N_{(\mathcal{N},M_{\mathcal{N}})} [\![trans''.ts/trans.ts \mid ts \in \mathbb{P}\, T_{\mathcal{N}}]\!]$$
$$\Sigma''_{\mathcal{N}} \;=\; \{\, trans''.ts \mid ts \in \mathbb{P}\, T_{\mathcal{N}}\}.$$

Processes *LHS* and *RHS* are once more constructed from the parallel combination of the relevant control process and (this time three) interleaved copies of the process corresponding to the given net. We extend the definitions of processes *LHS* and *RHS* as presented in Section 6.3 as follows:

$LHS(SU, test, \mathcal{N}, M_{\mathcal{N}}) \;=\;$
  if $(test == conflict)$ then $\ldots$

  else if $(test == dec)$ then
    $((N_{(\mathcal{N},M_{\mathcal{N}})} \;|\!|\!|\; N'_{(\mathcal{N},M_{\mathcal{N}})} \;|\!|\!|\; N''_{(\mathcal{N},M_{\mathcal{N}})}) \;|\!|_{\Sigma_{\mathcal{N}_S} \cup \Sigma'_{\mathcal{N}_S} \cup \Sigma''_{\mathcal{N}_S}}\; Control(left, SU, dec, \mathcal{N}))$

  else $\ldots$

$RHS(SU, test, \mathcal{N}, M_{\mathcal{N}}) \;=\;$
  if $(test == conflict)$ then $\ldots$

  else if $(test == dec)$ then
    $((N_{(\mathcal{N},M_{\mathcal{N}})} \;|\!|\!|\; N'_{(\mathcal{N},M_{\mathcal{N}})} \;|\!|\!|\; N''_{(\mathcal{N},M_{\mathcal{N}})}) \;|\!|_{\Sigma_{\mathcal{N}_S} \cup \Sigma'_{\mathcal{N}_S} \cup \Sigma''_{\mathcal{N}_S}}\; Control(right, SU, dec, \mathcal{N}))$

  else $\ldots$

These definitions will be further extended in Section 8 when we consider conflict-increasing confusion.

7.2 The *Control* Processes

Before the *check* event occurs, the *Control* processes used in the detection of conflict-decreasing confusion play the same role as the control processes used in the detection of conflict. That is, regardless of whether the process is controlling the left-hand side or the right-hand side, and regardless of whether it is controlling a safe net or an unsafe net, it ensures that the copies of the net are kept in step. Therefore, we simply extend the code for *Control* as introduced in Section 6.1 taking the third, double primed copy of the process into consideration.

$Control(LR, SU, test, \mathcal{N}) =$
  if $(test == conflict)$ then ...

  else if $(test == dec)$ then
    $(\,\square\, ts : \mathbb{P}\, T_{\mathcal{N}} \bullet trans.ts \rightarrow trans'.ts \rightarrow trans''.ts \rightarrow Control(LR, SU, dec, \mathcal{N})$
    $\square$
    $check \rightarrow AfterCheck(LR, SU, test, \mathcal{N}))$

  else ...

Once again, after the check event, the *Control* process behaves as its associated *AfterCheck* process since all parameters are preserved, and once again we will further extend these definitions in Section 8 when we consider conflict-increasing confusion.

7.3 The *AfterCheck* Processes

After the *check* event, for both safe and unsafe nets, the *AfterCheck* processes on both sides permit three events: first event $trans.\{t_1\}$ for some $t_1 \in T_{\mathcal{N}}$; second event $trans'.\{t_2\}$ for some $t_2 \in T_{\mathcal{N}}$ such that t_1 and t_2 conflict; and third event $trans''.\{t_3\}$ for some $t_3 \in T_{\mathcal{N}}$ that does not interfere with t_1.[9] Only after this point, having demonstrated the availability of t_1, t_2 and t_3, might the behaviour of the left-hand side and the right-hand side differ. Regardless of whether the net is safe or unsafe, the *AfterCheck* process on the left-hand side permits the event $trans''.\{t_2\}$, although this will be blocked by process $\mathrm{N}_{(\mathcal{N}, M_{\mathcal{N}})}''$ if t_2 is not enabled after t_3. Conversely, the process on the right-hand side always permits without obstruction from $\mathrm{N}_{(\mathcal{N}, M_{\mathcal{N}})}''$ the event $trans'''.\{t_2\}$ which will subsequently be renamed to $trans''.\{t_2\}$.[10]

$AfterCheck(LR, SU, test, \mathcal{N}) =$
  if $(test == conflict)$ then ...

  else if $(test == dec)$ then
    $(\,\square\, t_1 : T_{\mathcal{N}} \bullet trans.\{t_1\} \rightarrow$
      $\square\, t_2 : T_{\mathcal{N}} \mid Interfere(SU, \mathcal{N}, t_1, t_2) \bullet trans'.\{t_2\} \rightarrow$
        $\square\, t_3 : T_{\mathcal{N}} \mid IntFree(SU, \mathcal{N}, \{t_1, t_3\}) \bullet trans''.\{t_3\} \rightarrow$
          $(\text{ if } (LR == left) \text{ then } (trans''.\{t_2\} \rightarrow Stop)$
          $\text{else } (trans'''.\{t_2\} \rightarrow Stop)))$

  else ...

---

[9] Note once more that the definition of interference depends on whether the net is safe or unsafe.

[10] The purpose of the renaming is to avoid synchronisation with $\mathrm{N}_{(\mathcal{N}, M_{\mathcal{N}})}''$.

Once again we have extended the definition given in Section 3.5 and will finally complete the definition in Section 8.

7.4   The Test

Through synchronisation with the appropriate *Control* and *AfterCheck* processes we have constructed processes *LHS* and *RHS* so that, after the *check* event, if one side can perform trace $tr \frown \langle check, trans.\{t_1\}, trans'.\{t_2\}, trans''.\{t_3\}\rangle$ then so can the other. However, the right-hand side can always extend this trace with the event $trans'''.\{t_2\}$, to be renamed to $trans''.\{t_2\}$ but the left-hand side can it extend it with $trans''.\{t_2\}$ only if t_2 is still enabled after t_3, that is if conflict-decreasing confusion is *not* present. Hence, whenever conflict-decreasing confusion *is* present, the right-hand side will be able to execute a trace that the left-hand side can not. Model-checker FDR will detect this discrepancy and, incorporating the necessary renaming, the appropriate refinement check, that corresponding to either safe or unsafe nets, will fail.

$$LHS(safe, dec, \mathcal{N}_S, M_{\mathcal{N}_S}) \sqsubseteq_{\mathcal{T}}$$
$$(RHS(safe, dec, \mathcal{N}_S, M_{\mathcal{N}_S}))\,[[trans''.ts/trans'''.ts \mid ts \in \mathbb{P}\,T_{\mathcal{N}_S}]]$$

$$LHS(unsafe, dec, \mathcal{N}_U, M_{\mathcal{N}_U}) \sqsubseteq_{\mathcal{T}}$$
$$(RHS(safe, dec, \mathcal{N}_U, M_{\mathcal{N}_U}))\,[[trans''.ts/trans'''.ts \mid ts \in \mathbb{P}\,T_{\mathcal{N}_U}]]$$

8   Testing for Conflict-Increasing Confusion

Conflict-increasing confusion, like conflict-decreasing confusion, can arise when there is a mixture of concurrency and conflict. This time the conflict set of a given transition is *augmented* by the occurrence of another transition with which it does not interfere. Equivalently, we have conflict-increasing confusion in net $\mathcal{N}$ modelled by process $N_{(\mathcal{N}, M_{\mathcal{N}})}$ after sequence of transitions $tr \in \mathcal{T}[\![\,N_{(\mathcal{N}, M_{\mathcal{N}})}\,]\!]$ if we can find transitions $t_1, t_2, t_3 \in T_{\mathcal{N}}$ where t_1 and t_3 do not interfere but t_1 and t_2 do, such that t_1 and t_3 are all enabled after tr and such that t_2 is enabled after trace $tr \frown \langle trans.\{t_3\}\rangle$ but not after trace tr.

8.1   Processes LHS and RHS

The techniques for demonstrating the presence of conflict-*increasing* confusion are similar to those for demonstrating the presence of conflict-*decreasing* confusion. Once more both the left-hand side and the right-hand side are built from the parallel combination of a control process and an interleaving of the unprimed, primed and double-primed variants of the process corresponding to the given net. Since these processes have the same structure as their counterparts for detecting conflict-decreasing confusion, provided the appropriate parameters are passed on to the control process, we can re-use the same definition. The complete definitions of processes *LHS* and *RHS*, extended from those definitions given in Sections 6.3 and 7.1 are therefore as follows:

$LHS(SU, test, \mathcal{N}, M_{\mathcal{N}}) =$
   if $(test == conflict)$ then
      $((N_{(\mathcal{N}, M_{\mathcal{N}})} \parallel\!\parallel N'_{(\mathcal{N}, M_{\mathcal{N}})}) \parallel_{\Sigma_{\mathcal{N}_S} \cup \Sigma'_{\mathcal{N}_S}} Control(left, SU, conflict, \mathcal{N}))$

   else
      $((N_{(\mathcal{N}, M_{\mathcal{N}})} \parallel\!\parallel N'_{(\mathcal{N}, M_{\mathcal{N}})} \parallel\!\parallel N''_{(\mathcal{N}, M_{\mathcal{N}})}) \parallel_{\Sigma_{\mathcal{N}_S} \cup \Sigma'_{\mathcal{N}_S} \cup \Sigma''_{\mathcal{N}_S}} Control(left, SU, test, \mathcal{N}))$

$RHS(SU, test, \mathcal{N}, M_{\mathcal{N}}) =$
   if $(test == conflict)$ then
      $((N_{(\mathcal{N}, M_{\mathcal{N}})} \parallel\!\parallel N'_{(\mathcal{N}, M_{\mathcal{N}})}) \parallel_{\Sigma_{\mathcal{N}_S} \cup \Sigma'_{\mathcal{N}_S}} Control(right, SU, conflict, \mathcal{N}))$

   else
      $((N_{(\mathcal{N}, M_{\mathcal{N}})} \parallel\!\parallel N'_{(\mathcal{N}, M_{\mathcal{N}})} \parallel\!\parallel N''_{(\mathcal{N}, M_{\mathcal{N}})}) \parallel_{\Sigma_{\mathcal{N}_S} \cup \Sigma'_{\mathcal{N}_S} \cup \Sigma''_{\mathcal{N}_S}} Control(right, SU, test, \mathcal{N}))$

Note that the processes for detecting conflict differ in structure from their counterparts for detecting confusion only in the number of copies of the process corresponding to the given net.

8.2   The *Control* Processes

For both safe and unsafe nets, the identical behaviour of the left-hand side and the right-hand side before the *check* event can be captured in exactly the same way as when we were detecting conflict-increasing confusion. Therefore, provided we pass on the correct parameters we can once more re-use our definitions. It therefore follows that the full definition for the process *Control*, extended from the part definitions given in Sections 6.1 and 7.2 is as follows:

$Control(LR, SU, test, \mathcal{N}) =$
   if $(test == conflict)$ then
      $\Box\, ts : \mathbb{P}\, T_{\mathcal{N}} \bullet trans.ts \to trans'.ts \to Control(LR, SU, conflict, \mathcal{N})$
      $\Box$
      $check \to AfterCheck(LR, SU, test, \mathcal{N})$

   else
      $(\Box\, ts : \mathbb{P}\, T_{\mathcal{N}} \bullet trans.ts \to trans'.ts \to trans''.ts \to Control(LR, SU, test, \mathcal{N})$
      $\Box$
      $check \to AfterCheck(LR, SU, test, \mathcal{N}))$

8.3   The *AfterCheck* Processes

After the *check* event, for both safe and unsafe nets, the *AfterCheck* processes on both sides permit three events: first event $trans.\{t_1\}$ for some $t_1 \in T_{\mathcal{N}}$; second, event $trans''.\{t_3\}$ for some $t_3 \in T_{\mathcal{N}}$ such that t_1 and t_3 do not interfere; and third event $trans''.\{t_2\}$ for some $t_2 \in T_{\mathcal{N}}$ that interferes with t_1.[11] Only after this point, having demonstrated that t_1 is enabled and that t_3 and t_2 are

---

[11] Note once more that the definition of interference depends on whether the net is safe or unsafe.

enabled in sequence, might the behaviour of the left-hand side and the right-hand side differ. Regardless of whether the net is safe or unsafe, the *AfterCheck* process on the left-hand side permits the event $trans'.\{t_2\}$, although this will be blocked by process $N_{(\mathcal{N},M_\mathcal{N})}{}'$ if t_2 was not enabled before the occurrence of t_3. Conversely, the process on the right-hand side always permits without obstruction from $N_{(\mathcal{N},M_\mathcal{N})}{}'$ the event $trans'''.\{t_2\}$ which will subsequently be renamed to $trans'.\{t_2\}$.[12] The complete definition of process *AfterCheck*, extended from the part definitions given in Sections 6.2 and 7.3, is therefore

$AfterCheck(LR, SU, test, \mathcal{N}) =$
    if $(test == conflict)$ then $(\Box\, t_1 : T_\mathcal{N} \bullet trans.\{t_1\} \to$
        $(\,$if $(LR == left)$ then $Stop$
        else $(\Box\, t_2 : T_\mathcal{N} \mid Interfere(SU, \mathcal{N}, t_1, t_2) \bullet trans'.\{t_2\} \to Stop\,)))$

    else if $(test == dec)$ then
      $(\Box\, t_1 : T_\mathcal{N} \bullet trans.\{t_1\} \to$
        $\Box\, t_2 : T_\mathcal{N} \mid Interfere(SU, \mathcal{N}, t_1, t_2) \bullet trans'.\{t_2\} \to$
          $\Box\, t_3 : T_\mathcal{N} \mid IntFree(SU, \mathcal{N}, \{t_1, t_3\}) \bullet trans''.\{t_3\} \to$
            $(\,$if $(LR == left)$ then $(\,trans''.\{t_2\} \to Stop)$
            else $(\,trans'''.\{t_2\} \to Stop)))$

    else $(\Box\, t_1 : T_\mathcal{N} \bullet trans.\{t_1\} \to$
        $\Box\, t_2, t_3 : T_\mathcal{N} \mid Interfere(\mathcal{N}, t_1, t_2) \wedge IntFree(SU, \mathcal{N}, \{t_1, t_3\}) \bullet$
        $trans''.\{t_3\} \to trans''.\{t_2\} \to$
          $(\,$if $(LR == left)$ then $(\,trans'.\{t_2\} \to Stop)$
          else $(\,trans'''.\{t_2\} \to Stop)))$

If one side can perform trace $tr^\frown\langle check, trans.\{t_1\}, trans''.\{t_3\}, trans''.\{t_2\}\rangle$ then so can the other. However, the right-hand side can always extend this trace with the event $trans'''.\{t_2\}$, to be renamed to $trans'.\{t_2\}$, but the left-hand side can it extend it with $trans'.\{t_2\}$ only if t_2 is enabled before t_3, that is if conflict-increasing confusion is *not* present.

8.4   The Test

We have constructed our processes for safe and unsafe nets so that, subject to the appropriate re-naming, whenever conflict-decreasing confusion is present, the right-hand side will be able to execute a trace that cannot. Model-checker FDR will detect this discrepancy and the following refinement check, incorporating the necessary renaming, will fail.

$LHS(safe, inc, \mathcal{N}_S, M_{\mathcal{N}_S}) \sqsubseteq_T$
    $(\,RHS(safe, inc, \mathcal{N}_S, M_{\mathcal{N}_S})\,)\,[[trans''.ts / trans'''.ts \mid ts \in \mathbb{P}\, T_{\mathcal{N}_S}]]$

$LHS(unsafe, inc, \mathcal{N}_U, M_{\mathcal{N}_U}) \sqsubseteq_T$
    $(\,RHS(safe, inc, \mathcal{N}_U, M_{\mathcal{N}_U})\,)\,[[trans''.ts / trans'''.ts \mid ts \in \mathbb{P}\, T_{\mathcal{N}_U}]]$

---

[12] Once again, the purpose of the renaming is to avoid synchronisation with $N_{(\mathcal{N},M_\mathcal{N})}{}'$.

9 Discussion

In [5] we presented a translation from a *safe nets*, a simple subset of Petri nets, to CSP. Through this translation we demonstrated the surprising result that the CSP model-checker might be used to automatically detect instances of conflict and confusion in CSP. This result was surprising since the interleaving semantic models of CSP cannot distinguish between the concurrent execution of actions and the non-deterministic choice between the possible orders of their executions.

In this paper we have developed the work presented in [5]. We have extended the domain of our translation, removing the restriction on our Petri nets that places can contain at most one token, thereby significantly increasing the number of potential application domains. Once again we incorporated flow information, or presets and postsets of transitions, into our model in order to capture and detect the truly concurrent notions of conflict and confusion.

The Importance of Automatic Verification. In the development of critical systems standards dictate that it is necessary to first design and analyse abstract models of the system. Since concurrent systems have high levels of complexity making them especially vulnerable to errors, automating this process is of paramount importance. As observed by Clarke et al. in [7] and by Steiner et al. in [23], model-checking is an increasingly important technique in the verification and validation of the correctness of systems. As opposed to testing in which a pre-chosen selection of executions of the system are analysed, the model-checker exhaustively checks every reachable state in the system, thereby guaranteeing to find conflict and confusion if either is present.

Why Confusion is of Concern. Motivations for truly concurrent models over their interleaving counterparts are given in many papers on Petri nets, trace theory and pomsets e.g. [18]. However, as decentralisation, re-use and component-based specification become more prevalent we must pay particular attention to confusion. The developer of a component might exploit, indeed rely on, the fact that whenever one action is on the "menu" then so too is its companion action. However, as we have clearly demonstrated in previous sections, interference, arising from combining one component with another, might mean that the companion action is blocked. We demonstrated the problems that this might cause through a simple example, the parallel combination of an alarm system and a maintenance system, in the Discussion Section in [5].

Tractability of Verification. State space explosion is always a key concern when model-checking any system. When considering safe nets in [5], assuming a finite number of places in any given net, we could be certain that the number of tokens would be finite. Here, although we do not have that guarantee, most specifications of unsafe nets do give bounds on the number of tokens in each place. Further, it should be noted that using standard tricks of CSP [12], even systems with infinite state spaces can be model-checked. In these instances, however, the code would need to be modified: here, as we did in [5], we have chosen clarity over efficiency in our CSP models.

Related work. Whilst there has been little previous work translating from Petri Nets to CSP, there is a significant body of work in which the translation is performed in the other direction. Examples include [9] and [11]. In addition, there has also been a significant body of work translating from the process algebra CCS [15,14] to Petri Nets, including [22].

Conclusions. As systems get more and more complex there is a move towards building separate components for managing distinct parts of a system. Whilst factorisation is a useful technique, detection of confusion will become increasingly significant. It is therefore important that software engineers using CSP to develop distributed systems learn to recognise, detect and avoid building confusion into their systems.

References

1. Petri nets tool database. Available via URL http://www.daimi.au.dk/PetriNets/tools/
2. Bergstra, J.A., Klop, J.W.: Algebra of communicating processes with abstraction. Theoretical Computer Science, vol. 37(1) (1985)
3. Best, E., de Boer, F.S., Palamidessi, C.: Partial order and sos semantics for linear constraint programs. In: Garlan, D., Le Métayer, D. (eds.) COORDINATION 1997. LNCS, vol. 1282, Springer, Heidelberg (1997)
4. Bolton, C.: On the Refinement of State-Based and Event-Based Models. D.Phil., University of Oxford (2002)
5. Bolton, C.: Adding conflict and confusion to CSP. In: Fitzgerald, J.A., Hayes, I.J., Tarlecki, A. (eds.) FM 2005. LNCS, vol. 3582, Springer, Heidelberg (2005)
6. Bolton, C., Lowe, G.: A hierarchy of failures-based models. In: Proceedings of the 10th International Workshop on Expressiveness in Concurrency: EXPRESS'03 (2003)
7. Clarke, E., Grumberg, O., Peled, D.: Model-Checking. The MIT Press, Cambridge (1999)
8. Formal Systems (Europe) Ltd. Failures-Divergence Refinement FDR 2 User Manual, (1999) Available via URL: http://www.fsel.com/fdr2_manual.html
9. Goltz, U., Reisig, W.: CSP-programs as nets with individual tokens. In: Rozenberg, G. (ed.) Advances in Petri Nets 1984. LNCS, vol. 188, Springer, Heidelberg (1985)
10. Hoare, C.A.R.: Communicating Sequential Processes. Prentice-Hall, Englewood Cliffs (1985)
11. Kavi, K., Sheldon, F., Shirazzi, B., Hurson, A.: Reliability analysis of CSP specifications using petri nets and markov processes. In: Proceedings of 28th Annual Hawaii International Conference on System Sciences, IEEE, Los Alamitos (1995)
12. Lazic, R.: A Semantic Study of Data Independence with Applications to Model Checking. PhD thesis, University of Oxford (1999)
13. Mazurkiewicz, A.: Introduction to trace theory. In: Diekert, V., Rozenberg, G. (eds.) The book of traces, World Scientific, Singapore (1995)
14. Milner, R. (ed.): A Calculus of Communication Systems. LNCS, vol. 92. Springer, Heidelberg (1980)
15. Milner, R.: Communications and concurrency. Prentice-Hall, Englewood Cliffs (1989)

16. Olderog, E.-R.: Nets, Terms and Formulas: Three Views of Concurrent Processes and Their Relationship. Cambridge University Press, Cambridge (1991)
17. Petri, C.A.: Fundamentals of a theory of asynchronous information flow. In: Proceedings of IFIP, Congress'62, pp. 386–390 (1962)
18. Pratt, V.: On the composition of processes. In: Proceedings of 1982 ACM Symposium on Principles of Programming Languages (POPL) (1982)
19. Reisig, W.: Petri Nets. Springer, Heidelberg (1982)
20. Reisig, W., Rozenberg, G.: Informal introduction to petri nets. LNCS, vol. 1491. Springer, Berlin Heidelberg (1998)
21. Roscoe, A.W.: The Theory and Practice of Concurrency. Prentice-Hall, Englewood Cliffs (1997)
22. Schreiber, G.: Functional equivalences of petri nets. In: DeMichelis, G., Díaz, M. (eds.) Application and Theory of Petri Nets 1995. LNCS, vol. 935, Springer, Heidelberg (1995)
23. Steiner, W., Rushby, J., Sorea, M., Pfeifer, H.: Model checking a faulttolerant startup algorithm: From design exploration to exhaustive fault simulation. In: Proceedings of Dependable Systems and Networks (DSN 2004) (2004)
24. Störrle, H.: An evaluation of high-end tools for petri-nets. Technical Report 9802, Ludwig-Maximilians-Universität München (1997)
25. Winskel, G.: Events in Computation. D.Phil, University of Edinburgh (1980)

A Stepwise Development Process for Reasoning About the Reliability of Real-Time Systems

Larissa Meinicke[1,*] and Graeme Smith[2]

[1] Department of Computer Science, Åbo Akademi, Finland
[2] School of Information Technology and Electrical Engineering,
The University of Queensland, Australia

Abstract. This paper investigates the use of the probabilistic and continuous extensions of action systems in the development and calculation of reliability of continuous, real-time systems. Rather than develop a new semantics to formally combine the existing extensions, it investigates a methodology for using them together, and the conditions under which this methodology is sound. A key feature of the methodology is that it simplifies the development process by separating the probabilistic calculations of system reliability from the details of the system's real-time, continuous behaviour.

Keywords: action systems, refinement, probability, real-time, reliability.

1 Introduction

System reliability is an important characteristic of safety-critical and mission-critical systems. Informally, it may be defined as a measure of the ability of a system to satisfy its specification in certain operational conditions over a period of time [17].

McIver, Morgan and Troubitsyna [12] show how system reliability may be calculated from component reliability via a stepwise development process using probabilistic datatypes. Building on this work, Troubitsyna [18] develops a similar approach for probabilistic action systems [16]. These are an extension of action systems [2,3] in which actions may be expressed and composed using discrete probabilistic choices as well as demonic nondeterministic choices.

While Troubitsyna's approach allows development at an abstract level, it does not support the expression of real-time constraints, nor continuous behaviour. These behavioural aspects are, however, relevant in many safety-critical and mission-critical systems where software is embedded in a continuously changing physical environment.

Back, Petre and Porres [4] propose an extension of action systems for developing *hybrid systems*, i.e., those in which both discrete and continuous real-time behaviour coexist. It may therefore be of interest to develop an extension of action systems which combines both probabilistic and continuous action systems.

---

* The first author carried out part of this work while at the School of Information Technology and Electrical Engineering, The University of Queensland, Australia.

J. Davies and J. Gibbons (Eds.): IFM 2007, LNCS 4591, pp. 439–458, 2007.
© Springer-Verlag Berlin Heidelberg 2007

The semantics of the individual extensions are, however, quite different. Hence the semantic development would be non-trivial.

Rather than performing such a construction, in this paper we investigate the possibility of using probabilistic action systems and continuous action systems during the development of systems, *without* the development of a new action system extension. Not only does this allow us to use the existing semantics and definitions of refinement, but also allows us to simplify the overall development process: probabilistic calculations are performed independently of the continuous, real-time behaviour of the system being developed.

In our approach, probabilistic aspects of the program are first considered, and developed. Non-probabilistic behaviour is then extracted from the specification, and continuous behaviour is introduced and developed. Probabilistic calculations from the first part of the structured development process are then used to estimate system reliability. We demonstrate our approach by extending the probabilistic steam boiler example used by McIver, Morgan and Troubitsyna [12] to include a more realistic specification of real-time aspects.

In Section 2 we briefly describe the theory of action systems. This is followed by a brief introduction to both probabilistic action systems in Section 3, and continuous action systems in Section 4. In Section 5 we outline our methodology, and apply it to the probabilistic steam boiler case study. We discuss our approach, including its limitations, in Section 6.

2   Action Systems

Action systems [2,3] are a construct for reasoning about concurrent, reactive systems that can be analysed in the refinement calculus [6]. An action system is of the form

$$\|[\text{ var } x_1 : X_1; \ ...; \ x_n : X_n \bullet A_0; \text{ do } A_1 \ \| \ ... \ \| \ A_n \text{ od}]\|:< z_1 : Z_1; \ ...; \ z_m : Z_m >,$$

where each x_i is a local variable, and each z_j is a global variable. A_0 is an *initialisation action* that initialises the local variables without modifying the global variables. $A_1, ..., A_n$ are *actions* that operate on the combined local and global state space.

Each action A_i has a guard denoted by $\text{gd}.A_i$[1]: as long as $\text{gd}.A_i$ is satisfied, action A_i is said to be enabled, meaning that it can execute. The predicate $\neg\text{gd}.A_i$ thus models the states from which A_i is unable to be executed. Also, $\text{term}.A_i$ denotes the states from which action A_i terminates properly. The negation, $\neg\text{term}.A_i$, denotes the states from which action A_i is aborting.

The behaviour of an action system **A** may be informally described as follows: first the local variables are initialised then, while the guard of at least one action continues to hold, an enabled action is nondeterministically selected and executed. In this way, concurrent behaviour is expressed by interleaving actions.

---

[1] Throughout this paper we use the notation $f.x$ to denote the application of function f to argument x.

When no more actions are enabled, the action system terminates. If an aborting action is executed, then no more constraints are placed on future behaviour, that is, the action system itself aborts.

2.1   Semantics

The state space Σ_A of an action system $\mathbf{A}$ is a set of mappings from the names of variables in $\mathbf{A}$ to the values of their types. The local and global parts of this state space are denoted $local.\Sigma_A$ and $global.\Sigma_A$, respectively.

A trace semantics may be used to describe the reactive behaviour of action systems [5]. The trace semantics of an action system $\mathbf{A}$ is given in terms of sets of *behaviours* that $\mathbf{A}$ may produce, $beh.\mathbf{A}$. Each behaviour represents the "output" of one possible execution of A, where the "output" is represented by a sequence which records the states that are reached after the execution of each action. Formally, $beh.\mathbf{A}$ is of type $\mathbb{P}(seq_\top.\Sigma_A)$, where $seq_\top.\Sigma_A$ represents the set of all finite and infinite sequences of Σ_A, where the finite sequences may be appended with a special state $\top$, which represents termination. A behaviour b is defined to be *terminating* if it is finite and its last state is $\top$; it is *aborting* if it is finite and its last state is not $\top$; it is *nonterminating* if it is neither terminating nor aborting.

An action system $\mathbf{A}$ is refined by another action system $\mathbf{C}$, if the globally visible behaviour of $\mathbf{C}$ is able to be produced by $\mathbf{A}$. The globally visible view of a behaviour b is a *trace* $tr.b$ of type $seq_\top.(global.\Sigma_A)$. A trace of a behaviour is simply the behaviour with local states and all finite sequences of *stuttering* steps removed; a stuttering step is a step which does not modify the global state. Traces are defined as terminating, aborting or nonterminating in the same way as behaviours. Let $traces.\mathbf{A}$ denote the set of traces of action system $\mathbf{A}$, i.e., $\{b : beh.\mathbf{A} \bullet tr.b\}$.

Definition 1. *(from [5]). The trace refinement relation $\sqsubseteq_{tr}$ between two action systems $\mathbf{A}$ and $\mathbf{C}$ is defined as*

$$\mathbf{A} \sqsubseteq_{tr} \mathbf{C} \triangleq \forall t_C : traces.\mathbf{C} \bullet (\exists t_A : traces.\mathbf{A} \bullet t_A \preceq_{tr} t_C),$$

where $t_A \preceq_{tr} t_C$ if, neither t_A nor t_C is aborting and $t_A = t_C$, or t_A is aborting and is a prefix of t_C.

3   Probabilistic Action Systems

Probabilistic action systems [18] have the same general form as action systems. They differ because actions may be expressed and composed using both nondeterministic choice *and* discrete probabilistic choice: we write $A_1 \, {}_p\oplus A_2$ to mean that A_1 is executed with probability p and A_2 is executed with probability $1 - p$. For example, consider the action system

$$|[n := 0; \; \mathsf{do} \; n := n + 1 \; {}_a\oplus \mathsf{abort} \; \mathsf{od}]|: \langle n : \mathbb{N} \rangle. \tag{1}$$

It has one global variable n, which counts the number of times the action has been performed, and it has a probability of $1 - a$ of aborting on each iteration. Strictly, action systems are not allowed to specify initial values of global variables such as n. However, we do this as a shorthand for an initial action and a local "program counter" variable which would ensure the initial action is the first to occur and occurs exactly once.

It is possible to reason about the reliability of probabilistic action systems such as this one. Reliability is a measure of the ability of a system to satisfy its specification over a period of *time*, where *time* may be measured by some abstract parameter [17]. If we equate aborting with behaviour that falls outside the specification, then the reliability of (1) may be described by the function $R.n \triangleq a^n$, where $R.n$ specifies the probability the system has functioned correctly for at least n iterations.

Now consider a more complex system which tolerates N consecutive transient faults in a component which has an *availability* of $1 - c$, i.e., a probability of $1 - c$ of functioning correctly at any instant[2].

$$
\begin{aligned}
&\|[\ \mathbf{var}\ i : int \bullet \\
&\quad n, i := 0, 0; \\
&\quad \mathbf{do}\ \{i < N\};\ (i := i + 1\ {}_c\oplus i := 0);\ n := n + 1\ \mathbf{od} \\
&]\|: \langle n : \mathbb{N} \rangle
\end{aligned}
\tag{2}
$$

This probabilistic action system aborts when the assertion $i < N$ does not hold. To calculate its reliability, it is possible to use data refinement. Using the same reasoning presented by McIver, Morgan and Troubitsyna [12] for sequential probabilistic programs[3], it can be shown that (1) is data refined by (2) provided $a \le a'$, where a' is the largest solution for $x \in [0..1]$ of the equation

$$
x^N = (1 - c)(x^{N-1} + cx^{N-2} + \dots + c^{N-2}x + c^{N-1}).
\tag{3}
$$

Therefore, (2) is a refinement of a system which has reliability $R.n = a'^n$, where a' is calculated from parameters c and N, as shown above. Since system reliability is only improved by refinement (i.e., by refining aborting behaviour), this provides a lower bound for the reliability of (2), and for any of its refinements.

3.1   Semantics

To capture the reactive behaviour of probabilistic action systems they, like action systems, may be given a trace semantics [13].

A probabilistic action system **PA** may be seen to generate a set of *behaviour trees*, *behTree*.**PA**. These, similar to the behaviours of action systems, may be seen to represent the possible deterministic probabilistic executions of the system: that is, each behavior tree describes one way in which nondeterministic

---

[2] See [17], page 167, for a more detailed discussion of availability.

[3] The data refinement rule applied by McIver et al. in their proof [12] is applicable to probabilistic action systems whose actions are unguarded ($\mathsf{gd}.A = \mathsf{true}$), hence their proof is valid in a probabilistic action system setting.

choices between different probabilistic next-state distributions may been resolved during execution. Each behaviour tree is succinctly described by its expectation of producing any finite prefix of a behaviour, and can be used to describe a distribution over behaviours. Given a finite behaviour prefix s, and a behaviour tree t, prefixExpt.$t.s$ denotes the probability that the behaviour tree t will produce behaviour prefix s.

As for action systems, one probabilistic action system **PA** is refined by another **PC**, if the globally visible behaviour of **PC** is able to be produced by **PA**. The globally visible view of a behaviour tree t is a *trace tree*, $trTree.t$. Similar to the standard case, this is the behaviour tree t with all local states and finite sequences of stuttering steps removed. Like behaviour trees, trace trees are characterised by their expectation to produce any finite trace prefix. Let $trTree.$**PA** denote the set of trace trees of **PA**.

Definition 2. *(from [13]). The trace tree refinement relation $\sqsubseteq_\oplus$ between two probabilistic action systems* **PA** *and* **PC** *that share the same global state space Σ, is defined as*

$$\mathbf{PA} \sqsubseteq_\oplus \mathbf{PC} \triangleq \forall t_C : trTree.\mathbf{PC} \bullet (\exists t_A : trTree.\mathbf{PA} \bullet t_A \preceq_\oplus t_C),$$

where $t_A \preceq_\oplus t_C \triangleq \forall s : seq_T.\Sigma \bullet finite.s \Rightarrow$ prefixExpt.$t_A.s \le$ prefixExpt.$t_C.s$.

The prefix relation between trace trees, $\preceq_\oplus$, states that one trace tree t_A is a prefix of another t_C if, for any finite trace prefix s, the probability of t_C to achieve s is at least that of t_A. As for the standard case, this definition allows aborting behaviour to be refined by terminating or by producing further states. Since the set of trace trees are defined such that they are convex closed [13],

$$(\forall p : [0..1], t_1, t_2 : trTree.\mathbf{A} \bullet \text{prefixExpt.}t_1.\langle z_0 \rangle = \text{prefixExpt.}t_2.\langle z_0 \rangle \Rightarrow$$
$$(\exists t_3 : trTree.\mathbf{A} \bullet$$
$$(\forall s \bullet \text{prefixExpt.}t_3.s = p * \text{prefixExpt.}t_1.s + (1 - p) * \text{prefixExpt.}t_2.s)),$$

the definition of probabilistic action system refinement allows nondeterminism between trace trees to be refined by probabilistic choice.

4   Continuous Action Systems

Continuous action systems [4] are a variant of the action system formalism for modeling *hybrid systems*, i.e., systems with a discrete controller acting over a continuously evolving environment. They differ from action systems in that each local or global variable is a *timed stream*, i.e., a total function from the time domain, Time $\triangleq \mathbb{R}_+$, to the set of values the variable may assume. The value of such a variable x at time t is denoted $x.t$.

Timed stream variables are common in other formalisms for continuous, real-time systems [19,11,15,7] and capture both the past and future values of the variable in addition to its present value. In continuous action systems, the future behaviour of a variable at any point in time is a default behaviour only. This default behaviour may be changed by the subsequent occurrence of an action.

Additionally, continuous action systems support an implicit variable τ : Time denoting the current time[4]. Initially, $\tau = 0$ and its value is updated after each action to the time of the next enabled guard, if any. If no more guards will ever be enabled, τ is not updated and denotes the moment the last action occurred. The variable τ may be used in the initialisation and both the guards and statements of actions. To illustrate continuous action systems, we present an abstract specification of the controller of a steam boiler system [1].

The steam boiler system comprises the boiler and associated hardware such as water pumps and valves together with various sensors which report the state of the boiler to the controller. As it produces steam, the boiler loses water which can be replenished via a pump. It is the controller's job to monitor the level of the water in the boiler and activate or deactivate the pump as required. Whenever the water level is at or above a high-level boundary H, the pump should be deactivated to avoid the water level rising further. Conversely, whenever it is at or below a low-level boundary L, the pump should be activated. When the water level is between H and L, there are a number of strategies the controller could adopt.

Let M be the maximum possible rate of change of the water level, and δ_1 and δ_2 be times such that $0 < \delta_1 < \delta_2$ and $L + \delta_2 M < H - \delta_2 M$. The steam boiler controller is specified in Fig. 1, where the global variable w represents the boiler water level[5] and the local variable *next* denotes the time that the next action will occur. For brevity, we declare and use *next* as a discrete (non-stream) variable; replacing it with a timed-stream variable (as required by continuous action systems) is straightforward.

Initially, we assume the water level is within the bounds and will not go beyond the bounds before the first control action. This situation would be set up in the actual system before the controller is made operational. (As in Section 3, we allow global variables to be initialised as a shorthand.)

Each of the actions is guarded by the fact that τ must be equal to the local variable *next*. This variable is used to separate the occurrence of actions by a time in the range $\delta_1 \ldots \delta_2$[6]. This separation is sufficient to guarantee the requirement that the continuous action system does not allow *Zeno behaviour*, i.e., an infinite number of actions occurring in a finite time.

Nondeterministic assignments ($:\in$) on timed streams are interpreted as *future updates*. They cannot change the past behaviour of the variable (i.e., the behaviour before τ), but define its default future behaviour. Hence, the first action changes w so that from time τ (to the occurrence of the next action if any), the rate of change of w is between $-M$ and 0. This corresponds to the pump being deactivated. Similarly, the second action corresponds to the pump being

---

[4] This variable is named *now* in [4].

[5] We assume w is differentiable; this can be specified as in [8].

[6] The separation is based on relative, rather than absolute, times to allow for clock drift in an implementation.

$|(\textbf{var } next : \textsf{Time} \bullet$

$$w :\in \left\{ \begin{array}{l} w' : \textsf{Time} \to \mathbb{R} \mid w'.0 \in [L + \delta_2 M ... H - \delta_2 M] \wedge \\ \qquad\qquad (\forall\, t : \textsf{Time} \bullet \frac{dw'}{dt}.t \in [-M...M]) \end{array} \right\} ;$$

$next :\in [\delta_1...\delta_2];$

$\textbf{do } G \wedge w.\tau + \delta_2 M \geq H \to$

$$w :\in \left\{ \begin{array}{l} w' : \textsf{Time} \to \mathbb{R} \mid w'.\tau = w.\tau \wedge \\ \qquad\qquad (\forall\, t : \textsf{Time} \bullet \frac{dw'}{dt}.t \in [-M...0]) \end{array} \right\} ; \; U$$

$[\!]\; G \wedge w.\tau - \delta_2 M \leq L \to$

$$w :\in \left\{ \begin{array}{l} w' : \textsf{Time} \to \mathbb{R} \mid w'.\tau = w.\tau \wedge \\ \qquad\qquad (\forall\, t : \textsf{Time} \bullet \frac{dw'}{dt}.t \in [0...M]) \end{array} \right\} ; \; U$$

$[\!]\; G \wedge L + \delta_2 M < w.\tau < H - \delta_2 M \to$

$$w :\in \left\{ \begin{array}{l} w' : \textsf{Time} \to \mathbb{R} \mid w'.\tau = w.\tau \wedge \\ \qquad\qquad (\forall\, t : \textsf{Time} \bullet \frac{dw'}{dt}.t \in [-M...M]) \end{array} \right\} ; \; U$$

$\textbf{od}$

$)|: \langle w : \textsf{Time} \to \mathbb{R}\rangle$

where $G \triangleq \tau = next$, $U \triangleq next :\in [\tau + \delta_1...\tau + \delta_2]$.

Fig. 1. A steam boiler specification

activated, it changes w so that from time τ, the rate of change of w is between 0 and M. The final action allows any rate of change of w between $-M$ and M from time τ.

4.1   Semantics

Back et al. [4] provide a trace semantics for continuous action systems via a translation to action systems. However, as shown by Meinicke and Hayes [14], this does not support an intuitive definition of refinement. Hence, in this paper we adopt the alternative stream semantics developed in the latter paper. Under this semantics, the meaning of a continuous action system is expressed in terms of the timed streams of its local and global variables (other than τ).

For a continuous action system **CA** with state space Σ_{CA}, we let *streams*.**CA** denote the set of streams that may be produced by **CA**. Each stream is a mapping from the variables in $dom.\Sigma_{CA} - \{\tau\}$ to a possible timed stream of that variable. A stream s is aborting if it is a partial timed stream whose domain is a right-open interval. An aborting stream is not defined at the time of abortion so that refinements may modify this value. We use *aborting.s* to indicate whether or not s aborts. A formal definition of the function *streams* can be found in [14][7].

Let $tr.s$ denote the global behaviour of the stream s, i.e., where the domain of s is restricted to global variables only.

Definition 3. *(from [14]). The stream refinement relation $\sqsubseteq_{\mathrm{str}}$ between two continuous action systems **CA** and **CC**, is defined as*

$$\textbf{CA} \sqsubseteq_{\mathrm{str}} \textbf{CC} \triangleq \forall\, s_C : streams.\textbf{CC} \bullet (\exists\, s_A : streams.\textbf{CA} \bullet s_A \preceq_{\mathrm{str}} s_C),$$

---

[7] The definition of *streams*.**CA** is given by *behStreams*.(*actSys*.**CA**) in [14].

where $s_A \preceq_{str} s_C$ if, neither s_A nor s_C is aborting and $tr.s_A = tr.s_C$, or s_A is aborting and $tr.s_A$ is a prefix of $tr.s_C$.

5   Combining Probabilistic and Continuous Action Systems

In this section, we introduce our methodology for the combined use of probabilistic and continuous action systems. This allows us to use reliability calculations such as those in Section 3, in the development of continuous systems such as the steam boiler system of Section 4. We illustrate and motivate our approach using the steam boiler example.

We advocate a stepwise development approach, in which discrete, probabilistic behaviour of the overall system is first specified, and developed using a number of correctness preserving steps. During this phase the specification captures the required behaviour of the system and the environment at a very high level. System reliability may be calculated via data refinement, using the approach discussed in Section 3. Next the non-probabilistic part of the specification is extracted and translated into a continuous action system in which timing constraints are imposed, and continuous timed variables are introduced. Probabilistic results calculated in the first phase may then be related to the continuous specification. A process of refinement is then used to introduce further behavioural requirements to the non-probabilistic part of the specification, and develop it into an implementable specification.

In order for this approach to be practical and sound, after the probabilistic development phase, it must be possible to separate the specification into a probabilistic and non-probabilistic component so that the non-probabilistic part may be independently developed. Refinements of the non-probabilistic part of the specification must preserve refinement of the combined probabilistic and non-probabilistic specification. In the following sections we explain and verify the soundness of our approach in detail.

- We explain how the probabilistic action system (2) may be decomposed into a probabilistic and non-probabilistic specification, in which the non-probabilistic specification takes the form of an action system. We verify that action system trace refinements of the action system component, in combination with the probabilistic aspect of the specification, may be interpreted as refinements of the the original probabilistic action system, (2).
- Also, we demonstrate how continuous behaviour may be introduced to an action system, and how under certain conditions, refinement of the continuous action system refines the behaviour of the original action system.

5.1   The Probabilistic Steam Boiler

A probabilistic specification of the steam boiler system may be used to introduce reliability constraints. Consider a boiler with a faulty water sensor which may suffer from transient faults. If the sensor has an availability of $1 - c$, i.e., at any instant the sensor has a probability of $1 - c$ of returning a correct water level reading, and transient faults are detectable, then probabilistic action system (2) may be used to capture a design specification of the system. The design specification states that the system must be able to tolerate N consecutive transient faults in the water sensor. The data refinement outlined in Section 3 may be used to calculate the reliability of (2). At this point the specification is very abstract. In later steps, the abstract variable N will be calculated from other parameters which have not yet been introduced, and the abstract reliability calculation will be related to the timed behaviour.

5.2   Extracting the Non-probabilistic Behaviour

In our case study, the probabilistic choices in the initial specification represent the behaviour of hardware components in the system. After probabilistic calculations have been performed this behaviour does not need to be considered further and we may focus on developing the non-probabilistic part of the specification.

We may seek to represent the non-probabilistic part of a probabilistic action system as a standard action system with extra inputs that describe the behaviour of probabilistic parts of the specification. The action system should describe how the system should behave, given that the probabilistic part of the specification behaves according to the extra inputs. A probability distribution may be used to describe how the probabilistic inputs are chosen. For example, (2) could be rewritten as the combination of the standard action system

$$\|[\text{ var } i : int \bullet n, i := 0, 0;$$
$$\quad \text{do } \{i < N\}; \text{ if } f.n \text{ then } i := i + 1 \text{ else } i := 0 \text{ fi}; \ n := n + 1 \text{ od} \qquad (4)$$
$$]\|: \langle n : \mathbb{N}; \ f : \mathbb{N} \to \mathbb{B} \rangle,$$

and a probability measure $\mu_{(2)}$ which describes the distribution of the initial value of global variable f. Variable f describes the outcome of a series of independent, discrete probabilistic choices. Probability measure $\mu_{(2)}$ should be constructed so that it is defined on sample space $\mathbb{N} \to \mathbb{B}$, and σ-field $\mathcal{F}$, such that $\mathcal{F}$ is the least σ-field containing each set $\{v_f : \mathbb{N} \to \mathbb{B} \mid s \ll v_f\}$, for each finite prefix s of type $seq.\mathbb{B}$[8]. We should have that for each finite, non-empty prefix s, $\mu_{(2)} .\{v_f : \mathbb{N} \to \mathbb{B} \mid s \ll v_f\} = \Pi_{i:dom.s} d.(s.i)$, where $d = (\lambda b : \mathbb{B} \bullet \text{ if } b \text{ then } c \text{ else } 1 - c)$[9].

This method of describing a probabilistic action system as a standard action system with probabilistic inputs is reminiscent of some of the early sequential program semantics for probabilistic programs in which inputs to the program are probabilistic, but the program itself may not make stochastic moves [10]. Probabilistic action systems are, however, more complicated than this early work

---

[8] We write $s \ll v_f$ to denote that s is a prefix of v_f.

[9] For a summary of the relevant measure theory, and the construction of a similar measure, see [9].

because they allow for the modeling of both probabilistic *and* nondeterministic choices. In fact, this approach may be problematic when it is applied to probabilistic action systems in which both of these kinds of choice are present. The reason for this is that probabilistic action systems are ignorant of the outcome of a probabilistic choice until the choice statement has been executed. This is important since knowledge of the outcome of a probabilistic choice may be used to influence how nondeterministic choices are made. Consider the following probabilistic action system **A**

$$\begin{aligned}
&|[\ \textbf{var}\ i : \mathbb{B} \bullet n := 0; \\
&\quad \textbf{do}\ n = 0 \rightarrow (i := \textsf{true} \sqcap i := \textsf{false});\ n := n + 1 \\
&\quad []\ n = 1 \rightarrow (y := \textsf{true}\ {\textstyle\frac{1}{2}} \oplus y := \textsf{false});\ z := i;\ n := n + 1 \\
&\quad \textbf{od} \\
&]\!|: \langle n : \mathbb{N}, z : \mathbb{B}, y : \mathbb{B} \rangle.
\end{aligned}$$

We have that the nondeterministic choice made in the first action must be made without knowledge of the outcome of the probabilistic choice which is performed in the second action. If the outcome of the choice were known beforehand, as in the following probabilistic action system **A**′

$$\begin{aligned}
&|[\ \textbf{var}\ i, j : \mathbb{B} \bullet n := 0;\ (j := \textsf{true}\ {\textstyle\frac{1}{2}} \oplus j := \textsf{false}); \\
&\quad \textbf{do}\ n = 0 \rightarrow (i := \textsf{true} \sqcap i := \textsf{false});\ n := n + 1 \\
&\quad []\ n = 1 \rightarrow y, z := j, i;\ n := n + 1 \\
&\quad \textbf{od} \\
&]\!|: \langle n : \mathbb{N}, z : \mathbb{B}, y : \mathbb{B} \rangle,
\end{aligned}$$

then the behaviour of the probabilistic action system is quite different. For example, **A**′ may be trace refined by

$$\begin{aligned}
&|[\ \textbf{var}\ i, j : \mathbb{B} \bullet n := 0;\ (j := \textsf{true}\ {\textstyle\frac{1}{2}} \oplus j := \textsf{false}); \\
&\quad \textbf{do}\ n = 0 \rightarrow i := j;\ n := n + 1\ []\ n = 1 \rightarrow y, z := j, i;\ n := n + 1\ \textbf{od} \\
&]\!|: \langle n : \mathbb{N}, z : \mathbb{B}, y : \mathbb{B} \rangle,
\end{aligned}$$

whereas **A** may not. In order for us to model a probabilistic action system, such as **A**, as an action system with probabilistic inputs, we must be able to constrain the action system so that it retains ignorance of the probabilistic inputs until appropriate times.

In the next section we formalize how an action system of a particular form, in combination with a probabilistic input may be interpreted as a probabilistic action system. We then verify that trace refinement of the action system component guarantees refinement of the probabilistic action system interpretation. This demonstrates that (4) together with $\mu_{(2)}$ can be thought of as an alternative representation of the probabilistic action system (2). And that refinements of (4), in combination with the probabilistic input distribution, may be interpreted as refinements of the overall system, (2).

Soundness. Assume we are given an action system **A** with a global variable f of type $\mathbb{N} \rightarrow \mathbb{B}$ such that f is constant, and a global variable n of type $\mathbb{N}$. If f

describes the behaviour of probabilistic inputs, and for each action A of $\mathbf{A}$ and intermediate state σ, we use the value of n at σ to indicate that only the first $\sigma.n$ positions of f should be visible when A is executed from σ, then we may describe the different possible deterministic "global behaviours" of $\mathbf{A}$ from any initial state σ_g of type $\{f\} \lhd global.\Sigma_A$ by the following set of functions[10].

$$
\left\{
\begin{array}{l}
F : (\mathbb{N} \to \mathbb{B}) \to seq_\top.(\{f\} \lhd global.\Sigma_A) \mid \forall\, v_f : \mathbb{N} \to \mathbb{B} \bullet \\
\quad (\exists\, t : traces.\mathbf{A} \bullet \\
\qquad t.1 = (\sigma_g \cup \{f \mapsto v_f\}) \wedge F.v_f = (\lambda\, i : \mathrm{dom}.t \bullet \{f\} \lhd (t.i))) \wedge \\
\quad (\forall\, s \ll F.v_f \bullet size.s \geq 2 \Rightarrow \\
\qquad (\forall\, v_f' : \mathbb{N} \to \mathbb{B} \bullet \\
\qquad\quad [1..(penultimate.s).n] \lhd v_f = [1..(penultimate.s).n] \lhd v_f' \\
\qquad\quad \Rightarrow s \ll F.v_f'))
\end{array}
\right\}
$$

Each function F in this set describes how $\mathbf{A}$ might deterministically behave from σ_g depending on the different probabilistic inputs (described by f) that it may receive. To be precise, each function F maps each possible input value of f, v_f, to a trace of global variables (other than f) that may be produced by $\mathbf{A}$ from global initial state $(\sigma_g \cup \{f \mapsto v_f\})$. Each function F is constrained such that the traces assigned to different probabilistic input values are chosen such that the ignorance constraints placed by n are considered. For instance, consider some trace prefix s, of minimum length two. The choice to produce s should only be dependent on the first $[0..(penultimate.s).n]$ positions of f. This means that, if for some v_f, s is a prefix of $F.v_f$, then for all other values of f, v_f', that are the same as v_f up until the $(penultimate.s).n^{th}$ place, s must also be a prefix of $F.v_f'$.

Note that it is possible for n to be used to "incorrectly" specify constraints on how the probabilistic inputs f may be used. That is, n may be used to declare that from state σ, an action A must be performed independently of the positions of f from $\sigma.n + 1$ onwards, however A may make a choice that is explicitly dependent on these forbidden values. In this case the set of deterministic behaviours defined above may be empty, indicating that it is not implementable given the constraints specified. We discuss this point more later on.

If each value $f.i$ of the probabilistic input variable f is chosen according to some discrete probability distribution d_i, then a probability measure μ may be defined that describes f. The probability measure may be constructed so that it is defined on sample space $\mathbb{N} \to \mathbb{B}$, and σ-field $\mathcal{F}$, such that $\mathcal{F}$ is the least σ-field containing each set $\{v_f : \mathbb{N} \to \mathbb{B} \mid s \ll v_f\}$, for each finite prefix s of type $seq.\mathbb{B}$. We should have that, for each finite prefix s, $\mu.\{v_f : \mathbb{N} \to \mathbb{B} \mid s \ll v_f\} = \Pi_{i:dom.s}\, d_i.(s.i)$.

If we are given a measure μ that satisfies the above description, then we may describe how $\mathbf{A}$ in conjunction with μ may be interpreted as a probabilistic action system with global state space $\{f\} \lhd global.\Sigma_A$.

---

[10] We use $\lhd$ to represent domain subtraction, and $\lhd$ to denote domain restriction.

We start by specifying how μ in conjunction with a deterministic behaviour F, that is possible from some initial state σ_g, may be used to define a trace tree, $trTree.(\mu, F)$. Trace tree $trTree.(\mu, F)$ is defined such that for all finite trace prefixes s

$$\text{prefixExpt.}(trTree.(\mu, F)).s = \mu.\{v_f : \mathbb{N} \to \mathbb{B} \mid s \ll F.v_f\}.$$

That is, the expectation that $trTree.(\mu, F)$ will produce s is the probability in μ that a value of f is chosen which constructs prefix s, given the resolution of nondeterminism encoded by F. Note that by the definition of μ and F, each of the sets $\{v_f : \mathbb{N} \to \mathbb{B} \mid s \ll F.v_f\}$ must be measurable, and so this tree specification is well defined.

Let $pbeh.\mathbf{A}$ be the set of all deterministic behaviours F that may be produced from any initial state σ_g in $\{f\} \lhd global.\Sigma$. We define the set of trace trees that may be constructed from $\mathbf{A}$ given μ to be $trTree.(\mathbf{A}, \mu)$, which is the convex closure of the set

$$\{t \mid \exists F : pbeh.\mathbf{A} \wedge t = trTree.(\mu, F)\}.$$

The convex closure of the set is taken so that possible probabilistic refinements of the nondeterministic behaviour of the action system are included.

Definition 4. *Given an action system* $\mathbf{A}$*, and probability measure* μ*, as defined in the above text, we say that* $\mathbf{A}$ *is equivalent to probabilistic action system* $\mathbf{PA}$ *by* μ *when the trace trees constructed from* $\mathbf{A}$ *using* μ *are equal to those from* $\mathbf{PA}$*.*

$$\mathbf{A} \cong_\mu \mathbf{PA} \Leftrightarrow trTree.(\mathbf{A}, \mu) = trTree.\mathbf{PA}$$

It is straightforward to show that $(4) \cong_{\mu_{(2)}} (2)$. Furthermore, as shown below, if we refine (4) to an action system $\mathbf{C}$, there is a refinement $\mathbf{PC}$ of (2) such that $\mathbf{C} \cong_{\mu_{(2)}} \mathbf{PC}$. That is, under the interpretation given by $\mu_{(2)}$, any refinement of (4) refines the behaviour of (2) as desired. Of course when we refine the specification we should be careful not to refine it into an unimplementable specification. As mentioned earlier, this could be possible if we break the ignorance constraints specified by n.

Lemma 1. *Given action systems* $\mathbf{A}$ *and* $\mathbf{C}$ *containing global constant* f *and variable* n *and probability measure* μ *over* f*, we have that*

$$\mathbf{A} \sqsubseteq_{\text{tr}} \mathbf{C} \Rightarrow (\forall\, t_C : trTree.(\mathbf{C}, \mu) \bullet (\exists\, t_A : trTree.(\mathbf{A}, \mu) \bullet t_A \preceq_\oplus t_C)).$$

Proof. From the definition of convex closure over trace trees it is sufficient to show that

$$(\forall\, t_C : \{t \mid \exists F : pbeh.\mathbf{C} \bullet t = trTree.(\mu, F)\} \bullet$$
$$(\exists\, t_A : \{t \mid \exists F : pbeh.\mathbf{A} \bullet t = trTree.(\mu, F)\} \bullet t_A \preceq_\oplus t_C)).$$

Given $\mathbf{A} \sqsubseteq_{\mathrm{tr}} \mathbf{C}$, for any F_C from $pbeh.\mathbf{C}$, there exists a F_A from $pbeh.\mathbf{A}$, such that $(\forall f : \mathbb{N} \to \mathbb{B} \cdot F_A.f \preceq_{\mathrm{tr}} F_C.f)$. This implies that for any s, $\{f : \mathbb{N} \to \mathbb{B} \mid s \ll F_A.f\} \subseteq \{f : \mathbb{N} \to \mathbb{B} \mid s \ll F_C.f\}$, and hence $\mathsf{prefixExpt}.(trTree.(\mu, F_A)).s \leq \mathsf{prefixExpt}.(trTree.(\mu, F_C)).s$. $\qquad\square$

Theorem 1. *Given action systems* $\mathbf{A}$ *and* $\mathbf{C}$ *containing global constant* f *and variable* n, *and probability measure* μ *over* f, *for all probabilistic action systems* $\mathbf{PA}$

$$\mathbf{A} \cong_\mu \mathbf{PA} \wedge \mathbf{A} \sqsubseteq_{\mathrm{tr}} \mathbf{C} \Rightarrow (\exists\,\mathbf{PC} \cdot \mathbf{PA} \sqsubseteq_\oplus \mathbf{PC} \wedge \mathbf{C} \cong_\mu \mathbf{PC}).$$

Proof sketch. Given that $\mathbf{A} \cong_\mu \mathbf{PA}$, it is always possible to construct a probabilistic action system $\mathbf{PC}$ such that $\mathbf{C} \cong_\mu \mathbf{PC}$.

Hence, for such a probabilistic action system $\mathbf{PA}$, the theorem reduces to showing that $\mathbf{A} \cong_\mu \mathbf{PA} \wedge \mathbf{C} \cong_\mu \mathbf{PC} \wedge \mathbf{A} \sqsubseteq_{\mathrm{tr}} \mathbf{C} \Rightarrow \mathbf{PA} \sqsubseteq_\oplus \mathbf{PC}$.

$\qquad \mathbf{A} \sqsubseteq_{\mathrm{tr}} \mathbf{C}$
$\Rightarrow \hspace{6cm} \text{(Lemma 1)}$
$\qquad \forall\, t_C : trTree.(\mathbf{C}, \mu) \cdot (\exists\, t_A : trTree.(\mathbf{A}, \mu) \cdot t_A \preceq_\oplus t_C)$
$\Leftrightarrow \hspace{3cm} \text{(Definition 4 and assumptions } \mathbf{A} \cong_\mu \mathbf{PA} \text{ and } \mathbf{C} \cong_\mu \mathbf{PC})$
$\qquad \forall\, t_C : trTree.\mathbf{PC} \cdot (\exists\, t_A : trTree.\mathbf{PA} \cdot t_A \preceq_\oplus t_C)$
$\Leftrightarrow \hspace{6cm} \text{(Definition 2)}$
$\qquad \mathbf{PA} \sqsubseteq_\oplus \mathbf{PC} \hspace{6cm} \square$

5.3   Introducing Time and Continuous Behaviour

The next step in our approach is to add time and continuous variables to the action system (4). This is done by providing a continuous action system $\mathbf{CA}$ which preserves the untimed, discrete behaviour of (4). The abstract reliability calculation from the first development stage may be interpreted with respect to the timed behaviour.

We begin by rewriting (4) as a continuous action system where actions are separated by a finite, non-zero time. This separation is necessary for two reasons. Firstly, it ensures non-Zeno behaviour. Secondly, it disallows potential timings where actions occur simultaneously. This is necessary as the effect of only one action occurring at a particular time (the last of the actions occurring at that time in the trace) is observable under the continuous action system semantics [14]. Hence to preserve the action system behaviour, we want to restrict our continuous action system to one in which there are no simultaneous occurrences of actions.

For example, with the steam boiler system of Section 4 in mind, we could separate the actions of (4) by a time in the range $\delta_1 \mathinner{\ldotp\ldotp} \delta_2$ where δ_1 and δ_2 are times such that $0 < \delta_1 < \delta_2$. (As in Section 4, we allow variables to be declared and used as discrete (non-stream) variables as a shorthand.)

$|($ **var** $i : int;\ next : \mathsf{Time}\ \bullet$
$\qquad n, i := 0, 0;$
$\qquad next :\in [\delta_1...\delta_2];$
$\qquad$ **do** $\tau = next \rightarrow$
$\qquad\qquad \{i < N\};$ $\hfill(5)$
$\qquad\qquad next :\in [\tau + \delta_1...\tau + \delta_2];$
$\qquad\qquad$ **if** $f.n$ **then** $i := i + 1$ **else** $i := 0$ **fi**; $n := n + 1$
$\qquad$ **od**
$)|: \langle n : \mathbb{N};\ f : \mathbb{N} \rightarrow \mathbb{B} \rangle$

The addition of such timing information does not affect in any way the untimed behaviour of the specified system.

From this continuous action system, we can determine that while the action system has not aborted, the following invariant is maintained[11]:

$$(\forall t \leq \tau \bullet \lfloor \frac{t}{\delta_2} \rfloor \leq n.t \leq \lfloor \frac{t}{\delta_1} \rfloor).$$

So, given that the input function f behaves according to our original probabilistic calculations, we may determine that the reliability of our system at any time t, $R.t$, is such that $a^{\lfloor \frac{t}{\delta_1} \rfloor} \leq R.t \leq a^{\lfloor \frac{t}{\delta_2} \rfloor}$.

To develop (5) further requires the addition of other variables; in particular, continuous variables. For example, for the steam boiler system of Section 4, we need to introduce the global variable w denoting the water level. This can be done without affecting the existing behaviour by placing no constraints on w apart from that it assumes a nondeterministic value from its type initially and on each occurrence of an action.

$|($ **var** $i : int;\ next : \mathsf{Time}\ \bullet$
$\qquad n, i := 0, 0;$
$\qquad w :\in Time \rightarrow \mathbb{R};$
$\qquad next :\in [\delta_1...\delta_2];$
$\qquad$ **do** $\tau = next \rightarrow$
$\qquad\qquad \{i < N\};$ $\hfill(6)$
$\qquad\qquad w :\in Time \rightarrow \mathbb{R};$
$\qquad\qquad next :\in [\tau + \delta_1...\tau + \delta_2];$
$\qquad\qquad$ **if** $f.n$ **then** $i := i + 1$ **else** $i := 0$ **fi**; $n := n + 1;$
$\qquad$ **od**
$)|: \langle n : \mathbb{N};\ f : \mathbb{N} \rightarrow \mathbb{B};\ w : Time \rightarrow \mathbb{R} \rangle$

Other variables (both global and local) related to the particular system we are developing could be added in a similar fashion.

Finally, we would like to refine the behaviour of the added variables such as w to specify the desired system. This would enable us to express the system reliability in terms of the system's parameters (rather than the constant N).

---

[11] $\lfloor r \rfloor$ rounds down real number r to the nearest integer.

In order for this to be sound, however, we require that such a refinement of (6) refine the original behaviour of (4).

Soundness. First we formalise how the discretely changing state of a continuous action system may be given an action system interpretation. This is done by defining a mapping between streams and traces. We then prove that, under certain conditions, refinement of a continuous action system preserves refinement of the action system interpretation.

The state space of a continuous action system will, in general, include variables that do not behave discretely (i.e., they do not behave as a step function with finite changes of value within any finite interval). These variables are ignored when defining the action system interpretation. We therefore define a function res_Σ which restricts a stream to the variables in a state space Σ.

$$res_\Sigma.s \triangleq dom.\Sigma \lhd s,$$

where $\lhd$ is the domain restriction operator. We refer to the value of a stream s at time t as $s@t$, where

$$s@t \triangleq (\lambda\, v : dom.s \bullet s.v.t).$$

The trace corresponding to a stream s (which behaves discretely), $trace.s$, may be constructively defined as follows. Informally, the ith value of the trace describes the value of s after i discrete changes in its value. If s does not abort at time 0, then $trace.s.1$ describes the value of s at time 0. If s does abort at time 0, then $trace.s$ is the empty trace. Each subsequent value denotes the value of s the next time it changes. If there is no future time at which a change is made and the stream does not abort, then the next and last element in $trace.s$ is element $\top$, which denotes termination. If there is no future time that a change of state is made, and s aborts, then the subsequent value is not defined (that is, the trace aborts). Formally,

$$trace.s \triangleq \begin{cases} \langle\rangle, & \text{if } 0 \notin tdom.s \\ \langle s@0 \rangle \frown gettr.s.0, & \text{if } 0 \in tdom.s \end{cases}$$

where $tdom.s$ is the time domain of the variables in s and function $gettr.s$ takes as a parameter a time at which s modified the variables, and returns the rest of the trace produced from time t.

$$gettr.s.t \triangleq \begin{cases} \langle s@(min\,.(D.t)) \rangle \frown gettr.s.(min\,.(D.t)), & \text{if } D.t \neq \{\} \\ \langle \top \rangle, & \text{if } D.t = \{\} \text{ and } \neg aborting.s \\ \langle\rangle, & \text{if } D.t = \{\} \text{ and } aborting.s \end{cases}$$

where $D.t \triangleq \{t' : tdom.s \mid t' > t \land s@t' \neq s@t\}$.

We then define $trace_\Sigma$ to be a function which maps a stream to a corresponding trace over the state space Σ,

$$trace_\Sigma.s \triangleq trace.(res_\Sigma.s).$$

Definition 5. *A continuous action system* **CA** *preserves the global behaviour of an action system* **A** *with global state space* Σ *iff its set of streams maps via* $trace_\Sigma$ *to the set of traces of* **A**.

$$\mathbf{CA} \cong_\Sigma \mathbf{A} \Leftrightarrow \{t \mid \exists\, s : streams.\mathbf{CA} \bullet t = trace_\Sigma.s\} = traces.\mathbf{A}$$

It can be readily shown that (5) $\cong_\Sigma$ (4), and similarly that (6) $\cong_\Sigma$ (4) where $\Sigma \triangleq \{n \mapsto \mathbb{N}, f \mapsto (\mathbb{N} \to \mathbb{B})\}$.

What we need to show is under what conditions on a refinement **CC** of (6), there is a refinement **C** of (4) such that **CC** $\cong_\Sigma$ **C**. This ensures that the untimed, discrete behaviour of **CC** is a refinement of that of (4) as desired.

Lemma 2. *For all streams* s_A *and* s_C, *if* $s_A \preceq_{str} s_C$ *then, for any state space* Σ *over state variables which behave discretely in* s_A *and* s_C, $trace_\Sigma.s_A \preceq_{tr} trace_\Sigma.s_C$.

Proof. There are two cases to consider: either (i) s_A and s_C are not aborting and $tr.s_A = tr.s_C$, or (ii) s_A is aborting and $tr.s_A$ is a prefix of $tr.s_C$.

In case (i), since neither s_A nor s_C are aborting the timed traces $trace_\Sigma.s_A$ and $trace_\Sigma.s_C$ are not aborting by the definition of $trace$. Furthermore, since the global variables of s_A and s_C behave identically, the corresponding traces also behave identically, i.e., $trace_\Sigma.s_A = trace_\Sigma.s_C$.

In case (ii), s_A comprises partial timed streams whose domains are right-open intervals. Hence, $trace_\Sigma.s_A$ is an aborting timed trace by the definition of $trace$. Furthermore, since the global variables of s_C behave identically to those of s_A up to the time of abortion, the global variables of $trace_\Sigma.s_C$ behave identically to those $trace_\Sigma.s_A$ up to when it aborts. Hence, $trace_\Sigma.s_A$ is a prefix of $trace_\Sigma.s_C$.   □

Theorem 2. *For all continuous action systems* **CA** *and* **CC** *where global variables which behave discretely in* **CA** *also behave discretely in* **CC**, *and all action systems* **A**, *with global state space* Σ,

$$\mathbf{CA} \cong_\Sigma \mathbf{A} \wedge \mathbf{CA} \sqsubseteq_{str} \mathbf{CC} \Rightarrow (\exists\, \mathbf{C} \bullet \mathbf{A} \sqsubseteq_{tr} \mathbf{C} \wedge \mathbf{CC} \cong_\Sigma \mathbf{C}).$$

Proof sketch. Given that **CA** $\cong_\Sigma$ **A** and that global variables that behave discretely in **CA** also behave discretely in **CC**, it is always possible to construct an action system **C** such that **CC** $\cong_\Sigma$ **C**.

Hence, for such an action system **C**, the theorem reduces to showing that **CA** $\cong_\Sigma$ **A** $\wedge$ **CC** $\cong_\Sigma$ **C** $\wedge$ **CA** $\sqsubseteq_{str}$ **CC** $\Rightarrow$ **A** $\sqsubseteq_{tr}$ **C**.

    CA $\sqsubseteq_{str}$ **CC**

$\Leftrightarrow$ (Definition 3)

    $\forall\, s_C : streams.\mathbf{CC} \bullet (\exists\, s_A : streams.\mathbf{CA} \bullet s_A \preceq_{str} s_C)$

$\Rightarrow$ (Lemma 2)

    $\forall\, s_C : streams.\mathbf{CC} \bullet (\exists\, s_A : streams.\mathbf{CA} \bullet trace_\Sigma.s_A \preceq_{tr} trace_\Sigma.s_C)$

$\Leftrightarrow$ (Definition 5 and assumptions **CA** $\cong_\Sigma$ **A** and **CC** $\cong_\Sigma$ **C**)

    $\forall\, t_C : traces.\mathbf{C} \bullet (\exists\, t_A : traces.\mathbf{A} \bullet t_A \preceq_{tr} t_C)$

$\Leftrightarrow$ (Definition 1)

    A $\sqsubseteq_{tr}$ **C**   □

5.4   Refining the Real-Time Steam Boiler

We now refine our abstract continuous action system (6). This allows us to proceed towards an implementation and also allows us to re-express our previous reliability result in terms of the parameters of this implementation (instead of the abstract variable N).

The following refinement of (6) constrains the water level to be maintained in between the high (H) and low (L) level boundaries up until the time of abortion[12]. Like the steam boiler modeled in Section 4, this is achieved by adjusting the behaviour of the water level on each iteration, depending on a worst case prediction of where the water level may reach before the time of the next action.

$$
\begin{aligned}
&|(\ \textbf{var}\ i : int;\ next : \mathsf{Time}\ \bullet \\
&\quad n, i := 0, 0; \\
&\quad w :\in \left\{ \begin{array}{l} w' : \mathsf{Time} \to \mathbb{R} \mid w'.0 \in [L + \delta_2 M ... H - \delta_2 M] \wedge \\ \qquad\qquad\qquad (\forall\, t : \mathsf{Time} \bullet \frac{dw'}{dt}.t \in [-M...M]) \end{array} \right\} ; \\
&\quad next :\in [\delta_1...\delta_2]; \\
&\quad \textbf{do}\ G \wedge w.\tau + \delta_2 M \geq H \to \\
&\qquad \{i < N\}; \\
&\qquad w :\in \left\{ \begin{array}{l} w' : \mathsf{Time} \to \mathbb{R} \mid w'.\tau = w.\tau \wedge \\ \qquad\qquad (\forall\, t : \mathsf{Time} \bullet \frac{dw'}{dt}.t \in [-M...0]) \end{array} \right\} ;\ U \\
&\quad [\!]\ G \wedge w.\tau - \delta_2 M \leq L \to \\
&\qquad \{i < N\}; \\
&\qquad w :\in \left\{ \begin{array}{l} w' : \mathsf{Time} \to \mathbb{R} \mid w'.\tau = w.\tau \wedge \\ \qquad\qquad (\forall\, t : \mathsf{Time} \bullet \frac{dw'}{dt}.t \in [0...M]) \end{array} \right\} ;\ U \\
&\quad [\!]\ G \wedge L + \delta_2 M < w.\tau < H - \delta_2 M \to \\
&\qquad w :\in \left\{ \begin{array}{l} w' : \mathsf{Time} \to \mathbb{R} \mid w'.\tau = w.\tau \wedge \\ \qquad\qquad (\forall\, t : \mathsf{Time} \bullet \frac{dw'}{dt}.t \in [-M...M]) \end{array} \right\} ;\ U \\
&\quad \textbf{od} \\
&)|: \langle n : \mathbb{N};\ f : (\mathbb{N} \to \mathbb{B});\ w : \mathsf{Time} \to \mathbb{R}\rangle
\end{aligned}
$$

where

$$
\begin{aligned}
G &\triangleq \tau = next, \\
U &\triangleq next :\in [\tau + \delta_1...\tau + \delta_2]; \\
&\quad \textbf{if}\ f.n\ \textbf{then}\ i := i + 1\ \textbf{else}\ i := 0\ \textbf{fi};\ n := n + 1; \\
&\quad \{(\forall\, t \leq next \bullet L \leq w.t \leq H)\}.
\end{aligned}
$$

This refinement step is dependent on the assumption $\frac{H-L}{2} > \delta_2 M$. This ensures that the water level cannot cross either boundary before the next action occurs. If this were possible, the assertion in U would cause the system to abort at a time which was not possible in (6).

In an implementation we will be unable to access the water level directly. Instead when our system performs an action, it must use the value of a sensor reading that was taken at some earlier time. We introduce a local variable g to

---

[12] This may be ascertained from the assertion on the water level in U.

represent such a sensor reading. When the sensor provides a correct reading on a given loop iteration ($f.n$ is false), g is updated to be a reading within an error err of the water level that is taken between the time of the current action, and the next action. If the sensor does not provide a correct reading ($f.n$ is true) then g is unmodified from the previous reading. It is assumed that the initial reading of the water level is correct. The direct reference to the water level in the guards of the conditional statement is updated to reference the current reading of the water level, g. This refinement may be proven using the coupling invariant

$$g \in w.\tau \pm (\delta_2 M (i + 1) + err).$$

$|($ **var** $i : int;\ next : \mathsf{Time};\ g : \mathbb{R}\ \bullet$
  $\quad n, i := 0, 0;$
  $\quad w :\in \left\{ \begin{array}{l} w' : \mathsf{Time} \mid w'.0 \in [L + \delta_2 M \ldots H - \delta_2 M] \wedge \\ \qquad\qquad (\forall\, t : \mathsf{Time} \bullet \frac{dw'}{dt}.t \in [-M \ldots M]) \end{array} \right\};$
  $\quad next :\in [\delta_1 \ldots \delta_2];$
  $\quad g :\in w(\!|\ [0..next]\ |\!) \pm err;$
  $\quad \textbf{do}\ G \wedge g + \delta_2 M (i + 1) + err \geq H \rightarrow$
  $\qquad \{i < N\};$
  $\qquad w :\in \left\{ \begin{array}{l} w' : \mathsf{Time} \to \mathbb{R} \mid w'.\tau = w.\tau \wedge \\ \qquad\qquad (\forall\, t : \mathsf{Time} \bullet \frac{dw'}{dt}.t \in [-M \ldots 0]) \end{array} \right\};\ U$
  $\quad [\!]\ G \wedge g - \delta_2 M (i + 1) - err \leq L \rightarrow$
  $\qquad \{i < N\};$
  $\qquad w :\in \left\{ \begin{array}{l} w' : \mathsf{Time} \to \mathbb{R} \mid w'.\tau = w.\tau \wedge \\ \qquad\qquad (\forall\, t : \mathsf{Time} \bullet \frac{dw'}{dt}.t \in [0 \ldots M]) \end{array} \right\};\ U$
  $\quad [\!]\ G \wedge L + \delta_2 M (i + 1) + err < g < H - \delta_2 M (i + 1) - err \rightarrow$
  $\qquad \{i < N\};$
  $\qquad w :\in \left\{ \begin{array}{l} w' : \mathsf{Time} \to \mathbb{R} \mid w'.\tau = w.\tau \wedge \\ \qquad\qquad (\forall\, t : \mathsf{Time} \bullet \frac{dw'}{dt}.t \in [-M \ldots M]) \end{array} \right\};\ U$
  $\quad \textbf{od}$
$)|: \langle n : \mathbb{N};\ f : (\mathbb{N} \to \mathbb{B});\ w : \mathsf{Time} \to \mathbb{R} \rangle$

where

$\quad G \triangleq \tau = next,$
$\quad U \triangleq next :\in [\tau + \delta_1 \ldots \tau + \delta_2];$
$\qquad \textbf{if}\ f.n\ \textbf{then}\ i := i + 1\ \textbf{else}\ i := 0;\ g :\in w(\!|\ [\tau..next]\ |\!) \pm err\ \textbf{fi};$
$\qquad n := n + 1;$
$\qquad \{(\forall\, t \leq next \bullet L \leq w.t \leq H)\}.$

This refinement step is only valid if $N \leq \lfloor \frac{H - L - 2err}{2\delta_2 M} - 3/2 \rfloor$. This provides us with a correspondence between the abstract reliability parameter N, and the implementation. From this correspondence, and our earlier calculations we can deduce that the reliability of our implementation, or any further refinements, at any time t is at least $a^{\lfloor \frac{t}{\delta_1} \rfloor}$, where a is the greatest solution to the equation (3), given that $N = \lfloor \frac{H - L - 2err}{2\delta_2 M} - 3/2 \rfloor$. While the system has not failed, the water level is maintained within the appropriate limits.

6   Conclusion

In this paper, we have demonstrated how the probabilistic and continuous extensions of actions systems may be used in the development and calculation of reliability of continuous, real-time systems. This is achieved via behaviour-preserving mappings between probabilistic actions systems and action systems, and between action systems and continuous action systems. The first mapping allows properties of a probabilistic action system, in particular reliability results, to be carried over to an action system and any of its refinements. The second mapping allows such properties to be further carried over to a continuous action system and, under certain conditions, its refinements. While the second mapping is general enough to use with any action system, the first mapping appears to be more restrictive. It would be of interest to investigate the generality of this approach. If necessary, further methods for extracting the non-probabilistic part of a probabilistic action system, so that it may be independently developed, could be explored.

We consider the main benefit of our approach to be that it separates probabilistic reasoning from the rest of the development process. We have demonstrated our methodology by extending a probabilistic steam boiler case study [12] in which an unreliable component functions correctly at any time with a given probability, to include real-time considerations. It would also be of interest to investigate how it may be applied to other case studies in which there is a more complex interplay between probabilistic and real-time behaviour. It may not be possible, or sensible, in all cases to perform probabilistic reasoning independently of real-time behaviours.

Acknowledgements. This research was supported by Australian Research Council (ARC) Discovery Grant DP0558408, *Analysing and generating fault-tolerant real-time systems*. The authors are grateful to Ian Hayes, Kim Solin and the anonymous referees for helpful suggestions.

References

1. Abrial, J.-R., Börger, E., Langmaack, H.: Formal Methods for Industrial Applications: Specifying and Programming the Steam Boiler Control. LNCS, vol. 1165. Springer, Heidelberg (1996)
2. Back, R.J.R., Kurki-Suonio, R.: Decentralization of process nets with centralized control. In: 2nd ACM SIGACT-SIGOPS Symp. on Principles of Distributed Computing, pp. 131–142. ACM Press, New York (1983)
3. Back, R.J.R., Kurki-Suonio, R.: Distributed cooperation with action systems. ACM Trans. Program. Lang. Syst. 10(4), 513–554 (1988)
4. Back, R.J.R., Petre, L., Porres, I.: Generalizing action systems to hybrid systems. In: Joseph, M. (ed.) FTRTFT 2000. LNCS, vol. 1926, pp. 202–213. Springer, Heidelberg (2000)
5. Back, R.J.R., von Wright, J.: Trace refinement of action systems. In: Jonsson, B., Parrow, J. (eds.) CONCUR 1994. LNCS, vol. 836, pp. 367–384. Springer, Heidelberg (1994)

6. Back, R.J.R., von Wright, J.: Refinement Calculus: A Systematic Introduction. Springer, Heidelberg (1998)
7. Broy, M.: Refinement of time. In: Rus, T., Bertran, M. (eds.) AMAST-ARTS 1997, ARTS 1997, and AMAST-WS 1997. LNCS, vol. 1231, Springer, Heidelberg (1997)
8. Fidge, C.J., Hayes, I.J., Mahony, B.P.: Defining differentiation and integration in Z. In: Staples, J., Hinchey, M.G., Liu, S. (eds.) International Conference on Formal Engineering Methods (ICFEM '98), pp. 64–73. IEEE Computer Society Press, Los Alamitos (1998)
9. Hurd, J.: Formal Verification of Probabilistic Algorithms. PhD thesis, University of Cambridge (2002)
10. Kozen, D.: Semantics of probabilistic programs. Journal of Computer and System Sciences 22, 328–350 (1981)
11. Mahony, B.P., Hayes, I.J.: A case-study in timed refinement: A mine pump. IEEE Transactions on Software Engineering 18(9), 817–826 (1992)
12. McIver, A., Morgan, C., Troubitsyna, E.: The probabilistic steam boiler: a case study in probabilistic data refinement. In: Grundy, J., Schwenke, M., Vickers, T. (eds.) International Refinement Workshop/Formal Methods Pacific '98. Series in Discrete Mathematics and Theoretical Computer Science, pp. 250–265. Springer, Heidelberg (1998)
13. Meinicke, L.: Probabilistic action system trace semantics. Technical report, School of Information Technology and Electrical Engineering, The University of Queensland, Australia (2007)
14. Meinicke, L., Hayes, I.J.: Continuous action system refinement. In: Uustalu, T. (ed.) MPC 2006. LNCS, vol. 4014, pp. 316–337. Springer, Heidelberg (2006)
15. Scholefield, D., Zedan, H., Jifeng, H.: A specification-oriented semantics for the refinement of real-time systems. Theoretical Computer Science 131, 219–241 (1994)
16. Sere, K., Troubitsyna, E.: Probabilities in action systems. In: 8th Nordic Workshop on Programming Theory (1996)
17. Storey, N.: Safety-Critical Computer Systems. Addison-Wesley, Reading (1996)
18. Troubitsyna, E.: Reliability assessment through probabilistic refinement. Nordic Journal of Computing 6(3), 320–342 (1999)
19. Chaochen, Z., Hoare, C.A.R., Ravn, A.P.: A calculus of durations. Information Processing Letters 40, 269–271 (1991)

Decomposing Integrated Specifications for Verification

Björn Metzler

Department of Computer Science
University of Paderborn
Germany
D-33098 Paderborn, Germany
bmetzler@upb.de

Abstract. Integrated formal specifications are intrinsically difficult to (automatically) verify due to the combination of complex data and behaviour. In this paper, we present a method for *decomposing* specifications into several smaller parts which can be independently verified. Verification results can then be combined to make a global result according to the original specification.

Instead of relying on an *a priori* given structure of the system such as a parallel composition of components, we compute the decomposition by ourselves using the technique of *slicing*. With less effort, significant properties can be verified for the resulting specification parts and be applied to the full specification. We prove correctness of our method and exemplify it according to a specification from the rail domain.

Keywords: Integrated Formal Specifications, Decomposition, Compositional Verification, Program Slicing, Model Checking.

1 Introduction

Model checking [4] is a technique to automatically verify a program against certain requirements. For a representation of the system and a requirement most often specified in temporal logic, it aims at solving the question of whether the property is valid in the model or not.

Higher complexity of a program leads to a bigger state space of the model – the number of states actually grows exponentially with the size of the program description. This issue is known as the *state explosion problem* and is the subject of a lot of ongoing research. This especially applies to the context of integrated formal methods, where we combine complex data aspects with the behaviour of the system, the state space might become unmanageable and model checking is no longer possible. Different techniques such as data abstraction [6], partial order reduction [7] as well as symbolic [5] techniques have been developed to master this challenge. The common idea is the *reduction* of the explored state space.

J. Davies and J. Gibbons (Eds.): IFM 2007, LNCS 4591, pp. 459–479, 2007.

Other approaches to tackle the state explosion problem investigate *compositional* techniques. By using the intuitive composition of a system, the verification task can be reduced and local properties can be shown for parts of the system. In many cases, the given system is defined as the parallel composition of several modules like for example in [13]. Compositional reasoning can be applied: in case the components do not influence each other, we can immediately deduce properties of the full system from local properties of its components. Otherwise, the dependencies have to be taken into account and more complex techniques as *assume-guarantee reasoning* [8] are utilized. An application of these approaches assumes that the system specification is already given by a composition of several components. This is, however, not always the case. In particular, due to their complexity and necessity of modelling different aspects of a system, integrated specifications do in general not have the required shape.

In this paper, we do not assume that a given system description is intuitively composed of several components. Instead, we introduce a technique of how to reasonably decompose an integrated specification based on the global properties to be verified. Our approach does not require a certain shape of the specification and in addition makes an independent verification of the resulting specification parts possible. As an application in the context of high data complexity, this may enable us to automatically verify parts of the specification by sourcing out data-heavy behaviour to independent components.

Desired properties of a program will be described in the next-less part of the temporal logic LTL [14]. Our program specifications are written in the integrated formal method CSP-OZ [9], a combination of the formalisms CSP [12] for the *dynamic* behaviour and Object-Z [19] for the *static* behaviour of a system. The CSP part defines communication and an ordering of operations while the Object-Z part uses state variables and predicates to model the data aspects.

Our decomposition approach is based on the analysis technique of specification *slicing* [22]. In general, slicing removes parts from a specification which are irrelevant for a certain property under interest. Slicing has already been introduced for CSP-OZ [2]. In contrast to these approaches using operation elimination, our approach divides the set of *state variables* of the Object-Z part. We require that any property of a slice also holds for the original specification. As a main contribution, we are able to separate parts of the specification from each other and can independently verify them even though an intuitive decomposition is not given. The local verification results can subsequently be composed implying the global property. Figure 1 illustrates the decomposition.

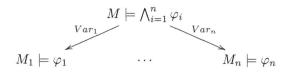

$$M \models \bigwedge_{i=1}^{n} \varphi_i$$

Var_1 Var_n

$$M_1 \models \varphi_1 \qquad \cdots \qquad M_n \models \varphi_n$$

Fig. 1. General approach

The paper is organized as follows: Section 2 introduces CSP-OZ by means of an example. We describe the operational semantics of our formalism and the temporal logic LTL. In Section 3, we introduce our approach of decomposing a specification. We present the reduction technique and illustrate the decomposition on our example. To show that the decomposition is reasonable, Section 4 explains how verification results for the decomposed specification can be applied to the full specification. Again, we use our example to illustrate the verification technique. Correctness of decomposition and verification technique will be shown. The last section concludes and discusses related and future work.

2   A Specification in CSP-OZ

To describe and illustrate CSP-OZ and to motivate our approach, we start with an example. A simplified version of a scenario in the domain of the rail cab project "Neue Bahntechnik Paderborn"[1] serves as the basis for the ongoing example of this paper. In this scenario, a number of shuttles circuit on a given route. The shuttles are coordinated by a control system.

Our general goal is to ensure safety for the whole scenario: by no means should the shuttles collide. To achieve this, we specify a very simple solution in CSP-OZ. Later, we describe the requirements in the temporal logic LTL and prove them by applying our technique.

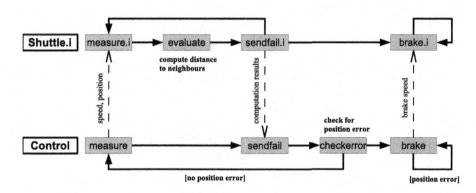

Fig. 2. Graphical representation of Shuttle specification

Figure 2 shows a graphical representation of the specifications protocol. The whole system can be situated in two different modes: initially, its non-error mode is executed starting with a communication of a shuttles current speed and position (*measure*). Parameter i is used for the addressing the shuttles. After the communication, each shuttle computes the distance to its neighbours, compares it to the minimal allowed distance (*evaluate*) and sends the result to the control system (*sendfail*). Next, the controller analyses the transmitted

---

[1] http://www.nbp-www.upb.de

values (*checkerror*). In case the distance between at least one pair of shuttles is too small, the control system initiates a break manoeuvre leading to a continuous execution of *brake*. Otherwise, the protocol restarts.

The system consists of two CSP-OZ class specifications for an arbitrary shuttle component (*Shuttle*[i]) and the control system (*Control*). A total number of N shuttles are composed in parallel without synchronization by using the CSP operator ||| for *interleaving*: $Shuttles = |||_{i=1,...,N} Shuttle[i]$

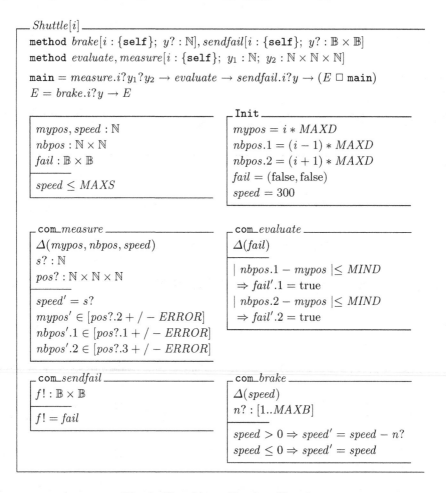

Fig. 3. Shuttle specification: Shuttles

For simplification, we will omit modulo computation. We compose *Shuttles* with the *Control* component by means of *synchronous parallel composition* described by the CSP operator ||. The set $S := \{measure, sendfail, brake\}$ is the synchronization alphabet, a subset of the set of *channels*. The full system is defined as $System = Shuttles \|_S Control$. Figure 3 and Figure 4 show the CSP-OZ specifications of an arbitrary shuttle i and the control system, respectively.

Every class specification has three parts: an interface (given by a number of channels for communication with its environment), a CSP part and an Object-Z part. The CSP part of a class identifies the dynamic aspects of the system. It defines a protocol describing all possible orders on its operation schedule. The protocol itself consists of a set of process equations. The Object-Z part describes the data aspects of the class. It consists of the state space, its initial configuration and a set of methods – one method for each channel of the class.

Control

method $brake[i? : ShuttleRef; \; y? : \mathbb{N}]$, $sendfail[i? : ShuttleRef; \; y? : \mathbb{B} \times \mathbb{B}]$
method $checkerror, measure[i? : ShuttleRef; \; y_1 : \mathbb{N} \times \mathbb{N} \times \mathbb{N}; \; y_2 : \mathbb{N}]$

$\mathbf{main} = |||_i \, measure.i?y_1?y_2 \rightarrow |||_i \, sendfail.i?y \rightarrow Q$
$Q = checkerror \rightarrow (B \; \Box \; \mathbf{main}), \quad B = |||_i \, brake.i?y \rightarrow B$

$pos : seq_1 \, \mathbb{N}$
$fail : seq_1 \, \mathbb{B} \times \mathbb{B}$
$err\_pos : \mathbb{Z}$
___
$\#pos = \#Sh$

Init
$\forall i \bullet fail(i) = (false, false)$
$err\_pos = -1$

---

com_sendfail
$\Delta(fail)$
$i? : ShuttleRef$
$f? : \mathbb{B} \times \mathbb{B}$
___
$fail'.i? = f?$

com_checkerror
$\Delta(err\_pos)$

if $(\exists j \in Sh \bullet fail(j-1).2 = true$
$\qquad\qquad\qquad \wedge fail(j).1 = true)$
then $err\_pos' = j$
else $err\_pos' = -1$

---

com_measure
$i! : ShuttleRef$
$p! : \mathbb{N} \times \mathbb{N} \times \mathbb{N}$
$s! : \mathbb{N}$
___
$err\_pos = -1$
$p! = (pos.(i!-1), pos.i!, pos.(i!+1))$

com_brake
$i! : ShuttleRef$
$n! : [1..MAXB]$
___
$err\_pos! = -1$
if $(i! \geq err\_pos)$ **then** $n! = MAXB$
else $n! = i!$

Fig. 4. Shuttle specification: Control

The Object-Z part contains the class' state space. The state space of a shuttle component includes the variables *mypos* (the shuttles current position), *speed* (the shuttles speed), *nbpos* (the positions of the shuttles predecessor and successor) and *fail* (the error evaluation result). In addition, the Object-Z part comprises the initial state schema **Init** and several **com** schemas describing the guards and effects of the respective methods.

Each schema has two parts: the upper part starts with a (possible empty) list of variables which are modified in the second part. It may also contain an optional list of input (described by '?') and output (described by '!') parameters according to the parameters of the channels. The lower part may include a set of predicates about the variables of the state space. We distinguish between primed and unprimed variables where a primed variable defines the variables value *after* execution of the method and an unprimed variable the value *before*. To determine if the execution of a method is blocked, its precondition [23]

$$pre \ op = \exists State, outputs \bullet op$$

is computed. In case an after state and output exists such that the precondition is satisfied, the event is *enabled* and its *effect* (also referred to as its *postcondition*) is computed. The effect of an event relates the current state with variable values after execution of the event.

For instance, schema *measure* of *Control* is blocked unless $err\_pos = -1$ is satisfied. The methods effect sets the state variables to the communicated values within a given tolerance. The communicated values have to satisfy the class invariant specifying that a shuttle cannot exceed a certain speed limit ($speed \leq MAXS$). To model the discrepancy between the communicated and the correct positions of the shuttles (the correct value may be effected by different kinds of tolerated errors and inaccuracies), we use a constant ($ERROR$).

2.1   Semantics of CSP-OZ: Labelled Kripke Structures

To describe requirements of a CSP-OZ specification, we need to define its model which is given by its operational semantics, *labelled Kripke structures*. In addition to normal Kripke structures, transitions are labelled with events of the class.

Definition 1. *(Labelled Kripke Structure) Let AP be a non-empty set of atomic propositions and E an alphabet of events. An event-labelled Kripke structure $K = (S, S_0, \rightarrow, L)$ over AP and E consists of a set of states S, a set of initial states $S_0 \subseteq S$, a transition relation $\rightarrow \subseteq S \times E \times S$ and a labelling function $L : S \rightarrow 2^{AP}$.*

To define the operational semantics for a CSP-OZ class, we introduce the necessary notations. The Object-Z part of a class will in the following be denoted by $Z = (State, \texttt{Init}, (\texttt{com\_}m)_{m \in M})$, where *State* is the state schema of the class, Init the initial state schema and M the set of all methods used in the Object-Z part. We use the alphabet $Events = \{m.i.o \mid m \in M, i \in in(m), o \in out(m)\}$ of all CSP events, consisting of the channel name m and optional values from the sets $in(m)$ and $out(m)$ of all input and output parameters of m. The CSP part neither restricts nor uses values of parameters, i.e. it is *data independent*. Communication is always one sided from the Object-Z part to the CSP part. V denotes the set of all variables of the state space of Z. $Var(m)$ is the set of variables the method m refers to or modifies.

The operational semantics of a class will be given in two steps: first, we define the labelled Kripke structure for the Object-Z part and then the same for the

CSP part. Let AP_O be the set of all atomic propositions over the Object-Z state space:

Definition 2. *(Kripke structure semantics of the Object-Z part)*
The Kripke structure semantics of the Object-Z part is defined as the labelled Kripke structure $K^{OZ} = (State, Init, \rightarrow_{OZ}, L^{OZ})$ *with the labelling function* L^{OZ} *mapping each state onto the set of atomic propositions over the Object-Z state space that are valid in this state, Init being the set of states that satisfy the Object-Z part's* Init *schema and the transition relation* $\rightarrow_{OZ} = \{(z, m.i.o, z') \mid$ com_$m(z, i, o, z')\}$ *relating pre (z) and post (z') states according to the definition of associated Object-Z methods.*

Atomic propositions are given by predicates over unprimed variables and parameters such as $speed > 0$ or $self = i?$ in our example. For the CSP part, we refer to the operational semantics of CSP. In addition, we introduce a *labelling function* for its Kripke structure: requirements may be dependent on the specifications behaviour and therefore only hold at specific locations. In case we want to refer to a certain location of the CSP part, we can use its label. Let PId be the set of process identifiers used in the CSP part with $PId \cap M = \emptyset$:

Definition 3. *(Kripke structure semantics of the CSP part)*
The Kripke structure semantics of the CSP part is defined as the labelled Kripke structure $K^{CSP} = (CSP, \{\texttt{main}\}, \rightarrow_{CSP}, L^{CSP})$ *with CSP denoting the set of all CSP terms,* main *being the only initial CSP term,* $\rightarrow_{CSP}$ *being the transition relation defined according to the operational semantics of CSP [17] and with the labelling function*

$$
L^{CSP}(P) = \begin{cases} \{at\_P\}, & P \in PId \\ \bigcup_i L^{CSP}(Q_i), & P = \|_i Q_i \\ \emptyset, & otherwise \end{cases}
$$

For example, a state $P\|Q$ would be associated with the labelling set $\{at\_P, at\_Q\}$, while $P\|(a \rightarrow Q)$ would be associated with $\{at\_P\}$.

We are now able to define the operational semantics of a CSP-OZ class by means of parallel composition of the Kripke structures of both parts. Note that we combine both labelling functions by unifying the labels:

Definition 4. *(Kripke structure semantics of a CSP-OZ class)*
The Kripke structure semantics of a CSP-OZ class C is the parallel composition of the semantics of the Object-Z part and the CSP part: $K = (State_C, Init_C, \rightarrow, L_C)$ *with* $State_C = State \times CSP$, $Init_C = Init \times \{\texttt{main}\}$, $L_C(z, P) = L^{OZ}(z) \cup L^{CSP}(P)$ *and*

$$
\rightarrow = \{((z, P), ev, (z', P')) \mid (ev \neq \tau, P \xrightarrow{ev}_{CSP} P', z \xrightarrow{ev}_{OZ} z') \vee \\ (ev = \tau, P \xrightarrow{\tau}_{CSP} P', z = z')\}
$$

2.2   Syntax and Semantics of Requirements: LTL-X

To model requirements for CSP-OZ classes, we use the next less part of the temporal logic LTL [14], called LTL-X. The operator X (nexttime) has to be eliminated since it precisely identifies the position of a state in which a certain property holds. In our approach, we deal with a technique not capable of identifying concrete states since the reduced and the full specification in general differ in the number of steps they perform.

Any LTL-X formula is defined over a set of atomic propositions AP. In our case, we will define AP to be the set of all atomic propositions of the CSP-OZ class, i.e. AP_O combined with the labelling of the CSP-part:

$$AP = AP_O \cup \{at\_P_1, \ldots, at\_P_k\} \text{ iff } PId = \{P_1, \ldots, P_k\}.$$

Definition 5. *(Syntax of LTL-X)*
The set of LTL-X formulae over AP is defined as the smallest set of formulae satisfying the following conditions:

- *$p \in AP$ is a formula,*
- *if φ_1 and φ_2 are formulae, so are $\neg \varphi_1$ and $\varphi_1 \vee \varphi_2$,*
- *if φ is a formula, so are $\Box \varphi$ (always) and $\Diamond \varphi$ (eventually),*
- *if φ_1 and φ_2 are formulae, so is $\varphi_1 \, \mathcal{U} \, \varphi_2$ (until).*

The other boolean connectives $\wedge$, $\Rightarrow$ and $\Longleftrightarrow$ can be derived from $\neg$ and $\vee$.

LTL-X formulae are interpreted over *paths* of labelled Kripke structures. Since we will deal with fairness conditions, we also introduce *fair* paths:

Definition 6. *([fair] path)*
*Let $K = (State_C, Init_C, \rightarrow, L_C)$ be the Kripke structure of a CSP-OZ class specification C. An infinite sequence $\pi = s_0 \, ev_0 \, s_1 \, ev_1 \ldots$ of states and events of this class is called a **path of** C iff $s_0 \in Init_C$ and $(s_i, ev_i, s_{i+1}) \in \rightarrow$. π is **fair** wrt. Events' $\subseteq$ Events iff $inf(\pi) \cap Events' \neq \emptyset$ with*

$$inf(\pi) = \{ev \in Events | \exists \text{ infinitely many } i \in \mathbb{N} : ev_i = ev\}.$$

$\pi[i]$ will be the notation for the state s_i and $\pi.i$ for event ev_i. π^i describes the suffix $s_i \, ev_i \, s_{i+1} \, ev_{i+1} \ldots$ of π. If we need to speak about the components of a specific state, we will write s_i as (z_i, P_i). The semantics of LTL-X is inductively defined as follows:

Definition 7. *(Semantics of LTL-X)*
Let π be a path of a labelled Kripke structure K over AP and φ a LTL formula. $\pi \vDash \varphi$ is inductively defined:

- *$\pi \vDash p$ iff $p \in L_C(\pi[0])$ with $p \in AP$,*
- *$\pi \vDash \neg \varphi$ iff $\pi \nvDash \varphi$,*
- *$\pi \vDash \varphi_1 \vee \varphi_2$ iff $\pi \vDash \varphi_1$ or $\pi \vDash \varphi_2$,*

$- \pi \vDash \Box\varphi$ iff $\forall i \bullet \pi^i \vDash \varphi$,

$- \pi \vDash \Diamond\varphi$ iff $\exists i \bullet \pi^i \vDash \varphi$,

$- \pi \vDash \varphi_1 \, \mathcal{U} \, \varphi_2$ iff $\exists k \bullet \pi^i \vDash \varphi_2$ and $\forall j < i \bullet \pi^j \vDash \varphi_1$.

A Kripke structure K satisfies φ ($K \vDash \varphi$) iff $\pi \vDash \varphi$ holds for all paths π of K. K *fairly* satisfies φ wrt. a set of events E ($K \vDash_E \varphi$) iff $\pi \vDash \varphi$ holds for all E-fair paths π of K. Sometimes we will speak about fairness wrt. to a set of methods $M' \subseteq M$ where M' is an abbreviation for the set *Events'*.

In our approach for decomposing a CSP-OZ class, we need to ensure that properties are preserved. This necessitates the notion of *simulation*:

Definition 8. *(Simulation)*
Let $K = (State_C, Init_C, \rightarrow, L_C)$ and $K' = (State_{C'}, Init_{C'}, \rightarrow', L_{C'})$ be the Kripke structures of two CSP-OZ class specifications C and C' such that $M' \subseteq M$ and $V' \subseteq V$. K' *simulates* K ($K \preceq K'$) if there is a relation $H \subseteq State \times State'$ such that the following conditions are satisfied:

1.) For all $s \in Init_C$ there exists $s' \in Init_{C'}$ such that $(s, s') \in H$.
2.) For all $(s_1, s_2) \in H$ with $(s_1, s_2) = ((z_1, P_1), (z_2, P_2))$
   a) $L^{OZ}(z_1) \cap AP'_O = L'^{OZ}(z_2)$ and $L^{CSP}(P_1) = L'^{CSP}(P_2)$
   b) $\forall (s_1, ev, s'_1) \in \rightarrow$:
      - if $ev \in Events'$ then $\exists s'_2 \in State_{C'}$ such that
        $(s_2, ev, s'_2) \in \rightarrow'$ and $(s'_1, s'_2) \in H$ or
      - if $ev \notin Events'$ then $(s'_1, s_2) \in H$.

If we talk about simulation in terms of CSP-OZ specifications, we will sometimes denote a simulation by using the class identifiers instead of the Kripke structures.

The notion of *stuttering equivalence* [4] bridges the gap between LTL-X and simulation. If a Kripke structure is simulated by a second one, their fair paths are stuttering equivalent. Stuttering equivalent paths satisfy the same LTL-X formulae. The following two statements describe this:

Lemma 1. *Let C and C' be CSP-OZ class specifications labelled over M and M' with $M' \subseteq M$ and $V' \subseteq V$. Let $C \preceq C'$. For every M'-fair path π of C there exists a path π' of C' such that π and π' are stuttering equivalent wrt. AP'.*

Lemma 2. *Let C and C' be CSP-OZ class specifications labelled over M and M' with $M' \subseteq M$ and $V' \subseteq V$. Let $C \preceq C'$. If an M'-fair path π of C is stuttering equivalent to a path π' of C', they satisfy the same LTL-X formulae, i.e.*

$$\forall \varphi : LTL\text{-}X \bullet \pi \vDash \varphi \iff \pi' \vDash \varphi$$

The proofs can be found in [21] and [4].

3 Decomposition

In this section, we describe and illustrate our decomposition technique. In the first place, we divide the set of *state variables* of a class. This leads to a decomposition on the level of *predicates*.

Even though this paper deals with the decomposition of a *specification*, a verification of a system starts with decomposing the system *requirements*. The focus in this paper lies on the former and not the latter aspect. However, we will give an example of how to intuitively decompose a requirement. A precise analysis will be part of our future work.

Consider an amount of n verification properties $\varphi_1, \ldots, \varphi_n$ written in LTL-X. In general, we partition the set of state variables V of the class into $n + 1$ subsets based on their occurrence in the requirements: V_v is defined to be the set of variables occurring in every requirement – it is therefore the set of commonly used state variables in any part of the specification. We will refer to them as the verification variables. Additionally, V_i denotes the set of the remaining state variables V_i occurring in the requirement φ_i. The variable sets $V_v \cup V_i$ then serve as the basis for the computation of the smaller specifications C_i. Figure 5 illustrates this approach.

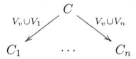

Fig. 5. Decomposition: General approach

To define C_i, we use a certain reduction technique, a variant of program slicing, called *weak* slicing [21]. We start with the quoted subset of state variables and first operate on the Object-Z part of the class. For every method, slicing leads to an elimination of predicates not related to the base variable set. More precisely, preconditions are relaxed but never strengthened. Postconditions can be eliminated in case they do not modify the respective variables, otherwise they are kept. More variables may be added to our base set due to indirect influence and to ensure correctness of the technique – we have to construct the *closure* of our base set.

Our slicing technique *over approximates* the system description meaning that the slices may have *less* behaviour than the original specification but not *more*, i.e. the following condition is satisfied: *If a property holds in the slice, it also holds in the full specification (under certain fairness constraints).*

As a consequence, we are able to do small proof steps by verifying properties for specifications C_i. The property preservation condition yields that C satisfies the conjunction of all properties. In addition, the verification effort is reduced.

3.1   Decomposing a CSP-OZ Specification: Weak Slicing

We will now explain the details of our decomposition approach for CSP-OZ specifications including the following steps: first, we partition the set of state variables of the class' Object-Z part wrt. to a set of requirements. For any of the variable sets we then define the (weak) slice of the specification: we recursively define the closure of the variable sets (i.e. the base sets additionally including indirectly dependent variables) and afterwards slice every method of the Object-Z part wrt. the closure set. Subsequently, we eliminate methods without remaining behaviour from any part of the class (using a projection function for the CSP part).

The intuitive idea behind V_v is that these variables describe the link between the slices of the specification. In some cases, this set can be empty. By $Var(\varphi)$ we denote the set of state variables occurring in a requirement φ specified in LTL-X.

Definition 9. *(state variable partitioning of a CSP-OZ class)*
*Let C be a CSP-OZ class specification over the set of state variables V and $\varphi_1, \ldots, \varphi_n$ be LTL-X requirements for (part of) C. A **state variable separation of C wrt. to** $\varphi_1, \ldots, \varphi_n$ is a partitioning of V into disjoint subsets*

$$V = V_v \uplus \biguplus_{i=1,\ldots,n} V_i \uplus V_r$$

where $V_v = \bigcap_{i=1}^{n} Var(\varphi_i)$, $V_i = Var(\varphi_i) \setminus V_v$ and V_r containing the variables not part of any requirement.

To include variables dependent on the base sets $V_v \cup V_i$, we recursively define the *closure* of a variable set. The closure may also add variables in V_r which are not part of any base set. In the following, let *post* m be the postcondition of a method m and $mod(m)$ denote the set of modified variables within m:

Definition 10. *(variable closure)*
Let C be a CSP-OZ class specification and V be the set of its state variables. For a set $W \subseteq V$ we recursively define $closure(W) \subseteq V$ as follows:

$$V_0 = W$$
$$V_{i+1} = V_i \cup \bigcup_{m \in M} close(m, V_i)$$

with $close(m, X) = \{Var(p) \mid p \in post\ m \wedge mod(p) \cap X \neq \emptyset\}$.

The definition basically says that we extend W with variables occurring in a not further decomposable expression p within a methods postcondition and influencing an arbitrary variable under interest. Note, that we do not add any variables to the base set according to guards: since we over approximate the specification, guards can be weakened. Therefore, we eliminate guards in case they do not solely refer to the variables under interest.

Next, we define the slice of an Object-Z method. According to the definition of the variable closure, we eliminate predicates not related to these variables. To achieve this, we refer to the syntax of Object-Z [19] for describing a method m of the Object-Z part. We refrain from giving a precise definition for every possible predicate of the Object-Z part but rather illustrate the general concept based on boolean connectives:

Definition 11. *(method slice)*
Let C be a CSP-OZ class specification, V be its set of state variables and $W \subseteq V$.
For a method $m \in M$ with

$$m = [DeltaList\ Declaration \mid pre\ m\ post\ m]$$

and $V' = closure(W)$ we define the method slice $sl(m)$ *of m as follows:*

$$sl(m) = [DeltaList\ Declaration' \mid \mathbf{n\_pre}(pre\ m, V')\ \mathbf{n\_post}(post\ m, V')]$$

with

$$\mathbf{n\_pre}(p, V') = \begin{cases} p & Var(p) \subseteq V' \\ true & otherwise \end{cases}$$

$$\mathbf{n\_pre}(pred_1 \vee pred_2, V') = \begin{cases} pred_1 \vee pred_2 & Var(pred_1 \vee pred_2) \subseteq V' \\ true & otherwise \end{cases}$$

$$\mathbf{n\_pre}(pred_1 \wedge pred_2, V') = \mathbf{n\_pre}(pred_1, V') \wedge \mathbf{n\_pre}(pred_2, V')$$

$$\mathbf{n\_post}(p, V') = \begin{cases} p & mod(p) \cap V' \neq \emptyset \\ true & otherwise \end{cases}$$

$$\mathbf{n\_post}(pred_1 \vee pred_2, V') = \mathbf{n\_post}(pred_1, V') \vee \mathbf{n\_post}(pred_2, V')$$
$$\mathbf{n\_post}(pred_1 \wedge pred_2, V') = \mathbf{n\_post}(pred_1, V') \wedge \mathbf{n\_post}(pred_2, V')$$
where $pred_1, pred_2$ describe predicates of the Object-Z state space and p an atomic
expression.

Let us take a closer look at this definition: the precondition of the sliced method is inductively defined as the precondition of the original method restricted to *closure(W)*. Since guards of a method must not be strengthened, we have to be careful in one specific case: we are not allowed to replace a disjunction of a guard with one of its components. In this case, we have to eliminate the whole precondition (as defined in the second case of **n_pre**). The postcondition will be retained in case we modify any variable under interest.

To illustrate the definition, consider a method $m = [\Delta(y) \mid x = true \vee y' = true\ ]$ with two boolean variables x and y and let $V' = \{y\}$. Since there is no precondition for this method, we only use the second part of our definition leading to $sl(m) = [\Delta(y) \mid true \vee y' = true]$, i.e. $sl(m) = [\Delta(y)]$. In case we replace $\vee$ by $\wedge$, the precondition of the method now evaluates to $x = true$. Since x is not a variable under interest, it is completely eliminated and solely the postcondition $y' = true$ remains leading to $sl(m) = [\Delta(y) \mid y' = true\ ]$.

In the definition of the method slice, we used *Declaration'* but did not refer to input and output parameters yet. It is possible, that predicates dealing with parameters are no longer present in its slice. In case a parameter is no longer used in the lower part of a method, we completely remove it from the whole method. This leads to a modification of the class interface and the CSP part. For simplification, we will denote events of the specification and its slice equally by keeping in mind that the slices methods may lack of some of its parameters.

It may sometimes be possible that every pre- and postcondition of a method will be eliminated. For example, consider the method *brake* in our running example: slicing wrt. to a set of variables not containing *speed* and *err_pos* leads to an empty method in both components. In this case, the method should be eliminated from the CSP part as well. This motivates the introduction of the *projection* [2] of the CSP part wrt. a set of (remaining) methods:

Definition 12. *(CSP projection)*
*Let P be the right side of a process definition from the CSP part and $M' \subseteq M$. The **projection** $\lfloor P \rfloor_{M'}$ of P wrt. to M' is defined inductively as follows:*

a) $\lfloor \text{SKIP} \rfloor_{M'} = \text{SKIP}$ and $\lfloor \text{STOP} \rfloor_{M'} = \text{STOP}$,
b) for any process identifier $P \in PId$ $\lfloor P \rfloor_{M'} = P$,

c) $\lfloor ev \to P \rfloor_{M'} = \begin{cases} \lfloor P \rfloor_{M'} & ev \notin Events' \\ ev \to \lfloor P \rfloor_{M'} & ev \in Events' \end{cases}$

d) $\lfloor P \circ Q \rfloor_{M'} = \lfloor P \rfloor_{M'} \circ \lfloor Q \rfloor_{M'}$ for any operator $\circ \in \{; , \|\|, \Box, \sqcap\}$.

After defining the reduction of the Object-Z part (Definition 11) and CSP part (Definition 12), we are now able to define the *weak slice* of a specification wrt. to a set of state variables:

Definition 13. *(weak slice)*
*Let C be a CSP-OZ class specification and let $W \subseteq V$. Let $V' = closure(W)$ based on Definition 10. The **weak slice** C_s of C is defined as the specification consisting of*

- *methods $M' = \{sl(m) | m \in M \wedge sl(m) \neq [\Delta()]\}$,*
- *inside the state schema only variables from V',*
- *$Init_C$ restricted to V',*
- *the projections of the CSP process definitions in C based on M'.*

To show simulation of the full specification by its slice, we need to deal with the operational semantics of CSP-OZ as defined in the last section. The next lemma describes that any execution of a method in a class C is also possible in its weak slice:

Lemma 3. *Let C be a CSP-OZ class specification, C_s be its weak slice wrt. to the variable set $W \subseteq V$ and $V' = closure(W)$. The transition relation of the Kripke structure $K^s = (State^s_C, Init^s_C, \to^s, L^s_C)$ of C_s with*

- *$State^s_C = \pi_{V'}[State] \times \lfloor [CSP] \rfloor_{M'}$,*
- *$Init^s_C = \pi_{V'}[Init] \times \lfloor \mathtt{main} \rfloor_{M'}$,*
- *$L^s_C(z, P) = L^{OZ}(z) \cup L^{CSP}(P)$*

is related to the transition relation of the full specification in the following way:

$$\forall (z, P) \in State_C, ev \in Events' \bullet$$
$$(z, P) \xrightarrow{ev} (z', P') \implies (\pi_{V'}(z), \lfloor P \rfloor_{M'}) \xrightarrow{ev}^s (\pi_{V'}(z), \lfloor P' \rfloor_{M'})$$

In case of $ev = m.i.o \notin Events'$, the given event has been eliminated from the specification and we obviously cannot show the property of Lemma 3. Otherwise, equivalent before states are able to execute the same events leading to equivalent after states. Due to lack of space, the proof will not be given here. Figure 6 illustrates the lemma.

Fig. 6. Illustration of Lemma 3

3.2   Decomposition of the Example

We want to illustrate our approach on the example from section 2. The full specification can be considered as two-piece: in the coordination mode, a repeated measuring and computing is performed. In case of a distance error, a break manoeuvre is initiated by the control system. In the following, we use the abbreviations S and C for *Shuttle* and *Control*.

Our main goal is to secure safetyness for the whole specification. A safety property can intuitively be described as

> *Whenever the distance between two shuttles is too small, all shuttles will eventually stop.*[2]

In LTL-X, this can be specified as $\varphi := \Box(\bigwedge_{i=1}^{N}(small\_dist(i) \rightarrow \Diamond all\_stop))$ where
$$small\_dist(i) := |S[i].mypos - S[i].nbpos.2| < MIND,$$
$$all\_stop := \bigwedge_{j=1}^{N} S[j].speed \le 0.$$

To verify the given requirement, we split it into two parts which can individually be verified for the slices of the specification which we will determine in the following:

> *Whenever the distance between two shuttles is too small, the control system is notified by the shuttles. In consequence, all shuttles will eventually stop.*

The notification about a possible error (communication of the *fail* vector) is the link between both parts of the specification. This can be used for our main goal φ: the formula is split into two implications with an inner part addressing the communication. LTL-X formulae for these properties are:

$$\psi_1 \qquad := \Box(\bigwedge_{i=1}^{N}(small\_dist(i)) \rightarrow (C.at\_Q \rightarrow fail\_set(i)))$$
$$\psi_2 \qquad := \Box(\bigwedge_{i=1}^{N}(C.at\_Q \rightarrow fail\_set(i)) \rightarrow \Diamond all\_stop)$$
$$fail\_set(i) := C.fail(i).2 \wedge C.fail(i+1).1$$

---

[2] For simplicity, we do not verify an assumption additionally stating that the shuttles do not collide.

We define the partitioning of the state variables according to Definition 9 into three sets V_v, V_d and V_r. The only state variable used in ψ_1 and ψ_2 is the variable $C.fail$. As a first step, we get

$$V_v = \{C.fail\},\ V_d = \{S[i].mypos, S[i].nbpos\}, V_r = \{S[i].speed\}$$

The closures of the base sets are defined next. Because of the dependency to $C.fail$ due to communication via method $sendfail$, $closure(V_v \cup V_d)$ additionally contains $S[i].fail$. A similar argument leads to adding $C.pos$ to $closure(V_v \cup V_d)$ and $C.err\_pos$ to $closure(V_v \cup V_r)$.

$Shuttle^d[i]$

method $evaluate, sendfail[i : \{\mathbf{self}\};\ f? : \mathbb{B} \times \mathbb{B}]$
method $measure[i : \{\mathbf{self}\};\ y : \mathbb{N} \times \mathbb{N} \times \mathbb{N}]$

$\mathbf{main} = measure.i?y \rightarrow evaluate \rightarrow sendfail.i?y \rightarrow (E\ \Box\ \mathbf{main}),\ E = E$

	Init
$mypos : \mathbb{N}$	$mypos = i * MAXD$
$nbpos : \mathbb{N} \times \mathbb{N}$	$nbpos = \ldots$
$fail : \mathbb{B} \times \mathbb{B}$	$fail = (\text{false}, \text{false})$

com_measure	
$\Delta(mypos, nbpos)$	$evaluate \,\hat{=}\, Shuttle[i].evaluate$
$pos? : \mathbb{N} \times \mathbb{N} \times \mathbb{N}$	$sendfail \,\hat{=}\, Shuttle[i].sendfail$
$mypos', nbpos' \in [\ldots]$	

$Control^d$

method $sendfail[i? : ShuttleRef;\ y? : \mathbb{B} \times \mathbb{B}]$
method $measure[i? : ShuttleRef;\ y : \mathbb{N} \times \mathbb{N} \times \mathbb{N}]$

$\mathbf{main} = \|\|_i\, measure.i?y \rightarrow \|\|_i\, sendfail.i?y \rightarrow Q$
$Q = (B\ \Box\ \mathbf{main}),\ B = B$

	com_measure
$pos : \text{seq}_1\, \mathbb{N}$	$i! : ShuttleRef,\ p! : \mathbb{N} \times \mathbb{N} \times \mathbb{N}$
$fail : \text{seq}_1\, \mathbb{B} \times \mathbb{B}$	$p! = (pos.(i! - 1), pos.i!, pos.(i! + 1))$
$\#pos = \#Sh$	

Init	
$\forall i \bullet fail(i) = (\text{false}, \text{false})$	$sendfail \,\hat{=}\, Control.sendfail$

Fig. 7. Specification: Data slice

$$closure(V_v \cup V_d) = \{C.fail, S[i].fail, S[i].mypos, S[i].nbpos, C.pos\}$$
$$closure(V_v \cup V_r) = \{C.fail, S[i].fail, S[i].speed, C.err\_pos\}$$

The partitioning is reasonable since it separates the variables dealing with positions and evaluation of the variable *fail* from the rest.

We will now decompose our shuttle specification into two parts: the part $System^d$ basically evaluating if any two shuttles have at least the minimal distance and the part $System^r$ describing the error mode. The decomposition is according to Definition 13 and based on the variable sets $V_v \cup V_d$ and $V_v \cup V_r$. The specifications are depicted in Figure 8 and Figure 7, respectively. Note, that $Control^d$ and $Shuttle[i]^d$ have divergent [17] processes E and B: after elimination of method *brake* from $brake \rightarrow B$, the process equation $B = brake \rightarrow B$ is projected on $B = B$. This does, however, not pose a problem for us.

The whole decomposition can also be seen as an outsourcing of the data-heavy behaviour from the rest of the specification as mentioned in the introduction: $System^r$ can be replaced by any scenario mainly dealing with the *result* of the distance evaluation without considering its details. An automatic verification of properties is thus better practicable since it needs to consider fewer data variables.

4   Verification

After introducing our technique of decomposing a specification, we will now explain how to use it to verify requirements written in LTL-X. We show, that the slice simulates the specification in terms of Kripke structures. Since simulation preserves temporal logic formulae as stated in Section 2, we are able to prove that properties of the slice also hold for the specification.

In case we talk about temporal logic properties, we sometimes have to require fairness wrt. the operation set of the slice since Lemma 1 only holds under fairness assumptions. We use the notations of Definition 6 and Definition 7. The following theorem states the core result of this paper and is based on Lemma 3:

Theorem 1. *Let C be a CSP-OZ class specification and C_s be its weak slice wrt. some $V' \subseteq V$ and $M' \subseteq M$. Then $C \preceq C_s$.*

Proof: Let $K = (State_C, Init_C, \rightarrow, L_C)$ and $K^s = (State_C^s, Init_C^s, \rightarrow^s, L_C^s)$ be the Kripke structures of C and C_s. We define

$$H := \{((z, P), (\pi_{V'}(z), \|P\|_{M'}) | z \in State, P \in CSP\}$$

and show the simulation conditions of Definition 8.

1.) Let $(z, \mathtt{main}) \in Init_C$. Then $(\pi_{V'}(z), \|\mathtt{main}\|_{M'}) \in Init_C^s$ and $((z, \mathtt{main}), (\pi_{V'}(z), \|\mathtt{main}\|_{M'})) \in H$ holds by definition.
2.) Let $((z_1, P_1), (z_2, P_2)) \in H$. By definition of H we get $P_2 = \|P_1\|_{M'}$ and $z_2 = \pi_{V'}(z_1)$.
   a) Since we project a state on the variable set V' according to the restricted set of atomic propositions, z_2 and the projection of z_1 are equally labelled.

__ $Shuttle^r[i]$ _____

method $brake[i : \{\texttt{self}\};\ n? : \mathbb{N}], measure[i : \{\texttt{self}\};\ y : \mathbb{N}]$

method $evaluate, sendfail[i : \{\texttt{self}\};\ f? : \mathbb{B} \times \mathbb{B}]$

main $= measure.i?y \rightarrow sendfail.i?y \rightarrow (E \ \Box\ \texttt{main}),\ E = brake.i?y \rightarrow E$

	__Init_____
$speed : \mathbb{N},\ fail : \mathbb{B} \times \mathbb{B}$	$speed = 300$
$speed \leq MAXS$	$fail = (\text{false, false})$

__com_measure_____	__com_sendfail_____
$\Delta(speed),\ s? : \mathbb{N}$	$f! : \mathbb{B} \times \mathbb{B}$
$speed' = s?$	$f! = fail$

	__com_evaluate_____
$brake \mathrel{\hat=} Shuttle[i].brake$	$\Delta(fail)$

__ $Control^r$ _____

method $brake[i? : ShuttleRef;\ n? : \mathbb{N}], sendfail[i? : ShuttleRef;\ y? : \mathbb{B} \times \mathbb{B}]$

method $checkerror, measure[i? : ShuttleRef;\ y : \mathbb{N}]$

main $= |||_i\, measure.i?y \rightarrow |||_i\, sendfail.i?y \rightarrow Q$

$Q = checkerror \rightarrow (B \ \Box\ \texttt{main}),\ B = |||_i\, brake.i?y \rightarrow B$

	__com_measure_____
$fail : \text{seq}_1\, \mathbb{B} \times \mathbb{B}$	$i! : ShuttleRef, s! : \mathbb{N}$
$err\_pos : \mathbb{Z}$	$err\_pos = -1$

__com_sendfail_____	
$\Delta(fail)$	$\texttt{Init} \mathrel{\hat=} Control.\texttt{Init}$
$i? : ShuttleRef,\ f? : \mathbb{B} \times \mathbb{B}$	$checkerror \mathrel{\hat=} Control.checkerror$
$fail'.i? = f?$	$brake \mathrel{\hat=} Control.brake$

Fig. 8. Specification: Reduction slice

Moreover, the labelling of the CSP part is accordingly since we do not eliminate any process identifiers.

b) If $((z_1, P_1), ev, (z_1', P_1')) \in \rightarrow$, we have to distinguish two cases:
   - $ev \in Events'$: let $(z_2', P_2') := (\pi_{V'}(z_1'), \lfloor\!\lfloor P_1'\rfloor\!\rfloor_{M'})$. $((z_1', P_1'), (z_2', P_2')) \in H$ holds. $((\pi_{V'}(z_1), \lfloor\!\lfloor P_1\rfloor\!\rfloor_{M'}), ev, (\pi_{V'}(z_1'), \lfloor\!\lfloor P_1'\rfloor\!\rfloor_{M'})) \in \rightarrow'$ holds due to Lemma 3 (cp. Figure 6).

- $ev \notin Events'$: we have to show that $((z_1', P_1'), (z_2, P_2)) \in H$ holds, i.e. $\pi_{V'}(z_1') = \pi_{V'}(z_1)$ and $\|P_1'\|_{M'} = \|P_1\|_{M'}$. Since $ev \notin Events'$, $sl(m) = [\Delta()]$ holds. According to Definition 11, no variable of V' is modified within ev. We get $z_1.v = z_1'.v$ for all $v \in V'$, i.e. $\pi_{V'}(z_1') = \pi_{V'}(z_1)$. For the CSP part, the only interesting case is $P_1 = ev \rightarrow P_1'$. But then we get $\|P_1'\|_{M'} = \|P_1\|_{M'}$ due to $ev \notin M'$. □

Next, we show that the conjunction of the verified requirements for a set of n slices is satisfied for the source specification:

Theorem 2. Let C be a CSP-OZ class specification and C_i with $i = \{1, \ldots, n\}$ be weak slices of C wrt. to $V_i \subseteq V$ and $M_i \subseteq M$. Let $M^* := \bigcap_{i=1}^n M_i$. Then the following holds for all LTL-X properties φ_i[3]:

$$(\bigwedge_{i=1}^n C_i \vDash_{M_i} \varphi_i) \rightarrow (C \vDash_{M^*} \bigwedge_{i=1}^n \varphi_i)$$

Proof: Let $C_j \vDash_{M_j} \varphi_j$ with $1 \le j \le n$. Assume there is a fair (wrt. to M^*) path $\pi \in paths(C)$ such that $\pi \nvDash \varphi_j$. Since $C \preceq C_j$ based on Theorem 1, we can apply Lemma 1: in particular, π is fair wrt. M_j, so we can construct a stuttering equivalent path π' of π for C_j. π' satisfies φ_j by assumption and π, π' satisfy the same LTL-X formulae (Lemma 2), i.e. $\pi \vDash \varphi_j$ holds. That is a contradiction to our assumption. □

The next theorem shows that the fairness restriction is not necessary for every class of requirements. For invariance properties (properties which have to hold in every step of a computation), we can drop the fairness condition.

Theorem 3. Let C be a CSP-OZ class specification and C' be its weak slice wrt. to $V' \subseteq V$ and $M' \subseteq M$. Then the following holds for all properties $p \in AP'$:

$$C' \vDash_{M'} \Box p \rightarrow C \vDash \Box p$$

The proof basically uses the idea that from a certain point on, an unfair path wrt. V' does only execute methods outside of M'. If this path would not satisfy $\Box p$, it would either violate it before or after this point, where both cases lead to a contradiction. We omit the complete proof due to lack of space.

4.1   Verification of the Example

We will now explain how to use our technique to verify the property φ (s. Section 3) for the shuttle specification. Figure 9 illustrates the application of our results.

In a first step, a verification of ψ_1 for $System^d$ and ψ_2 for $System^r$ (both formulae according to Section 3) is necessary. In general, we have to decide if the verification can be achieved automatically by a model checker or manually by for example using deductive proof techniques. The detailed verification is not part

---

[3] Obviously, φ_i may only use variables of V_i.

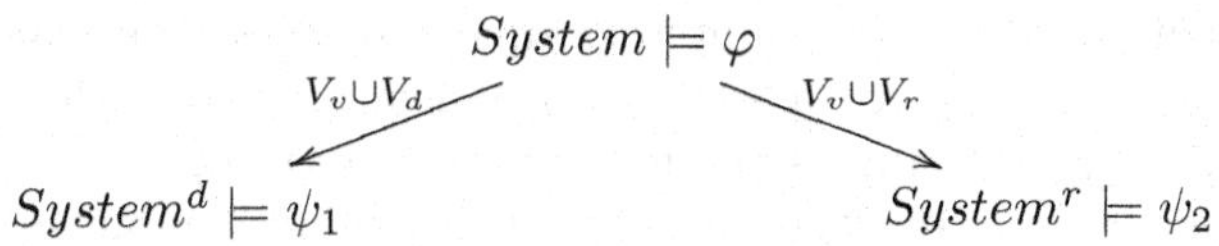

$$System \models \varphi$$

$$V_v \cup V_d \qquad\qquad V_v \cup V_r$$

$$System^d \models \psi_1 \qquad\qquad System^r \models \psi_2$$

Fig. 9. Verification of Shuttle specification

of this work. However, our separation of the data-heavy part from the rest of the specification motivates a manual verification of ψ_1 and an automatic verification of ψ_2. In general, this is one achievement of our approach - if a data-heavy part can be separated from a larger specification, manual verification needs only be performed for this specific part.

To apply our approach, we assume that $System^d \models_{M_d} \psi_1$ and $System^r \models_{M_r} \psi_2$ have been shown where $M_r = M \setminus \{evaluate\}$ and $M_d = M \setminus \{checkerror, brake\}$. Since ψ_1 is an invariance property, we apply Theorem 2 and Theorem 3 yielding that $System \models_{M_r} (\psi_1 \wedge \psi_2)$. $\varphi = (\psi_1 \wedge \psi_2)$ holds because of $\Box(\psi_1 \wedge \psi_2) = \Box\psi_1 \wedge \Box\psi_2$. Since there are no unfair traces wrt. M_r in the whole specification (the only event of $M \setminus M_r$, $evaluate$, can not continuously be executed), we get $System \models \varphi$ without any fairness requirement.

5 Conclusion

This paper has presented an approach to decompose and verify specifications written in the integrated formal method CSP-OZ. The main focus was to divide the state space of a specification and therefore simplify verification. We achieved our goal by using the technique of weak slicing and showed how the slices enable us to verify requirements for the specification with less effort. Moreover, we applied our results to an example in the rail domain.

Related Work. *Slicing* was first introduced by Weiser [22]. In model checking and specifically in the context of reducing the state space of a program, it was amongst others applied in [11]. In object orientation, slicing has been applied to Java programs with the goal to automatically remove irrelevant code.

Verification for IFMs undergoes intensive research. For CSP∥B, a coupling of the B method with CSP, Treharne and Schneider explored compositional proof techniques [18] by using the model checker FDR [16] for verification of CSP processes. Mota and Sampaio analysed deadlock freedom [15] for specifications written in CSP-Z again by using FDR for model checking purposes. Similar approaches can be found for Circus [24], a combination of CSP and Z with a refinement calculus.

The use of slicing for verification of Object-Z specifications has first been examined in [3]. The approach uses slicing in a non-decompositional manner by construction of *one* slice and has later been extended to CSP-OZ [2]. The resulting specification has to ensure that a property is satisfied if and only if it is satisfied in the full specification. This leads to slices much closer to the specification while wrong counterexamples (so-called false negatives) are not possible. Weak slicing for a simple formalism aligned with CSP-OZ has been introduced in [21] serving as the foundation of our approach.

We adopt some of the approaches, but instead of computing one specification slice, we split the specification into several slices. In contrast to the former approach, slicing is applied in the context of decomposing the specification and the requirement. Verification techniques such as assume guarantee reasoning [8] or formal verification techniques for temporal logic [14] have already been explored and will be part of further research.

Future Work. In a recent field of research for a complete decomposition and verification technique for CSP-OZ, this paper is intended to provide the basic concept. There are many follow-up steps to be taken, with some of them described next.

Our technique is based on a decomposition of the systems requirements. The state variable sets of different slices should preferably be independent from each other. Keeping that in mind, an elaboration of a reasonable method for separating verification properties requires a more precise and less intuitive analysis of the dependency structure of the Object-Z state space. In [2], the program dependence graph for CSP-OZ specifications is used to determine the data and control dependencies between methods of a class. We aim at a similar analysis for our weak slicing technique.

Verification of CSP-OZ specifications is the main objective of the whole approach. For the case, that automatic techniques are adequate, model checkers such as FDR [10] or SAL [20] can be used. If verification necessitates manual proof strategies, decompositional techniques as assume-guarantee based reasoning [8], deductive approaches such as in [14] or invariant based techniques as explained in [1] are applicative.

Some further steps include checking the feasibility of counterexamples as presented in [21], an analysis of our approach on behalf of object oriented concepts of CSP-OZ, and furthermore we aim to expand it to real time extensions of CSP-OZ.

References

1. Brückner, I., Metzler, B., Wehrheim, H.: Optimizing slicing of formal specifications by deductive verification. Nordic Journal of Computing 13(1–2), 22–45 (2006)
2. Brückner, I., Wehrheim, H.: Slicing an Integrated Formal Method for Verification. In: Lau, K.-K., Banach, R. (eds.) ICFEM 2005. LNCS, vol. 3785, pp. 360–374. Springer, Heidelberg (2005)
3. Brückner, I., Wehrheim, H.: Slicing Object-Z Specifications for Verification. In: Treharne, H., King, S., Henson, M.C., Schneider, S. (eds.) ZB 2005. LNCS, vol. 3455, pp. 414–433. Springer, Heidelberg (2005)
4. Clarke, E., Grumberg, O., Peled, D.: Model checking. MIT Press, Cambridge (1999)
5. Clarke, E., Grumberg, O., Jha, S., Lu, Y., Veith, H.: Counterexample-guided abstraction refinement for symbolic model checking. J. ACM 50(5), 752–794 (2003)

6. Clarke, E.M., Grumberg, O., Long, D.E.: Model checking and abstraction. ACM Transactions on Programming Languages and Systems 16(5), 1512–1542 (1994)
7. Clarke, E.M., Grumberg, O., Minea, M., Peled, D.: State space reduction using partial order techniques. STTT 2(3), 279–287 (1999)
8. de Roever, W.P., Hanneman, U., Hooiman, J., Lakhneche, Y., Poel, M., Zwiers, J., de Boer, F.: Concurrency Verification. Cambridge University Press, Cambridge, UK (2001)
9. Fischer, C.: CSP-OZ: A Combination of Object-Z and CSP. In: Formal Methods for Open Object-Based Distributed Systems (FMOODS'97), vol. 2, pp. 423–438. Chapman & Hall, Sydney (1997)
10. Fischer, C., Wehrheim, H.: Model-checking CSP-OZ specifications with FDR. In: IFM, pp. 315–334 (1999)
11. Hatcliff, J., Dwyer, M.B., Zheng, H.: Slicing Software for Model Construction. Higher-Order and Symbolic Computation 13(4), 315–353 (2000)
12. Hoare, C.A.R.: Communicating Sequential Processes. CACM 21, 666–677 (1978)
13. Kupferman, O., Vardi, M.Y.: Modular model checking. In: de Roever, W.-P., Langmaack, H., Pnueli, A. (eds.) COMPOS 1997. LNCS, vol. 1536, pp. 381–401. Springer, Heidelberg (1998)
14. Manna, Z., Pnueli, A.: Temporal verification of reactive systems: safety. Springer, Berlin Heidelberg (1995)
15. Mota, A., Sampaio, A.: Model-checking CSP-Z. In: Astesiano, E. (ed.) ETAPS 1998 and FASE 1998. LNCS, vol. 1382, pp. 205–220. Springer, Heidelberg (1998)
16. Roscoe, A.W.: Model-checking csp. pp. 353–378 (1994)
17. Roscoe, A.W.: The Theory and Practice of Concurrency. Prentice-Hall, Englewood Cliffs (1998)
18. Schneider, S., Treharne, H.: Verifying controlled components. IFM, pp. 87–107 (2004)
19. Smith, G. (ed.): The Object-Z Specification Language. Kluwer Academic Publishers, Dordrecht (2000)
20. Smith, G., Wildman, L.: Model checking Z specifications using SAL. In: Treharne, H., King, S., Henson, M.C., Schneider, S. (eds.) ZB 2005. LNCS, vol. 3455, pp. 85–103. Springer, Heidelberg (2005)
21. Wehrheim, H.: Incremental slicing. In: Liu, Z., He, J. (eds.) ICFEM 2006. LNCS, vol. 4260, pp. 514–528. Springer, Heidelberg (2006)
22. Weiser, M.: Program slicing. In: Proceedings of the 5th International Conference on Software Engineering, pp. 439–449. IEEE Computer Society Press, Los Alamitos (1981)
23. Woodcock, J., Davies, J.: Using Z – Specification, Refinement, and Proof. Prentice-Hall, Englewood Cliffs (1996)
24. Woodcock, J.C.P., Cavalcanti, A.L.C.: The Semantics of Circus. In: Bert, D., Bowen, J.P., Henson, M.C., Robinson, K. (eds.) B 2002 and ZB 2002. LNCS, vol. 2272, pp. 184–203. Springer, Heidelberg (2002)

Validating Z Specifications Using the PROB Animator and Model Checker

Daniel Plagge and Michael Leuschel

Softwaretechnik und Programmiersprachen
Institut für Informatik, Universität Düsseldorf
Universitätsstr. 1, D-40225 Düsseldorf
{plagge,leuschel}@cs.uni-duesseldorf.de

Abstract. We present the architecture and implementation of the PROZ tool to validate high-level Z specifications. The tool was integrated into PROB, by providing a translation of Z into B and by extending the kernel of PROB to accommodate some new syntax and data types. We describe the challenge of going from the tool friendly formalism B to the more specification-oriented formalism Z, and show how many Z specifications can be systematically translated into B. We describe the extensions, such as record types and free types, that had to be added to the kernel to support a large subset of Z. As a side-effect, we provide a way to animate and model check records in PROB. By incorporating PROZ into PROB, we have inherited many of the recent extensions developed for B, such as the integration with CSP or the animation of recursive functions. Finally, we present a successful industrial application, which makes use of this fact, and where PROZ was able to discover several errors in Z specifications containing higher-order recursive functions.

1   Introduction

Both B [1] and Z [2,26] are formal mathematical specification notations, using the same underlying set theory and predicate calculus. Both formalisms are used in industry in a range of critical domains.

The Z notation places the emphasis on human-readability of specifications. Z specifications are often documents where ambiguities in the description of the system are avoided by supporting the prose with formal statements in Z. LaTeX packages such as $f$uzz [25] exists to support type setting and checking those documents. The formal part of a specification mainly consists of schemas which describe different aspects of a system using set theory and predicate logic. The schema calculus—a distinct feature of Z—enables system engineers to specify complex systems by combining those schemas.

B was derived from Z by Jean-Raymond Abrial (also the progenitor of Z) with the aim of enabling tool support. In the process, some aspects of Z were removed and replaced, while new features were added (notably the ASCII Abstract Machine Notation). We will discuss some of the differences later in depth.

J. Davies and J. Gibbons (Eds.): IFM 2007, LNCS 4591, pp. 480–500, 2007.
© Springer-Verlag Berlin Heidelberg 2007

In a nutshell, B is more aimed at refinement and code generation, while Z is a more high-level formalism aimed for specification. This is, arguably, why B has industrial strength tools, such as Atelier-B [27] and the B-toolkit [5]. Recently the PROB model checker [19] and refinement checker [20] have been added to B's list of tools. Similar tools are lacking for Z, even though there are recent efforts to provide better tool support for Z [24].

In this paper we describe the challenge of developing a Z version of PROB, capable of animating and model checking realistic Z specifications. We believe an animator and model checker is a very important ingredient for formal methods; especially if we do not formally derive code from the specification (as is common in Z [13,12]). This fact is also increasingly being realised by industrial users of formal methods.

At the heart of our approach lies a translation of Z specifications into B, with the aim of providing an integrated tool that is capable to validate both Z and B specifications, as well as inheriting from recent refinements developed for B (such as the integration with CSP [8]). One motivation for our work comes from an industrial example, which we also describe in the paper.

2   Specifications in Z

First we give a brief introduction to the Z notation. We want to describe the structure of Z specifications, especially how this differs from specifications in B as supported by PROB. The interested reader can find a tutorial introduction to Z inside the Z reference manual [26]. A more comprehensive introduction with many examples is [16].

2.1   A Brief Description of Z

Usually, a specification in Z consists of informal prose together with formal statements. In a real-life applications, the prose part is at least as important as the formal part, as a specification has to be read by humans as well as computers.

Usually, one describes state machines in Z, i.e., one defines possible states as well as operations that can change the state. The Z syntax can be split into two: a notation for discrete mathematics (set theory and predicate calculus) and a notation for describing and combining *schemas*, called the schema calculus.

For illustration, we use the simple database of birthdays (Fig. 1) from [26]. The first line in the example is a declaration [*NAME, DATE*] which simply introduces *NAME* and *DATE* as new basic types, without providing more information about their attributes (like generics in some programming languages). We can also see three boxes, each with a name on the upper border and a horizontal line dividing it into two parts. These boxes define the so-called schemas. Above the dividing line is the declaration part, where variables and their types are introduced, and below a list of predicates can be stated.

Without additional description, the purpose of each schema in the example is not directly apparent. We use the first schema *BirthdayBook* to define the state

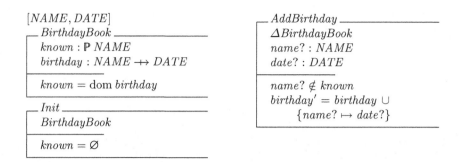

Fig. 1. The birthday book example

space of our system. *Init* defines a valid initial state and the schema *AddBirthday* is the description of an operation that inserts a new name and birthday into the database.

We describe the schemas in more detail. In *BirthdayBook* we have two variables: *known* is a set of names and *birthday* is a partial function that maps names to a date. The predicate states that *known* is the domain of the partial function, i.e., the set of names that have an entry in the function. A possible state of our system consists of values for these two variables which satisfy the predicate.

The declaration part of the *Init* schema contains a reference to the schema *BirthdayBook*. This imports all *BirthdayBook*'s variable declarations and predicates into *Init*. The predicate says that *known* is empty. Together with the predicate of *BirthdayBook* this implicitly states that the domain of *birthday* is empty, resulting in an empty function.

The schema defining the operation *AddBirthday* contains two variables with an appended question mark. By convention, variables with a trailing ? (resp. !) describe inputs (resp. outputs) of operations, thus *name?* and *date?* are inputs to the operation. The first line of the schema is $\Delta BirthdayBook$. This includes all declarations and predicates of *BirthdayBook*, as previously seen in *Init*. Additionally the variable declarations are included with a prime appended to their name, representing the state after the execution of the operation. The predicates are also included a second time where all occurring variables have a prime appended. To clarify this, we show the *expanded* schema:

```
__ AddBirthday _____
  known, known' : ℙ NAME
  birthday, birthday' : NAME ⇸ DATE
  name? : NAME
  date? : DATE
_____
  known = dom birthday ∧ known' = dom birthday'
  name? ∉ known
  birthday' = birthday ∪ {name? ↦ date?}
```

The schema thus defines the relation between the state before and after executing the operation *AddBirthday*. Accordingly the unprimed variables refer to the state before and the primed ones to the state after the execution. The effect of *AddBirthday* is that the function *birthday* has been extended with a new entry. But, together with the predicates from *BirthdayBook*, it is (again implicitly) stated that *name?* should be added to *known*.

Instead of the schema boxes there is also a shorter equivalent syntax. E.g., *Init* can also be defined with *Init* $\widehat{=}$ [*BirthdayBook* | *known* = $\varnothing$]. In addition to inclusion, as seen in the example, the schema calculus of Z provides more operators to combine schemas. E.g., the conjunction of two schemas $R \widehat{=} S1 \wedge S2$ merges their declaration part in a way that the resulting schema R has the variables of both schemas $S1$ and $S2$, and its predicate is the logical conjunction of both original predicates. The schema calculus is a very important aspect of the Z notation, because it makes Z suitable for describing large systems by handling distinct parts of it and combining them.

2.2 Some Differences Between Z and B

PROZ is an extension of PROB, a tool that animates specifications in B. To make use of its core functionality, we need to translate a Z specification into PROB's internal representation of a B machine. To illustrate the fundamental issues and problems, we describe some of the major differences between Z and B using our example.

Figure 2 shows the birthday book example as a B machine. Aside from the ASCII notation, one difference is the use of keywords to divide the specification into multiple sections. The **VARIABLES** section defines that **known** and **birthday** are the variables making up the state. There is an explicit initialisation and in the **OPERATIONS** section the operation **AddBirthday** is described. In a Z specification, on the other hand, the purpose of each schema must be explained in the surrounding prose.

If we look closer at the **INITIALISATION** section in the example, we see that both **known** and **birthday** are set to $\varnothing$. This is unlike the Z schema *Init* in Fig. 2, where only *known* = $\varnothing$ is stated and the value of *birthday* is implicitly defined.

```
MACHINE BirthdayBook
SETS NAME;DATE
VARIABLES known,birthday
INVARIANT
 known:POW(NAME) & birthday:NAME+->DATE & known=dom(birthday)
INITIALISATION known,birthday := {},{}
OPERATIONS
  AddBirthday(name,date) = PRE name:NAME & date:DATE & name/:known THEN
    birthday(name) := date || known := known \/ {name}
  END
END
```

Fig. 2. The birthday book example in B

Also in the definition of the operation `AddBirthday` both variables are changed explicitly. Generally in B all changes to variables must be stated explicitly via generalised substitutions. All other variables are not changed, whereas in Z every variable can change, as long its values satisfy the predicates of the operation.

Another noteworthy difference is the declaration of an invariant in the B machine. An invariant in B is a constraint that must hold in every state. To prove that a machine is consistent it has to be proven that the initialisation is valid and that no operation leads to an invalid state if applied to a valid state. In Z the predicate of the state's schema is also called invariant, but unlike B the operations implicitly satisfy it by including the state's schema. Errors in a B specification can lead to a violation of the invariant. A similar error in Z leads to an operation not being enabled, which in turn can lead to deadlocks.

2.3   Translating Z to B

The notation of substitutions often results in specifications that are easier to animate than higher-level Z specifications. Hence, at the heart of PROZ is a systematic translation of Z schemas into B machines.

Figure 3 contains such a B translation of the birthday book Z specification, as computed by our tool (to make the specification more readable we use Z style identifiers, i.e., ending with ', ? or !, even though strictly speaking this is not valid B syntax). As can bee seen, we have identified that the variables *birthday* and *known* form part of the state, their types are declared in the invariant. The initialisation part is a translation of the expanded *Init* schema. One operation *AddBirthday* with two arguments *date?* and *name?* has been identified, a translation of the expanded *AddBirthday* schema can be found in the WHERE clause of its ANY statement. There are also several references to a constant *maxentries*. We added it and a constraint $\# known \leq maxentries$ to demonstrate the handling of axiomatic definitions (cf. Section 3.1).

The B machine from Figure 3 can be fed directly into PROB, for animation and model checking. However, Z has also two data types, free types and schema types, that have no counterpart in B. This means that some aspects of Z cannot be effectively translated into B machines, and require extensions of PROB. In the next section we present the overall architecture of our approach, as well as a formal explanation of how to derive a B model from a Z specification.

3   Architecture and the PROZ Compiler

In the previous section we have examined the basic ingredients of Z specifications, and have highlighted why Z specifications are inherently more difficult to animate and model check than B specifications. In this and the next section we explain how we have overcome those issues; in particular:

  – How to analyse the various schemas of Z specification, identifying the state of a Z specification, the state-changing operations and the basic user-defined data types (cf. Section 3.1).

```
MACHINE z_translation
SETS NAME;DATE
CONSTANTS maxentries
PROPERTIES
    (maxentries:INTEGER) & (maxentries>=5)
VARIABLES birthday, known
INVARIANT
    (birthday:POW(NAME*DATE)) & (known:POW(NAME))
INITIALISATION
  ANY birthday', known'
    WHERE
        (known':POW(NAME)) & (birthday':(NAME+->DATE))
      & (known'=dom(birthday')) & (card(known')<=maxentries)
      & (known'={})
    THEN
      birthday, known := birthday', known'
  END
OPERATIONS
  AddBirthday(date?, name?) =
    PRE (name?:NAME)
      & (date?:DATE)
      THEN
        ANY birthday', known'
          WHERE
              (known:POW(NAME)) & (birthday:(NAME+->DATE))
            & (known=dom(birthday)) & (card(known)<=maxentries)
            & (known':POW(NAME)) & (birthday':(NAME+->DATE))
            & (known'=dom(birthday')) & (card(known')<=maxentries)
            & (name?/:known) & (birthday'=(birthday\/{(name?,date?)}))
          THEN
            birthday, known := birthday', known'
        END
    END
END
```

Fig. 3. The translated birthday book example

- How to deal with the fact that Z specifications do not specify all changes to variables explicitly.
- How to deal with the new data types provided by Z.
- How to deal with new operators and constructs.

Overall Architecture. PROZ is an extension of PROB that supports Z specifications which can be parsed by the *f*UZZ typechecker. Those specifications are given as a LATEX file. When the user loads a specification into PROZ, the following steps are performed (see also Figure 4):

1. The specification is typechecked with *f*UZZ. *f*UZZ writes the formal content of the specification into a file which then is parsed by PROZ.

2. The different components of the specification (definition of constants, state, initialisation and operations) are identified.
3. All schemas are expanded and normalised, i.e., all schema inclusions are resolved and the type declarations of variables are strictly separated from constraints on their values.
4. PROZ then translates the specification to an internal representation of a B machine (with some small extensions, which are discussed later in the paper).
5. After the translation process PROB treats the specification the same way as other B machines are treated (with some extensions having been added to the PROB kernel).

Most of the expressions in Z have a direct counterpart in B, for those the translation in point 4 is just a conversion from one syntax into another. Some cases where there is more logic need in the translation process or where we extended the PROB interpreter are presented in Section 3.3. The support of two Z data types as discussed in the next section affects the translation process and requires extensions to the kernel as well.

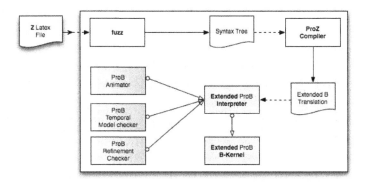

Fig. 4. Overview of PROZ Architecture

3.1   Identifying Components of the Specification

As we have seen in the previous sections, the purpose of the schemas in a specification is not stated formally. But to interpret a given specification for animation and model checking, we must identify which schemas describe the state space, the initialisation and the operations. To be able to do so, we require that the specification satisfies some rules:

- There must be a schema called *Init* for initialisation.
- *Init* includes exactly one other schema. The included schema will be taken as the description of the state space.
- A schema with all variables of the state and their primed versions, that is not included by any other schema, will be used as an operation.

The rules can be applied to the birthday book example in Fig. 1: There is a schema *Init* which includes *BirthdayBook*. Thus *Init* is the initialisation of the state which consists of *BirthdayBook*'s variables *known* and *birthday*. Expanding *AddBirthday* shows that it has all variables of the state and also the primed versions *known'* and *birthday'*. It is not included by any other schema. Thus PROZ would identify *AddBirthday* as an operation.

In the next two paragraphs we present two other components of a specification that are used by PROZ and explain how they relate to existing features of PROB.

Invariant. As seen in the comparison in Sect. 2.2, the B invariant has no direct counterpart in Z. But it can be useful to search for states that violate a certain property by model checking. To make this feature available for Z specifications, PROZ looks for a schema named *Invariant*. If such an invariant is given, its predicate is checked for every visited state in an animation or in model checking. The predicate is then used analogously to the invariant in B.

Axiomatic definitions. In our short introduction to Z we did not describe how global constants can be introduced in Z by *axiomatic definitions*. Like schemas, axiomatic definitions consist also of a declaration and a predicate part, but their declared variables can be used throughout the specification without a schema inclusion. E.g., we can define a constant *maxentries* which value is at least 5 with the axiomatic definition

$$
\begin{array}{|l}
\hline
maxentries : \mathbb{Z} \\
\hline
maxentries \geq 5 \\
\end{array}
$$

We interpret axiomatic definitions analogously to how PROB interprets the sections CONSTANTS and PROPERTIES in a B machine: The very first step of an animation or model checking—before the initialisation of the state variables—consists in finding values for the constants which satisfy the predicates of the axiomatic definitions. After this step the predicates of the axiomatic definitions can be ignored. To illustrate how the axiomatic definitions are handled, we added the definition above to the birthday book example and appended the predicate $\# known \leq maxentries$ to the schema *BirthdayBook* before translating the specification to the result in Figure 3.

3.2   Translating Initialisation and Operations from Z to B

The *initialisation* schema *Init* consists of the declaration of all state variables and a predicate I. We annotate T_v as the type of variable v.

$$
\begin{array}{|l}
\hline
\textit{Init} \\
\hline
x_1 : T_{x_1}; \ \ldots; x_n : T_{x_n} \\
\hline
I \\
\hline
\end{array}
$$

In B, the initialisation is a generalised substitution to all variables of the abstract machine. We can state "choose any values that satisfy I" with an ANY statement:

ANY $x'_1, \ldots, x'_n$
    WHERE $x'_1 \in T_{x_1} \wedge \ldots \wedge x'_n \in T_{x_n} \wedge$
    I'
    THEN $x_1, \ldots, x_n := x'_1, \ldots, x'_n$
END

Beside the predicate I, the WHERE clause of the ANY contains the type declaration of the variables. The types T_v and the predicate I are translated from Z to B syntax. Most of the types, predicates and expressions in Z have a direct counterpart in B and can be translated directly. In section 3.3 we show how we extended the B interpreter to support other constructs.

An *operation* schema Op declares in addition to the state variables $x_1, \ldots, x_n$ their primed counterparts $x'_1, \ldots, x'_n$ and variables for input $i_1?, \ldots, i_k?$ and output $o_1!, \ldots, o_l!$. The predicate P describes the effect of the operation.

$\boxed{\begin{array}{l} Op \\ \hline x_1 : T_{x_1}; \ \ldots; x_n : T_{x_n} \\ x'_1 : T_{x_1}; \ \ldots; x'_n : T_{x_n} \\ i_1? : T_{i_1}; \ \ldots; i_k? : T_{i_k} \\ o_1! : T_{o_1}; \ \ldots; o_l! : T_{o_l} \\ \hline P \end{array}}$

PROZ translates such a schema to a B operation of the form

$o^*_1!, \ldots, o^*_l! \leftarrow Op(i_1?, \ldots, i_k?) =$
    PRE $i_1 \in T_{i_1} \wedge \ldots \wedge i_k \in T_{i_k}$ THEN
        ANY $x'_1, \ldots, x'_n, o_1!, \ldots, o_l!$
            WHERE $x'_1 \in T_{x_1} \wedge \ldots \wedge x'_n \in T_{x_n} \wedge o_1! \in T_{o_1} \wedge \ldots \wedge o_l! \in T_{o_l} \wedge$
            P
            THEN $x_1, \ldots, x_n, o^*_1!, \ldots, o^*_l! := x'_1, \ldots, x'_n, o_1!, \ldots, o_l!$
        END
    END
END

Like in the initialisation the central part of the operation is an ANY statement with the predicate P, but additionally we have to consider the possible result values. The surrounding PRE statement is just for declaring the types of the operation's arguments.

Often operations change only a subset of the state variables. PROZ checks if terms like $x = x'$ occur in the predicate P. If such a term is found, we know that x does not change and so we can remove the substitution $x := x'$. Also we can replace all occurrences of x' by x in P. Then x' is not used anymore in the statement and can be removed. If parts of the state or the complete state are not modified by an operation, the expression $\theta S = \theta S'$ is often used, where S is a schema containing all variables that should not change. ΞS is an abbreviation for including ΔS and stating $\theta S = \theta S'$. Those expressions are transformed into $s_1 = s_1' \wedge \ldots \wedge s_n = s_m'$ with $s_1, \ldots, s_m$ as the variables of S. This way the simplification of the ANY statement is also working with θ-expressions.

3.3   New Constructs and Operators

Some constructs of Z's mathematical language do not have a direct counterpart in B, and below we show how we have treated those.

Translation of Comprehension Sets. A comprehension set has the form $\{ Decl \mid Pred \}$ and specifies a set with a declaration of variables and a predicate. E.g., the expression $\{ i : \mathbb{N} \mid i \geq 5 \}$ is the set of all numbers greater or equal to 5. This kind of comprehension sets is also supported by B, but Z has an extended syntax of the form $\{ Decl \mid Pred \bullet Expr \}$. E.g., the set $\{ i : \mathbb{N} \mid i \geq 5 \bullet i \ast i \}$ is the set of all square numbers greater or equal to 25. We translate such comprehension sets as follows. Let T be the type of $Expr$, then we express $\{ Decl \mid Pred \bullet Expr \}$ by $\{ v : T \mid (\exists Decl \mid v = Expr \wedge Pred) \}$ and translate this into B.

Extensions to the B Interpreter. The following expressions are not easily translatable to B (or would entail a considerable efficiency penalty), and hence extensions were made to the PROB interpreter to support an extended B syntax:

- We added an **if**-expression to the standard B syntax. While B contains a substitution IF − THEN − ELSE, it can not be used as an expression that yields a value. The **if** expression of Z resembles to the ternary ? : operator known in C or Java.
- The **let** in Z can be used as an expression or as a predicate. Both can not be stated directly in B, which again only has the **LET** as a substitution.
- The operations $\restriction$ (extraction) and $\upharpoonright$ (filter) on sequences are defined with the function *squash*. We added the *squash* function to the interpreter.
- We added the definite description quantifier μ.

4   New Types

To deal with the Z specifications we have seen so far, it was sufficient to translate Z to B, possibly with some some syntactic extensions. There are, however, two important features of Z which cannot be effectively dealt with in that way: Z's schema and free types. Supporting those features in an effective manner requires a fundamental addition to the core datatypes of the PROB kernel.

Overview of the PROB-kernel. The PROB kernel is responsible for storing and finding values for the values of the variables in a specification. In order to avoid naive enumeration of possible values, the PROB kernel is written in Prolog works in multiple phases (controlled by Prolog's `when` co-routining mechanism). In the first phase, only deterministic propagations are performed (e.g., the predicate $x = 1$ will be evaluated but the predicates $x \in I\!N$ will suspend until they either become deterministic or until the second phase starts). In the second phase, a restricted class of non-deterministic enumerations will be performed. For example, the predicate $x \in \{a, b\}$ will suspend during the first phase but will lead to two solutions $x = a$ and $x = b$ during the second phase. In the final phase, *all* variables, parameters and constants that are still undetermined (or partially determined) are enumerated.

New Data types. Adding a new basic data type to the kernel requires the extension of four Prolog predicates: `equal_object` to check two objects for equality, `not_equal_object` to check two objects for disequality, one predicate to type check an object and one predicate to enumerate all possible values of an object given its type. So far the kernel supported basic user-defined types (defined in B's SET clause), integers, pairs and sets (relations are represented as sets of pairs). Below, we present two new data types, schema types and free types, which are needed for Z.

4.1   Schema Types

In Z each schema defines a new data type, a *schema type* which resembles record types known from other languages. Basically, a record data value $rec(f)$ consists of a list $f = [n_1/v_1, \ldots, n_k/v_k]$ of field names n_i along with values v_i for each field. We require that all field names are sorted alphabetically. Two record values are identical iff they have the exact same field names and all field values are identical. In the kernel this gives rise to two new inference rules:

$$\frac{x_1 = y_1 \quad \ldots \quad x_k = y_k \qquad n_1 < n_2 < \ldots < n_k}{rec([n_1/x_1, \ldots, n_k/x_k]) = rec([n_1/y_1, \ldots, n_k/y_k])}$$

$$\frac{x_i \neq y \qquad 0 \leq i \leq k \qquad n_1 < n_2 < \ldots < n_k}{rec([n_1/x_1, \ldots, n_i/x_i, \ldots, n_k/x_k]) \neq rec([n_1/x_1, \ldots, n_i/y, \ldots, n_k/x_k])}$$

The type of a record contains the name of the fields and the types of each field. This gives rise to two new inference rules for type inference and enumeration, where we use the k-ary type constructor *Record* for records with k-fields:

$$\frac{x_1 : \tau_1 \quad \ldots \quad x_k : \tau_k \qquad n_1 < n_2 < \ldots < n_k}{rec([n_1/x_1, \ldots, n_k/x_k]) : Record(n_1/\tau_1, \ldots, n_k/\tau_k)}$$

$$\frac{x_1 \in enum(\tau_1) \quad \ldots \quad x_k \in enum(\tau_k) \qquad n_1 < n_2 < \ldots < n_k}{rec([n_1/x_1, \ldots, n_k/x_k]) \in enum(Record(n_1/\tau_1, \ldots, n_k/\tau_k))}$$

Classical B does not have a record type, but a record type extension and syntax has been introduced by the tool Atelier-B [27].[1] In extending the kernel, PROB now also supports those records in B.

---

[1] See also [11] for a theoretical foundation of records.

Note that in Z, possible instances of a schema type (the *bindings*) can be further constrained by the predicates of the schema. E.g. the schema

$$ExampleRecord \cong [\, x, y : \mathbb{Z} \mid x < y \,]$$

can be used as a record with the constraint $x < y$. The kernel does not support this directly, instead an unconstrained record $[\, x, y : \mathbb{Z} \,]$ can be used. We show how the constraints can be preserved in the translation process by *normalisation*.

PROZ normalises all schemas of a specification, i.e. it strictly separates type information and additional predicates on the instances. E.g. the normalised form of the schema $[\, x : \{1, 2, 3\} \,]$ is $[\, x : \mathbb{Z} \mid x \in \{1, 2, 3\} \,]$. Given a normalised schema $A \cong [\, Decl \mid Pred \,]$, we define $A^* \cong [\, Decl \,]$ as the schema with just the type information and without any additional constraints. If A is used as a type for a variable v, in the normalisation process it is split into the type A^* and the additional constraint $v \in \{\, Decl \mid Pred \bullet \theta A \,\}$. Because the type A^* does not have further constraints, it's supported by the kernel. The constraint had been made explicit by the normalisation and can be translated to B. The used θ-operator creates an instance of type A. We can translate it directly to a record constructor.

4.2 Free Types

Another feature of the Z notation is the definition of *free types*. E.g.,

$$T ::= empty \mid value\langle\!\langle \{1, 2, 3\} \rangle\!\rangle$$

defines a new data type T with a constant value *empty* and a constructor function *value* which maps values from $\{1, 2, 3\}$ to T. Contrary to schema types, free types can also be recursive, as in the following example, defining a binary tree with integers:

$$BinTree ::= empty \mid leaf\langle\!\langle \mathbb{Z} \rangle\!\rangle \mid node\langle\!\langle BinTree \times \mathbb{Z} \times BinTree \rangle\!\rangle$$

In Z, free types are only syntactic sugar and can also be expressed with axiomatic definitions and basic types. But for the purpose of animating the specification it is essential for efficiency to implement this type directly.

There is no counterpart for free types in B, so we extended the PROB core. The representation of data values and the inference rules for equality and typing are similar to record types; one just needs to also store the constructor used (e.g., in the case of T above we need to know whether we are in the case *empty* or in the case *value*). Two free type data values are thus identical iff they have the same constructor and if the values for that constructor are identical.

Free type definitions can be made recursive, so the implementation of enumeration must prevent the generation of infinitely many values. We solved this by introducing a maximum recursion depth when enumerating free types. The maximum is adjustable by the user. The introduction of a maximum recursion depth has the effect that the model checker might not find all possible solutions (similarly to integer variables whose enumeration is restricted to MININT..MAXINT).

The PROB interpreter is extended by a constructor *FreeConstructor* for creating instance values of free types. The arguments are the free type, the case (*empty* or *value* in the T example) and the tuple containing the arguments to the constructor. Also there is the inverse of the constructor *FreeDestructor*, which takes a free type instance and returns the type, the case and the tuple of arguments. Finally, we have a predicate *FreeCase* that takes the identifier of a case and a free type instance as arguments and evaluates to true if the free type value has the given case.

The kernel itself does not support constraints on the values of a constructor. In the T example above the type of the constructor *value* is $\mathbb{Z}$ but the domain constrained to $\{1, 2, 3\}$. Like with the schema types, the constraints have to be handled separately in the translation. This is done by normalisation as follows.

Given a free type F of the form

$$F ::= c_1 \mid \ldots \mid c_n \mid d_1 \langle\!\langle S_1 \rangle\!\rangle \mid \ldots \mid d_m \langle\!\langle S_m \rangle\!\rangle$$

we define the type F^* which has just the type information of F without other constraints, where T_i is the underlying type of S_i (e.g. $S_i = \{1, 2, 3\} \Rightarrow T_i = \mathbb{Z}$):

$$F^* ::= c_1 \mid \ldots \mid c_n \mid d_1^* \langle\!\langle T_1 \rangle\!\rangle \mid \ldots \mid d_m^* \langle\!\langle T_m \rangle\!\rangle$$

Then we convert F and the constructors d_i, $1 \leq i \leq m$ to

$$\begin{aligned} F ==\ & \{\, x : F^* \mid \\ & x \in \operatorname{ran} d_1^* \Rightarrow d_1^{*\sim}(x) \in S_1 \wedge \ldots \wedge x \in \operatorname{ran} d_m^* \Rightarrow d_m^{*\sim}(x) \in S_m \,\} \\ d_i ==\ & (\lambda\, x : T_i \mid x \in S_i \bullet d_i^*(x)) \end{aligned}$$

The schema normalisation transforms a variable v of type F to a variable of type F^* and adds the constraint $v \in F$.

The transformed example would be

$$\begin{aligned} T^* ::=\ & empty \mid value^* \langle\!\langle \mathbb{Z} \rangle\!\rangle \\ T ==\ & \{\, x : T^* \mid x \in \operatorname{ran} value^* \Rightarrow value^{*\sim}(x) \in \{1, 2, 3\} \,\} \\ value ==\ & (\lambda\, x : \mathbb{Z} \mid x \in \{1, 2, 3\} \bullet value^*(x)) \end{aligned}$$

Finally, expressions of the form $x \in \operatorname{ran} d_i^*$ are translated to the predicate *FreeCase*(F, d_i^*, x) and constructor calls of the form $d_i^*(x)$ are translated to *FreeConstructor*(F^*, d_i^*, x) (resp. the inverse $d_i^{*\sim}(y)$ is translated to the expression *FreeDestructor*(F^*, d_i^*, y)). The result can then be dealt with by the extended PROB interpreter and kernel.

5   Case study

The case study was inspired by a real industrial example. The specifications are very high level and, using the guidelines from [13], were not destined to be refined into code. These Z specifications thus[2] provide a particular challenge for our tool. Below we present two sub-components of the system, the challenges in animating and validating them, as well as an indication on the errors located by our tool.

5.1   Route Calculation

The *route calculation* component is a key component of the overall system, containing several intricate algorithmic aspects. It is important to ascertain the correctness of the algorithms (e.g., before proceeding with an implementation).

This system component calculates routes through a given geometry. The geometry (mainly places and roads) is stored in the system state. The main part of the specification consists of the definition of a function that takes a route as input. The input route is a sequence that starts and ends with a place and between both is a list of places or roads. The result of the function is the *expansion* of the route, i.e. the sequence of all places that lie between the first and the last place. E.g., in the given geometry in figure 5 the expansion of $\langle Bicester, A34, M4, Swindon \rangle$ is $\langle Bicester, Oxford, NewburyRoundabout, Swindon \rangle$. For sake of simplicity we ignore below the connections which are not roads. The expansion function is constructed by combining several other functions, which do not work directly on the input route. Instead a record is created that contains the original route, information about which part has already been

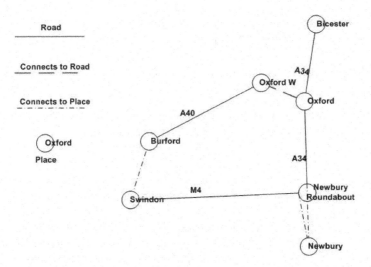

Fig. 5. An example geometry

---

[2] Some of the features of B, such as generalised union, are rarely used in formal refinements as the existing B provers do not support them very well. It is our experience that formal B specifications that are refined to code are easier to animate than more liberal specifications.

processed, the result so far, and a set of errors. An error could be "no connection found", for example. A recursive function (Fig. 6) expands every single element in the route until the complete route is expanded or an error is found. In total the specification consists of 8 function definitions which are combined to calculate the result. Most of these functions are defined by comprehension sets.

Due to the complexity of the defined functions, it was not feasible to enumerate them (i.e., to store all possible inputs and outputs). Fortunately, PROB [22] has the ability to compile these kind of definitions into *symbolic* closures, which are evaluated and expanded on demand. For example, given a set comprehension $S = \{x \mid x \in I\!\!N \Rightarrow P\}$ and the condition $y \in S$ the Kernel will "only" check that P holds for $x = y$ and *not* compute the entire set S. A similar situation arises for lambda abstractions. Take for example, $f = \lambda x.(x \in I\!\!N \mid E)$. In that case, to evaluate $f(y)$ the Kernel "only" evaluates E with y substituted for x and *not* the entire function f.[3] The kernel, even supports recursive function definitions, such as the one presented in Fig. 6.

Storing comprehensions sets and λ-expressions symbolically was an essential feature to allow the animation of the specification. By integrating PROZ into PROB we inherit this feature, which allows us to validate this specification.

ExpandElems

    $ExpandElemexpandElems : Expansion \nrightarrow Expansion$

$expandElems = \{ \, \Delta Expansion \mid$
    $\theta Expansion' = \textbf{if } error \neq \varnothing \vee currentElem \notin \mathrm{dom}\, proposedRoute$
      $\textbf{then } \theta Expansion$
      $\textbf{else } expandElems(expandElem(\theta Expansion)) \; \bullet$
    $\theta Expansion \mapsto \theta Expansion' \, \}$

Fig. 6. Example: The recursive definition of the function *expandElems*

To make an animation possible, the system was initialised with test data that describes a map with six cities. Running the animation the user can simply click on the *AddElement* operations to construct an input and sees immediately the result. Figure 7 shows a screenshot of the animator after entering the route "Newbury $\rightarrow$ A34 $\rightarrow$ Bicester". In the middle the list of enabled operations can be seen where the *Expand* operation contains the solution (which is truncated in the screenshot).

The animation of the specification quickly exhibited one error in the specification. For each road a sequence of places to which it connects is stored in the geometry. When a route contains a road, the entry and exit points are calculated and the section between both is appended to the result. But under certain circumstances the section was appended in the wrong direction so that

---

[3] Some expressions, however, will require the computation of the entire function (e.g., $dom(f) \subseteq SetA$). In those circumstances the kernel converts the symbolic form into explicit form.

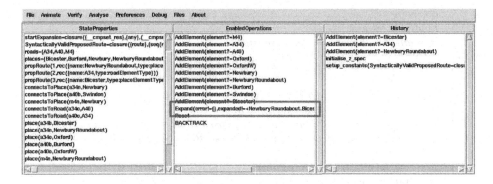

Fig. 7. Animation of the route calculation

the route "Newbury → A34 → Bicester" was calculated to "Newbury → Bicester → Oxford → Newbury → Bicester" instead of the much simpler correct solution "Newbury → Oxford → Bicester".

Figure 8 shows the function containing the error. The result of the expression (in the third **let** expression)

$$(\textbf{if } entry > exit \textbf{ then } exit \mathinner{.\,.} entry \textbf{ else } entry \mathinner{.\,.} exit) \upharpoonright roadPlaces(r)$$

are all places on the road r that are between $entry$ and $exit$. If $roadPlaces(r)$ is the sequence $\langle a, b, c, d, e \rangle$, $entry$ is 4 and $exit$ is 2, than the result is $\langle b, c, d \rangle$. Although the case $entry > exit$ is covered explicitly in the specification, it has been forgotten to reverse the resulting sequence to $\langle d, c, b \rangle$.

For this application we did not yet use the model checking facilities of PROZ, because we have no further properties about the result of the algorithm (and hence no way to automatically check the correctness of the result). But the animator alone gives the user a powerful tool to get more insight in the behaviour of a specification, as the quick detection of errors showed.

5.2   Network Protocol

A second important component of the overall system implements access control to a shared resource, employing a simple network protocol. A number of work-stations are connected via a network and share are critical resource. Whenever a workstation wants to access the resource it has to send a request to the other workstations. The protocol should assure that only one workstation can be in the critical section at the same time.

The specification distinguishes between the state and behaviour of the work-stations and the the state and behaviour of the underlying middleware.

The specification of the middleware is the description of an existing system. Its state space consists of a sent and received buffer for each workstation. Messages can be added to a sent buffer, transferred between workstations and removed from a received buffer to deliver it to the workstation.

┌─ *ExpandRoad* ──
│ *FindConnections*
│ *expandRoad* : *Expansion* ⇸ *Expansion*
├──
│ *expandRoad* = {*r* : *ElementName*; *ExpansionOp* |
│   *r* ∈ *RoadName* ∧
│   (*proposedRoute*(*currentElem*)).*type* = *roadElementType* ∧
│   (*proposedRoute*(*currentElem*)).*name* = *r* ∧
│   (**let** *entries* == *findConnections*(*r*, *proposedRoute*(*currentElem* − 1));
│   *exits* == *findConnections*(*r*, *proposedRoute*(*currentElem* + 1)) •
│   ((*entries* = ∅ ∨ *exits* = ∅)
│   ∧ *error*′ = {*noConnection*} ∧ *expandedRoute*′ = ⟨⟩) ∨
│   (**let** *entry* == *min*(*entries*); *exit* == *min*(*exits*) •
│   (**let** *placesToAdd* == (**if** *entry* > *exit* **then** *exit* .. *entry*
│   **else** *entry* .. *exit*) ↾ *roadPlaces*(*r*) ⨟ *place* •
│   *expandedRoute*′ = **if** *last expandedRoute* = *head placesToAdd*
│   **then** *expandedRoute* ⌢ *tail placesToAdd*
│   **else** *expandedRoute* ⌢ *placesToAdd* ∧
│   *error*′ = ∅))) •
│   *θExpansion* ↦ *θExpansion*′}
└──

Fig. 8. The definition of the function *expandRoad* containing an error

The specification of the workstation defines their current states (*idle*, *waiting*, *editing* or *failed*) and their operations. They can send requests to the other workstations, read their responses, read other requests and send responses.

The components from both parts of the definitions are combined by using the schema calculus. Especially the pipe operator (≫) was used to connect operations, where the result of one operation serves as the input for another operation. E.g. when a workstation sends a request, the operation describing the workstation behaviour outputs a message that is taken by a middleware operation as input:

$$RequestOK \mathrel{\widehat{=}} RequestWorkstationOK \gg AcceptMsgMiddleware$$

A screenshot of the animator is shown in Fig. 9. On the left side the current state is displayed. It can be seen that workstation 1 is waiting for a response of workstation 2, workstation 2 is in editing mode and workstation 3 is idle. Also a message is still in the sent buffer of workstation 1.

Free types are used in the specification for distinguishing the different modes of a workstation. *wsIdle* and *wsEditing* are constants of the free type, whereas *wsWaiting* is a constructor, e.g. *wsWaiting*({1, 3}) refers to the state "waiting for workstations 1 and 3".

First we used the model checker to find deadlocks in the protocol. It found a deadlock that was caused by an error in the specification. It was possible that a workstation could ignore a rejected request. The same error caused a situation where more than one workstation was in the critical section.

Fig. 9. Animation of the network protocol

We added an *Invariant* schema to the specification to check automatically if more than one workstation is in the editing mode (*wsState* is a function defined in the schema *Workstations* that maps each workstation to its mode, and the operator $\triangleright$ is used to restrict it to all entries which map to *wsEditing*):

$$Invariant \; \widehat{=} \; [\; Workstations \; | \; \#(wsState \triangleright \{wsEditing\}) \leq 1 \,]$$

The model checker was able to find states where the invariant was violated. Another error was found: Every response to a request was treated as if it was a grant, even rejections.

The model checker was not able to do an exhaustive search of the state space because the message buffers in the model are not limited.

6   Discussion, Related and Future Work

Limitations Z is a very large and extensive formal method, with many features and extension. While we provide a tool that can animate a considerable subset of Z, some of Z's features are obviously not yet supported:

- Bags (multisets) are not supported.
- Some expressions like disjoint and partition are not yet implemented.
- Generic definitions cannot be used in a specification yet. We plan to support them by determining with wich types a generic definition is used, and then creating for each such type a separate axiomatic definition.

Related and Future Work. On the theoretical side, there are several works discussing the relationship and translations between Z and B [9,10] or weakest precondition semantics [4].

On the practical side, several animators for Z exist, such as [29], which presents an animator for Z implemented in Mercury, as well as the Possum animation tool [14]. Another animator for Z is ZANS [17]. It has been developed in C++ and unlike PROB only supports deterministic operations (called explicit in [17]). The more recent Jaza tool by Mark Utting [28] looks very promising. There has also been a recent push [24] to provide more tool support for Z. However, to our knowledge, no existing Z animator can deal with the recursive higher-order functions present in our case study.

The most closely related work on the B side is [6,3,18], which uses a special purpose constraint solver over sets (CLPS) to animate B and Z specifications using the so-called BZ-Testing-Tools. However, the focus of these tools is test-case generation and not verification, and the subset of B that is supported is comparatively smaller (e.g., no set comprehensions or lambda abstractions, constants and properties nor multiple machines are supported).

Another very popular tool for validating specifications and models is Alloy [15], which makes use SAT solvers (rather than constraint solving). However, the specification language of Alloy is first-order and thus cannot be applied "out of the box" to our motivating industrial example.

Conclusion. In this paper we presented PROZ, a tool for animating and model checking Z specifications. We pursued an approach to translate Z specifications to B, reusing the existing PROB toolset as much as possible. Some extensions to the PROB core were required (e.g., for free types and schema types), after which we have obtained an integrated tool that is now capable to animate and validate Z and B specifications. In principle our tool could now validate combined B/Z specifications,[4] and as a side effect we have added support for B specifications with records. By integrating PROZ with PROB our tool has also inherited from the recent developments and improvements originally devised for B, such as visualisation of large state spaces [23], integration with CSP [8], symmetry reduction [21], and symbolic validation of recursive functions [22].

Our tool was successfully applied to examples which were based on industrial specifications and also revealed several errors. Especially PROZ's ability to store comprehensions sets symbolically was essential to make the animations of those specifications possible.

Acknowledgements. We would like to thank Anthony Hall for his very helpful contributions and feedback on the paper.

References

1. Abrial, J.-R.: The B-Book. Cambridge University Press, Cambridge (1996)
2. Abrial, J.-R., Schuman, S.A., Meyer, B.: Specification language. In: McKeag, R.M., Macnaghten, A.M. (eds.) On the Construction of Programs: An Advanced Course, pp. 343–410. Cambridge University Press, Cambridge (1980)
3. Ambert, F., Bouquet, F., Chemin, S., Guenaud, S., Legeard, B., Peureux, F., Utting, M., Vacelet, N.: BZ-testing-tools: A tool-set for test generation from Z and B using constraint logic programming. In: Proceedings of FATES'02, Formal Approaches to Testing of Software, pp. 105–120, August 2002, Technical Report, INRIA (2002)
4. Ana Cavalcanti, J.W.: A weakest precondition semantics for z. The. Computer Journal 41(1), 1–15 (1998)

---

[4] It is not clear to us whether this has any practical benefit.

5. U.B-Core (UK) Limited, Oxon. B-Toolkit, On-line manual (1999) Available at http://www.b-core.com/ONLINEDOC/Contents.html

6. Bouquet, F., Legeard, B., Peureux, F.: CLPS-B - a constraint solver for B. In: Katoen, J.-P., Stevens, P. (eds.) ETAPS 2002 and TACAS 2002. LNCS, vol. 2280, pp. 188–204. Springer, Heidelberg (2002)

7. Bowen, J.P.: Formal Specification and Documentation using Z. International Thomson Computer Press (1996)

8. Butler, M., Leuschel, M.: Combining CSP and B for specification and property verification. In: Fitzgerald, J.A., Hayes, I.J., Tarlecki, A. (eds.) FM 2005. LNCS, vol. 3582, pp. 221–236. Springer, Heidelberg (2005)

9. Diller, A., Docherty, R.: Z and abstract machine notation: A comparison. In: User, Z. (ed.) Z User Workshop, pp. 250–263 (1994)

10. Dunne, S.: Understanding object-z operations as generalised substitutions. In: Boiten, E.A., Derrick, J., Smith, G.P. (eds.) IFM 2004. LNCS, vol. 2999, pp. 328–342. Springer, Heidelberg (2004)

11. Evans, N., Butler, M.: A proposal for records in event-b. In: Misra, J., Nipkow, T., Sekerinski, E. (eds.) FM 2006. LNCS, vol. 4085, pp. 221–235. Springer, Heidelberg (2006)

12. Hall, A.: Correctness by construction: Integrating formality into a commercial development process. In: Eriksson, L.-H., Lindsay, P.A. (eds.) FME 2002. LNCS, vol. 2391, pp. 224–233. Springer, Heidelberg (2002)

13. Hall, J.A.: Seven myths of formal methods. IEEE Software 7(5), 11–19 (1990)

14. Hazel, D., Strooper, P., Traynor, O.: Requirements engineering and verification using specification animation. Automated Software Engineering 00, 302 (1998)

15. Jackson, D.: Alloy: A lightweight object modelling notation. ACM Transactions on Software Engineering and Methodology (TOSEM) 11, 256–290 (2002)

16. Jacky, J.: The Way of Z: Practical Programming with Formal Methods. Cambridge University Press, Cambridge (1997)

17. Jia, X.: An approach to animating Z specifications. Available at http://venus.cs.depaul.edu/fm/zans.html

18. Legeard, B., Peureux, F., Utting, M.: Automated boundary testing from Z and B. In: Eriksson, L.-H., Lindsay, P.A. (eds.) FME 2002. LNCS, vol. 2391, pp. 21–40. Springer, Heidelberg (2002)

19. Leuschel, M., Butler, M.: Pro B: A model checker for B. In: Araki, K., Gnesi, S., Mandrioli, D. (eds.) FME 2003. LNCS, vol. 2805, pp. 855–874. Springer, Heidelberg (2003)

20. Leuschel, M., Butler, M.: Automatic refinement checking for B. In: Lau, K.-K., Banach, R. (eds.) ICFEM 2005. LNCS, vol. 3785, pp. 345–359. Springer, Heidelberg (2005)

21. Leuschel, M., Butler, M., Spermann, C., Turner, E.: Symmetry reduction for B by permutation flooding. In: Julliand, J., Kouchnarenko, O. (eds.) B 2007. LNCS, vol. 4355, pp. 79–93. Springer, Heidelberg (2006)

22. Leuschel, M., Cansell, D., Butler, M.: Validating and animating higher-order recursive functions in B. Submitted; preliminary version presented at Dagstuhl Seminar 06191 Rigorous Methods for Software Construction and Analysis (2006)

23. Leuschel, M., Turner, E.: Visualizing larger states spaces in P ro B. In: Treharne, H., King, S., Henson, M.C., Schneider, S. (eds.) ZB 2005. LNCS, vol. 3455, pp. 6–23. Springer, Heidelberg (2005)

24. Malik, P., Utting, M.: CZT: A framework for Z tools. In: Treharne, H., King, S., Henson, M.C., Schneider, S. (eds.) ZB 2005. LNCS, vol. 3455, pp. 65–84. Springer, Heidelberg (2005)

25. Spivey, J.M.: The Fuzz Manual. `http://spivey.oriel.ox.ac.uk/mike/fuzz`
26. Spivey, J.M.: The Z Notation: A Reference Manual. Prentice Hall International Series in Computer Science, vol. 2. Prentice-Hall, Englewood Cliffs (1992)
27. Steria, F.: Aix-en-Provence. Atelier B, User and Reference Manuals (1996) Available at http://www.atelierb.societe.com/index_uk.html
28. Utting, M.: Data structures for Z testing tools. In FM-TOOLS 2000 conference, July 2000, in TR 2000-07, Information Faculty, University of Ulm (2000)
29. Winikoff, M., Dart, P., Kazmierczak, E.: Rapid prototyping using formal specifications. In: Proceedings of the 21st Australasian Computer Science Conference, Perth, Australia, February 1998, pp. 279–294 (1998)

Verification of Multi-agent Negotiations Using the Alloy Analyzer

Rodion Podorozhny[1], Sarfraz Khurshid[2], Dewayne Perry[2], and Xiaoqin Zhang[3]

[1] Texas State University, San Marcos, TX 78666
rp31@txstate.edu
[2] The University of Texas, Austin, TX 78712
{khurshid,perry}@ece.utexas.edu
[3] The University of Massachusetts, North Dartmouth, MA 02747
x2zhang@umassd.edu

Abstract. Multi-agent systems provide an increasingly popular solution in problem domains that require management of uncertainty and a high degree of adaptability. Robustness is a key design criterion in building multi-agent systems. We present a novel approach for the design of robust multi-agent systems. Our approach constructs a model of the design of a multi-agent system in Alloy, a declarative language based on relations, and checks the properties of the model using the Alloy Analyzer, a fully automatic analysis tool for Alloy models. While several prior techniques exist for checking properties of multi-agent systems, the novelty of our work is that we can check properties of coordination and interaction, as well as properties of complex data structures that the agents may internally be manipulating or even sharing. This is the first application of Alloy to checking properties of multi-agent systems. Such unified analysis has not been possible before. We also introduce the use of a formal method as an integral part of testing and validation.

1 Introduction

Multi-agent systems provide an increasingly popular solution in problem domains that require management of uncertainty and high degree of adaptability. Robustness is a key design criterion in building multi-agent systems.

A common definition of a multi-agent system (MAS) [26] stipulates that an agent is an autonomous, interacting and intelligent (i.e. optimizing its actions) entity. Any MAS is a distributed system but not every distributed system can be categorized as a MAS by the above mentioned definition.

Management of uncertainty via adaptability and an ability to provide a satisficing solution to otherwise intractable problems are distinguishing features of multi-agent systems compared to centralized or other distributed systems. An agent knows of a great variety of methods to solve their local tasks, and it can tailor a method of achieving a goal according to resource availability for data processing, information exchanges and sources of information. Agents, due to their interactions, are capable of influencing the choices of methods both by themselves and by other agents due to recognition of various kinds of relationships between their subtasks that can be generalized as redundancy,

J. Davies and J. Gibbons (Eds.): IFM 2007, LNCS 4591, pp. 501–517, 2007.

facilitation and enabling [19]. Agents can decide the degree to which an environment state, their own state, and their partial knowledge about states of other agents influence the amount of their contribution to the solution of a task imposed on the whole MAS. Unlike components of other distributed systems, an agent can refuse a request or can choose not to answer. At the same time, other agents are prepared to deal with a possibility that their requests will be refused or not answered. This freedom of choice, in a way, defines an agent's autonomy and distinguishes it from a component in a conventional distributed system. Thus, due to the above mentioned capabilities, agents are able to adapt their solution methods to the dynamics of the environment [17].

Some MAS have explicit specifications of interaction protocols between the agents. There has been a plethora of work on verification of MAS systems. Such approaches as model-checking ([27], [21], [16], [3]), Petri-nets and situation-calculus [8] have been applied to MAS verification. The vast majority of recent work on MAS verification are various applications of model checking that take into account peculiarities of properties that are desired to be verified in a MAS. The peculiarities of such properties usually are a consequence of bounded rationality in agents. Thus the set of operators (modalities) for property specifications is often extended to include such operators as agent *beliefs, desires, intentions*. Once such additional operators are introduced, usually a method is suggested to map a property specification that uses these MAS-specific operators into a formalism understood by off-the-shelf model-checkers, e.g. into the propositional LTL.

Examples of properties might be: "every request for a quote is answered within 4 time steps" [3], "for all paths in each state if agent *Train1* is in the tunnel then agent *Train1* knows that agent *Train2* is not in the tunnel" [16], "when sender is about to send an acknowledgment then it knows that the receiver knows the value of the bit that was most recently sent" [21] and "some agent A_i eventually comes to believe that A_j intends that A_i believes variable a has the value 10" [27].

As we can see from these examples most properties are some sort of reachability properties on a state transition model of a MAS. The use of model checking for these properties is understandable since it is essentially an efficient brute-force global state transition graph reachability analysis. ConGolog [8] uses situation calculus which is also most suited for the specification and analysis of event sequences, not data structures.

One lightweight formal method that is particularly suitable for checking properties of data structures is Alloy.

Most of the prior applications of the Alloy Analyzer have abstracted away from properties of multi-threaded systems. We explore the use of Alloy in designing, testing and validating a class of distributed systems known as the *multi-agent systems* (MAS). In particular we focus on exploring the suitability of the Alloy Analyzer to checking structurally rich properties of MAS.

In case of a model checking approach one needs to generate a number of particular instances of data structures either by hand or by writing a dedicated generator. For complex data structures the size of such an enumeration can be prohibitively large. Moreover, writing a generator correctly can itself be error-prone [22]. In contrast, the Alloy approach allows verification of rich structural properties, such as acyclicity of a binary tree, via capturing them in a simple first-order logic formula based on intuitive path expressions.

We explore an application of Alloy with its relational logic specification language to multi-agent systems specifically focusing on properties of data structures in addition to event sequences. We expect to be able to check properties of the following format: "if agent A receives a data structure that satisfies property ϕ then eventually agent A will enter state σ_a if it believes that agent B is in state σ_b", "if agent A is in state σ_a and its task structure τ_1 satisfies property ϕ_1 then on reception of data structure m (from agent B) agent A will modify τ_1 with some part of m such that τ_1 will preserve property ϕ_1" and so on.

We also propose the use of a formal method for checking actual behavior of a system as exhibited by its execution traces against a behavior of its model. This is done in addition to the usual application of a formal method for verification of the system's model. Thus we integrate a formal method into testing and validation activities of a software design and analysis process.

We make the following contributions:

- **Checking multi-agent systems.** We present an approach to check a *utility-based reasoning* multi-agent system using a lightweight formal method;
- **Alloy application.** We present a novel application of the Alloy tool-set in checking rich properties that represent structural constraints in a multi-threaded scenario; and
- **Adequacy checking.** Our approach allows checking the adequacy of a given test suite against a relational specification.

2   Brief Overview of Alloy

As software systems steadily grow in complexity and size, designing such systems manually becomes more and more error-prone. The last few years have seen a new generation of design tools that allow formulating designs formally, as well as checking their correctness to detect crucial flaws that, if not corrected, could lead to massive failures.

The Alloy tool-set provides a software design framework that enables the modeling of crucial design properties as well as checking them. Alloy [13] is a first-order, declarative language based on relations. The Alloy Analyzer [15] provides a fully automatic analysis for checking properties of Alloy models.

The Alloy language provides a convenient notation based on path expressions and quantifiers, which allow a succinct and intuitive formulation of a range of useful properties, including rich structural properties of software. The Alloy Analyzer performs a bounded exhaustive analysis using propositional satisfiability (SAT) solvers. Given an Alloy formula and a *scope*, i.e., a bound on the universe of discourse, the analyzer translates the Alloy formula into a boolean formula in conjunctive normal form (CNF), and solves it using an off-the-shelf SAT solver.

The Alloy tool-set has been used successfully to check designs of various applications, such as Microsoft's Common Object Modeling interface for interprocess communication [5], the Intentional Naming System for resource discovery in mobile networks [1], and avionics systems [7], as well as designs of cancer therapy machines [14].

The Alloy language provides a convenient notation based on path expressions and quantifiers, which allow a succinct and intuitive formulation of a range of useful properties, including rich structural properties of software. Much of Alloy's utility, however, comes from its fully automatic analyzer, which performs a bounded exhaustive analysis using propositional satisfiability (SAT) solvers. Given an Alloy formula and a *scope*, i.e., a bound on the universe of discourse, the analyzer translates the Alloy formula into a boolean formula in conjunctive normal form (CNF), and solves it using an off-the-shelf SAT solver.

We present an example to introduce the basics of Alloy.

Let us review the following Alloy code for a DAG definition:

```
module models/examples/tutorial/dagDefSmall

sig DAG {
  root: Node,
  nodes: set Node,
  edges: Node -> Node
}
sig Node {}
```

The keyword `module` names a model. A `sig` declaration introduces a set of (indivisible) atoms; the signatures `DAG` and `Node` respectively declare a set of DAG atoms and a set of node atoms. The *fields* of a signature declare relations. The field `root` defines a relationship of type `DAG x Node` indicating that only one node can correspond to a DAG by this relationship. The absence of any keyword makes `size` a total function: each list must have a size. The field `nodes` has the same type as `nodes` but maps a DAG onto a set of nodes defining a partial function. Alloy provides the keyword `set` to declare an arbitrary relation. The field `edges` maps a DAG onto a relationship, i.e. on a set of tuples `Node x Node`, thus defining edges.

The following *fact* constrains a graph to be a DAG:

```
fact DAGDef {
  nodes = root.*edges
  all m: Node | m !in m.^edges
}
```

The operator '`*`' denotes reflexive transitive closure. The expression `root.*edges` represents the set of all nodes reachable from the root following zero or more traversals along the `edge` field. A universally quantified (`all`) formula stipulates that no atom m of signature `Node` can appear in traversals originating for that atom m. The operator ^ denotes transitive closure.

Here are some other common operators not illustrated by this example. Logical implication is denoted by '`=>`'; '`<=>`' represents bi-implication. The operator '`-`' denotes set difference, while '`#`' denotes set cardinality and '`+`' - set union.

To instruct the analyzer to generate a DAG with 6 nodes, we formulate an empty predicate and write a `run` command:

```
pred generate() {}

run generate for 6 but 1 DAG
```

The scope of 6 forces an upper bound of 6 nodes. The `but` keyword specifies a separate bound for a signature whose name follows the keyword. Thus we restrict a generated example to 1 DAG.

3   Subject System Details

As the subject of our analysis we have chosen a cooperative multi-agent system with explicit communication and with a utility-based proactive planning/scheduling.

A multi-agent system is cooperative if it can be assumed that agents strive to collectively contribute to reaching some common goal. In such a cooperative MAS, agents are willing to sacrifice their local optimality of actions if they are convinced (e.g. via a negotiation) that such a sacrifice will help increase the global optimality of the combined actions in the whole MAS. For simplicity we also assume there are no malicious agents in the chosen MAS.

3.1   Property Examples Derived from Requirements

We can describe several properties informally at this stage, before we fix the assumptions of the MAS design further.

Some of the informal properties that are likely to be useful for such a negotiation:

1. negotiation must terminate;
2. the utility of the agreed upon combination of schedules must eventually increase throughout the course of negotiation even though occasional decreases are allowed; i.e. the negotiation must eventually converge on some choice of schedules that provides a local optimum of the combined utility (here local is used in the sense of restrictions on action set and time deadline, not in the sense of local to a single agent);
3. if agent B (the one who is requested to do an additional task) agrees to accomplish the task at a certain point in negotiation then it cannot renege on that agreement in the course of subsequent negotiation (somewhat related to the need to converge); and,
4. the beliefs of one agent about an abstraction of partial state of another agent obtained as a result of negotiation should not contradict the actual state of that other agent.

3.2   Experiment Design

The experiment design is illustrated as derivation relationships between the software process artifacts in Fig. 1. The system requirements are used to derive a test suite and specify the intended behavior as properties. The subject MAS system is run on the test suite thus producing traces. The Alloy model of the system includes the representation of traces. This model is then verified against the formally specified properties and the properties that check correspondence of the traces to the results of the verification. Thus we check if the model satisfies the properties and if a sample of actual behavior highlighted by the test suite does not contradict the ideal behavior of the model.

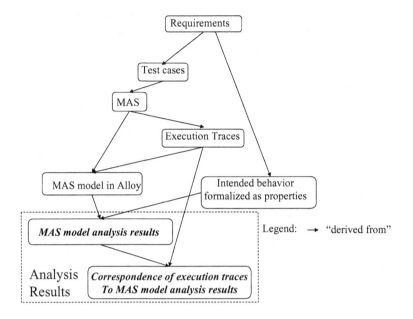

Fig. 1. Experiment design

3.3 Choice of the Analyzed System

Next we will provide greater detail about the design of the chosen MAS. This detail will let us illustrate the task allocation problem introduced generally above and to formalize a property. The chosen system has been developed in the MAS laboratory headed by Prof. Victor Lesser at the University of Massachusetts, Amherst. This MAS is a mature utility-based reasoning multi agent system that has been extensively used and validated. It has been used as a testbed for a great number of experiments and technology transfer demonstrations in the area of MAS ([23], [24], [11], [12], [18], [9], [10]). This MAS is not restricted to a particular problem domain. It applies the utility-based reasoning to abstract tasks with generalized relationships. Thus we expect that the results obtained from its analysis can be useful for other utility-based systems. In this system an agent is combined of several components that include a problem solver and a negotiation component, among others. The problem solver provides a schedule based on a current set of task structures assigned for execution. The negotiation component drives the execution of negotiation protocols, it is aware of protocol specifications and keeps track of current states of negotiation instances undertaken by its agent. The task structures are specified in the TÆMS language [6]. The schedules are provided by the Design-To-Criteria (DTC) scheduler ([25]) developed by Dr. Tom Wagner which is invoked as part of the agent's problem solver component operation. The DTC takes as input a task structure in TÆMS and a utility function specification and provides as output a set of schedules ranked by their utilities.

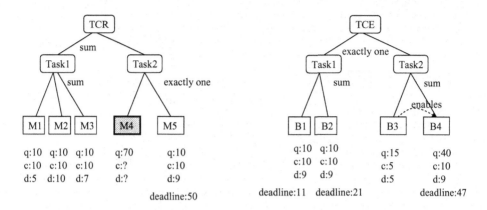

Fig. 2. Pre-negotiation task structures

In this system a simplified description of an agent's cycle is as follows:

1. *Local scheduling*: in response to an event requesting a certain task to be performed, obtain a number of high ranked schedules by utility;
2. *Negotiation*: conduct negotiation(s) within a predefined limit of time; and,
3. *Execution*: start execution of the schedule chosen as a result of negotiation(s).

The actual cycle of agent's operation is more complex as an agent can react to various kinds of events that it can receive at any of the mentioned cycle stages.

3.4   Relation Between Protocol FSMs, Task Structures, Offers and Visitations

Next we describe the task allocation problem in terms of this design. More details about the cooperative negotiation example can be found in [28]. The negotiation protocol of an agent starting the negotiation (agent *A*), the contractor, is given in Fig. 4. The negotiation protocol of an agent responding to the request (agent *B*), the contractee, is given in Fig. 5.

Let us assume that agent *A* needs a certain non-local task (this means that an agent is not capable of doing that task even though it appears in one of its task structures) to be performed by some other agent. The negotiation's goal is to increase the combined utility of actions of both agents by choosing a particular way to perform the non-local task at a particular time.

In the description that follows we mention the concepts of a protocol FSM, task structures, offers and execution paths encoded in visitations. These concepts are related to one another in the following way.

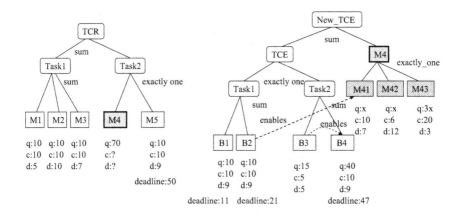

Fig. 3. Post-negotiation task structures

The design of the particular MAS we are analyzing contains a module called an agent [23]. This module itself is an aggregate of several submodules. One of these submodules is the "Negotiation" submodule and it is responsible for encapsulating knowledge about various protocols known to an agent. These protocols are encoded as FSMs with states corresponding to abstractions of the states of an agent in negotiation and transitions attributed with trigger conditions and actions. A sequence of visitations corresponds to a path from a start node of such a protocol FSM to one of the final nodes.

A task structure of an agent captures its knowledge about multiple ways in which a certain task can be accomplished. The root of a task structure corresponds to a task that an agent is capable of accomplishing. The leaves of a task structure correspond to atomic actions in which both the set and partial order can vary to reflect the way to accomplish an assigned task in a "utility-increasing" (but not guaranteed to be optimal) way. As an agent progresses through a negotiation protocol according to an FSM, the agent's task structure changes to reflect the agent's changing knowledge about other agent's state throughout that negotiation. Thus there are certain properties imposed on a task structure that must hold while an agent is in certain states of a negotiation protocol FSM.

A collection of task structures determines an agent's functionality analogously to a set of function signatures that define an interface of a module. The roots of task structures serve a similar purpose to function signatures at the agent level of abstraction of describing a software system. An outside event corresponding to a request to accomplish a certain task triggers an agent's reasoning about whether it can accomplish that task considering an agent's knowledge about the way to accomplish that task, that agent's state, the environment state and partial states of some other agents in the same MAS. The result of that reasoning is the current schedule that "interweaves" instances of atomic actions from various tasks currently assigned to that agent in a time-oriented partial order. That current schedule can be changed dynamically, as it is being executed, in response to agents' changing opinion about the most reasonable schedule for a certain moment in time.

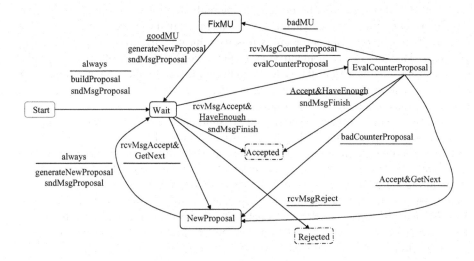

Fig. 4. Contractor's FSM

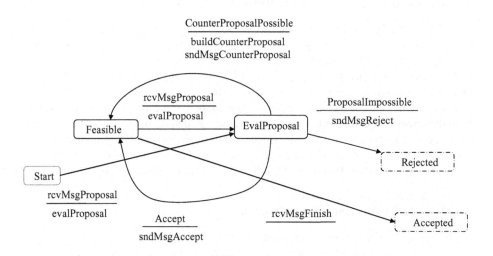

Fig. 5. Contractee's FSM

We do not consider execution of schedules, but focus only on the negotiation phase in which schedules always cover future time intervals.

An offer is a data structure generated by actions associated with FSM transitions. An offer encapsulates the parameters of a particular schedule formed on the basis of the agents' task structures, such as quality achieved, start time and finish time. The agents negotiate over these parameters.

Another submodule of an agent is "Communication". The "Negotiation" submodule relies on "Communication" in a fashion similar to how a networking application relies on TCP/IP protocols. The design intentionally separated the concern of ensuring reliable communication and naming mechanisms from the concern of ensuring that a certain "utility-increasing" protocol is followed during a negotiation between a pair of agents. Thus the issues of identifying agents to communicate with for a particular purpose were separated from the "negotiation" submodule by the authors of the MAS system we analyze. This was done to simplify their own analysis, to separate concerns. Our Alloy specification reflects that separation.

In a way, the task structure specifies all possible behaviors of an agent responsible for achieving the goal embodied by a task structure's root. During the stages of *Local scheduling* and *Negotiation* the task structure can be modified, thus modifying specification of a set of behaviors of an agent during an *Execution* stage. The behavior of an agent during the stages of *Local scheduling* and *Negotiation* is static, i.e. it is not modified during run-time. A schedule agreed upon as a result of *Negotiation* is a selected behavior (execution path) from a set of behaviors that was modified at run-time (represented by a task structure; to be performed in the *Execution* stage). Thus a property we describe below checks certain well-formedness of a behavior specification modified at run-time and correctness of an implementation responsible for the modification.

3.5   Details of the Task Allocation Problem in the Chosen Design

Let us go over a possible scenario of agents' interactions in regard to a task allocation problem for the sake of illustration. This kind of interaction between agents is quite common in any utility-based reasoning MAS. In Fig. 2 we see two task structures. Suppose one task structure, with the root TCR, was assigned to agent *A*, the other, TCE, was assigned to agent *B*. Before the negotiation the striped methods (M4 and its children) are not part of the TCE structure. This assignment can be due to requests sent from the environment (e.g. a human or other automated system). TCE and TCR turned out to be non-leaf nodes with elaborations. Upon receiving task assignments agent *A* sent TCR structure to its local scheduler, agent *B* did the same for TCE.

Let us suppose agent *A* receives the following schedules from its scheduler:

– M1, M2, M3, M4 - highest utility
– M1, M2, M3, M5 - lower utility, feasible

Agent *B* receives the following schedule: B3, B4 that has the highest utility.

Next, agent *A* identifies M4 in its best schedule as non-local. It sends a request to agent *B* to do it. The fact that agent *A* knows that *B* can do M4 is hardwired for the example without loss of generality for the negotiation analysis results. The request initiates an instance of negotiation. Agent *A* plays the role of a *Contractor*, agent *B* - that of a *Contractee*. Agent *B* must see whether it can do M4 by the deadline agent *A* needs it, while accomplishing its current task TCE within the constraints. This is done by modifying the "currently reasoned about" structure and submitting it to the scheduler that will report if such a schedule is possible and, if yes, then with what utility.

The TCE structure must be modified preserving its well-formedness constraints (e.g. functional decomposition remains a tree); and forcing an M4 into a schedule by choosing appropriate quality of M4 that reflects the combined utility of both schedules (chosen by *A* and by *B*). Fig. 3 shows agent *B*'s task structure updated with an M4. The quality attribute of M4 must be such that the scheduler of agent *B* must produce feasible (though not necessarily high ranking) schedules that contain M4 and still accomplish the original TCE task.

Even if the agent *B*'s local scheduler returns an acceptable schedule (which has M4 in it and the original TCE is accomplished with the constraints on time and quality), agent *A* can request to make a tighter fit. Therefore if its scheduler found a feasible schedule that includes M4, agent *B* (*Contractee*) is supposed to transition to state "Feasible" (Fig. 5) and wait for agent *A* to send another proposal with a "tighter" deadline on M4's execution or a "finish" message. This means that agent *B* must have modified its task structure to include M4. On the contrary, if there is not a single feasible schedule that can include M4 then agent *B* is supposed to transition to state "Rejected". If agent *B* reaches state "Rejected" then its post task structure TCE' is unchanged from the pre TCE.

With this description in mind we can rephrase this property in terms of the TÆMS structures and negotiation protocol specifications in Figures 4 and 5 as:

After agent *B* reaches state "Feasible" at least once its task structure must contain a subtree corresponding to task M4 and M4 must appear in a feasible schedule returned to agent *A*.

In this example the Contractee's FSM has been simplified for the sake of this illustration. For additional details about this example please refer to [28].

4   Alloy Specification for the Negotiation Model

Our approach implies modeling particular paths traversed in the agents' negotiation finite state machines (FSMs) in response to certain testcases. Thus we check an abstraction of an execution path in a particular implementation. Both FSMs contain cycles. If a cycle diameter can be modeled with the scope that can be processed by the Alloy analyzer then we can iteratively check a certain property on an execution path that corresponds to multiple iterations of a cycle.

The negotiation protocols and task structures described in section 3 had to be simplified to have a tractable scope for the Alloy analyzer. The simplifications include:

1. ignoring attributes of task structures nodes (quality, duration, cost);
2. ignoring attributes of offers (mutual utility gain, cost, earliest start time);
3. ignoring attributes of schedules (start time and finish time of actions); and,
4. simplifying task structures by removing intermediate nodes (e.g. no Task_1, Task_2) and reducing the number of leaf nodes (e.g. only B1 and B3 left in agent *B*'s task structure).

The actual models used for analysis also contain only those atoms that are necessary for verifying a property at hand. Thus transitions that were not traversed by a modeled execution path and associated states were removed.

This amount of simplification was necessary to make the analysis feasible. Earlier we constructed a more detailed Alloy specification of the analyzed system. The Alloy analyzer was not able to cope with such a specification. We had to reduce its size gradually while still keeping the analysis useful. We expect that the next generation of the Alloy analyzer, Kodkod [20], would be able to deal with a larger specification.

The resultant Alloy model of the MAS for the purpose of verifying our assertions consists of 3 modules. One module, `negProtocol12_1abridgeDataProp`, models the FSMs, visitations of transitions through the FSMs (paths specified by transitions) and assertions. Two more modules model the data structures manipulated by the agents - their task structures and schedules. Let us briefly go over the Alloy models in these modules.

The `negProtocol12_1abridgeDataProp` defines signatures for `State`, `Transition`, `Visitation` and `Offer`. Thus an FSM is modeled by constraining atoms of `State` and `Transition` signatures via the "fact" construct. A `Transition` signature contains fields for source and destination states, a set of visitations of that transition by a path and a set of transitions outgoing from the destination state of the transition. The `treeDefSmall` module models a task structure of an agent. The `schedDefSmall` module models a schedule data structure of an agent. It imports the `treeDefSmall` so that schedule items can reference the nodes of task structures. The consistency of the model has been successfully checked with an empty stub predicate. The analyzer found a solution.

```
abstract sig State {}

abstract sig Transition {
  source, dest: State,
  visit: set Visitation,
  nextTrans: set Transition
}

fact Injection { all t, t': Transition | t.source =
                    t'.source && t.dest =
                    t'.dest => t = t' }

abstract sig Visitation {
  trans: lone Transition,
  nextVisit: lone Visitation,
  offer: lone Offer
}
fact VisTransConsistent {
  all visitation: Visitation | visitation in
    visitation.trans.visit
}
```

5   Alloy Specification for the Properties

The paths of execution of the two negotiation protocols are represented by atoms of the `Visitation` signature. Thus it is via these atoms that we express a property that can be informally phrased as "If agent *A* is led to believe by a certain sequence of communications that agent *B* reaches a certain state then agent *B* should have indeed reached that state, having been subjected to the same changes of observed environment as agent *A*". This informal statement pinpoints such a feature of agents in a MAS as bounded rationality. The property checks for consistency between a certain abstraction of other agent's state (agent *B*) that a certain agent (*A*) obtains via communication. In the case of the particular system we used the communication is explicit. By modeling

```
module models/examples/tutorial/treeDefSmall

abstract sig Tree {
  root: Node,
  nodes: set Node,
  edges: Node -> Node
}

{
  nodes = root.*edges
  all m: Node | m !in m.^edges
}

abstract sig Node {}

one sig TCR,  M3, M4, M5, TCE, B1, B3, New_TCE extends Node{}

one sig AgentB_preTaskStrucTCE extends Tree {} fact
AgentB_preTaskStrucTCEDef {
  AgentB_preTaskStrucTCE.root = TCE
  AgentB_preTaskStrucTCE.nodes = TCE + B3
  AgentB_preTaskStrucTCE.edges = TCE->B3
}

one sig AgentB_postTaskStrucTCE extends Tree {} fact
AgentB_postTaskStrucTCEDef {
  AgentB_postTaskStrucTCE.root = New_TCE
  AgentB_postTaskStrucTCE.nodes = New_TCE + TCE + B1 +   M4
  AgentB_postTaskStrucTCE.edges = New_TCE->TCE +
   New_TCE->M4 + TCE->B1
}
```

the environment sensed by agents we could allow for checking such properties based on implicit communication.

More specifically, in view of the simplifications we made, a property of this kind can be informally restated as "if agent *A* reaches state `EvalCounterProposal` then agent *B* should have reached state `Wait2` and beginning since that state, agent *B*'s current schedule data structure should have contained an instance of atomic action M4". Below we can see how this property is formally expressed in the Alloy's relational algebra. The assertion has been successfully checked. No counterexamples were found for the path containing visitations that corresponded to the expected states and data structure conditions. Conversely, once an inconsistency between agent *A*'s belief and agent *B*'s state and data structures has been introduced into visitations, the analyzer pinpointed a possible counterexample.

We have also translated an Alloy specification of this property into a dynamic assertion in Java using a systematic translation approach [2]. Thus we were able to dynamically check the conformance of an implementation to the Alloy specification. We also showed the utility of the Alloy Analyzer by making sure that an assertion in the Alloy specification is right and then mechanically translating that assertion into a dynamic assertion in Java implementation.

```
module models/examples/tutorial/schedDefSmall open
models/examples/tutorial/treeDefSmall

abstract sig SchedItem {
  activity:  Node
}
```

```
one sig SchedItemM3 extends SchedItem{} fact SchedItemM3Def {
  SchedItemM3.activity = M3
}

one sig SchedItemM4 extends SchedItem{} fact SchedItemM4Def {
  SchedItemM4.activity = M4
}

one sig SchedItemM5 extends SchedItem{} fact SchedItemM5Def {
  SchedItemM5.activity = M5
}

one sig SchedItemB1 extends SchedItem{} fact SchedItemB1Def {
  SchedItemB1.activity = B1
}

one sig SchedItemB3 extends SchedItem{} fact SchedItemB3Def {
  SchedItemB3.activity = B3
}

abstract sig Sched {
  items: set SchedItem,
  precedenceRel: SchedItem -> SchedItem
}

one sig AgentAschedWithNL extends Sched {} fact
AgentAschedWithNLDef {
  AgentAschedWithNL.items = SchedItemM3 + SchedItemM4
  AgentAschedWithNL.precedenceRel =
     SchedItemM3->SchedItemM4
}

one sig AgentAschedWithOutNL extends Sched {} fact
AgentAschedWithOutNLDef {
  AgentAschedWithOutNL.items = SchedItemM3 + SchedItemM5
  AgentAschedWithOutNL.precedenceRel =
     SchedItemM3->SchedItemM5
}

one sig AgentBschedWithNL extends Sched {} fact
AgentBschedWithOutNLDef {
  AgentBschedWithOutNL.items = SchedItemB1 + SchedItemM4
  AgentBschedWithOutNL.precedenceRel =
     SchedItemB1->SchedItemM4
}

one sig AgentBschedWithOutNL extends Sched {} fact
AgentBschedWithNLDef {
  AgentBschedWithNL.items = SchedItemB3
}

assert AgentAbeliefCompliesWithAgentBState {
  (some visitation: Visitation |
    visitation.trans.dest = EvalCounterProposal) =>
     (some visitation': Visitation |
       visitation'.trans.dest = Wait2 &&
         M4 in visitation'.offer.agentBTaskTree.nodes)
}
```

6 Specification Difficulties

The main difficulty is keeping the Alloy model under a tractable scope while checking useful properties. In the case of the design of this particular MAS the protocols are specified via FSMs with loops. Thus we can check properties only within the scope of the FSM's diameter. Other difficulties are due to highly dynamic, hard to predict behavior of sensing agents. One has to classify the dynamics of the environment sensed by the agents and check the properties within each such situation. For instance, in the example used in this paper we can classify the situations based on combinations of "best" schedules of the 2 agents with regard to including the non local task (M4) into their schedules. Some of the possible combinations (for all cases agent A has M4 in its best schedule):

- agent B does not have M4 in its best schedule; the local utility of agent B's schedule outweighs the combined utility if agent B is forced to do M4;
- agent B does not have M4 in its best schedule; the local utility of agent B's schedule is below the combined utility if agent B is forced to do M4;
- agent B has M4 in its best schedule too, but not within the timeframe agent A needs M4 to be finished
- agent B has M4 in its best schedule too, it is within the timeframe agent A needs M4 to be finished

It should be possible to provide an Alloy model so that these combinations would not have to be specified explicitly. Instead, the Alloy analyzer itself would check over all the alternatives it sees in the model. A straightforward approach of modeling the attributes of the nodes in the agents' task structures results in too large a scope for the Alloy to handle. Perhaps the attribute values should be abstracted as features of the task structures, not as numerical values.

7   Conclusions and Future Work

We have created and validated a model for verifying data structure rich properties of a cooperative multi-agent system using a manually created execution path. To our knowledge, our work is the first application of the Alloy analyzer for checking properties of a multi-agent system. Moreover, this example illustrates how the use of Alloy's formal reasoning capability can be integrated into the testing and validation activities of software development.

Another step might be checking a property on all interior paths of a loop in an FSM. One more interesting property would involve checking if an elaboration of the non-local task is "interwoven" in one of the many alternative ways into the task structure of an agent. We expect that checking such a more complicated and a more realistic case might highlight Alloy's advantage due to the declarative nature of its relational algebra. It would also be interesting to see whether CSP-based models and tools (FDR) or B CSP models would be useful for checking properties of negotiation in MAS systems with explicit communication.

Acknowledgments

We would like to express our deep gratitude to Prof. Victor Lesser (UMass, Amherst) for his help with the negotiation protocol example implemented in the multi-agent system simulator and helpful comments.

References

1. Adjie-Winoto, W., Schwartz, E., Balakrishnan, H., Lilley, J.: The design and implementation of an intentional naming system. In: 17th ACM Symposium on Operating Systems Principles (SOSP), Kiawah Island, December 1999, ACM Press, New York (1999)
2. Al-Naffouri, B.: An algorithm for automatic generation of run-time checks from alloy specification. Advanced Undergraduate Project Report, Massachusetts Institute of Technology (2002)
3. Alechina, N., Logan, B.: Verifying bounds on deliberation time in multi-agent systems. In: EUMAS, pp. 25–34 (2005)
4. Becker, B., Beyer, D., Giese, H., Klein, F., Schilling, D.: Symbolic invariant verification for systems with dynamic structural adaptation. In: Proceedings of the 28th International Conference on Software Engineering (ICSE 2006), Shanghai, May 20-28, 2006, pp. 72–81. ACM Press, New York (2006)
5. Box, D.: Essential COM. Addison-Wesley, Reading (1998)
6. Decker, K.: TAEMS: A Framework for Environment Centered Analysis & Design of Coordination Mechanisms. In: O'Hare, G., Jennings, N. (eds.) Foundations of Distributed Artificial Intelligence, January 1996, Ch. 16, pp. 429–448. Wiley Inter-Science, Chichester (1996)
7. Dennis, G.: TSAFE: Building a trusted computing base for air traffic control software. Master's thesis, Massachusetts Institute of Technology (2003)
8. Gans, G., Jarke, M., Lakemeyer, G., Vits, T.: SNet: A modeling and simulation environment for agent networks based on i* and ConGolog. In: Bussler, C.J., McIlraith, S.A., Orlowska, M.E., Pernici, B., Yang, J. (eds.) CAiSE 2002 and WES 2002. LNCS, vol. 2512, pp. 328–343. Springer, Heidelberg (2002)
9. Horling, B., Lesser, V.: Using Diagnosis to Learn Contextual Coordination Rules. Proceedings of the AAAI-99 Workshop on Reasoning in Context for AI Applications, July 1999, pp. 70–74 (1999)
10. Horling, B., Lesser, V., Vincent, R., Bazzan, A., Xuan, P.: Diagnosis as an Integral Part of Multi-Agent Adaptability. Proceedings of DARPA Information Survivability Conference and Exposition, January 2000, pp. 211–219 (2000)
11. Horling, B., Mailler, R., Lesser, V.: Farm: A Scalable Environment for Multi-Agent Development and Evaluation. In: Lucena, C., Garcia, A., Romanovsky, A., Castro, J., Alencar, P.S.C. (eds.) Software Engineering for Multi-Agent Systems II. LNCS, vol. 2940, pp. 171–177. Springer, Heidelberg (2004)
12. Horling, B., Vincent, R., Mailler, R., Shen, J., Becker, R., Rawlins, K., Lesser, V.: Distributed Sensor Network for Real Time Tracking. Proceedings of the 5th International Conference on Autonomous Agents, June 2001, pp. 417–424 (2001)
13. Jackson, D.: Software Abstractions: Logic, Language and Analysis. MIT Press, Cambridge (2006)
14. Jackson, D., Jackson, M.: Separating Concerns in Requirements Analysis: An Example. In: chapter Rigorous development of complex fault tolerant systems, Springer, Heidelberg (To appear)
15. Jackson, D., Schechter, I., Shlyakhter, I.: ALCOA: The Alloy constraint analyzer. In: 22nd International Conference on Software Engineering (ICSE), Limerick, Ireland (June 2000)
16. Kacprzak, M., Lomuscio, A., Penczek, W.: Verification of multiagent systems via unbounded model checking. In: Kudenko, D., Kazakov, D., Alonso, E. (eds.) Adaptive Agents and Multi-Agent Systems II. LNCS (LNAI), vol. 3394, pp. 638–645. Springer, Heidelberg (2004)
17. Lesser, V.: Reflections on the Nature of Multi-Agent Coordination and Its Implications for an Agent Architecture. Autonomous Agents and Multi-Agent Systems 1, 89–111 (1998)

18. Lesser, V., Atighetchi, M., Benyo, B., Horling, B., Raja, A., Vincent, R., Wagner, T., Ping, X., Zhang, S.X.: The Intelligent Home Testbed. Proceedings of the Autonomy Control Software Workshop (Autonomous Agent Workshop) (January 1999)
19. Lesser, V., Decker, K., Wagner, T., Carver, N., Garvey, A., Horling, B., Neiman, D., Podorozhny, R., Prasad, M.N., Raja, A., Vincent, R., Xuan, P., Zhang, X.: Evolution of the GPGP/TAEMS Domain-Independent Coordination Framework. Autonomous Agents and Multi-Agent Systems 9(1), 87–143 (2004)
20. Torlak, E.: http://web.mit.edu/~emina/www/kodkod.html
21. van der Hoek, W., Wooldridge, M.: Model checking knowledge and time. In: Bošnački, D., Leue, S. (eds.) Model Checking Software. LNCS, vol. 2318, pp. 95–111. Springer, Heidelberg (2004)
22. Vaziri, M.: Finding Bugs Using a Constraint Solver. PhD thesis, Computer Science and Artificial Intelligence Laboratory, Massachusetts Institute of Technology (2004)
23. Vincent, R., Horling, B., Lesser, V.: Agent Infrastructure to Build and Evaluate Multi-Agent Systems: The Java Agent Framework and Multi-Agent System Simulator. In: Wagner, T.A., Rana, O.F. (eds.) Infrastructure for Agents, Multi-Agent Systems, and Scalable Multi-Agent Systems. LNCS (LNAI), vol. 1887, pp. 102–127. Springer, Heidelberg (2001)
24. Wagner, T., Horling, B.: The Struggle for Reuse and Domain Independence: Research with TAEMS, DTC and JAF. In: Proceedings of the 2nd Workshop on Infrastructure for Agents, MAS, and Scalable MAS (Agents 2001) (June 2001)
25. Wagner, T., Lesser, V.: Design-to-Criteria Scheduling: Real-Time Agent Control. In: Proceedings of AAAI 2000 Spring Symposium on Real-Time Autonomous Systems, pp. 89–96 (March 2000)
26. Weiss, G. (ed.): Multiagent systems: a modern approach to distributed artificial intelligence. MIT Press, Cambridge (1999)
27. Wooldridge, M., Fisher, M., Huget, M.-P., Parsons, S.: Model checking multi-agent systems with mable. In: Falcone, R., Barber, S., Korba, L., Singh, M.P. (eds.) AAMAS 2002. LNCS (LNAI), vol. 2631, pp. 952–959. Springer, Heidelberg (2003)
28. Zhang, X., Podorozhny, R.M., Lesser, V.: Cooperative, MultiStep Negotiation Over a Multi-Dimensional Utility Function. In: Proceedings of the IASTED International Conference on Artificial Intelligence and Soft Computing (ASC 2000), pp. 136–142 (2000)

Integrated Static Analysis for Linux Device Driver Verification

Hendrik Post and Wolfgang Küchlin

University of Tübingen, Germany
{post,kuechlin}@informatik.uni-tuebingen.de
http://www-sr.informatik.uni-tuebingen.de

Abstract. We port verification techniques for device drivers from the Windows domain to Linux, combining several tools and techniques into one integrated tool-chain. Building on ideas from Microsoft's *Static Driver Verifier* (SDV) project, we extend their specification language and combine its implementation with the public domain bounded model checker CBMC as a new verification back-end. We extract several API conformance rules from Linux documentation and formulate them in the extended language SLICx. Thus SDV-style verification of temporal safety specifications is brought into the public domain. In addition, we show that SLICx, together with CBMC, can be used to simulate preemption in multi-threaded code, and to find race conditions and to prove the absence of deadlocks and memory leaks.

1 Introduction

Correctness and API conformance are especially important for the development of device drivers. Errors in driver code may easily lead to inconsistent data, security leaks and system downtime. For Windows XP it is claimed that errors in device drivers cause 85% of system crashes [1]. Microsoft's *Static Driver Verifier* (SDV) [2] has been reported to be successful in automatic, high-precision bug-finding in this domain, but its application is currently limited to Windows.

Our work aims at carrying the work of the SDV project over into the public domain, extending and adapting it in the process. Our verification target are Linux device drivers, our verification back-end is the source code bounded model checker CBMC, and our tool-chain is implemented as a plug-in to the Eclipse integrated program development environment. The combination of specifications and driver code follows the well-known paradigm of Aspect Oriented Programming (AOP). SLICx rules embody the aspect correctness. SLICx rules are translated into C code snippets that are injected into the device driver source code automatically. The modified sources are then checked at compile time by the CBMC [3] model checker for the existence of execution paths to certain error states.

Although the implementation of device drivers is crucial for the correctness of operating systems, it is a task that is commonly not performed by operating

J. Davies and J. Gibbons (Eds.): IFM 2007, LNCS 4591, pp. 518–537, 2007.

system developers but by third party device manufacturers. With Linux, this task is even distributed further among a large community of volunteers. As these people are not in direct contact with the developers of the operating system kernel itself, it is desirable to thoroughly check device drivers before adding them to an operating system distribution. Note that Linux is increasingly used in enterprise critical, high-availability environments such as IBM mainframes, or in safety critical real-time settings.

In this work we describe the integration and adaptation of verification solutions to make automatic Linux Device Driver verification possible. Our approach builds on, and extends, SDV which implements API conformance checks for drivers adhering to the *Windows Driver Model* (WDM). SLIC [4], the specification language of SDV, allows to specify temporal safety properties. The temporal safety properties are encoded as an automaton that is associated with a driver's source code during the verification process. SLIC rules, which are attached to appropriate points (*join points* in AOP parlance) in the source code, trigger transitions in the automaton, and SDV's model checker SLAM [5] verifies temporal properties such as the reachability of error states. The developers of SDV report large numbers of errors discovered with their tool [2].

The question we deal with in this work is whether any concept similar to SDV may be implemented in the public domain with reasonable effort such that it works on Linux device drivers. To accomplish this, API rules for Linux must be found and formulated, a SLIC processor and AOP-style code weaver— capable of handling Linux sources and SLIC rules simultaneously—must be implemented, and a suitable model checker must be selected. Our decision was to choose CBMC [3] as model checker and to build and integrate the remaining tools based on the Eclipse IDE. More details concerning our integrated tool-chain called *Avinux* are reported in [6].

First, we created and implemented a new language SLICx that is an extension of SDV's specification language SLIC. Essentially, SLIC statements can only manipulate an associated safety automaton, while SLICx rules may contain full C expressions including calls to other Linux functions. Thus they come much closer to supporting the full AOP paradigm: the driver state can be manipulated including ways that reflect the preemption of the driver by interrupt handlers.

Next we extracted API conformance rules from the Linux documentation and implemented them in SLICx, which gives us similar functionality for Linux as SDV provides for Windows.

The second part of our contribution is the formulation of checks that significantly extend those reported for SDV. Memory safety analysis is enabled by CBMC directly. We extend these built-in checks by a new rule that covers memory leaks. We can prove the absence of deadlocks by checking whether all lock acquisitions follow a common acquisition order (not necessarily known in advance). This check is also implemented as a SLICx rule. We complement this complete rule with a sound rule that forbids recursive locking.

Another new rule enforces the absence of race conditions. This rule is implemented by exploiting a synergy between SLICx and CBMC: using an AOP-style

SLICx code manipulation rule, unprotected access to a shared memory location is reduced to a memory safety violation which CBMC can detect. The preemption of a device driver by an interrupt handler function is simulated sequentially by inserting a call to the handler at appropriate points in the driver's source, again using the AOP-style code transformation power of our SLICx implementation. This rule adds support for (some) multithreaded programs, though SLIC itself covers only sequential programs.

The organization of the paper is as follows. In Section 2 the general setting of software verification solutions is reviewed. Having clarified the dependencies between different verification entities, we describe the adaptation of SDV for Linux in Section 3. Our specification language SLICx is compared with SLIC in Section 3.1. The verification backend CBMC is reviewed in Section 3.2. The adaptation part ends with a discussion of the problems creating operating system models for Linux and the presentation of an SDV-style API rule example. Section 4 presents features beyond the capabilities of SDV. Section 5 discusses our experiences applying our solution to real drivers. We conclude with a brief overview of related works in Section 6. Examples for processed drivers and for formulated SLICx rules are provided on our project website[1].

2   On Programs, Specifications, Hazards and Specification Implementations

A typical verification process involves 5 components:

- A *program* to be verified (e.g. a device driver).
- A *hazard* we want to avoid (e.g. API misuse, race conditions, memory leaks).
- A *specification* that (semi-)formalizes how the problem can be avoided (e.g. API documentation).
- An *implementation of a specification* that can be checked by the engine (e.g. rules in SLIC or SLICx, pre- or postconditions).
- An *engine* that tells us if the program models the specification implementation (e.g. model checker, theorem prover).

Both, specification and its implementation, may suffer from imprecision issues that may be classified as *soundness* and *completeness* issues:

1. Is the specification, respectively its implementation,*complete* such that each hazard is surely covered—i.e. do false negatives occur?
2. Are specification and its implementation *sound* with respect to the hazard—i.e. no false positives are reported?

One example of a typical hazard is *dereferences of* NULL *pointers*. A specification that forbids such accesses globally would be sound and complete. A partial specification requiring that a dynamically allocated object should not be used after it has been passed to free() is sound, but incomplete with respect to the

---

[1] http://www-sr.informatik.uni-tuebingen.de/~post/avinux

hazard. A specification that forbids any memory accesses would be unsound, but complete.

We consider API rules as (partial) specifications. Although API misuse can also be considered to be a hazard itself.

Different verification settings exist:

– The absence of hazards should be enforced.
– API conformance should be enforced—i.e. API misuse is an hazard.
– API usage analysis is necessary to detect hazards.
– API usage analysis is sufficient to detect hazards.
– API usage analysis complements the detection of hazards.

The first two points represent the conservative interpretation of the verification task. Our experience in doing verification on Linux device drivers has led to solutions that fall into the latter categories. Therefore we concentrate on formulating and applying API rules rather than providing direct solutions.

3   Adapting SDV

We use the same basic verification architecture as in SDV: A driver is instrumented with a specification implementation in the rule (specification) language SLIC and with an operating system model. The resulting annotated driver contains a `main` function provided by the operating system model. Finally, the verification engine analyzes the code starting with `main` (Figure 1).

It is tempting to think that SDV is applicable to Linux Device Driver source code as well as Windows drivers since both are C programs. However, we found the following problems that prohibit the direct application:

– The SLIC compiler (annotation tool) is not available and, if it were available, it might not support the unofficial Linux C dialect.
– No formal rules exist for Linux. We found only sparse API documentation.
– Are Linux APIs similar to WDM APIs? Or are they too broad or complex to be specified in SLIC?
– In contrast to WDM specifying a tight driver framework for Windows, Linux does not enforce a common driver structure. Hence, how can an operating system model be obtained?

We treat the first problems by

– Replacing the verification backend from SDV by the bounded source code model checker CBMC [3] for C (Subsection 3.2).
– Reimplementing the specification language SLIC and its annotation component (Subsection 3.1).
– Discovering and implementing rules for Linux.

The problem of creating an environment model automatically is not yet solved, but discussed in Subsection 3.3. In the remaining part of this section our SLIC dialect SLICx is presented. Additionally we review the features of the verification backend CBMC. We omit SDV-style API rules for Linux as we will later present advanced rules in Section 4.

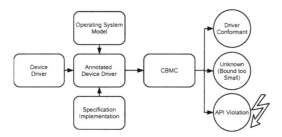

Fig. 1. The verification architecture resembles the architecture found in SDV, BLAST [7] and other tools. A driver is instrumented by a specification implementation and an operating system model. In our project, the resulting C code is then checked by CBMC.

3.1 Extending SLIC to SLICx

SLIC [4] is an interface specification language for sequential C programs. In SLIC, temporal safety properties are encoded as an event-driven automaton where events are limited to the events {call, entry, exit, return} of a C function.

The state of the automaton is encoded as a **state** component. The state and the transfer (transition) functions can be translated into C code. This code provides a specification aspect that is injected into the original driver. Errors are reported in SLIC by a call to a reserved statement **abort**. The star (∗) expression denotes a non-deterministic choice implemented in most static analysis tools. Transfer functions in SLIC may only read the driver's state, the parameters of the corresponding C function (numbered from $1 to $n) and the function's return value. Write operations are only permitted on state variables and only once per variable.

A notable way of expressing universal quantification with SLIC is the *universal quantification trick*. If a specification involves universal quantification over a potentially infinite set of dynamically allocated objects, the SLIC state monitors one non-deterministically chosen object. In this manner, the model checker may independently check for all single objects if calls on them violate the specification. The trick is extensively used in SLIC. To the best of our knowledge this mechanism has been introduced in the Bandera project [8]. An example for the application of our dialect SLICx and the universal quantification trick is given in Figure 2.

The setting in which we are operating is that we do not have access either to the SLIC annotation component or to a version of the Static Driver Verifier that supports custom SLIC rules. Therefore we were forced to reimplement a compiler that translates and injects SLIC specifications. Thus, we were free to create a language SLICx which extends SLIC such that it reflects our needs better than the original version. SLICx features the following extensions: function call expressions, write operations to all memory locations, loops and multiple writes to the same memory location.

One key idea in SLIC was that all transfer functions, manipulating the safety automaton, are necessarily terminating. Termination in SLIC is ensured by code restrictions. We have removed these code restrictions to make rule code even more C-like. Transfer functions violating the termination bound are handled by unwinding assertions. SLICx moves closer toward the *Aspect Oriented Programming* paradigm that was already hidden in SLIC. Having broken the restrictions of SLIC, SLICx rule code may now allocate new variables and manipulate the original driver's source on a larger scale. The extensions are necessary for the functional extensions of SDV in Section 4. A grammar of SLICx is given in Table 1.

3.2   Verification Engine CBMC

SDV's verification engine SLAM is not available for custom modifications and custom rules, thus we chose CBMC which supports many low-level C operations found in Linux device drivers.

CBMC [3] is a bounded model checker intended to be used for the analysis of C programs and Verilog descriptions. When running in C analysis mode, it translates ANSI-C programs into propositional logic. Loops and recursions are handled by code unwinding. CBMC supports pointer arithmetic, integer operators, type casts, side effects, function calls, calls through function pointers, non-determinism, assumptions, assertions, arrays, structs, named unions and dynamic memory. CBMC itself is capable of finding double-free and use-after-free errors besides bounds and pointer validity checking.

```
1: int main(void)
2: {
3:   buffer_t *b1
       = malloc(10);
// ...
5: }
```

```
state{
  void *which_buffer
    = NULL;
  int allocated
    = 0;
}
malloc.exit{
  if(*) {
    which_buffer
      = $return;
    allocated = 1;
  }
}
```

```
void *which_buffer=NULL;
int allocated=0;
void *__malloc(int s) {
  ...
  ret = malloc(s);
  if(nondet_bool()) {
    which_buffer = ret;
    allocated = 1;
  }...
}
  ...
3:   buffer_t *b1
       = __malloc(10);
```

Fig. 2. The excerpt illustrates the universal quantification trick implemented in SLICx. The left column lists the original driver code. The middle column contains the SLICx rule, while the last column contains the annotated driver. The original function call in line 3 is replaced by a call to a wrapper function __malloc. In this wrapper function—after calling the original function—one buffer is randomly chosen to be monitored. Its state is stored in the flag allocated. nondet_bool is CBMC's implementation of *.

Table 1. An EBNF like grammar for SLICx. The comment column summarizes differences to SLIC.

Syntax		Comment
S ::=	$(extDecl)^*$ $[state]$ $transFun^*$	
$state$ ::=	**state** { $fieldDecl^+$ }	
$fieldDecl$ ::=	$fieldType\ id\ =\ expr$; | **enum** { id (, id)$^+$ } $id = id$;	
$fieldType$ ::=	**int *** | **int** | **void ***	Reduced set of possible types for state fields.
$transFun$ ::=	$pattern\ stmt$	
$pattern$ ::=	id . $event$	
$event$ ::=	**call** | **return** | **entry** | **exit**	
$stmt$ ::=	$id\ =\ expr$;	Parallel assignments removed.
	| **if** ($choose$) $stmt$ [**else** $stmt$] | **abort** $string$; | **reset**; | **halt**;	
	| $cStmt$	We allow all possible C statements instead of a reduced set.
$choose$ ::=	***** | $expr$	
$expr$ ::=	$cExpr$	All C expressions are accepted.
id ::=	$C\_identifier$ | **\$** int | **\$ return** | **\$** $C\_identifier$	

3.3   An Operating System Model for Linux

Drivers sometimes cannot be analyzed without using an artificial operating system model that invokes a driver's service routines and simulates callbacks to the core. Moreover such a model usually implements a life cycle for a device driver. One abstract example is shown in Figure 3. For the Windows Driver Framework such a generic model has been developed [2]. For Linux, generic use-cases cannot be created that easily because Linux is lacking a common driver framework and architecture. Hence, empirical results for Linux Device Drivers can be obtained only by investing additional manual effort.

3.4   Example: RCU-API Checking

The RCU algorithm was implemented for the Linux kernel to gain speed-ups for shared complex data types like lists. The main idea is to avoid synchronization

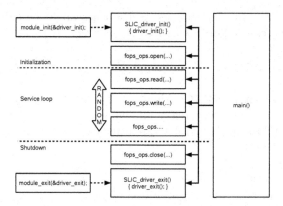

Fig. 3. An abstract life cycle of a Linux Device Driver module. The `module_init` and `module_exit` macros mark the functions that are called first and last. Using preprocessor macros, we transform them into uniformly named functions that may be called from our main function.

operations whenever possible. Disregarding the internal implementations of the algorithm, we extracted a partial black box specification from the kernel documentation: *If a list element is deleted from an RCU list by a call to* `list_del_rcu`, *this element may not be deallocated prior to a call to* `synchronize_rcu` *or* `call_rcu`. Here we must annotate calls to the above functions as well as calls to `kfree()` in order to track the memory-state of the list.

With SLICx, CBMC, and a new rulebase, we have a similar system as SDV. Section 4 gives our results that concern extensions to SDV's capabilities. Implementation aspects of our integrated tool-chain are summarized in [6]. Other examples can be obtained through our website.

4 Beyond SDV

The following extended features are also covered by our integrated solution, but not by CBMC or SDV:

1. Proving the absence of memory leaks.
2. Sequential simulation of preemption.
3. Absence of deadlocks.
4. Race condition detection.

The above features are not new by themselves, but we find it notable that they can be integrated into the above adaptation of SDV directly. We list our implementations below and classify them as sound, respectively complete, with respect to the described hazards.Some SLICx rule implementations are available for download from our website.

The specifications of the rules were extracted from the kernel documentations included in vanilla distributions [9] and from [10]. As the APIs of the Linux kernel may change with each subversion, the rules might be subject to change. Our kernel reference version is 2.6.18.

4.1 Memory

Memory Safety with CBMC. Memory safety—i.e. the avoidance of invalid accesses to memory areas—is already implemented in CBMC. However, CBMC only supports generic memory-related specifications that must be true for all programs written in C:

- Dereferences of NULL pointers.
- Dereferences of pointers to deallocated objects.
- Dereferences of pointers to objects that were not initialized within the scope of analysis.
- Accesses beyond an object's bounds within memory—e.g. after the last element of an array.
- Calls to function pointers with an offset.

Memory Leaks (ML). Dynamic objects are allocated by means of kmalloc() and some minor variations of it. A module must deallocate this memory by kfree() if it is no longer in use. A situation where deallocation is necessary is described by the following two conditions:

- Module initialization has failed or the module is unloaded
- and the memory is at that time not used by other modules or the kernel.

As most modules are unloadable and design principles impose that memory is only deallocated in the module where it is allocated this scenario covers most Linux drivers. The description is sound but not complete. For example memory leaks may also occur in modules that cannot be unloaded and are successfully initialized.

We call this rule 'Memory Leak' (ML). Figure 3 shows a possible life cycle that must be implemented as part of the operating system model. Specifications that refer to the life cycle of a driver can also be found as part of the SDV rulebase. Our contribution is to adapt this idea to cover memory leaks.

The universal quantification trick is used to monitor one non-deterministically chosen[2] object. We track the objects allocation status. In Linux initialization and unload functions are marked by module_init respectively by module_exit. If one of these functions ends the allocation status is checked. This check may lead to false-positives if memory is allocated and deallocated in two different modules. Linux coding rules disencourage these cases so one may expect not to find false positives. False negatives result from the fact that module unloading is not necessary for the occurrence of memory leaks.

---

[2] The object is chosen at allocation time, hence its state is allocated.

4.2   Preemption Simulation (PS)

Many problems in operating system software arise from parallel executions. In order to extend our rules to cover these concurrent traces, we simulate concurrent execution by non-deterministic executions of interrupts and other functions. The sequential simulation idea in operating systems was introduced by the tool KISS [11]. KISS simulates slightly more parallel szenarios, but it is unknown if the presented techniques are applicable for the complex parallelism found in Linux. Other tools like TCBMC [12] cover even more traces but have only be applied to small examples.

The complete and correct modeling of all possible concurrent executions within a Linux device driver requires a large and detailed operating system model. It is unknown if a device driver running on such a vast environment can be verified. If it can be done the question arises whether the manual annotation overhead is feasible for the large set of drivers a Linux kernel contains.

Following the spirit of SDV we establish a fully automatic, feasible analysis of concurrency. Therefore we pose the following design constraints:

- No manual annotation per driver should be necessary.
- One concurrency model must be applicable for all drivers.
- The model checker does not need to support parallelism.

Because of our design goals and the complexity of full thread parallelism we reduce the task to partially simulate preemption. Our solution is incomplete but sound as we carefully model API semantics.

To simulate preemption by interrupts, we annotate function calls with a non-deterministic call to the interrupt handler. The call to the handler is guarded by a check whether the interrupt is enabled and registered.

In general this mechanism is applicable to all entry functions in modules that may be called concurrently in uni- and multi-processor environments. We have implemented this mechanism for the small class of USB input devices such that concurrent calls to drivers may preempt running ones. These functions are guarded by flags that indicate that the callback function has been registered. Tests show that CBMC is capable of handling our sort of parallelism for the USB drivers, though we did not expose new errors during the tests.

A common error in device driver initialization is that interrupts and callback functions may be called as soon as they are registered [10]. With our technique we have detected artificially introduced errors in USB inout drivers.

The sequential simulation of concurrency is implemented as a SLICx rule. It provides a concurrent setting for the following checks for race conditions and deadlocks.

4.3   Sound Locking (AL)

The commonly cited locking rule 'Alternating Locking' (AL) refers to the requirement that for each lock instance, lock and unlock operations must be performed in an alternating manner. If a lock object is requested twice without unlocking a deadlock occurs. This specification is sound, but clearly incomplete with respect to deadlocks. This rule can be implemented in a similar way as in the original SLIC language [4]. We extended the rule to cover all different locking and unlocking operations.

4.4   Complete Locking (LO)

The sound rule AL is complemented by a second rule that is complete with respect to deadlocks [3]. The 4 Coffman conditions [13] describe necessary requirements that must be true in order to produce a deadlock.

Three of the Coffman conditions are true due to the Linux locking implementation. Therefore the only option to avoid deadlocks is to enforce that the fourth condition is not true: deadlocks can only occur if there is a circular wait for locks. To prevent this, we require that locks are requested in a strict locking order. We present a SLICx rule that monitors this requirement and is therefore complete with respect to deadlocks (in the locking API).

The rule is named 'Lock order' (LO) and is implemented via a non-deterministically chosen pair of lock objects similar to the universal quantification trick. For each watched lock a status flag is introduced that monitors the locked / unlocked state of this lock. Moreover, a flag is introduced that stores the order of acquisitions for the chosen pair of locks. If it never happens that any pair of locks is acquired in more than one order, we may assume that a circular wait is not induced by the locks. Fig. 4 shows an excerpt from our locking rule.

If the lock order were specified in the API, each thread could be checked separately. Of course, preemption simulation must be added to both rules.

Linux kernel handbooks [10, p. 122] encourage developers to maintain a strict looking order. Our experiences show that for lock sets defined in a module a strict locking order is kept. It is unknown if this requirement holds for lock sets that are used in different modules.

4.5   Race Conditions (UA)

A race condition may occur if two threads of control access a shared memory location and at least one of them writes a new value into it. Instead of finding race conditions directly, we propose a conservative rule that is complete but unsound with respect to races. The difference to other race checking tools is that we implement race checking with the standard means provided by CBMC and SLICx while each tool does not offer a notion of parallelism or race-checking by itself. The rule is called 'Unprotected Access' (UA).

Our solution covers the following common setting: *A dynamically allocated* struct *shall be protected from accesses without prior acquisitions of a lock that protects it.* We reverse this requirement: an unlock operation prohibits all further accesses to this struct and its members up to the next lock operation. Memory accesses cannot be directly annotated with either SLIC or SLICx. CBMC also

---

[3] Completeness refers to the spinlock part of the API.

```
spin_lock.exit{                          irq_return_t interrupt_handler() {
   // case 1: parameter is the first          spin_lock(lock2);
   // monitored lock                          spin_lock(lock1);
   if(which_first_lock!=NULL &&               ...
      ($1 == which_first_lock)){              spin_unlock(lock1);
      if (first_lock_locked==0){              spin_unlock(lock2);
         if (second_lock_locked==1) {    }
            if (!order_set) {
               first_before_second = 0;  void device_read() {
               order_set = 1;               spin_lock(lock1);
            } else                           if (nondet_bool())
               if (first_before_second) {       interrupt_handler();
               abort "Lock order viol.";      spin_lock(lock2);
               }                              if (nondet_bool())
         }                                       interrupt_handler();
         first_lock_locked = 1;            // ...
      } else {                              spin_unlock(lock2);
         abort "Double acquire!";           if (nondet_bool())
      }                                         interrupt_handler();
   // case 2: parameter is the second       spin_unlock(lock1);
   // monitored lock                        if (nondet_bool())
   ...                                          interrupt_handler();
}                                        }
```

Fig. 4. (l) Excerpt from the specification implementation of the locking restriction (LO). The `which__lock` pointers track the pair of locks that is currently monitored. `order_set` tracks if one lock order has been determined on the current trace. (r) This example shows a common locking situation between an interrupt handler and a driver service function. Both functions operate on a pair of locks, but the interrupt handler uses a different locking order. Using partial simulation of the preemption, this deadlock is discovered by our toolchain.

offers no way to insert additional checks for each memory access. We therefore exploit the built-in memory checks from CBMC.

Consider the code excerpt in Figure 5. The `struct driver` is protected by the spinlock `lock`. Possible driver code is presented on the left. Line 4 contains an unprotected access that may lead to data races if the code is reentrant. The application of the rule (right) inserts the unnumbered lines into the driver's code where

- `which_lock` refers to the lock that is monitored.
- `$1` refers to the first parameter of the lock / unlock functions. We use a shortcut and replace it on the left side by `&lock` as it is the only lock instance that occurs in the example.
- `while(1);` terminates the execution due to the bounded model checking.

In order to make CBMC report the access in line 4, we non-deterministically call `free` on `driver`. CBMC's memory checking ensures that all memory accesses

```
  // annotation omitted
  1: spin_lock(&lock);
  2: driver->request_nr++;                    spin_lock.entry {
  3: spin_unlock(&lock);                        if (which_lock==$1) {
  // nondet_bool() implements *                   if (object_destroyed==1)
     if (which_lock==&lock) {                        // Terminate trace
        if (nondet_bool()) {                            while(1);
           object_destroyed = 1;                }
           free(driver);                     }
        }
     }                                       spin_unlock.exit {
  // invalid access:                           if(which_lock==$1) {
  4: driver->request_nr++;                       if(*) {
  5: spin_lock(&lock);                              object_destroyed = 1;
     if (which_lock==&lock) {                       kfree(which_object);
        if (object_destroyed) while(1);         }
     }                                         }
  6: driver->request_nr++;                   }
  7: spin_unlock(&lock);
  // annotation omitted
```

Fig. 5. (l) A code example for race condition dectection. The code in unnumbered lines on the left side is inserted by the SLICx rule on the right side (r).

occurring after free will be reported (line 4). Additionally we want to prohibit false positives that arise when the previously deallocated struct is locked—i.e. protected—again in line 5. This restoration of the object's state is achieved by a termination of the current execution if driver had been deallocated before. An additional complication is that reallocations of driver could occur between line 3 and 4. This problem can be solved by annotating allocation functions.

We summarize that our rule detects races under the described common circumstances. The rule implementation is sound and complete, but the specification is not sound, but complete.

The relationship between locks and protected structs can be heuristically inferred from Linux conventions as locks are commonly embedded in the structs they protect.

In order to cover accesses prior to any locking operation, we modify memory allocation functions like kmalloc such that they may non-deterministically set the pointer to NULL. If such a pointer reaches a lock operation the trace is also terminated.

4.6   Additional Techniques

Specification by implementation. Some pre- and postconditions of functions cannot be encoded in either SLICx or with CBMC's checks. One example is the memcpy(target_buffer, source_buffer, length) function that copies bytes from a source buffer to a target buffer. One precondition for `memcpy` is that the buffer sizes are greater than `length`. However, the size of the buffers cannot be inferred for dynamically allocated arrays or objects passed using pointer casts. Our solution to the problem is that we annotate calls to `memcpy` with its C implementation. The implementation iterates over all bytes by pointer arithmetic and hence CBMC will detect invalid accesses if the loop unwinding bound is large enough. A better solution would be to provide access to the buffer sizes stored in CBMC's internal model. Since the source code of CBMC has been recently released, we will be able to patch CBMC such that SLICx rules may access object sizes by new keywords.

Runtime Testing. As the SLICx rules are directly inserted into Linux kernel sources, runtime testing can be achieved easily. The rules are meant for static analysis but rely only on one aspect that is not available for runtime-testing: non–determinism. However the API of CBMC for non-determinism could be implemented by random generators. Though it is an arbitrary selection of test cases it should work without any further modifications. We have used SLICx to patch a recent Linux kernel (2.6.20.4). The patch implements a check that the second parameter of the function `kmem_cache_free` is not `NULL`. Instead of using `assert` we have used the kernel macro `BUG_ON` for runtime testing. Running the kernel did not lead to any bug reports.

5 Empirical Results

We performed the following small case studies: Testing rules on artificial drivers, rediscovering errors from a case study [14] and finding double-free errors in Linux drivers. For artificially created drivers our specification worked without any manual intervention besides writing the driver. Before presenting results on real drivers, we briefly review problems performing modular analysis.

5.1 Modularity Issues

One might expect that checking of API properties is trivial if the verification backend is powerful and efficient enough. Our experiences show that modular analysis faces serious problems when checking function call specifications. Moreover, it is hardly possible to check memory violations as all external data objects are passed by, potentially invalid, references. A detailed analysis of the problems with modular device driver analysis is given in [15]. It is inherently difficult to do automatic modular analysis on device drivers.

Basically, three solutions to the unknown environment problem exist. The first solution is to include large parts of the Linux kernel. The resulting model will be too large for bit-level precision model checking, but light-weight code checking may still be successfully applied. One example for this strategy can be found in [16]. We found that for CBMC the performance bottleneck lies in the model generation. One possible reason is that code unwinding increases the size of the code by an exponential factor.

Another approach is to construct a generic environment for device drivers as done in SDV. For Linux the architecture and interfaces for device drivers are less uniform than in the Windows Device Driver Framework. No common Linux driver model is implemented that supports a generic operating system model as implemented in SDV[4].

For the data environment aspect some tools exist (e.g. [17]), but many C extensions of the Linux kernel code seem to prevent a direct application [15]. We are currently working on automatic environment construction specialized on Linux device drivers. An early prototype enabled us to check some device drivers for known memory violations.

5.2   Results on Real Drivers

If the verification process is not fully automated as it is in SDV, it is time consuming to find unknown bugs within the large set of Linux source files. A detailed study of this problem is given by Mühlberg and Lüttgen [14] who critically evaluated the applicability of BLAST [7] on Linux Device Drivers. The authors managed to reproduce some known errors with considerable manual effort. We took some of their examples and tried our solution to rediscover the same bugs. Our verification process works as follows:

1. Configuration of the Linux kernel such that the relevant modules are built.
2. Manual implemention of a SLICx interface rule to be checked in SLICx.
3. Automatic annotation of all drivers with the above rule.
4. Automatic annotation of subsystems or other source files that are involved.
5. Compilation of the Linux kernel using additional header files and the code preprocessing tool CIL [18].
6. Manually selecting relevant source code files that are automatically merged with CIL.
7. Code simplification with a custom automatic script [19].
8. Manual creation of a `main` function simulating the operating system's use of the driver.
9. Automatic data environment creation for `main`.
10. Running CBMC on `main`.

After annotating, preprocessing, merging and enriching the driver, the verification is performed by CBMC. Our tool-chain rediscovered most bugs mostly without manual intervention. Compared to the results given in [14] the manual effort seems to be significantly reduced. Besides rediscovering known errors we have launched a first check for double-free errors. Due to an incomplete environment and some minor CBMC bugs, our tool reported 95 issues. For this case study we can only report one real error. More results and details on performed case studies can be obtained through our project website.

---

[4] A generic device driver model exists in Linux, but many drivers do not use it yet. Moreover the model is subject to extensions and modifications for different subsystems.

```
int main(void)
{
  SLIC_driver_init();
  struct scsi_cmnd cmd;
  struct scsi_device scsidev ;
  struct Scsi_Host host;
  spinlock_t host_lock;
// ...
// API preconditon
  __SLIC_spin_lock_init(&host_lock);
  __SLIC_spin_lock(&host_lock);
// continued on right side...
```

```
// Introduce aliasing
  host.host_lock = &host_lock;
  scsidev.host = &host;
  cmd.device = &scsidev;
  cmd.sc_request = &sc_req;
// Call the erronous function
  ata_scsi_queuecmd(&cmd,
         ... scsi_finish_command);
  SLIC_driver_exit();
  return (0);
}
```

Fig. 6. A manually constructed operating system model tuned to one error hidden in a SCSI subsystem component. If memory safety checks are enabled, the data environment has to be initialized as well.

6 Related Work

The contribution of this work is the integration of several verification aspects into one tool chain. SDV is clearly a predecessor of our approach. SDV has a domain that is focussed on a fixed set of some 60 API conformance rules for Windows Driver Model drivers. A second set of 40 rules for the Kernel-Mode Driver Framework has also been developed. SDV's backend, SLAM, is a model checker that is integrated into a Counter Example Guided Abstraction Refinement (CEGAR) loop. SDV itself cannot analyze memory safety, concurrent programs with shared memory, bit-level and integer operations [2]. We use an extended specification language together with a novel and extended rule base for Linux. We employ a verification engine that has a built-in support for checking memory safety and bit-level operations. We extend the work by rules that can only be implemented by using SLICx in combination with CBMC. This paper concentrates on the specification, specification application and integration aspects and therefore we do not discuss the numerous verification techniques and their implementations in greater detail.

Verification Engines. As a back-end we chose the bounded model checker CBMC [3]. Other C source code model checkers are BLAST [7] and MAGIC [20]. A case study on Linux sources using a heuristic checker is given in [16]. Other approaches include MOPS [21] and abstract interpretation [22]. We omit examples for runtime analysis tools and tools based on theorem proving techniques.

We chose to use CBMC as it supports a wide range of C features, a fact that is crucial when automatic processing of rough device driver code must be achieved. Some new tools for analyzing C source code are: F-Soft [23], Cascade [24] and the work in [25] which extends the analysis of C programs to recursive calls and message passing synchronization. We plan to test if these tools are embeddable in our tool-chain as well.

Separation logic [26] provides a promising approach to improve reasoning about low-level programs. To the best of our knowledge it has not been tested on large real-world systems written in C.

API Specification Languages for C. The specification language strongly resembles the *Aspect Oriented Programming* paradigm. With SLICx, we do not formally restrict the code in transfer functions: we allow function calls, recursion and memory allocation. Several other verification tools feature an integrated specification language (for example BLAST [7]).

Operating System Interface Specification Implementations. To the best of our knowledge the SDV project has the only other available specification implementation for systems software APIs used by device drivers. SDV's specifications target the Windows Driver Model framework and are hence not immediately applicable to Linux drivers.

A specification implementation for the Linux Standards Base [27] is developed in the Olver Project [28]. The project targets interfaces between the Linux kernel and user level software. The project includes formal specifications of more than one thousand functions imposed by the Linux Standard Base meant for automatic model based implementation testing.

Several specifications of user space APIs are analyzed with model checking technology in [29].

Practical Results on Linux Device Driver Verification. There have been several works on bug finding or verification of Linux device drivers: BLAST is a source code level model checker for C. Though BLAST does implement powerful techniques, its practical applicability has been criticized in [14].

CBMC's manual explicitly uses a Linux device driver as an example for verification, but the presented code is a high-level abstraction. Besides, CBMC does not offer specifications other than memory safety checking, division by zero and assertions.

D. Engler et al. published several papers presenting results from Linux kernels (e.g. [16], [30]). The presented techniques are effective and efficient, but do not guarantee soundness or completeness and could therefore be classified as heuristic approaches.

SATURN [31] is a SAT-based checking tool that has reported several bugs in the Linux kernel.

7   Summary

We have ported the SDV approach to Linux. We successfully extended the specification language and implemented a compiler for SLICx. CBMC is integrated in our approach such that SLICx features are transformed into C code that uses CBMC's specification and modeling directives. We extracted several API-rules and implemented them in SLICx. Our specifications may be used for checking Linux device drivers as long as the problems of modular verification can be solved. A general limitation of our approach is fact the we employ a bounded model checker. Hence our contributions are only sound and complete disregarding limitations in the analysis backend CBMC.

SLICx and CBMC allow us to formulate several new rules that significantly extend the application area of SDV. Rules are presented for sound and complete deadlock detection. Race conditions are covered by a complete rule. From a practitioner's point of view, the sound detection of memory leaks is also a notable contribution. On a large domain on unloadable device driver the rule can be considered complete.

The simulation of multithreaded executions is achieved with SLICx allowing to preemption at a higher precision—fewer false positives—automatically.

We have gained new insights into the dependence between hazards, API-specifications and rules that implement these specifications.

The solutions have been proven to be effective on small, artificially created driver models. For some examples we were able to even apply the techniques to rediscover known bugs in real Linux drivers. Due to problems concerning environment model we could only present some new errors. We believe that providing Linux operating system models will lead to a solution that resembles or even extends the success of SDV for the Linux domain.

Acknowledgement. We would like to thank Carsten Sinz, Friedrich Meissner and Matthias Sauter for helpful discussions and comments on this topic. Friedrich Meissner and Matthias Sauter have substantially contributed on the implementation part of this work. Friedrich Meissner has implemented the SLICx compiler as a part of his master thesis [32]. Besides helpful discussions, Reinhard Bündgen contributed by organizing an early internship at IBM.

References

1. Swift, M.M., Bershad, B.N., Levy, H.M.: Improving the reliability of commodity operating systems. In: 19th ACM Symp. on Operating Systems Principles, Proc., pp. 207–222. ACM Press, New York (2003)
2. Ball, T., Bounimova, E., Cook, B., Levin, V., Lichtenberg, J., McGarvey, C., Ondrusek, B., Rajamani, S.K., Ustuner, A.: Thorough static analysis of device drivers. ACM SIGOPS Oper. Syst. Rev. 40(4), 73–85 (2006)
3. Clarke, E., Kroening, D., Lerda, F.: A tool for checking ANSI-C programs. In: Jensen, K., Podelski, A. (eds.) TACAS 2004. LNCS, vol. 2988, pp. 168–176. Springer, Heidelberg (2004)
4. Ball, T., Rajamani, S.K.: SLIC: A specification language for interface checking. Technical report, Microsoft Research (2001)
5. Various: The SLAM Project (2006) http://research.microsoft.com/slam/
6. Post, H., Sinz, C., Küchlin, W.: Avinux: Towards automatic verification of Linux device drivers (2007) Available at
   http://www-sr.informatik.uni-tuebingen.de/~post/avinux
7. Henzinger, T.A., Jhala, R., Majumdar, R., Sutre, G.: Software verification with blast. In: Ball, T., Rajamani, S.K. (eds.) Model Checking Software. LNCS, vol. 2648, pp. 235–239. Springer, Heidelberg (2003)

8. Corbett, J.C., Dwyer, M.B., Hatcliff, J., Laubach, S., Păsăreanu, C.S., Robby, Z.H.: Bandera: extracting finite-state models from Java source code. In: Software Engineering, 22nd Intl. Conf., Proc., pp. 439–448. ACM Press, New York (2000)
9. Various: Linux kernel releases (Available online under http://www.kernel.org)
10. Corbet, J., Rubini, A., Kroah-Hartman, G.: Linux Device Drivers, 3rd edn. O'Reilly Media, Inc. (2005)
11. Qadeer, S., Wu, D.: KISS: keep it simple and sequential. In: ACM SIGPLAN Conf. on Programming Language Design and Implementation, Proc., vol. 39, pp. 14–24. ACM Press, New York (2004)
12. Rabinovitz, I., Grumberg, O.: Bounded model checking of concurrent programs. pp. 82–97
13. Coffman, E.G., Elphick, M., Shoshani, A.: System deadlocks. ACM Comput. Surv. 3(2), 67–78 (1971)
14. Mühlberg, J.T., Lüttgen, G.: Blasting Linux Code. In: Brim, L., Haverkort, B., Leucker, M., van de Pol, J. (eds.) FMICS 2006 and PDMC 2006. LNCS, vol. 4346, pp. 211–226. Springer, Heidelberg (2007)
15. Post, H., Küchlin, W.: Automatic data environment construction for static device drivers analysis. In: Conf. on Specification and verification of component-based systems, Proc., pp. 89–92. ACM Press, New York (2006)
16. Yang, J., Twohey, P., Engler, D., Musuvathi, M.: Using model checking to find serious file system errors. ACM Trans. Comput. Syst. 24(4), 393–423 (2006)
17. Sen, K., Marinov, D., Agha, G.: CUTE: a concolic unit testing engine for c. In: Wermelinger, M., Gall, H. (eds.) ESEC/SIGSOFT FSE, pp. 263–272. ACM Press, New York (2005)
18. Necula, G.C., McPeak, S., Rahul, S.P., Weimer, W.: Cil: Intermediate language and tools for analysis and transformation of c programs. In: Horspool, R.N. (ed.) CC 2002 and ETAPS 2002. LNCS, vol. 2304, pp. 213–228. Springer, Heidelberg (2002)
19. Sauter, M.: Automatisierung und Integration regelbasierter Verifikation für Linux Gerätetreiber. Master's Thesis (To appear, 2007)
20. Chaki, S., Clarke, E., Groce, A., Jha, S., Veith, H.: Modular verification of software components in C. In: Software Engineering. 25th Intl. Conf., Proc, pp. 385–395. IEEE Computer Society, Washington, DC (2003)
21. Chen, H., Wagner, D.: MOPS: an infrastructure for examining security properties of software. In: Atluri, V. (ed.) ACM Intl. Conf. on Computer and Communications Security, Proc., pp. 235–244. ACM, New York (2002)
22. Cousot, P.: Abstract interpretation. ACM Comput. Surv. 28(2), 324–328 (1996)
23. Ivancic, F., Yang, Z., Ganai, M.K., Gupta, A., Shlyakhter, I., Ashar, P.: F-Soft: Software verification platform. [33], pp. 301–306
24. Sethi, N., Barrett, C.: Cascade: C assertion checker and deductive engine. In: Ball, T., Jones, R.B. (eds.) CAV 2006. LNCS, vol. 4144, pp. 166–169. Springer, Heidelberg (2006)
25. Chaki, S., Clarke, E.M., Kidd, N., Reps, T.W., Touili, T.: Verifying concurrent message-passing C programs with recursive calls. In: Hermanns, H., Palsberg, J. (eds.) TACAS 2006 and ETAPS 2006. LNCS, vol. 3920, pp. 334–349. Springer, Heidelberg (2006)
26. Reynolds, J.C.: Separation logic: A logic for shared mutable data structures. In: LICS, pp. 55–74. IEEE Computer Society, Los Alamitos (2002)
27. Various: Linux standard base project (Available online under http://www.linuxbase.org)

28. Various: The OLVER project (Available under `http://linuxtesting.org`)
29. Chen, H., Dean, D., Wagner, D.: Model checking one million lines of C code. In: NDSS, The Internet Society (2004)
30. Engler, D., Ashcraft, K.: RacerX: effective, static detection of race conditions and deadlocks. In: 19th ACM Symp. on Operating Systems Principles, Proc., pp. 237–252. ACM Press, New York (2003)
31. Xie, Y., Aiken, A.: Scalable error detection using boolean satisfiability. In: 32nd ACM SIGPLAN-SIGACT Symp. on Principles of Programming Languages, Proc., pp. 351–363. ACM Press, New York (2005)
32. Meissner, F.: Regelbasierte Spezifikation von Linux Kernel-Schnittstellen mit SLIC. Master's Thesis (To appear, 2007)
33. Etessami, K., Rajamani, S.K. (eds.): CAV 2005. LNCS, vol. 3576, pp. 6–10. Springer, Heidelberg (2005)

Integrating Verification, Testing, and Learning for Cryptographic Protocols[*]

M. Oostdijk[1,4], V. Rusu[2], J. Tretmans[1,3], R.G. de Vries[1],
and T.A.C. Willemse[1,4]

[1] Radboud University, Nijmegen, NL
[2] Irisa/Inria Rennes, FR
[3] Embedded Systems Institute, Eindhoven, NL
[4] Eindhoven University of Technology, NL
[5] Riscure, Delft, NL

Abstract. The verification of cryptographic protocol *specifications* is an active research topic and has received much attention from the formal verification community. By contrast, the black-box testing of actual *implementations* of protocols, which is, arguably, as important as verification for ensuring the correct functioning of protocols in the "real" world, is little studied. We propose an approach for checking secrecy and authenticity properties not only on protocol specifications, but also on black-box implementations. The approach is compositional and integrates ideas from verification, testing, and learning. It is illustrated on the Basic Access Control protocol implemented in biometric passports.

1 Introduction

The verification of cryptographic protocols has been an active research topic for at least the last two decades. Early approaches consisted in developing dedicated logics for specification and inference rules [1,2,3], which a user applied "by hand". More recently, automatic, or, at least, computer-assisted techniques have emerged. These include model checking [4,5], theorem proving [6,7] and combinations of these two techniques [8]. Other approaches are based on term rewriting techniques [9] sometimes combined with abstract interpretation [10,11,12]. The above list, albeit incomplete, shows that most formal verification techniques have been applied, or adapted to, cryptographic protocol verification.

The situation is quite different in the area of testing of black-box implementations of protocols[1]. A thorough search of computer science research bibliographies revealed only a few related works. Closest to ours is [14], where an executable implementation is instrumented (hence, it is not really a black box) to detect violations of security properties. In other works [15,16], various source-code verification techniques have been applied to source-code implementations.

---

[*] This work was done while the second author was visiting the university of Nijmegen.
[1] Here, by "implementation" we mean black-box executable code, which is controllable/observable only through some interfaces, e.g., like in conformance testing [13].

J. Davies and J. Gibbons (Eds.): IFM 2007, LNCS 4591, pp. 538–557, 2007.
© Springer-Verlag Berlin Heidelberg 2007

All these works assume in one way or another that some kind of source code of the protocol is available, which may not always be the case.

Outside the academic world, practitioners have also developed empirical approaches for testing security protocols. The tester (or "cracker") will try to find whatever information might leak from a protocol implementation, by applying ad-hoc techniques such as sending arbitrary messages, trying to overflow buffers, or attempting to break cryptography by brute force. Some of these techniques were tried when testing the new Dutch biometric passport [17].

Clearly, there are differences between verification and testing techniques for cryptographic protocols. Some are the usual differences between the two: formal verification may prove either presence or absence of errors in specifications, while testing may only prove the presence of errors in implementations. Other differences are specific to the present field of interest:

- in verification, specifications are often very partial, in the sense that only some inputs and outputs are specified. Of course, only the specified behaviour, together with that of an implicit "intruder", e.g., following the so-called Dolev-Yao model [18] can be verified. This amounts to saying that the intruder does not "try" to feed the honest agents with messages that they do not " expect" (i.e., whose reception is not specified in the protocol).
- testing for security is not limited to the behaviour of the protocol as described by an (incomplete) specification; rather, the protocol's behaviour outside the specification is also targeted, in the hope that violations of security properties will be observed.

The two techniques are different, yet complementary: verification proves correctness of the specification against a given set of security properties, whereas testing checks correctness of the implementation with respect to the specification and, outside the specification, with respect to the security properties. In this paper we propose an approach that builds on this complementarity and, moreover, performs *learning* from implementations to "complete" the incomplete specifications. The approach can be roughly described as follows:

1. the protocol's specification is automatically verified against a given set of security properties (e.g., secrecy and authenticity properties);
2. if the properties hold on the protocol's specification, we proceed with the learning step, which consists in augmenting each agent's specification with a set of new behaviours, obtained by testing/interacting with their respective implementations; then, the process continues at Step 1;
3. otherwise, the verification finds a violation of a property on the protocol's specification, and produces a counterexample. Then, we attempt to execute the counterexample on the black-box implementation:
   (a) if the attempt succeeds, a violation of a property on the protocol's global implementation has been found, and the procedure terminates.
   (b) if the attempt does not succeed, the last learning step is responsible; hence, it is modified, and the process is continued at Step 2.

The global procedure can terminate by reporting a violation of a security property by the protocol's implementation, or when all "representative" traces up to a certain length have been learned. In the latter case, the conclusion is that the implementation satisfies the security properties, provided that the testing/learning was "exhaustive". This "exhaustiveness" condition is formally defined in the paper, and notions of soundness and (theoretical) completeness of the approach are formally defined and proved.

The rest of the paper is organised as follows. In Section 2 we introduce the model of IOSTS (Input-Output Symbolic Transition Systems), which we use for writing specifications of cryptographic protocols. In Section 3 we present the ingredients of our approach: verification of security properties (secrecy, authentication) expressed using observers (which are IOSTS augmented with certain acceptance conditions) against protocol specifications expressed as parallel compositions of IOSTS; and learning new behaviours of a specification by testing a black-box implementation of the protocol and observing/interpreting the results. In Section 4 our approach integrating verification, testing, and learning is defined. The approach is demonstrated on the Basic Access Control protocol, which is part of the security mechanisms implemented in biometric passports [19].

2   Models

The IOSTS model (*Input/Output Symbolic Transition Systems*) is inspired from I/O automata [20]. We specialise here IOSTS for modelling security protocols. The symbolic data that our protocol-oriented IOSTS manipulate are of three main *sorts*: the sort $\mathcal{M}$ of *messages*, the sort $\mathcal{K}$ of *keys*, and the sort $\mathcal{N}$ of *nonces*. Keys and nonces are subsorts of messages. We define a *composition* (i.e., concatenation) function $".": \mathcal{M} \times \mathcal{M} \mapsto \mathcal{M}$ as well the decomposition of a composed message into its components, using the usual axiomatic way. We also define a (symmetrical) *encryption function* $"\{\}_-": \mathcal{M} \times \mathcal{K} \mapsto \mathcal{M}$, with the property that $\{\{m\}_k\}_k = m$, for all $m : \mathcal{M}$ and $k : \mathcal{K}^2$. We enrich this signature with the usual Boolean sort, and obtain a simple equational theory, with the usual notion of *terms* (closed as well as with free variables). We denote by *free(trm)* the set of free variables of a term *trm*. Each term has a *smallest sort* (with the convention that the sorts $\mathcal{M}$, $\mathcal{K}$, and $\mathcal{N}$ are ordered such that $\mathcal{K}$ and $\mathcal{N}$ are *smaller* than $\mathcal{M}$). We shall need the following notion: a term trm_1 is *sort-compatible* with a term trm_2 if the smallest sort of trm_1 is smaller than or equal to the smallest sort of trm_2. The semantics of closed terms is given by the usual *initial algebra* of our signature.

2.1   Syntax of IOSTS

Definition 1 (IOSTS). *An IOSTS is a tuple* $\langle V, P, C, \Theta, L, l^0, \Sigma^?, \Sigma^!, \Sigma^\tau, \mathcal{T} \rangle$ *where*

---

[2] In this paper we only use symmetrical encryption. If needed, asymmetrical encryption can also be defined in a similar way.

- V *is a finite set of* state variables[3], P *is a finite set of* formal parameters, *and* C *is a finite set of* symbolic constants, *all of which can be of any of the above sorts* $\mathcal{M}$, $\mathcal{K}$, *or* $\mathcal{N}$.
- Θ *is the* initial condition, *a term of Boolean sort, with free*$(\Theta) \subseteq V$,
- L *is a nonempty, finite set of* locations *and* $l^0 \in L$ *is the* initial location,
- $\Sigma^?$ *is a set of* input actions, $\Sigma^!$ *is a set of* output actions, *and* Σ^τ *is a set of* internal actions. *For each action* $a \in \Sigma^? \cup \Sigma^!$, *its* formal parameter list *par*$(a) = \langle p_1, \ldots, p_k \rangle \in P^k$ $(k \in \mathbb{N})$ *is a tuple of pairwise distinct formal parameters. We say that the action* a carries *the formal parameters in par*(a). *By convention, internal actions* $\tau \in \Sigma^\tau$ *carry no parameters.*
- T *is a nonempty, finite set of* transitions. *Each transition is a tuple* $\langle l, a, G, A, l' \rangle$ *made of:*
  - *a location* $l \in L$, *called the* origin *of the transition;*
  - *an action* $a \in \Sigma^? \cup \Sigma^! \cup \Sigma^\tau$ *called the* action *of the transition;*
  - *a term* G *of Boolean sort, with free*$(G) \subseteq V \cup P$, *called the* guard;
  - *an* assignment A, *which is a set of expressions of the form* $(x := A^x)_{x \in V}$ *such that, for each* $x \in V$, A^x *is a term that is sort-compatible with* x, *and free*$(A^x) \cap P \subseteq$ *free*(G);
  - *a location* $l' \in L$ *called the* destination *of the transition.*

For an IOSTS $\mathcal{S}$ we shall denote by V_S its set of state variables, by C_s its set of symbolic constants, by L_s its set of locations, etc. In graphical representations of IOSTS, the identifiers of input actions are followed by the the the "?" symbol, and the identifiers of output actions are followed by the "!" symbol. These symbols are not part of the action's name, but are only used to easily identify inputs and outputs. Input and output actions are also called *visible* or *observable* actions; this in contrast with *internal* actions, which are not observable from the environment. Guards that are identically *true* are not depicted, and a variable not present in the assignments of a transition is assumed to be left unmodified.

The difference between state variables, constants and formal parameters is that a state variable's value can be modified, whereas a symbolic constant's value cannot. However, both state variables and constants always *have* values, while a formal parameter, say, p, has a value only during the instantaneous firing of the transition labelled by the action carrying p[4].

Example 1. The two IOSTS depicted in Figure 1 describe, respectively the behaviour of a terminal (in the left-hand side) and of a biometric passport (in the right hand side), executing the Basic Access control protocol [19]. This protocol is designed to ensure that the passport and the terminal mutually authenticate, and generate a certain secret session key, by which all communication between the two - after successful completion of Basic Access Control - will be encrypted.

Initially, both passport and terminal know a certain key K (different from the session key), which is a symbolic constant. The terminal initiates the protocol by sending a certain command, Get_Chal!, to the passport. Upon reception, the

---

[3] Not to be confused with the free variables appearing in terms of our signature.
[4] Cf. Section 2.2 on the formal semantics of IOSTS.

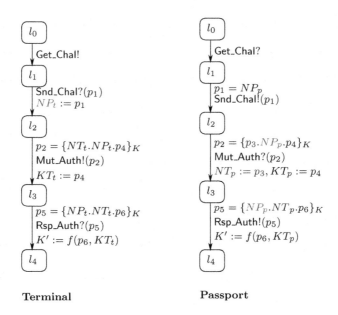

Terminal   **Passport**

Fig. 1. Sample IOSTS: Basic Access Control in the Biometric Passport

passport replies by a Snd_Chal! response, carrying a formal parameter p_1 of sort nonce, whose value is equal to NP_p, the passport's nonce (a symbolic constant). The terminal receives this value and memorises it in its state variable NP_t, which is the terminal's copy of the passport's nonce. (State variables/symbolic constants of the passport are subscripted by p, those of the terminal, by t.)

Then, the terminal sends a Mut_Auth! output, carrying a formal parameter $p_2 = \{NT_t.NP_t.p_4\}_K$, that is, an encryption under K of a sequence consisting of: the terminal's nonce NT_t (a symbolic constant), the previously memorised passport's nonce NP_t, and a certain arbitrary value p_4 of sort $\mathcal{K}$. The value p_4 is stored in the terminal's variable KT_t containing so-called *key material* (to be used later). The passport accepts the output only if, on the passport's side, the formal parameter p_2 contains, under the encryption with the same key K, the passport's nonce NP_p, surrounded by two arbitrary values: p_3 and p_4. On the same transition, these values are stored, respectively, in the state variables NT_p, i.e., the passport's copy of the terminal's nonce, and KT_p (*key material*).

Next, the passport outputs a Rsp_Auth! response, together with a formal parameter p_5, of the form $p_5 = \{NP_p.NT_p.p_6\}_K$, i.e., an encryption with the same original key K of a concatenation of the nonces NP_p and NT_p, together with an arbitrary value p_6, to serve as *key material* of the passport. This response is accepted by the terminal only if it is able to decrypt and decompose its formal parameter p_5 and to find, at the beginning, its copies NP_t, NT_t of the nonces.

Finally, on their last transitions, both passport and terminal compute a new session K' as a function f, not specified here, of the key material exchanged [19].

Note that the behaviour of the passport and terminal in Basic Access Control is not completely specified by the above IOSTS (which closely follows the informal documents [19]). For example, nothing is said about what happens if a Get_Chal? input is received in a location different from l_0, or if the formal parameter carried by the Mut_Auth! output is not of the expected form. Later in the paper we shall make this specification more "complete" by means of *learning*.

2.2   Semantics of IOSTS

The semantics of IOSTS is described in terms of labelled transition systems.

Definition 2. *An input-output labelled transition system (IOLTS) is a tuple* $\langle S, S^0, \Lambda^?, \Lambda^!, \Lambda^\tau, \rightarrow \rangle$ *where* S *is a possibly infinite set of* states, $S^0 \subseteq S$ *is the possibly infinite set of* initial states, $\Lambda^?$, $\Lambda^!$, *and* Λ^τ *are possibly infinite sets of* input, output, *and* internal *actions, respectively, and* $\rightarrow \subseteq S \times (\Lambda^? \cup \Lambda^! \cup \Lambda^\tau) \times S$ *is the* transition relation.

Intuitively, the IOLTS semantics of an IOSTS $\langle V, C, P, \Theta, L, l^0, \Sigma^?, \Sigma^!, \Sigma^\tau, \mathcal{T} \rangle$ explores the reachable tuples of values (hereafter called *valuations*) of the variables of the IOSTS. Let $\mathcal{V}$ denote the set of valuations of the state variables, and Π denote the set of valuations of the formal parameters P. Then, for a term E with $\mathit{free}(E) \subseteq V \cup P$, and for $\nu \in \mathcal{V}$, $\pi \in \Pi$, we denote by $E(\nu, \pi)$ the value obtained by evaluating E after substituting each state variable by its value according to ν, and each formal parameter by its value according to π. In particular, when the term E does not include parameters, i.e., $\mathit{free}(E) \subseteq V$, the value obtained by evaluating E after substituting each state variable by its value according to ν is denoted by $E(\nu)$. For $P' \subseteq P$ and for $\pi \in \Pi$, we denote by $\pi_{P'}$ the restriction of the valuation π to a subset set $P' \subseteq P$ of parameters, and let $\Pi_{P'} \triangleq \{\pi_{P'} | \pi \in \Pi\}$.

Definition 3. *The semantics of an IOSTS* $\mathcal{S} = \langle V, C, P, \Theta, L, l^0, \Sigma^?, \Sigma^!, \Sigma^\tau, \mathcal{T} \rangle$ *is an IOLTS* $[\![\mathcal{S}]\!] = \langle S, S^0, \Lambda^?, \Lambda^!, \Lambda^\tau, \rightarrow \rangle$, *defined as follows:*

- *the set of states is* $S = L \times \mathcal{V}$,
- *the set of initial states is* $S^0 = \{\langle l_0, \nu \rangle | \Theta(\nu) = true\}$,
- *the set of input actions, also called the set of* valued inputs, *is the set* $\Lambda^? = \{\langle a, \pi' \rangle | a \in \Sigma^?, \pi' \in \Pi_{par(a)}\}$,
- *the set of output actions, also called the set of* valued outputs, *is the set* $\Lambda^! = \{\langle a, \pi' \rangle | a \in \Sigma^!, \pi' \in \Pi_{par(a)}\}$,
- *the set of internal actions is* $\Lambda^\tau = \Sigma^\tau$,
- $\rightarrow$ *is the smallest relation in* $S \times (\Lambda^? \cup \Lambda^! \cup \Lambda^\tau) \times S$ *defined by the following rule:*

$$\frac{t: \langle l, a, G, A, l' \rangle \in \mathcal{T} \quad \pi \in \Pi \quad \nu \in \mathcal{V} \quad G(\nu, \pi) = true \quad \pi' = \pi_{par(a)} \quad \nu' = A(\nu, \pi)}{\langle l, \nu \rangle \xrightarrow{\langle a, \pi' \rangle} \langle l', \nu' \rangle}$$

The rule says that the transition t is fireable when control is in its origin location l, and its guard G is satisfied by the valuation ν of the state variables and π of the formal parameters. If this is the case, then the system moves to the destination location l, and the assignment A maps (ν, π) to ν', *via* the valued action $\langle a, \pi' \rangle$, where π' restricts the valuation π to the formal parameters $par(a)$ carried by the action a (if any; remember that internal actions do not carry parameters). Intuitively, this is because $par(a)$ are the only formal parameters "visible" from the environment. In the sequel, we let $\Lambda \triangleq \Lambda^? \cup \Lambda^! \cup \Lambda^\tau$.

Definition 4 (Execution). *An execution fragment is a sequence of alternating states and valued actions* $s_0 \alpha_0 s_1 \alpha_1 ... \alpha_{n-1} s_n \in S \cdot (\Lambda \cdot S)^*$ *such that* $\forall i = 0, n - 1, s_i \xrightarrow{\alpha_i} s_{i+1}$. *An execution is an execution fragment starting in an initial state. We denote by* $Exec(\mathcal{S})$ *the set of executions of the IOLTS* $[\![\mathcal{S}]\!]$.

Definition 5 (Trace). *The* trace *$trace(\rho)$ of an execution ρ is the projection of ρ on the set $\Lambda^! \cup \Lambda^?$ of valued actions. The set of traces of an IOSTS $\mathcal{S}$ is the set of all traces of all executions of $\mathcal{S}$, and is denoted by* $Traces(\mathcal{S})$.

We shall sometimes need to restrict the traces of an IOSTS in a given *environment*. This operation, together with the *parallel product* operation, defined below, allows for communication of values between IOSTS and enables us to formally define the interactions between agents in a protocol. These interactions ar similar to those encountered, e.g., in coordination models such as Linda [21].

Intuitively, an environment is an unordered channel connected to an IOSTS, and may contain, zero, one, or several instances or each valued action in $\Lambda^! \cup \Lambda^?$ (hence the multiset structure):

Definition 6 (environment). *For an IOSTS $\mathcal{S}$, an environment is a multiset* $\mathcal{E} : \Lambda^! \cup \Lambda^? \to \mathbb{N}$ *of valued inputs and outputs of the IOSTS.*

Then, the traces of an IOSTS that are "admissible" in an environment are those traces obtained by taking valued inputs from the environment and adding valued outputs to it. In the following definition, $\cup$ and $\setminus$ denote the usual union and difference operations on multisets.

Definition 7 (traces in environment). *A trace $\sigma \in Traces(\mathcal{S})$ is admissible in an environment $\mathcal{E} \in \mathbb{N}^{\Lambda^! \cup \Lambda^?}$ if the pair $(\sigma, \mathcal{E})$ belongs to the following recursively defined admissibility relation:*

- *Any pair $(\epsilon, \mathcal{E})$ where ϵ denotes the empty trace, is admissible,*
- *if $(\sigma, \mathcal{E})$ is admissible, $\alpha \in \Lambda^!$ is a valued output, and $\sigma \cdot \alpha \in Traces(\mathcal{S})$, then $(\sigma \cdot \alpha, \mathcal{E} \cup \{\alpha\})$ is admissible,*
- *if $(\sigma, \mathcal{E})$ is admissible, $\alpha \in \Lambda^?$ is a valued input, $\alpha \in \mathcal{E}$, and $\sigma \cdot \alpha \in Traces(\mathcal{S})$, then $(\sigma \cdot \alpha, \mathcal{E} \setminus \{\alpha\})$ is admissible.*

We denote by $Traces(\mathcal{S}, \mathcal{E})$ the set of traces of $\mathcal{S}$ that are admissible in the environment $\mathcal{E}$.

Lemma 1 (Monotonicity of admissible traces). *For all IOSTS $\mathcal{S}_1$, $\mathcal{S}_2$ and environment $\mathcal{E}$: if $Traces(\mathcal{S}_1) \subseteq Traces(\mathcal{S}_2)$ then $Traces(\mathcal{S}_1, \mathcal{E}) \subseteq Traces(\mathcal{S}_2, \mathcal{E})$.*

2.3   Parallel Product

The *parallel product* of two IOSTS S_1, S_2 will be used in specification and verification (for defining the protocol, and its interaction with the intruder and with "observers" for security properties). The parallel product operation is defined only for *compatible* IOSTS, defined as follows:

Definition 8. *Two IOSTS S_1,S_2 are compatible if $V_{s_1} \cap V_{s_2} = \emptyset$, $P_1 = P_2$ and $C_1 = C_2$.*

Definition 9 (Parallel Product). *The parallel product $S = S_1 \| S_2$ of two compatible IOSTS $S_i = \langle V_i, P_i, C_i, \Theta_i, L_i, l_i^0, \Sigma_i^?, \Sigma_i^!, \Sigma_i^\tau, T_i \rangle$ $(i = 1, 2)$ is the IOSTS defined by the following components: $V = V_1 \cup V_2$, $P = P_1 = P_2$, $C = C_1 = C_2$, $\Theta = \Theta_1 \wedge \Theta_2$, $L = L_1 \times L_2$, $l^0 = \langle l_1^0, l_2^0 \rangle$, $\Sigma^! = \Sigma_1^! \cup \Sigma_2^!$, $\Sigma^? = \Sigma_1^? \cup \Sigma_2^?$, $\Sigma^\tau = \Sigma_1^\tau \cup \Sigma_2^\tau$. The set T of symbolic transitions of the parallel product is the smallest set satisfying the following rules:*

$$\frac{\langle l_1, a_1, G_1, A_1, l_1' \rangle \in T_1, \quad l_2 \in L_2}{\langle \langle l_1, l_2 \rangle, a_1, G_1, A_1 \cup (x := x)_{x \in V_2}, \langle l_1', l_2 \rangle \rangle \in T}$$

$$\frac{\langle l_2, a, G_2, A_2, l_2' \rangle \in T_2, \quad l_1 \in L_1}{\langle \langle l_1, l_2 \rangle, a_2, G_2, A_2 \cup (x := x)_{x \in V_1}, \langle l_1, l_2' \rangle \rangle \in T}$$

The parallel product allows each IOSTS to fire its transitions independently of the other one. We also note that the parallel product is associative and commutative (up to the names of locations).

Example 2. The Basic Access Control protocol depicted in Fig. 1 can be formally modelled as *Traces(Terminal‖Passport, ∅)*, that is, as the traces of the parallel composition of *Terminal* and *Passport* that are admissible in the empty environment ∅ (cf. Definition 7). This initially empty environment is enriched by the outputs of the agents, which also consume inputs from it. We shall see in the next section that the full protocol, including the intruder, can be modelled in a similar manner.

Lemma 2 (Monotonicity of traces in the parallel product). *For three IOSTS S_1, S_1', S_2 such that S_1, S_2 are compatible and S_1', S_2 are compatible, if $Traces(S_1') \subseteq Traces(S_1)$ then $Traces(S_1' \| S_2) \subseteq Traces(S_1 \| S_2)$.*

In the sequel, whenever two IOSTS are composed by the parallel product operation, we implicitly assume that they are compatible.

3   Verification, Testing, and Learning

In this section we present the ingredients of our approach, which are verification, testing, and learning. The approach itself is presented in the next section.

3.1   Expressing Security Properties Using Observers

We represent security properties, such as secrecy and authentication, using *observers*, which are IOSTS equipped with a set of *recognising* locations. Observers can be seen as an alternative to, e.g., temporal logics and, for some temporal logics such as LTL, formulas can be translated into "equivalent" observers; see, e.g., [22] for a transformation of *safety* LTL formulas into observers.

Definition 10 (recognised traces). *Let $F \subseteq L$ be a set of locations of an IOSTS S. An execution ρ of S is recognised by F if the execution terminates in a state in $F \times V$. A trace is recognised by F if it is the trace of an execution recognised by F. The set of traces of an IOSTS S recognised by a set F of locations is denoted by $Traces(S, F)$.*

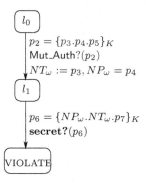

Fig. 2. Observer ω for the authentication to Terminal

Example 3. The passport authenticates itself to the terminal by demonstrating its ability to decrypt the terminal's nonce, and by sending that nonce (within is an encrypted tuple of messages) back to the terminal by the Rsp_Auth command. The observer depicted in Figure 2 expresses a scenario where the *intruder* gains enough information in order to authenticate itself to the terminal. The observer starts by observing the Mut_Auth? input from the terminal, and, by decrypting the parameter p_2 of the input (which is an encrypted sequence of three messages), it memorises the first and second messages in the sequence in its variables NT_ω and NP_ω, respectively. Then, the observer waits for a certain **secret?** input, emitted only by the *intruder* (defined below), carrying a parameter of the form $\{NP_\omega.NT_\omega.p_7\}_K$. Intuitively, when the intruder emits this parameter, it can also emit Rsp_Auth($\{NP_\omega.NT_\omega.p_7\}_K$), hence, it can also authenticate itself to the terminal. Hence, upon reception of the **secret?** input, the observer enters its *Violate* location, which expresses the violation of the authentication property.

In addition to authentication properties, secrecy properties (and in general all *safety* properties) can be defined using observers in a similar way.

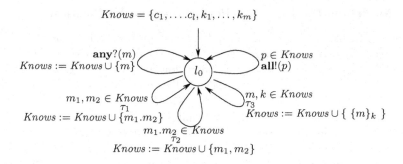

Fig. 3. Template IOSTS for generic intruder

Definition 11 (recognised traces of product). *For IOSTS $\mathcal{S}$ and ω and $F \subseteq L_\omega$ a subset of locations of ω, we denote by $Traces(\mathcal{S}||(\omega, F))$ the set of recognised traces $Traces(\mathcal{S}||\omega, L_s \times F)$.*

Lemma 3 (monotonicity of recognised traces). *For IOSTS $\mathcal{S}_1, \mathcal{S}_2, \omega$, and $F \subseteq L_\omega$, if $Traces(\mathcal{S}_1) \subseteq Traces(\mathcal{S}_2)$ then $Traces(\mathcal{S}_1||(\omega, F)) \subseteq Traces(\mathcal{S}_2||(\omega, F))$.*

3.2   The Intruder

The Basic Access Control protocol will be modelled as a parallel product between the terminal and passport IOSTS, depicted in Figure 1, together with observers for security properties (such as that depicted in Figure 2) and an intruder, whose general structure is given in Figure 3 as a "template" IOSTS. A "template" IOSTS is just like an IOSTS, except that it has "generic" actions, which are abbreviations for any (input, output) actions in a given set of actions.

The generic intruder depicted in Figure 3 reacts to "any" input **any?**(m), by adding the formal parameter m to the variable *Knows*, which is a state variable encoding the intruder's current knowledge. This state variable is initialised as a certain set $\{c_1, , \ldots, c_l, k_1, \ldots k_m\}$ ($l, m \geq 1$) of symbolic constants. The constants c_i will be used as *nonces*, whereas the constants k_j will be used as *keys*[5]. The knowledge of the intruder is then closed under the concatenation, deconcatenation, and encryption operations, which is modelled by the transitions labelled by the internal action τ_1, τ_2, and τ_3, respectively. For example, the transition labelled τ_3 in Figure 3 can be fired whenever some message m and key k belong to the current knowledge *Knows*, and, by firing the transition, the intruder adds the encrypted message $\{m\}_k$ to its knowledge. The intruder sends messages by the **all!**(p) output, where p is any term in the current knowledge.

The above model of the intruder corresponds to the Dolev-Yao model [18], with a few limitations: finitely many nonces and keys, and symmetrical encryption only. The full Dolev-Yao model can also be encoded as a template IOSTS.

---

[5] Finitely many nonces is a usual approximation in cryptographic protocol verification. Infinitely many nonces can be generated by using a function symbol *nonce* : $\mathbb{N} \mapsto \mathcal{N}$.

3.3   Modelling the Protocol, Performing the Verification

We now have all the ingredients for defining the protocol and its verification. We specify the protocol as the *admissible traces* in the empty environment $\emptyset$ (cf. Definition 7) of the *parallel product* (cf. Definition 9) $Terminal\|Intruder\|Passport$, where *Terminal* and *Passport* are the IOSTS depicted in Fig. 1, and *Intruder* is obtained from the template depicted in Fig. 3 by letting **any?** denote any element in the set $\{\mathsf{Get\_Chal?}, \mathsf{Snd\_Chal?}, \mathsf{Mut\_Auth?}, \mathsf{Rsp\_Auth?}\}$, and **all!** denote any element in $\{\mathsf{Get\_Chal!}, \mathsf{Snd\_Chal!}, \mathsf{Mut\_Auth!}, \mathsf{Rsp\_Auth!}, \mathbf{secret!}\}$. We let initially $Knows = \{c_1, k_1\}$, where c_1 is a symbolic constant of sort $\mathcal{N}$ and k_1 is a symbolic constant of type $\mathcal{K}$. That is, the intruder uses one nonce to send to the terminal, and has one key k_1. Note that the traces of the product have been restricted to those admissible in the empty environment $\emptyset$, to which the agents (including the intruder) add outputs, and from which agents consume inputs.

Once the specifications of the two agents and of the intruder are known, and once the property is expressed by an observer ω with a set *Violate* of recognising locations, the verification problem becomes: decide whether

$$Traces([Terminal\|Intruder\|Passport\|(\omega, Violate)], \emptyset) = \emptyset \qquad (1)$$

where, for an IOSTS $\mathcal{S}$ and an observer $(\omega, Violate)$, we denote (cf. Definition 11) by $Traces(\mathcal{S}\|(\omega, Violate))$ the set of recognised traces $Traces(\mathcal{S}\|\omega, L_s \times Violate)$.

To decide whether Equality (1) holds, we proceed as follows: we translate the IOSTS *Terminal*, *Intruder*, and *Passport* into the language of the Maude tool [23]. We choose this particular tool because it is well adapted to modelling IOSTS and their parallel compositions. Then, Maude's rewriting engine checks whether the *Violate* location, or set of locations, of the observer are reachable in the parallel composition of the modules. If yes, then the property is violated, otherwise, the property holds. Of course, in general (in the presence of loops), the reachability analysis may not terminate. Hence, for practical reasons, we restrict the analysis to traces of a certain length $n \in \mathbb{N}$, which is a parameter of our global approach (including verification, testing, and learning). The protocol depicted in Figure 1 does satisfy the property defined by the observer depicted in Figure 2. Below is an example of a negative result.

Example 4. Consider the IOSTS $Terminal_1$ in Fig. 4, which is very much like *Terminal* (Fig. 1) except for the fact that, in the guard of the transition from l_2 to l_3, the variable NP_t equals NT_t. That is, instead of sending back its own nonce as it should, $Terminal_1$ sends back the *same* nonce it received from the passport[6]. Then, the intruder may just copy the message p_2 and send it back *via* a Rsp_Auth! command, which the terminal accepts as "valid" authentication. In this way, the intruder manages to "fake" the identity of the passport. The intruder also generates a **secret!** output with the same parameter

---

[6] Note that, in the correct protocol in Fig. 1, on the transition from l_2 to l_3 of *Terminal*, we have $NP_t \neq NT_t$: by the protocol's semantics, we have $NP_t = NP_p$, and by the initial algebra semantics, the constants NP_p and NT_t are different as no equality between has been specified.

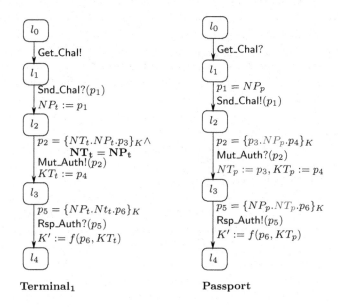

Fig. 4. Erroneous protocol, which violates authentication property

as Rsp_Auth!, which makes the observer enter its *Violate* location; formally, we
have $Traces([Terminal_1 || Intruder || Passport || (\omega, Violate)], \emptyset) \neq \emptyset$.

3.4 Learning by Testing

Another ingredient of our approach is *testing/learning*. Intuitively, each agent's
specification, say, A, may be "augmented" using information obtained by interacting with the corresponding (unknown) implementation I_A. If a trace $\sigma_A \in$
$Traces(I_A) \setminus Traces(A)$ is observed, then transitions are added to A, such as
to include the trace σ_A, called thereafter an *example*; and this part of the
learning process is called *adding examples*. The ultimate goal of the *adding examples* process is that, eventually, $Traces(I_A) \subseteq Traces(A)$ and $Traces(I_B) \subseteq$
$Traces(B)$ hold, in which case no more examples can be added. In general, infinitely many examples, in the above sense, must be added before the process
terminates[7].

---

[7] There are two sources of infinity: infinite *breadth* due to the values of the parameters
carried by the actions, and infinite length (or depth) of the traces. In order to make
this process finite we can resort to *uniformity* and *regularity* hypotheses [24]. In our
context, *uniformity hypotheses* say that the valued inputs can be partitioned into
finitely many classes, and that it is enough to stimulate the implementation with one
input in each class in order to obtain all possible (equivalent) outputs; and *regularity
hypotheses* state that it is enough to bound the length of the testing/learning step
to a certain natural number n.

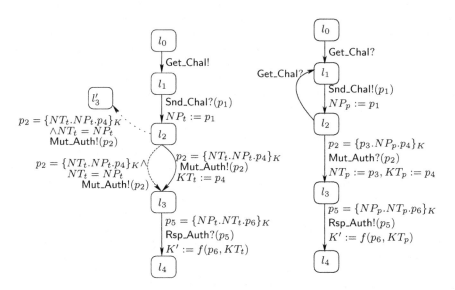

Fig. 5. Terminal (left) and Passport (right), after learning

Example 5. Assume that, by interacting with the passport's implementation[8] we obtain the *example* that, after the first time the nonce was sent via the Snd_Chal! output, a new Get_Chal? input results in sending the nonce once again. Then, we add to the specification the transition labelled Get_Chal? from l_2 to l_1. The resulting specification *Passport$_2$* of the passport is depicted in the right-hand side of Figure 5. Next, assume that, by interacting with the terminal, we discover that the Mut_Auth! command emits a sequence in which the first element is equal to the terminal's copy NP_t of the passport's nonce. Then, we add a transition to the specification; the left-hand side of Figure 5 shows two possibilities for adding the new transition (drawn with dashed, and dotted lines, respectively): either to a new location l'_3, or to the existing location l_3. We denote by *Terminal$_2$* the IOSTS obtained by adding the latter transition (depicted using a dashed line).

The second part of the learning process deals with *removing counterexamples*. Let again A and B denote the honest agents in a protocol and C denote the intruder. Then, as seen in Section 2, the protocol is modelled by the set of traces $Traces(A||C||B, \emptyset)$, and a *counterexample* is a trace $\sigma \in Traces(A||C||B, \emptyset)$, which violates the property φ, and which is not in $Traces(I_A||I_C||I_B, \emptyset)$. That is, a trace showing that φ is not satisfied by the protocol's global specification, but that cannot be "reproduced" on the protocol's implementation. The existence of such "spurious" counterexamples indicates that the learning was imperfect; they have to be removed from the specifications A, B in order to "fix" the learning.

Example 6. We have seen in Example 4 that if the terminal re-uses the nonce of the passport instead of its own in its Mut_Auth output (as does *Terminal$_2$* in

---

[8] Due to confidentiality issues about the case study, these examples are fictitious.

the left-hand side of Figure 5), the protocol is incorrect as it is able to "authenticate" the intruder via the Rsp_Auth input. Then, a model checker generates a trace σ, illustrating the authentication property's violation, which, if the protocol's *implementation* does not violate our property, is not reproducible on the implementation. That is, σ is a *counterexample* for the property described by the observer in Fig. 2.

We now give more details on the *adding examples* and *removing counterexamples* procedures. These procedures are only one way, among many, to perform learning. We do not know of any existing learning techniques for infinite-states systems such as IOSTS, but for finite-state automata such techniques exist [25].

Adding examples. The intuition is that we want to preserve as much as possible the control structures of the honest agent's current specifications A, B. Let $\sigma_A \in Traces(I_A) \setminus Traces(A)$. Then, σ_A can be decomposed as $\sigma_A = \sigma'_A \cdot \alpha \cdot \sigma''_A$, where $\sigma'_A \in Traces(A)$, $\alpha \in \Lambda_A^? \cup \Lambda_A^!$, $\sigma'_A \cdot \alpha \notin Traces(A)$, and $\sigma''_A \in (\Lambda_A^? \cup \Lambda_A^!)^*$. Then, let $\alpha = \langle a, \pi \rangle$, let $\langle l, \nu \rangle$ be any state of $[\![A]\!]$ in which the IOLTS $[\![A]\!]$ may be after firing the sequence σ'_A. We add one new transition t to the IOSTS A in order to "include" the valued action $\alpha = \langle a, \pi \rangle$. The transition t has:

- origin l;
- action a;
- guard G, chosen by the user to be some predicate G on the variables V_A and parameters P_A such that $G(\nu, \pi) = true$; by default, G is chosen to be the *complement* of the union of the conditions under which a may be fired in l;
- assignments are also chosen by the user - by default, the identity assignments $(x := x)_{x \in V_A}$;
- the destination is defined as follows:
  - if, by choosing the destination of t to be a location $l' \in L_A$, the whole sequence σ_A becomes a trace of the resulting IOSTS, then we let the destination of t be l'; if several choices are possible for l', then one is chosen;
  - otherwise, we let the destination of t be a new location $l'' \notin L_A$.

In the right-hand side of Figure 5, the transition t labelled Get_Chal? from l_2 to l_1 has been added to the passport's specification, as a result of the observation that, after one Snd_Chal! output, a new Get_Chal? input produces another Snd_Chal!. Here, the existing location l_1 has been chosen as the destination of t. The left-hand side of Figure 5 shows two different ways of adding a transition to the terminal's specification: the transition drawn with a dashed line goes to an existing location, whereas the one depicted with a dotted line goes to a newly created location.

Removing counterexamples. This procedure is called whenever the last call to *adding examples* leads to a violation of the property under verification by the the protocol's augmented specification. (It is assumed that the protocol is initially correct, hence, any counterexample may only exist because of the last added example.) Hence, removing counterexamples consists in undoing the effect of the last "adding examples" operation, and in proposing another way of adding the last example (in terms of the transition t to be added to one of the agent's specifications). A marking mechanism is used to ensure that a different choice is proposed if the removing counterexamples operation is called repeatedly for the same example. These procedures are illustrated in the next section.

4   Our Approach

The proposed approach deals with the problem of establishing whether or not $I_A||I_C||I_B \models \varphi$ holds, for *black-box* implementations I_A, I_B of the honest agents and I_C of the intruder, assumed to have some (unknown) representations in terms of finite or infinite IOLTS (Input-Output Labelled Transition Systems), and a security property φ represented using an observer $(\omega, Violate)$[9].

The corresponding specifications of the agents are denoted by A, B, C. We assume that $Traces(I_C) = Traces(C)$, that is, our model of the intruder is correct. The approach is presented in Figure 6 in pseudocode.

The outer while loop is executed as long as a certain Boolean flag inconclusive holds true. The flag is set to false and will be reset to true if the function's inner while loop, described below, fails to deliver a "conclusive" result.

The inner while loop can be executed as long as $A||C||B \models \varphi$. The latter formula denotes a verification problem, to be solved by means of model checking as described in Section 3.3. In each iteration of the inner while loop, one of the two honest agent's specifications, A and B (in alternation) is augmented using the add-example mechanism informally described in Section 3.4. The inner while loop may terminate in two situations: when, after a number of iterations, the done() function returns true (intuitively, this happens if all "representative" traces up to a bounded length have been explored *and* $A||C||B \models \varphi$ still holds); or when $A||C||B \models \varphi$ fails to hold.

– in the first situation, the result is that *if the learning process was* exhaustive *i.e., such that* $Traces(I_A) \subseteq Traces(A)$ and $Traces(I_B) \subseteq Traces(B)$ holds, the conclusion is that *the property* φ *also holds on the protocol's implementation.* That is, we have established the correctness of the protocol's implementation without actually executing it. This is a consequence of the *theoretical completeness* theorem given below.

   Note that, since I_A, I_B are black boxes, the hypothesis that $Traces(I_A) \subseteq Traces(A)$ and $Traces(I_B) \subseteq Traces(B)$ cannot, in general, be validated. It is only possible to increase our confidence in the validity of the hypothesis, by performing as many iterations of the while loop as possible and by systematically testing as many sequences of inputs/outputs as possible[10].

---

[9] Remember from Section 3 that $A||B||C \models \varphi$ iff $Traces([A||B||C||(\omega, Violate)], \emptyset) = \emptyset$.

[10] Under *regularity* and *uniformity* hypotheses on the data types [24], only a finite set of traces need to satisfy the trace-inclusion hypotheses, which becomes checkable.

```
function VerifyTestLearn(A, B, C, IA, IB, IC, φ)
    inconclusive := true
    turn := A
    while inconclusive do
        inconclusive := false
        while A||C||B ⊨ φ and not done() do
            if turn = A then
                choose σA ∈ Traces(IA) \ Traces(A)
                A := add-example(A, σA)
            else
                choose σB ∈ Traces(IB) \ Traces(B)
                B := add-example(B, σB)
            endif
          turn := next(turn)
        endwhile
        if done() //by assumption, done() = true => A||C||B ⊨ φ
            return
            "Traces(IA) ⊆ Traces(A) ∧ Traces(IB) ⊆ Traces(B) ⇒ IA||IC||IB ⊨ φ"
        else // implicitly, after while loop done() = false => A||C||B ⊭ φ
            choose(σ ∈ Traces(A||C||B, ∅) ∩ {σ|σ ⊭ φ})
            if is-executable(σ, IA||IC||IB) return "IA||IC||IB ⊭ φ'"
            else
                if turn = B
                    A := remove-counterexample(A, σA)
                else
                    B := remove-counterexample(B, σB)
                endif
            endif
            inconclusive := true
        endif
    endwhile
end.
```

Fig. 6. Our approach

– on the other hand, if, after a number of executions, $A||C||B \models \varphi$ does not
   hold any more, we obtain a trace σ, which is a sequence of interactions
   between the intruder and the honest agents, demonstrating that the security
   property is violated. There are again two cases:
   • if σ is *executable* on the implementation, that is, if it is possible to repro-
     duce it on $I_A||I_C||I_B$ - where, e.g., the intruder's implementation I_C is
     replaced by a test execution engine - then the protocol's implementation
     also violates the property. Note that we have obtained an information
     about the protocol's *implementation* mostly by using informations ob-
     tained by *verifying* the protocol's *specification*. Of course, it is necessary
     to ensure that the trace σ obtained by verification is executable by the
     implementation; but we execute just *one* trace, obtained *via the capabil-
     ities of a model checker of exploring "all" the possible traces of a model.*

This is arguably, more efficient for finding errors than directly executing and monitoring the *implementation* $I_A||I_C||I_B$ (with all the execution traces induced by the intruder's implementation!) in the hope of detecting an error.

- otherwise, the trace σ found on the protocol's specification cannot be executed on the protocol's implementation, and we have a *spurious counterexample* in the sense given in Section 3.4. This means that the learning performed during the inner `while` loop was incorrect. Then, the `remove-counterexample` procedure just undoes the effect of the last `add-example` procedure, and proposes another way of including the last example. A marking mechanism is employed to ensure that a future attempt to add the same example trace gives a different result.

Example 7. Assume that we have performed one whole iteration of the inner `while` loop in the procedure described in Figure 6, and that, after the testing/learning phase, the passport, which plays the role of agent A, is that depicted in Figure 5 (right). This augmented specification of the passport, together with the intruder, and the initial specification of the terminal, i.e., that depicted in Figure 1 (left), satisfies the property represented by the observer depicted in Figure 2. Then, a new iteration of the inner `while` loop is started, and it is now the terminal's turn to "learn" new behaviours. Assume that in this phase we "learn" the transition depicted with a dashed line in Figure 5 (left). Then, as seen in Example 4 the protocol now violates the property, and we are presented with a counterexample showing how the property is violated. If the counterexample is executable on the global protocol's implementation, then, the procedure terminates with a conclusive (negative) answer. Otherwise, the *remove counterexample* procedure takes over and replaces the transition depicted with a dashed line in Figure 5 with the one depicted with a dotted line, and the process continues until, e.g., all the (finitely many) traces of the agent's specifications, satisfying adequate *uniformity* and *regularity* hypotheses, have been learned.

We now give the main theorem, stating the method's theoretical completeness. Inttuitively, it says that if the models of the agents in a protocol are sufficiently precise, then the results obtained on the models also hold on the implementation.

Theorem 1 (theoretical completeness). *Consider three IOSTS A, B, and C, such that C is an intruder as described in Section 3.2. Let φ be a safety property with the corresponding observer, $(\omega, violate)$, as described in Section 3.1, and assume that A, B, C, and ω are pairwise compatible IOSTS (cf. Definition 8). Let also I_A, I_B, I_C be the (unknown) models for the implementations of the honest agents and of the intruder, which are IOLTS such that $\Lambda^!_{I_A} = \Lambda^!_{[A]}$, $\Lambda^?_{I_A} = \Lambda^?_{[A]}$, $\Lambda^!_{I_B} = \Lambda^!_{[B]}$, $\Lambda^?_{I_B} = \Lambda^?_{[B]}$, $\Lambda^!_{I_C} = \Lambda^!_{[C]}$, $\Lambda^?_{I_C} = \Lambda^?_{[C]}$. Finally, assume that $A||C||B \models \varphi$ as defined in Section 3.3. Then, we have the valid implication $Traces(I_A) \subseteq Traces(A) \wedge Traces(I_B) \subseteq Traces(B) \Rightarrow I_A||I_C||I_B \models \varphi$.*

This theorem says that, when the procedure returns '$Traces(I_A) \subseteq Traces(A) \wedge Traces(I_B) \subseteq Traces(B) \Rightarrow I_A||I_C||I_B \models \varphi$" then this is really the case. As a result, using standard conformance testing, one can ensure that the collaborating agents meet the required (security) properties. As the completeness result does not require that the composition of the agents is tested, a major advantage of our method is that the test effort can be distributed over several companies, i.e. each agent can be certified by a different company (or several). On the one hand, this reduces the required test effort per company and the amount of information that a company needs for testing, and, on the other hand, a distributed certification mechanism can have a significant positive impact on the trust one has in the agents and the system as a whole. Note that *soundness* - i.e., when the procedure says that the protocol's implementation violates a property, then this is really the case - is trivial by construction.

5   Conclusion and Future Work

We propose an approach for checking security properties (such as secrecy and authenticity properties), as well as other, general-purpose temporal logic properties, on black-box implementations of cryptographic protocols. The approach integrates ideas from verification, black-box testing, and learning.

Specifications of agents are given as IOSTS (Input-Output Symbolic Transition Systems), and the implementations of all the agents in the protocol are black boxes, assumed to have some unknown representations in terms of finite or infinite IOLTS (Input-Output Labelled Transition Systems). Security properties and other temporal logic properties are represented using *observers*, which are IOSTS equipped with a set of dedicated locations that are entered when the corresponding property is violated. The verification is then standard state-space exploration, and the learning consists in adding transitions to the honest agents' specifications by observing so-called *examples*, that is, traces of an agent's implementation that are not in the corresponding specification. Learning also consists in *removing counterexamples*, when a trace violating a property on the protocol's specification cannot be reproduced on the implementation.

The method is *sound*, as it only says that a property is violated by a protocol's implementation when such a violation has actually been found. It is also *theoretically complete*, in the sense that, if the learning is *exhaustive* (i.e., if the traces of the agent's implementations are included in the traces of the corresponding specifications obtained by learning) and if the property holds on the protocol's global specification, then the property also holds on the protocol's implementation. Of course, the trace-inclusion hypothesis between a black-box implementation and a white-box specification cannot be established in general, but confidence in it can be increased by increasing the amount of testing and learning. We are investigating connections with ideas from the area of testing of processes with data [24] where it is shown that if some *regularity* and *uniformity* hypotheses hold on the data, then a complete finite test suite can be given.

The method is *compositional* in the testing/learning parts: *adding examples* and *removing counterexamples* operate on each agent, not on the composition of the agents. The benefit of a compositional approach is the usual one (the ability to deal with larger state spaces). From a security point of view, certifying a system by testing each agent in isolation has its benefits too: on the one hand, only isolated pieces of a (possibly proprietary) system have to be made available to a company for testing, and on the other hand, testing for security properties such as secrecy and authentication become a less ad-hoc activity.

We illustrate our method on the Basic Access Control protocol implemented in biometric passports. Some of the examples presented in the paper are simplified instances of actual experiments that we performed with actual passports [17]; the present paper formalises and enhances the empirical testing methodology that we used in [17].

Finally, our method is not limited, in principle, to cryptographic protocols or security properties. Cryptographic protocols are interesting here because they have "small" specifications, which are typically incomplete and for which it makes sense to attempt completion by means of learning techniques.

References

1. Burrows, M., Abadi, M., Needham, R.M.: A logic of authentication. ACM Trans. Comput. Syst. 8(1), 18–36 (1990)
2. Gong, L., Needham, R.M., Yahalom, R.: Reasoning about belief in cryptographic protocols. In: IEEE Symposium on Security and Privacy, pp. 234–248 (1990)
3. Abadi, M., Gordon, A.D.: A calculus for cryptographic protocols: The spi calculus. Inf. Comput. 148(1), 1–70 (1999)
4. Lowe, G.: Casper: A compiler for the analysis of security protocols. Journal of Computer Security 6(1-2), 53–84 (1998)
5. Armando, A., Basin, D.A., Boichut, Y., Chevalier, Y., Compagna, L., Cuéllar, J., Drielsma, P.H., Héam, P.-C., Kouchnarenko, O., Mantovani, J., Mödersheim, S., von Oheimb, D., Rusinowitch, M., Santiago, J., Turuani, M., Viganò, L., Vigneron, L.: The avispa tool for the automated validation of internet security protocols and applications. In: Etessami, K., Rajamani, S.K. (eds.) CAV 2005. LNCS, vol. 3576, pp. 281–285. Springer, Heidelberg (2005)
6. Paulson, L.C.: The inductive approach to verifying cryptographic protocols. Journal of Computer Security 6(1-2), 85–128 (1998)
7. Hughes, J., Warnier, M.: The coinductive approach to verifying cryptographic protocols. In: Wirsing, M., Pattinson, D., Hennicker, R. (eds.) Recent Trends in Algebraic Development Techniques. LNCS, vol. 2755, pp. 268–283. Springer, Heidelberg (2003)
8. Gunter, E.L., Felty, A.P. (eds.): TPHOLs 1997. LNCS, vol. 1275, pp. 19–22. Springer, Heidelberg (1997)
9. Denker, G., Millen, J.K.: Modeling group communication protocols using multiset term rewriting. Electr. Notes Theor. Comput. Sci., vol. 71 (2002)
10. Genet, T., Klay, F.: Rewriting for cryptographic protocol verification. In: McAlleste, D.A. (ed.) Automated Deduction - CADE-17. LNCS, vol. 1831, pp. 271–290. Springer, Heidelberg (2000)
11. Bozga, L., Lakhnech, Y., Périn, M.: Pattern-based abstraction for verifying secrecy in protocols. In: Garavel, H., Hatcliff, J. (eds.) ETAPS 2003 and TACAS 2003. LNCS, vol. 2619, pp. 299–314. Springer, Heidelberg (2003)

12. Monniaux, D.: Abstracting cryptographic protocols with tree automata. Sci. Comput. Program. 47(2-3), 177–202 (2003)
13. ISO/IEC 9646. Conformance Testing Methodology and Framework (1992)
14. Jeffrey, A.S.A., Ley-Wild, R.: Dynamic model checking of C cryptographic protocol implementations. In: Workshop on Foundations of Computer Security and Automated Reasoning for Security Protocol Analysis (fcs'06) (2006)
15. Goubault-Larrecq, J., Parrennes, F.: Cryptographic protocol analysis on real C code. In: Cousot, R. (ed.) VMCAI 2005. LNCS, vol. 3385, pp. 363–379. Springer, Heidelberg (2005)
16. Bhargavan, K.: Provable implementations of security protocols. In: IEEE Symposium on Logic in Computer Science (LICS 2006), pp. 345–346 (2006)
17. Breunesse, C.-B., Hubbers, E., Koopman, P., Mostowski, W., Oostdijk, M., Rusu, V., de Vries, R., van Weelden, A., Schreur, R.W., Willemse, T.: Testing the dutch e-passport, Technical report, Radboud University, Nijmegen, The Netherlands (2006)
18. Dolev, D., Yao, A.C.: On the security of public key protocols. In: Proceedings of the IEEE 22nd Annual Symposium on Foundations of Computer Science, pp. 350–357 (1981)
19. Technical advisory group on Machine-Readable travel documents. Pki for machine-readable travel documents, version 1.1. Technical report, International Civil Aviation Organization (October 2004)
20. Lynch, N., Tuttle, M.: Introduction to IO automata. CWI Quarterly, vol. 3(2) (1999)
21. Carriero, N., Gelernter, D.: Linda in context. Commun. ACM 32(4), 444–458 (1989)
22. Kupferman, O., Vardi, M.Y.: Model checking of safety properties. Formal Methods in System Design 19(3), 291–314 (2001)
23. Clavel, M., Durán, F., Eker, S., Lincoln, P., Martí-Oliet, N., Meseguer, J., Talcott, C.: The maude 2.0 system. In: Nieuwenhuis, R. (ed.) RTA 2003. LNCS, vol. 2706, pp. 76–87. Springer, Heidelberg (2003)
24. Gaudel, M.-C., James, P.R.: Testing algebraic data types and processes: A unifying theory. Formal Asp. Comput. 10(5-6), 436–451 (1998)
25. Angluin, D.: Inference of reversible languages. Journal of the ACM 29(3), 741–765 (1982)

Translating FSP into LOTOS and Networks of Automata[*]

Gwen Salaün[1,*], Jeff Kramer[2], Frédéric Lang[1], and Jeff Magee[2]

[1] INRIA, Centre de Recherche Rhône-Alpes / VASY, Montbonnot, France
`salaun@lcc.uma.es, Frederic.Lang@inria.fr`
[2] Imperial College, London, UK
`{j.kramer,j.magee}@imperial.ac.uk`

Abstract. Many process calculi have been proposed since Robin Milner and Tony Hoare opened the way more than 25 years ago. Although they are based on the same kernel of operators, most of them are incompatible in practice. We aim at reducing the gap between process calculi, and especially making possible the joint use of underlying tool support. FSP is a widely-used calculus equipped with LTSA, a graphical and user-friendly tool. LOTOS is the only process calculus that has led to an international standard, and is supported by the CADP verification toolbox. We propose a translation from FSP to LOTOS. Since FSP composite processes are hard to encode into LOTOS, they are translated into networks of automata which are another input language accepted by CADP. Hence, it is possible to use jointly LTSA and CADP to validate FSP specifications. Our approach is completely automated by a translator tool we implemented.

1 Introduction

Process calculi (or process algebras) are abstract description languages to specify concurrent systems. The process algebra community has been working on this topic for 25 years and many different calculi have been proposed. At the same time, several toolboxes have been implemented to support the design and verification of systems specified with process calculi. However, although they are based on the same kernel of operators, most of them are incompatible in practice. In addition, there is no connection between calculi and very few bridges between existing verification tools. Our goal is to reduce the gap between the different formalisms, and to propose some bridges between existing tools to make their joint use possible.

We focus here on the process calculi FSP and LOTOS. FSP [16] is a widely-used and expressive process calculus conceived to make the writing of specifications easier and concise. FSP is supported by LTSA, a user-friendly tool which allows to compile FSP specifications into finite state machines known as LTSs (Labelled

---

[*] G. Salaün currently works at Universidad de Málaga, Spain.

J. Davies and J. Gibbons (Eds.): IFM 2007, LNCS 4591, pp. 558–578, 2007.

Transition Systems), to visualise and animate LTSs through graphical interfaces, and to verify LTL properties. On the other hand, LOTOS is an ISO standard [13], which has been applied successfully to many application domains. LOTOS is more structured than FSP, and then adequate to specify complex systems possibly involving data types. LOTOS is equipped with CADP [9], a verification toolbox for asynchronous concurrent systems. CADP allows to deal with very large state spaces, and implements various verification techniques such as model checking, compositional verification, equivalence checking, distributed model checking, etc.

To sum up, the simplicity of FSP makes it very accessible to everyone, whereas LOTOS requires a better level of expertise. In addition, CADP is a rich and efficient verification toolbox which can complement basic analysis possible with LTSA. We propose to translate FSP specifications into LOTOS to enable FSP users to access the verification means available in the CADP toolbox. Since some FSP constructs for composite processes are difficult to encode into LOTOS (for instance synchronisations between complex labels or priorities), they have been encoded into the EXP format which is another input format of CADP. EXP allows the description of networks of automata using parallel composition, but also supports renaming, hiding and priorities.

Our goal is not to replace LTSA, since LTSA is convenient to debug and visualise graphically simple examples, but to extend it with supplementary verification techniques such as those mentioned before. Furthermore, we choose a high-level translation between process calculi, as most as possible, instead of low-level connections with CADP (through the OPEN/CÆSAR application programming interface [7] for instance) because (i) we preferred to keep the expressiveness of the specification and then make the translation of most behavioural operators easier, (ii) high-level models are necessary to use some verification techniques available in CADP, such as compositional verification, (iii) verification of the generated LOTOS code can benefit from the numerous optimisations implemented in the CÆSAR.ADT and CÆSAR [6,12,11] compilers of LOTOS available in CADP, which would be too expensive to re-implement at the FSP level.

The translation from FSP to LOTOS/EXP is completely automated in a translator tool we implemented (about 25,000 lines of code). This tool was validated on many examples (more than 10,000 lines of FSP) to ensure that the translation is reliable. As regards semantics, our translation preserves a branching equivalence relation [22] which is stronger than observational equivalence.

The remainder of this paper is organised as follows. Section 2 gives short introductions to FSP, LOTOS, and EXP. Section 3 presents some preliminary definitions that are used in the remainder of the paper. Sections 4 and 5 describe respectively the translation of FSP sequential processes into LOTOS and of FSP composite processes into EXP. In Section 6, we present our tool and its validation. Section 7 illustrates how LTSA and CADP can be used jointly on a simple system. Section 8 ends with some concluding remarks. More details about this work are given in an INRIA technical report [15].

2   FSP, LOTOS, and EXP

We start with a short description of FSP (Finite State Processes, see [16] for a more complete presentation of the language). FSP can define (i) constants, ranges, and sets, (ii) basic (*i.e.*, sequential) and composite processes, (iii) safety and progress properties (not handled in this work). In the grammar of FSP basic processes below, an upper case identifier P refers to a process identifier, X (or x) is a variable, *act* is a string label, and V is an expression involving arithmetic, comparison, and logical operators with variables. We discard in this paper local process definitions as well as the visibility operateur "@", dual of the hiding operator, although the full expressiveness of FSP is taken into account in the translator we implemented (see Section 6).

$$
\begin{aligned}
P_B ::= \, & P(X_1{=}V_1, \dots, X_k{=}V_k) = B && \textit{process definition} \\
& +\{A_{e1}, \dots, A_{en}\} && \textit{alphabet extension} \\
& /\{A'_{r1}/A_{r1}, \dots, A'_{rn}/A_{rn}\} \setminus \{A_{h1}, \dots, A_{hn}\} && \textit{relabel + hide} \\
B ::= \, & \texttt{stop} \mid \texttt{end} \mid \texttt{error} \mid P(V_1, \dots, V_n) && \textit{terminations + process call} \\
& \mid \, \texttt{if } V \texttt{ then } B_1 \texttt{ else } B_2 && \textit{if-then-else structure} \\
& \mid \, \texttt{when } V_1 \, S_1 \rightarrow B_1 \mid \dots \mid \texttt{when } V_n \, S_n \rightarrow B_n && \textit{choice} \\
& \mid \, P_1(V_{11}, \dots, V_{1k}) ; \dots ; P_n(V_{n1}, \dots, V_{nl}) ; B && \textit{sequential composition} \\
S ::= \, & A_1 \rightarrow \dots \rightarrow A_k && \textit{sequence of labels} \\
A ::= \, & L_1 \dots L_n && \textit{label} \\
L ::= \, & act && \textit{action} \\
& \mid \, V \mid x : V && \textit{expression} \\
& \mid \, \{A_1, \dots, A_n\} \mid x : \{A_1, \dots, A_n\} && \textit{set of labels} \\
& \mid \, [V_1..V_2] \mid x : [V_1..V_2] && \textit{range}
\end{aligned}
$$

FSP has an expressive syntax to represent labels A, A_1, etc. Each label is thus the concatenation of lower-case identifiers *act*, expressions V, and integers within a range "$[V_1..V_2]$" where V_1 and V_2 are integer expressions. A variable x may be associated to some labels, which allows to reuse them later in the behaviour. A basic process definition consists of a process name P, a set of parameters $X_1, \dots, X_k$ with default values $V_1, \dots, V_k$, and a sequential behaviour B. This behaviour can be either relabeled, "A'_{ri}/A_{ri}" meaning that each label in A_{ri} renames into labels A'_{ri} (a single label may rename into several labels, thus yielding several transitions), or hidden to the environment, which corresponds to relabeling into the special action τ. FSP uses label prefix matching while applying hiding and relabeling operators. The *alphabet* of a process consists of the set of labels (possibly renamed) occurring in B and the supplementary labels in "$\{A_{e1}, \dots, A_{en}\}$". The stop, end, and error behaviours correspond to deadlock, successfull termination, and erroneous termination. Process call and *if-then-else* have a standard semantics. The "|" operator denotes a choice in which every branch "$S_i \rightarrow B_i$" whose condition V_i evaluates to true may execute nondeterministically; S_i corresponds to a sequence of labels. Finally, a sequential composition is made up of a list of process calls requiring that all these processes terminate. FSP composite processes are defined as follows:

$$P_C ::= \|P(X_1{=}V_1,\ldots,X_k{=}V_k) = C \qquad\qquad\quad \textit{process definition}$$
$$\gg \{A_{p1},\ldots,A_{pn}\} \setminus \{A_{h1},\ldots,A_{hn}\} \qquad \textit{priority + hide}$$
$$|\;\; \|P(X_1{=}V_1,\ldots,X_k{=}V_k) = C \qquad\qquad\quad \textit{process definition}$$
$$\ll \{A_{p1},\ldots,A_{pn}\} \setminus \{A_{h1},\ldots,A_{hn}\} \qquad \textit{priority + hide}$$
$$C ::= SL \;\; P(V_1,\ldots,V_n) \;/\{A'_{r1}/A_{r1},\ldots,A'_{rn}/A_{rn}\} \;\; \textit{process call + relabel}$$
$$|\;\; SL \;\; (C_1\|\ldots\|C_n) \;/\{A'_{r1}/A_{r1},\ldots,A'_{rn}/A_{rn}\} \;\; \textit{parallel compo. + relabel}$$
$$|\;\; \text{if } V \text{ then } C_1 \text{ else } C_2 \qquad\qquad\qquad \textit{if-then-else structure}$$
$$SL ::= \{A_1,\ldots,A_m\} :: \{A_1,\ldots,A_n\} : \qquad\qquad \textit{sharing / labeling}$$

A composite process definition consists of a name "$\|P$" (the symbol "$\|$" indicating that P belongs to the class of composite processes), a set of parameters $X_1,\ldots,X_k$ with default values $V_1,\ldots,V_k$, and a composite behaviour C. Priorities can be assigned to labels in C, "$\gg$" (respectively "$\ll$") meaning that labels in "$\{A_{p1},\ldots,A_{pn}\}$" have lower (respectively higher) priority than all other labels occurring in C. A composite behaviour may be either a call to a basic process, a parallel composition of composite behaviours synchronising on the intersection of their alphabets, or a deterministic choice between composite processes. Relabeling and hiding are also possible using a syntax similar to basic processes. At last, FSP contains two original operators named *process labeling* "$:$" and *process sharing* "$::$" which are always used subsequently (first sharing then labeling, see the grammar above). Process labeling "$\{A_1,\ldots,A_n\}:C$" generates an interleaving of as many instances of C as there are labels in "$\{A_1,\ldots,A_n\}$". All the labels of each instance are prefixed by the label of "$\{A_1,\ldots,A_n\}$" associated to this instance. Process sharing "$\{A_1,\ldots,A_m\}::C$" replaces each label l occurring in C by a choice between labels "$\{A_1 l,\ldots,A_m l\}$". As an illustration, the resulting automata for "$\|$C1 = {a,b}:P" and "$\|$C2 = {a,b}::P" are given below with "P = comm.END".

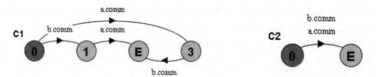

Example 1. The following specification describes a semaphore. The process ACCESS simulates a client which accesses the critical section protected by the process SEMAPHORE. The system, called SEMADEMO, is made up of the semaphore in charge of three resources a, b, c, and of the process which wants to access them.

```
SEMAPHORE(N=0)  = SEMA[N],
SEMA[v:0..1]    = ( up -> SEMA[v+1] | when (v>0) down -> SEMA[v-1] ).
ACCESS          = ( mutex.down -> critical -> mutex.up -> ACCESS ).
||SEMADEMO      = ( {a,b,c}:ACCESS || {a,b,c}::mutex:SEMAPHORE(1) ).
```

LOTOS (Language Of Temporal Ordering Specification) is a specification language standardised by ISO [13]. It combines definitions of abstract data types and algebraic processes. The full syntax of a process is the following:

```
process P [G_1, ..., G_m] (X_1:S_1, ..., X_n:S_n) : func :=
    B  where block_1, ..., block_p
endproc
```

A process defines a list of formal gates $G_{i \in \{1,...,m\}}$ and of parameters $X_{j \in \{1,...,n\}}$ of sort S_j. Each $block_{k \in \{1,...,p\}}$ denotes a data type or process definition. The functionality $func$ of a process is `exit` if it ends by an `exit` behaviour, or `noexit` otherwise. The process behaviour B is formalised in the following grammar. We present only operators that are required for our translation:

$$
\begin{array}{lll}
B ::= & \texttt{exit} & \textit{termination} \\
     | & G\ O_1\ \ldots\ O_n\ \texttt{[V]}\ \texttt{;}B\ |\ \texttt{i;}B & \textit{action prefix} \\
     | & \texttt{[}V\texttt{]->}B & \textit{guarded behaviour} \\
     | & B_1\ \texttt{[]}\ B_2 & \textit{choice} \\
     | & B_1\texttt{>>}B_2 & \textit{sequential composition} \\
     | & \texttt{hide}\ G_1,\ldots,G_n\ \texttt{in}\ B & \textit{hiding} \\
     | & P\texttt{[}G_1,\ldots,G_n\texttt{]}(V_1,\ldots,V_m) & \textit{process call} \\
     | & \texttt{choice}\ X : T\ \texttt{[]}\ B & \textit{choice on values} \\
O ::= & \texttt{!}V\ |\ \texttt{?}X : T & \textit{emission / reception} \\
V ::= & X\ |\ f(V_1,\ldots,V_n) & \textit{value expression}
\end{array}
$$

Gate identifiers G may be complemented with a set of parameters called offers. An *offer* has either the form "$!V$" which corresponds to the emission of a value V, or the form "$?X : T$" which means the reception of a value of sort T in a variable X. A single action can contain several offers, and these offers can be complemented by a guard which constrains the received values. For instance, "`COMM?X:Int[X==1]`" means that 1 is the only value that can be received in `X`. The guarded behaviour "$[V]->B$" means that B is executed only if the boolean expression V evaluates to true. The sequential composition "$B_1>>B_2$" executes first B_1 until it reaches an exit, then B_2 is executed. Hiding masks gates within a behaviour, thus producing an hidden event written `i`. Cyclic behaviours may be defined using tail-recursive process calls. The choice on values "`choice` $X : T$ `[]` B" generates a choice between behaviours $B_{V_1}, \ldots, B_{V_n}$ where $V_1, \ldots, V_n$ are all the values of sort T, and variable X is instantiated with value V_1 in B_{V_1}, with value V_2 in B_{V_2}, etc.

The main differences between FSP and LOTOS resides in the treatment of labels. On the one hand, LOTOS labels are structured in the form of a static (*i.e.*, determined at compile time) gate, possibly followed by dynamic (*i.e.*, computed at run-time) offers. Label hiding and label synchronisation are determined uniquely by the gate. On the other hand, no such distinction between gate and offers exists in FSP, where hiding and synchronization depend on full labels, computed at run-time by concatenation of sub-labels and replacement of variables. This difference constitutes the main difficulty of the translation.

Fortunately, CADP also provides a tool for communicating automata, called EXP.OPEN [14], whose input language (EXP) features more flexible label handling mechanisms than LOTOS. EXP allows to describe parallel compositions of finite state machines using several parallel composition operators, synchronisation vectors, as well as renaming, hiding, cutting, and priority operators. We present the part of the EXP language that is used in this paper. $L_1, L_1', \ldots$ represent labels, which are merely character strings.

$$
\begin{aligned}
B ::=\ &\texttt{total rename}\ L_1 \rightarrow L'_1, \ldots, L_n \rightarrow L'_n\ \texttt{in}\ B\ \texttt{end rename} && \textit{rename} \\
\mid\ &\texttt{total hide}\ L_1, \ldots, L_n\ \texttt{in}\ B\ \texttt{end hide} && \textit{hide} \\
\mid\ &\texttt{total cut}\ L_1, \ldots, L_n\ \texttt{in}\ B\ \texttt{end cut} && \textit{cut} \\
\mid\ &\texttt{total prio all but}\ L_1, \ldots, L_n > L'_1, \ldots, L'_k\ \texttt{in}\ B\ \texttt{end prio} && \textit{priority (1)} \\
\mid\ &\texttt{total prio}\ L_1, \ldots, L_n > \texttt{all but}\ L'_1, \ldots, L'_k\ \texttt{in}\ B\ \texttt{end prio} && \textit{priority (2)} \\
\mid\ &B_1 |||B_2 && \textit{interleaving} \\
\mid\ &\texttt{label par}\ L_1, \ldots, L_m\ \texttt{in}\ B_1 || \ldots ||B_n\ \texttt{end par} && \textit{par. compo.} \\
\mid\ &\texttt{label par}\ V_1, \ldots, V_m\ \texttt{in}\ B_1 || \ldots ||B_n\ \texttt{end par} && \textit{vect. compo.} \\
V ::=\ &(L_1|_-) * \ldots * (L_n|_-) \rightarrow L && \textit{vector}
\end{aligned}
$$

Rename and hide respectively define a set of labels to be renamed, and a set of labels to be hidden in behaviour B. The $\texttt{cut}$ operator is used to cut the transitions that carry some given labels in a transition system. Priority expresses that a set of labels have a higher priority than another set of labels. "$\texttt{all but}\ L_1, \ldots, L_n$" represents all labels except $L_1, \ldots, L_n$. We introduce three forms of parallel composition: "$B_1|||B_2$" means that B_1 and B_2 run in parallel without synchronising, "$\texttt{label par}\ L_1, \ldots, L_m\ \texttt{in}\ B_1||\ldots||B_n$" means that $B_1, \ldots, B_n$ run in parallel and synchronise all together on labels $L_1, \ldots, L_m$, and "$\texttt{label par}\ V_1, \ldots, V_m\ \texttt{in}\ B_1||\ldots||B_n$" means that they synchronise following the constraints expressed by the synchronisation vectors $V_1, \ldots, V_m$. Precisely, a vector "$l_1 * \ldots * l_n \rightarrow l$" produces a transition labeled l if all B_i such that "$l_i \neq \_$" execute all together a transition labeled l_i. EXP.OPEN provides alternative semantics for the $\texttt{hide}$, $\texttt{rename}$, $\texttt{cut}$, $\texttt{prio}$, and $\texttt{par}$ operators, the precise semantics used in this paper being determined by the $\texttt{total}$ (which means that a label matches if it matches a regular expression entirely) and $\texttt{label}$ (which means that processes synchronise on full labels, and not only on the gate part of the label) keywords. Finally, we mention SVL [8] (Script Verification Language), which allows a high-level and concise description of the calls to the different CADP tools.

3 Preliminary Definitions

3.1 Environment

When translating an FSP specification into LOTOS/EXP, we need to propagate along the abstract syntax tree of the FSP specification, information collected during the tree traversal. This information is called an environment and is made of the following objects:

- E is a partial function associating expressions to variables, represented as a set of couples of the form "$x \mapsto v$". Environment E will be used during the translation to store variables defined in FSP labels but also process parameters and constant definitions. E is initialised with constant definitions which are global to all processes.
- S is a set of labels used with the "$::$" FSP operator, to be shared between the parallel processes.

- L is a label coming from the ":" FSP operator, to be distributed as prefix over the parallel processes.
- R is a relabeling relation represented as a set of elements of the form "$l \mapsto \{l_1, \ldots, l_k\}$", which associates sets of new labels to old labels.
- H is a set of labels to be hidden.
- X is a mapping from variables to sets of labels, represented as a set of elements of the form "$x \mapsto s$", where s is either a range "(v_1, v_2)" or a set of labels "$\{l_1, \ldots, l_k\}$".

An environment is a tuple "$\langle E, M, X \rangle$" where M is a list of tuples "$\langle S, L, R, H \rangle$". We now define some functions used thereafter to formalise the translation. Function dom applies to R such that: $dom(\{l_1 \mapsto s_1, \ldots, l_k \mapsto s_k\}) = \{l_1, \ldots, l_k\}$ where $s_{i \in \{1,\ldots,k\}}$ are sets of labels. The dispatching function $\mapsto_d$ associates every element of one source set to all the elements of a target set:

$$\{l_1, \ldots, l_k\} \mapsto_d \{l'_1, \ldots, l'_k\} = \{l_1 \mapsto \{l'_1, \ldots, l'_k\}, \ldots, l_k \mapsto \{l'_1, \ldots, l'_k\}\}$$

Function $\otimes$ concatenates elements of two sets:

$$\{l_1, \ldots, l_k\} \otimes \{m_1, \ldots, m_p\} = \{l_1 m_1, \ldots, l_1 m_p, \ldots, l_k m_1, \ldots, l_k m_p\}$$

Function pm is a prefix matching test, which takes as input a label l and a set of labels, and returns $true$ if one of the labels in the list is a prefix for l:

$$pm(l, \{l_1, \ldots, l_n\}) = (\exists i \in \{1, \ldots, n\})(\exists l') \, l = l_i l'$$

Function $newlab$ takes as input a label l and returns the set of labels after relabeling by R:

$$newlab(l, \{l_1 \mapsto s_1, \ldots, l_k \mapsto s_k\}) = \{l'_i l' | (\exists i \in \{1, \ldots, k\}) \, l = l_i l' \wedge l'_i \in s_i\}$$

3.2 Expressions

Function $f2l_e$ translates FSP expressions (which are of type integer or string) into LOTOS expressions substituting the values of variables *wrt.* environment E:

$$f2l_e(x, E) = E(x)$$
$$f2l_e(f(V_1, \ldots, V_n), E) = f(f2l_e(V_1, E), \ldots, f2l_e(V_n, E))$$

Function $vars$ extracts the variables appearing in an expression:

$$vars(x) = \{x\}$$
$$vars(f(V_1, \ldots, V_n)) = vars(V_1) \cup \ldots \cup vars(V_n)$$

Function $type$ computes the type of an expression, that is either Int or String. This function is standard, and therefore not defined here.

3.3 Translation of a Label

The translation of an FSP label is not easy because FSP labels involve different notions that have no direct counterpart in LOTOS, namely sets, ranges, complex expressions, and variable definitions. Moreover, hiding or renaming of a label can only be made after flattening this high-level notation, as computed by LTSA while generating transition systems from FSP specifications. Consequently, we define two functions, $flatten$ and $flatten_x$, to translate an FSP label into a set of LOTOS labels. Function $flatten$ expands all the variables appearing in the label, whereas $flatten_x$ translates as often as possible into LOTOS variables the variables defined in the FSP label. In the following, function $flatten$ is used instead of the less space-consuming $flatten_x$ one when hiding or renaming has to be applied on the label.

We start with the definition of the $flatten$ function which is called with an environment E associating one value to every variable appearing in FSP, and returns a set of couples *(label, environment)*. In case a variable is assigned several values (as defined in an FSP range or set), $flatten$ generates as many labels and environments as there are values associated to the variable. At this abstract level, all the label portions are stored in a list using the *cons* and *nil* operator. A variable is defined only once in an FSP specification, so union between variable environments can be used instead of an overloading operation.

$flatten(L_1 \ldots L_n, E) =$
    $\{(cons(l_1, l_{11}), E_{11} \cup E_1), \ldots, (cons(l_1, l_{1m}), E_{1m} \cup E_1), \ldots,$
    $(cons(l_k, l_{k1}), E_{k1} \cup E_k), \ldots, (cons(l_k, l_{kl}), E_{kl} \cup E_k)\}$
where $\{(l_1, E_1), \ldots, (l_k, E_k)\} = flatten_l(L_1, E),$
    $\{(l_{11}, E_{11}), \ldots, (l_{1m}, E_{1m})\} = flatten(L_2 \ldots L_n, E_1),$ and
    $\{(l_{k1}, E_{k1}), \ldots, (l_{kl}, E_{kl})\} = flatten(L_2 \ldots L_n, E_k).$

The terminal case is defined on an empty list ε as: $flatten(\varepsilon, E) = \{(nil, E)\}$

Function $flatten_l$ flattens a portion of label. In case of an expression indexed by a variable, environment E is extended with the variable x and its value v obtained after evaluation by $f2l_e$.

$flatten_l(act, E) = \{(act, E)\}$
$flatten_l(V, E) = \{(v, E)\}$
$flatten_l(x : V, E) = \{(v, \{x \mapsto v\} \cup E)\}$
where $v = f2l_e(V, E).$

In case of sets of labels, all the labels are expanded, and environments updated if necessary.

$flatten_l(\{A_1, \ldots, A_n\}, E) =$
    $\{(l_{11}, E_{11}), \ldots, (l_{1k}, E_{1k}), \ldots, (l_{n1}, E_{n1}), \ldots, (l_{nm}, E_{nm})\}$
$flatten_l(x : \{A_1, \ldots, A_n\}, E) =$
    $\{(l_{11}, \{x \mapsto l_{11}\} \cup E_{11}), \ldots, (l_{1k}, \{x \mapsto l_{1k}\} \cup E_{1k}), \ldots,$
    $(l_{n1}, \{x \mapsto l_{n1}\} \cup E_{n1}), \ldots, (l_{nm}, \{x \mapsto l_{nm}\} \cup E_{nm})\}$
where $\{(l_{11}, E_{11}), \ldots, (l_{1k}, E_{1k})\} = flatten(A_1, E),$ and
    $\{(l_{n1}, E_{n1}), \ldots, (l_{nm}, E_{nm})\} = flatten(A_n, E).$

In case of ranges, all the integer expressions are computed from the range.

$flatten_l([V_1..V_2], E) = \{(v_1, E), \ldots, (v_r, E)\}$
$flatten_l(x : [V_1..V_2], E) = \{(v_1, \{x \mapsto v_1\} \cup E), \ldots, (v_r, \{x \mapsto v_r\} \cup E)\}$
where $v_1 = f2l_e(V_1, E)$, $r = (f2l_e(V_2, E) - f2l_e(V_1, E)) + 1,$ and
    $(\forall i \in \{1, \ldots, r - 1\})\ v_{i+1} = v_i + 1.$

Example 2. The FSP label "`lab[x:1..2]`" is translated using $flatten$ as two abstract LOTOS labels (see Section 7 for the concrete notation): "$cons(lab, cons(1, nil))$" and "$cons(lab, cons(2, nil))$".

Function $flatten_x$ generates LOTOS labels keeping variables when the label is not concerned by relabeling or hiding. Function $flatten_x$ returns a set of tuples

"(l, E, X)" where l is a label, E is a variable environment, and X binds variables which are kept while translating to a range of integer values, or a set of labels.

$$flatten_x(L_1 \ldots L_n, E, X) = \{(cons(l_1, l_{11}), E_{11} \cup E_1, X_{11} \cup X_1), \ldots,$$
$$(cons(l_1, l_{1m}), E_{1m} \cup E_1, X_{1m} \cup X_1), \ldots, (cons(l_k, l_{k1}), E_{k1} \cup E_k, X_{k1} \cup X_k),$$
$$\ldots, (cons(l_k, l_{kl}), E_{kl} \cup E_k, X_{kl} \cup X_k)\}$$
$$flatten_x(\varepsilon, E, X) = \{(nil, E, X)\}$$
where $\{(l_1, E_1, X_1), \ldots, (l_k, E_k, X_k)\} = flatten_{xl}(L_1, E, X),$
$$\{(l_{11}, E_{11}, X_{11}), \ldots, (l_{1m}, E_{1m}, X_{1m})\} = flatten_x(L_2 \ldots L_n, E_1, X_1),$$
$$\{(l_{k1}, E_{k1}, X_{k1}), \ldots, (l_{kl}, E_{kl}, X_{kl})\} = flatten_x(L_2 \ldots L_n, E_k, X_k),$$

Function $flatten_{xl}$ translates a portion of an FSP label into a portion of a LOTOS label. All the variables appearing in the FSP label are kept taking advantage of the expressiveness of LOTOS offers. Thus, an FSP set or range is translated as the variable at hand, and the set or range is stored in X that will be used during the translation of the full label to generate a guard constraining the value of the variable. If a variable is part of an expression to be translated, a new variable (y below) is kept in place of this expression.

$$flatten_{xl}(act, E, X) = \{(act, E, \emptyset)\}$$
$$flatten_{xl}(V, E, X) =$$
$$\begin{cases} \{(y, \{y \mapsto y\} \cup E, \{y \mapsto (v, v)\})\} & \text{if } \exists z \in vars(V) \ \wedge \ z \in X \\ \{(v, E, \emptyset)\} & \text{otherwise} \end{cases}$$
$$flatten_{xl}(x{:}V, E, X) =$$
$$\begin{cases} \{(y, \{x \mapsto v, y \mapsto y\} \cup E, \{y \mapsto (v, v)\})\} & \text{if } \exists z \in vars(V) \ \wedge \ z \in X \\ \{(v, \{x \mapsto v\} \cup E, \emptyset)\} & \text{otherwise} \end{cases}$$
where $v = f2l_e(V, E)$.

When translating sets and ranges, several labels with environments E and X are generated. In case a variable x appears as index of the set (resp. range), x is kept as a variable in E and the environment X is extended with all the possible values that can be computed for x from the set (resp. range).

$$flatten_{xl}(\{A_1, \ldots, A_n\}, E, X) = \{(l_{11}, E_{11}, X_{11}), \ldots, (l_{1k}, E_{1k}, X_{1k}), \ldots,$$
$$(l_{n1}, E_{n1}, X_{n1}), \ldots, (l_{nm}, E_{nm}, X_{nm})\}$$
$$flatten_{xl}(x{:}\{A_1, \ldots, A_n\}, E, X) =$$
$$\{(x, \{x \mapsto x\} \cup E, \{x \mapsto \{l_{11}, \ldots, l_{1k}, \ldots, l_{n1}, \ldots, l_{nm}\}\})\}$$
where $\{(l_{11}, E_{11}, X_{11}), \ldots, (l_{1k}, E_{1k}, X_{1k})\} = flatten_x(A_1, E, X),$ and
$$\{(l_{n1}, E_{n1}, X_{n1}), \ldots, (l_{nm}, E_{nm}, X_{nm})\} = flatten_x(A_n, E, X).$$
$$flatten_{xl}([V_1..V_2], E, X) =$$
$$\begin{cases} \{(y, \{y \mapsto y\} \cup E, \{y \mapsto (v_1, v_r)\})\} & \text{if } \exists z \in (vars(V_1) \cup vars(V_2)) \wedge z \in X \\ \{(v_1, E, \emptyset), \ldots, (v_r, E, \emptyset)\} & \text{otherwise} \end{cases}$$
$$flatten_{xl}(x{:}[V_1..V_2], E, X) = \{(x, \{x \mapsto x\} \cup E, \{x \mapsto (v_1, v_r)\})\}$$
where $v_1 = f2l_e(V_1, E)$, $r = (f2l_e(V_2, E) - f2l_e(V_1, E)) + 1$, and
$$(\forall i \in \{1, \ldots, r-1\}) \ v_{i+1} = v_i + 1.$$

Example 3. The FSP label "`lab[x:1..2]`" is translated using $flatten_x$ in LOTOS as "$cons(lab, cons(x, nil))$" with a guard "$(x \geq 1) \wedge (x \leq 2)$" which restricts the values of x. Both pieces of specification generate exactly the same labels.

3.4   Hiding or Renaming

Function *horr* tests if a set of flattened labels is concerned by hiding or renaming, and is used while translating sequences of labels to decide if variables may be kept (use of $flatten_x$) or not (use of $flatten$) in the LOTOS code. The list of tuples "$\langle S, L, R, H \rangle$" is applied starting by the first tuple since this list is built adding in head, and tuples have to be applied starting by the most recent one.

$$horr(\{l_1, \ldots, l_k\}, [\langle S_1, L_1, R_1, H_1 \rangle, \ldots, \langle S_n, L_n, R_n, H_n \rangle]) =$$
$$\bigvee\nolimits_{i \in \{1, \ldots, q\}, j \in \{1, \ldots, k\}}$$
$$(\ pm(s_i ml_j, H_1) \lor pm(s_i ml_j, dom(R_1))$$
$$\lor\ horr(\{s_i ml_j\}, [\langle S_2, L_2, R_2, H_2 \rangle, \ldots, \langle S_n, L_n, R_n, H_n \rangle])\ )$$

where $S_1 = \{s_1, \ldots, s_q\}$, and $L_1 = m$.

4   Translating FSP Sequential Processes into LOTOS

This section presents function $f2l_p$ which translates a sequence of labels, and function $f2l_b$ which generates LOTOS code for FSP sequential processes.

4.1   Sequence of Labels

The translation of a sequence depends if labels have to be modified (renamed or hidden) during the translation: if it is the case, they are flattened using the *flatten* function; otherwise variables are kept and function $flatten_x$ is used. We also recall that an FSP label may correspond to several labels in LOTOS. Therefore, the translation of a label may generate a choice in LOTOS with as many branches as labels computed by *flatten* or $flatten_x$.

Hiding or relabeling required. More formally, it means that $horr(\{l_1, \ldots, l_h\}, M) = true$ where $\{(l_1, E_1), \ldots, (l_h, E_h)\} = flatten(A_1, E)$.

$$f2l_p(A_1 \to \ldots \to A_k \to B, \langle E, M, X \rangle) =$$
$$f2l_l(apply(l_1, M))\ seq(l_1, M)\ f2l_p(A_2 \to \ldots \to A_k \to B, \langle E_1 \cup E, M, X \rangle)$$
$$[]\ \ldots\ []$$
$$f2l_l(apply(l_h, M))\ seq(l_h, M)\ f2l_p(A_2 \to \ldots \to A_k \to B, \langle E_h \cup E, M, X \rangle)$$
$$f2l_p(B, \langle E, M, X \rangle) = f2l_b(B, \langle E, M, X \rangle)$$

The last rule applies when the sequence of labels is empty. Function $f2l_b$ dedicated to the translation of sequential processes is defined in the sequel. Function *apply* computes a set of labels resulting of the application in sequence of the list of tuples on a label. Note that relabeling may replace a single label by several ones, and that prefixing, relabeling and hiding are successively applied.

$$apply(l, [\langle S_1, L_1, R_1, H_1 \rangle, \ldots, \langle S_n, L_n, R_n, H_n \rangle]) =$$
$$apply(l_1', [\langle S_2, L_2, R_2, H_2 \rangle, \ldots, \langle S_n, L_n, R_n, H_n \rangle])$$
$$\cup\ \ldots\ \cup$$
$$apply(l_k'', [\langle S_2, L_2, R_2, H_2 \rangle, \ldots, \langle S_n, L_n, R_n, H_n \rangle])$$

where $S_1 = \{s_1, \ldots, s_q\}$, $L_1 = m$, $\{l_1, \ldots, l_p\} = \{s_1 ml, \ldots, s_q ml\}$,
$\{l_1', \ldots, l_r'\} = apply_R(l_1, R_1) \cup apply_R(l_p, R_1)$, and
$\{l_1'', \ldots, l_k''\} = apply_H(l_1', R_1) \cup apply_H(l_r', R_1)$.

Functions $apply_R$ and $apply_H$ are resp. in charge of renaming and hiding.

$$apply_R(l, R) = \begin{cases} newlab(l, R) & \text{if } pm(l, dom(R)) \\ l & \text{otherwise} \end{cases}$$

$$apply_H(l, H) = \begin{cases} i & \text{if } pm(l, H) \\ l & \text{otherwise.} \end{cases}$$

Function $f2l_l$ generates a LOTOS choice from a set of labels.

$$f2l_l(\{l_1, \ldots, l_n\}) = \begin{cases} l_1 & \text{if } n = 1 \\ l_1\text{;exit [] } \ldots \text{ [] } l_n\text{;exit} & \text{otherwise} \end{cases}$$

Function seq chooses the LOTOS sequential composition "$\gg$" as sequence operator when this operator is preceded by a behaviour (a choice among several labels), and the LOTOS action prefix ";" when preceded by a single label.

$$seq(l, M) = \begin{cases} \gg & \text{if } |apply(l, M)| > 1 \\ ; & \text{otherwise} \end{cases}$$

No hiding or relabeling required. In this case, there is $horr(\{l_1, \ldots, l_m\}, M) = false$ where $\{(l_1, E_1), \ldots, (l_m, E_m)\} = flatten(A_1, E)$.

$f2l_p(A_1 \to \ldots \to A_k \to B, \langle E, M, X \rangle) =$
  $f2l_l(apply(l_1, M), X_1 \cup X) \, seq(l_1, M, X_1 \cup X)$
    $f2l_p(A_2 \to \ldots \to A_k \to B, \langle E_1 \cup E, M, X_1 \cup X \rangle)$
  [] $\ldots$ []
  $f2l_l(apply(l_h, M), X_h \cup X) \, seq(l_h, M, X_h \cup X)$
    $f2l_p(A_2 \to \ldots \to A_k \to B, \langle E_h \cup E, M, X_h \cup X \rangle)$
$f2l_p(B, \langle E, M, X \rangle) = f2l_b(B, \langle E, M, X \rangle)$
where $\{(l_1, E_1, X_1), \ldots, (l_h, E_h, X_h)\} = flatten_x(A_1, E, X)$.

Extra variables in X generated while flattening labels using $flatten_x$ (see for instance the second rule of $flatten_{xl}$, page 566) are not considered below because they make the notation concise but are not used in the following of the behaviour.

$f2l_l(\{l_1, \ldots, l_n\}, X) =$
$$\begin{cases} l_1 & \text{if } n = 1 \\ l_1\,[G]\text{;exit}(x_1, \ldots, x_p) \text{ [] } \ldots \text{ [] } l_n\,[G]\text{;exit}(x_1, \ldots, x_p) & \text{otherwise} \end{cases}$$
where $X = \{x_1 \mapsto D_1, \ldots, x_p \mapsto D_p\}$, and
    $G = f2l_t(x_1 \mapsto D_1) \wedge \ldots \wedge f2l_t(x_p \mapsto D_p)$.

Function $f2l_t$ generates guards from tuples of X. These guards are used to constrain the values of variables introduced in the translation of labels.

$f2l_t(x \mapsto (v_1, v_2)) = (x \geq v_1) \wedge (x \leq v_2)$
$f2l_t(x \mapsto \{l_1, \ldots, l_k\}) = (x = l_1) \vee \ldots \vee (x = l_k)$

Finally, function seq makes the variable passing explicit when the LOTOS sequential composition "$\gg$" is chosen as sequence operator. This is mandatory compared to the expanded translation of labels since variables are preserved here and can be used in the rest of the behaviour.

$$seq(l, M, X) = \begin{cases} \gg \text{ accept } x_1 : T_1, \ldots, x_p : T_p \text{ in} & \text{if } |apply(l, M)| > 1 \\ ; & \text{otherwise} \end{cases}$$
where $X = \{x_1 \mapsto D_1, \ldots, x_p \mapsto D_p\}$, and $T_1 = type(x_1), \ldots, T_p = type(x_p)$.

4.2   Sequential Processes

FSP sequential processes are translated into LOTOS processes. FSP allows the definition of local processes which are translated as local processes into LOTOS as well. We only present the translation of a process without local definitions, although this structuring is taken into account into the tool we have implemented (see Section 6). Now, we define the translation from FSP to LOTOS as a function $f2l_b$. Function $func$ computing the process functionality is defined in [15]. Note also that only two concrete LOTOS gates are generated by our translation: EVENT which prefixes all the regular FSP labels, and EVENT_ERROR which is used to encode the FSP error termination.

$f2l_b(P(X_1=V_1,\ldots,X_k=V_k) = B + \{A_{e1},\ldots,A_{en}\}$
$\quad /\{A'_{r1}/A_{r1},\ldots,A'_{rn}/A_{rn}\} \setminus \{A_{h1},\ldots,A_{hn}\}, \langle E, M, X\rangle) =$
$\quad\quad$ process P [EVENT,EVENT_ERROR] $(X_1 : T_1,\ldots,X_k : T_k) : func(B)$:=
$\quad\quad\quad f2l_b(B, \langle E_0, [\langle\emptyset,\emptyset,R_0,H_0\rangle,M], X\rangle)$
$\quad\quad$ endproc

where $T_1 = type(V_1),\ldots,T_k = type(V_k)$, $E_0 = \{X_1 \mapsto V_1,\ldots,X_k \mapsto V_k\} \cup E$,
$\quad\quad \{(l_{r11}, E_{r11}),\ldots,(l_{r1k}, E_{r1k})\} = flatten(A_{r1}, E)$,
$\quad\quad \{(l'_{r11}, E'_{r11}),\ldots,(l'_{r1k}, E'_{r1k})\} = flatten(A'_{r1}, E)$,
$\quad\quad \{(l_{rn1}, E_{rn1}),\ldots,(l_{rnk}, E_{rnk})\} = flatten(A_{rn}, E)$,
$\quad\quad \{(l'_{rn1}, E'_{rn1}),\ldots,(l'_{rnk}, E'_{rnk})\} = flatten(A'_{rn}, E)$,
$\quad\quad R_0 = \{\{l_{r11},\ldots,l_{r1k}\} \mapsto_d \{l'_{r11},\ldots,l'_{r1k}\},\ldots,$
$\quad\quad\quad\quad\quad \{l_{rn1},\ldots,l_{rnk}\} \mapsto_d \{l'_{rn1},\ldots,l'_{rnk}\}\}$,
$\quad\quad \{(l_{h11}, E_{h11}),\ldots,(l_{h1k}, E_{h1k})\} = flatten(A_{h1}, E)$,
$\quad\quad \{(l_{hn1}, E_{hn1}),\ldots,(l_{hnk}, E_{hnk})\} = flatten(A_{hn}, E)$, and
$\quad\quad H_0 = \{l_{h11},\ldots,l_{h1k},\ldots,l_{hn1},\ldots,l_{hnk}\}$.

Usual terminations (stop and end) have direct equivalent in LOTOS. The error termination is translated using a P_ERROR process whose behaviour is an endless loop on an EVENT_ERROR label.

$f2l_b(\text{stop}, \langle E, M, X\rangle) = \text{stop}$
$f2l_b(\text{end}, \langle E, M, X\rangle) = \text{exit}$
$f2l_b(\text{error}, \langle E, M, X\rangle) = \text{P\_ERROR [EVENT\_ERROR]}$

A process call is translated as is with as parameter its list of arguments.

$f2l_b(P(V_1,\ldots,V_n), \langle E, M, X\rangle) =$
$\quad P$ [EVENT,EVENT_ERROR] $(f2l_e(V_1, E),\ldots,f2l_e(V_n, E))$

The if structure is encoded as a LOTOS choice with two branches respectively encoding the then and else part of the FSP behaviour.

$f2l_b(\text{if } V \text{ then } B_1 \text{ else } B_2, \langle E, M, X\rangle) =$
$\quad [f2l_e(V, E)] \text{-> } f2l_b(B_1, \langle E, M, X\rangle)$
$\quad []$
$\quad [\neg f2l_e(V, E)] \text{-> } f2l_b(B_2, \langle E, M, X\rangle)$

The FSP choice is translated into a LOTOS choice with guards.

$f2l_b(\text{when } V_1 S_1 \to B_1 | \ldots | \text{when } V_n S_n \to B_n, \langle E, M, X\rangle) =$
$\quad [f2l_e(V_1, E)] \text{-> } f2l_p(S_1 \to B_1, \langle E, M, X\rangle)$
$\quad [] \ldots []$
$\quad [f2l_e(V_n, E)] \text{-> } f2l_p(S_n \to B_n, \langle E, M, X\rangle)$

Last, a sequential composition is translated similarly in LOTOS.

$$f2l_b(P_1(V_{11}, \ldots, V_{1k}) ; \ldots ; P_n(V_{n1}, \ldots, V_{nl}) ; B, \langle E, M, X \rangle) =$$
$$P_1 \texttt{[EVENT,EVENT\_ERROR]} (f2l_e(V_{11}, E), \ldots, f2l_e(V_{1k}, E)) \gg \ldots \gg$$
$$P_n \texttt{[EVENT}, \ldots] (f2l_e(V_{n1}, E), \ldots, f2l_e(V_{nl}, E)) \gg f2l_b(B, \langle E, M, X \rangle)$$

No variables are passed along the LOTOS sequential composition because processes involved in the composition are independent of each other: each process has to terminate correctly before starting the next one. In addition, LOTOS local processes are generated for each process called in the sequential composition. This is needed to apply the environment (and possible renaming or hiding) to the definitions of referred processes. As an example, process P_1 is translated as follows, where $\hat{P}_1$ is the process definition of P_1:

process P_1 [EVENT,EVENT_ERROR] $(X_1 : T_1, \ldots, X_k : T_k) : func(\hat{P}_1)$:=
    $f2l_b(\hat{P}_1, \langle E_0, M, X \rangle)$
endproc
where $T_1 = type(V_1), \ldots, T_k = type(V_k)$, $E_0 = \{X_1 \mapsto V_1, \ldots, X_k \mapsto V_k\} \cup E$.

5 Translating FSP Composite Processes into EXP

Encoding FSP composite processes into LOTOS is tedious for several reasons:

- LOTOS hiding and synchronisation constructs operate on gates, whereas FSP constructs operate on full labels (which are gates + offers in LOTOS).
- LOTOS has no renaming operator. The only way to rename a gate in LOTOS is to instantiate a process with an actual gate different from the formal one. Such a renaming is not always satisfactory, because it only permits injective renaming (different gates cannot be renamed into the same gate), whereas non-injective renaming is allowed in FSP.
- LOTOS does not have a priority operator. The only way to express it is by refactoring the specification to only allow labels with high priority to be executed when necessary.

Consequently, we chose to translate FSP composite processes into the EXP format instead of LOTOS. Translation of an FSP composite process into EXP is made up of three steps. First, all the FSP sequential processes are translated into LOTOS using function $f2l_b$ presented in Section 4. This translation takes into account the possible parameters coming with the process call. Then, SVL [8] scripts are automatically derived to generate a BCG file (which is a computer representation for state/transition models) for each sequential process translated into LOTOS. These BCG descriptions of processes are used in the last step, namely the translation of FSP composite processes into EXP.

Function $f2l_c$ translates composite processes into EXP specifications. The abstract notation "$l.*$" matches labels with l as prefix, and is used to take the prefix matching into account while hiding labels. The environment is only used during the translation of composite processes to store values of process parameters. This is due to the top-down approach our translation is based on, and to the fact that all the FSP operators are directly expressed in EXP.

$f2l_c(\ \|P(X_1{=}V_1,\ldots,X_k{=}V_k)\ =$
$\qquad C \gg \{A_{p1},\ldots,A_{pn}\} \setminus \{A_{h1},\ldots,A_{hn}\}, \langle E,M,X \rangle\ ) =$
$\qquad$ `total hide` $l_{h11}, l_{h11}.*, \ldots, l_{h1k}, l_{h1k}.*,$
$\qquad\qquad\qquad\qquad \ldots, l_{hn1}, l_{hn1}.*, \ldots, l_{hnk}, l_{hnk}.*$ `in`
$\qquad\quad$ `total prio all but` $l_{p11},\ldots,l_{p1k},\ldots,l_{pn1},\ldots,l_{pnk}$ `>`
$\qquad\qquad\qquad\qquad l_{p11},\ldots,l_{p1k},\ldots,l_{pn1},\ldots,l_{pnk}$ `in`
$\qquad\qquad f2l_c(C, \langle E_0,M,X \rangle)$
$\qquad\quad$ `end prio`
$\qquad$ `end hide`
$f2l_c(\ \|P(X_1{=}V_1,\ldots,X_k{=}V_k)\ =$
$\qquad C \ll \{A_{p1},\ldots,A_{pn}\} \setminus \{A_{h1},\ldots,A_{hn}\}, \langle E,M,X \rangle\ ) =$
$\qquad$ `total hide` $l_{h11}, l_{h11}.*, \ldots, l_{h1k}, l_{h1k}.*, \ldots,$
$\qquad\qquad\qquad\quad l_{hn1}, l_{hn1}.*, \ldots, l_{hnk}, l_{hnk}.*$ `in`
$\qquad\quad$ `total prio` $l_{p11},\ldots,l_{p1k},\ldots,l_{pn1},\ldots,l_{pnk}$ `>`
$\qquad\qquad$ `all but` $l_{p11},\ldots,l_{p1k},\ldots,l_{pn1},\ldots,l_{pnk}$ `in`
$\qquad\quad f2l_c(C, \langle E_0,M,X \rangle)$
$\qquad\quad$ `end prio`
$\qquad$ `end hide`
`where` $T_1 = type(V_1),\ldots,T_k = type(V_k)$, $E_0 = \{X_1 \mapsto V_1,\ldots,X_k \mapsto V_k\} \cup E$,
$\qquad \{(l_{h11}, E_{h11}),\ldots,(l_{h1k}, E_{h1k})\} = flatten(A_{h1}, E)$,
$\qquad \{(l_{hn1}, E_{hn1}),\ldots,(l_{hnk}, E_{hnk})\} = flatten(A_{hn}, E)$,
$\qquad \{(l_{p11}, E_{p11}),\ldots,(l_{p1k}, E_{p1k})\} = flatten(A_{p1}, E)$, and
$\qquad \{(l_{pn1}, E_{pn1}),\ldots,(l_{pnk}, E_{pnk})\} = flatten(A_{pn}, E)$.

As regards the translation of a process call into EXP, process P is duplicated in as many interleaved processes P as there are labels in the labeling set with all the labels of process P prefixed by one label of this set, respectively m_1, m_2, etc. The "`label par`" statement is used below for renaming purposes, since the **rename** statement existing in EXP does not allow to rename a single label into several labels (thus producing several transitions from a single one). Therefore, we use synchronisation vectors (usually used for synchronisation purposes) to rename labels ($vectors_r$), and to prefix all the labels of the process by the labels defined in S ($vectors_p$). Function $alpha$ computing the alphabet of a process is defined in [15].

$f2l_c(SL\ P(V_1,\ldots,V_n)\ /\{A'_{r1}/A_{r1},\ldots,A'_{rn}/A_{rn}\}, \langle E,M,X \rangle) =$
$\qquad$ `label par` $vectors_r(R_0, alpha(SL\ P(V_1,\ldots,V_n), \langle E,M,X \rangle))$ `in`
$\qquad\quad$ `label par`
$\qquad\qquad vectors_p(\{s_1,\ldots,s_k\}, \{m_1\} \otimes alpha(P(V_1,\ldots,V_n), \langle E,M,X \rangle))$ `in`
$\qquad\qquad\quad f2l_{pr}(P(V_1,\ldots,V_n), \langle E,M,X \rangle)$
$\qquad\quad$ `end par`
$\qquad\quad$ `|||...|||`
$\qquad\quad$ `label par`
$\qquad\qquad vectors_p(\{s_1,\ldots,s_k\}, \{m_p\} \otimes alpha(P(V_1,\ldots,V_n), \langle E,M,X \rangle))$ `in`
$\qquad\qquad\quad f2l_{pr}(P(V_1,\ldots,V_n), \langle E,M,X \rangle)$
$\qquad\quad$ `end par`
$\qquad$ `end par`

where $\{s_1, \ldots, s_k\} = flatten_{sh}(SL, E)$, $\{m_1, \ldots, m_p\} = flatten_{lb}(SL, E)$,
$$\{(l_{11}, E_{11}), \ldots, (l_{1k}, E_{1k})\} = flatten(A_{r1}, E),$$
$$\{(l'_{11}, E'_{11}), \ldots, (l'_{1k}, E'_{1k})\} = flatten(A'_{r1}, E),$$
$$\{(l_{n1}, E_{n1}), \ldots, (l_{nk}, E_{nk})\} = flatten(A_{rn}, E),$$
$$\{(l'_{n1}, E'_{n1}), \ldots, (l'_{nk}, E'_{nk})\} = flatten(A'_{rn}, E), \text{ and}$$
$$R_0 = \{\{l_{11}, \ldots, l_{1k}\} \mapsto_d \{l'_{11}, \ldots, l'_{1k}\}, \ldots,$$
$$\{l_{n1}, \ldots, l_{nk}\} \mapsto_d \{l'_{n1}, \ldots, l'_{nk}\}\}.$$

Functions $flatten_{sh}$ and $flatten_{lb}$ flatten the sets of labels used as prefixes:
$$flatten_{sh}(\{A_1, \ldots, A_m\}::\{A_1, \ldots, A_n\}:, E) = flatten(\{A_1, \ldots, A_m\}, E)$$
$$flatten_{lb}(\{A_1, \ldots, A_m\}::\{A_1, \ldots, A_n\}:, E) = flatten(\{A_1, \ldots, A_n\}, E)$$

Auxiliary functions $f2l_{pr}$, $vectors_r$, and $vectors_p$ are now defined. Function $f2l_{pr}$ refers to the BCG file generated previously from the LOTOS code if it is a sequential process, or calls the $f2l_c$ function if it is a composite process. We present a simplified version of $f2l_{pr}$ since a same process can be referred several times with different parameters. In our translator tool, we indexed such processes with numbers to distinguish their different instances.

$$f2l_{pr}(P(V_1, \ldots, V_n), \langle E, M, X \rangle) =$$
$$\begin{cases} \text{"}P.bcg\text{"} & \text{if } is\_sequential(P) \\ f2l_c(P(\hat{X}_1{=}V_1, \ldots, \hat{X}_n{=}V_n){=}\hat{P}, \langle E, M, X \rangle) & \text{otherwise} \end{cases}$$

where $\hat{X}_{i \in \{1, \ldots, n\}}$ refers to formal parameter identifiers, and $V_{i \in \{1, \ldots, n\}}$ refer to actual values for them.

Function $vector_r$ generates vectors with as left part a single element corresponding to the label to rename, and as right part its new name. Labels which are not concerned by relabeling preserve their original name.

$$vectors_r(R, \{l_1, \ldots, l_p\}) =$$
$$\begin{cases} l_1 \;\text{->}\; l_1, \, vectors_r(R, \{l_2, \ldots, l_p\}) & \text{if } newlab(l_1, R) = \emptyset \\ l_1 \;\text{->}\; n_1, \ldots, l_1 \;\text{->}\; n_q, \, vectors_r(R, \{l_2, \ldots, l_p\}) & \text{otherwise} \end{cases}$$

where $\{n_1, \ldots, n_q\} = newlab(l_1, R)$.

Function $vector_p$ generates vectors with as left part the label to extend, and derives from it a new label with a prefix taken into a set of prefixes. All the combinations are computed for the set of labels and prefixes in input. Function cat corresponds to the concatenation of lists.

$$vectors_p(\{s_1, \ldots, s_k\}, \{l_1, \ldots, l_p\}) =$$
$$l_1 \;\text{->}\; cat(s_1, l_1), \ldots, l_1 \;\text{->}\; cat(s_k, l_1), \, vectors_p(\{s_1, \ldots, s_k\}, \{l_2, \ldots, l_p\})$$

Similarly to the translation of a process call, for a parallel composition, interleaving of processes is derived, as well as renaming and prefixing using respectively $vectors_r$ and $vectors_p$ functions. Synchronisation sets are made explicit. Below, the composite process C_1 synchronise with the rest of the involved processes on labels $I_1, \ldots, I_q$.

$f2l_c(SL \ (C_1||\ldots||C_n) \ /\{A'_{r1}/A_{r1}, \ldots, A'_{rn}/A_{rn}\}, \langle E, M, X \rangle) =$
```
label par I_1,...,I_q in
    (
          label par vectors_r(R_0, alpha(SL C_1, <E, M, X>)) in
             label par
```

$vectors_p(\{s_1, \ldots, s_k\}, \{m_1\} \otimes alpha(C_1, \langle E, M, X \rangle))$ in
$\quad f2l_c(C_1, \langle E, M, X \rangle)$
$\quad$ end par
$\quad$ end par
|||...|||
label par $vectors_r(R_0, alpha(SL\ C_1, \langle E, M, X \rangle))$ in
$\quad$ label par
$\qquad vectors_p(\{s_1, \ldots, s_k\}, \{m_p\} \otimes alpha(C_1, \langle E, M, X \rangle))$ in
$\qquad f2l_c(C_1, \langle E, M, X \rangle)$
$\quad$ end par
$\quad$ end par
)
|| $f2l_c(SL\ (C_2||\ldots||C_n)\ /\{A'_{r1}/A_{r1}, \ldots, A'_{rn}/A_{rn}\}, \langle E, M, X \rangle)$
end par
where $\{I_1, \ldots, I_q\} = alpha(SL\ C_1\ /\{A'_{r1}/A_{r1}, \ldots, A'_{rn}/A_{rn}\}, \langle E, M, X \rangle),$
$\qquad \cap\ alpha(SL\ (C_2||\ldots||C_n)\ /\{A'_{r1}/A_{r1}, \ldots, A'_{rn}/A_{rn}\}, \langle E, M, X \rangle),$
$\qquad \{s_1, \ldots, s_k\} = flatten_{sh}(SL, E),\ \{m_1, \ldots, m_p\} = flatten_{lb}(SL, E),$
$\qquad \{(l_{r11}, E_{r11}), \ldots, (l_{r1k}, E_{r1k})\} = flatten(A_{r1}, E),$
$\qquad \{(l'_{r11}, E'_{r11}), \ldots, (l'_{r1k}, E'_{r1k})\} = flatten(A'_{r1}, E),$
$\qquad \{(l_{rn1}, E_{rn1}), \ldots, (l_{rnk}, E_{rnk})\} = flatten(A_{rn}, E),$
$\qquad \{(l'_{rn1}, E'_{rn1}), \ldots, (l'_{rnk}, E'_{rnk})\} = flatten(A'_{rn}, E),$ and
$\qquad R_0 = \{\{l_{r11}, \ldots, l_{r1k}\} \mapsto_d \{l'_{r11}, \ldots, l'_{r1k}\}, \ldots,$
$\qquad\qquad \{l_{rn1}, \ldots, l_{rnk}\} \mapsto_d \{l'_{rn1}, \ldots, l'_{rnk}\}\}.$
The if construct is translated as for sequential processes.
$f2l_c(\text{if } V \text{ then } C_1 \text{ else } C_2, \langle E, M, X \rangle) =$
$$\begin{cases} f2l_c(C_1, \langle E, M, X \rangle) & \text{if } f2l_e(V, E) \\ f2l_c(C_2, \langle E, M, X \rangle) & \text{otherwise} \end{cases}$$

6 Tool and Validation

Translator Tool. We developed an automatic translator from FSP to LOTOS using the SYNTAX and LOTOS NT compiler construction technologies [10]. The tool consists of about 5,000 lines of SYNTAX, 20,000 lines of LOTOS NT, and 500 lines of C. This implementation was split into two main steps: (i) parsing the FSP language and storing the result into an abstract syntax tree, (ii) translating the abstract syntax tree into semantically equivalent LOTOS code. The parsing task was difficult since SYNTAX accepts only LALR(1) grammar as input. Therefore, the abstract FSP grammar as formalised in [16] was refined to a concrete grammar free of ambiguities. We validated the translator on about 10,500 lines of FSP specifications (approx. 2,400 FSP processes) that we reused from [16] or wrote ourselves. In the latter case, we tried to systematically explore all the expressiveness that allows the FSP notation to ensure robustness of our translation. These 10,500 lines of FSP correspond after translation to about 72,000 lines of LOTOS, 2,000 lines of SVL, and 8,000 lines of EXP. This large number of LOTOS lines has two main explanations: (i) LOTOS is more verbose than FSP, for instance there are more keywords, or gates have to be made explicit; (ii) although we keep variables as often as possible, our translation of FSP sequential processes may flatten labels whereas FSP allows a concise notation for them.

Correctness of the Translation. It is essential to preserve the semantics of the source language after translation into the target one. Indeed, any verification performed with CADP on the specification obtained after translation has to be valid for the initial specification. Our translation preserves semantics of both process calculi *wrt.* a branching equivalence relation [22]. Branching equivalence is the strongest of the weak equivalences found in the literature. Unlike strong equivalence, branching equivalence does not require a strict matching of τ transitions. This is exactly what we need since sequential composition in LOTOS induces τ transitions which do not appear in the semantics of FSP. Semantics preservation modulo branching equivalence is important as it ensures that the properties restricted to visible actions (*e.g.,* safety and fair liveness) verified on the LOTOS specification are indeed properties of the FSP specification. One drawback of branching equivalence might be that it does not preserve τ cycles. For instance, two systems can be branching equivalent even if one system contains a τ cycle which does not appear in the other. However, our translation ensures that all the τ cycles in the FSP specification are preserved in the LOTOS one, and no new cycle is introduced.

We checked on all the examples that we used for validation that branching equivalence is preserved by our translation. For each specification, this test is performed on LTSs generated by LTSA and CADP *wrt.* the semantics of their respective notations. It was verified automatically using BISIMULATOR [2] for nontrivial examples. BISIMULATOR is a tool of the CADP toolbox which allows to verify the most common notions of behavioural equivalences. The equivalence test cannot be applied directly because FSP labels generated by LTSA and LOTOS labels generated by CADP do not follow the same syntactic conventions. Additionally, the FSP hidden event `tau` corresponds to i in LOTOS, and the LOTOS termination event `exit` has no counterpart in FSP. However, CADP allows to systematically transform an LTS with FSP conventions into one with LOTOS conventions, by renaming and cutting labels that match some predefined regular expressions.

7   Application

In this section, we focus on the specification of a semaphore. We present several refinements of this specification, and show how the use of LTSA is complemented by the use of CADP based on the translation from FSP to LOTOS/EXP. The starting point is the specification of the semaphore given in FSP in Example 1. The resulting automaton is made up of 7 states and 9 transitions.

A first refinement is to extend the number of resources ("{a,b,c}" but also "{1,2,3}") being concerned by the mutual exclusion as well as the number of accesses. This result is obtained by this new specification:

```
||SEMADEMO1 = (  {a,b,c}:ACCESS
```

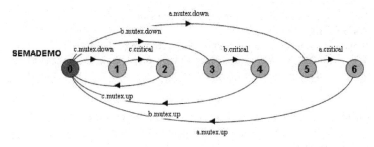

```
          || {a,b,c,[1..3]}::mutex:SEMAPHORE(1) || [1..3]:ACCESS ).
```

from which LTSA generates an automaton with 13 states and 18 transitions. The next step aims at duplicating both semaphores so that each semaphore is in charge of a single resource.

```
||SEMADEMO2 =
  (  {a,b,c}:ACCESS                || {a,b,c}::mutex:SEMAPHORE(1)
  || [1..3]::mutex:SEMAPHORE(1)    || [1..3]:ACCESS   ).
```

The resulting automaton contains 49 states and 126 transitions and becomes difficult to analyse visually, because all the transitions between resources "{a,b,c}" and "{1,2,3}" are interleaved. The last refinement defines the specification as a composition of two composite processes being dedicated to one resource.

```
||C_P = ( {a,b,c}:ACCESS || {a,b,c}::mutex:SEMAPHORE(1) ).
||C_Q = ( [1..3]:ACCESS  || [1..3]::mutex:SEMAPHORE(1)  ).
||SEMADEMO3 = ( C_P || C_Q ).
```

The automaton generated by LTSA has the same number of states and transitions as the former system, but it is impossible to claim that both specifications (SEMADEMO2 and SEMADEMO3) are equivalent. At this level, we use the translation to check this equivalence with the CADP toolbox. We show first some pieces of the code obtained by our translation. The FSP process SEMAPHORE is translated as follows in LOTOS:

```
process SEMAPHORE [EVENT,EVENT_ERROR] (N:Int): noexit :=
  SEMA [EVENT,EVENT_ERROR] (N)
where
  process SEMA [EVENT,EVENT_ERROR] (N:Int): noexit :=
    EVENT !CONS(UP,NIL); SEMA[EVENT,EVENT_ERROR](N+POS(1))
    []
    [V>POS(0)]-> EVENT !CONS(DOWN,NIL); SEMA[EVENT,EVENT_ERROR](N-POS(1))
  endproc
endproc
```

The concrete notation for LOTOS labels is slightly different from the abstract notation we introduced in Section 3. Indeed, a label is systematically represented by the EVENT gate followed by an offer consisting of a list of items of types Int and String, using the following data type:

```
type  Label is IntegerNumber, String
sorts Label
opns  CONS (*! constructor *) : String, Label -> Label
      CONS (*! constructor *) : Int, Label    -> Label
      NIL  (*! constructor *) :                -> Label
endtype
```

If variables appear in one label, the LOTOS choice construct is used to distinguish variables and regular string labels. For instance, the FSP label "lab[x:1..2]" is translated in LOTOS using the aforementioned concrete syntax as:

```
choice X:Int []
    EVENT !CONS (LAB, CONS (X, NIL)) [(X>=POS(1)) and (X<=POS(2))]
```

Now we show a piece of EXP code generated for the C_P process defined in the SEMADEMO3 system. Processes ACCESS and SEMAPHORE synchronise on the set of labels appearing at the beginning of the EXP description. This example shows how prefixing labels of ACCESS by B is done using synchronisation vectors, and how the exit label is cut within sequential processes.

```
label par
    "EVENT !CONS (A, CONS (MUTEX, CONS (DOWN, NIL)))",
    "EVENT !CONS (A, CONS (MUTEX, CONS (UP, NIL)))",
    "EVENT !CONS (B, CONS (MUTEX, CONS (DOWN, NIL)))", ...
in
    label par
        "EVENT !CONS (MUTEX, CONS (DOWN, NIL))"
                -> "EVENT !CONS (B, CONS(MUTEX, CONS (DOWN, NIL)))",
        "EVENT !CONS (CRITICAL, NIL)"
                -> "EVENT !CONS (B, CONS (CRITICAL, NIL))" ,
        "EVENT !CONS (MUTEX, CONS (UP, NIL))"
                -> "EVENT !CONS (B, CONS (MUTEX, CONS (UP, NIL)))"
    in
        total cut exit in "ACCESS.bcg" end cut
    end par
    ||
    ... total cut exit in "SEMAPHORE.bcg" end cut  ...
end par
```

Processes SEMADEMO2 and SEMADEMO3 translated into LOTOS/EXP have been checked strongly equivalent using the BISIMULATOR tool of the CADP toolbox. We illustrated here the use of equivalence checking on FSP designs, but other CADP verification techniques can be used to complement LTSA validation, such as distributed, compositional, or on-the-fly verification to tackle the state explosion problem, or efficient model checking techniques available in EVALUA-TOR [17]. Last, the debugging stage using CADP does not add any complexity for designers because labels used in counter-examples may be translated in FSP format (see Section 6) using renaming facilities available in CADP.

8   Concluding Remarks

In this paper, our motivation was to reduce the gap between existing tool support for process calculi. We chose here the popular process calculus FSP and the international standard LOTOS. FSP is based on an expressive and concise notation. Therefore, we proposed a translation from FSP to LOTOS (and EXP) to make the joint use of LTSA and CADP possible for FSP users. The translation is completely automated by a tool we implemented. This translator will be integrated in a future release of the CADP toolbox.

As regards related work, to the best of our knowledge, the only proposals focusing on high-level translations between process algebras have been made in the hardware area [20,23]. Their common goal is to allow verification of asynchronous circuits and architectures. Beyond that, the most related set of works are those advocating the encoding of process calculi (mainly ACP, CCS, CSP and their dialects) into higher-order logics, inputs of theorem provers such as HOL, PVS, ISABELLE [18,4,21,1] or into the B method [3]. Motivations of these works are to take advantage of the formal verification means available for the target formalism. Theorem proving allows to fight the state explosion problem and to deal with infinite automata, but is not suitable to prove temporal properties. We preferred model checking because it makes verification steps easier thanks to a full automation and its adequacy to automata-based models.

A first future work is to apply our approach on complex systems, such as web service models described first in BPEL or WS-CDL, and then automatically translated into FSP for analysis purposes [5]. In this case, many interacting services can involve huge underlying state spaces which can be generated and minimised using the optimised means of CADP. Moreover, equivalence checking available in CADP can help in web services to ensure that an abstract specification of a problem and its solution described as a composition of services are equivalent [19]. Another perspective is to take FSP safety and progress properties into account, and to translate them into regular alternation-free mu-calculus formulas, input format of the on-the-fly model checker EVALUATOR [17].

References

1. Basten, T., Hooman, J.: Process Algebra in Pvs. In: Cleaveland, W.R. (ed.) ETAPS 1999 and TACAS 1999. LNCS, vol. 1579, pp. 270–284. Springer, Heidelberg (1999)
2. Bergamini, D., Descoubes, N., Joubert, C., Mateescu, R.: Bisimulator: A Modular Tool for On-the-Fly Equivalence Checking. In: Halbwachs, N., Zuck, L.D. (eds.) TACAS 2005. LNCS, vol. 3440, pp. 581–585. Springer, Heidelberg (2005)
3. Butler, M.: Csp2B: A Practical Approach to Combining Csp and B. Formal Aspects of Computing 12(3), 182–198 (2000)
4. Dutertre, B., Schneider, S.: Using a Pvs Embedding of Csp to Verify Authentication Protocols. In: Gunter, E.L., Felty, A.P. (eds.) TPHOLs 1997. LNCS, vol. 1275, pp. 121–136. Springer, Heidelberg (1997)
5. Foster, H., Uchitel, S., Magee, J., Kramer, J.: Tool Support for Model-Based Engineering of Web Service Compositions. In: Proc. of ICWS'05, pp. 95–101. IEEE Computer Society Press, Los Alamitos (2005)

6. Garavel, H.: Compilation of Lotos Abstract Data Types. In: Proc. of FORTE'89, pp. 147–162. North-Holland, Amsterdam (1989)
7. Garavel, H.: Open/Cæsar: An Open Software Architecture for Verification, Simulation, and Testing. In: Steffen, B. (ed.) ETAPS 1998 and TACAS 1998. LNCS, vol. 1384, pp. 68–84. Springer, Heidelberg (1998)
8. Garavel, H., Lang, F.: Svl: A Scripting Language for Compositional Verification. In: Proc. of FORTE'01, pp. 377–394. Kluwer, Dordrecht (2001)
9. Garavel, H., Lang, F., Mateescu, R.: An Overview of Cadp 2001. EASST Newsletter 4, 13–24 (2001)
10. Garavel, H., Lang, F., Mateescu, R.: Compiler Construction Using Lotos nt. In: Horspool, R.N. (ed.) CC 2002 and ETAPS 2002. LNCS, vol. 2304, pp. 9–13. Springer, Heidelberg (2002)
11. Garavel, H., Serwe, W.: State Space Reduction for Process Algebra Specifications. Theoretical Computer Science 351(2), 131–145 (2006)
12. Garavel, H., Sifakis, J.: Compilation and Verification of Lotos Specifications. In: Proc. of PSTV'90, pp. 379–394. North-Holland, Amsterdam (1990)
13. ISO. Lotos: a Formal Description Technique based on the Temporal Ordering of Observational Behaviour. Technical Report 8807, International Standards Organisation (1989)
14. Lang, F.: Exp.Open 2.0: A Flexible Tool Integrating Partial Order, Compositional, and On-The-Fly Verification Methods. In: Romijn, J.M.T., Smith, G.P., van de Pol, J. (eds.) IFM 2005. LNCS, vol. 3771, pp. 70–88. Springer, Heidelberg (2005)
15. Lang, F., Salaün, G.: Translating Fsp into Lotos and Networks of Automata. Technical report, INRIA (2007)
16. Magee, J., Kramer, J.: Concurrency: State Models & Java Programs. Wiley, Chichester (1999)
17. Mateescu, R., Sighireanu, M.: Efficient On-the-Fly Model-Checking for Regular Alternation-Free Mu-Calculus. Science of Comp. Progr. 46(3), 255–281 (2003)
18. Nesi, M.: Formalising a Value-Passing Calculus in Hol. Formal Aspects of Computing 11(2), 160–199 (1999)
19. Salaün, G., Bordeaux, L., Schaerf, M.: Describing and Reasoning on Web Services using Process Algebra. In: Proc. of ICWS'04, pp. 43–51. IEEE Computer Society Press, Los Alamitos (2004)
20. Salaün, G., Serwe, W.: Translating Hardware Process Algebras into Standard Process Algebras: Illustration with Chp and Lotos. In: Romijn, J.M.T., Smith, G.P., van de Pol, J. (eds.) IFM 2005. LNCS, vol. 3771, pp. 287–306. Springer, Heidelberg (2005)
21. Tej, H., Wolff, B.: A Corrected Failure-Divergence Model for Csp in Isabelle/Hol. In: Jones, C.B. (ed.) FME 1997. LNCS, vol. 1313, pp. 318–337. Springer, Heidelberg (1997)
22. van Glabbeek, R.J., Weijland, W.P.: Branching Time and Abstraction in Bisimulation Semantics. Journal of the ACM 43(3), 555–600 (1996)
23. Wang, X., Kwiatkowska, M.Z., Theodoropoulos, G.K., Zhang, Q.: Towards a Unifying Csp approach to Hierarchical Verification of Asynchronous Hardware. ENTCS, vol. 128, pp. 231–246 (2005)

Common Semantics for Use Cases and Task Models

Daniel Sinnig[1], Patrice Chalin[1], and Ferhat Khendek[2]

[1] Department of Computer Science and Software Engineering,
Concordia University, Montreal, Quebec, Canada
{d_sinnig,chalin}@encs.concordia.ca
[2] Department of Electrical and Computer Engineering,
Concordia University, Montreal, Quebec, Canada
khendek@ece.concordia.ca

Abstract. In this paper, we introduce a common semantic framework for developing and formally modeling use cases and task models. Use cases are the notation of choice for functional requirements specification and documentation, whereas task models are used as a starting point for user interface design. Based on their intrinsic characteristics we devise an intermediate semantic domain for use cases and for task models, respectively. We describe how the intermediate semantic domain for each model is formally mapped into a common semantic domain which is based on sets of partial order sets. We argue that a two-step mapping results in a semantic framework that can be more easily validated, reused and extended. As a partial validation of our framework we provide a semantics for ConcurTaskTrees (CTT) one of the most popular task model notations as well as our own DSRG use case formalism. Furthermore we use the common semantic model to formally define a satisfiability relation between task model and use case specifications.

Keywords: Use cases, task models, requirements, formal semantics, partial order sets, labeled transition systems.

1 Introduction

User Interface (UI) design and the engineering of functional requirements are generally carried out by different teams using different methodologies, processes and lifecycles [1]. Since both disciplines have their own models and theories, often the respective artifacts are created independently of each other; as a result there arises:

- Duplication in effort during development and maintenance due to redundancies / overlaps in the (independently) developed UI and software engineering models.
- Possible conflicts during implementation as both processes do not have the same reference specification and thus may result in inconsistent designs.

A process allowing for UI design to follow as a logical progression from functional requirements specification does not exist.

Use cases are the artifacts of choice for functional requirements specification and documentation [2] while UI design typically starts with the identification of user tasks, and context requirements [3]. Our primary research goal is to define an integrated

J. Davies and J. Gibbons (Eds.): IFM 2007, LNCS 4591, pp. 579–598, 2007.

methodology for the development of use cases and task models within an overall software process. A prerequisite of this initiative is the definition of a formal framework for handling use case models and task models. The cornerstone for such a formal framework is a common semantic domain for both notations.

Figure 1 illustrates how our framework promotes a two-step mapping from a particular use case or task model notation to the common semantic domain which is based on *sets of partial order sets*. The common semantic model will serve as a reference for tool support and will be the basis for the definition of a satisfiability relation between a use case specification and a task model specification. A definition of the latter is given in this paper.

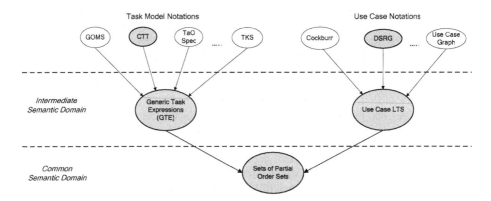

Fig. 1. Two-Step Semantic Mapping

The main reason behind a two-step mapping, rather than a direct mapping, is to provide a semantic framework that can be more easily validated, reused and extended. The intermediate semantic domains have been carefully chosen by taking into consideration the intrinsic characteristics of task models and use cases, respectively, so that the mappings to the intermediate semantic domains are straightforward and intuitive: task models are mapped into what we call Generic Task Expressions (GTE); use cases are mapped to Use Case Labeled Transition Systems (UC-LTS). Since the second level mappings to sets of posets are more involved, the intermediate semantic domains have been chosen so as to be as simple as possible, containing only the necessary core constructs. As a consequence of this two-step semantic definition, we believe that our framework can be easily extended to incorporate new task model or use case notations by simply defining a new mapping to the intermediate semantic domain.

In this paper, we focus on providing concise definitions of both the intermediate semantic domains for use cases and task models and the common semantic model. As concrete examples of mappings, we illustrate how ConcurTaskTree (CTT) [4] specifications and DSRG-style use cases (defined in the next section) are mapped to the intermediate semantic domains. This is followed by a formalization of the second level mappings of GTEs and UC-LTSs into the sets of posets.

The remainder of this paper is organized as follows. In Section 2 we provide necessary background information by reviewing and contrasting use cases and task models. Section 3 discusses related work with respect to the definition of semantics of scenario-based notations. Section 4, formally defines our semantic framework. Finally, in Section 5 we conclude and provide an outlook of future work.

2 Background

In this section we remind the reader of the key characteristics of use cases and task models. For each model we present a particular notation, and an illustrative example. Finally, both models are compared and main commonalities and differences are contrasted.

2.1 Use Case Models

A use case captures the interaction between actors and the system under development. It is organized as a collection of related success and failure scenarios that are all bound to the same goal of the primary actor [5]. Use cases are typically employed as a specification technique for capturing functional requirements. They document the majority of software and system requirements and as such, serve as a contract (of the envisioned system behavior) between stakeholders [2].

Every use case starts with a header section containing various properties of the use case. The core part of a use case is its main success scenario, which follows immediately after the header. It indicates the most common ways in which the primary actor can reach his/her goal by using the system. A use case is completed by specifying the use case extensions. These extensions constitute alternative scenarios which may or may not lead to the fulfillment of the use case goal. They represent exceptional and alternative behavior (relative to the main success scenario) and are indispensable to capturing full system behavior. Each extension starts with a condition (relative to one or more steps of the main success scenario), which makes the extension relevant and causes the main scenario to "branch" to the alternative scenario. The condition is followed by a sequence of action steps, which may lead to the fulfillment or the abandonment of the use case goal and/or further extensions. From a requirements point of view, exhaustive modeling of use case extensions is an effective requirements elicitation device.

Different notations at different degrees of formality have been suggested as a medium to capture use cases. The extremes range from purely textual constructs written in prose language [2] to entirely formal specification written in Z [6], or as Abstract State Machines (ASM) [7, 8]. While the use of narrative languages makes use case modeling an attractive tool to facilitate communication among stakeholders, prose language is well known to be prone to ambiguities and leaves little room for advanced tool support.

Therefore, in this paper we take up a compromise solution, which enforces a formal structure (needed for the definition of formal semantics) but preserves the intuitive nature of use case. In particular, we have developed an XML Schema

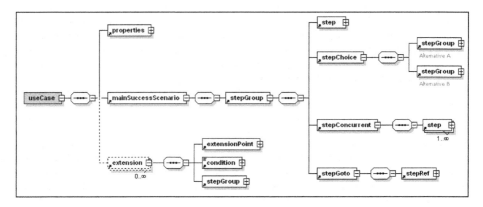

Fig. 2. DSRG Use Case Meta Model

(depicted in Figure 2), which acts as a meta model for use cases. As such, it identifies the most important use case elements, defines associated mark-up and specifies existing containment relationships among elements. We refer to use cases that correspond to the schema presented in Figure 2 as "DSRG-style use cases".

Most relevant for this paper is the definition of the *stepGroup* element as it captures the behavioral information of the use case. As depicted, the *stepGroup* element consists of a sequence of one of the following sub elements:

- The *step* element denotes an atomic use case step capturing the primary actor's interactions or system activities.
- The *stepChoice* element denotes the alternative composition of two *stepGroup* elements.
- The *stepConcurrent* element entails a set of (atomic) *step* elements, whose execution order is not defined.
- The *stepGoto* element denotes an arbitrary branching to another *step*.

We note that the *stepGroup* element is part of the *mainSuccessScenario* as well as the *extension* element. The latter additionally contains a condition and a reference to one or many steps stating *why* and *when* the extension may occur.

In order to generate a readable representation of the use case XML document we use XSLT style sheets [9]. Figure 3 depicts the generated HTML presentation of a sub-function level use case for a "Login" function. Note that we will be using the same "Login" example throughout this paper, and for the sake of simplicity, have kept the complexity of the use case to a minimum.

2.2 Task Models

User task modeling is by now a well understood technique supporting user-centered UI design [4]. In most UI development approaches, the task set is the primary input to the UI design stage. Task models describe the tasks that users perform using the application, as well as how the tasks are related to each other. The origin of most task modeling approaches can be traced back to activity theory [10], where a human

Use Case: Login

Properties

- **Primary Actor**: <u>Customer</u>
- **Goal**: <u>Customer</u> logs into the program.
- **Level**: Sub-function

Main Success Scenario

1. Primary Actor indicates that he/she wishes to log-in to the system.
2. Primary Actor *performs the following in abritrary order.*
   - 2.1 The Primary Actor provides the user name.
   - 2.2 The Primary Actor provides the password.
3. Primary Actor confirms the provided data.
4. System authenticates the Primary Actor.
5. System informs the Primary Actor that the Login was successful.
6. System grants access to the Primary Actor based on his/her access levels.

Extensions

4a. The provided username or/and password is/are invalid:
   - 4a1. System informs the Primary Actor that the provided username or/and password is/are invalid
   - 4a2. System denies access to the Primary Actor.

Fig. 3. Generated HTML Presentation of the "Login" Use Case

operator carries out activities to change part of the environment (artifacts) in order to achieve a certain goal [11]. Like use cases, task models describe the user's interaction with the system. The primary purpose of task models is to systematically capture the way users achieve a goal when interacting with the system [12]. More precisely, the task model specifies how the user makes use of the system to achieve his/her goal but also indicates how the system supports the user tasks.

Various notations for task models exits. Among the most popular ones are ConcurTaskTrees (CTT) [4], GOMS [13], TaO Spec [14], and TKS [15]. Even though all notations differ in terms of presentation, level of formality, and expressiveness they share the following common tenet: Tasks are hierarchically decomposed into sub-tasks until an atomic level has been reached. Atomic tasks are also called actions, since they are the tasks that are actually carried out by the user or the system. The execution order of tasks is determined by operators that are defined between peer tasks.

Figure 4 shows a CTT visualization of the "Login" task model. The figure illustrates the hierarchical break down and the temporal relationships between tasks involved in the "Login" functionality (depicted in the use case of Section 2.1). An indication of task types is given by the symbol used to represent tasks. In CTT the execution order between tasks is defined by temporal operators. Various temporal operators exist; examples include: enabling (>>), choice ([]), iteration (*), and disabling ([>].A complete list of the CTT operators together with an informal definition of their interpretation can be found in [4]. In Section 4.2 we will assign

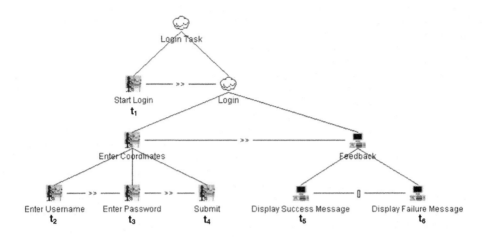

Fig. 4. "Login" Task Model

formal semantics to CTT task models by defining a mapping to the intermediate semantic domain of generic task expressions.

2.3 Use Cases vs. Task Models: A Comparison

In the previous two sections, the main characteristics of use cases and task models were discussed. In this section, we compare both models and outline noteworthy differences and commonalities.

Both, use cases and task models, belong to the family of scenario-based notations and as such capture sets of usage scenarios of the system. On the one hand, a use case specifies system behavior by means of a main success scenario and any corresponding extensions. On the other hand, a task model specifies system interaction within a single "monolithic" task tree. In theory, both notations can be used to describe the same information. In practice however, use cases are mainly employed to document functional requirements whereas task models are used to describe UI requirements/design details. Based on this assumption we identify three main differences which are pertinent to their purpose of application:

1. Use cases capture requirements at a higher level of abstraction whereas task models are more detailed. Hence, the atomic actions of the task model are often lower level UI details that are irrelevant (actually contraindicated [2]) in the context of a use case. We note that due to its simplicity, within our example, this difference in the level of abstraction is not explicitly visible.
2. Task models concentrate on aspects that are relevant for UI design and as such, their usage scenarios are strictly depicted as input-output relations between the user and the system. Internal system interactions (i.e. involvement of secondary actors or internal computations) as specified in use cases are not captured.
3. If given the choice, a task model may only implement a subset of the scenarios specified in the use case. Task models are geared to a particular user interface and

as such must obey its limitations. E.g. a voice user interface will most likely support less functionality than a fully-fledged graphical user interface.

3 Related Work

For scenario-based notations, the behavioral aspects of a system (capturing the ordering and relations between the events) represent the important features to describe. While several different formalisms have been proposed for scenario-based notations, in what follows we briefly discuss three prominent approaches, namely: process algebras, partial orders and graph structures.

Process Algebra has been widely used to define *interleaving* semantics of scenario-based notations [17-19]. The International Telecommunication Union (ITU) has published a recommendation for the formal semantics of basic Message Sequence Charts (MSCs) based on the Algebra of Communicating Processes (ACP) [20, 18]. This work is a continuation of preliminary research work by Mauw and Reniers [17]. In more recent work, Xu et. al. also suggest a process algebraic semantics for use case models, with the overall goal of formalizing use case refactoring [19]. In their approach, scenarios are represented as basic MSCs. The authors assign meaning to a particular use case scenario (episode) by partially adapting the ITU MSC semantics.

Formalisms suitable for the definition of *non-interleaving* semantics are based on partial orders. For example, Zheng et. al. propose a non-interleaving semantics for timed MSC 2000 [21, 22] based on timed labeled partial order sets (lposets). Partial order semantics for (regular, un-timed) MSCs has been proposed by Alur [23], and Katoen and Lambert [24]. Alur et. al. propose a semantics for a subset of MSCs that restricts MSC event types to message events only.

Mizouni et. al. propose use case graphs as an intermediate notation for use cases [25]. Use case graphs are directed, potentially cyclic graphs whose edges represent use case steps and nodes represent system states. This allows for a natural representation of the order in which actions are to be performed. Structural operational semantics for CTT task models are defined in [26]. In particular Paternò defines a set of inference rules to map CTT terms into labeled transition systems.

The semantic framework proposed in this paper is inspired by the lposet approach proposed in [22]. Similar to the approach in [22], our semantic framework is based on sets of partial order sets. The main motivation for this choice was the quest for a true, non-interleaving, model of concurrency. System behavior is represented as causally inter-related events based on a partial order relation. Events, that are not causally related, are seen as concurrent. In addition, similar to the work in [25], we employ labeled graph structures (Use Case LTS) as an intermediate notation for use cases. Preliminary results towards the definition of a common semantic model for use cases and task models were reported in [27]. In this paper we complete and define our framework as a two-step mapping process, provide a formal semantics for all CTT expressions, and formalize the mapping from DSRG-style use cases to partial order sets using the intermediary notation of Use Case LTS.

4   Semantics for Use Cases and Task Models

In the previous section we have studied key characteristic of use cases and task models and reviewed relevant related work. In this section we re-employ this information to define a common formal semantics for use cases and task models. We start with the definition of the intermediate semantic domains. Then we define the common semantic model based on sets of partial order sets and specify the corresponding mappings from the intermediate domains. We conclude the section by providing a formal definition of a *satisfiability* relation based on the common semantic model.

4.1   Intermediate Semantic Domain for Use Cases

In this section we define an intermediate semantic domain, UC-LTS, for use cases and specify how DSRG-style use cases are transformed into UC-LTS.

Definition 1: (UC-LTS). *A use case labeled transition system* (UC-LTS) is defined by the tuple (S, Q, q_0, F, T), where:

S is the set of labels of atomic use case steps.

Q is a set of states.

$q_0 \in Q$ is the initial state.

$F \subseteq S$ is the set of final states.

$T = Q \times 2^S \times Q$ is the set of transitions.

We have defined UC-LTS in order to capture easily and intuitively the nature of use cases. A use case primarily describes the execution order of user and system actions in the form of use case steps. From a given state, the execution of a step leads into another state. Sometimes, the execution order of two or more steps is not important or just abstracted away for the purpose of the description. In UC-LTS the execution of a step is denoted by a labeled transition, from a source state to a target state. The transition labels serve as references to the corresponding steps in the original use case. The execution order of use case steps is modeled using transition sequences, where the target state of a transition serves as a source state of the following transition.

Contrary to LTSs, the labels in the UC-LTS are sets. For a given transition, if this set contains more than one label, then no specific execution order exists between the corresponding use case steps. This partial order semantics reflects better the nature of use cases.

In what follows we illustrate how use cases in DSRG style are transformed to the intermediate UC-LTS form. As the mapping turns out to be quite straightforward we will only sketch out the main translation principles. Given a UC-LTS consisting of a single state q_0 and a DSRG-style use case specification, iterate through the steps of *stepGroup* of the Main Success Scenario. For each found element, perform the following (depending on the type), using q_0 as a starting state:

- *Step:* Create a new state q_{new} and define the following transition: $(q_{last}, \{label\}, q_{new})$ where q_{last} is the last state that has been created and 'label' is a (unique) identifier of the currently visited use case step. If there exists an extension for the currently visited step then, using q_{new} as a starting state, recursively repeat the same procedure for each step defined in the *stepGroup* of the extension.

*   ***stepChoice***: For each of the two entailed *stepGroup* elements recursively re-perform this procedure with q_{last} as a starting state.

*   ***stepConcurrent***: Create a new state q_{new} and define the following transition: (q_{last}, L, q_{new}) where q_{last} is the last state that has been created and L is the set of labels of all the step elements entailed in the *stepConcurrent* element. If there exist an extension for the *stepConcurrent* element then, using q_{new} as a starting state, recursively repeat the same procedure for each step defined in the *stepGroup* of the extension.

*   ***stepGoto:*** Continue with the target step referenced in *stepGoto* element. If the target step has been already visited then replace q_{last} with the target step and update all transition definitions that included q_{last}, accordingly.

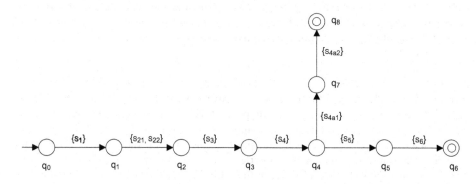

Fig. 5. Intermediate UC-LTS corresponding to the "Login" Use Case

Figure 5 illustrates the UC-LTS generated from the use case of Figure 3. Note that the transition between state q_1 and state q_2 has been annotated with labels of two use case steps, denoting the concurrent execution of use case step 2.1 and step 2.2. It is also to be noted that starting from state q_4 two transitions are defined, denoting the execution of step 5 in the main success scenario and alternatively the execution of step 4a1 defined in extension 4.

4.2   Intermediate Semantic Domain for Task Models

In this section we define an intermediate semantic domain for task models called Generic Task Expressions (GTE) and specify how a CTT specification (possibly including "Disabling" and "Suspend / Resume") is mapped into a corresponding GTE specification. In Section 2.2 we noted that tasks are commonly decomposed into subtasks and sub-subtasks until an atomic level is reached. For the definition of GTE we adopted the same paradigm and define a task expression as either an atomic action or a composition of (sub) task expression.

Definition 2: (Generic Task Expression). A generic task expression T is recursively defined as follows:

(1) An atomic action α is a generic task expression ($\alpha \in$ T)
(2) If ψ and ρ are generic task expressions ($\psi, \rho \in$ T) then

$$\psi^{Opt},$$
$$\psi^{Rep},$$
$$\psi\ \_\|\ \rho,$$
$$\psi\ \_[]\ \rho,$$
$$\psi\ \_>>\ \rho,$$

are also generic task expressions.

Please note that the operator precedence is reflected by the order of their enumeration in Definition 2. Operators listed at a higher position have a higher precedence than operators listed at a lower position. Intuitively the meaning of the operators is as follows: The binary operators _>>, _||, and _[] denote the sequential, concurrent or alternative composition of two generic task expressions. The unary operators 'Opt' and 'Rep' denote the optional or the iterative (zero to infinitely many times) execution of a generic task expression.

In what follows we demonstrate how CTT task models are mapped to GTE. More precisely, we assign for each CTT task expression a corresponding denotation expressed in GTE. At the atomic level, we define that *CTT leaf tasks* correspond to *atomic GTE expressions (α).* At the composite level, CTT expressions entailing basic operators are mapped in a one-to-one manner to the corresponding GTE expressions. As depicted in Table 1, the only exception is the "Order_Independency" operator which is translated into the shallow interleaving of its operands. In order to illustrate the basic mapping, let us use again the "Login" task model from Section 2.2. According to the definitions of Table 1 the CTT specification is mapped into the following GTE specification: t_1 _>> t_2 _>> t_3 _>> t_4 _>> (t_5 _[] t_6).

Unfortunately, the mappings of the complex binary operators *disabling* and *suspend/resume* are not straightforward and require a pre-processing of their operands.

Table 1. Mappings of Basic CTT Operators into GTE

CTT Expression			GTE Expression
$t_1 >> t_r$	(Enabling)	=	t_1 _>> t_r
$t_1 \mathrel{|||} t_r$	(Concurrency)	=	t_1 _|| t_r
$t_1 [] t_r$	(Choice)	=	t_1 _[] t_r
$t*$	(Iteration)	=	t^{Rep}
(t)	(Optional)	=	t^{Opt}
$t_1 \mathrel{|+|} t_r$	(Order Indepen.)	=	$(t_1$ _>> $t_r)$ _[] $(t_r$ _>> $t_1)$

Intuitively the meaning of the *disabling* operator is defined as follows: Both tasks specified by its operands are enabled concurrently. As soon as the first (sub) task specified by the second operand is executed, the task specified by the first operand becomes disabled. If the execution of the task(s) specified by the first operand is completed (without interruption) the task(s) specified by the second operand are subsequently executed. In other words, none of the (sub) tasks of the first operand must necessarily be executed, whereas the execution of the tasks of the second operand is mandatory. Hence, a term including the *disabling* operator can be rewritten as the "optionalization" of all tasks involved in the first operand, followed by the execution of the second operand.

For the purpose of "optionalizing" the first operand we have defined the unary auxiliary operator *Deep Optionalization* ({ }). As inductively defined in Table 2, the application of the operator defines every subtask of its target task expression as optional. However if the subtasks are executed, they have to be executed in their pre-defined order. The final mapping of the disabling operator to an AGT expression, using the Deep Optionalization operator can be found in Table 3. We note that the definition of the CTT *disabling* operator has been inspired by the disabling operator of the LOTOS process algebra [28]. Yet, the interpretation of both operators is *not* identical. In particular, in LOTOS the subsequent execution of the second operand, after completion of the first one is not allowed.

Table 2. Inductive Definitions of "Deep Optionalization" and "Interleaved Insertion"

(Unary) Deep Optionalization { }		(Binary) Interleaved Insertion $\oplus$	
$\{\alpha\}$	$= \alpha^1$	$\alpha \oplus t_i$	$= t_i \_{>>} \alpha$
$\{t_l \_{>>} t_r\}$	$= (\{t_l\} \_{>>} (\{t_r\})^{Opt})^{Opt}$	$(t_l \_{>>} t_r) \oplus t_i$	$= (t_l \oplus t_i) \_{>>} (t_r \oplus t_i)$
$\{t_l \| t_r\}$	$= (\{t_l\})^{Opt} \| (\{t_r\})^{Opt}$	$(t_l \| t_r) \oplus t_i$	$= (t_l \oplus t_i) \| (t_r \oplus t_i)$
$\{t_l \_{[]} t_r\}$	$= (\{t_l\} + \{t_r\})^{Opt}$	$(t_l \_{[]} t_r) \oplus t_i$	$= (t_l \oplus t_i) \_{[]} (t_r \oplus t_i)$
$\{t^{Opt}\}$	$= (\{t\})^{Opt}$	$(t^{Opt} \oplus t_i)$	$= (t \oplus t_i)^{Opt}$
$\{t^{Rep}\}$	$= t^{Rep} \_{>>} (\{t\})^{Opt}$	$(t^{Rep} \oplus t_i)$	$= (t \oplus t_i)^{Rep}$

The interpretation of the *suspend/resume* operator is similar to the one of the *disabling* operator. Both tasks specified by its operands are enabled concurrently. At any time the execution of the first operand can be interrupted by the execution of the first (sub) task of the second operand. In contrast to *disabling*, however, the execution of the task specified by the first operand is only suspended and will (once the execution of the second operand is complete) be reactivated from the state reached before the interruption [4]. At this point, the task specified by the first operand may continue its execution or may be interrupted again by the execution of the second operand.

Table 3. Mappings of Disabling and Suspend/Resume into GTE

CTT Expression			GTE Expression
$t_l [> t_r$	(Disabling)	$=$	$(\{t_l\})^{Opt} \_{>>} t_r$
$t_l \|> t_r$	(Suspend/Resume)	$=$	$t_l \oplus (t_r^{Rep})$

---

[1] α denotes an atomic action.

In order to model this behavior, we have defined the auxiliary binary operator *Interleaved Insertion* (⊕). As defined in Table 2 it "injects" the task specified by its second operand at any possible position in between the (sub) tasks of the first operand. Using the auxiliary operator it is now possible to define a mapping from a *suspend/resume* CTT expression to a corresponding GTE expression (Table 3).

4.3   Common Semantic Domain Based on Sets of Posets

This section defines the second-level mapping of our semantic framework. We start by providing necessary definitions. Next we present a semantic function that maps GTE specifications into the common semantic domain. Finally we specify an algorithm that generates a set of posets from a UC-LTS.

4.3.1   Notations and Definitions

The common semantic domain of our framework is based on sets of partial order sets (posets). In what follows we provide definitions of the involved formalisms and specify a set of operations needed for the semantic mapping. It is also in this section, where we propose a notion of refinement between two sets of posets specifications.

Definition 3: (Poset). A partially ordered set (poset) is a tuple $(E, \leq)$, where

E is a set of events, and

$\leq \subseteq E \times E$ is a partial order relation (reflexive, anti-symmetric, transitive) defined on E. This relation specifies the causal order of events. We will use the symbol $\varnothing_{poset}$ to denote the empty poset with $\varnothing_{poset} = (\varnothing, \varnothing)$. Further we will use the symbol e_{poset} to denote a poset containing a single event e $(e_{poset} = (\{e\}, \{(e,e)\}))$.

In order to be able to compose posets we define the following operations:

Definition 4: (Binary Operations on Posets). The binary operations: *sequential composition* (.) and *parallel composition* (∥) of two posets p and q are defined as[2]:

Let $p = (E_p, \leq_p)$ and $q = (E_q, \leq_q)$ with $E_p \cap E_q = \varnothing$ then:

$p.q = (E_p \cup E_q, (\leq_p \cup \leq_q \cup \{(e_p, e_q) \mid e_p \in E_p \text{ and } e_q \in E_q\})^*)$

$p \| q = (E_p \cup E_q, \leq_p \cup \leq_q)$

We define semantics for GTE and UC-LTS using the following operations over sets of posets.

Definition 5.1: (Binary Operators on Sets of Posets). For two sets of posets P and Q, *sequential composition* (.), *parallel composition* (∥), and *alternative composition* (#) are defined as follows:

$P . Q = \{ p_i . q_j \mid p_i \in P \text{ and } q_j \in Q \}$

$P \| Q = \{ p_i \| q_j \mid p_i \in P \text{ and } q_j \in Q \}$

$P \# Q = P \cup Q$

---

[2] Note that R* denotes the reflexive, transitive closure of R.

Definition 5.2: (Repeated Sequential Composition). The *repeated sequential composition* of a set of posets P is defined as:

$$P^0 = \{\emptyset_{poset}\}$$
$$P^n = P^{n-1}.\, P \ \text{ for } n > 0$$
$$P^* = P.\, P.\, \cdots$$

Definition 5.3: (Iterated Alternative Sequential Composition). The *iterated alternative sequential composition* of a set of posets P is defined as:

$$P_\#^0 = \{\emptyset_{poset}\}$$
$$P_\#^n = P^0 \# P^1 \# \ldots \# P^n$$
$$P_\#^* = P^0 \# P^1 \# \ldots$$

Also fundamental to our model is the notion of a *trace*. A trace corresponds to one particular scenario defined in the original use case or task model specification. In the following we define the set of traces for a given poset, and for a given set of posets.

Definition 6: (Trace). A *trace* t of a poset $p = (E, \leq)$ is defined as a (possibly infinite) sequence of events from E such that

$$\forall \ (i, j \text{ in the index set of } t) \bullet i < j \Rightarrow \neg(\, t(j) \leq t(i) \,) \text{ and}$$
$$\bigcup t(i) = E$$

where $t(i)$ denotes the ith event of the trace.

Definition 7: (Set of All Traces of a Poset). The set of all traces of a poset p is defined as:
$$tr(p) = \{\, t \mid t \text{ is a trace of } p \,\}.$$

Definition 8: (Set of All Traces of a Set of Posets). The set of all traces of a set of posets P is defined as:

$$Tr(P) = \bigcup_{p_i \in P} tr(p_i)$$

Using the set of all traces as a basis, we can define refinement among two sets of posets through trace inclusion.

Definition 9: (Refinement). A set of posets Q is a refinement of a set of posets P if, and only if

$$Tr\,(Q) \subseteq Tr\,(P)$$

The refining specification is more restricted (in terms of possible orderings of events) than the refined specification. Or, in other words, the refining specification has less partial orders than the refined specification. In Section 4.4 we will re-use the definition of refinement to specify a satisfiability relation between two task model or use case specifications.

4.3.2 Mapping GTE Specifications to Sets of Posets

This section specifies how a generic task expression is mapped into a corresponding set of posets. For this purpose we define a (compositional) semantic function in the common denotational style. As given in Definition 10, an atomic generic task expression (denoted by α) is mapped into a set containing a single poset, which in turn consists of a single element only. Composite task expressions are represented by sets of posets, which are composed using the composition operators, defined in the previous section.

Definition 10: Let t, t_1, t_2 be abstract task expressions, then the mapping to sets of partial order sets is defined as follows:

$$\mathcal{M} \llbracket \alpha \rrbracket = \{\alpha_{poset}\}$$
$$\mathcal{M} \llbracket t_1 \_{>>} t_2 \rrbracket = \mathcal{M} \llbracket t_1 \rrbracket \, . \, \mathcal{M} \llbracket t_2 \rrbracket$$
$$\mathcal{M} \llbracket t_1 \_\| t_2 \rrbracket = \mathcal{M} \llbracket t_1 \rrbracket \, \| \, \mathcal{M} \llbracket t_2 \rrbracket$$
$$\mathcal{M} \llbracket t_1 \_[] t_2 \rrbracket = \mathcal{M} \llbracket t_1 \rrbracket \, \# \, \mathcal{M} \llbracket t_2 \rrbracket$$
$$\mathcal{M} \llbracket t^{Opt} \rrbracket = \mathcal{M} \llbracket t \rrbracket \, \# \, \{\varnothing_{poset}\}$$
$$\mathcal{M} \llbracket t^{Rep} \rrbracket = \mathcal{M} \llbracket t \rrbracket_\#^*$$

In what follows we illustrate the application of the semantic function by applying it to the "Login" generic task expression of the previous section. The overall application of

$$\mathcal{M} (t_1 \_{>>} t_2 \_{>>} t_3 \_{>>} t_4 \_{>>} (t_5 \_[] t_6)$$

can be further decomposed, by successively applying the definition of $\_{>>}$ and $\_[]$. As a result, we obtain the following expression:

$$\mathcal{M} (t_1). \, \mathcal{M} (t_2). \, \mathcal{M} (t_3). \, \mathcal{M} (t_4).(\mathcal{M} (t_5) \, \# \, \mathcal{M} (t_6)).$$

By mapping the atomic tasks into the corresponding sets of posets and by performing the required set compositions we obtain the following:

$$\{(\{t_1, t_2, t_3, t_4, t_5\}, \{(t_1, t_2), (t_2, t_3), (t_3, t_4), (t_4, t_5)\}^*),$$
$$(\{t_1, t_2, t_3, t_4, t_6\}, \{(t_1, t_2), (t_2, t_3), (t_3, t_4), (t_4, t_6)\}^*)\}$$

The first poset denotes the scenario of a successful login and the second poset represents a scenario of login failure.

4.3.3 Transforming UC-LTS to Sets of Posets

In this section we demonstrate how UC-LTS specifications (as defined in Section 4.1) are mapped into the common semantic model. For this purpose we have devised an algorithm that generates a set of posets from a given UC-LTS specification. Table 4 gives the corresponding pseudo code. We note that the main idea for the algorithm stems from the well-known algorithm that transforms a deterministic finite automaton into an equivalent regular expression [29]. However, as described in the following, instead of step-wise composition of regular expressions, we compose sets of posets.

Table 4. Algorithm Transforming a UC-LTS to a Set of Posets

(1)	var tt:SPOSET[][] with all array elements initialized to $\{\emptyset_{sposet}\}$ **for each** transition (q_s, X, q_e) in T **do** $tt[q_s, q_e] := \{(X, id\ X)\}$ where $id\ X = \{(l, l) \mid l \in X\}$ **od**
(2)	**for** each state q_i in $Q - (F \cup \{q_0\})$ **do**
(3)	**for each** pair of states q_n and q_k with $n \neq i$ & $k \neq i$ and $X, Y \in 2^S$ such that $(q_n, X, q_i) \in T$ and $(q_i, Y, q_k) \in T$ **do**
(4)	var tmp:SPOSET $tmp := tt[q_n, q_i] . tt[q_i, q_i]^*_{\#} . tt[q_i, q_k]$

(5)	**if** $\exists V \in 2^S$ such that $(q_n, V, q_k) \in T$ **then**
	        $tmp := tmp \# tt[q_n, q_k]$
	      endif

(6)	$T := T \cup \{ (q_n, \emptyset, q_k) \}$
(7)	$tt[q_n, q_k] := tmp$ **od**
(8)	$Q = Q - \{q_i\}$ **od**

(9)	var result:SPOSET $:= \emptyset$
	 for each q_f in F **do**
	    if result $= \emptyset$ **then**
	      result $:= tt[q_0, q_f]$
	    else
	      result $:=$ result $\# tt[q_0, q_f]$
	    endif
	 od

(10)	**if** $\exists W \in 2^S$ such that $(q_0, W, q_0) \in T$ **then**
	    result $:=$ result $\# tt[q_0, q_0]$
	 endif
	 return result

The procedure starts (1) with the creation of the transition table (a two-dimensional array ('tt')) populated with all transitions of the given UC-LTS specification. Indexed by a source and a target state a table cell contains a set of posets constructed from the label(s) associated to the representative transition. In most cases the set of posets will contain a single poset, which in turn consists of a single element representing *one* use case step. Only, if multiple labels were associated with the transition, indicating the concurrent or unordered execution of use case steps, the set of posets will contain a poset which consists of several elements. Those elements, however, are not causally related.

The core part of the algorithm consists of two nested loops. The outer loop (2) iterates through all states of the UC-LTS (except for the initial and the final states) whereas the inner loop (3) iterates through all pairs of incoming and outgoing transitions for a given state.

For each found pair, we perform the following: Compute (and temporarily store) the sequential composition of the following three sets of posets (4):

1. Set of posets associated to the incoming transition
2. Result of the *iterated alternative sequential composition* (Definition 5.2) of the poset associated to a possible self-transition defined over the currently visited state. If such a self transition does not exist then the iterative alternative composition yields $\emptyset_{sposet}$.
3. Set of posets associated to the outgoing transition.

Next we examine whether there exists a transition from the source state of the incoming transition to the target state of the outgoing transition. If yes (5), the temporary stored set of posets is overwritten by the choice composition of the set of posets denoted by the found existing transition and the former "value" of the temporary store. Then (6) we add a new transition from the source state of the incoming transition to the target state of the outgoing transition. In addition (7) we populate the corresponding cell in the transition table with the temporary stored set of posets.

Back in the outer loop, we eliminate (8) the currently visited state from the UC-LTS and proceed with the next state. Once the UC-LTS consists of only the initial state and the final states we exit the outer loop and perform the following two computations, in order to obtain the final result. First (9) we perform a choice composition of the sets of posets indexed by all the transitions from the initial state to a final state. Second, if the initial state additionally contains a self loop (10) then we add the set of posets denoted by that self loop to the before-mentioned choice composition.

If we apply our algorithm to the example "Login" UC-LTS of section 4.1 we obtain the following set of posets:

{
$(\{s_1, s_{21}, s_{22}, s_3, s_4, s_5, s_6\}, \{(s_1, s_{21}), (s_1, s_{22}), (s_{21}, s_3), (s_{22}, s_3), (s_3, s_4), (s_4, s_5), (s_5, s_6)\}*)$,
$(\{s_1, s_{21}, s_{22}, s_3, s_4, s_{4a1}, s_{4a2}\}, \{(s_1, s_{21}), (s_1, s_{22}), (s_{21}, s_3), (s_{22}, s_3), (s_3, s_4), (s_4, s_{4a1}), (s_{4a1}, s_{4a2})\}*)$
}

The first poset represents the main success scenario in the original "Login" use case whereas the second poset represents the scenario where extension 4a ("The provided username or/and password is/are invalid") is taken. We note that the events e_{21} and e_{22} are not related by the partial order relation. Hence, a valid trace (see Definition 6) can contain e_{21} and e_{22} in any order. This correlates to the original use case specification where the primary actor may perform step 2.1 and step 2.2 in arbitrary order.

4.4 Satisfiability Between Use Cases and Task Models

The common semantic domain defined in the previous sections is the essential basis for the formal definition of a satisfiability relation between two specifications. Such a notion of satisfiability applies equally well between artifacts of a similar nature (e.g. two use cases) as it does between use cases and task models. Our definition of satisfiability is as follows: *A specification 'X' satisfies another specification 'Y' if every scenario of 'X' is also a valid scenario of 'Y'.*

Within our semantic framework, a scenario of a use case or task model corresponds to a trace (Definition 6) in the corresponding set of posets. Hence a task model or use case specification satisfies another specification if the set of all traces (Definition 8) of the former is a subset of the set of all traces of the latter. One precondition for the application of the definition is that both sets of posets are based on the same event 'alphabet'. This can be achieved by renaming the events of the refined specification to their corresponding counterparts in the refining specification. Moreover, if a task model specification is compared with a use case specification, all events representing internal use case steps need to be removed. As pointed out in Section 2.3 task models focus on aspects that are relevant for UI design and as such abstract from internal system interactions.

For illustration purposes, we will formally determine whether the specification of the "Login" task model satisfies the specification of the "Login" use case. As a first step we need to unify the event alphabets. In the case of the "Login" use case steps 4, 4a1 and 6 represent internal (UI irrelevant) system interactions and hence are to be deleted. Moreover, the events representing use case steps must be renamed after the events representing the corresponding tasks in the task model.

Table 5. Mappings of Disabling and Suspend/Resume into GTE

Set of Posets representing "Login" UC (after Event Mapping)
$\{(\{t_1, t_2, t_3, t_4, t_5\}, \{(t_1, t_2), (t_1, t_3), (t_2, t_4), (t_3, t_4), (t_4, t_5)\}*),$
$(\{t_1, t_2, t_3, t_4, t_6\}, \{(t_1, t_2), (t_1, t_3), (t_2, t_4), (t_3, t_4), (t_4, t_6)\}*)\}$
Set of Posets representing the "Login" Task Model
$\{(\{t_1, t_2, t_3, t_4, t_5\}, \{(t_1, t_2), (t_2, t_3), (t_3, t_4), (t_4, t_5)\}*),$
$(\{t_1, t_2, t_3, t_4, t_6\}, \{(t_1, t_2), (t_2, t_3), (t_3, t_4), (t_4, t_6)\}*)\}$

As depicted by Table 5, it can be easily seen that every trace of the set of posets representing the task model is also a trace of the set of posets (after the event mapping) of the use case. Hence, according to the definition above, we can conclude that the "Login" task model satisfies the "Login" use case.

5   Conclusion and Future Work

In this paper we have presented a common semantic framework for use cases and task models. The main motivation behind our research is the need for an integrated development methodology where task models are developed as logical progressions from use case specifications. Our semantic framework is based on a two-step mapping from a particular use case or task model notation to the common semantic domain of *sets of partial order sets*. We argue that a two-step mapping results in a semantic framework that can be more easily validated, reused and extended.

The intermediate semantic domains have been carefully chosen by taking into consideration the intrinsic characteristics of task models and use cases, respectively. In particular we defined a Use Case Labeled Transition System as an intermediate semantic domain for use cases. It was demonstrated that UC-LTS allow for a natural representation of the order in which actions are to be performed. In the case of task models we defined generic task expressions (GTE) as an intermediate semantic domain. Similar to tasks, a generic task expression is hierarchically composed of sub-task expressions using a set of standard operators. Hence the mapping from a concrete task model to GTE remains straightforward and intuitive. In order to (partially) validate our approach we used the framework to define a semantics for CTT task models, including complex operators such as "disabling" and "suspend/resume". We also demonstrated how DSRG-style use cases are mapped into a set of partially order sets. Finally we used our semantic framework to provide a formal definition of satisfiability between use case and task model specifications. According to the definition, a use case or task model specification satisfies another specification if every scenario of the former is also a valid scenario of the latter.

Thus far, we concentrated on capturing sets of usage scenarios. As future work, we are aiming at further extending our semantic framework. One such extension is the introduction of different event types. The main motivation for such an extension is that in task modeling (e.g. CTT), one often distinguishes between different task *types*. Examples are: "data input", "data output", "editing", "modification", or "submit". As a consequence, rules to further restrict the definition of a valid trace may need to be defined. An example of such a rule may be the condition that an event of type "data input" must always be followed by a corresponding event of type "submit". Another extension of the semantic model deals with the capturing of state information. State information is often employed in a use case to express and evaluate conditions. For example the pre-condition of a use case denotes the set of states in which the use case is to be executed. In addition, every use case extension is triggered by a condition that must hold before the steps defined in the extension are executed. In order to be able to evaluate conditions, the semantic model must provide means to capture the notion of the state and should be able to map state conditions to the appearance of events.

Further avenues deal with the extension of the proposed definition of a satisfiability relation for use case and task model specifications. Such an extended definition may take into account different event types and the refinement of state conditions. Moreover, we envision that refinements, and proofs of satisfiability, can ideally be aided by tools, supporting the verification. We are currently investigating how our approach can be translated into the specification languages of existing model checkers and theorem provers.

Acknowledgments. This work is partially supported by the Natural Sciences and Engineering Research Council of Canada (NSERC) in the form of a Postgraduate Scholarship for D. Sinnig and Discovery Grants for P. Chalin and F. Khendek.

References

1. Seffah, A., Desmarais, M.C., Metzger, M.: Software and Usability Engineering: Prevalent Myths, Obstacles and Integration Avenues. In: Human-Centered Software Engineering—Integrating Usability in the Software Development Lifecycle, Springer, Heidelberg
2. Cockburn, A.: Writing effective use cases. Addison-Wesley, Boston (2001)
3. Pressman, R.S.: Software engineering: a practitioner's approach. McGraw-Hill, Boston, MA (2005)

4. Paternò, F.: Model-Based Design and Evaluation of Interactive Applications. Springer, Heidelberg (2000)
5. Larman, C.: Applying UML and patterns: an introduction to object-oriented analysis and design and the unified process. Prentice Hall PTR, Upper Saddle River, NJ (2002)
6. Butler, G., Grogono, P., Khendek, F.: A Z Specification of Use Cases. In: Proceedings of APSEC 1998, pp. 94–101 (1998)
7. Grieskamp, W., Lepper, M., Schulte, W., Tillman, N.: Testable use cases in the abstract state machine language. In: Proc. APAQS'01, Asia-Pacific Conference on Quality Software (2001)
8. Barnett, M., Grieskamp, W., Schulte, W., Tillmann, N., Veanes, M.: Validating Use Cases with the AsmL Test Tool in Proceedings of QSIC 2003 (Third International Conference on Quality Software) (November 2003)
9. XSLT, XSL Transformations Version 2.0 [Internet], Available from Accessed: December 2006. Last Update: November 2006 http://www.w3.org/TR/xslt20/
10. Kuutti, K.: Activity theory as a potential framework for human-computer interaction research (chapter) In: Context and consciousness: activity theory and human-computer interaction, Massachusetts Institute of Technology, pp. 17–44
11. Dittmar, A., Forbrig, P.: Higher-Order Task Models. In: Proceedings of Design, Specification and Verification of Interactive Systems 2003, Funchal, Madeira Island, Portugal, pp. 187–202 (2003)
12. Souchon, N., Limbourg, Q., Vanderdonckt, J.: Task Modelling in Multiple contexts of Use. In: Proceedings of Design, Specification and Verification of Interactive Systems, Rostock, Germany, pp. 59–73 (2002)
13. Card, S., Moran, T.P., Newell, A.: The Psychology of Human Computer Interaction (1983)
14. Dittmar, A., Forbrig, P., Stoiber, S., Stary, C.: Tool Support for Task Modelling - A Constructive Exploration. In: Proceedings of Design, Specification and Verification of Interactive Systems 2004 (July 2004)
15. Johnson, P., Johnson, H., Waddington, R., Shouls, A.: Task Related Knowledge Structures: Analysis, Modelling and Application. In: Jones, D.M., Winder, R. (eds.) People and Computers IV, Manchester, pp. 35–62. Cambridge University Press, Cambridge (1988)
16. Sinnig, D., Chalin, P., Khendek, F.: Consistency between Task Models and Use Cases. To Appear in Proceedings of Design, Specification and Verification of Interactive Systems, Salamanca, Spain (March 2007)
17. Mauw, S., Reniers, M.A.: An Algebraic Semantic of Basic Message Sequence Charts. In Computer Journal, 37 (1994)
18. ITU-T, Recommendation Z.120- Message Sequence Charts, Geneva (1996)
19. Xu, J., Yu, W., Rui, K., Butler, G.: Use Case Refactoring: A Tool and a Case Study. In: Proceedings of APSEC 2004, Busan, Korea, pp. 484–491 (2004)
20. Baeten, J.C.M., Weijland, W.P.: Process algebra. Cambridge University Press, Cambridge (1990)
21. ITU-T, Recommendation Z.120- Message Sequence Charts, Geneva (1999)
22. Zheng, T., Khendek, F.: Time consistency of MSC-2000 specifications, in Computer Networks, June 2003, vol. 42(3). Elsevier, Amsterdam (2003)
23. Alur, R., Holzmann, G.J., Peled, D.: An Analyzer for Message Sequence Charts. In: Software - Concepts and Tools, vol. 17, pp. 70–77 (1996)
24. Katoen, J.P., Lambert, L.: Pomsets for Message Sequence Charts, in Proceedings of FBT-VS 1998, Cottbus, Germany, Shaker Verlag, pp. 197–207 (1998)

25. Mizouni, R., Salah, A., Dssouli, R., Parreaux, B.: Integrating Scenarios with Explicit Loops. In: Proceedings of NOTERE, 2004, Essaidia Morocco (2004)
26. Paternò, F., Santoro, C.: The ConcurTaskTrees Notation for Task Modelling, Technical Report at CNUCE-C.N.R. (May 2001)
27. Sinnig, D., Chalin, P., Khendek, F.: Towards a Common Semantic Foundation for Use Cases and Task Models, to appear in Electronic Notes in Theoretical Computer Science (ENTCS) (2007)
28. Brinksma, E., Scollo, G., Steenbergen, C.: LOTOS specifications, their implementations, and their tests. In: Proceedings of IFIP Workshop Protocol Specification, Testing, and Verification VI, pp. 349–360 (1987)
29. Linz, P.: An introduction to formal languages and automata. Jones and Bartlett Publishers, Sudbury, MA (1997)

Unifying Theories of Objects

Michael Anthony Smith[1,2] and Jeremy Gibbons[1]

[1] Oxford University, UK
`Michael.Smith@kellogg.ox.ac.uk`
[2] Systems Assurance Group, QinetiQ, UK
`Jeremy.Gibbons@comlab.ox.ac.uk`

Abstract. We present an approach to modelling Abadi–Cardelli-style object calculi as Unifying Theories of Programming (UTP) *designs*. Here we provide a core object calculus with an operational *small-step evaluation rule* semantics, and a corresponding UTP model with a denotational *relational predicate* semantics. For clarity, the UTP model is defined in terms of an operand stack, which is used to store the results of subprograms. Models of a less operational nature are briefly discussed. The consistency of the UTP model is demonstrated by a structural induction proof over the operations of the core object calculus. Overall, our UTP model is intended to provide facilities for encoding both object-based and class-based languages.

1 Introduction

Hoare and He's Unifying Theories of Programming (UTP) [6] can be used to formally define how results produced in one formal model can be translated as assumptions to another formal model. Essentially, programs are considered to be predicates that relate the values of their observable input and output variables (their alphabet). For example, the increment program $x := x + 1$ is typically defined by the relational predicate $x' = x + 1$, where predicate variables x and x' denote the input and output values of the program variable x. In general, the alphabet of a program P is denoted by αP; it is the disjoint union of P's input and output sets ($in\alpha P$ and $out\alpha P$ respectively), which in the case of the example is the set $\{x, x'\}$.

This basic relational model has been specialised to reflect the semantics of various programming paradigms and languages, such as: imperative programs without subroutines; reactive systems for simple message-based concurrency; and class-based object orientation [4,2,11]. Here, we consider a variant of the Abadi–Cardelli-style untyped object calculus (ς-calculus) [1]. We hope that, by providing an encoding of the ς-calculus in the UTP, we can provide facilities for modelling and relating a wide range of object-oriented (OO) languages. In particular, we take an object-based rather than class-based approach, following Abadi and Cardelli, providing both object values and references through the use of a heap. We do not discuss delegation, inheritance, or other mechanisms for sharing methods, since these can be implemented in terms of our primitives; nor

J. Davies and J. Gibbons (Eds.): IFM 2007, LNCS 4591, pp. 599–618, 2007.

again, following Abadi and Cardelli, do we support evolution of object interfaces, although it would be trivial to remove this restriction.

In the remainder of this section we introduce the notion of a UTP design and some notation that is too cumbersome to introduce when it is required. The paper then presents our variant of the object calculus, its stack-based UTP model, the consistency of this model, and some concluding remarks.

1.1   Designs in Unifying Theories of Programming

A *UTP design* specialises the general model of programming within the UTP by adding the notion of program termination. It introduces two special model variables Π_{OK} and Π_{OK}' to denote when a program is ready to start and when a program has terminated, respectively.

Definition 1 (UTP design). *A design predicate $p \vdash P$ states that the program represented by the relational predicate P will successfully terminate whenever it has been started in an input state that satisfies input assumption (precondition) predicate p.*

$$p \vdash P \ \ \widehat{=} \ \ (\Pi_{OK} \wedge p) \Rightarrow (\Pi_{OK}' \wedge P)$$

$$\alpha(p \vdash P) \ \ \widehat{=} \ \ \alpha P \cup \{\Pi_{OK}, \Pi_{OK}'\}$$

where $\quad \alpha p \subseteq in\alpha P \quad$ *and* $\quad \Pi_{OK}, \Pi_{OK}' \notin \alpha P$.

This definition of a UTP design is taken from [4]. It updates the original definition in [6] by ensuring that "the assumption is a precondition, containing only undashed [input] variables [... which ...] corresponds exactly to the third healthiness condition" of [6, page 84]. The remainder of the UTP design language is now summarised as follows:

skip	to represent the program whose outputs are unchanged;
chaos	to represent the program whose outputs are arbitrary;
miracle	to represent the program whose outputs are always correct;
var x	to introduce variable x (i.e. add it to the alphabet);
end x	to complete variable x (i.e. remove it from the alphabet);
$x_{i=1}^k := e_{i=1}^k$	to assign the evaluation of each e_i to x_i simultaneously;
$P \,\fatsemi\, Q$	to compose subprograms P and Q sequentially;
$P \triangleleft b \triangleright Q$	to execute P when b is true, and Q otherwise;
$P \sqcap Q$	to choose non-deterministically between P and Q;
$b * P$	to iterate subprogram P whilst b is true;
$\mu z \bullet P[z]$	to establish the weakest fixed point of recursive program P.

where the meta variables

b, e	denote a boolean value and a general expression respectively;
P, Q	denote UTP relational predicates (e.g. designs);
x, y	denote variables (in this case program variables);
z	denotes the special fixed point variable;
$P[z]$	denotes a relational predicate P that may contain the variable z.

The miracle program is not implementable; it and chaos are useful for reasoning about program, as they are the bottom and top of the design refinement lattice respectively. For further information on UTP designs refer to [4,6,12].

1.2 Design Frame and Compilation Notation

We now introduce two utility notations. First, design frames are introduced to simplify the definitions of relational predicates that affect only some of the variables within an alphabet.

Definition 2 (Design Frame). *Let V be a set of program variables. A design with frame V has the form $V : (p \vdash P)$, denoting the predicate $p \vdash P \wedge w' = w$, where the vector w contains the logical and program variables within the input alphabet of $p \vdash P$ except those in the set V (i.e. $\{x \mid x \in w\} = in\alpha(p \vdash P) \setminus V$).*

Second, the compilation of a source language term t with subterms $t_1, \ldots, t_k$ is denoted by $\langle\!\langle t\{t_{i=1}^k\}\rangle\!\rangle^{\mathrm{M}}$, where M represents an optional compilation mode. We use this notation for compiling the heap extended core ς-calculus ($\mathcal{O}_{\mathrm{CH}}$-calculus) into the UTP operand stack model ($\mathcal{U}_{\mathrm{SH}}$) below.

1.3 Operational Reduction Rule Notation

The semantics of object calculus operations is defined in terms of a collection of small-step evaluation-rules. These rules are similar to those in [10] except that they include a notion of a general context (Γ), which is essentially used to denote those *specific* contexts that are irrelevant to a given rule. A specific context, such as the heap in the $\mathcal{O}_{\mathrm{CH}}$-calculus (Section 2.3), can be selected and set as follows:

$\{\mathrm{HEAP} \mapsto H\}$	Let H denote the HEAP context.
$\{\mathrm{HEAP} \leftarrowtail H\}$	Set the HEAP context to the value of H.

The objective of the evaluation rules is to provide the circumstances under which a term t in a context Γ can evaluate in one step to a term t' in context Γ'; such one-step evaluations are denoted by $\Gamma \bullet t \longrightarrow \Gamma' \bullet t'$, where $\_ \bullet \_$ denotes the context-term pair binder and $\_ \longrightarrow \_$ denotes an individual evaluation step. It is now possible to define the rule representation as follows:

$$\frac{\langle condition_1\rangle \quad \ldots \quad \langle condition_n\rangle}{\langle concluded\ term\ evaluation\ step\rangle} \text{RULENAME} \quad \boxed{\langle optional\ side\ condition\rangle}$$

where $condition_i$ may be either a logical constraint or an evaluation step.

2 The Object Calculi

The $\mathcal{O}_{\mathrm{CH}}$-calculus we consider in this paper is an extension of the ς-calculus presented in Chapter 6 of Abadi and Cardelli's book on objects [1]. We now provide a brief summary of the ς-calculus (Section 2.1), which is followed by our arithmetic and heap extensions (Sections 2.2 and 2.3 respectively).

2.1   Abadi–Cardelli Untyped Object Calculus

The Abadi–Cardelli ς-calculus introduces the notion of an object, as a collection of labelled methods that can be updated and selected as follows.

$[^{k}_{i=1}\, l_i = m_i]$	denotes an object value – a partial map from labels to methods, where method m_i is identified by label l_i.
$\varsigma(x)\, e$	denotes a method whose body is defined by the expression e, which may itself contain one or more instances of the self variable (identifier) x.
$o.l \Leftarrow m$	denotes a method update operation, which generates a new object by taking a copy of the object o and replacing the method identified by label l with the method m.
$o.l$	denotes a method selection operation, which evaluates the body of the method with label l in object o, after each instance of the method's *self* variable has been replaced by a copy of the invoking object o.

where the meta-variables

o, l denote an object and a label value respectively;

m denotes a method;

e, x denote an expression and the self identifier (variable/expression).

Note that a ς-calculus expression is either an object value, variable identifier, or an application of the method selection or update operators. In particular, neither a label nor a method is considered to be a value-expression.

Method Update. The base case for the method update operations can now be defined by the following small-step evaluation rule.

$$\frac{l \in o}{\Gamma \bullet o.l \Leftarrow m \longrightarrow \Gamma \bullet \ulcorner o \oplus \{l \mapsto m\} \urcorner}\ \text{UpdM}$$

where

$l \in o$	label l is in the domain of object o.
$o_1 \oplus o_2$	object map o_1 is overridden by object map o_2.
$\ulcorner e \urcorner$	the meta-expression e.

There is one other small-step evaluation rule, which ensures that the evaluable argument (i.e. expression argument) of the method update operation is evaluated prior to the operation being applied.

$$\frac{\Gamma \bullet e \longrightarrow \Gamma' \bullet e'}{\Gamma \bullet e.l \Leftarrow m \longrightarrow \Gamma' \bullet e'.l \Leftarrow m} \ \ \textsc{UpdM-1}$$

Method Invocation (or Selection). The base case for the method invocation operations of the ς-calculus can be defined by the following rule.

$$\frac{l \in o}{\Gamma \bullet o.l \longrightarrow \Gamma \bullet \ulcorner b \{x \leftarrowtail o\} \urcorner} \ \ \textsc{InvM} \quad \boxed{\begin{array}{l} m \mathrel{\hat{=}} o(l) \\ \varsigma(x)\, b \doteq m \end{array}}$$

where

$o(l)$	is the method of object o with label l.
$m \mathrel{\hat{=}} e$	defines variable m to be the evaluation of meta-expression e.
$\varsigma(x)\, b \doteq m$	binds x and b to the self-variable and body of method m.
$b \{x \leftarrowtail o\}$	the substitution of object o for free variable x in term b.

The rule for evaluating an evaluable argument before the base rule can be applied is defined in precisely the same manner as that of the method update operation.

2.2   Core Object Calculus ($\mathcal{O}_{\mathrm{c}}$-Calculus)

The core ς-calculus ($\mathcal{O}_{\mathrm{c}}$-calculus) introduces field assignment, integer literals, and some basic arithmetic operators.

$o.l := e$	denotes the operation that evaluates the expression e to a value v, then applies the method update operation $o.l \Leftarrow \varsigma(\_)\, v$.
i	denotes a (literal) integer value.
$\Box(e_{i=1}^k)$	denotes a k-ary operation on literal values (e.g. binary "+").

The following rules specify the base cases for both of the above operations.

$$\frac{}{\Gamma \bullet \Box(v_{i=1}^k) \longrightarrow \Gamma \bullet \ulcorner \Box(v_{i=1}^k) \urcorner} \ \ \textsc{LitOp} \quad \boxed{v_{i=1}^k \in \mathrm{dom}(\Box)}$$

$$\frac{l \notin o}{\Gamma \bullet o.l := v \longrightarrow \Gamma \bullet \ulcorner o \oplus \{l \mapsto \varsigma(\_)\, v\} \urcorner} \ \ \textsc{FldA}$$

The other cases for these operations ensure that their evaluable arguments are processed in a left to right order.

$$\frac{\Gamma \bullet e_n \longrightarrow \Gamma' \bullet e_n'}{\Gamma \bullet \Box(v_{i=1}^{n-1}, e_{i=n}^k) \longrightarrow \Gamma' \bullet \Box(v_{i=1}^{n-1}, e_n', e_{i=n+1}^k)} \ \ \textsc{LitOp-N}$$

$$\frac{\Gamma \bullet e_1 \longrightarrow \Gamma' \bullet e_1'}{\Gamma \bullet e_1.l := e_2 \longrightarrow \Gamma' \bullet e_1'.l := e_2} \ \ \textsc{FldA-1}$$

$$\frac{\Gamma \bullet e \longrightarrow \Gamma' \bullet e'}{\Gamma \bullet o.l := e \longrightarrow \Gamma' \bullet o.l := e'} \ \ \textsc{FldA-2}$$

2.3 Heap-Extended Object Calculus ($\mathcal{O}_{\text{CH}}$-Calculus)

The $\mathcal{O}_{\text{CH}}$-calculus introduces a copy-based heap storage model [10], where the heap is a partial map from abstract locations to values. Here the contents of an abstract location can be read (dereferenced) or updated (assigned) via atomic operations that take copies of the source values. The new constants and operators introduced by this model now follow.

ℓ_i denotes an abstract location on the heap and an allocated reference value.

null   denotes the null (i.e. unallocated) reference value.

¿   denotes the unset value.

fresh   denotes the operation that results in the location of a newly allocated heap entry, whose contents are unset.

$*r$ denotes the operation that takes a copy of the contents in heap location r.

$r *= v$ denotes the assignment, by copy, of value v to location r.

where r, v, and i are reference, general, and integer values respectively.

The following rules specify the base cases for the fresh, dereference, and assignment (reference update) operators. The other cases for these operators are defined to follow the usual left to right evaluation order, in a similar manner to those of the $\mathcal{O}_{\text{C}}$-calculus operators.

$$\frac{}{\Gamma\{\text{HEAP} \mapsto H\} \bullet \text{fresh} \longrightarrow \Gamma\{\text{HEAP} \leftarrowtail H'\} \bullet r} \; \text{FRESH} \qquad \boxed{\begin{array}{l} r \mathrel{\hat{=}} \text{fresh}_{\text{LOC}}(\text{dom } H) \\ H' \mathrel{\hat{=}} H \oplus \{r \mapsto \text{¿}\} \end{array}}$$

$$\frac{r \in H}{\Gamma\{\text{HEAP} \mapsto H\} \bullet *r \longrightarrow \Gamma \bullet H(r)} \; \text{DEREF}$$

$$\frac{r \in H}{\Gamma\{\text{HEAP} \mapsto H\} \bullet r *= v \longrightarrow \Gamma\{\text{HEAP} \leftarrowtail H \oplus \{r \mapsto v\}\} \bullet r} \; \text{UPDL}$$

where $\text{fresh}_{\text{LOC}}$ is a meta-function that takes a set of location values and returns a location that is not within this set.

3 The Operand Stack Model ($\mathcal{U}_{\text{SH}}$) of the $\mathcal{O}_{\text{CH}}$-Calculus

The UTP operand stack model ($\mathcal{U}_{\text{SH}}$) extends the notion of a UTP design with an operand stack for storing intermediate results, and a heap map for storing dynamically allocated values in abstract heap locations. Formally this stack and heap are denoted by the UTP context variables ΠSTK, ΠHEAP, $\Pi\text{STK}'$, and $\Pi\text{HEAP}'$, which represent the input and output states (values) of the operand stack and heap storage respectively.

The contents of the stack are the semantic entities that represent the operands of the $\mathcal{O}_{\text{CH}}$-calculus operations, i.e. the integers, objects, labels, methods, and (heap) locations. The idea is that following the execution of a subprogram the top value on the stack represents its result.

The heap storage (map) context is essentially taken from the $\mathcal{O}_{\text{CH}}$-calculus, the main differences being in the changes to its name and the precise representation of its contents (values). In particular, the restriction that the heap can only contain values is kept; thus unlike the stack a heap cannot contain labels or methods. An alternative *trace-based* approach to modelling the $\mathcal{O}_{\text{CH}}$-calculus is the subject of current work as discussed in Section 5.2.

3.1   Literal Value Programs

The simplest object calculus program is represented by a literal value, which is also the final result value of the program. Therefore, the compilation of such an $\mathcal{O}_{\text{CH}}$-calculus program must result in the $\mathcal{U}_{\text{SH}}$ design ($\mathcal{E}\ sv$) that pushes a single *stack-value* (sv) – i.e. a label, a method or a value – onto the operand stack.

$$\mathcal{E}\ sv \ \widehat{=}\ \{\Pi_{\text{STK}}\} : (\ \text{true} \vdash \Pi_{\text{STK}}' = \langle sv \rangle \frown \Pi_{\text{STK}}\ )$$

The compilation of a literal value lv to the $\mathcal{U}_{\text{SH}}$ is now defined in stages by the following two compilation rules. Here, the first rule compiles the value to a UTP program, whereas the second rule compiles the value to a UTP expression.

$$\langle\!\langle lv \rangle\!\rangle \ \widehat{=}\ \mathcal{E}\langle\!\langle lv \rangle\!\rangle^{\text{E}} \qquad \langle\!\langle lv \rangle\!\rangle^{\text{E}} \ \widehat{=}\ lv$$

Note that these compilation rules produce $\mathcal{U}_{\text{SH}}$ texts, which can then be converted into a $\mathcal{U}_{\text{SH}}$ program by applying the semantic meaning brackets as follows.

$$[\![\,t\,]\!] \ \widehat{=}\ t$$

where t is a *valid* output of the program compilation process. This amounts to being in a subset of the available $\mathcal{U}_{\text{SH}}$ operations, whose syntactic forms are amenable to the structural definition of functions involving scope of variables. For example, the free-variable substitution function in Section 3.5 is defined in terms of such a structural definition.

3.2   Modelling Object Values and Method Definitions

In the $\mathcal{U}_{\text{SH}}$ an object value is defined as a map from labels to methods. This is denoted by $\{{}_{i=1}^{k}\ l_i \mapsto m_i\}$, where k represents the number of object methods m_i with distinct labels l_i. The compilation of an object value is similar to that of literal values.

$$\langle\!\langle [{}_{i=1}^{k}\ l_i = m_i] \rangle\!\rangle \ \widehat{=}\ \mathcal{E}\langle\!\langle [{}_{i=1}^{k}\ l_i = m_i] \rangle\!\rangle^{\text{E}}$$
$$\langle\!\langle [{}_{i=1}^{k}\ l_i = m_i] \rangle\!\rangle^{\text{E}} \ \widehat{=}\ \{{}_{i=1}^{k}\ \langle\!\langle l_i \rangle\!\rangle^{\text{E}} \mapsto \langle\!\langle m_i \rangle\!\rangle^{\text{E}}\}$$

A method is defined as a pair of compiled program texts that represent the method's *self* variable and body. It is denoted by $(\!|\ x, P\ |\!)$, where the scope of the *self* variable x is the program text P. Methods cannot occur as top level programs as they are not considered to be values, thus they only have an evaluation moded compilation scheme.

$$\langle\!\langle \varsigma(x)\,e \rangle\!\rangle^{\text{E}} \;\; \widehat{=} \;\; (\!|\; \langle\!\langle x \rangle\!\rangle^{\text{E}}, \langle\!\langle e \rangle\!\rangle \;|\!)$$

where a variable is represented by itself in both the program and declaration (literal evaluation) contexts.

$$\langle\!\langle x \rangle\!\rangle \;\; \widehat{=} \;\; x \qquad\qquad \langle\!\langle x \rangle\!\rangle^{\text{E}} \;\; \widehat{=} \;\; x$$

Note that a variable by itself is not a valid program, but it may be the entire contents of a method's body (i.e. a compiled program text). Such variables are substituted by their values, prior to the program text being extracted to a $\mathcal{U}_{\text{SH}}$ subprogram. Details of the program text variable-substitution and extraction processes are presented in the discussion of method invocation (Section 3.5).

3.3   Command Expressions

In the $\mathcal{O}_{\text{CH}}$-calculus, almost all the programming operations are expressions. Such expressions are converted into UTP commands by evaluating each of their arguments, whose results are stored in the operand stack (Π_{STK}), and then applying an appropriate stack transformation command.

The $\mathcal{U}_{\text{SH}}$ stack transformation operation $\text{trans}(f, k)$ takes a k-parameter function f, which defines the operation being modelled, and constructs a UTP program that applies this function to the top k contents of the operand stack. Care must be taken to ensure that the parameters are in the order that they are going to appear on the operand stack, as this may not be the same as the left-to-right declaration order.

Given that the meta-variables $x_1, \ldots, x_k$ represent the arguments for function f, then the updated stack can be modelled by $\langle f(x_1, \ldots, x_k) \rangle \frown (\text{tail}^k \, \Pi_{\text{STK}})$, assuming that: it has started ($\Pi_{\text{OK}} = \text{true}$); there are sufficient arguments ($k \le \#\Pi_{\text{STK}}$); and these arguments are in the domain of the function being modelled ($(x_1, \ldots, x_k) \in f$).

$$
\begin{aligned}
&\text{trans}(f, k) \;\; \widehat{=} \\
&\quad \exists\, x_{i=1}^{k} \bullet (\\
&\qquad (k \le \#\Pi_{\text{STK}}) \;\wedge\; (\forall_{i=1}^{k}\, x_i = \text{head}(\text{tail}^{k-i}\, \Pi_{\text{STK}})) \;\wedge\; (x_{i=1}^{k}) \in f \\
&\qquad \vdash \\
&\qquad \Pi_{\text{STK}}' = \langle f(x_{i=1}^{k}) \rangle \frown (\text{tail}^k\, \Pi_{\text{STK}}) \\
&\quad)
\end{aligned}
$$

Having defined the transformation function, the next step is to provide a $\mathcal{U}_{\text{SH}}$ operation that evaluates the arguments for this function and then applies this function to these arguments. Note that these arguments range over acceptable *stack values*, so may include labels and methods, which are considered to be values for the purpose of the argument evaluation. Therefore, the arguments consist of stack values and general expressions $(se_1, \ldots, se_k)$.

$$\mathsf{cmdExp}(f, (se_{i=1}^k)) \;\; \widehat{=} \;\; (\overset{\circ}{\underset{i=1}{9}}^{k} \langle\!\langle se_i \rangle\!\rangle) \,\text{\fontsize{1em}{1em}\selectfont\ensuremath{\stackrel{\circ}{,}}}\, \mathsf{trans}(f, k)$$

Example 1. The $\mathcal{O}_{\mathrm{CH}}$-calculus addition operation can be modelled in terms of the cmdExp operation as follows:

$$\langle\!\langle e_1 + e_2 \rangle\!\rangle \;\; \widehat{=} \;\; \mathsf{cmdExp}((\_ + \_), (\langle\!\langle e_1 \rangle\!\rangle, \langle\!\langle e_2 \rangle\!\rangle))$$
$$= \;\; \langle\!\langle e_1 \rangle\!\rangle \,\text{\ensuremath{\stackrel{\circ}{,}}}\, \langle\!\langle e_2 \rangle\!\rangle \,\text{\ensuremath{\stackrel{\circ}{,}}}\, \mathsf{trans}((\_ + \_), 2)$$

3.4 Method Updates and Field Assignments

Method update in the $\mathcal{O}_{\mathrm{CH}}$-calculus is compiled in two parts: first, the terms representing the arguments are compiled; and second, they are combined by an appropriate method update transformation function.

$$\langle\!\langle e_1.e_2 \Leftarrow m \rangle\!\rangle \;\; \widehat{=} \;\; \mathsf{cmdExp}(methUpd, (\langle\!\langle e_1 \rangle\!\rangle, \langle\!\langle e_2 \rangle\!\rangle, \mathcal{E}\langle\!\langle m \rangle\!\rangle))$$

where:

$$methUpd = \{ \; (o, l, m) \mapsto o \oplus \{l \mapsto m\} \mid \\ (o, l, m) \in Object \times Label \times Method \wedge l \in o \\ \}$$

A field assignment is compiled in a similar manner.

$$\langle\!\langle e_1.e_2 := e_3 \rangle\!\rangle \;\; \widehat{=} \;\; \mathsf{cmdExp}(fldUpd, (\langle\!\langle e_1 \rangle\!\rangle, \langle\!\langle e_2 \rangle\!\rangle, \langle\!\langle e_3 \rangle\!\rangle))$$

where:

$$fldUpd = \{ \; (o, l, v) \mapsto o \oplus \{l \mapsto (\!(\_, v)\!)\} \mid \\ (o, l, v) \in Object \times Label \times Value \wedge l \in o \\ \}$$

3.5 Method Invocation

Method invocation in the $\mathcal{O}_{\mathrm{CH}}$-calculus is compiled in two parts. First an object-member pair is constructed from the invocation arguments: a pair of expressions (e_1 and e_2) representing an object (o) and a label (l). This is achieved by retrieving the method with label l from object o. The second part performs the actual method invocation, using a generic method call command (call). It executes the body of the method where the method's self variable has been instantiated with the calling object's value.

$$\langle\!\langle e_1.e_2 \rangle\!\rangle \;\; \widehat{=} \;\; \mathsf{cmdExp}(omPair, (\langle\!\langle e_1 \rangle\!\rangle, \langle\!\langle e_2 \rangle\!\rangle)) \,\text{\ensuremath{\stackrel{\circ}{,}}}\, \mathsf{call}$$

where:

$$omPair = \{(o, l) \mapsto (o, o(l)) \mid (o, l) \in Object \times Label\}$$

Before formally defining the generic call command, it is worth presenting two helper functions, for method extraction and self variable substitution. Both these functions are defined by cases, where the first case that matches is taken. The $ext(t, z)$ constructs a program that can be represented by program text t once the fixed point variable z has been instantiated.

$$
\begin{aligned}
ext(t, z) &\;\widehat{=}\; [\![extInner(t, z)]\!] \\
extInner(\mathsf{call}, z) &\;\widehat{=}\; z \\
extInner(t\{_{i=1}^{k} t_i\}, z) &\;\widehat{=}\; t\{_{i=1}^{k} extInner(t_i, z)\} \\
extInner(t, z) &\;\widehat{=}\; t
\end{aligned}
$$

The following $\mathcal{U}_{\mathrm{SH}}$ substitution function ($t\{\!| x \leftarrow sv |\!\}$) performs the same role as that of its $\mathcal{O}_{\mathrm{CH}}$-calculus counterpart, in that it replaces all free occurrences of the program variable x with the stack-value sv in the program text t.

$$
\begin{aligned}
x\{\!| x \leftarrow sv |\!\} &\;\widehat{=}\; sv \\
(\!| x, t |\!)\{\!| x \leftarrow sv |\!\} &\;\widehat{=}\; (\!| x, t |\!) \\
t\{_{i=1}^{k} t_i\}\{\!| x \leftarrow sv |\!\} &\;\widehat{=}\; t\{_{i=1}^{k} t_i\{\!| x \leftarrow sv |\!\} \} \\
t\{\!| x \leftarrow sv |\!\} &\;\widehat{=}\; t
\end{aligned}
$$

Note that this definition assumes that both the variable x and the stack-value sv have a textual representation. Both variables and literal values are their own texts. This leaves methods and object stack values. As a method is modelled by its text and an object is a partial map from labels to method texts, it is possible to define a straightforward function (text) for taking these values to an equivalent program text.

We are now in a position to define the call command. It is defined as the least fixed point of the apply function, which substitutes the self object o in the method text t for its self variable x.

$$\mathsf{call} \;\widehat{=}\; \mu z \bullet \mathsf{apply}(z)$$

where

$$
\begin{aligned}
\mathsf{apply}(z) \;\widehat{=}\; &(\;\exists o, x, t \mid (o, (\!| x, t |\!)) = \mathsf{head}\, \Pi_{\mathrm{STK}} \bullet \\
&\qquad \mathsf{pop}\,_9^\circ\, \mathsf{ext}(t\{\!| x \leftarrow \mathsf{text}(o) |\!\}, z) \\
&) \\
&\triangleleft \#\Pi_{\mathrm{STK}} > 0 \wedge (\mathsf{head}\, \Pi_{\mathrm{STK}}) \in Object \times Method \triangleright \\
&\mathsf{chaos}
\end{aligned}
$$

3.6 Modelling the Heap Operations

The $\mathcal{U}_{\mathrm{SH}}$ model of a heap mirrors that of the $\mathcal{O}_{\mathrm{CH}}$-calculus, where the location, unset and null values are shared semantic entities between the models.

Fresh Operator. The $\mathcal{O}_{\text{CH}}$-calculus fresh operation is compiled to its $\mathcal{U}_{\text{SH}}$ mirror.

$$\langle\!\langle\,\text{fresh}\,\rangle\!\rangle \ \widehat{=} \ \text{fresh}$$

The fresh command creates a new location on the heap, which is initialised to the explicit unset value; it then pushes the value of this new location onto the operand stack.

$$\text{fresh} \ \widehat{=} \ \exists\, r \mid r = \text{fresh}_{\text{LOC}}(\text{dom}\,\varPi_{\text{HEAP}}) \ \bullet$$
$$\varPi_{\text{STK}}, \varPi_{\text{HEAP}} := \langle r \rangle \ \frown \ \varPi_{\text{STK}}, \varPi_{\text{HEAP}} \oplus \{r \mapsto \, \xi\}$$

Note that this operation deliberately uses the same fresh location generation function as in the $\mathcal{O}_{\text{CH}}$-calculus, as it simplifies the consistency proof between the models. Without this we would have to have a notion of heap equivalence.

Dereference Operator. The dereference $\mathcal{O}_{\text{CH}}$-calculus operation is compiled by evaluating the expression representing the heap location, then applying the $\mathcal{U}_{\text{SH}}$'s command for dereferencing the current result.

$$\langle\!\langle\,*e\,\rangle\!\rangle \ \widehat{=} \ \langle\!\langle\,e\,\rangle\!\rangle \,\fatsemi\, \text{deref}$$

The heap dereference command (deref), takes the heap location on the top of the stack and replaces it with a copy of the associated heap value.

$$\text{deref} \ \widehat{=} \ \{\varPi_{\text{STK}}\} : ($$
$$\#\varPi_{\text{STK}} > 0 \wedge (\text{head}\,\varPi_{\text{STK}}) \in \varPi_{\text{HEAP}}$$
$$\vdash$$
$$\varPi_{\text{STK}}' = \langle \varPi_{\text{HEAP}}(\text{head}\,\varPi_{\text{STK}}) \rangle \ \frown \ (\text{tail}\,\varPi_{\text{STK}})$$
$$)$$

Heap Update Operator. The heap update $\mathcal{O}_{\text{CH}}$-calculus operation is compiled by evaluating its arguments in a left to right order, storing their results into a single location-value pair, and then applying the model of the heap update operation.

$$\langle\!\langle\,e_1 \mathrel{*=} e_2\,\rangle\!\rangle \ \widehat{=} \ \text{cmdExp}(lvPair, (\langle\!\langle\,e_1\,\rangle\!\rangle, \langle\!\langle\,e_2\,\rangle\!\rangle)) \,\fatsemi\, \text{update}$$

where $lvPair$ is a variant of the identity function whose domain elements are defined to be the location-value pairs.

$$lvPair = \{(r, v) \mapsto (r, v) \mid (r, v) \in Location \times Value\}$$

The reason for combining the location and value into a pair, is so that it has the same form as the heap extended result-value and constant-map UTP models of the $\mathcal{O}_{\text{CH}}$-calculus. This helps to highlight the semantic, rather than syntactic, differences between the models. These alternative models are discussed briefly in Section 5.2.

The heap update command consumes the location-value pair on the top of the stack, assigns the new value to the existing heap location, and then pushes the heap location onto the stack.

$$
\begin{aligned}
\mathsf{update} \;\; \widehat{=} \;\; (\;\; &\exists\, r, v \mid (r, v) = \mathsf{head}\, \varPi_{\mathrm{STK}} \bullet \\
& \varPi_{\mathrm{STK}}, \varPi_{\mathrm{HEAP}} := \langle r \rangle \frown (\mathsf{tail}\, \varPi_{\mathrm{STK}}), \varPi_{\mathrm{HEAP}} \oplus \{ r \mapsto v \} \\
& \triangleleft\, r \in \varPi_{\mathrm{HEAP}} \,\triangleright \\
& \mathsf{chaos} \\
) \;\; & \\
\triangleleft\, \#\varPi_{\mathrm{STK}} & > 0 \;\; \wedge \;\; (\mathsf{head}\, \varPi_{\mathrm{STK}}) \in Location \times Value \,\triangleright \\
\mathsf{chaos} &
\end{aligned}
$$

4   Consistency of the Operand Stack Model

We now demonstrate that the $\mathcal{U}_{\mathrm{SH}}$ denotational semantics is consistent with the $\mathcal{O}_{\mathrm{CH}}$-calculus operational semantics via a structural induction over the object calculus' terms — specifically, that the denotational semantics of an $\mathcal{O}_{\mathrm{CH}}$-calculus operation is the same as that of its result. The commuting diagram in Figure 1 illustrates the structure of the proof that the semantic models for an object calculus operation op with k subterms are consistent, where:

se_i is the ith subexpression of the original operation.

sv_i is the ith subterm of the operation after its arguments (i.e. stack values) have been evaluated in the correct order.

$\llbracket t \rrbracket^{\mathrm{M}}$ is the the combination of the compilation and semantic meaning functions (i.e. $\llbracket\, \langle\!\langle t \rangle\!\rangle^{\mathrm{M}} \,\rrbracket$), where M is the compilation mode.

Γ_i is the ith object calculus run-time context variable.

$A0$ is the assumption that the subterms can be evaluated in the correct order. Note this assumption also guarantees the consistency of the sub-term mappings (i.e. $\bigvee_{i=1}^{k} \langle\!\langle sv_i \rangle\!\rangle = \mathcal{E}\, sv_i$).

$A1$ is the assumption that the arguments are in the domain of the operation being modelled (i.e. $(sv_{i=1}^{k}) \in op$).

$A2$ is the assumption that the result of executing the operation with arguments $sv_{i=1}^{k}$ is the expression e.

$\rightarrow, \twoheadrightarrow$ are the one-step and multi-step $\mathcal{O}_{\mathrm{CH}}$-calculus operations.

$\downarrow$ is a compilation and/or semantic evaluation function.

$=, \parallel$ are two different representations of the equality relation, for horizontal and vertical display contexts respectively.

The left hand square of the commuting diagram in Figure 1 is essentially the same for every operator being checked, as it mirrors the use of the induction

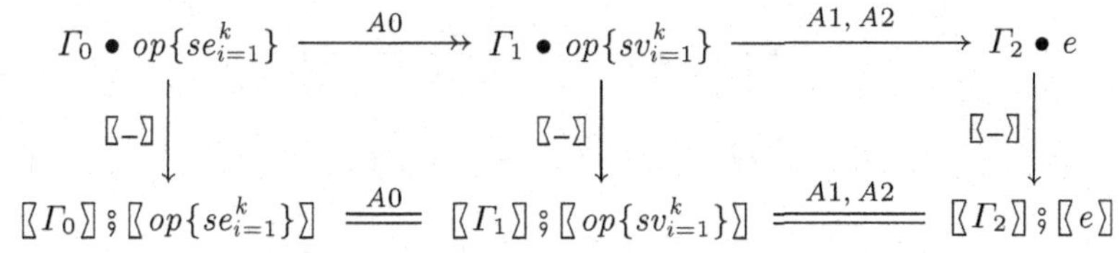

$$\Gamma_0 \bullet op\{se_{i=1}^k\} \xrightarrow{\;\;A0\;\;} \Gamma_1 \bullet op\{sv_{i=1}^k\} \xrightarrow{\;\;A1,\,A2\;\;} \Gamma_2 \bullet e$$

$$[\![-]\!] \downarrow \qquad\qquad\qquad [\![-]\!] \downarrow \qquad\qquad\qquad [\![-]\!] \downarrow$$

$$[\![\Gamma_0]\!] \,\mathring{,}\, [\![op\{se_{i=1}^k\}]\!] \overset{A0}{=\!=\!=\!=} [\![\Gamma_1]\!] \,\mathring{,}\, [\![op\{sv_{i=1}^k\}]\!] \overset{A1,\,A2}{=\!=\!=\!=} [\![\Gamma_2]\!] \,\mathring{,}\, [\![e]\!]$$

Fig. 1. Commuting diagram principle

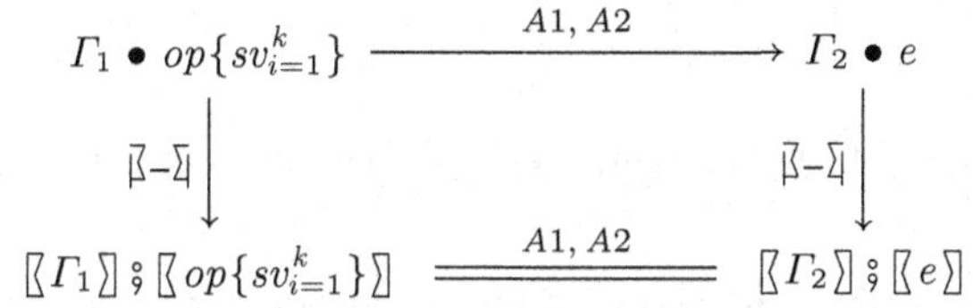

$$\Gamma_1 \bullet op\{sv_{i=1}^k\} \xrightarrow{\;\;A1,\,A2\;\;} \Gamma_2 \bullet e$$

$$[\![-]\!] \downarrow \qquad\qquad\qquad [\![-]\!] \downarrow$$

$$[\![\Gamma_1]\!] \,\mathring{,}\, [\![op\{sv_{i=1}^k\}]\!] \overset{A1,\,A2}{=\!=\!=\!=} [\![\Gamma_2]\!] \,\mathring{,}\, [\![e]\!]$$

Fig. 2. Commuting diagram practice

hypothesis, that an operation's arguments (subterms) can be evaluated success-fully. Therefore, in practice this aspect of the diagram is omitted, as illustrated in Figure 2.

The remainder of this section presents a representative sample of the consistency proofs; space limits preclude completeness.

4.1   Scalar Value Operations

The $\mathcal{O}_{\mathrm{CH}}$-calculus provides a variety of arithmetic operations that take scalar values and return a scalar value. Further, as all of these operations are system-atically translated into the $\mathcal{U}_{\mathrm{SH}}$, it is possible to present a generic proof that these operations are consistently modelled.

The commuting diagram in Figure 3 outlines the structure of the proof that a generic infix binary operator $(\_ \odot \_)$, over scalar values in the $\mathcal{O}_{\mathrm{CH}}$-calculus, has a consistent denotational semantics. Here we assume that:

A1   The scalar values sv_1 and sv_2 are in the domain of the infix operator; i.e. $(sv_1, sv_2) \in (\_ \odot \_)$.

A2   The scalar value sv_3 is the result of evaluating the binary operator; i.e. $sv_3 = sv_1 \odot sv_2$.

In Figure 3's commuting diagram, $L1$ denotes the first lemma (Lemma 1). It is the key step in this consistency proof, which demonstrates that a command ex-pression has the expected semantics. Essentially, this commuting diagram forms a template for all the $\mathcal{O}_{\mathrm{CH}}$-calculus operations that are defined as command ex-pressions in the $\mathcal{U}_{\mathrm{SH}}$. In particular, field assignment and method update are also covered by this proof template.

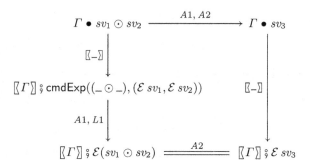

Fig. 3. Generic binary operation commuting diagram

Command expression lemma. The command expression lemma demonstrates that the effect of applying a command-expression command to a function f, with *pre-evaluated* arguments $sv_{i=1}^k$, is the same as the effect of applying the evaluation command to the result of the function f on its arguments. It assumes that the arguments are in the domain of the function (i.e. $(sv_{i=1}^k) \in f$). Note that a *pre-evaluated* argument is an operand-stack value (i.e. a label, method definition or a value).

Lemma 1 (Command Expression Lemma)

$$(sv_{i=1}^k) \in f \quad \Rightarrow \quad \mathsf{cmdExp}(f, (\underset{i=1}{\overset{k}{}} \mathcal{E}\, sv_i)) = \mathcal{E}(f(sv_{i=1}^k))$$

Note that within the following proof, the left-hand-side of the initial implication is added as an assumption to the proof context.

$\mathsf{cmdExp}(f, (\overset{k}{\underset{i=1}{}} \mathcal{E}\, sv_i))$

$=$ .... Defn. of cmdExp

$(\overset{\circ k}{\underset{9\, i=1}{}} \mathcal{E}\, sv_i) \,\mathring{9}\, \mathsf{trans}(f, k)$

$=$ .... Defn. of $\mathcal{E}$

$(\overset{\circ k}{\underset{9\, i=1}{}} (\mathsf{true} \vdash \Pi_{\mathrm{STK}'} = \langle sv_i \rangle \frown \Pi_{\mathrm{STK}}))\mathring{9}$
$\mathsf{trans}(f, k)$

$=$ .... Defn. of $\mathring{9}$

$(\mathsf{true} \vdash \Pi_{\mathrm{STK}'} = \langle \overset{k}{\underset{i=1}{}} sv_{k+1-i} \rangle \frown \Pi_{\mathrm{STK}})\mathring{9}$ and predicate logic
$\mathsf{trans}(f, k)$

$=$ .... Defn. of trans

$(\mathsf{true} \vdash \Pi_{\mathrm{STK}'} = \langle \overset{k}{\underset{i=1}{}} sv_{k+1-i} \rangle \frown \Pi_{\mathrm{STK}})\mathring{9}$
$\exists\, x_{i=1}^k \bullet \#\Pi_{\mathrm{STK}} \geq k \wedge$
$\quad (\forall_{i=1}^k\ x_i = \mathsf{head}(\mathsf{tail}^{k-i}\, \Pi_{\mathrm{STK}})) \wedge$
$\quad (x_{i=1}^k) \in f$
$\vdash$
$\quad \Pi_{\mathrm{STK}'} = \langle f(x_{i=1}^k) \rangle \frown (\mathsf{tail}^k\, \Pi_{\mathrm{STK}})$

$$= \quad \dots\dots\dots\dots\dots\dots\dots\dots\dots\dots\dots\dots\dots\dots\dots\dots\dots\dots \quad \text{Defn. of } \fatsemi$$

$$\#(\langle_{i=1}^{k} sv_{k+1-i}\rangle \frown \Pi_{\text{STK}}) \geq k \wedge \qquad \text{and predicate logic}$$
$$(\forall_{i=1}^{k} \ sv_i = \mathsf{head}(\mathsf{tail}^{k-i} \ \Pi_{\text{STK}})) \wedge$$
$$(sv_{i=1}^{k}) \in f$$
$$\vdash$$

$$\Pi_{\text{STK}}' = \langle f(sv_{i=1}^{k})\rangle \frown \mathsf{tail}^{k}(\langle_{i=1}^{k} sv_{k+1-i}\rangle \frown \Pi_{\text{STK}})$$

$$= \quad \dots\dots\dots\dots\dots\dots\dots\dots\dots\dots\dots\dots\dots\dots\dots\dots\dots\dots \quad \text{Predicate logic}$$

$$(sv_{i=1}^{k}) \in f \vdash \Pi_{\text{STK}}' = \langle f(sv_{i=1}^{k})\rangle \frown \Pi_{\text{STK}}$$

$$= \quad \dots\dots\dots\dots\dots\dots\dots\dots\dots\dots\dots\dots\dots\dots\dots\dots\dots\dots \quad A1, \text{ i.e. } (sv_{i=1}^{k}) \in f$$

$$\mathsf{true} \vdash \Pi_{\text{STK}}' = \langle f(sv_{i=1}^{k})\rangle \frown \Pi_{\text{STK}}$$

$$= \quad \dots\dots\dots\dots\dots\dots\dots\dots\dots\dots\dots\dots\dots\dots\dots\dots\dots\dots \quad \text{Defn. of } \mathcal{E}$$

$$\mathcal{E}(f(sv_{i=1}^{k}))$$

4.2 Method Invocation

The commuting diagram in Figure 4 demonstrates that the $\mathcal{O}_{\text{CH}}$-calculus method invocation is consistent with one unwinding of the fixed-point function (call) that defines method invocation, where:

A1   The label l of object o has the method $\varsigma(x)\,e$;

A2   The compilation of substitution process is defined as:

$$\langle\!\langle e\{x \leftarrow o\}\rangle\!\rangle \quad \widehat{=} \quad \mathsf{ext}(\langle\!\langle e\rangle\!\rangle\{x \leftarrow \langle\!\langle o\rangle\!\rangle^{\text{E}}\}, \mathsf{call})$$

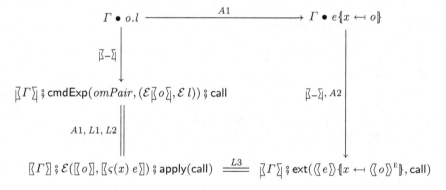

Fig. 4. Method invocation commuting diagram

The consistency diagram in Figure 4 relies on three lemmas: the command expression lemma (Lemma 1); the unwinding lemma (Lemma 2), which uses the fixed-point definition to provide a single unwinding; and the method call lemma (Lemma 3), which demonstrates that this unwinding is correct. We now state and prove the remaining two lemmas.

Recall that the method call operation is defined as the fixed point of an apply function ($\mu z \bullet \mathsf{apply}(z)$). The structure of this definition leads to the following unwinding lemma.

Lemma 2 (Unwinding Lemma)

$$\mathsf{call} = \mathsf{apply}(\mathsf{call})$$

Proof

$$\mathsf{call}$$
$$=\ \dotfill\ \text{Defn. of } \mathsf{call}$$
$$(\mu\, z \bullet \mathsf{apply}(z))$$
$$=\ \dotfill\ \text{Defn of fixed point } \mu$$
$$\mathsf{apply}(\mu\, z \bullet \mathsf{apply}(z))$$
$$=\ \dotfill\ \text{Defn. of } \mathsf{call}$$
$$\mathsf{apply}(\mathsf{call})$$

Method call lemma. Informally the method call lemma says that the effect of applying the call command is equivalent to the effect of applying one iteration of this command to itself.

Lemma 3 (Method Call Lemma)

$$\mathcal{E}(\llbracket o \rrbracket^{\mathrm{E}}, \llbracket \varsigma(x)\, e \rrbracket)\ \mathring{,}\ \mathsf{apply}(\mathsf{call})\quad =\quad \mathsf{ext}(\langle\!\langle e \rangle\!\rangle \{x \hookleftarrow \langle\!\langle o \rangle\!\rangle^{\mathrm{E}}\}, \mathsf{call})$$

Proof

$$\mathcal{E}(\llbracket o \rrbracket^{\mathrm{E}}, \llbracket \varsigma(x)\, e \rrbracket)\ \mathring{,}\ \mathsf{apply}(\mathsf{call})$$
$$=\ \dotfill\ \text{Defn. of } \llbracket \varsigma(x)\, e \rrbracket$$
$$\mathcal{E}(\llbracket o \rrbracket^{\mathrm{E}}, (\!|\ x, \langle\!\langle e \rangle\!\rangle\ |\!))\ \mathring{,}\ \mathsf{apply}(\mathsf{call})$$
$$=\ \dotfill\ \text{Defn. of } \mathcal{E}$$
$$(\mathbf{true} \vdash \Pi_{\mathrm{STK}}' = \langle(\llbracket o \rrbracket^{\mathrm{E}}, (\!|\ x, \langle\!\langle e \rangle\!\rangle\ |\!))\rangle \frown \Pi_{\mathrm{STK}})\mathring{,}$$
$$\mathsf{apply}(\mathsf{call})$$
$$=\ \dotfill\ \text{Defn. of } \mathsf{apply}$$
$$(\mathbf{true} \vdash \Pi_{\mathrm{STK}}' = \langle(\llbracket o \rrbracket^{\mathrm{E}}, (\!|\ x, \langle\!\langle e \rangle\!\rangle\ |\!))\rangle \frown \Pi_{\mathrm{STK}})\mathring{,}$$
$$(\ (\ \exists\, o_1, x_1, t_1 \mid (o_1, (\!|\ x_1, t_1\ |\!)) = \mathsf{head}\, \Pi_{\mathrm{STK}} \bullet$$
$$\qquad \mathsf{pop}\ \mathring{,}\ \mathsf{ext}((\!|\ t_1\{x_1 \hookleftarrow \mathsf{text}(o_1)\}\ |\!), \mathsf{call})$$
$$\ )$$
$$\ \lhd\ \#\Pi_{\mathrm{STK}} > 1\ \wedge\ (\mathsf{head}\, \Pi_{\mathrm{STK}}) \in \mathit{Object} \times \mathit{Method}\ \rhd$$
$$\ \mathsf{skip}$$
$$\ )$$
$$=\ \dotfill\ \text{Defn. of } \mathsf{pop}$$
$$(\mathbf{true} \vdash \Pi_{\mathrm{STK}}' = \langle(\llbracket o \rrbracket^{\mathrm{E}}, (\!|\ x, \langle\!\langle e \rangle\!\rangle\ |\!))\rangle \frown \Pi_{\mathrm{STK}})\mathring{,}$$
$$(\ (\ \exists\, o_1, x_1, t_1 \mid (o_1, (\!|\ x_1, t_1\ |\!)) = \mathsf{head}\, \Pi_{\mathrm{STK}} \bullet$$
$$\qquad (\#\Pi_{\mathrm{STK}} > 1 \vdash \Pi_{\mathrm{STK}}' = \mathsf{tail}\, \Pi_{\mathrm{STK}})\mathring{,}$$
$$\qquad \mathsf{ext}((\!|\ t_1\{x_1 \hookleftarrow \mathsf{text}(o_1)\}\ |\!), \mathsf{call})$$
$$\ )$$
$$\ \lhd\ \#\Pi_{\mathrm{STK}} > 1\ \wedge\ (\mathsf{head}\, \Pi_{\mathrm{STK}}) \in \mathit{Object} \times \mathit{Method}\ \rhd$$
$$\ \mathsf{skip}$$
$$\ )$$

$=$ .... Defn. of $\,_9^{\circ}$
$$(\;\exists\, o_1, x_1, t_1 \mid (o_1, (\!|\; x_1, t_1\;|\!)) = (\![o]\!]^{\mathrm{E}}, (\!|\; x, \langle\!\langle e \rangle\!\rangle\;|\!)) \;\bullet$$ and predicate logic
$$(\mathit{true} \vdash \Pi_{\mathrm{STK}}' = \Pi_{\mathrm{STK}})_9^{\circ}$$
$$\mathsf{ext}((\!|\; t_1\{\!|x_1 \leftharpoonup \mathsf{text}(o_1)\}\!|\;|\!)), \mathsf{call})$$
$$)$$
$$\lhd \mathit{true} \;\wedge\; (\![o]\!]^{\mathrm{E}}, (\!|\; x, \langle\!\langle e \rangle\!\rangle\;|\!)) \in \mathit{Object} \times \mathit{Method} \rhd$$
$$\mathsf{skip}$$

$=$ .... Defn. of $(\_\lhd\_\rhd\_)$
$$\exists\, o_1, x_1, t_1 \mid (o_1, (\!|\; x_1, t_1\;|\!)) = (\![o]\!]^{\mathrm{E}}, (\!|\; x, \langle\!\langle e \rangle\!\rangle\;|\!)) \;\bullet$$ and predicate logic
$$(\mathit{true} \vdash \Pi_{\mathrm{STK}}' = \Pi_{\mathrm{STK}})_9^{\circ}$$
$$\mathsf{ext}((\!|\; t_1\{\!|x_1 \leftharpoonup \mathsf{text}(o_1)\}\!|\;|\!)), \mathsf{call})$$

$=$ .... One point rule
$$\mathsf{skip}_9^{\circ}$$ and defn of skip
$$\mathsf{ext}((\!|\; \langle\!\langle e \rangle\!\rangle\{\!|x \leftharpoonup \mathsf{text}((\![o]\!]^{\mathrm{E}})\}\!|\;|\!)), \mathsf{call})$$
$=$ .... skip unit of $(\_\,_9^{\circ}\_)$
$$\mathsf{ext}((\!|\; \langle\!\langle e \rangle\!\rangle\{\!|x \leftharpoonup \langle\!\langle o \rangle\!\rangle^{\mathrm{E}}\}\!|\;|\!)), \mathsf{call})$$ and defn. of text

4.3   Fresh Heap Locations

The commuting diagram in Figure 5 outlines the structure of the proof that the fresh operator in the $\mathcal{O}_{\mathrm{CH}}$-calculus has a consistent denotational semantics. Here we assume that:

A1   The initial $\mathcal{O}_{\mathrm{CH}}$-calculus context-heap value is H_0.
A2   The expression $\mathsf{fresh}_{\mathrm{LOC}}(\mathrm{dom}\, H_0)$ evaluates to ℓ_j.
A3   The context-heap value H_1 is $H_0 \oplus \{\ell_j \mapsto \text{¿}\}$.

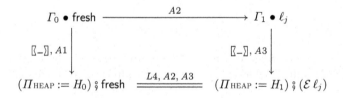

Fig. 5. Fresh operator commuting diagram

Lemma 4 (Fresh location lemma)

$$(\Pi_{\mathrm{HEAP}} := H_0)\,_9^{\circ}\, \mathsf{fresh} \;=\; (\Pi_{\mathrm{HEAP}} := H_1)\,_9^{\circ}\, (\mathcal{E}\, \ell_j)$$

Proof

$$(\Pi_{\mathrm{HEAP}} := H_0)\,_9^{\circ}\, \mathsf{fresh}$$

$$= \quad \cdots\cdots\cdots\cdots\cdots\cdots\cdots\cdots\cdots\cdots\cdots\cdots\cdots\cdots\cdots\cdots\cdots \quad \text{Defn. of fresh}$$
$$(\Pi_{\text{HEAP}}' = H_0)\,\mathring{,}$$
$$(\ \exists\, r \mid r = \text{fresh}_{\text{LOC}}(\text{dom}\ \Pi_{\text{HEAP}}) \bullet$$
$$\qquad \Pi_{\text{STK}}, \Pi_{\text{HEAP}} := \langle r \rangle \frown \Pi_{\text{STK}}, \Pi_{\text{HEAP}} \oplus \{r \mapsto \imath\}$$
$$)$$
$$= \quad \cdots\cdots\cdots\cdots\cdots\cdots\cdots\cdots\cdots\cdots\cdots\cdots\cdots\cdots\cdots\cdots\cdots \quad \text{Defns. of }\mathring{,}\text{ and }:=$$
$$\exists\, r \mid r = \text{fresh}_{\text{LOC}}(\text{dom}\ H_0) \bullet$$
$$\qquad \Pi_{\text{STK}}, \Pi_{\text{HEAP}} := \langle r \rangle \frown \Pi_{\text{STK}}, H_0 \oplus \{r \mapsto \imath\}$$
$$= \quad \cdots\cdots\cdots\cdots\cdots\cdots\cdots\cdots\cdots\cdots\cdots\cdots\cdots\cdots\cdots\cdots\cdots \quad A2$$
$$\exists\, r \mid r = \ell_j \bullet$$
$$\qquad \Pi_{\text{STK}}, \Pi_{\text{HEAP}} := \langle r \rangle \frown \Pi_{\text{STK}}, H_0 \oplus \{r \mapsto \imath\}$$
$$= \quad \cdots\cdots\cdots\cdots\cdots\cdots\cdots\cdots\cdots\cdots\cdots\cdots\cdots\cdots\cdots\cdots\cdots \quad \text{1-point rule \& }A3$$
$$\Pi_{\text{STK}}, \Pi_{\text{HEAP}} := \langle \ell_j \rangle \frown \Pi_{\text{STK}}, H_1$$
$$= \quad \cdots\cdots\cdots\cdots\cdots\cdots\cdots\cdots\cdots\cdots\cdots\cdots\cdots\cdots\cdots\cdots\cdots \quad \text{Defns. of }\mathring{,}\text{ and }\mathcal{E}$$
$$(\Pi_{\text{HEAP}} := H_1)\,\mathring{,}\,(\mathcal{E}\ \ell_j)$$

5 Conclusions and Related Work

In this paper we have provided a UTP encoding of an Abadi–Cardelli-style ς-calculus with an explicit heap model, along with a proof of its consistency. It is straightforward to add several other features, such as direct support for eagerly evaluated untyped lambda calculus (λ-calculus) functions, and for treating labels as values. In the former case, this amounts to relaxing the restriction on the definition of the $\mathcal{U}_{\text{SH}}$'s call operator, to accept any value-method pair rather than an object-method pair. The latter case amounts to treating labels as values, and adding operations for conditional execution and for checking whether an object contains a method with a given label.

5.1 Related Work

Hoare and He's UTP [6,12] provides a rich model of programs as relational-predicates. Abadi and Cardelli's ς-calculi [1] provides an alternative model of programs as objects. Our contribution is to model the Abadi–Cardelli notion of an object in the UTP, which provides: a simple untyped object calculus with a relational-predicate denotational semantics; and the UTP with an object-based model of object-orientation. Further, as the UTP already has several models of concurrency, this encoding provides the potential for adding one (or more) of these concurrency models to the ς-calculus.

This is not the first time object-oriented ideas have been added to (or modelled in) the UTP. In particular, there have been several works that model class-based object-orientation, such as [4,2,11]. These differ fundamentally from our approach, as each object is considered to be an instance of a class, rather than a class being a special sort of object. In particular, within our approach objects need not be associated with a class. This opens the possibility of considering prototype-based languages, such as Self.

Within the more general field of predicative programming [5], another notion of object-orientation has been modelled [9]. It defines objects as a combination of their attributes and behaviour, where each attribute (field) has a unique address and the details of its behaviour (methods) are defined by its type (e.g. class). This approach is similar to that of Abadi and Cardelli's imperative ς-calculus [1], except that in this case both methods and fields are bound to objects. Further, the $\mathcal{O}_{\mathrm{CH}}$-calculus deliberately separates the heap and object representations, to gain a measure of orthogonality between concerns. An earlier version of this predicative programming model [8] did not use addresses in the definition of an object, but was still essentially class-oriented in its outlook.

Alternative approaches to modelling references (pointers) in the UTP have been provided in [7,3]. The former of these approaches was the inspiration for the *trace* model that is briefly discussed in Section 5.2. The latter of these approaches uses path-based equivalence classes to identify variables that share the same reference, which are referred to as *entity groups*. Preliminary results of the on-going work in this area suggest that our trace-based model is also essentially an entity group model, which ought to enable us to unify these ideas.

5.2   On-Going Work

The operand-stack model of the $\mathcal{O}_{\mathrm{CH}}$-calculus is arguably too operational in nature. In order to address this issue three further models have been constructed, the *result-value*, *constant-map*, and *trace* models. For reasons of space we can only provide a brief description of these models.

Result-value Model. This replaces the stack with a single value that represents the result of executing an $\mathcal{O}_{\mathrm{CH}}$-calculus model, and intermediate results are stored in temporary variables, which are introduced and completed in the usual UTP manner. The one significant complication introduced by this model is the need to manage the scope of its alphabets – specifically the requirement to hide the intermediate result variables from the *execution* of a subprogram. This follows from two observations: first, that a subprogram's execution is independent of the result – but not side-effecting heap updates – of a previous subprogram; and second, that the weakest fixed point semantics of method invocation requires the alphabets both before and after any method invocation to be the same.

Constant-Map Model. This extends the result-value model by updating the representation of a method (and its invocation). Here a method is represented by a triple: a *self* variable; a program-text *body*; and a *map* from the free variables within that body to their values. Such values may be updated during the method invocation process, which recursively updates all free instances of a method's self variable, within both its own and its inner-method variable maps. The idea is that by the time of a method's invocation, all the free-variables within a method's body have a defined value in their associated variable map; and that this variable map is used to introduce read-only (constant) variables for the scope of the method's definition.

Trace Model. This takes a fundamentally different approach from that presented in this paper, in that it models variables, values, and heap locations, in terms of a directed graph that can be represented by a set of trace sets. This approach was inspired by trace-based pointers in [7] and is also similar to the entity-group work in [3]. Essentially, it came from the motivation of using the ideas presented in these UTP models on the $\mathcal{O}_{\mathrm{CH}}$-calculus. Here, each entity group is represented by an equivalence class, which is the set of traces that defines a node of the directed graph. There are several complicating factors, not least of which is that in the $\mathcal{O}_{\mathrm{CH}}$-calculus not all values have locations (nor should they).

Having said that the trace-based model is fundamentally different from the others, it also has some striking similarities to the constant-map model; specifically, that the layout of the graph essentially mirrors the structure of the variables and the heap of the constant-map model. With a little extra work, we can make use of the constant-map model's variable-maps to provide a named path (trace) to any location within the graph.

References

1. Martin Abadi and Luca Cardelli. *A Theory of Objects.* Springer, 1996.
2. A.L.C. Cavalcanti, A.C.A. Sampaio, and J.C.P. Woodcock. Unifying classes and processes. *Software and System Modelling*, 4(3):277–296, 2005.
3. Ana Cavalcanti, Will Harwood, and Jim Woodcock. Pointers and records in the unifying theories of programming. In Steve Dunne and Bill Stoddart, editors, *First International Symposium on Unifying Theories of Programming*, volume 4010 of *Lecture Notes in Computer Science*. Springer-Verlag, 2006.
4. Jifeng He, Zhiming Liu, and Xiaoshan Li. Towards a refinement calculus for object systems. Research Report 251, UNU/IIST, P.O. Box 3058, Macau, May 2002.
5. Eric C.R. Hehner. *A Practical Theory of Programming.* Springer-Verlag, 1993. Electronic edition freely available on line from: www.cs.utoronto.ca/~hehner/aPToP.
6. C.A.R. Hoare and J. He. *Unifying Theories of Programming.* Computer Science. Prentice Hall, 1998.
7. C.A.R. Hoare and Jifeng He. A trace model for pointers and objects. In 13th *European Conference on Object-Oriented Programming*, pages 1–17, 1999.
8. Ioannis T. Kassios. Objects as predicates. Technical report, Computer Systems Research Group, University of Toronto, 2004.
9. Ioannis T. Kassios. *A Theory of Object Oriented Refinement.* PhD thesis, University of Toronto, 2006.
10. Benjamin C. Pierce. *Types and Programming Languages.* MIT Press, 2002.
11. Thiago Santos, Ana Cavalcanti, and Augusto Sampaio. Object-orientation in UTP. In Steve Dunne and Bill Stoddart, editors, *First International Symposium on Unifying Theories of Programming*, volume 4010 of *Lecture Notes in Computer Science*, pages 20–38. Springer-Verlag, 2006.
12. J.C.P. Woodcock and A.L.C. Cavalcanti. A tutorial introduction to designs in unifying theories of programming. In *IFM 2004: Integrated Formal Methods*, volume 2999 of *Lecture Notes in Computer Science*, pages 40–66. Springer-Verlag, 2004. Invited tutorial.

Non-interference Properties for Data-Type Reduction of Communicating Systems*

Tobe Toben

Carl von Ossietzky Universität Oldenburg, Germany
toben@informatik.uni-oldenburg.de

Abstract. An increasing interest in "Systems of Systems", that is, Systems comprising a varying number of interconnected sub-systems, raises the need for automated verification techniques for dynamic process creation and a changing communication topology. In previous work, we developed a verification approach that is based on finitary abstraction via Data-Type Reduction. To be effective in practice, the abstraction has to be complemented by non-trivial assumptions about valid communication behaviour, so-called non-interference lemmata.

In this paper, we mechanise the generation and validation of these kind of non-interference properties by integrating ideas from communication observation and counter abstraction. We thereby provide a fully automatic procedure to substantially increase the precision of the abstraction.

We explain our approach in terms of a modelling language for dynamic communication systems, and use a running example of a car platooning system to demonstrate the effectiveness of our extensions.

1 Introduction

The current trend of *mobile computing* induces complex systems that comprise a varying number of interconnected sub-systems, for example in ad-hoc networking [6] where mobile devices detect other devices within a certain scanning range and autonomously maintain networks of arbitrary size. Similar principles are nowadays employed in traffic control systems, e.g. the European Train Control System [18] defines so-called Radio Block Controllers (RBC) along the track that are dynamically contacted by trains entering their communication range. From the viewpoint of an RBC, the responsibility for spontaneously appearing trains adds a new level of complexity when designing safety-critical systems.

Not surprisingly, automatic verification of systems with dynamic process creation and destruction is an active research problem. As the number of involved process within the system is a priori unbounded, finitary abstraction is applied

---

* This work was partly supported by the German Research Council (DFG) as part of the Transregional Collaborative Research Centre "Automatic Verification and Analysis of Complex Systems" (SFB/TR 14 AVACS).

J. Davies and J. Gibbons (Eds.): IFM 2007, LNCS 4591, pp. 619–638, 2007.

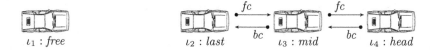

Fig. 1. Snapshot of the car platooning system where car ι_1 approaches a platoon. After detecting and merging with car ι_2, a platoon of size four will be established.

to obtain a manageable representation of the infinite state system. As demonstrated in the literature [5,20], in particular the technique of Data-Type Reduction (DTR) [12] is suitable for systems with dynamic process creation. Up to now, it is however an open problem how DTR can effectively be refined in order to reduce the large amount of spurious behaviour stemming from the abstraction.

In this paper, we devise an automatic procedure for excluding a typical source for spurious behaviour in abstractions of communicating systems, namely message interferences. We show that the observation of the communication history allows to identify invalid communication even if the actual status of a communication partner is blurred by the abstraction. We demonstrate our approach in terms of a modelling language for *Dynamic Communication Systems* (DCS) [2], a proper extension of *Communicating Finite State Machines* [3] by process creation and dynamic link topologies. The following example system will be used throughout the paper in order to demonstrate the ideas of our approach.

Running Example "Car Platooning". Another real-world example of a DCS is the car platooning scenario as studied in the PATH project [9]. There, cars travelling on a highway are supposed to form *car platoons*, i.e. to establish series of interlinked cars driving with only little distance. The main manoeuvres are *merge*, i.e. a car joins an existing platoon, and *split*, i.e. a platoon is separated into unconnected cars again. Figure 1 depicts a snapshot of the car platooning system. Every car is aware of its current state, i.e. whether it is not involved in a platoon (*free*), the last car in a platoon (*last*), the first car in a platoon (*head*) or somewhere in the middle of a platoon (*mid*). The platoon itself is organised as a doubly-linked list of wireless communication channels, where a car knows its front car under the name *fc* and its back car under the name *bc*.

Analysis Approach. Due to the unbounded number of participating processes, DCS are infinite state systems. In [5,20], Data-Type Reduction (DTR) has been shown to be a valuable abstraction for system with dynamic process creation and destruction, and in [2] we already sketched how DTR applies to the special case of DCS models.

DTR belongs to the category of *heterogeneous* abstraction techniques [22] which allow different parts of the system to be abstracted using different degrees of precision. The characteristic of DTR is that it maintains the *full degree of precision* for a fixed and finite set of processes, and *completely* dismisses information of any other processes. That is, DTR follows spotlight principle [19] by focusing on a finite set of processes and abstracting the rest into one *summary process* that represents the behaviour of *any* unfocused process.

The advantage of employing these two extrema of precision is that the abstract transition relation can be easily computed by a syntactical transformation of the system [5]. This is in contract to homogeneous abstraction techniques like predicate abstraction [16] where the computation of the abstraction itself is the performance bottleneck. However, the disadvantage of entirely abstracting the behaviour of unfocused processes is a large amount of spurious behaviour, i.e. runs in the abstracted system that are not present in the original system. The spurious behaviour stems from invalid interferences of abstracted processes with concrete processes. [5] suggests to exclude these unwanted interferences by adding so-called non-interference lemmata which are of the form

"If some process sends something to me, then it is allowed to do so."

It is however not obvious whether and how concrete instances of this pattern can automatically be inferred from the system. Furthermore, once they are found, the validity of these lemmata has to be proven to be correct for the original (and thus infinite state) system as additional verification tasks.

In this paper, we devise a technique to automatically generate and integrate non-interference properties into the DTR abstraction. For this purpose, we keep track of *valid* interferences of the summary process. Roughly spoken, for each message m and concrete process ι, we count the number of summarised processes that currently may send m to ι. To keep this information finite, we count up to a finite number and fall back to uncertainty only if this number is exceeded, i.e. we apply a variant of Counter Abstraction [11] to that part of the system that normally is completely blurred in the DTR approach.

The process counters themselves are updated based on the communication between concrete processes and the summary process. The reason why this kind of communication observation gives enough information in order to precisely update the process counter is that a communicating system usually exhibits a causal relationship among the messages, e.g. if a car sends a *split* command to me, then I have requested a *merge* from it beforehand, and in between no *split* commands have been exchanged. Thus, a concrete car sending a *merge* message to the summary process will increase the counter for valid *split* interferences from the summary, and the reception of a *split* from the summary process will decrease this counter again.

This paper makes two contributions. Firstly, as a continuation of our work in [2], we provide a formal definition of DTR for DCS models. Secondly, our main contribution is a method to automatically generate and integrate non-interference properties into the abstraction by combining Data-Type Reduction with a variant of Counter Abstraction.

Structure. Section 2 introduces a concise modelling language for Dynamic Communication Systems (DCS), based on the concepts defined in [2]. Section 3

explains our approach for analysing DCS models in detail. We start in subsection 3.1 by formally defining the technique of Data-Type Reduction for DCS models, and motivate the need for further refinement of the abstraction. Subsection 3.2 then describes our method to automatically obtain this kind of refinement. Section 4 discusses related work, and Sect. 5 concludes.

2   Dynamic Communication Systems

In [2], we introduce *DCS protocols* as a modelling language for *Dynamic Communication Systems*, basically as an extension of Communicating Finite State Machines [3] by dynamic creation of processes and dynamic topologies. Thereby, DCS provides for an alternative to the well-known π-calculus [13] in which the important language constructs of DCS only appear in an encoded form and are not directly accessible for a tailored analysis (cf. [2]). In this paper, we define a restricted synchronous variant of DCS protocols that still contains the relevant features for both adequately modelling DCS and explaining our approach.

DCS Overview. A global DCS state, called topology, comprises a set of processes. Each process is described by its unique identity and its configuration, that is, its local state and its links to other processes. A topology can be extended by adding a process in an initial configuration to it. On the other hand, a process can disappear from a topology if it is in a fragile configuration (see below).

The behaviour of each of the processes is defined in terms of a *DCS protocol* and each process operates on a sole copy of this protocol description, similarly to instances of classes in object-oriented modelling. A DCS protocol defines the set of *states* a process can assume, the set of *channels* by which a process can link itself to other processes and the set of *messages* a process can send and receive. Transitions among the states are annotated by sending and reception of messages over channels. A sent message always includes the identity of the sender process, and the receiver process can store the attached identity into one of its channels. This is the mechanism to establish links between processes. To remove an existing link to another process, each transition has a boolean *reset flag* indicating whether the corresponding channel is cleared after taking this transition. To bootstrap the linking procedure as sketched above, a process can receive a so-called *external message* that carries some identity from the set of currently existing processes.

Definition 1 (DCS Protocol). *A DCS Protocol is a tuple*

$$\mathsf{P} = (Q, A, \Omega, \chi, \Sigma, \Sigma_X, succ)$$

where

- *Q is a finite set of states,*
- *$A \subseteq Q$ is the set of initial states,*
- *$\Omega \subseteq Q$ is the set of fragile states,*

- χ is a finite set of channel names,
- Σ is a finite set of message names,
- $\Sigma_X \subseteq \Sigma$ is the set of external message names, and
- $succ \subseteq Q \times \chi \times \{!, ?\} \times \Sigma \times \mathbb{B} \times Q$ is the successor relation.   ◇

For a transition $tr = (q, c, sr, m, r, q') \in succ$, we use $q(tr)$, $c(tr)$, $sr(tr)$, $m(tr)$, $r(tr)$, and $q'(tr)$ to denote the respective components of tr. The transition tr is called a send transition if $sr = !$ and a receive transition if $sr = ?$. The effect of a send transition is to send the message m to the process stored in channel c. The effect of a receive transition is to store the identity of the sender of message m in channel c. In both cases, the process then moves from state q to q' and clears the channel c iff the reset flag r is $true$ (cf. Def. 2 below for a formal definition).

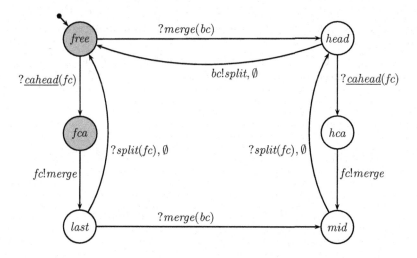

Fig. 2. DCS Protocol for platoon merge and split. For channel c and message m, a send transition is written in the form '$c!m$' and a receive transition as '$?m(c)$'. If the reset flag r is set for a transition, this is indicated by the '$\emptyset$' symbol.

The Running Example. Figure 2 shows the DCS protocol 'platoon' implementing the merge and split manoeuvres. It comprises six states, two channels and three messages where *free* is the single initial state and the (gray marked) states *free* and *fca* are fragile states. The (underlined) message *cahead* is an external message.

The *merge manoeuvre* starts when a process in state *free* (a car not involved in a platoon) or in state *head* (the head of a platoon) receives the external message *cahead* (car ahead). It stores the attached identity in its channel *fc* (front car). The process then proceeds to state *last* (the last car in a platoon) resp. state *mid* (in the middle of a platoon) if it can synchronise with the process denoted by its *fc* channel on message *merge*. The process receiving the *merge* message proceeds from state *free* to *head* resp. from *last* to *mid*, thereby storing the received identity in its channel *bc* (back car). Repeating these protocol steps allows to build platoons of arbitrary lengths.

The *split manoeuvre* is initiated the head of the platoon by synchronising on *split* with its back car on the transition from *head* to *free*. It thereby removes the process from its *bc*-channel. The back car clears its *fc*-channel on reception of *split*. If it is in state *last*, it moves to state *free* and the platoon is completely split. If it is in state *mid*, it becomes the new head of the platoon and itself initiates the splitting of the remaining platoon.

DCS Configurations. For the rest of this paper, let *Id* be a countably infinite set of process identities. Given a DCS protocol $\mathsf{P} = (Q, A, \Omega, \chi, \Sigma, \Sigma_X, succ)$, a configuration of P is a tuple

$$(q, C)$$

where $q \in Q$ is a state and $C : \chi \rightharpoonup Id$ is a partial evaluation of the channels. A configuration is called initial if $q \in A$ and $C(c)$ is undefined for all $c \in \chi$. A configuration is called fragile if $q \in \Omega$. The set of all configurations of P is denoted by $\mathcal{L}(\mathsf{P})$.

Having defined a (local) configuration of a DCS protocol, a global configuration, called topology, of P is a partial function $T : Id \rightharpoonup \mathcal{L}(\mathsf{P})$. The idea is that the domain of T, written $\mathsf{dom}(T)$, describes the set of processes existing in T, and $T(\iota)$ yields the (local) configuration of each $\iota \in \mathsf{dom}(T)$. The set of all topologies of P is denoted by $\mathcal{T}_{Id}(\mathsf{P})$.

The Running Example. The snapshot presented in Fig. 1 corresponds to the following topology

$$\begin{aligned} T_S = [\iota_1 &\mapsto (\mathit{free}, [\,]), \iota_2 \mapsto (\mathit{last}, [\mathit{fc} \mapsto \iota_3]), \\ \iota_3 &\mapsto (\mathit{mid}, [\mathit{fc} \mapsto \iota_4, \mathit{bc} \mapsto \iota_2]), \iota_4 \mapsto (\mathit{head}, [\mathit{bc} \mapsto \iota_3])] \end{aligned} \tag{1}$$

with $\mathsf{dom}(T_S) = \{\iota_1, \iota_2, \iota_3, \iota_4\} \subset Id$.

DCS Semantics. We now specify under which conditions a DCS topology can evolve. As already sketched, a topology can be extended by a new process, an existing process can disappear, a process can receive an external message and processes can communicate among each other.

Definition 2 (Topology Evolution). *Let* $\mathsf{P} = (Q, A, \Omega, \chi, \Sigma, \Sigma_X, succ)$ *be a DCS protocol. Two topologies* $T, T' \in \mathcal{T}_{Id}(\mathsf{P})$ *evolve, written* $T \to T'$, *if exactly one of the following four conditions is satisfied:*

Process Appearance (PA). *A process* $\iota \in Id$ *freshly appears, i.e.* $\mathsf{dom}(T') = \mathsf{dom}(T) \dot\cup \{\iota\}$ *and* $T'(\iota)$ *is initial.*

External Message (EM). *A process* $\iota \in \mathsf{dom}(T)$ *in configuration* $T(\iota) = (q, C)$ *receives an external message on transition* $(q, c, ?, m, r, q') \in succ$ *with* $m \in \Sigma_X$, *i.e.* $T'(\iota) = (q', C')$ *with*

$$C' = \begin{cases} C|_{\mathsf{dom}(C) \setminus \{c\}} & \mathit{if}\ r = \mathit{true} \\ C[c \mapsto \iota'] & \mathit{if}\ r = \mathit{false} \end{cases}$$

for some $\iota' \in \mathsf{dom}(T)$ *with* $\iota' \neq \iota$.

Process Synchronisation (PS). *Two processes $\iota_s, \iota_r \in \mathsf{dom}(T)$ with $T(\iota_s) = (q_s, C_s)$ and $T(\iota_r) = (q_r, C_r)$ with $C_s(c_s) = \iota_r$ synchronise on transitions $(q_s, c_s, !, m, r_s, q_s'), (q_r, c_r, ?, m, r_r, q_r') \in succ$, i.e. $T'(\iota_s) = (q_s', C_s')$ and $T'(\iota_r) = (q_r', C_r')$ with*

$$C_s' = \begin{cases} C_s|_{\mathsf{dom}(C_s)\setminus\{c_s\}} & \text{if } r_s = \text{true} \\ C_s & \text{if } r_s = \text{false} \end{cases}$$

and

$$C_r' = \begin{cases} C_r|_{\mathsf{dom}(C_r)\setminus\{c_r\}} & \text{if } r_r = \text{true} \\ C_r[c_r \mapsto \iota_s] & \text{if } r_r = \text{false}. \end{cases}$$

Process Disappearance (PD). *A process $\iota \in \mathsf{dom}(T)$ disappears, i.e. $T' = T|_{\mathsf{dom}(T)\setminus\{\iota\}}$ and $T(\iota)$ is fragile.*

In each of the four cases, all processes not involved in the current topology evolution are required to remain the same. $\diamond$

A sequence of topologies $(T_i)_{i \in \mathbb{N}_0}$ with $T_i \rightarrow T_{i+1}$ for all $i \in \mathbb{N}_0$ and T_0 being the initial topology, i.e. $\mathsf{dom}(T_0) = \emptyset$, is called a run of P. The semantics of P, denoted $[\![P]\!]_{Id}$, is the set of all runs of P. We explicitly use the subscript Id to denote the concrete semantics which employs an *infinite* set of available identities in contrast to modifications of the semantics in later sections.

The Running Example. In Fig. 3, we exemplarily sketch a run of the DCS protocol platoon from Fig. 2. Starting at the initial topology, two processes enter the scene. The first one then receives an external message carrying the identity of the second one. Both then agree on the merge transition and become a platoon of size two. The head of the platoon then decides to split again, and disappears from the scene afterwards.

3 Analysis of Dynamic Communication Systems

We are interested in the formal verification of properties of DCS that can be expressed as universally quantified first-order formulae in prenex form, i.e.

$$\forall p_1, \ldots, p_n . \phi$$

where ϕ is some temporal formula using variables p_1 to p_n, but with no further quantification. For example, a desirable property of the platooning system is

$$\forall p_1, p_2 . \mathsf{G}\ (p_1.bc = p_2 \rightarrow p_2.fc = p_1) \tag{2}$$

that is, for all two processes p_1 and p_2, it is always the case that when process p_1 has p_2 as its back car, then p_2 has p_1 as its front car. For lack of space, we have to refer the reader to [2] for a detailed description of the DCS property language called METT.

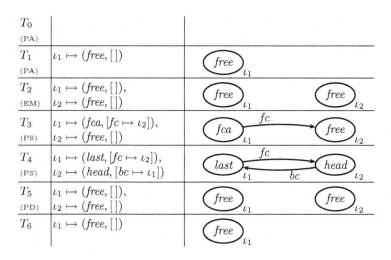

Fig. 3. Concrete run of platoon. The first column names the topology and the kind of evolution (cf. Def. 2) to the next topology. The second column shows the topology in a formal notation and the third column visualises it in a graph notation.

However, formal analysis of DCS protocols faces the problem that the semantics of a DCS protocol is an infinite set of runs, due to the infinite set of available identities. A straight-forward approach to enable automated verification is the restriction to a *finite* subset of identities. In general, considering only a subset of identities $Id' \subseteq Id$ for a DCS protocol P means that the *Process Appearance* condition in Def. 2 only picks identities from Id'. We thereby obtain the underapproximated semantics, denoted $[\![P]\!]_{Id'}$. As every run with identities Id' is also a run with identities Id, we have

$$[\![P]\!]_{Id'} \subseteq [\![P]\!]_{Id}$$

for any $Id' \subseteq Id$ (especially if Id' is a *finite* subset of Id). Thus the technique of underapproximation is good for finding errors in the protocol by limiting the analysis to a finite set of processes, e.g. check if two cars in isolation adhere to property (2). However, as any influences from processes from $Id \setminus Id'$ are disregarded, the absence of unwanted behaviour in general can not be guaranteed by considering only finitely many processes. For example, to show that a car platoon behaves correctly under any influence of arbitrarily many other cars, we need something stronger.

3.1 Data-Type Reduction for DCS

Data-Type Reduction yields a finite state representation of an infinite state system by applying the spotlight principle [19], that is, focus on a finite set of processes and represent these processes precisely. Any information about the rest, i.e. the processes "in the shadows", is completely dismissed. To provide a sound overapproximation of the system, a special identity $\perp$ is introduced to summarise the behaviour of any process that is not in the focus of the spotlight. Concrete processes will still be able to communicate with $\perp$, but no information about $\perp$ will be stored. DTR was originally introduced for the verification of parameterised systems [12], and has been demonstrated to be suitable for systems with unbounded dynamic creation and destruction in [5]. In the following, we formally describe how DTR applies to Dynamic Communication Systems as defined in the previous section.

Abstract DCS Configurations. For the rest of the paper, let $Id' \subset Id$ be a finite subset of identities. Given a protocol $\mathsf{P} = (Q, A, \Omega, \chi, \Sigma, \Sigma_X, succ)$, an *abstract configuration* of P is a tuple $(q, C^\sharp)$ where $q \in Q$ is a state and $C^\sharp : \chi \rightharpoonup Id' \cup \{\perp\}$ is a partial evaluation of the channels. The set of all abstract configurations of P is denoted by $\mathcal{L}^\sharp(\mathsf{P})$. An abstract topology of P is a partial function $T^\sharp : Id' \rightharpoonup \mathcal{L}^\sharp(\mathsf{P})$, and the set of all abstract topologies of P is denoted by $\mathcal{T}^\sharp_{Id'}(\mathsf{P})$.

The DTR abstraction of a topology $T \in \mathcal{T}_{Id}(\mathsf{P})$ with respect to Id', denoted $\alpha_{Id'}(T)$, is basically a restriction of the domain of T to Id'. Additionally, all remaining local configurations (q, C) in $\mathsf{ran}(T|_{Id'})$ are modified such that each channel $c \in \chi$ with $C(c) \in Id \setminus Id'$ is set to $C(c) = \perp$.

The Running Example. The DTR abstraction of the topology (1) of Fig. 1 with respect to $\{\iota_1, \iota_2, \iota_3\}$ yields the abstract topology

$$[\iota_1 \mapsto (free, [\,]), \iota_2 \mapsto (last, [fc \mapsto \iota_3]), \iota_3 \mapsto (mid, [fc \mapsto \perp, bc \mapsto \iota_2])], \qquad (3)$$

that is, ι_4 has disappeared from the domain and the fc link of ι_3 is set to $\perp$.

DTR Semantics of DCS. The evolution of abstract topologies is based on the evolution of concrete topologies as defined in Def. 2 as follows. Firstly, two modification are to be made, namely that *Process Appearance* only creates processes from the finite set Id', and *External Messages* can also carry the abstract identity $\perp$. Secondly, the possibility to synchronise a concrete process with $\perp$ is added, such that messages can be send to and received from the abstract process.

Definition 3 (DTR Topology Evolution). *Let $\mathsf{P} = (Q, A, \Omega, \chi, \Sigma, \Sigma_X, succ)$ be a DCS protocol. Two topologies $T^\sharp_1, T^\sharp_2 \in \mathcal{T}^\sharp_{Id'}(\mathsf{P})$ evolve under DTR, written $T^\sharp_1 \rightsquigarrow T^\sharp_2$, if $T^\sharp_1 = T^\sharp_2$, or $T^\sharp_1 \rightarrow T^\sharp_2$ by (PS) or (PD) as defined in Def. 2, or if exactly one of the following conditions is satisfied:*

Process Appearance (PA). *A process $\iota \in Id'$ freshly appears, i.e. $\mathsf{dom}(T^\sharp_2) = \mathsf{dom}(T^\sharp_1) \dot\cup \{\iota\}$ and $T^\sharp_2(\iota)$ is initial.*

External Message (EM). *A process $\iota \in \mathsf{dom}(T^\sharp_1)$ in configuration $T^\sharp_1(\iota) = (q, C^\sharp_1)$ receives an external message on transition $(q, c, ?, m, r, q') \in succ$ with $m \in \Sigma_X$, i.e. e $T^\sharp_2(\iota) = (q', C^\sharp_2)$ with*

$$C^\sharp_2 = \begin{cases} C^\sharp_1|_{\mathsf{dom}(C^\sharp_1) \setminus \{c\}} & \text{if } r = true \\ C^\sharp_1[c \mapsto \iota'] & \text{if } r = false \end{cases}$$

for some $\iota' \in \mathsf{dom}(T^\sharp) \cup \{\perp\}$ with $\iota' \neq \iota$.

Send to Summary (SS). *A process* $\iota \in \mathsf{dom}(T_1^\sharp)$ *in configuration* $T_1^\sharp(\iota) = (q_s, C_1^\sharp)$ *with* $C_1^\sharp(c_s) = \bot$ *synchronises with* $\bot$ *on transitions*

$$tr_s = (q_s, c_s, !, m, r_s, q_s') \in succ$$
$$tr_r = (q_r, c_r, ?, m, r_r, q_r') \in succ$$

i.e. $T_2^\sharp(\iota) = (q_s', C_2^\sharp)$ *with*

$$C_2^\sharp = \begin{cases} C_1^\sharp|_{\mathsf{dom}(C_1^\sharp)\setminus\{c_s\}} & \textit{if } r_s = \textit{true} \\ C_1^\sharp & \textit{if } r_s = \textit{false}. \end{cases}$$

Receive from Summary (RS). *A process* $\iota \in \mathsf{dom}(T_1^\sharp)$ *in configuration* $T_1^\sharp(\iota) = (q_r, C_1^\sharp)$ *synchronises with* $\bot$ *on transitions*

$$tr_s = (q_s, c_s, !, m, r_s, q_s') \in succ$$
$$tr_r = (q_r, c_r, ?, m, r_r, q_r') \in succ$$

i.e. $T_2^\sharp(\iota) = (q_r', C_2^\sharp)$ *with*

$$C_2^\sharp = \begin{cases} C_1^\sharp|_{\mathsf{dom}(C_1^\sharp)\setminus\{c_r\}} & \textit{if } r_r = \textit{true} \\ C_1^\sharp[c_r \mapsto \bot] & \textit{if } r_r = \textit{false}. \end{cases}$$

In each case, all processes not involved in the current topology evolution are required to remain the same.   ◇

A sequence of abstract topologies $(T_i^\sharp)_{i\in\mathbb{N}_0}$ with $T_i^\sharp \rightsquigarrow T_{i+1}^\sharp$ for all $i \in \mathbb{N}_0$ and $T_0^\sharp$ being the initial topology, i.e. $T_0^\sharp = T_0$, is called an abstract run of P. The abstract semantics of P, denoted $[\![\mathsf{P}]\!]_{Id'}^\sharp$, is the set of all abstract runs of P.

The Running Example. An abstract run of platoon with a single identity ι_1 is shown in Fig. 4. Clearly, the *under*approximated semantics with a single identity does not comprise a topology where the single process reaches the state *last* as there is no other process to merge with.

Note that Def. 3.(RS) reveals the very coarse abstraction employed by the DTR approach, as no constraints about the relation between $\bot$ and the receiver process ι are required. The summary process $\bot$ can send any message, as long there is a corresponding sending transition tr_s *somewhere* in the DCS protocol. However, the benefit of DTR is that computing the abstract system is as easy as computing the underapproximated system, as Def. 3 only considers the local information of finitely many processes.

DTR provides a sound abstraction for DCS as follows. The abstraction of a concrete run $\sigma = (T_i)_{i\in\mathbb{N}_0} \in [\![\mathsf{P}]\!]_{Id}$, denoted $\alpha_{Id'}(\sigma)$, is the sequence of abstracted topologies $(\alpha_{Id'}(T_i))_{i\in\mathbb{N}_0}$. Then we have:

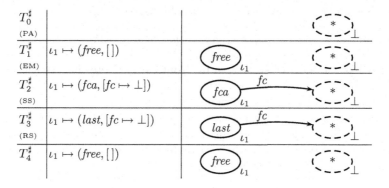

Fig. 4. Abstract run of platoon. The first column names the topology and the kind of evolution (cf. Def. 3) to the next topology. The second column shows the topology in a formal notation and the third column visualises it in a graph notation.

Theorem 1 (Soundness of DTR abstraction). *Let* P *be a DCS protocol. The abstraction of each concrete run of* P *is an abstract run of* P, *i.e.*

$$\sigma \in [\![P]\!]_{Id} \implies \alpha_{Id'}(\sigma) \in [\![P]\!]^{\sharp}_{Id'} \qquad \qquad \diamond$$

Proof. For any $T_1, T_2 \in \mathcal{T}_{Id}(P)$, we can show $T_1 \to T_2 \implies \alpha_{Id'}(T_1) \rightsquigarrow \alpha_{Id'}(T_2)$ by close examination of the four cases from Def. 2. It is straight-forward to see that the abstract evolution to $\alpha_{Id'}(T_2)$ according to Def. 3 preserves the same information concerning the summary process $\bot$ as the abstraction of the concrete topology T_2 does, namely links to $\bot$ but no information about $\bot$ itself.   □

Theorem 1 states any behaviour of a finite subset of identities Id' that is possible in the concrete semantics, is also possible in the abstract semantics. Note that this kind of behaviour preservation is best suited to analyse universally quantified DCS properties of the form $\forall p_1, \ldots, p_n \, . \, \phi$, as these properties express relationships among *finitely many* processes. In fact, the heuristic of the DTR approach to determine the set of concretely represented processes is to choose $Id' \subset Id$ such that $|Id'| = n$. If ϕ can be proven correct for a concrete binding of p_i to Id', symmetry arguments allow to conclude the correctness of the whole first-order formula for the original system. This concluding step is known under the term Query Reduction [21].

However, DTR abstraction is not complete, i.e. in general there are abstract runs $\sigma^{\sharp}$ in $[\![P]\!]^{\sharp}_{Id'}$ for which no concrete run $\sigma \in [\![P]\!]_{Id}$ with $\alpha_{Id'}(\sigma) = \sigma^{\sharp}$ exists. Moreover, the maximal coarse abstraction of unfocused processes allows for a *large* amount of spurious behaviour, that in practice often prevents to successfully prove relevant properties of the systems via DTR (cf. [2]).

The Running Example. To see an example of such spurious behaviour, consider the topology T_4 as shown in Fig. 3. The abstract evolution according to Def. 3 allows the abstract process to send a *split* message to process ι_1, i.e. the topology

$$[\iota_1 \mapsto (last, [fc \mapsto \iota_2]), \iota_2 \mapsto (head, [bc \mapsto \iota_1])] \qquad (4)$$

may evolve under DTR by Def. 3.(RS) to the topology

$$[\iota_1 \mapsto (\textit{free}, [\,]), \iota_2 \mapsto (\textit{head}, [bc \mapsto \iota_1])], \tag{5}$$

that is, ι_1 has "stealthily" split from his front car ι_2. Note that we thereby have reached a topology violating property (2), but we do not a priori know whether we encountered spurious or valid behaviour in order to reach this topology. By *manually* investigation of the platoon protocol, we can identify the interference of the summary as *spurious* as only the front car is supposed to initiate the splitting from its back car. In the setting above however, some car completely unrelated to car ι_1 has requested the split.

Wrapping Up. Intuitively, DTR turns the falsification capabilities of the underapproximated semantics into a proper verification techniques by putting the isolated finite set of identities into an environment that summarises an arbitrary number of other processes. However, this summary process shows in general more behaviour than the processes it summarises. Thus to be effective for verification, DTR abstraction needs a sound refinement of the summary process' behaviour. As sketched in the introduction, the integration of non-interference lemmata gives a good intuition of "what to do", but it does not provide a method of "how to do so". In the next section, we show how to automatically generate non-interference properties that effectively eliminate spurious behaviour from DTR abstractions, thus turning the manual investigation sketched above into an automatic procedure.

3.2   Refining Data-Type Reduction by Process Counting

The spurious example from the last section shows that the DTR abstraction allows for message interferences of completely unrelated processes. Intuitively, the reason for this artifact of the abstraction is that no information about the relation from summarised processes to concrete processes, i.e. no links from $\bot$ to processes from Id', is maintained.

However, a characteristic of DCS is that links are established via message communication, thus the validity of a message interference from $\bot$ to some $\iota' \in Id'$ depends on prior communication among ι' and $\bot$. We exploit this fact by maintaining information about the summary process in terms of messages that have been "enabled" by prior communication between $\bot$ and processes from Id'.

For this, note that we can (statically) derive from a DCS protocol which messages are next to be send over some channel c if a process is in state q. Consider the DCS example depicted in Fig. 5. The next messages a process in state q_2 can send over channel c_1 are m_a and m_b. From state q_5, the next enabled message for channel c_1 is only m_b. Thus a concrete process ι' sending m_1 to $\bot$ enables the set $\{m_a, m_b\}$, and sending m_2 enable the set $\{m_b\}$. Note that both sets can be enabled in one topology (although one process cannot be in state q_2 and q_5 simultaneously) as $\bot$ represents *multiple* processes. In addition to communication from ι' to $\bot$, also $\bot$ sending a message that has been enabled

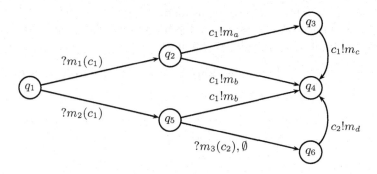

Fig. 5. Artificial DCS Protocol to demonstrate the concept of enabled messages

before alters the set of enabled messages. Clearly, sending back m_a to ι' will *disable* the complete set $\{m_a, m_b\}$. The consequence of sending back m_b to ι' is more difficult to see, as we cannot decide whether this particular sending of m_b has been enabled by itself upon reception of m_2, or together with m_a by reception of m_1. Thus both alternatives have to be considered, i.e. one possible update of enabled message is to disable the set $\{m_b\}$, the other to disable the set $\{m_a, m_b\}$. Sending messages from $\perp$ to Id may also *enable* new message sending, e.g. sending message m_a will enable the set $\{m_c\}$. As a final remark, note that sending m_3 to $\perp$ must no enable $\{m_d\}$ as the channel c_2 is cleared upon reception of m_3.

Unfortunately, we cannot maintain the complete information of enabled message sets as described above, as one set can be enabled many times at once. For example, process ι' sending m_2 twice enables the set $\{m_b\}$ twice, namely for two different processes represented by $\perp$. A natural solution to avoid infinite counting is to do finite counting up to some K and fall back to uncertainty if the counter exceeds K, i.e. to apply Counter Abstraction [11].

Formalising the approach. In the following, let $\mathsf{P} = (Q, A, \Omega, \chi, \Sigma, \Sigma_X, succ)$ be a DCS protocol. A sequence of transitions $tr_0 tr_1 \ldots tr_n$ is called a transition path of P if $q'(tr_i) = q(tr_{i+1})$ for all $0 \le i < n$. The set of all paths of P is denoted by $Paths(\mathsf{P})$. The set $E_{\mathsf{P}}(q, c)$ determines the set of messages which are the next to be send over channel c if a process is in state q, according to $succ$.

$$E_{\mathsf{P}}(q, c) = \{m \in Msgs \mid \exists tr_0 tr_1 \ldots tr_n \in Paths(\mathsf{P}) : q(tr_0) = q \land c(tr_n) = c \land$$
$$m(tr_n) = m \land sr(tr_n) = ! \land \forall 0 \le i < n : c(tr_i) \neq c\}$$

For each concretely represented process $\iota' \in Id'$ and set of messages $M \subseteq \Sigma$, we keep track of those processes from $Id \setminus Id'$ that are able to send some $m \in M$ to ι'. That is, given a concrete topology $T \in \mathcal{T}_{Id}(\mathsf{P})$, we define the set of potential communication partners (CP) for $\iota' \in Id$ and $M \subseteq \Sigma$ as

$$CP_T(\iota', M) := \{\iota \in Id \setminus Id' \mid T(\iota) = (q, C) \land \exists c \in \chi : C(c) = \iota' \land M = E_{\mathsf{P}}(q, c)\}.$$

The keep the information finite, we do not keep track of the process identities themselves, but rather we only *count* the number of processes in each set

$CP_T(\iota', M)$ up to a finite number K as follows. Let $\mathbb{N}_K := \{0, 1, \ldots, K, \infty\}$. The order $\leq_K$ is defined on $\mathbb{N}_K$ as $n_1 \leq_K n_2$ iff $n_2 = \infty$ or $n_1 \leq n_2 \leq K$. Addition and subtraction in $\mathbb{N}_K$ are defined as follows:

$$n_1 \oplus_K n_2 := \begin{cases} \infty & \text{if } n_1 = \infty \vee n_2 = \infty \vee n_1 + n_2 > K \\ n_1 + n_2 & \text{else} \end{cases}$$

$$n_1 \ominus_K n_2 := \begin{cases} \infty & \text{if } n_1 = \infty \\ 0 & \text{if } n_1 \neq \infty \wedge n_2 = \infty \vee n_1 - n_2 < 0 \\ n_1 - n_2 & \text{else} \end{cases}$$

A *process counter* of P assigns a value to a pair of identity and set of messages, i.e. it is a function $\Pi : (Id \times 2^\Sigma) \to \mathbb{N}_K$. The set of all process counters of P is denoted $\mathcal{PC}(\mathsf{P})$. Given two process counters $\Pi_1, \Pi_2 \in \mathcal{PC}(\mathsf{P})$, we say that the counter Π_1 is smaller than Π_2, written $\Pi_1 \preceq_K \Pi_2$, if $\Pi_1((\iota, M)) \leq_K \Pi_2((\iota, M))$ for all $\iota \in Id'$ and $M \subseteq \Sigma$. The addition of Π_1 and Π_2, denoted $\Pi_1 \oplus_K \Pi_2$, is defined pointwise as $(\Pi_1 \oplus_K \Pi_2)((\iota, M)) := \Pi_1((\iota, M)) \oplus_K \Pi_2((\iota, M))$ for all $\iota \in Id'$ and $M \subseteq \Sigma$.

For a given concrete topology $T \in \mathcal{T}_{Id}(\mathsf{P})$, we compute the *derived* process counter with respect to Id', written $\pi_{Id'}(T)$, for $\iota' \in Id'$ and $M \subseteq \Sigma$ as

$$\pi_{Id'}(T)((\iota', M)) = \begin{cases} \infty & \text{if } |CP(\iota', M)| > K \\ |CP(\iota', M)| & \text{else.} \end{cases}$$

Figure 6 depicts a topology with two sets of communication partners. We assume that the processes $\iota_3, \iota_4, \iota_6, \iota_7$ are in a situation that allows them to send some message from M_1 to ι_1 in the future. For ι_2, the processes ι_7 and ι_8 may send some message from M_2. When abstracting this topology, only the process counter will be maintained, e.g. for $K = 3$ we obtain $\Pi((\iota_1, M_1)) = \infty$ and $\Pi((\iota_2, M_2)) = 2$.

Using process counters. The derived process counter represents the most precise information we can get from a topology T in terms of process counting. Unfortunately, when performing the abstract evolution according to Def. 3 we cannot compute the derived process counter *directly* as we have no information about the configurations of processes from $Id \setminus Id'$. Thus the main problem to be solved is how to (precisely) update the process counter based on the information that is present in the abstract topology evolution. As sketched in the beginning of the section, a concretely represented process sending a messages to $\bot$, i.e. to some process $Id \setminus Id'$ in the original system, will enable $\bot$ to communicate with ι' afterwards, as it can store the identity Id' in one of its channel. That is, the corresponding counters for the enabled messages have to be increased.

On the other hand, a counter for a pair of process ι' and set of messages M has to be decreased after $\bot$ has sent a message $m \in M$ to ι'. However, if the channel is not cleared when sending m, then other messages may now be enabled which are next to be send according to the DCS protocol.

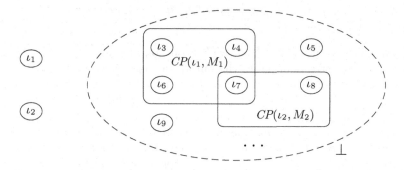

Fig. 6. Communication Partners in a concrete topology. After abstracting with respect to ι_1 and ι_2, only the process counter will be preserved in order to provide a finite characterisation of the summary process $\perp$.

Maintaining a precise process counter allows to eliminate spurious interferences as $\perp$ is now only allowed to send message m to ι' if there is a set of messages M with $m \in M$ for which the counter of the pair ι' and M is *not zero*.

Formalising the ideas sketched above, we define the refined DTR topology evolution that modifies and respects the status of the process counter as follows.

Definition 4 (Refined DTR Topology Evolution). *Let* P *be a DCS protocol. Two topologies* $T_1^\sharp$, $T_2^\sharp \in \mathcal{T}_{Id'}^\sharp(\mathsf{P})$ *and two process counters* $\Pi_1, \Pi_2 \in \mathcal{PC}(\mathsf{P})$ *evolve under DTR, written* $(T_1^\sharp, \Pi_1) \rightsquigarrow (T_2^\sharp, \Pi_2)$, *if* $(T_1^\sharp, \Pi_1) = (T_2^\sharp, \Pi_2)$, *or* $T_1^\sharp \rightsquigarrow T_2^\sharp$ *by (PA), (EM), (PS), or (PD) as defined in Def. 3 and* $\Pi_1 = \Pi_2$, *or if exactly one of the following conditions is satisfied:*

Refined Send to Summary (rSS). *A process* $\iota \in \mathrm{dom}(T)$ *synchronises with* $\perp$ *on transitions* tr_s, tr_r *as defined in Def. 3.(SS) and*

$$\Pi_2 = \begin{cases} \Pi_1 & \text{if } r(tr_r) = \text{true} \\ \Pi_1[(\iota, E) \mapsto \Pi_1((\iota, E)) \oplus_K 1] & \text{if } r(tr_r) = \text{false} \end{cases}$$

where $E = E_\mathsf{P}(q'(tr_r), c(tr_r))$.

Refined Receive from Summary (rRS). *A process* $\iota \in \mathrm{dom}(T)$ *synchronises with* $\perp$ *on transitions* tr_s, tr_r *as defined in Def. 3.(RS) if there exists a set of messages* M *with* $m(tr_s) \in M$ *such that*

$$\Pi_1((\iota, M)) \geq 1$$

and

$$\Pi_2 = \begin{cases} \Pi_1[(\iota, M) \mapsto \Pi_1((\iota, M)) \ominus_K 1] & \text{if } r(tr_s) = \text{true} \\ \Pi_1[(\iota, M) \mapsto \Pi_1((\iota, M)) \ominus_K 1][(\iota, E) \mapsto \Pi_1((\iota, E)) \oplus_K 1] & \text{else} \end{cases}$$

where $E = E_\mathsf{P}(q'(tr_s), c(tr_s))$.

In each case, all processes not involved in the current topology evolution are required to remain the same.   ◇

To explain a run of P under refined DTR evolution, we have to specify the initial process counter corresponding to the initial topology. Note that the initial process counter may not be zero for all pairs of processes and messages, although the initial topology does not comprise any processes. The reason is that, at any time, processes summarised by $\bot$ may receive an external message carrying a process identity from Id' and thus may communicate with ι' afterwards. Unfortunately, external messages to $\bot$ are not visible under DTR evolution, thus the initial process counter has to cater for this communication possibilities by enabling an arbitrary number of those messages that follow the reception of external messages in the DCS protocol. In the running example, sending *merge* messages from $\bot$ to some concrete process ι' must always be possible, as a process summarised by $\bot$ may always receive an external message *cahead* carrying the identity ι'. Thus we define the *initial* process counter of P as

$$\Pi_0((\iota', M)) := \begin{cases} \infty & \text{if } \exists tr \in succ : m(tr) \in \Sigma_X \wedge r(tr) = false \wedge \\ 0 & \text{else} \qquad\qquad\qquad M = E_\mathsf{P}(q'(tr), c(tr)) \end{cases}$$

for all $\iota' \in Id'$ and $M \subseteq \Sigma$.

A sequence of abstract topologies and observers $((T_i^\sharp, \Pi_i))_{i \in \mathbb{N}_0}$ with $(T_i^\sharp, \Pi_i) \rightsquigarrow (T_{i+1}^\sharp, \Pi_{i+1})$ for all $i \in \mathbb{N}_0$ and $T_0^\sharp$ being the initial topology, i.e. $T_0^\sharp = T_0$, and Π_0 being the initial observer, is called a refined abstract run of P. The refined abstract semantics of P, denoted $[\![\mathsf{P}]\!]_{Id}^{\sharp R}$, is the set of all its refined abstract runs.

The Running Example. Two examples of process counter updating can be obtained by "replaying" the abstract runs from the previous section under the refined abstract evolution. Figure 7 shows the refined abstract run corresponding to Fig. 4. The important observation is that the (rSS) evolution to topology T_3 increase the counter for the pair ι_1 and $\{split\}$ to one, as *split* is in $E_\mathsf{P}(head, bc)$. The subsequent sending of *split* to ι_1 is thereby enabled in (rRS). For the spurious run from the last section however, we expect the refinement via process counting to obey the evolution from topology (4) to (5). As up to topology (4) no communication with the summary has taken place, the process counter is still the initial one. Especially the counter for the pair ι_1 and $\{split\}$ is zero, thus the summary is not allowed to take this[1] transition to reach topology (5).

We observe from Def. 4 that if the evolution (rRS) is possible with some process counter Π, it is also possible with all process counters Π' with $\Pi \preceq_K \Pi'$. This motivates the following lemma.

Lemma 1. *Let $T_1^\sharp, T_2^\sharp \in \mathcal{T}_{Id'}^\sharp(\mathsf{P})$ and $\Pi_1, \Pi_2 \in \mathcal{PC}(\mathsf{P})$. If $(T_1^\sharp, \Pi_1) \rightsquigarrow (T_2^\sharp, \Pi_2)$, then for all $\Pi_1' \in \mathcal{PC}(\mathsf{P})$ with $\Pi_1 \preceq_K \Pi_1'$ there exists $\Pi_2' \in \mathcal{PC}(\mathsf{P})$ such that $(T_1^\sharp, \Pi_1') \rightsquigarrow (T_2^\sharp, \Pi_2')$ and $\Pi_2 \preceq_K \Pi_2'$.*   ◇

---

[1] Actually, the refinement blocks *all* spurious interferences leading to a violation of (2) such that (2) can be proven to be correct for the platooning system by our method.

$T_0^\sharp$ (PA)		$\Pi_0((\iota_1, \{merge\})) = \infty$
$T_1^\sharp$ (EM)	$\iota_1 \mapsto (free, [\,])$	$\Pi_1((\iota_1, \{merge\})) = \infty$
$T_2^\sharp$ (rSS)	$\iota_1 \mapsto (fca, [fc \mapsto \bot])$	$\Pi_2((\iota_1, \{merge\})) = \infty$
$T_3^\sharp$ (rRS)	$\iota_1 \mapsto (last, [fc \mapsto \bot])$	$\Pi_3((\iota_1, \{merge\})) = \infty$ $\Pi_3((\iota_1, \{split\})) = 1$
$T_4^\sharp$	$\iota_1 \mapsto (free, [\,])$	$\Pi_4((\iota_1, \{merge\})) = \infty$

Fig. 7. Refined abstract run of platoon. The first column names the topology and the kind of evolution (cf. Def. 4) to the next topology. The second column shows the topology in a formal notation and the third column shown the process counter for those entries that are not zero.

We are now ready to prove the soundness of the refined DTR abstraction. The crucial point is to see that the process counter is updated in such a manner that it does not block any valid message sendings from the summarised process.

Theorem 2 (Soundness of Refined DTR abstraction). *Let* P *be a DCS protocol. Each concrete run of* P *has an abstract counterpart in the refined abstract semantics of* P, *i.e. there exist process counters* Π_i *such that*

$$(T_i)_{i \in \mathbb{N}_0} \in [\![P]\!]_{Id} \implies ((\alpha_{Id'}(T_i), \Pi_i))_{i \in \mathbb{N}_0} \in [\![P]\!]_{Id'}^{\sharp R} \qquad \diamondsuit$$

Proof. We show that $H \subseteq \mathcal{T}_{Id}(P) \times (\mathcal{T}_{Id'}^\sharp(P) \times \mathcal{PC}(P))$ with

$$(T, (T^\sharp, \Pi)) \in H \iff \alpha_{Id'}(T) = T^\sharp \wedge (\pi_{Id'}(T) \oplus_K \Pi_0) \preceq_K \Pi$$

is a simulation relation, that is, for all $T_1 \in \mathcal{T}_{Id}(P)$ and $(T_1^\sharp, \Pi_1) \in (\mathcal{T}_{Id'}^\sharp(P) \times \mathcal{PC}(P))$ with $H((T_1, (T_1^\sharp, \Pi_1)))$ we have

$$\forall T_2 \in \mathcal{T}_{Id}(P) : T_1 \to T_2 \ \exists (T_2^\sharp, \Pi_2) \in (\mathcal{T}_{Id'}^\sharp(P) \times \mathcal{PC}(P)) :$$
$$(T_1^\sharp, \Pi_1) \rightsquigarrow (T_2^\sharp, \Pi_2) \wedge H((T_2, (T_2^\sharp, \Pi_2))).$$

Let $T_1, T_2 \in \mathcal{T}_{Id}(P)$ with $T_1 \to T_2$. By lemma 1 we are left to show the existence of a process counter $\Pi_2 \in \mathcal{PC}(P)$ with $(\pi_{Id'}(T_2) \oplus_K \Pi_0) \preceq_K \Pi_2$ such that

$$(\alpha_{Id'}(T_1), \pi_{Id'}(T_1) \oplus_K \Pi_0) \rightsquigarrow (\alpha_{Id'}(T_2), \Pi_2).$$

We distinguish between the four cases (PA), (EM), (PS), (PD) of concrete topology evolution of Def. 2. In Def. 3, the refined abstract evolution for the cases (PA), (PD), (EM) do not evaluate the current status of process counter but requires it to remain the same. We thus set $\Pi_2 = \pi_{Id'}(T_1) \oplus_K \Pi_0$ in these cases. The same applies to the (PS) case when either $\{\iota_s, \iota_r\} \subseteq Id'$ or $\{\iota_s, \iota_r\} \subseteq Id \setminus Id'$, i.e. communication is only among concrete resp. summarised processes. Two cases for (PS) are left:

(1) $\iota_s \in Id', \iota_r \in Id \setminus Id'$, i.e. a concrete process sends $m(tr_s)$ to the summary process. The case for $r(tr_r) = true$ is trivial as neither a change in the derived process counter nor in the evolution of $\pi_{Id'}(T_1)$ happens. If $r(tr_r) = false$, we set $\Pi_2 := (\pi_{Id'}(T_1) \oplus_K \Pi_0)[(\iota, E) \mapsto \Pi((\iota, E)) \oplus_K 1]$ with $E = E_P(q'(tr_r), c(tr_r))$ according to Def. 3.(rSS). In T_2, the effect of ι_s sending the message $m(tr_s)$ to ι_r is that the communication partner sets $CP_{T_2}(\iota, M)$ with $m(tr_r) \in M$ may be extended by process ι_r. By definition of the derived process counter, this ensures $(\pi_{Id'}(T_2) \oplus_K \Pi_0) \preceq_K \Pi_2$.

(2) $\iota_s \in Id \setminus Id', \iota_r \in Id'$, i.e. the summary process sends $m(tr_s)$ to the concrete process ι_r. As $T_1 \to T_2$, there exists a message set $M \subseteq \Sigma$ with $m(tr_s) \in M$ such that the set of communication partners $CP_{T_1}(\iota_r, M)$ is not the empty set. Thus $(\pi_{Id'}(T_1) \oplus_K \Pi_0)((\iota_r, M)) \geq 1$, and we have $\alpha_{Id'}(T_1) \rightsquigarrow \alpha_{Id'}(T_2)$.

For showing the existence of Π_2, we set Π_2 according to Def. 3.(rRS). Again, the derived process counter $\pi_{Id'}(T_2)$ is changed in the same manner as Π_2. Especially the reduction of the process counter for the pair ι_r and m is safe as ι_s disappears from the corresponding partner sets $CP_{T_2}(\iota_r, M)$ for $m(tr_s) \in M$ when computing the derived process counter for T_2.

To conclude the proof, we have to show that there exists an abstract topology $T^\sharp$ and a process counter Π for the initial topology T_0 such that $(T_0, (T^\sharp, \Pi)) \in H$. As $\alpha_{Id'}(T_0) = T_0$ and $\pi_{Id'}(T_0)((\iota, M)) = 0$ for all $\iota \in Id'$ and $M \subseteq \Sigma$, we set $T^\sharp = T_0$ and $\Pi = \Pi_0$. This setting implies $H(T_0, (T^\sharp, \Pi))$. □

Tool support. Note that the integration of process counting into the DTR abstraction can be conducted fully automatically. For a given DCS protocol P, we calculate the sets $E_P(q, c)$ and adjust the abstract transition relation according to Def. 4. Recently, we have extended the DCS verification framework of Rakow [15] by our method and were able to establish properties like (2) for the car platooning example using standard tools like the SPIN model-checker [8].

Assessment. This section has shown that the observation of communication sequences allows us to derive information about the existence of communication partners in the abstracted part of the system. By our method, we are able to automatically establish properties that DTR alone is not able to prove.

However, the demonstrated approach is not able to eliminated all spurious message interferences. Firstly, the sets of communication partners only denote a *potential* communication. It is possible that a message sending that is enabled by prior communication is in fact not executable in the original system, e.g. if the process always gets blocked before. Nevertheless, the summary process is always allowed to send a message that has been enabled. Secondly, the process counter falls back to uncertainty if the counter exceeds K. The scenario is possible when there is a source of unrestricted sendings in the system, e.g. a concrete process sending perpetually messages without waiting for any answers. We however expect that such kind of polling only occurs in the low-level physical layer, but not on the high-level negotiation protocols addressed by DCS protocols. We thus conjecture that counting up to $K = 1$ is already sufficient for reasonable DCS protocols.

4   Related Work

In the literature, analyses of systems that comprise an unbounded number of processes are mainly developed in terms of a parameterised system $S(N)$, that is, a parallel composition of N identical finite processes. The task is to prove properties of $S(N)$ for every $N > 1$. Various verification approaches have been proposed, e.g. based an network invariants [10], counter abstraction [14], environment abstraction [4], or symmetry reduction [7]. However, parametrised systems have no means of changing the connection topology and basically communicate via a global shared memory. The problem of a changing link structures is mainly addressed in the area of shape analysis [17]. However, the links are only among *data cells*, i.e. the connected nodes do not exhibit a local behaviour. Dynamic Communication Systems (DCS) combine the two difficulties of unbounded processes and dynamic connections and hence require new verification techniques. The verification of Java programs with dynamic thread creation is addressed in [23], based on a 3-valued logic framework. This approach is restricted to safety properties, while Data-Type Reduction is able to preserve liveness properties on the concrete part of the system. We have sketched the verification of DCS already in [2] by combining Data-Type Reduction with global system invariants that denote all possible communication topologies. These invariants are computed by a new form of abstract interpretation of graph transformation rules [1]. This approach is currently worked out in more detail. The ideas presented in this paper present an alternative approach and we have to investigate how both relate to each other in terms of effectiveness and performance.

5   Conclusion

Reducing the number of message interferences substantially increases the applicability of Data-Type Reduction for communicating systems of systems. We demonstrate that the observation of communication sequences allows us to obtain valuable information about valid communication partners that is normally dismissed by the abstraction. We thereby extend the idea of manually inferring and adding non-interference lemmata for DTR refinement to a fully automatic procedure. The extension itself is based on a variant of Counter Abstraction.

Future work has to evaluate the approach in terms of effectiveness and performance for larger systems. We furthermore work on a formal characterisation of the "degree of improvement" of DTR by our method, and identify subclasses of DCS where the refinement leads to a *complete* abstraction technique.

References

1. Bauer, J.: Analysis of Communication Topologies by Partner Abstraction. PhD thesis, Universität des Saarlandes (2006)
2. Bauer, J., Schaefer, I., Toben, T., Westphal, B.: Specification and Verification of Dynamic Communication Systems. In: Goossens, K., Petrucci, L. (eds.) Proc. ACSD 2006, Turku, Finland, June 2006, IEEE, New York (2006)

3. Brand, D., Zafiropulo, P.: On Communicating Finite-State Machines. Journal of the Association for Computing Machinery 30(2), 323–342 (1983)
4. Clarke, E.M., Talupur, M., Veith, H.: Environment Abstraction for Parameterized Verification. In: Emerson, E.A., Namjoshi, K.S. (eds.) VMCAI 2006. LNCS, vol. 3855, pp. 126–141. Springer, Heidelberg (2005)
5. Damm, W., Westphal, B.: Live and let die: LSC-based verification of UML-models. Science of Computer Programming 55(1–3), 117–159 (2005)
6. Frodigh, M., Johansson, P., Larsson, P.: Wireless Ad Hoc Networking: The Art of Networking without a Network. Ericsson Review, 4 (2000)
7. Gyuris, V., Sistla, A.P.: On-the-Fly Model Checking Under Fairness that Exploits Symmetry. Formal Methods in System Design 15(3), 217–238 (1999)
8. Holzmann, G.J.: The SPIN model checker: Primer and reference manual. Addison Wesley, Reading, MA (2004) HOL g 03:1 1.Ex
9. Hsu, A., Eskafi, F., Sachs, S., Varaiya, P.: The Design of Platoon Maneuver Protocols for IVHS. PATH Research Report UCB-ITS-PRR-91-6, Inst. of Transportation Studies, University of California (April 1991) ISSN 1055-1425
10. Kesten, Y., Pnueli, A., Shahar, E., Zuck, L.D.: Network Invariants in Action. In: Brim, L., Jančar, P., Křetínský, M., Kucera, A. (eds.) CONCUR 2002. LNCS, vol. 2421, pp. 101–115. Springer, Heidelberg (2002)
11. Lubachevsky, B.D.: An Approach to Automating the Verification of Compact Parallel Coordination Programs I. Acta Inf. 21, 125–169 (1984)
12. McMillan, K.L.: A methodology for hardware verification using compositional model checking. Science of Computer Programming 37, 279–309 (2000)
13. Milner, R.: Communicating and Mobile Systems: The Pi Calculus. CU Press, Cambridge, MA (1999)
14. Pnueli, A., Xu, J., Zuck, L.: Liveness with (0,1,infty)-Counter Abstraction. In: Hunt Jr., W.A., Somenzi, F. (eds.) CAV 2003. LNCS, vol. 2725, pp. 107–133. Springer, Heidelberg (2003)
15. Rakow, J.: Verification of Dynamic Communication Systems. Master's thesis, Carl von Ossietzky Universität Oldenburg (April 2006)
16. Graf, S., Saidi, H.: Construction of Abstract State Graphs with PVS. In: Grumberg, O. (ed.) CAV 1997. LNCS, vol. 1254, pp. 72–83. Springer, Heidelberg (1997)
17. Sagiv, S., Reps, T.W., Wilhelm, R.: Parametric Shape Analysis via 3-Valued Logic. ACM Transactions on Programming Languages and Systems, 22 (2001)
18. UNISIG. SUBSET 026-Chapter 3; Version 2.2.2 (SRS) (March 2002) http://www.aeif.org/ccm/default.asp
19. Wachter, B., Westphal, B.: The Spotlight Principle. On Combining Process-Summarising State Abstractions. In: Cook, B., Podelski, A. (eds.) VMCAI 2007. LNCS, vol. 4349, pp. 182–198. Springer, Heidelberg (2007)
20. Westphal, B.: LSC Verification for UML Models with Unbounded Creation and Destruction. In: Visser, W., Cook, B., Stoller, S. (eds.) Proc. SoftMC 2005, July 2005. ENTCS, vol. 144(3), pp. 133–145. Elsevier B.V, Amsterdam (2005)
21. Xie, F., Browne, J.C.: Integrated State Space Reduction for Model Checking Executable Object-oriented Software System Designs. In: Kutsche, R.-D., Weber, H. (eds.) ETAPS 2002 and FASE 2002. LNCS, vol. 2306, pp. 64–79. Springer, Heidelberg (2002)
22. Yahav, E., Ramalingam, G.: Verifying safety properties using separation and heterogeneous abstractions. In: Proc. of the ACM SIGPLAN 2004 conference on Programming language design and implementation, pp. 25–34. ACM Press, New York (2004)
23. Yahav, E.: Verifying safety properties of concurrent Java programs using 3-valued logic. ACM SIGPLAN Notices 36(3), 27–40 (2001)

Co-simulation of Distributed Embedded Real-Time Control Systems*

Marcel Verhoef[1], Peter Visser[2], Jozef Hooman[3], and Jan Broenink[2]

[1] Chess, P.O. Box 5021, 2000 CA Haarlem and Radboud University Nijmegen,
Institute of Computing and Information Sciences, P.O. Box 9010,
6500 GL Nijmegen, The Netherlands
`Marcel.Verhoef@chess.nl`
[2] University of Twente, Control Engineering, Department of Electrical Engineering,
Mathematics and Computer Science, P.O. Box 217, 7500 AE Enschede,
The Netherlands
`P.M.Visser@utwente.nl, J.F.Broenink@utwente.nl`
[3] Embedded Systems Institute, P.O. Box 513, 5600 MB Eindhoven and
Radboud University Nijmegen, Institute of Computing and
Information Sciences
`hooman@cs.ru.nl`

Abstract. Development of computerized embedded control systems is difficult because it brings together systems theory, electrical engineering and computer science. The engineering and analysis approaches advocated by these disciplines are fundamentally different which complicates reasoning about e.g. performance at the system level. We propose a lightweight approach that alleviates this problem to some extent. An existing formal semantic framework for discrete event models is extended to allow for consistent co-simulation of continuous time models from within this framework. It enables integrated models that can be checked by simulation in addition to the verification and validation techniques already offered by each discipline individually. The level of confidence in the design can now be raised in the very early stages of the system design life-cycle instead of postponing system-level design issues until the integration and test phase is reached. We demonstrate the extended semantic framework by co-simulation of VDM++ and bond-graph models on a case study, the level control of a water tank.

Keywords: simulation, continuous time, discrete event, VDM++, bond graphs.

1 Introduction

Computers that are intimately coupled to the environment which they monitor and control are commonly referred to as embedded systems. We focus on the class

---

* This work has been carried out as part of the Boderc project under the responsibility of the Embedded Systems Institute. This project was partially supported by the Dutch Ministry of Economic Affairs under the Senter TS program.

J. Davies and J. Gibbons (Eds.): IFM 2007, LNCS 4591, pp. 639–658, 2007.

of embedded systems that control a physical process in the real world. We refer to these systems as embedded control systems. Examples are the control unit of a washing machine and the fuel injection system in a private car. Embedded control systems execute an algorithm that ensures the correct behavior of the system as a whole. The common element of all these systems is that timeliness is of concern. Control actions have to be taken *on time* to keep the physical process in the required state. I.e., embedded control systems are real-time systems.

This is in particular true for the class of high-tech systems such as for instance wafer steppers and high-volume printers and copiers. The productivity of these machines, which is often their most important selling point, depends on the performance of the embedded control system. Typically, these complex machines are composed of several subsystems that need to work together to get the job done, which may require multi-layer and distributed control. For example, each subsystem may have its own embedded control system to perform its specific function while another, dedicated, subsystem coordinates the system as a whole by telling the other subsystems what to do and when. It is not hard to imagine that the design of the control strategy for these systems is challenging.

This is complicated by the fact that systems are often developed out-of-phase. Typically, mechanical design precedes electronics design which precedes software design. Although there is a trend towards concurrent engineering to reduce development time, the lead times for mechanical design and engineering typically still exceed those of electronics and software. System level design considerations are validated during the test and integration phase, which may cause significant delays in the project if an important issue was overlooked. Software is often the only part of the system that can be changed at this late stage. These late changes can cause a significant increase in the complexity of the software, especially when a carefully designed software architecture is violated to compensate for some unforeseen problems in the hardware. Hence, it is important to get as much feedback as possible in the earliest stages of the system design life-cycle, to prevent this situation.

Model-based design addresses this challenge. Reasoning about system-level properties is enabled by creating abstract, high-level and multidisciplinary models of the system under construction. Mono-disciplinary models typically allow optimization of single aspects of the design, while multidisciplinary models allow reasoning about fitness for purpose across multiple system aspects. Suppose, for instance, that the position of a sheet of paper in the paper path of a printer is measured with a sensor that generates an interrupt when the edge of the sheet is observed. High interrupt loads can occur on the embedded control system if these sensors are placed physically close together, because they are triggered right after one another. A very powerful processor may be required in order to deal with this sudden peak load, in particular when a short response time must be guaranteed for each event. There is a clear trade-off between spatial layout and performance in this example. Analysis of multidisciplinary models provides valuable insight into the design such that these trade-offs can be made in a structured way, earlier, and with more confidence.

This approach was studied in the BODERC project [1] in which the authors participated. We observed that creating multidisciplinary models is far from trivial. The notations and the engineering and analysis approaches that are advocated by the involved disciplines are different and the resulting models are typically not at the same level of abstraction. Henzinger and Sifakis [2] even claim that these are fundamental problems and that a new mathematical foundation is required to reason about these integrated multidisciplinary models. The approach taken in this paper is different. We would like to be able to combine the state of the art in each discipline in a useful and consistent way. In other words, we want to construct multidisciplinary models from mono-disciplinary models. We are certainly not the first to propose this idea but we believe that our solution to this problem is novel.

Contribution of this paper. We have reconciled the semantics of two existing formal notations such that system models, which are composed of sub-models written in either language, can be conveniently studied in combination. We also demonstrate how this is achieved in practice by tool coupling. The result is a light-weight modeling approach that enables construction of multidisciplinary models that can be simulated, in addition to the analysis techniques already available for each sub-model individually. Moreover, the reconciled semantics ensures reliable simulation results which can be obtained with little effort.

Structure of this paper. An overview of the current state of practice is presented in Section 2. Modeling and analysis of embedded control systems is discussed by introducing a motivating case study in Section 3. The results of the simulation using the tool coupling are shown in Section 4. The semantic integration is presented from a formal perspective in Section 5. Finally, we look at related and future work and we draw conclusions in Section 6.

2   Current State of Practice in Academia and Industry

The importance of model-based design is widely recognized and we observe that many contenders, typically originating from a specific discipline, are extending their techniques to cater for this wider audience. Matlab/Simulink is an example of this trend. In combination with their Stateflow and Real-time Workshop add-on products, they provide a tool chain for embedded systems design and engineering. It is particularly well-suited for fine grained controller design. This is not surprising because the roots of the tools are firmly based in systems theory. Stateflow can be used to model the control software using finite state machines. However, this technique is not very convenient for specifying complex algorithms. One has to write so-called S-functions or provide a piece of C-code in order to execute the Stateflow model. Timing is idealized by the assumption that all transitions take a fixed amount of timer ticks. Scheduling and deployment of software on a distributed system cannot easily be described and analyzed. Henriksson [3] designed and implemented the TrueTime toolkit on top of Simulink which provides a solution for describing scheduling and deployment, but the software models remain at a low abstraction level. We believe that these tools are *not* acceptable to the embedded software engineer at large, because insufficient support is provided for modern software engineering approaches to design and implement complex real-time software.

A similar situation arises from IBM Rational Technical Developer (formerly known as Rational Rose Real-time) and I-Logix Rhapsody. These software development environments are increasingly used in real-time embedded systems development [4]. They provide modeling capabilities based on the Unified Modeling Language (UML) and the System Modeling Language (SysML) and are supported by mature development processes (RUP and Harmony respectively). Both tools aim to develop executable models that are deployed on the target system as soon as possible to close the design loop. This requires the model to evolve to a low level of abstraction early in the design process in order to achieve that goal. Actions are coded directly in the target (programming) language and timing can be specified by using so-called timer objects provided by the modeling framework. However, their resolution and accuracy is determined by the services of the operating system running on the target platform, they are not part of the modeling language. Moving code from one platform to another might lead to completely different timing behavior. Similarly, task priorities and scheduling are implementation specific. We believe that these tools are *not* acceptable to the control engineer at large, because no support is provided to design and analyze the control laws that the system should implement.

Is it possible to support control and software engineers using a single method or tool? Several attempts have been made to unify both worlds. For example, Hooman, Mulyar and Posta [5] have co-simulated Rose Real-time software models with control laws specified in Matlab/Simulink. They removed the platform dependent notion of time in Rose Real-time by providing a platform neutral notion of time instead. This is achieved by development of an interface that sits in between Rose Real-time and Simulink, which exposes the software simulator of Rose Real-time to the Simulink internal clock. While this is a step forward, it also shows that Rose Real-time is not very suitable for the co-simulation of control systems, because it lacks a suitable notion of simulation time and the run-to-completion semantics does not allow interrupts due to relevant events of the physical system under control. I-Logix has recently announced integration of Rhapsody with Simulink but the technical details have not yet been unveiled.

Lee et al [6] propose a component based, actor oriented approach. They define a framework in which all components are concurrent and interact by sending messages according to some communication protocol. The communication protocol and the concurrency policies together are called the model of computation. Ptolemy-II [6] is a system-level design environment that supports heterogeneous modeling and design using this approach. It supports several domains, each of which is based on a particular model of computation, such as for example discrete event, synchronous data flow, process networks, finite state machines and communicating sequential processes. They can be combined at liberty to describe the system under investigation. This approach seems to be a major step forward for model based design of real-time embedded systems, but paradoxically, it does not appeal to either control engineers or software engineers. Perhaps the approach proposed by Ptolemy-II upsets the current way of working so much that it is considered too high a risk to use in an industrial environment. Currently, only simulation is offered as a means of model validation and synthesis is under development for some domains. Verification of Ptolemy-II models is not yet possible because the semantics of actors has not been formally defined.

3   Modeling and Analysis of Embedded Control Systems

The complexity of embedded control design and analysis is probably best explained by means of a motivating example. We use the level control of a water tank in this paper. This example is small and simple, but it contains all the basic elements of an embedded control system. These elements are presented in detail in this section. An overview of the case study is presented in Figure 1. The case study concerns a water tank that is filled by a constant input flow f_I and can be emptied by opening a valve resulting in an output flow f_O. The volume change is described by equations (1) and (2), where A is the surface area of the tank bottom, V is the volume, g is the gravitation constant, ρ is the density of liquid and R is the resistance of the valve exit.

From the system theoretic point of view, we distinguish the *plant* and the *controller* of an embedded control system, as shown in Fig. 2. The plant is the physical entity in the real world that is observed and actuated by the controller. More accurately, we study feedback control in this paper. Feedback controllers compute and generate a control action that keeps the difference between the observed plant state and its desired value, the so-called set-point, within a certain allowed margin of error at all times. The plant is a dynamic system that is usually described by differential equations if in the continuous time (CT) domain or by difference equations if it is described in the discrete time (DT) domain.

The water tank case study is an example of a continuous time system, described by differential equation (1). Controllers observe some property of the plant and they change the state of the plant by performing a control action, according to some control law. This control law keeps the system as a whole in some desired state. In our case study, the water level is observed by three

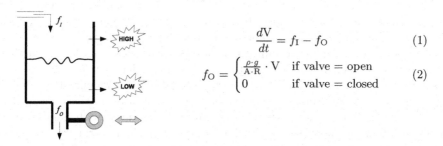

$$\frac{dV}{dt} = f_I - f_O \tag{1}$$

$$f_O = \begin{cases} \frac{\rho \cdot g}{A \cdot R} \cdot V & \text{if valve = open} \\ 0 & \text{if valve = closed} \end{cases} \tag{2}$$

Fig. 1. The water tank level control case study

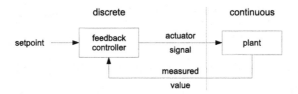

Fig. 2. System theoretic view of a control system

sensors: a pressure sensor at the bottom of the tank which measures the current water level continuously and two discrete sensors that raise an alarm if a certain situation occurs. The top sensor informs us when the water level exceeds the high water mark and the bottom sensor fires if the water level drops below the low water mark. The aim of the controller is to keep the water level between the low and high watermark. The controller can influence the water level by opening or closing a valve at the bottom of the tank. We assume that the valve is either fully open or fully closed. Plant modeling and controller descriptions are discussed in more detail in the following sections.

3.1   Plant Modeling

For modeling the plant of the embedded control system, we use so-called bond graphs [7,8] in this paper. Bond graphs are directed graphs, showing the relevant dynamic behavior of the system. Vertices are the sub-models and the edges, which are called *bonds*, denote the ideal (or idealized) exchange of energy. Entry points of the sub-models are the so-called *ports*. The exchange of energy through a port (p) is always described by two implicit variables, effort $(p.e)$ and flow $(p.f)$. The product of these variables is the amount of energy that flows through the port. For each physical domain, such a pair of variables can be specified, for example: voltage and current, force and velocity. The half arrow on the vertex at the bonds shows the positive direction of the flow of energy, and the perpendicular stroke indicates the computational direction of the two variables involved. They connect the energy flows to the two variables of the bond. The equations that define the relationship between the variables are specified as real equalities, not as assignments. Port variables obtain a computational direction (one as input, the other as output) by means of computational causal analysis on the graph. This efficient algorithm ensures that the underlying set of differential equations can be solved deterministically by rewriting the equations as assignment statements such that a consistent evaluation order is enforced whenever a solution is calculated. Bond graphs are physical-domain independent, due to analogies between the different domains on the level of physics. Mechanical, electrical, hydraulic and other system parts can all be modeled with bond graphs. Bond graphs may be mixed with block diagrams in a natural way to cover the information domain. Control laws are usually specified with block diagrams and the plant is specified with bond graphs to model a controlled mechatronic

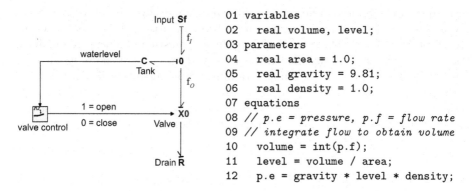

```
01 variables
02    real volume, level;
03 parameters
04    real area = 1.0;
05    real gravity = 9.81;
06    real density = 1.0;
07 equations
08 // p.e = pressure, p.f = flow rate
09 // integrate flow to obtain volume
10    volume = int(p.f);
11    level = volume / area;
12    p.e = gravity * level * density;
```

Fig. 3. The bond graph plant model of the water tank case study

system. Figure 3 shows the bond graph plant model of the water tank case study. The S_f element is the input flow f_I. The C element describes the water tank, the equations are next to the figure. The R element describes the drain. The X0 element is a so-called switching junction which describes the valve. When the valve is opened, a flow f_O will be drained from C. There is no flow from C when the valve is closed.

Differential equations are the general format for representing dynamic systems mathematically. For specifying a plant model many continuous-time representations exist, e.g., bond graph models, ideal physical models, block and flow diagrams and so on. A common property is that all these model types are directly related to a set of differential equations. For the subset of linear time-invariant plant models, alternative description techniques exist, such as the s-plane, frequency response and state-space formats [9].

System theory has provided many analysis techniques for time-invariant linear models and design techniques for their associated controllers, for which certain properties can be proven to hold. However, real world systems often tend to be nonlinear and time varying. The task of the control engineer is to find a suitable linearization such that system theory can still be applied to design a controller. Alternatively, simulation can be used if the dynamic system can be described by a collection of so-called ordinary differential equations. This includes the linear time-invariant models mentioned earlier, as well as non-linear and time varying differential equations. Partial differential equations can be approximated by lumped parameter models in ordinary differential equations and also non-deterministic (or stochastic) models can be simulated. Although simulation can never provide hard answers, it is often used because it can address a much larger class of problems than linear analysis. For example, it can be used to determine whether a linearized model is a good abstraction of the original non-linear model, since both models can be simulated.

The basic method used in simulation is to solve a differential equation numerically instead of analytically. Approximations of the solution are computed by means of integration of the differential equations. These numerical integration techniques are commonly referred to as "solvers" and they exist in many flavors. Examples of well-known solvers are Euler, Runge-Kutta and Adams-Bashforth [10,11]. These solvers belong to the class of fixed step size integration algorithms. Also many variable step size algorithms exist and selection of the right solver is non-trivial and requires a good understanding of the model itself. For example, variable step size solvers are typically required when the dynamic system is described by (combined CT and) DT models. In addition, since an approximation of the solution is computed, an integration error is introduced. This error might lead to instability if the solver, and its parameters, are not carefully selected.

3.2   Controller Description

According to Cassandras and Lafortune [12], a system belongs to the class of discrete event systems if the state can be described by a set of discrete values and state transitions are observed at discrete points in time. We adopt this definition here. Discrete event models can be used to describe the behavior of digital computers, which implement certain control laws. Computers execute instructions based on a discrete clock. The result of an instruction becomes available after a certain number of clock ticks has elapsed. Sensor input samples and actuator output values are seen as discrete events in this model of computation.

In order to bridge the gap between continuous time and discrete event simulation, we obviously need to introduce the notion of events in the continuous time solver. Here, we distinguish two different event types: a) state events and b) time events. State events occur when the solution of a differential equation reaches some value p. Time events occur when the solver has reached some time t. Consider a solver that produces a sequence of time steps $time$ and a sequence of solutions $state$ for variable x then we can declare events as follows

$$\text{REE}\,(x,p) \;\stackrel{def}{=}\; state\,(x, n-1) - p < 0 \;\wedge\; state\,(x, n) - p \geq 0 \qquad (3)$$

$$\text{FEE}\,(x,p) \;\stackrel{def}{=}\; state\,(x, n-1) - p > 0 \;\wedge\; state\,(x, n) - p \leq 0 \qquad (4)$$

$$\text{TE}\,(t) \;\stackrel{def}{=}\; time\,(n-1) < t \;\wedge\; time\,(n) = t \qquad (5)$$

whereby n is the index used in both sequences. The event REE is the so-called rising edge zero crossing and FEE is the falling edge zero crossing. The zero crossing functions of the solver ensure that $time(n)$ is an accurate approximation within user-defined bounds. The time event TE is generated as soon as the solver has exactly reached time t, whereby the solver ensures that the solution x in $state(x, n)$ at $time(n) = t$ is an accurate approximation. For our case study, we define two edge triggered events: REE $(level, 3.0)$ and FEE $(level, 2.0)$, whereby $level$ is a shared continuous time variable that represents the height of the water level in the tank. This variable is declared on line 2 of Fig. 3 and line 4 of Fig. 5. An event is declared as a normal equation in 20-SIM [13] as shown in Fig. 4. In this example, we increment a simple event counter eue and inform the CT solver that the DE model needs to be updated, by setting the variable fireDES.

We use VDM++ [14] in this paper to describe the controller. We extended this notation in earlier work [15] such that the behavior of distributed embedded

```
// check for the upper water level limit
if (eventup(level - 3.0)) then
      eue = eue + 1;
      fireDES = true;
end;
```

Fig. 4. The REE (*level*, 3.0) event in 20-SIM

real-time systems can be analyzed by means of discrete event simulation. Here we assume a single processor system `cpu1` that executes the controller presented in Fig. 5. The shared continuous sensor and actuator variables *level* and *valve* are declared on Line 4 and 5. Whenever *level* is read, it contains the actual value of the corresponding continuous time variable on line 11 of Fig. 3. Similarly, whenever *valve* is assigned a value, it changes the state of X0 in Fig. 3.

We demonstrate that two styles of control can be specified: event driven control and time triggered control. For event driven control, two asynchronous operations, *open* and *close* are defined in lines 8 and 11 respectively. The former will be the handler for the REE (*level*, 3.0) event and the latter is the handler for the FEE (*level*, 2.0) event. In other words, these asynchronous operations will be called automatically whenever the corresponding event fires. This will cause the creation of a new thread. This thread will die as soon as the operation is completed. In VDM++, all statements have a default duration, which can be redefined using the **duration** and **cycles** statements. The duration statement on line 9 states that opening the valve in this case takes 50 *msec*. The cycles statement on line 12 denotes that closing the valve takes 1000 cycles. Assuming this

```
01  class Controller
02
03  instance variables
04     static public level : real;
05     static public valve : bool := false   -- default is closed
06
07  operations
08     static public async open: () ==> ()
09     open () == duration(0.05) valve := true;
10
11     static public async close: () ==> ()
12     close () == cycles(1000) valve := false;
13
14     loop: () ==> ()
15     loop () ==
16        if level >= 3 then valve := true -- check high water mark
17        else if level <= 2 then valve := false; -- check low water mark
18
19  threads
20     periodic(1.0,0,0,1.0)(loop)
21
22  sync
23     mutex(open, close, loop)
24
25  end Controller
```

Fig. 5. The controller description in VDM++

class is deployed on a processor with a capacity of 100000 cycles per second, then executing `valve := false` will take $10\,msec$. Note that the result of the assignment is available *after* this time has passed. Time triggered control is provided by the *loop* operation in line 14-17. The `periodic` clause in line 20 states that the operation *loop* is called periodically, once per second, starting at $t = 1\,sec$. Note that we use the default statement durations here. Finally, the `mutex` clause on line 23 states that the three operations are declared mutually exclusive. This implies that only one operation call can be active at any time and they cannot be interrupted by each other. All threads that do not meet this requirement are blocked until the currently executing operation call is completed.

4   Tool Support

We implemented a discrete event simulator to execute VDM++ models as described in the previous section, as a proof of concept. We coupled this tool to the 20-SIM [13] continuous time simulator for dynamic systems. This tool has the ability to make calls to user-defined libraries from within the simulation. We implemented a simple DLL in C++ to exchange arbitrary sequences of double precision reals over a TCP/IP connection. The same library is used in the VDM++ simulator to set-up a connection. The progress of time in the simulators on either end of the connection is synchronized by exchanging the current time, time steps, actuator and sensor values and events, whereby the current time is always strict monotone increasing. In this section we will focus on the construction and use of the interface. In the next section we will look at the semantics in more detail.

The behavior of the interface is shown in the UML sequence diagram in Fig. 7. We use an XML configuration file to describe the information that is exchanged over the link, the interface is completely model independent. For brevity, we use an informal description as presented in Fig. 6. The keywords `sensor` and `actuator` are defined as perceived from the perspective of the discrete event simulator. Basically, we define a `sensor[]` array, an `actuator[]` array and an `event[]` array. These arrays provide the bindings for all variables and events. The `abort` keyword is used to stop the simulation, in addition to other tool specific stop criteria that may be defined, and gives control back to the user, for example to inspect the state of the model.

The XML configuration file is read by both simulations when the interface is started, indicated by `initialize` in Fig. 7. When a message is sent from

```
sensor[1] = cpu1.Controller'level
actuator[1] = cpu1.Controller'valve
event[1] = REE(level,3.0) -> cpu1.Controller'open
event[2] = FEE(level,2.0) -> cpu1.Controller'close
event[3] = TE(15.0) -> abort
```

Fig. 6. The interface configuration file

VDM++ to 20-SIM, indicated as `updateCT` in Fig. 7, the message contains the current time T, the target time step t_s, and the value of each defined actuator variable at T from `actuator[]`. So, for our case study only three values are exchanged in this direction for every step. Upon arrival, the operation `updateCTmodel` calls the continuous time solver and tries to perform the time step t_s. Either this time was reached or the solver stopped due to an event that occurred at t_r. When a message is sent from 20-SIM to VDM++, indicated as `updateDE` in Fig. 7, the message contains the current time T, the realized time step $t_r \leq t_s$, the value of each defined sensor variable at $T+t_r$ from `sensor[]`, followed by a monotone increasing counter for each declared `event[]`. This counter is incremented when the event occurred at $T+t_r$. This allows us to monitor the integrity of the interface. Several events can be detected at the same time, but an event can only occur once per iteration. Six values are offered when a message is sent from 20-SIM to VDM++ in this model. Upon arrival, the operation `updateDEmodel` processes all events, updates the shared continuous variables and performs a simulation step on the discrete event model, after which we iterate.

Figure 8 shows a simulation run for our case study, whereby we have disabled all state events. In other words, we are studying the periodic control loop behavior (lines 14-17 in Fig. 5). The top screen shows the evolution of the *level* sensor variable. The middle screen shows the evolution of the *valve* actuator variable. The bottom screen shows when the controller has been active, by means of a counter which is increased whenever the VDM++ model makes a time step. It resembles a staircase profile because the execution times of a single instruction are small compared to the changes in the water level. However, if we zoom in, we can actually see how much time is spent in the control loop. Notice that the

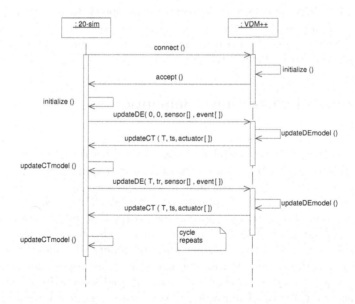

Fig. 7. Tool interface behavior as a UML sequence diagram

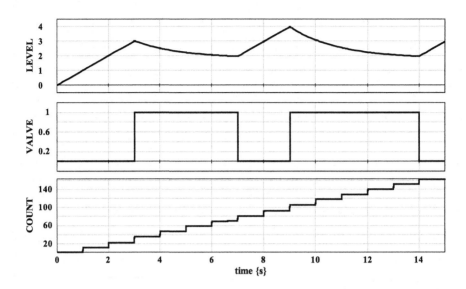

Fig. 8. Visualization of a co-simulation run of the water tank case study

discrete controller is indeed invoked every second, but the control actions, for example at $t = 4\,sec$ are slightly delayed, as expected. Moreover, observe that the valve was not opened at $t = 8\,sec$ because *level* was 2.96 at that time. The overshoot would have been substantially smaller if event based control was used here. We can change many system parameters in the discrete event simulator and observe their impact, such as the processor speed, task switch overheads, and the scheduling policy, without modifying the model shown in Fig. 5. Similarly, we can change parameters in 20-SIM, such as the input flow rate, the liquid density, the resistance of the valve exit, etc.

5   Reconciled Operational Semantics

There are many techniques available from computer science that can be used to create discrete event models. Two-phase labeled transition systems are commonly used, whereby state and time transitions are explicitly distinguished. Assuming some initial state, in the first phase, the successor state is computed and then time elapses in the second phase after which the process is repeated. We have presented an abstract operational semantics for distributed embedded real-time systems in VDM++ in [15] which is also based on this approach. In this paper, we extend this abstract formal semantics to allow for consistent co-simulation with continuous time models. The tool support described in the previous section conforms to the formal operational semantics presented here. One of the key features of our work is that state modifications computed in phase one are made visible after the time step in phase two has been completed, in order to guarantee consistency in the presence of shared continuous variables and arbitrary interleaving of multiple, concurrent, labeled transition systems.

The main aim of the operational semantics is to formalize the interaction between the discrete event simulator, which executes a control program, and a solver for a continuous time plant model. Hence we have omitted many details of the VDM++ model such as the links between nodes, message transfer along these links, the definition of classes, including explicit definitions of synchronous and asynchronous operations, guards and a concept to define periodic threads. The operational semantics of these concepts can be found in [15]. In contrast with this previous work, we will focus in this section on communication by means of global variables and events, since this is used to model the interaction between continuous time and discrete event models. In Sect. 5.1 we define the syntax of a simple imperative language which serves as an illustration of the basic concepts, without trying to be complete. The operational semantics of this language is defined in Sect. 5.2.

5.1   Syntax

The distributed architecture of an embedded control program can be represented by so-called nodes. Let *Node* be the set of node identities. Nodes are used to represent computation resources such as processors. On each node a number of concurrent threads are executed in an interleaved way. In addition, execution is interleaved with steps of a solver.

Threads can be created dynamically, e.g., to deal with events received from the solver. Let *Thread* be the set of thread identities, including dormant threads that can be made alive when a new thread is created. Function $node : Thread \rightarrow Node$ denotes on which node each thread is executing. Each thread executes a sequential program, that is, a statement expressed in the language of Table 1.

Let *Value* be a domain of values, such as the real numbers $\mathbb{R}$. Assume given a set of variables $Var = InVar \cup OutVar \cup LVar$ where *InVar* is the set of input/sensor variables, *OutVar* is the set of output/actuator variables, and *LVar* a set of local variables. The input and output variables are global and shared between all threads and the continuous model. Hence, they can also be accessed by the solver, which may read the actuator variables and write the sensor variables. Let $IOVar = InVar \cup OutVar$. Let $Time = \mathbb{R}$ be the time domain. The syntax of our sequential programming language is given in Table 1, with $c \in Value$, $x \in Var$, and $d \in Time$.

The execution of basic statements such as skip and assignment $x := e$ takes zero time, except for the **duration**(d) statement which represents a time step of d time units. For each thread, any sequence of statements between two successive duration statements is executed atomically in zero time. However, the execution of such a sequence might be interleaved with statements of other threads or a step of the solver. Concerning the shared IO-variables in *IOVar* this means that we have to ensure atomicity explicitly. Hence, we introduce a kind of *transaction* mechanism to guarantee consistency in the presence of arbitrary interleaving of steps. Thread *thr* is only allowed to modify IO-variable x if there is no transaction

Table 1. Syntax of Statements

Value Expression	$e ::= c \mid x \mid e_1 + e_2 \mid e_1 - e_2 \mid e_1 \times e_2$
Boolean Expression	$b ::= e_1 = e_2 \mid e_1 < e_2 \mid \neg b \mid b_1 \vee b_2$
Statement	$S ::= \textbf{skip} \mid x := e \mid \textbf{duration}(d) \mid S_1 \,;\, S_2 \mid$
	$\textbf{if } b \textbf{ then } S_1 \textbf{ else } S_2 \textbf{ fi} \mid \textbf{while } b \textbf{ do } S \textbf{ od}$

in progress by any other thread. The transaction is committed as soon as the thread performs a time step. This will be explained in detail in Defs. 2 and 5.

Let *SeqProg* be the set of sequential programs of the form $S \,;\, E$, where E is an auxiliary statement which is used to denote termination of a thread.

The solver may send events to the control program. Let *Event* be a set of events. They may be defined by the primitives REE (x, p), FEE (x, p), and TE (t), as proposed in Eqs. 3-5. Assume that an event handler has been defined for each event, i.e., a sequential program, and a node on which this statement has to be executed (as a new thread), denoted by the function *evhdlr* : *Event* $\rightarrow$ *SeqProg* $\times$ *Node*.

5.2 Operational Semantics

To define the operational semantics, we first introduce a *configuration C* in Def. 1 to capture the state of affairs at a certain point in the execution of our model. Next, we define the so-called *variant* of a configuration in Def. 2. The notion of a *step*, denoted by $C \longrightarrow C'$ for configurations C and C', is defined in Def. 3, using Defs. 4, 5, and 6. This finally leads to a set of runs of the form $C_0 \longrightarrow C_1 \longrightarrow C_2 \longrightarrow \cdots$ in Def. 7, which provides the abstract formal operational semantics of simulating a control program in parallel with a solver of a continuous time model.

Definition 1 (Configuration). A *configuration C* contains the following fields:

- *instr* : *Thread* $\rightarrow$ *SeqProg*
  the remaining program to be executed by each thread.
- *curthr* : *Node* $\rightarrow$ *Thread*
  yields for each node the currently executing thread.
- *status* : *Thread* $\rightarrow$ {*dormant, alive*}
  thread status; a thread can be created by making a dormant thread alive.
- *lval* : *LVar* $\times$ *Thread* $\rightarrow$ *Value*
  denotes the value of each local variable for each thread.
- *ioval* : *IOVar* $\rightarrow$ *Value*
  denotes the committed value of each sensor and actuator variable.
- *modif* : *IOVar* $\times$ *Thread* $\rightarrow$ *Value* $\cup$ {$\bot$}
  to denote the values of sensor and actuator variables that have been modified by a thread and for which the transaction has not yet been committed (by executing a duration statement). The symbol $\bot$ denotes that the value is

undefined, i.e., the thread did not modify the variable in a non-committed transaction.
- now : $Time$ to denote the current time.   □

For a configuration C, we use the notation $C(f)$ to obtain its field f, such as $C(instr)$. We define a few suitable abbreviations:

- $cur(C, n)$ denotes the current thread on node n, i.e. $C(curthr)(n)$
- $exec(C, thr)$ expresses that thr is executing, i.e., there exists an $n \in Node$ such that $cur(C, n) = thr$.

We define the notion of a variant to express configuration modifications.

Definition 2 (Variant). The *variant* of a configuration C with respect to a field f and a value v, denoted by $C[f \mapsto v]$, is defined as

$$(C[f \mapsto v])(f') = \begin{cases} v & \text{if } f' = f \\ C(f') & \text{if } f' \neq f \end{cases} \tag{6}$$

Similarly for field parts, such as variants of mapping $ioval$.   □

We define the value of an expression e in a configuration C which is evaluated in the current thread on a node n, denoted by $[\![e]\!](C, n)$. The main point is the evaluation of a variable:

$$[\![x]\!](C, n) = \begin{cases} C(modif)(x, cur(C, n)) & \text{if } x \in IOVar, C(modif)(x, cur(C, n)) \neq \bot \\ C(ioval)(x) & \text{if } x \in IOVar, C(modif)(x, cur(C, n)) = \bot \\ C(lval)(x, cur(C, n)) & \text{if } x \in LVar \end{cases}$$

The other cases are trivial, e.g., $[\![e_1 \times e_2]\!](C, n) = [\![e_1]\!](C, n) \times [\![e_2]\!](C, n)$ and $[\![c]\!](C, n) = c$. It is also straightforward to define when a Boolean expression b holds in the current thread of a configuration C on a node n, denoted by $[\![b]\!](C, n)$. For instance, $[\![e_1 < e_2]\!](C, n)$ iff $[\![e_1]\!](C, n) < [\![e_2]\!](C, n)$, and $[\![\neg b]\!](C, n)$ iff not $[\![b]\!](C, n)$.

Definition 3 (Step). $C \longrightarrow C'$ is called a *step* if and only if it corresponds to the execution of a statement (Def. 4), performing a time step (Def. 5), or a context switch (Def. 6).   □

Definition 4 (Execute Statement). A step $C \longrightarrow C'$ corresponds to the execution of a statement if and only if there exists at least one executing thread thr with $exec(C, thr)$ such that $C(instr)(thr) = S_1 ; S_2$, allowing $S_2 = E$, and one of the following clauses holds:

- $S_1 = \textbf{skip}$. The skip statement does not have any effect except that the statement is removed from the instruction sequence
  $C' = C[instr(thr) \mapsto S_2]$.
- $S_1 = x := e$. We distinguish two cases, depending on the type of variable x.

- If $x \in IOVar$ we require that there is no transaction in progress by any other thread: for all thr' with $thr' \neq thr$ we have $C(modif)(x, thr') = \bot$. Then the value of e is recorded in the modified field of thr:
  $$C' = C[instr(thr) \mapsto S_2, modif(x, thr) \mapsto [\![\, e \,]\!](C, n)]$$
  As we will see later, all values belonging to thread thr in $C(modif)$ are removed and bound to the variables in $C(ioval)$ as soon as thread thr completes a time step (Def. 5). This corresponds to the intuition that the result of a computation is available only at the end of the time step that reflects the execution of a piece of code.
- If $x \in LVar$ then we change the value of x in the current thread:
  $$C' = C[instr(thr) \mapsto S_2, lval(x, thr) \mapsto [\![\, e \,]\!](C, n)]$$

- $S_1 = \mathbf{if}\ b\ \mathbf{then}\ S_{11}\ \mathbf{else}\ S_{12}\ \mathbf{fi}$. If $[\![\, b \,]\!](C, n)$ then we have
  $C' = C[instr(thr) \mapsto S_{11}\ ;\ S_2]$, otherwise $C' = C[instr(thr) \mapsto S_{12}\ ;\ S_2]$.

- $S_1 = \mathbf{while}\ b\ \mathbf{do}\ S\ \mathbf{od}$. If $[\![\, b \,]\!](C, n)$ then we have
  $C' = C[instr(thr) \mapsto S\ ;\ \mathbf{while}\ b\ \mathbf{do}\ S\ \mathbf{od}\ ;\ S_2]$, otherwise we obtain
  $C' = C[instr(thr) \mapsto S_2]$.

Observe that the execution of these statements does not affect now, that is, $C(now) = C'(now)$. □

Definition 5 (Time Step). A step $C \longrightarrow C'$ is called a *time step* only if all current threads are ready to execute a duration instruction or have terminated. More formally, for all thr with $exec(C, thr)$, $C(instr)(thr)$ is of the form $\mathbf{duration}(d)\ ;\ S$ or equals E. Then the definition of a time step consists of three parts: (1) the definition of the requested duration of the time step, (2) the execution of this time step by the solver, leading to intermediate configuration C_s (3) updating all durations of all current threads, dealing with events generated by the solver, and committing all variables of the current threads.

1. Time may progress with a number of time units which is smaller than or equal to all durations of all current threads. Hence, the requested length of the time step is defined by
   $t_s = min\{d \mid \exists\, thr, S : exec(C, thr) \land C(instr)(thr) = \mathbf{duration}(d)\ ;\ S\}$.
2. If $t_s > 0$ the solver tries to execute a time step of length t_s in configuration C. Concerning the variables, the solver will only use the *ioval* field, ignoring the *lval* and *modif* fields. It will only read the actuator variables in $OutVar$ and it may write the sensor variables in $InVar$ in field *ioval*. As soon as the solver generates one or more events, its execution is stopped. This leads to a new configuration C_s and a set of generated events $EventSet$. Since the solver takes a positive time step, $C(now) < C_s(now) \leq C(now) + t_s$, and if $C_s(now) < C(now) + t_s$ then $EventSet \neq \emptyset$. Moreover, $C_s(f) = C(f)$ for $f \in \{instr, curthr, status, lval, modif\}$.

   If $t_s = 0$ then the solver is not executed and $C_s = C$, $EventSet = \emptyset$. This case is possible because we allow $\mathbf{duration}(0)$ to commit variable changes, as shown in the next point.

3. Starting from configuration C_s and *EventSet*, next the durations are decreased with the actual time step performed, new threads are created for the event handlers, and finally for threads with zero durations the transactions are committed.

   Let $t_r = C_s(now) - C(now)$ be the time step realized by the solver. For each event $e \in EventSet$ with $evhdlr(e) = (S_e, n_e)$, let thr_e be a fresh - not yet used - thread identity with status *dormant* and $node(thr_e) = n_e$.

   We define an auxiliary function $NewInstr(C, t_r) : Thread \to SeqProg$ which decreases durations, removes zero durations, and installs event handlers:
   $NewInstr(C, t_r)(thr) =$
   $$\begin{cases} duration(d - t_r)\,;\ S & \text{if } exec(C, thr),\ C(instr)(thr) = duration(d)\,;\ S, \\ & \quad \text{and } d > t_r \\ S & \text{if } exec(C, thr) \text{ and } C(instr)(thr) = duration(t_r)\,;\ S \\ S_e & \text{if } thr = thr_e \text{ for some } e \in EventSet \\ C(instr)(thr) & \text{otherwise} \end{cases}$$

   Next define a function to awake the new threads for event handlers:
   $$NewStatus(C)(thr) = \begin{cases} alive & \text{if } thr = thr_e \text{ for some } e \in EventSet \\ C(status)(thr) & \text{otherwise} \end{cases}$$

   Let $ActDurZero = \{thr \mid exec(C, thr) \text{ and } C(instr)(thr) = duration(t_r)\,;\ S\}$ be the set of threads which will have a zero duration after this time step. For these threads the transactions are committed and the values of the modified variables are finalized. This is defined by two auxiliary functions:
   $NewIoval(C)(x) =$
   $$\begin{cases} v & \text{if } \exists\, thr \in ActDurZero \text{ and } C(modif)(x, thr) = v \neq \bot \\ C(ioval)(x) & \text{otherwise} \end{cases}$$

   Note that at any point in time at most one thread may modify the same global variable in a transaction. Hence, there exists at most one thread satisfying the first condition of the definition above, for a given variable x. The next function resets the modified field.
   $$NewModif(C)(x, thr) = \begin{cases} \bot & \text{if } thr \in ActDurZero \\ C(modif)(x, thr) & \text{otherwise} \end{cases}$$

   Then $C' = C_s[\ instr \mapsto NewInstr(C_s, t_r),\ status \mapsto NewStatus(C_s),$
   $ioval \mapsto NewIoval(C_s),\ modif \mapsto NewModif(C_s)]$
   Observe that $C'(now) = C_s(now) = C(now) + t_r$ with $t_r \leq t_s$. $\qquad\square$

Definition 6 (Context Switch). A step $C \longrightarrow C'$ corresponds to a context switch iff there exists a thread thr which is alive and not running, and which has a non-empty program, that is, $\neg exec(C, thr)$, $C(status)(thr) = alive$, and $C(instr)(thr) = S \neq E$. Then thr becomes the current thread and a duration of δ_{cs} time units is added to represent the context switching time:
$C' = C[\ instr(thr) \mapsto \textbf{duration}(\delta_{cs})\,;\ S, curthr(node(thr)) \mapsto thr\ ]$ $\qquad\square$

Note that more than one thread may be eligible as the current thread on a node at a certain point in time. In that case, a thread is chosen nondeterministically in our operational semantics. Fairness constraints or a scheduling strategy may be added to enforce a particular type of node behavior, such as for example rate monotonic scheduling.

Definition 7 (Operational Semantics). The operational semantics of our model is the set of execution sequences of the form $C_0 \longrightarrow C_1 \longrightarrow C_2 \longrightarrow \cdots$, where each pair $C_i \longrightarrow C_{i+1}$ is a step (Def. 3) and the initial configuration C_0 all current threads are *alive* and the *modif* field is $\perp$ everywhere. Finally, to avoid Zeno behaviour, we require that for any point of time t there exists a configuration C_i in the sequence with $C_i(now) > t$. $\qquad\qquad\square$

6 Concluding Remarks

A multidisciplinary modeling approach shall provide sufficient means of abstraction to support all mono-disciplinary views in order to be industrially applicable. A solid semantic foundation of the combination of these views is required to support meaningful and reliable analysis of the heterogenous model. We believe that this can be achieved by taking a "best of both worlds" approach whereby the software discipline uses a formal specification technique. Firstly because it provides abstraction mechanisms that allow high-level specification and secondly because its well-defined semantics provides a platform independent description of the model behavior that can be analyzed properly. Software models as advocated by IBM Rational Technical Developer and I-Logix Rhapsody are, in our opinion, not suited for this purpose in particular because they lack a suitable notion of abstraction, time and deployment. We showed how tool integration can be achieved based on the formal semantics proposed in this paper, which we applied to a case study. Note however that the approach taken here is not specific to any tool in particular. Our approach has been applied to a larger case study: the distributed controller of a paper path of a printer [16].

Nicolescu et al [17] propose a software architecture for the design of continuous time / discrete event co-simulation tools for which they provide an operational semantics in [18]. Our work is in fact an instantiation of that architecture, however, with a difference. Their approach is aimed at connecting multiple simulators on a so-called simulation bus, whereas we connect two simulators using a point-to-point connection. They use Simulink and SystemC whereas we use 20-SIM and VDM++ to demonstrate the concept. The type of information exchanged over the interfaces is identical (the state of continuous variables and events). They have used formal techniques to model properties of the interface, whereas we have integrated the continuous time interface into the operational semantics of a discrete event system. We believe that our approach is stronger because a weak semantics for the discrete event model may still yield unexpected simulation results even though the interface is proven to work consistently. An in-depth comparison of both approaches is subject for further study.

The interface between the continuous time and discrete event models seems to be convenient when resilience of a system is studied. Early experiments performed in collaboration with Zoe Andrews at the Centre for Software Reliability at Newcastle University have shown that it is possible to use this interface for fault injection. Values and events exchanged over this interface can be dropped, inserted, modified, delayed and so on to represent the failure mode of a sensor or actuator, such as for example "stuck at x". The advantage of this approach is that the failure model can remain orthogonal to the continuous time and the discrete event models. These system models need no longer be obscured by explicit failure mode modeling in either plant or controller, which usually clobbers the specification. We certainly plan to explore this further.

In summary, the approach is to bring realistic time-aware models of software, executed on a possibly distributed hardware architecture, into the realm of control engineering without enforcing a certain model of computation a priori. We propose to use formal specification techniques to provide suitable software models required for this approach, mainly in order to manage complexity such that small, abstract and high-level models can be created. This is essential in the early phases of the system design life-cycle, where changes are likely to occur while working under severe time pressure. We provide a system level approach for modeling computation, communication and control with support and flexibility for the decision making during the early phases of the system-design life cycle, whereby the trade-offs can be investigated by co-simulation.

Acknowledgments. The authors wish to thank Job van Amerongen, Zoe Andrews, Peter van den Bosch, Erik Gaal, Peter Gorm Larsen, Frits Vaandrager and the anonymous reviewers for their valuable comments to this paper and support for this work.

References

1. Boderc: Model-based design of high-tech systems. Final report. Embedded Systems Institute, P.O. Box 513, 5600 MB Eindhoven, NL (2006) Available on-line at `http://www.esi.nl/boderc`
2. Henzinger, T.A., Sifakis, J.: The embedded systems design challenge. In: Misra, J., Nipkow, T., Sekerinski, E. (eds.) FM 2006. LNCS, vol. 4085, pp. 1–15. Springer, Heidelberg (2006)
3. Henriksson, D.: Flexible Scheduling Methods and Tools for Real-Time Control Systems. PhD thesis, Lund Institute of Technology, Department of Automatic Control (2003) `http://www.control.lth.se/truetime/`
4. Douglas, B.P.: Real-Time UML Workshop for Embedded Systems. Embedded Technology. Newnes. Elsevier, Amsterdam (2007)
5. Hooman, J., Mulyar, N., Posta, L.: Coupling Simulink and UML models. In: Lakhnech, Y., Yovine, S. (eds.) FORMATS 2004 and FTRTFT 2004. LNCS, vol. 3253, pp. 304–311. Springer, Heidelberg (2004)

6. Davis, J., Galicia, R., Goel, M., Hylands, C., Lee, E., Liu, J., Liu, X., Muliadi, L., Neuendorffer, S., Reekie, J., Smyth, N., Tsay, J., Xiong, Y.: Ptolemy-II: Heterogeneous concurrent modeling and design in Java. Technical Memorandum UCB/ERL No. M99/40, University of California at Berkeley (1999)
7. Karnopp, D.C., Margolis, D.L., Rosenberg, R.C.: System Dynamics: Modeling and Simulation of Mechatronic Systems, 3rd edn. Wiley-Interscience, Chichester (2000)
8. Breedveld, P.: Multibond-graph elements in physical systems theory. Journal of the Franklin Institute 319, 1–36 (1985)
9. Ledin, J.: Simulation Engineering - Build Better Embedded Systems Faster. Embedded Systems Programming. CMP Books (2001)
10. Hairer, E., Nørsett, S.P., Gerhard., W.: Solving ordinary differential equations I: Nonstiff problems, 2nd edn. Springer, Heidelberg (1993)
11. Hairer, E., Wanner, G.: Solving ordinary differential equations II: Stiff and differential-algebraic problems, 2nd edn. Springer, Heidelberg (1996)
12. Cassandras, C.G., Lafortune, S.: Introduction to Discrete Event Systems. Kluwer Academic Publishers, Dordrecht (1999)
13. ControlLab Products: 20-sim (2006) http://www.20sim.com
14. Fitzgerald, J., Larsen, P.G., Mukherjee, P., Plat, N., Verhoef, M.: Validated Designs for Object-oriented Systems. Springer, Heidelberg (2005) http://www.vdmbook.com
15. Verhoef, M., Larsen, P.G., Hooman, J.: Modeling and validating distributed embedded real-time systems with VDM++. In: Misra, J., Nipkow, T., Sekerinski, E. (eds.) FM 2006. LNCS, vol. 4085, pp. 147–162. Springer, Heidelberg (2006), http://dx.doi.org/10.1007/11813040_11
16. Visser, P., Verhoef, M., Broenink, J., Hooman, J.: Co-simulation of continuous-time/discrete-event systems as vehicle for embedded system design trade-off's (Submitted, 2007)
17. Nicolescu, G., Boucheneb, H., Gheorghe, L., Bouchhima, F.: Methodology for efficient design of continuous/discrete-events co-simulation tools. In: Anderson, J., Huntsinger, R. (eds.) High Level Simulation Languages and Applications - HLSLA. SCS, San Diego, CA, pp. 172–179 (2007)
18. Gheorghe, L., Bouchhima, F., Nicolescu, G., Boucheneb, H.: Formal definitions of simulation interfaces in a continuous/discrete co-simulation tool. In: Proc. IEEE Workshop on Rapid System Prototyping, pp. 186–192. IEEE Computer Society Press, Los Alamitos (2006) http://doi.ieeecomputersociety.org/10.1109/RSP.2006.18

Author Index

Lecture Notes in Computer Science

For information about Vols. 1–4464

please contact your bookseller or Springer

Vol. 4507: F. Sandoval, A. Prieto, J. Cabestany, M. Graña (Eds.), Computational and Ambient Intelligence. XXVI, 1167 pages. 2007.

Vol. 4506: D. Zeng, I. Gotham, K. Komatsu, C. Lynch, M. Thurmond, D. Madigan, B. Lober, J. Kvach, H. Chen (Eds.), Intelligence and Security Informatics: Biosurveillance. XI, 234 pages. 2007.

Vol. 4505: G. Dong, X. Lin, W. Wang, Y. Yang, J.X. Yu (Eds.), Advances in Data and Web Management. XXII, 896 pages. 2007.

Vol. 4504: J. Huang, R. Kowalczyk, Z. Maamar, D. Martin, I. Müller, S. Stoutenburg, K.P. Sycara (Eds.), Service-Oriented Computing: Agents, Semantics, and Engineering. X, 175 pages. 2007.

Vol. 4501: J. Marques-Silva, K.A. Sakallah (Eds.), Theory and Applications of Satisfiability Testing – SAT 2007. XI, 384 pages. 2007.

Vol. 4500: N. Streitz, A. Kameas, I. Mavrommati (Eds.), The Disappearing Computer. XVIII, 304 pages. 2007.

Vol. 4499: Y.Q. Shi (Ed.), Transactions on Data Hiding and Multimedia Security II. IX, 117 pages. 2007.

Vol. 4497: S.B. Cooper, B. Löwe, A. Sorbi (Eds.), Computation and Logic in the Real World. XVIII, 826 pages. 2007.

Vol. 4496: N.T. Nguyen, A. Grzech, R.J. Howlett, L.C. Jain (Eds.), Agent and Multi-Agent Systems: Technologies and Applications. XXI, 1046 pages. 2007. (Sublibrary LNAI).

Vol. 4495: J. Krogstie, A. Opdahl, G. Sindre (Eds.), Advanced Information Systems Engineering. XVI, 606 pages. 2007.

Vol. 4494: H. Jin, O.F. Rana, Y. Pan, V.K. Prasanna (Eds.), Algorithms and Architectures for Parallel Processing. XIV, 508 pages. 2007.

Vol. 4493: D. Liu, S. Fei, Z. Hou, H. Zhang, C. Sun (Eds.), Advances in Neural Networks – ISNN 2007, Part III. XXVI, 1215 pages. 2007.

Vol. 4492: D. Liu, S. Fei, Z. Hou, H. Zhang, C. Sun (Eds.), Advances in Neural Networks – ISNN 2007, Part II. XXVII, 1321 pages. 2007.

Vol. 4491: D. Liu, S. Fei, Z.-G. Hou, H. Zhang, C. Sun (Eds.), Advances in Neural Networks – ISNN 2007, Part I. LIV, 1365 pages. 2007.

Vol. 4490: Y. Shi, G.D. van Albada, J. Dongarra, P.M.A. Sloot (Eds.), Computational Science – ICCS 2007, Part IV. XXXVII, 1211 pages. 2007.

Vol. 4489: Y. Shi, G.D. van Albada, J. Dongarra, P.M.A. Sloot (Eds.), Computational Science – ICCS 2007, Part III. XXXVII, 1257 pages. 2007.

Vol. 4488: Y. Shi, G.D. van Albada, J. Dongarra, P.M.A. Sloot (Eds.), Computational Science – ICCS 2007, Part II. XXXV, 1251 pages. 2007.

Vol. 4487: Y. Shi, G.D. van Albada, J. Dongarra, P.M.A. Sloot (Eds.), Computational Science – ICCS 2007, Part I. LXXXI, 1275 pages. 2007.

Vol. 4486: M. Bernardo, J. Hillston (Eds.), Formal Methods for Performance Evaluation. VII, 469 pages. 2007.

Vol. 4485: F. Sgallari, A. Murli, N. Paragios (Eds.), Scale Space and Variational Methods in Computer Vision. XV, 931 pages. 2007.

Vol. 4484: J.-Y. Cai, S.B. Cooper, H. Zhu (Eds.), Theory and Applications of Models of Computation. XIII, 772 pages. 2007.

Vol. 4483: C. Baral, G. Brewka, J. Schlipf (Eds.), Logic Programming and Nonmonotonic Reasoning. IX, 327 pages. 2007. (Sublibrary LNAI).

Vol. 4482: A. An, J. Stefanowski, S. Ramanna, C.J. Butz, W. Pedrycz, G. Wang (Eds.), Rough Sets, Fuzzy Sets, Data Mining and Granular Computing. XIV, 585 pages. 2007. (Sublibrary LNAI).

Vol. 4481: J. Yao, P. Lingras, W.-Z. Wu, M. Szczuka, N.J. Cercone, D. Ślęzak (Eds.), Rough Sets and Knowledge Technology. XIV, 576 pages. 2007. (Sublibrary LNAI).

Vol. 4480: A. LaMarca, M. Langheinrich, K.N. Truong (Eds.), Pervasive Computing. XIII, 369 pages. 2007.

Vol. 4479: I.F. Akyildiz, R. Sivakumar, E. Ekici, J.C.d. Oliveira, J. McNair (Eds.), NETWORKING 2007. Ad Hoc and Sensor Networks, Wireless Networks, Next Generation Internet. XXVII, 1252 pages. 2007.

Vol. 4478: J. Martí, J.M. Benedí, A.M. Mendonça, J. Serrat (Eds.), Pattern Recognition and Image Analysis, Part II. XXVII, 657 pages. 2007.

Vol. 4477: J. Martí, J.M. Benedí, A.M. Mendonça, J. Serrat (Eds.), Pattern Recognition and Image Analysis, Part I. XXVII, 625 pages. 2007.

Vol. 4476: V. Gorodetsky, C. Zhang, V.A. Skormin, L. Cao (Eds.), Autonomous Intelligent Systems: Multi-Agents and Data Mining. XIII, 323 pages. 2007. (Sublibrary LNAI).

Vol. 4475: P. Crescenzi, G. Prencipe, G. Pucci (Eds.), Fun with Algorithms. X, 273 pages. 2007.

Vol. 4474: G. Prencipe, S. Zaks (Eds.), Structural Information and Communication Complexity. XI, 342 pages. 2007.

Vol. 4472: M. Haindl, J. Kittler, F. Roli (Eds.), Multiple Classifier Systems. XI, 524 pages. 2007.

Vol. 4471: P. Cesar, K. Chorianopoulos, J.F. Jensen (Eds.), Interactive TV: a Shared Experience. XIII, 236 pages. 2007.

Vol. 4470: Q. Wang, D. Pfahl, D.M. Raffo (Eds.), Software Process Dynamics and Agility. XI, 346 pages. 2007.

Vol. 4469: K.-c. Hui, Z. Pan, R.C.-k. Chung, C.C.L. Wang, X. Jin, S. Göbel, E.C.-L. Li (Eds.), Technologies for E-Learning and Digital Entertainment. XVIII, 974 pages. 2007.

Vol. 4468: M.M. Bonsangue, E.B. Johnsen (Eds.), Formal Methods for Open Object-Based Distributed Systems. X, 317 pages. 2007.

Vol. 4467: A.L. Murphy, J. Vitek (Eds.), Coordination Models and Languages. X, 325 pages. 2007.

Vol. 4466: F.B. Sachse, G. Seemann (Eds.), Functional Imaging and Modeling of the Heart. XV, 486 pages. 2007.

Vol. 4465: T. Chahed, B. Tuffin (Eds.), Network Control and Optimization. XIII, 305 pages. 2007.